THE BICENTENNIAL EDITION
OF THE
WORKS OF JOHN WESLEY

General Editor RICHARD P. HEITZENRATER

Textual Editor FRANK BAKER

*The Directors of the Bicentennial Edition of
the Works of John Wesley
gratefully acknowledge the financial support of
The Trustees of the Ruck Trust
together with auxiliary grants from
The University of Durham
and the Commissions on Archives and History of
The Northern New Jersey Conference
and
The Southern Indiana Conference
of the United Methodist Church
in the preparation of this volume.*

THE WORKS OF
JOHN WESLEY

VOLUME 18

═══

JOURNAL AND DIARIES

I

(1735–38)

EDITED BY

W. REGINALD WARD

(JOURNAL)

AND

RICHARD P. HEITZENRATER

(MANUSCRIPT JOURNALS AND DIARIES)

ABINGDON PRESS

NASHVILLE

1988

The Works of John Wesley, Volume 18
JOURNAL AND DIARIES, I, 1735–38

Library of Congress Cataloging in Publication Data

(Revised for vol. 18)

Wesley, John, 1703-1791
The works of John Wesley.

Vol. 18 edited by W. Reginald Ward and Richard P. Heitzenrater.
Includes bibliographical references.
Contents: v. 1. Sermons I, 1-33 — v. 2. Sermons II, 34-70 — [etc.] — v. 18. Journal and diaries I (1735-38)
  1. Methodist Church—Collected works. 2. Theology—Collected works—18th century. I. Outler, Albert Cook, 1908-   . II. Ward,W. Reginald (William Reginald) III. Heitzenrater, Richard P., 1939-   . IV. Title.
BX8217.W5 1984   230'.7   83-22434

ISBN 0-687-46213-4 (v. 4)
ISBN 0-687-46212-6 (v. 3)
ISBN 0-687-46211-8 (v. 2)
ISBN 0-687-46210-X (v. 1)

THE MONOGRAM USED ON THE CASE AND HALF-TITLE IS
ADAPTED BY RICHARD P. HEITZENRATER FROM ONE OF
JOHN WESLEY'S PERSONAL SEALS

MANUFACTURED BY THE PARTHENON PRESS AT
NASHVILLE, TENNESSEE, UNITED STATES OF AMERICA

THE BICENTENNIAL EDITION OF
THE WORKS OF JOHN WESLEY

This edition of the works of John Wesley reflects the quickened interest in the heritage of Christian thought that has become evident during the last half-century. A fully critical presentation of Wesley's writings had long been a desideratum in order to furnish documentary sources illustrating his contribution to both catholic and evangelical Christianity.

Several scholars, notably Professor Albert C. Outler, Professor Franz Hildebrandt, Dean Merrimon Cuninggim, and Dean Robert E. Cushman, discussed the possibility of such an edition. Under the leadership of Dean Cushman, a Board of Directors was formed in 1960 comprising the deans of four sponsoring theological schools of Methodist-related universities in the United States: Drew, Duke, Emory, and Southern Methodist. They appointed an Editorial Committee to formulate plans, and enlisted an international and interdenominational team of scholars for the Wesley Works Editorial Project.

The works were divided into units of cognate material, with a separate editor (or joint editors) responsible for each unit. Dr. Frank Baker was appointed textual editor for the whole project, with responsibility for supplying each unit editor with a critically developed, accurate Wesley text. The text seeks to represent Wesley's thought in its fullest and most deliberate expression, in so far as this can be determined from the available evidence. Substantive variant readings in any British edition published during Wesley's lifetime are shown in appendices to the units, preceded by a summary of the problems faced and the solutions reached in the complex task of securing and presenting Wesley's text. The aim throughout is to enable Wesley to be read with maximum ease and understanding, and with minimal intrusion by the editors.

This edition includes all Wesley's original or mainly original prose works, together with one volume devoted to his *Collection of Hymns* (1780) and another to his extensive work as editor and publisher of extracts from the writings of others. An essential feature of the project is a Bibliography outlining the historical settings of the works published by Wesley and his brother Charles, sometimes jointly, sometimes separately. The Bibliography also offers full analytical data for identifying each of the two thousand editions of these 450 items that were published during the lifetime of John Wesley, and notes the location of copies. An index is supplied for each unit, and a General Index for the whole edition.

The Delegates of the Oxford University Press agreed to undertake publication, but announced in June 1982 that because of severe economic problems they would regretfully be compelled to withdraw from the enterprise with the completion in 1983 of Vol. 7, the *Collection of Hymns*. Abingdon Press offered its services, beginning with the publication of the first volume of the *Sermons* in 1984, the bicentennial year of the formation of American Methodism as an autonomous church. The new title now assumed, however, refers in general to the bicentennial of Wesley's total activities as author, editor, and publisher, from 1733 to 1791, especially as summarized in the first edition of his collected works in thirty-two volumes, 1771–74.

Dean Robert E. Cushman of Duke University undertook general administration and promotion of the project until 1971, when he was succeeded as President by Dean Joseph D. Quillian, Jr., of Southern Methodist University, these two universities having furnished the major support and guidance for the enterprise. During the decade 1961–70, the Editorial Committee supervised the task of setting editorial principles and procedures, and general editorship was shared by Dr. Eric W. Baker, Dean William R. Cannon, and Dean Cushman. In 1969 the Directors appointed Dr. Frank Baker, early attached to the project as bibliographer and textual editor for Wesley's text, as Editor-in-Chief also. Upon Dean Quillian's retirement in 1981, he was succeeded as President of the project by Dean James E. Kirby, Jr., also of Southern Methodist University. In 1986 the Directors appointed Richard P. Heitzenrater as General Editor to begin the chief editorship of the project with the *Journal and Diaries* unit.

Other sponsoring bodies have been successively added to the original four: The United Methodist Board of Higher Education and Ministry, The Commission on Archives and History of The United Methodist Church, and Boston University School of Theology. For the continuing support of the sponsoring institutions the Directors express their profound thanks. They gratefully acknowledge also the encouragement and financial support that have come from the historical Societies and Commissions on Archives and History of many Annual Conferences, as well as the donations of The World Methodist Council, The British Methodist Church, private individuals, and foundations.

On June 9, 1976, The Wesley Works Editorial Project was incorporated in the State of North Carolina as a nonprofit corporation. In 1977, by-laws were approved governing the appointment and duties of the Directors, their Officers, and their Executive Committee.

The Board of Directors

President: James E. Kirby, Dean of Perkins School of Theology, Southern Methodist University, Dallas, Texas

Vice-President: Robert E. Cushman, The Divinity School, Duke University, Durham, North Carolina

Secretary: Donald H. Treese, Associate General Secretary of The Division of the Ordained Ministry, The United Methodist Board of Higher Education and Ministry, Nashville, Tennessee

Treasurer: Thomas A. Langford, The Divinity School, Duke University, Durham, North Carolina

General Editor: Richard P. Heitzenrater, Perkins School of Theology, Southern Methodist University, Dallas, Texas

Textual Editor: Frank Baker, The Divinity School, Duke University, Durham, North Carolina

James M. Ault, Bishop of The United Methodist Church, Pittsburgh, Pennsylvania

Dennis M. Campbell, Dean of The Divinity School, Duke University, Durham, North Carolina

William R. Cannon, Candler School of Theology, Emory University, Atlanta, Georgia

Rupert E. Davies, Bristol, England

Joe Hale, General Secretary of The World Methodist Council, Lake Junaluska, North Carolina

Richard Nesmith, Dean of Boston University School of Theology, Boston, Massachusetts

PREFACE

No man can complete a work on the scale of the present edition of Wesley's *Journal* without incurring more obligations than can be acknowledged in a preface. It is right, however, to mention that I have had the constant assistance of the textual editor, Professor Baker, and the general editor, Professor Heitzenrater; that my Durham colleagues have patiently withstood endless interrogation on particular points; and that helpful assistance has been rendered by Dr. John Walsh, the Rev. Henry D. Rack, Professor Jan van den Berg, Dr. Thomas Munk, Dr. David Hempton, Roy Huddleston, and the archivists of the Moravian Church Archives in Herrnhut and of the Representative Church Body in Dublin. Various readers have kindly helped me with comments on the introduction, including, amongst others not already mentioned, Dr. Anne Orde, Professor Patrick Collinson, and Professor Richard Watson. Miss Joan Grant has been a typist of exemplary stamina and accuracy. In our sister city of Durham in America, Professor Baker pays testimony to the skilled and devoted assistance over many years of Miss Ruby Bailey as typist and Mrs. Enid Hickingbotham as assistant copy-editor. To all, I am most grateful. To the reader I should say that the principal object of the introduction to a document of this kind ought to be to locate its position in the history of the *genre*, and that has been my object here. Readers whose principal concern is to discover what the *Journal* may reveal about Wesley as a man are invited to proceed directly to that section of the introduction.

W. R. W.

CONTENTS

xi

Contents

ILLUSTRATIONS

Permission for reproduction of illustrations:
    1,3,6—Bridwell Library, Southern Methodist University
        2—Drew University Library
    4,5—Hargrett Rare Book and Manuscript Library, University of Georgia
      Libraries
7,8,9,10—Methodist Archives, The John Rylands University Library of
      Manchester

SIGNS, SPECIAL USAGES, ABBREVIATIONS

[ ]   Indicate editorial insertions or substitutions in the original text, or (with a query) doubtful readings.

< >   Indicate conjectural readings in manuscripts where the original text is defective.

. . .   Indicate a passage omitted by the writer from the original and so noted by Wesley, usually by dash.

[. . .]   Indicate a passage omitted silently by Wesley from a text he was quoting, to which the present editor is drawing attention; the brackets are not used in editorial annotations and introductions.

(( ))   Enclose passages within a manuscript struck through for erasure.

[[ ]]   Enclose passages supplied by the present editors from cipher or shorthand, from an abstract or similar document in the third person, or reconstructed from secondary evidence.

a,b,c   Small superscript letters indicate footnotes supplied by Wesley.

1,2,3   Small superscript figures indicate footnotes supplied by the editor.

Cf.   Before a scriptural or other citation by Wesley, indicates that he was quoting with more than minimal inexactness, yet nevertheless displaying the passage as a quotation.

See   Before a scriptural citation indicates an undoubted allusion or a quotation which was not displayed as such by Wesley, and which is more than minimally inexact.

Wesley's publications. Where a work by Wesley was first published separately, its title is italicized; where it first appeared within a different work such as a collected volume, the title appears within quotation marks. References such as '*Bibliography*, No. 3' are to the forthcoming Bibliography in this edition (Vols. 33–34), which has a different numbering system from Richard Green's *Wesley Bibliography*.

Book-titles in Wesley's text are italicized if accurate, and given in roman type with capitals if inaccurate. If a title consists of only one generic word which forms a major part of the original title, it is italicized; but if it is inaccurate (such as 'Sermons' for a volume entitled *Discourses*), it is printed in lower case roman.

Abbreviations. In addition to many common and fairly obvious abbreviations, the following are used in the notes: A[nswer], Conf[erence], Meth[odis]m, Meth[odist], Q[uestion], Wes[leyan].

Works and institutions frequently cited are abbreviated thus:

BCP   The Book of Common Prayer, London, 1662.

Signs, Special Usages, Abbreviations

Bibliography	Frank Baker, *A Descriptive and Analytical Bibliography of the Publications of John and Charles Wesley* (in preparation), Vols. 33–34 in this edn.
Curnock	Nehemiah Curnock, ed., *The Journal of the Rev. John Wesley, A.M.*, 8 vols., London, Epworth Press, 1938.
CWJ	Thomas Jackson, ed., *The Journal of the Rev. Charles Wesley, M.A.*, 2 vols., London, Wes. Meth. Bookroom, 1849.
Jackson	Thomas Jackson, ed., *The Works of the Rev. John Wesley*, 4th edn., 14 vols., London, Mason, 1840–42.
JW	John Wesley (1703–91).
JWJ	John Wesley's *Journal.*
Loeb	The Loeb Classical Library, London, Heinemann; Cambridge, Mass., Harvard Univ. Press.
OED	Sir James A. H. Murray et al., *A New English Dictionary on Historical Principles*, 11 vols., Oxford, Clarendon Press, 1884–1933.
SPCK	Society for Promoting Christian Knowledge.
SPG	Society for the Propagation of the Gospel.
Telford	John Telford, ed., *The Letters of the Rev. John Wesley*, 8 vols., London, Sharp, 1931.
Works (1771–74)	John Wesley, *The Works of the Rev. John Wesley, M.A.*, 32 vols., Bristol, Pine, 1771–74.
WHS	*The Proceedings of the Wesley Historical Society*, 1898– .

INTRODUCTION

JOHN WESLEY'S *Journal* has always been used as a major source for the life of its writer, but it has become a problematic one. It stands as a monument to a literary genre now lost. Though the *Journal* in its entirety has been available in print for almost two centuries, its editors have established almost nothing about the methods and motives of its composition (or even the date it first appeared). Still more important, no effort has been made to locate this huge document in the context of literary history.[1] The *Journal* undoubtedly contains evidences for the man, but its evidences and, still more, its reticences make sense chiefly in the light of the common expectations of the writer and his original readers. Quarrying for Wesley in the *Journal* is a circuitous affair, and the nature of the indirect approach for which it calls emerges with the greatest ultimate clarity from a circuitous approach to the *Journal*. To establish the historical 'location' of the *Journal* is to establish also what may be reasonably expected from it for Wesley biography and to give a sharper profile to the style of editing it requires.

I. AUTOBIOGRAPHY BEFORE WESLEY AND DURING HIS EARLIER YEARS

THOUGH the *Oxford English Dictionary* traces the word 'autobiography' only from 1809, autobiographical writing is a genre of immense antiquity: Georg Misch found it necessary to begin his *Geschichte der Autobiographie* with the Assyrians. When Wesley tried his hand at this vein, the vitality of autobiography was being attested by substantial changes of form and content and by a vast increase in the numbers of those who were prepared to make an

---

[1] Cf., e.g., the engaging but unsystematic account of the *Journal* given in John Butt and Geoffrey Carnall, *The Mid-Eighteenth Century*, Vol. 8 in *Oxford History of English Literature* (Oxford, 1979), pp. 276-78, with Georg Misch, *Geschichte der Autobiographie* (Frankfurt, 1907–69), 4(Pt. 2):793-94, which nobly attempts to establish the international context but omits mention of the *Journal* in favour of Thomas Jackson's *Lives of Early Methodist Preachers*. W. Matthews, *British Autobiographies* (Berkeley, 1955), p. 323, excludes the *Journal* in favour of J. A. Léger, *John Wesley's Last Love* (London, 1910). The whole subject is briefly treated by G. A. Benrath in *Theologische Realenzyklopädie*, IV.772-89.

attempt to write it. The growing army of men and women who would now commit something of their experience and history to a diary or journal certainly implies a growing will to imagine, delimit, and affirm a self, and, eclectic in his style of journal writing as in his theology, Wesley embodied features of the styles of many of his contemporaries and predecessors in his own work. This is important because of two of the constraints under which he wrote. Unlike the *Journal,* the bulk of the autobiographical writing in Wesley's time and earlier was not written for publication; much did not appear in print until the nineteenth century, and much remains in manuscript. A large measure of the interest of these private Lives as a source for historical psychology lies in the fact that they were written independently of each other, and their very existence is evidence of a ground-swell of imaginative effort which led ultimately to the publication of the influential examplars in this style, Rousseau's *Confessions* (published posthumously in 1782), Goethe's *Dichtung und Wahrheit* (1811–33), or Johann Herder's attempt to comprehend autobiography in a scheme of thought preoccupied with ideas of history, of the individual and humanity. And of course autobiographical self-representation, published or unpublished, was all the time closely linked with other attempts to represent a self in novels, biography, and letters.[2]

To mention the superb work *Dichtung und Wahrheit* in relation to Wesley's *Journal* is to compare like with unlike in terms of personal self-revelation. The truth is that Wesley's *Journal* has much more in common with its literary predecessors than with its successors. The second constraint under which he wrote was that he was in no way encouraged to surpass his predecessors by the limited expectations of the theoreticians of the genre, who were indeed unable even to classify the materials they had inherited. Editors of autobiographies claimed for their wares greater authenticity than biographies by another hand[3] which either

---

[2] Not all biography found its way into print. In the evangelical world A. G. Spangenberg, who found great difficulty in holding his theological viewpoint in harness with his genuine veneration for Zinzendorf, was compelled only by use of the lot first to write and then to publish his *Life* of the Count (G. Reichel, *August Gottlieb Spangenberg* [Tübingen, 1906], pp. 215-19; reprint in *Nikolaus Ludwig von Zinzendorf: Materialien und Dokumente* [Hildesheim, 1971], Reihe 2, Bd. 13). Of the remarkable *Lives* of Zinzendorf from an enlightenment viewpoint that by Schrautenbach (1782) was not published till 1851 (reprint, 1972), and that by Schachmann (1786) was not given general circulation till 1981.

[3] A. Cocchi, 'Foreword of the Italian Editor' to the first edition of the *Vita di Benvenuto*

gushed like a funeral panegyric[4] or, inhibited by envy or lack of material, said too little.[5] The earliest writer, to my knowledge, who attempted to give some shape to the subject, Gottfried Wagner, who produced a dissertation on *Scriptores qui de sua ipsi vita exposuerunt* (Wittenberg, 1716), shared this general view, for he provided the minimum of biographical data for the authors admitted to his catalogue, and fleshed out the bare bones with quotations from their autobiographies, clearly regarded as superior material. That autobiography might not even be clearly distinguished from biography was illustrated, as Wesley began to write, by Gabriel Wilhelm Götten in a kind of academic "Who's Who" which had many successors.[6] He solicited from his authors brief accounts of their life and writings with a view to reworking them himself. By this device he might achieve unity of treatment and stamp the work with his own judgment. This view, that the business of the autobiographer was to supply true facts for the biographer, was even lower than that which had marked the autobiographies of scholars in the past; it was supported by historians who thought that the evidence of reliable participants was to be preferred to other sources only in cases of doubt and after strict examination;[7] it was upheld by encyclopaedists[8] and exploited by authors in straits. Richard Baxter even prepared *Reliquiae Baxterianae; or, Mr. Richard Baxter's Narrative of the Most*

Cellini (Naples, 1728), trans. Goethe, *Goethes Werke*, (Weimar, 1887–1919), Abtl. I, 43:3-8.

[4] 'D. Phil. Jacob Speners eigenhändig aufgesetzter Lebens-Lauff', Heinrich Anselm von Ziegler und Kliphausen, *Continuirter historischer Schau-Platz und Labyrinth der Zeit* (Leipzig, 1718), p. 856a.

[5] Foreword of Friedrich Heinrich Theunen to Jacob Friedrich Reimann, *Eigene Lebens-Beschreibung* (Brunswick, 1745), pp. [1, 8].

[6] Gabriel Wilhelm Götten, *Das jetzt-lebende gelehrte Europa*, 3 vols, (Braunschweig, Hildesheim, and Celle, 1735–40; reprint, Hildesheim, 1977), 1:[21], [23], [25-26]. Among Götten's German successors was one who performed a similar service for the British: Jeremiah David Reuss, *Alphabetical Register of All the Authors Actually Living in Great Britain, Ireland, and the United Provinces of North America* (Berlin and Stettin, 1791). Jonathan Edwards's *Life of David Brainerd* (1749), which was re-edited by John Wesley, was an immensely successful biography composed principally of autobiographical journal material; the new Yale edition (1985) tips the balance back towards autobiography by incorporating much material from Brainerd which Edwards excluded.

[7] Henry St. John, Viscount Bolingbroke, *Letters on the Study and Use of History* (London, 1752), I.134-37; and Lenglet du Fresnoy, *A New Method of Studying History*, trans. R. Rawlinson (London, 1728), pp. 212-17, 221-25.

[8] J. H. Zedler, *Grosses vollständiges Universal-Lexicon aller Wissenschaften und Künste* (Halle und Leipzig, 1735; reprint, Graz, 1961), Vol. 13, cols. 284-85 (Art. *Histoire*).

Memorable Passages of his Life and Times[9] for literary executors to lick into shape after his death. The licking resulted in changes being made in the texts of what was in fact a file of documents, without any gain in coherence or readability, and when in 1702 Calamy came to prepare a memorial to the great man which might not be stillborn,[10] he turned Baxter's first-person account into a third-person narrative in which only the clash of styles indicates where the Puritan Baxter ends and the Augustan Calamy begins.

Lives of scholars formed a large part of the published work in this field,[11] and Wesley's *Journal* has a kinship with them in more than the fact of publication. Scholars were noted for a professional clannishness. Humanists recorded each other for posterity in memorial addresses from the sixteenth century onwards, and it was usual for a man's life to be prefixed or appended to posthumous editions of his works.[12] In Wesley's day, for example, John Gillies prefixed a full-scale *Life* of George Whitefield to the *Works* of that notable preacher.[13] The conflicts which began in the Reformation period gave articulate scholars every reason to state their own case against detractors, ahead of what might be done on their behalf by writers of memorials or obituarists. Melanchthon let it be known that Luther had intended writing an autobiographical introduction to the second part of the complete edition of his works, but had not lived to complete the task.[14] A whole life-history might seem a necessary

[9] (London, 1696).

[10] Edmund Calamy, *An Abridgement of Mr. Baxter's History of his Life and Times* (London, 1702); J. M. Lloyd Thomas, ed., *The Autobiography of Richard Baxter* (Everyman edn., London, 1931), pp. xxx-xxxvii. Calamy's *Historical Account of my Own Life*, not edited by J. T. Rutt till 1829, also blurred the line between biography and autobiography by including a good deal of material (ch. 1) about the church fathers and English notabilities derived from letters and biographies, on the grounds that 'whereas there is a vast multitude of volumes extant (even enow to make a tolerable library) of the epistles of men of letters, it is easy to observe, that they have very generally been as much esteemed as any part of their works' (*Historical Account*, I.4). On the general problem of Baxter's autobiography see W. M. Lamont, *Richard Baxter and the Millennium* (London, 1979), p. 79.

[11] For a more theoretical treatment in this vein see Günter Niggl, *Geschichte der deutschen Autobiographie im 18. Jahrhundert: Theoretische Grundlegung und literarische Entfaltung* (Stuttgart, 1977).

[12] Erasmus arranged in his will for his executors, in lieu of other celebrations, to publish a complete edition of his works with a biography written by Beatus Rhenanus and dedicated to Charles V. *Omnia opera D. Erasmi*, 19 vols. (Basel, 1540–42).

[13] *The Works of the Reverend G. W. . . . to which is Prefixed an Account of His Life* [by J. Gillies], 6 vols. (London, 1771–72).

[14] *Opera quae supersunt omnia*, 28 vols., ed. C. G. Bretschneider, in *Corpus Reformatorum*, (Halle, 1834, etc.), Vol. 6, col. 155.

part of an intellectual defence; equally a polemical occasion might be a necessary excuse for publishing as distinct from writing it. Numerous in the sixteenth century, autobiographies of this kind continued down to Wesley's day. One notable seventeenth-century example of this was afforded by Johann Valentin Andreae (1586–1654), the great champion of the kingdom of God in Württemberg.[15] Andreae was a man who combined many of the intellectual forces of his age with much passion of his own and an obsession with the complexity and fragility of life. Reflection of this kind enabled him to make an innovation in the literary form to which Wesley did not aspire, combining topical and chronological treatment of his life within the same structure. He succeeded in treating the first thirty-four years of his life in two general chapters and then went over to a diary form to give a fresh impression of annual or six-monthly periods. This kind of writing was still not strong on well-defined form; Misch notes that Andreae's description of his annals as 'the rhapsody of his life' recurs in both Shaftesbury and Schleiermacher,[16] and it could well be applied to Wesley's *Journal*.

One large group of spiritual writers of a scholarly kind stood not far behind Wesley himself. Anna Maria van Schurman, the devout blue-stocking of the Netherlands (1607–78),[17] Wesley read more than once, finding her 'perhaps a woman of the strongest understanding that the world ever saw'.[18] She wrote in Latin to obtain a wider readership. But the rest of this group were French and owed their need for defence to the curious religious history of France in the later seventeenth century. The Bourbons had been as late as the Habsburgs in espousing the Counter-Reformation as an ideological platform, but remarkable results then followed. A genuine religious revival in the mid-seventeenth century, followed by the creation of the most powerful state-machine in Europe, an organization of crushing weight,

---

[15] Andreae's *Vita* was edited by F. H. Rheinwald (Berlin, 1849); a German translation appeared in D. F. Seybold, *Selbstbiographen berühmter Männer*, Vol. III (Wintherthur, 1799). On Andreae, see Heinrich Hermelink, *Geschichte der evangelischen Kirche in Württemberg von der Reformation bis zur Gegenwart* (Stuttgart, 1949), pp. 138-47; and Hartmut Lehmann, *Pietismus und weltliche Ordnung in Württemberg von 17. bis zum 20. Jahrhundert* (Stuttgart, 1969), pp. 22-23.

[16] Misch, *Geschichte der Autobiographie*, 4(Pt. 2):687.

[17] Anna Maria van Schurman, *Encleria seu Melioris Partis electio* (Altonae ad albim, 1673). See A. Ritschl, *Geschichte des Pietismus* (Bonn, 1880–86; reprint, Berlin, 1966), I.206-8.

[18] Curnock I.453n.; JWJ, Feb. 14, 1774.

produced in the early eighteenth century near-unanimity in church attendance (if the Easter Communion figures may be taken as a guide), a level of practice which France had never attained before and which neither France nor any other major state was to reach again. In this process, French writers added to the common stock of mankind a remarkable body of religious literature, but churchmen of whatever sort found it increasingly difficult to harmonize the claims not merely of God and mammon, but of king and pope, authority and conscience. To those who went to the wall, autobiography was a necessary defence. The writers of Port Royal, who had already translated the *Confessions* of St. Augustine and St. Teresa, began a series of confessions in express imitation of those of the church fathers.[19] This effort, however, did not generate autobiography of quality, for the Jansenists succumbed to the doctrine of Pascal that avoiding speaking of oneself, avoiding even using the words 'I' and 'me', was part of the annihilation of self-love.

A different form of self-defence was required by Mme. Guyon (1648–1717) whose writings, together with those of her adherent and publicist Pierre Poiret, the reformed preacher at Metz,[20] were of real consequence to Wesley, as to the pietists in Germany. Mme. Guyon, the offspring of Provençal aristocracy, and later in touch with the great aristocratic ladies of Paris in the days of the Fronde, appeared at the court of Louis XIV in the eighties as the official struggle against quietism was beginning. Begun in prison, her autobiography has the double interest of setting forth her clash with authority, and analysing the special peculiarities of her spiritual way, which she distinguished from that of the body of mystical literature she had mastered: a purely inward movement which supplanted the images of metaphor, appearance, or ecstasy. Mme. Guyon's assertion that rapturous devotion was the true human condition and the enduring constitution of her inner life had an autobiographical as well as religious signif-

---

[19] C. A. Sainte-Beuve, *Port Royal* (Paris, 1840), I.425.

[20] *La Vie de Mme J. M. B. de la Mothe-Guyon écrite par elle-même* (Paris, 1791). In 1694 Mme. Guyon submitted her MS to Bossuet, who put it before the bishops' conference. A first draft was burned at the behest of her spiritual director. The work was finally published in 1720 by Pierre Poiret. On Poiret see Gustav A. Krieg, *Der mystische Kreis, Wesen und Werden der Theologie Pierre Poirets* (Göttingen, 1979). On Mme. Guyon see Heinrich Heppe, *Geschichte der quietistischen Mystik in der katholischen Kirche* (Berlin, 1875; reprint, Hildesheim, 1978).

icance and was echoed even in Rousseau and Schopenhauer.[21]

Founders of new religious movements were under special pressure to explain or defend themselves in this kind of way. George Fox's *Journal* was indeed published posthumously by a committee,[22] but its title, *A Journal or Historical Account of the Life, Travels, Sufferings, Christian Experiences, and Labour of Love in the Work of the Ministry*, linked it with that special and voluminous literature of Quaker sufferings which the Society of Friends made it its business to elicit[23] and which helped to make its Meeting for Sufferings a notable political pressure group.[24] The Quakers offered Wesley abundant instruction in securing constitutional redress for bad treatment. In Germany there was no such support for religious dissidence, and Johann Wilhelm Petersen (1649–1727) and his wife Johanna Eleonora (née von Merlau) (1644–1724), both of whom broke from their moorings, offered what explanation they could in published autobiographies. Petersen had been a professor at Rostock and a superintendent in Lübeck and then Lüneburg, but a career in the religious establishments was closed to him by chiliastic visions of the restoration of all things. The psychological analysis of pietist autobiography was of no consequence to Petersen, who had a series of direct visions to relate, visions which disclosed the meaning of the apocalypse.[25] Eleonora Petersen, who had first published her autobiography in 1689 to explain why she had gradually turned from the noble world to devotion to Christ, republished it in 1719 as a supplement to her husband's life, enlarged by a series of dreams and chiliastic meditations.[26]

---

[21] Arthur Schopenhauer, *Die Welt als Wille und Vorstellung*, in *Sämtliche Werke*, 9 vols. (Zürich, 1977), 1:446-71.

[22] *A Journal or Historical Account of the Life, Travels, Sufferings, Christian Experiences, and Labour of Love in the Work of the Ministry of. . . George Fox*, ed. W. Penn (London, 1694–98).

[23] *Brief Accounts* and *Particular Accounts of the Late and Present Sufferings of the People called Quakers* (London, 1680, etc.) were legion, as were biographical compendia to the same effect. By 1725 the Quakers had published over 80 religious confessions and journals. Luella M. Wright, *The Literary Life of the Early Friends, 1650–1725* (New York, 1932), pp. 110, 237-38.

[24] N. C. Hunt, *Two Early Political Associations* (Oxford, 1961), pp. 1-112.

[25] *Lebensbeschreibung Johannis Wilhelm-Petersen* (2nd edn., n.p., 1719). See also Walter Nordman, 'Die Eschatologie des Ehepaares Petersen, ihre Entwicklung und Auflösung'; *Zeitschrift des Vereins für Kirchengeschichte der Provinz Sachsen und des Freistaates Anhalt* (1930), 26:83-108; (1931), 27:1-19; and F. Groth, *Die "Wiederbringung aller Dinge" im Württembergischhen Pietismus* (Göttingen, 1984), pp. 38-59.

[26] The autobiography was first published as an appendix to *Gespräche des Hertzens mit Gott*, Aufgesetzet von Johanna Eleonora Petersen (Ploen, 1689), pp. 235-95; and

Another apologia which Wesley seems not to have encountered was that of Zinzendorf, published in 1746 under the title ΠΕΡΙ ΕΑΥΤΟΥ: *Das ist Naturelle Reflexiones.*[27] Public attacks upon the Moravians reached a violent climax in the 1740s just when attacks on English Methodism began to abate. Zinzendorf took the aristocratic line that polemic was a profession for mere scholars, but had ultimately to make a number of replies. The *Naturelle Reflexiones* was a fascinating and curious performance. Much of the book was cast in the modish form of the literary journal, the style which Germany had embraced so enthusiastically from *The Tatler* and *The Spectator.*[28] The title was an appeal against the intellectual traditions of Lutheranism to new currents of sensibility; yet Zinzendorf was somehow to defend himself without vulgar personal disclosure.[29] The feat was triumphantly brought off with the bland assertion that 'I have not the convenience of being one of those people who are either governed by feeling or just amused by feeling. I am one of the thinking people, one of those who think very abstractly, think very quickly, and whose thoughts cohere so closely as to leave no room for concrete images between them. I do not reject feeling. . . . But I am in no way to be reckoned among those who look upon feeling as a talent.'[30] The unifying theme of his life is *Condescendenz*—not just aristocratic superiority, but a consistent disposition to peaceful dealings with critics. This quality was compared by Zinzendorf himself to the 'charity' of 1 Cor. 13, a grace which as a minimum made it 'impossible to hate what is impossible to love'.[31] He presented a series of scenes from his past constructed on this principle, and when he came to the point in time where the method would no longer work, conducted his

reappeared as *Leben Frauen Johannä Eleonorä Petersen . . . als ein zweyter Theil zu Ihres Ehe-Herrn Lebens-Beschreibung beygefüget* (n.p., 1719).

[27] Reprinted in Nikolaus Ludwig von Zinzendorf, *Ergänzungsbände zu den Hauptschriften* (Hildesheim, 1964), Bd. 4.

[28] See Wolfgang Martens, *Die Botschaft der Tugend: Die Aufklärung im Spiegel der deutschen Moralischen Wochenschriften* (Stuttgart, 1971).

[29] And certainly not disclosure of the kind which had lately emerged from a revival milieu in M. Adam Bernd, *Eigene Lebens-Beschreibung* (Leipzig, 1738; new edn. by Volker Hoffmann, Munich, 1973). In this work Bernd, a melancholic given to suicide attempts, tried to provide his readers, especially those with medical expertise, with material for research into his miserable condition to the tune of more than 400 pages of economical modern type and, rather unsuccessfully, to combine physiological explanations of his own with religious interpretations of punishment for sin and tempting God.

[30] *Naturelle Reflexiones*, p. 4.

[31] Ibid., p. 16.

controversy mostly without mentioning names, thus moving back towards the unpretentious kind of autobiography derived from the family chronicle. Moreover Zinzendorf's method reveals as well as conceals; if in the end he always fell out with men of independent mind, he had a striking ability to make a good first impression, and the autobiography helps to show how this was done. Wesley's *Journal* could quite easily have been bounded by this literary genre. In fact his closest approximation to it came in his *Short History of the People called Methodists* (1781),[32] and this, as the *Journal* shows,[33] he used as preaching material, especially late in life when he needed educative and expository matter. Indeed in the *Naturelle Reflexiones* and its appendices, Zinzendorf included materials which could have stood independently as a short history of the Moravians, much in Wesley's vein.[34]

Both Zinzendorf and Wesley belonged to that family of related religious movements commonly called pietist, which reacted against the scriptural objectivity of the doctrines of salvation as they were upheld in Protestant Orthodoxy, both Lutheran and Reformed;[35] and there were many of this kind who in the eighteenth century began to wish to realize the history of salvation not only as an objective and outward fact but as an event of the soul. This enabled them to add a dimension to autobiographical writing of an entirely different order from the defensive tracts we have been discussing and formed one of many links between them and the last great Protestant religious movement, the wave of international Puritanism of the first half of the seventeenth century.

Whether or not the custom of requiring testimonies of an interior work of grace from prospective church members originated in America has been much debated;[36] certainly

---

[32] *Bibliography*, No. 420.i (see Vol. 9 of this edn.; Jackson, XIII.303-81).

[33] E.g., JWJ, May 18, 1788.

[34] *Naturelle Reflexiones*, pp. 131-44; Beilage 2, pp. 33-62.

[35] In this essay the word 'Orthodoxy' appears in upper case where the reference is to the parties, both Lutheran and Reformed, which developed the theology of the early Reformers into a highly articulated doctrinal system. With Orthodoxy in this sense the pietists and promoters of religious revival were frequently in severe conflict. There is no reference in this introduction to any of the Orthodox churches, nor is any judgment made here as to the orthodoxy (in lower case) of any of the eighteenth-century parties.

[36] Edmund S. Morgan, *Visible Saints: The History of a Puritan Idea* (New York, 1963), p. 73; G. F. Nuttall, *Visible Saints: The Congregational Way, 1640–1660* (Oxford, 1957), pp. 111-12. On Puritan conversion narratives generally, especially in America, see Patricia Caldwell, *The Puritan Conversion Narrative: The Beginnings of American Expression* (Cambridge, Eng., 1983).

testimonies of this sort were required in Rotterdam and England before the English Civil War, and they became characteristic of the Congregational as distinct from the Presbyterian churches. In so far as Puritanism was 'a movement towards immediacy, towards direct communion with God through his Holy Spirit, in independence of all outward and creaturely aids',[37] it was always likely to take this turn; even in churches, like that of Scotland, which did not require of members a testimony to the work of grace within, diaries of God's dealings with the soul burgeoned in numbers unknown amongst, for example, Roman Catholics.[38] During the Civil War testimonies of religious experience were published in great numbers,[39] testimonies which took classic shape in Bunyan's *Grace Abounding*.[40] The requirement of testimonies of this kind could still be assumed as normative in America by Cotton Mather in 1702,[41] but it was already a question whether it was bruising to individuals and incapable of taking a satisfactory literary form. Certainly the authentication of religious experience in the light of well-known Puritan patterns[42] began to look uncommonly like a new legalism. Right at the beginning indeed, Henry Walker, ironmonger, had offered the liberal encouragement that there were 216 signs, the possession of any one of which ought to convince a man that he was indeed a child of God,[43] but in the middle of the eighteenth century Jonathan Edwards was admitting that the effect of the systematization of the Christian life to which the requirement of testimonies had given rise was that 'many persons seem to be prejudiced against affections and experiences that come in by such a method as has been insisted upon by many divines; . . . they look upon all such

[37] G. F. Nuttall, *The Holy Spirit in Puritan Faith and Experience* (2nd edn., Oxford, 1947), pp. 91-92.

[38] Ibid., p. 7 and n. 5.

[39] E.g., John Beadle, *Diary of a Thankful Christian* (London, 1656), and the titles listed in Nuttall, *Visible Saints*, p. 111, n. 2. See also L. D. Lerner, 'Puritanism and the Spiritual Autobiography', *Hibbert Journal* (1956–57), 54:373-86.

[40] See below, pp. 32-33.

[41] Cotton Mather, *Magnalia Christi Americana; or, The Ecclesiastical History of New-England; from its First Planting, in the Year 1620, unto the Year of our Lord 1698* (3rd edn., Hartford, 1853; reprint, Edinburgh, 1979), II.226-27.

[42] Summarized by Morgan (*Visible Saints*, p. 72) as 'knowledge, conviction, faith, combat, and true, imperfect assurance'; and by Lerner ('Puritanism', p. 374) as 'serious childhood, sinful youth, legal righteousness often preceded by a struggle, and final illumination'.

[43] *The Sermon of Henry Walker, Ironmonger* (London, 1642), quoted in Caldwell, *Puritan Conversion Narrative*, pp. 153-54.

schemes, laying down such methods and steps to be of men's devising; . . . what they have experienced is insensibly strained to bring all to an exact conformity to the scheme established.'[44]

This embarrassment was immensely eased at the beginning of the Great Awakening by Whitefield's preaching of the new birth. For the experience of regeneration seemed to validate reformed doctrine, and reformed doctrine appeared demonstrably to trigger off the experience of regeneration, for no converts were observed where the pulpit was in possession of 'dead and Arminian time-servers'. The most profound analysis of the experience, Jonathan Edwards's *Treatise on Religious Affections*, entered every possible *caveat*, but came in the end to an aesthetic conclusion. Regeneration was an apprehension of beauty, an inner harmony achieved by the experiential discovery of the 'divine sweetness' at a level unknown to the 'reason' of the deist.[45] And this sense of beauty had its autobiographical model in *The Life and Diary of the Rev. David Brainerd*, the missionary to the Indians, which Edwards prepared for publication[46] and Wesley abridged for his own flock.[47] Important as Edwards was for Wesley, the latter's own religious experience was not quintessentially aesthetic, and he had to produce some exemplary reply from the standpoint of the 'time-serving Arminian'. This was a demand which left its mark on the *Journal*, and still more on the *Arminian Magazine*. The *Magazine* contained numerous obituaries in which a cursory account of the life introduced an extended narrative of the triumphant death; the most telling answer to the equation of Arminianism with deadness was the evidence of victory in extremis. The failures in the Reformed tradition adequately to link life and conversion led Edwards to complain of a new legalism; paradoxically they helped to push Wesley into an overemphasis on the significance of death.

Wesley himself might have been surprised at this charge, for he certainly regarded himself as offering a release from the tyranny

[44] Jonathan Edwards, *Treatise on Religious Affections* (1746), in S. E. Dwight and E. Hickman, eds., *Works* (London, 1834; reprint, Edinburgh, 1974), I.252, 255, 324. *An Extract* from this treatise appeared in Wesley's *Works* (1773), Vol. XXIII, but seems not to have been published separately in Wesley's lifetime. 'Out of this dangerous heap, wherein much wholesome food is mixed with deadly poison, I have selected many remarks and admonitions which may be of great use to the children of God' (Jackson, XIV.270).

[45] Edwards, *Works*, I.281.

[46] Ibid., II.313-458.

[47] *An Extract of the Life of the late Rev. Mr. David Brainerd* (Bristol, 1748; reprinted 7 times before 1839); *Bibliography*, No. 310 (see Vol. 16 of this edn.).

of death in popular religion as it is known to us through the chap-books. The figure of death in the twopenny godlies was a 'pedagogue . . . pointing a bony finger at the way to conversion', more potent in his power to condemn than Christ was to save.[48] Seventeenth-century Englishmen were as obsessed with death as their fellows in New England,[49] and English Puritans must cope with the obsession as best they might. In their work, biography and autobiography were important because examples were held to be more important than precepts, and they were able, within a common framework of doctrine, to illustrate the variety of God's electing strategy, his dealings with endlessly different individuals. After 1660 the fruits of two generations of Puritan teaching about the management of experimental religion were reaped in a host of biographies and autobiographies. What had been in the 1630s and 1640s a handful of lives of preachers prefacing their collected works or appended to their funeral sermons became a spate of productions by laymen, including many substantial collections of mass biography,[50] as the full fruits were reaped of diary-keeping and a long tradition of practical divinity.[51] Some of the autobiographies of preachers have considerable resemblance to the secular family chronicles to which reference will be made later; but there are attempts, however ineffective, to link the story with the ways of God. The Rev. Ralph Josselin offered 'a thankful observacon of divine providence and goodness towards me';[52] Adam Martindale drew out the spiritual significance of his tale with a series of moralizing notes in proverbial form at the end of each chapter and compressed his conversion experience into a single sentence.[53] Henry Newcome, in a work which necessarily found much more room for politics than Wesley's *Journal*,

---

[48] Margaret Spufford, *Small Books and Pleasant Histories* (London, 1981), pp. 136, 207.

[49] See David E. Stannard, *The Puritan Way of Death* (New York, 1977).

[50] A number of these were made by Samuel Clarke (1599–1683), who held that 'collected lives' like those assembled by Plutarch and Melchior Adams had much better staying power than small individual biographical essays. His *Lives of Sundry Eminent Persons in this Later Age* (1683), much bowdlerized and modified, was included by Wesley in his *Christian Library* (1749–55), vols. 26 and 27 (see vols. 15 and 16 in 1822 edn.).

[51] Owen C. Watkins, to whom this paragraph is indebted, lists over 200 titles, several of them being substantial collections of Clarke's kind. *The Puritan Experience* (London, 1972).

[52] E. Hockliffe, ed., *The Diary of the Rev. Ralph Josselin, 1616–1683* (London, 1908). On Josselin see also A. Macfarlane, *The Family Life of Ralph Josselin, a 17th Century Clergyman* (London, 1970), and *The Diary of Ralph Josselin* (Oxford, 1976).

[53] R. Parkinson, ed., *The Life of Adam Martindale Written by Himself*, Chetham Society 4 (Manchester, 1845; reprint, New York, 1968), p. 36.

indicated his conversion in less than a line ('I had notable stirrings in my heart').[54] Laymen might enlarge more fully and beat their pastors into print; but from an early date (Watkins reckons 1666) even their accounts were published almost exclusively after death. The belief that exceptional initiatives by the Holy Spirit were at hand, which had been so powerful during the Civil War, was in decline. It was Quakers who sat lightest to the letter of Scripture and who most strenuously resisted the weight of institutionalism in the name of the leadings of the Spirit, and it was Quakers who continued longest to publish the experience of individuals.

While the Reformed tradition had been struggling with the problem of describing and analysing an interior work of grace, important developments in the art of autobiography had taken place in that family of religious movements in Central Europe to which Methodism was as nearly related as it was to the Reformed tradition. These developments left their mark even on Wesley's *Journal;* for in some of the most moving pages he relates the testimonies of Christian David and his friends, the original pioneers of the settlement on Zinzendorf's estates at Herrnhut.[55] Precisely because pietism retained a vivid Reformation repudiation of works-righteousness and because it came speedily into conflict with the champions of Orthodoxy, Lutheran and Reformed, it could not be content with the impersonal and defensive tradition of German scholarly autobiography, and had to create a new kind of confessional literature. In varying degrees this literature had to answer the dogmatic charges of the Orthodox and the spiritual anxieties of the faithful created by the sheer militancy of the Orthodox insistence on their exclusive possession of the Lutheran tradition and their endless wrangling over what were and what were not things indifferent.[56] Somehow the pietists must dig deeper than most of the biographical and autobiographical literature in the field.

P. J. Spener's autobiography[57] made notably little progress in

---

[54] R. Parkinson, ed., *The Autobiography of Henry Newcome, M. A.*, Chetham Society 26-27 (Manchester, 1852), I.13.

[55] JWJ, Aug. 10, 1738.

[56] Ritschl, *Geschichte des Pietismus*, II.174, 191, 193, 261-62, 292, 411-13, 451, 521, 541.

[57] P. J. Spener, *Eigenhändig aufgesetzter Lebens-Lauff* in Ziegler und Kliphausen, *Continuirter historischer Shau-Platz*, pp. 856-62. The work was originally written between 1683 and 1686.

the new direction. He gave a narrative of his studies and professional career, presented as the fruit of providential leading, followed it up with a static account of his activities and failures as pastor and preacher, and concluded with a general confession of sin and request for forgiveness addressed to God and the congregation. In other words he simply arranged three traditional autobiographical forms of *curriculum vitae*, portrait, and *confessio* in series, and, in so far as he imparted a personal character to the work, it is to be found in a general tone of self-accusation.

Spener's form was, moreover, ill-suited to those accounts of conversion and the new birth which became the stock-in-trade of the pietist movement; the decisive breakthrough here as in so many other matters was achieved by August Hermann Francke (1663–1727). In 1690 and 1691 Francke cast his religious experience into the form of a history of conversion,[58] structured in precise phases and presented as a pattern of a whole conversion system.[59] Francke's scheme was a revival of the tradition of Augustine and Luther in a special form. Francke gave dynamic shape to his spiritual analysis; conviction of sin was followed by anxiety, by despair of faith, the desire for redemption, and wrestling in prayer. Then came a powerful penitential struggle (or *Busskampf*) and a shattering breakthrough to illumination and certainty of faith. Francke, one of the most remarkable organizers the Christian church has ever known, imparted an organized shape to the Christian life by which the individual Christian might hope to feel his spiritual pulse and test his progress with assurance, or later the Methodist class-leader might test that of the members of society in his care. Francke had been through a process of the sort he described, and believed that if men were to be moved at all, it would be by personal examples of this kind. His basic scheme served as the foundation of innumerable pietist diaries of daily self-observation, and these came to be supplemented by summary interpretations of the individual's conversion story. Both these forms were much used by pietists

---

[58] *August Hermann Franckens . . . Lebenslauff.* Reprinted in August Hermann Francke, *Werke in Auswahl*, ed. Erhard Peschke (Berlin, 1969), pp. 5-29. Peschke (p. 3) gives useful notes as to the confusion of autobiographical material relating to Francke in print and in the archive of the Franckesche Stiftungen.

[59] This system owed something to Arndt's attempts to rescue a living faith from a dead confessionalism (Ritschl, *Geschichte des Pietismus*, II.111) and is more fully described in E. Hirsch, *Geschichte des neueren evangelischen Theologie* (5th edn., Gütersloh, 1975), II.157-60.

outside the orbit of Halle, and, while the strict form of the Franckean conversion struggle did not always stand its ground, pietists found it hard to break away from because of their instinctive desire for a coherent and dramatic form in which to cast their conversion experiences.

Exactly as scholarly biography and autobiography had taken collective form, so did the new form of evangelical confession, the literary medium assisting a transition in social reality. For there is no doubt that the new religious movements exemplified in a high degree the ways men adapted to the decline of corporative *(ständisch)* society. Men found it increasingly difficult to locate themselves and their mutual relations within the framework of the inherited collective organization of society, but were abundantly ingenious in replacing lost community by new forms of fellowship; 'clubbability' became the order of the day, from the coffee-house to the class-meeting. The academic "Who's Who" of eighteenth-century Germany was from one point of view a device by which an intellectual guild reinforced its cohesion and prospects of survival in an age unwilling to regard learning as the monopoly of *academe* and well able to find alternatives to the methods long practised by academic theologians, logicians, and natural philosophers. The collective biography or autobiography of the regenerate suggested that the new-born enjoyed both an historical pedigree and a present fellowship, however hollow the forms of ecclesiastical Orthodoxy might become. To this double sense of community and separateness Wesley's *Journal* was in due course to contribute; the overt forms of collective biography and autobiography which he and his successors were to create contributed still more. The itinerant Methodist preacher sustained a very distinctive lifestyle; the autobiographies which Wesley collected for the *Arminian Magazine* and which were republished as the *Lives of Early Methodist Preachers*,[60] the obituaries of the preachers who died in the work, annually published in the *Minutes* of Conference from 1777, and collected in such works as Charles Atmore's *Methodist Memorial* (1801), powerfully reinforced their common conviction of being a living order in a society in which the old corporativeness (including that of the clergy) was in decay.

There were of course problems in a stance and a literature in

[60] The most useful edition of which is the fourth, in 6 vols. (London, 1871–72).

which cohesiveness was the fruit of self-conscious separation from mankind at large. There was bound to be discomfort in the position of those Methodist preachers who wished to claim at one and the same time that they were ministers in the church of Christ like any other, and yet that in life and calling they were unlike any other. Comparable problems had been present with this sort of literature from its origins in eighteenth-century Germany.

The most notable collection was that of Johann Heinrich Reitz, his *Historie der Wiedergebohrnen*.[61] Its object was indicated by a copious subtitle: 'Examples of godly Christians, famous and little known, of both sexes and all classes, how they were first called by God and then converted, and, after many struggles and anxieties, were brought by the spirit and the word of God to faith and peace of conscience'. Reitz provided an international gallery of the regenerate which enabled him to present the pietists as the lineal successors, not only of that Lutheran most of all devoted to the *studium pietatis*, Johann Arndt, but of mystics like Jacob Boehme and of the whole Puritan movement. (Among the numerous British names in his compendium are John Knox, Richard Baxter, and John Bunyan, together with Anthony Horneck, the famous German minister at the Savoy.) The problem which Reitz could not solve was how to demonstrate that this impressive communion of saints was a single fellowship on the principles of Francke's pattern of conversion. The more autobiographical material he introduced, the more he had mechanically to force it to shape, and the less likely he was either to fulfil his object of enabling each of his readers to judge where he stood in relation to the kingdom of God or to advance the understanding of biography.

These failures, however, did not deter Christian Gerber, a pietist pastor at Lockwitz, from attempting the task again with a history of the regenerate in Saxony.[62] This work was a product of the peculiar and intense piety of Upper Lusatia and aimed to continue the work of a sixteenth-century preacher at Zittau which

[61] When this was first published is not quite clear; the edition used was the fifth, published at Berleburg in 1724, a fourth edition appeared at Wesel in 1717, and a second in 1707. An alternative to this collection, published with the official commendation of the Halle divinity faculty, was produced by Erdmann Heinrich, Count Henckel, *Die letzten Stunden einiger der evangelischen Lehre zugethanen* (1st edn., Halle, 1720; 4th edn., much enlarged, in 4 parts, Halle, 1746).

[62] Christian Gerber, *Historie derer Wiedergebohrnen in Sachsen*, 6 parts (Dresden/Leipzig, 1725–29).

was still in use, Bruno Quino's *Disce Mori* (1582). It hoped to avoid the 'fanaticism' of Reitz and, against the Saxon Orthodoxy threatening Lusatia since the annexation of that province in 1623, maintained that 'the dear God does not solely acknowledge us evangelicals as his own and absolutely reject Papists and Reformed. . . . No. No. He has among other religions still his children and his worshippers.' Above all the work stated clearly on the lines of Spener the nature and necessity of the new birth and offered balm to anxious souls by listing eight signs of the new birth, by the possession of which a man might know assuredly that he was born again. Then with the pietist propensity to replace one legalism by another, Gerber undermined his whole object by adding that a man must examine himself daily, for if he lacked even one of the eight signs, he could have no assurance that he was safe. This depressing effect could only be deepened by the catalogue of saints which followed. The first and most prominent position was given to electors of Saxony and to leading figures in the state, army, and aristocracy.

Yet the personal confession of the conversion experience remained indispensable to the movements of evangelical piety. It was a prime evidence of spiritual vitality, it became the staple of the love-feast and the stock-in-trade of the magazines in both autobiographical and biographical forms. The journals helped once more to standardize autobiographical expression, and did so just as another very striking attempt fell under a cloud. No one had come nearer to institutionalizing the personal confession than the Moravians. Their bands and societies, like the bands and classes of early Methodism, met for mutual edification and confession, but, in a way which was singular to them, having received confessions in writing or by word of mouth, they bound them up and preserved them in what were called *Bandenbucheln* or *Bandenbriefen*.[63] Many of these volumes accumulated in the Archive of the Unity at Herrnhut, and it may be one of the signs of Spangenberg's efforts to rescue the Moravians from the 'time of sifting' and push them back toward Lutheran Orthodoxy that, when efforts were made to go through the archive after 1760, many of these volumes of confessions were destroyed, and the

---

[63] On this form of literature see Gottfried Schmidt, 'Die Bunden oder Gesellschaften im alten Herrnhut', *Zeitschrift für Brüdergeschichte* (1909), 3:145-207 (espec. 175-79). Reprint in *Nikolaus Ludwig von Zinzendorf: Materialien und Dokumente* (Hildesheim, 1973), Reihe 3, Bd. 1.

Moravian synods of 1764, 1769, and 1775 recommended destruction of materials of this kind, even when they turned up in private hands.

This iconoclasm makes it impossible to know how this form of confession developed, but from the middle of the eighteenth century the Moravian community was creating and preserving other forms of autobiographical confession. The *Jungerhaus-Diarium* (1747–60) and the *Gemein-Nachrichten* (1760–1819) were weekly productions for the Unity laboriously duplicated by hand. They included communications from the central offices of the church, but also excerpts from the diaries of individual congregations, including addresses, sermons, and funeral panegyrics. An analysis of the personal material in these publications has shown[64] that in the early years the diaries of the individual congregations included brief single-page personal notices in the third person simply recording the dates and outer events of the subject's life and embodying no personal material emanating from him. The archive at Herrnhut is said to contain 20,000 autobiographical notices of this sort.[65]

From 1755, columns of *Personalia* were included which in numerical succession embraced rather longer biographies of up to eight pages. These entries recorded details of religious awakening and spiritual life, and some of them quite clearly depended on autobiographical material submitted by the subjects and copied and preserved in Herrnhut. From 1757 autobiographies in the first person began to appear. At first only conversion stories were cited from the autobiographical narratives; and material about the subject's labours in the congregation or on the mission field was supplied in the third person by another hand (just like the supplementary matter added to many of the *Lives of Early Methodist Preachers* and funeral addresses at Basel),[66] even where it derived from autobiographical sources. The decisive and edifying thing was the conversion experience, and this appeared in the first person. By the end of the 1760s life-stories in the first person predominated, and difficulties in the spiritual life, the

[64] Niggl, *Die deutsche Autobiographie*, pp. 62-66.

[65] Misch, *Geschichte der Autobiographie*, 4(Pt. 2):810.

[66] Rolf Hartmann, *Das autobiographische in der Basler Leichenrede* (Basel, 1963), pp. 51-54. The German-language literature in this vein is enormous; 240,000 funeral sermons have been traced for the period 1570–1770, two-thirds of them stylized eulogies of deceased from the middle and upper-middle classes. R. Lenz, ed., *Leichenpredigten: Eine Bestandsaufnahme* (Marburg, 1980).

faithfulness of the Saviour, and devotional matters dear to the Moravians, were the principal substance; these were sufficient to permit the appearance of individual psychological nuances. The personal narrative normally concluded with the narrator's acceptance into the congregation and admission to Communion. A short appendix in the third person contained the bare bones of the subject's professional career and details of his last illness and death.

From the beginning of the seventies the picture changed again, and the autobiography in the first person began to include a much more general account of the subject's work within the community, and hence to reduce the conversion story to a much smaller proportion of the whole. It was now possible for individuals to extend and vary the treatment to a much greater degree. The process of conversion might now be altogether released from the straitjacket of the Franckean pattern of the ebb and flow of the emotions, of spiritual sickness and dryness, and the therapeutic presence of the Saviour. The dramatic contrast now was between the unworthiness of the narrator and the faithfulness of Jesus. This form of autobiography was the preferred form of the sisters of the Moravian community, most especially in the 1770s and 1780s when, in the outside world, the rage for sensibility was at its peak. To this vogue the community was clearly responding. Some narratives, by contrast, preserved a balance between the account of the interior conversion and that of the outward events of life. Both might be enriched in detail, and Niggl found that in occasional cases the writers were able to suggest a connection between the outward circumstances and the inner change, though not of a causative kind.

In the 1780s and 1790s the balance changed still further, and the weight came mostly to be put upon service to the congregation, entry to the community being reduced to a brief notice of standard leadings of grace. What mattered now was the travels and labours in European and overseas communities, the adventures, successes, and persecutions; these were indeed leavened by praises to the Saviour for his redeeming help and by narratives of encounters with the great of this world, especially Zinzendorf. Whether this transformation is the secularization of the type, as Niggl suggested, or the natural development in a community that now recruited substantially from the children of members rather than from the world, we need not here inquire.

The *Lives* of the Moravians were no longer guides to the management of experimental religion, but educational tracts in the history of the community and their missions, and as such they were republished in the nineteenth century, much as Wesley's *Journal* and the *Lives of Early Methodist Preachers* were republished in England.

The inability of the Moravians effectively to combine their various traditions of self-understanding was perhaps most dramatically demonstrated in the case of Zinzendorf's henchman and successor, August Gottlieb Spangenberg. In 1784 he wrote an account of his life which began with only a short and formal description of his early life and conversion and then launched into its main theme, his long years of service to the Brethren, both in Germany and in the North American mission. Here the tradition of professional autobiography was dominant; conversion was not so much the culmination as the commencement of the life that mattered and appeared almost as a concession to a past tradition of confessional practice. Awkward attempts were indeed made to hold the two things together by references to acts of grace and answers to prayer, and other statements of religious experience. In all this Spangenberg had very little literary success; the work remains an account of the history of the Brethren from the standpoint of their leader, with unassimilated intrusions, fittingly concluded by an exhortation to his fellows to return to their first simplicity. The disjunction is the more striking in that in 1789 Spangenberg wrote a second life, designed to be read as his spiritual testimony at his funeral. The narrative of his years in office now disappeared in favour of a general confession and request for absolution by the Brethren. Published side by side in the *Gemein-Nachrichten* of the Brethren in 1792, the two lives of Spangenberg stood as a monument to the unreconciled traditions of autobiography within his community.

The Moravian experience was mirrored in the history of pietistic autobiography generally. The notion that the crux of spiritual autobiography was conversion came out most clearly in the case of a man, J. C. Edelmann,[67] who finally repudiated

[67] *Johann Christian Edelmanns von ihm selbst aufgesetzter Lebenslauf.* This work was written in three parts 1749–53, when Edelmann had been granted political asylum in Berlin by Frederick the Great on condition that he did not go into print. It was edited by C. R. W. Klose (Berlin, 1829). Reprint in Edelmann, *Sämtliche Schriften*, Vol. 12 (Stuttgart, 1976). On Edelmann see also Walter Grossmann, *Johann Christian Edelmann: From Orthodoxy to Enlightenment* (The Hague, 1976).

evangelical conversion altogether and moved all the way from revivalism to rationalism. Edelmann's autobiography belongs in one sense to the defensive category for it was occasioned by irony and sarcasm towards his critics. All the more remarkably, therefore, Edelmann's apology for his own passage into free thought, with no irony at all, takes the shape of a pietist conversion drama. His pilgrimage from biblical faith to 'true Christianity' and on to recognizing the divinity of reason is cast into a time of preparation, the struggle for faith, and 'the powerful breakthrough of a new birth'.[68] He also keeps up a trust in Providence, and the guidance of inner voices and chance passages in books.

Of course, even in Francke himself, two-thirds of what was intended as a conversion account was taken up with details of his studies and early career, which bore neither on the understanding of his conversion nor on the exemplary purposes of the tract. Francke tried to fit this early history into his theme of the rival claims of God and the world, but this framework was constantly sacrificed to what he had to say about the proper education of children and the details of the teachers, lectures, and disputations of his academic career. A considerable passage devoted to a detailed history of the *Collegium Philobiblicum* and his translation of Molinos, included for purposes of self-defence, has to be artificially retained within the general scheme by being reckoned part of the life of the world.[69] Francke's problem was one which led religious autobiography in two different directions. The tradition of religious confession on the Augustinian pattern had to start from the assumption of sin and reach its climax in conversion; the tradition of the professional autobiography, especially that of the scholars, envisaged a steady development from the student years into public achievement, however sharply that progress might be interrupted by conflict and disappointment. And in a real sense this was also true of those who could not or would not describe their religious experience in terms of the *Busskampf* and could rest on Spener's explicit assurance that not every soul need suffer the pains of hell at the decisive moment.[70] If the conversion experience was not in fact to be climactic, Francke's whole notion of autobiography was turned upside

[68] Ibid., p. 276.
[69] Francke, *Lebenslauff* in *Werke in Auswahl*, pp. 17-23.
[70] Ritschl, *Geschichte des Pietismus*, II.113-14.

down. A brief introduction might indicate a gradual turning from
the world and might not even involve a confession of sin. The
decision for God might be an undramatic affair and the point
where the meat of the story might commence; for it was now that
conflict with the world and genuine temptation could begin. In
short, this kind of autobiography, like the academic *Life*, began
from a premise not of sin but of innocence, however much its
author's growth might be ascribed to unmerited grace.

Francke's heritage was variously developed among his
followers. Johann Georg Hamann's autobiography (1758–59) is
the first in the German literature of confession to establish some
real connection between events in the world and events within.
He was also assisted by a recent experience of religious
awakening to preserve some balance between his introduction
and the process of conversion.[71] He could treat his past as God's
testing and guidance and, introducing prayers at regular intervals,
take the process through the new birth of the present moment and
project it into the future. The spiritual framework drew together
past, present, and future, and enabled Hamann in each part of his
autobiography to interweave descriptions of his personal circle
and travels with penitential statements and prayers. Hamann did
not limit his self-observation to the conversion process, but gave
it emphasis by a more detailed and touching narrative. Moreover
he was able to present the outward events of his life—his change
of profession and travels—as the consequences of spiritual
unrest, and could thus combine a good deal of realistic detail with
psychological analysis and present them both as the work of God.

If Hamann developed Francke's scheme, two other pietist
scholars overlaid it with different things. The *Life* of Joachim
Lange (1670–1744),[72] a theology professor at Halle, relates his
spiritual doubts as a student but contains no conversion in the
ordinary sense of the word. Lange's main theme, the continually
preserving grace of God, enables him to describe how difficulties
were overcome but not to build his story around the towering
crisis of the new birth. Indeed even the organizing notion of the
leadings of grace wears thin as Lange broaches the themes of

---

[71] Johann Georg Hamann, 'Gedanken über meinen Lebenslauf' in *Sämtliche Werke*, ed.
Josef Nadler (Vienna, 1950), II.9-54.

[72] D. *Joachim Langens . . . Lebenslauf, zur Erweckung seiner in der Evangelischen Kirche
stehenden, und ehemal gehabten vielen und mehrtesten Zuhörer, von ihm selbst verfasset*
(Halle/Leipzig, 1744). One of Lange's hymns was translated by Wesley.

professional autobiography, finally publishing his story in the hope of checking the decline in the number of his pupils.[73] Lange's life-story offers the opportunity to defend the rise of Halle and its religious party and to advertise and describe his own professional labours and success; but it is the didactic production of a teacher, not the confession of a child of sin, by grace plucked from the burning.

This process was taken much further in the autobiography (1762–72) of the Württemberger pietist, Friedrich Christoph Oetinger (1702–82).[74] Oetinger created an intellectual system of the utmost difficulty,[75] a new map of knowledge eked out with the aid of cabbalistic ideas acquired from the ghetto in Frankfurt, and his *Life* was subtitled 'the genealogy of the real ideas of a divine'. In describing his decision to devote himself to theological study, Oetinger went so far as to compare himself with Augustine hesitating before conversion; but this crisis of faith had little significance for the organization of the autobiography, and could have none for an essay properly described as an intellectual genealogy. In the first half of the book the dispensations of Providence were introduced to explain his theological meanderings and errors, and 'guidance' of this kind, along with philosophy and Scripture, formed one of the three pillars of his intellectual system. In the second part of the autobiography, when Oetinger has discovered the *philosophia sacra,* he dispenses with the framework of Providence and expounds his intellectual system by way of contrast with others in the field. Thus in the end this particular life-story develops into the general style of scholarly autobiography, its distinguishing characteristics being its unpolemical tone and its description of the genesis of a system of thought.

The pietists thus made a significant contribution within strict limits to the history of spiritual autobiography, and their success and their limitations help to explain some problematic features in Wesley's *Journal.* They conceived a dramatic climax to life, a striking way of envisaging its setting in the purpose of God and its response to the Saviour's call. By introducing the exalted dimension of salvation, they had also to develop an insight into the

[73] Ibid., Vorrede.

[74] Oetinger's *Selbstbiographie* was first edited by Julius Hamberger (Stuttgart, 1845) and more recently by Julius Roessle (Metzingen, 1961).

[75] See Sigrid Grossmann, *Friedrich Christoph Oetingers Gottesvorstellung* (Göttingen, 1979).

depths within, which entirely eluded the secular retailers of picaresque adventures. In addition they palpably added to the impulses which led men to imagine a self and seek to portray it. The sheer bulk of the surviving evangelical self-representation and confession is a broad hint of the huge volume of class-meeting testimony and the like which never moved from oral to literary form. But the pietists were not able to make the new birth central to life as a whole, except for special purposes of restricted scope within the community where the new birth took place. As we have seen, Spangenberg's own funeral address differed markedly from his autobiography, in that the conversion experience was central in the one case and relatively peripheral in the other. Whether this was due to insufficient intellectual independence to make a break from the inherited traditions of autobiography requiring a chronological framework; to insufficient insight for showing how the rest of life was determined by the new birth; to the possibility that the Moravians had set themselves an insoluble problem and that life, not least intellectual life, is too evolutionary to be fitted into the Franckean scheme; may here be left undetermined.

But the problem that has much exercised Wesley critics, why the conversion narrative plays so small a role in the *Journal*, may be seen in this context to be in a large measure an unreal one. Whether there was room for a radical conversion analysis in a journal so largely devoted to self-justification as were Wesley's early extracts may be doubted; it is quite certain that he fully shared the difficulties of the pietists in combining narrative with interior analysis and made the problem absolutely insoluble for himself by choosing the device of occasional publication. Much more highly worked, despite its title, than a daily diary, it was debarred by serialization from offering the personal overview which might be expected from a reflective autobiography; the more so, because the birthday soliloquies of Wesley's later years were given up to gratitude to his Maker and hearty self-congratulation for health, strength, and the continued ability to work. In short, the biographical problem of the personal significance of Wesley's conversion and the literary problem of its significance to the *Journal* are two distinct issues.

One reason why the conversion narrative plays a relatively small part in the *Journal* as it was ultimately completed is that Wesley included a great deal of material familiar to readers of his day from lay and unprofessional writing; and some account, however brief, must be given of this. The overwhelming bulk of the older material concerned (as did Wesley's *Journal*) the outward events of the writer's life. The oldest and most widespread form since the later Middle Ages had been the writing of house- and family-books. This had especially characterized the great free cities of Europe where an individual's place in a social group had seemed to support rather than stifle self-representation, and the family-book flourished side by side with the municipal chronicle. These writings, intended for the descendants of the family and not for publication, came to include family portraits and were influenced by the form of published biography from ancient or more recent times. Cornelius Nepos, Petrarch, the modern writers of funeral sermons, obituaries, and the like, had created a stable form of *curriculum vitae*, characteristics, and, for the learned, lists of publications—a form which could be developed in various ways. And if the famous early examples of this style are from Italy and Germany, by the seventeenth century it was widespread among the English aristocracy, most famously perhaps in the autobiography of Lord Herbert of Cherbury.[76] Well into the eighteenth century much autobiographical writing kept up this character of a private chronicle.

Amongst the categories of writing that sprouted from this root in immense profusion were narratives of travel and adventure,[77] a literature which found its fictional counterpart in the most successful novel of the eighteenth century, Defoe's *Robinson Crusoe*.[78] Travel diaries and journals are of very great antiquity (Marco Polo's journal was written in 1298)[79] and have grown steadily in autobiographical interest over the centuries. They have varied greatly in nature with the social standing of the writer.

[76] Sidney Lee, ed., *The Autobiography of Edward, Lord Herbert of Cherbury*, (2nd edn., London [1906]).

[77] For the English language, see E. G. Cox, *Reference Guide to the Literature of Travel*, 3 vols. (Seattle, 1935–49).

[78] *Robinson Crusoe* was first published in England in 1719 and never looked back. So many editions and bowdlerizations were published in colonial America that a recent historian, Jay Fliegelmann, in *Prodigals and Pilgrims* (Cambridge, 1982), pp. 67-83, has been tempted to use them as an index of the national pulse. The novel appeared in German dress the year after its first appearance in London (*Das Leben und die gantz ungemeine Begebenheiten . . . des Robinson Crusoe* [Hamburg, 1720]) and did very well up to the middle of the century. Some of Defoe's attitudes had been anticipated in Germany by Christian Thomasius. Arnold Hirsh, *Bürgertum und Barock im deutschen Roman* (Köln/Graz, 1957), p. 86.

[79] *The Travels of Marco Polo*, trans. and ed. Ronald Latham (London, 1958), p. xvi.

One group of these writings in which eighteenth-century Britain was sadly lacking was the journals of itinerant working-men.[80] Germany, however, produced a few, including the autobiography of Johann Dietz (*c.* 1735), field surgeon and court-barber to the Great Elector.[81] Dietz claimed in the upper-class manner to have been requested by his friends to publish the stories he quite clearly intended for the delight of the public. There was also the *Reyss- und Lebensbeschreibung* of a Bohemian chancery clerk, Johan Caspar Hammerschmid, who gave an account of his experiences at the wars with the Austrian army in the late 1680s.[82]

Some of the problems which cropped up in Dietz are reminiscent of those encountered in Wesley. In form Dietz's work has much in common with the traditional house-chronicle, and when he sought to break up his material by a certain number of chapter headings, he put the emphasis upon the traditional stages in the life of an artisan (upbringing, instruction, travels, attaining master's status, and marriage). Wesley, of course, did not rise to chapter headings at all, but by publishing in instalments of some seventy modern pages upwards, he kept the portions of his narrative within bounds. Dietz's second problem was that of cramming the experiences his enthusiasm for narrative led him to relate into a religious framework designed to show the workings of Providence from his birth onwards. Wesley escaped this only to encounter it in another form. He had indeed a keen sense of Providence, and amongst his pre-enlightenment characteristics was a very sharp eye for special providences;[83] but he did not, on the whole, strive for a suprahistorical framework for his narrative. On the other hand, while his main burden, once the initial defensiveness was past, was the work of grace as he participated in it, he was a considerable raconteur of sights seen, places visited, natural curiosities encountered or heard of, and the merest trifle could trigger him into a passionate defence of Mary Queen of Scots, Richard III, or some other of his heroes

[80] Though the diaries of a teacher of clockmaking and of a wigmaker are noted in W. Matthews, *British Diaries* (2nd edn., Gloucester, Mass., 1967), pp. 60-61; see also his *British Autobiographies*, p. 24. The diaries and autobiographies of soldiers and sailors, however, are very numerous.

[81] Meister Johann Dietz, *Mein Lebenslauf*, ed. E. Consentius (Ebenhausen bei München, 1915, and later edns.). An English translation was published by Bernard Miall under the title *Master Johann Dietz* (London, 1923).

[82] Ed. V. O. Ludwig in *Jahrbuch des Stiftes Klosterneuburg* (1915), 7(1):7-66.

[83] JWJ, Oct. 20, 1770; July 6, 1781.

and heroines. Wesley, in short, like a growing number of his contemporaries and their immediate forbears, was moved by a passion for narrative too great to be effectively embraced within his main theme and, despite reworking his entries, ended up by including a great deal of unassimilated material.[84] And, as in Dietz, some of this arose from the desire to meet a public demand for entertainment.

The literature of travel and adventure worked its way up in society, especially in the military line. Military autobiography had been common in Spain in the early seventeenth century, and it had given much to and taken a good deal from the picaresque novel. Spanish infantrymen and captains became stock figures in both kinds of literature. Naturalism rather than reflection, the endemic violence of low life, were the order of the day. In seventeenth-century France the great aristocracy, both Catholic and Protestant, produced their military *Lives*.[85] In Germany Götz von Berlichingen wrote (after 1544) an autobiography full of vigour, which Goethe eventually made into something much more famous,[86] and in Wesley's lifetime an interesting narrative that bursts the bounds of the conventional military history and approximates to the adventure story was produced by Zinzendorf's stepfather, the Baron von Natzmer, a field-marshal in the Prussian army.[87] At the top of the social scale there were the narratives of the soldier-kings, and especially those of Sweden. Charles IX wrote a chronicle of his pilgrimage in rhyming Swedish verse, while Gustavus Adolphus set out to write an autobiography embodying a Christian view of history, but got no further than his father's accession.[88] The adventure stories of kings eventually tailed away into their political testaments, a form of composition to which the kings of England, by the eighteenth century much preoccupied with the grimy details of electoral and parliamentary management, never rose.

[84] How this problem might descend to details comes out in the way Wesley in his diary will note occasions of special blessing with an exclamation mark (!), while Dietz would draw attention to maxims he felt especially important by a nota bene (N.B.).

[85] Blaise de Monluc, *Commentaires, 1521–1576*, ed. P. Courteault (Paris, 1964). The work was substantially revised by the author, 1571–77; see Theodore Agrippa d'Aubigné, *Mémoires*, ed. L. Lalanne (Paris, 1854).

[86] H. S. M. Stuart, ed., *The Autobiography of Götz von Berlichingen* (London, 1956). Goethe's play was entitled *Geschichte Gottfriedens von Berlichingen* (1771).

[87] Eugenia Gräfin Ballestrem, ed., *Memoiren des Freiherrn Dubislav Gneomar von Natzmer* (Berlin, 1881).

[88] Misch, *Geschichte der Autobiographie*, 4(Pt. 2):609.

The upper classes, however, had other forms of adventure to relate. The French court in the eighteenth century gave rise to numerous memoirs with a biographical content. The abundance of this literature reveals the conviction that an acquaintance with political passion and intrigue was indispensable for a practical understanding of life. The most important document in this vein was the memoirs of the Cardinal de Retz (1614–79), one of the leading actors of the Fronde.[89] A familiar of the Paris salons, acquainted with the work of Molière and Corneille, versed in the philosophy of Descartes, de Retz in Renaissance style set the arts to work on his behalf. But he was above all a politician aiming for political effect. The object of self-representation now was not the desire to understand, nor delight in holding up a mirror to the self, nor even enthusiasm for narrative of this kind, but the urge to continue the struggle by other means.

This object was perfectly apparent to one of his English successors in the genre, Lord Hervey (1686–1743), who professed an intention of avoiding the egotism which disfigures the memoirs of Cardinal de Retz and Bishop Burnet, 'those ecclesiastical heroes of their own romances'.[90] Hervey, however, had his own egotism, the notion of fulfilling the function of the chorus in an ancient drama,[91] and part of the entertainment of the *Memoirs* is provided by Hervey's discovery that he was not up to his ambition. Bishop Burnet (1643–1715) was also an avowed propagandist for the Whig and Protestant cause during some of its most difficult years. The perspective of his *History of his Own Times*,[92] by no means entirely of Burnet's own creation, not only haunted British politics for much of the eighteenth century, but lingered in the minds of the leaders of the religious revival in ways

[89] M. Allem, ed., *Mémoires du Cardinal de Retz* (Paris, 1939). The memoirs were first published in 1717. A modern English translation was edited by David Ogg for Everyman's Library (London, 1906).

[90] John, Lord Hervey, *Some Materials towards Memoirs of the Reign of King George II*, ed. Romney Sedgwick (London, 1931), I.2.

[91] Ibid., I.3. For another political diary by a contemporary of Hervey which is valuable for Wesley himself, see the *Diary of Viscount Percival, afterwards First Earl of Egmont*, 3 vols. (London, Historical MSS Commission, 1920-23); henceforth 'Egmont, *Diary*'.

[92] Gilbert Burnet, *History of his Own Times* (1st edn., London, 1724–34); ed. H. C. Foxcroft in 3 vols. (Oxford, 1897–1902). Burnet's Protestant view was also expressed in *Some Letters Containing an Account of what Seemed most Remarkable in Travelling through Switzerland, Italy, some Parts of Germany, etc., in the years 1685 and 1686* (3rd edn., Amsterdam, 1688); e.g., on p. 64 he gives an account of the expulsion of Protestants from the Dereeggental in 1685.

that (quite wrongly) seem surprising to the modern commentators. When Howell Harris raised his volunteer company for the defence of the east coast in the Seven Years War, he understood himself as Burnet had done, to be defending a beleaguered Protestantism.[93] Horace Walpole, who developed Hervey's genre on the greatest scale in his memoirs of the reigns of George II and George III, so clearly wrote for effect that he is not an easy source to use for ordinary historical purposes. The problem with him is to know at any given moment what is the desired effect uppermost in his mind, a display of personal cleverness, the paying-off of old scores, or the furthering of a political cause.[94]

In most respects Wesley's *Journal* is remote from the court memoir and its derivatives. He has no secrets to reveal, is prudentially as well as loyally discreet in what he relates even of conversations with bishops, and is blessedly free from the complicated ego of Horace Walpole. His sphere of action as well as his political views were of the 'country' rather than the court; indeed, even when he was not acting upon the fringes of England (or beyond the Pale of Ireland), he was putting down roots in urban centres, the City of London, Bristol, Newcastle, where anti-court sentiments were strong. Yet, like the other examples of this genre, Wesley's *Journal* was the narrative of a man of action describing his actions rather than himself and writing for effect. The *Journal* was defensive in the short run, but in the long run it had the aggressive intention of changing the religious situation by authenticating a particular kind of religious appeal.[95] Moreover Wesley was not going to have his readers (any more than his hearers) go astray by putting their trust in sound doctrine or in riches or even in a cause for which he was to sacrifice a great deal, that of Christian perfection.

The final category of autobiographical writing of the upper classes was that of travel. The upper classes travelled as part of their education, travelled on state business and in the armed forces, and travelled for fun; and the narratives in which they set

---

[93] See T. Beynon, ed., *Howell Harris, Reformer and Soldier, 1714–1773* (Caernarvon, 1958).

[94] Horace Walpole, *Memoirs of the Reign of King George II*, ed. Lord Holland, 3 vols. (London, 1846); also Walpole, *Memoirs of the Reign of King George III*, ed. Sir Denis Le Marchant and G. F. R. Barker, 4 vols. (London, 1894); and *The Last Journals of Horace Walpole*, ed. J. Doran and A. F. Steuart, 2 vols. (London, 1890).

[95] This goes rather beyond the valid point about self-instruction made in G. A. Starr, *Defoe and Spiritual Autobiography* (Princeton, 1965), p. 32.

they had seen and learned are legion. Many such diaries are still being recovered from private papers and are proving, among other things, a useful source for the history of diplomacy.[96] Travel narratives were among Wesley's favourite reading, and the endlessly varied motives for their composition spoke volumes about their authors.

Boswell published a *Journal of a Tour to Corsica* (1768)[97] in enthusiasm for the work of a hero of classical stature, Pasquale Paoli, in civilizing a rude people; a book which inspired Wesley in turn. A voluminous literature, purporting to be scientific, in which the works of travellers were prominent, gathered round the question whether the infant republic in America deserved approbation or not. Whether the American climate was better or worse than that of the rest of the known world, whether species of animals known in Europe degenerated under the depressing influences of American life, or whether to be American was ipso facto to be bigger and better, were momentous questions which seemed involved in the justice or otherwise of American independence; they much engaged the writers, and had Jefferson on his Paris embassy (1784–89) importing hairless and rebarbative specimens of American big game as collateral to his political cause. Europeans were worth studying too. Did the modern inhabitants (good or bad) of Greece and Rome cast fresh light upon their classical forebears so familiar to educated Europeans in books? Robert Wood[98] and Tobias Smollett[99] had no doubt that they did.

Travel also proved that Papists were superstitious and priest-ridden and, perhaps more significant, that the Russians, hitherto known chiefly through press reports based on information gathered in the Netherlands,[1] were so degraded by despotic government as to be incapable of setting their affairs to rights by

[96] Jeremy Black, 'British Travellers in Europe in the Early Eighteenth Century', *Dalhousie Review* (1981–82), 61:655-67; and *The British and the Grand Tour* (London, 1985).

[97] James Boswell, *The Journal of a Tour to Corsica; and Memoirs of Pascal Paoli*, ed. M. Bishop (London, 1951).

[98] Robert Wood, *A Comparative View of the Ancient and Present State of the Troade: to which is Prefixed an Essay on the Original Genius of Homer* (London, 1767). This edition is unpaginated and in fact lacks the 'Comparative View'. Under 'Homer's manner', Wood traced the same social behaviour as he had himself observed.

[99] Tobias Smollett, *Travels through France and Italy* (London, 1766), I.325-27.

[1] Jeremy Black, 'Russia and the British Press, 1720–1740', *British Journal for Eighteenth-Century Studies* (1982), 5:85-92.

revolution or otherwise.[2] And the eighteenth century had a wealth of more exotic travel literature, created by those well below the top of the social pyramid, but enjoyed by high and low. Wesley would have enjoyed Anson's *Journal*[3] had it introduced God into history more often, but was irked by Hawkesworth's edition of the journals of Cook and others in the South Seas.[4] Hawkesworth catered for a market which considered that the sexual life was more uninhibitedly enjoyed in those southern latitudes. The economic improvers, most of all Arthur Young, travelled and garnered their observations in didactic memoirs, and at least one able historian, Archdeacon Coxe, produced a serious study both of landscape and political institutions in his *Sketches . . . of Swisserland.*[5]

Clearly Wesley's *Journal* has much in common with the travel narratives. Constantly on the move, he reported in his journals both the fruits of special inquiries, particularly the journey to Herrnhut to inquire whether sinless perfection really existed in this world, and his more general observations on his rounds. In particular he had a sharp eye for economic improvement, whether agricultural (as in Ulster)[6] or industrial (as in the Potteries),[7] and an interest in geological oddities strangely compounded of genuine scientific curiosity and antiscientific prejudice.[8]

Misch, who was given to organizing his vast learning around arbitrary assumptions of national character, believed that there was an English tradition in autobiography, that it was created in the seventeenth century as England moved towards a free constitution (and the civic foundations of the old family memorials gradually crumbled on the continent), that its great characteristic was realism, an accumulation of details characteristic of a positivist frame of mind, and that it was closely linked with that sense of family solidarity which led Lucy Hutchinson

[2] William Richardson, *Anecdotes of the Russian Empire* (London, 1784).

[3] George Anson, *Voyage Round the World* (London, 1748); JWJ, Oct. 29, 1755.

[4] John Hawkesworth, *An Account of the Voyages . . . for Making Discoveries in the Southern Hemisphere*, 3 vols. (London, 1773); JWJ, July 6, 1781.

[5] William Coxe, *Sketches of the National, Civil, and Political State of Swisserland* (London, 1779).

[6] JWJ, July 19, 1756.

[7] Ibid., Mar. 28, 1781. Cf. Wesley's attitude to Matthew Boulton, which was cautiously ambivalent (ibid., Mar. 22, 1774); but he clearly admired the final achievement, especially the gardens! (ibid., July 12, 1782).

[8] Ibid., June 2, 1755.

and Anne Fanshawe[9] to acquaint their families with the merits of their husbands.[10] His account is open to doubt. The march of England in the seventeenth century towards constitutional liberty was more obvious to Misch than it is to us (or for that matter than it was to Bunyan, incarcerated in Bedford jail and 'really possessed with the thought of death, that oft I was as if I was on the Ladder, with the Rope about my neck').[11] Nor does family life rank high among the themes of eighteenth-century autobiography, for most of its well-known practitioners were single. Boswell of course was married; Colley Cibber barely mentions his wife, and refers to his marriage mockingly as an economic folly and 'Leap in the Dark';[12] and Wesley, though wed in 1751, scarcely began to make a marriage. Again Bunyan's account of his conversion experience in *Grace Abounding* took the form of the testimony to the work of grace required of aspirants to membership of dissenting congregations, with its characteristic conventions,[13] and assisted by its publication to harden the conventions of the style still further.[14]

One very important feature of this hardening was, so to speak, antinational, for Bunyan put his own stamp on the tradition

[9] Lucy Hutchinson, *Memoirs of the Life of Colonel Hutchinson*, ed. C. H. Firth (London, 1906); and *Memoirs of Ann Lady Fanshawe*, ed. H. C. Fanshawe (London, 1907), p. 1. These memoirs were written in 1676.

[10] Misch, *Geschichte der Autobiographie*, 4(Pt. 2):787-88. A more down-to-earth analysis is provided by Paul Delany, *British Autobiography in the Seventeenth Century* (London, 1969).

[11] John Bunyan, *Grace Abounding in the Chief of Sinners* (Oxford standard authors edn., London, 1966), p. 102. *Grace Abounding* was first published at London in 1666.

[12] Patricia Meyer Spacks, *Imagining a Self: Autobiography and the Novel in Eighteenth-Century England* (Cambridge, Mass., 1976), p. 202.

[13] It has been further argued by W. Y. Tindall, *John Bunyan, Mechanick Preacher* (New York, 1934), p. 221, that *Grace Abounding* followed the conventional form of the ministerial autobiography, in the tripartite division into conversion, calling, and ministry, though the two latter sections are compressed into a single and slight passage of a dozen pages. Bunyan, in short, like pietists and Moravians, did not succeed in getting beyond that statement of his conversion experience required for church membership to any substantial analysis of its significance for the rest of his life.

[14] This is borne out in a modest English counterpart to the German collections of Rietz and Gerber, Charles Doe's *Collection of Experience of the Work of Grace* (London [1700]). Doe's own autobiography, which is included in the collection, departs from the rule in dealing mainly with his spiritual experiences after he became a Baptist, and with the contemplation of the minute fore-ordination of Providence (p. 53): 'I was travelling to a fair, and about the middle of a field, thirty-five miles off London, I saw a kind of bug crawling across my path, and immediately there started into my mind, did God, do you think, from before the foundation of the world, decree or fore-appoint that this little creeping creature and I should meet in this place at this time, or that I should come to London to meet this thus?'

deriving from John Foxe that Luther was an expert doctor of anxious souls, and introduced the notion that Luther's personal spiritual struggle was the archetype of the conversion-struggle generally:

> One day [he acquired] a book of *Martin Luther*, his comment on the *Galatians*, so old that it was ready to fall piece from piece, if I did but turn it over. Now I was pleased much that such an old book had fallen into my hand; the which when I had but a little way perused, I found my condition in his experience, so largely and profoundly handled, as if his Book had been written out of my heart; this made me marvel: for thus thought I, this man could not know anything of the state of Christians now, but must needs write of the Experience of former days. . . . This methinks I must let fall before all men, I do prefer this book of Mr. *Luther* upon the *Galatians* (excepting the Holy Bible) before all the books that I have ever seen, as most fit for a wounded conscience.[15]

Charles Wesley was not converted by reading Luther on Galatians because Bunyan recommended it; by this time pietists and evangelicals almost everywhere had found that the 'old books' of the Reformation spoke to their condition as more recent Orthodoxy did not, and conversion through the *Preface* to Romans or the commentary on Galatians was almost de rigueur.[16] But the heavy evangelical reinforcement of Bunyan's view, not least in Wesley's *Journal*, made Luther's spiritual struggle normative with the regenerate in England, virtually for the first time, and paved the way for that later staple of evangelical preaching, the sermon which in three points moved from Paul to Luther to John Wesley.

In all these respects the seventeenth century bequeathed to its successors a firmer sense of form rather than a sharper realism—E. Calamy indeed found it necessary to begin his life story with a history of autobiography itself[17]—but there was realism amongst the diarists who, achieving only posthumous publication, won a literary reputation exceeded only by Bunyan among contemporaries and proved of enduring value as historical

[15] *Grace Abounding*, pp. 42-43. No doubt this view of the matter aided Bunyan's enormous circulation in the northern half of the Holy Roman Empire, and his impact upon pietists, for many of whom, as for Bunyan (p. 10), religious experience had been shaped by reading Lewis Bayley's *Praxis Pietatis* in one of the numerous languages in which it appeared.

[16] Martin Schmidt, 'Luthers Vorrede zum Römerbrief im Pietismus'; rev. and enlarged version in Schmidt, *Wiedergeburt und neuer Mensch: Gesammelte Studien zur Geschichte des Pietismus* (Witten, 1969), pp. 299-330.

[17] E. Calamy, *Historical Account of my Own Life* (London, 1829), I.1-51.

material. When it is said that in the later seventeenth century, English history and English literature were closer together than at any other time, the reference is primarily to the diarists. John Evelyn (1620–1706),[18] who has no more idea than the other autobiographers of the period that the first few years of life may be more formative than whole decades later, does at least recount what he can remember of his childhood and spares us his ancestors.[19] He then launches into his travels in Europe in very conventional style. Evelyn began early in life to jot down memoranda on the blank pages of almanacs, and very much later (E. S. de Beer thinks after 1660)[20] he copied them into his 'Kalendarium', adding material from newspapers and pamphlets. The final result suggests that Evelyn the diarist was probably a good deal duller than Evelyn the man; but if the method cannot be described as realistic, it is hard to imagine one that can.

The recluse, Narcissus Luttrell (1657–1732), took one side of Evelyn's realism to an extreme, becoming an annalist who chronicled the activities of the world quite largely from newspapers,[21] while Samuel Pepys (1633–1713) achieved literary immortality by garnering all manner of curious facts and experiences and retailing them, not merely with delight, but with a breath-taking honesty that eluded the great Augustine and most of his successors in the line of confessional literature.[22] Unlike Evelyn and Wesley who ground on with their journals to the end of very long lives, Pepys gained in freshness by keeping his diary for only nine years, 1660–69, as a relatively young man. What he wrote reveals him, not merely as a butterfly sipping every flower from sin to salvation, but as a man with as solid a work to accomplish as had Wesley himself in his different way. And even Wesley's *Journal*, one of whose claims to note is enormous scale, yields the palm in terms of sheer volume to the diary of Samuel Pepys.

Volume and realism, rather in the Luttrell manner, also

---

[18] E. S. de Beer, ed., *The Diary of John Evelyn*, 6 vols. (Oxford, 1955).

[19] As Lord Herbert of Cherbury did not. *The Autobiography of Edward, Lord Herbert of Cherbury*, pp. 2–9.

[20] *The Diary of John Evelyn*, 1:46.

[21] Narcissus Luttrell, *A Brief Historical Relation of State Affairs from September 1678 to April 1714*, 6 vols. (Oxford, 1857).

[22] Portions of Pepys's diary were first published in 1825. The whole has now received the accolade of superlative editing (in 11 vols.) by Robert Latham and William Matthews (London, 1970–83).

characterized the Oxford gossips of an older generation than Wesley, Anthony Wood (1632–95) and Thomas Hearne (1678–1735). Wesley would doubtless have considered them both rather idle monks, but Wood was able to show the Germans a thing or two in the matter of collective academic biography[23] and left a mass of manuscript jottings of a personal kind as well as notes from printed sources which, two centuries after his death, filled five volumes of the *Life and Times of Anthony Wood*.[24] Thomas Hearne, even more embittered than Wood, was observing, vituperating, and above all collecting, throughout Wesley's time in Oxford.[25] Hearne, a Jacobite, could maintain political views of pure fantasy,[26] but he was not behind more sober men in grasping that England was a great outdoor museum of antiquity and that the assembling and cataloguing of a mass of fragments of information would provide the keys to unlock much of the past.

Realism of all these kinds (as well as other things) is certainly a feature of Wesley's *Journal*. Professor Outler has maintained with some force that what transformed Wesley from a failed missionary into a successful outdoor evangelist was the realistic observation that when he preached after the manner of Jonathan Edwards he got results after the manner of Jonathan Edwards;[27] that he was saved not as Peter Böhler recommended by preaching faith till he had it, but by preaching faith till he observed that other people had it. The sharpness of Wesley's observation of abnormal psychical phenomena is matched by his awareness of normal gifts which ordinary people had in an unusual degree,[28] by a painful familiarity with mobs and how to deal with them, and an unwillingness to romanticize country life.[29] He taxes his editors by the range of his topographical references, the range of his reading,[30] the range of events he reports. And if his diarist predecessors found no objection to adding the realism of the

[23] Anthony Wood, *Athenae Oxonienses: An Exact History of All the Writers and Bishops who have had their Education in the University of Oxford from 1500 to 1690* (London, 1691–92; reprinted in 1721, 1813-20, and 1848). Wood also wrote extensively on the history of the colleges and the University of Oxford.

[24] Ed. A. Clark (Oxford, 1891–1900).

[25] Thomas Hearne, *Remarks and Collections*, 11 vols. (Oxford, 1885–1921).

[26] On Hearne as a politician see W. R. Ward, *Georgian Oxford* (Oxford, 1958).

[27] Albert C. Outler, ed., *John Wesley* (New York, 1964), pp. 15-17.

[28] JWJ, Mar. 22, 1768.

[29] Ibid., Nov. 5, 1766.

[30] See Onra K. Boshears, Jun., 'John Wesley, the Bookman: a Study of his Reading Interests in the Eighteenth Century' (Ph.D. thesis, University of Michigan, 1972).

newspapers to their own miscellanies, neither did Wesley; even if, in one instance, an engaging piece of newspaper 'realism' was in fact rubbish.[31]

There was not a great deal of Anglican journal-writing before Wesley, and the shapelessness of what there was made it easier for him to pursue realism rather than form. In the hands of a better, more reflective, and more inspired artist, Wesley's method could also issue in that remarkable realistic biography, Boswell's *Life of Johnson*. For Boswell the biographer was, in the first instance, Boswell the diarist with an eye to the telling detail, the significant incident. What was unusual, perhaps unique, in Boswell's relation to Johnson was the degree to which the author was able to cross-question, to 'bring out', the subject of his study. In one of its aspects Wesley's *Journal* was a collective biography of the early Methodist movement, replaced in this respect by other and later publications. But Wesley the itinerant was in too big a hurry and too authoritarian to incorporate in the *Journal* the fruits of his education of preachers and flock. The contrast between the triviality of his Conference reports and the monumental importance ascribed to the institution of the Conference by later Wesleyan ecclesiologists is very striking. That Wesley did 'bring out' (especially in Conference) some of those whose lives he briefly recorded and whose funeral sermons he so often preached is clear from the high degree of loyalty which, on the whole, he commanded. The evidence of it, however, survives more often in the *Letters* than in the *Journal*.

---

[31] JWJ, Feb. 24, 1773.

FROM an early stage, though not quite from the beginning, Wesley put himself in that small category of autobiographers who wrote for publication. The early diaries had a mixed character, being part engagement diary, part record, part a means of self-examination, and part the management of the small change of daily business (Wesley's laundry lists are legion—he had no intention of relying on the honesty or accuracy of the college washer-woman). In Georgia, however, Wesley had to write great journal-letters home, some of which duplicate or supplement what he ultimately published, and will be found below. Here, like missionaries generally, he felt the need of the prayers and interest of friends at home, even though the Georgia Trustees ran him on a somewhat looser rein, as regards reporting home, than later missionary societies were to contemplate. Even these letters were written for restricted publication, in the sense of extended private circulation. As a foreign correspondent of the *Gentleman's Magazine* he put into print a fuller version of a conference with the Chickasaw Indians which was later to appear in the *Journal*,[32] but (as Wesley himself made no bones in his preface) he might never have published the *Journal* as it stands 'had not Captain Williams's affidavit, published as soon as he had left England, laid an obligation upon me to do what in me lies in obedience to that command of God, "Let not the good which is in you be evil spoken of." ' In short, as in so much published autobiographical writing, there were strong defensive motives in the public appearance of the first extracts. Wesley must justify himself against charges of misconduct in Georgia, and a broad view of his whole mission there was not an inappropriate way of doing so.

This situation persisted though the charges and the critics changed. The second *Journal* is prefaced by the statement: 'That "men revile me, and say all manner of evil against me"; that "I am become as it were a monster unto many"; . . . this gives me, with regard to myself, no degree of uneasiness. . . . But it does give me

---

[32] *Gentleman's Magazine* (1737), VII.318-19; cf. JWJ, July 20, 1736. Wesley published a letter appealing for help in the same periodical (ibid., p. 575) in Sept. 1737.

a concern with regard to those who by this artifice of the devil are prevented from hearing that "word which is able to save their souls".'[33] Now it was a question of clearing the Moravians from unjust charges in the press, but also of flying a kite indicating the position he had already taken up against Molther on the 'stillness' controversy in the period which had elapsed between the termination of this *Journal* on August 12, 1738, and its publication just over two years later. In the third *Journal* it is a different complaint. Wesley acknowledged that his friends stood up for him loyally, but his critics discredited their testimony by saying, 'I suppose you are a Methodist too.' The object now was to set out the work of God as it was going on in the land, and to illustrate its power in instantaneous conversions.[34] By the time Wesley had resolved to publish *Journal* 4, extending from November 1739 to September 1741, he had allowed a further three years to pass from the conclusion of the narrative. He now thought it right to invite a full-dress confrontation with the Moravians, and the journal which follows, though mainly given up to the grounds of his dissatisfaction with a religious community he still much admired, also contains an account of his breach with Calvinists.

There were no more prefaces, but though the main theme of the fifth journal is a plain narrative of the progress of the movement, it is full of Wesley's encounters with polemical individuals[35] and of his view of the way he got the better in this controversy or that. It is also defensive in that it contains Wesley's statement of his case against the severe treatment he received at the hands of mobs, especially at Wednesbury, and against inadequate law enforcement by the magistrates. By the end of the *Journal* Wesley was presenting himself as enjoying a continual triumph; but even here the defensive note was occasionally struck,[36] and, more positively, Wesley was able to present his case against separation from the Church of England.[37] And in the half-century between, there were innumerable occasions on which Wesley used his *Journal* to rebut attacks, to draw a line between himself and those from whom he differed, and to expound his own views.

Yet Wesley was not a German professor maintaining a line

[33] See below, *Journal* 2, Pref., ¶1.
[34] See *Journal* 3 (Vol. 19 in this edn.), Pref., ¶¶3-6.
[35] JWJ, Nov. 3, 1742.
[36] E.g., ibid., Apr. 8, 1787; Sept. 9, 1790.
[37] E.g., ibid., Apr. 12, 1789.

against public criticism, and if he had been, the *Journal* would have been much shorter and less varied. There is a greater resemblance between Wesley's *Journal* and some of those produced by the founders of new religious communities and movements, most of all perhaps with the journal of George Fox. But Wesley was never an out-and-out controversialist like Fox, and the burden of his complaint during the early years of his outdoor ministry was that men were unwilling to take him for the loyal establishment-man that he really was. He was also more fortunate than Fox in the age in which he lived. It is notorious that though Wesley in his earlier years suffered his full toll of mob violence and many of his preachers were rough-housed within an inch of their lives, only one, William Seward, was actually martyred—Wesley refers to 'the surprising news' of his death in 1740;[38] and it seems unlikely that the stone-throwing which cost Seward his life was intended to do so.

Miscarriages of justice there were, but the eighteenth-century mob had an acute sense of the limits of violence the upper classes would tolerate. Even supposing Wesley's methods were bad for the Church of England, the upper classes did not want the old order in the establishment at the price of popular pogroms[39] any more than in some parts of the country they wanted church towers to stay up at the price of the level of church rates required to maintain them, or than in Parliament they wanted a bishop in America at the price they would have to pay to introduce him. Fox, by contrast, survived into the White Terror of the Restoration period when the upper classes were prepared to use mob force, not merely to eject clergy, but to kill. The difference in the historical context of the two men, quite apart from the difference in their attitudes, was sufficient to guarantee a marked difference between their journals.

Wesley's hybrid *Journal* partakes very fully of the character of upper-class *res gestae,* although in his case they are (mostly) *res gestae christianae;* unlike many writers of this class, he wrote for publication and, especially at first, for substantially defensive reasons. Moreover, from early modern times journals had arisen from diary jottings on odd sheets of paper or the margins of

---

[38] Ibid., Oct. 27, 1740.
[39] See further on this subject J. D. Walsh, 'Methodism and the Mob in the Eighteenth Century', *Studies in Church History* (1972), 8:213-27.

books, and especially in almanacs when they became available in cheap printed form. These contained domestic, professional, and purely personal experiences and moods; but they also contained notices of the weather and of public events of the kind for which newspapers came eventually to cater[40] and which, as we have seen, later diarists did not scruple to transcribe from newspapers. The longer Wesley's *Journal* continued, the more like a newspaper it became, and the more the religious news it contained was varied by items of entertainment or general education in the newspaper manner. It is indeed noteworthy that George Whitefield, who commenced his *Journals* along with Wesley, let them lapse quite quickly, and allowed them to be replaced by newspapers run by his friends on both sides of the Atlantic.[41] Wesley was slow to exploit the opportunities afforded by the development of the eighteenth-century press, as the community he gathered was slow to modify and adapt the forms of publication which he created. Eighteenth-century Methodism produced nothing like the moral weeklies which went with such a swing in England and Germany, nor did Wesley's Methodism produce a newspaper.

Failing this, however, the occasional publication of the *Journal* offered considerable advantages to Wesley personally. If one of Wesley's weaknesses was to believe that nothing was done properly unless he did it himself, it must be admitted that when, in the last years of his life, his connexion took up publishing on a broader scale, events were to bear out his fears; and the business remained a headache long after his death. What was quite certain was that Wesley could not maintain the itinerant oversight of his connexion and publish even a weekly newspaper himself. With an occasional pause for breath in the carefully guarded quiet of the suburban homes of leading London Methodists, he could write up his *Journal* and get it off to the printer in batches. Delays of two

---

[40] Misch, *Geschichte der Autobiographie*, 4(Pt. 2):600.

[41] Whitefield published seven journals covering the period 1737–41, and prefaced them with two substantial 'Account[s] of God's dealings with George Whitefield, 1714–37', reprinting the whole in 1756. A modern edition including a hitherto unpublished journal (1744–45) was published at London in 1960. Friends of Whitefield, however, published papers, as short-lived as the Great Awakening they reported; William McCulloch, *The Glasgow Weekly History* (Glasgow, 1741–42); Thomas Prince, Jun., *The Christian History* (Boston, Mass., 1743–44); and James Robe, *The Christian Monthly History* (Edinburgh, 1743–44). There were also Calvinistic Methodist journals published, 1740–45, under successive titles: *The Christian's Amusement*, *The Weekly History*, and *An Account of the Progress of the Gospel*.

or three years between instalments might have positive advantages; they might allow the heat of controversy to cool and permit him to retouch his entries (an opportunity which Wesley did not always use to attain greater accuracy).

The *Journal* proved a reasonably good commercial proposition. Not much is known of its circulation, but in later years the print order varied from 1,500 to 3,000 copies,[42] and there was no great backlog of unsold stock at the time of Wesley's death. Wesley needed to make some money from publication, if only because he had helped to bring about his brother Charles's wedding with Sarah Gwynne in 1749 by settling on him a modest income from literary profits.[43] The *Journal* was no great money-spinner, but it must have kept in the black, and it lasted far longer than the emphemeral Whitefieldite newspapers.

The *Journal* also allowed Wesley to participate in the literature of confession as the movements of revival and renewal in Germany had developed it and to do so in a curious way. Wesley's conversion narrative, which is fitted into the *Journal* under the dates May 24 and 25, 1738, lacks the systematic shape of Franckean conversion, but it is very like the conversion experiences of the Moravians who helped to nurse him into and through the crisis. And coming into print as it did, in the middle of the second *Journal*, and prefacing the visit to Herrnhut which fills the rest of that *Journal*, it was, on its much greater scale, not unlike the narratives which the Moravians circulated among themselves in the middle of the century. Here too, the early trials led up to the climax of conversion and (in their case) to entry into the Moravian society.[44] By keeping up the *Journal* to within a few months of his death, however, Wesley reduced the conversion narrative to an insignificant proportion of a huge work running to a million words, of which the principal theme was his service to the Kingdom of God and the gathering of the Methodist people.

---

[42] The earlier journals were all reprinted four or five times each, and the main run (*Journals* 7–17) averaged three editions each (WHS [1933], 22:61). An indication of Wesley's notion of a print run is given in WHS (1959), 32:45. On the other hand, serial production put the *Journal* in the class of ephemera, and reasonable circulation did not mean that readers kept the back numbers. Wesley reprinted his obituary account of the religious experience of Jane Murray (*Journal*, July 31, 1741) in *Arminian Magazine* (1781), IV.153, 'because the tracts [i.e., *Journals*] from which most of these accounts are taken are not in many hands'.

[43] Thomas Jackson, *The Life of Charles Wesley* (London, 1841), I:519-21.

[44] The resemblance is the closer as, after their first publication, these two Journals were always printed and bound together.

Thus, again on his own vast scale, Wesley once more mirrored what had now happened to the Moravian confession (as in the case of Spangenberg discussed above) in which a formal conversion narrative briefly introduced a lengthy account of service to the community.

He had now also successfully built in his own version of the collective histories of the regenerate published in Germany. The *Journal* is full of thumb-nail sketches of the new birth, the victorious lives, and triumphant deaths of saints young and old, which showed implicitly the marks of regeneration a man might expect to discover in himself, and which were set off by equally numerous cameos of backsliders. The historical pedigree of the regenerate of his own day Wesley shifted off in the main to his *Christian Library*, with its heavy emphasis on Puritanism, and to the Conference *Minutes*;[45] but at least once in the *Journal* (in the entry for Sept. 4, 1775) he claimed to be fulfilling 'to the fourth generation' the Cornish ministry of the ejected Puritan, Thomas Tregosse.

Wesley's fondness for the narrative traditions commoner in other forms of autobiographical writing enabled him enormously to enlarge the scale of his work and vastly to improve it as an historical source. It enabled the ordinary Methodist of his day to form an impression of how the religious society to which he belonged had come into being and what its leader was about. But it sustained delusions among posterity that not only were Methodist preachers exclusively those who were in connexion with Wesley, but that Methodist people were those who had voluntarily sought out his pastoral oversight, long after this idea had lost any practical meaning. It gave a general support to a view of Methodist life from the centre outwards beyond what was warranted by the facts or by the welfare of the community. And it meant that Wesley's narrative shared the same psychological limitations of the genre at large, a literary form here bolstering the incipient Pelagianism of Wesley's view of sin and his excessive optimism about Christian perfection. Wesley bequeathed to historians a controversy about the significance of his conversion because he shared the inability of the Moravians to give literary

[45] R. C. Monk, *John Wesley: His Puritan Heritage* (London, 1960), *passim*, espec. pp. 32-46; Conference *Minutes* for 1758 in WHS, Pub. 1 (Bennet Minutes), p. 72; and Sermon 68, 'The Wisdom of God's Counsels',§§10-12 (2:556-58 in this edn.). Note, however, his remarks on the precisionism of the Puritans in JWJ, Mar. 13, 1747.

form to the determination of his later existence by the new birth; certainly no new loss was occasioned by his turn from analysis to narrative. That Wesley was capable of describing a personal crisis in very sharp and direct prose was demonstrated by the narrative he wrote of the frustration of his hopes of marrying Grace Murray;[46] but the contretemps surrounding this affair was damaging enough in the inner councils of Methodism without being broadcast in the *Journal.* The conventional surface narrative was safer as well as easier; and, unlike more sophisticated autobiographers, Wesley did not have to terminate his story early in his life.

What Wesley was capable of writing (though not publishing) about personal relations in the case of Grace Murray, illuminates vividly what he did not write at all. He did not participate in the great developments in autobiographical writing which took place in his later years. It was impossible on doctrinal grounds for him to attempt anything of the kind undertaken by Rousseau. The notion that the inward eye could reveal the original innocence of the individual menaced by the corruptions of social existence was not possible, even to a Wesley who emerged from a strong anti-Walpole milieu and was not politically well-disposed towards the interests of government until all things sacred seemed endangered by the outbreak of the American War of Independence.[47]

He converged with Rousseau indeed in certain common interests, but from a quite different starting point. Each was passionately interested in education. Apart from his own schools at Kingswood, on which he lavished such pains, Wesley would never miss a chance to visit the schools of the Misses Owen at Publow, of Miss Bishop at Keynsham, of Miss Bosanquet at Leytonstone ('exactly *Pietas Hallensis* in miniature')[48] and Cross Hall near Batley, of Miss Price at Worcester, of the Misses

---

[46] JWJ, Sept. 24, 1749. The narrative excluded from the *Journal* is most conveniently to be read in Léger, *John Wesley's Last Love.* The sharpness of Wesley's prose in this instance sprang clearly from the mortification he felt. He took pride in living, on the whole, on a very even plane, avoiding both the heights and the doldrums of personal existence (JWJ, June 28, 1776). There is at least one striking example in the *Journal* (under June 4, 1772), however, in which his prose style took wing and vigour under the clear sense of exaltation inspired in him by the revival in Weardale.

[47] Like so many other independents, Wesley was finally converted to the court by the discovery that there were worse things in a wicked world than the government, and by the blandishments of Pitt (Telford, VIII.113).

[48] JWJ, Dec. 1, 1764.

Yeoman of Sheriffhales ('several of the children are under strong drawings'),[49] of Lady Maxwell near Edinburgh where the children were afflicted by the Scots' vice of *ambitiosa paupertas*,[50] of Miss Teulon at Highgate;[51] and there were others. At some of them Wesley privately supported children. The reason for this concern was not that childhood offered adults a special opportunity to elicit the gifts nature had bestowed, but that childhood was a very active area of the Holy Spirit's operation.[52]

Eighteenth-century commentators might vary in their estimate of childhood religion; they could not disregard it. Reports of the training of child-prophets among the hard-pressed Huguenots of the Cevennes[53] had been capped by news of the 'revolt of the children' in Silesia over the winter of 1707–8,[54] their day-long camp-meetings in the snow, and the well-publicized evidence that Halle could actually educate children towards the *Busskampf*. Children and young people were prominent again in the reports of Jonathan Edwards's awakening at Northampton, Massachusetts.[55] Good men, however cautious, were loathe (as in the case of the French prophets) to take up the stance that God could not act in the way these precociously devout children alleged. Wesley was quite sure that God did so act. His concern with the revivals among the boys at Kingswood, which the modern historians of that school find so embarrassing,[56] is well known. Actual examination of children who claimed conversion in these contagious juvenile revivals convinced him, not merely that the results might be as genuine as those claimed by the regenerate of maturer years,[57] but that the very young might be blessed with the adult fruits of the Spirit.[58]

---

[49] Ibid., Mar. 24, 1785; Mar. 25, 1782.   [50] Ibid., May 31, 1782.

[51] Ibid., Dec. 13, 1787; Dec 15, 1788.

[52] Compare a somewhat different theological assessment of Wesley's pedagogy in Manfred Marquardt, *Praxis und Prinzipien der Sozialethik John Wesleys* (Göttingen, 1977), pp. 70-78.

[53] Hillel Schwartz, *The French Prophets* (Berkeley, 1980), pp. 17-21.

[54] W. R. Ward, 'Power and Piety: the Origins of Religious Revival in the Early Eighteenth Century', *Bulletin of the John Rylands University Library of Manchester* (1980), 63:240.

[55] Jonathan Edwards, *A Faithful Narrative of the Surprising Work of God in the Conversion of Many Hundred Souls in Northampton*, in *Works*, I.347, 360-63.

[56] A. G. Ives, *Kingswood School in Wesley's Day and Since* (London, 1970), pp. 60-63.

[57] JWJ, Apr. 12, 1779.

[58] 'Thirteen or fourteen little maidens in one class are "rejoicing in God their Saviour". And are as serious and staid in their whole behaviour as if they were thirty or forty years old' (JWJ, Apr. 12, 1785). 'Many children [in Weardale] have had far deeper experience,

It seems, moreover, that in the economy of the Spirit the conversion of the children was a quite usual preface to the conversion of their elders. The great revival of Epworth in 1782 began among children gathered there for employment in textile factories, and it fizzled out, in no small measure, because recession reduced juvenile employment and scattered the labour force.[59] Children played a key role in revivals at Stockton and Manchester, in Cornwall and in Cork.[60] Wesley was not blind to the importance of parental influence upon the staying-power of young converts[61] but held that the reverse process was just as significant. For the Holy Spirit to use the young to convert adults was a good deal less remarkable than for the Holy Spirit overnight to turn the unregenerate young into the regenerate adult. Nor is there much doubt that Wesley would have said of the schools in which revivals were worked up as well as prayed down, what he said of Richard Henderson's lunatic asylum at Hanham, between Bristol and Bath: 'He has a peculiar art of governing his patients; not by fear but by love. The consequence is, many of them speedily recover, and love him ever after.'[62]

So vast was the disparity between Wesley's general intellectual frame of reference and that of Rousseau that no point of contact could be established between them, even on the common ground of their passion for the education of the young. Rousseau, commencing from a premise of the natural innocence of children, could look to the gradual unfolding of their gifts; Wesley, convinced of their unregeneracy, clung to the evidences that the Holy Spirit could and did overcome not only natural depravity, but also other natural limitations of the young. To Rousseau, Wesley's view would have seemed to characterize the general swindle of religious orthodoxy; to Wesley, Rousseau's view was actually cynical: 'I read with much expectation a celebrated book, Rousseau upon *Education* [*Émile*]. But how was I disappointed! Sure a more consummate coxcomb never saw the sun! How amazingly full of himself! . . . But I object to his temper more than to his judgment: he is a mere misanthrope, a cynic all over.'[63] And Wesley's inability to grapple with Rousseau was a mark of his

and more constant fellowship with God, than the oldest man or woman at Everton which I have seen or heard of' (ibid., June 5, 1772).
[59] Ibid., May 14, 1782; May 28, 1784.   [60] Ibid., June 8, 1784; May 6, 1785.
[61] Ibid., Apr. 12, 1780; June 4, 1772.   [62] Ibid., Sept. 29, 1781.
[63] Ibid., Feb. 3, 1770; cf. May 31, 1774.

more general inability to emulate the pioneers of the new autobiography.

For in one way or another all of them moved beyond the notion of mere narration, however realistic, to that of development; and in varying degrees to the development of the self, the movement of the times, and the relation between the two. This was a level of sophistication to which the *Journal* never rose, even after it had outlived its mainly defensive functions. In so far as Wesley entered into the Enlightenment, he was capable of complex historical judgments which might lead to the idea of development: late in life he was prepared to assert that his contemporaries were no less devout than their forebears at the time of the Reformation, and considerably less cruel.[64] He was also not averse to applying to his own movement those gospel analogues which suggested continuous growth: 'I was now considering how strangely the grain of mustard seed, planted about fifty years ago, has grown up. It has spread through all Great Britain and Ireland, the Isle of Wight, and the Isle of Man; then to America from the Leeward Islands, through the whole continent, into Canada and Newfoundland. And the societies in all these parts walk by one rule, knowing religion is holy tempers.'[65] This was an optimistic judgment upon a community in which, within twelve months, the American Methodists were to leave Wesley's own name out of the Conference minutes; and much of Wesley's difficulty arose from the fact that it was very hard for him to combine realism with a genuinely historical view in which concepts like 'growth' and 'development' might gain real substance.

Wesley mellowed as an old man, the mellowing eased by the degree to which he became an accepted public institution. No one could possibly regard him as a threat to the public order after his violent counterblast to American resistance. If he was now subject to public reproach, it was that he prayed with one arm extended to the Lord, the other extended to Lord North expectant of a bribe[66] (which conspicuously failed to arrive). Wesley was mindful enough of the change in atmosphere. Once he had had to face the mobs; now people came to hear him in

---

[64] Sermon 102, 'Of Former Times' (3:440-53 in this edn.).

[65] JWJ, Mar. 24, 1785.

[66] 'A Letter to Wesley on his Address to the Americans', *Gentleman's Magazine* (1775), XLV.561.

throngs, if only that they might see him while they still had the chance.[67] Once church doors had been closed to him; now he had more invitations to churches and meeting-houses than he could accept.[68] All this was perhaps the growth of the mustard tree. But if one looked a little closer at what really concerned Wesley, the springs of religious vitality in individuals and communities, the picture was far more variegated. It was not just that the reasons why one individual was converted and the next was not were as inscrutable as they had always been; there was no obvious reason why a congregation might be full of life at one time and enjoying the sleep of the grave a few years later, still less why one year should be especially favourable to the preaching of the gospel and the next should not. It is not possible to plot a religious cycle from Wesley's comments in the *Journal*, but it is equally impossible to mistake his awareness of the ebb and flow of the tides of the Spirit which were to be a feature of Methodist life till the end of the nineteenth century. There was no mustard tree here.

That Wesley succeeded no better than most subsequent historians with one of the most difficult of all forms of life-experience history would not have mattered to the task he had in hand, had it not lain so close to the challenge no eighteenth-century evangelist could refuse. That challenge was how to distinguish spirits, or at any rate religious affections. For the practitioners of religious revival were in an apologetic and pastoral embarrassment. They wished to claim their place in a great international movement, and draw encouragement from it—even Wesley did so, though he was not subject to the theological pressure felt by the moderate Calvinists to justify 'offers of grace';[69] yet their unity was always fraught by sharp and unpredictable internal conflicts. They wished to champion the claims of new birth, of 'living' faith, against the demands of the old Orthodoxies, yet there were some forms of religious awakening— of which the French Prophets were the outstanding example—which were (more or less) unacceptable to all of them all the time, and other forms unacceptable to at least some of them some of the time. Moreover, each party in the revival movement knew from experience within its own ranks that

[67] JWJ, Aug. 10, 1788.
[68] Ibid., Jan. 19, 1783.
[69] On this subject see W. R. Ward, 'The Baptists and the Transformation of the Church, 1790–1830', *Baptist Quarterly* (1973), 25:167-84.

religious awakening was contagious and that some of what 'caught', however apparently genuine, was counterfeit; or, as they might have said, it was the devil mimicking the work of God. And, as we have seen, at the individual level the question was an acute pastoral problem, for no one could stop the faithful asking whether they were saved or the evangelists putting the same question to the flock. What basis of common discourse could there be? Whether they accepted the Franckean analysis of conversion or not, they could not dispense with an understanding of the marks of the new birth. Or, to put it at its lowest, was Gerber right to arrive at eight marks of the new birth and to insist that unless a man had them all he was not safe?[70] These questions were not historians' questions, but they involved the assessment of historical phenomena, and to answer them might have been eased by historical understanding.

The *Journal* reveals Wesley grappling with these questions in an empirical rather than a scientific spirit and seeking by short cuts to arrive at the laws governing the freedom of the Spirit:

The whole congregation was earnestly attentive. But not above one or two cried out. And I did not observe any that fainted away, either then or in the morning. I have generally observed more or less of these outward symptoms to attend the beginning of a general work of God. So it was in New England, Scotland, Holland, Ireland, and many parts of England. But after a time they gradually decrease, and the work goes on more quietly and silently. Those whom it pleases God to employ in his work ought to be quite passive in this respect. They should *choose* nothing, but leave entirely to him all the circumstances of his own work.[71]

Scarcely had Wesley established that the normal progress of the Spirit was from abnormal psychical phenomena to the normal, than he began to have doubts:

None now were in trances, none cried out; none fell down or were convulsed. Only some trembled exceedingly; a low murmur was heard. And many were refreshed with the 'multitude of peace'. The danger *was* to regard *extraordinary* circumstances too much, such as outcries, convulsions, visions, trances, as if these were *essential* to the inward work, so that it *could not* go on without them.

---

[70] See above, sect. I (at n. 62).

[71] JWJ, Aug. 6, 1759. Ralph Erskine commented: 'What influence these sharp awakenings may have upon the body I pretend not to explain. But I make no question Satan, so far as he gets power, may exert himself on such occasions, partly to hinder the good work in the persons who are thus touched with the sharp arrows of conviction, and partly to disparage the work of God, as if it tended to lead people to distraction.' A. C. H. Seymour, *The Life and Times of Selina, Countess of Huntingdon*, 2 vols. (London, 1840), I.398n.

Perhaps the danger *is* to regard them too little, to condemn them altogether; to imagine they had nothing of God in them, and were an hindrance to his work. Whereas the truth is: (1) God suddenly and strongly convinced many that they were lost sinners, the natural consequences whereof were sudden outcries, and strong bodily convulsions. (2) To strengthen and encourage them that believed, and to make his work more apparent, he favoured several of them with divine dreams, others with trances and visions. (3) In some of these instances, after a time, nature mixed with grace. (4) Satan likewise mimicked *this work of God* in order to discredit the *whole work*. And yet it is not wise to give up *this part*, any more than to give up the *whole*. At first it was doubtless wholly from God. It is partly so at this day. And he will enable us to discern how far in every case the work is *pure*, and where it *mixes* or *degenerates*. Let us even suppose that in some few cases there was a mixture of *dissimulation*. . . . The shadow is no disparagement of the substance, nor the counterfeit of the real diamond.[72]

These passages bring out very clearly the degree to which Wesley felt that he must choose between realism and history, that the extraordinary variety of religious phenomena was better interpreted in the light of the unlimited freedom of God than by relating one thing with another and both with more general historical circumstances.

This retreat from the brink was powerfully reinforced by the conviction that the thought-world of the Bible, or thought-worlds to be found in the Bible, were obligatory for the awakened Christian of the eighteenth century, and urgently needed as a protest against what Wesley saw as the unrealistic, unscientific, unhistorical, premature dogmatism of the Enlightenment. He would raise his voice against the sceptics who had persuaded the educated everywhere to surrender a belief in witches. 'They well know (whether Christians know it or not), that the giving up witchcraft is in effect giving up the Bible. And they know, on the other hand, that if but one account of the intercourse of men with separate spirits be admitted, their whole castle in the air (deism, atheism, materialism) falls to the ground.'[73] Indeed, not merely religious realism, but even history itself, seemed to require the witches. 'I cannot give up to all the Deists in Great Britain the existence of witchcraft till I give up the credit of all history, sacred and profane.'[74]

It was the same story with special providences. Having had a wet week out from London in which he was only once caught by

[72] JWJ, Nov. 25, 1759.
[73] Ibid., May 25, 1768; cf. July 4, 1770.
[74] Ibid., May 23, 1776.

the rain, he noted, 'Poor reasoners! who think any instance of providence too *small* to be observed or acknowledged!'[75] A process composed in any great degree of special providences is, of course, incapable of historical understanding, yet this is what Wesley seemed to ask for when he condemned the historian William Robertson for 'writing a history with so very little of Christianity in it. Nay, he seems studiously to avoid saying anything which might imply that he believes the Bible.'[76] Wesley had a lifelong enthusiasm for noting, and often seeking explanations for, strange natural phenomena. Unlike the Quaker, Thomas Story (1670–1742), he did not exclude them from his *Journal* 'as subjects of too light and insignificant a nature' to mix with 'things appertaining to religion, and the world to come'.[77] And he could not have been the sensible man he was without heeding such scientific explanations as were available.[78] He thought poorly of William Lilly, the seventeenth-century astrologer.[79] But feeling that God was being driven out of the world by scientific law, he felt bound to protest against the presumption of natural philosophers who claimed to have more phenomena in their net than in fact they had, and, being an adept rhetorician, he would pile on the agony. 'I looked over the *Transactions* of the Royal Society. Is not that a little too severe—

Turpe est difficiles habere nugas?

If this be true, and if it had been well considered, would half of these *Transactions* have had a being? Nay, were men convinced of this, what would become of the greater part of all the philosophical experiments in Europe?'[80]

Here Wesley was kicking a body of scientific experiment presumed to be down. But in another case (assuming his diagnosis to be correct) he represented the cause of science against the scientists.

---

[75] Ibid., Oct. 20, 1770.   [76] Ibid., July 6, 1781.

[77] *A Journal of the Life of Thomas Story: Containing an Account of his Remarkable Convincement of, and Embracing the Principles of Truth as Held by the People called Quakers* (Newcastle upon Tyne, 1747), p. ii.

[78] 'A round pillar, narrowest at the bottom, of a whitish colour, rose out of the sea near Mousehole, and reached the clouds. . . . It had a strong sulphurous smell. It dragged with it abundance of sand and pebbles from the shore, and then went over the land, conveying with it corn, furze, or whatever it found in its way.' The sulphurous smell invited supernatural explanation; Wesley's comment was, 'It was doubtless a kind of water-spout; but a water-spout on land, I believe, is seldom seen.' JWJ, Sept. 17, 1760.

[79] Ibid., Oct. 18, 1763.   [80] Ibid., Jan. 28, 1769.

Reflecting today on the case of a poor woman who had a continual pain in her stomach, I could not but remark the inexcusable negligence of most physicians in cases of this nature. They prescribe drug upon drug, without knowing a jot of the matter concerning the root of the disorder. And without knowing this they cannot cure, though they can murder, the patient. Whence came this woman's pain? (which she would never have told had she never been questioned about it.) From fretting for the death of her son. And what availed medicines while that fretting continued? Why then do not all physicians consider how far bodily disorders are caused or influenced by the mind? And in those cases which are utterly out of their sphere, call in the assistance of a minister—as ministers, when they find the mind disordered by the body, call in the assistance of a physician?

Then Wesley's rhetoric carried him once again a step too far. 'But why are these cases out of their sphere? Because they know not God. It follows, no man can be a thorough physician without being an experienced Christian.'[81]

It is only fair to Wesley to note that he himself laid no claim to the powers of spiritual healing, which on at least one occasion were attributed to him by others,[82] and that he was prepared meekly to accept surprises offered by scientists, especially if they seemed to enhance the drama of salvation. 'I read Mr. Huygens's *Conjectures on the Planetary World.* He surprised me. I think he clearly proves that the moon is not habitable; that there are neither

Rivers nor mountains on her spotty globe;

that there is no sea, no water on her surface, nor any atmosphere. And hence he very rationally infers that "neither are any of the secondary planets inhabited". And who can prove that the primary are? I *know* the earth is. Of the rest I know nothing.'[83]

If it was necessary to keep an eye on the scientist lest he claim too much for his still modest expertise or expel God from his universe, the prospects for the historical understanding of religious awakening must be regarded as far more precarious. On occasion, like other bad drivers, Wesley was prepared to ascribe his own incompetence on the road to the intervention of 'both evil and good angels . . . : how large we do not know now, but we

[81] Ibid., May 12, 1759; cf. A. W. Hill, *John Wesley among the Physicians* (London, 1958).
[82] JWJ, May 31, 1785.
[83] Ibid., Sept. 20, 1759. Only a little earlier Wesley had been ready rather brusquely to conclude that all systems of astronomy were dubious and that the whole of what was valuable in the astronomy of his day had been familiar to the ancients (ibid., Feb. 10, 1757).

shall know hereafter.'[84] His comments on religious phenomena are not usually unhistorical in this sense, but embody an empiricism so short-range as to be altogether *unwissenschaftlich* and markedly resembling the trite moralism which is the most tedious feature of the *Journal*.

Why did congregations decline? Wesley can produce explanations like rabbits from a hat. At Epworth this was due to the misconduct of preachers and the neglect of Methodist hymns and doctrines.[85] The cogency of this explanation is undermined less by the other explanations Wesley adduced for other places and times than by the fact that he was quite prepared to ride different hobby-horses at the same time. One of these was the absolute necessity of the early preaching at 5 a.m. At Lisburn in 1765, Wesley found that this 'had been discontinued for three years. And this alone would account for the scattering of the people, and the deadness of them that remained.'[86] Twenty years later he was appalled to find the early preaching given up at Stroud and the whole neighbourhood. 'If this be the case while I am alive, what must it be when I am gone? Give this up, and Methodism too will degenerate into a mere sect, only distinguished by some opinions and modes of worship'[87]—a description perhaps apt enough for a Methodism principally marked by a custom which (in the event) required more stamina than either preachers or congregations could muster. And what Wesley could attempt by harrying he would not fail to try. At Chester the custom also lapsed '"Because the people will not come, or at least, not in the winter." If so, "the Methodists are a fallen people." Here is proof. They have lost "their first love", and they never will or can recover it till they "do the first works".' What was the sense of securing preaching-houses for the next generation of a people of this kind? 'Let all the preachers that are still alive to God join together as one man, fast and pray, lift up their voice as a trumpet, [requiring] . . . rising in the morning, without which neither their souls nor their bodies can long remain in health.'[88] So near at hand as Liverpool 'I found a people much alive to God, one cause of which was that they have preaching several mornings a week, and prayer-meetings on the rest.'[89] It proved generally impossible to rouse the Scots early in

---

[84] Ibid., June 20, 1774; see accompanying notes under that date.
[85] Ibid., May 11, 1751.
[86] Ibid., May 4, 1765.
[87] Ibid., Mar. 15, 1784.
[88] Ibid., Apr. 5, 1784.
[89] Ibid., Apr. 7, 1784.

the morning; but the Scots' intransigence made no impression on Wesley's self-confidence about his nostrum, for notwithstanding this fatal flaw in their make-up, he was in many northern places able to win an inexplicably enthusiastic response.[90]

After Wesley's death Methodist societies did very much better without the early preaching than ever they had done with it; and even in his lifetime, finding some congregations 'sermon-proof',[91] he had heavily worked a different line of explanation. At the same time as Lisburn was under the hammer for dropping early preaching, Bristol was also declining. 'One reason is, Christian perfection has been little insisted on. And wherever this is not done, be the preachers ever so eloquent, there is little increase, either in the number or the grace of his hearers.'[92] At Bradford ten years later the cause thrived: 'this I always observe—wherever a work of sanctification breaks out the whole work of God prospers.'[93] At Launceston in Cornwall 'the preachers had given up the Methodist testimony. Either they did not speak of perfection at all (the peculiar doctrine committed to our trust), or they spoke of it only in general terms, without urging the believers to "go on to perfection", and to expect it every moment. And wherever this is not earnestly done, the work of God does not prosper.'[94] But there was much the same trouble in Scotland, where preachers were told, 'You must not preach such doctrine here. The doctrine of perfection is not calculated for the meridian of Edinburgh.'[95]

The use of the doctrine of Christian perfection as a device for historical explanation did not square with the things Wesley was concurrently saying about early preaching, and it had drawbacks of its own. It very easily became circular, as when Wesley accused the society at Limerick of doing no good because they had no zeal;[96] and, at least where individuals were concerned, Christian perfection might fall victim to physical upsets. 'I was desired to see one that, after she had been filled with peace and joy in believing, was utterly distracted. I soon found it was a merely

[90] Ibid., Apr. 26, May 5-6, 11, 1784.

[91] Ibid., Oct. 31, 1781.

[92] Ibid., Sept. 30, 1765. In 1790 the charge was phrased slightly differently as 'want of self-denial' (ibid., Mar. 13, 1790).

[93] Ibid., Aug. 4, 1775.

[94] Ibid., Aug. 15, 1776.

[95] Ibid., June 17, 1779.

[96] Ibid., May 17, 1775.

natural case—a temporary disorder common to women at that period of life.'[97]

And the belief in sanctification raised other apparently insoluble questions of an historical kind. Like all the practitioners of religious awakening (however prickly themselves), Wesley held that the old Orthodoxies, Lutheran and Reformed, had promised more than they could deliver and had burdened Christendom with a precision 'of opinions and strife of words'[98] from which it was now important to get away. The essence of Christianity (to use a later phrase) consisted not in doctrinal scrupulosity (even about Christian perfection) but in holy dispositions. 'How hard it is to fix, even on serious hearers, a lasting sense of the nature of true religion! Let it be right opinions, right modes of worship, or anything rather than right tempers!'[99] To the end of his life he would beat the drum that all that was required of members of the Methodist society was a real desire to flee from the wrath to come; their opinions doctrinal (e.g., upon predestination) or liturgical (for or against infant baptism) or ecclesiastical (episcopal or presbyterian) might be what they would. This liberal or latitudinarian position always gilded the Methodist lily somewhat, and Wesley could display a very catholic or establishmentarian repugnance when he encountered pluralism in a wider society—at Frome, for example. 'The people here seem more alive than most I have seen in the circuit. And this is the more strange because in this town only there is such a mixture of men of all opinions—Anabaptists, Quakers, Presbyterians, Arians, Antinomians, Moravians, and what not. If any hold to the truth in the midst of all these, surely the power must be of God.'[1] Indeed, an infallible recipe for religious decay was the appearance of 'mongrel Methodists',[2] a breed whose hardiness Wesley in fact pleaded when it suited him and when he was obsessed with Christian perfection as a principle of explanation.

Vociferously as he might maintain that he had accepted the care of a religious society rather than created a church, Wesley understood very clearly that the growth of his movement to substantial proportions presupposed the gradual development and extension of religious choice in British society (a choice even more vividly illustrated by the rapid change of course of his

97 Ibid., Feb. 19, 1777. 98 Ibid., Oct. 22, 1771; cf. ibid., Mar. 25, 1777.
99 Ibid., Dec. 11, 1785.
1 Ibid., Sept. 29, 1768. 2 Ibid., Apr. 11, 1768.

movement after his death and by the concurrent growth of an English Roman Catholicism). He knew that the same liberty of choice which brought adherents into the movement would take some of them out again whatever doctrine, discipline, or devotion were inculcated, and that the choices both to come in and to go out were socially conditioned. The difficulty was to establish the way the conditioning was effected.

Wesley's failure to work out an historical understanding of a question so central to his mission is less remarkable than his strenuous efforts to do so. Wesley began with a proposition which perhaps owed more to literary convention and Aristotelian and scriptural assumptions (Prov. 30:8-9) than to observation: 'How unspeakable is the advantage, in point of common sense, which middling people have over the rich! There is so much paint and affectation, so many unmeaning words and senseless customs among people of rank.'[3] Little more is heard of the 'middling sort', and Wesley's normal dichotomy was between rich and poor. There was a 'stiffness'[4] about some of the aristocracy which boded ill, and both Scripture and observation convinced Wesley that only 'a few of the rich and noble are called';[5] 'Oh how hardly shall these enter into the kingdom.'[6] Wesley enjoyed gentry society of the more wholesome sort, happily noted the presence of 'the rich' at his meetings and, notwithstanding his advocacy of the necessity of field-preaching,[7] was anxious that his preachers should always preach in the Exchange at Kinsale, premises fit for the more genteel element in the town.[8] The least class-conscious of men, Wesley professed delight at the idea of the evangelization of the upper classes 'if it were done by the ministry of others. If I might choose, I should still (as I have done hitherto) preach the gospel to the poor,'[9] even (as he put it in a rather different proposition) to 'the outcasts of men'.[10]

---

[3] Ibid., June 29, 1758. According to Henry Moore (*Life of Wesley*, 1824-25, II.346n.), Wesley had the same disappointments with the middling sort as with the rich: 'Mr. Wesley has repeatedly observed to me that he could rarely keep professional men, either in law or medicine, long in the society.'

[4] Ibid., Feb. 7, 1772. This was the impression left on Wesley by Blenheim.

[5] Ibid., Nov. 17, 1759.   [6] Ibid., Apr. 15, 1764.

[7] Ibid., Sept. 23, 1759; July 17, 1762. Wesley nevertheless found field preaching 'a cross' (ibid., Sept. 6, 1772).

[8] Ibid., Aug. 7, 1760.

[9] Ibid., Nov. 17, 1759. Perhaps this is a broad hint that Whitefield and the Countess of Huntingdon should get on with their own business.

[10] Ibid., Sept 4. 1763.

Various factors influenced this choice which (partly through the agency of the *Journal* itself) was deeply etched into the psychology of the Methodist community. In part, Wesley, like the Methodist community after him, was being disingenuous; certainly in Ireland his mission worked downward from the gentry class and outward from the garrison in a way that would have been unthinkable in England. In part Wesley was subject to the spiritual and literary pressure of the Scripture texts in which the preaching of the gospel to the poor was one of the signs of the day of the Lord.[11] But in part his choice turned on the empirical observation that 'everywhere we find the labouring part of mankind the readiest to receive the gospel.'[12] Even in Ireland Wesley found that at Belfast his audience 'were all poor; the rich . . . "cared for none of these things"';[13] and the implication is clear that this was because they were rich and not because they were Presbyterian (notwithstanding that at Lisburn three days later he 'had many rich and genteel hearers').[14] But 'religion must not go "from the greatest to the least", or the power would "appear to be of men".'[15]

The grand simplicities of Wesley's dichotomy between rich and poor were confused also on the side of the poor. Not all the poor were receptive. The mobs were not the problem, for Wesley assumed (to a degree beyond what was warranted by the facts) that the mobs were manipulated by their betters, an assumption supported by the success of his own authoritarian attitude towards disorder. The difficulty was rather that even among the social groups with whom Wesley established the closest rapport, such as coal miners, there was no consistency of response. 'The poor colliers at Plessey [Northumberland, were] . . . a pattern to all the county,'[16] and the contrast between the colliers of Kingswood (among whom the work had begun) and those at Gateshead aroused a good deal of asperity. 'In earnestness the colliers of Gateshead utterly shame the colliers of Kingswood, scarce thirty of whom think it worth while to hear the word of God on a week-day! Not even when I preach.'[17] 'At three

[11] Matt. 11:5.
[12] JWJ, Oct. 21, 1771.
[13] Ibid., Apr. 21, 1762. Wesley fared ill at Belfast; on a later visit he found some sensible men in a congregation 'remarkably stupid and ill-mannered' (ibid., July 3, 1771).
[14] Ibid., Apr. 24, 1762.
[15] Ibid., May 25, 1764.
[16] Ibid., May 19, 1764.
[17] Ibid., June 6, 1759.

I preached to the poor colliers in Gateshead Fell. How do these shame the colliers at Kingswood! flocking from all parts on the week-days as well as Sundays, such a thirst have they after the good word.'[18] But the contrast could be equally marked much nearer to Gateshead than Kingswood. 'I . . . preached at the east end of [Sunderland] to a huge multitude, the greater part of whom had little thought of God or devil. Thence we returned to Gateshead Fell, where there was a multitude of another kind, ripe for the whole gospel.'[19]

Would the distinction between Tyne and Wear or between rich and poor be reproduced within the Methodist community itself? Wesley half hoped, half feared, that it would. He was justly proud of what conversion and spiritual fellowship could do for ordinary people. 'We had a love-feast. I could not but observe the manner wherein several of them spoke, one after the other. Not only the matter, but the language: the accent, the tone of voice, wherewith illiterate persons, men and women, young and old spoke, were such as a scholar needeth not to be ashamed of. "Who teacheth like him"?'[20] From a human point of view, many of the fruits of conversion may be regarded as the consequences of rendering people who had never been articulate about anything, articulate about their religious experience. Wesley was not as didactic about the prospects of social mobility as Franklin, but he certainly believed that those who developed socially useful qualities, who became 'so remarkably diligent in business, and at the same time of so quiet a spirit, and so calm and civil in their behaviour',[21] were likely to be rewarded.

His first thought was that a wealthy congregation would corrupt the preachers. In 1755 he reckoned that York was 'the richest society, number for number, which we have in England. I hope this place will not prove (as Cork has for some time done) the Capua of our preachers.'[22] But clearly the principal impact of riches must be on those who possessed them, and Wesley gave vent to endless complaints that Methodism was involved in a self-defeating mission of redeeming its converts not merely from, but to, the world, and thus losing those it had once saved. 'Satan

---

[18] Ibid., Apr. 18, 1765.   [19] Ibid., July 5, 1766.

[20] Ibid., Feb. 6, 1785.

[21] Ibid., Jan. 16, 1764.

[22] Ibid., June 9, 1755 (cf. July 18, 1759). The comforts of Capua were the downfall of Hannibal.

will surely endeavour to overthrow the present work of God. Riches swiftly increase on many Methodists, so called. What but the mighty power of God can hinder their "setting" their "hearts upon them"? And if so, the life of God vanishes away.'[23] 'Many swiftly increase in goods. And I fear very few sufficiently watch and pray that they "may not set their hearts upon them".'[24] At Aughrim and Tyrellspass in Ireland the societies in 1785 were 'wellnigh shrunk into nothing! Such is the baleful influence of riches! The same effect we find in every place. The more men increase in goods (very few excepted) the more they decrease in grace.'[25] Only at Mevagissey did he see 'a very rare thing—men swiftly increasing in substance, and yet not decreasing in holiness'.[26] The problem was the worse because Wesley had no illusions about the evils of a society suffering chronic underemployment; for him economic growth was genuine improvement,[27] be the spiritual peril what it might.

Wesley in short was struggling to understand a situation in which religious allegiance itself bore the marks of greater liberty and of social mobility. His repeated allegations that the prosperous moved out of Methodism solely from love of the world are not credible; many have always done so, and some have done so for religious reasons. What the new circumstances required was to take advantage of the new liberty to recruit, and to create a spiritual appeal not invalidated by social change and social mobility. At the first level Wesley was certainly a tireless evangelist and in the *Journal* bequeathed to his community a monument to the fact. For a generation after his death, with the rigidity of social institutions shaken by the French Revolution, political tension, and dearth, his community exploited the new openings on a scale undreamed of by Wesley himself, and on a considerable scale for a further generation beyond that. But if failure of nerve, low morale, or other circumstances checked the recruiting drive as it did in the 1850s, or in the generation which began in the 1950s, then the movement quickly revealed the

[23] Ibid., July 11, 1764.
[24] Ibid., Apr. 4, 1780; cf. Oct. 20, 1764.
[25] Ibid., Apr. 25, 1785.
[26] Ibid., Aug. 27, 1776.
[27] Cf. his paean upon the causes of the late eighteenth-century increase of population which Wesley mistakenly believed was as great in England as in America (ibid., May 1, 1776). He was, of course, nearer the truth than contemporaries who did not recognize the great growth in population.

consequences of the 'leakage' which, in common with all other religious communities, it had to face, and which was a consequence of the very freedom of choice exploited by Methodist evangelism. Wesley had some success in dealing with this problem: the class-meeting, the bands, the love-feast and prayer-meetings for conversions, all contributing something to the cause of spiritual fellowship and growth, and all adapting the principles of 'clubbability' in response to the decline of corporative society. In truth Wesley was not as hard pressed on this front as were his successors; they saw no option but to build dikes of discipline, of churchmanship, of the ghetto and its private subculture, against the tide of social mobility, and they went the way of Canute.

It is, moreover, only justice to Wesley to note that he did himself less than justice in the *Journal*, that the literary and the biographical problems again diverge. As we have seen, he struggled for some historical understanding of what he was about, but could arrive at only very short-range explanations of what he observed. Realism, it seemed, could be sustained only by turning one's back on secondary causes.[28] Yet Wesley's empiricism, short-range as it might be on paper, was wide-ranging enough in practice. He managed to shake off the burden of Orthodox system by the notion of 'our' doctrines, i.e., doctrines not invented by Methodists but found by them especially effective in practice. He applied empiricism to the cultivation of the spiritual life, holding, like Francke and (in their different way) the Moravians, that there was a shape to the Christian life by which a man (perhaps with the help of his class-leader) might empirically check his progress towards Christian perfection. And he clearly managed, on empirical principles, to construct a Christian community able to perform specific functions at particular times and places, unimpeded by a sense that past models were in some way normative.

Even the sacraments might find fresh power in this frame of reference. Wesley's well-known notion of the Eucharist as a 'converting ordinance' was not simply a way of pleading in eighteenth-century terms for more frequent reception; the Holy Communion was empirically found to be a converting ordinance

---

[28]As Bolingbroke put it: 'Naked facts without the causes that produced them are not sufficient to characterize action or counsels.' *Letters on the Study and Use of History*, I.166.

in a way which still awaits its historian. And much the same might be said of Baptism. 'I baptized a gentlewoman at the Foundery, and the peace she immediately found was a fresh proof that the outward sign, duly received, is always accompanied with the inward grace.'[29] 'I baptized a young woman brought up an Anabaptist. And God bore witness to his ordinance, filling her heart at the very time with peace and joy unspeakable.'[30]

It was in one sense a merit that Wesley's power to observe outran his power to explain. Two major questions he formulated still await historical treatment. The first was the difference created by the role of religious establishment in the one case where establishment tried to use revival.

What an amazing difference is there in the manner wherein God has carried on his work in England and in America! There, above an hundred of the established clergy, men of age and experience, and of the greatest note for sense and learning in those parts, are zealously engaged in the work. Here almost the whole body of the aged, experienced, learned clergy are zealously engaged against it; and few, but a handful of raw young men, engaged in it, without name, learning, or eminent sense. And yet by that large number of honourable men the work seldom flourished above six months at a time, and then followed a lamentable and general decay before the new revival of it; whereas that which God hath wrought by these despised instruments has continually increased for fifteen years together; and at whatever time it has declined in any one place, has more eminently flourished in others.[31]

Though Wesley used Gillies's *Historical Collections*, an attempt to update the Acts of the Apostles in the history of the revival,[32] and though he had made substantial use of Bengel's *Gnomon* as a basis for his own *Notes upon the New Testament*, he clearly did not know that the experience of his own movement was fairly closely paralleled in Württemberg. Probably nothing would have deterred him from ascribing the setbacks in Scotland and New England to the simple fact that the leaders were Presbyterians, too keen on confessional niceties, too committed to a learned ministry,[33] and unwilling to preach Christian perfection.[34] If Wesley's answer smacks slightly of sour grapes, the question was well put and awaits scholarly historical inquiry.

---

[29] JWJ, Feb. 5, 1760.   [30] Ibid., Dec. 26, 1785.

[31] Ibid., Feb. 28, 1753. Wesley makes the same point at greater length on June 17, 1755.

[32] Ibid., July 24, 1755.

[33] This may refer to the fact that Wesley had recently supported Gilbert Tennent's College of New Jersey, later Princeton. Ibid., Oct. 26, 1754.

[34] Ibid., July 23, 1755.

Wesley also perceived the wavelike movement which characterized the whole history of revival, though he had no intellectual mechanism with which to interpret it except the liberty of God. He might not have been pleased to learn that latter-day advertisers have, for lucre, and the guardians of public health, for defence against contagion, explored mathematically the process he very precisely describes:

But how is it that in almost every place, even where there is no lasting fruit, there is so great an impression made at first upon a considerable number of people? The fact is this: Everywhere the work of God rises higher and higher till it comes to a point. Here it seems for a short time to be at a stay. And then it gradually sinks again. All this may be easily accounted for. At first curiosity brings many hearers. At the same time God draws many by his preventing grace to hear his word, and comforts them in hearing. One then tells another. By this means, on the one hand, curiosity spreads and increases, and, on the other, drawings of God's Spirit touch more hearts, and many of them more powerfully than before. He now offers grace to all that hear, most of whom are in some measure affected, and more or less moved with approbation of what they hear, desire to please God, and goodwill to his messenger. These principles, variously combined and increasing, raise the general work to its highest point. But it cannot stand here, for in the nature of things curiosity must soon decline. Again, the drawings of God are not followed, and thereby the Spirit of God is grieved. The consequence is, he strives with this and this man no more, and so his drawings end. Thus both the natural and supernatural power declining, most of the hearers will be less and less affected. Add to this that, in the process of the work, "it must be that offences will come". Some of the hearers, if not preachers also, will act contrary to their profession. Either their follies or faults will be told from one to another, and lose nothing in the telling. Men once curious to hear will now draw back; men once drawn, having stifled their good desires, will disapprove what they approved before, and feel dislike instead of goodwill to the preacher. Others who were more or less convinced will be afraid or ashamed to acknowledge that conviction. And all these will catch at ill stories (true or false) in order to justify their change. When by this means all who do not savingly believe have quenched the Spirit of God, the little flock goes on from faith to faith; the rest sleep on and take their rest. And thus the number of hearers in every place may be expected first to increase and then decrease.[35]

Here Wesley describes very fully a complex phenomenon, recognizes that even in the revival of the work of God 'supernatural' forces do not abrogate 'natural' forces, and in effect leaves it to his successors to inquire further.

[35] Ibid., July 13, 1756; cf. Apr. 12, 1785.

If Wesley's inability to achieve a sense of history and of development gave his *Journal* a somewhat old-fashioned look and limited its capacity for self-revelation, he could not write a million words about his activities without revealing something of himself. Wesley's biographers have on the whole concentrated on the earlier *Journals*, apparently believing that the conversion story and the launching of the Methodist movement provided the real elements of substance and drama,[36] while the later narratives, like Wesley's biennial visitations of the connexion, simply covered the ground again. In fact, though Wesley himself goes out of his way at times to create an impression of déja vu, and though he noted changes in the times without perceiving a pattern of growth, it is the later *Journals* (from *Journal* 8, and especially from *Journal* 11, onwards to *Journal* 21) which most illuminate his reaction to the world about him.

The advice he gave in 1770 on safe horse-riding (which he admitted did not apply to every horse) in some ways applied as much to himself as his mount. 'Near thirty years ago I was thinking, "How is it that no horse ever stumbles while I am reading?" (History, poetry, and philosophy I commonly read on horseback, having other employment at other times.) No account can possibly be given but this—because then I throw the reins on his neck. I then set myself to observe. And I aver that in riding above an hundred thousand miles, I scarce ever remember any horse (except two that would fall head over heels anyway) to fall or make a considerable stumble, while I rode *with a slack rein.*'[37] The truth is that, activist as he was, Wesley learned how to ride himself with a slack rein, or as he put it, to cultivate 'evenness of temper. I *feel* and I *grieve;* but by the grace of God, I *fret* at nothing.'[38]

This was an enormous improvement on the Mr. Primitive Christianity of Oxford and Georgia, and it permitted him not merely to improve his mind between other engagements but to enjoy himself. In later life Wesley never missed an opportunity to visit stately homes, and most especially their gardens. The great

---

[36] This is true even of recent writing, e.g., S. Ayling, *John Wesley* (London, 1979).
[37] Ibid., Mar. 21, 1770.
[38] Ibid., June 28, 1776.

gardens at Stourhead,[39] Stowe, and Cobham[40] were assiduously visited, assessed, and compared; and Wesley went far towards compiling a primitive Baedeker of great gardens for his flock. Two things are striking about his comment. He much preferred the landscaping of the gardens to the often fussy, dirty, or trivial architectural items with which they were adorned (indeed in Wesley's view one of the great features of the poet Shenstone's garden at Leasowes was that it was almost free of these excrescences);[41] and, except in the case of the very greatest gardens, he could not resist spoiling the reader's participation in his evident enjoyment by commonplace moralizing about the vanity of riches. The Earl of Donegal laid out 'large and elegant gardens. But his only son proved an idiot.'[42] Edward Walter created splendid gardens at Dorking, but they passed to his son-in-law, who lived in another county, with 'not so much as "the beholding them with his eyes"'.[43] Even Shenstone grossly overspent on expectation of promises of preferment. 'But nothing was performed till he died at forty-eight—probably of a broken heart!' 'What a pity [the Duke of Northumberland] must leave all these, and die like a common man.'[44]

This wearisome habit of trite moralism, even about a form of conspicuous waste which he thoroughly enjoyed, is a point to be watched in the *Journal* because Wesley was apt to slip into it in ways which make him appear a good deal more anti-intellectual than he was. On his first visit to the British Museum, Wesley, the man with an amateur interest in everything, reported with some enthusiasm on the varied collections 'which the indefatigable Sir Hans Sloane, with such vast expense and labour, procured in a life of four-score years'.[45] On his second visit, made, perhaps unwillingly, 'at the desire of some of my friends', the moralist was not to be put down. 'What account will a man give to the Judge of quick and dead for a life spent in collecting all these?'[46] To one old

---

[39] Ibid., Sept. 12, 1776.

[40] Ibid., Oct. 8, 13, 1779.

[41] Ibid., July 13, 1782. Shenstone's walks were nevertheless lined with commemorative urns.

[42] Ibid., May 15, 1758.

[43] Ibid., Feb. 20, 1783.

[44] Ibid., May 21, 1766.

[45] Ibid., Dec. 12, 1759.

[46] Ibid., Dec. 22, 1780. Compare the comment on Colchester Castle: 'Seat of ancient kings! British and Roman! Once dreaded far and near. But what are they now? Is not "a living dog better than a dead lion"?' (ibid., Dec. 29, 1758).

intellectual loyalty Wesley remained on the whole true. As an angry young man he could not see 'why a man of tolerable understanding may not learn in six months' time more of solid philosophy than is commonly learned at Oxford in four (perhaps seven) years'.[47] But from Wesley, the aged sage, alma mater earned at least a back-handed compliment (and one which his editors removed in 1794): 'Well, bad as they are, Oxford and Cambridge are not Utrecht yet.'[48]

Some of Wesley's dislike of the garden furniture sprang from a prejudice against 'temples', and some from a robust challenge to 'all mankind to reconcile statues with nudities either to common sense or decency',[49] a challenge which extended to those who included even the most animated nudes in paintings of scripture scenes,[50] or perhaps still worse, clothing in bright colours.[51] The landscape garden in Wesley's younger days was designed upon principles of Lockean psychology. Locke had explained that sense stimuli provided the mind with simple ideas which might be subsequently combined, compared, and associated into more complex ones. The landscape gardeners set out to assist processes of both kinds, their prospects and their furniture assuming 'some of the functions of albums and commonplace books, philosophical *vademecum* and *memento mori*'. They served as 'aids to reflection, . . . introspection, and worship, giving us says Addison, "a great insight into the contrivance and wisdom of Providence", and suggesting "innumerable subjects for Meditation".'[52] Though Wesley's mind was well furnished to appreciate the literary message of the early eighteenth-century garden, he seems in fact to have had no time for it and was in one sense ahead of some of his contemporaries in being prepared for the less importunate styles associated with Capability Brown. For Wesley's criticisms of garden follies sprang from an aesthetic rather than a moral chastity. One of the ways in which he entered into the Enlightenment was his delight in a landscape gardening

[47] Ibid., Mar. 4, 1747.
[48] Ibid., Aug. 26, 1786.
[49] Ibid., Sept. 12, 1776.
[50] Ibid., Feb. 7, 1772. The painter is Rubens.
[51] Ibid., Oct. 9, 1781. The painting was a representation of the raising of Lazarus, at that time (but no longer) in Winchester Cathedral.
[52] Maynard Mack, *The Garden and the City* (Toronto, 1969), pp. 22-23; see also J. D. Hunt, *The Figure in the Landscape* (Baltimore, 1976); W. B. Carnochan, *Confinement and Flight* (Berkeley, 1977); and Ronald Paulsen, *Literary Landscape* (New Haven, 1982).

in which art strove to appear as nature unassisted, an object which could only be frustrated by the bric-à-brac of a bogus antiquity. But the disjunction between literature and perception in Wesley had its penalty. The constraints of the garden eventually led writers like Gray into the Scottish mountains, to an admiration for Ossian and the wilder grandeurs of nature, even to talk of renting a house in Switzerland. Wesley too was bowled over by Ossian, but could never come to terms with crag and torrent.[53]

That what Wesley wanted was indeed art and not nature in the raw is the consistent message of his comment on the landscape at large, a comment which reveals an uncomfortable disjunction in his mind between his understanding of revival and his perception of the world in which it took place. 'One of the finest prospects in the world' was the Vale of Evesham; the Carse of Gowrie was 'that lovely valley', 'the fruitfullest valley in the kingdom'.[54] In each of these cases, as in the great park of the stately home, improvement had done its saving work.

How un-Rousseauesque or unclassical all this was is apparent from the clarity with which Wesley observed the way, given an opportunity, English farmers sweated themselves and exploited their labourers, while Irish landlords injured their tenants.

I have thought much on the huge encomiums which have been for many ages bestowed on a *country life*. How have all the learned world cried out—
> *O fortunati nimium, sua si bona norint,*
> *Agricolae.*
But after all what a flat contradiction is this to universal experience! See the little house, under the wood, by the riverside. There is *rural life* in perfection. How happy, then, is the farmer that lives there! Let us take a detail of his happiness. He rises with or before the sun, calls his servants, looks to his swine and cows; and then to his stable and barns. He sees to the ploughing and sowing his ground, in winter or in spring. In summer and autumn he hurries and sweats among his mowers and reapers. And where is his happiness in the meantime? . . . Our eyes and ears may convince us, there is not a less happy body of men in all England than the country farmers. In general their life is supremely dull; and it is usually unhappy, too. For of all people in the kingdom, they are the most discontented; seldom satisfied either with God or man.[55]

Rural insurrection, even in Ulster, came as no surprise. 'Lord Donegal, the proprietor of almost the whole country, came hither

---

[53] See Wesley's just comment on Westminster Abbey: 'I once more took a serious walk through the tombs in Westminster Abbey. What heaps of unmeaning stone and marble!' (JWJ, Feb. 16, 1764). For *Ossian*, see ibid., July 17, 1767; May 15, 1784.
[54] Ibid., July 9, 1777; May 23, 1774; May 1, 1784.   [55] Ibid., Nov. 5, 1766.

to give his tenants new leases. But when they came, they found
two merchants of the town had taken their farms over their heads;
so that multitudes of them, with their wives and children, were
turned out to the wide world. It is no wonder that as their lives
were now bitter to them, they should fly out as they did.'[56]

Yet the outcome of such cooperation as could be got between
God and man, between land, labour, and capital, was a thing of
beauty. 'No sooner did we enter Ulster [from Co. Cavan] than we
observed the difference. The ground was cultivated just as in
England, and the cottages, not only neat, but with doors,
chimneys, and windows.'[57] If the legend that neatness and tidiness
are Protestant virtues has any substance at all, Wesley not merely
admired the Protestant ethic, he enforced it. 'I exhorted the little
society [at Derry] to avoid sloth, prodigality, and sluttishness, and
on the contrary to be patterns of diligence, frugality, and
cleanliness.'[58] And in one of the few landscape set-pieces that
Wesley gives, he finds the charm in the softer foreground, the
green vale, the 'interposed pastures or fields of corn', the Dyfi
valley, rather than Cader Idris.[59]

Taking horse early in the morning, we rode over the rough mountains of
Radnorshire and Montgomeryshire into Merionethshire. In the evening I was
surprised with one of the finest prospects, in its kind, that I ever saw in my life.
We rode in a green vale, shaded with rows of trees, which made an arbour for
several miles. The river laboured along on our right hand, through broken rocks
of every size, shape, and colour. On the other side of the river the mountain rose
to an immense height, almost perpendicular. And yet the tall, straight oaks
stood, rank above rank, from the bottom to the very top; only here and there,
where the mountain was not so steep, were interposed pastures or fields of corn.
At a distance, as far as the eye could reach, as it were by way of contrast,
                    A mountain huge uprear'd
                    Its broad bare back,
with vast, rugged rocks hanging over its brow, that seemed to nod, portending
ruin.[60]

[56] Ibid., June 15, 1773.
[57] Ibid., July 19, 1756.
[58] Ibid., May 22, 1765.
[59] Wesley had a shot at writing a natural theology in a work derived largely from the Jena
theologian, J. F. Buddeus. Here Wesley felt bound to find evidence of divine wisdom in
mountains, and saw it in two things: (1) that mountains decanted water downhill to its
proper place, the plains; and (2) that divine wisdom ordained that 'all countries throughout
the world should enjoy the great benefit of mountains placed here and there, at due and
proper distances', i.e., not too frequently for comfort! See *A Survey of the Wisdom of God in
the Creation* (2nd edn., Bristol, 1770), II.23-24; *Bibliography*, No. 259, Vol. 17 of this edn.
[60] Ibid., Aug. 5, 1747.

This last phrase was more than a romantic conceit and more than the pessimistic metaphor of a man who had some bad experiences in the hills. These included getting so lost in a crossing of the Lake District over a mountain 'the like to which I never beheld either in Wales or Germany', that it is no longer possible to determine his route.[61] Wesley could not bear mountains, and, as will later appear from the notes, his sensibilities could be reinforced by that eighteenth-century theology which envisaged the earth as a sort of egg which at the Flood had burst open to release the waters within, leaving the jagged edges of the shell as the world's mountains, 'portending ruin' in an ultimate sense. Like most men of his generation Wesley lacked a sense of scale where hills were concerned—Arthur's Seat at Edinburgh which barely topped eight hundred feet was to him 'an exceeding high mountain'[62]—but the important truth was that mountains of whatever size were 'rough' and 'horrid', and were not in any way redeemed by the work of grace which so often flourished in hill communities where deference was at a discount.

'What has God wrought in the midst of these rough mountains,' notes Wesley of the modest hills of Haworth.[63] Weardale was better still. 'I have not found so deep and lively a work in any other part of the kingdom as runs through the whole circuit, particularly in the vales that wind between these horrid mountains.'[64] There were similar rewards in the 'horrid mountains' of Todmorden and Heptonstall,[65] and even at Buxton, to which he 'clambered over the mountains'.[66] Wesley's unease surfaced most clearly at Chapel-en-le-Frith in the High Peak, where the hills reminded him of John Burton's paraphrase of Ps. 104, 'The hills are a refuge for the wild goats,' the wild goats on this occasion being the congregation. 'It is chiefly among these enormous mountains that so many have been awakened, justified, and soon after perfected in love. But even while they are full of love, Satan strives to push many of them to extravagance. This appears in several instances: (1) Frequently three or four, yea, ten or twelve, pray aloud all together. (2) Some of them, perhaps many, scream all together as loud as they possibly can. (3)

[61] Ibid., Apr. 18, 1761.
[63] Ibid., July 12, 1761.
[65] Ibid., Apr. 18, 1776.

[62] Ibid., June 16, 1766.
[64] Ibid., June 3, 1768.
[66] Ibid., Sept. 1, 1783.

Some of them use improper, yea, indecent expressions in prayer.
(4) Several drop down as dead, and are as stiff as a corpse. But in
a while they start up and cry, "Glory! Glory!" perhaps twenty
times together. Just so do the French Prophets, and very lately the
Jumpers in Wales, bring the real work into contempt.'[67] The hills
had nodded portending ruin only too effectively. Small wonder
that the only 'wonderful mountains' to Wesley were the small hills
near Keighley, while 'the first mountains in Europe' were the
Douglas hills in southern Scotland, for they were 'clothed with
grass to the very top'.[68]

If Wesley's pragmatism would take him into the hills against
every sensibility and instinct, how did he shape up to the missions
in Scotland and Ireland (the history of which has still to be
written), missions which took him still further from the green and
well-ordered England he loved? It must be said that Wesley never
arrived at a view of Scotland, had no consistent mission strategy,
and bequeathed to his successors a confusion still worse
confounded in the age of Valentine Ward and Jabez Bunting.[69]
From the beginning Wesley was something of an outsider in
Scotland. He found 'such a peculiar oddness in their manner of
building',[70] and was 'most surprised at the entertainment [i.e.,
accommodation] we met with in every place, so far different from
common report'.[71] Ecclesiastically speaking his position was in
many ways ambiguous. At the time of the Cambuslang revival in
1741, Whitefield had been invited to Scotland by Scots of
Cameronian bent, only to find himself abused on arrival as a
devotee of episcopacy and prelacy by those who had summoned
him. This was a risk which Wesley also ran, and it was sufficient
to confine his contacts almost exclusively to the Kirk.

Wesley, nevertheless, was a man who drew comfort in print
from the steady progress of his own revival movement as
compared with spasmodic explosions of those with substantial
backing inside the Presbyterian establishment of New England
and selective support inside that of Scotland. In addition, unlike

[67] Ibid., Apr. 3, 1786.
[68] Ibid., May 31, 1757.
[69] W. R. Ward, 'Scottish Methodism in the Age of Jabez Bunting', *Records of the Scottish
Church History Society* (1978), 20:47-63.
[70] JWJ, Apr. 24, 1751.
[71] This surprise persisted into the next visit when 'we had not only everything we
wanted, but everything readily and in good order, and as clean as I ever desire.' Ibid., Apr.
15, 1753.

Whitefield, he was a resolute Arminian, and the hazard of serious theological warfare was realized in 1765 when John Erskine, minister of Old Greyfriars Church in Edinburgh, published eleven letters against Wesley by James Hervey, made worse, as Wesley believed, by interpolations from the antinomian William Cudworth.[72] Wesley described the Scottish evangelicals in his *Journal* as 'the Scotch bigots [who] were beyond all others, placing Arminianism (so called) on a level with deism and the Church of England with that of Rome. Hence they not only suffered in themselves and their brethren a *bitter zeal*, but applauded themselves therein, in showing the same spirit against all who differed from them as the Papists did against our forefathers. With pride, bitterness, and bigotry, *self-indulgence* was joined.'[73] This blast was directed principally, no doubt, against the Associate Presbytery, but it embraced the nascent evangelical party in the Kirk.

All the more remarkable then that Wesley always had good friends among the Scots clergy, that John Gillies, the minister of College Kirk, Glasgow, should give him his early invitations to Scotland and arrange his itineraries,[74] and that Wesley should enjoy the ear of a much larger slice of the Scottish aristocracy (especially on the distaff side)[75] than was ever disposed to him in England.[76] It was equally remarkable that for the four years 1763–66 Wesley made it his business to be in Edinburgh at the time the General Assembly (a body he professed to care little for) was meeting. This was partly because the Assembly 'drew together, not the ministers only, but abundance of the nobility and gentry, [and] many of both sorts were present' at Wesley's meetings;[77] but it is hard not to believe that Wesley was hoping for something from the Assembly itself. Of what this was he gives not the least hint, and it is clear that nothing was forthcoming.

Wesley judged the Scottish countryside upon familiar English principles. Dundee and Dumfries passed muster: 'I observe a

[72] See ibid., Apr. 23, 1765.

[73] Ibid., June 23, 1755.

[74] *Letters*, Mar. 24, 1761; Telford, IV.141-42; Thomas Jackson, *Lives of Early Methodist Preachers*, 6 vols. (London, 1871), V.156.

[75] Besides the famous cases of Lady Maxwell and Lady Glenorchy, see below for Lady Henrietta Hope, the Countess of Leven, Lady Banff, and others.

[76] Wesley himself was appointed Chaplain to the Countess of Buchan in 1768. WHS (1915), 10:91-92.

[77] JWJ, May 29, 1763; May 28, 1764; Apr. 26, 1765; and May 26, 1766.

spirit of improvement prevails in Dundee, and all the country round about it. Handsome houses spring up on every side. Trees are planted in abundance. Wastes and commons are continually turned into meadows and fruitful fields. There wants only a proportionable improvement in religion and this will be one of the happiest countries in Europe.'[78] Dumfries benefited from road improvement and was 'beautifully situated; but as to wood and water, and gently rising hills, etc., is, I think the neatest, as well as the most civilized town that I have seen in the kingdom'.[79] In Greenock, on the other hand, the spirit of improvement was booming on a scale which distressed Wesley's tidy mind: 'It is built very much like Plymouth Dock and has a safe and spacious harbour. The trade and inhabitants, and consequently the houses, are increasing swiftly. And so is cursing, swearing, drunkenness, Sabbath-breaking, and all manner of wickedness.'[80]

If, however, English analogies could be stretched to the assessment of Scots towns, they could not be extended to the Scots themselves. Wesley's critique of the Scot as believer has a muddy quality which sprang partly from his continued foreignness and partly from the fact that the success of the Scots kirk and parish schools in putting down roots in lowland parishes and producing a peasantry who, at their best, were both devout and literate was by no means reproduced in other parts of the country. There was much of the English caricature in Wesley's view of the Scots, a view which was never nuanced by region. 'They *know everything*. So they *learn nothing*';[81] they '*hear* much, *know* everything, and *feel* nothing'.[82] In Glasgow he found a girl 'as ignorant of the nature of religion as an Hottentot. And many such I have found in Scotland—able to read, nay, and repeat the catechism, but wholly unacquainted with true religion, yea, and all genuine morality.'[83] At Aberdeen Wesley fared well with the academics, 'but there were many rude, stupid creatures round about them who knew as little of reason as of religion—I never saw such brutes in Scotland before. One of them threw a potato.'[84] Yet even Aberdeen deserved a back-handed compli-

[78] Ibid., May 1, 1784.
[80] Ibid., Apr. 20, 1772.
[82] Ibid., May 12, 1774.
[83] Ibid., June 18, 1766.
[84] Ibid., May 1, 1768.

[79] Ibid., May 13, 1788.
[81] Ibid., May 31, 1764.

ment. 'A company of strolling players, who have at length found place here also, stole away the gay part of the hearers. Poor Scotland! Poor Aberdeen! This only was wanting to make them as completely irreligious as England.'[85] Another visit to Glasgow produced a better impression. 'So much of the form of religion is here still as is scarce to be found in any town in England. There was once the power too. And shall it not be again? Surely the time is at hand.'[86]

But let Wesley cross the border into Northumberland, and he heaved a sigh of relief. 'What a difference between an English and a Scotch congregation! These [at Alnwick] judge themselves rather than the preacher; and their aim is, not only to know, but to love and obey.'[87] Wesley's view of the Scots was thus a pastiche of two entirely contradictory English caricatures; in the one the Scot was a knowledgeable but pert and conceited sermon-taster, in the other he was beyond the pale of civilization altogether. On the best assessment they were 'the best hearers in Europe',[88] but on the Lord's Day only.[89] Much the same stereotypes governed Wesley's assessment of the labours of the Scots ministers he canvassed so hard. In 1772 he found the Glasgow ministers led by Gillies 'to be pious as well as sensible men'.[90] But Wesley's blanket verdict on their work was that their services were dull, 'full as formal as any in England',[91] while their sermons were soporific rather than awakening, containing 'much truth, but . . . no more likely to awaken one soul than an Italian opera',[92] lacking 'application, . . . [and] likely to do as much good as the singing of a lark'.[93] This was a pity, for no people resented 'plain dealing' less than the Scots.[94] Wesley had criticized David Brainerd, the melancholic Reformed missionary to the Red Indians (a version of whose *Journal* he published for the Methodist people), 'for prescribing to God the way wherein he [God] should work';[95] he had no such scruple in prescribing to even the 'pious' ministers of the Kirk.

---

85 Ibid., Apr. 26, 1768.
87 Ibid., May 23, 1772.
89 Ibid., May 28, 1790.
90 Ibid., Apr. 23, 1772.
91 Ibid., May 16, 19, 1776.
92 Ibid., May 15, 1774.
93 Ibid., June 13, 1779.
94 Ibid., May 29, 1763; Aug. 4, 1767.
95 Ibid., Dec. 4, 1749.

86 Ibid., Apr. 26, 1765.
88 Ibid., May 13, 1788

Perhaps after all, as a country politician turned courtier, he had fallen victim to one piece of country propaganda he repudiated only in 1778. 'For many years I had heard the King severely blamed for "giving all places of trust and profit to Scotchmen". And this was so positively and continually affirmed that I had no doubt of it. To put the matter beyond all possible dispute, the writer appeals to the Court Calendar of the present year, which contains the names of all those that hold places under the King. And hereby it appears that of four hundred and fifty odd places, just *eight* are possessed by Scotchmen; and of the one hundred and fifty-one places in the Royal Household, *four* are possessed by Scots, and no more.'[96]

If Wesley lacked a convincing strategy for Scotland, he gives few clues as to what he thought he was about in Ireland. The journals of his Irish tours are full, but are constructed entirely on old-fashioned principles of adventurous *res gestae* and are almost without general reflection. Wesley faced Ireland in much the same frame of mind as Scotland; of course the circumstances were different, and in the end the harvest, though disappointing, was greater. In Ireland as in Scotland, Wesley hoped to find some trace of the well-ordered England he loved. Dublin, where his journeys began, was mean and depressing, though Trinity College won a commendation with 'two little quadrangles, and one about as large as that of New College, Oxford'.[97] And Dublin reproduced in a more acute form the troubles Wesley encountered in Edinburgh; his flock was disturbed, on the one side, by both the forces in possession in the church establishment and by the evangelicals of that allegiance, and on the other side, by the foreign intrusions which loomed so large in eighteenth-century Irish history, and especially by the Moravians. It is very odd that Wesley, who was hoping for signs of Englishness (this eventually slipped out at Coleraine where the roads were miserable, 'but the company there made amends for them. We met with a right English society, in spirit, in carriage, and even in dress.')[98] and priming himself for incursions into the outer

---

[96] Sept. 7, 1778.

[97] Ibid., Aug. 21, 1747.

[98] Ibid., June 3, 1789. It proved that there was a better market for Englishness in Ireland than in Scotland. The *Minutes* of the Irish Conference of 1787 were enlivened by a request for guidance on the correct way to pronounce certain English vowels (R. Gillespie, *Wild as Colts Untamed: Methodism and Society in Lurgan 1750–1975* [Lurgan, 1977], p. 10). As late

darkness by strenuous application to the Protestant historians of Ireland, did not discover Ulster (where 'the ground was cultivated just as in England' and Newry was like Liverpool)[99] for a decade.

His earlier journeys took him due west across the centre of the country to Athlone and then in a great sweep southwards, in the course of which permanent strongholds were established in Cork and Bandon. The reason for this probably was that Wesley, like later Protestant evangelists in Ireland, underestimated the difficulty of his task, though he clearly perceived the issue of nationality involved. 'I stayed at home, and spoke to all that came. But I found scarce any Irish among them. At least ninety-nine in an hundred of the native Irish remain in the religion of their forefathers. The Protestants, whether in Dublin or elsewhere, are almost all transplanted lately from England. Nor is it any wonder that those who are born Papists generally live and die such, when the Protestants can find no better ways to convert them than penal laws and Acts of Parliament.'[1] Those better ways Wesley attempted to provide; but even after a quarter of a century of effort, he could still assert that 'if the parish ministers were zealous for God, the Protestants in Ireland would soon outnumber the Papists.'[2] Hope burned regardless, and in 1775 in the region of Derry he could perceive 'a wonderful reformation spreading throughout this whole country, for several miles around. Outward wickedness is gone; and many, young and old, witness that the kingdom of God is within them.'[3]

It was of course the case that the Catholic cause in Ireland was at its lowest ebb in the middle of the eighteenth century, that Wesley had no difficulty in attracting Catholic hearers to his earlier meetings, and that at this stage, before the Catholic revival had begun, Wesley's hopes of converting Irish whose Catholicism was purely nominal were more reasonable than those of the often

as 1813 it was reported that Methodists 'often aspire to the English speech and manners of their Rev. John Wesley and successive leaders' (John Gamble, *A View of Society and Manners in the North of Ireland in . . . 1812* [London, 1813], quoted in Gillespie, *Wild as Colts*, p. 10). Gamble also believed that the Methodists of Clones adopted not only the accent of Thomas Coke, who was virtually perpetual president of the Irish Conference after Wesley's death, but also 'the short hair, combed sleek behind the ears, the sanctified look, and musical tones . . . of their renowned teacher' (John Gamble, *Sketches of History, Politics, and Manners* [London, 1810], pp. 159, 160).

[99] Ibid., July 19, 1756.
[1] Ibid., Aug. 15, 1747.
[2] Ibid., May 13, 1771.
[3] Ibid., May 31, 1775.

ferocious Protestant evangelists of the two generations after his death. There was, however, a gulf which it would be a mistake to regard as racial, but which went very deep, separating Wesley from the Catholic Irish, a gulf not paralleled in the case of even the more barbaric Scots. Wesley found the Irish 'indolent' (which implied 'squalid')[4] and 'fickle'.[5] He was driven almost speechless by the tendency to exaggerate and the 'pompous accounts' of even the Methodists;[6] his reaction to the level of truthfulness of the rest may be imagined.

There was a lack of sympathy as well as of knowledge in Wesley's approach to the Irish which did not bode well; and his chief impact upon the 'national' problem in Ireland was to acquire a strong following among the unassimilated foreign Protestants—Huguenots and Palatines—who had been planted in Ireland after having to leave their own homelands in the late seventeenth, and early part of the eighteenth, century. Here Wesley found a much more palatable ethos. 'These have quite a different look from the natives of the country, as well as a different temper. They are a serious, thinking people. And their diligence turns all their land into a garden.'[7] They prospered, or, if they fell out with their landlord, they emigrated to America;[8] 'there is no cursing or swearing, no Sabbath-breaking, no drunkenness, no alehouse in any of them [their towns of Killeheen, Ballingrane, and Courtmatrix]. How will these poor foreigners rise up in the judgment against those that are round about them!'[9] German-language populations of this kind, deprived of their church but clinging to their Luther Bible,[10] had been the first to generate religious revival in Central Europe,[11] and after a poor start[12] a flame was kindled among them in Ireland

---

[4] Ibid., May 26, 1769.

[5] Ibid., Feb. 17, 1781.

[6] Ibid., Mar. 16, 1748; May 29, 1778.

[7] Ibid., June 4, 1762. Cf. W. E. H. Lecky, *History of Ireland in the Eighteenth Century*, 5 vols. (London, 1892), I.351-52; A. W. Hutton, ed., *Arthur Young's Tour in Ireland* (London, 1892), I.368, 377-79, 386-87; II.34.

[8] JWJ, July 16, 1760; June 14, 1765; and May 21, 1767.

[9] Ibid., July 9, 1760.

[10] Methodism was eventually introduced into the American colonies by two Palatines from Ireland, Philip Embury and Barbara Heck. A half-length portrait of the latter depicts her piously clasping her Bible, the *Luther* Bible. E. S. Bucke, ed., *The History of American Methodism*, 3 vols. (New York/Nashville, 1964), I.13-14.

[11] Ward, 'Power and Piety', pp. 238-50.

[12] JWJ, June 23, 1758.

'such as was never seen before. Many in every place have been deeply convinced, many converted to God, and some perfected in love. Some societies are doubled in number, some increased six or even tenfold. All the neighbouring gentry were likewise gathered together.'[13] The Huguenots at Portarlington had a church and pastor, and at one point Wesley seems to be saying that revivalism was the order of the day there too. 'I have sometimes thought Mr. Whitefield's action was violent; but he is a mere post to Mr. Caillard,' their pastor.[14]

The very existence of the Roman Catholic Ireland on which Wesley made so little impact nevertheless eased his passage among Protestants across St. George's Channel, much as the re-emergence of Cameronianism in Scotland had facilitated his entrée into the Kirk. The Protestant cause needed every watchman upon the walls it could muster, and although in the early days Methodists were rough-housed by Protestant as well as Catholic mobs, Wesley was on the whole well received. Moreover, confronted as it was by an unmistakable mission-field, the Church of Ireland, whatever its defects as a pastoral agency for the nation, was in places preparing better things already. Wesley found Dr. Hort, the rector of Longford, 'a learned, sensible, pious man, and a pattern both for clergy and laity'.[15] Arthur Grueber, rector of Athlone, preached excellently on 'the necessity of the religion of the heart',[16] a theme dear to Wesley, who believed that righteousness, peace, and joy in the Holy Spirit 'must be *felt* or they have no being'.[17] Then there was Philip Skelton, rector of Devonish and Trory (1759–66) and Fintona (1766–87), 'as extraordinary a man as Mr. [William] Law'; whose works and conversation Wesley admired equally.[18] In later years the Wesleyan line came to be that although Skelton's 'classes for religious instruction, and . . . faithful preaching . . . , alarmed the fears and raised the moral tone of many . . . , yet that able and laborious divine not having clear views of the method of a sinner's justification, few, if any, received the forgiveness of sins.'[19] Skelton was, however, well fitted to play John the Baptist to

13 Ibid., May 13, 1789.
14 Ibid., June 24, 1750.
15 Ibid., June 9, 1760.
16 Ibid., Aug. 9, 1752.
17 Ibid., Aug. 12, 1771.
18 Ibid., June 14, 1771; Apr. 21, 1783.
19 C. H. Crookshank, *History of Methodism in Ireland* (Belfast, 1885), I.215-16.

Wesley's Messiah: 'A brighter day . . . was about to dawn on the church in this neighbourhood.'

And there were the congenial learned clergy of the North, Dr. Wilson, rector of Newton Stewart, an Orientalist,[20] and Dr. Leslie of Tanderagee near Armagh, whose well-designed property so nearly corresponded to Wesley's view of heaven that he almost forgot his ritual warning against the vanity of this world's goods: 'A pleasanter spot I never saw. It lies on the top of a fruitful hill, . . . and commands the whole view of a lovely country, east, west, north, and south; and it is laid out with the finest taste imaginable. The ground I took for a park I found was an orchard, tufted with fruit-trees and flowering shrubs, and surrounded with a close, shady walk. I spent another hour with the amiable family this morning; and it was an hour I shall not soon forget. But it will never return! For one, if not more, of that lovely company are since removed to Abraham's bosom.'[21] Felicity must not get out of hand. And, less reliably, there were the evangelicals, men like Edward Smyth, and the Hon. and Rev. Walter Shirley. In Ireland, much more than in England, Wesley could be accepted as an auxiliary to the establishment, not to mention a pleasing change of cultivated company from distant parts.

Much more striking, however, once the early flounderings were past, was the degree to which Wesley came to depend on contacts, not indeed amongst the absentee aristocracy, whose gardens were more familiar to him than their persons, but among the gentry and other men of property. These were so numerous and are so fully illustrated in the notes below, as to need no further emphasis here.[22] Some of them were apparently chance contacts like the 'gentleman of Ballyrane, near Wexford, [who] told me, if I would preach at his house the next evening, he would meet me on the road with a fresh horse. So I complied, though it was some miles out of the way.'[23] But in total the number is so great as to make it clear that Wesley's self-consciously asserted English mission to the poor was in Ireland refracted through the Protestant gentry class. This was probably not a matter of

---

[20] JWJ, May 29, 1789.

[21] Ibid., June 25, 1778. Compare this with Wesley's comment on the view from Croagh Patrick: 'As most of it is waste and uncultivated, the prospect is not very pleasing' (ibid., May 24, 1762).

[22] See, e.g., ibid., May 18, 24, 1762; Apr. 26, 1785.

[23] Ibid., Apr. 21, 1773 (the horse was not a success; see Apr. 22, 1773).

calculation (though it clearly helped in the maintenance of order); the English as well as the Protestant element in the gentry class spoke to the same element in Wesley.

The other factor in preserving law and order in Ireland which was usually absent in England was the garrison; and it is striking how much of Wesley's ministry there was devoted to the troops. In more than one case conversions among the troops were the agency of conversions among the civilian population;[24] at least one distinguished Methodist preacher was recruited from the Irish garrison;[25] and when Wesley preached at Waterford, 'the major of the Highland Regiment standing behind me, with several of his officers, many of the soldiers before me, and the sentinel at the entrance of the court',[26] or inside the castle at Charlemont with all the soldiers drawn up,[27] or inside the barracks at Limerick or Athlone or Cappaquin,[28] he was making absolutely clear where he stood in relation to the Ascendancy. More generally, the skyline in small Irish towns was distinguished from that of their English counterparts by four prominent features, the distillery, the barracks, the court-house, and the jail. Law enforcement in Ireland being a far more tense affair even in Wesley's lifetime than in England, his habitual preaching in the court-house must have had a chilling effect upon the Roman Catholic population. (Taking advantage of the growing number of new English town halls, as Wesley did in his later years, was a different matter.) And when at Birr he preached out-of-doors before the memorial to the Duke of Cumberland, the Butcher of Culloden, on its 58-foot column, and built a chapel by the court-house, jail, and excise office,[29] he made what he thought was the content of the gospel quite unmistakable and, despite recruiting a handful of ex-Catholic preachers, guaranteed that he could reap no great Catholic harvest.

The great perplexity in Ireland, however, in Wesley's later lifetime, was to know *how* to be establishmentarian. Although, as in Scotland, the major forms of dissent remained a market closed to him, he found it easiest to acquire followers (especially in Dublin) who had some grievance against the existing order, so

---

[24] Ibid., July 3, 1750; Apr. 29, 1787.
[25] Joseph Burgess, a quartermaster; *Wesleyan Methodist Magazine* (1840), 63:537-56.
[26] JWJ, Apr. 26, 1775.   [27] Ibid., June 20, 1778; June 15, 1787.
[28] Ibid., May 11, 1773; Apr. 17, 1789; and May 1, 1789.
[29] See note to ibid., Apr. 26, 1785.

that to the end of his days he was clutching at straws 'that they will not easily be so prejudiced against the Church as they were in time past',[30] and enforcing at length 'the original design of the Methodists, viz., not to be a distinct party, but to stir up all parties, Christians or heathens, to worship God in spirit and in truth, but the Church of England in particular, to which they belonged from the beginning'.[31] The outbreak of the American War of Independence and the final destruction of the American part of the old colonial system evoked a vivid response in Ireland which altogether overshadowed the nonconformist tub-thumping in England. Wesley welcomed the formation of the Volunteers[32] as an anti-Catholic measure, and even preached before them in their uniforms,[33] with no inkling of their subsequent political pretensions, which he found in the last degree unwelcome.[34]

Moreover Wesley's violent reaction to American resistance, so profitable to him politically in England, could not be wished away for the sake of Irish sensibilities. Wesley had recourse in this difficulty to a sort of jeremiad in reverse.[35] In the jeremiad a preacher piled up the sins of congregation and community, calling for repentance before the wrath of God was meted out. In his *Compassionate Address* Wesley sought to give a fillip to morale by arguing that, black as the domestic and international situations were, they were not as menacing as critics insisted; and, what was more, a God who would spare Sodom should ten righteous men be found in it, would certainly spare a Britain in every part of which religious revival was gaining ground.[36] Wesley, in short, set himself against the Catholic community, and also against those Anglican and Presbyterian forces that wished to use the wartime embarrassments of the imperial government to free Ireland from at least some of the drawbacks of colonial status.

The situation actually produced by the Catholic revival after Wesley's death was already casting its shadow before; by that time most of Wesley's work in the south was destroyed, leaving

---

[30] Ibid., July 3, 1785.
[31] Ibid., Apr. 12, 1789.
[32] Ibid., Apr. 26, 1778.
[33] Ibid., May 3, 1778.
[34] See *Letters*, June 2, 1785; Telford, VII.272.
[35] See below, notes to JWJ, May 9, 17, 1778.
[36] Confronted by a similar problem in the Jacobite rebellion of 1745, Wesley had reacted in exactly the opposite way; his advice to the Mayor of Newcastle was, not just to keep his powder dry, but to keep sin off the streets. JWJ, Sept. 21, 1745.

substantial strongholds only in Dublin, Cork, Bandon, and amongst the Palatines. In the north, Methodism made little impact upon Presbyterian communities and thrived under the wing of the Irish Church, partaking of its Orange sentiment; yet it broke up rather than remain a religious society within the Church. By this time, too, Methodist connexionalism had also taken steam out of the Irish revival. From an early date it had proved impossible to get English Methodist preachers to accept Irish appointments; while the Irish—not merely connexional celebrities like Henry Moore, Wesley's literary executor and biographer; Adam Clarke, the polymath; and William Myles, the denominational historian; but many eloquent preachers with Irish flair—had been lured to the lusher pastures of the English work. All in all it is remarkable that the Methodist flock in Ireland in the early nineteenth century was as numerous and as steadfast as it was. Wesley's testy verdict in 1784 was unnecessarily and uncharacteristically ungracious: 'You want lively, zealous, active preachers. And, to tell you a melancholy truth, few of our elder preachers are of this character. You must look for zeal and activity among the young preachers. I am greatly scandalized at this, that a preacher fifty years old is but half a preacher.'[37] Those who made something out of the confusions of Wesley's Irish mission deserved better than this.

[37] See *Letters*, June 21, 1784; Telford, VII.222.

A N
EXTRACT

FROM THE

Rev. Mr. JOHN WESLEY's.

JOURNAL,

With Regard to the

AFFIDAVIT

MADE BY

Captain *ROBERT WILLIAMS*.

Doth our Law judge any Man before it hear him?
John vii. 51.

LONDON:
Printed in the YEAR MD.CC.XLI.

THE date when the *Journal* first appeared is now a good deal more certain than the way it was written. The publication of the first *Journal* has been generally ascribed to 1738 or 1739, the latter date being favoured because of the reference in the preface to 'Captain Williams's Affidavit, published as soon as he had left England', which contained charges against Wesley's conduct in Georgia, to which the *Journal* was to reply. That affidavit was sworn by Williams before the Mayor of Bristol on March 14, 1739. Professor Baker has shown in the *Bibliography* to this edition and elsewhere[38] that this date is Old Style and should now be reckoned as 1740, that Williams did not get to London from Georgia till November 1739, and that the affidavit was probably printed quickly as a broadsheet.[39] When Wesley first knew of the broadsheet is unknown, for there is a gap in his diary from November 10, 1739, until April 13, 1740, but as soon as the diary reopens it is clear that he was actively preparing the *Journal* (on which he had been working intermittently for a year) for the press. On May 12 he corrected the proofs and on May 23 'writ Preface to Journal'. This was a substantial job, for it included a transcription of 'a plain account of the rise of that little Society in Oxford, which has been so variously represented', promised in the preface. This material was set up in type after the first part of the *Journal* was printed, and the whole was published probably before Wesley left Bristol on June 2, 1740 (to deal with the crisis caused by the Moravians in the London society), and certainly before Charles Wesley replaced him there on June 21 and reported that 'the Journals are no longer called for here.'[40] This dating also adds precision to the first statement in Wesley's preface, that 'it was in pursuance of an advice given by Bishop Taylor, in his *Rules for Holy Living and Dying*, that about fifteen

---

[38] F. Baker, 'The Birth of John Wesley's Journal', *Methodist History* (1970), 8:25-32.

[39] Ibid., p. 27 and n. 7. Both Wesley and Whitefield refer to this broadsheet, *The Life and Conversation of that Holy Man Mr. John Wesley during his Abode in Georgia: The Affidavit of Mr. Robert Williams, of the City of Bristol, Merchant*, the only known copy of which is in the Bodleian Library, Oxford (Rawlinson MSS, J. fol.5). This is described by both Whitefield and Wesley as a reprint and was dated by the former to June 22, 1741.

[40] CWJ, I.242; *Letters*, 26:18 in this edn. Wesley's response was to advertise his *Journal* in the *London Evening Post*, July 29, 1740.

years ago I began to take a more exact account than I had done before of the manner wherein I spent my time, writing down how I had employed every hour'; he had begun his Oxford diary on April 5, 1725, a fraction over fifteen years before he penned his first preface on May 23, 1740.[41]

By this time, as we have seen, Wesley was in full conflict with the Moravians; the preface to the second part of the *Journal* detailing his dealings with them was dated September 29, 1740, and it was published in late October or early November. This was the last time that Wesley was in a hurry with the publication of his *Journal.* In the ordinary way, he would allow almost four years to pass between the events last recorded in a *Journal* and its publication, and real haste was made only in the period of confusion about his literary remains which followed his death; his executors brought out *Journal* 21 within a few months of that event, and only a year after his last entry on October 24, 1790. This usual delay between event and print must be constantly borne in mind by the reader, and it is frequently referred to in the notes below. The passage of time is sometimes briefly referred to: 'Some months since, John Smith, now with God, was pressed in spirit. . .'.[42] Sometimes it leads to the compression or contraction of an important matter in the light of later knowledge: 'I met several serious clergymen. I have long desired that there might be an open, avowed union between all who preach those fundamental truths, original sin and justification by faith, producing inward and outward holiness. But all my endeavours have been hitherto ineffectual. God's time is not fully come.'[43] On this point more would have been desirable; but, by contrast, the passage of time could open Wesley's lips as well as seal them: 'hearing an exceeding strange story, I sent for the person herself, Grace Paddy, a well-bred, sensible young woman. I can speak of her now without restraint, as she is safe in Abraham's bosom.'[44]

Preparing the *Journal* long after the event betrayed Wesley into

---

[41] This was not the end of Williams's accusations. He reprinted this broadside in the summer of 1741, and there were further reprints and a pamphlet in the summer of 1742. Whitefield, now at odds with Wesley on many things, loyally stood by him where the Georgia charges were concerned, and Wesley defended himself further with a twelve-page extract from his printed *Journal* in 1741 and two *Letters to Captain Robert Williams* in July and Oct. 1742.

[42] JWJ, July 4, 1771.
[43] Ibid., Mar. 16, 1764.
[44] Ibid., Sept. 8, 1765.

innumerable mistakes, quite apart from those to which he was in any case prone (Wesley teases his editors by gross carelessness about proper names; William Cookworthy is referred to as Clotworthy;[45] foreign names are commonly rendered by conventions peculiar to Wesley himself; Buonamici, for example, appearing as Bonavici,[46] and the bulk of the Dutch names encountered in the visits of 1783 and 1786 are inventions of his own). In March 1778, having described his visitation of the society at Bristol, Wesley is led by association of ideas to add events which took place at the following Conference and afterwards: 'This year I myself (which I have seldom done) chose the preachers for Bristol; and these were plain men and likely to do more good than has been done in one year for these twenty years.'[47] Sometimes the passage of time leads Wesley to abbreviate his narrative erroneously. At Halifax in 1784 he records: 'The house would in no wise contain the people; yet the wind was so high that I could not preach abroad.'[48] It is clear, however, from the independent accounts of both Joseph Benson and William Ripley that he preached out of doors twice, once at noon when he was unable to make himself properly heard and again in the evening 'upon a table before our garden', this time very successfully.

There are also errors which may be Wesley's, but may be uncorrected printer's errors. One which is probably Wesley's occurs twice in *Journals* 10 and 11. 'I read with the preachers this week the Glasgow abridgment of Mr. Hutchinson's *Works*, wherein the abridgers have expressed with surprising exactness not only his sense, but his very spirit.'[49] Here Wesley seems to have been misled by his polemic against John Hutchinson (four Journal entries above)[50] into attributing to him another book he did not like; the author in question was actually an Ulster Presbyterian, later Professor of Moral Philosophy at Glasgow, Francis Hutcheson. Occasionally the diary shows that the *Journal* is in error, as, for example, in the case of the *Journal* entry for March 1, 1786, which is an inaccurate conflation of the diary

---

[45] Ibid., Apr. 22, 1779.
[46] Ibid., Feb. 15, 1773.
[47] Ibid., Mar. 9, 1778.
[48] Ibid., July 11, 1784, and note.
[49] Ibid., Nov. 22, 1756; July 31, 1758.
[50] Ibid., Oct. 26, 1756.

entries for March 1-3. It is only fair to Wesley to note that errors of this kind are commonest at the very end of his life and in *Journal* 21 which he did not live to see through the press.[51]

There is another category of error which raises more fundamental questions about the way in which the *Journal* as we have it was constructed, and of this group three examples will suffice. On February 14, 1772, Wesley notes, 'I began to execute a design which had long been in my thoughts, to print as accurate an edition of my works as a bookseller would do.' Alas, the note itself illustrated Wesley's difficulties in securing the accurate production of his work. For the new edition of his works had been begun in 1771 and was completed in thirty-two volumes by 1774, long before the publication of this *Journal* in 1777. This may be a simple error occasioned by the passage of time, but it has the appearance of an entry accurately prepared for February 1771 (the preface to the *Works* is dated March 1771) and wrongly inserted.

Something of this kind has clearly happened in the other two cases. Under April 2, 1762, in the middle of the narrative of an Irish journey there is inserted a large set-piece obituary of Grimshaw of Haworth. The insertion is less remarkable than the perfectly accurate statement that Grimshaw was born in 1708 and 'departed, April the 7th, in the fifty-fifth year of his age, and the twenty-first of his eminent usefulness', i.e., in *1763*. Whether Wesley was short of material to fill the requisite sheets for *Journal* 12; whether he thought so notable a death ought not to go unnoticed in the *Journal* for the further four or five years until *Journal* 13 saw the light, or whether he simply made a mistake in assembling slabs of ready prepared material, is not clear.

The third example is also odd. In 1784 Wesley visited Bridlington and Beverley on successive days. Under the second day he relates: 'We stopped at a little town, where Mr. Osbaldeston lately lived, a gentleman of large fortune, whose lady was as gay and fashionable as any. But suddenly she ran from east to west. She parted with all her clothes, dressed like a servant, and

---

[51] Two cases where Wesley's redaction has gone to pieces are: (1) Aug. 22, 1786, where a visit to a wrongly named and now unidentifiable Dutchman is recorded, which the diary shows to have taken place on Aug. 23; and (2) Aug. 19, 1786; 'Joseph Bradford preached at six in the morning at Mon Plaisir les Terres to a numerous congregation.' Mon Plaisir and Les Terres are not only different places, but are situated at opposite ends of the town of St. Peter Port, Guernsey.

scarce allowed herself the necessities of life. But who can convince her that she is going too far? I fear nothing less than Omnipotence.'[52] The 'little town' is certainly Hunmanby, where there was a small Methodist society and where from 1770 the manor was held by Humphrey Brooke Osbaldeston, whose eccentric wife was Catherine, the daughter of Sir Joseph Pennington, Bt. It is not clear why Wesley relates the story in the past tense (*Journal* 20 was published in 1789). Nor is it clear when the visit to Hunmanby took place. The diary and the independent account of William Ripley show that on the day of the entry, Wesley was in Beverley (south of Bridlington) much too early to have taken in Hunmanby (to the north) on the way. It has been suggested (and it is not impossible) that Wesley visited Hunmanby on the previous day while at Bridlington. The diary, however, shows that Wesley was heavily engaged in Bridlington morning, afternoon, and evening; so the suggestion is not attractive. The story has the appearance of a ready-made piece, perhaps a sermon illustration, which Wesley was prompted to include in the *Journal* at a point where he was visiting the *Sitz im Leben*. If this is so, it is a reminder that we have no way of gauging how far the selection of material for the *Journal* was influenced in a general way by the things which were uppermost in Wesley's mind at the time when each part was prepared for the press.

The reader may now well ask why, since every published part was described as *An Extract of the Rev. Mr. John Wesley's Journal*, the textual prehistory of the publication may not simply be elucidated by reference to the manuscript Journal from which the *Extracts* came. The answer to this question is that no such journal exists, and that it is in the last degree unlikely that it ever did. Wesley liked a holocaust: 'I employed all my leisure hours this week in revising my letters and papers. Abundance of them I committed to the flames. Perhaps some of the rest may see the light when I am gone'[53]—but what was destroyed was a good deal less than a large journal; and when in 1774 Wesley was wakened in the night at the Foundery and found the place in imminent danger of being overwhelmed by a great fire in a timber-yard nearby, he records that, 'perceiving I could be of no use, I took my diary and my papers, and retired to a friend's house.'[54] There is no mention of a journal.

---

[52] Ibid., June 22, 1784.   [53] Ibid., Jan. 20, 1765.
[54] Ibid., Nov. 13, 1774.

All his adult life Wesley kept a diary, most of which survives, down to 1741. The present editors' original intention was to include the whole of this material, much of which requires to be deciphered from various systems of shorthand, abbreviation, and code, in the first volume of this edition of the *Journal*.[55] Publishing difficulties, however, led at a late stage to the decision to deal subsequently with the earlier part of this material in a separate volume. That volume will reveal that, like the later transcripts with which Curnock had more success, the diary was basically a brief record and engagement diary, expanded somewhat, but not greatly, in the 1730s when Wesley became anxious to use the document as a means of self-examination, at least as regards the profitable use of time. Entries such as 'necessary talk', 'good talk (necessary)', 'religious talk' abound. This is the document to which Wesley refers in the preface to Extract 1 of the *Journal* as being kept till the time he left England. He then adds: 'The variety of scenes which I then past through induced me to transcribe from time to time the more material parts of my diary, adding here and there such little reflections as occurred to my mind. Of this journal, thus occasionally compiled, the following is a short extract; it not being my design to relate all those particulars which I wrote for my own use only.'

The diary, in short, went on, but, as is the way with missionaries on foreign station, Wesley prepared for various recipients other fuller accounts, many of which overlapped at least in part. From them the column (referred to above) in the *Gentleman's Magazine* and (when a public defence of his conduct in Georgia was called for) the first part of the *Extracts* were both constructed. How nearly that published portion corresponded to what he was preparing in the year before Robert Williams's charges were made public, it is impossible to know;[56] but since Wesley believed his record would bear examination, and substantial portions of it were already in the hands of others, the probability is that much of what he prepared remained unchanged.

Some of this material is in journal form, and it was finally dressed up by Curnock for publication as a Voyage Journal, six

[55] Curnock (I.72) claimed to have had the key to the cipher revealed to him in a dream; not a completely accurate dream, one may conclude, since Curnock's longhand transcripts of the shorthand were at times shorter than the original.

[56] See notes in the Diary such as Apr. 6, 1739: 'At home; writ journal.'

Savannah Journals, and five Frederica Journals. These twelve journals were an editorial fabrication, as were also the materials he referred to as once 'in existence': the 'many copies and several versions of the Georgia Journal, possibly also of the Second Extract'.[57] The manuscripts which lie behind the first *Journal* are explained and published in collated form in the Appendix to the present volume. Briefly summarized they consist of the following.

1. Voyage journal, Oct. 14, 1735–Feb. 16, 1735/36 (three extant manuscript copies and one formerly known, now lost, none of which is in Wesley's hand).
2. Georgia journals, Mar. 7, 1735/36–Dec. 16, 1737 (five extant manuscripts, all in Wesley's hand, covering different segments of the period and written for different audiences).[58]

Of these items, three were not known to Curnock, but even their addition to the list does not substantiate his notion of 'many copies and several versions of the Georgia Journal' as it was later published. The extant papers represent the working up of material, sometimes for different purposes, of different overlapping periods. Taken together, these manuscripts fill out in an interesting way the extracts which Wesley chose to publish in 1740. The sheer bulk of material available in these manuscripts and the amount of duplication among them, however, make it difficult to display them easily in conjunction with the *Journal* as first published. Curnock adopted the very worst solution, which was to incorporate the material available to him into the text published by Wesley (admittedly with the warning signal of square brackets), describing the result as the twelve journals mentioned above, which were neither written nor published by Wesley or anyone else. The solution attempted here is to edit Wesley's *Journal* as it appeared in print, and in an appendix to incorporate the supplementary manuscript matter, indicating the relation of the documents to each other.

Editing the *Journal* as it appeared in print is, it must be admitted, an infelicitous description of the preparation of the text by the textual editor for the unit editor. The editions of the *Journal* published in Wesley's lifetime were full of mistakes, and those extracts from the *Journal* included in the edition of Wesley's

[57] Curnock, I.vii.

[58] For further descriptions and locations of these manuscripts see below, Introduction to the Appendix.

Works begun in 1771 were reprints of the first edition, *Journal* 8, to Wesley's disgust, being omitted by the negligence of the printer. In 1808, Conference directed the connexional editor, Joseph Benson, to prepare another edition of Wesley's *Works*. So far as the *Journal* was concerned this was marked by unexplained omissions; perhaps worst of all, the printer overlooked the various tables of *errata* prepared by Wesley himself. In 1828 the celebrated Thomas Jackson began his edition of the *Works*, which ran finally to fourteen volumes. In Jackson's view the business of the editor was to assist the reader by producing a good text, but to do no more. Jackson's text was a good one, but it still contained very large numbers of small errors, which were steadily reduced in successive editions. Curnock took as his starting point the fifth edition of Jackson.

The text here edited represents an attempt to establish a good modern text based on the stemma of the eighteenth-century editions and incorporating important variant readings. The publishing history for *Journal* 1 is as follows:

A	Bristol, Farley [1740]
Ae	errata slip in some copies
AW	London, Strahan [*Bibliography*, No. 19.i] (Printed extract, June 25–Dec. 22, 1737)
B	2nd, Bristol, Farley, 1743
C	3rd, Bristol, Pine, 1765
D	Bristol, Pine, 1774 (*Works*, Vol. 26)
De	errata page printed later
Dm	Wesley's manuscript corrections
E	5th, London, Hawes, 1775

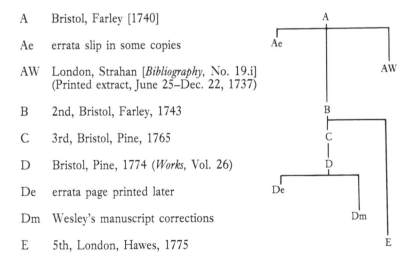

The text of the later Journals is established in the same way, *mutatis mutandis*.

As we have seen, Curnock believed that in addition to several versions of the Georgia Journal there had once been several copies, all lost to him, of the second Journal. The loss he thought 'the more remarkable because in all probability Wesley sent copies of his German Journal home for the information of friends, and it is in the highest degree probable that he communicated a journal account of his conversion to his mother, to his brother Samuel, and to Mr. [John] Clayton.'[59] Here again Curnock confuses two different things. No doubt Wesley wrote up extended passages while he was abroad for use in his *Journal;* indeed the elaborate documentation which he provided about the community at Herrnhut could not have been reproduced from memory assisted only by brief diary entries.[60] Even if the very formal testimonies of Christian David and his friends were given (in the form in which Wesley renders them) from their written submissions to the community archive, rather than in conversation (as Wesley reports), Wesley must have taken lengthy notes while he was at Herrnhut.[61] It is equally possible that he wrote extended journal-type letters home, though there is no longer any trace of these, and the register of correspondence accompanying Vol. I of the *Letters* in the present edition suffers at this point from there being no diary extant for that period. But even the possibility of his having written journal letters from Germany does not mean that Wesley wrote several copies of the *Journal* he printed in the autumn of 1740, still less that he wrote a much fuller Journal from which he later printed *Extracts.*

A number of later journal letters are extant, which Curnock hailed as fragments of another, perhaps the lost, larger version of the *Journal.*[62] Wesley himself notes that, 'knowing . . . that it was an entertainment above the taste of our evening congregation, I read some select letters at five in the morning to those who desired to hear them. And many of them were not a little comforted, and established in the ways of God.'[63] The reading of letters which were either edifying in themselves or contained encouraging news of the progress of the gospel was a familiar practice in evangelical circles, and it is quite clear that the *Journal* contained material which had been, or was intended to be, used in

[59] Curnock, I.ix. [60] Given in JWJ under Aug. 10, 1738.
[61] The material in J. J. Moser, *Altes und Neues aus dem Reich Gottes* (Frankfurt/Leipzig, 1733-39), 3:24 (cf. also Christian David, *Beschreibung und zuverlässige Nachricht von Herrnhut* [1735], pp. 98ff.), encourages the supposition that the original pioneers prepared written statements for visitors; but long afterwards Wesley's own version was reprinted at Halle. O. Uttendörfer, *Zinzendorf und die Mystik* (Berlin [1952]), p. 70, n. 2.
[62] For examples of these see Curnock, III.341-45; IV.148-49, 250-53.
[63] JWJ, Aug. 4, 1760.

this way.[64] That occasional letters of this sort survive containing material which might also be drawn upon for the production of the *Journal* is not evidence for the existence of a fuller Journal from which the published version consisted literally of extracts.

What seems to have happened, and what happened in Georgia on a larger scale and in a more complicated way, was that Wesley faithfully kept his brief daily diary and from time to time wrote up portions of it on a much larger scale with a view to use in the *Journal* later.[65] When William Ripley was travelling with Wesley across Yorkshire in June 1784, he saw the material at this stage.

Having got a glance at his Journal, I find he says: 'In Whitby I found the life that Darlington enjoyed for a season; great congregations and at parting such a select society as I have not seen since I left London.' He speaks well of the Bay of Robin Hood, only they had suffered much by differences among themselves. 'This week,' he says, 'I have entered on my eighty-second year, and I am as well and as able to labour as I was forty years ago. Nay, I am stronger than at twenty-one, and freed from those toothaches and headaches.' This he ascribes all to God's great goodness and the people's prayers.[66]

The general accuracy of what Ripley reports is borne out by the *Journal* entries for June 19 ('I met such a select society as I have not seen since I left London') and the good précis he gives of Wesley's account of the frictions in the society at Robin Hood's Bay. Ripley's account of Wesley's birthday thanksgiving also bears the clear marks of Wesley's *ipsissima verba* as they were

---

[64] The notion that Wesley kept on producing his *Journal* because of its converting power is strikingly absent from the sources; but a near-conversion through reading the *Journal* was reported in *Arminian Magazine* (1781), IV.251, and Thomas Rankin held that: 'I had been led to think, if I really was called of God to preach, the Divine power would attend the word in a very remarkable manner, in the conviction and conversion of sinners. This arose from reading Messrs. Wesley's and Whitefield's *Journals*; as also in hearing Mr. Whitefield myself. . . . [After various disappointments he made a special effort to meet Wesley himself.] As I had read all Mr. Wesley's Works, and in particular his *Journals*, I had formed a very high opinion of him; and the moment I distinctly saw him, and heard his voice, such a crowd of ideas rushed upon my mind as words cannot express. The union of soul I there felt with him was indescribable.' Jackson, *Early Methodist Preachers*, V.165, 167.

[65] See, e.g., Diary, July 8, 1784: '2 Writ journal; prayed' (cf. Mar. 31, 1736). A number of these narratives survive. One was printed by Professor Baker in support of a somewhat different theory of journal construction in WHS (1980), 42:93-100. H.M. Muhlenberg's *Journal* was constructed in a similar way, though being a business record and propaganda for fund-raisers much more than Wesley's Journal, it was written up more often. *The Journal of Henry Melchior Muhlenberg*, trans. Theodore G. Tappert and John Doberstein (Philadelphia, 1942-58), 1:x-xii.

[66] WHS (1904), 4:130. A similar example at a later stage of Journal preparation is given in *Wesleyan Methodist Magazine* (1911), 134:787-90.

finally published in the entry for June 28, 1784. What did not appear in the published *Journal* was the critical remark about the Darlington society, which was presumably removed at the later editorial stage; and what does not appear in Ripley's account is the suspect story about Hunmanby noted above[67] and a careful set-piece in which Wesley accounts for the ebbing of the revival at Epworth.[68]

These two self-contained passages, it may reasonably be assumed, were not in the papers which Ripley saw. When, indeed, Wesley talks of 'my diary and my papers',[69] he is talking of the material from which the *Journal* was constructed for the press at a late stage; the reason for the strange anomalies like the obituary of Grimshaw or the Hunmanby story, which appear like geological intrusions, is that the 'papers' included documents other than those expanded on Wesley's rounds, introduced into the printed version sometimes in error, sometimes on rather dubious grounds of relevance, sometimes because of the preoccupations of the moment. Sometimes, as in the case of the Epworth revival analysis, they were introduced as matters on which more thought was required than could be immediately given on a preaching round. This was the mass of loose paper Wesley was prepared to burn when a *Journal* was in print; and the printed *Journal* might fairly be described as 'extracts', since it was of briefer compass than the 'papers' on which it was based.

This view is borne out by the one Journal to survive in the intermediate state, written up (more or less) for the press, but not subject to the final redaction for publication, *Journal* 21. This was published after Wesley's death by his literary executors. They declared that 'there are unavoidable chasms in this *Journal,* owing to some parts being mislaid,' in particular a two-month gap between December 24, 1787 and February 25, 1788, a fact which confirms the hypothesis that loose papers were involved and that the Journal was not written in bound volumes like the diary. It is clear, too, that *Journal* 21 is written on a larger scale than even the fullest of Wesley's recent Journals.[70]

Is it then possible to infer from the special character of *Journal* 21 on what principles Wesley's final editorial ax was usually wielded? To the explanations offered by Wesley's literary executors,

[67] JWJ, June 22, 1784. [68] Ibid., June 28, 1784. [69] Ibid., Nov. 13, 1771.
[70] The following table gives the number of months (rounded to the nearest month)

Thomas Jackson in his edition added, 'It should also be stated, that this part of the Journal contains some passages which it is probable Mr. Wesley would never have committed to the press, and for the publication of which he should not be made responsible.'[71] If Jackson implied that Wesley was guilty of harsh judgments which would not have survived his second thoughts, he miscalculated entirely; *Journal* 21 is suffused with the same autumn sunshine that gently gilded all the later Journals. It is true that Wesley describes with some asperity the unwillingness of the London preachers to get up for the five o'clock preaching,[72] but he had always found it hard to bear that men younger than himself should not equal his own stamina. Some janglings in the London society over the management of pews are reported, but in terms quite familiar to readers of the *Journal;* at that point the lacuna in the *Journal* occurs, and the narrative is resumed only where Wesley takes leave of the society for what he felt might be the last time.

What Jackson regretted were probably statements very inconvenient to the ecclesiastical politicians of his own day, such as the gracious reference to John Hampson, Jun., who had left the connexion to become a curate in Sunderland,[73] and who subsequently incensed the connexional management by bringing out a fresh and independent *Life* of Wesley immediately after his death. There were forceful statements of the need of Methodists to remain within the Church of England, but also the blunt reference to the curate of Epworth who 'is not a pious man, but rather an enemy to piety, who frequently preaches against the truth, and those that hold and love it, [and] I cannot with all my influence persuade them either to hear him, or to attend the Sacrament administered by him. If I cannot carry this point even while I live, who then can do it when I die?'[74] To the defenders of the pastoral office in the age of Bunting and Jackson, this acceptance of the flock's determination to vote with its feet must have sounded like abdication, if not the sin against the Holy Ghost.

covered by the last journals, together with the number of pages of print required by Jackson's unannotated text:

Journal 17	28 months	62 pp.
Journal 18	43 months	96 pp.
Journal 19	37 months	73 pp.
Journal 20	46 months	100 pp.
Journal 21	50 months	161 pp.

[71] Jackson, IV.339.   [72] JWJ, Jan. 9, 1787.
[73] Ibid., June 1, 1788.   [74] Ibid., July 6, 1788.

The major difference between *Journal* 21 and its predecessors is that it contains none of the blocks of prepared material from newspapers or from Wesley's own files with which he had diversified the narrative of so many journals in the past.[75] To this extent *Journal* 21 is *shorter* than it would have been had Wesley lived to the point where he decided to prepare it for the press. As a confident young man in his mid-sixties, Wesley had nailed his colours to the mast: 'I abridged Dr. Watts's pretty *Treatise on the Passions.* His hundred and seventy-seven pages will make an useful tract of four-and-twenty. Why do persons who treat the same subjects with me write so much larger books? Of many reasons, is not this the chief? We do not write with the same view. Their *principal end* is to get money; my *only one* to do good.'[76] This programme—itself a good example of Wesley's direct and economical prose, rising only twice to words of three syllables—when stripped of its personal prickliness, amounted to a pitch for a subcommercial market in which size and price were all-important.

The evidence of *Journal* 21 is that, after the practice of a long lifetime, this economy of style still cost Wesley a big effort, put in on the eve of going to press. To judge by precedent, had Wesley revised his last Journal for the press he would have included more material and still produced a text one-third shorter than that which we have.[77] He would certainly have pruned the account of his voyage home from the Netherlands[78] and gushed less about the Mayor of Cork,[79] both 'passages which [to adapt Jackson] it is more than probable Mr. Wesley would never have committed to the press'. But at the end of the pruning he would still have had to cut a good many entries altogether. The final outcome would indeed have been *An Extract of the Rev. Mr. John Wesley's Journal.*

---

[75] This introduction of anecdotes was also a feature of Wesley's preaching and one which attracted hostile comment. 'Many have remarked that when he fell into anecdote and storytelling, which was not seldom, his discourses were little to the purpose. The remark is true. We have scarcely ever heard from him a tolerable sermon in which a story was introduced.' John Hampson, Jun., *Memoirs of the late Rev. John Wesley, A.M., with a Review of his Life and Writings, and a History of Methodism*, 3 vols. (Sunderland, 1791), III.170.

[76] JWJ, Feb. 17, 1769.

[77] The Journals were priced at between 8*d.* and 1*s.*; *Journal* 21 cost 1*s.* 6*d.* See *Bibliography*, No. 23, Table, Wesley's Journal. Thomas Coke and Henry Moore remark: 'Many . . . who knew and loved [Wesley] are not able to purchase the Journals, though the price is not considerable' (*Life of Wesley* [2nd edn., London, 1792], p. vii).

[78] JWJ, Sept. 2-3, 1786. [79] Ibid., May 12, 1787.

THE posthumous influence of the *Journal* as a whole upon Wesley's biographers was highly paradoxical; the more they departed from its form, the more they depended on its substance, and vice versa. The first biographer, John Hampson, Jun.[80] (a former itinerant), set out to give an independent assessment of Wesley, which by its very independence should imply the grounds that had sufficed him and his father for separation. In this enterprise the *Journal* was indispensable, but could not be the controlling influence; and, so far as the last years of Wesley's life were concerned, Hampson's *Life* and the last *Journal* were racing neck and neck towards publication.[81] Two official *Lives* followed, the first, knocked off by Thomas Coke and Henry Moore[82] in a few weeks, was designed to undo the putative damage created by Hampson and to brace the preachers to ensure that, though 'the god of this world has hitherto triumphed over every revival of true religion', he would not do so on this occasion. Coke and Moore had access to most of the corpus of Wesley's published material and relied very heavily on the text of the *Journal*. Yet their inability or unwillingness to manage the bulky sources in the time available meant that the balance which Wesley achieved in the *Journal* eluded them altogether. It is, moreover, difficult to avoid the feeling that they were creating a myth of a young Wesley according to canons which were shortly to be applied to the creation of a German myth of a 'young' Luther, and a generation later to myths of 'young' reformers and nationalists of all kinds. At the time of the indulgence controversy Luther was a middle-aged thirty-four; at the time of his conversion, Wesley was almost a middle-aged thirty-five. Each, however, could be presented as 'youthfully' outwitting the forces in possession of church and

---

[80] Hampson, *Memoirs* (see above, n. 75). It must have been galling to the official biographers that Hampson's sprightly *Memoirs* received the accolade of instant translation into German (*Leben Johann Wesleys*, trans. August Hermann Niemeyer [Halle, 1793]); theirs never did. The German edition included Hampson's attack on Coke and Moore written after the publication of his English edition.

[81] So far as sources went, Hampson's main contribution was early Wesley family correspondence which had passed into private hands (Hampson, *Memoirs*, I.iv).

[82] Coke and Moore, *Life of Wesley*.

state, and for the biographers of each this was a convenient way of circumventing the embarrassment of assessing their legacy.

In the *Journal*, however, Wesley had got to 1746 in the first six Extracts (what would in the end amount to about one quarter of his total material); by this time Georgia, conversion, and Herrnhut were well behind, his movement was established, and many of its organizational peculiarities were in place. Ten further Extracts took him to September 1773, by which time another stage of consolidation had been marked by the commencement of the first complete edition of the *Works*, and Wesley was being far more free than of old with his views on non-theological matters. The last instalments (one quarter) of the *Journal* covered the rapid expansion of the last seventeen years of Wesley's life and the crises created by the American War. It was in order for Wesley's biographers to dwell more fully on the young Wesley, personally unknown to their contemporaries, to introduce material about his family which had been no concern of the *Journal*, to enlarge on the Oxford years and the importance of the conversion. But Coke and Moore used almost a third of their space to bring their hero to the point of conversion in May 1738, just over a third for his main ministry down to the Deed of Declaration in 1784, and the remainder for Ireland, Scotland, America, and a general assessment, including an account of Wesley's last illness and death, which could not be covered by his own text. Coke and Moore, in short, relied heavily on the *Journal*, but stamped on the material they drew from it a quite different and less satisfactory shape and proportion.

Exactly the same was true of the *Life* attempted by another of Wesley's literary executors, John Whitehead, M.D.,[83] who, in a work of some merit, used well over half his space to get Wesley converted, and having consumed three-quarters of his space in getting to 1751, was constrained feebly to confess that 'the materials for this life are so abundant, without having recourse to Mr. Wesley's printed works; and the present volume begins to fill up so very fast, that I shall be obliged in future to take but little notice of the journeys of this laborious and successful minister of Christ.'[84] This was particularly ruinous for Whitehead who, instead of producing the apologetic official life which had been

---

[83] John Whitehead, *The Life of the Rev. John Wesley, M.A.*, 2 vols. (London, 1793–96).
[84] Ibid., II.265-66.

hoped for, forfeited his society membership by using the biography as a vehicle for a slashing attack on Methodist separation from the Church and on Wesley's ordinations in particular. 'Thus we see that Mr. Wesley's principle and practice in this affair directly oppose each other. If his principle was true, his practice was bad; if his practice was good, his principle was false: they cannot both stand good together. It is painful to see him fall into such a *dilemma*, which we have not seen before in the whole course of his life.'[85] A catastrophe so important, so unaccountable a 'hodge-podge of inconsistencies',[86] was far too significant to tuck in at the end of a work overwhelmingly devoted to Wesley's youth, too complex for the shorthand attribution to the great man's being 'biased by persuasion'. And by imposing this shape, so unsuited to his polemical purposes, upon his material, Whitehead actually increased his dependence on the *Journal*, which formed a much larger proportion of the total material available to him for the years of Wesley's youth than it did for the old age in which, as it seemed to the ex-preacher, everything had gone wrong.

In the biographies of the next generation, published or written in the 1820s, a substantial change is perceptible in the influence of the *Journal* upon form and substance. Robert Southey's *Life*, based on the whole range of printed materials available when he wrote,[87] is much less directly dependent on the substance of the *Journal* than those of his predecessors, but in general shape and proportion much closer to the *Journal* than they. Southey has Wesley born and born again in about one sixth of his space; about the same is needed at the end to deal with America and sum up after the Deed of Declaration (1784); the substance of the book is given to the general ministry of Wesley and to the subtitle, 'the rise and progress of Methodism'. For Southey, who wished to state a case against Methodism, knew that if the charges were to lie they must be made against the general tenor of the movement. That Wesley 'encouraged enthusiasm and extravagance, lent a ready ear to false and impossible relations, and spread superstition as well as piety, would hardly be denied by the candid and judicious among his own people'; these weaknesses,

[85] Ibid., II.423.
[86] Ibid., II.420.
[87] Robert Southey, *The Life of Wesley and the Rise and Progress of Methodism* (1st edn., London, 1820; edn. here used by Maurice H. Fitzgerald, London, 1925).

however, were being healed by the saving processes of time. But 'they who consider the wide-spreading schism to which [Methodism] has led, and who know that the welfare of the country is vitally connected with its Church Establishment, may think that the evil overbalances the good';[88] and in Southey's view this hazard had been real, if unperceived, in the movement from an early date. It was not, as Whitehead had broadly hinted, a question of 'the conduct of two or three preachers, or of a few individuals in the societies'.[89]

Southey's *Life* attracted great salvoes from the Methodist connexional leaders, who maintained that he saw 'religion in its peace, power, and purity, as set forth not only in the writings of Mr. Wesley, but of the Fathers of the Church of England, . . . as a *mental disease* of the most pitiable description'; Wesley was chronically subject to a form of it 'which with the pertinacity of a cuckoo, he [Southey] calls ENTHUSIASM, without once defining the term'.[90] In particular, Henry Moore, as Wesley's last surviving literary trustee, produced a vast official *Life* on twice the scale of the one he had hastily drafted with Thomas Coke more than a generation before. The increase in scale and the passage of time enabled Moore to master and introduce a greater variety of materials than in his previous biography; but the proportions of the work are strikingly similar to those of 1792, and it was these which had driven him into heavy reliance upon the *Journal*. Moore was determined, moreover, not merely to give Whitehead a drubbing, but to borrow heavily from him; and this could only underline the importance of the *Journal* to the substance (though not the form) of the work.

If Moore had hardly moved from the position of the 1790s, this could not be said of a younger luminary of the connexion, the author of its principal text-book in divinity, the *Theological Institutes*,[91] Richard Watson. He attempted a more popular reply to Southey, which was nevertheless a substantial and scholarly book and partook of many of the qualities of the work he sought to rebut.[92] Like Southey, Watson had passed Wesley's conversion by

---

[88] Ibid., II.334.   [89] Whitehead, *Wesley*, II.507.   [90] Moore, I.xii-xiii.
[91] Richard Watson, *Theological Institutes*, 6 parts (London, 1823–29).
[92] Richard Watson, *The Life of the Rev. John Wesley, A.M.* (1st edn., London, 1831; edn. here used, 6th edn. London, 1839). Watson had written an elaborate critical review of Southey's biography when it first appeared: *Observations on Southey's "Life of Wesley"*, *being a Defence of the Character, Labours, and Opinions of Mr. Wesley* (London, 1820).

the time he had trod one-sixth of his course, an economy the more remarkable in that he wished to defend a Pauline interpretation of Wesley's conversion against the 'several philosophic solutions' of Southey. The Deed of Declaration, the American ordinations, and the usual concluding discussions required a fifth of the space; all the rest was devoted to the general story. Watson believed that Methodism stood, as Southey hinted it fell, by its general record. And, like Southey, Watson believed that in the long run it was inherent in Methodism to separate from the Church, and to Wesley's credit that 'dissent has never been formally professed by the body', and for obvious reasons. 'The first is, that the separation of the society from the Church did not in any degree result from the principles assumed by the professed Dissenters . . . ; the second, that a considerable number of Methodists actually continue in the communion of the Church to this day; and the third, that to leave that communion is not in any sense a condition of membership with us.'[93] In short, the most appropriate form in which to discuss the life of Wesley in connection with a disestablishment controversy which had barely existed in his day was a treatment of the great man's ministry as a whole, proportioned much as it had been in the *Journal.*

How this notion took root leads the discussion back to its beginning, for the next two landmarks of Wesley scholarship were Luke Tyerman's *Life* and Curnock's edition of the *Journal.* Tyerman's huge three-decker[94] retains its importance, despite vociferous prejudices sometimes indulged even at the expense of his hero,[95] because of the great range of original material on which it was based and which it contrived to print. Thanks to Tyerman, manuscript sources now lost may still be consulted either in his text or in his voluminous manuscript transcriptions. All the more striking, therefore, that a work which moved as far as it was able from dependence on the *Journal* as a source, adopted a kind of journal form, being written as a succession of annual chronicles the general balance of which did not greatly differ from that of Wesley. Tyerman, moreover, found, as students of newspaper

---

[93] Watson, *Wesley*, pp. 462-63.

[94] Luke Tyerman, *The Life and Times of John Wesley* (1st edn., London, 1870–71; edn. here used, London, 1890).

[95] 'John Wesley was a dupe. Grace Murray was a flirt. John Bennet was a cheat. Charles Wesley was a sincere, but irritated, impetuous, and officious friend.' Ibid., II.55.

sources habitually find, that whatever the drawbacks of the chronicle, it has one considerable advantage; it illuminates the way diverse problems impinge concurrently upon the hero. This line of thought could be taken only one stage further. The fundamental mistake made by Nehemiah Curnock in designing the Standard Edition of the *Journal* was to envisage the task less as editing an historical source (Wesley's text), than of adorning that text with all the materials he could mobilize for a Wesley biography. Tyerman, with considerable success, had used the journal form to write a richly documented biographical chronicle; Curnock attempted to use the text of the *Journal* as the basis for a biographical and denominational compendium, and this was much less effective.

An editor must in candour make plain his procedures to his readers and hence cannot avoid stating a position towards the work which for three-quarters of a century has been justly entitled the 'Standard Edition' of the *Journal.* Nehemiah Curnock, who prepared that edition, put subsequent editors in his debt, and with all his numerous faults was not a stupid or ignorant man. No useful purpose could be served by cataloguing his errors; for no editor will prove infallible in assembling the myriad details required for a work on this scale. Nor should Curnock be held strictly accountable for the errors in Volumes 7 and 8 of the work which appeared the year after his death in 1915. John Telford says that Curnock 'had written most of the final notes, prepared the Appendix and much of the additional matter; so that the whole work has been carried out under his editorship'.[96] This seems to mean that Telford did not check, and perhaps felt debarred from altering, Curnock's final copy, notwithstanding that it contains some of the editor's less gentlemanly gaffes. A long quotation from Moore's *Life of Wesley,* for example, is given an incomplete reference, perhaps because it is both abbreviated and altered without notice.[97] A footnote reference to the *Dictionary of National Biography* article on Dr. William Falconer does not help the inquirer, as the name is entirely misspelled.[98] And in Volume 8, Curnock, who was not above appropriating other men's footnotes without acknowledg-

---

[96] Curnock, VIII.349.   [97] Ibid., VII.43, n. 2.   [98] Ibid., VII.205, n. 1.
[99] E.g., ibid., VI.227, n. 3, lifted with minor adjustments from Luke Tyerman's *Oxford Methodists* (London, 1873), pp. 61-62; and VI.172, n. 1, lifted inaccurately from WHS (1905), 5:77.

ment,[99] appropriated one without checking that it contained a serious error in a reference.[1] These points merely underline what is clear on other grounds, that Curnock, though a learned, was also an unscholarly man, and they do not extend to the most important point of all, the main design of the work.

Curnock, as we have seen, set himself two tasks which, though closely related in his mind, were neither of them strictly involved in his editorial responsibilities but nevertheless determined his editorial style. He wished to create a large biographical memorial to Wesley, so far as possible in his own words. Where that was not possible, as in the case of his dying days, the words of Elizabeth Ritchie could be added in an appendix;[2] or where there was a gap in the *Journal*, there could be a footnote account of what 'must constantly have been in [Wesley's] thoughts', in Curnock's own words.[3] Material from Wesley himself must, where possible, be incorporated into the text, even if, as was doubtless the case once or twice, Wesley had made the deliberate decision to exclude it. It was in the same spirit, wishing to leave no memorial stone to his hero's capacity for work unturned, that Curnock elaborately footnoted the letters that Wesley wrote,[4] whether they illuminated the *Journal* text or not (and they fall overwhelmingly into the latter category), or whether they were available to his readers or not. The very frequent footnote, 'See new ed. of *Wesley Letters*',[5] indicates an innocence about his connexion's celerity in scholarly publishing, surprising in so seasoned a campaigner. Curnock had been dead sixteen years before Telford's edition of the *Letters* had been completed.

He was also raising a monument to the denomination he served, and here the issues were less clear-cut. Curnock believed, truly enough, that the Wesleyan Methodist Church of his day had sprung from the labours of his hero recorded in the *Journal*, and believed also that the gates of hell would not prevail against it. His footnotes give the impression that he thought that wherever Methodism was planted, it became a permanent part of the church catholic, and he found the appearance of a village name in the text of the *Journal* a legitimate reason to footnote whatever

---

[1] Curnock, VIII.41, n. 1, lifted from WHS (1907), 6:82. The reference to *Methodist Magazine* (1803) should be to *Methodist Magazine* (1808).

[2] Curnock, VIII.131-44.

[3] Ibid., VI.170, n. 2.

[4] Ibid., V.243, n. 1; 264, n.3.

[5] E.g., ibid., VI.513, n. 1.

biographical or other material he could find relating to the place, whether it had any relevance to the text or not.[6]

There is, it must be admitted, a considerable grey area here where judgments will differ. A crucial factor in the development of early Methodism was the availability of hospitality for Wesley and his preachers. Where a bed was regularly to be had, the itinerants would call and a society was likely to be formed. In terms of editing the *Journal*, this often means (whether Wesley comments on the fact or not) that he is to be found in one place rather than another because hospitality was offered there. In due course one of the less pleasant forms of social distinction that came to prevail in Methodism was the distinction between those often somewhat more substantial people who regularly entertained the preachers and were associated with them, and those who did not. Curnock took this system for granted and used his footnotes to create memorials to those who sustained it long after Wesley's death. It is but fair to Curnock to recognize that this particular cause evoked some of his best notes, some of them embodying source material and personal reminiscences now no longer available.

No editor will now share Curnock's confidence in the future of English Methodism, central or local, to the point of regarding this kind of memorial-building as an adjunct to the editing of the *Journal*. On the other hand, the creation of a hospitality network was crucial to the early development of the Methodist movement, and some knowledge of it helps the reader to understand the *Journal*. The present editor has followed Curnock in attempting to elucidate cases of this kind, but not of the more general sort. His decisions in these cases are in one sense arbitrary and might not be followed exactly by any other scholar; but he hopes that they will on the whole be found reasonable. There is a similar problem a generation later in the *Journal*, when the age of chapel-building begins. Where an account of the origins of a chapel or society is needed to elucidate the text of the *Journal*, the editor has endeavoured to provide it; but he has not followed Curnock in celebrating Methodist 'chapelicity' on any heroic scale.

Two other features of Curnock's editing will find no defenders. Curnock was almost incapable of giving references to

---

[6] An example where it has no relevance at all is ibid., V.44.

published material in usable, let alone scholarly, form. Like any editor of the *Journal*, he had to make extensive use of the labours of Methodist local historians, the best of whom embodied a splendid nineteenth-century flowering of Wesley's eighteenth-century empiricism, capitalized much less by the connexion than by recent scholarship. Curnock, who assumed that his readers had this material at their finger-tips, frequently presented titles in such a way that they could not be traced in a library catalogue, and still more frequently presented the title of a work differently each time he referred to it. It is particularly important to avoid this in the case of local history, for the great British copyright libraries are so establishmentarian as to have overlooked much material of this kind. All the more important, therefore, for the inquirer to know at once that his failure to locate a title implies that the work is not in the collection and is not simply the result of his own inadequate reference. It is earnestly hoped that this difficulty will not beset users of the present edition and that Curnock's most fanciful references, such as the manuscript Life of Benson,[7] actually a valuable correspondence between William Smith and Joseph Benson preserved in the connexional archives, have been entirely eliminated.

Then, secondly, Curnock's title page attributed the work to him, 'assisted by experts'. Many of these were named by him in the preface, or by Telford in the appendix: men like Richard Green, Harrison Rigg, Henry S. Foster, W. C. Sheldon, and Telford himself. Many more, unnamed, were contributors to the *Proceedings of the Wesley Historical Society.* One of the reasons why that publication has been less useful than it might have been to historians over the generations is that its principal object at first was to elicit material to assist the editor of Wesley's *Journal,* and contributors got into the way of presenting fragments useful to an editor but less significant for more general purposes. Many of these fragments were used by Curnock, and have been found invaluable by the present editor. The *Proceedings* also gave scope to Methodist notions of team-work and made it possible to farm out particular tasks, the tracing of English quotations, the translation of classical quotations, the tracing of books referred to in the text, Wesley being as cavalier about titles as Curnock, and with much more excuse. It is but justice to the memory of this

[7] E.g., ibid., VI.513, n.2.

platoon of departed 'experts' to say that they were much better scholars than Curnock, who mangled some of what they did for him, and in one important instance failed to use it: where references are required to titles mentioned in the text, Curnock will generally supply not the title, but a reference to the *Proceedings of the Wesley Historical Society*, a private publication. In the present edition those titles are supplied, and it is much to the credit of those long-deceased contributors to the *Proceedings* that, though their work does not always meet the standards of the British Library cataloguers, it never fails to guide a student to the book.

The present editor, therefore, has been happy in the assistance, not only of many friends and colleagues mentioned in the preface, but also of the experts at Curnock's disposal. To mention this is to point to a revolution in the state of scholarship over the last three-quarters of a century. Curnock's 'experts' were all learned ministers and laymen of his own denomination, and he clearly expected his readers to be of the same stable; the only others interested in the *Journal* were a handful of literary scholars. That this kind of assistance is still very freely and generously forthcoming is a matter of gratitude; but the editor must now turn to Germans who know about Melanchthon, to Scandinavians who know about shipping, to Dutchmen familiar with Dutch evangelicalism, and to archivists of many kinds who understand their holdings. International scholarship has permitted the view that unique as Wesley's *Journal* is, it has a recognizable place in the general development of autobiographical writing; and the work of lay scholarship, British and foreign, impinges at untold points on Wesley's astounding range of interests. It has indeed saved us from the twin abominations of a Wesleyan Wesley who was the premise of a tedious ecclesiology and an ecumenical Wesley who can with equal tedium be relied on to form the middle term between any ecclesiastical opposites whatever. Scholarship of the modern kind makes its contribution to an edition, and it exacts its price. It is no longer possible to edit the *Journal* without considering what it can contribute as an historical document to modern scholarship, as well as what that scholarship can contribute to the understanding of the *Journal*. A modern edition is therefore every bit as provisional, as *zeitgebunden*, as was Curnock's; the notes which follow may be as gossipy as his, but the gossip is intended for other ears.

No editor will ever identify all the persons named in the *Journal*. In this edition it has been possible to extend the range of identification well beyond the limits attained by Curnock, and it is hoped that this work will encourage students to improve the quality and enlarge the number of biographical notices. The problems involved in publishing on the scale required by this edition of the *Works* unfortunately mean a considerable delay before readers can hope to receive an index for the *Journal;* to ease their difficulty biographical notices will normally be provided the first time a character is mentioned; and there will be many cross-references later. Topography was a matter to which Curnock gave little attention; here topographical notices will be frequent. Several places (e.g., Plessey, Northumberland) mentioned in the *Journal* have disappeared from the map, and many in Ireland have changed their name. Moreover, topographical information frequently illuminates the text, and that is the controlling object of annotation. Topographical notes are therefore provided on very many of those places mentioned in the text which will not be found on maps of modest scale; these are not generally cross-referenced. It is unhappily the case that places, like persons, are not all to be identified, especially as the unit beloved by the British topographers (like Samuel Lewis) was the parish; and Wesley often writes in a familiar and not always accurate way about the hamlet or even smaller social units. Lastly, explanatory notes, some of them substantial, are provided on matters of consequence, and many of these are cross-referenced.

To accompany Wesley on his pilgrimage through two-thirds of the eighteenth century, on journeys which extended from Georgia to Upper Lusatia, from Derry to Deal, and from Aberdeen to Land's End, is taxing for an editor who cannot count on the life-span of his subject; for the reader it should not be less than a liberal education. To 'locate' Wesley's *Journal* must in candour contribute one thing more to a liberal education: it must convey a reminder that the last generation of the eighteenth century was to produce both biography and autobiography of an entirely new order of excellence and to pursue ends which Wesley did not set himself. Some of these developments emerge from a sample of the work new in his later years.

The most sensational example of the new style, Rousseau's *Confessions*, began to appear in 1781–82, not long after his death; it had been pronounced in advance by Wieland to be of a quite different order of importance from those of Marcus Aurelius and Augustine,[8] and led that professed model of philosophic tranquillity, David Hume, to take defensive measures before a word appeared.[9] Posthumously published though they were, the *Confessions* appeared at the height of the author's influence, when sensibility was in full vogue. And their claims were not modest. 'I have entered on a performance which is without example, whose accomplishment will have no imitator. I mean to present my fellow-mortals with a man in all the integrity of nature; I know my heart and have studied mankind; I am not made like anyone I have been acquainted with, perhaps like no one in existence. . . . Whenever the last trumpet shall sound I will present myself before the sovereign Judge with this book in my hand, and loudly

---

[8] C. M. Wieland, *Gesammelte Werke*, ed. J. J. Gruber (Leipzig, 1826), 32:67.

[9] As it transpired Hume died before the *Confessions* appeared, and the *Confessions* stopped short just before the period of Rousseau's quarrel with Hume, perhaps because of his promise 'that there will never escape from him, in speech or writing, a single word of complaint respecting the misfortunes which have befallen him in England: that he will never speak of M. Hume, or that he will never speak of him but with honour.' *Original Letters of J. J. Rousseau* (London, 1799), p. 192. But Rousseau went on brooding over what he took to be Hume's malice, and his views were posthumously published in *Rousseau Juge de Jean-Jacques*. J. J. Rousseau, *Oeuvres* (Geneva, 1782–89), 21:252-53, 257-58. E. C. Messner, *The Life of David Hume* (Oxford, 1970), pp. 536-37.

proclaim, Thus I have acted; these were my thoughts; such was I. With equal freedom and veracity I have related what was laudable or wicked, I have concealed no crimes, added no virtues.'[10] This last, however, was an artificial concession to form. Rousseau's *Confessions* were, in the traditional sense of the word, bound to be a misnomer; he had nothing to confess but innocence.

Mankind at large might, as the *Contrat Social* proclaimed, have been born free, but was now everywhere in chains; Rousseau, on the other hand, was the offspring of an idyllic marriage, had grown up in a Swiss idyll, and, beginning free, was now (very nearly) as free as it was possible to imagine. If Bunyan wrote his testimony to gain the freedom of the narrow bounds of a Baptist congregation, Rousseau could be assured of the freedom of the world to come; he was troubled less by fear of hell than by defects of memory.[11] The harmless youthful amours which Wesley concealed in the shorthand and code of his early diaries,[12] Rousseau could puff out to half a volume. And if he thought 'the termination of a love affair is good for nothing unless it partakes of the romantic,' if his love-letters contained 'pathetic expressions . . . sufficient to have split a rock', and at the departure of Miss Vulson he 'would have thrown [himself] into the water, and . . . absolutely rent the air with [his] cries',[13] why be shy? Exaggerated sensibilities were not merely a luxury to which all were entitled; they were a perception of reality denied by the harsher rationalism of the Enlightenment. Richard Baxter would have turned in his grave to learn that all this could be justified by his own principle, that 'self-examination is but the means of self-knowledge. . . . Go to, therefore, examine and prove yourself.'[14]

Yet there were shadows, perhaps actual darkness, in Rousseau, and he had no revolutionary desire to break with the Enlightenment. Self-observation was the only way to a knowledge of mankind, and autobiography was the only way to set it forth. Mankind understood itself so little because individuals had not looked within and compared what they found with what they knew of at least one other individual. The difficulty was that the

---

[10] *The Confessions of Jean Jacques Rousseau*, Eng. trans. (London, Glaisher [1918]), p. 1.
[11] Ibid., p. 215.
[12] These are to form Vol. 32 in this edn.
[13] Rousseau, *Confessions*, p. 21.
[14] Richard Baxter, *The Mischiefs of Self-Ignorance, and the Benefits of Self-Acquaintance* (London, 1662), p. 2.

man who lived in society could not break through to the truth because he could never break free from the general make-believe. What was needed, and what Rousseau claimed to offer, was a basic turning away from the outside world to an artistic enjoyment of the inner life, a turn which would be a solvent of the religious and moral counterfeits of the past. Shaking off social convention and discovering the original goodness of human nature had brought him to peace and happiness; and the *Confessions* did not so much state this principle as reveal it to the reader. 'Did I take upon myself to decide, and say to the reader, "Such is my character", he might think that if I did not endeavour to deceive him, I at least deceived myself; but in recounting simply all that has happened to me, all my actions, thoughts, and feelings, I cannot lead him into an error, unless I do it wilfully, which by this means I could not easily effect.'[15] Rousseau invites induction, and offers an illustration of an individual self in the course of its development. And although Rousseau had earlier talked of the circumstances which led to personal development,[16] he had in *La Nouvelle Héloïse*, like Samuel Richardson, developed a novel-form which had as its theme conflicts of passions, not psychologically analysed but hinted at through the movement of feelings. It was not circumstances but the natural passions, of the heart (the kind of thing which, in another context, the quietists had explored) which conditioned the development of the individual. In the *Confessions*, Rousseau found for this view, not a fictional, but an autobiographical form and reached the peak of his literary achievement.

Such a form of self-revelation was unthinkable to Wesley. His views on child-raising, his demand for the disciplining, even breaking, of the naturally unregenerate infant will, were sharpened by all the self-confidence of a childless adult (he thought that even his formidable mother could not be trusted not to spoil her grandchildren).[17] And Rousseau's successors in the art of autobiography found other problems with him which helped to shape the development of the genre. That theme, however, goes far beyond our present purpose of establishing the limits of Wesley's achievement, which we may illustrate in three

[15] Rousseau, *Confessions*, p. 134.
[16] Misch, *Geschichte der Autobiographie*, 4(Pt. 2):847.
[17] Philip Greven, *The Protestant Temperament* (New York, 1977), p. 27.

very different cases of Benjamin Franklin, Edward Gibbon, and Johann Wolfgang Goethe.

Benjamin Franklin (1706–90) was an almost exact contemporary of Wesley, and his *Autobiography* (first illicitly published in part in France in 1791 and then in retranslations into English and half a dozen other European languages)[18] has a good deal in common with Wesley's *Journal* despite the differences in their theological viewpoint. For in some ways Franklin came from similar stock, and what he offered was a secularized, 'enlightened', version of the old Puritan confession. 'My first collection [he writes] was of John Bunyan's Works in separate little Volumes. I afterwards sold them to enable me to buy R. Burton's Historical Collections; they were small Chapman's books and cheap, 40 to 50 in all.' He read his father's library of polemical divinity and later regarded it as time lost. Like very many modern autobiographers, he derived great advantage from application to Plutarch's *Lives,* and, in the best Enlightenment vein, he had a penchant for scientific inquiry of the kind where calculation was involved and a strong preference for actual, as distinct from imputed, righteousness. 'There was also a Book of Defoe's, called an Essay on Projects, and another of Dr. Mather's called Essays to do Good,[19] which perhaps gave me a Turn of Thinking that had an influence on some of the principal future events of my Life.'[20]

The difference between Franklin and Wesley is aptly illustrated by their common interest in electricity. For some years Wesley carried an electrical contraption about with him, electrified people by the thousand, and in the spirit of the empiric wrote a small treatise explaining that the practice was beneficial to their health.[21] Franklin was only slightly ahead of Wesley in seeing

[18] By the time John Bigelow published the first edition based on the original MS (Philadelphia, 1868), more than 150 editions of the kind described had appeared. A scholarly parallel-text edition was produced by Max Farrand and others as *The Autobiography of Benjamin Franklin: A Restoration of a 'Fair Copy'* (Berkeley and Los Angeles, 1949). The edition used here is the even better one sponsored by the American Philosophical Society and Yale University and edited by Leonard W. Labaree and others (New Haven, 1964).

[19] Cotton Mather, *Bonifacius: An Essay upon the Good, that is to be Devised and Designed by Those who Desire . . . to do the Good while they Live* (Boston, 1710).

[20] Franklin, *Autobiography*, pp. 57-58.

[21] JWJ, Nov. 9, 1756; Oct. 31, Nov. 1, 1759. How empirical in the unscientific sense was Wesley's interest in electricity may be illustrated by his assertion that the life of his preacher John Prickard was saved when he was struck by lightning by his being wet through (JWJ, July 23, 1777). Wesley believed that this prophylactic was commended by

the interest of the subject, but he submitted papers to the Royal Society, demonstrated that lightning was electricity, and his work in the field, *Experiments and Observations on Electricity* (3 parts, London, 1751–54), consisting mostly of reprints of his scientific papers, attained international celebrity.[22] The difference between Franklin and Rousseau came out in the powerfully didactic line of the former, which the latter, his gaze fixed steadily upon the natural innocence within, neither could nor would rival. Rousseau's society was the great corrupter of natural virtue; that of Franklin would certainly reward those who organized themselves rationally.

At his most didactic Franklin presents, in a manner reminiscent of the Puritans or the young Wesley, a table of all the thirteen virtues (commencing with temperance and ending with 'Humility—imitate Jesus and Socrates') and how to acquire them.[23] This didactic tone, long thought appropriate for American schoolchildren, has always been unpalatable to some of Franklin's critics; Mark Twain, indeed, robustly accused him of being 'full of animosity towards boys', and, having 'a malevolence which is without parallel in history, he would work all day and then sit up at nights and let on to be studying algebra by the light of a smoldering fire, so that all other boys might have to do that also, or else have Benjamin Franklin thrown up to them.'[24] (What he would have said had Wesley been the prescribed pabulum for the American young makes an interesting speculation.)

It was, however, precisely Franklin's vigorous didacticism which in the eyes of the most highbrow German critics constituted his great superiority over Rousseau. Kant was quoted as saying that there could be nothing worse than the man who wanted to tell everything;[25] Friedrich Schlegel thought that people who wrote autobiographies like Rousseau were suffering

Franklin himself (ibid., Feb. 17, 1753), though this is the exact opposite of what he said. See Benjamin Franklin, *Experiments and Observations on Electricity* (London, 1751), pp. 24, 36.

[22] Franklin, *Autobiography*, pp. 240-46.   [23] Ibid., pp. 149-52.

[24] Mark Twain, 'The Late Benjamin Franklin', *The Galaxy* (1870), 10:138-39; quoted in Franklin, *Autobiography*, p. 15. For modern scepticism about Franklin's autobiography, see Melvin H. Buxbaum, *Benjamin Franklin and the Zealous Presbyterians* (University Park, Pa., 1975).

[25] *Biographie . . . Theodor Gottlieb von Hippel, zum Theil von ihm selbst verfasst: Aus Schlichtegrolls Nekrolog (auf die Jahre 1796/97, [Gotha, 1800/01]) besonders abgedrucket* (Gotha, 1801), p. 345.

nervous illness;[26] Schleiermacher thought that the confession was pointless from the standpoint both of the reader and the writer—the former must work for his own general point of view, the latter was not capable of the necessary self-analysis without destroying his inner life.[27] Franklin appeared to be the answer to the Rousseau-disease. Johann Herder, who had so far recommended only old biographies as sources for the history of mankind, was now possessed of the idea that autobiography ought to be of moral and political use and seized on the early French version of Franklin as 'an antitype to Rousseau's Confessions' and a great 'school of industry, common sense, and decency'.[28] His advice to Adolf Heinrich Friedrich von Schlichtegroll, who in 1791 began a great series of annual volumes containing notices of remarkable personalities who had died during the year,[29] was that he should include only those who had contributed substantially to the good of mankind and represent them so far as possible in their own words, written or spoken.[30] Who better to fill the bill than Franklin? He was not merely purported to go about doing good, but actually did so and vigorously explained how others might equal not only his benevolence but also his felicity. Certainly the pirated French translation of Franklin had no sooner appeared in 1791 than Herder, Goethe, and their friends organized the 'Friday Club', whose objects and rules were based on Franklin's mutual improvement society, the Junto.[31] And if Franklin afforded ammunition against the memory and idiom of Rousseau, he had also afforded at least an outline of his progress from Calvinism to deism. Development had not been a characteristic of autobiographical writing and was not a feature of Wesley's *Journal*.

Edward Gibbon (1737–94) received one of the more flattering of Friedrich Schlegel's categorizations of autobiographers, being

---

[26] *Athenäum: Eine Zeitschrift von August Wilhelm Schlegel und Friedrich Schlegel,* Vol. 1, Pt. 2, No. 1, p. 51; reprint in Hans Eichner, ed., *Kritische Friedrich Schlegel Ausgabe* (Munich, 1967), 2:196.

[27] Ibid., p. 223.

[28] Herder thought him 'the noblest popular writer of our century' and longed for even one European nation to read and accept his principles. Johann Gottfried Herder, *Humanitätsbriefe* (1793), 1-2; B. Suphan, ed., *Werke* (Berlin, 1877–1913), 17:7, 8.

[29] *Nekrolog enthaltend Nachrichten von dem Leben merkwürdiger, in diesem Jahr verstorbener Personen,* 22 vols. (Gotha, 1791–1806).

[30] Herder, *Werke,* 17:19.

[31] Beatrice M. Victory, *Benjamin Franklin and Germany* (Philadelphia, 1915), p. 119. Franklin's works were first translated into German by G. T. Wenzel at Dresden, 1780.

'one of the born historians who are themselves only the material of historical art'.[32] He represents part of the reaction against Rousseau in that, in a real sense, he failed to write an autobiography. Between 1788 and 1793 he wrote no less than six drafts of a life. In 1796, two years after his death, his friend and literary executor, John Holroyd, the first Earl of Sheffield, published two volumes of his *Miscellaneous Works*, and in traditional style, prefixed to them a memoir. This memoir, however, as Sheffield clearly explained, was a composite affair, pieced together by himself from the six documents bequeathed by Gibbon.[33] This version, which necessarily excluded much of Gibbon's material, was so skilfully done and so delighted readers and critics that it went on being republished by scholarly editors and presses into the present century, long after the full extent of Sheffield's labours and omissions had been made known. Gibbon's *Memoirs*, therefore, are a distinguished example of the process of biographical reworking of autobiographical material which we have already noticed.

The fact that in their finished state they are not the work of Gibbon himself is a point of consequence. For Gibbon failed to find a form that satisfied him for the memoir he wished to write, and that memoir was to be essentially a public life, that of an historian.[34]

In the prayers of the Church our personal concerns are judiciously reduced to the threefold distinction of *mind, body,* and *estate*. The sentiments of the mind excite and exercise our social sympathy; the review of my moral and literary character is the most interesting to myself and to the public; and I may expatiate without reproach on my private studies, since they have produced the public writings which can alone entitle me to the esteem and friendship of readers. The pains and pleasures of the body, how important soever to ourselves, are an indelicate topic of conversation. . . .[35] The experience of the world inculcates a discreet reserve on the subject of our estate.[36]

[32] See above, n. 15.

[33] No detailed analysis of the textual origins of the work which soon assumed an independent life as Gibbon's *Memoirs of My Life and Writings* is required here. The original documents were edited by John Murray as *The Autobiographies of Edward Gibbon* (London, 1896). They are discussed and used as the basis of a longer reconstitution of Gibbon's life in Edward Gibbon, *Memoirs of My Life*, ed. Georges A. Bonnard (London, 1966), the version used here.

[34] The differences between the drafts are discussed by Spacks, *Imagining a Self*, pp. 92-126.

[35] Like Wesley, Gibbon suffered from a painful and prominent hydrocele; unlike him he says nothing of it in his autobiographical papers. It was, however, a fact of importance; the operation on it cost him his life.

[36] Gibbon, *Memoirs of My Life*.

Yet too much discretion on a worldly point would make it impossible to explain how his public character, that of an historian, had been achieved. 'In circumstances more indigent or more wealthy, I should never have accomplished the task, or acquired the fame, of an historian: that my spirit would have been broken by poverty and contempt, and that my industry might have been relaxed in the labour and luxury of a superfluous fortune. Few works of merit have been executed either in a garret or a palace.'[37] There were black days before his father's death opened to him 'the first of earthly blessings, Independence',[38] when a largely wasted youth seemed likely to be followed by an aimless middle age.

In the end, all turned out for the best. Becoming an historian enabled him to attain distinction and to be a spectator at the same time. Even his youthful exile in the Pays de Vaud had paid dividends; plain fare strengthened his constitution, 'seclusion from Engish society' did wonders for his French, adapting to a total change of milieu and culture revived his love of reading, and he wasted no more time on 'the horse, the favourite of my countrymen'.[39] Providence provides no framework for the story: 'I have drawn a high prize in the lottery of life . . . the double fortune of my birth in a free and enlightened country in an honourable and wealthy family is the lucky chance of an unit against millions,'[40] and though Gibbon is unable to say that he was in any sense 'meant' to be an historian, he would assert with emphasis that 'I *know* by experience that from my early youth I aspired to the character of an historian.'[41] And he held that it was legitimate to look into his ancestry, not in the spirit of the old family chronicles, but to illustrate how the odds had swung his way in the lottery of life and how his own intellectual enthusiasms had been foreshadowed by some of his more eccentric forbears.[42]

In the nature of the case, such a story could not be didactic in the manner of Franklin—'my own amusement is my motive and will be my reward'[43]—and, if in the manner of Rousseau, he offered 'truth, naked, unblushing truth',[44] the story of the making of an historian could not be told at all on Rousseau's basis of perception of the natural passions of the heart. And though

[37] Ibid., p. 153.   [38] Ibid., p. 137, 154-55.   [39] Ibid., pp. 70-72.
[40] Ibid., p. 186.   [41] Ibid., p. 119.   [42] Ibid., p. 11.
[43] Ibid., p. 1.   [44] Ibid.

Gibbon failed to hone his memoir to the polished form he wished,[45] he conveyed through his fragments a sense of development, not only the making of an historian and the making of a success, but the making of felicity: 'Twenty happy years have been animated by the labour of my history.'[46]

What Rousseau's critics had so far failed to do was to overcome the radical disjunction which his method implied between the autobiographer and his times. If self-knowledge arose principally from the inward gaze, and the outer world represented largely a principle of corruption, this disjunction was not to be avoided. Franklin might have said something on this score had he carried his autobiography to the later date when he became involved in public events of the first importance; but his slight treatment of events in the Seven Years War does not suggest that he thought outward events had as powerful effect upon him as his own system of self-discipline, or that public life mattered to the autobiographer more than as a sphere for the exercise of his principles of active benevolence. Gibbon, in phrases only too famous, maintained that 'the captain of the Hampshire grenadiers (the reader may smile) has not been useless to the historian of the Roman empire', and that 'the eight sessions I sat in parliament were a school of civil prudence, the first and most essential virtue of an historian'; but he was being educated for profitable scholarly seclusion, 'the idle and insignificant spectator of the agitations of the state and the business of the world'.[47] Though offering hints on how the lottery of life had helped him to become a historian, Gibbon did not fully harness the historian and the autobiographer within himself, any more than he achieved an autobiographical form to his satisfaction.

Gibbon had, however, been symptomatic of a major shift in outlook, the attainment of an historical perspective. In Germany a combination of events and personal accidents led to this being applied to autobiography in a way certainly unprecedented and perhaps unequalled. German national sentiment had no focus in political or confessional institutions and had gradually been attracted to German culture, a culture whose attractiveness had

---

[45] Gibbon's memoirs sparkle not only with highly polished phrases—e.g., 'the Catholic superstition which is always the enemy of reason is often the parent of taste'—but also with the pursuit of 'polished and amiable people'. Ibid., p. 125.

[46] Ibid., p. 187.

[47] Ibid., pp. 117, 156.

been enhanced by the Enlightenment and the historical studies it had promoted. Then came the shattering blows of the revolutionary and Napoleonic wars which made it impossible to take any of the old institutional landmarks for granted any longer. How, moreover, was the confessional character of autobiography to preserve a connection with truth? (Goethe's later title, *Dichtung und Wahrheit*, cast a long shadow before.) Either, it seemed, the autobiographer must give up the idea of confession and be content with descriptive writing, or the confession must be supplemented by historical or psychological material. In other words it looked as if every autobiographer needed an editor, as Herder maintained in 1795,[48] or even a biographer, as the psychologist Friedrich August Carus held in 1808.[49]

Autobiographers, however, began to try their hand. Some of the Moravian religious confessions began to widen their scope so as to include psychological considerations,[50] and a scholar like Johann Stephen Pütter, the Göttingen public lawyer, attempted to delineate his own scholarly life in connection with public events and a century of historical development. In Pütter, however, the weight is still overwhelmingly upon the academic *curriculum vitae*, and the excursions into politics are obtained at the expense of an almost total neglect of interior experience.[51] Other writers of professional autobiography introduced narrative elements from the old lives of adventure, some of which, the lives of soldiers and of artisans, had concerned themselves with public events. The object now, however, was to use the narrative to cast light on the development of the writer,[52] and in this respect the autobiographers were getting close to the contemporary novel. At their best those of the new style could attempt a simultaneous presentation of the individual, the world, and the age, and trace the marks of the age upon the individual.[53] The limitations of the

---

[48] Herder, *Humanitätsbriefe* (1795) V, no. 54; *Werke*, 17:265.

[49] Friedrich August Carus, *Der Psychologie: Nachgelassene Werke* (2nd edn., Leipzig, 1823), 2:358-60.

[50] Niggl, *Die deutsche Autobiographie*, pp. 122-23.

[51] Johann Stephen Pütter, *Selbstbiographie zur dankbaren Jübelfeier seiner 50 jährigen Professorstelle zu Göttingen* (Göttingen, 1798). Pütter deserves a minor footnote in British history, for his three-volume *Historical Development of the Present Political Constitution of the Germanic Empire* was translated into English by Josiah Dornford (London, 1790) as an antidote to the untimely insularity of his fellow-countrymen (see pp. i-xi).

[52] E.g., Carl Friedrich Bahrdt, *Geschichte seines Lebens seiner Meinungen und Schicksale: von ihm selbst geschrieben*, 4 pts. (Vienna/Berlin, 1790–91).

[53] J. G. Seume, *Mein Leben* (Leipzig, 1813); reprint in Werner Kraft, ed., *Prosaschriften*

new professional autobiography lay in the fact that these interconnections, and the background to the life of the individual, were still illustrated by individuals and circumstances chiefly chosen from a narrow sphere of experience on an exemplary basis. But as Bunyan and Pepys had made two old autobiographical conventions into memorable achievements, Goethe was able to unite the new achievements of scholarly autobiography with other developments to create one of the greatest landmarks of the art, *Dichtung und Wahrheit.*

Goethe (1749–1832) had had a lifelong acquaintance, indeed preoccupation, with literature of this sort. Born in Frankfurt when the long reign of Orthodoxy was beginning to crumble, he was early connected with the Moravians, those energetic practitioners of confessional autobiography. As a mature scholar he was familiar with the whole European development from Augustine onwards, with Hieronymous Cardano, Benvenuto Cellini, and Montaigne, right up to his contemporaries. Nor was he concerned simply to read in this vein. He used Götz von Berlichingen's *Lebens-Beschreibung* as the basis for his historical drama, he encouraged Johann Heinrich Jung-Stilling to write his autobiography and helped to get it published,[54] he translated and

(Cologne, 1962), pp. 53-164. Seume claimed the honour of helping the king of England to lose the American colonies (ibid., p. 8).

[54] The various instalments of Johann Heinrich Jung-Stilling's autobiography are now conveniently collected in his *Lebensgeschichte*, ed. G. A. Benrath (Darmstadt, 1984). Partial Engl. trans. R. O. Moon, *Jung-Stilling: His Biography* (London [1938]); see also *Heinrich Stilling*, trans. S. Jackson (Bristol, 1835–36). The life of Jung-Stilling (1740–1817), a generation later than Wesley, seems to have been overlooked by Wesley scholars, but from a standpoint of both literary and biographical comparison there is much of interest in it. Jung-Stilling rose from nothing to be both an eye surgeon and an economist of note and wrote an autobiography of a coherence unmatched by Wesley. Goethe notes how his intense, winsome but narrow pietism attracted even the testy Herder: 'That Herder's power of attraction had as much effect on others as on me, I should scarcely mention, had I not to remark that it extended itself particularly to Jung, commonly called Stilling. Even Herder behaved toward him with more forbearance than toward the rest of us. . . . Jung's narrowness was accompanied by so much goodwill, his urgency with so much softness and earnestness, that a man of intelligence could certainly not scoff at him or turn him into ridicule' (*Dichtung und Wahrheit*, Bk. 10; Eng. trans. John Oxenford, *The Autobiography of Johann Wolfgang von Goethe*, ed. K. J. Weintraub [Chicago, 1974], 2:22-23). In later life, however, finding Jung mortified by the failure of an operation he had performed on the eyes of Herr von Lersner, Goethe rejected Jung-Stilling's views and milieu with some asperity: 'The things sympathetic persons of this kind love most to talk of are the so-called awakenings and conversions to which we will not deny a certain psychological value. They are properly what we call in scientific and poetical matters an *aperçu*: the perception of a great maxim which is always a genius-like operation of the mind; we arrive at it by pure intuition, that is, by reflection, neither by learning nor tradition. . . . I was glad to let

wrote a commentary on the *Life* of Benvenuto Cellini, reviewed the autobiography of Johannes von Muller, and wrote forewords to the *Memoirs* of Sachse and Mämel. He had also given a good deal of thought to biography and to the theory of what autobiography might be supposed to be, concluding that it required a much more active interchange between the ego and the world than his predecessors had understood or than he himself had once acknowledged.

Moreover, taking up themes from other styles of autobiography, he required a 'joyful' confession of the writer's own value in an unembarrassed narrative of his success and the great moments of his life; the writer should also instruct posterity by a faithful account of times past, the personal presentation of the truth in all this opening the possibility of his work becoming an independent art form.[55] The final impulse to act exemplified the interplay between the individual, times present, and conventions past for which Goethe called.[56] The death of Schiller and the political catastrophe of the German states in 1806 intensified Goethe's preoccupation with history and his feeling that the period since the outbreak of the French Revolution had constituted a major historical revolution. The other side of this great watershed was lost forever except in so far as it could be preserved as the experienced past of himself and others. This mission might offer private enjoyment and instruction for his circle; but it was in principle a public obligation, and, unlike the bulk of the autobiographical writing of the past, it must be written for publication to instruct the nation in the 'revolutions of the moral, aesthetic, and philosophical culture' he had witnessed.[57]

Finally, there came a request from a friend: 'The first thing we ask of you, then, is that you set your works—which in the new edition have been arranged according to certain inner relations—in chronological order, and that you bring together in

everyone interpret as he pleased and work out the riddle of his days; but this way of ascribing to an immediate divine influence all the good that after a rational manner occurs to us in our chanceful life, seemed to me too presumptuous, and the habit of regarding the painful consequences of the hasty acts and omissions of our own thoughtlessness or conceit, as a divine judgment, did not at all suit me.' *Dichtung und Wahrheit*, Bk. 16; Eng. trans., *Autobiography of Goethe*, 2:322-23.

[55] On all this see Ursula Wertheim, 'Zu Problemen von Biographie und Autobiographie in Goethes Ästhetik', in her *Goethe Studien* ([East] Berlin, 1968), pp. 89-126.

[56] Goethe prefixed a motto to the work from Neander: 'Man does not learn unless he is thrashed.'

[57] Goethe to Franz Bernhard von Bucholtz, Feb. 11, 1814; *Werke*, Abtl. IV, 24:153.

their interdependence both the circumstances of life, and the states of mind which furnished the subject matter, as well as the influences which worked upon you and—not less important—the theoretical principles you followed. If you direct this effort to a rather narrow circle, something may come of it that could be both useful and pleasing to a wider one.'[58] Here, in German style, was the old conventional demand for the biographical or autobiographical preface to a scholar's collected works.

Both the preparation and the conclusion of Goethe's work, however, showed that something entirely unconventional was on foot. In a way infinitely removed from what was possible to a man devoted to Wesley's style of life, he set about collecting biographical data, examining old diaries and letters, writing to friends for their reminiscences, working through the poetry of an earlier age, his own and that of others, and getting up the history, not only of Germany, but also of Europe in the eighteenth century. This was the preface to a series of skeletons where Goethe worked out the way in which the history of the Reich and of European politics and society generally could be made the framework, not only of his own life, but of the multitude of details of which it was composed. What made this such a formidable, indeed, in Goethe's own words, 'an almost impossible task',[59] was his determination that the person to be related to this vast context should not be a static but a developing being, in a way the Wesley of the *Journal* (as distinct from the Wesley of real life), notwithstanding conversion and the pursuit of Christian perfection, was not.[60] How difficult it was even for Goethe to keep a grip upon this came out in his own preface: 'What is demanded is that the individual know both himself and his century—himself insofar as he has remained the same in all circumstances, the century inasmuch as it sweeps both the willing and the unwilling along with it, determining and forming them so that it can truthfully be said that any man, had he been born a mere ten years earlier or later might, as far as his own formation and his outward achievements are concerned, have become an entirely different

---

[58] Goethe, *Autobiography*, 1:2b.

[59] Ibid., 1:2c.

[60] The conclusion of Robert A. Fothergill, *Private Chronicles: A Study of English Diaries* (London, 1974), p. 24, that Wesley '*is* his work; he has no personal life', is based on the assumption that the Wesley of the *Journal* and the Wesley of real life were identical, a curious conclusion from the historian of the private chronicle.

person.'[61] Here the self is presented at once as unchangeable and as the passive product of circumstances.

The union of life and times, both conceived in terms of development, was nevertheless achieved by Goethe, inevitably with consequences for his place in the history of the genre, and inevitably at a certain cost. In substance though not in word, Goethe is the severest of all the critics of Rousseau—it has to be the self related to the world, and the world has primarily to be not that of the general historian but the world (broadly conceived nevertheless) related to Goethe and his circle. That this world was primarily the world of letters was entirely appropriate and in no way a premise for the wilder flights of *Geistesgeschichte*. Goethe's belief that the individual was in some way an example of the general, also kept the two poles of his study together and preserved him from Rousseauesque introversion. This stance meant that Goethe must renounce the direct confession after the manner of the Moravians. If his poetry has sprung from life and has a confessional character, the object of the autobiography was to reveal the origins of the poetry. The self-portrait consists in showing his critical reception of the artistic, scholarly, philosophical, and religious currents of the time and his own interventions in this outside world.

But as Goethe moved towards the end of his work in the spring and summer of 1813, the shattering events of the War of Liberation and the defeat of Napoleon disturbed this relatively orderly pattern and drove him to more direct confession. 'There are few biographies which can represent a pure, quiet, steady progress of the individual. Our life, as well as that whole in which we are contained, is in an incomprehensible manner composed of freedom and necessity. That which we would do is a prediction of what we shall do, under all circumstances. But these circumstances lay hold on us in their own fashion. The *what* lies in us, the *how* seldom depends on us, after the *wherefore* we dare not ask, and on this account we are rightly referred to the *quia*.'[62] This doctrine was at loggerheads with the proverb prefixed to Part 3 of the *Autobiography* ('Care is taken that trees do not grow into the sky')[63] and with a foreword Goethe wrote to this part saying that his original intention was to construct his biography on the logical

[61] Goethe, *Autobiography*, 1:2c.
[62] Ibid., 2:95.
[63] Ibid., 2:61.

pattern of the laws of plant development; this foreword Goethe now left unprinted.[64]

By the time Goethe had come to the last book, this random force of circumstance had grown to 'the immense and incomprehensible', a force which 'seemed to sport at will with the necessary elements of our existence. . . . In the impossible alone did it appear to find pleasure, while it rejected the possible with contempt. To this principle, which seemed to come in between all other principles, I gave the name of the Demonic.' From this Goethe could find no refuge in artistic creation. The demonic was only too fully embodied in the popular heroes of the age. 'Seldom if ever do the great men of an age find their equals among their contemporaries, and they are overcome by nothing but the universe itself; and it is from the observation of this fact that the strange but most striking proverb must have arisen, *Nemo contra Deum nisi Deus ipse.*'[65] It was time for Goethe to draw his great work to a close.

Practical considerations indeed pointed in the same direction. Books 1–15 were published or ready for the publisher in May 1814, and much of the rest was already in draft by 1816. But in fact Books 16–20 were not completed till Goethe's last year, were published posthumously, and took Goethe's story only up to the time he accepted a post at Weimar in 1775. Remarkable as his achievement was, he could not continue it, as Wesley continued his simple chronicle to the point where failing strength compelled him to put it down.[66] Nor is it clear that this was the fault of the demonic. The last part of Goethe's autobiography was heavily centred on his love for Lili Schönemann, and he found it hard to work on this while she was still alive. By the same token it was difficult to be candid about the Weimar years while the actors were still on the stage. The dialectic between man and his times might reveal much, but could not be allowed to reveal all. Ultimately, Goethe, like Wesley, escapes from his autobiography.

---

[64] *Werke*, Abtl. I, 28:356-57.
[65] Goethe, *Autobiography*, 2:423, 425.
[66] The Journal in draft form which Wesley's executors found possible to publish continued to within six months, and the diary to within six days, of his death.

AN EXTRACT

OF THE

Rev. Mr. JOHN WESLEY'S

JOURNAL

From his Embarking for GEORGIA

To his Return to LONDON.

What shall we say then?——That Israel which follow'd after the Law of Righteousness, hath not attained to the Law of Righteousness.—— Wherefore? Because they sought it not by Faith, but as it were by the Works of the Law. Rom. ix. 30, 31.

BRISTOL:

Printed by S. and F. FARLEY.

And sold at the New School-House in the Horse-Fair; and by the Booksellers in Town and Country.

The Preface

1. It was in pursuance of an advice given by Bishop Taylor, in his *Rules for Holy Living and Dying*,[1] that about fifteen years ago I began to take a more exact account than I had done before of the manner wherein I spent my time, writing down how I had 5 employed every hour.[2] This I continued to do, wherever I was, till the time of my leaving England. The variety of scenes which I then passed through induced me to transcribe from time to time the more material parts of my diary, adding here and there such little reflections as occurred to my mind. Of this journal, thus 10 occasionally compiled, the following is a short extract;[3] it not being my design to relate all those particulars which I wrote for my own use only, and which would answer no valuable end to others, however important they were to me.

2. Indeed I had no design or desire to trouble the world with 15 any of my little affairs; as can't but appear, to every impartial mind, from my having been so long 'as one that heareth not',[4] notwithstanding the loud and frequent calls I have had to answer for myself. Neither should I have done it now had not Captain Williams's affidavit,[5] published *as soon as he had left England*, laid 20

---

[1] Jeremy Taylor's 'first general instrument of Holy Living' was 'Care of our time', and he provided twenty-three 'rules for employing our time' profitably. See J. Taylor, *The Rule and Exercises of Holy Living* (19th edn., London, 1703), pp. 6-13.

[2] The first extract from the *Journal* is undated but was published about the end of May 1740. In the spring of 1725 Wesley had begun to keep a diary.

[3] Wesley sent his voyage journal to James Hutton, son of the Rev. John Hutton, the neighbour and friend of his brother Samuel Wesley in Westminster. The reading of the journal and letters led to the formation of a society in Hutton's house. Daniel Benham, *Memoirs of James Hutton* (London, 1856), pp. 12-13; cf. *Wesleyan Methodist Magazine* (1857), 80:158.

[4] Cf. Ps. 38:14.

[5] Capt. Robert Williams, who held a 500-acre lot in Georgia and caused much trouble to the Georgia Trustees on the score of his conveyance and his desire for Negro slaves (Egmont, *The Journal of the Earl of Egmont*, ed. Robert G. McPherson [Athens, Ga., 1962], p. 307) and who was trying to establish his credit with commercial connections in Bristol (A. D. Candler, *Colonial Records of the State of Georgia*, 18 vols. [Atlanta, 1904–8], IV.29, V.658), swore an affidavit before the Mayor of Bristol, Mar. 14/25, 1740, accusing Wesley of absconding when given bail to answer bills brought against him by the grand jury in Savannah. Whitefield took some trouble to clear Wesley from this charge (Curnock, VIII.256-58), which is said to have been due to Wesley's animosity against slavery. The affidavit and other documents relating to the case were published in *The Progress of*

an obligation upon me to do what in me lies in obedience to that
command of God, 'Let not the good which is in you be evil spoken
of.'[6] With this view I do at length 'give an answer to every man that
asketh me a reason of the hope which is in me',[7] that in all these
5 things 'I have a conscience void of offence towards God and
towards man.'[8]

3. I have prefixed hereto a letter wrote several years since,
containing a plain account of the rise of that little Society in
Oxford which has been so variously represented. Part of this was
10 published in 1733,[9] but without my consent or knowledge. It now
stands as it was wrote, without any addition, diminution, or
amendment, it being my only concern herein nakedly to 'declare
the thing as it is'.[10]

4. Perhaps my employments of another kind may not allow me
15 to give any farther answer to them who 'say all manner of evil of
me falsely',[11] and seem to 'think that they do God service'.[12]
Suffice it that both they and I shall shortly 'give an account to him
that is ready to judge the quick and the dead'.[13]

Methodism in Bristol: or the Methodist Unmasked (Bristol, 1743). Later in the year Williams
prepared papers against the Georgia Trustees, who expected trouble from him in
Parliament. He subsequently opened a store in Port Royal, Carolina (Candler, *Colonial
Records*, V.561-62, 658). For evidence that JW's *Journal*, designed to vindicate him against
these charges, was not published till the summer of 1740, see Frank Baker, 'The Birth of
John Wesley's Journal' in *Methodist History* (1970), 8:25-32.

6 Cf. Rom. 14:16.
7 Cf. 1 Pet. 3:15.
8 Cf. Acts 24:16.
9 In *The Oxford Methodists; Being some Account of a Society of Young Gentlemen in that City
so Denominated* (London, Roberts, 1733), which has sometimes been attributed to William
Law.
10 Cf. Job 26:3.
11 Cf. Matt. 5:11.
12 Cf. John 16:2.
13 1 Pet. 4:5.

Oxon, Oct, [19], 1732[14]

Sir,[15]

The occasion of my giving you this trouble is of a very extraordinary nature. On Sunday last I was informed (as no doubt you will be e'er long) that my brother and I had killed your son; 5 that the rigorous fasting which he had imposed upon himself, by our advice, had increased his illness and hastened his death. Now though, considering it in itself, 'it is a very small thing with me to be judged by man's judgment,'[16] yet as the being thought guilty of so mischievous an imprudence might make me less able to do the 10 work I came into the world for, I am obliged to clear myself of it by observing to you, as I have done to others, that your son left off fasting about a year and a half since, and that it is not yet half a year since I began to practise it.[17]

I must not let this opportunity slip of doing my part towards 15 giving you a juster notion of some other particulars relating both to him and myself which have been industriously misrepresented to you.

In March last he received a letter from you which, being not able to read, he desired me to read to him; several of the 20 expressions whereof I perfectly remember, and shall do till I too am called hence. I then determined that if God was pleased to take away your son before me I would justify him and myself, which I now do with all plainness and simplicity, as both my character and cause require. 25

In one practice for which you blamed your son I am only concerned as a friend, not as a partner. That therefore I shall consider first. Your own account of it was in effect this:

> He frequently went into poor peoples' houses in the villages about Holt, called their children together, and instructed them in their duty to God, their 30

---

[14] Charles Wesley's transcript of this letter is dated Oct. 18, 1732; all contemporary editions incorrectly give the date as 1730. John Wesley's diary clearly indicates the letter was written Oct. 19-20, 1732. Cf. Oxford diary, Wed., Oct. 19, 1732, and the reference to Clayton in JW's *A Short History of Methodism*, §4 (*Bibliography*, No. 264; see Vol. 9 of this edn.).

[15] Richard Morgan (*c.* 1679-1742), Second Remembrancer in the Court of Exchequer, Dublin. He was educated at Hart Hall, Oxford, and the Middle Temple, London. His son William was one of the original circle of Oxford Methodists; his younger son Richard was placed under Wesley's tuition in 1733 and subsequently converted.

[16] 1 Cor. 4:3.

[17] In 1725 JW had resolved to fast on the last Wednesday of every month (Oxford diary, Dec. 1, 1725), but had not stuck to this resolution. Changing his practice in various ways

neighbour, and themselves. He likewise explained to them the necessity of private as well as public prayer, and provided them with such forms as were best suited to their several capacities. And being well apprised how much the success of his endeavours depended on their goodwill towards him, to win upon their
5 affections he sometimes distributed among them a little of that money which he had saved from gaming, and the other fashionable expenses of the place.

This is the first charge against him; upon which all that I shall observe is, that I will refer it to your own judgment whether it be fitter to have a place in the catalogue of his faults, or of those
10 virtues for which he is 'now numbered among the sons of God'.[18]

If all the persons concerned in 'that ridiculous Society, whose follies you have so often heard repeated' could but give such a proof of their deserving the glorious title[a] which was once bestowed upon them, they would be contented that their 'lives',
15 too, 'should be counted madness, and their end thought to be without honour'.[19] But the truth is, their title to holiness stands upon much less stable foundations; as you will easily perceive when you know the ground of this wonderful outcry, which, it seems, England is not wide enough to contain.

20 In November 1729, at which time I came to reside at Oxford, your son, my brother, myself, and one more,[20] agreed to spend three or four evenings in a week together. Our design was to read over the classics, which we had before read in private, on common nights, and on Sunday some book in divinity. In the summer
25 following Mr. M[organ] told me he had called at the jail to see a man who was condemned for killing his wife, and that, from the talk he had with one of the debtors, he verily believed it would do much good if anyone would be at the pains of now and then speaking with them. This he so frequently repeated that on the
30 24th of August, 1730, my brother and I walked with him to the Castle. We were so well satisfied with our conversation there that

---

[a] 'The Holy Club'.

under the influence of John Clayton, JW began from the first Friday in June 1732 to fast till at least 3 p.m. every Wednesday and Friday (see Oxford diaries, Vol. 32 in this edn.).
[18] Cf. Wisd. 5:5.
[19] Cf. Wisd. 5:4.
[20] Robert Kirkham, son of Lionel Kirkham of Stanton, Gloucester, cleric, matriculated at Merton College, Oxford, July 12, 1727, aged 19; B.C.L. 1735. One of Wesley's letters (25:245 in this edn.) and his Oxford diary indicate that Kirkham's change of behaviour in early 1730 and his consequent close association with the Oxford Methodists were simultaneous with the beginning of regular meetings of the group; he was much in JW's company during that time. He died in 1767.

we agreed to go thither once or twice a week; which we had not done long before he desired me to go with him to see a poor woman in the town who was sick. In this employment too, when we came to reflect upon it, we believed it would be worth while to spend an hour or two in a week, provided the minister of the 5 parish in which any such person was were not against it. But that we might not depend wholly on our own judgments I wrote an account to my father[21] of our whole design; withal begging that he, who had lived seventy years in the world, and seen as much of it as most private men have ever done, would advise us whether we 10 had yet gone too far, and whether we should now stand still or go forward.

Part of his answer, dated Sept. 21, 1730, was this:

And now, as to your own designs and employments, what can I say less of them than, *Valde probo*,[b] and that I have the highest reason to bless God that he 15 has given me two sons together at Oxford, to whom he has given grace and courage to turn the war against the world and the devil, which is the best way to conquer them. They have but one more enemy to combat with, the flesh; which if they take care to subdue by fasting and prayer, there will be no more for them to do but to proceed steadily in the same course, and expect the crown which 20 fadeth not away.[22] You have reason to bless God, as I do, that you have so fast a friend as Mr. M[organ], who, I see, in the most difficult service is ready to break the ice for you. You do not know of how much good that poor wretch who killed his wife has been the providential occasion. I think I must adopt Mr. M[organ] to be my son, together with you and your brother Charles; and when I have such 25 a ternion to prosecute that war wherein I am now *miles emeritus*,[23] I shall not be ashamed when they speak with their enemies in the gate.

I am afraid lest the main objection you make against your going on in the business with the prisoners may secretly proceed from flesh and blood. For 'who can harm you if you are followers of that which is' so 'good,'[24] and which will be 30 one of the marks by which the Shepherd of Israel will know his sheep at the last day? Though if it were possible for you to suffer a little in the cause, you would have a confessor's reward. You own, none but such as are out of their senses would be prejudiced against your acting in this manner, but say, 'These are they that need a physician.'[25] But what if they will not accept of one who will be 35

---

[b] 'I greatly approve.'

---

[21] Samuel Wesley, Sen. (1662–1735), second son of John Wesley. Educated in London for the Independent ministry, 1678–83; and at Exeter College, Oxford, 1684–88; B.A. 1688. Ordained deacon 1688, priest 1689/90; rector of South Ormsby, 1691–95, rector of Epworth, 1695–1735, and of Wroot, 1722–34.

[22] See 1 Pet. 5:4.

[23] 'A worn-out soldier'.

[24] Cf. 1 Pet. 3:13.

[25] Cf. Matt. 9:12.

welcome to the poor prisoners? Go on then, in God's name, in the path to which
your Saviour has directed you, and that track wherein your father has gone
before you! For when I was an undergraduate at Oxford I visited those in the
Castle there, and reflect on it with great satisfaction to this day. Walk as
5 prudently as you can, though not fearfully, and my heart and prayers are with
you.

Your first regular step is to consult with him (if any such there be) who has a
jurisdiction over the prisoners, and the next is to obtain the direction and
approbation of your bishop. This is Monday morning, at which time I shall
10 never forget you. If it be possible, I should be glad to see you all three here in the
fine end of the summer. But if I cannot have that satisfaction, I am sure I can
reach you every day, though you were beyond the Indies. Accordingly, to him,
who is everywhere, I now heartily commit you, as being,

Your most affectionate and joyful father.

15   In pursuance of these directions I immediately went to Mr.
Gerard,[26] the Bishop of Oxford's chaplain, who was likewise the
person that took care of the prisoners when any were condemned
to die (at other times they were left to their own care). I proposed
to him our design of serving them as far as we could, and my own
20 intention to preach there once a month if the bishop approved of
it. He much commended our design, and said he would answer
for the bishop's approbation, to whom he would take the first
opportunity of mentioning it. It was not long before he informed
me he had done so, and that his lordship not only gave his
25 permission, but was greatly pleased with the undertaking, and
hoped it would have the desired success.

Soon after, a gentleman of Merton College, who was one of our
little company, which now consisted of five persons,[27] acquainted
us that he had been much rallied the day before for being a
30 member of 'The Holy Club', and that it was become a common
topic of mirth at his college, where they had found out several of
our customs to which we were ourselves utter strangers. Upon
this I consulted my father again, in whose answer were these
words:

[26] Apparently Joseph Gerard, matriculated at Oriel College 1718, aged 18, ordained
1727 to serve as curate of Cuddesdon, becoming rector of St. Martin's, Oxford in 1729,
and vicar of Banbury in 1734. The Bishop was John Potter (1674?–1747) Bishop of
Oxford, 1715–37; Archbishop of Canterbury, 1737–47. Potter ordained JW deacon 1725,
priest 1728.
[27] To the original four—the Wesley brothers, Robert Kirkham (the 'gentleman of
Merton College'), and William Morgan—the latter now introduced John Boyce
(matriculated at Christ Church 1727, aged 16, M.A. 1735), son of Sir John Boyce, Mayor
of Oxford in 1727–28.

Dec. 1 [1730]

This day I received both yours,[28] and this evening, in the course of our reading,[29] I thought I found an answer that would be more proper than any I myself could dictate; though since it will not be easily translated I send it in the original. 2 Cor. 7:4. Πολλή μοι καύχησις ὑπὲρ ὑμῶν· πεπλήρωμαι τῇ παρακλήσει, ὑπερπερισσεύομαι τῇ χαρᾷ.[c] What would you be? Would you be angels? I question whether a mortal can arrive to a greater degree of perfection than steadily to do good, and for that very reason patiently and meekly to suffer evil. For my part, on the present view of your actions and designs, my daily prayers are that God would keep you humble; and then I am sure that if you continue to 'suffer for righteousness' sake',[30] though it be but in a lower degree, 'the Spirit of God and of glory' shall in some good measure 'rest upon you'.[31] Be never weary of well-doing; never look back, for you know the prize and the crown are before you. Though I can scarce think so meanly of you as that you would be discouraged with 'the crackling of thorns under a pot'.[32] Be not high-minded, but fear. Preserve an equal temper of mind under whatever treatment you meet with from a not very just or well-natured world. Bear no more sail than is necessary, but steer steady. The less you value yourselves for these unfashionable duties (as there is no such thing as works of supererogation), the more all good and wise men will value you, if they see your actions are of a piece; or, which is infinitely more, he by whom actions and intentions are weighed will both accept, esteem, and reward you.[33]

Upon this encouragement we still continued to sit[34] together as usual; and to confirm one another, as well as we could, in our resolutions to communicate as often as we had an opportunity (which is here once a week) and to do what service we could to our acquaintance, the prisoners, and two or three poor families in the, town. But the outcry daily increasing, that we might show what ground there was for it, we proposed to our friends, or opponents, as we had opportunity, these, or the like questions:

---

[c] 'Great is my glorying of you: I am filled with comfort. I am exceeding joyful.'

[28] I.e., JW's reply of Nov. 23 to the letter of his father of Sept. 21, 1730, and probably another by Charles Wesley, neither of which is extant.

[29] The first and second editions read, 'in our course of our reading'; 1765 and 1774, 'in the course of our reading'; 1775, 'in our course of reading'. Whitehead, *Wesley*, I.425, gives the text presented here as the version of the original letter by Samuel Wesley.

[30] 1 Pet. 3:14.

[31] Cf. 1 Pet. 4:14.

[32] Eccles. 7:6.

[33] A further passage in this letter is quoted in Moore, *Wesley*, I.171: 'I hear my son John has the honour of being styled the "Father of the Holy Club": if it be so, I am sure I must be the grandfather of it; and I need not say that I had rather any of my sons should be so dignified and distinguished than to have the title of His Holiness.'

[34] 1774, 'meet'.

I. Whether it does not concern all men of all conditions to imitate him, as much as they can, 'who went about doing good'?[35]

Whether all Christians are not concerned in that command, 'while we have time let us do good to all men'?[36]

5 Whether we shall not be more happy hereafter, the more good we do now?

Whether we can be happy at all hereafter unless we have according to our power 'fed the hungry, clothed the naked, visited those that are sick, and in prison',[37] and made all these actions subservient to a higher purpose, even the saving of souls from death?

10 Whether it be not our bounden duty always to remember that he did more for us than we can do for him, who assures us, 'Inasmuch as ye have done it unto one of the least of these my brethren, ye have done it unto me'?[38]

II. Whether upon these considerations we may not try to do good to our acquaintance? Particularly, whether we may not try to convince them of the 15 necessity of being Christians?

Whether of the consequent necessity of being scholars?

Whether of the necessity of method and industry in order to either learning or virtue?

Whether we may not try to persuade them to confirm and increase their 20 industry by communicating as often as they can?

Whether we may not mention to them the authors whom we conceive to have wrote best on those subjects?

Whether we may not assist them as we are able, from time to time, to form resolutions upon what they read in those authors, and to execute them with 25 steadiness and perseverance?

III. Whether, upon the considerations above mentioned, we may not try to do good to those that are hungry, naked, or sick? In particular, whether, if we know any necessitous family, we may not give them a little food, clothes, or physic, as they want?

30 Whether we may not give them, if they can read, a Bible, Common Prayer Book, or *Whole Duty of Man?*

Whether we may not now and then inquire how they have used them, explain what they don't understand, and enforce what they do?

Whether we may not enforce upon them more especially the necessity of 35 private prayer, and of frequenting the church and sacrament?

Whether we may not contribute what little we are able toward having their children clothed and taught to read?

Whether we may not take care that they be taught their catechism, and short prayers for morning and evening?

40 IV. Lastly, Whether, upon the considerations above mentioned, we may not try to do good to those that are in prison? In particular, whether we may not release such well-disposed persons as remain in prison for small sums?

Whether we may not lend smaller sums to those that are of any trade, that they may procure themselves tools and materials to work with?

45 Whether we may not give to them who appear to want it most a little money, or clothes, or physic?

---

[35] Acts 10:38.
[37] Matt. 25:35-36.

[36] Cf. Gal. 6:10.
[38] Matt. 25:40.

Whether we may not supply as many as are serious enough to read with a Bible and *Whole Duty of Man?*

Whether we may not, as we have opportunity, explain and enforce these upon them, especially with respect to public and private prayer, and the Blessed Sacrament?[39]   5

I do not remember that we met with any person who answered any of these questions in the negative, or who even doubted whether it were not lawful to apply to this use that time and money which we should else have spent in other diversions. But several we met with who increased our little stock of money for the   10 prisoners and the poor by subscribing something quarterly to it; so that the more persons we proposed our designs to, the more were we confirmed in the belief of their innocency, and the more determined to pursue them in spite of the ridicule which increased fast upon us during the winter. However, in spring I   15 thought it could not be improper to desire farther instructions from those who were wiser and better than ourselves; and accordingly (on May 18, 1731) I wrote a particular account of all our proceedings to a clergyman of known wisdom and integrity.[40] After having informed him of all the branches of our design as   20 clearly and simply as I could, I next acquainted him with the success it had met with, in the following words:

Almost as soon as we had made our first attempts this way, some of the men of wit in Christ Church entered the list[s] against us, and between mirth and anger made a pretty many reflections upon the 'Sacramentarians', as they were   25 pleased to call us. Soon after, their allies at Merton changed our title, and did us the honour of styling us 'The Holy Club'. But most of them being persons of well-known characters, they had not the good fortune to gain any proselytes from the *Sacrament,* till a gentleman, eminent for learning, and well esteemed for piety, joining them, told his nephew that if he dared to go to the weekly   30 communion any longer he would immediately turn him out of doors. That argument indeed had no success: the young gentleman communicated next

---

[39] Though these questions mainly inculcate good works, they imply, particularly in pt. 3, a view of what the interior Christian life should be, which was much more fully developed in 'A Scheme of Self-Examination used by the first Methodists in Oxford', developed during this period but first published in *Arminian Magazine* (1781), IV.319 (Jackson, XI.521-23).

[40] This is shown by Wesley's diary to be Joseph Hoole, vicar of Haxey, Lincs., 1712–36; rector of St. Anne's, Manchester, 1736–45; died Nov. 27, 1745, and buried at St. Anne's; took M.A. from Sidney Sussex College, 1727. He appears to have obtained his Manchester preferment through friendship and marriage connection with John Byrom and (with Charles Wesley) was one of those who supported the publication of Byrom's shorthand system. Amongst his publications was a *Guide to Communicants* (1739). Cf. C. W. Bardsley, *Memorials of St. Ann's Church, Manchester* (Manchester, 1877), pp. 50-69.

week; upon which his uncle, having again tried to convince him that he was in
the wrong way, by shaking him by the throat to no purpose, changed his method,
and by mildness prevailed upon him to absent from it the Sunday following, as
he has done five Sundays in six ever since.[41] This much delighted our gay
5 opponents, who increased their numbers apace; especially when, shortly after,
one of the seniors of the college, having been with the Doctor,[42] upon his return
from him sent for two young gentlemen severally, who had communicated
weekly for some time, and was so successful in his exhortations that for the
future they promised to do it only three times a year. About this time there was a
10 meeting (as one who was present at it informed your son) of several of the
officers and seniors of the college, wherein it was consulted what would be the
speediest way to stop the progress of enthusiasm in it. The result we know not,
only it was soon publicly reported that Dr. Terry[43] and the censors were going to
blow up 'The Godly Club'. This was now our common title, though we were
15 sometimes dignified with that of 'The Enthusiasts', or 'The Reforming Club'.

Part of the answer I received was as follows:

Good Sir,
   A pretty while after the date yours came to my hand. I waived my answer till I
had an opportunity of consulting your father, who, upon all accounts, is a more
20 proper judge of the affair than I am. But I could never find a fit occasion for it. As
to my own sense of the matter, I confess I cannot but heartily approve that
serious and religious turn of mind that prompts you and your associates to those
pious and charitable offices; and can have no notion of that man's religion or
concern for the honour of the university that opposes you as far as your design
25 respects the colleges. I should be loath to send a son of mine to any seminary
where his conversing with virtuous young men, whose professed design of
meeting together at proper times was to assist each other in forming good
resolutions, and encouraging one another to execute them with constancy and
steadiness, was inconsistent with any received maxims or rules of life among the
30 members. As to the other branch of your design, as the town is divided into
parishes, each of which has its proper incumbent, and as there is probably an
ecclesiastic who has the spiritual charge of the prisoners, prudence may direct
you to consult them. For though I dare not say you would be too officious should
you of your own mere motion seek out the persons that want your instructions

----

[41] The original punctuation of the first two editions ends the letter to Hoole here, but
also encloses within quotation marks the passage, 'gay opponents . . . "The Reforming
Club"'. The actual extent of the letter to Hoole is obscured by the fact that it is printed
continuously within the letter to Morgan. The probability is, however, that the parenthetic
clause below, referring to 'your son', was inserted for the benefit of Morgan (for Hoole had
no son at Oxford at that time), and that Wesley's letter to Hoole continues until JW
introduces the reply to it.

[42] Dr. Terry, on whom see n. 43 below.

[43] 'Terry' was added in manuscript by Wesley in his own annotated copy of the *Works*.
Thomas Terry (c. 1678–1735) was Regius Professor of Greek in Oxford, 1712–35, Canon
of Christ Church, 1713–35, Chaplain to the King and rector of Chalfont St. Giles,
1712–35. He had formerly been tutor to Lord Harley and was a well-known Harleyite
politician.

and charitable contributions, yet should you have the concurrence of their proper pastor, your good offices would be more regular and less liable to censure.

Your son was now at Holt; however, we continued to meet at our usual times, though our little affairs went on but heavily 5 without him. But at our return from Lincolnshire, in September last, we had the pleasure of seeing him again; when, though he could not be so active with us as formerly, yet we were exceeding glad to spend what time we could in talking and reading with him. It was a little before this time my brother and I were at London, 10 when going into a bookseller's shop (Mr. Rivington's in St. Paul's Churchyard[44]), after some other conversation he asked us whether we lived in town; and upon our answering, 'No; at Oxford': 'Then, gentlemen', said he, 'let me earnestly recommend to your acquaintance a friend I have there, Mr. Clayton, of 15 Brasenose.'[45] Of this, having small leisure for contracting new acquaintance, we took no notice for the present. But in the spring following (April 20 [1732]) Mr. Clayton meeting me in the street, and giving Mr. Rivington's service, I desired his company to my room, and then commenced our acquaintance. At the first 20 opportunity I acquainted him with our whole design, which he immediately and heartily closed with; and not long after, Mr. M[organ] having then left Oxford, we fixed two evenings in a week to meet on, partly to talk upon that subject, and partly to read something in practical divinity. 25

The two points whereunto, by the blessing of God, and your son's help, we had before attained, we endeavoured to hold fast: I mean, the doing what good we can, and in order thereto communicating as often as we have opportunity. To these, by the advice of Mr. Clayton, we have added a third—the observing the 30

[44] Charles Rivington (1688–1742) who acquired the premises of Thomas Chiswell in Paternoster Row in 1711 and became the leading theological publisher. An intimate friend of the Wesley brothers, he published JW's translation of Thomas à Kempis, *The Christian's Pattern* (1735), and one of Whitefield's earliest works, *The Nature and Necessity of a New Birth in Christ* (1737).

[45] Orig., 'Brazen-Nose'. John Clayton (1709–73), son of William Clayton, bookseller, Manchester. Matriculated at Brasenose College, Oxford, July 17, 1725; B.A. 1729; M.A. 1732. A high churchman, he joined the Oxford Methodists and exerted a considerable influence upon the formulation of their views of spiritual practice. He helped Wesley compile his first publication, *A Collection of Forms of Prayer* (1733). Curate of Sacred Trinity, Salford, 1733; chaplain of Manchester Collegiate Church, 1740–60; fellow, 1760–73. When the Young Pretender occupied Manchester in 1745, Clayton publicly advocated his cause, and prayed for the Stuarts in the Collegiate Church.

fasts of the Church, the general neglect of which we can by no means apprehend to be a lawful excuse for neglecting them. And in the resolution to adhere to these, and all things else which we are convinced God requires at our hands, we trust we shall
5 persevere till he calls us too to give an account of our stewardship. As for the names of 'Methodists', 'Supererogation Men', and so on, with which some of our neighbours are pleased to compliment us, we do not conceive ourselves to be under any obligation to regard them, much less to take them for arguments. To the law
10 and to the testimony[46] we appeal, whereby we ought to be judged. If by these it can be proved we are in an error, we will immediately and gladly retract it. If not, we 'have not so learned Christ'[47] as to renounce any part of his service, though men should 'say all manner of evil against us',[48] with [no] more judgment and as little
15 truth as hitherto. We do indeed use all the lawful means we know to prevent 'the good which is in us' from being 'evil spoken of';[49] but if the neglect of known duties be the one condition of securing our reputation, why, fare it well. We know whom we have believed, and what we thus lay out he will pay us again. Your son
20 already stands before the judgment-seat of him who judges righteous judgment, at the brightness of whose presence the clouds remove; his eyes are open, and he sees clearly whether it was 'blind zeal and a thorough mistake of true religion that hurried him on in the error of his way',[50] or whether he acted like a
25 faithful and wise servant, who, from a just sense that his time was short, made haste to finish his work before his Lord's coming, that when 'laid in the balance' he might not 'be found wanting'.[51]

I have now largely and plainly laid before you the real ground of all the strange outcry you have heard; and am not without hope
30 that by this fairer representation of it than you probably ever received before, both you and the clergyman you formerly mentioned may have a more favourable opinion of a good cause, though under an ill name. Whether you have or no, I shall ever

---

[46] Isa. 8:20. [47] Eph. 4:20.
[48] Cf. Matt. 5:11. [49] Cf. Rom. 14:16.
[50] Cf. Richard Morgan's letter of Mar. 15, 1732, to his son William, chiding him for his associations with 'that ridiculous society': 'I could not but advise with a wise, pious, and learned clergyman. He told me that he has known the worst of consequences follow from such blind zeal, and plainly satisfied me that it was a thorough mistake of true piety and religion. . . . He concluded that . . . as soon as your judgment improved . . . you would see the error of the way you was in . . .' (MS extract prepared by Charles Wesley; at Drew University, Madison, New Jersey).
[51] Cf. Dan. 5:27.

acknowledge my best services to be due to yourself and your family, both for the generous assistance you have given my father,[52] and for the invaluable advantages your son has (under God) bestowed on,

Sir,

Your ever obliged,

And most obedient servant.

5

On the Death of
Mr. Morgan of Christ Church.
By the Rev. Mr. Samuel Wesley.[53]

10

We fools counted his life madness.[54]

If aught beneath them happy souls attend,
Let Morgan hear the triumph of a friend,
And hear well-pleas'd. Let *libertines* so gay
With careless indolence despise the lay;
Let critic wits, and fools for laughter born
Their verdict pass with supercilious scorn;
Let jovial crowds, by[55] wine their senses drown'd,
Stammer out censure in their frantic round;
Let yawning sluggards faint dislike display,
Who, while they trust tomorrow, lose today;
Let such as these the sacred strains condemn;
For 'tis true glory to be hiss'd by them.

15

20

[52] Both Richard Morgan and his son subscribed to Samuel Wesley's *Dissertationes in librum Jobi* (1735).

[53] Samuel Wesley, Jun. (1691–1739), eldest child of Samuel Wesley, rector of Epworth. Educated at Westminster School (1704–11) and Christ Church, Oxford, he was usher at Westminster School (1713–33) and Master of Blundell's School, Tiverton (1733–39). A friend and protégé of Atterbury (by whom he was ordained), he was well known for his poetry in London literary circles, and published this elegy in *Poems on Several Occasions* (1736). JW read the proof-sheets in Georgia, and seems to have quoted the poem from them, his version showing a considerable number of small variant readings (which have been noted) from that which was finally published. Samuel Wesley is said to have been personally acquainted with Richard Morgan in London.

[54] Cf. Wisd. 5:4. (JW has added this motto.)

[55] 1736, 'in'.

Wise in his prime, he waited not for[56] noon,
Convinc'd that mortal 'never liv'd too soon'.
As if foreboding then his little stay,
He made his morning bear the heat of day.
5 Fix'd, while unfading glory he pursues,
No ill to hazard, and no good to lose.
No fair occasion glides unheeded by,
Snatching the golden moments as they fly,
He by few fleeting hours ensures eternity.

10 Friendship's warm beams his artless breast inspire,
And tend'rest rev'rence for a much-lov'd sire.
He dar'd for Heav'n this flatt'ring world forego,
Ardent to teach, as diligent to know.
Unwarp'd by sensual views, or vulgar aims,
15 By idle riches, or by idler names.
Fearful of sin in every close disguise,
Unmov'd by threat'ning, or by glozing lies.
Seldom indeed the wicked came so far,
Forc'd by his piety to defensive war;
20 Whose zeal for other men's salvation shown,
Beyond the reach of Hell secur'd his own.
Glad'ning the poor, where'er his steps he turn'd,
Where pin'd the orphan, or the widow mourn'd;
Where prisoners sigh'd beneath guilt's horrid stain,
25 The worst confinement, and the heaviest chain.
Where death's sad shade th' uninstructed sight
Veil'd with thick darkness in the land of light.
Our Saviour thus fulfill'd his great design,
(If human we may liken to divine)[57]
30 Heal'd each disease that bodies frail endure,
And preach'd th' unhop'd-for gospel to the poor.[58]

---

[56] 1736, 'till'.
[57] 1736, '(for human may be likened to divine)'.
[58] Here the 1736 *Poems* adds:

> Nor yet the priestly function he invades,
> 'Tis not his sermon, but his life, persuades.
> Humble and teachable to Church he flies,
> Prepar'd to practise, not to criticize.
> Then only angry, when a wretch conveys
> The deists' poison in the gospel phrase.

To means of grace the last respect he show'd,
Nor sought new paths, as wiser than his God:
Their sacred strength preserv'd him from extremes
Of empty outside, or enthusiast dreams;
Whims of Molinos,[59] lost in rapture's mist,   5
Or Quaker, late-reforming Quietist.

He knew that works our faith must here employ,
And that 'tis Heaven's great business to enjoy.
Fix'd on that Heav'n, he death's approaches saw,
Nor vainly murmur'd at our nature's law: 10
Repin'd not that his youth so soon should go,
Nor griev'd for fleeting pleasures here below.
Of sharpest anguish scorning to complain,
He fills with mirth the intervals of pain.
Not only unappall'd, but joyful,[60] sees   15
The dark, cold passage that must lead to peace;
Strong with immortal bloom secure to rise,
The tears for ever banish'd from his eyes.

Who now regrets his early youth would spend
The life so nobly that so soon should end?   20
Who blames the stripling for performing more
Than doctors grave, and prelates of threescore?
Who now esteems his fervour indiscreet,
His prayers too frequent, or his alms too great?
Who thinks, where blest he reigns beyond the sky,   25
His crown too radiant, or his throne too high?
Who but the fiend, who once his course withstood,
And whisper'd: 'Stay till fifty to be good'?
Sure, if believ'd, t' obtain his hellish aim,
Adjourning to the time that never came.   30

---

[59] Miguel de Molinos (*c.* 1640–97), Spanish quietist, whose spiritual teaching on attaining perfection by the annihilation of the will led to disturbances among religious, and to his own condemnation and imprisonment. Molinos had considerable influence upon German pietists, and his *Spiritual Guide* was included, much abridged, in JW's *Christian Library*, Vol. XXXVIII.

[60] 1736, 'cheerful'.

Journal

From October 14, 1735, to February 1, 1737/38

Tuesday, October 14, 1735. Mr. Benjamin Ingham,[1] of Queen's College, Oxford, Mr. Charles Delamotte,[2] son of a
5 merchant in London, who had offered himself some days before, my brother Charles Wesley, and myself, took boat for Gravesend,[3] in order to embark for Georgia.[4] Our end in leaving our native country was not to avoid want (God having given us plenty of temporal blessings), nor to gain the dung or dross of

---

[1] Benjamin Ingham (1712–72), son of William Ingham of Ossett, near Dewsbury. Matriculated at Queen's College, Oxford, 1730; B.A. 1734; ordained 1735. One of the most active Oxford Methodists, he accompanied the Wesley brothers to Georgia. On his return he became a prominent evangelist in the North and Midlands and, joining the Moravians, became severed from the Wesleys; an attempt to unite his societies with theirs in 1755 did not succeed. He separated from the majority of his own societies on adopting Sandemanian views in 1760. He married Lady Margaret Hastings, daughter of the Earl of Huntingdon, 1741.

[2] Charles Delamotte (c. 1714–96), son of T. Delamotte, sugar baker, of Blendon House, Bexley, Kent, who was also a Middlesex magistrate. How he became acquainted with JW is unknown, but, hearing that Wesley was going to Georgia, Delamotte resolved to accompany him as a servant. In Georgia he opened a school for free instruction in the elements of religion. He returned to England in 1738, became a Moravian and settled at Barton-upon-Humber, where he died. His mother, two sisters, and his brother William, who became the first Methodist in Cambridge, were converted by the influence of Ingham and Charles Wesley; George Whitefield unsuccessfully proposed marriage to his sister Elizabeth.

[3] 'Gravesend being within the jurisdiction of the port of London, all outward-bound ships . . . were here obliged to undergo a second clearing. . . . Outward-bound vessels take in their pilots here, and all vessels entering the port of London take in pilots from this place for the navigation of the river.' Samuel Lewis, *A Topographical Dictionary of England*, 4 vols. (4th edn., London, 1840), II.287.

[4] The colony of Georgia was organized by Trustees led by James Edward Oglethorpe under a charter received from George II in 1732. The objects were to provide a buffer against Spanish power in Florida; to give a chance to imprisoned debtors from English jails; and to assist persecuted Protestants (proposals to exclude Catholics and Jews soon had to be dropped). The Trustees received considerable grants from private philanthropists and Parliament, and divided the money into funds for establishing the colony, for religion, for agriculture, for schools, and for transporting German and Swiss settlers. An old friend of Samuel Wesley, Oglethorpe pressed JW to accompany the second party of emigrants and to undertake a mission to the Indians. The plans for the social organization of the colony by grants of 50-acre plots to the settlers proved as difficult to implement as those for pastoral oversight. By 1751, when the Trustees relinquished their rights to the Crown, the growth of a class of large landowners was drawing the colony into the circle of the Southern plantation aristocracy.

riches or honour; but singly this—to save our souls,[5] to live wholly to the glory of God. In the afternoon we found the *Simmonds* off Gravesend, and immediately went on board.

Wednesday and Thursday we spent with one or two of our friends, partly on board and partly on shore, in exhorting one 5 another to 'shake off every weight, and to run with patience the race set before us'.[6]

Fri. 17. I began to learn German, in order to converse with the Moravians, six and twenty of whom we had on board.[7] On Sunday, the weather being fair and calm, we had the morning 10 service on quarter-deck. I now first preached extempore, and then administered the Lord's Supper to six or seven communicants. A little flock. May God increase it!

Mon. 20. Believing the denying ourselves, even in the smallest instances, might by the blessing of God be helpful to us, we 15 wholly left off the use of flesh and wine, and confined ourselves to vegetable food, chiefly rice and biscuit.[8] In the afternoon David Nitschmann,[9] Bishop of the Moravians, and two others, began to learn English. O may we be not only of one tongue, but of one mind and of one heart!   20

[5] In JW's summonses to his friends the presence of the Indians looms large. Ever since the preaching of John Eliot had enjoyed some success in the 17th century, Indian missions, the conversion of the apparently unconvertible, had seemed the touchstone of God's presence with the Protestant churches. It was still believed by Jonathan Edwards (*Works*, ed. H. Rogers, S. E. Dwight, and E. Hickman [London, 1837], I.600) that the devil, alarmed by the success of the early church, led the Indians into America that he 'might quietly possess them' himself. Edwards's account of the later Indian Missions in the *Life of David Brainerd* was abridged for Methodist readers by JW himself (1768). But JW had privately assured Dr. John Burton, one of the Georgia Trustees responsible for his sailing: 'My chief motive, to which all the rest are subordinate, is the hope of saving my own soul. I hope to learn the true sense of the gospel of Christ by preaching it to the heathens' (*Letters*, 25:439 in this edn.).

[6] Cf. Heb. 12:1.

[7] These emigrants were accurately described as Germans, for although they originated in various villages in Bohemia and Moravia, and had constituted themselves a religious community known for short as the Moravians (on whom see below, n. 9), they were German-speaking. A great part of the migration from Bohemia and Moravia in these years was, however, Czech; and though many of these passed through Gross Hennersdorf, a parish belonging to Zinzendorf's aunt, Henrietta von Gersdorf, and adjacent to his own property, their religious and political history was very different. The Herrnhut migrants, being German, had no national cause to defend against the public authorities in Germany, and dealt with their discomforts by religious revival and a mission to the universal church.

[8] Wesley uses the spelling normal until the eighteenth century, 'bisket', which still governs the pronunciation.

[9] David Nitschmann (1696–1772), consecrated bishop of the Moravians in 1735. United into a unique spiritual fellowship by a religious revival, the refugees on Zinzendorf's estates at Herrnhut laid claim to being the Renewed Church of the United

Tue. 21. We sailed from Gravesend. When we were past about half the Goodwin Sands, the wind suddenly failed. Had the calm continued till ebb, the ship had probably been lost. But the gale sprung up again in an hour, and carried us into the Downs.

5 We now began to be a little regular. Our common way of living was this: from four in the morning till five each of us used private prayer. From five to seven we read the Bible together, carefully comparing it (that we might not lean to our own understandings) with the writings of the earliest ages. At seven we breakfasted. At

10 eight were the public prayers. From nine to twelve I usually learned German, and Mr. Delamotte, Greek. My brother writ sermons,[10] and Mr. Ingham instructed the children. At twelve we met to give an account to one another what we had done since our last meeting, and what we designed to do before our next.[11] About

15 one we dined. The time from dinner to four we spent in reading to those of whom each of us had taken charge, or in speaking to them severally, as need required. At four were the evening prayers, when either the Second Lesson was explained (as it always was in the morning), or the children were catechized and

20 instructed before the congregation. From five to six we again used private prayer. From six to seven I read in our cabin to two or three of the passengers (of whom there were about eighty English on board), and each of my brethren to a few more in theirs. At seven I joined with the Germans in their public service, while Mr.

25 Ingham was reading between the decks to as many as desired to hear. At eight we met again, to exhort and instruct one another. Between nine and ten we went to bed, where neither the roaring of the sea nor the motion of the ship could take away the refreshing sleep which God gave us.

30 Fri. 24. Having a rolling sea, most of the passengers found the

Brethren; the appointment of Nitschmann, himself born at Zauchtental in Moravia, was one of the signs of their formal reconstitution. Nitschmann had travelled to Georgia with JW on the *Simmonds* and was on good terms with him. Proceeding to America a second time in 1740, he founded the Moravian settlement at Bethlehem, Pa., and was in charge of the American work, 1740–44. After much travelling to and from Europe in pursuit of financial assistance, he retired to live in Bethlehem in 1761.

[10] Charles Wesley had been ordained Sept. 21 and 29, 1735 (with some reluctance on his part and under pressure from JW and Dr. Burton), only just before sailing. His new stock of sermons (some copied from JW's) was put to use when the ship was forced into Cowes (see below, Nov. 20, 1735).

[11] The friends are here fulfilling the Oxford rules, and, when JW was not able to consult his friends, he maintained the spirit of the rules by consulting Moravian elders. At least where marriage was concerned, the discipline of mutual consultation was preserved in the *Twelve Rules of a Helper* (1744; Jackson, VIII.309-10).

effects of it. Mr. Delamotte was exceeding sick for several days; Mr. Ingham for about half an hour. My brother's head ached much. Hitherto, it has pleased God, the sea has not disordered me at all; nor have I been hindered one quarter of an hour from reading, writing, composing, or doing any business I could have 5 done on shore.

During our stay in the Downs[12] some or other of us went, as often as we had opportunity, on board the ship that sailed in company with us,[13] where also many were glad to join in prayer and hearing the Word. 10

Friday, October 31. We sailed out of the Downs. At eleven at night I was waked by a great noise. I soon found there was no danger. But the bare apprehension of it gave me a lively conviction what manner of men those ought to be who are every moment on the brink of eternity. 15

Saturday, November 1. We came to St. Helen's harbour,[14] and the next day into Cowes Road.[15] The wind was fair, but we waited for the man-of-war, which was to sail with us.[16] This was a happy opportunity of instructing our fellow-travellers. May he whose seed we sow give it the increase! 20

Sun. 16. Thomas Hird, and Grace his wife, with their children, Mark, aged twenty-one, and Phoebe, about seventeen, late Quakers, were, at their often repeated desire, and after careful instruction, admitted to baptism.[17]

Thur. 20. We fell down into Yarmouth Road;[18] but the next day 25 were forced back to Cowes. During our stay here there were

---

[12] 'The Downs: the part of the sea within the Goodwin Sands, off the east coast of Kent, a famous rendezvous for ships. (It lies opposite to the eastern end of the North Downs.)' *OED.*

[13] The *London Merchant*, Capt. Thomas, with a large party of refugee Salzburgers, led by Friedrich von Reck from Windhausen, together with a few English.

[14] St. Helen's was a small town and parish in the Isle of Wight bounded on the east by the Channel, on the north by Spithead, and on the south by Brading Harbour, where perhaps the *Simmonds* put in. St. Helen's had long been suffering from encroachments by the sea. Lewis, *England*, II.400.

[15] Cowes was a flourishing seaport built on each bank of the River Medina. Its excellent harbour afforded shelter to ships in stormy weather and enabled them to sail out to the east or the west according to the direction of the wind. Lewis, *England*, I.638.

[16] The sloop *Hawk*, Capt. Gascoigne, the naval escort of the convoy.

[17] Thomas Hird, a dyer, was 42, his wife Grace, 39. Hird became constable at Frederica in 1739. He was authorized to set up a brewhouse, and in 1743 petitioned for a grant of Hird's Island, discovered and improved by him. Candler, *Colonial Records*, V.708.

[18] Yarmouth was a market town and parish on the River Yar. Until the advent of steamboats the route from Lymington to Yarmouth 'was considered the safest and most expeditious passage' to the Isle of Wight. Lewis, *England*, IV.634.

several storms, in one of which two ships in Yarmouth Road were lost.

The continuance of the contrary winds gave my brother an opportunity of complying with the desire of the minister of 5 Cowes,[19] and preaching there three or four times. The poor people flocked together in great numbers. We distributed a few little books among the more serious of them, which they received with all possible expressions of thankfulness.

Fri. 21. One recovering from a dangerous illness desired to be 10 instructed in the nature of the Lord's Supper.[20] I thought it concerned her to be first instructed in the nature of Christianity, and accordingly fixed an hour a day to read with her in Mr. Law's *Treatise on Christian Perfection.*[21]

Sun. 23. At night I was waked by the tossing of the ship and 15 roaring of the wind, and plainly showed I was unfit, for I was unwilling to die.

Tuesday, December 2. I had much satisfaction in conversing with one that was very ill and very serious. But in a few days she recovered from her sickness and from her seriousness together.[22] 20 Sun. 7. Finding nature did not require so frequent supplies as we had been accustomed to, we agreed to leave off suppers; from doing which we have hitherto found no inconvenience.

Wednesday, December 10. We sailed from Cowes, and in the afternoon passed the Needles. Here the ragged rocks, with the 25 waves dashing and foaming at the foot of them, and the white side of the island rising to such a height, perpendicular from the beach, gave a strong idea of him that 'spanneth the heavens, and holdeth the waters in the hollow of his hand'![23]

Today I spoke closely on the head of religion to one I had 30 talked with once or twice before.[24] Afterwards she said, with many

<hr/>

[19] Thomas Troughear (1681–1761), vicar of Carisbrooke (in which parish Cowes was situated) 1722, and rector of Northwood. Matriculated at Queen's College, Oxford, 1701; fellow 1712–24.

[20] Anne, wife of Richard Lawley; see MS journal in Appendix below, and JW's list of the passengers, Wesley College, Bristol.

[21] William Law, *A Practical Treatise upon Christian Perfection,* first published 1726, of which JW published an extract in 1743 (*Bibliography,* No. 77).

[22] MS journal: 'Mrs. Moore, one of Mr. Oglethorpe's servants', who from JW's list of passengers must have been Mary, wife of Francis Moore, who became Recorder of Frederica, and in 1744 published *A Voyage to Georgia begun in the Year 1735.*

[23] Cf. Isa. 40:12; 48:13.

[24] Beata, wife of Thomas Hawkins, surgeon, who became the First Bailiff at Frederica. He was 24, she 22.

tears, 'My mother died when I was but ten years old. Some of her last words were, "Child, fear God; and though you lose me you shall never want a friend." I have now found a friend, when I most wanted, and least expected one.'

From this day to the fourteenth, being in the Bay of Biscay, the sea was very rough. Mr. Delamotte and many others were more sick than ever; Mr. Ingham, a little; I, not at all. But the fourteenth being a calm day, most of the sick were cured at once.

Thur. 18. One who was big with child, in a high fever, and almost wasted away with a violent cough, desired to receive the Holy Communion before she died. At the hour of her receiving she began to recover, and in a few days was entirely out of danger.[25]

Sun. 21. We had fifteen communicants, which was our usual number on Sundays. On Christmas Day we had nineteen; but on New Year's Day, fifteen only.

Thursday, January 15, 1736. Complaint being made to Mr. Oglethorpe of the unequal distribution of the water among the passengers, he appointed new officers to take charge of it. At this the old ones and their friends were highly exasperated against us, to whom they imputed the change. But 'the fierceness of man shall turn to thy praise.'[26]

Sat. Jan. 17. Many people were very impatient at the contrary wind. At seven in the evening they were quieted by a storm. It rose higher and higher till nine. About nine the sea broke over us from stem to stern, burst through the windows of the state cabin where three or four of us were, and covered us all over, though a bureau sheltered me from the main shock. About eleven I lay down in the great cabin, and in a short time fell asleep, though very uncertain whether I should wake alive, and much ashamed of my unwillingness to die. O how pure in heart must he be who would rejoice to appear before God at a moment's warning! Toward morning 'He rebuked the winds and the sea, and there was a great calm.'[27]

Sun. 18. We returned God thanks for our deliverance, of which a few appeared duly sensible. But the rest (among whom were most of the sailors) denied we had been in any danger. I

---

[25] Anne, wife of John Welch, a carpenter. He was 35, she 26. They settled at first in Frederica, with their son James, aged 5, but in 1740 moved to Carolina.

[26] Ps. 76:10 (BCP).

[27] Matt. 8:26.

could not have believed that so little good would have been done by the terror they were in before. But it cannot be that they should obey God from fear, who are deaf to the motives of love.

Fri. 23. In the evening another storm began. In the morning it
5 increased, so that they were forced to let the ship drive. I could not but say to myself, 'How is it that thou hast no faith?'[28] being still unwilling to die. About one in the afternoon, almost as soon as I had stepped out of the great cabin door, the sea did not break as usual, but came with a full, smooth tide over the side of the
10 ship. I was vaulted over with water in a moment, and so stunned that I scarce expected to lift up my head again till the sea should give up her dead. But, thanks be to God, I received no hurt at all. About midnight the storm ceased.

Sun. 25. At noon our third storm began. At four it was more
15 violent than any before. Now indeed we could say, 'The waves of the sea were mighty and raged horribly.'[29] They 'rose up to the heavens above, and clave down to hell beneath'.[30] The winds roared round about us, and (what I never heard before) whistled as distinctly as if it had been a human voice. The ship not only
20 rocked to and fro with the upmost violence, but shook and jarred with so unequal, grating a motion, that one could not but with great difficulty keep one's hold of anything, nor stand a moment without it. Every ten minutes came a shock against the stern or side of the ship, which one would think should dash the planks in
25 pieces. At this time a child, privately baptized before, was brought to be received into the Church.[31] It put me in mind of Jeremiah's buying the field when the Chaldeans were on the point of destroying Jerusalem,[32] and seemed a pledge of the mercy God designed to show us, even in the land of the living.

30 We spent two or three hours after prayers in conversing suitably to the occasion, confirming one another in a calm submission to the wise, holy, gracious will of God. And now a storm did not appear so terrible as before. Blessed be the God of all consolation!

35 At seven I went to the Germans. I had long before observed the great seriousness of their behaviour. Of their humility they had given a continual proof, by performing those servile offices for the

---

[28] Cf. Mark 4:40.
[29] Cf. Ps. 93:5 (BCP).   [30] Cf. Ps. 107:26.
[31] The diary affords no sure clue to the identity of this child.
[32] The field of Hanameel, the purchase of which is described in Jer. 32:1-15.

other passengers which none of the English would undertake; for which they desired, and would receive, no pay, saying it was good for their proud hearts, and their loving Saviour had done more for them. And every day had given them occasion of showing a meekness which no injury could move. If they were pushed, 5 struck, or thrown down, they rose again and went away; but no complaint was found in their mouth. There was now an opportunity of trying whether they were delivered from the spirit of fear, as well as from that of pride, anger, and revenge. In the midst of the psalm wherewith their service began the sea broke 10 over, split the mainsail in pieces, covered the ship, and poured in between the decks, as if the great deep had already swallowed us up. A terrible screaming began among the English. The Germans calmly sung on. I asked one of them afterwards, 'Was you not afraid?' He answered, 'I thank God, no.' I asked, 'But were not 15 your women and children afraid?' He replied mildly, 'No; our women and children are not afraid to die.'

From them I went to their crying, trembling neighbours, and pointed out to them the difference in the hour of trial between him that feareth God and him that feareth him not. At twelve the 20 wind fell. This was the most glorious day which I have ever hitherto seen.

Mon. 26. We enjoyed the calm. I can conceive no difference comparable to that between a smooth and a rough sea except that which is between a mind calmed by the love of God and one torn 25 up by the storms of earthly passions.

Thursday, January 29. About seven in the evening we fell in with the skirts of a hurricane. The rain as well as the wind was extremely violent. The sky was so dark in a moment that the sailors could not so much as see the ropes, or set about furling the 30 sails. The ship must in all probability have overset had not the wind fell as suddenly as it rose. Toward the end of it we had that appearance on each of the masts which (it is thought) the ancients called Castor and Pollux. It was a small ball of white fire, like a star.[33] The mariners say it appears either in a storm (and then 35 commonly upon the deck) or just at the end of it; and then 'tis usually on the masts or sails.

Fri. 30. We had another storm, which did us no other harm

[33] Castor and Pollux were held in Greek mythology to be the patron gods of sailors, who identified their presence with the phenomenon here described, which occurred in thundery weather, and which was later known as St. Elmo's fire, or corona discharge.

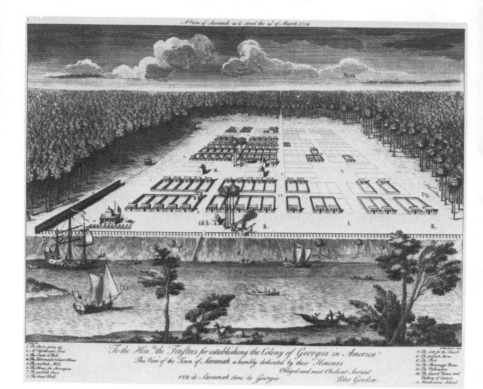

A View of Savanah as it stood the 29.th of March. 1734

than splitting the fore-sail. Our bed being wet, I laid me down on the floor and slept sound till morning. And I believe I shall not find it needful to go to bed (as it is called) any more.

Sunday, February 1. We spoke with a ship of Carolina; and Wednesday 4, came within soundings. About noon the trees were 5 visible from the mast, and in the afternoon from the main deck. In the Evening Lesson were these words, 'A great door and effectual is opened.'[34] O let no one shut it!

Thursday, February 5. Between two and three in the afternoon God brought us all safe into the Savannah River. We cast anchor 10 near Tybee Island, where the groves of pines running along the shore made an agreeable prospect, showing, as it were, the bloom of spring in the depth of winter.

Fri. 6. About eight in the morning we first set foot on American ground. It was a small, uninhabited island, over against Tybee. 15 Mr. Oglethorpe[35] led us to a rising ground, where we all kneeled down to give thanks. He then took boat for Savannah. When the rest of the people were come on shore, we called our little flock together to prayers. Several parts of the Second Lesson, Mark 6, were wonderfully suited to the occasion; in particular the account 20 of the courage and sufferings of John the Baptist, our Lord's directions to the first preachers of his gospel, and their toiling at sea and deliverance with those comfortable words, 'It is I, be not afraid.'[36]

Saturday, February 7. Mr. Oglethorpe returned from 25 Savannah with Mr. Spangenberg, one of the pastors of the Moravians.[37] I soon found what spirit he was of, and asked his

[34] 1 Cor. 16:9.
[35] James Edward Oglethorpe (1696–1785), philanthropist and founder of Georgia (on which see above, Oct. 14, 1735, n. 4), third and youngest surviving son of Sir Theophilus Oglethorpe. Served as a volunteer in eastern Europe under Prince Eugene and was familiar with Habsburg policies of frontier settlement. Chairman of parliamentary commission on debtors' prisons, 1729, his interest in pauperism was one of the motives which led him to the colonization of Georgia. M.P. for Haslemere, 1722–54, he acted at first with the Jacobites, but defended Lancashire against them in 1745. Accused by Cumberland of misconduct, he was acquitted in court martial. Variously described in the thirties as a 'very obstinate Tory' and 'Old Whig', he is now regarded as a doubtful supporter of the ministry. J. B. Owen, *Rise of the Pelhams* (London, 1957), pp. 6, 70, 209.
[36] Mark 6:50.
[37] August Gottlieb Spangenberg (1704–92), a member of the original party of Moravians in Georgia, and throughout his life the driving force of the Moravian work in America. A parson's son from Klettenberg/Harz, he was converted as a student at Jena and turned from law to theology. Becoming a separatist, he made contact with Zinzendorf in 1727, and became the leading figure in his group at Jena. Called to the theology faculty

advice with regard to my own conduct. He said, 'My brother, I must first ask you one or two questions. Have you the witness within yourself? Does the Spirit of God bear witness with your spirit that you are a child of God?'[38] I was surprised, and knew not

5　what to answer. He observed it, and asked, 'Do you know Jesus Christ?' I paused, and said, 'I know he is the Saviour of the world.' 'True', replied he, 'but do you know he has saved you?' I answered, 'I hope he has died to save me.' He only added, 'Do you know yourself?' I said, 'I do.' But I fear they were vain words.

10　　Mon. 9. I asked him many questions, both concerning himself and the small remains of the Moravian Church.[39] The substance of his answers was this:

At eighteen years old I was sent to the University of Jena,[40] where I spent some years in learning languages, and the vain philosophy which I have now long been

15　labouring to forget. Here it pleased God, by some that preached his word with power, to overturn my heart. I immediately threw aside all my learning but what tended to save my soul. I shunned all company, and retired into a solitary place, resolving to spend my life there. For three days I had much comfort here; but on the fourth it was all gone. I was amazed, and went for advice to an experienced

20　Christian. When I came to him I could not speak. But he saw my heart, and advised me to go back to my house, and follow the business providence called me to. I went back, but was fit for nothing. I could neither do business nor join in any conversation. All I could say to anyone was Yes, or No. Many times I could not say that, nor understand the plainest thing that was said to me. My friends

25　and acquaintance looked upon me as dead, came no more to me, nor spoke about me.

When I grew better I began teaching some poor children. Others joining with me, we taught more and more, till there were above thirty teachers and above two hundred scholars. I had now invitations to other universities. But I could not

and Orphan House at Halle in 1732, he was roughly dismissed in 1733, when he became a major colleague of Zinzendorf at Herrnhut, and took charge of Schwenckfelders in America. In the 1750s he spent most of his time in Europe consolidating the theological position and finances of the Moravian community of which, after Zinzendorf's death in 1760, he became the leader. Gerhard Reichel, *August Gottlieb Spangenberg, Bischof der Brüderkirche* (Tübingen, 1906); reprint in *Nikolaus Ludwig von Zinzendorf: Materialien und Dokumente*, Reihe 2, Bd. 13 (1975).

[38] See Rom. 8:16.

[39] 1765 and 1775, 'the Church at Hernhuth' (i.e., Herrnhut).

[40] Jena, founded in 1558 by the Saxon house when the University of Wittenberg had been almost extinguished by war emergencies, remained one of the successful Reformation foundations and, at the time of which Spangenberg speaks, was noted for a somewhat old-fashioned attitude to classical education and, in theology, for the efforts of Buddeus to steer a middle course between Orthodoxy and pietism. K. Biedermann, *Die Universität Jena* (Jena, 1858); and F. Paulsen, *Geschichte der gelehrnten Unterrichts* (Leipzig, 1896–97), I.244-46, 542.

accept of any; desiring only, if it were the will of God, to be little and unknown. I had spent some years thus when Professor Breithaupt of Halle died.[41] Being then pressed to remove thither, I believed it was the call of God, and went. I had not been long there before many faults were found both with my behaviour and preaching; and offences increased more and more till, after half a year, a petition 5 against me was sent to the King of Prussia, who sent an order to the commander at Halle, in pursuance whereof I was warned to leave the city in forty-eight hours. I did so, and retired to Herrnhut,[42] to Count Zinzendorf.[43]

The village of Herrnhut[44] contains about a thousand souls, gathered out of many nations. They hold fast the discipline, as well as the faith and practice, of 10 the apostolical church. I was desired by the brethren there last year to conduct sixteen of them to Georgia, where two lots of ground are assigned us, and with them I have stayed ever since.

[41] Halle, founded in 1694 as a rival to Leipzig and a much-needed Lutheran university in the central territories of the Elector of Brandenburg, was the first really modern university in Germany and had a strong practical bent to its scholarship. It was marked from the beginning not only by the political ambitions of Brandenburg-Prussia, but also by a mixture of early-Enlightenment and pietist academic influences (Thomasius in jurisprudence, Francke and Wolff in theology). It was Francke who secured the appointment of Joachim Justus Breithaupt (1658–1732) who had early made contact with the pietists and had already held theological chairs at Kiel and Erfurt. A scholarly theologian of confirmed pietist bent, he was central to the theology faculty till his death; but he received church preferment and is regarded as principally significant for his practical activity. The balance between pietism and rationalism at Halle remained precarious and much influenced by political considerations. After Breithaupt's death his appointment was occupied jointly by Spangenberg and S. J. Baumgarten (Martin Schloemann, *Siegmund Jacob Baumgarten* [Göttingen, 1974], p. 37); the latter introduced into theology the philosophical concepts of Wolff, who, expelled in 1723, himself returned in 1740. These wider considerations underlay the offence given to the theologians (especially Joachim Lange and the officials of the Orphan House) by Spangenberg's tactless championship of Zinzendorf while he held a fellowship at Halle and led to his expulsion.

[42] I.e., 'the Lord's ward' (or 'flock'). Founded on Zinzendorf's estate at Berthelsdorf, Saxony, in 1722 by Christian David. Here as elsewhere, Wesley spells it 'Hernhuth'.

[43] Nikolaus Ludwig von Zinzendorf (1700–60) belonged to the imperial nobility closely connected with Halle, where he was educated; but he showed considerable originality in religious inspiration. Even as a student he had formed the Order of the Grain of Mustard Seed, whose members bound themselves to be a leaven amongst all Christians, regardless of church connections, to succour the persecuted, and to carry the gospel to the heathen overseas, objects which remained prominent amongst the Moravians. Regarded from an early stage as *Vorsteher*, or *Ordinarius* of the Moravian community, Zinzendorf was consecrated its second bishop in 1737 and retained practical control of the movement till his death. Unable to cooperate for long with men of independent mind, Zinzendorf's attempt to steer between confessionalism and rationalism and his innovations in liturgy and community life have remained of interest to the modern commentators.

[44] Herrnhut, attracting Bohemian and Moravian migrants of German tongue (see above, Oct. 17, 1735, n. 7), offered at least a temporary home for Germans from many parts, including Silesia and Poland. Fears of large gatherings of emigrants in various parts of Upper Lusatia increased the hostility of the Saxon authorities in church and state towards the settlement at Herrnhut.

I asked whither he was to go next. He said, 'I have thoughts of going to Pennsylvania.[45] But what God will do with me I know not. I am blind. I am a child. My Father knows, and I am ready to go wherever he calls.'

5   Fri. 13. Some of the Indians sent us word of their intention to come down to us. In our course of reading today were these words: 'Thus saith the Lord of hosts, It shall yet come to pass that there shall come people, and the inhabitants of many cities. And the inhabitants of one city shall go to another, saying, Let us go

10 speedily to pray before the Lord, and to seek the Lord of hosts; I will go also. Yea, many people and strong nations shall come to seek the Lord of hosts, and to pray before him.'[a]

Saturday, February 14. About one Tomochichi,[46] his nephew Toonahowi,[47] his wife Sinauky, with two more women, and two or

15 three Indian children, came on board. As soon as we came in they all rose, and shook us by the hand, and Tomochichi (one Mrs. Musgrove[48] interpreted) spoke as follows:

---

[a] Zech. 8:20-22 [This was not included in the BCP lessons for the day].

---

[45]For half a century, the principal point of disembarkation of the large German emigration to America was Philadelphia, and they remained very numerous in Pennsylvania, especially at Germantown. The community of Schwenckfelders, dislodged from Silesia by persecution and dislodged again from Herrnhut by political menaces, had left for Pennsylvania in 1733, where there were already Mennonites and other sectaries of German and Dutch extraction. Zinzendorf hoped to establish among them a single supra-confessional communion.

[46]Among various spellings this is the most generally accepted form; JW used the form 'Tomo-Chachi'. Tomochichi, reputed to be 90 in 1734, was the mico or chief of the Yamacraw Indians, a branch of the Creek Indians, settled four miles from Savannah. In 1734 Oglethorpe took him and his wife to England because of the chief's reputation of being 'a very prudent man, and of great use in pacifying differences and making other Indian Nations our friends' (Egmont, *Journal*, p. 108). He was to be taught English and Christianity and to confirm a peace, and Oglethorpe presented them to the king and queen (Egmont, *Diary*, II.112-32). He died in 1739, was buried with military honours in the great square of Savannah, and was commemorated in an ode by Samuel Wesley. His portrait was included in Urlsperger's *Ausführliche Nachricht von der Saltzburgischen Emigranten*, and is reprinted by Angelika Marsch, *Die Salzburger Emigration in Bildern* (2nd edn., Weissenhorn, 1979), plate 137.

[47] Orig., 'Thleeanouchee'; variously spelled in the copies of Wesley's MS voyage journal: Toanoh, Tooanohooi, Tooanohooy, Toonahowhi, and Toonahowi.

[48] Mary Musgrove (died *c*. 1760), 'Queen of the Creeks' and indispensable as an interpreter and diplomat with the Indians, was the half-Indian wife of John Musgrove, a white settler, trader, and interpreter, who took up Lot 45 in Savannah Feb. 1, 1732/33, but died in 1735. Mrs. Musgrove herself received a grant of 500 acres promised to her husband and was described in the Earl of Egmont's MS list of settlers as 'the best interpreter in the Trustees' service, and in good circumstances'. In 1736 she married

'I am glad you are come. When I was in England I desired that some would speak *the Great Word* to me. And my nation then desired to hear it. But now we are all in confusion. Yet I am glad you are come. I will go up and speak to the wise men of our nation. And I hope they will hear. But we would not be made Christians 5 as the Spaniards make Christians. We would be taught before we are baptized.'

I answered, 'There is but one, he that sitteth in heaven, who is able to teach man wisdom. Though we are come so far, we know not whether he will please to teach you by us or no. If he teaches 10 you, you will learn wisdom; but we can do nothing.' We then withdrew.

Sun. 15. Another party of Indians came.[49] They were all tall, well-proportioned men, and had a remarkable softness in their speech, and gentleness in their whole behaviour. In the afternoon 15 they all returned home but three, who stayed to go with Mr. Oglethorpe.

Monday, February 16. Mr. Oglethorpe set out for the new settlement on the Altamaha River.[50] He took with him fifty men, besides Mr. Ingham, Mr. Hermsdorf,[51] and the three Indians. 20

Thur. 19. My brother and I took boat, and, passing by Savannah, went up to pay our first visit in America to the poor *heathens*. But neither Tomochichi nor Sinauky were at home. Coming back, we waited upon Mr. Causton,[52] the Chief

Jacob Matthews, who died in 1742. Benhamin Ingham lived on her farm to learn the Indian language and reported in 1737 that Mrs. Musgrove was leaving for Carolina with her new husband, a commander of the rangers (Egmont, *Diary*, II.129-30, 172, 196, 422-23; cf. below, Dec. 2, 1737, §16). In 1742 she married Thomas Bosomworth, who began as Secretary for Indian affairs and ended as a disreputable land speculator. E. M. Coulter, 'Mary Musgrove, "Queen of the Creeks": a chapter of early Georgia troubles', *Georgia Historical Quarterly* (1927), XI.1-30; and E. Merton Coulter and Albert B. Saye, eds., *A List of the Early Settlers of Georgia* (Athens, Ga. 1949), p. 90 (henceforth 'Coulter and Saye').

[49] MS journal: 'of the Savannah nation'.

[50] I.e., Darien; JW's spelling is 'Alatamaha'.

[51] Capt. Hermsdorf, a military attaché to Oglethorpe, who later served with him on a military expedition against the Spaniards in Florida, was apparently an officer permitted to serve by the Prussian government, and is to be distinguished from Johann Christian Adolf von Hermsdorf (1709–67), a Moravian also in Georgia 1735–37, on whom see Martin Schmidt, *John Wesley: A Theological Biography*, 2 vols. in 3 (Eng. trans., London, 1962–73). I.284-85n.

[52] Thomas Causton, a calico printer at the time of his emigration to Georgia in Nov. 1732, became third, second, and then head bailiff in Georgia, and storekeeper, 1733–39. He was an admittedly violent and dictatorial man, confronted with a difficult situation and unruly people. He was subject to endless complaints of taking the best land, falsifying

Magistrate of Savannah. From him we went with Mr. Spangenberg to the Moravian brethren. About eleven we returned to the boat, and came to our ship about four in the morning.

5   Sat. 21. Mary Welch,[53] aged eleven days, was baptized according to the custom of the first church and the rule of the Church of England, by immersion. The child was ill then, but recovered from that hour.

Tue. 24. Mr. Oglethorpe returned. The day following I took
10   my leave of most of the passengers of the ship, who all appeared serious. It may be all the seed is not fallen upon stony ground.

In the evening I went to Savannah again, whence Mr. Spangenberg, Bishop Nitschmann, and Andrew Dober[54] went up with us to Mrs. Musgrove's, to choose a spot for the little house
15   which Mr. Oglethorpe had promised to build us. Being afterward disappointed of our boat, we were obliged to pass the night there. But wherever we are it is the same thing, if it be the will of our Father which is in heaven.

At our return the next day (Mr. Quincy[55] being then in the

accounts, mismanaging justice, and being unfair in his dealing in bills of exchange; the President and Council of Carolina complained that he interfered with the rum trade to their own settlements, and the grand jury of Savannah sent a remonstrance against him in 1737. In 1738 the Georgia Trustees deprived him of his storekeeper's place and then ordered Oglethorpe to arrest him. But Causton always had his defenders, and the bitter complaints brought against him by JW and Charles Delamotte were balanced by favourable testimony from Charles Wesley. Egmont, *Diary*, II.313, 467-68, 513-14 (*et passim*); CWJ, I.33-34; Coulter and Saye; P. Tailfer, *et al.*, *A True and Historical Narrative of the Colony of Georgia* (Charlestown, 1741), *passim* (N.B.: the enumeration of pages here is very different from that of the reprint, ed. Clarence L. Ver Steeg, published by the Wormsloe Foundation [Athens, Univ. of Georgia Press, 1960], which incorporates the Earl of Egmont's very lengthy running commentary).

[53] Mary Welch, daughter of James and Anne Welch, passengers on the *Simmonds*.

[54] Johann Andreas Dober, a potter aged 27, and his wife were among the Moravians on the *Simmonds*. In his MS journal for Oct. 20, Wesley calls him 'Ant. Dober'. He became the schoolmaster at Highgate and persuaded Zinzendorf, in opposition to the advice of the pietists at Halle, to negotiate the dispatch of a party of Moravians to Georgia (Benham, Hutton, pp. 23-24). He returned to Europe in 1740 (Coulter and Saye).

[55] Samuel Quincy, a native of Boston, Mass., was educated at 'the college in New England' (Harvard), a London dissenting academy, and Cambridge; after preaching for the Independents and Presbyterians he was ordained in the Church of England and served at Southwold, Suffolk. He was already in ill odour with the Trustees for failing to correspond with the Society for Propagation of the Gospel (hereafter SPG), for abandoning his flock on a six-months' visit to relatives in New York, for inadequately attending to his work, and for being 'in league with the malcontents of our Province'. Failing to get Westley Hall to travel out with JW to replace him, the Georgia Trustees grasped at Quincy's desire to return to England to join his wife, who would not go to America, and replaced him by Wesley, who reported adversely on his attention to duty.

house wherein we afterwards were), Mr. Delamotte and I took up our lodging with the Germans. We had now an opportunity, day by day, of observing their whole behaviour; for we were in one room with them from morning to night, unless for the little time I spent in walking. They were always employed, always cheerful 5 themselves, and in good humour with one another. They had put away all anger and strife and wrath and bitterness and clamour and evil-speaking. They walked worthy of the vocation wherewith they were called,[56] and adorned the gospel of our Lord in all things.[57]   10

Saturday, February 28. They met to consult concerning the affairs of their church, Mr. Spangenberg being shortly to go to Pennsylvania, and Bishop Nitschmann to return to Germany. After several hours spent in conference and prayer, they proceeded to the election and ordination of a bishop.[58] The great 15 simplicity as well as solemnity of the whole almost made me forget the seventeen hundred years between, and imagine myself in one of those assemblies where form and state were not, but Paul the tent-maker or Peter the fisherman presided; yet with the demonstration of the Spirit and of power.[59]   20

Sun. 29. Hearing Mr. Oglethorpe did not come any more to

Various unspecified charges were made against Quincy's character (though Oglethorpe maintained that his only fault was 'marrying a native woman to an Englishman'), and in 1737 the SPG refused to support him in South Carolina (Egmont, *Diary*, II, *passim;* Egmont, *Journal, passim*), where he served at St. John's, Colleton, 1742–45, St. George's, Dorchester, 1746–47, and St. Philip's, Charleston, 1747–49. He published a volume of sermons at Boston in 1750, and in the following year the SPG would have sent him back to South Carolina if his health had permitted. E. L. Pennington, 'The Rev. Samuel Quincy, SPG, Missionary', *Georgia Historical Quarterly* (1927), XI.157-65.

[56] See Eph. 4:1.

[57] See Titus 2:10. The Georgia Trustees had been informed by the SPCK that 'these Moravians are a lot of enthusiasts,' but Charles Wesley soon reported from Georgia that 'the most laborious, cheapest workers and best subjects in Georgia are the Moravians, who have among them also the best carpenters'; Benjamin Ingham held that 'these people of Count Zinzendorf's are the most pious and perfect people he ever saw or read of since the Apostle's times', and it became clear that they were model settlers (Egmont, *Diary*, II.133, 313, 333, 491; III.57). However, they would not arm in defence of the colony and left in 1740.

[58] JW was in error in reporting the ordination of a bishop (Adelaide L. Fries, *The Moravians in Georgia, 1735–40* [Raleigh, 1905], pp. 134-35; J. Taylor Hamilton, *A History of the Church known as the Moravian Church or Unitas Fratrum* [Bethlehem, Pa., 1900], p. 80). Nitschmann (n. 9 above) ordained Anton Seiffert (1712–85), as pastor (JW met him again in 1783). The incident is of interest as probably the first ordination *by* a Protestant bishop on the American continent. JW later found theological reasons to justify what he thought he saw here, viz., presbyteral election and ordination of a bishop.

[59] See 1 Cor. 2:4.

Savannah before he went to Frederica, I was obliged to go down
to the ship again (Mr. Spangenberg following me thither), and
receive his orders and instructions on several heads. From him
we went to public prayers; after which we were refreshed by
5 several letters from England. Upon which I could not but observe
how careful our Lord is to repay whatever we give up on his
account. When I left England I was chiefly afraid of two things:
one, that I should never again have so many faithful friends as I
left there; the other, that the spark of love which began to kindle
10 in their hearts would cool and die away. But who knoweth the
mercy and power of God! From ten friends I am awhile secluded,
and he hath opened me a door into the whole Moravian church.
And as to the very persons I left behind, his Spirit is gone forth so
much the more, teaching them not to trust in man, but 'in him that
15 raiseth the dead',[60] 'and calleth the things that are not, as though
they were'.[61]

About four, having taken leave of Mr. Spangenberg, who was
the next morning to set out for Pennsylvania, I returned to
Savannah.

20 Saturday, March 6. I had a long conversation with John
Regnier,[62] the son of a gentleman who, being driven out of France
on account of his religion, settled at Vevey[63] in Switzerland, and
practised physic there. His father died while he was a child. Some
years after he told his mother he was desirous to leave
25 Switzerland, and to retire into some other country, where he
might be free from the temptations which he could not avoid
there. When her consent was at length obtained he agreed with a
master of a vessel, with whom he went to Holland by land, thence
to England, and from England to Pennsylvania. He was provided
30 with money, books, and drugs, intending to follow his father's
profession. But no sooner was he come to Philadelphia than the
captain, who had borrowed his money before, instead of repaying
it, demanded the full pay for his passage, and under that pretence

---

[60] Cf. 2 Cor. 1:9.
[61] Cf. Rom. 4:17.
[62] Orig., 'Reinier'; John Francis Regnier, who came to America in 1728. He went to
Germany in 1738, becoming a member of the Herrnhaag congregation, but by 1743 was
back in Pennsylvania, criticizing the Moravians. See Georg Neisser, *A History of the
Beginnings of the Moravian Work in America* (Bethlehem, Pa., 1955), pp. 75-76, which refers
for further details to Sachse, *The German Sectarians of Pennsylvania, 1708-42*, I.192-95,
and J. P. Fresenius, *Bewährte Nachrichten von Herrenhutischen Sachen* (4 vols., Frankfurt,
1746-51), I.327-479, etc.
[63] Orig., 'Vivay'.

seized on all his effects. He then left him in a strange country, where he could not speak to be understood, without necessaries, money, or friends. In this condition he thought it best to sell himself for a servant, which he accordingly did, for seven years. When about five were expired he fell sick of a lingering illness, which made him useless to his master; who, after it had continued half a year, would not keep him any longer, but turned him out to shift for himself. He first tried to mend shoes, but soon after joined himself to some French Protestants, and learned to make buttons. He then went and lived with an Anabaptist; but soon after hearing an account of the Moravians in Georgia, walked from Pennsylvania thither, where he found the rest which he had so long sought in vain.

Sunday, March 7. I entered upon my ministry at Savannah, by preaching on the Epistle for the day, being the thirteenth of the First of Corinthians. In the Second Lesson, Luke 18, was our Lord's prediction of the treatment which he himself (and consequently his followers) was to meet with from the world; and his gracious promise to those who are content *nudi nudum Christum sequi:*[64] 'Verily I say unto you, There is no man that hath left house or friends or brethren or wife or children for the kingdom of God's sake, which shall not receive manifold more in this present time, and in the world to come everlasting life.'[65]

Yet notwithstanding these plain declarations of our Lord, notwithstanding my own repeated experience, notwithstanding the experience of all the sincere followers of Christ whom I have ever talked with, read, or heard of; nay, and the reason of the thing, evincing to a demonstration that all who love not the light must hate him who is continually labouring to pour it in upon them; I do here bear witness against myself that when I saw the number of people crowding into the church, the deep attention with which they received the Word, and the seriousness that afterwards sat on all their faces, I could scarce refrain from giving the lie to experience and reason and Scripture all together. I could hardly believe that the greater, the far greater part of this attentive, serious people, would hereafter trample under foot that Word, and say all manner of evil falsely of him that spake it. O

---

[64] 'Naked to follow a naked Christ', an expression of Jerome (*Epistles*, No. 125), embraced by Bernard of Clairvaux and Francis of Assisi. Cf. Wesley's edn. of Thomas à Kempis, *The Christian's Pattern*, III.xxxvii.3 (*Bibliography*, No. 4).
[65] Cf. Luke 18:29-30.

who can believe what their heart abhors? Jesus, Master, have mercy on us! Let us love thy cross! Then shall we believe. 'If we suffer with thee, we shall also reign with thee!'[66]

[Monday, March 8.] This evening one of the Moravians,[67] who 5 had been long ill of a consumption, found himself much worse. On my mentioning it to Bishop Nitschmann he smiled and said, 'He will soon be well; he is ready for the Bridegroom.'

Sunday, March 14. Having before given notice of my design to do so every Sunday and holiday, according to the rules of our 10 Church, I administered the Holy Communion to eighteen persons. Which of these will endure to the end?

Monday, March 15. Mr. Quincy going for Carolina, I removed into the minister's house. It is large enough for a larger family than ours, and has many conveniences, besides a good garden. I 15 could not but reflect on the well-known epigram: Ἀγρος Ἀχαιμενίδου γενόμην ποτε νῦν δὲ Μενίππου.[68] How short a time will it be before its present possessor is removed! Perhaps to be no more seen!

Sun. 28. A servant of Mr. Bradley's[69] sent to desire to speak 20 with me. Going to him, I found a young man, ill, but perfectly sensible.[70] He desired the rest to go out, and then said, 'On Thursday night, about eleven, being in bed, but broad awake, I heard one calling aloud, "Peter! Peter Wright!" And looking up, the room was as light as day, and I saw a man in very bright clothes

---

[66] Cf. 2 Tim. 2:12.

[67] Jacob Franck, a Moravian vintager from Heppack in Württemberg, who was 31 when he came over on the *Simmonds* with Wesley. See Wesley's diary; Wesley's list of passengers (in Adam Clarke, *Memoirs of the Wesley Family* (London, 1836), II.175-77, corrected from orig. in Wesley College, Bristol); Coulter and Saye; and Neisser, *Moravian Work.*

[68] Lucian, *Epigram*, 13: 'I was once the field of Achaemenides and am now Menippus.' The epigram continues: 'and I shall continue to pass from one man to another. For Achaemenides once thought he possessed me, and Menippus again thinks he does; but I belong to no man, only to fortune.' W. R. Paton, *The Greek Anthology*, III.39.

[69] William Bradley, who was dispatched by the Georgia Trustees to teach agriculture, should have travelled out with the Wesleys, but 'lost his passage from Cowes by going to Portsmouth to seek for a midwife to attend the passengers to Georgia, there being six women on board who will lie in within a month and nobody to assist them.' He, however, caught the next boat and arrived in Feb. 1736 (Egmont, *Diary*, II.216, 221; Egmont, *Journal*, pp. 123, 319). He obtained very large grants of land in Georgia and Carolina, but became embroiled with his Georgia creditors, stole cattle, and after a number of unsuccessful attempts, absconded to Carolina in 1740. Candler, *Colonial Records*, IV.581-82; Coulter and Saye, p. 51.

[70] Peter Wright, a servant to William Bradley, and who arrived in Georgia with him. Coulter and Saye, p. 58.

stand by the bed, who said, "Prepare yourself, for your end is nigh"; and then immediately all was dark as before.' I told him the advice was good, whencesoever it came. In a few days he recovered from his illness. His whole temper was changed, as well as his life; and so continued to be till after three or four weeks he relapsed, and died in peace.

Tuesday, March 30. Mr. Ingham, coming from Frederica, brought me letters pressing me to go thither. The next day Mr. Delamotte and I began to try whether life might not be as well sustained by one sort as by variety of food. We chose to make the experiment with bread, and were never more vigorous and healthy than while we tasted nothing else.[71] 'Blessed are the pure in heart,'[72] who, whether they eat or drink, or whatever they do, have no end therein but to please God! To them all things are pure. Every creature is good to them, and nothing to be rejected. But let them who know and feel that they are not thus pure, use every help and remove every hindrance, always remembering, 'He that despiseth little things shall fall by little and little.'[73]

Sunday, April 4. About four in the afternoon, I set out for Frederica in a piragua (a sort of flat-bottomed barge).[74] The next evening we anchored near Skidaway Island,[75] where the water at flood was twelve or fourteen foot deep. I wrapped myself up from head to foot in a large cloak to keep off the sand-flies, and lay down on the quarter-deck. Between one and two, I waked under water, being so fast asleep that I did not find where I was till my

[71] Moore related a story which he had from JW himself, that Oglethorpe, asking Wesley to dine, said: 'Mr. Wesley, there are some here who have a wrong idea of your abstemiousness. They think you hold the eating of animal food and drinking wine to be unlawful. I beg that you will convince them of the contrary.' Wesley took a little of each but was confined for five days by a fever (Moore, *Wesley*, I.311). Dr. Cheyne, whose regimen Wesley seems to have adopted ('the natural order . . . for all those who would cultivate and maintain clear heads and quick senses to the last, is from their birth till fifteen to persevere in a gradually increasing temperate diet, without fermented liquors; from fifteen to fifty to be only temperate in animal foods and fermented liquors; after fifty to give up animal food suppers and fermented liquors; after sixty to give up all animal food; and then about every ten years after to lessen about a quarter of their vegetable food'), complained of being a victim to a similar calumny: 'Some persons have industriously and designedly spread it about that I was of opinion that a sole strict vegetable, or milk and seed diet, was the best and fittest for all persons, climates, and ages, without exception or limitation' (G. Cheyne, *An Essay on Regimen* [London, 1740], pp. xxx, x, xii).

[72] Matt. 5:8.   [73] Ecclus. 19:1.

[74] There are many forms of this Spanish name for a dug-out canoe, including 'pettiawga', which Wesley uses here (see *OED*).

[75] Contrary to the normal practice then and now, Wesley here and elsewhere spells the word 'Skidoway'.

mouth was full of it. Having left my cloak, I know not how, upon deck, I swam round to the other side of the piragua, where a boat was tied, and climbed up by the rope without any hurt more than wetting my clothes. Thou art the God of whom cometh salvation:
5 thou art the Lord by whom we escape death.

The winds were so contrary that on Saturday 10, we could but just get over against Doboy Island, twenty miles from Frederica, but could not possibly make the creek, having a strong tide also against us. Here we lay beating off till past one, when the
10 lightning and rain, which we had long seen at a distance, drove down full upon us; till after a quarter of an hour the clouds parted, some passing on the right, and some on the left, leaving us a clear sky, and so strong a wind right after us as in two hours brought us to Frederica.

15 A little before we landed I opened my Testament on these words, 'If God be for us, who can be against us?'[76] Coming on shore I found my brother exceeding weak,[77] having been for some time ill of a flux. But he mended from the hour he saw me. *This* also 'hath God wrought'![78]

20 Sunday, April 11. I preached at the new storehouse, on the first verse of the Gospel for the day: 'Which of you convinceth me of sin? And if I say the truth, why do you not believe me?'[79] There was a large congregation, whom I endeavoured to convince of unbelief, by simply proposing the conditions of salvation as they
25 are laid down in Scripture, and appealing to their own hearts whether they believed they could be saved on no other terms.

In every one of the six following days I had some fresh proofs of the absolute necessity of following that wise advice of the Apostle: 'Judge nothing before the time, until the Lord come, who both
30 will bring to light the hidden things of darkness, and will make manifest the counsels of the hearts.'[80]

Saturday, April 17. We set out for Savannah, and reached it on Tuesday evening. O blessed place, where, having but one end in

---

[76] Rom. 8:31.

[77] Charles Wesley's flock had been 'ill of the bloody flux' (dysentery), and, after a period of fever, he himself became very ill. He records that when 'Mr. Delamotte and my brother landed . . . my strength was so exhausted I could not have read prayers once more'. The following day: 'I had just recovered strength enough to consecrate at the Sacrament; the rest my brother discharged.' CWJ, I.16-18.

[78] Num. 23:23.

[79] John 8:46.

[80] 1 Cor. 4:5.

view, dissembling and fraud are not; but each of us can pour out his heart without fear into his brother's bosom!

Not finding as yet any door open for the pursuing our main design,[81] we considered in what manner we might be most useful to the little flock at Savannah. And we agreed: first, to advise the 5 more serious among them to form themselves into a sort of little society,[82] and to meet once or twice a week, in order to reprove, instruct, and exhort one another; second, to select out of these a smaller number for a more intimate union with each other, which might be forwarded, partly by our conversing singly with each, 10 and partly by inviting them all together to our house; and this accordingly we determined to do every Sunday in the afternoon.

Wednesday, May 5. I was asked to baptize a child of Mr. Parker's, Second Bailiff of Savannah;[83] but Mrs. Parker told me, 'Neither Mr. P[arker] nor I will consent to its being dipped.' I 15 answered, 'If you "certify that your child is weak, it will suffice" (the rubric says) "to pour water upon it".'[84] She replied, 'Nay, the child is not weak, but I am resolved it shall not be dipped.' This argument I could not confute. So I went home, and the child was baptized by another person. 20

Sun. 9. I began dividing the public prayers according to the original appointment of the church (still observed in a few places

---

[81] The mission to the Indians.

[82] In these arrangements, encouraged by the Moravians, was foreshadowed the later class-meetings and select bands of Methodism. Wesley himself, in 'A Short History of the People called Methodists' (1781, §9; see Vol. 9 of this edn.), acknowledged their significance: 'On Monday, May 1 [1738], our little society began in London. But it may be observed, the first rise of Methodism (so called) was in November 1729, when four of us met together at Oxford; the second was at Savannah, in April 1736, when twenty or thirty persons met at my house; the last was at London, on this day.'

[83] Henry Parker, linen draper, who arrived in Savannah in 1733. He became third, second, and later head bailiff, succeeding Thomas Causton in these offices. He earned many good opinions: 'a tolerable magistrate', a sensible man, not 'of a rough or harsh temper'; but in 1739 the Trustees dismissed him from all his offices for 'abetting the application for Negroes, as also his character for drunkenness, and degrading his post, together with his being the leading man in courts of law', which might enable him to block a prosecution of Thomas Causton. In 1740, however, being assured that he 'has left drinking', the Trustees reappointed him head bailiff. Egmont, *Diary*, II.194, 494; III.54, 57, 70, 76, 119, 124, 139, 217; Coulter and Saye, p. 39.

[84] Wesley is here seeking to apply the rubric of the first Prayer Book of Edward VI (1549), believing it to be of more primitive usage than that of 1662. 'In England . . . [immersion of infants] remained the rule until towards the end of the 16th century, although affusion was allowed "if the child be weak"' (G. Harford and M. Stevenson, *The Prayer Book Dictionary* [London, 1925], p. 79). The Wesleys' scruples in this matter seem to have been singular to themselves, and it is notable that in his own *Sunday Service . . . in North America* (1784) the rubric simply required affusion.

in England).[85] The morning service began at five; the communion office (with the sermon) at eleven; the evening service about three. And this day I began reading prayers in the court-house, a large and convenient place.

5   Mon. 10. I began visiting my parishioners in order, from house to house; for which I set apart the time when they can't work, because of the heat, viz., from twelve till three in the afternoon.

Sunday, May 16. We were surprised in the evening by my brother, just come from Frederica.[86] After some conversation we
10   consulted how the poor people there might be taken care of during his absence. And it was at last agreed that Mr. Ingham and I should take our turns in assisting them; and the first was allotted me. Accordingly on Tuesday 18, I walked to Thunderbolt, whence the next afternoon we set out in a small boat. In the
15   evening we touched at Skidaway, and had a small but attentive congregation[87] to join with us in Evening Prayer.

Saturday, May 22. About four in the afternoon we entered upon Doboy Sound. The wind, which was right ahead, was so high when we were in the middle of it, and the sea so rough, being
20   driven in at the inlet, that the boat was on the point of sinking every moment. But it pleased God to bring us safe to the other side in half an hour, and to Frederica the next morning. We had public prayers at nine, at which nineteen persons were present, and (I think) nine communicants.

25   Fri. 28. I read the commendatory prayer[88] by Mr. Germain,[89]

[85] JW again follows the arrangements of the Prayer Book of 1549, which divided the prayers into Matins, Communion, and Evensong. But the rule of the Church required only three celebrations per annum; the level generally aimed at in country parishes in the eighteenth century was only four; and although in Oxfordshire a number of country parishes achieved monthly celebration, it is clear that the whole Prayer Book programme was not often carried out.

[86] Charles Wesley had come by boat to Thunderbolt and walked the remaining 5 miles to Savannah, 'whither the Indian traders were coming down to meet me and take out licences. I was overjoyed at my deliverance out of this furnace [Frederica], and not a little ashamed of myself for being so.' CWJ, I.27.

[87] To whom Charles Wesley had ministered on his way to Savannah, and for whom he had promised to try to contrive a monthly supply.

[88] 'A commendatory prayer for a sick person at the point of departure', one of three prayers inserted in the 1662 Prayer Book at the close of the Office for the Visitation of the Sick.

[89] Michael Germain, son of Michael Germain who died on the day of arrival in Feb. 1736, had been committed to prison by Oglethorpe on Mar. 21 for shooting on a Sunday; his wife had clashed with Charles Welsey for refusing baptism by immersion for her baby, and tried to secure an allowance from the Georgia Trustees after her husband's death. CWJ, I.2, 4; Egmont, *Diary*, III.115; Candler, *Colonial Records*, II.287, 298; Coulter and Saye, pp. 18, 75.

who lay at the point of death. He had lost his speech and his senses. His eyes were set, neither had he any discernible motion but the heaving of his breast. While we stood round him he stretched out his arms, rubbed his head, recovered his sight, speech, and understanding; and immediately sending for the bailiffs, settled the affairs of his family, and then lay down and died.

At the first service on Sunday, May 30, were only five, at the second twenty-five. The next day I made Mr. Lascelles's[90] will; who, notwithstanding his great weakness, was quite revived when any mention was made of death or of eternity.

Tuesday, June 1. After praying with him I was surprised to find one of the most controverted questions in divinity, disinterested love, decided at once by a poor, old man without education or learning, or any instructor but the Spirit of God. I asked him what he thought of paradise—to which he had said he was going. He said, 'To be sure, it is a fine place. But I don't mind that. I don't care what place I am in. Let God put me where he will, or do with me what he will, so I may but set forth his honour and glory.'

Thursday, June 3. Being Ascension Day, we had the Holy Communion, but only Mr. Hird's family[91] joined with us in it. One reason why there were no more was because a few words which a woman[92] had inadvertently spoken had set almost all the town in a flame. Alas! How shall a city stand that is thus divided against itself![93] Where there is no brotherly love, no meekness, no forbearing or forgiving one another; by envy, malice, revenge, suspicion, anger, clamour, bitterness, evil-speaking, without end! Abundant proof that there can be no true love of man unless it be built on the love of God.

Sun. 6. Calling on Mr. Lascelles, and asking how he did, 'My departure (said he) I hope is at hand.' I asked, 'Are you troubled at that?' He replied, 'Oh no; to depart and to be with Christ is far better. I desire no more of this bad world. My hope and my joy

---

[90] Henry Lascelles, Jun., son of Henry Lascelles, surgeon; both came over at the same time as JW, though not in the same ship. Lascelles's hut had been completely burned out on Apr. 9, 1736 (CWJ, I.17).

[91] Cf. above, Nov. 16, 1735, n. 17. In his diary of the voyage to Georgia, JW listed the Hird family as Thomas, Grace, Mark, and Phoebe Hird. Hird became constable at Frederica and was regarded by Causton as a trouble-maker. Mrs. Hird had befriended Charles Wesley in his illness. CWJ, I.10, 16, 17, 21; Egmont, *Diary*, II.423.

[92] Mrs. Thomas Hawkins.

[93] Cf. Matt. 12:25.

and my love is there.' The next time I saw him he said, 'I desire nothing more than for God to forgive my many and great sins. I would be humble. I would be the humblest creature living. My heart is humble and broken for my sins. Tell me, teach me, what
5 shall I do to please God? I would fain do whatever is his will.' I said, 'It is his will you should suffer.' He answered, 'Then I *will* suffer. I will gladly suffer whatever pleases him.'

Mon. 7. Finding him weaker I asked, 'Do you still desire to die?' He said, 'Yes; but I dare not pray for it, for fear I should
10 displease my heavenly Father. His will be done. Let him work his will, in my life or in my death.'

Thur. 10. We began to execute at Frederica what we had before agreed to do at Savannah. Our design was, on Sundays in the afternoon and every evening after public service, to spend
15 some time with the most serious of the communicants in singing,[94] reading, and conversation. This evening we had only Mark Hird. But on Sunday Mr. Hird and two more desired to be admitted. After a psalm and a little conversation, I read Mr. Law's *Christian Perfection*[95] and concluded with another psalm.

20 Saturday, June 12. Being with one who was very desirous to converse with me, 'but not upon religion',[96] I spoke to this effect: 'Suppose you was going to a country where everyone spoke Latin and understood no other language, neither would converse with any that did not understand it; suppose one was sent to stay here a
25 short time, on purpose to teach it you; suppose that person, pleased with your company, should spend his time in trifling with you, and teach you nothing of what he came for—would that be well done? Yet this is our case. You are going to a country where everyone speaks the love of God. The citizens of heaven
30 understand no other language. They converse with none who do not understand it. Indeed none such are admitted there. I am sent from God to teach you this. A few days are allotted us for that purpose. Would it then be well done in me, because I was pleased with your company, to spend this short time in trifling, and teach
35 you nothing of what I came for? God forbid! I will rather not

---

[94] In the possibilities of this devotional practice JW had been encouraged by the Moravians. Hymn-books were not in regular use in the Church of England; at the gathering here described only psalms were sung in the Anglican manner.

[95] First edn., 'we read the *Christian Perfection*'.

[96] Possibly Mrs. Patterson, who was ill, or Mrs. Hawkins, who 'invited' him (see diary entry for June 12 in Appendix below).

converse with you at all. Of the two extremes this is the best.'

Wednesday, June 16. Another little company of us met—Mr. Reed,[97] Davison,[98] Walker,[99] Delamotte, and myself. We sung, read a little of Mr. Law, and then conversed. Wednesdays and Fridays were the days we fixed for constant meeting. 5

Thur. 17. An officer of the man-of-war, walking just behind me[1] with two or three of his acquaintance, cursed and swore exceedingly, by upon my reproving him seemed much moved, and gave me many thanks.

Sat. 19. Mr. Oglethorpe returned from the south, and gave 10 orders on Sunday the 20th that none should profane the day (as was usual before) by fishing or fowling upon it. In the afternoon sermon I summed up what I had seen or heard at Frederica inconsistent with Christianity, and consequently with the prosperity of the place. The event was as it ought: some of the 15 hearers were profited, and the rest deeply offended.

This day, at half an hour past ten, God heard the prayer of his servant, and Mr. Lascelles, according to his desire, was 'dissolved that he might be with Christ'.[2]

Tue. 22. Observing much coldness in Mr. [Horton]'s[3] 20 behaviour, I asked him the reason of it. He answered, 'I like nothing you do. All your sermons are satires on particular

---

[97] Mr. and Mrs. Reed came out to Georgia on the same boat as the Wesleys; Charles Wesley slept in a corner of their hut at Frederica. CWJ, I.14.

[98] Samuel Davison, chairman, who was sent out with his wife and daughter by the Trustees as a maker of stocks for guns, arrived in Georgia at the same time as JW. Subsequently he was made second constable at Frederica and overseer of the Trust's servants. Charles Wesley, to whom Davison was 'my good Samaritan', reported to the Trustees that 'though a Presbyterian, [he was] one of the best of my parishioners.' Davison, who feared that the lack of pastoral care would prove ruinous to the civilizing of the next generation of Georgians, quickly fenced his property and built a three-storey brick house. CWJ, I.4, 13, 17; Egmont, *Diary*, II.170, 180, 313, 411; III.72, 74, 75, 158; Coulter and Saye, p. 12.

[99] Thomas Walker, carpenter, who came at the same time as JW and settled on Lot 10N; appointed second bailiff of Frederica, 1742. Candler, *Colonial Records*, V.655; Coulter and Saye, p. 55.

[1] 1743 onwards, 'a man-of-war, . . . behind us'.

[2] Cf. 2 Cor. 5:1; Phil. 1:23; see also below, July 10, 1736, when Wesley echoes this Scripture for himself.

[3] William Horton, former subsheriff of Herefordshire, now a settler at Jekyll Island, magistrate and commander of the militia at Frederica. There had been friction between him and JW on religious grounds on the boat. On June 6, 1737, Horton with three others was made trustee of a 300-acre lot at Frederica, to raise a maintenance for a minister (Curnock, I.121, 234). Taken to court and acquitted on a charge of felony, Horton believed that JW was maintaining an agitation of the Frederica freeholders against him. Egmont, *Journal*, p. 320; Coulter and Saye, p. 79; Egmont, *Diary*, II.449.

persons. Therefore I will never hear you more. And all the people are of my mind. For we won't hear ourselves abused.

'Beside[s], they say they are Protestants. But as for you, they can't tell what religion you are of. They never heard of such a religion before. They don't know what to make of it. And then, your private behaviour—All the quarrels that have been here since you came have been 'long of you. Indeed there is neither man nor woman in the town who minds a word you say. And so you may preach long enough; but nobody will come to hear you.'

He was too warm for hearing an answer. So I had nothing to do but to thank him for his openness, and walk away.

Wed. 23. I had a long conversation with Mr.——[4] upon the nature of true religion. I then asked him why he did not endeavour to recommend it to all with whom he conversed. He said, 'I did so once; and for some time I thought I had done much good by it. But I afterwards found they were never the better, and I myself was the worse. Therefore now, though I always strive to be inoffensive in my conversation, I don't strive to make people religious, unless those that have a desire to be so, and are consequently willing to hear me. But I have not yet (I speak not of you or your brother) found one such person in America.'

'He that hath ears to hear, let him hear!'[5] Mark the tendency of this accursed principle![6] If you will speak only to those who are 'willing to hear', see how many you will turn from the error of their ways! If therefore, striving to do good, you have done hurt, what then? So did St. Paul. So did the Lord of life. Even his word was 'the savour of death', as well as 'the savour of life'.[7] But shall you therefore strive no more? God forbid! Strive more humbly, more calmly, more cautiously. Do not strive *as you did before*—but strive, while the breath of God is in your nostrils!

Being to leave Frederica in the evening, I took the more notice of these words in the Lesson for the day: 'Whereunto shall I liken the men of this generation . . . ? They are like unto children sitting in the market-place, . . . and saying, We have piped unto you, and ye have not danced; we have mourned to you, and ye

[4] Perhaps Oglethorpe, the most likely person among those with whom JW's diary shows him to have conversed that day from 8:30 to 10:45 a.m

[5] Matt. 11:15, etc.

[6] The principle of speaking only to those willing to hear was said to have been adopted by many Moravians.

[7] Based on 2 Cor. 2:16, where the terms are applied to the Christian's relation to God and to 'them that perish'.

have not wept. For John the Baptist came neither eating bread nor drinking wine; and ye say, He hath a devil. The Son of man is come eating and drinking; and ye say, Behold a gluttonous man, and a wine-bibber, a friend of publicans and sinners.'[b]

About eleven at night we took boat. And on Saturday 26, about one in the afternoon, came to Savannah. O what do we want here, either for life or godliness! If suffering, God will send it in *his* time.

Sunday, June 27. About twenty joined with us in Morning Prayer. An hour or two after, a large party of Creek Indians came, the expectation of whom deprived us of our place of public worship,[8] in which they were to have their audience.

Wed. 30. I hoped a door was opened for going up immediately to the Choctaws, the least polished, i.e., the least corrupted, of all the Indian nations. But upon my informing Mr. Oglethorpe of our design, he objected, not only the danger of being intercepted, or killed by the French there; but much more the inexpediency of leaving Savannah destitute of a minister. These objections I related to our brethren in the evening, who were all of opinion, 'We ought not to go yet.'

Thursday, July 1. The Indians had an audience, and another on Saturday, when Chigilly,[9] their headman, dined with Mr. Oglethorpe. After dinner I asked the grey-headed old man what he thought he was made for. He said, 'He that is above knows what he made us for. We know nothing. We are in the dark. But white men know much. And yet white men build great houses, as if they were to live for ever. But white men can't live for ever. In a little time white men will be dust as well as I.' I told him, 'If red men will learn the Good Book, they may know as much as white

---

[b] Luke 7[:31-34].

---

[8] Services were normally held in the court-house, now requisitioned for the reception of the Indians (see diary entry in Appendix below). The Moravians lent their meeting-house.

[9] Headman of the Choctaw Indians. In 1739 Oglethorpe negotiated a formal treaty of alliance between the King and Chigilly on behalf of the Creeks and other Indians as part of the general defence against the Spanish (Curnock, VIII.317). Like most Indian names, found variously spelled both in that day and this—Chekelli, Chigelley, Chikillie, and JW's usual spelling (as here, orig.), Chicali. John Pitts Corry, *Indian Affairs in Georgia, 1732–56* (Philadelphia, 1936), p. 124; Robert Wright, *Memoir of Oglethorpe* (London, 1867), p. 213; L. F. Church, *Oglethorpe: a Study of Philanthropy in England and Georgia* (London, 1932), p. 136; L. E. Ivers, *British Drums on the Southern Frontier* (Chapel Hill, 1974), p. 40; see also below, Dec. 2, 1737, JW's report to the Trustees, §28.

men. But neither we nor you can understand that book unless we are taught by him that is above; and he will not teach unless you avoid what you already know is not good.' He answered, 'I believe that; he will not teach us while our hearts are not white. And our
5 men do what they know is not good. They kill their own children. And our women do what they know is not good. They kill the child before it is born. Therefore he that is above does not send us the Good Book.'

Hearing the younger of the Miss Boveys was not well, I called
10 upon them this evening.[10] I found she had only the prickly heat, a sort of rash very common here in summer. We soon fell into serious conversation, after I had asked if they did not think they were too young to trouble themselves with religion yet. And whether they might not defer it ten or a dozen years. To which
15 one of them replied, 'If it will be reasonable ten years hence to be religious, it is so now; I am not for deferring one moment.'

Wednesday, July 7. I called there again, being determined now to speak more closely. But meeting company there, *prudence* induced me to put it off till another opportunity.

20 Thur. 8. Mr. O[glethorpe] being there, and casually speaking of sudden death, Miss Becky said, 'If it was the will of God, I should choose to die without a lingering illness.' Her sister said, 'Are you then always prepared to die?' She replied, 'Jesus Christ is always prepared to help me. And little stress is to be laid on such
25 a preparation for death as is made in a fit of sickness.'

Saturday, July 10. Just as they had done drinking tea Mrs. Margaret,[11] seeing her colour change, asked if she was well. She did not return any answer; and Dr. Tailfer[12] soon after going by, she desired him to step in, and said, 'Sir, my sister, I fear, is not
30 well.' He looked earnestly at her, felt her pulse, and replied,

---

[10] Margaret and Rebecca Bovey were two unmarried daughters of a Georgia settler who died in 1735. In the same year they secured Lot 33 in Savannah, forfeited by Thomas Pratt on his return to England. Rebecca was on the point of marrying an unscrupulous Dutch adventurer named Appee when she suddenly died on July 10, 1736. Margaret married James Burnside on Mar. 12, 1736/37, lived with him at Rotten Possum, and died Sept. 26, 1742. She supported JW in his work and defended him in the controversy over Sophy Hopkey.

[11] I.e., Margaret Bovey.

[12] Patrick Tailfer, M.D., one of the authors of *A True and Historical Narrative*: a 'saucy fellow and ringleader' for the importation of liquor and slaves, who for a time had a 500-acre lot by the Cowpen (Egmont, *Journal*, p. 103). 'Went away to Carolina for fear of the Spaniards', August 31, 1740 (Candler, *Colonial Records*, V.395; Coulter and Saye, p. 98). First edn., 'Talfer'; appears in 1774 *Works* as 'Talser'.

'Well, madam! Your sister is dying.' However, he thought it not impossible bleeding might help. She bled about an ounce, leaned back, and died.

As soon as I heard of it I went to the house, and begged they would not lay her out immediately, there being a possibility, at least, she might only be in a swoon; of which indeed there was some slight hope, she not only being as warm as ever, but having a fresh colour in her cheeks, and a few drops of blood starting out upon bending her arm. But there was no pulse and no breath; so that having waited some hours we found her 'spirit was indeed returned to God that gave it'.[13]

I never saw so beautiful a corpse in my life. Poor comfort to its late inhabitant! I was greatly surprised at her sister. There was in all her behaviour such an inexpressible mixture of tenderness and resignation. The first time I spoke to her she said, 'All my afflictions are nothing to this. I have lost not only a sister, but a friend. But 'tis the will of God. I rely on him and doubt not but he will support me under it.'

This evening we had such a storm of thunder and lightning as I never saw before, even in Georgia. This voice of God, too, told me I was not fit to die; since I was afraid rather than desirous of it! O when shall I wish to be dissolved and to be with Christ?[14] When I love him with all my heart.

Almost the whole town was the next evening at the funeral, where many doubtless made a world of good resolutions. O how little trace of most of these will be left in the morning! 'Tis a true saying, 'Hell is paved with good intentions.'[15]

Tuesday, July 20. Five of the Chickasaw Indians (twenty of whom had been in Savannah several days) came to see us, with Mr. Andrews,[16] their interpreter. They were all warriors, four of them headmen. The two chief were Paustoobee and Mingo Mattaw.[17] Our conference was as follows:

---

[13] Cf. Eccles. 12:7.

[14] Cf. above, June 19, 1736.

[15] Cf. John Ray, *English Proverbs*, 1670; and Wesley's Sermon 2, *The Almost Christian*, II.9 (2:140-41 in this edn.).

[16] Almost certainly Thomas Andrews, who employed 8 men and 70 horses in trade with the Creek and Chickasaw nations. *A Brief Account of the Causes that have Retarded the Progress of the Colony of Georgia* (London, 1743), p. 38.

[17] JW reported this conference very fully to the Georgia Trustees (Egmont, *Journal*, pp. 177-78) and to *Gentleman's Magazine* (May 1737), VII.318-19. For the text which contains many minor variants, see *Letters*, 25:464-66 in this edn. In *Gentleman's Magazine* the leading Indians appear as Postubee and Mingomawtaw.

Q: Do you believe there is One above, who is over all things?

Paustoobee answered, We believe there are four beloved things above: the clouds, the sun, the clear sky, and he that lives in the clear sky.

Q: Do you believe there is but One that lives in the clear sky?

5   A: We believe there are two with him, three in all.

Q: Do you think he made the sun, and the other beloved things?

A: We cannot tell. Who hath seen?

Q: Do you think he made you?

A: We think he made all men at first.

10   Q: How did he make them at first?

A: Out of the ground.

Q: Do you believe he loves you?

A: I don't know. I cannot see him.

Q: But has he not often saved your life?

15   A: He has. Many bullets have gone on this side, and many on that side, but he would not let them hurt me. And many bullets have gone into these young men, and yet they are alive.

Q: Then, can't he save you from your enemies now?

A: Yes, but we know not if he will. We have now so many enemies round about

20   us that I think of nothing but death. And if I am to die, I shall die, and I will die like a man. But if he will have me to live, I shall live. Though I had ever so many enemies, he can destroy them all.

Q: How do you know that?

A: From what I have seen. When our enemies came against us before, then

25   the beloved clouds came for us. And often much rain, and sometimes hail, has come upon them, and that in a very hot day. And I saw, when many French and Choctaws and other nations came against one of our towns. And the ground made a noise under them, and the beloved ones in the air behind them. And they were afraid, and went away, and left their meat and drink and their guns. I tell no

30   lie. All these saw it too.

Q: Have you heard such noises at other times?

A: Yes, often; before and after almost every battle.[18]

Q: What sort of noises were they?

A: Like the noise of drums and guns and shouting.

35   Q: Have you heard any such lately?

A: Yes; four days after our last battle with the French.

Q: Then you heard nothing before it?

A: The night before I dreamed; I heard many drums up there, and many trumpets there, and much stamping of feet and shouting. Till then I thought we

40   should all die. But then I thought the beloved ones were come to help us. And the next day I heard above a hundred guns go off before the fight began.[19] And I said, 'When the sun is there, the beloved ones will help us, and we shall conquer our enemies.' And we did so.

Q: Do you often think and talk of the beloved ones?

45   A: We think of them always, wherever we are. We talk of them and to them, at

---

[18] *Gentleman's Magazine* adds: '(Here Mr. Andrews said that he had often heard them himself, and so had all the traders.)'

[19] *Gentleman's Magazine* adds: '("as did I", said Mr. Andrews)'.

home and abroad; in peace, in war, before and after we fight; and indeed
whenever and wherever we meet together.

Q: Where do you think your souls go after death?

A: We believe the souls of red men walk up and down near the place where
they died, or where their bodies lie. For we have often heard cries and noises 5
near the place where any prisoners had been burned.

Q: Where do the souls of white men go after death?

A: We can't tell. We have not seen.

Q: Our belief is that the souls of bad men only walk up and down, but the
souls of good men go up. 10

A: I believe so too. But I told you the talk of the nation.

(Mr. Andrews: They said at the burying[20] they knew what you was doing. You
was speaking to the beloved ones above to take up the soul of the young woman.)

Q: We have a book that tells us many things of the beloved ones above. Would
you be glad to know them? 15

A: We have no time now but to fight. If we should ever be at peace, we should
be glad to know.

Q: Do you expect ever to know what the white men know?

(Mr. Andrews: They told Mr. O[glethorpe] they believe the time will come
when the red and the white men will be one.) 20

Q: What do the French teach you?

A: The French black kings[c] never go out. We see you go about. We like that.
That is good.

Q: How came your nation by the knowledge they have?

A: As soon as ever the ground was sound and fit to stand upon, it came to us, 25
and has been with us ever since. But we are young men. Our old men know
more. But all of them do not know. There are but a few; whom the Beloved One
chooses from a child, and is in them, and takes care of them and teaches them.
They know these things. And our old men practise; therefore they know. But I
don't practise; therefore I know little. 30

Monday, July 26. My brother and I set out for Charleston, in
order to his embarking for England.[21] But the wind being contrary
we did not reach Port Royal, forty miles from Savannah, till
Wednesday evening. The next morning we left it. But the wind
was so high in the afternoon, as we were crossing the neck of St. 35
Helena Sound, that our oldest sailor cried out, 'Now everyone

---

[c] So they call the priests.

---

[20] *Gentleman's Magazine*: 'of Miss Bovey' (see above, July 11, 1736).

[21] The previous day, July 25, Charles Wesley had resigned his secretaryship, though
Oglethorpe tried to dissuade him and assured him he could do his business in London in
three days (CWJ, I.35). The object of returning to England was to secure additional
manpower and money for the mission, and Charles, having been less successful in
Georgia even than John, who was now much in Oglethorpe's confidence, was chosen to
pursue it. No one knew at this point that he would never return to Georgia. Charleston
(spelled 'Charlestown' by Wesley), the port of embarkation, is in South Carolina.

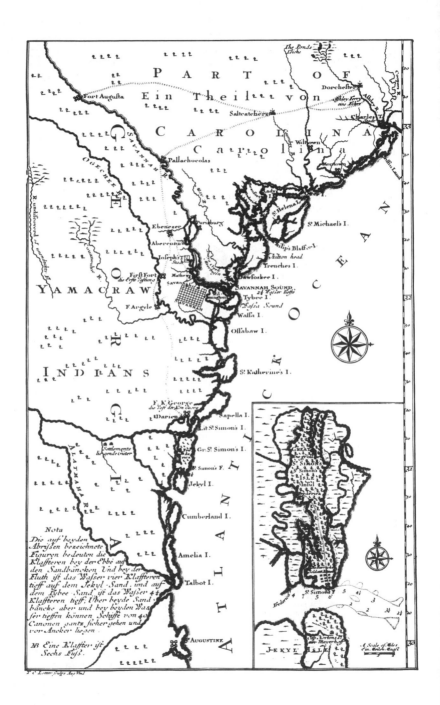

must take care for himself.' I told him God would take care for us all. Almost as soon as the words were spoken, the mast fell. I kept on the edge of the boat, to be clear of her when she sunk (which we expected every moment), though with little prospect of swimming to shore against such a wind and sea. But 'How is it that thou hadst no faith?'[22] The moment the mast fell, two men caught it and pulled it into the boat; the other three rowed with all their might, and God 'gave command to the winds and seas',[23] so that in an hour we were safe on land.

Saturday, July 31. We came to Charleston. The church is of brick but plastered[24] over like stone. I believe it would contain three or four thousand persons. About three hundred were present at the morning service the next day (when Mr. Garden[25] desired me to preach); about fifty at the Holy Communion. I was glad to see several Negroes at church; one of whom told me she was there constantly, and that her old mistress (now dead) had many times instructed her in the Christian religion. I asked her what religion was. She said she could not tell. I asked if she knew what a soul was. She answered, 'No.' I said, 'Don't you know there is something in you different from your body? Something you can't see or feel?' She replied, 'I never heard so much before.' I added, 'Do you think, then, a man dies altogether as a horse dies?' She said, 'Yes, to be sure.' O God, where are thy tender mercies? Are they not over all thy works?[26] When shall the Sun of Righteousness arise on these outcasts of men, with healing in his wings![27]

Monday, August 2. I set out for the Lieutenant-Governor's seat,[28] about thirty miles from Charleston, to deliver Mr. Oglethorpe's letters. It stands very pleasantly on a little hill, with a

[22] Cf. Mark 4:40.

[23] Luke 8:25.

[24] Wesley used the form 'plaistered', obsolescent during the eighteenth century. Samuel Johnson did not recognize it in his *Dictionary*, though it is found in his writings.

[25] Alexander Garden (1685–1756), a Scotsman in Anglican orders, went to Charleston in 1719, becoming rector of St. Philip's church and the Bishop of London's commissary in South Carolina. In 1740 he began a furious controversy with George Whitefield and constituted what is said to have been the first ecclesiastical court in the colonies to take proceedings against him. JW sent a copy of his sermon on *Free Grace* (1739), implicitly attacking Whitefield's doctrines, to Commissary Garden at this time. Garden's son, of the same name, a distinguished doctor, botanist, and correspondent of Linnaeus, gave his name to the *Gardenia florida*.

[26] See Ps. 145:9.

[27] See Mal. 4:2.

[28] The lieutenant-governor was Thomas Broughton, who died on Nov. 22, 1737.

vale on either side, in one of which is a thick wood; the other is planted with rice and Indian corn. I designed to have gone back by Mr. Skene's,[29] who has about fifty Christian Negroes. But my horse tiring, I was obliged to return the straight way to
5 Charleston.

I had sent the boat we came in back to Savannah, expecting a passage thither myself in Colonel Bull's;[30] his not going so soon, I went to Ashley Ferry on Thursday, intending to walk to Port Royal. But Mr. Bellinger[31] not only provided me a horse, but rode
10 with me himself ten miles, and sent his son with me to Combahee Ferry, twenty miles farther; whence, having hired horses and a guide, I came to Beaufort (on Port Royal)[32] the next evening. We took boat in the morning, but the wind being contrary, and very high, did not reach Savannah till Sunday in the afternoon.

15 Finding Mr. Oglethorpe was gone, I stayed only a day at Savannah, and leaving Mr. Ingham and Delamotte there, set out on Tuesday morning for Frederica. In walking to Thunderbolt I was in so heavy a shower that all my clothes were as wet as if I had gone through the river. On which occasion I can't but observe
20 that vulgar error concerning the hurtfulness of the rains and dews of America. I have been thoroughly wet with these rains more than once, yet without any harm at all. And I have lain many nights in the open air and received all the dews that fell. And so, I believe, might anyone, if his constitution was not impaired by the
25 softness of a genteel education.

At Thunderbolt we took boat, and on Friday, August 13, came

---

[29] Alexander Skene (Wesley spells the name 'Skeen'), a wealthy landowner from Barbados, was one of the councilmen of South Carolina. He was the first planter to agree to the attempted conversion of his slaves by the SPG missionaries. This had been in 1715. M. Eugene Sirmans, *Colonial South Carolina* (Chapel Hill, 1966), pp. 99, etc.; Richard P. Sherman, *Robert Johnson, Proprietary and Royal Governor of South Carolina* (Columbia, 1966).

[30] William Bull (1683–1755), a native of South Carolina, President of the South Carolina Council and friend of Oglethorpe, was lieutenant-governor of South Carolina, 1738–55. His seat was at Ashley Hall, 2 miles from Ashley Ferry. Bull was much concerned with the supply of cattle to Georgia, and its defence; on Feb. 24, 1736, he had visited Wesley in Savannah.

[31] Orig., 'Belinger'. The Bellingers were an old dissenting family in South Carolina. This one was probably William Bellinger, a planter of Ashepoo Ferry, South Carolina, with whom JW was in frequent contact in the course of the next year (Candler, *Colonial Records*, II.363). In 1723 he had been appointed captain of a troop of men commissioned to build Fort Prince George, better known as Palachacola Garrison, north of Purrysburg on the east side of the Savannah River (Ivers, pp. 23-25; Sirmans, pp. 72, 98n.).

[32] I.e., Port Royal Island.

to Frederica, where I delivered to Mr. O[glethorpe] the letters I had brought from Carolina. The next day he set out for Fort St. George.[33] From that time I had less and less prospect of doing good at Frederica, many there being extremely zealous and indefatigably diligent to prevent it, and few of the rest daring to 5 show themselves of another mind, for fear of their displeasure.[34]

Sat. 28. I set apart (out of the few we had) a few books towards a library at Frederica. In the afternoon I walked to the fort on the other side of the Island. About five we set out homeward, but my guide not being perfect in the way, we were soon lost in the 10 woods. We walked on, however, as well as we could, till between nine and ten, when, being heartily tired and thoroughly wet with dew, we lay down and slept till morning.

About daybreak on Sunday the 29th we set out again, endeavouring to walk straight forward, and soon after sunrise 15 found ourselves in the Great Savannah, near Frederica. By this good providence I was delivered from another fear, that of lying in the woods, which experience showed was to one in tolerable health a mere 'lion in the way'.[35]

Thursday, September 2. I set out in a sloop, and about ten on 20 Sunday morning came to Skidaway, which (after reading prayers and preaching to a small congregation) I left, and came to Savannah in the evening.

Mon. 13. I began reading, with Mr. Delamotte, Bishop Beveridge's *Pandectae canonum conciliorum.*[36] Nothing could so 25 effectually have convinced us that both particular and 'general councils may err, and have erred'; and that 'things ordained by them as necessary to salvation have neither strength nor authority unless they be taken out of Holy Scripture.'[37]

Mon. 20. We ended (of which also I must confess I once 30

---

[33] See Aug. 2, 1736, and n. 31.

[34] By this time the scandal surrounding JW's relations with Sophia Hopkey had broken.

[35] Prov. 26:13.

[36] William Beveridge (1637–1708), vicar of Ealing, 1661–72, and of St. Peter's, Cornhill, 1672; Canon of Chichester, 1673, and of St. Paul's, 1674; Prebendary of Canterbury, 1684. Joined with Horneck and others in forming Religious Societies. Refused the See of Bath and Wells vacated by the deprivation of Thomas Ken, 1691, but accepted St. Asaph, 1704. The book here referred to, *Codex canonum ecclesiae primitivae vindicatus ac illustratus* (London, 1678), was a collection of the apostolic canons and decrees of councils received by the Greek church, together with canonical epistles of the Fathers, and evidenced what is now regarded as '(in places misguided) erudition'. F. L. Cross, ed., *Oxford Dictionary of the Christian Church* (London, 1974), p. 164.

[37] Cf. Thirty-nine Articles, Art. XXI, 'Of the Authority of General Councils'.

thought more highly than I ought to think) the Apostolical Canons; so called, as Bishop Beveridge observes, 'because partly grounded upon, partly agreeing with, the traditions delivered down from the apostles'. But he observes farther (in the 159th
5 page of his *Codex canonum ecclesiae primitivae*—and why did he not observe it in the first page of the book?), 'They contain the discipline used in the church at the time when they were collected, not when the Council of Nicaea met; for then many parts of it were useless and obsolete.'[38]

10 Tuesday, October 12. We considered if anything could yet be done for the poor people of Frederica. And I submitted to the judgment of my friends, which was, that I should take another journey thither; Mr. Ingham undertaking to supply my place at Savannah for the time I should stay there. I came thither on
15 Saturday the 16th, and found few things better than I expected. The morning and evening prayers, which were read for a while after my leaving the place, had been long discontinued, and from that time everything grew worse and worse, not many retaining any more of the form than of the power of godliness.[39]

20 I was at first a little discouraged, but soon remembered the word which cannot fail: 'Greater is he that is in you than he that is in the world.'[40] I cried to God to 'arise and maintain his own cause',[41] and after the evening prayers were ended invited a few to my house (as I did every night while I stayed in Frederica). I read
25 to them one of the exhortations of Ephraem Syrus,[42] the most awakening writer (I think) of all the ancients. We concluded our reading and conversation with a psalm, and, I trust, our God gave us his blessing.

Mon. 18. Finding there were several Germans at Frederica
30 who, not understanding the English tongue, could not join in our public service, I desired them to meet at noon in my house, which they did every day at noon from thenceforward. We first sung a German hymn, then I read a chapter in the New Testament, then explained it to them as well as I could. After another hymn we
35 concluded with prayer.

[38] The quotations represent JW's rather free recollections of passages on pp. 12, 159 of Beveridge's *Codex*. According to Curnock (I.277, n. 1), the study of the *Codex canonum* was prescribed for missionaries by the SPG.

[39] See 2 Tim. 3:5.   [40] 1 John 4:4.

[41] Ps. 74:23 (BCP).

[42] A prolific Syrian writer (*c.* 306–73). JW sometimes (as here) uses the form 'Ephrem', elsewhere (as in *An Address to the Clergy*, I.2) 'Ephraim'.

Mon. 25. I took boat, and after a slow and dangerous passage came to Savannah on Sunday the 31st.

Tuesday, November 23. Mr. Oglethorpe sailed for England, leaving Mr. Ingham, Mr. Delamotte, and me at Savannah, but with less prospect of preaching to the Indians than we had the first day we set foot in America. Whenever I mentioned it, it was immediately replied, 'You can't leave Savannah without a minister.' To this indeed my plain answer was, 'I know not that I am under any obligation to the contrary. I never promised to stay here one month. I openly declared both *before, at, and ever since* my coming hither, that I neither would nor could take charge of the English any longer than till I could go among the Indians.' If it was said, 'But did not the Trustees of Georgia appoint you to be minister of Savannah?' I replied, 'They did; but it was not done by my solicitation: it was done without either my desire or knowledge. Therefore I cannot conceive that appointment to lay me under any obligation of continuing there any longer than till a door is opened to the heathens. And this I expressly declared at the time I consented to accept of that appointment.' But though I had no other obligation not to leave Savannah now, yet that of love I could not break through; I could not resist the importunate request of the more serious parishioners to watch over their souls yet a little longer, till someone came who might supply my place. And this I the more willingly did because the time was not come to preach the gospel of peace to the heathens, all their nations being in a ferment; and Paustoobee and Mingo Mattaw having told me, in terms, in my own house, 'Now our enemies are all about us, and we can do nothing but fight; but if the beloved ones should ever give us to be at peace, then we would hear *the Great Word*.'[43]

Thursday, December 9. Hearing of one dangerously ill,[44] I went to her immediately. She told me that she had many things to say; but her weakness prevented her saying them then; and the next day God required her soul of her.

Wed. 22. Mr. Delamotte and I, with a guide, set out to walk to the Cowpen. When we had walked two or three hours our guide told us plainly he did not know where we were. However, believing it could not be far off, we thought it best to go on. In an hour or two we came to Cypress Swamp, which lay directly across

---

[43] Cf. Wesley's interview with the Indians, July 20, 1736.
[44] Mrs. Clark.

our way. There was not time to walk back to Savannah before
night, so we walked through it, the water being about breast-high.
By that time we had gone a mile beyond it, we were out of all path;
and it being now past sunset, we sat down, intending to make a
5 fire and to stay there till morning; but finding our tinder wet, we
were at a stand. I advised to walk on still; but my companions,
being faint and weary, were for lying down, which we accordingly
did about six o'clock. The ground was as wet as our clothes,
which (it being a sharp frost) were soon froze together; however, I
10 slept till six in the morning. There fell a heavy dew in the night,
which covered us over as white as snow. Within an hour after
sunrise we came to a plantation, and in the evening, without any
hurt, to Savannah.

    Tue. 28. We set out by land with a better guide for Frederica.
15 On Wednesday evening we came to Fort Argyle, on the bank[45] of
the River Ogeechee.[46] The next afternoon we crossed Canoochee[47] River in a small canoe, our horses swimming by the side of
it. We made a fire on the bank and, notwithstanding the rain, slept
quietly till the morning.

20   Saturday, January 1, 1737. Our provisions fell short, our
journey being longer than we expected; but having a little
barbecued bear's flesh (i.e., dried in the sun), we boiled it and
found it wholesome food. The next day we reached Darien, the
settlement of the Scotch Highlanders—a sober, industrious,
25 friendly, hospitable people, whose minister, Mr. Macleod,[48] is a
serious, resolute, and (I hope) a pious man.

---

[45] All contemporary editions read 'back', but an errata slip present in some copies of the
first edition alters this to 'bank'.

[46] Orig., 'Ogeechy'.

[47] Orig., 'Cooanoochy'.

[48] The Scottish Presbyterian minister variously described in the documents as the Rev.
G., the Rev. Hugh, or the Rev. John Macleod, and listed in Hew Scott, *Fasti Ecclesiae
Scoticanae* (Edinburgh, 1915–28), 7:664, as John M'Leod, native of Skye, and brother of
Roderick, minister of Bracadale, acknowledged by George Whitefield as a 'worthy
minister of the Scotch Church' (*Journals* [London, 1960], p. 161); he had been ordained
by the Edinburgh presbytery in 1735 and had gone to Georgia at the same time as JW to
minister to the 45 Scots families at Darien (later New Inverness); he exchanged his
personal land grant into an endowment for a minister (Egmont, *Journal*, p. 6). But the
settlers proved restive, and Macleod himself moved to Charleston in 1741, 'having left his
flock out of discontent, and labour'd to induce the rest also to desert' (Candler, *Colonial
Records*, V.556). He wrote 'such letters against the Society that the Scotch Incorporate
Society had resolved to pay for no other minister at Darien' (Coulter and Saye, p. 87). In
his diary for Jan. 2, 1737, Wesley spells his name as it was doubtless pronounced,
'Macloud'.

On Monday evening we left Darien, and on Wednesday 5, came to Frederica. Most here were, as we expected, cold and heartless: we found not one who retained his first love. O send forth thy light and thy truth, that they may guide them![49] Let them not yet follow their own imaginations![50]

After having 'beaten the air'[51] in this unhappy place for twenty days, on January 26, I took my final leave of Frederica. It was not any apprehension of my own danger (though my life had been threatened many times) but an utter despair of doing good there, which made me content with the thought of seeing it no more.

In my passage home, having procured a celebrated book, the Works of Nicholas Machiavelli,[52] I set myself carefully to read and consider it. I began with a prejudice in his favour, having been informed he had often been misunderstood and greatly misrepresented. I weighed the sentiments that were less common, transcribed the passages wherein they were contained, compared one passage with another, and endeavoured to form a cool, impartial judgment. And my cool judgment is, that if all the other doctrines of devils which have been committed to writing since letters were in the world were collected together in one volume, it would fall short of this; and that should a prince form himself by this book, so calmly recommending hypocrisy, treachery, lying, robbery, oppression, adultery, whoredom, and murder of all kinds, Domitian or Nero would be an angel of light compared to that man.

Monday, January 31. We came to Savannah. Tuesday, February 1, being the anniversary feast on account of the first convoy's landing in Georgia, we had a sermon and the Holy Communion. Thursday 24, it was agreed Mr. Ingham should go for England, and endeavour to bring over (if it should please God) some of our friends to strengthen our hands in his work. Saturday 26, he left Savannah.

By Mr. Ingham I writ to Dr. Bray's Associates,[53] who had sent a parochial library to Savannah. It is expected of the ministers who

---

[49] See Ps. 43:3. [50] See Jer. 9:14.

[51] Cf. 1 Cor. 9:26.

[52] A third edition of the *Works of the Famous Nicolas Machiavel* (the spelling of the name adopted by JW himself, here and JWJ, Apr. 14, 1756), translated into English by Henry Nevile, had been published in one volume at London, 1720.

[53] Thomas Bray (1656–1730), the founder of the SPG, being in 1695 appointed the Bishop of London's commissary in Maryland and finding that the only recruits to Anglican livings in Maryland were too poor to buy books, made the help of the bishop in providing

receive these to send an account to their benefactors of the method they use in catechizing the children and instructing the youth of their respective parishes. That part of the letter was as follows:

5   Our general method is this: A young gentleman who came with me[54] teaches between thirty and forty children to read, write, and cast accounts. Before school in the morning, and after school in the afternoon, he catechizes the lowest class, and endeavours to fix something of what was said in their understandings as well as their memories. In the evening he instructs the larger
10   children. On Saturday, in the afternoon, I catechize them all. The same I do on Sunday before the evening service. And in the church, immediately after the Second Lesson, a select number of them having repeated the Catechism and been examined in some part of it, I endeavour to explain at large and to enforce that part, both on them and the congregation.
15   Some time after the evening service as many of my parishioners as desire it meet at my house (as they do also on Wednesday evening) and spend about an hour in prayer, singing, and mutual exhortation. A smaller number (mostly those who design to communicate the next day) meet here on Saturday evening; and a few of these come to me on the other evenings, and pass half an hour in the
20   same employment.

Friday, March 4. I writ the Trustees for Georgia an account of our year's expense, from March 1, 1736, to March 1, 1737; which, deducting extraordinary expenses (such as repairing the parsonage house, and journeys to Frederica), amounted for Mr.
25   Delamotte and me to £44. 4s. 4d.[55]

From the directions I received from God this day touching an affair of the greatest importance,[56] I could not but observe (as I had done many times before) the entire mistake of those who assert, 'God will not answer your prayer unless your heart be
30   wholly resigned to his will.' My heart was not wholly[57] resigned to his will. Therefore, not daring to depend on my own judgment, I cried the more earnestly to him to supply what was wanting in me. And I know, and am assured, he heard my voice and did send forth his light and his truth.[58]

libraries a condition of his going out. He subsequently projected a scheme for establishing parochial libraries in every deanery of England and Wales, and before his death over eighty were established there, thirty-nine in North America, and many others in other overseas settlements. In 1723 he founded a body called 'Dr. Bray's Associates for founding Clerical Libraries and supporting Negro Schools' to continue his work after his death.
[54] Charles Delamotte.   [55] See *Letters*, 25:496-98 in this edn.
[56] He had cast lots concerning the Sophy Hopkey affair and received the answer, 'Think of it no more.' See below in Appendix, diary entry for March 4.
[57] First edn., 'entirely'.   [58] See Ps. 43:3.

Thur. 24. A fire broke out in the house of Robert Hows,[59] and in an hour burned it to the ground. A collection was made for him the next day, and the generality of the people showed a surprising willingness to give a little out of their little for the relief of a necessity greater than their own.

About this time Mr. Lacy[60] of Thunderbolt called upon me; when observing him to be in a deep sadness, I asked what was the reason of it. And a terrible one indeed he gave in the relation following:

In 1733 David Jones, a saddler, a middle-aged man, who had for some time before lived at Nottingham, being at Bristol, met a person there who, after giving him some account of Georgia, asked whether he would go thither; adding, his trade (that of a saddler) was an exceeding good trade there, upon which he might live creditably and comfortably. He objected his want of money to pay his passage and buy some tools which he should have need of. The gentleman (Capt. W.)[61] told him he would supply him with that and hire him a shop when he came to Georgia, wherein he might follow his business and so repay him as it suited his convenience. Accordingly to Georgia they went, where, soon after his arrival, his master (as he now styled himself)[62] sold him to Mr. Lacy, who set him to work with the rest of his servants in clearing land. He commonly appeared much more thoughtful than the rest, often stealing into the woods alone. He was now sent to do some work on an island three or four miles from Mr. Lacy's great plantation. Thence he desired the other servants to return without him, saying he would stay and kill a deer. This was on Saturday. On Monday they found him

---

[59] Robert Hows, sawyer, parish clerk of Savannah, and an active class-leader. JW applied to the Georgia Trustees on his behalf, and they agreed that the cost of rebuilding his house should be defrayed from the fund for religious uses. However, in 1739, having signed the petition of freeholders against the misgovernment of the province, Hows returned to England, making over his lot to the Trustees for the use of Whitefield's Orphan House before returning with Whitefield to Pennsylvania. William Stephens declared that Hows did so well from the various charities that he gave up improving his land and that when he went to England after the death of his wife, 'he disposed of his two children (most unnaturally as I conceive), and against the will of their grandparents, to the unity of the Moravian Brethren'. Candler, *Colonial Records*, IV.394, 478; Coulter and Saye, p. 24.

[60] Roger Lacy (died 1738), who had prepared an abortive scheme to set up silk manufacture in Georgia with charity children, obtained a 500-acre grant at Thunderbolt and contributed to the defence of the new colony by building a fort and manufacturing potash. Agent to the Cherokees, he did well out of Indian trading and the surreptitious employment of Negroes in agriculture. The evidence of Wesley's diary suggests that the interview took place on Mar. 4, 1736/37, and makes it clear that he and Lacy were mutually sympathetic on religious matters. Egmont, *Diary*, II.141; Egmont, *Journal*, pp. 23, 25, 201, 215, 237; Tailfer, *Narrative*, p. 77; Candler, *Colonial Records*, IV.179; Coulter and Saye, p. 81.

[61] The parenthetic addition appears only in the *Works* (1774) and probably indicated the same Capt. Robert Williams who attempted to defame Wesley and thus precipitated the publication of the first extract from his *Journal*.

[62] First edn., 'him'.

on the shore, with his gun by him, and the forepart of his head shot to pieces. In his pocket was a paper book, all the leaves whereof were fair, except one, on which ten or twelve verses were written; two of which were these (which I transcribed thence from his own handwriting):

5   Death could not a more sad retinue find;
            Sickness and pain before, and darkness all behind![63]

Sunday, April 3, and every day in this great and holy week, we had a sermon and the Holy Communion. Monday 4, I began learning Spanish in order to converse with my Jewish
10 parishioners,[64] some of whom seem nearer the mind that was in Christ than many of those who call him Lord.

Tue. 12. Being determined, if possible, to put a stop to the proceedings of one in Carolina who had married several of my parishioners without either banns or licence, and declared he
15 would do so still,[65] I set out in a sloop for Charleston. I landed there on Thursday, and related the case to Mr. Garden, the

[63] John Norris, *Miscellanies*, 'The Meditation', st. 2. Wesley included the poem in *A Collection of Moral and Sacred Poems* (1744), I.74. It seems almost certain that the suicide had penned the first two stanzas of the poem, of which these are the closing lines.

[64] A party of Portuguese Jews had settled at Savannah, all but one of whom had left by 1741, owing, it was variously reported, to their inability to farm profitably without Negro slaves or to the fact that the Portuguese Inquisition had been instructed to leave them unmolested if they returned (Egmont, *Diary*, III.188, 218). Actually Wesley had already been learning Spanish for 8 months. In his diary for June 28, 1736, he noted, 'Began Spanish', and this new venture after a weekend visit to Frederica may well have been sparked by a religious talk with his Jewish friend, Dr. Samuel Núñez, on June 24. This somewhat fitful study was enthusiastically renewed on Apr. 4, 1737, once again through the instrumentality of Núñez, who apparently became his chief mentor and religious colleague during the following months.

[65] This was apparently the clergyman at Purrysburg who had recently married (without banns) both Margaret Bovey and Sophy Hopkey, precipitating the controversy which forced Wesley's retreat from Georgia. It has sometimes been conjectured that the culprit was the Rev. Edward Dyson, the drunken chaplain at Port Royal, to whom JW handed over ecclesiastical authority at Frederica, Sept. 7, 1737 (W. W. Manross, *Fulham Papers* [Oxford, 1965], pp. 146-47). The evidence of Wesley's diary, however, points strongly to the Rev. Henry Chiffelle. He certainly was in charge of the episcopal parish of St. Peter's, Purrysburg, after its formation in 1747 until 1758, and apparently for a few years before that, after the departure of the original French clergyman, Joseph Bugnion (Frederick Lewis Weis, *The Colonial Churches and the Colonial Clergy of the Middle and Southern Colonies* [Lancaster, Mass., 1938], pp. 79, 86; cf. Fulham MSS, X.229, and 'Letters to the Bishop of London from the Commissaries in South Carolina', ed. George W. Williams, in *South Carolina Historical Magazine* [1977], 78:146-47, 216-17). There were a few freelance clergy around, some of whom were eventually removed as having insufficient credentials or talents, like Lawrence O'Neill of Christ Church, Berkeley (Weis, p. 33; Williams, p. 234), and it is just possible that one of these was the offender at Purrysburg. Wesley easily discovered the culprit's name—if he had not known it already—and wrote both to him and to the Bishop of London about his ecclesiastical improprieties. The double wedding had taken place on Saturday, March 12, 1737, and both couples attended

Bishop of London's Commissary, who assured me he would take care no such irregularity should be committed for the future.

Sun. 17. Mr. Garden (to whom I must ever acknowledge myself indebted for many kind and generous offices) desiring me to preach, I did so, on those words of the Epistle for the day, 'Whatsoever is born of God overcometh the world.'[66] To that plain account of the Christian state which these words naturally led me to give, a man of education and character seriously objected (what is indeed a great truth), 'Why, if this be Christianity, a Christian must have more courage than Alexander the Great.'

Tue. 19. We left Charleston; but meeting with stormy and contrary winds, after losing our anchor, and beating out at sea all night, on Thursday 21, we with some difficulty got back into Charleston harbour.

Fri. 22. It being the time of their annual Visitation, I had the pleasure of meeting with the clergy of South Carolina;[67] among whom in the afternoon there was such a conversation for several hours on 'Christ our Righteousness'[68] as I had not heard at any Visitation in England, or hardly on any other occasion.

Sat. 23. Mentioning to Mr. Thompson, minister of St. Bartholomew's, near Ponpon,[69] my being disappointed of a passage home by water, he offered me one of his horses if I would go by land, which I gladly accepted of. He went with me twenty

worship under Wesley the following day in Savannah. On March 15, Wesley's diary records the first of these two letters 'to Mr. Chiffele' (spelled phonetically in shorthand 'chiefly'). On March 21 he wrote to him again. Chiffelle's reply was quite unrepentant, so that on April 4 Wesley set off for Charleston to complain in person to the bishop's commissary, Alexander Garden, who promised to put things right.

[66] 1 John 5:4.

[67] There were about a dozen clergy in South Carolina at this time; in North Carolina, originally part of the same colony, the Church of England was established but did not often boast more than a single priest.

[68] Cf. Rom. 10:4.

[69] Rev. Thomas Thompson, incumbent of St. Bartholomew's parish, South Carolina, 1734–45, and of St. George's, South Carolina, 1744–46; he had been ordained in 1730, and resigned in 1746 (*Calendar of Letters preserved at the United Society for the Propagation of the Gospel* [List and Index Society, Special Series, 5], p. 89; cf. Manross, *Fulham Papers*, pp. 144-46, 149-50). There was no church in St. Bartholomew's parish however, but Thompson served two chapels of ease. One of these was at Ashepoo, the other a wooden building at Ponpon, near which he lived and in which Wesley preached for him on April 24 to a congregation of seventy. The Ashepoo chapel (in which Thompson presumably preached that day) has gone. The building at Ponpon was replaced by a brick chapel in 1754, of which the fallen ruins still remain in eastern Colleton County (*Colonial Churches of South Carolina*, n.d., p. [4]).

miles, and sent his servant to guide me the other twenty to his house. Finding a young Negro there, who seemed more sensible than the rest, I asked her how long she had been in Carolina. She said two or three years; but that she was born in Barbados, and
5 had lived there in a minister's family from a child. I asked whether she went to church there. She said, 'Yes, every Sunday—to carry my mistress's children.' I asked what she had learned at church. She said, 'Nothing: I heard a deal, but did not understand it.' 'But what did your master teach you at home?' 'Nothing.' 'Nor your
10 mistress?' 'No.'

I asked, 'But don't you know that your hands and feet, and this you call your body, will turn to dust in a little time?' She answered, 'Yes.' 'But there is something in you that will not turn to dust, and this is what they call your soul. Indeed, you can't see your soul,
15 though it is within you, as you can't see the wind, though it is all about you. But if you had not a soul in you, you could no more see, or hear, or feel, than this table can. What do you think will become of your soul, when your body turns to dust?' 'I don't know.' 'Why, it will go out of your body, and go up there, above
20 the sky, and live always. God lives there. Do you know who God is?' 'No.' 'You can't see him, any more than you can see your own soul. It is he that made you and me, and all men and women, and all beasts and birds, and all the world. It is he that makes the sun shine, and rain fall, and corn and fruits to grow out of the ground.
25 He makes all these for us. But why do you think he made us, what did he make you and me for?' 'I can't tell.' 'He made you to live with himself, above the sky. And so you will, in a little time—if you are good. If you are good, when your body dies your soul will go up, and want nothing, and have whatever you can desire. No
30 one will beat or hurt you there. You will never be sick. You will never be sorry any more, nor afraid of anything. I can't tell you, I don't know, how happy you will be; for you will be with God.'

The attention with which this poor creature listened to instruction is inexpressible. The next day she remembered all,
35 readily answered every question, and said she would ask him that made her to show her how to be good.

Sun. 24. I preached twice at Ponpon Chapel, on the thirteenth chapter of the First Epistle to the Corinthians. O how will even these men of Carolina, who come eight, ten, or twelve miles to
40 hear the gospel, rise in judgment against those who hear it not, when it is preached at their own doors!

Wed. 27. I came to Mr. Bellinger's plantation at Chulifinny,[70] where the rain kept me till Friday. Here I met with an half Indian (one that had an Indian mother and a Spanish father) and several Negroes who were very desirous of instruction. One of them said, 'When I was at Ashley Ferry I went to church every Sunday.'[71] But here we are buried in the woods. Though if there was any church within five or six miles, I am so lame I can't walk, but I would crawl thither.'

Mr. Bellinger sent a Negro lad with me to Purrysburg,[72] or rather to the poor remains of it. O how hath God stretched over this place 'the lines of confusion and the stones of emptiness'![73] Alas for those whose lives were here vilely cast away, through oppression, through divers plagues and troubles! O earth! How long wilt thou hide their blood? How long wilt thou cover thy slain?[74]

This lad too I found both very desirous and very capable of instruction. And perhaps one of the easiest and shortest ways to instruct the American Negroes in Christianity would be first to inquire after and find out some of the most serious of the planters. Then, having inquired of them which of their slaves *were best inclined*, and understood English, to go to them from plantation to plantation, staying as long as appeared necessary at each. Three or four gentlemen in Carolina I have been with that would be sincerely glad of such an assistant, who might pursue his work with no more hindrances than must everywhere attend the preaching of the gospel.

Saturday 30. I came to Savannah and found my little flock in a

[70] The names of both Chulifinny Creek, which Wesley sought to cross on April 29 on his way to Purrysburg, and of Bellinger's plantation were later changed to Tillifinny, which the creek still bears (appreciation to Prof. George W. Williams, Duke University, for this information).

[71] The minister was the Rev. William Guy, M.A., whom Wesley had met in Charleston, and with whom he and Thompson travelled part of the way on April 23. He had been ordained in 1713, served in South Charleston, 1712–13, St. Helena parish on Port Royal Island, 1714–15, Charleston, 1716–17, and St. Andrew's parish on the Ashley River from 1719 until his death in 1751. *Calendar of Letters* (USPG), p. 87.

[72] A township up the Savannah River, named for the leader of the French-Swiss immigrants for whom it was laid out in 1731 on a site selected by their leader, Jean Pierre Purry. It was first served by a French-Swiss clergyman, Joseph Bugnion, who left by 1735. *Isa.* 34:11.

[73] Isa. 34:11.

[74] See Isa. 26:21. In the context of black slavery, there is little doubt that Wesley is referring to horrible cruelties practised by some slave-masters, which he and his brother Charles had first met with in South Carolina as Charles was returning to England. CWJ, Aug. 2, 1736; cf. JW, *Thoughts upon Slavery* (1774), III.11.

better state than I could have expected, God having been pleased greatly to bless the endeavours of my fellow-labourer[75] while I was absent from them.

Wednesday, May 18. I discovered the first convert to Deism
5 that (I believe) has been made here. He was one that for some time had been zealously and exemplarily religious. But indulging himself in harmless company, he first made shipwreck of his zeal, and then of his faith. I have since found several others that have been attacked. They have as yet maintained their ground. But I
10 doubt the devil's apostles are too industrious to let them long halt between two opinions.[76]

Wed. 25. I was sent for by one who had been several years of the Church of Rome,[77] but was now deeply convinced (as were several others) by what I had occasionally preached of the
15 grievous errors that Church was in, and the great danger of continuing a member of it. Upon this occasion I could not but reflect on the many advices I had received to beware of the increase of popery—but not one (that I remember) to beware of the increase of infidelity. This was quite surprising when I
20 considered: (1) that in every place where I have yet been the number of the converts to popery bore no proportion to the number of the converts to infidelity; (2) that as bad a religion as popery is, no religion is still worse, a baptized infidel being always found upon the trial twofold worse than even a bigotted Papist; (3)
25 that as dangerous a state as a Papist is in with regard to eternity, a Deist is in a yet more dangerous state, if he be not (without repentance) an assured heir of damnation; and lastly, [4] that as hard as it is to recover a Papist, it is still harder to recover an infidel: I myself having known many Papists, but never one Deist,
30 reconverted.

May 29, being Whitsunday, four of our scholars, after having been instructed daily for several weeks, were, at their earnest and repeated desire, admitted to the Lord's Table. I trust their zeal hath stirred up many to remember their Creator in the days of
35 their youth, and to redeem the time, even in the midst of an evil and adulterous generation.[78]

---

[75] Charles Delamotte.
[76] The deist proselytizer may have been William Aglionby, whom JW refused as a godfather at a baptism: see the ninth charge against him on Dec. 22, 1736.
[77] Apparently Mrs. Elizabeth Fallowfield, wife of John, a naval officer who arrived in 1734.
[78] See Eccles. 12:1; Eph. 5:16; Matt. 12:39.

Indeed about this time we observed the Spirit of God to move upon the minds of many of the children. They began more carefully to attend to the things that were spoken both at home and at church, and a remarkable seriousness appeared in their whole behaviour and conversation. Who knows but some of them 5 may 'grow up to the measure of the stature of the fullness of Christ'?[79]

June 25.[80] Mr. Causton (the storekeeper and chief magistrate of Savannah) was seized with a slow fever. I attended him every day (as I did any of my parishioners who were in any painful or 10 dangerous illness) and had a good hope, from the thankfulness he showed, that my labour was not in vain.

Sunday, July 3. Immediately after the Holy Communion I mentioned to Mrs. Williamson[81] (Mr. Causton's niece) some

[79] Cf. Eph. 4:13.

[80] In 1741 Wesley published a series of excerpts from this printed *Extract* in order to defend himself from the attacks of Capt. Robert Williams (see *Bibliography*, No. 19.i). These excerpts are exact reprints (except for the last paragraph where two minor alterations are introduced) of the entries for June 25, July 3, 6, 23, 27 (part), Aug. 3, 8, 9, 10, 11 (part), 16, [18], 22, Sept. 2, 3, Oct. 7, Nov. 3, Dec. 2 (omitting the second paragraph). This 12-page document reproduced all the essential elements of the Sophy Williamson controversy from pp. 42-67 of the original edition and was entitled, *An Extract from the Rev. Mr. John Wesley's Journal, with regard to the Affidavit made by Captain Robert Williams.*

[81] Née Sophia Christiana Hopkey, niece of Mrs. Causton. When this case came before the Georgia Trustees in Dec. 1737, Mrs. Williamson's husband, William, 'enclosed . . . the copy of a letter wrote by Mr. Wesley to his wife, accusing her of lying, breach of faith, etc.; and also enclosed his wife's deposition wherein she swears that he offered to marry her, and on that condition to make fasting and frequent communion easy to her, and to abandon his design of preaching among the Indians, but to fix himself in Savannah'. Thomas Causton neatly linked the political and personal objections to JW in a letter to the Trustees. 'When it was heard that the marriage [between Miss Hopkey and Williamson] was intended, Mr. Wesley came to Mrs. Causton and discovered with grief and tears that he himself desired to marry her. After the marriage he appear'd inconsolable, sometimes wanting to see her, but at other times promised he never would. But on this occasion he refused her the Sacrament, and became an advocate for every discontented person he met with. His refusal of giving her the Sacrament subjected him to a presentment of the Grand Jury, which Mr. Causton would have prevented, but for his own imprudency in publishing many pretended reasons for the refusal, and justifying the same by saying he had the authority so to do, from the Trustees; and for insinuating that Mr. Williamson had been guilty of something very notorious which in due time he would make appear. After the Grand Jury had found the bills against him, he (Causton) obtain'd an order of court to stay all prosecutions against Mr. Wesley, till the Trustees should be acquainted therewith and their pleasure known.' Mr. Causton adds that the people suspected Mr. Wesley was sent by the Trustees with instructions to enforce some particular designs, which they, the Trustees, were apprehensive would be disagreeable to the people, and that he was to represent to them all such as acted contrary or opposed his measures (Candler, *Colonial Records*, V.60-61). To Egmont it seemed that JW 'was in love with Mrs. Williamson before she married, and has acted indiscreetly with respect to her, and perhaps with respect to

things which I thought reprovable in her behaviour. At this she appeared extremely angry, said she did not expect such usage from me, and at the turn of the street (through which we were walking home) went abruptly away. The next day Mrs. Causton
5 endeavoured to excuse her, told me she was exceedingly grieved for what had passed the day before, and desired me to tell her in writing what I disliked; which I accordingly did the day following.

But first I sent Mr. Causton the following note:

Sir,
10   To this hour you have shown yourself my friend; I ever have and ever shall acknowledge it. And it is my earnest desire that he who hath hitherto given me this blessing would continue it still.

But this cannot be unless you will allow me one request, which is not so easy an one as it appears: 'Don't condemn me for doing in the execution of my office
15 what I think it my duty to do.'

If you can prevail upon yourself to allow me this, even when I act without respect of persons, I am persuaded there will never be, at least not long, any misunderstanding between us. For even those who seek it shall, I trust, find no occasion against me, 'except it be concerning the law of my God'.[82]
20 July 5, 1737

Wed. 6. Mr. Causton came to my house with Mr. Bailiff Parker[83] and Mr. Recorder,[84] and warmly asked, 'How could you possibly think I should condemn you for executing any part of your office?' I said short, 'Sir, what if I should think it the duty of
25 my office to repel one of your family from the Holy Communion?' He replied, 'If you repel me or my wife, I shall require a legal reason. But I shall trouble myself about none else. Let them look to themselves.'

Sat. 9. Meeting with a Frenchman of New Orleans on the

others, which is a great misfortune to us, for nothing is more difficult than to find a minister to go to Georgia who has any virtue and reputation' (Egmont, *Diary*, II.451). William Williamson was clearly a difficult character, claiming to have succeeded Christie as Recorder of Savannah for a brief period, 1739–40, when his authority was revoked (Candler, *Colonial Records*, IV.589). In 1741 he was provost marshal in Carolina (ibid., V.560).
82 Cf. Dan. 6:5.
83 Henry Parker (see above, May 5, 1736, n. 83).
84 Thomas Christie, merchant, aged 32 when he emigrated in Nov. 1732; recorder of Savannah till made bailiff, 1739. He was already accused of illicit retailing of rum and, after further charges of 'living in open adultery' and not properly completing his accounts with the Trustees, was suspended from his office in 1740. He was said to be 'in open adultery with Turner's wife, and guilty of other faults'. Egmont, *Diary*, II.172; III.123, 125; William Stephens, *Journal of the Proceedings in Georgia* (London, 1742; reprint, Atlanta, 1906–8), II.235; Coulter and Saye, pp. 9–10; *Letters*, 26:88-90 in this edn.

Mississippi, who had lived several months among the Chickasaws,[85] he gave us a full and particular account of many things
which had been variously related. And hence we could not but
remark what is the religion of nature, properly so called, or that
religion which flows from natural reason, unassisted by 5
revelation. And that, even in those who have the knowledge of
many truths, and who converse with their beloved ones day and
night. But too plainly does it appear by the fruits that 'the gods of
these heathens too are but devils'.[86]

The substance of his account was this: 10

Some years past the Chickasaws and French were friends. The French were
then mingled with the Natchez[87] Indians, whom they used as slaves, till the
Natchez made a general rising and took many of the French prisoners. But soon
after a French army set upon them, killed many, and carried away the rest.
Among those that were killed were some Chickasaws, whose death the 15
Chickasaw nation resented; and soon after, as a French boat was going through
their country, they fired into it and killed all the men but two. The French
resolved on revenge, and orders were given for many Indians and several parties
of white men to rendezvous on the 26th of March, 1736, near one of the
Chickasaw towns. The first party, consisting of fifty men, came thither some 20
days before the time. They stayed there till the 24th, but none came to join them.
On the 25th they were attacked by two hundred Chickasaws. The French
attempted to force their way through them. Five or six and twenty did so; the rest
were taken prisoners. The prisoners were sent two or three to a town to be
burned. Only the commanding officer and one or two more were put to death on 25
the place of the engagement.

I (said he) and one more were saved by the warrior who took us. The manner
of burning the rest was, holding lighted canes to their arms and legs and several
parts of their bodies for some time, and then for a while taking them away. They
likewise stuck burning pieces of wood into their flesh all round, in which 30
condition they kept them from morning till evening. But they commonly beat
them before they burn them. I saw the priest that was with us carried to be
burned; and from head to foot he was as black as your coat with the blows which
they had given him.

I asked him, 'What was their manner of life?' He said, 'They do 35
nothing but eat and drink and smoke from morning till night, and
in a manner from night till morning. For they rise at any hour of
the night when they wake, and after eating and drinking as much
as they can, go to sleep again.' See *The Religion of Nature* truly
Delineated![88]
40

[85] Orig., 'Chicasaws'.   [86] Cf. Ps. 96:5 (BCP).
[87] Orig., 'Nautchee'.

[88] JW is playing upon the title of William Wollaston's work, *The Religion of Nature
Delineated* (first published 1722), which he had read in 1733. Wollaston constructed a

Sat. 23. Reflecting on the state I was now in, I could not but observe in a letter to a friend:[89] 'How to attain to the being crucified with Christ I find not, being in a condition I neither desired nor expected in America—in ease, and honour, and
5   abundance. A strange school for him who has but one business, γύμναζειν ἑαυτὸν πρὸς ἐυσέβιαν.[d]
Wed. 27. I rejoiced to meet once more with that good soldier of Jesus Christ, August Spangenberg, with whom on Monday, August 1, I began my long-intended journey to Ebenezer. In the
10 way I told him the calm we had so long enjoyed was now drawing to an end; that I hoped he would shortly see I was not (as some had told him) a respecter of persons, but was determined (God being my helper) to behave indifferently to all, rich or poor, friends or enemies. I then asked his advice as to the difficulty I
15 foresaw, and resolved, by God's grace, to follow it.[90]
  In the evening we came to New Ebenezer, where the poor Salzburgers are settled.[91] The industry of this people is quite

---

[d]'To exercise himself unto godliness' [cf. 1 Tim. 4:7].

philosophical approach to religion and morality without the need for divine revelation, and here as at the beginning of this entry Wesley implies the poverty of 'that religion which flows from natural reason, unassisted by revelation'.

[89] Timothy Cutler (1684–1765), first President of Yale, 1719–22; created a sensation by taking episcopal orders, 1723; rector of Christ Church, Boston, Mass., 1723 till his death. See *Letters*, 25:515, 522-23 in this edn.

[90] This refers almost certainly to JW's determination to exercise ecclesiastical discipline over Sophy Williamson in spite of the serious repercussions hinted at in his conversation with Thomas Causton on July 6.

[91] Attempts by Baron Leopold von Firmian, elected Archbishop of Salzburg in 1727, to establish Catholic conformity in his diocese led to a diplomatic *cause célèbre* and to the discovery of a large, and hitherto unknown, Protestant population in his territory. They began to be seized with religious revival, and 25,000 were expelled over the winter of 1730–31. Twenty thousand of these were acquired as settlers by the King of Prussia, but one small party went to the Netherlands, and a settlement for another in Georgia was negotiated by Samuel Urlsperger, Senior of Augsburg, a corresponding member of the SPCK and former minister of the Savoy Chapel in London; he later wrote their history. On this episode generally, see Gerhard Florey, *Geschichte der Salzburger Protestanten und ihrer Emigration, 1731/2* (Vienna, 1977). The Georgia party settled in 1734 at Ebenezer, some twenty miles NW of Savannah, moving in 1736 six miles east to New Ebenezer beside the Savannah River, just upstream from Purrysburg, on the opposite (South Carolina) bank. The background to the visit of JW and Spangenberg from the side of the Salzburgers is fully sketched by Bolzius and Gronau in Samuel Urlsperger, *Detailed Reports on the Salzburger Emigrants who Settled in America*, ed. G. F. Jones, 8 vols. (Athens, Ga., 1968-85), esp. 4:92-93, 102, 117-19, 135. Embarrassments with both visitors inhibited them, however, from reporting the visit itself. The two pastors fully sustained the feud of Halle with Spangenberg, even in the New World; and while they thought well of Wesley in general, they were disturbed by the trickle of English settlers seeking to evade Wesley's marriage discipline by applying to them for the rite.

surprising. Their sixty huts are neatly and regularly built; and all the little spots of ground between them improved to the best advantage. On one side of the town is a field of Indian corn; on the other are the plantations of several private persons: all which together one would scarce think it possible for a handful of people 5 to have done in one year.

Wed. 3. We returned to Savannah. Sunday 7, I repelled Mrs. Williamson from the Holy Communion. And Monday 8, Mr. Recorder of Savannah issued out the warrant following:

Georgia, Savannah Ss.[92] 10
To all Constables, Tithingmen, and others, whom these may concern:
You, and each of you, are hereby required to take the body of John Wesley,[93] Clerk;
And bring him before one of the bailiffs of the said town, to answer the complaint of William Williamson[94] and Sophia his wife, for defaming the said 15 Sophia, and refusing to administer to her the Sacrament of the Lord's Supper, in a public congregation, without cause; by which the said William Williamson is damaged one thousand pounds sterling. And for so doing this is your warrant, certifying what you are to do in the premises.
Given under my hand and seal the 8th day of Aug. *Anno Dom.* 1737. 20
Tho. Christie

Tue. 9. Mr. Jones,[95] the constable, served the warrant, and carried me before Mr. Bailiff Parker and Mr. Recorder. My answer to them was that the giving or refusing the Lord's Supper being a matter purely ecclesiastical, I could not acknowledge their 25 power to interrogate me upon it. Mr. Parker told me, 'However, you must appear at the next court holden for Savannah.' Mr. Williamson (who stood by) said, 'Gentlemen, I desire Mr. Wesley may give bail for his appearance.' But Mr. Parker immediately replied, 'Sir, Mr. Wesley's word is sufficient.' 30

Wed. 10. Mr. Causton ('from a just regard', as his letter expressed it, 'to the friendship which had subsisted between us till this affair') required me to give the reasons in the court-house why I repelled Mrs. Williamson from the Holy Communion. I answered, 'I apprehend many ill consequences may arise from so 35 doing. Let the case be laid before the Trustees.'

---

[92] The meaning of this abbreviation is obscure, but may mean 'Sessions' (of the Grand Jury).
[93] 1740, 1741, 'Westley'.   [94] On whom see above, July 3, 1737, n. 81.
[95] Noble Jones, carpenter, who had arrived from England in 1733. Charles Wesley, among others, made complaints about him, and Oglethorpe removed him from his positions of surveyor and first constable in 1738. Egmont, *Diary*, II.287, 313; III.1.

Thur. 11. Mr Causton came to my house, and among many other sharp words said, 'Make an end of this matter. Thou hadst best. My niece to be used thus! I have drawn the sword, and I will never sheathe it till I have satisfaction.'

5   Soon after he added, 'Give the reasons of your repelling her, before the whole congregation.' I answered, 'Sir, if you insist upon it, I will; and so you may be pleased to tell her.' He said, 'Write to her, and tell her so yourself.' I said, 'I will'; and after he went I wrote as follows:

10   To Mrs. Sophia Williamson.
    At Mr. Causton's request I write once more. The rules whereby I proceed are these:
    'So many as intend to be partakers of the Holy Communion shall signify their names to the Curate, at least some time the day before.'[96] This you did
15   not do.
    'And if any of these . . . have done any wrong to his neighbours by word or deed, so that the congregation be thereby offended, the Curate . . . shall advertise him that in any wise he presume not to come to the Lord's Table until he hath openly declared himself to have truly repented.'[97]
20   If you offer yourself at the Lord's Table on Sunday I will advertise you (as I have done more than once) wherein you 'have done wrong'. And when you have 'openly declared yourself to have truly repented' I will administer to you the mysteries of God.
    August 11, 1737   John Wesley

25   Mr. Delamotte carrying this, Mr. Causton said, among many other warm sayings, 'I am the person that am injured. The affront is offered to me, and I will espouse the cause of my niece. I am ill used, and I will have satisfaction, if it be to be had in the world.'
    Which way this satisfaction was to be had I did not yet conceive.
30   But on Friday and Saturday it began to appear, Mr. Causton declaring to many persons that Mr. Wesley had repelled Sophy from the Holy Communion, purely out of revenge, because he had made proposals of marriage to her, which she rejected and married Mr. Williamson.
35   I could not but observe the gracious providence of God in the course of Lessons all this week. On Monday evening God spake to us in these words: 'Call to remembrance the former days, [. . .] in which you endured a great fight of afflictions; partly whilst ye were made a gazing-stock, both by reproaches and afflictions,

---

[96] BCP, Communion, opening rubrics.
[97] Ibid.

and partly whilst ye became companions of them that were so used. . . . Cast not away therefore your confidence, which hath great recompense of reward. For ye have need of patience, that after ye have done the will of God ye might receive the promise.'[98]

The Evening Lesson on Tuesday was the eleventh of the Hebrews, in reading which I was more particularly encouraged by his example who 'chose rather to suffer affliction with the people of God than to enjoy the pleasures of sin for a season; esteeming the reproach of Christ greater riches than the treasures of Egypt.'[99]

The Lesson on Wednesday began with these words: 'Wherefore, seeing we are compassed about with so great a cloud of witnesses, let us lay aside every weight . . . and run with patience the race that is set before us, looking unto Jesus, the author and finisher of our faith, who for the joy that was set before him endured the cross, despising the shame, and is set down at the right hand of the throne of God.'[1]

In the Thursday Lesson were these comfortable words: 'I will never leave thee nor forsake thee. So that we may boldly say, The Lord is my helper, and I will not fear what man shall do unto me.'[2]

The words of St. James, read on Friday, were, 'Blessed is the man that endureth temptation.'[3] And those on Saturday, 'My brethren, have not the faith of our Lord Jesus Christ . . . with respect of persons.'[4]

I was only afraid lest those who were weak should 'be turned out of the way';[5] at least so far as to forsake the public 'assembling of themselves together'.[6] But I feared where no fear was. God took care of this also. So that on Sunday 14, more were present at the morning prayers than had been for some months before. Many of them observed those words in the First Lesson, 'Set Naboth on high among the people; and set two men, sons of Belial, before him, to bear witness against him.'[7]

Tue. 16. Mrs. Williamson swore to and signed an affidavit,

---

[98] Heb. 10:32-33, 35-36.
[99] Cf. Heb. 11:25-26.
[1] Heb. 12:1-2.
[2] Heb. 13:5-6.
[3] Jas. 1:12.
[4] Jas. 2:1.
[5] Heb. 12:13.
[6] Cf. Heb. 10:25.
[7] 1 Kgs. 21:9-10.

insinuating much more than it asserted, but asserting that Mr. Wesley had many times proposed marriage to her, all which proposals she had rejected. Of this I desired a copy. Mr. Causton replied, 'Sir, you may have one from any of the newspapers in
5   America.'

On Thursday or Friday was delivered out a list of twenty-six men who were to meet as a grand jury on Monday the 22nd. But this list was called in the next day, and twenty-four names added to it. Of this grand jury (forty-four of whom only met), one was a
10 Frenchman who did not understand English, one a Papist, one a *professed infidel,*[8] three Baptists, sixteen or seventeen others, dissenters, and several others who had personal quarrels against me, and had openly vowed revenge.

To *this* grand jury, on Monday the 22nd, Mr. Causton gave a
15 long and earnest charge 'to beware of spiritual tyranny, and to oppose the new illegal authority which was usurped over their consciences'. Then Mrs. Williamson's affidavit was read; after which Mr. Causton delivered to the grand jury a paper entitled, 'A List of Grievances, *presented by* the Grand Jury for Savannah
20 this _____ day of Aug. 1737.' This the majority of the grand jury altered in some particulars and on Thursday, September 1, delivered it again to the court, under the form of two presentments, containing ten bills, which were then read to the people.

Herein they asserted, upon oath,

25 That John Wesley, Clerk, had 'broken the laws of the realm, contrary to the peace of our sovereign lord the King, his crown and dignity',
   1. By speaking and writing to Mrs. Williamson, against her husband's consent;
   2. By repelling her from the Holy Communion;
30 3. By not declaring his adherence to the Church of England;
   4. By dividing the morning service on Sundays;
   5. By refusing to baptize Mr. Parker's child otherwise than by dipping, except the parents would certify it was weak, and not able to bear it;
   6. By repelling Wm. Gough[9] from the Holy Communion;

---

[8] To this, Tailfer's *Narrative,* p. 35, replied: 'Mr. Westly [*sic*] asserts in his Journal printed at Bristol 1739 . . . [that] there were a professed atheist and deist in the number; but for our parts we know of neither.'

[9] William Gough, arrived 1733; tithingman, 1736. Tailfer, *Narrative,* p. 30, alleged that 'William Gaff who had once communicated, and always conformed to his [JW's] regulations . . . was at last found out by Mr. Wesley to have been baptized by a Presbyterian Dissenter. The same thing was propos'd to him [public recantation and rebaptism]; but Mr. Gaff, not inclinable to go that length, was ever thereafter excluded

7. By refusing to read the Burial Service over the body of Nathanael Polhill;[10]
8. By calling himself 'Ordinary'[11] of Savannah;
9. By refusing to receive Wm. Aglionby[12] as a godfather, only because he was not a communicant;
10. By refusing Jacob Matthews[13] for the same reason; and baptizing an Indian trader's child with only two sponsors.

(This, I own, was wrong; for I ought at all hazards to have refused baptizing it till he had procured a third.)

Fri. 2. Was the third court at which I appeared since my being carried before Mr. P[arker] and the Recorder.

I now moved for an immediate hearing on the first bill, being the only one of a civil nature, but it was refused. I made the same motion in the afternoon, but was put off till the next court-day.

On the next court-day I appeared again, as also at the two courts following, but could not be heard, 'because (the Judge said) Mr. Williamson was gone out of town'.

The sense of the minority of the grand jurors themselves (for they were by no means unanimous) concerning these presentments, may appear from the following paper, which they transmitted to the Trustees.

To the Honourable the Trustees for Georgia.
Whereas two presentments have been made, the one of August 23, the other of August 31, by the grand jury of Savannah in Georgia, against John Wesley, Clerk.

---

from the Communion.' JW's diary notes that he talked 'of Sacrament' with Mrs. Gough on Aug. 20, 1737. An 'idle fellow', Gough 'ran to South Carolina' (with Wesley) Dec. 3, 1737, where he died as a teacher. Candler, *Colonial Records*, IV.603; Coulter and Saye, p. 76 (which also, on p. 66, lists James Campbell as 'an idle fellow' who 'ran away with the Rev. Mr. John Wesley, Dec. 3, 1737').

[10] Nathanael Polhill (died July 1737) lived with his elder brother Edward and his sisters on Lot 194 in Savannah.

[11] 'An ecclesiastical person having jurisdiction attached to his office. In the Church of England the ordinary is usually the archbishop or archdeacon, but in earlier times the range was much wider and included abbots, prelates, officials and vicars-general, and holders of peculiar jurisdictions including canons and prebendaries. The parish priest has some measure of ordinary jurisdiction, which he may not delegate except by permission of his own ordinary.' J. S. Purvis, *Dictionary of Ecclesiastical Terms* (London, 1962), p. 133.

[12] William Aglionby, attorney, originally of Westminster [and granted 100 acres (Candler, *Colonial Records*, II.157)], was at loggerheads with Causton for interfering in the course of justice, and was regarded by the authorities of the colony as an inveterate agitator. Dying as he lived, a deist, on Aug. 23, 1738, he refused to allow Whitefield to pray with him, and the latter in consequence refused to read the burial service over him. Candler, *Colonial Records*, IV.188-89.

[13] In 1736, Jacob Matthews became the second husband of Mary Musgrove (see above, Feb. 14, 1736, n. 48); he died June 6, 1742.

We whose names are underwritten, being members of the said grand jury, do humbly beg leave to signify our dislike of the said presentments; being by many and divers circumstances thoroughly persuaded in ourselves that the whole charge against Mr. Wesley is an artifice of Mr. Causton's, designed rather to
5 blacken the character of Mr. Wesley than to free the colony from religious tyranny, as he was pleased in his charge to us to term it. But as these circumstances will be too tedious to trouble your honours with, we shall only beg leave to give the reasons of our dissent from the particular bills.

With regard to the first bill, we do not apprehend that Mr. Wesley acted
10 against any law by writing or speaking to Mrs. Williamson, since *it does not appear to us that the said Mr. Wesley has either spoke in private or wrote to the said Mrs. Williamson, since March 12,*^e *except one letter of July the 5th, which he wrote at the request of her aunt, as a pastor, to exhort and reprove her.*

The second we do not apprehend to be a true bill, because we humbly
15 conceive Mr. Wesley did not assume to himself any authority contrary to law. For we understand every person intending to communicate should 'signify his name to the Curate at least some time the day before',[14] which Mrs. Williamson did not do; although Mr. Wesley had often in full congregation declared he did insist on a compliance with that rubric, and *had before repelled divers persons for*
20 *noncompliance therewith.*

The third we do not think a true bill, because several of *us* have been his hearers when he has declared his adherence to the Church of England, in a stronger manner than by a formal declaration; by explaining and defending the Apostles', the Nicene, and the Athanasian Creeds, the Thirty-nine Articles, the
25 whole Book of Common Prayer, and the Homilies of the said Church; and because we think a formal declaration is not required but from those who have received institution and induction.

The fact alleged in the fourth bill we cannot apprehend to be contrary to any law in being.
30 The fifth we do not think a true bill, because we conceive Mr. Wesley is justified by the rubric, viz., 'If they (the parents) certify that the child is weak, it shall suffice to pour water upon it'[15]—intimating (as we humbly suppose) it shall not suffice if they do not certify.

The sixth cannot be a true bill, because the said William Gough, being one of
35 our members, was surprised to hear himself named without his knowledge or privity; and did publicly declare it was no grievance to him, because the said John Wesley had given him reasons with which he was satisfied.

The seventh we do not apprehend to be a true bill, for Nathanael Polhill was an Anabaptist, and desired in his lifetime that he might not be interred with the
40 office of the Church of England. And farther, we have good reason to believe that Mr. *Wesley was at Frederica*, or on his return thence, *when Polhill was buried.*

As to the eighth bill we are in doubt, as not well knowing the meaning of the word 'Ordinary'. But for the ninth and tenth we think Mr. Wesley is sufficiently justified by the Canons of the Church, which forbid 'any person to be admitted

---

^e The day of her marriage.

[14] See JW's letter to her, Aug. 11, 1737.
[15] BCP, Baptism, rubric at naming.

godfather or godmother to any child before the said person has received the Holy Communion';[16] whereas William Aglionby and Jacob Matthews had never certified Mr. Wesley that they had received it.

This was signed by twelve of the grand jurors, of whom three were constables, and six more tithingmen; who consequently would have made a majority had the jury consisted, as it regularly should have done, of only fifteen members, viz., the four constables and eleven tithingmen.

Friday, September 30. Having ended the Homilies,[17] I began reading Dr. Rogers's[18] eight sermons to the congregation, hoping they might be a timely antidote against the poison of infidelity which was now with great industry propagated among us.

October the 7th, I consulted my friends whether God did not call me to return to England. The reason for which I left it had now no force, there being no possibility as yet of instructing the Indians; neither had I as yet found or heard of any Indians on the continent of America who had the least desire of being instructed. And as to Savannah, having never engaged myself, either by word or letter, to stay there a day longer than I should judge convenient, nor ever taken charge of the people any otherwise than as in my passage to the heathens, I looked upon myself to be fully discharged therefrom by the vacating of that design. Besides, there was a probability of doing more service to that unhappy people in England than I could do in Georgia, by representing without fear or favour to the Trustees the real state the colony was in. After deeply considering these things they were unanimous that 'I ought to go; but not yet.' So I laid the thoughts of it aside for the present, being persuaded that when the time was come, God would 'make the way plain before my face'.[19]

---

[16] Cf. *Canons and Constitutions Ecclesiastical* (1604; henceforth *'Canons'*), Canon 29: '. . . neither shall any person be admitted godfather or godmother to any child at christening or confirmation, before the said person so undertaking hath received the Holy Communion.'

[17] *Certain Sermons or Homilies appointed by the King's Majesty* (1547; henceforth *'Homilies'*), of which a 'Second Book' was issued in 1571.

[18] John Rogers (1679–1729), vicar of Buckland 1704, and rector of Wringham 1716; he also held several lectureships at churches in the City of London. He first obtained celebrity in attacking Bishop Hoadly in *A Discourse of the Visible and Invisible Church of Christ* (1719; read by JW in 1733), and in 1726 became chaplain to the Prince of Wales, later George II. The eight sermons used here by JW (and first read by him in 1731) were published in 1727 with a preface attacking Anthony Collins the deist, under the title, *The Necessity of Divine Revelation and the Truth of the Christian Religion*. Many of his sermons were collected and published after his death by Dr. John Burton, one of the Georgia Trustees.

[19] Ps. 5:8 (BCP).

Saturday, October 15. Being at Highgate, a village five miles from Savannah, consisting of (all but one) French families, who, I found, knew but little of the English tongue, I offered to read prayers there in French every Saturday in the afternoon. They
5 embraced the offer gladly. On Saturday the 22nd, I read prayers in German likewise to the German villagers of Hampstead,[20] and so continued to do, once a week. We began the service (both at Highgate and Hampstead) with singing a psalm. Then I read and explained a chapter in the French or German Testament and
10 concluded with prayers and another psalm.

Saturday, October 29. Some of the French of Savannah were present at the prayers at Highgate. The next day I received a message from them all, that as I read prayers to the French of Highgate, who were but few, they hoped I would do the same to
15 those of Savannah, where there was a large number who did not understand English. Sunday 30, I began so to do; and now I had full employment for that holy day. The first English prayers lasted from five till half an hour after six. The Italian (which I read to a few Vaudois)[21] began at nine. The second service for the English
20 (including the sermon and the Holy Communion) continued from half an hour past ten till about half an hour past twelve. The French service began at one. At two I catechized the children. About three began the English service. After this was ended I had the happiness of joining with as many as my largest room would
25 hold in reading, prayer, and singing praise. And about six the service of the Moravians began, at which I was glad to be present, not as a teacher, but a learner.

Thursday, November 3. I appeared again at the court holden on that day; and again at the court held Tuesday, November 22,
30 on which day Mr. Causton desired to speak with me. He then read me some affidavits which had been made September 15 last past, in one of which it was affirmed that I then abused Mr. Causton in his own house, calling him liar, villain, and so on. It was now likewise repeated before several persons (which indeed I
35 had forgot), that I had been reprimanded at the last court for an enemy to, and hinderer of, the public peace.

I again consulted my friends, who agreed with me that the time

---

[20] Also a few miles south of Savannah.
[21] A few Piedmontese were brought over to superintend the silk industry, which developed mainly among the Salzburgers in New Ebenezer but was almost defunct by the end of the century.

we looked for was now come. And the next morning [Nov. 23], calling on Mr. Causton, I told him I designed to set out for England immediately. I set up an advertisement in the great square to the same effect, and quietly prepared for my journey.

Friday, December 2. I proposed to set out for Carolina about noon, the tide then serving. But about ten the magistrates sent for me and told me I must not go out of the province, for I had not answered the allegations laid against me. I replied, 'I have appeared at six or seven courts successively in order to answer them. But I was not suffered so to do, when I desired it time after time.' They then said, however, I must not go, unless I would give security to answer those allegations at their court. I asked, 'What security?' After consulting together about two hours the recorder showed me a kind of bond, engaging me, under a penalty of fifty pounds, to appear at their court when I should be required. He added, 'But Mr. Williamson too has desired of us that you should give bail to answer his action.' I then told him plainly, 'Sir, you use me very ill, and so you do the Trustees. I will give neither any bond, nor any bail at all. You know your business, and I know mine.'

In the afternoon the magistrates published an order requiring all the officers and sentinels[22] to prevent my going out of the province, and forbidding any person to assist me so to do. Being now only a prisoner at large, in a place where I knew by experience every day would give fresh opportunity to procure evidence of words I never said and actions I never did, I saw clearly the hour was come for leaving this place; and as soon as evening prayers were over, about eight o'clock, the tide then serving, I shook off the dust of my feet and left Georgia, after having preached the gospel (not as I ought, but as I was able) one year and nearly nine months.

During this time I had frequent opportunities of making many observations and inquiries concerning the real state of this province (which has been so variously misrepresented), the English settlements therein, and the Indians that have intercourse with them. These I minuted down from time to time; a small extract of which I have subjoined.

1. Georgia[23] lies in the 30th and 31st degree of north latitude.

---

[22] Orig., 'centinel', the normal (but not uniform) spelling which JW used throughout his life, even in his *Journal* entries for Apr. 26, 1775, and May 1, 1789.

[23] Parts of JW's description of Georgia (originally drawn up for the Georgia Trustees in

The air is generally clear, the rains being much shorter, as well as heavier, than in England. The dews are very great. Thunder and lightning are expected almost every day in May, June, July, and August. They are very terrible, especially to a stranger. During those months, from ten in the morning to four in the afternoon, the sun is extremely scorching. But the sea-breeze generally blows from ten till three or four. The winter is nearly of the same length as in England. But the midday sun is always warm, even when the mornings and evenings are very sharp, and the nights piercing cold.

2. The land is of four sorts, pine-barren, oak-land, swamp, and marsh. The pine-land is of far the greatest extent, especially near the sea-coasts. The soil of this is a dry, whitish sand, producing shrubs of several sorts, and between them a spiry, coarse grass, which cattle do not love to feed on. But here and there is a little of a better kind, especially in the savannahs (so they call the low, watery, meadows which are usually intermixed with pine-lands). It bears naturally two sorts of fruit, hurtleberries[24] (much like those in England) and chincapin[25] nuts—a dry, harsh nut, about the size of a small acorn. A laborious man may in one year clear and plant four or five acres of this land. It will produce the first year from two to four bushels of Indian corn, and from four to eight of Indian pease per acre. The second year it usually bears half as much; the third, less; the fourth, nothing.

3. Vines, mulberries, and peach trees it bears well. The white mulberry is not good to eat. The black is about the size of a blackberry, and has much the same flavour. In fresh pine-land Indian potatoes[26] grow well (which are more luscious and larger than the Irish). And so do watermelons and sewee beans,[27] about

---

Sept. 1737, and delivered to them after his return to England [Egmont, *Journal*, pp. 306-9]), were reproduced in a pamphlet bitterly hostile to him, Tailfer's *Narrative*, pp. 67-71. For a more favourable account, cf. *An Impartial Inquiry into the State and Utility of the Province of Georgia* (London, 1741).

[24] The same as whortleberry or bilberry in England, and similar to the blueberry or 'huckleberry' in America.

[25] Orig., 'chincopin'; 'the dwarf chestnut . . . a native of Virginia and the adjacent states, a shrubby tree . . . with a small, very sweet nut.' *OED*.

[26] This is a name used for the giant sunflower, *Helianthus giganteus*; JW probably had in mind another giant sunflower, *Helianthus tuberosus*, known also as 'Jerusalem artichoke', which has edible tuberous roots and was 'one of the few plants cultivated by the North American Indians'. Norman Taylor, ed., *Taylor's Encyclopedia of Gardening* (Boston, 1948), p. 1081.

[27] Apparently soy-beans, as is noted in *OED*, which cites only this example from Wesley.

the size of our scarlet, to be shelled and eaten like Windsor beans.

4. Oak-land commonly lies in narrow streaks between pine-land and some swamp, creek, or river. The soil is a blackish sand, producing several kinds of oak (though none exactly like the English), bay, laurel,[28] ash, walnut, sumac trees,[29] gum trees (a sort of sycamore),[30] dog trees (covered in spring with large white flowers),[31] and many hickory trees,[32] which bear a bad kind of walnut. In the moistest part of this land some persimmon trees[33] grow (which bear a sort of yellow, clear, luscious plum), and a few mulberry and cherry trees. The common wild grapes are of two sorts, both red. The fox-grape grows two or three only on a stalk, is thick-skinned, large-stoned, of a harsh taste, and of the size of a small Kentish cherry. The cluster-grape is of a harsh taste too, and about the size of a white currant.

5. This land requires much labour to clear; but when it is cleared it will bear any grain, for three, four, or sometimes five years, without laying any manure upon it. An acre of it generally bears ten bushels of Indian corn, besides five of pease, in a year. So that this at present is justly esteemed the most valuable land in the province.

6. A swamp is any low, watery place which is covered with trees or canes. They are here of three sorts: cypress-, river-, and cane-swamps. Cypress-swamps are mostly large ponds, in and round which cypresses grow. Most river-swamps are overflown[34] every tide by the river which runs through or near them. If they were drained they would produce good rice; as would the cane-swamps also, which in the meantime are the best feeding for all sorts of cattle.

7. The marshes are of two sorts: soft marsh, which is all a quagmire, and absolutely good for nothing; and hard marsh, which is a firm but barren sand, bearing only sour[35] rushes.

---

[28] Orig., 'lawrel'.

[29] Trees of the genus *Rhus*, different varieties of which produced materials for tanning and staining leather, and for varnish.

[30] I.e., sweet gum.

[31] I.e., dogwood.

[32] Orig., 'hickary'. There were many species of hickory in the southern colonies, the most important being the pecan, though this did not reach its present excellence until after grafting had begun a century later. JW apparently tried one of the bitter varieties.

[33] Orig., 'porsimmon-trees'; the American date-plum.

[34] This now archaic usage continued until after JW's death. *OED* cites an example from Southey (1818).

[35] Orig., 'sower'.

Marshes of both sorts abound on the sea islands, which are very
numerous, and contain all sorts of land. And upon these chiefly,
near creeks and runs of water, juniper trees and cedars grow.

5   8. Savannah stands on a flat 'bluff' (so they term any highland
hanging over a creek or river)[36] which rises forty-five feet
perpendicular from the river, and commands it several miles both
upward and downward. The soil is a white sand for above a mile
in breadth, south-east, and north-westward. Beyond this,
eastward, is a river-swamp; westward a small wood, in which was
10   the old Indian town. On the other side of the river is a marshy
island covered with large trees. South-west of the town is a large
pine-barren, which extends backward to a branch of the
Altamaha River.

9. St. Simons Island, having on the south-east the Gulf of
15   Florida, on the other sides branches of the Altamaha, is about a
hundred miles south of Savannah, and extends in length about
twenty, in breadth from two to five miles. On the west side of it, on
a low bluff, stands Frederica, having woods to the north and
south; to the east, partly woods, partly savannahs, and partly
20   marshes. The soil is mostly a blackish sand. There is not much
pine-land on the island, the greatest part being oak-land,
intermixed with many savannahs and old Spanish or Indian fields.

10. On the sea-point, about five miles south-east of the town, is
the fort where the soldiers are stationed. But the storehouse[37] in
25   Frederica better deserves that name, being encompassed with
regular ramparts of earth and a palisaded ditch, and mounted
with cannon, which entirely command the river.

11. About twenty miles north-west from St. Simons is Darien,
the settlement of the Scotch Highlanders, a mile from Fort King
30   George, which was built about seventeen, and abandoned about
eleven years since. The town lies on the mainland, close to a
branch of the Altamaha, on a bluff thirty feet above the river,
having woods on all sides. The soil is a blackish sand. They built
at first many scattered huts; but last spring (1736), expecting the
35   Spaniards, they built themselves a large fort, and all retired within
the walls of it.

12. Augusta, distant from Savannah one hundred and fifty

[36] *OED* cites this passage as its earliest example of this usage, which JW employs
frequently.
[37] The first edition (only) reads, 'The But-Storehouse', which is plausible, yet altered in
the errata to the revised text.

miles, and five from old Savannah town,[38] is designed to stand in an old Indian field, on a bluff about thirty feet high. A small fort of wooden piles was built there in 1737, but no house was then built, nor any more ground cleared than Mr. Lacy[39] and his men found so. 5

13. Old Ebenezer, where the Salzburgers settled at first, lies twenty-five miles west of Savannah. A small creek runs by the town down to the river, and many brooks run between the little hills: but the soil is a hungry, barren sand, and upon any sudden shower the brooks rise several feet perpendicular, and overflow 10 whatever is near them. Since the Salzburgers removed, two English families have been placed there; but those too say that the land is good for nothing, and that the creek is of little use, it being by water twenty miles to the river, and the water generally so low in summer-time that a boat cannot come within six or seven miles 15 of the town.

14. New Ebenezer, to which the Salzburgers removed in March 1736, lies six miles eastward from the old, on a high bluff near the Savannah River. Here are some tracts of fruitful land, though the greatest part of that adjoining to the town is 20 pine-barren. The huts, sixty in number, are neatly and regularly built; the little piece of ground allotted to each for a garden is everywhere put to the best use, no spot being left unplanted. Nay, even one of the main streets, being one more than was as yet wanted, bore them this year a crop of Indian corn. 25

15. About ten miles east of this, on a creek, three miles from the river, was the village of Abercorn. Ten families settled here in 1733, but it is now without inhabitant. Four miles below the mouth of Abercorn Creek is Josephstown, the settlement of two Scotch gentlemen.[40] A mile below was Sir Francis Bathurst's 30

---

[38] Savannah Town or New Windsor was the site of Fort Moore, maintained by South Carolina, on the east bank of the river. Ivers, *British Drums on the Southern Frontier*, pp. 8, 75.

[39] Capt. Roger Lacy and his rangers built Fort Augusta on the west bank of the Savannah River in the summer of 1737. It was named for a royal princess. Upon Lacy's death, Aug. 3, 1738, the garrison came under the command of Lt. Richard Kent, one of Oglethorpe's favourite officers. Ivers, *British Drums*, pp. 75-77; Sarah B. G. Temple and Kenneth Coleman, *Georgia Journeys* (Athens, Ga., 1961), pp. 274-75.

[40] John Mackay and Patrick Mackay were each granted 500 acres at Josephstown in 1735. John died a few months later. Patrick was commissioned captain by Oglethorpe and made agent to the Creeks. Because he provoked an Indian attack, the trustees discharged him. Three of Patrick's brothers also settled at Josephstown, which was sometimes known as Captain's Bluff. Coulter and Saye; Ivers, *British Drums*, pp. 33, 37, 39, 48-49, 75, 85.

plantation.[41] And a quarter of a mile from this, Walter Augustin's settlement.[42] But both these are left without inhabitant.

16. A mile below this is Captain Williams's[43] plantation; a mile from thence, Mrs. Matthew's[44] (late Musgrove), commonly
5 known by the name of Cowpen; adjoining to which is the land belonging to Captain Watson,[45] on which is an unfinished house, swiftly running to ruin. A mile from this is Irene,[46] a house built for an Indian school in the year 1736. It stands on a small round hill, in a little piece of fruitful ground, given by the Indians to Mr.
10 Ingham. The Indian town is within a furlong of it.

17. Five miles south-west of Savannah, on a small rise, stands the village of Highgate. It has pine-land on three sides, and a swamp on the fourth. Twelve families were placed here in 1733, nine whereof remain there. A mile eastward of this is Hampstead,
15 settled with twelve families also, a little before Highgate, five of which are still remaining.

[41] Sir Francis Bathurst (died 1756), younger son of Sir Benjamin Bathurst and Francis, second daughter of Sir Allen Apsley. On emigrating to Georgia where he settled with a son and two daughters at 'Westbrook', Dec. 1734, Bathurst was presented with £100 by his brother Allen, first Lord Bathurst, the prominent Tory politician. In Georgia JW officiated at Francis Bathurst's second marriage on July 18, 1736 (to Mary Pember, widow) and buried his mother-in-law on Oct. 29, 1736 (Curnock, I.247, 278). By June 1738 young Bathurst was back in England, explaining to the Georgia Trustees that 'having lost his father and mother-in-law (Sir Francis Bathurst and his lady), his wife could not bear the thoughts of staying in the country' (Egmont, *Diary*, II.493).

[42] Walter Augustin had come from Cat's Island, S.C., in 1735, and perhaps returned there. He had received a grant of 500 acres, settled with a family of 6, and erected a 'very good saw-mill' at a cost of £800, which was 'often blown up by the water, being ill-situated'. He quitted before Jan. 1739. Coulter and Saye, p. 62; Egmont, *Diary*, II.196, 205, 358; Tailfer, *Narrative*, p. 73.

[43] Robert Williams, who settled with 40 servants at Llandiloe and was reckoned to have lost £2000 in four years. Tailfer, *Narrative*, p. 93.

[44] Cf. above, Sept. 1, 1737, n. 13. Tailfer describes the settlement as 'Mr. Jacob Matthews's plantation (formerly Mrs. Musgrove's)'. *Narrative*, p. 73.

[45] Joseph Watson, a former sailor, an 'insolent, vile man', the drunken partner of the late John Musgrove, and interpreter to the Indians, was put on trial on a charge of having killed an Indian with rum and was confined as a lunatic. Charles Wesley reported to the Georgia Trustees that he was 'really disturbed in his senses', and that 'he had six years before been mad on account of his mistress's jilting him', but JW seems to have been sympathetic to him, signed a petition on his behalf, and when, after his wife's appeal to the Privy Council, he was released, admitted him to Communion. Coulter and Saye, p. 101; Egmont, *Diary*, II.141, 160, 313, 367-68, 375, 409, 487; Curnock, I.186, 237, 241, 242, 320, 397-98; *A Brief Account of the Causes that have Retarded the Progress of the Colony of Georgia* (London, 1743), p. 58.

[46] 'A little below this creek is a place called Irene, where Mr. John Wesly [*sic*] built a pretty good house for an Indian school; but he soon wearied of that undertaking, and left it' (Tailfer, *Narrative*, p. 74); see Delores B. Floyd, *New Yamacraw and the Indian Mound Irene* (Savannah, 1936).

18. Six miles south-east of Savannah is Thunderbolt. Three families are settled here, near a small, ruinous fort. Four miles south of this is the Island of Skidaway, on the north-east point whereof ten families were placed in 1733–34 (a small fort was built here likewise), but nine of them are either dead or removed to other places. A small creek divides Skidaway from Tybee Island, on the south-east part of which, fronting on the inlet, the lighthouse is built. Ten families were settled here in 1734, but they are part dead, and part removed, so that the island is now again without any fixed inhabitant.

19. Twelve miles southward from Savannah (by land) is Mr. Houston's[47] plantation; and forty or fifty miles from him, up Ogeechee River, that where Mr. Sterling[48] for some time lived. Fort Argyle stands twenty miles from this, on a high bluff, by the River Ogeechee. 'Tis a small, square, wooden fort, musket-proof. Ten freeholders were settled near it; but eight of them are gone, and the land they had cleared, lying wasted, will in a few years be as it was before.

20. The southermost[49] settlement in Georgia is Fort St. Andrews. It stands fifty miles south of Frederica, on the south-west side of Cumberland Island, upon a high neck of land, which commands the river both ways. The walls are of wood, filled up with earth, round which are a ditch and a palisade.

21. 'Tis hard to pick out any consistent account of the Georgian Indians from the contradictory relations of their traders. The following is extracted, partly from those wherein all, or the generality of them, agree, partly from the relations of such as have been occasionally amongst them, and have no interest in making them better or worse than they are.

22. Of the Georgian Indians in general it may be observed that

---

[47] James Houston, a clerk in Thomas Causton's stores, who also owned a plantation at Skidaway. Apparently because of altering Causton's accounts he fled when Causton was removed from his office of storekeeper, returned, and in 1739 left for good.

[48] William Sterling, gentleman, settled in Savannah County with a party of Scots, but finding that agriculture was unprofitable without Negro labour and that a 'saucy' correspondence with the Georgia Trustees did not produce him a large grant on Wilmington Island, he withdrew with the 'Scotch club' to Carolina, 'for fear of the Spaniards' (Coulter and Saye, p. 97; Egmont, *Diary*, II.199; III.125, 132, 168, 174, 201-2; Candler, *Colonial Records*, IV.465, 655). Tailfer describes the party as one of 25 servants, and ascribes their failure to the cost of fortifying the remote southern settlement (*Narrative*, pp. 65, 74).

[49] This word was in currency with 'southernmost' in the eighteenth century, but was gradually replaced by it in the nineteenth (cf. *OED*).

they are not so properly nations as tribes or clans, who have wandered thither at different times, perhaps expelled [from] their native countries by stronger tribes; but how or when they cannot tell, being none of them able to give any rational account of
5 themselves. They are inured to hardship of all kinds, and surprisingly patient of pain. But as they have no letters, so they have no religion, no laws, no civil government. Nor have they any kings or princes, properly speaking, their 'micos'[50] or headmen having no power either to command or punish, no man obeying
10 them any farther than he pleases. So that everyone doth what is right in his own eyes; and if it appears wrong to his neighbour the person aggrieved usually steals on the other unawares, and shoots him, scalps him, or cuts off his ears; having only two short rules of proceeding—to do what he will, and what he can.
15   23. They are likewise all, except (perhaps) the Choctaws, gluttons, drunkards, thieves, dissemblers, liars. They are implacable, unmerciful; murderers of fathers, murderers of mothers, murderers of their own children; it being a common thing for a son to shoot his father or mother because they are old
20 and past labour; and for a woman either to procure abortion, or to throw her child into the next river, because she will go with her husband to the war. Indeed husbands, strictly speaking, they have none; for any man leaves his wife (so called) at pleasure, who frequently, in return, cuts the throats of all the children she has
25 had by him. Whoredom they account no crime, and few instances appear of a young Indian woman's refusing anyone. Nor have they any fixed punishment for adultery; only if the husband take his wife with another man he will do what he can to both, unless speedily pacified by the present of a gun or a blanket.
30   24. The Choctaws only have some appearance of an entire nation, possessing a large extent of land, eight or nine hundred miles west of Savannah, and many well-inhabited towns. They are said to have six thousand fighting men, united under one head. At present they are in league with the French, who have
35 sent some priests among them, by whom (if one may credit the Choctaw traders) ten or twelve have been baptized.
    25. Next to these, to the north-east, are the Chickasaws. Their country is flat, full of meadows, springs, and rivers. In their fields,

---

[50] Contemporary manuscripts spell the word variously, and JW uses 'meeko', though 'mico' is the accepted spelling in Webster's *International Dictionary* (1961); it is not found in *OED*.

though six or seven hundred miles from the sea, are found sea-shells in great numbers. They have about nine hundred fighting men, ten towns, and one 'mico' (at least) in every one. They are eminently gluttons, eating, drinking, and smoking all day and almost every night. They are extreme indolent and lazy, 5 except in war: then they are the most indefatigable and the most valiant of all the Indians. But they are equally cruel with the rest, torturing and burning all their prisoners, whether Indian or European.

26. East of them, in the latitude of 35° and 36°, about three or 10 four hundred miles from Savannah, lie the Cherokees.[51] Their country is very mountainous, fruitful, and pleasant. They have fifty-two towns and above three thousand fighting men. In each town are three or more headmen, who keep up a sort of shadow of government, having power to set the rest to work, and to punish 15 such as will not join in the common labour. They are civil to strangers, and will do anything for them, *for pay*, being always willing, for a small piece of money, to carry a message for fifty or sixty miles, and if required, a heavy burden too.[52] But they are equally cruel to prisoners with the Chickasaws, though not 20 equally valiant. They are seldom intemperate in drinking but when they can be so on free cost.[53] Otherwise love of drink yields to covetousness, a vice scarce[54] to be found in any Indian but a Cherokee.

27. The Yuchis[55] have only one small town left (near two 25 hundred miles from Savannah) and about forty fighting men. The Creeks have been many times on the point of cutting them off. They are indeed hated by most, and despised by all the other nations, as well for their cowardice as their superlative diligence in thieving and for outlying all the Indians upon the continent. 30

28. The Creek Indians are about four hundred miles from Savannah. They are said to be bounded to the west by the Choctaws, to the north by the Chickasaws, to the east by the Cherokees, and to the south by the Altamaha River. They have many towns, a plain well watered country, and fifteen hundred 35

---

[51] Orig., 'Cherikee'.
[52] Wesley's uniform spelling was 'burthen'.
[53] For this obsolete phrase (now 'cost free') see *OED*, and 11:379, 433 in this edn.
[54] For this abverbial use of 'scarce' cf. Sermon 104, 'On Attending the Church Service' (1787), §17 (3:471 in this edn.). In the second and subsequent editions (whether at the insistence of Wesley or one of his assistants is unknown) it was changed to 'scarcely'.
[55] Orig., 'Uchees'.

fighting men. They have often three or four micos in a town; but without so much as the shadow of authority, only to give advice, which everyone is at liberty to take or leave. But age and reputation for valour and wisdom have given Chigilly,[56] a mico of
5 the Coweta Town, a more than ordinary influence over the nation—though not even the show of regal power. Yet neither age, wisdom, nor reputation can restrain him from drunkenness. Indeed all the Creeks, having been most conversant with white men, are most infected with insatiate love of drink,[57] as well as
10 other European vices. They are more exquisite dissemblers than the rest of their countrymen. They know not what friendship or gratitude means. They show no inclination to learn anything, but least of all Christianity, being full as opiniated[58] of their own parts and wisdom as either modern Chinese or ancient Roman.

15 Saturday, December 3. We came to Purrysburg early in the morning, and endeavoured to procure a guide for Port Royal. But none being to be had, we set out without one, an hour before sunrise. After walking two or three hours we met with an old man, who led us into a small path, near which was a line of 'blazed'[59]
20 trees (i.e., marked by cutting off part of the bark), by following which, he said, we might easily come to Port Royal in five or six hours.

We were four in all; one of whom intended to go for England with me, the other two to settle in Carolina.[60] About eleven we
25 came into a large swamp, where we wandered about until near two. We then found another 'blaze', and pursued it till it divided into two; one of these we followed through an almost impassable thicket, a mile beyond which it ended. We made through the thicket again, and traced the other 'blaze' till that ended too. It
30 now grew toward sunset, so we sat down, faint and weary, having had no food all day except a gingerbread cake which I had taken in my pocket. A third of this we had divided among us at noon; another third we took now; the rest we reserved for the morning; but we had met with no water all the day. Thrusting a stick into
35 the ground, and finding the end of it moist, two of our company

---

[56] See July 1, 1736, and n. 9.   [57] First edn., 'drunkenness'.

[58] This word and 'opinionated' were both in use, but 'opiniated' was gradually becoming obsolete; cf. JWJ, Dec. 26, 1740.

[59] This is the earliest example of this use of the word noted by *OED*.

[60] Two of these were apparently William Gough and James Campbell (see above, Sept. 1, 1737, n. 9), and the third perhaps a Frenchman from Purrysburg (see below, Dec. 22, 1737).

fell a digging with their hands, and at about three feet depth found water. We thanked God, drank, and were refreshed. The night was sharp; however, there was no complaining among us, but after having commended ourselves to God, we lay down close together, and (I at least) slept till near six in the morning.

Sunday, December 4. God renewing our strength, we arose neither faint nor weary, and resolved to make one trial more to find a path to Port Royal. We steered due east; but finding neither path nor blaze, and the woods growing thicker and thicker, we judged it would be our best course to return, if we could, by the way we came. The day before, in the thickest part of the woods, I had broke many young trees, I knew not why, as we walked along; these we found a great help in several places where no path was to be seen; and between one and two God brought us safe to Benjamin Arieu's house, the old man we left the day before.

In the evening I read French prayers to a numerous family, a mile from Arieu's; one of whom undertook to guide us to Port Royal. In the morning we set out. About sunset we asked our guide if he knew where he was. Who frankly answered, 'No.' However, we pushed on till about seven we came to a plantation, and the next evening (after many difficulties and delays) we landed on Port Royal Island.

Wed. 7. We walked to Beaufort; where Mr. Jones (the Minister of Beaufort),[61] with whom I lodged during my short stay here, gave me a lively idea of the old English hospitality. On Thursday Mr. Delamotte came, with whom on Friday 9th I took boat for Charleston. After a slow passage by reason of contrary winds, and some conflict (our provisions falling short) with hunger as well as cold, we came thither early in the morning on Tuesday the 13th. Here I expected trials of a different kind, and far more dangerous. For contempt and want are easy to be borne, but who can bear respect and abundance?

Wed. 14. Being desired to read public prayers,[62] I was much

---

[61] Lewis Jones was incumbent of St. Helena, Beaufort, 1725–44, when he died. He preached a thanksgiving sermon at Charleston on the occasion of Oglethorpe's arrival with the original Georgia settlers. He bequeathed £100 to support a free school at Beaufort.

[62] By the Rev. William Orr, a former Presbyterian minister, who had been ordained by the Bishop of London in Sept. 1736, and was now assistant to the Rev. Alexander Garden, the bishop's commissary in South Carolina. On previous occasions Wesley had also officiated at St. Philip's for Garden, who seems to have been absent when JW arrived on Dec. 13.

refreshed with those glorious promises contained both in the seventy-second Psalm and in the First Lesson, the fortieth chapter of Isaiah. Yea, 'they that wait upon the Lord shall renew their strength, and mount up with wings as eagles; they shall run
5 and not be weary; they shall walk, and not faint!'[63]

In the afternoon, visiting a dying man,[64] we found him still full of the freshest advices—and busy in settling the affairs of the Czarina, Prince Thamas, and the Ottoman Porte.[65] How natural then is the thought:

10 　　　　　　　　　*Quae cura nitentes*
　　　　　Pascere equos, eadem sequitur tellure repostos?[66]

For if a soul quivering on the verge of life has still leisure for these impertinencies, one might almost believe the same dreams would continue, even in the sleep of death!

15 Fri. 16. I parted from the last of those friends who came with me to America, Mr. Charles Delamotte, from whom I had been but a few days separate since October 14, 1735.[67]

Sun. 18. I was seized with a violent flux, which I felt came not before I wanted it. Yet I had strength enough given to preach once
20 more to this careless people; and a few 'believed our report'.[68]

Thur. 22. I took my leave of America (though, if it please God, not for ever), going on board the *Samuel*, Capt. Percy, Commander, with a young gentleman who had been a few months in Carolina, one of my parishioners of Savannah, and a
25 Frenchman, late of Purrysburg, who was escaped thence with the

---

[63] Cf. Isa. 40:31.

[64] Almost certainly Samuel Eveleigh, a prominent merchant and councilman whom JW had met on each of his two earlier visits. Wesley uses the phrase 'settling the affairs of' ironically, in the sense of 'putting the world to rights'. The Eastern Question was fully reported in the *South Carolina Gazette* in 1737. The same journal contained a notice of Eveleigh's death 'after a tedious indisposition' on Mar. 30, 1738.

[65] The reference is to the struggle of the Ottoman Turks to keep their position across the lines of communication, on the one hand, from Moscow to the Middle East, and on the other, from the Danube plain to the eastern Mediterranean; this involved conflict with, among others, Tamasp, Shah of Persia, 1731–32, and Anna, Czarina of Russia, 1730–40.

[66] Virgil, *Aeneid*, vi.654-55. In the 'Latin Sentences Translated' appended to Vol. XXXII of his *Works* (1774), Wesley gave his own translation (or rather, paraphrase): 'The same desires which they cherished on earth remain in the world of spirits.'

[67] Delamotte sailed for England on June 1, 1738, impressing Egmont on his arrival as 'an implacable enemy to Mr. Causton, our Magistrate, as much as he is a fast friend to all the malcontents in our colony'. Egmont, *Diary*, III.1.

[68] Isa. 53:1.

skin of his teeth.[69] Saturday 24,[70] we sailed over Charleston bar, and about noon lost sight of land.

The next day the wind was fair, but high, as it was on Sunday 25, when the sea affected me more than it had done in the sixteen weeks of our passage to America. I was obliged to lie down the greatest part of the day, being easy only in that posture.

Mon. 26. I began instructing a Negro lad in the principles of Christianity. The next day I resolved to break off living delicately and return to my old simplicity of diet, and after I did so, neither my stomach nor my head much complained of the motion of the ship.

Wed. 28. Finding the unaccountable apprehensions of I know not what danger (the wind being small, and the sea smooth) which had been upon me several days, increase, I cried earnestly for help, and it pleased God as in a moment to restore peace to my soul.

Let me observe hereon, (1) that not one of these hours ought to pass out of my remembrance, till I attain another manner of spirit, a spirit equally willing to glorify God by life or by death; (2) that whoever is uneasy on any account (bodily pain alone excepted) carries in himself his own conviction that he is so far an unbeliever. Is he uneasy at the apprehension of death? Then he believeth not that 'to die is gain'.[71] At any of the events of life? Then he hath not a firm belief that 'all things work together for his good'.[72] And if he bring the matter more close, he will always find, beside the general want of faith, every particular uneasiness is evidently owing to the want of some particular Christian temper.

Sunday, January 1, 1738. All in the ship (except the captain and the steersman) were present both at the morning and the evening service, and appeared as deeply attentive as even the poor people of Frederica did, while the Word of God was new to their ears. And it may be one or two among these likewise may 'bring forth fruit with patience'.[73]

Mon. 2. Being sorrowful and very heavy (though I could give no particular reason for it) and utterly unwilling to speak close to

[69] See above, Sept. 1, 1737, n.9.
[70] Possibly 'Fri. 23'; see following paragraph (there is no diary or MS journal for this period).
[71] Phil. 1:21.
[72] Cf. Rom. 8:28.
[73] Luke 8:15.

any of my little flock (about twenty persons), I was in doubt whether my neglect of them was not one cause of my own heaviness. In the evening, therefore, I began instructing the cabin-boy, after which I was much easier.

5   I went several times the following days with a design to speak to the sailors, but could not. I mean, I was quite averse from speaking—I could not see how to make an occasion, and it seemed quite absurd to speak without. Is not this what men commonly mean by, 'I could not speak'? And is this a sufficient 10 cause of silence, or no? Is it a prohibition from the good Spirit? Or a temptation from nature or the evil one?

    Fri. 6. I ended the abridgment of Mr. de Renty's life.[74] O that such a life should be related by such a historian! Who by inserting all, if not more than all the weak things that holy man ever said or 15 did, by his commendation of almost every action or word which either deserved or needed it not, and by his injudicious manner of relating many others which were indeed highly commendable; has cast the shade of superstition and folly over one of the brightest patterns of heavenly wisdom.

20   Sat. 7. I began to read and explain some passages of the Bible to the young Negro. The next morning another Negro who was on board desired to be a hearer too. From them I went to the poor Frenchman, who, understanding no English, had none else in the ship with whom he could converse. And from this time I read and 25 explained to him a chapter in the Testament every morning.

    Sun. 8. In the fullness of my heart I wrote the following words:[75]

By the most infallible of proofs, inward feeling, I am convinced:

    1. Of unbelief, having no such faith in Christ as will prevent my heart from 30 being troubled; which it could not be if I believed in God, and rightly believed also in him [i.e., Christ].

    2. Of pride, throughout my life past, inasmuch as I thought I had what I find I have not.

---

[74] Published by JW as *An Extract of the Life of Monsieur de Renty, a late Nobleman of France* (1741; see *Bibliography*, No. 43). He abridged this version from an English translation by Edward Sheldon (1658; reissued, 1684) of a French life of the Roman Catholic Gaston Jean Baptiste de Renty (1611–49) by J. B. S. Juré. Other lives of this French and Spanish mystic, who JW felt was a kindred spirit, exercised a great influence in the Reformed and Lutheran churches. Cf. M. Schmidt, 'Die Biographie des Französischen Grafen Gaston Jean-Baptiste de Renty (1611–1649) und ihre Aufnahme im 18. Jahrhundert', in *Wiedergeburt und neuer Mensch* (Witten, 1969), pp. 390-438.

[75] Wesley transcribes part of this document in his letter of Oct. 30, 1738, to his brother Samuel. See *Letters*, 25:575-78 in this edn.

3. Of gross irrecollection, inasmuch as in a storm I cry to God every moment, in a calm, not.

4. Of levity and luxuriancy of spirit, recurring whenever the pressure is taken off, and appearing by my speaking words not tending to edify; but most, by my manner of speaking of my enemies.   5

'Lord save, or I perish!'[76] Save me,

1. By such a faith as implies peace in life and in death.

2. By such humility as may fill my heart from this hour for ever with a piercing, uninterrupted sense, *Nihil est quod hactenus feci*,[f] having evidently built without foundation.   10

3. By such a recollection as may cry to thee every moment, especially when all is calm, Give me faith or I die; give me a lowly spirit; otherwise *Mihi non sit suave vivere*.[g]

4. By steadiness, seriousness, σεμνότης,[77] sobriety of spirit, avoiding as fire every word that tendeth not to edifying, and never speaking of any who oppose me, 15 or sin against God, without all my own sins set in array before my face.

This morning, after explaining those words of St. Paul, 'I beseech you, brethren, by the mercies of God, that ye present your bodies a living sacrifice, holy, acceptable to God',[78] I exhorted my fellow-travellers with all my might to comply with 20 the Apostle's direction. But *leaving them afterwards to themselves*, the seriousness they showed at first soon vanished away.

On Monday 9, and the following days, I reflected much on that vain desire which had pursued me for so many years, of being in solitude in order to be a Christian. I have now, thought I, solitude 25 enough. But am I therefore the nearer being a Christian? Not if Jesus Christ be the model of Christianity. I doubt indeed I am much nearer that mystery of Satan which some writers affect to call by that name. So near that I had probably sunk wholly into it had not the great mercy of God just now thrown me upon reading 30 St. Cyprian's *Works*.[79] 'O my soul, come not thou into their

[f] 'I have done nothing hitherto.' [Cf. Kempis, *De Imitatione Christi*, I.xix.1: 'Adiuva me, Domine Deus, . . . et da mihi nunc hodie perfecte incipere, quia nihil est quod hactenus feci.' JW's own edition of *The Christian's Pattern* (1735), translates: 'Help me, O Lord God, . . . and grant that I may now this day begin perfectly: for that which I have done hitherto is nothing.']

[g] 'Let life be a burden to me.' [Cf. Terence, *Heauton Timorumenos* (The Self-Tormentor), *l.* 482 (III.i.73), 'Tibi autem porro ut non sit suave vivere'—'how it will embitter all your future life' (Loeb).]

[76] Cf. Matt. 8:25.

[77] 'Honesty', in 1 Tim. 2:2; 'gravity' in 1 Tim. 3:4, Titus 2:7.

[78] Rom. 12:1.

[79] St. Cyprian, Bishop of Carthage, martyred A.D. 258, a great upholder of church discipline and order. JW's correspondence makes clear his continued respect for Cyprian

secret!'[80] 'Stand thou in the good old paths.'[81]

Fri. 13. We had a thorough storm, which obliged us to shut all close, the sea breaking over the ship continually. I was at first afraid; but cried to God and was strengthened. Before ten I lay
5 down, I bless God, without fear. About midnight we were awaked[82] by a confused noise of seas and wind and men's voices, the like to which I had never heard before. The sound of the sea breaking over and against the sides of the ship I could compare to nothing but large cannon or American thunder. The rebounding,
10 starting, quivering motion of the ship much resembled what is said of earthquakes. The captain was upon deck in an instant. But his men could not hear what he said. It blew a proper hurricane; which beginning at south-west, then went west, north-west, north, and in a quarter of an hour round by the east to the
15 south-west point again. At the same time the sea running (as they term it) mountain high, and that from many different points at once, the ship would not obey the helm; nor indeed could the steersman, through the violent rain, see the compass. So he was forced to let her run before the wind, and in half an hour the
20 stress of the storm was over.

About noon the next day it ceased. But first I had resolved, God being my helper, not only to preach it to all, but to apply the Word of God to every single soul in the ship; and if but one, yea, if not one of them will hear, I know 'my labour is not in vain'.[83]

25 I no sooner executed this resolution than my spirit revived, so that from this day I had no more of that fearfulness and heaviness which before almost continually weighed me down. I am sensible one who thinks the being *in orco*,[84] as they phrase it, an indispensable preparative for being a Christian, would say I had
30 better have continued in that state, and that this unseasonable relief was a curse, not a blessing. Nay, but who art thou, O man,

---

both in these matters and as a controversial writer against the popes. In 1745 JW arranged to keep sets of his works in Latin in London, Bristol, and Newcastle. Cf. JWJ, Aug. 27, 1729.

[80] Gen. 49:6.

[81] Jer. 6:16.

[82] First edn., 'waked', possibly a typographical error.

[83] Cf. 1 Cor. 15:58.

[84] 'In the infernal regions', a phrase which JW had probably met in the Latin mystic writers. In his diary for Feb. 14, 1735, JW had described the young George Whitefield, passing through severe spiritual depression, as 'in Orco'; similarly with Mr. Appee during JW's first month in Georgia (see diary entry for Mar. 17, 1736 in Appendix below).

who in favour of a wretched hypothesis thus blasphemest the good gift of God? Hath he not himself said, 'This also is the gift of God, if a man have power to rejoice in his labour'?[85] Yea, God setteth his own seal to his weak endeavours, while he thus 'answereth him in the joy of his heart'.[86]

Tue. 24. We spoke with two ships, outward bound, from whom we had the welcome news of our wanting but 160 leagues of the Land's End. My mind was now full of thought, part of which I writ down as follows:

I went to America to convert the Indians; but Oh! who shall convert me? Who, what is he that will deliver me from this evil heart of unbelief? I have a fair summer religion. I can talk well; nay, and believe myself, while no danger is near: but let death look me in the face, and my spirit is troubled. Nor can I say, 'To die is gain!'[87]

I have a sin of fear, that when I've spun
My last thread, I shall perish on the shore![88]

I think verily, if the gospel be true, I am safe. For I not only have given, and do give, all my goods to feed the poor; I not only give my body to be burned, drowned, or whatever God shall appoint for me, but I follow after charity (though not as I ought, yet as I can) if haply I may attain it. I *now* believe the gospel is true. 'I show my faith by my works,'[89] by staking my all upon it. I would do so again and again a thousand times, if the choice were still to make. Whoever sees me sees I *would* be a Christian. Therefore 'are my ways not like other men's ways'.[90] Therefore I have been, I am, I am content to be, 'a by-word, a proverb of reproach'.[91] But in a storm I think, 'What if the gospel be not true?' Then thou art of all men most foolish. For what hast thou given thy goods, thy ease, thy friends, thy reputation , thy country, thy life? For what art thou wandering over the face of the earth? A dream, 'a cunningly devised fable'?[92] O who will deliver me from this fear of death![93] What shall I do? Where shall I fly from it? Should I fight against it by thinking, or by not thinking of it? A wise man advised me some time since, 'Be still and go on.' Perhaps this is best, to look upon it as my cross; when it comes, to let it humble me, and quicken all my good resolutions, especially that of praying without ceasing; and at other times to take no thought about it, but quietly to go on 'in the work of the Lord'.[94]

---

[85] Cf. Eccles. 5:19.
[86] Eccles. 5:20.
[87] Phil. 1:21.
[88] John Donne, 'A Hymn to God the Father'. The poem is included in Walton's life of Donne, which JW abridged for his *Christian Library*, having read it in Nov. 1731.
[89] Cf. Jas. 2:18.
[90] Cf. Isa. 55:8.
[91] Cf. Deut. 28:37; Jer. 24:9, etc.
[92] Cf. 2 Pet. 1:16.
[93] See Rom. 7:24.
[94] 1 Cor. 15:58.

We went on with a small, fair wind,[95] till Thursday in the afternoon, and then sounding, found a whitish sand at seventy-five fathom. But having had no observation for several days, the Captain began to be uneasy, fearing we might either get
5   unawares into the Bristol Channel, or strike in the night on the rocks of Scilly.

Sat. 28. Was another cloudy day; but about ten in the morning (the wind continuing southerly) the clouds began to fly just contrary to the wind, and to the surprise of us all sunk down under
10 the sun, so that at noon we had an exact observation; and by this we found we were as well as we could desire, about eleven leagues south of Scilly.

[95] On Wed., Jan. 25, Wesley prepared a second memorandum on his spiritual condition, of which the manuscript is extant in Wesley College, Bristol:

Μὴ κλυδωνιζόμενοι παντὶ ἀνέμῳ τῆς διδαχῆς.
['not tossed to and fro by every wind of doctrine', cf. Eph. 4:14].
Second Paper.
Different views of Christianity are given, (1) by the Scripture, (2) the Papists, (3) the Lutherans and Calvinists, (4) the English Divines, (5) the Essentialist Nonjurors, (6) the Mystics.

Jan. 25, 1738

1. For many years have I been tossed about by various winds of doctrine. I asked long ago, What must I do to be saved? The Scripture answered, 'Keep the commandments. Believe, hope, love; follow after these tempers till thou hast fully attained, that is, till death, by all those outward works and means which God hath appointed, by walking as Christ walked.'

2. I was early warned against laying, as the Papists do, too much stress either on outward works or on a faith without works, which, as it does not include, so it will never lead to, true hope or charity. Nor am I sensible that to this hour I have laid too much stress on either, having from the very beginning valued both faith, the means of grace, and good works, not on their own account, but as believing God, who had appointed them, would by them bring me in due time to the mind that was in Christ.

3. But before God's time was come I fell among some Lutheran and Calvinist authors, whose confused and indigested accounts magnified faith to such an amazing size that it quite hid all the rest of the commandments. I did not then see that this was the natural effect of their overgrown fear of popery, being so terrified with the cry of 'merit and good works' that they plunged at once into the other extreme. In this labyrinth I was utterly lost, not being able to find out what the error was, nor yet to reconcile this uncouth hypothesis either with Scripture or common sense.

4. The English writers, such as Bishop Beveridge, Bishop Taylor, and Mr. Nelson, a little relieved me from these well-meaning, wrong-headed Germans. Their accounts of Christianity I could easily see to be, in the main, consistent both with reason and Scripture. Only when they interpreted Scripture in different ways I was often much at a loss. And again there was one thing much insisted on in Scripture—the unity of the Church—which none of them I thought clearly explained, or strongly inculcated.

5. But it was not long before Providence brought me to those who showed me a sure rule for interpreting Scripture, viz., *consensus veterum*—'quod ab omnibus, quod ubique, quod semper creditum'. At the same time they sufficiently insisted upon a due

Sun. 29. We saw English land once more, which about noon appeared to be the Lizard Point. We ran by it with a fair wind, and at noon the next day made the west end of the Isle of Wight.

Here the wind turned against us, and in the evening blew fresh, so that we expected (the tide being likewise strong against us) to be driven some leagues backward in the night; but in the morning, to our great surprise, we saw Beachy Head just before us, and found we had gone forwards near forty miles.

Toward evening was a calm; but in the night a strong north wind brought us safe into the Downs. The day before Mr. Whitefield[96] had sailed out, neither of us then[97] knowing anything

regard to the One Church at all times and in all places. Nor was it long before I bent the bow too far the other way: (1) by making antiquity a co-ordinate (rather than subordinate) rule with Scripture; (2) by admitting several doubtful writings as undoubted evidences of antiquity; (3) by extending antiquity too far, even to the middle or end of the fourth century; (4) by believing more practices to have been universal in the ancient Church than ever were so; (5) by not considering that the decrees of one provincial synod could bind only that province, and the decrees of a general synod only those provinces whose representatives met therein; (6) by not considering that most of those decrees were adapted to particular times and occasions, and consequently when those occasions ceased, must cease to bind even those provinces.

6. These considerations insensibly stole upon me as I grew acquainted with the mystic writers, whose noble descriptions of union with God and internal religion made everything else appear mean, flat, and insipid. But in truth they made good works appear so too; yea, and faith itself, and what not? These gave me an entire new view of religion, nothing like any I had had before. But alas! It was nothing like that religion which Christ and his apostles lived and taught. I had a plenary dispensation from all the commands of God. The form ran thus: 'Love is all; all the commands beside are only means of love; you must choose those which you feel are means to you, and use them as long as they are so.' Thus were all the bands burst at once. And though I could never fully come into this, nor contentedly omit what God enjoined, yet, I know not how, I fluctuated between obedience and disobedience: I had no heart, no vigour, no zeal in obeying; continually doubting whether I was right or wrong, and never out of perplexities and entanglements. Nor can I at this hour give a distinct account how or when I came a little back toward the right way. Only my present sense is this: all the other enemies of Christianity are triflers; the mystics are the most dangerous of all its enemies. They stab it in the vitals, and its most serious professors are most likely to fall by them. May I praise him who hath snatched me out of this fire likewise, by warning all others that it is set on fire of hell.

[96] George Whitefield (1714–70), formerly one of the Oxford Methodists and already an evangelist, had accepted an offer from the Georgia Trustees to be minister of Savannah and noted in his *Journals* (pp. 120-21): 'Anyone must needs think I should have been glad to have heard from Mr. Wesley, as he went by Deal; but I considered God ordered all things for the best. . . .' In fact JW arrived before Whitefield had left, and after casting lots, wrote to him advising him to abandon his mission to Georgia. Whitefield's letter declining to do so is printed in Luke Tyerman, *The Life of the Rev. George Whitefield* (2nd edn., London, 1890), I.115.

[97] 1743 onwards, 'then' added.

of the other. At four in the morning we took boat, and in half an hour landed at Deal, it being Wednesday, February 1, the anniversary festival in Georgia for Mr. Oglethorpe's landing there.

5   It is now two years and almost four months since I left my native country in order to teach the Georgian Indians the nature of Christianity. But what have I learned myself in the meantime? Why (what I the least of all suspected), that I who went to America to convert others, was never myself converted to God.[h] 'I am not

10 mad', though I thus speak, but 'I speak the words of truth and soberness';[98] if haply some of those who still *dream* may *awake*, and see that as I am, so are they.

    Are they read in *philosophy?* So was I. In ancient or modern *tongues?* So was I also. Are they versed in the science of *divinity?* I

15 too have *studied* it many years. Can they *talk* fluently upon spiritual things? The very same could I do. Are they plenteous in *alms?* Behold, I gave all my goods to feed the poor.[99] Do they give of their *labour* as well as of their *substance?* I have laboured more abundantly than they all. Are they willing to *suffer* for their

20 brethren? I have thrown up my friends, reputation, ease, country; I have put my life in my hand, wandering into strange lands; I have given my body to be devoured by the deep, parched up with heat, consumed by toil and weariness, or whatsoever God should please to bring upon me. But does all this (be it more or less, it

25 matters not) make me acceptable to God? Do all I ever did or can *know, say, give, do,* or *suffer,* justify me in his sight? Yea, or 'the constant use of all the means of grace'?[1]—which nevertheless is meet, right, and our bounden duty.[2] Or that 'I know nothing of myself,'[3] that I am, as touching outward, moral righteousness,

30 blameless? Or (to come closer yet) the having a *rational conviction* of all the truths of Christianity? Does all this give me a claim to the holy, heavenly, divine character of *a Christian?* By no means. If the oracles of God are true, if we are still to abide by 'the law and the

---

[h] I am not sure of this [added in errata to Vol. XXVI (1774)].

[98] Cf. Acts 26:25.
[99] See 1 Cor. 13:3.
[1] For Wesley's understanding of this, one of his key phrases, see his Sermon No. 16, 'The Means of Grace' (1746), especially its introductory comment (1:376-97 in this edn.).
[2] BCP, Communion, Vere dignum.
[3] 1 Cor. 4:4.

testimony',[4] all these things, though when ennobled by faith in Christ they are holy, and just, and good, yet without it[i] are 'dung and dross',[5] meet only to be purged away by 'the fire that never shall be quenched'.[6]

This then have I learned in the ends of the earth, that I am 'fallen short of the glory of God';[7] that my whole heart is 'altogether corrupt and abominable',[8] and consequently my whole life (seeing it cannot be that 'an evil tree' should 'bring forth good fruit');[9] that 'alienated' as I am 'from the life of God',[10] I am 'a child of wrath',[j] an heir of hell;[11] that my own works, my own sufferings, my own righteousness, are so far from reconciling me to an offended God, so far from making any atonement for the least of those sins, which 'are more in number than the hairs of my head',[12] that the most specious of them need an atonement themselves or they cannot abide his righteous judgment; that 'having the sentence of death'[13] in my heart, and having nothing *in* or *of* myself to plead, I have no hope, but that of being justified freely 'through the redemption that is in Jesus';[14] I have no hope, but that if I seek I shall find Christ and 'be found in him, not having my own righteousness, but that which is through the faith of Christ, the righteousness which is of God by faith.'[15]

If it be said that I have faith (for many such things have I heard, from many miserable comforters), I answer, So have the devils—*a sort* of faith; but still they are strangers to the covenant of promise. So the apostles had even at Cana in Galilee, when Jesus first 'manifested forth his glory';[16] even then they, in a sort, 'believed on him';[17] but they had not then 'the faith that overcometh the world'.[18] The faith I want is,[k] 'a sure trust and confidence in God, that through the merits of Christ my sins are

---

[i] I had even then the faith of a *servant*, though not that of a *son* [added in errata, 1774.]
[j] I believe not [added in errata, 1774; cf. Eph. 2:3].
[k] The faith of a *son* [added in errata, 1774].

---

[4] Isa. 8:20.
[5] Cf. 1 Macc. 2:62, 'dung and worms'.
[6] Mark 9:43, 45. 1775 omits, 'meet . . . quenched'.
[7] Rom. 3:23. [8] Cf. Ps. 53:2, 4 (BCP).
[9] Cf. Matt. 7:18; Luke 6:43. [10] Eph. 4:18.
[11] 1775 omits 'that "alienated" . . . hell'.
[12] Cf. Ps. 139:18; Matt. 10:30.
[13] Cf. 2 Cor. 1:9. [14] Rom. 3:24.
[15] Phil. 3:9. [16] John 2:11.
[17] Ibid. [18] Cf. 1 John 5:4.

forgiven, and I reconciled to the favour of God'.[19] I want that faith which St. Paul recommends to all the world, especially in his Epistle to the Romans; that faith which enables everyone that hath it to cry out, 'I live not, but Christ liveth in me; and the life which I now live, I live by faith in the Son of God, who loved me and gave himself for me.'[20] I want that faith which none can have without knowing that he hath it (though many *imagine* they have it who have it not). For whosoever hath it is 'freed from sin';[21] 'the whole body of sin is destroyed'[22] in him. He is freed from fear, 'having peace with God through Christ, and rejoicing in hope of the glory of God'.[23] And he is freed from doubt, 'having the love of God shed abroad in his heart through the Holy Ghost which is given unto him';[24] which 'Spirit itself beareth witness with his spirit, that he is a child of God'.[25]

---

[19] *Homilies*, 'Of Salvation', Pt. III. This is the definition of faith which Wesley quotes most frequently. Cf. *An Earnest Appeal*, §59 (11:68-69 in this edn.).

[20] Cf. Gal. 2:20.

[21] Rom. 6:7.

[22] Cf. Rom. 6:6.

[23] Cf. Rom. 5:1-2.

[24] Cf. Rom. 5:5.

[25] Cf. Rom. 8:16.

A N

EXTRACT

OF THE

Rev. Mr. JOHN WESLEY'S

JOURNAL

From FEBRUARY 1. 1737-8.

To his Return from GERMANY.

For this Cause I obtain'd Mercy, that in me first JESUS-CHRIST *might shew forth all Long-suffering, for a Pattern to them which should hereafter believe on Him to Life everlasting.* 1 Tim. i. 16.

L O N D O N:

Printed by W. STRAHAN, and Sold at the Foundery near *Upper Moorfields*, and at JAMES HUTTON's, at the *Bible* and *Sun* without *Temple-Bar*.

M. DCC. XL.

The Preface

1. That 'men revile me and say all manner of evil against me,'[1] that 'I am become as it were a monster unto many,'[2] that the zealous of almost every denomination cry out, 'Away with such a
5 fellow from the earth';[3] this gives me, with regard to myself, no degree of uneasiness.[4] For I know the Scripture must be fulfilled, 'If they have called the master of the house Beelzebub, how much more them of his household!'[5] But it does give me a concern with regard to those who by this artifice of the devil are prevented from
10 hearing that 'word which is able to save their souls'.[6]

2. For the sake of these, and indeed of all who desire to hear the truth of those things which have been so variously related, I have been induced to publish this farther account. And I doubt not but it will even hence appear to all candid and impartial judges, 'that *I*
15 *have* hitherto lived in all good conscience toward God'.[7]

3. I shall be easily excused, by those who either 'love' or seek 'the Lord Jesus in sincerity',[8] for speaking so largely of the Moravian church, 'a city' which ought to be 'set upon an hill'.[9] Their light hath been too, too long hid 'under a bushel'.[10] It is high
20 time it should at length break forth and 'so shine before men that' others also 'may glorify their Father which is in heaven'.[11]

4. If any should ask, 'But do you think even this church is perfect, "without spot or wrinkle or any such thing"?'[12] I answer plainly, 'No; though I trust it will be, when "patience has had its
25 perfect work".'[13] But neither do I think it right to entertain the world with the spots of God's children.[14]

5. It has been farther asked whether I imagine God is to be found only among them. I reply, 'By no means. I know there is a God in England, and we need not go to seek him in strange lands.'

---

[1] Cf. Matt. 5:11.   [2] Ps. 71:6 (BCP).   [3] Acts 22:22.
[4] Between the close of this part of the *Journal* on Aug. 12, 1738, and its publication on Sept. 29, 1740, JW had been involved in controversy with Molther on 'stillness' and had seceded with his adherents from Fetter Lane to form the United Societies at the Foundery. Capt. Williams had also published the affidavit against him which led to the publication of the first part of the *Journal* (see Preface to JWJ 1, n. 5). These controversies influenced not merely the tone of the preface, but the selection of extracts from the Journal.
[5] Matt. 10:25.   [6] Cf. Jas. 1:21.
[7] Cf. Acts 23:1.   [8] Cf. Eph. 6:24.
[9] Cf. Matt. 5:14.   [10] Cf. Matt. 5:15.
[11] Matt. 5:16.   [12] Eph. 5:27.
[13] Cf. Jas. 1:4.   [14] See Deut. 32:5.

I know that in our *own* he is very nigh unto all that call upon him;[15] and therefore I think those unwise (to say no more) who run to inquire after him in Holland or Germany.

6. When I went, the case was widely different. God had not then 'made bare his arm'[16] before us as he hath now done, in a manner (I will be bold to say) which had not been known either in Holland or Germany at that time when he, who ordereth all things wisely, according to the counsels of his own will,[17] was pleased by me to open the intercourse between the English and the Moravian Church.[18]

7. The particular reason which obliged me to relate so much of the conversation I had with those holy men is this. In September 1738, when I returned from Germany, I exhorted all I could to follow after that great salvation which is through faith in the blood of Christ; waiting for it 'in all the ordinances of God',[19] and in 'doing good, as they had opportunity, to all men'.[20] And many found the beginning of that salvation, 'being justified freely',[21] having 'peace with God through Christ, rejoicing in hope of the glory of God',[22] and having 'his love shed abroad in their hearts'.[23]

8. But about September 1739, while my brother and I were absent, certain men crept in among them unawares, greatly 'troubling and subverting their souls';[24] telling them they were in a delusion, that they had deceived themselves, and had *no true faith* at all. 'For (said they) none has any justifying faith who has ever any doubt or fear (which you know you have), or who has not a clean heart, which you know you have not; nor will you ever have it till you leave off using the means of grace (so called), till you leave off running to church and sacrament, and praying, and singing, and reading either the Bible, or any other book. For you can't *use* these things without *trusting* in them. Therefore, till you leave them off, you can never have true faith; you can never till then trust in the blood of Christ.'

9. And this doctrine, from the beginning to this day, has been

---

[15] See Ps. 145:18. [16] Isa. 52:10. [17] See Eph. 1:11.

[18] Wesley here refers to the outbreak of revival at Kingswood, in response to his preaching from Apr. 1739. The tone of his comment reflects his somewhat Pentecostalist tendencies at the time; he was quite wrong in supposing there had not been similar displays of spiritual power in many parts of Germany from Silesia to the Lower Rhine in the course of the previous generation (cf. above, Oct. 17, 1735, n. 7; July 27, 1737, n. 91) while in the Netherlands theologians of various bents were seeking to promote a livelier piety.

[19] Cf. Luke 1:6. [20] Cf. Gal. 6:10. [21] Rom. 3:24.
[22] Cf. Rom. 5:1-2. [23] Cf. Rom. 5:5. [24] Cf. Acts 15:24.

taught as the doctrine of the Moravian Church. I think therefore it is my bounden duty to clear the Moravians from this aspersion. And the more because I am perhaps the only person now in England that both *can* and *will* do it. And I believe it is the peculiar
5 providence of God that I *can;* that two years since the most eminent members of that church should so fully declare both their experience and judgment touching the very points now in question.

10. The sum of what has been asserted, as from them, is this:
10 (1) 'That a man *can't have any degree* of justifying faith till he is wholly freed from all doubt and fear, and till he has (in the full, proper sense) a new, a clean heart.'

(2) 'That a man *may not use* the ordinances of God, the *Lord's Supper* in particular, before he has such a faith as excludes
15 all doubt and fear, and implies a new, a clean heart.'

In flat opposition to this I assert:

(1) 'That a man *may have a degree* of justifying faith before he is wholly freed from all doubt and fear, and before he has (in the full, proper sense) a new, a clean heart.'
20 (2) 'That a man *may use* the ordinances of God, the *Lord's Supper* in particular, before he has such a faith as excludes all doubt and fear, and implies a new, a clean heart.'

I further assert, 'This I learned (not only from the English, but also) from the Moravian Church.'
25 And I hereby openly and earnestly call upon that church (and upon Count Zinzendorf in particular, who I trust is not ashamed or afraid to avow any part of the gospel of Christ) to correct me and explain themselves, if I have misunderstood or misrepresented them.

30 London, Sept. 29, 1740   John Wesley[25]

[25] While JW was here stating his position in relation to the Moravians, they were stating a position toward him at their synod of Gotha, 1740: 'The difference between those zealous servants of God, who, in Germany, by some were called Pietists, in England, Methodists, in France, Jansenists, in Italy and Spain, Quietists, in the Roman Church in general often known by the character of preacher of repentance and ascetics, but in the Protestant Church generally thought Mystics, on the one side, and our Oeconomy on the other, is this, the former either strive for an alteration of behaviour, or the thoughts, or both; or for an alteration in the religious worship; or are for abolishing all the external parts: we preach nothing but the Crucified Christ for the heart; and we think that when anyone gets hold of him, all that is idle vanishes away from such a person, and all necessary good comes, together with the living and abiding impression of the loving and faithful Lamb of God who was once a mortal man in reality.' The German original of this passage is to be found in the appendix to the *Naturelle Reflexiones*, p. 37; Nikolaus Ludwig von Zinzendorf, *Ergänzungsbände zu dem Hauptschriften*, Vol. 4.

Journal

From February 1, 1737/38, to September 16, 1738

Wednesday, February 1. After reading prayers and explaining a portion of Scripture to a large company at the inn, I left Deal, and came in the evening to Faversham.[1]

I here read prayers and explained the Second Lesson to a few of those who were called Christians but were indeed more savage in their behaviour than the wildest Indians I have yet met with. Fri. 3. I came to Mr. Delamotte's at Blendon,[2] where I expected a cold reception. But God had prepared the way before me; and I no sooner mentioned my name than I was welcomed in such a manner as constrained me to say, 'Surely God is in this place, and I knew it not!'[3] 'Blessed be ye of the Lord! Ye have shown more kindness in the latter end than at the beginning.'[4]

In the evening I came once more to London, whence I had been absent two years and near four months.

Many reasons I have to bless God, though the design I went upon did not take effect, for my having been carried into that strange land, contrary to all my preceding resolutions. Hereby I trust he hath in some measure 'humbled me and proved me, and shown me what was in my heart'.[5] Hereby I have been taught to 'beware of men'.[6] Hereby I am come to know assuredly that if 'in all our ways we acknowledge' God he will, where reason fails, 'direct our paths',[7] by lot[8] or by the other means which he

---

[1] Wesley spells the name 'Feversham', a familiar contemporary variant. Faversham was a respectable seaport and market town on the East Swale, noted for its production of gunpowder.

[2] Doubtless to deliver messages from Charles Delamotte.

[3] Cf. Gen. 28:16.

[4] Cf. Ruth 3:10.

[5] Cf. Deut. 8:2.

[6] Matt. 10:17.

[7] Cf. Prov. 3:6.

[8] There is a fittingness in the fact that this, the first explicit reference in the *Journal* to sortilege, occurs in an entry commencing with a visit to the Delamotte household; for it appears from the diary and MS journal material that on Mar.4, 1737, JW had cast lots in the presence of Charles Delamotte whether he should marry Sophy Hopkey. Having drawn the lot 'Think of it no more', he writes: 'We cast lots once again to know whether I ought to converse with her any more. And the direction I received from God was, "Only in the presence of Mr. Delamotte" ' (see Appendix). Wesley's earlier diaries indicate that he had begun using lots at Oxford as early as February 1735 as a means of determining God's

knoweth. Hereby I am delivered from the fear of the sea, which I had both dreaded and abhorred from my youth.

Hereby God has given me to know many of his servants; particularly those of the church of Herrnhut. Hereby my passage
5 is opened to the writings of holy men in the German, Spanish, and Italian tongues.[9] I hope too some good may come to others hereby. All in Georgia have heard the word of God. Some have believed, and begun to run well. A few steps have been taken towards publishing the glad tidings both to the African and
10 American heathens. Many children have learned 'how they ought to serve God',[10] and to be useful to their neighbour. And those

direction in particular questions. In the agreement JW's party made as they were setting out for Georgia not to act without mutual consultation, the understanding was 'that in case of an equality [of voices], after begging God's direction, the matter shall be decided by lot' (Curnock, I.127n.).

In the commentary he gives on the Moravian constitution (below, Aug. 1738, §16) JW notes that 'they have a peculiar esteem for lots; and accordingly use them both in public and private, to decide points of importance, when the reasons brought on each side appear to be of equal weight. . . .' In *The Principles of a Methodist Farther Explained* (1746), IV.3-4 (Vol. 9 of this edn.), JW modestly justified the practice, claiming no more than that he had received 'assistance and direction' by lots in cases of great mental distress. A knowledge of the limitations to sortilege which JW kept in mind did not, however, reconcile George Whitefield to the facts that JW had used it to try to prevent his returning to Georgia and also to determine to preach and print the polemic against him in the sermon on *Free Grace* (1739) (Whitefield, *Works*, IV.56-57).

[9] JW's reading as a young man was confined to works written or translated into English, French, and the biblical and classical languages, but it is clear from the diary that in Georgia he began to work hard at German, Spanish (which he needed for diplomatic as well as spiritual purposes), and Italian (see diary entries for Oct. 17, 1735; June 28, 1736; Apr. 19, 1737); see also R. P. Heitzenrater, 'John Wesley and the Oxford Methodists' (Ph.D. Dissertation, Duke University, 1972), pp. 493-526. An abiding memorial to his lifelong enthusiasm for German was provided by the 33 translations of German hymns and his salty comment on a poem by Voltaire (JWJ, Oct. 11, 1756) that 'by him I was more than ever convinced that the French is the poorest, meanest language in Europe; that it is no more comparable to the German or Spanish than a bagpipe is to an organ.' His Spanish studies in 1736 seem to have given rise to a metrical version of a Spanish paraphrase of Ps. 63 later published (see George Osborn, ed., *Poetical Works of John and Charles Wesley*, 13 vols. [London, 1868–72], I.174-76; see also Curnock, I.240). His studies seem not to have proceeded successfully; the following year he reports: 'I began learning Spanish, in order to converse with my Jewish parishioners' (JWJ, Apr. 4, 1737); in 1736 he hired a Spanish interpreter (JWJ, Jan. 5); and the versions of the Spanish authors appearing in JW's *Christian Library* were made from French translations. His Italian enabled him to read prayers in the vernacular to a small congregation of Vaudois (JWJ, Oct. 30, 1737), but, beyond this passage, is not heard of after his return from Georgia.

[10] In Georgia, JW prepared a children's catechism and catechized children and adults frequently. This quotation seems to be a reminiscence of the questions in the BCP Catechism, following the recital of the Ten Commandments:

What dost thou chiefly learn by the commandments?
Answer. I learn two things: my duty towards God, and my duty towards my neighbour.

whom it most concerns have an opportunity of knowing the true state of their infant colony, and laying a firmer foundation of peace and happiness to many generations.

Sat. 4. I told my friends some of the reasons which a little hastened my return to England. They all agreed it would be proper to relate them to the Trustees of Georgia.

Accordingly the next morning I waited on Mr. Oglethorpe, but had not time to speak on that head. In the afternoon I was desired to preach at St. John the Evangelist's.[11] I did so on those strong words, 'If any man be in Christ, he is a new creature.'[12] I was afterwards informed, many of the best in the parish were so offended that I was not to preach there any more.

Mon. 6. I visited many of my old friends, as well as most of my relations. I find the time is not yet come when I am to be 'hated of all men'.[13] O may I be prepared for that day!

Tue. 7. (A day much to be remembered.) At the house of Mr. Weinantz,[14] a Dutch merchant, I met Peter Böhler,[15] Schulius,[16] Richter,[17] and Wenzel Neisser,[18] just then landed from Germany.

[11] At Millbank, Westminster.

[12] 2 Cor. 5:17. Probably part of this sermon was later incorporated in one of Wesley's 'standard' sermons, *On Sin in Believers*, first published in 1763 (see 1:314-34 in this edn.).

[13] Matt. 10:22.

[14] Francis Wynantz (before 1700–74), a Danzig merchant naturalized in England by the Act of 5 Geo. II, c. 4. In 1732 he entered the movement of the French prophets with which he was connected through his father-in-law Portales. In 1732 he was a correspondent of Spangenberg and Zinzendorf. J. van den Berg, 'John Wesley's Contacten met Nederland', *Nederlands Archief voor Kergeschiendnis*, N.S. (1971), 52:45-47; Hillel Schwartz, *The French Prophets* (Berkeley, 1980), pp. 205, 209-10, 291, 314; *The Genealogist*, N.S. 22 (1905).

[15] Peter Böhler (1712–75) was persuaded by Zinzendorf on a visit to Jena to join the Moravians and was made tutor to his son; Zinzendorf's first act as bishop was to ordain him to the Moravian ministry. He was now called from Jena and was on his way to Georgia and a mission to the Negroes of Carolina.

[16] George Schulius, a convert of Böhler, was appointed his assistant on his Carolina mission for work among the Negroes and was with him in London before leaving. He died at Savannah, July 24, 1739.

[17] Abraham Ehrenfried Richter, already known as an 'aged brother', spent some six months in London ministering chiefly to the few Germans who were united there by Zinzendorf. A Stralsund merchant of considerable substance in the time of Charles XII of Sweden, he had subsequently become much impoverished. In 1734 when Zinzendorf proposed going to Stralsund to consult the theologians there, he received a request from Richter to provide a tutor for his children, and in due course stayed with him. Richter then joined the Brethren, became an evangelist in western Germany, and, arriving in Algiers as a teacher to Christian slaves at a time of plague in Feb. 1740, died July 10, 1740. See A. G. Spangenberg, *Leben des Herrn Nicolaus Ludwig Grafen . . . von Zinzendorfs* (Barby, 1773–75), pp. 828-30; reprint in *Nikolaus Ludwig von Zinzendorf: Materialien und Dokumente*, Reihe 2, Bd. 1-8 (1971).

[18] Friedrich Wenzel Neisser (1716–77), son of Augustin Neisser (see below, Aug. 1738, n. 22) whose early evidence of capacity during his education at Herrnhut led

Finding they had no acquaintance in England, I offered to procure them a lodging, and did so near Mr. Hutton's,[19] where I then was. And from this time I did not willingly lose any opportunity of conversing with them while I stayed in London.

5   Wed. 8. I went to Mr. Oglethorpe again, but had no opportunity of speaking as I designed. Afterwards I waited on the Board of Trustees, and gave them a short but plain account of the state of the colony:[20] an account, I fear, not a little differing from those which they had frequently received before, and for which I

10   have reason to believe some of them have not forgiven me to this day.[21]

Sun. 12. I preached at St. Andrew's, Holborn, on 'Though I give all my goods to feed the poor, and though I give my body to be burned, and have not charity, it profiteth me nothing.'[22] 'O hard

15   sayings! Who can hear them?'[23] Here too (it seems) I am to preach no more.

Wed. 15. I waited on the Trustees again, and gave them in writing the substance of what I had said at the last Board. Whatsoever farther questions they asked concerning the state of

20   the province I likewise answered to the best of my knowledge.[24]

Zinzendorf to take him into his service and to accompany him on journeys to the Wetterau (1736), Livland, and England (1737). He was subsequently dispatched to various parts of Europe and America on the business of the Brethren and remained active in their constitutional affairs. He wrote a considerable number of hymns, a few of which continued in general use. He became the ninth bishop of the Renewed Unity in 1746. Orig., 'Wensel Neiser', and 'Wensel Neusser' in JW's transcription of his autobiography (see below, Aug. 1738).

[19] The Wesley's London home was with the Huttons (see Preface to JWJ 1, n. 3). James Hutton had become the leading figure among the English Moravians.

[20] 'Mr. Wesley . . . attended us [the Georgia Trustees]; he acquainted us that about one hundred idle persons in Georgia have within two months left the colony. That the inhabitants were last year able to furnish corn of their own produce to supply the wants of half the colony. That the country is very healthy. That the Saltzburgers for their part had cultivated one hundred and fifty acres. That Piercy, our gardener, had left it on some distaste with Mr. Causton, and the garden now under no care and half the trees dead.' Egmont, *Diary*, II.466.

[21] 'and for . . . this day' added from the second edition onwards.

[22] Cf. 1 Cor. 13:3. This sermon was also preached on his arrival at Savannah in 1736 (Sermon 149, 'On Love', in Vol. 4 of this edn.). It concludes with a reference to the death of his father, who in 1689 had been ordained by Bishop Compton in St. Andrew's, Holborn, a church founded in the thirteenth century, rebuilt by Wren, and rebuilt a second time after being gutted in the Second World War.

[23] Cf. John 6:60.

[24] The Egmont *Diary* (II.467) says that the Trustees did no other business than prepare a petition to the Commons, but Charles Wesley records (CWJ, I.81) that the following day 'Mr. Oglethorpe told me, "Your brother must have a care. There is a very strong spirit raising against him. People say he is come over to do mischief to the colony. He will be

Fri. 17. I set out for Oxford with Peter Böhler, where we were kindly received by Mr. Sarney,[25] the only one now remaining here of many who at our embarking for America were used to 'take sweet counsel together',[26] and rejoice in 'bearing the reproach of Christ'.[27]

Sat. 18. We went to Stanton Harcourt, to Mr. Gambold,[28] and found my old friend recovered from his mystic delusion, and convinced that St. Paul was a better writer than either Tauler[29] or Jacob Boehme.[30] The next day I preached once more at the Castle (in Oxford) to a numerous and serious congregation.

called upon for his reasons why he left the people." I answered, "Sir, he has been twice before at the Board for that purpose, but was not asked that question, and therefore had no opportunity to answer it. He will attend them again on Wednesday morning." I waited on his Lordship of London, and informed him of my brother's return. He spoke honourably of him; asked many questions about Georgia, and the Trustees; forgot his usual reserve, and dismissed me very kindly.'

[25] John Sarney, with whom JW had corresponded while in Georgia (Wesley several times refers to 'Sarney' in his Oxford diaries during the winter of 1734/35). Charles Wesley notes, Sept. 28, 1738, 'I called on my friend that *was*, John Sarney, now entirely estranged by the offence of the cross' (CWJ, I.131). A John Sarney, Register to the Commissioners for Hackney Coaches, died Apr. 22, 1773 (*Gentleman's Magazine*, XLIII.204). Peter Böhler wrote to Zinzendorf of this journey: 'I travelled with the two brothers, John and Charles Wesley, from London to Oxford. The elder, John, is a good-natured man: he knew he did not properly believe on the Saviour, and was willing to be taught. His brother is at present very much distressed in his mind, but does not know how he shall begin to be acquainted with the Saviour.' *Weselyan Methodist Magazine* (1854), 77:687.

[26] Cf. Ps. 55:14.

[27] Cf. Heb. 13:13.

[28] John Gambold (1711–71), son of William Gambold, an Anglican clergyman who died in 1728 while his son was at Christ Church, Oxford. Gambold was reduced to religious melancholia by his father's death, introduced himself to Charles Wesley, and through him was brought into the circle of Oxford Methodists. Though impressed by JW, he was bent on mystical ways of his own. Ordained in 1733, he became vicar of Stanton Harcourt, 1735, a small parish four and one-half miles west of Oxford. Here Kezia Wesley, JW's youngest sister, was a member of his household, 1736–38. Now introduced by JW to the Moravians, he became interpreter for Zinzendorf's addresses, and in 1741, coming under the influence of Philip Henry Molther, he first broke with JW and then resigned his living. In 1743 he married Elizabeth, daughter of Joseph Walker of Littletown, Yorks.; in 1743 he became preacher at Fetter Lane and devoted himself to unsuccessful schemes for the reconciliation of the Moravians and the Church of England. In 1754 he was consecrated a Moravian bishop. He had much to do with the reorganization of Moravianism after Zinzendorf's death. After turning to Moravianism he was long estranged from JW who, however, continued to regard him as a sensible man.

[29] Johann Tauler (*c.* 1300–61), German Dominican mystic, who propounded a practical mystical teaching grounded in Thomist doctrine. Unity with God was to be desired for its fruits in charity and self-sacrifice. So popular in his lifetime that numerous spurious works were attributed to him, Tauler was posthumously esteemed by Luther.

[30] Orig., 'Behmen'. Jacob Boehme (1575–1624), theosophical writer. A shoemaker at Görlitz, he lived in a state of religious exaltation, reporting his mystical experiences in abstruse language from Paracelsus, astrological, and other sources in works published

All this time I conversed much with Peter Böhler, but I understood him not; and least of all when he said, *Mi frater, mi frater, excoquenda est ista tua philosophia*—My brother, my brother, that philosophy of yours must be purged away.

5 Mon. 20. I returned to London. On Tuesday I preached at Great St. Helen's,[31] on 'If any man will come after me, let him deny himself, and take up his cross daily and follow me.'[32]

Wed. 22. I was with the Trustees again, to whom I then gave a short account (and afterwards delivered it to them in writing) of 10 the reasons why I left Georgia.[33]

Sun. 26. I preached at six at St. Lawrence's,[34] at ten in St. Katherine Cree Church,[35] and in the afternoon at St. John's, Wapping.[36] I believe it pleased God to bless the first sermon most, because it gave most offence; being indeed an open defiance of 15 that mystery of iniquity which the world calls 'prudence',

mostly after his death. The English Behmenists were absorbed into Quakerism. For a later encounter of JW with the works of Boehme, see JWJ, June 4, 1742. JW preferred the spelling (and apparently the pronunciation) 'Behmen', though he occasionally used 'Behme'.

[31] Bishopsgate Street, a church which existed in the twelfth century, and in the grounds of which a nunnery was built in the thirteenth century. The nave was extended to match that of the nuns' church built alongside, an arrangement which produced the present very unusual double nave. The conventual buildings were not dismantled till 1799. The incumbent William Butler, LL.B. (1713–73) appointed Thomas Broughton to a lectureship associated with it on the recommendation of George Whitefield.

[32] Luke 9:23.

[33] Egmont records: 'Confined at home by a cold whereby I could not attend the Georgia Board, where the day's business was to receive Mr. Wesley's complaints of the usage he received at Georgia, and which obliged him to come for England. He gave the Trustees that met several papers and certificates for his justification, whereby it appeared indeed that he was guilty of indiscretion, but that Causton our head bailiff was much more to blame, and he charged upon him many particulars of gross mal-administration which must be inquired into. Mr. Vernon took him home to dinner, and in company of Mr. Hales examined him more particularly as to Causton's bad behaviour as a magistrate, which they took down in writing to be discoursed of at the Board.' Egmont, *Diary*, II.467.

[34] Probably St. Lawrence's, Jewry, 'a neat edifice' rebuilt 1670–87 by Wren, and restored with many changes after the Second World War.

[35] Orig., 'St. Katherine's Creed-Church.' St. Katherine Cree, Leadenhall St., in 1280 referred to as 'St. Katherine de Christchurch at Alegate', and 1303 as 'Sanctae Katerinae Trinitatis'. Creechurch means Christchurch, and Christchurch refers to the Priory of Holy Trinity within the precincts of which St. Katherine stood. Only the tower is early, and the bulk of the building, completed under the patronage of Laud and consecrated by him, is reckoned the most important church in London between Jones and Wren (Pevsner, *London* [2nd edn., London, 1962], 1:149). The church is now the headquarters of the Industrial Christian Fellowship.

[36] St. John's, Wapping, 'a rather curious structure with huge dormers and a low tower', replaced by another building in the mid-eighteenth century, of which only the tower now remains. Mervyn Blatch, *A Guide to London's Churches* (London, 1978), p. 178.

grounded on those words of St. Paul to the Galatians, 'As many as desire to make a fair show in the flesh, they constrain you to be circumcised, only lest they should suffer persecution for the cross of Christ.'[37]

Mon. 27. I took coach for Salisbury, and had several opportunities of conversing seriously with my fellow-travellers. But endeavouring to mend the wisdom of God by the worldly wisdom of prefacing sermons with light conversation, and afterwards following that advice of the mystics, 'Leave them to themselves,'[38] all I had said was written on the sand. 'Lord, lay not this sin to my charge!'[39]

Tue. 28. I saw my mother once more.[40] The next day I prepared for my journey to my brother at Tiverton.[41] But on Thursday, March 2nd, a message that my brother Charles was dying at Oxford[42] obliged me to set out for that place immediately. Calling at an odd house[43] in the afternoon, I found several persons there who seemed well-wishers to religion, to whom I spake plainly; as I did in the evening both to the servants and strangers at my inn.

With regard to my own behaviour,[44] I now renewed and wrote down my former resolutions:

1. To use absolute openness and unreserve[45] with all I should converse with.

2. To labour after continual seriousness, not willingly indulging myself in any the least levity of behaviour, or in laughter—no, not for a moment.

3. To speak no word which does not tend to the glory of God; in particular, not a tittle[46] of worldly things. Others may, nay must. But what is that to thee? And,

---

[37] Gal. 6:12.

[38] No specific instance of this has been identified.

[39] Cf. Acts 7:60.

[40] At the house of Westley Hall, who had married Martha Wesley, and held property and a living at Salisbury.

[41] JW's elder brother, Samuel, was Master of Blundell's School, Tiverton, 1733–39.

[42] Charles Wesley noted in his *Journal* (I.83) on Feb. 27 that 'the scale seemed to turn for life,' and on the following day he wrote an account of his recovery to his brother, but addressed it to Tiverton. The letter concludes: 'One consequence of my sickness you will not be sorry for—its stopping my sudden return to Georgia.'

[43] Apparently used in the sense of 'solitary', 'standing by itself'; retained in Yorkshire dialect. See *OED*, A.II.5.

[44] It was during this period of reflection that JW composed an account of his relations with Sophia Hopkey in Georgia, which he finished transcribing on March 12, 1738.

[45] *OED* cites no example of this word before 1751.

[46] 1774, 'not to talk'.

4. To take no pleasure which does not tend to the glory of God, thanking God every moment for all I do take, and therefore rejecting every sort and degree of it which I feel I cannot so thank him *in* and *for.*

5　Sat. 4. I found my brother at Oxford, recovering from his pleurisy; and with him Peter Böhler. By whom (in the hand of the great God) I was on Sunday the 5th clearly convinced of unbelief, of the want of 'that faith whereby alone we are saved',[47] with the full, Christian salvation.[48]

10　Immediately it struck into my mind, 'Leave off preaching. How can you preach to others, who have not faith yourself?' I asked Böhler whether he thought I should leave it off or not. He answered, 'By no means.' I asked, 'But what can I preach?' He said, 'Preach faith *till* you have it, and then, *because* you have it,

15　you *will* preach faith.'

Accordingly, Monday 6, I began preaching this new doctrine, though my soul started back from the work. The first person to whom I offered *salvation by faith alone* was a prisoner under sentence of death. His name was Clifford.[49] Peter Böhler had

20　many times desired me to speak to him before. But I could not prevail on myself so to do, being still (as I had been many years) a zealous asserter of *the impossibility of a death-bed repentance.*

Fri. 10. Peter Böhler returned to London. Tuesday 14, I set out for Manchester, with Mr. Kinchin,[50] Fellow of Corpus

25　Christi, and Mr. Fox,[51] late a prisoner in the city prison. Between

---

[47] Cf. Acts 4:12.　　　　[48] 'with . . . Salvation' was added in 1774, errata sheet.

[49] Böhler's own notes link the visit to the otherwise unknown malefactor directly with the dramatic conversation reported by Wesley above. 'I took a walk with the elder Wesley, and asked him about his spiritual state. He told me that he sometimes felt certain of his salvation, but sometimes he had many doubts; that he could only say this, "If what stands in the Bible be true, then I am saved." Thereupon I spoke with him very fully; and earnestly besought him to go to the opened fountain, and not to mar the efficacy of free grace by his unbelief. . . . Later in the evening Wesley and other students met, and we had a religious conversation. The case of a prisoner who had been condemned to death gave me occasion to speak of the duty of seeking souls for the Saviour.' J. P. Lockwood, *Memorials of the Life of Peter Böhler* (London, 1868), pp. 73-74.

[50] Charles Kinchin (*c.* 1711–42), fellow of Corpus Christi College, Oxford, rector of Dummer, Hants., 1735, an earnest Oxford Methodist for whom Whitefield and Hervey did duty on occasion in his parish. He took charge of the prison work in Oxford for the Methodists when the Wesley brothers went to Georgia. Under the influence of Böhler and other Moravians, resigned his fellowship and parish, 1739, with a view to becoming an itinerant preacher.

[51] Fox and his wife became soundly converted and wished to serve in Georgia. JW, however, opposed their moving, for a society met in their house, and the cause was short of support in Oxford. See *Letters*, 25:580, 587-89 in this edn.

five and six we called at Chapel on the Heath,[52] where lived a poor
man, sometime prisoner in the Castle of Oxford. He was not at
home; but his wife came to us, to whom Mr. Kinchin spoke a few
words, which so melted her heart that she burst out into tears, and
we went on rejoicing and praising God.   5

About eight, it being rainy and very dark, we lost our way; but
before nine came to Shipston,[53] having rode over, I know not how,
a narrow foot-bridge, which lay across a deep ditch near the town.
After supper I read prayers to the people of the inn, and explained
the Second Lesson; I hope, not in vain.   10

The next day we dined at Birmingham, and soon after we left it
were reproved for our negligence there (in letting those who
attended us go without either exhortation or instruction) by a
severe shower of hail. At Hednesford,[54] about five, we
endeavoured to be more faithful; and all who heard seemed   15
serious and affected.

In the evening we came to Stafford. The mistress of the house
joined with us in family prayer. The next morning one of the
servants appeared deeply affected, as did the ostler[55] before we
went. Soon after breakfast, stepping into the stable, I spake a few 20
words to those who were there. A stranger who heard me said,
'Sir, I wish I was to travel with you,' and when I went into the
house followed me, and began abruptly, 'Sir, I believe you are a
good man, and I come to tell you a little of my life.' The tears
stood in his eyes all the time he spoke, and we hoped not a word   25
which was said to him was lost.

At Newcastle, whither we came about ten, some to whom we
spoke at our inn were very attentive, but a gay young woman that
waited on us, quite unconcerned. However, we spoke on. When
we went away she fixed her eyes, and neither moved nor said one   30

---

[52] Perhaps Heath (or Hethe), a small parish 4 miles N. by E. from Bicester.

[53] Shipston on Stour, formerly one of the largest sheep markets in the county; in
Wesley's day a decayed market town and parish 16 miles S. by W. from Warwick.

[54] Orig., 'Hedgeford,' here and Mar. 21, 1737/38. The name as JW gave it was
preserved in Hedgford Pool, a large lake, and the Hedgford hills where race-horses were
trained. Hednesford was a small township in the parish of Cannock, 4 miles SW. by S.
from Rugeley.

[55] Wesley's manuscript (as revealed by the first edition) seems to have read 'hostler',
though from the second edition this was changed to 'ostler'. However, on other occasions
(July 18, 1743; June 15, 1750; Aug. 26, 1763) the alternate form 'hostler' appears in all
editions, although on July 25, 1764, the first edition reads 'ostler'. Both forms have
remained current, but it seems almost certain that JW himself preferred 'hostler', though
probably pronounced with a silent *h* and *t*.

word, but appeared as much astonished as if she had been one risen from the dead.

Coming to Holmes Chapel[56] about three, we were surprised at being shown into a room where a cloth and plates were laid; soon
5 after, two men came in to dinner. Mr. Kinchin told them, if they pleased, that gentleman would ask a blessing for them. They stared, and *as it were* consented; but sat still while I did it, one of them with his hat on. We began to speak on turning to God, and went on, though they appeared utterly regardless. After a while
10 their countenances changed, and one of them stole off his hat, and laying it down behind him said, all we said was true; but he had been a grievous sinner, and not considered it as he ought; but he was resolved, with God's help, now to turn to him in earnest. We exhorted him and his companion, who now likewise drank in
15 every word, to cry mightily to God that 'he would send them help from his holy place'.[57]

Being faint in the evening, I called at Altrincham,[58] and there light[59] upon a Quaker, well skilled in, and therefore (as I soon found) sufficiently fond of, controversy. After an hour spent
20 therein (perhaps not in vain) I advised him to dispute as little as possible, but rather to follow after holiness, and walk humbly with his God.

Late at night we reached Manchester. Friday the 17th we spent entirely with Mr. Clayton, by whom, and the rest of our friends
25 here, we were much refreshed and strengthened. Mr. Hoole, the Rector of St. Ann's Church, being taken ill the next day, on Sunday 19, Mr Kinchin and I officiated at Salford Chapel[60] in the morning, by which means Mr. Clayton was at liberty to perform the service at St. Ann's; and in the afternoon I preached there on
30 those words of St. Paul, 'If any man be in Christ, he is a new creature.'[61]

---

[56] Orig., 'Holmes-Chappel'.   [57] Cf. Ps. 20:2.

[58] 1740, 'Alteringham'; 1743 onwards, 'Altringham'. Altrincham was a prosperous market town in the parish of Bowdon, 7 miles N. by E. from Knutsford.

[59] The past tense of 'light' would today be 'lit', but JW employs 'light' in all 5 contemporary editions with no correction in the printed errata or in his own revised copy of his *Works*. He apparently used 'light upon' in the same sense as the example 'lighted upon' quoted from the 1701 edition of Thomas Stanley's *History of Philosophy* in *OED*, II.10.d (where this passage from Wesley needs amending as a 1738 usage from 'lit' to 'light, 'lit' being a revision made after Wesley's death). Cf. July 6, 1741.

[60] I.e., Holy Trinity, Salford, a non-parochial chapel of which Clayton was perpetual curate.

[61] 2 Cor. 5:17. A sermon on this text appears as Sermon 13 (1:314-34 of this edn.).

Early in the morning we left Manchester, taking with us Mr. Kinchin's brother,[62] for whom we came, to be entered at Oxford. We were fully determined to lose no opportunity of awakening, instructing, or exhorting any whom we might meet with in our journey. At Knutsford,[63] where we first stopped, all we spake to thankfully received the word of exhortation. But at Talk-o'-th'-Hill,[64] where we dined, she with whom we were was so much of a gentlewoman that for near an hour our labour seemed to be in vain. However, we spoke on. Upon a sudden she looked as one just awaked out of sleep. Every word sunk into her heart. Nor have I seen so entire a change both in the eyes, face, and manner of speaking of anyone in so short a time.

About five, Mr. Kinchin riding by a man and woman double-horsed,[65] the man said, 'Sir, you ought to thank God it is a fair day; for if it rained, you would be sadly dirty with your little horse.' Mr. Kinchin answered, 'True. And we ought to thank God for our life and health, and food and raiment, and all things.' He then rode on. Mr. Fox following, the man said, 'Sir, my mistress would be glad to have some more talk with that gentleman.' We stayed, and when they came up began to search one another's hearts. They came to us again in the evening at our inn at Stone, where I explained both to them and many of their acquaintance who were come together that great truth, 'Godliness hath the promise both of this life, and of that which is to come.'[66]

Tue. 21. Between nine and ten we came to Hednesford. Just then one was giving an account of a young woman who had dropped down dead there the day before. This gave us a fair occasion to exhort all that were present 'so to number their own days, that they might apply their hearts unto wisdom'.[67]

In the afternoon one overtook us whom we soon found more inclined to speak than to hear. However, we spoke, and spared not. In the evening we overtook a young man, a Quaker, who

[62] Stephen Kinchin, son of Augustine Kinchin of Woodmancott, Hants. Matriculated at Trinity College, Oxford, Mar. 23, 1737/38, aged 16.

[63] Knutsford was a substantial market town and parish 25 miles NE. by E. from Chester.

[64] Orig., 'Talk-in-the-Hill'. Talk-o'-th'-Hill was a chapelry in the parish of Audley, then on the main road north and commanding a view into nine counties.

[65] Both riding on one horse. *OED* notes for this practice 'ride double', and of a horse, 'to carry double' (B.1.c), but gives no example of 'double-horse' or 'double-horsed'.

[66] Cf. 1 Tim. 4:8.   [67] Cf. Ps. 90:12.

afterwards came to us to our inn at Henley, whither he sent for the rest of his family to join with us in prayer; to which I added, as usual, the exposition of the Second Lesson. Our other companion went with us a mile or two in the morning, and then
5 not only spoke less than the day before, but took in good part a serious caution against talkativeness and vanity.

An hour after, we were overtook by an elderly gentleman, who said he was going to enter his son at Oxford. We asked, 'At what college?' He said he didn't know, having no acquaintance there
10 on whose recommendation he could depend. After some conversation he expressed a deep sense of the good providence of God, and told us he knew God had cast us in his way, in answer to his prayer. In the evening we reached Oxford, rejoicing in our having received so many fresh instances of that great truth, 'In all
15 thy ways acknowledge him, and he shall direct thy paths.'[68]

Thur. 23. I met Peter Böhler again, who now amazed me more and more, by the account he gave of the fruits of living faith—the holiness and happiness which he affirmed to attend it. The next morning I began the Greek Testament again, resolving to abide
20 by 'the law and the testimony',[69] and being confident that God would hereby show me 'whether' this 'doctrine was of God'.[70]

Sun. 26. I preached at Whitam[71] on 'the new creature',[72] and went in the evening to a society in Oxford, where (as my manner then was at all societies) after using a collect or two, and the
25 Lord's Prayer, I expounded a chapter in the New Testament, and concluded with three or four more collects and a Psalm.

Mon. 27. Mr. Kinchin went with me to the Castle, where, after reading prayers and preaching, on 'It is appointed for all men once to die,'[73] we prayed with the condemned man,[74] first in
30 several forms of prayer, and then in such words as were given us in that hour. He kneeled down in much heaviness and confusion, having 'no rest in his bones, by reason of his sins'.[75] After a space he rose up and eagerly said, 'I am now ready to die. I know Christ

---

[68] Prov. 3:6.
[69] Cf. Isa. 8:20.
[70] Cf. John 7:17.
[71] Apparently Wytham, Berks., a small parish 3 miles northwest of Oxford.
[72] 2 Cor. 5:17; Gal. 6:15.
[73] Cf. Heb. 9:27.
[74] Doubtless Clifford, mentioned above, Mar. 6, 1738.
[75] Cf. Ps. 38:3 (BCP).

has taken away my sins, and there is no more condemnation for me.' The same composed cheerfulness he showed when he was carried to execution; and in his last moments he was the same, enjoying a perfect peace, in confidence that he was 'accepted in the Beloved'.[76]

Saturday, April 1. Being at Mr. Fox's society, my heart[77] was so full that I could not confine myself to the forms of prayer, which we were accustomed to use there. Neither do I purpose to be confined to them any more, but to pray indifferently, with a form or without, as I may find suitable to particular occasions.[78]

Sun. 2. Being Easter Day, I preached in our College chapel on 'The hour cometh and now is, when the dead shall hear the voice of the Son of God, and they that hear shall live.'[79] I preached in the afternoon, first at the Castle, and then at Carfax,[80] on the same words. I see the promise. But it is afar off.

Believing it would be better for me to wait for the accomplishment of it in silence and retirement, on Monday 3, I complied with Mr. Kinchin's desire, and went to him at Dummer in Hampshire.[81] But I was not suffered to stay here long; being earnestly pressed to come up to London, if it were only for a few days. Thither therefore I returned on Tuesday 18th.

Sat. 22. I met Peter Böhler once more. I had now no objection to what he said of the nature of faith, viz., that it is (to use the words of our Church), 'A sure trust and confidence which a man hath in God, that through the merits of Christ *his* sins are

---

[76] Eph. 1:6.

[77] 1740, 'soul'.

[78] For this practice of extempore prayer they 'were greatly censured by some persons, particularly by their brother Samuel'. Moore, *Wesley*, I.377; J. Priestley, ed., *Original Letters by the Rev. John Wesley and his Friends* (Birmingham, 1791), p. 96.

[79] John 5:25.

[80] St. Martin's Church and Thomas Broughton's house were both at Carfax; the former seems the more probable location of the sermon, especially since the diary entry 'Carfax' (as in this case) usually designated St. Martin's.

[81] The Kinchin family at this moment (the brothers Charles, Stephen, and James, their sister Molly, and Charles's wife Esther) divided the time between the rectory at Dummer and the house of their father Augustine at Woodmancott, a few miles away. JW's friends were frequently drawn to Dummer by Charles's need for curates during his periods of college residence; JW, however, was now there for a fortnight rethinking his personal position. This reconsideration was doubtless not assisted by the acute illness of Molly, with whom he spent a good deal of time during this visit (see diary in Appendix). The occasion of the earnest summons to London is not known, but the diary indicates he went to Oxford on the 17th, and when he set out for London on the morning of the 19th, he 'ran' part of the way to Beaconsfield.

forgiven, and *he* reconciled to the favour of God.'[82] Neither could
I deny either the happiness or holiness which he described as
fruits of this living faith. 'The Spirit itself beareth witness with
our spirit that we are the children of God,'[83] and 'He that
5 believeth hath the witness in himself,'[84] fully convinced me of the
former; as 'Whatsoever is born of God doth not commit sin',[85] and
'Whosoever believeth is born of God,'[86] did of the latter. But I
could not comprehend what he spoke of *an instantaneous work.*[87] I
could not understand how this faith should be given in a moment;
10 how a man could *at once* be thus turned from darkness to light,
from sin and misery to righteousness and joy in the Holy Ghost. I
searched the Scriptures again touching this very thing,
particularly the Acts of the Apostles: but to my utter astonishment
found scarce any instances there of other than *instantaneous*
15 conversions—scarce any other so slow as that of St. Paul, who
was three days in the pangs of the new birth. I had but *one* retreat
left, viz., '*Thus,* I grant, God wrought in the *first* ages of
Christianity; but the times are changed. What reasons have I to
believe he works in the same manner now?'
20   But on Sunday 23, I was beat out of this retreat too, by the
concurring evidence of several living witnesses, who testified
God *had thus wrought in themselves;* giving them in a moment such
a faith in the blood of his Son as translated them out of darkness
into light, out of sin and fear into holiness and happiness. Here
25 ended my disputing. I could now only cry out, 'Lord, help thou
my unbelief!'[88]
    I asked P[eter] Böhler again whether I ought not to 'refrain
from teaching others'. He said, 'No; do not hide in the earth the
talent God hath given you.' Accordingly on Tuesday 25, I spoke
30 clearly and fully at Blendon, to Mr. Delamotte's family, of the
nature and fruits of faith. Mr. Broughton[89] and my brother were

---

[82] JW's reminiscence of his favourite definition of 'true faith' from the *Homilies*, 'Of Salvation', Part III.

[83] Rom. 8:16.   [84] 1 John 5:10.

[85] Cf. 1 John 3:9.   [86] Cf. 1 John 5:1.

[87] Böhler professed to have undergone instantaneous conversion and regarded this as normal.

[88] Cf. Mark 9:24. The diary entry indicates that Wesley was 'convinced that faith c[onvert]s at once' (see Appendix).

[89] Thomas Broughton (1712–77), son of Thomas Broughton of Oxford; matriculated at University College, Oxford, Dec. 17, 1731, aged 19; B. A. 1736/37; fellow of Exeter College, Oxford, 1734–41; rector of Wootton, Surrey, 1753–77. An Oxford Methodist, and drawn for a time towards the Moravians, Broughton was separated from the Wesleys

there. Mr. Broughton's great objection was, he could never think that I had not faith, who had done and suffered such things.[a] My brother was very angry, and told me I did not know what mischief I had done by talking thus. And indeed it did please God then to kindle a fire, which I trust shall never be extinguished. 5

On Wednesday 26, the day fixed for my return to Oxford, I once more waited on the Trustees for Georgia; but being straitened for time was obliged to leave the papers for them which I had designed to give into their own hands. One of these was the instrument whereby they had appointed me minister of 10 Savannah; which, having no more place in those parts, I thought it not right to keep any longer.[90]

P[eter] Böhler walked with me a few miles, and exhorted me not to stop short of the grace of God. At Gerrards Cross I plainly declared to those whom God gave into my hands 'the faith as it is 15 in Jesus';[91] as I did the next day to a young man I overtook on the road, and in the evening to our friends at Oxford. A strange doctrine, which some, who did not care to contradict, yet knew not what to make of; but one or two, who were thoroughly bruised by sin, willingly heard, and received it gladly. 20

In the day or two following I was much confirmed in 'the truth that is after godliness'[92] by hearing the experiences of Mr. Hutchins[93] (of Pembroke College) and Mrs. Fox[94]—two living witnesses that God *can* (at least, if he *does* not always) give that faith whereof cometh salvation in a moment, as lightning falling 25 from heaven.

Monday, May 1. The return of my brother's illness obliged me

---

[a] He was in the right. I certainly then had the faith of a *servant*, though not the faith of a son [added in 1775; cf. addition to 1774 edn. of JWJ, Feb. 1, 1738, n. i].

by questions of church order. He was Lecturer of All Hallows, Lombard Street, and was secretary of the SPCK, 1743–77. Wrote *Serious Advice and Warning to Servants, more especially those of the Nobility and Gentry* (1746) and sermons.

[90] Egmont noted: 'Mr. John Wesley, our minister at Savannah, left us with his licence for performing ecclesiastical service at Savannah, which we took for a resignation, and therefore resolved to revoke his commission. In truth the Board did it with great pleasure, he appearing to us to be a very odd mixture of a man, an enthusiast, and at the same time a hypocrite, wholly distasteful to the greater part of the inhabitants, and an incendiary of the people against the magistracy.' Egmont, *Diary*, II.481; cf. Egmont, *Journal*, p. 350.

[91] Cf. 1 Tim. 3:13.

[92] Cf. Titus 1:1.

[93] John Hutchings, son of Richard Hutchings of Woollmiston, Som., pleb.; matriculated at Pembroke College, May 30, 1734, aged 18; B.A. 1738.

[94] See above, Mar. 10, 1738, n. 51.

again to hasten to London. In the evening I found him at James Hutton's, better as to his health than I expected, but strongly averse from what he called 'the new faith'.

5 This evening our little society began,[95] which afterwards met in Fetter Lane. Our fundamental rules were as follows:

In obedience to the command of God by St. James,[96] and by the advice of Peter Böhler, it was agreed by us—

1. That we will meet together once a week to 'confess our faults one to another, and pray for one another that we may be 10 healed'.

2. That the persons so meeting be divided into several 'bands', or little companies, none of them consisting of fewer than five or more than ten persons.

3. That everyone in order speak as freely, plainly, and 15 concisely as he can, the real state of his heart, with his several temptations and deliverances, since the last time of meeting.

4. That all the bands have a conference at eight every Wednesday evening, begun and ended with singing and prayer.

5. That any who desire to be admitted into this society be 20 asked, What are your reasons for desiring this? Will you be entirely open, using no kind of reserve? Have you any objection to any of our orders? (which may then be read).

6.[97] That when any new member is proposed everyone present speak clearly and freely whatever objection he has to him.

25 7. That those against whom no reasonable objection appears be, in order for their trial, formed into one or more distinct bands, and some person agreed on to assist them.

8. That after two months' trial, if no objection then appear, they be admitted into the society.

30 9. That every fourth Saturday be observed as a day of general intercession.

10. That on the Sunday sennight[98] following be a general love-feast, from seven till ten in the evening.

---

[95] The debates of nineteenth-century Methodist ecclesiologists on this society are no longer of interest. It was a Church of England society with love-feasts and bands, and from it sprang both the Moravian society which became the Moravian Church, and also the first Methodist 'United Societies', which retained the Anglican connection.

[96] See first rule, which paraphrases Jas. 5:16.

[97] The first two editions numbered the rules 1-5, 7-12, corrected in 1765 to 1-11.

[98] Orig., 'seven-night'. In the *Letters* (where the bulk of Wesley's uses of the archaism are to be found) the word is almost always spelled 'sennight', but once 'sen'night', and once 'sevennight'. Cf. JWJ, Sept. 16, 1744, where the editions from 1779 onwards use 'se'nnight'.

11. That no particular member be allowed to act in anything contrary to any order of the society; and that if any persons, after being thrice admonished, do not conform thereto, they be not any longer esteemed as members.

Wed. 3. My brother had a long and particular conversation 5 with Peter Böhler. And it now pleased God to open his eyes,[99] so that he also saw clearly what was the nature of that one, true, living faith, whereby alone 'through grace we are saved'.[1]

Thur. 4. Peter Böhler left London in order to embark for Carolina. O what a work hath God begun since his coming into 10 England![2] Such an one as shall never come to an end till heaven and earth pass away.

Friday and Saturday I was at Blendon. They now 'believed our report'.[3] O may 'the arm of the Lord' be speedily 'revealed'[4] *unto them!*   15

Sunday 7. I preached at St. Lawrence's in the morning; and afterwards at St. Katherine Cree Church.[5] I was enabled to speak strong words at both, and was therefore the less surprised at being informed I was not to preach any more in either of those churches.   20

Tue. 9. I preached at Great St. Helen's, to a very numerous congregation, on 'He that spared not his own Son, but delivered him up for us all, how shall he not with him also freely give us all things?'[6] My heart was now so enlarged to declare the love of God to all that were oppressed by the devil, that I did not wonder in the 25 least when I was afterwards told, 'Sir, you must preach here no more.'

Wed. 10. Mr. Stonehouse,[7] Vicar of Islington, was convinced

---

[99] CWJ (I.85-86) makes it plain that his conversion had proceeded less rapidly than this reference might suggest. On May 1st he said: 'Now I have demonstration against the Moravian doctrine that a man cannot have peace without assurance of his pardon. I now have peace, yet cannot say of a surety that my sins are forgiven'; and a week after Peter Böhler had left London: 'I . . . confessed my unbelief and want of forgiveness, but declared my firm persuasion that I should receive the atonement before I died.'

[1] Cf. Eph. 2:5, 8.

[2] This exclamation was added from 1743 (2nd edn.) onwards.

[3] Isa. 53:1.

[4] Ibid.

[5] See above, Feb. 26, 1738, n. 35.

[6] Rom. 8:32. Wesley's controversial sermon, *Free Grace* (1739) was preached from this text (see 3:542-63 in this edn.).

[7] George Stonehouse (1714–93), son of Francis Stonehouse of Hungerford Park, Berks., arm.; matriculated at Pembroke College, Oxford, 1729; M.A. 1736; vicar of Islington 1738–40, when he sold the living which belonged to his family. He married

of 'the truth as it is in Jesus'.[8] From this time till Saturday 13, I was sorrowful and very heavy, being neither able to read nor meditate, nor sing, nor pray, nor do anything. Yet I was a little refreshed by Peter Böhler's letter, which I insert in his own words.

5   Charissime et suavissime Frater,
       Intentissimo amore te diligo, multum tui recordans in itinere meo, optando et precando ut quam primum viscera misericordiae crucifixi Iesu Christi, tui gratia iam ante 6000 annos commota, menti tuae appareant: ut gustare et tunc videre possis, quam vehementer te Filius Dei amaverit et hucusque amet, et ut
10 sic confidere possis in eo omni tempore, vitamque eius in te et in carne tua sentire. Cave tibi a peccato incredulitatis, et si nondum vicisti illud, fac ut proximo die illud vincas, per sanguinem Iesu Christi. Ne differ, quaeso, credere tuum in Iesum Christum; sed potius promissionum eius quae pertinent ad miserandos peccatores, coram facie eius benigna sic mentionem fac, ut non
15 aliter possit quam praestare tibi, quod multis aliis praestitit. O quam multus, quam magnus, quam ineffabilis, quam inexhaustus, est illius amor! Ille certe iamiam paratus est ad auxilium, et nihil potest illum offendere nisi incredulitas nostra. Crede igitur. Fratrem tuum Carolum et Hall,[9] nomine meo saluta multum; et admonete vos invicem ad credendum, et tunc ambulandum coram
20 facie Domini ἀκριβῶς et ad pugnandum contra diabolum et mundum νομιμῶς, et ad crucifigendum et conculcandum peccatum omne sub pedibus nostris, quantum nobis datum est per gratiam secundi Adami, cuius vita excedit mortem prioris Adami, et cuius gratia antecellit corruptionem et damnationem prioris Adami.
25   Dominus tibi benedicat. Permane in fide, amore, doctrina communione sanctorum, et breviter, in omni quod habemus in novo foedere. Ego sum et maneo

In Agris Southamptonianis,   Tuus indignus frater,
    Die 8vo Maii, 1738   Petrus Böhler

Mary, daughter of Sir John Crispe. Cooperating actively with the Moravians, he became a committee member for Hutton's Society for the Furtherance of the Gospel, 1741, and frequently conducted love-feasts. His relations with the Moravians ceased in 1744 or 1745, and he retired to East Brent, where he remained in JW's view a wealthy eccentric. His wife, who had been adopted as a daughter by Zinzendorf, continued in the Moravian work and before her death in 1751 made large contingent benefactions. Benham, *Hutton*, pp. 267-71.

   [8] Cf. Eph. 4:21.

   [9] Westley Hall (1711–76), son of Thomas Hall of Salisbury; matriculated at Lincoln College, Oxford, 1731. A pupil of JW, but left without taking a degree, being ordained 1734. About the same time he became secretly engaged to JW's eldest sister, Martha; a few months later he proposed marriage to Kezia, the younger sister, and was accepted. Thereupon Martha revealed their engagement, and he married her at once. In 1735 he arranged to accompany JW to Georgia, but took a curacy at Wootton, Wilts., 1735, moving to Fisherton, Salisbury, 1736. Kezia and her mother came to reside with the family, who all moved to London in 1739 to assist in the organization of the Methodist society. In 1741 he adopted Moravian tenets, and, returning to Salisbury in 1743, formed a new religious society, quarrelling with his wife because she refused to leave the Church of England with

(I love you greatly, and think much of you in my journey, wishing and praying that the tender mercies of Jesus Christ the crucified, whose bowels were moved toward you more than six thousand years ago, may be manifested to your soul: that you may taste, and then see, how exceedingly the Son of God has loved you, and loves you still, and that so you may continually trust in him, and feel his 5 life in yourself. Beware of the sin of unbelief; and if you have not conquered it yet, see that you conquer it this very day, through the blood of Jesus Christ. Delay not, I beseech you, to believe in *your* Jesus Christ; but so put him in mind of his promises to poor sinners that he may not be able to refrain from doing for you what he hath done for so many others. O how great, how inexpressible, how 10 unexhausted is his love! Surely he is now ready to help; and nothing can offend him but our unbelief. . . .[10]

The Lord bless you! Abide in faith, love, teaching, the communion of saints, and briefly, in all which we have in the New Testament. I am

Your unworthy brother 15
Peter Böhler)

Sun. 14. I preached in the morning at St. Ann's,[11] Aldersgate; and in the afternoon at the Savoy Chapel,[12] free salvation by faith

his congregation. Successful as a field preacher, he became a deist and advocated polygamy. In 1747 he took leave of his Salisbury followers, and in 1750–51 disturbed Charles Wesley's prayer-meetings in Bristol. He briefly migrated to the West Indies with a mistress. After returning to England he seems to have engaged in literary work and clerical duty. In valetudinarian old age he calculated: '12 Sons and 6 Daughters—only 3 living 1774' (WHS [1906], 5:149-50).

[10] The ellipsis indicates that Wesley's free translation did not include this part of the letter, which may be translated thus: 'Believe, therefore. Greet heartily in my name your brother Charles and Hall; and admonish one another to believe and then to walk circumspectly before the Lord, and to fight lawfully against the devil and the world, and to crucify and trample under your feet all sin, as much as this is given to you by the grace of the second Adam, whose life outweighs the death of the first Adam, and whose grace cancels the corruption and condemnation entailed by the first Adam.'

[11] The church of St. Anne and St. Agnes, Aldersgate Street, was first mentioned in the thirteenth century. It was completely destroyed (along with St. John Zachary next door) in the Great Fire, but was rebuilt by Wren, 1676–87, and absorbed the parish of St. John Zachary. It suffered extensive bomb damage in 1940 and was substantially rebuilt (1963–68) in the style which preceded its Victorian restorations. It now houses St. John's Evangelical Lutheran Church of London, with services in Esthonian, Latvian, and English. Blatch, *London's Churches*, pp. 22-26.

[12] The Savoy Hospital, already decaying, never recovered from the Great Fire of 1661; the chaplains did not reside again and in 1670 obtained an act enabling them to redevelop sites on building leases. The hospital was finally dissolved in 1702, but various foreign chapels continued in the precincts until the building of Waterloo Bridge in 1817. The Savoy Chapel itself dated from early in the sixteenth century and in Horneck's time was very ill-endowed. After the burning of the church of St. Mary-le-Strand in 1564, the Savoy Chapel was opened to the parishioners till their church was rebuilt in 1717, and hence was commonly but erroneously known as St. Mary le Savoy. Horneck gathered a great congregation there, and preached for the relief of French Protestants on the revocation of the Edict of Nantes. W. J. Loftie, *Memorials of the Savoy* (London, 1878), pp. 151-93.

in the blood of Christ. I was quickly apprised that at St. Ann's, likewise, I am to preach no more.

So true did I find the words of a friend,[13] wrote to my brother about this time:

5   I have seen upon this occasion, more than ever I could have imagined, how intolerable the doctrine of faith is to the mind of man, and how peculiarly intolerable to *religious* men. One may say the most unchristian things, even down to Deism; the most enthusiastic things, so they proceed but upon mental raptures, lights, and unions; the most severe things, even the whole rigour of

10 ascetic mortification: all this will be forgiven. But if you speak of faith in such a manner as makes Christ a Saviour to the utmost, a most universal help and refuge; in such a manner as takes away glorying, but adds happiness to wretched man; as discovers a greater pollution in the best of us than we could before acknowledge, but brings a greater deliverance from it than we could before

15 expect: if anyone offers to talk at this rate, he shall be heard with the same abhorrence as if he was going to rob mankind of their salvation, their Mediator, or their hopes of forgiveness. I am persuaded that a Montanist or a Novatian, who from the height of his purity should look down with contempt upon poor sinners, and exclude them from all mercy, would not be thought such an

20 overthrower of the gospel as he who should learn from the Author of it to be a friend of publicans and sinners, and to sit down upon the level with them as soon as they begin to repent.

    But this is not to be wondered at. For all *religious* people have such a quantity of righteousness, acquired by much painful exercise, and formed at last

25 into current habits; which is their wealth, both for this world and the next. Now all other schemes of religion are either so complaisant as to tell them they are very rich, and have enough to triumph in; or else only a little rough, but friendly in the main, by telling them their riches are not yet sufficient, but by such arts of self-denial and mental refinement they may enlarge the stock. But the doctrine

30 of faith is a downright robber. It takes away all this wealth, and only tells us it is deposited for us with somebody else, upon whose bounty we must live like mere beggars. Indeed they that are truly beggars, vile and filthy sinners till very lately, may stoop to live in the dependent condition: it suits them well enough. But they who have long distinguished themselves from the herd of vicious wretches, or

35 have even gone beyond *moral* men; for them to be told that they are either not so well, or but the same needy, impotent, insignificant vessels of mercy with the others: this is more shocking to reason than transubstantiation. For reason had rather resign its pretensions to judge what is bread or flesh than have this honour wrested from it, to be the architect of virtue and righteousness. But

40 where am I running? My design was only to give you warning that, wherever you go, 'this foolishness of preaching'[14] will alienate hearts from you, and open mouths against you.

---

[13] John Gambold. Fuller versions of the letter are given in Whitehead, *Wesley*, II.75-77; and Moore, *Wesley*, I.380-82. The holograph, dated June 23, 1738, and endorsed by JW, is in the Methodist Archives, Manchester.

[14] Cf. 1 Cor. 1:21.

Fri. 19. My brother had a second return of his pleurisy. A few of us spent Saturday night in prayer. The next day, being Whitsunday, after hearing Dr. Heylyn[15] preach a truly Christian sermon (on 'They were all filled with the Holy Ghost'[16]—and so, said he, may *all you* be, if it is not your own fault), and assisting 5 him at the Holy Communion (his curate being taken ill in the church), I received the surprising news that my brother had found rest to his soul. His bodily strength returned also from that hour.[17] 'Who is so great a God as our God?'[18]

I preached at St. John's Wapping at three, and at St. Benet's,[19] 10 Paul's Wharf, in the evening. At these churches likewise I am to preach no more. At St. Antholin's I preached for the last time[20] on the Thursday following.

Monday, Tuesday, and Wednesday I had continual sorrow and heaviness in my heart; something of which I described, in the 15 broken manner I was able, in the following letter to a friend:[21]

O why is it that so great, so wise, so holy a God, will use such an instrument as me! Lord, 'let the dead bury their dead!'[22] But wilt thou send the dead to raise the dead? Yea, thou sendest whom thou *wilt* send, and showest mercy by whom

---

[15] John Heylyn (1685?–1759), the 'Mystic Doctor', son of John Heylyn of Chelsea, saddler and army contractor. Educated at Westminster School and Trinity College, Cambridge; M.A. 1714, D.D. 1728. First rector of St. Mary-le-Strand, 1724–59; rector of Sunbury, 1742–47; prebendary of Westminster, 1743–59. Wesley (who spells the name 'Heylin') read his work as early as 1732, using it with the Oxford Methodists. He read Heylyn's edition of devotional tracts in Georgia (which he later prescribed for reading by his preachers; see *Minutes* of Conference, 1746), and used Heylyn's *Theological Lectures* (1749) as one of the sources for his *Explanatory Notes upon the New Testament* (1755). JW had also arranged to prepare an edition of Thomas à Kempis with him, according to John Byrom (*Remains*, Chetham Society 34 [Manchester, 1855], p. 542).

[16] Acts 2:4; 4:31.

[17] Again the report was premature, though from this Whitsunday Charles Wesley began to make rapid progress towards the resolution of his spiritual malaise. He records: 'I now found myself at peace with God, and rejoiced in hope of loving Christ. . . . I saw that by faith I stood. . . . I went to bed still sensible of my own weakness . . . yet confident of Christ's protection.' CWJ, I.92.

[18] Ps. 77:13.

[19] Orig., 'St. Bennett's', St. Benet's, Paul's Wharf, now the Metropolitan Welsh Church, was first mentioned in 1111, destroyed in the Great Fire, and rebuilt by Wren, 1677-85, in red and blue brick with Portland stone dressings. One of the most attractive of Wren's churches, it escaped damage in the Second World War, but suffered a fire in the organ and galleries in 1971. St. Antholin's, Bridge Row, was a Wren church demolished in the 1870s, the proceeds of the sale of the site contributing to the restoration of St. Mary Aldermary in 1875–76. Blatch, *London's Churches*, p. 126.

[20] 'for the last time' omitted 1743 onwards.

[21] Identity not known, but possibly John Gambold.

[22] Matt. 8:22; Luke 9:60.

thou *wilt* show mercy! Amen! Be it then according to thy will! If thou speak the word, Judas shall cast out devils.

I feel what you say (though not enough) for I am under the same condemnation. I see that the whole law of God is holy and just and good. I know
5 every thought, every temper of my soul ought to bear God's image and superscription. But how am I fallen from the glory of God! I feel that 'I am sold under sin'.[23] I know that I too deserve nothing but wrath, being full of all abominations; and having no good thing in me to atone for them, or to remove the wrath of God. All my works, my righteousness, my prayers, need an
10 atonement for themselves. So that my mouth is stopped. I have nothing to plead. God is holy; I am unholy. God is a consuming fire; I am altogether a sinner, meet to be consumed.

Yet I hear a voice (and is it not the voice of God?) saying, 'Believe, and thou shalt be saved.'[24] 'He that believeth is passed from death unto life.'[25] 'God so
15 loved the world that he gave his only begotten Son, that whosoever believeth on him should not perish, but have everlasting life.'[26]

O let no one deceive us by vain words, as if we had already attained this faith![b] By its fruits we shall know. Do we already feel 'peace with God',[27] and 'joy in the Holy Ghost'?[28] Does his 'Spirit bear witness with our spirit, that we are the
20 children of God'?[29] Alas, with *mine* he does not. Nor, I fear, with yours. O thou Saviour of men, save us from trusting in anything but *thee*! Draw us after thee! Let us be emptied of ourselves, and then fill us with all peace and joy in believing, and let nothing separate us from thy love in time or in eternity!

What occurred on Wednesday 24, I think best to relate at large,
25 after premising what may make it the better understood.[30] Let him that cannot receive it ask of the Father of lights that he would give more light both to him and me.

1. I believe, till I was about ten years old I had not sinned away

---

[b] I.e., the proper Christian faith [added in 1774 errata].

---

[23] Rom. 7:14.
[24] Cf. Acts 16:31.
[25] Cf. John 5:24.
[26] John 3:16.
[27] Rom. 5:1.
[28] Rom. 14:17.
[29] Cf. Rom. 8:16.
[30] It was JW's custom to write memoranda, sometimes lengthy, upon important events, and what follows is undoubtedly such a document, prepared as an independent statement, and later incorporated into the *Journal*. That it is a contemporary document is shown by the entry on June 8, together with that of June 13, 1739, relating how in the previous June, before leaving for Germany, he had read to his mother 'a paper . . . containing a short account of what had passed in [his] own soul till within a few days of that time'. This does not preclude the possibility that the document may have undergone some revision before being included in the *Journal* almost two years later.

that 'washing of the Holy Ghost'[31] which was given me in baptism, having been strictly educated and carefully taught that I could only be saved *by universal obedience, by keeping all the commandments of God,* in the meaning of which I was diligently instructed.[32] And those instructions, so far as they respected outward duties and sins, I gladly received and often thought of. But all that was said to me of inward obedience or holiness I neither understood nor remembered. So that I was indeed as ignorant of the true meaning of the law as I was of the gospel of Christ.

2. The next six or seven years were spent at school;[33] where, outward restraints being removed, I was much more negligent than before even of outward duties, and almost continually guilty of outward sins, which I knew to be such, though they were not scandalous in the eye of the world. However, I still read the Scriptures, and said my prayers, morning and evening. And what I now hoped to be saved by, was, (1) *not being so bad as other people;* (2) *having still a kindness for religion;* and (3) *reading the Bible, going to church, and saying my prayers.*

3. Being removed to the university[34] for five years, I still said my prayers both in public and private, and read with the Scriptures several other books of religion, especially comments on the New Testament. Yet I had not all the while so much as a notion of inward holiness; nay, went on habitually and (for the most part) very contentedly, in some or other known sin: indeed with some intermissions and short struggles, especially before and after the Holy Communion, which I was obliged to receive thrice a year. I cannot well tell what I hoped to be saved by now, when I was continually sinning against the little light I had, unless by those transient fits of what many divines taught me to call 'repentance'.

4. When I was about twenty-two[35] my father pressed me to enter into holy orders. At the same time, the providence of God directing me to Kempis's *Christian Pattern,* I began to see that true religion was seated in the heart and that God's law extended to all our thoughts as well as words and actions. I was, however, very angry at Kempis for being *too strict,* though I read him only in

---

[31] Cf. Titus 3:5.
[32] This process is described below, in Susanna Wesley's own words; JWJ, Aug. 1, 1742 (letter of July 24, 1732; cf. 25:330-31 in this edn.).
[33] At Charterhouse, 1714–20.
[34] Matriculated at Christ Church, Oxford, July 18, 1720; B.A. 1724.
[35] I.e., *c.* 1725.

Dean Stanhope's translation.[36] Yet I had frequently much sensible comfort in reading him, such as I was an utter stranger to before. And meeting likewise with a religious friend,[37] which I had never had till now, I began to alter the whole form of my
5 conversation and to set in earnest upon *a new life*. I set apart an hour or two a day for religious retirement. I communicated every week. I watched against all sins,[38] whether in word or deed. I began to aim at and pray for inward holiness. So that now, *doing so much and living so good a life*, I doubted not but I was a good
10 Christian.

5. Removing soon after to another college,[39] I executed a resolution which I was before convinced was of the utmost importance, shaking off at once all my trifling acquaintance. I began to see more and more the value of time. I applied myself
15 closer to study. I watched more carefully against actual sins; I advised others to be religious, according to that scheme of religion by which I modelled my own life. But meeting now with Mr. Law's *Christian Perfection*[40] and *Serious Call*[41] (although I was much offended at many parts of both, yet) they convinced me
20 more than ever of the exceeding height and breadth and depth of the law of God. The light flowed in so mightily upon my soul that everything appeared in a new view. I cried to God for help and resolved not to prolong the time of obeying him as I had never done before. And by my continued *endeavour to keep his whole law*,
25 inward and outward, *to the utmost of my power*, I was persuaded

[36] *The Christian's Pattern: or a Treatise of the Imitation of Christ. To which are added meditations and prayers for sick persons*, by George Stanhope (London, 1699), and many subsequent editions. Beginning in 1735, JW issued several editions of Thomas à Kempis based largely on the 1677 translation of John Worthington (see *Bibliography*, Nos. 4, 45, etc.).

[37] At the time JW admitted to being 'advised to read Thomas à Kempis over' (JW to his mother, May 28, 1725, *Letters*, 25:162-64 in this edn.), he had been visiting the rectory at Stanton, where he was friendly with the rector's daughter, Sally Kirkham, whom he called by her nickname Varanese. The introduction to Kempis may well have been made in the rectory, but Curnock's attempts (I.12-16) to show that it was made by Sally Kirkham and to infer that she was the unnamed 'religious friend' are inadequately substantiated. As good and as inconclusive a case could be made out for Robin Griffiths.

[38] 1740, 'sin'.

[39] JW was elected a fellow of Lincoln College, Oxford, on Mar. 17, 1725/26.

[40] *A Practical Treatise upon Christian Perfection* (1726) of which JW published an extract in 1743 (*Bibliography*, No. 77).

[41] *A Serious Call to a Devout and Holy Life* (1729, or at the earliest Nov. 1728). For JW's introduction to these works see WHS (1969-70), 37:78-82, 143-50, 173-77. Wesley also published an extract of this work in 1744 (*Bibliography*, No. 86).

that I should be accepted of him, and that I was even then in a state of salvation.[c]

6. In 1730 I began visiting the prisons, assisting the poor and sick in town, and doing what other good I could by my presence or my little fortune to the bodies and souls of all men. To this end I abridged myself of all superfluities, and many that are called necessaries of life. I soon became 'a byword'[42] for so doing, and I rejoiced that 'my name was cast out as evil.'[43] The next spring I began observing the Wednesday and Friday fasts, commonly observed in the ancient church, tasting no food till three in the afternoon.[44] And now I knew not how to go any farther. I diligently strove against all sin. I omitted no sort of self-denial which I thought lawful. I carefully used, both in public and in private, all the means of grace at all opportunities. I omitted no occasion of doing good. I for that reason suffered evil. And all this I knew to be nothing unless as it was directed toward inward holiness. Accordingly this, the image of God, was what I aimed at in all, by doing his will, not my own. Yet when, after continuing some years in this course, I apprehended myself to be near death, I could not find that all this gave me any comfort, nor any assurance of acceptance with God. At this I was then not a little surprised, not imagining I had been all this time building on the sand,[d] nor considering that 'other foundation can no man lay than that which is laid by God, even Christ Jesus.'[45]

7. Soon after, a contemplative man[46] convinced me still more than I was convinced before, that outward works are nothing, being alone; and in several conversations instructed me how to

---

[c] And I believe I was [added as a footnote in 1775].
[d] Not so: I was right, as far as I went [added as a footnote in 1775].

---

[42] Deut. 28:37, etc.
[43] Cf. Luke 6:22.
[44] These were the 'stations', or stationary fasts, so called because they came on specific occasions every week, instead of being movable, like those observed on days differing each year according to the date of Easter. JW had been rather unsuccessful in his early efforts at fasting; this new attempt to link himself with the church universal, begun on June 2, 1732, was one of several ways in which the High Church tendencies of John Clayton began to influence the life of the Oxford friends. See Heitzenrater, 'John Wesley', pp. 162-63, 365-67.
[45] Cf. 1 Cor. 3:11.
[46] No certain identification is possible, but it is noteworthy that on July 3, 1732, JW paid his first visit to William Law, who set him reading the *Theologia Germanica* (Diary, July 3 and 31, 1732; JW to William Law, May 20, 1738, *Letters*, 25:546-48 in this edn.).

pursue inward holiness, or a union of the soul with God. But even of his instructions (though I then received them as the words of God) I cannot but now observe, (1) that he spoke so incautiously against *trusting in outward works* that he discouraged me from 5 *doing* them at all; (2) that he recommended (as it were, to supply what was wanting in them) *mental prayer*, and the like exercises, as the most effectual means of purifying the soul and uniting it with God. Now these were, in truth, as much *my own works* as visiting the sick or clothing the naked, and the 'union with God' thus 10 pursued was as really *my own righteousness* as any I had before pursued under another name.

8. In this *refined* way of trusting to my own works and my own righteousness (so zealously inculcated by the mystic writers),[47] I dragged on heavily, finding no comfort or help therein, till the 15 time of my leaving England.[48] On shipboard, however, I was again active in outward works; where it pleased God of his free mercy to give me twenty-six of the Moravian brethren for companions, who endeavoured to show me a more excellent way.[49] But I understood it not at first. I was too learned and too wise. So that it 20 seemed foolishness unto me. And I continued preaching, and following after, and trusting in that righteousness whereby no flesh can be justified.

9. All the time I was at Savannah I was thus 'beating the air'.[50] Being ignorant of the righteousness of Christ, which by a living 25 faith in him bringeth salvation 'to every one that believeth',[51] I sought to establish my own righteousness, and so laboured in the fire all my days. I was now properly 'under the law';[52] I knew that 'the law' of God was 'spiritual';[53] 'I consented to it that it was good.'[54] Yea, 'I delighted in it, after the inner man.'[55] Yet was I 30 'carnal, sold under sin'.[56] Every day was I constrained to cry out, 'What I do, I allow not; for what I would I do not, but what I hate, that I do.'[57] 'To will is indeed present with me; but how to perform that which is good, I find not.'[58] For 'the good which I would, I do

---

[47] The third edition of 1765 onwards omitted a passage present within the parentheses in 1740, 1743: 'whom I declare in my cool judgment, and in the presence of the most high God, I believe to be one great antichrist'.
[48] Oct. 14, 1735.
[49] See 1 Cor. 12:31.
[50] Cf. 1 Cor. 9:26.
[51] Rom. 1:16.
[52] Rom. 6:14, 15.
[53] Cf. Rom. 7:14.
[54] Cf. Rom. 7:16.
[55] Cf. Rom. 7:22.
[56] Rom. 7:14.
[57] Cf. Rom. 7:15.
[58] Cf. Rom. 7:18.

not; but the evil which I would not, that I do.'[59] 'I find a law, that when I would do good, evil is present with me,'[60] even the 'law in my members warring against the law of my mind', and still 'bringing me into captivity to the law of sin'.[61]

10. In this vile, abject state of bondage to sin[62] I was indeed fighting continually, but not conquering. Before, I had willingly served sin: now it was unwillingly, but still I served it. I fell and rose and fell again. Sometimes I was overcome and in heaviness. Sometimes I overcame and was in joy. For as in the former state I had some foretastes of the terrors of the law, so had I in this of the comforts of the gospel. During this whole struggle between nature and grace (which had now continued above ten years) I had many remarkable returns to prayer, especially when I was in trouble; I had many sensible[63] comforts, which are indeed no other than short anticipations of the life of faith. But I was still 'under the law', not 'under grace'[64] (the state most who are called Christians are content to live and die in); for I was only 'striving with',[65] not 'freed from sin'.[66] Neither had I 'the witness of the Spirit with my spirit'.[67] And indeed could not; for I 'sought it not by faith, but (as it were) by the works of the law'.[68]

11. In my return to England, January 1738, being in imminent danger of death, and very uneasy on that account, I was strongly convinced that the cause of that uneasiness was unbelief, and that the gaining a true, living faith, was the 'one thing needful'[69] for me. But still I fixed not this faith on its right object: I meant only faith in God, not faith in or through Christ. Again, I knew not that I was *wholly void of this faith*, but only thought *I had not enough* of it. So that when Peter Böhler, whom God prepared for me as soon as I came to London, affirmed of true faith in Christ (which is but one) that it had those two fruits inseparably attending it,

---

[59] Rom. 7:19.
[60] Cf. Rom. 7:21.
[61] Rom. 7:23.
[62] 1775, 'In this state'.
[63] Wesley normally used the word 'sensible' in its primary meaning of 'perceptible by the senses' rather than that of 'making sense', which Samuel Johnson claimed in 1755 was used only in 'low conversation' (see *OED*, IV.14).
[64] Rom. 6:14, 15.
[65] Cf. Heb. 12:4.
[66] Rom. 6:7.
[67] Cf. Rom. 8:16.
[68] Rom. 9:32.
[69] Cf. Luke 10:42.

'dominion over sin, and constant peace from a sense of forgiveness', I was quite amazed, and looked upon it as a new gospel. If this was so, it was clear I had not faith. But I was not willing to be convinced of this. Therefore I disputed with all my
5   might and laboured to prove that faith might be where these were not, especially where that sense of forgiveness was not. For all the Scriptures relating to this I had been long since taught to construe away, and to call all 'Presbyterians' who spoke otherwise. Besides, I well saw no one could (in the nature of things) have such a sense
10 of forgiveness and not *feel* it. But I felt it not. If then there was no faith without this,[e] all my pretensions to faith dropped at once.

12. When I met Peter Böhler again, he readily consented to put the dispute upon the issue which I desired, viz., Scripture and experience. I first consulted the Scripture. But when I set aside
15 the glosses of men, and simply considered the words of God, comparing them together and endeavouring to illustrate the obscure by the plainer passages, I found they all made against me, and was forced to retreat to my last hold,[70] that experience would never agree with the *literal interpretation* of those Scriptures. Nor
20 could I therefore allow it to be the true till I found some living witnesses of it. He replied, he could show me such at any time; if I desired it, the next day. And accordingly the next day he came again with three others, all of whom testified of their own personal experience that a true, living faith in Christ is
25 inseparable from a sense of pardon for all past, and freedom from all present sins. They added with one mouth that this faith was the gift, the free gift of God, and that he would surely bestow it upon every soul who earnestly and perseveringly sought it. I was now thoroughly convinced. And, by the grace of God, I resolved to
30 seek it unto the end, (1) by absolutely renouncing all dependence, in whole or in part, upon *my own* works or righteousness, on which I had really grounded my hope of salvation, though I knew it not, from my youth up; (2) by adding to 'the constant use of all the' other 'means of grace',[71] continual prayer for this very thing,
35 justifying, saving faith, a full reliance on the blood of Christ shed

---

[e] There is no *Christian* faith without it [added as a footnote in 1775].

[70] I.e., stronghold. For a similar example of this usage see *Some Remarks on Mr. Hill's Farrago Double-Distilled* (1773), §13.

[71] For the source of this phrase in the BCP, see editorial introduction to Sermon 16, 'The Means of Grace', 1:377 in this edn.

for *me;* a trust in him as *my* Christ, as *my* sole justification, sanctification, and redemption.

13. I continued thus to seek it (though with strange indifference, dullness, and coldness, and unusually frequent relapses into sin) till Wednesday, May 24. I think it was about five this morning that I opened my Testament on those words: Τὰ μέγιστα ἡμῖν καὶ τίμια ἐπαγγέλματα δεδώρηται, ἵνα γένεσθε θείας κοινωνοὶ⁷² φύσεως—'There are given unto us exceeding great and precious promises, even that ye should be partakers of the divine nature.'ᶠ Just as I went out I opened it again on those words, 'Thou art not far from the kingdom of God.'⁷³ In the afternoon I was asked to go to St. Paul's. The anthem was, 'Out of the deep have I called unto thee, O Lord. Lord, hear my voice. O let thine ears consider well the voice of my complaint. If thou, Lord, wilt be extreme to mark what is done amiss, O Lord, who may abide it? But there is mercy with thee; therefore thou shalt be feared. [. . .] O Israel, trust in the Lord: For with the Lord there is mercy, and with him is plenteous redemption. And he shall redeem Israel from all his sins.'⁷⁴

14. In the evening I went very unwillingly to a society in Aldersgate Street,⁷⁵ where one was reading Luther's Preface to the Epistle to the Romans.⁷⁶ About a quarter before nine, while he

---

ᶠ 2 Pet. 1:4.

---

⁷² Orig., κοινοινοι.
⁷³ Mark 12:34.
⁷⁴ Ps. 130:1-4, 7-8 (BCP).
⁷⁵ Moravian sources (extensively quoted in Curnock, I.475n.) suggest that this was a society which met weekly in Nettleton Court, Aldersgate Street. Among its members was James Hutton; Whitefield had ministered there in 1737; and Peter Böhler formed them into bands. The Wesley brothers were staying at different addresses nearby at the time. The reader is thought to be William Holland (died 1761) a devout Anglican who now introduced the Wesley brothers to Luther's commentaries on Galatians and Romans. He was a founding member of the Fetter Lane Society, and on its division in 1740 threw in his lot with the Moravians. He became one of their leading officers and preachers, succeeding Viney in charge of the Moravian settlement at Fulneck, Yorkshire. Holland had been induced by the Brethren to give up a substantial painting concern for their activities, but wishing to keep a closer Anglican connection than they wished, he first returned to business and then left them in 1747. Benham, *Hutton*, pp. 89, 153; JWJ, Nov. 28, 1747.
⁷⁶ This work, which had already been instrumental in the conversion of the elder Francke, was *A Methodicall Preface prefixed before the Epistle of S. Paule to the Romanes, very necessary and profitable for the better understanding of it. Made by the right reverend father and faithfull servant of Christ Jesus, Martin Luther, now newly translated out of Latin into English by W[illiam] W[ilkinson]* (London [1594]), and subsequently reprinted). Here Luther explains that 'those remnants of sinne are not layde to our charge, by reason of fayth which

was describing the change which God works in the heart through faith in Christ, I felt my heart strangely warmed. I felt I did trust in Christ, Christ alone for salvation, and an assurance was given me that he had taken away *my* sins, even *mine*, and saved *me* from the
5 law of sin and death.[77]

15. I began to pray with all my might for those who had in a more especial manner despitefully used me and persecuted me.[78] I then testified openly to all there what I now first felt in my heart. But it was not long before the enemy suggested, 'This cannot be
10 faith; for where is thy joy?' Then was I taught that *peace and victory over sin are essential to faith in the Captain of our salvation;*[79] *but that as to the transports of joy* that usually attend the beginning of it, especially in those who have mourned deeply, *God sometimes giveth, sometimes withholdeth them, according to the counsels of his own*
15 *will.*[80]

16. After my return home I was much buffeted with temptations; but cried out, and they fled away. They returned again and again. I as often lifted up my eyes, and he 'sent me help from his holy place'.[81] And herein I found the difference between
20 this and my former state chiefly consisted. I was striving, yea fighting with all my might under the law, as well as under grace. But then I was sometimes, if not often, conquered; now, I was always conqueror.

17. Thursday, May 25. The moment I awaked, 'Jesus,[82]
25 Master,' was in my heart and in my mouth; and I found all my strength lay in keeping my eye fixed upon him, and my soul waiting on him continually. Being again in St. Paul's in the afternoon, I could taste the good word of God in the anthem, which began, 'My song shall be always of the loving-kindness of
30 the Lord: with my mouth will I ever be showing forth thy truth from one generation to another.'[83] Yet the enemy injected a fear,

continually wrastleth with the desires of the fleishe . . . not to be under the lawe is this, that out harts are to be made newe by the spirit, through fayth, that freely, willingly, and of our owne accorde, we may doo that which the lawe requires, though there were no law at all' (cf. J. T. McNeill, 'Luther at Aldersgate', *London Quarterly & Holborn Review* [1939], 164:200-217). Luther's original preface, not to be confused with his commentary on Romans, is to be found in *Luthers Werke* (Weimar Ausgabe), *Deutsche Bibel*, VII.2-27 (1931).

[77] See Rom. 8:2.
[78] See Matt. 5:44.   [79] See Heb. 2:10.
[80] See Eph. 1:11 (1740 omitted 'own').
[81] Cf. Pss. 20:2; 24:3; Heb. 9:12.
[82] 1740, 'Jesu', probably a printer's error.   [83] Ps. 89:1 (BCP).

'If thou dost believe, why is there not a more sensible change?' I answered (yet not I), 'That I know not. But this I know, I have *now peace with God*,[84] and *I sin not today*, and Jesus my Master has forbid me to take thought for the morrow.'[85]

18. 'But is not *any* sort of *fear*', continued the tempter, 'a proof that thou dost not believe?' I desired my Master to answer for me, and opened his book upon those words of St. Paul, 'Without were fightings, within were fears.'[86] Then inferred I, well may fears be within *me;* but I must go on, and tread them under my feet.[87]

Friday, May 26. My soul continued in peace, but yet in heaviness, because of manifold temptations. I asked Mr. Töltschig[88] the Moravian what to do. He said, You must not fight with them as you did before, but flee from them the moment they appear, and take shelter in the wounds of Jesus. The same I learned also from the afternoon anthem, which was, 'My soul truly waiteth still upon God; for of him cometh my salvation. He verily is my strength and my salvation; he is my defence, so that I shall not greatly fall. [. . .] O put your trust in him always, ye people; pour out your hearts before him, for God is our hope.'[89]

Sat. 27. Believing one reason of my want of joy was want of time for prayer, I resolved to do no business till I went to church in the morning, but to continue pouring out my heart before him. And this day my spirit was enlarged; so that though I was now also assaulted by many temptations, I was more than conqueror,

[84] See Rom. 5:1.
[85] See Matt. 6:34.
[86] 2 Cor. 7:5.
[87] This aspect of his conversion JW expounded at length in a letter to his older brother Samuel, Oct. 30, 1738 (*Letters*, 25:575-78), and in verse published jointly by him and his brother Charles:

> I wrestle not now, But trample on sin,
> For with me art thou, And shalt be within,
> Whilst stronger and stronger In Jesus's power,
> I go on to conquer, Till sin is no more.

Hymns and Sacred Poems (1742), p. 120; cf. *A Collection of Hymns* (1780), 7:322 in this edn.
[88] Johann Töltschig (1703–64), one of the original founders of the Brethren community at Herrnhut. The son of a Moravian property-owner hostile to the revival, he was converted in 1723 by Christian David, and went to Herrnhut with the Nitschmanns, 1724. After a period of manual work he was sent with David Nitschmann to Holland and England to advocate the cause of the Brethren with the influential. He was overseer to the Brethren in Georgia, 1734–38. From 1739 he was occupied in founding and supervising Moravian communities in England and Ireland. JW normally, as here, spelled his name 'Telchig'.
[89] Ps. 62:1-2, 8 (BCP).

gaining more power thereby to trust and to rejoice in God my Saviour.

Sun. 28. I waked in peace, but not in joy. In the same even quiet state I was till the evening, when I was roughly attacked in a large 5 company as an enthusiast, a seducer, and a setter-forth of new doctrines.[90] By the blessing of God I was not moved to anger, but after a calm and short reply went away, though not with so tender a concern as was due to those who were seeking death in the error of their life.[91]

10 This day I preached in the morning at St. George's, Bloomsbury, on 'This is the victory that overcometh the world,

---

[90] This episode is described in a letter from Mrs. E. Hutton to Samuel Wesley, June 6, 1738, she having offered hospitality in her house to the Wesleys' meetings after Samuel Wesley, who had been entertaining them, left town: '. . . your brother John seems to be turned a wild enthusiast, or fanatic, and, to our very great affliction, is drawing our two children into these wild notions, by their great opinion of Mr. John's sanctity and judgment. It would be a great charity to many other honest well-meaning simple souls, as well as to my children, if you could either confine, or convert, Mr. John when he is with you. For after his behaviour on Sunday the 28th May, when you hear it, you will think him not quite a right man.

'Without ever acquainting Mr. Hutton with any of his notions or designs, when Mr. Hutton had ended a sermon of Bishop Blackall's, which he had been reading in his study to a great number of people; Mr. John got up, and told the people that five days before he was not a Christian, and this he was as well assured of as that five days before he was not in that room, and the way for them all to be Christians was to believe, and own, that they were not now Christians. Mr. Hutton was much surprised at this unexpected injudicious speech, but only said, "Have a care, Mr. Wesley, how you despise the benefits received by the two sacraments." I not being in the study when this speech was made, had heard nothing of it when he came into the parlour to supper, where were my two children, two or three other of his deluded followers, two or three ladies who board with me, my niece, and two or three gentlemen of Mr. John's acquaintance, though not got into his new notions.

'He made the same wild speech again, to which I made answer, if you was not a Christian ever since I knew you, you was a great hypocrite, for you made us all believe you was one. He said, when we had renounced everything but faith, and then got into Christ, then, and not till then, had we any reason to believe we were Christians; and when we had so got Christ, we might keep him, and so be kept from sin. Mr. Hutton said, "If faith only was necessary to save us, why did our Lord give us that divine sermon?" Mr. John said, that was *the letter that killeth.* "Hold", says Mr. Hutton, "you seem to know not what you say. Are our Lord's words the letter that killeth?" Mr. John said, "If we had no faith". Mr. Hutton replied, "I did not ask you how we should receive it. But why our Lord gave it; as also the account of the judgment in the twenty-fifth of St. Matthew, if works are not what he expects, but faith only?"

'Now it is a most melancholy thing to have not only our children, but many others, to disregard all teaching, but by such a spirit as comes to some in dreams, to others in such visions as will surprise you to hear of. If there cannot be some stop put to this, and he can be taught true humility, the mischief he will do wherever he goes among the ignorant, but well-meaning Christians, will be very great. . . .' Priestley, *Original Letters,* pp. 68-70; reprinted in Benham, *Hutton,* pp. 34-35.

[91] See Wisd. 1:12.

even our faith',[92] and in the afternoon at the chapel in Long Acre, on God's justifying the ungodly—the last time (I understand) I am to preach at either. 'Not as I will, but as thou wilt'![93]

Mon. 29. I set out for Dummer with Mr. Wolf,[94] one of the first-fruits of Peter Böhler's ministry in England. I was much 5 strengthened by the grace of God in him: yet was his state so far above mine that I was often tempted to doubt whether we had one faith. But, without much reasoning about it, I held here: 'Though his be *strong* and mine *weak*, yet that God hath given *some degree* of faith even to me I know by its fruits. For I have *constant peace*, not 10 one uneasy thought. And I have *freedom from sin*, not one unholy desire.'

Yet on Wednesday did I grieve the Spirit of God, not only by not 'watching unto prayer',[95] but likewise by speaking with sharpness instead of tender love, of one that was not sound in the 15 faith. Immediately God hid his face and I was troubled; and in this heaviness I continued till the next morning, June 1, when it pleased God, while I was exhorting another, to give comfort to *my* soul, and (after I had spent some time in prayer) to direct me to those gracious words, 'Having therefore boldness to enter into 20 the holiest by the blood of Jesus, . . . let us draw near with a true heart in full assurance of faith.[. . .] Let us hold fast the profession of our faith without wavering (for he is faithful that promised), and let us consider one another, to provoke unto love and to good works.'[96]   25

Saturday, June 3. I was so strongly assaulted by one of my old enemies that I had scarce strength to open my lips, or even to look up for help. But after I had prayed, faintly, as I could, the temptation vanished away.

Sunday 4 was indeed a feast day. For from the time of my rising 30 till past one in the afternoon I was praying, reading the Scriptures, singing praise, or calling sinners to repentance. All these days I

[92] 1 John 5:4. St. George's, Bloomsbury (1730–31) was a porticoed Hawksmoor church, done in the general style of St. George's, Hanover Square (1721–24). Pevsner, *London*, 1:449; Blatch, *London's Churches*, p. 263.

[93] Matt. 26:39.

[94] 'A poor, simple barber', who appears as Shepherd Wolfe in the Moravian lists; he signed Hutton's letter to Zinzendorf requesting the stationing of Peter Böhler in England, May 2, 1738 (Benham, *Hutton*, pp. 33, 39), and was expelled from JW's Society for disowning the Church of England, June 13, 1739 (CWJ, I.153).

[95] Cf. 1 Pet. 4:7.

[96] Heb. 10:19, 22-24.

scarce remember to have opened the Testament but upon some great and precious promise. And I saw more than ever that the gospel is in truth but one great promise, from the beginning of it to the end.

5   Tue. 6. I had still more comfort, and peace, and joy; on which I fear I began to presume. For in the evening I received a letter from Oxford which threw me into much perplexity. It was asserted therein that no doubting could consist with the least degree of true faith; that whoever at any time felt any doubt or fear

10 was not *weak in faith*, but had *no faith* at all; and that none hath any faith till the law of the Spirit of life has made him *wholly* free from the law of sin and death.

Begging of God to direct me, I opened my Testament on 1 Cor. 3, verse 1, etc., where St. Paul speaks of those whom he

15 terms 'babes in Christ', who were 'not able to bear strong meat', nay (in a sense) 'carnal';[97] to whom nevertheless he says, 'Ye are God's building,'[98] 'Ye are the temple of God.'[99] Surely, then these men had *some degree* of faith, though it is plain their faith was but *weak*.

20 After some hours spent in the Scripture and prayer I was much comforted. Yet I felt a kind of soreness in my heart, so that I found my wound was not fully healed. O God, save thou me, and all that are 'weak in the faith', from 'doubtful disputations'![1]

Wednesday, June 7. I determined, if God should permit, to

25 retire for a short time into Germany. I had fully purposed before I left Georgia so to do, if it should please God to bring me back to Europe. And I now clearly saw the time was come. My weak mind could not bear to be thus sawn asunder. And I hoped the conversing with those holy men who were themselves living

30 witnesses of the full power of faith, and yet able to bear with those that are weak, would be a means, under God, of so stablishing my soul, that I might 'go on from faith to faith, and from strength to strength'.[2]

Thur. 8. I went to Salisbury to take leave of my mother.[3] The

35 next day I left Sarum, and on Saturday came to Stanton Harcourt.

---

[97] Cf. 1 Cor. 3:1-3.   [98] 1 Cor. 3:9.
[99] 1 Cor. 3:16.   [1] Rom. 14:1.
[2] Cf. Ps. 84:7; Rom. 1:17.

[3] JW read to his mother the statement of his religious experience given above under May 24. How this same document was used by his critics to distress her is related below, June 13, 1739. Cf. J. Nichols, *Literary Anecdotes of the Eighteenth Century*, 9 vols. (London, 1812–15), V. 220, 233, 240, 242.

Having preached faith in Christ there on Sunday 11, I went on to Oxford;[4] and thence on Monday to London, where I found Mr. Ingham just setting out. We went on board the next day, Tuesday 13, and fell down to Gravesend that night. About four in the afternoon on Wednesday we lost sight of England. We reached 5 the Maas[5] at eight on Thursday morning, and in an hour and a half landed at Rotterdam.

We were eight in all, five English and three Germans.[6] Dr. Koker,[7] a physician of Rotterdam, was so kind when we set forward in the afternoon as to walk an hour with us on our way. I 10 never before saw any such road as this. For many miles together it is raised for some yards above the level, and paved with a small sort of brick, as smooth and clean as the mall at St. James's. The walnut trees stand in even rows on either side, so that no walk in a gentleman's garden is pleasanter. About seven we came to 15 Gouda,[8] where we were a little surprised at meeting with a treatment which is not heard of in England. Several inns utterly refused to entertain us, so that it was with difficulty we at last found one where they did us the favour to take our money for some meat and drink, and the use of two or three bad beds. They 20 pressed us much in the morning to see their church, but were displeased at our pulling off our hats when we went in, telling us we must not do so; it was not the custom there. It is a large old building, of the Gothic kind, resembling some of our English cathedrals. There is much history-painting in the windows, 25

---

[4] JW preached the same sermon at St. Mary's in the afternoon as he had preached at Gambold's church in the morning, the famous sermon *Salvation by Faith*, which he subsequently placed as No. 1 in the collected *Sermons* (1746), dated incorrectly as June 18.

[5] Orig., 'Maese'.

[6] In addition to Wesley and Benjamin Ingham, the Englishmen apparently comprised John Browne (see July 19), John Holmes, tailor (died 1780), Richard Viney, tailor, and the Germans Johann Töltschig, Gottlob Hauptmann (see July 19), and one other.

[7] Johannes de Koker (1696–1752) a Mennonite and Rotterdam doctor who obtained his medical qualification under Boerhaven. A leading member of the Rotterdam Collegiants, he stressed their central tenets of love and tolerance. Belonging to their pietistic rather than their rational wing, he brought the Moravians to Rotterdam, but ultimately concluded that certain aspects of their movement were in conflict with 'the plain gospel', and that one authoritarian utterance of Zinzendorf was 'no language for a humble child of Jesus'. But he also thought that the professions of tolerance in JW's *The Character of a Methodist* (1742; which he read with great interest)—'as to all opinions which do not strike at the root of Christianity, we think and let think'—were not tolerant enough. Koker kept up a correspondence with JW till at least 1749 (see JWJ, Nov. 10, 1749), and was probably but not quite certainly the translator of some of his tracts into Dutch (J. van den Berg, 'Wesley's Contacten', pp. 48-61 *passim*).

[8] Orig., 'Goudart'.

which, they told us, is greatly admired. About eight we left
Gouda, and in a little more than six hours reached Ijsselstein.[9]
Here we were at Baron Watteville's,[10] as at home. We found
with him a few German brethren and sisters, and seven or eight of
5 our English acquaintance, who had settled here some time
before. They lodged just without the town, in three or four little
houses, till one should be built that would contain them all.
Saturday 17 was their intercession day.[11] In the morning some of
our English brethren desired me to administer the Lord's
10 Supper. The rest of the day we spent with all the brethren and
sisters, in hearing the wonderful work which God is beginning to
work over all the earth, in making our requests known unto him,
and giving him thanks for the mightiness of his kingdom.

At six in the morning we took boat. The beautiful gardens lie
15 on both sides of the river for great part of the way to Amsterdam,
whither we came about five in the evening. The exact neatness of
all the buildings here, the nice cleanness of the streets (which we
were informed, were all washed twice a week), and the canals
which run through all the main streets, with rows of trees on
20 either side, make this the pleasantest city which I have ever seen.
Here we were entertained with truly Christian hospitality by Mr.
Deknatel,[12] a minister of the Mennonists, who suffered us to want

[9] Orig., 'Ysselstein'.

[10] Friedrich, Baron Watteville (1700–77), born at Bern, son of a father who left the
Swiss republic because of his pietistic views. He was educated at Halle where he met his
contemporary Zinzendorf, one of whose most trusted friends and business advisers he
became from his student days on. He received Moravian refugees at Herrnhut and
persuaded Zinzendorf to establish the settlement there. He took a leading part in the
revival at Herrnhut and also in the establishment of the Moravian community at
Heerendyk near Ijsselstein. He became a Moravian bishop 1743, presided over the
Moravian Reformed tropus in the same year, and had general charge of the reformed wing
of the movement (See Johannes Grosse, *Studien über Friedrich von Watteville* [Halle,
1914]). In 1744 Watteville adopted Johann Michael Langguth as his son, in the following
year obtaining an imperial diploma confirming the adoption and providing for the son to
enter into the dignity of Watteville. It was this John, Baron Watteville, who in 1746
married Benigna, Countess of Zinzendorf, daughter of the Moravian leader, and with
Leonard Dober took charge of the Lutheran side of the work. Wesley's itinerary in the
Netherlands and Germany (as at home) was substantially influenced by the availability of
hospitality, the hosts being Moravians or their connections.

[11] At Heerendyk and other Moravian settlements an order of Intercessors offered
prayer and thanksgiving in turn during twenty-four hours, meeting weekly to learn the
needs of the congregation.

[12] Orig., 'Decknatel'. Johannes Deknatel (1698–1759), a leading Mennonite minister
in Amsterdam, who brought about an evangelical revival among a religious community
tending to unitarianism and was actively concerned to bring about a union among the
scattered Baptists of Hungary. He gave financial assistance to the Moravians, but

nothing while we stayed here, which was till the Thursday
following. Dr. Barkhausen[13] (a physician, a Muscovite[14] by nation)
who had been with Mr. Deknatel for some time, showed us
likewise all possible kindness. 'Remember them, O Lord, for
good!'[15]   5

Mon. 19. I was at one of the societies, which lasted an hour and
an half. About sixty persons were present. The singing was in
Low Dutch (Mr. Deknatel having translated into Low Dutch part
of the Herrnhut Hymn-book),[16] but the words were so very near
the German that any who understood the original might   10
understand the translation. The expounding was in High Dutch.
I was at another of the societies on Tuesday, where were present
about the same number. On Wednesday one of our company
found a sheep that had been lost—his sister, who had lived here
for some time with one whom she loved too well, as he did her.   15
But they were now both resolved, by the grace of God (which they
accordingly executed without delay), 'to pluck out the right eye,
and cast it from them'.[17]

Thurs. 22. We took boat at eight in the evening, and landing at
four in the morning, walked on to Jutphaas,[18] which we left about   20
two, having now another boy added to our number. A little before
eight we came to Buren,[19] a small, ill-built city, belonging to the
Prince of Orange. Setting out early in the morning we came to
Nijmegen,[20] the last town in Holland, about two in the afternoon;
and leaving it at four, came before eight to an inn two hours short   25
of Kleve.[21]

Sun. 25. After spending an hour in singing and prayer, we

ultimately instituted lawsuits against them. His portrait is preserved in the Archiv der
Brüder-Unität at Herrnhut (hereafter 'Herrnhut Archiv').

[13] Otto Barkhausen probably had no doctor's degree. He came with Zinzendorf to
Holland in Dec. 1736, and became tutor to Deknatel's children. He became one of the
first 'assistants' of the Amsterdam Moravian congregation, 1738. There is correspondence from him in Herrnhut Archiv, MSS R.10.Aa.11.35-46.

[14] Muscovy, Muscovite (from Moscow) were frequently used from Shakespeare's day
for Russia, Russian (see *OED*). Cf. *A Farther Appeal*, III.31: 'They no more pretended to
belong to the Church of England than to the Church of Muscovy' (11:313 in this edn.).

[15] Cf. Neh. 13:31.

[16] *Das Gesangbuch der Gemeine in Herrnhuth* (1735) from which JW had translated four
hymns in Georgia. Henry Bett, 'The Earliest Methodist Hymns and Tunes', *Wesleyan
Methodist Magazine* (1910), 133:452-56.

[17] Cf. Matt. 5:29.

[18] Orig., 'Uutfass'.

[19] Orig., 'Beurn'.

[20] Orig., 'Nimwegen'.

[21] Orig., 'Cleve'.

walked till near noon before we could meet with any refreshment.
The road would have appeared exceeding pleasant, being broad
and straight, with tall trees on either side, had not weariness and
rain prevented. We hoped to reach Rheinberg[22] in the evening,
5 but could not; being obliged to stop two hours short of it, at a little
house where many good Lutherans were concluding the Lord's
day (as is usual among them) with fiddling and dancing!

Mon. 26. We breakfasted at Rheinberg, left it at half an hour
past ten, and at four came to Urdingen.[23] Being much tired, we
10 rested here, so that it was near ten at night before we came to
Neuss.[24] Having but a few hours' walk from hence to Cologne,[25]
we went thither easily, and came at five the next evening into the
ugliest, dirtiest city I ever yet saw with my eyes.

Wed. 28. We went to the cathedral, which is mere heaps upon
15 heaps; a huge, misshapen thing, which has no more of symmetry
than of neatness belonging to it. I was a little surprised to observe
that neither in this, nor in any other of the Romish churches
where I have been, is there properly speaking any such thing as
joint worship; but one prays at one shrine or altar, and another at
20 another, without any regard to or communication with one
another. As we came out of the church a procession began on the
other side of the churchyard. One of our company scrupling to
pull off his hat, a zealous Catholic presently cried out, 'Knock
down the Lutheran dog.' But we prevented any contest by retiring
25 into the church.

Walking on the side of the Rhine in the afternoon, I saw, to my
great surprise (for I have always thought, before, no Romanist of
any fashion believed anything of the story), a fresh painting, done
last year at the public expense, on the outside of the city wall, 'in
30 memory of the bringing in the heads of the three kings',[26] says the
Latin inscription, 'through the gate adjoining'; which indeed, in
reverence (it seems) to them, has been stopped up ever since.

At four we took boat, when I could not but observe the decency
of the Papists above us who are called 'Reformed'. As soon as ever
35 we were seated (and so every morning after) they all pulled off

[22] Orig., 'Reinberg'.
[23] Orig., 'Urding'.
[24] Orig., 'Neus'.
[25] Orig., 'Cölen', representing the German 'Köln'.
[26] Curnock notes (II.9, n.1) that these skulls are shown in the cathedral on rare occasions.

their hats, and each used by himself a short prayer for our prosperous journey. And this justice I must do to the very boatmen (who upon the Rhine are generally wicked even to a proverb): I never heard one of them take the name of God in vain, or saw anyone laugh when anything of religion was mentioned. So that I believe the glory of *sporting with sacred things* is peculiar to the English nation!

We were four nights on the water, by reason of the swiftness of the stream, up which the boat was drawn by horses. The high mountains on each side of the river, rising almost perpendicular, and yet covered with vines to the very top, gave us many agreeable prospects; a religious house, or old castle, every now and then appearing on the brow of one of them. On Sunday evening, July 2, we came to Mainz;[27] and Monday the 3rd, at half an hour past ten, to Frankfurt.[28]

Faint and weary as we were, we could have no admittance here, having brought no passes with us, which indeed we never imagined would have been required in a time of settled general peace. After waiting an hour at the gates we procured a messenger, whom we sent to Mr. Böhler[29] (Peter Böhler's father), who immediately came, procured us entrance into the city, and entertained us in the most friendly manner. We set out early in the morning on Tuesday the 4th, and about one came to Marienborn.[30] But I was so ill that after talking a little with Count Zinzendorf I was forced to lie down the rest of the day.

The family at Marienborn consists of about ninety persons, gathered out of many nations. They live for the present in a large house hired by the Count, which is capable of receiving a far greater number; but are building one, about three (English) miles off, on the top of a fruitful hill.[31] 'O how pleasant a thing it is for brethren to dwell together in unity!'[32]

---

[27] Orig., 'Mentz'.   [28] Orig., 'Frankfort', as always with Wesley.

[29] Johann Konrad Böhler, a brewer, and a burgher of the city, who in 1736 became comptroller at the Corn-Office.

[30] Marienborn-bei-Büdingen was a large house some 25 miles from Frankfurt, rented from the Count of Ysenburg-Meerholz, to which Zinzendorf retreated when banished from his estates at Berthelsdorf in Saxony. Here he created educational charities for children and a settlement, known as the Pilgrim Congregation.

[31] This building when finished was called Herrnhaag. It was intended as a refuge for Brethren from Reformed territories and grew rapidly, becoming a place where many who worked in Moravian mission fields withdrew for a period, and others were trained and sent out.

[32] Cf. Ps. 133:1.

Thur. 6. The Count carried me with him to the Count of Solms,[33] where I observed with pleasure the German frugality. Three of the young Countesses (though grown up) were dressed in linen, the Count and his son in plain cloth. At dinner the next day a glass of wine and a glass of water were set by everyone, and if either was emptied, a second. They all conversed freely and unaffectedly. At ten at night we took coach again, and in the morning reached Marienborn.

I lodged with one of the brethren at Eckershausen, an English mile from Marienborn, where I usually spent the day, chiefly in conversing with those who could speak either Latin or English; not being able (for want of more practice) to speak German readily. And here I continually met with what I sought for, viz., living proofs of the power of faith: persons 'saved from *inward as well as outward* sin',[34] by 'the love of God shed abroad in their hearts';[35] and from all doubt and fear by the abiding 'witness of the Holy Ghost given unto them'.[36]

Sun. 9. The Count preached in the old castle at Ronneburg[37] (about three English miles from Marienborn), where is also a small company of those who seek the Lord Jesus in sincerity. Wednesday 12, was one of the conferences for strangers; where one of Frankfurt proposing the question, Can a man be justified, and not know it?, the Count spoke largely[38] upon it, to this effect:

---

[33] There were about this time eight Counts of Solms (*The Present State of Germany* [London, 1738], II.35), with whom the connection of the Zinzendorf family was one of friendship before it was sealed by marriage and was central to the pietist interest among the imperial counts. Zinzendorf's grandmother, Henrietta Catherine, had been an intimate friend of Benigna, the widowed Countess of Solms-Laubach in Wildenfels, who had been born Countess of Promnitz, the celebrated pietist family of Sorau. She was the grandmother of Erdmuthe Dorothea who became Zinzendorf's wife. When Benigna (an intimate of Spener and described by him as an ornament of the church) died in 1702, Henrietta Catherine acted as mother towards her son, Friedrich Ernst, Count of Solms-Wildenfels. JW's correspondence (*Letters*, 25:557-58 in this edn.) shows that he visited Utphe, south of Wetzlar, the seat of Carl Otto, Count of Solms-Utphe (1673–1743), the second son of Benigna. He had enjoyed a brief diplomatic career in the early years of the century, partly in the service of Prussia. He was the most intimate friend of that pillar of South German pietism, Count Henry XXIV of Reuss, into whose family Zinzendorf married. Hans-Walter Erbe, *Zinzendorf und der fromme hohe Adel seiner Zeit* (Leipzig, 1928), pp. 144-50; F. W. Barthold, *Die Erweckten im protestantischen Deutschland* (Darmstadt, 1968; reprinted from Friedrich von Raumer, ed., *Historische Taschenbuch* [1852–53]), pp. 166-70.

[34] Cf. Matt. 1:21.

[35] Cf. Rom. 5:5.

[36] Cf. ibid.

[37] Orig., 'Runneberg'. This was a third property in the area taken over by Zinzendorf.

[38] 1774 errata, 'largely, and scripturally'.

1. Justification is the forgiveness of sins.
2. The moment a man flies to Christ he is justified.
3. And has peace with God, but not always joy.
4. Nor perhaps may he know he is justified till long after.
5. For the assurance of it is distinct from justification itself.[g]   5
6. But others may know he is justified by his power over sin, by his seriousness, his love of the brethren, and his 'hunger and thirst after righteousness',[39] *which alone proves the spiritual life to be begun.*
7. To be justified is the same thing as to be born of God.[h]
8. When a man is awakened, he is begotten of God; and his fear and sorrow   10 and sense of the wrath of God are the pangs of the new birth.

I then recollected what Peter Böhler had often said upon this head, which was to this effect:

1. When a man has living faith in Christ, then is he justified.
2. This is always given in a moment.   15
3. And in that moment he has peace with God.
4. Which he cannot have without knowing that he has it.
5. And being born of God, he sinneth not.[40]
6. Which deliverance from sin he cannot have without knowing that he has it.

Saturday 15 was the intercession day, when many strangers   20 were present from different parts. On Monday 17, having stayed here ten days longer than I intended (my first design being only to rest one or two days), I proposed setting out for Herrnhut; but Mr. Ingham desiring me to stay a little longer, I stayed till Wednesday 19, when Mr. Hauptmann[41] (a native of Dresden),   25

---

[g] 'Most true' [comment added by JW in his own copy of the 1774 edn.].

[h] (Not so) [added in text of 1774]; 'No: this is a mistake' [added as a footnote in 1775].

---

[39] Matt. 5:6.

[40] Cf. JW to Charles Wesley, July 7, 1738 (*Letters*, 25:557-58 in this edn.): 'The spirit of the Brethren is beyond our highest expectations. Young and old, they breathe nothing but faith and love, at all times and in all places. I do not therefore concern myself with smaller points, that touch not the essence of Christianity, but endeavour (God being my helper) to grow up in these, after the glorious examples set before me; having already seen with my own eyes more than one hundred witnesses of that everlasting truth, "Everyone that believeth hath peace with God, and is freed from sin, and is in Christ a new creature." See therefore, my brethren, that none of you receive the grace of God in vain!'

[41] See above, June 15, 1738, n. 6. Gottlob Hauptmann (1708–94) was born near Dresden, the son of a shoemaker, becoming himself a joiner by trade. He travelled in the course of business all over western Europe, and only encountered the Moravians in London in 1738. He caught up with JW and Browne in Mariendorf, reached Herrnhut on August 23, and joined the Unity in November. In 1741 he returned to London, and spent the rest of his life in the service of Moravian congregations in England, with one of which, Risley, Beds., he died. He was ordained deacon at Herrnhaag in 1747 (information from Herrnhut Archiv).

Mr. Browne,[42] and I set out together.

We breakfasted at Gelnhausen,[43] an old, unhandsome town,
dined at Anfenau[44] (where is a strange instance of moderation, a
church used every Sunday both by the Papists and the Lutherans
5 alternately and, notwithstanding some sharp showers of rain, in
the evening reached Steinau. Thursday 20 we dined at Bronzell,[45]
and passing through Fulda in the afternoon (where the Duke has
a pleasant palace), travelled through a delightful country of hills
and vales, and in the evening came to Rückers.[46] The next night
10 (after having had the most beautiful prospect which I think I ever
saw, from the top of a high hill, commanding a vast extent of
various land on every side) we, with some difficulty, and many
words, procured a poor accommodation at an inn in Marksuhl.[47]
Saturday 22, having passed through Eisenach in the morning, we
15 came through a more level open country to Saxe-Gotha in the
afternoon, a neat, pleasant city, in which the Prince's palace is
indeed a fine building. We stopped an hour here with a friendly
man, and in the evening came to Tüttleben;[48] and thence in the
morning to Erfurt, where we were kindly entertained by Mr.
20 Reinhardt,[49] to whom we were directed by some of the brethren at
Marienborn. In the afternoon we came to Weimar,[50] where we
had more difficulty to get through the city than is usual, even in
Germany, being not only detained a considerable time at the gate,
but also carried before I know not what great man (I believe the
25 Duke[51]) in the square; who, after many other questions, asked
what we were going so far as Herrnhut for. I answered, 'To see
the place where the Christians live.'[52] He looked hard, and let us
go.

[42] John Browne, woollen draper, born 1712; warden of the Fetter Lane congregation,
and later a member of the Yorkshire settlement and Moravian minister at Ballymena. He
signed Hutton's letter to Zinzendorf, May 2, 1738, requesting the appointment of Böhler
to London. Benham, *Hutton*, pp. 89, 97.

[43] Orig., 'Gehlenhausen'.   [44] Orig., 'Offenau'.
[45] Orig., 'Braunsal'.   [46] Orig., 'Rickhersch'.
[47] Orig., 'Marksul'.   [48] Orig., 'Ditleben'.

[49] Orig., 'Reinhart'. In view of the way this character is introduced, and of JW's
notorious casualness in reproducing foreign names, this is less likely to be the pietist
professor Tobias Jakob Reinharth (1684–1743), advocate at Erfurt from 1710 and rector
of the university, 1735–43, than one Reichard with whom Moravians often lodged in
Erfurt. See Herrnhut Archiv, MS R.21.A.112a.II:10.

[50] Orig., 'Weymar'.

[51] If this were the duke, it would be Wilhelm Ernst August, Duke of Weimar, 1728–49.

[52] The line, 'And show me where the Christians live', appeared in a hymn JW annexed
to the second edition of his *Earnest Appeal* (1743; see 11:91 in this edition), and like this
answer in the *Journal* may reflect JW's reading of Antoinette Bourignon in Georgia. She is

Mon. 24. We came early to Jena,[53] which lies at the bottom of several high, steep, barren hills. The students here are distinguished from the townsmen by their swords. They do not live together in colleges (nor indeed in any of the German universities) as we do in Oxford and Cambridge, but are scattered 5 up and down the town, in lodging- or boarding-houses. Those of them to whom we were recommended behaved as brethren indeed. O may brotherly kindness, and every good word and work, abound among them more and more!

At Jena the stone pillars begin, set up by the Elector of Saxony, 10 and marking out every quarter of a German mile to the end of his electorate. Every mile is a large pillar, with the names of the neighbouring towns, and their distances inscribed. It were much to be wished that the same care were taken in England, and indeed in all countries. 15

We left Jena early on Tuesday, reached Weissenfels[54] in the evening, and Merseburg[55] on Wednesday morning. Having a desire to see Halle (two German miles off) we set out after breakfast, and came thither at two in the afternoon. But we could not be admitted into the town when we came. The King of 20 Prussia's tall-men,[56] who kept the gates, sent us backward and forward, from one gate to another, for near two hours. I then thought of sending in a note to Professor Francke,[57] the son of that August Hermann Francke[58] whose name is indeed as

said, as a child, to have 'asked her parents "Where are the Christians? *Let us go to the country where the Christians live.*"' *Light of the World* (London, 1863), p. xvi.

[53] On the circumstances of the foundation of the university at Jena, see above, Feb. 9, 1736 (on Spangenberg's training there, n. 40). Offering a progressive science in a Christian framework, Jena had attained a new scholarly significance in the latter part of the previous century, and, being cheaper than Wittenberg and Leipzig, was the principal academic resort of the Protestant minorities of Silesia, Poland, Bohemia, and the Siebenburgen. Particularly in Silesia, Jena had helped to breed a liberal kind of pietism, not unlike that of JW himself. See Hildegard Zimmerman, *Caspar Neumann und die Entstehung der Frühaufklärung* (Witten, 1969), p. 33 *et passim*.

[54] Orig., 'Weizenfeltz'.   [55] Orig., 'Merseberg'.

[56] Frederick William I, King of Prussia, had a passion for recruiting *lange Kerle*, tall fellows, from all over Europe, not merely for the royal body-guard, the Potsdam grenadiers, but for other regiments as well.

[57] Gotthilf August Francke (1696–1769) succeeded to the leadership of his father's work at Halle and maintained it in a similar spirit, though failing state support under Frederick II heralded the decline of Hallesian pietism. A professor at the university from 1707, G. A. Francke was celebrated for his support of the growing Lutheran church in Pennsylvania and missions in India and the East Indies.

[58] August Hermann Francke (1663–1727), the most celebrated of the pietists of the second generation and creator of the famous institutions at Halle (see below, n. 61). He

precious ointment. O may I follow him, as he did Christ! And 'by manifestation of the truth commend myself to every man's conscience in the sight of God'![59]

He was not in town. However, we were at length admitted into the orphan-house, that amazing proof that 'all things are' still 'possible to him that believeth.'[60] There is now a large yearly revenue for its support, beside what is continually brought in by the printing-office, the books sold there, and the apothecary's shop, which is furnished with all sorts of medicines. The building reaches backward from the front in two wings, for, I believe, a hundred and fifty yards. The lodging chambers for the children, their dining-room, their chapel, and all the adjoining apartments, are so conveniently contrived, and so exactly clean, as I have never seen any before. Six hundred and fifty children (we were informed) are wholly maintained there, and three thousand (if I mistake not) taught. Surely such a thing neither we nor our fathers have known, as this great thing which God hath done here![61]

Thur. 27. We returned to Merseburg, and at five in the evening came to the gates of Leipzig. After we had sent in our pass, and waited an hour and an half, we were suffered to go to a bad inn in the town.

Fri. 28. We found out Mr. Marschall[62] and the other gentlemen

---

was a great organizer also of theological studies (he founded the first exegetical monthly), of the principles of pedagogy, and of the spiritual life. He sustained a correspondence and a published output even larger than that of Wesley and nourished hopes of world-wide social regeneration.

[59] Cf. 2 Cor. 4:2.   [60] Mark 9:23.

[61] JW's account reflects the prestige which the orphan-house gave to children's charities right through the evangelical world (not merely at Newcastle and Savannah). This huge establishment was the work not of faith only, but of extensive privileges granted by the Prussian government with a view to services to the state, and of large commercial operations. It was less a charity than the headquarters of Francke's campaign for universal social regeneration. The 'printing office' was not merely a large publishing concern intended to help finance the orphan-house, but an instrument of the pietist mission equipped with German, Latin, Greek, Hebrew, Syriac, Ethiopian, and Slavonic type. The 'apothecary's shop' had similar objects; based on a laboratory to test pharmaceutical prescriptions and alchemist recipes, it aimed to manufacture medical products for 'whole cities and provinces', and advertised its output in Latin, French, English, Dutch, and Greek. Francke's universal objects included not merely industry, but trade as well.

[62] Either Johann Ludwig von Marschall (1720–1800) or his brother Friedrich Wilhelm von Marschall (1721–1802), sons of the commandant of the Stolpen garrison, both of whom were studying at the University of Leipzig in 1738, and both of whom visited Herrnhut the same year. Friedrich Wilhelm entered the Moravian community in 1740 and had a distinguished career in it in Holland, England, and America. He was one of the constitutional committee formed to manage the community's affairs after the death of

of the university to whom we were directed. They were not wanting in any good office while we stayed, and in the afternoon went with us an hour forward in our journey.

After a pleasant walk on Saturday, on Sunday 30, about seven in the morning, we came to Meissen. In Meissen Castle the German chinaware is made, which is full as dear as that imported from the Indies; and as finely shaped, and beautifully coloured, as any I have ever seen. After breakfast we went to church. I was greatly surprised at all I saw there: at the costliness of apparel in many, and the gaudiness of it in more; at the huge fur caps worn by the women, of the same shape with a Turkish turban,[63] which generally had one or more ribbons[64] hanging down to a great length behind. The minister's habit was adorned with gold and scarlet, and a vast cross both behind and before. Most of the congregation sat (the men generally with their hats on, at the prayers as well as sermon) and all of them stayed during the Holy Communion, though but very few received. Alas, alas! What a *Reformed* country is this!

At two in the afternoon we came to Dresden, the chief city of Saxony. Here also we were carried for above two hours from one magistrate or officer to another, with the usual impertinent solemnity, before we were suffered to go to our inn. I greatly wonder that common sense and common humanity (for these doubtless subsist in Germany as well as England) do not put an end to this senseless, inhuman usage of strangers, which we met with at almost every German city, though more particularly at Frankfurt, Weimar, Halle, Leipzig, and Dresden. I know nothing that can reasonably be said in its defence in a time of full peace, being a shameful breach of all the common, even heathen laws of hospitality. If it be a custom, so much the worse; the more is the pity, and the more the shame.

In the evening we saw the palace the late Elector was building when God called him away.[65] The stonework he had very near

Zinzendorf. Johann Ludwig also entered the community in 1740 and, apart from brief visits to Germany and England (1743–44), served it exclusively in different parts of the Holy Roman Empire.

[63] Orig., 'turband'; apparently the most common of many contemporary spellings. Cf. JW's *Explanatory Notes upon the New Testament*, Rev. 9:7n.

[64] Orig., 'ribbands'.

[65] Frederick Augustus I, 'the Strong' (1670–1733), Elector of Saxony and King of Poland, who drained the resources of Saxony by his ambitions to claim the Polish crown and to lead a life of pleasure which involved expensive building programmes and art patronage.

finished, and some of the apartments within. It is a beautiful and magnificent design; but all is now swiftly running to ruin. The new church on the outside resembles a theatre. It is eight-square,[66] built of fine freestone.[67] We were desired also to
5 take notice of the great bridge, which joins the new with the old town; of the large brass crucifix upon it, generally admired for the workmanship; and the late King Augustus's statue on horseback, which is at a small distance from it. Alas! Where will all these things appear when 'the earth and the works thereof shall be
10 burned up'?[68]

Between five and six the next evening (having left Mr. Hauptmann with his relations in Dresden) we came to Neustadt, but could not procure any lodging in the city. After walking half an hour we came to another little town, and found a sort of an inn
15 there; but they told us plainly we should have no lodging with them, for they did not like our looks.

About eight we were received at a little house in another village, where God gave us sweet rest.

Tuesday, August 1. At three in the afternoon I came to
20 Herrnhut, about thirty English miles from Dresden. It lies in Upper Lusatia, on the border of Bohemia, and contains about an hundred houses, built on a rising ground, with evergreen woods on two sides, gardens and cornfields on the others, and high hills at a small distance. It has one long street, through which the great
25 road from Zittau to Löbau goes. Fronting the middle of this street is the orphan-house, in the lower part of which is the apothecary's shop, in the upper the chapel, capable of containing six or seven hundred people. Another row of houses runs at a small distance from either end of the orphan-house, which accordingly divides
30 the rest of the town (beside the long street) into two squares. At the east end of it is the Count's house,[69] a small, plain building, like the rest, having a large garden behind it, well laid out, not for show, but for the use of the community.

[66] I.e., octagonal, a form which JW came strongly to approve for churches. His normal word was 'octagon', for noun and adjective.

[67] The Frauenkirche, dedicated to the Virgin Mary, built 1726–43. This church, built as a court chapel in Italian style by an Italian architect and craftsmen, marked the conversion of the dynasty to Roman Catholicism to gain the Polish crown. No ordinary court chapel, it was the biggest church in Saxony and, restored after the aerial bombardment at the end of the Second World War, is now the Roman Catholic cathedral in Dresden.

[68] Cf. 2 Pet. 3:10.

[69] I.e., Zinzendorf. The house is now a rehabilitation centre for handicapped children.

We had a convenient lodging assigned us in the house appointed for strangers; and I had now abundant opportunity of observing whether what I had heard was enlarged by the relators, or was neither more nor less than the naked truth.

I rejoiced to find Mr. Hermsdorf[70] here, whom I had so often 5 conversed with in Georgia. And there was nothing in his power which he did not do to make our stay here useful and agreeable. About eight we went to the public service, at which they frequently use other instruments with their organ. They began (as usual) with singing. Then followed the expounding, closed by 10 a second hymn. Prayer followed this; and then a few verses of a third hymn, which concluded the service.

Wed. 2. At four in the afternoon was a love-feast of the married men, taking their food with gladness and singleness of heart, and with the voice of praise and thanksgiving. 15

Thursday 3 (and so every day at eleven), I was at the Bible conference, wherein Mr. Müller[71] (late master of a great school in Zittau till he left all to follow Christ) and several others read together, as usual, a portion of Scripture in the original. At five was the conference for strangers, when several questions 20 concerning justification were resolved. This evening Christian David[72] came hither. O may God make him a messenger of glad tidings.

On Friday and Saturday (and so every day in the following week) I had much conversation with the most experienced of the 25

---

[70] Johann Christian Adolf von Hermsdorf (1709–67), who accompanied the Herrnhuters to Georgia in 1735, sailing with JW on the *Simmonds*. Although closely associated with Zinzendorf and the Herrnhut community, he was not officially received into it until 1741. He became a devotee of what the Moravians called 'liturgical existence'. A MS account of his life preserved at Herrnhut is fully summarized by Schmidt, *Wesley*, I.284-85n.

[71] Gottfried Polycarp Müller (1684–1747), son of a pastor of Stolberg. He studied philosophy, theology, Greek, and oriental languages at Leipzig and Altdorf; he undertook cabbalistic studies in Holland, making contact with the French Protestant mystic, Pierre Poiret, and with revival circles in England (1706–8). Returning to Leipzig he attained distinction in a wide range of studies, seeking to free scholarship, especially in philosophy and politics, from its tutelage to Lutheran Orthodoxy. He became rector of the Gymnasium at Zittau, 1723. His contacts with Zinzendorf from 1729 brought him into conflict with the church and civic authorities. He resigned his rectorate in 1738. At the beginning the brethren distrusted his philosophy but elected him bishop in North America in Zinzendorf's place, 1740. He founded educational institutions in America and Germany.

[72] Christian David (1691–1751), carpenter, born Senftleben (Moravia), the most original of the early collaborators of Zinzendorf. Travelling in the course of his work, he was first a Roman Catholic, then, attempting to become a Jew, he underwent an

brethren concerning the great work which God had wrought in their souls, purifying them by faith; and with Martin Dober,[73] and the other teachers and elders of the church, concerning the discipline used therein.

5   Sun. 6. We went to church at Berthelsdorf,[74] a Lutheran village about an English mile from Herrnhut. Two large candles stood lighted upon the altar. The Last Supper was painted behind it; the pulpit was placed over it, and over that, a brass image of Christ on the cross.

10   The minister[75] had on a sort of pudding-sleeve gown, which covered him all round. At nine began a long voluntary on the organ, closed with a hymn, which was sung by all the people sitting (in which posture, as is the German custom, they sung all that followed). Then the minister walked up to the altar, bowed,
15 sung these Latin words, *Gloria in excelsis Deo,* bowed again, and went away. This was followed by another hymn, sung as before, to the organ, by all the people. Then the minister went to the altar again, bowed, sung a prayer, read the Epistle, and went away. After a third hymn was sung he went a third time to the altar, sung
20 a versicle (to which all the people sung a response), read the third chapter to the Romans, and went away. The people having then sung the Creed in rhyme, he came and read the Gospel, all

evangelical conversion at Görlitz, confirmed by the preaching of Steinmetz at Teschen. Restlessly returning to his native country as a revival preacher, he persuaded many descendants of the old Unity of the Brethren to emigrate. In 1722 he joined with Zinzendorf and helped created the first settlement at the Hutberg by Berthelsdorf. Later, not always with the agreement of the Brethren, he traversed Moravia, Germany, Livonia, Switzerland, Holland, Greenland, and America. For his autobiography, see below, JWJ, Aug. 1738.

[73] Martin Dober (1702–48), one of the earliest helpers at Herrnhut, much employed by the Brethren in diplomacy and theological advocacy. He opposed the views of Konrad Dippel and accompanied Zinzendorf to obtain a favourable opinion of the Brethren from the theological faculty at Tübingen, 1733. He was sent as a deputy to Holstein, 1736, and Sweden, 1741. Made a bishop at Herrnhaag, 1744.

[74] Orig., 'Bertholdsdorf'. Berthelsdorf was, and still is, the site of the parish church for Herrnhut.

[75] Johann Andreas Rothe (1688–1758) was early connected with pietistic circles in Görlitz, his native territory. In 1722 he was called by Zinzendorf to the living of Berthelsdorf, returning to Hermsdorf bei Görlitz, 1737. In his first decade at Berthelsdorf, he was actively engaged with Zinzendorf in the development of the community of the Brethren and the preparation of catechisms and hymn-books (among his own hymns being *Ich habe nun den Grund gefunden,* translated by JW as 'Now I have found the ground wherein'; see *A Collection of Hymns,* 7:308-9 in this edn.). He wrote a comprehensive exegetical appendix to the Ebersdorf Bible and was a revival preacher. Increasing disagreements with Zinzendorf and a turning to establishment views led him to break with the Brethren in 1737.

standing. Another hymn followed, which being ended the minister in the pulpit used a long extemporary prayer, and afterwards preached an hour and a quarter on a verse of the Gospel. Then he read a long intercession and general thanksgiving, which before twelve concluded the service.

After the evening service at Herrnhut was ended, all the unmarried men (as is their weekly custom) walked quite round the town, singing praise with instruments of music; and then on a small hill, at a little distance from it, casting themselves into a ring, joined in prayer. Thence they returned into the great square, and a little after eleven commended each other to God.

Tue. 8. A child was buried. The burying ground (called by them *Gottes Acker*, i.e. God's ground) lies a few hundred yards out of the town, under the side of a little wood. There are distinct squares in it for married men and unmarried; for married and unmarried women; for male and female children, and for widows. The corpse was carried from the chapel, the children walking first; next the 'orphan-father'[76] (so they call him who has the chief care of the orphan-house) with the minister of Berthelsdorf; then four children bearing the corpse, and after them, Martin Dober and the father of the child. Then followed the men, and last the women and girls. They all sung as they went. Being come into the square where the male children are buried, the men stood on two sides of it, the boys on the third, and the women and girls on the fourth. There they sung again; after which the minister used (I think, read) a short prayer, and concluded with that blessing, 'Unto God's gracious mercy and protection I commit you.'[77]

Seeing the father (a plain man, a tailor by trade) looking at the grave, I asked, 'How do you find yourself?' He said, 'Praised be the Lord, never better. He has taken the soul of my child to himself. I have seen, according to my desire, his body committed to holy ground. And I know that when it is raised again, both he and I shall be ever with the Lord.'

Several evenings this week I was with one or other of the private bands.[78] On Wednesday and Thursday I had an

---

[76] The German *Waisenvater* now means the director of an orphanage.

[77] Cf. Num. 6:24-26, and BCP, Visitation of the Sick, Commendation and Aaronic Blessing.

[78] Before going to Herrnhut, Wesley had come across Moravian bands and societies in England, founded by Peter Böhler, and had himself been a member of a band before his conversion experience. Moravian societies, like the ones Wesley would develop, were compulsory for members and embraced those of various stages of religious experience;

opportunity of talking with Michael Linner,[79] the eldest of the church, and largely with Christian David, who, under God, was the first planter of it.

5 Four times also I enjoyed the blessing of hearing him [i.e. Christian David] preach during the few days I spent here; and every time he chose the very subject which I should have desired had I spoken to him before. Thrice he described the state of those who are 'weak in faith',[80] who are justified, but have not yet a new, clean heart; who have received forgiveness through the blood of 10 Christ, but have not received the indwelling of the Holy Ghost. This state he explained once from, 'Blessed are the poor in spirit; for theirs is the kingdom of heaven';[81] when he showed at large from various Scriptures that many are children of God and heirs of the promises long before their hearts are softened by holy 15 *mourning,* before they are *comforted* by the abiding witness of the Spirit, melting their souls into all gentleness and *meekness;* and much more before they are renewed in all that *righteousness* which they 'hungered and thirsted'[82] after; before they are 'pure in heart'[83] from all self and sin, and *merciful* as their Father which is 20 in heaven is merciful.[84]

A second time he pointed out this state from those words, 'Who shall deliver me from the body of this death? I thank God, Jesus Christ our Lord.'[85] 'There is therefore now no condemnation to them which are in Christ Jesus.'[86] Hence also he at large both 25 proved the existence and showed the nature of that intermediate state which most experience between that bondage which is described in the seventh chapter of the Epistle to the Romans, and the full glorious liberty of the children of God described in the eighth and in many other parts of Scripture.

---

and the bands (like Wesley's) were voluntary associations of the converted for fellowship and mutual confession. But whereas Wesley's classes were mixed gatherings of members of local societies, Moravian classes were division of 'choirs' of the settlement at Herrnhut in which the members were already distinguished by age, sex, and marital status. J. E. Hutton, 'Methodist Bands: their Origin and Nature', *Wesleyan Methodist Magazine* (1911), 134:197-202.

[79] Michael Linner (1692–1760), brother of Martin Linner (see below, Aug. 1738, n. 24), a member of the communal court of justice at Herrnhut which had oversight of business and trade. He was born in Schönau (Moravia) and died in Herrnhut, though his death is not noticed in the church book.

[80] Rom. 4:19.
[81] Matt. 5:3.
[82] Cf. Matt. 5:6.
[83] Matt. 5:8.
[84] See Luke 6:36.
[85] Rom. 7:24-25.
[86] Rom. 8:1.

This he yet again explained from the Scriptures which describe
the state the apostles were in from our Lord's death (and indeed
for some time before) till the descent of the Holy Ghost at the day
of Pentecost. They were then 'clean,' as Christ himself had borne
them witness, 'by the word which he had spoken unto them'.[87] 5
They then *had faith*, otherwise he could not have prayed for them
that their 'faith might not fail'.[88] Yet they were not properly
converted; and they were not *delivered from* the spirit of fear; they
had not *new hearts;*[89] neither had they received 'the gift of the Holy
Ghost'.[90] 10

The fourth sermon which he preached, concerning the ground
of our faith, made such an impression upon me that when I went
home I could not but write down the substance of it, which was as
follows:

The word of reconciliation[91] which the apostles preached as the foundation of 15
all they taught was that 'we are reconciled to God, not by our own works, nor by
our own righteousness, but wholly and solely by the blood of Christ.'

But you will say, Must I not grieve and mourn for my sins? Must I not humble
myself before God? Is not this just and right? And must I not first do this before
I can expect God to be reconciled to me? I answer, It is just and right. You must 20
be humbled before God. You must have a broken and a contrite heart. But then
observe. This is not your own work. Do you grieve that you are a sinner? This is
the work of the Holy Ghost. Are you contrite? Are you humbled before God? Do
you indeed mourn, and is your heart broken within you? All this worketh the
selfsame Spirit. 25

Observe again, this is not the foundation. It is not this by which you are
justified. This is not the righteousness, this is no part of the righteousness by
which you are reconciled unto God. You grieve for your sins. You are deeply
humbled. Your heart is broken. Well. But all this is nothing to your justification.
The remission of your sins is not owing to this cause, either in whole or in part. 30
Your humiliation and contrition has no influence on that. It has no connection
with it. Nay, observe farther, that it *may* hinder your justification, that is, if you
build anything upon it, if you think, I must be *so or so* contrite. I must grieve *more*,
before I can be justified. Understand this well. To think you must be *more*
contrite, *more* humbled, *more* grieved, *more* sensible of the weight of sin, before 35
you can be justified; is to lay your contrition, your grief, your humiliation for the
foundation of your being justified—at least for a part of the foundation.
Therefore it hinders your justification; and a hindrance it is which must be
removed before you can lay the right foundation. The right foundation is, not

[87] Cf. John 15:3.
[88] Cf. Luke 22:32.
[89] 1765, 1774 (only) omitted 'they were . . . fear', reading, 'Yet they had not in the full
sense new hearts.'
[90] Acts 2:38.
[91] 2 Cor. 5:19.

your contrition (though that is not your *own*), not *your* righteousness, nothing of *your own;* nothing that is wrought *in you* by the Holy Ghost; but it is something *without* you, viz., the righteousness and the blood of Christ.

5 For this is the word: 'To him that believeth on God that justifieth the ungodly, his faith is counted for righteousness.'[92] See ye not that the foundation is nothing *in us?* There is no connection between God and the ungodly. There is no tie to unite them. They are altogether separate from each other. They have nothing in common. There is nothing less or more in the ungodly to join them to God. Works, righteousness, contrition? No. Ungodliness only. This then do, if
10 you will lay a right foundation. Go straight to Christ with all your ungodliness. Tell him, Thou, whose eyes are as a flame of fire searching my heart, seest that I am ungodly. I plead nothing else. I do not say I am humble or contrite; but I am ungodly. Therefore bring me to him that justifieth the ungodly. Let thy blood be the propitiation for me. For there is nothing in me but ungodliness.

15 Here is a mystery. Here the wise men of the world are lost, are taken in their own craftiness. This the learned of the world cannot comprehend. It is foolishness unto them: sin is the only thing which divides men from God. Sin (let him that heareth understand) is the only thing which unites them to God, i.e. the only thing which moves the Lamb of God to have compassion upon, and by
20 his blood to give them access to the Father.

This is 'the word of reconciliation'[93] which we preach. This is the foundation which never can be moved. By faith we are built upon this foundation. And this faith also is the gift of God. It is his free gift, which he now and ever giveth to everyone that is willing to receive it. And when they have received this gift of
25 God, then their hearts will melt for sorrow that they have offended him. But this gift of God lives in the heart, not the head. The faith of the head, learned from men or books, is nothing worth. It brings neither remission of sins nor peace with God. Labour then to believe with your whole heart. So shall you have redemption through the blood of Christ. So shall you be cleansed from all sin.
30 So shall ye go on from strength to strength, being renewed day by day in righteousness and all true holiness.

Saturday 12, was the intercession day, when many strangers were present, some of whom came twenty or thirty miles. I could gladly have spent my life here; but my Master calling me to labour
35 in another part of his vineyard, on Monday 14, I was constrained to take my leave of this happy place, Martin Dober and a few others of the brethren walking with us about an hour. O when shall THIS Christianity cover the earth, as the 'waters cover the sea'![94]

40 To hear in what manner 'God out of darkness commanded this light to shine'[95] must be agreeable to all those in every nation who

[92] Cf. Rom. 4:5.
[93] 2 Cor. 5:19.
[94] Isa. 11:9; Hab. 2:14.
[95] Cf. 2 Cor. 4:6.

can testify from their own experience, 'The gracious Lord hath so done his marvellous acts that they ought to be had in remembrance.'[96] I shall therefore here subjoin the substance of several conversations which I had at Herrnhut, chiefly on this subject. And may many be incited hereby to give praise 'unto him 5 that sitteth upon the throne, and unto the Lamb, for ever and ever'![97]

It was on August 10th (Old Style) that I had an opportunity of spending some hours with Christian David. He is a carpenter by trade, more than middle-aged, though I believe not fifty yet.[98] 10 Most of his words I understood well; if at any time I did not, one of the brethren who went with me explained them in Latin. The substance of what he spoke I immediately after wrote down, which was as follows:

When I was young I was much troubled at hearing some affirm that the Pope 15 was antichrist.[99] I read the Lutheran books writ against the Papists, and the popish books writ against the Lutherans. I easily saw that the Papists were in the wrong; but not that the Lutherans were in the right. I could not understand what they meant by being justified by faith, by faith alone, by faith without works. Neither did I like their talking so much of Christ. Then I began to think, How 20 can Christ be the Son of God? But the more I reasoned with myself upon it, the more confused I was, till at last I loathed the very name of Christ. I could not bear to mention it. I hated the sound of it; and would never willingly have either read or heard it. In this temper I left Moravia, and wandered through many countries, seeking rest, but finding none. 25

In these wanderings I fell among some Jews. Their objections against the New Testament threw me into fresh doubts. At last I set myself to read over the Old Testament, and see if the prophecies therein contained were fulfilled. I was soon convinced they were. And thus much I gained, a fixed belief that Jesus was the Christ. 30

But soon after a new doubt arose: Are the New Testament prophecies fulfilled? This I next set myself to examine. I read them carefully over, and could not but see every event answered the prediction; so that the more I compared the

---

[96] Cf. Ps. 111:4 (BCP).

[97] Rev. 5:13.

[98] He was in fact 47. The sheer space given by JW to Christian David's preaching and autobiography testifies to the impact which they made. David's personal struggle for religious and theological maturity had already had a great influence on the Moravian Brethren, encouraging them to hold together an objective emphasis upon the work of Christ with a pietistic sense of his indwelling. The texts which David now chose to expound dealt with issues all of which had preoccupied JW during the past six months. Schmidt concluded that it was this preaching which prepared JW for conversion and that he owed more to David than to anyone, Peter Böhler only excepted. Schmidt, *Wesley*, I.295-96.

[99] David was raised as a Roman Catholic (see above, Aug. 3, 1738, n. 72).

one with the other, the more fully I was convinced that 'all Scripture was given by inspiration of God.'[1]

Yet still my soul was not in peace. Nor indeed did I expect it till I should have openly renounced the errors of popery; which accordingly I did at Berlin. I now
5 also led a very strict life. I read much, and prayed much. I did all I could to conquer sin; yet it profited not; I was still conquered by it. Neither found I any more rest among the Lutherans than I did before among the Papists.

At length, not knowing what to do, I listed myself a soldier. Now I thought I should have more time to pray, and read, having with me a New Testament and
10 a hymn-book. But in one day both my books were stole. This almost broke my heart. Finding also in this way of life all the inconveniences which I thought to avoid by it, after six months I returned to my trade, and followed it two years. Removing then to Görlitz in Saxony, I fell into a dangerous illness. I could not stir hand nor foot for twenty weeks. Pastor Schwedler[2] came to me every day.
15 And from him it was that the gospel of Christ came first with power to my soul.

Here I found the peace I had long sought in vain; for I was assured *my* sins were forgiven. Not indeed all at once, but by degrees; not in one moment, nor in one hour. For I could not immediately believe that I *was* forgiven, because of the mistake I was then in concerning forgiveness. I saw not then that the first
20 promise to the children of God is, 'Sin shall no more reign over you'; but thought I was to *feel it in me* no more from the time it was forgiven. Therefore, although I had the mastery over it, yet I often feared it was not forgiven, because it still *stirred in me,* and at some times 'thrust sore at me that I might fall'.[3]

Because, though it did not *reign,* it did *remain* in me; and I was continually
25 *tempted,* though not *overcome.* This at that time threw me into many doubts; not understanding that the devil *tempts,* properly speaking, only those whom he perceives to be escaping from him. He need not tempt his own. For they 'lie in the wicked one'[4] (as St. John observes) and do his will with greediness. But those whom Christ is setting free he tempts day and night, to see if he can recover
30 them to his kingdom. Neither saw I then that the 'being justified' is widely different from the having the 'full assurance of faith'.[5] I remembered not that our Lord told his apostles before his death, 'Ye are clean';[6] whereas it was not till many days after it that they were fully assured, by the Holy Ghost then received, of their reconciliation to God through his blood. The difference between these
35 fruits of the Spirit was as yet hid from me; so that I was hardly and slowly convinced I had the one, because I had not the other.

[1] Cf. 2 Tim. 3:16.
[2] Orig., 'Sleder'. Johann Christian Schwedler (1672–1730), pastor at Niederwiesa, Upper Lusatia, on the Silesian frontier, 1701–30, a church erected to accommodate Silesian Protestants across the border, among whom he won an unrivalled reputation; he was a celebrated writer of spiritual lyrics, many of which were collected in books of devotion and the hymn-books of Löbau and Württemberg. By nature an eloquent peasant advocate of 'heart-religion', often preaching for eight or nine hours, he was educated at the gymnasium at Zittau and under Carpzov at Leipzig. From an early date he assisted Protestant refugees, including the first Moravians, frequently acting on behalf of Zinzendorf's grandmother.
[3] Ps. 118:13.
[4] Cf. 1 John 5:19.
[5] Cf. Rom. 3:24, etc.; Heb. 10:22.   [6] John 13:10.

When I was recovered from my illness I resolved to return into Moravia, and preach Christ to my relations there. Thence I came back to Görlitz, where I continued five years, and there was a great awakening both in the town and country round about. In this space I made two more journeys into Moravia, where more and more came to hear me, many of whom promised to come to me, wherever I was, when a door should be opened for them.

After my return from my third journey Count Zinzendorf sent to Görlitz, the minister of Berthelsdorf being dead, for Mr. Rothe, who was in a gentleman's family there, to be minister of that place. Mr. Rothe told him of me, and he writ to me to come to him. And when I came said, 'Let as many as will of your friends come hither; I will give them land to build on, and Christ will give the rest.' I went immediately into Moravia and told them God had now found out a place for us. Ten of them followed me then; ten more the next year; one more in my following journey. The Papists were now alarmed, set a price upon my head, and levelled the house I had lodged in, even with the ground. I made however eleven journeys thither in all, and conducted as many as desired it to this place, the way to which was now so well known that many more came of themselves.

Eighteen years ago we built the first house. We chose to be near the great road rather than at Berthelsdorf (for the Count gave us our choice), hoping we might thereby find opportunities of instructing some that travelled by us. In two years we were increased to a hundred and fifty, when I contracted an intimate acquaintance with a Calvinist, who after some time brought me over to his opinions touching election and reprobation;[7] and by me were most of our brethren likewise brought over to the same opinions. About this time we were in great straits, wherewith many were much dejected. I endeavoured to comfort them with the sense of God's love towards them. But they answered, 'Nay, it may be he hath no love toward us; it may be we are not of the election, but God hated us from eternity, and therefore he has suffered all these things to come upon us.' The Count, observing this, desired me to go to a neighbouring minister, Pastor Steinmetz,[8] and talk with him fully on that head, 'Whether Christ died for all.' I did so, and by him God fully convinced me of that important truth. And not long after the Count desired we might all meet

[7] Johann Georg Heitz, Zinzendorf's estate manager, who was Zürich Reformed by religious profession and who, after settling the Moravians at Herrnhut, left the Count's service because of religious disagreements. For a time Christian David also moved his house out of the village. H. C. Hahn and H. Reichel, eds., *Zinzendorf und die Herrnhuter Brüder* (Hamburg, 1977), pp. 63-67.

[8] Johann Adam Steinmetz (1689–1762), Silesian Lutheran pastor (and son of a pastor) in Töpliwoda (1717) and Teschen (1720), where his preaching had a powerful effect among Moravians, awakening (even among those few whose spiritual biographies were collected by JW) Christian David, Zacharias Neisser, and David Schneider. When he had to leave Teschen because of Jesuit opposition, Zinzendorf had him appointed pastor and superintendent at Neustadt/Aisch (1729). In 1732 he became General Superintendent of the duchy of Magdeburg and abbot of Klosterbergen, where he continued the educational work begun by Breithaupt on Hallesian lines. He kept in touch with Zinzendorf and helped him formulate his criticism of the Halle position. He maintained links between German and American pietism, and originated the pietistic Magdeburg hymn-book of 1738. He wrote an introduction to the German translation of Doddridge's *Family Expositor* (Biel, 1755).

together, and consider these things thoroughly. We met accordingly at his house, and parted not for three days. We opened the Scriptures, and considered the account which is given therein of the whole economy of God with man, from the creation to the consummation of all things. And by the blessing of God we
5 came all to one mind; particularly in that fundamental point that 'he willeth all men to be saved, and to come to the knowledge of his truth.'[9]

Sometime after the Jesuits told the Emperor that the Count was gathering together all the Moravians and Bohemians, forming them into one body, and making a new religion.[10] Commissioners were immediately sent to Herrnhut to
10 examine the truth of this. The substance of the final answer returned through them to the Emperor was as follows:

An Extract of the Public Instrument Signed at Herrnhut in August, 1629[11]

1. We believe the Church of the Bohemian and Moravian Brethren, from
15 whom we are descended, to have been a holy and undefiled Church, as is owned by Luther and all other Protestant divines, who own also that our doctrine agrees with theirs. But our discipline they have not.

2. But we do not rest on the holiness of our ancestors; it being our own continual care to show that we are passed from death unto life, by worshipping
20 God in spirit and in truth. Nor do we account any man a brother unless he has either preserved inviolate the covenant he made with God in baptism, or, if he has broken it, been born again of God.

3. On the other side, whosoever they are who being sprinkled by the blood of Christ are sanctified through faith, we receive them as brethren, although in
25 some points they may differ from us. Not that we can renounce or give up any doctrine of God contained in Holy Writ, the least part of which is dearer unto us than thousands of gold and silver.

3. Discipline we judge to be necessary in the highest degree for all those who have any knowledge of divine truth; and we can therefore in no wise forsake that
30 which we have received from our forefathers. Yet if it should ever be (which

---

[9] Cf. 1 Tim. 2:4.

[10] I.e., a religious body other than the Roman Catholic, Lutheran, or Reformed, for which toleration had been provided by the Peace of Westphalia (1648), or the Anabaptists who had acquired unofficial toleration in a few places. Hence the attempt in the documents which follow to establish the Moravians' continuity of life and doctrine with recognized religious bodies of the Empire. David's reference is to Carl Regent, *Unpartheyische Nachricht von der in Laussnitz überhand nehmenden . . . neuen Sect* (Breslau, 1729); reprint in *Nikolaus Ludwig von Zinzendorf: Materialien und Dokumente*, Reihe 2, Bd. 14 (1976).

[11] A much fuller extract of the notarial document signed at Herrnhut on Aug. 12, 1729, and further signed by Zinzendorf on Aug. 28, 1729, is given in the *Büdingische Sammlung einiger in die Kirchenhistorie einschlagender sonderlich neuerer Schrifften*, 3 vols. (Büdingen, 1742–45), I.3-23, and has a somewhat more negative tone than the brief excerpts here given by David. The document formed a sort of constitution for the settlement at Herrnhut, there being as yet no constitution of the Moravian Church. On the literary history of the reports here given by JW see above, Introduction, IV. n. 61.

God forbid) that any of us should speak or act perverse things, we could only say, with St. John, 'They went forth from us, but were not of us; for if they had been of us they would have continued with us.'[12]

4. The public worship of God at Berthelsdorf, which we have hitherto frequented, we are the less able now to forsake, because we have there an 5 assembly of true believers, a doctrine free from error, and a pastor who, 'having laboured much in the word, is worthy of double honour'.[13] Therefore we have no cause to form any congregation separate from this; especially seeing we both use that liberty which Christ hath purchased for us, and so often experience the power of the doctrine which is taught there, and agree with the evangelical 10 Protestants (i.e., Lutherans) in all truths of importance. As for the controverted points, which require a subtle wit, we either are ignorant of them, or despise them.

5. The name of brethren and sisters we do not reject, as being agreeable both to Scripture and to Christian simplicity. But we do not approve of being called 15 by the name of any man; as knowing, we 'have one Father, even him which is in heaven'.[14]

In 1732 we were again required to give an account of ourselves. This was then done in the manner following:

An Extract of the Letter wrote by the Church of Herrnhut 20
to the President of Upper Lusatia, 24 Jan., 1732[15]

1. None can be ignorant of the religion of our ancestors who have read the history of John Hus.[16] Some of his followers endeavoured to repel force by force. The rest, having better learned Christ, obtained leave of George Podibrad, King of Bohemia,[17] to retire and live apart. Retiring accordingly, in the year 25

---

[12] 1 John 2:19.   [13] Cf. 1 Tim. 5:17.
[14] Cf. Matt. 23:9.

[15] Complaints against the community at Herrnhut brought the Privy Council at Dresden to institute an inquiry under the governor of Görlitz, Zinzendorf's relative, Georg Ernst von Gersdorf. This and the previous document were among the material produced for his inspection.

[16] Orig., 'Huss'. John Hus (c. 1369–1415), born of a Bohemian peasant family, who in 1402 became rector of the University of Prague. Influenced by the doctrines of Wycliffe (whose *Trialogus* he translated into Czech), he called for reform. Temporarily aided by the existence of rival claimants to the papacy, Huss was excommunicated by John XXIII in 1411, took refuge with his supporters among the nobility, and appealed against the pope to a general council. Having left for the Council of Constance with a pledge of safe-conduct from the emperor, Hus was imprisoned and died at the stake. He became a national hero, and the schism he introduced into the nation was perpetuated by the Hussite wars. In 1920 the church in the new Czechoslovakia appealed to his tradition, much in the manner of the Moravians here.

[17] George of Poděbrady (1420–71), elected king of Bohemia, 1458, the last native Czech monarch, a man of great diplomatic and administrative skill. He exterminated the Taborites in 1452 and also persecuted the Brotherhood, which, however, obtained sufficient protection from the substantial classes of Bohemia and Moravia to increase to several hundred congregations by the end of the century.

1453, to a place on the borders of Silesia and Moravia, they lived in peace till the time of Luther and Calvin, with both of whom, as with their followers, they maintained a friendly intercourse; especially when, by the providence of God, they were placed among those of either opinion.

5   2. In the year 1699 Daniel Ernst Jablonski,[18] grandson to Amos Comenius,[19] the last bishop of the Moravians, was consecrated bishop of the United Brethren in Moravia, Bohemia, and Poland, in a synod regularly assembled. To him Count Zinzendorf signified that several of the Moravian brethren, having escaped from the tyranny of the Papists, were so joined to the Lutherans, whose
10 doctrine they approved, as nevertheless to retain their ancient discipline. His entire approbation of this Bishop Jablonski testified to the Count in several letters.

3. It must be acknowledged that many of our ancestors, about the beginning of the Reformation, from fear of man, did not openly confess the truth. And
15 hence it was that the Romish pastors bore with them; being little concerned what their private opinions were. But hence it also was that, continually using dissimulation, and not walking in simplicity, they were no longer fervent in spirit, as of old time, neither could they find any peace to their souls.

4. It was in the year 1715 that a soldier of the Emperor's, lately discharged,[20]
20 came to Schleu,[21] a village of which the Jesuits are lords, and began to talk with Augustin Neisser and his brother.[22] He sharply reproved their hypocrisy in

[18] Orig., 'David Ernest Jablonsky'. Daniel Ernst Jablonski (1660–1741) was born near Danzig to a family of refugee Brethren and educated at the gymnasium at Lissa (Poland) and the University of Frankfurt-on-Oder, also visiting Dutch and English universities. He became pastor of the reformed congregation at Magdeburg (*c.* 1680), before returning to a pastoral charge and the rectorate of a school at Lissa, the main centre of the Brethren in Poland. In 1691 he became a court chaplain at Königsberg, and in 1693 at Berlin, enjoying considerable influence. He supported Leibnitz's plan for an academy of sciences (becoming president in 1733) and became eminent in OT and Talmudic studies. He sought to promote unity between the Reformed and Lutheran churches. Through his agency, a refuge for Moravians was preserved first at Lissa and later in Prussia. He tried to resolve confessional disputes among Polish Protestants. From the beginning he was sympathetic to the new foundation of the Brethren at Herrnhut and, himself consecrated bishop among the Brethren at the Synod of Lissa (1699), conferred the episcopal office upon Nitschmann (1735) and Zinzendorf (1737).

[19] Johannes Amos Comenius (1592–1671), ministered among the Moravians in Bohemia and Poland. In the course of study and to avoid persecution, he travelled widely in England, Sweden, Germany, Hungary, and Holland. Celebrated as an educationist, he was deeply influenced by the spiritual hope of uniting all religions in Christian love. To this end schools were to form men into images of Christ by the organic development of all elements of the divine wisdom.

[20] Christian David himself.

[21] Orig., 'Sehl'.

[22] Augustin Neisser, one of five brothers of Sehlen in Moravia, who were supplied with books, put in touch with the preachers at Teschen, and converted by Christian David in 1717. In 1722 David brought news of the refuge on Zinzendorf's estates, and Augustin with his brother Jacob, both cutlers, left with their families and their cousin Michael Jaeschke, becoming known amongst the Brethren as the 'firstlings of Herrnhut'. The three brothers left behind, George, Hans, and Wenzel, encountered great difficulties with their Jesuit lords, but succeeded in following their brothers with their families in August 1723. Augustin became a vice-elder at Herrnhut in 1730.

pretending to be Romanists, and dissembling the true faith. Yet they 'conferred with flesh and blood'[23] till the year 1722, when at length they forsook all and retired into Upper Lusatia. They left their three brothers behind them, who were soon after cast into prison, and grievously persecuted by the Papists; so that as soon as ever a door was opened they also left all and followed their brothers 5 into Lusatia. The same did many others soon after, as finding no safety either for body or soul in their own country. Whence about the same time Michael and Martin Linner,[24] and the Haberlands,[25] were driven out, with their families, after having suffered the loss of all things, for not conforming to the Romish worship, and for receiving those they called 'heretics' into their houses.   10

5. But the brethren at Kühnewald[26] were treated with still greater severity. All their books were taken away; they were compelled by the most exquisite torments to conform to the popish superstitions and idolatries; and in the end cast into, and kept in, the most loathsome prisons: whereby David Schneider,[27] the Nitschmanns, and many others, were constrained also to leave their country, 15 and all that they had. These are the plain reasons of our leaving Moravia, of which your Excellency desired an account from us.

In the meantime we found a great remissness of behaviour had crept in among us. And indeed the same was to be found in most of those round about us, whether Lutherans or Calvinists, so insisting on faith as to forget, at least in 20 practice, both holiness and good works.

Observing this terrible abuse of preaching Christ *given for us*, we began to insist more than ever on Christ *living in us*. All our exhortations and preaching turned on this; we spoke, we writ, of nothing else. Our constant inquiries were: 'Is Christ formed *in you*? Have you a new heart? Is your soul renewed in the 25 image of God? Is the whole body of sin destroyed in you? Are you fully assured,

[23] Cf. Gal. 1:16.

[24] Martin Linner (1701–33), brother of Michael (see above, Aug. 9-10, 1738, n. 79), elected elder of the church at Herrnhut in place of Melchior Nitschmann, 1730, but resigned his office after a perilous journey into Moravia, 1731. Commemorated in verse by Zinzendorf.

[25] Numerous Haberlands appear both in the succession of secret Protestantism in Moravia and in the open work of the Herrnhuters. George Haberland, born 1675 at Schönau in Moravia, is reported as a man 'diligent in reading the Scriptures', who helped to keep the faith alive. Julia Haberland's proposed marriage to John Töltschig (see above, May 26, 1738, n. 88) was put to the lot in 1732. Michael Haberland was one of the first Moravian party in Georgia, 1734. A Haberland, later a labourer in Livonia, was present at James Hutton's ordination as deacon, 1749. Benham, *Hutton*, p. 241.

[26] Christian David returned to Kühnewald in Moravia, one of the centres of surviving Moravian religious practice, in 1723, and worked a considerable revival there which led to the imprisonment of numerous of its adherents.

[27] Descended from former Moravian ministers, Schneider was an early pillar of revived Protestantism in Zauchtental, suffering imprisonment for his faith; he secured release under what were held to be miraculous circumstances (T. Boys, *The Suppressed Evidence* [London, 1832], p. 269) and fled the country. Before he could settle at Herrnhut in 1725, he acted as a schoolmaster at Sorau till his family could escape. He congratulated Francke on the effects of the dissemination of his writings in Moravia through Steinmetz at Teschen (Eduard Winter, *Die tchechische und slovakische Emigration in Deutschland im 17. und 18. Jahrhundert: Beiträge zur Geschichte der hussitchen Tradition* [(East) Berlin, 1955], pp. 251-52). For Schneider's testimony, see below, Aug. 1738.

beyond all doubt or fear, that you are a child of God? In what manner and at what moment did you receive that full assurance?' If a man could not answer all these questions, we judged he had no true faith. Nor would we permit any to receive the Lord's Supper among us till he could.

5 In this persuasion we were when I went to Greenland[28] five years ago. There I had a correspondence by letter with a Danish minister, Hans Egede,[29] on the head of justification. And it pleased God to show me by him (though he was by no means a holy man, but openly guilty of gross sins) that we had now leaned too much to this hand, and were run into another extreme: that 'Christ in us' and 10 'Christ for us' ought indeed to be both insisted on, but first and principally 'Christ for us', as being the ground of all. I now clearly saw we ought not to insist on anything we *feel*, any more than anything we *do*, as if it were necessary previous to justification or the remission of sins. I saw that least of all ought we so to insist on the full assurance of faith, or the destruction of the body of sin, 15 and the extinction of all its motions, as to exclude those who had not attained this from the Lord's Table,[30] or to deny that they had any faith at all. I plainly perceived this full assurance was a distinct gift from justifying faith, and often not given till long after it; and that justification does not imply that sin should not *stir* in us, but only that it should not *conquer*.

20 And now first it was that I had that full assurance of my own reconciliation to God through Christ. For many years I had had the forgiveness of my sins, and a measure of the peace of God; but I had not till now that witness of his Spirit which shuts out all doubt and fear. In all my trials I had always a confidence in Christ, who had done so great things for me. But it was a confidence mixed with 25 fear: I was afraid *I had not done enough*. There was always something dark in my soul till now. But now the clear light shined; and I saw that what I had hitherto so constantly insisted on, the *doing* so much and *feeling* so much, the long repentance and preparation for believing, the bitter sorrow for sin, and that deep contrition of heart which is found in some, were by no means essential to 30 justification. Yea, that wherever the free grace of God is rightly preached, a sinner in the full career of his sins will probably receive it, and be justified by it, before one who insists on such previous preparation.

---

[28] 1740–74, 'Groenland'.

[29] Name added, 1775 only. Hans Egede (1686–1758), a Danish Lutheran missionary, hoped from 1708 to be able to take the gospel to the descendants of the ancient Norse settlers on the east coast of Greenland. When in 1721 he was finally able to go there, no such people could be discovered, and he turned to the Eskimos, offering a medical as well as an evangelistic mission. Zinzendorf, like many other pietists, had had connections with the Danish court since his youth, and when the Nitschmann brothers (see Neisser, *Moravian Work*, pp. 62-63) were dispatched thither in 1727, they returned with a MS account of Egede's work. A reversal of Danish royal policy in 1730, which led to a withdrawal from Greenland, and the news that Egede's missionary efforts were on the verge of failure led to the dispatch of Christian David and two other Moravians to Greenland in 1733. But at first, physical and linguistic difficulties, together with the doctrinal disputes here referred to, isolated the Moravian missionaries. No real harvest was reaped for another decade. See Finn Gad, *The History of Greenland*, Vol. 2 (Montreal, 1973).

[30] Curnock (II.35, n. 4) notes that Molther taught this doctrine and that JW was excluded from the Lord's Table at Marienborn because he had not attained the full assurance of faith. Cf. Benham, *Hutton*, p. 40.

At my return to Herrnhut I found it difficult at first to make my brethren sensible of this, or to persuade them not to insist on the assurance of faith as a necessary qualification for receiving the Lord's Supper. But from the time they were convinced, which is now three years since, we have all chiefly insisted on Christ 'given for us'.[i] This we urge as the principal thing, which if we rightly 5 believe, Christ will surely be 'formed in us'. And this preaching we have always found to be accompanied with power, and to have the blessing of God following it. By this believers receive a steady purpose of heart, and a more unshaken resolution to endure with a free and cheerful spirit whatsoever our Lord is pleased to lay upon them. 10

The same day I was with Michael Linner, the eldest of the church, the sum of whose conversation was this:

The Church of Moravia was once a glorious church; but it is now covered with thick darkness. It is about sixteen years ago that I began to seek for light. I had a New Testament which I constantly read; upon which I often said to 15 myself, 'This says I ought to be humble, and meek, and pure in heart. How comes it that I am not so?' I went to the best men I knew, and asked, 'Is not this the Word of God? And if so, ought I not to be such as this requires, both in heart and life?' They answered, 'The first Christians indeed were such; but it was impossible for *us* to be so perfect.' This answer gave me no satisfaction. I knew 20 God could not mock his creatures by requiring of them what he saw it was impossible for them to perform. I asked others, but had still the same answer, which troubled me more and more.

About fourteen years ago I was more than ever convinced that I was wholly different from what God required me to be. I consulted his Word again and 25 again; but it spoke nothing but condemnation; till at last I could not read, nor indeed do anything else, having no hope and no spirit left in me. I had been in this state for several days, when being musing by myself, those words came strongly into my mind, 'God so loved the world that he gave his only begotten Son, to the end that all who believe in him should not perish, but have 30 everlasting life.'[31] I thought, 'All? Then I am one. Then he is given for *me*. But I am a sinner. And he came to save sinners.' Immediately my burden dropped off, and my heart was at rest.

But the full assurance of faith I had not yet; nor for the two years I continued in Moravia. When I was driven out thence by the Jesuits I retired hither, and was 35 soon after received into the church. And here after some time it pleased our Lord to manifest himself more clearly to my soul, and give me that full sense of acceptance in him which excludes all doubt and fear.

Indeed the leading of the Spirit is different in different souls. His more usual method, I believe, is to give in one and the same moment the forgiveness of sins 40

---

[i] I dare not say this is right [added as a footnote in 1774, the 'not' in the errata, as also by JW in his own copy].

[31] Cf. John 3:16.

and a full assurance of that forgiveness. Yet in many he works as he did in me—giving first the remission of sins, and after some weeks or months or years the full assurance of it.[32]

This great truth was farther confirmed to me the next day by
5 the conversation I had with David Nitschmann,[33] one of the teachers or pastors of the church, who expressed himself to this effect:

In my childhood I was very serious, but as I grew up was so careless that at eighteen years old I had even forgot to read. When I found this I was startled. I
10 soon learned again, and then spent much time in reading and prayer. But I knew nothing of my heart till at about the age of twenty-six I bought a Bible, and began to read the New Testament. The farther I read the more I was condemned. I found a law which I did not, could not keep. I had a will to avoid all sin; but the power I had not. I continually strove; but was continually conquered. The thing
15 which 'I would I did not'; but what I would not have done, that I did.[34] In this bondage I was when I fell into a fit of sickness, during my recovery from which I felt a stronger desire than ever to avoid all sin. At the same time I felt the power. And sin no longer reigned over me.
    But soon after I fell into grievous temptations, which made me very uneasy.
20 For though I yielded not to them, yet they returned again and again, as fast as they were conquered. Then it came into my mind, 'I take all this pains to serve God. What if there be no God? How do I know there is?' And on this I mused more and more, till I said in my heart, 'There is no God.'
    In this state I was when I came to Herrnhut about fourteen years ago. And
25 every day for a full year, from morning to night, I groaned under this unbelief. Yet I prayed continually, unbelieving as I was; particularly one Sunday when, being in the church of Berthelsdorf, and quite weary of hearing so much of him whose very being I did not believe, I vehemently said, 'O God, if thou be a God, thou must manifest thyself, or I cannot believe it.' In walking home I thought of
30 an expression of Pastor Rothe's, 'Only *suppose* these things are so: *suppose* there be a God.' I said to myself, 'Well, I will, I *do* suppose it.' Immediately I felt a strange sweetness in my soul, which increased every moment till the next morning. And from that time, if all the men upon earth, and all the devils in hell, had joined in denying it, I could not have doubted the being of a God, no, not for
35 one moment. This first sweetness lasted for six weeks, without any intermission.
    I then fell into doubts of another kind. I believed in God; but not in Christ. I opened my heart to Martin Dober, who used many arguments with me, but in vain. For above four years I found no rest by reason of this unbelief; till one day, as I was sitting in my house, despairing of any relief, those words shot into me,
40 'God was in Christ, reconciling the world to himself.'[35] I thought, 'Then God and Christ are one.' Immediately my heart was filled with joy; and much more at the remembrance of these words which I now felt I *did believe:* 'The Word was

[32] Cf. this experience with that of Christian David in the previous testimony.
[33] See above, Oct. 20, 1735, n. 9.
[34] Cf. Rom. 7:15.
[35] 2 Cor. 5:19.

with God, and the Word was God.' 'And the Word was made flesh, and dwelt among us.'[36]

Yet in a few days I was troubled again. I believed Christ was the Saviour of the world. But I could not call him *my* Saviour, neither did I believe he would save *me*. And one day, as I was walking across the square, that text came strongly into my mind, 'The unbelieving shall have their part in the lake which burneth with fire and brimstone.'[37] I returned home, terrified beyond expression, and instantly began crying out to our Saviour, telling him I deserved no less than hell, and gave myself up, if it were his will, to suffer what I had deserved. In a moment I found a gleam of hope that he *would* have mercy even on me.

But this in a short time vanished away, and my uneasiness returned again. Many endeavoured to persuade me that I had, but I knew I had not, a right faith in Christ. For I had no confidence in him; nor could I lay hold upon him as *my* Saviour. Indeed reading one day (in Arndt's *True Christianity*)[38] that 'if all the sins of all the men upon earth were joined in one man, the blood of Christ was sufficient to cleanse that man from all sin,' I felt for a time comfort and peace. But it was but for a time, and then I was overwhelmed as before with sadness and unbelief. And I was oppressed almost beyond my strength, when a year ago[j] I went into this little wood. At first I was tempted to break out into impatience; but then I thought, Our Saviour knows best, nor would he suffer this trouble to continue so long if he did not see it was good for me. I delivered myself wholly into his hands, to dispose of according to his good pleasure. In that hour I saw that all who believe in him are reconciled to God through his blood, and was assured that I was thereby reconciled, and numbered among the children of God. And from that hour I have had no doubt or fear, but all peace and joy in believing.

[j] N.B. I.e., in the year 1737, several years before which he was elected one of the four public teachers of the Church; which office he retains to this day. Now which of the two consequences will you choose (for one or the other is unavoidable), either that a man may preach the gospel (yea, and with the demonstration of the Spirit) who has no faith, or that a man who has a degree of true faith may yet have doubts and fears?

The account given of him when in the midst of these doubts and fears, in a treatise wrote by one of the brethren, and published in the year 1735, runs in the following words: 'The third of our teachers is a shoemaker, a Moravian, "an Israelite indeed, in whom there is no guile", who has had a good testimony of all the brethren. This man endeavours in the most pathetic manner to inculcate true sincerity and uprightness of heart; and acknowledges his own misery and corruption first, before he applies himself to others. He then endeavours to beat down all the false rests and deceitful supports in the Christian warfare. He declares how one ought to come to Christ, viz., with an humble spirit, without self-flattery, not being ashamed to confess our sins, nor yet standing still or dwelling too long upon complaining of our depravity and misery; but taking courage to venture on the grace of God in Christ Jesus; and calling upon him, in tears and prayers, till he avenge us of our adversaries.' [The last two paragraphs were omitted in 1774 and 1775.]

[36] John 1:1, 14.
[37] Rev. 21:8.
[38] Johann Arndt (1555–1621), pastor in north Germany and from 1611 General Superintendent for Lüneburg. His *Four* [later *Six*] *Books of True Christianity* (1604–10), was the first popular devotional work of German Lutheranism and had a powerful after-effect on the literature and piety of the Lutheran world, not least in the early stages of the revival.

Some of the circumstances of this uncommon relation were made more clear to me by the account I received in the afternoon from a student at Herrnhut, Albinus Theodorus Feder.[39]

I (said he) for three years fought against sin with all my might, by fasting and
5 prayer and all the other means of grace. But notwithstanding all my endeavours I gained no ground; sin still prevailed over me; till at last, not knowing what to do farther, I was on the very brink of despair. Then it was that having no other refuge left I fled to my Saviour as one lost and undone, and that had no hope but in his power and free mercy. In that moment I found my heart at rest, in good
10 hope that my sins were forgiven; of which I had a stronger assurance six weeks after, when I received the Lord's Supper here. But I dare not affirm I am a child of God; neither have I the seal of the spirit. Yet I go on quietly doing my Saviour's will, taking shelter in his wounds from all trouble and sin, and knowing he will perfect his work in his own time.
15   Martin Dober, when I described my state to him, said he had known very many believers who, if asked the question, would not have dared to affirm that they were the children of God. And he added, It is very common for persons to receive remission of sins, or justification through faith in the blood of Christ, before they receive the full assurance of faith, which God many times withholds
20 till he has tried whether they will work together with him in the use of the first gift. Nor is there any need (continued he, Dober) to incite anyone to seek that assurance by telling him the faith he has is nothing. This will be more likely to drive him to despair than to encourage him to press forward. His single business, who has received the first gift, is *credendo credere et in credendo perseverare*
25 (to believe on, and to hold fast that whereunto he hath attained), to go on, doing his Lord's will, according to the ability God hath already given; cheerfully and faithfully to use what he has received, without solicitude for the rest.

In the conversation I afterwards had with Augustin Neisser a knife-smith (another of the pastors or teachers of the church,
30 about sixty years of age), as also with his brothers, Wenzel[40] and Hans[41] Neisser, the nature of true faith and salvation was yet farther explained to me.
Augustin Neisser spoke to this effect:

By experience I know that we cannot be justified through the blood of Christ
35 till we feel that all our righteousness and good works avail nothing toward our

[39] Albinus Theodorus Feder from Vogtland was sent in 1739, while still a student, on a mission to St. Thomas, and was drowned on Jan. 17, 1740, before arriving. Letters by him and diary material about the mission are to be found in the *Büdingische Sammlung*, I.561-628; II.489-92.
[40] Wenzel Neisser the elder (cf. Feb. 7, 1738, n. 18), who in 1728 had been sent with Töltschig and David Nitschmann on a fruitless mission to England in the hope of negotiating a connection with the SPCK (Spangenberg, *Zinzendorf*, p. 484). In the index to Hamilton, *Moravian Church*, he is confused with his nephew Friedrich Wenzel.
[41] Orig., 'Hantz'.

justification. Therefore what men call 'a good life' is commonly the greatest of all hindrances to their coming to Christ. For it will not let them see that they are lost, undone sinners; and if they see not this they cannot come unto him.

Thus it was with me. I led a good life from a child. And this was the great hindrance to my coming to Christ. For, abounding in good works, and diligently 5 using all the means of grace, I persuaded myself for thirteen or fourteen years that all was well, and I could not fail of salvation. And yet I cannot say my soul was at rest, even till the time when God showed me clearly that my heart was as corrupt, notwithstanding all my good works, as that of an adulterer or murderer. Then my self-dependence withered away. I wanted a Saviour, and fled naked to 10 him. And in him I found true rest to my soul, being fully assured that all *my* sins were forgiven. Yet I cannot tell the hour or day when I first received that full assurance. For it was not given me at first, neither at once; but grew up in me by degrees. But from the time it was confirmed in me I have never lost it, having never since doubted, no, not for a moment. 15

What Wenzel Neisser said was as follows:

From a child I had many fits of seriousness, and was often uneasy at my sins. This uneasiness was much increased about fifteen years since by the preaching of Christian David. I thought the way to get ease was to go and live among the Lutherans, whom I supposed to be all good Christians. But I soon found, they, 20 as well as the Papists, were carnal, worldly-minded men. About thirteen years ago I came from among them to Herrnhut; but was still as uneasy as before. Which I do not wonder at now (though I did then); for all this time, though I saw clearly I could not be saved but by the death of Christ, yet I did not trust in that *only* for salvation, but depended on my own righteousness *also*, as the joint 25 condition of my acceptance.

After I was settled here, seeing the great diversity of sects wherewith we were surrounded, I began to doubt whether any religion was true. For half a year these doubts perplexed me greatly; and I was often just on the point of casting off all religion and returning to the world. The fear of doing this threw me into a 30 deeper concern than ever I had been in before. Nor could I find how to escape, for the more I struggled, the more I was entangled. I often reflected on my former course of life, as more desirable than this. And one day, in the bitterness of my soul, besought our blessed Saviour at least to 'restore me to that state which I was in before I left Moravia'. In that moment he manifested himself to 35 me, so that I could lay hold on him as *my* Saviour, and showed me it is *only* the blood of Christ which cleanseth us from all sin. This was ten years since, and from that hour I have not had one doubt of my acceptance. Yet I have not any transports of joy. Nor had I when he thus revealed himself unto me. Only I well remember that manifestation of himself was like a cool, refreshing wind to one 40 that is fainting away with sultry heat. And ever since my soul has been sweetly at rest, desiring no other portion in earth or heaven.

I was awakened (said Hans Neisser) by my grandfather, when a child, and by him carefully instructed in the New Testament. I married young, and being from that time weak and sickly, was the more earnest to work out my salvation. 45 And nineteen or twenty years ago I had a strong confidence in our Saviour, and

was continually warning others against trusting in themselves, in their own righteousness or good works. Yet I was not free from it myself. I did not trust in him *only* for acceptance with God. And hence it was that, not building on the right foundation, the blood and righteousness of Christ alone, I could not gain a
5 full victory over my sins, but sometimes conquered them, and sometimes was conquered by them. And therefore I had not a full or constant peace, though I was commonly easy, and hoping for mercy.

Sixteen years ago (on Saturday next) I came to my brother Augustin at Herrnhut. There was then only one little house here. Here I continued eight
10 years in much the same state, thinking I trusted in Christ alone, but indeed trusting partly in his and partly in my own righteousness. I was walking one day in this little wood, when God discovered my heart to me. I saw I had till that hour trusted in my own righteousness, and at the same time that I had no righteousness at all, being altogether corrupt and abominable, and fit only for
15 the fire of hell. At this sight I fell into bitter grief, and an horrible dread overwhelmed me, expecting nothing (as I saw I deserved nothing else) but to be swallowed up in a moment. In that moment I beheld the Lamb of God, taking away my sins. And from that time I have had redemption through his blood, and full asurance of it. I have that peace in him which never fails, and which admits
20 of no doubt or fear. Indeed I am but a little one in Christ; therefore I can receive as yet but little of him. But from his fullness I have enough; and I praise him, and am satisfied.

In the three or four following days I had an opportunity of talking with Zacharias Neisser (cousin to Hans), David
25 Schneider,[42] Christoph Demuth,[43] Arvid Gradin[44] (now at Constantinople), and several others of the most experienced brethren. I believe no preface is needful to the account they gave of God's dealings with their souls, which I doubt not will stir up

[42] See above, Aug. 1738, n. 27.

[43] Christoph Demuth, bandbox-maker, visited emigrants from Salzburg in Lithuania 'who afterwards were often visited at the request of some minister by the brethren travelling that way to Livonia' (Cranz, *Ancient and Modern History of the Brethren* [London, 1780], p. 239; orig. German edn. [Barby, 1771], pp. 316-17). He established links between the Berlin Moravians and Herrnhut in 1726 and was with his wife in Bethlehem, Pa., in 1743 (Hamilton, *Moravian Church*, p. 10; Hamilton, ed., *Bethlehem Diary*, pp. 172, 178, 184, 207, 215).

[44] Arvid Gradin (1704–54), born Wiks, Sweden, son of a clergyman. Came under pietist influence, 1724, and in the 1730s had contact with Dippelianism. He was won to Herrnhut by reading a book and by a personal visit. On Mar. 24, 1740, he was dispatched with Frederick Cossart to Constantinople to negotiate with the Greek Church through personal interviews with the Patriarch. The negotiations were fruitless, but he served as chaplain to the Swedish embassy. In 1741 the Marienborn synod sent him with Martin Dober on an evangelistic mission in Sweden and Norway, which finally obtained the approval of the Archbishop of Stockholm. He was imprisoned in Russia on a diplomatic mission to the Holy Synod, 1743. He wrote a short history of the United Brethren which was translated into English in 1743 and sold by James Hutton (see N. Bohman, *Svenska Män och Kvinnor* [Stockholm, 1942–55], 3: 80). For Gradin's theological views see Gösta Hök, *Zinzendorf's Begriff der Religion* (Uppsala Universitets Årsskrift, 1948), 6:147-52.

many, through his grace, to 'glorify their Father which is in heaven'.[45]

I was born (said Zacharias Neisser) on the borders of Moravia, and was first awakened by my cousin Wenzel, who soon after carried me to hear Mr. Steinmetz, a Lutheran minister about thirty (English) miles off. I was utterly 5 astonished. The next week I went again. After which, going to him in private, I opened my heart, and told him all my doubts, those especially concerning popery. He offered to receive me into communion with him, which I gladly accepted of; and in a short time after I received the Lord's Supper from his hands. While I was receiving I felt Christ had died for *me*. I knew I was 10 reconciled to God. And all the day I was overwhelmed with joy, having those words continually on my mind, 'this day is salvation come to my house: I *also* am a son of Abraham.'[46] This joy I had continually for a year and a half, and my heart was full of love to Christ.

After this I had thoughts of leaving Moravia. I was convinced it would be 15 better for my soul. Yet I would not do it, because I got more money here than I could elsewhere. When I reflected on this I said to myself, 'This is mere covetousness. But if I am covetous I am not a child of God.' Hence I fell into deep perplexity, nor could I find any way to escape out of it. In this slavery and misery I was for five years, at the end of which I fell sick. In my sickness my heart 20 was set at liberty, and peace returned to my soul. I now prayed earnestly to God to restore my health, that I might leave Moravia. He did restore it, and I immediately removed to Herrnhut. After I had been here a quarter of a year, the Count preached one day upon the nature of sanctification. I found I had not experienced what he described, and was greatly terrified. I went to my cousin 25 Wenzel, who advised me to read over the third, fourth, and fifth chapters of the Epistle to the Romans. I did so. I had read them an hundred times before, yet now they appeared quite new, and gave me such a sight of God's justifying the ungodly as I never had had before. On Sunday I went to church at Berthelsdorf, and while we were singing those words, *'Wir glauben auch in Jesum Christ'*[47] ('we 30 believe also in Jesus Christ'), I clearly saw him as my Saviour. I wanted immediately to be alone, and to pour out my heart before him. My soul was filled with thankfulness, and with a still, soft, quiet joy, such as it is impossible to express. I had full assurance that 'my Beloved was mine and I was his,'[48] which has never ceased to this day. I see by a clear light what is pleasing to him, and I do 35 it continually in love. I receive daily from him peace and joy; and I have nothing to do but to praise him.

The most material part of David Schneider's account now was this:

Both my father and mother feared God, and carefully instructed me in the 40 Holy Scriptures. I was from a child earnestly desirous to follow their instructions, and more so after my father's death. Yet as I grew up many sins got the dominion over me; of which God began to give me a sense by the preaching

---

[45] Cf. Matt. 5:16.
[47] By Luther.
[46] Cf. Luke 19.9.
[48] Cf. S. of S. 2:16.

of Pastor Steinmetz; who speaking one day of drunkenness, to which I was then addicted, I was so grieved and ashamed that for several days I could not bear to look anyone in the face. It pleased God afterwards to give me, though not all at once, a sense of my other both outward and inward sins. And before the time of
5   my coming out of Moravia I knew that my sins were forgiven. Yet I can't fix on any particular time when I knew this first. For I did not clearly know it at once; God having always done everything in my soul by degrees.

When I was about twenty-six I was pressed in spirit to exhort and instruct my brethren. Accordingly many of them met at my house, to read, pray, and sing
10 psalms. They usually came about ten or eleven, and stayed till one or two in the morning. When Christian David came to us we were much quickened and comforted, and our number greatly increased. We were undisturbed for two years. But then the Papists were informed of our meeting. Immediately search was made. All our books were seized, and we were ordered to appear before the
15 consistory. I was examined many times; was imprisoned, released, and imprisoned again five times in one year. At last I was adjudged to pay fifty rix-dollars[49] and suffer a year's imprisonment. But upon a rehearing the sentence was changed, and I was ordered to be sent to the galleys. Before this sentence was executed I escaped out of prison, and came to Sorau[50] in Silesia.
20 Many of my brethren followed me, and here for near ten years I taught the children in the orphan-house. I soon sent for my wife and children. But the magistrates had just then ordered that the wives and children of all those who had fled should be taken into safe custody. The night before this order was to be executed she escaped and came to Sorau.
25 Soon after some of my brethren, who had been there, pressed me much to remove to Herrnhut, Christian David in particular, by whose continued importunity I was at length brought to resolve upon it. But all my brethren at Sorau were still as strongly against it as I myself had formerly been. For a whole year I was struggling to break from them, or to persuade them to go too. And it
30 cost me more pains to get from Sorau than it had done to leave Moravia.

At length I broke loose and came to Herrnhut, which was about three years ago. Finding I could scarce subsist my family here by hard labour, whereas at Sorau all things were provided for me, I grew very uneasy. The more uneasy I was, the more my brethren refrained from my company;[k] so that in a short time I
35 was left quite alone. Then I was in deep distress indeed. Sin revived and almost got the mastery over me. I tried all ways, but found no help. In this miserable state I was about a year ago, when the brethren cast lots concerning me, and were thereby directed to admit me to the Lord's Table. And from that hour my soul received comfort, and I was more and more assured that I had an advocate
40 with the Father, and that I was fully reconciled to God by his blood.

---

[k] This was cruel and unchristian [footnote in 1774; replaced in 1775 by, 'This was utterly wrong'].

---

[49] A silver coin used in some European countries during this period (e.g., the German *Reichstaler* and the Swedish *Riksdaler*), the value varying between two and five shillings at the time.

[50] The seat of the celebrated pietist family of imperial counts, the Promnitzes, related by marriage to Zinzendorf. On them see Barthold, *Die Erweckten im protestantischen Deutschland*, pp. 227-40.

Christoph Demuth spoke to this effect:

My father was a pious man from his youth. He carefully instructed all his children. I was about fifteen when he died. A little before he died, having been all his lifetime under the law, he received at once remission of sins and the full witness of the Spirit. He called us to him and said, 'My dear children, let your 5 whole trust be in the blood of Christ. Seek salvation in this, and in this alone, and he will show you the same mercy he has to me. Yea, and he will show it to many of your relations and acquaintance, when his time is come.'

From this time till I was twenty-seven years old I was more and more zealous in seeking Christ. I then removed into Silesia, and married. A year after I was 10 much pressed in spirit to return and visit my brethren in Moravia. I did so. We had the New Testament, our Moravian hymns, and two or three Lutheran books. We read and sung and prayed together, and were much strengthened. One day, as we were together at my house, one knocked at the door. I opened it, and it was a Jesuit. He said, 'My dear Demuth, I know you are a good man, and 15 one that instructs and exhorts your friends. I must see what books you have.' And going into the inner room he found the Testament and the rest together. He took them all away; nor did we dare to hinder him. The next day we were summoned before the consistory, and after a long examination ordered to appear in the church before the congregation on the following Sunday. There 20 they read a long confession of faith, and afterwards bid us say, 'In the name of the Father, and of the Son, and of the Holy Ghost.' We did so, though not knowing what they meant. They then told us we had abjured the Lutheran errors, and called the blessed Trinity to witness that we assented to that confession of faith. My heart sunk within me when I heard it. I went home, but 25 could find no rest. I thought I had now denied my Saviour, and could expect no more mercy from him. I could not bear to stay in Moravia any longer, but immediately returned into Silesia. There I continued six years, but there too I was perpetually terrified with the thoughts of what I had done. I often inquired after my brethren whom I had left in Moravia. Some of them, I heard, were 30 thrown into prison, and others escaped to a little village in Lusatia called Herrnhut. I wished I could go to that place myself; and at last, meeting with one who had the same desire, we agreed to go together. But our design being discovered, he was apprehended and thrown into prison. Expecting the same treatment, I earnestly prayed that God would show me a token for good. Immediately my soul 35 was filled with joy, and I was ready to go to prison or to death.

Two days passed, and no man asked me any question; when, doubting what I ought to do, I went into a neighbouring wood, and going into a little cave fell on my face and prayed, 'Lord, thou seest I am ready to do what thou wilt. If it be thy will I should be cast into prison, thy will be done. If it be thy will that I should 40 leave my wife and children, I am ready. Only show me thy will.' Immediately I heard a loud voice saying, *'Fort, fort, fort'* ('Go on, go on'). I rose joyful and satisfied; went home and told my wife it was God's will I should now leave her; but that I hoped to return in a short time, and take her and my children with me. I went out of the door, and in that moment was filled with peace, and joy, and 45 comfort.

We had above two hundred miles to go (thirty-five German) and neither I nor my friend who went with me had one kreutzer.[1] But God provided things convenient for us, so that in all the way we wanted nothing.

In this journey God gave me the full assurance that my sins were forgiven. This was twelve years ago, and ever since it has been confirmed more and more, 5 by my receiving from him every day fresh supplies of strength and comfort.

By comparing my experience with that of others you may perceive how different ways God leads different souls. But though a man should be led in a way different from that of all other men, yet if his eye be at all times fixed on his Saviour; if his constant aim be to do his will; if all his desires tend to him; if in all 10 trials he can draw strength from him; if he fly to him in all troubles, and in all temptations find salvation in his blood—in this there can be no delusion. And whosoever is thus minded, however or whenever it began, is surely reconciled to God through his Son.

Arvid Gradin, a Swede, born in Dalecarlia,[51] spoke to this 15 purpose:

Before I was ten years old I had a serious sense of religion, and great fervour in prayer. This was increased by my reading much in the New Testament; but the more I read, the more earnestly I cried out, 'Either these things are not true, or we are not Christians.' About sixteen my sense of religion began to decline, by 20 my too great fondness for learning, especially the oriental tongues, wherein I was instructed by a private preceptor, who likewise did all that in him lay to instruct me in true divinity.

At seventeen I went to the University of Uppsala,[52] and a year or two after was licensed to preach. But at twenty-two, meeting with Arndt's *True Christianity*, I 25 found myself was not a Christian. Immediately I left off preaching, and betook myself wholly to philosophy. This stifled all my conviction for some years; but when I was about twenty-seven they revived and continued the year after, and I was desired to be domestic tutor to the children of the Secretary of State.[53] I now felt I was 'carnal, sold under sin',[54] and continually struggled to burst the bonds, 30 till (being about thirty-one years old) I was unawares entangled in much worldly business. This cooled me in my pursuit of holiness; yet for a year and a half my heart was never at peace. Being then in a bookseller's shop, I saw the account of the church at Herrnhut. I did not think there could be any such place, and asked the bookseller if that was a real account. His answer, that it was 'no more than 35 the plain truth', threw me into deep thought and fervent prayer, that God would bring me to that place. I went to the Secretary, and told him I did not design to stay at Uppsala, having a desire to travel. He said he had a desire his son should travel, and was glad of an opportunity to send him with me. I was grieved, but

---

[1] A small coin of about a halfpenny value.

---

[51] Dalecarlia or Dalarne, an old Swedish province now comprised in Kopparberg.
[52] Orig., 'Upsal'.
[53] Olaf Carlsson (1669–1745), Secretary of State, 1728; created Baron Cederström, 1731; to whose family he was private tutor, 1731–36. *Svenskt Biografiskt Lexikon* (Örebro and Stockholm, 1857–1907), 8:115 seq.
[54] Rom. 7:14.

knew not how to refuse anything to my patron and benefactor. Accordingly we left Uppsala together, and after a year spent in several parts of Germany, went through Holland into France, and so to Paris, where we spent another year. But I was more and more uneasy till I could be disengaged from my charge, that I might retire to Herrnhut. In our return from France, my pupil's elder brother, 5 returning from Italy, met us at Leipzig. I immediately writ to his father, and having obtained his consent delivered him into his hands. April 23, 1738 (N[ew] S[tyle]) I came hither. Here I was as in another world. I desired nothing but to be cleansed inwardly and outwardly from sin by the blood of Christ. I found all here laying the same foundation. Therefore though I did not think with them in all 10 points of doctrine, I waived these, and singly pursued reconciliation with God through Christ.[55]

On the 22nd of May last I could think of nothing but, 'He that believeth hath everlasting life.'[56] But I was afraid of deceiving myself, and continually prayed I might not build without a foundation. Yet I had a sweet, settled peace, and for 15 five days this Scripture was always in my thoughts. On the 28th those words of our Lord were as strongly impressed upon me, 'If ye, being evil, know how to give good gifts to your children, how much more shall your heavenly Father give the Holy Ghost to them that ask him.'[57] At the same time I was incessantly carried out to ask that he would give me the witness of his Spirit. On the 29th I 20 had what I asked of him, viz., the $\pi\lambda\eta\rho o\phi o\rho i\alpha$ $\pi i\sigma\tau\epsilon\omega\varsigma$[58] which is:

'Requies in sanguine Christi. Firma fiducia in Deum et persuasio de gratia divina; tranquillitas mentis summa, atque serenitas et pax; cum absentia omnis desiderii carnalis, et cessatione peccatorum etiam internorum. Verbo, cor quod antea instar maris turbulenti agitabatur, in summa fuit requie, instar maris 25 sereni et tranquilli.'[59]

('Repose in the blood of Christ. A firm confidence in God, and persuasion of his favour; serene peace and steadfast tranquillity of mind, with a deliverance from every fleshly desire, and from every outward and inward sin. In a word, my heart, which before was tossed like a troubled sea, was still and quiet, and in a 30 sweet calm.')

In the present discipline of the church of Herrnhut, all which is alterable at the discretion of the superiors, may be observed:

    I.   The officers of it.
    II. The division of the people.   35
    III. The conferences, lectures, and government of the children.
    IV. The order of divine service.

---

[55] Curnock notes (II.48, n. 6) that Gradin received the offer of a chair at Uppsala soon after arriving at Herrnhut, but declined it.

[56] John 3:36; 6:47.

[57] Luke 11:13.

[58] Heb. 10:22, 'the full assurance of faith'.

[59] This is apparently Gradin's own statement in Latin, as taken down by Wesley, and translated by him below, although it may possibly be a quotation from some other author.

I. The officers are: (1) The *Eldest* of the whole church; beside whom there is an Eldest of every particular branch of it. There is also a distinct Eldest over the young men, and another over the boys; a female Eldest over the women in general, and another
5 over the unmarried, and another over the girls. (2) The *Teachers*, who are four. (3) The *Helpers* (or *Deaccns*). (4) The *Overseers* (or *Censors*), eleven in number at Herrnhut. (5) The *Monitors*, who are eleven likewise. (6) The *Almoners*, eleven also. (7) The *Attenders* on the sick, seven in number. (8) Lastly, the *Servants*, or
10 deacons of the lowest order.

II. The people of Herrnhut are divided: (1) Into five male classes, viz., the little children, the middle children, the big children, the young men, and the married. The females are divided in the same manner. (2) Into eleven classes, according to
15 the houses where they live; and in each class is an Helper, an Overseer, a Monitor, an Almoner, and a Servant. (3) Into about ninety Bands, each of which meets twice at least, but most of them three times a week, to 'confess their faults one to another, and pray for one another, that they may be healed'.[60]

20 III. The rulers of the church, i.e., the Elders, Teachers, and Helpers (all chosen by the congregation),[61] have a conference every week, purely concerning the state of souls, and another concerning the institution of youth. Beside which they have one every day concerning outward things relating to the church.

25 The Overseers, the Monitors, the Almoners, the Attenders on the sick, the Servants, the Schoolmasters, the young men, and the children, have likewise each a conference once a week, relating to their several offices and duties.

Once a week also is a conference for strangers; at which any
30 person may be present, and propose any question or doubt which he desires to have resolved.

In Herrnhut is taught reading, writing, arithmetic, Latin, Greek, Hebrew, French, English, history, and geography.

There is a Latin, French, and an English lecture every day, as
35 well as an historical and geographical one. On Monday, Wednesday, Friday, and Saturday is the Hebrew lecture, the Greek on Tuesday and Thursday.

---

[60] Cf. Jas. 5:16.
[61] The parenthetic phrase was omitted from the 1774 edition.

In the orphan-house the larger children rise at five (the smaller between five and six). After a little private prayer they work till seven. Then they are at school till eight, the hour of prayer. At nine those who are capable of it learn Latin, at ten French. At eleven they walk. At twelve they dine all together, and walk[62] till one. At one they work or learn writing; at three arithmetic; at four history; at five they work; at six sup and work; at seven, after a time spent in prayer, walk; at eight the smaller children go to bed, the larger go to the public service. When this is ended they work again till (at ten) they go to bed.

IV. Every morning at eight is singing and exposition of Scripture; and commonly a short prayer.

At eight in the evening there is commonly only mental prayer,[m] joined with the singing and expounding.

The faithful afterwards spend a quarter of an hour in prayer, and conclude with the kiss of peace.

On Sunday morning the service begins at six; at nine the public service at Berthelsdorf. At one the Eldest gives separate exhortations to all the members of the church, divided into fourteen little classes for that purpose, spending about a quarter of an hour with each class. At four begins the evening service at Berthelsdorf, closed by a conference in the church. At eight is the usual service; after which the young men, singing praises round the town, conclude the day.

On the first Saturday in the month the Lord's Supper is administered. From ten in the morning till two the Eldest speaks with each communicant in private concerning the state of his soul. At two they dine, then wash one another's feet, after which they sing and pray. About ten they receive in silence without any ceremony, and continue in silence till they part at twelve.

On the second Saturday is the solemn prayer day for the children; the third is the day of general intercession and thanksgiving; and on the fourth is the great monthly conference of all the superiors of the church.

For the satisfaction of those who desire a more full account I have added—

---

[m] This is unscriptural [footnote in 1774].

[62] All editions except 1774, 'work', apparently an error.

An Extract of the Constitution of the Church of the Moravian
Brethren at Herrnhut, laid before the Theological Order at
Württemberg[63] *in the Year 1733.*

1. They have a *Senior,* or *Eldest,* who is to assist the church by his counsel and
5 prayers, and to determine what shall be done in matters of importance. Of him is
required that he be well experienced in the things of God, and witnessed to by
all for holiness of conversation.

2. They have *Deacons,* or *Helpers,* who are, in the private assemblies, to
instruct; to take care that outward things be done decently and in order; and to
10 see that every member of the church grows in grace and walks suitably to his
holy calling.

3. The *Pastor* or *Teacher* is to be an overseer of the whole flock, and every
person therein; to baptize the children diligently to form their minds, and bring
them up 'in the nurture and admonition of the Lord';[64] when he finds in them a
15 sincere love of the cross, then to receive them into the church. To administer the
Supper of the Lord. To join in marriage those who are already married to
Christ. To reprove, admonish, quicken, comfort, as need requires. To declare
the whole counsel of God; taking heed at all times to speak as the oracles of God,
and agreeably to the analogy of faith. To bury those who have died in the Lord;
20 and to keep that safe which is committed to his charge, even the pure doctrine
and apostolical discipine which we have received from our forefathers.

4. We have also another sort of *Deacons* who take care that nothing be wanting
to the orphan-house, the poor, the sick, and the strangers. Others again there
are who are peculiarly to take care of the sick; and others, of the poor. And two of
25 these are entrusted with the public stock, and keep accounts of all that is
received or expended.

5. There are women who perform each of the above-mentioned offices
among those of their own sex; for none of the men converse with them besides
the Eldest, the Teacher, and one, or sometimes two, of the Deacons.

30 6. Towards magistrates, whether of a superior or inferior rank, we bear the
greatest reverence. We cheerfully submit to their laws; and even when many of
us have been spoiled of their goods, driven out of their houses, and every way
oppressed by them, yet they resisted them not, neither opening their mouths nor
lifting up their hand against them. In all things which do not immediately
35 concern the inward, spiritual kingdom of Christ, we simply, and without
contradicting, obey the higher powers. But with regard to conscience, the liberty
of this we cannot suffer to be any way limited or infringed. And to this head we

---

[63] Orig., 'Wirtemberg', the earlier spelling—not to be confused with Luther's
Wittenberg, in spite of the 1775 misprint, 'Wittenberg'. In 1733 Zinzendorf went to
Württemberg to create a good impression of his work at Herrnhut in the theology faculty at
Tübingen, for whom this document was prepared. It was on this visit that Zinzendorf and
Bengel (one of the leading figures in Württemberger pietism who never accepted a
university appointment) were brought together by Oetinger, and each acquired a lasting
distaste for the other and his views. On this see Gottfried Mälzer, *Bengel und Zinzendorf*
(Witten, 1968), and his *Johann Albrecht Bengel: Leben und Werk* (Stuttgart, 1970). From this
visit Zinzendorf, however, obtained the opinion from the theological faculty that the
principles of the Brethren were consistent with the Augsburg Confession, a diplomatic
asset to set against the suspicion of the Saxon church-government.
[64] Eph. 6:4.

refer whatever directly and in itself tends to hinder the salvation of souls; or whatsoever things Christ and his holy apostles (who we know meddled not with outward worldly things) took charge of and performed as necessary for the constituting and well-ordering of his church. In these things we acknowledge no head but Christ; and are determined, God being our helper, to give up not only our goods (as we did before) but life itself, rather than this liberty which God hath given us.

7. As it behoves all Christians not to be slothful in business, but diligently to attend the works of their calling, there are persons chosen by the church to superintend all those who are employed in outward business. And by this means also many things are prevented which might otherwise be an occasion of offence.

8. We have also *Censors* and *Monitors*. In those experience and perspicacity, in these wisdom and modesty, are chiefly required. The *Censors* signify what they observe (and they observe the smallest things) either to the *Deacons* or *Monitors*. Some *Monitors* there are whom all know to be such; others who are secretly appointed, and who, if need require, may freely admonish, in the love of Christ, even the rulers of the church.

9. The church is so divided that first the husbands, then the wives, then the widows, then the maids, then the young men, then the boys, then the girls, and lastly the little children, are in so many distinct classes; each of which is daily visited, the married men by a married man, the wives by a wife, and so of the rest.[n] These larger are also (now) divided into near ninety smaller classes or Bands,[65] over each of which one presides who is of the greatest experience. All these *Leaders* meet the Senior every week, and lay open to him and to the Lord whatsoever hinders or furthers the work of God in the souls committed to their charge.

10. In the year 1727 four and twenty men, and as many women, agreed that each of them would spend an hour in every day in praying to God for his blessing on his people; and for this purpose both the men and women chose a place where any of their own sex who were in distress might be present with them. The same number of unmarried women, of unmarried men, of boys, and of girls,[66] were afterwards, at their desire, added to them; who pour out their souls before God, not only for their own brethren, but also for other churches and persons that have desired to be mentioned in their prayers. And this perpetual intercession has never ceased day or night since its first beginning.

11. And as the members of the church are divided according to their respective states and sexes, so they are also with regard to their proficiency in the knowledge of God. Some are dead, some quickened by the spirit of God. Of these, some again are untractable, some diligent, some zealous, burning with

---

[n] This work all the married brethren and sisters, as well as all the unmarried, perform in their turns.

---

[65] Though the classes are clearly different from those which JW later instituted in England, the bands were on the lines he followed first in Georgia and then in England (see above, Aug. 8-10, 1738, n. 78).

[66] Remarkable gifts of public prayer in boys and girls had been exhibited in Silesia (whence some of the first settlers at Herrnhut had come) in the spontaneous emergence of camp-meetings *(Feldgottesdienste)* in 1707.

their first love; some babes, and some young men. Those who are still dead are visited every day. And of the babes in Christ especial care is taken also, that they may be daily inspected and assisted to grow in grace, and in the knowledge of our Lord Jesus.

5   12. In the orphan-house about seventy children are brought up, separate according to their sex. Beside which several experienced persons are appointed to consult with the parents touching the education of the other children. In teaching them Christianity we make use of Luther's Catechism, and study the amending their wills as well as understanding; finding by experience that when

10 their will is moved they often learn more in a few hours than otherwise in many months. Our little children we instruct chiefly by hymns, whereby we find the most important truths most successfully insinuated into their minds.

13. We highly reverence marriage, as greatly conducive to the kingdom of Christ. But neither our young men nor women enter into it till they assuredly

15 know they are married to Christ. When any know it is the will of God that they should change their state, both the man and woman are placed for a time with some married persons, who instruct them how to behave so that their married life may be pleasing to God. Then their design is laid before the whole church, and after about fourteen days they are solemnly joined, though not otherwise

20 habited than they are at other times. If they make any entertainment (which is not always), they invite only a few intimate friends, by whose faithful admonitions they may be better prepared to bear their cross and fight the good fight of faith. If any women is with child, not only especial mention is made of her in the public prayers, but she is also exhorted in private wholly to give herself

25 up into the hands of her faithful Creator. As soon as a child is born, prayer is made for it, and if it may be it is baptized in the presence of the whole church. Before it is weaned it is brought into the assembly on the Lord's days.

14. Whoever either of the male or female children seek God with their whole heart, know their sins are forgiven,⁰ and obey the truth, are not used to be much

30 incited to come to the Lord's Supper, neither are they forbidden so to do if they desire it. We think it enough to teach our children just conceptions of it, and the difference between this food of the soul and that milk which they every day receive of Christ. They then publicly declare the sentiments of their hearts concerning it. They are afterwards examined⁶⁷ both in private by the pastor, and

35 also in public; and then, after an exhortation by the *Senior*, are by him through laying on of hands added to the church and *confirmed.* The same method is used with those who renounce the papal superstitions, or who are turned from the service of Satan to God; and that, if they desire it, although they are not young; yea, though they are well stricken in years.

40 15. Once or twice a month, either at Berthelsdorf, or if it may be at Herrnhut, all the church receives the Lord's Supper. It cannot be expressed how greatly the power of God is then present among us. A general confession of sins is made

---

⁰ This was the order of the church till Christian David's return from Greenland; see p. 63 [i.e, pp. 280-81 above].

---

⁶⁷ The 1774 *Works* omitted most of the first half of the paragraph, including the footnote, reading: '14. Whoever either of the male or female children seek God with their whole heart need not be much incited to come to the Lord's Supper. Before they receive they are examined.'

by one of the brethren in the name of all. Then a few solid questions are asked; which when they have answered, the absolution or remission of sins is either pronounced to all in general, or confirmed to every particular person by the laying on of hands. The Seniors first receive; then the rest in order, without any regard had to worldly dignity, in this, any more than in any other of the solemn 5 offices of religion. After receiving, all the men (and so the women) meet together to renew their covenant with God, to seek his face, and exhort one another to the patience of hope and the labour of love.

16. They have a peculiar esteem for lots, and accordingly use them both in public and private to decide points of importance, when the reasons brought on 10 each side appear to be of equal weight. And they believe this to be then the only way of wholly setting aside their own will, of acquitting themselves of all blame, and clearly knowing what is the will of God.

17. At eight in the morning, and in the evening, we meet to pray to and praise God, and to read and hear the Holy Scriptures. The time we usually spend in 15 sleep is from eleven at night till four in the morning. So that, allowing three hours a day for taking the food both of our bodies and souls, there remain sixteen for work. And this space those who are in health spend therein with all diligence and faithfulness.

18. Two men keep watch every night in the street,[68] as do two women in the 20 women's apartment; that they may pour out their souls for those that sleep; and by their hymns raise the hearts of any who are awake to God.

19. For the farther stirring up the gift which is in us, sometimes we have public, sometimes private love-feasts; at which we take a moderate refreshment, with gladness and singleness of heart, and the voice of praise and thanksgiving. 25

20. If any man among us, having been often admonished, and long forborne, persists in walking unworthy of his holy calling, he is no longer admitted to the Lord's Supper. If he still continues in his fault, hating to be reformed, the last step is, publicly, and often in the midst of many prayers and tears, to cast him out of our congregation. But great is our joy if he then see the error of his ways, so 30 that we may receive him among us again.

21. Most of our brethren and sisters have in some part of their life experienced holy mourning and sorrow of heart; and have afterwards been assured that 'there was no more condemnation for them,'[69] being 'passed from death unto life'.[70] They are therefore far from fearing to die, or desiring to live 35 on earth; knowing that to them 'to die is gain',[71] and being confident that they are the care of him whose are the 'issues of life and death'.[72] Wherefore they depart as out of one chamber into another. And after the soul has left its habitation their remains are deposited in the earth appointed for that purpose. And the survivors are greatly comforted, and rejoice over them, with a 'joy the world knoweth not 40 of'.[73]

---

[68] 1740, 1743, 1775, 'streets'.   [69] Cf. Rom. 8:1.

[70] John 5:24.   [71] Phil 1:21.

[72] BCP, Visitation of the Sick, prayer for a sick child; cf. Ps. 68:20 and Prov. 4:28.

[73] Cf. John 14:27-28; 1 John 3:1. It is somewhat strange that in spite of a title-page which promises an extract covering his *Journal* until 'his return from Germany', the extract in fact breaks off here, even though what remained could have been accommodated in the pages of a complete gathering. In fact readers had to wait two years for the remaining six pages, prefixed to the third extract.

APPENDIX

MS JOURNALS AND DIARIES

EDITORIAL INTRODUCTION

As was pointed out in the Introduction above, these volumes are primarily intended to reproduce the *Journal* which Wesley himself prepared and published. Both for literary and historical purposes, however, it is important to present at least some of the material which lies behind the published work. This is especially true of his opening 'Extract'. Wesley's Oxford diaries and memoranda will be published in Vol. 32 of this edition, but the remainder (including those arising during his Georgia and later ministries) will be presented in association with the published *Journals* relating to those periods. It would be unduly awkward to present three types of material (in addition to footnotes) on one page. Therefore the diaries and manuscript journals are printed in this appendix, one above the other under their corresponding dates; appropriate annotations will be found at the proper place with the published *Journal.*

The Manuscript Journals

(a) The Voyage to Georgia: Oct. 14, 1735–Feb. 16, 1736

Unlike the manuscript journals which cover the period he spent in Georgia (for which we have multiple copies in Wesley's hand), the holograph of the journal Wesley wrote summarizing his voyage over from England seems long ago to have vanished, as have the letters which he wrote about the voyage to various friends and relatives. We do have, of course, the narrative that was incorporated into his first published *Journal,* surely based on this missing manuscript journal. It seems certain that several copies of the voyage documents were made at various times by his companions. Only four seem to have survived into this century, however.

One of these was apparently made by Benjamin Ingham. This was used by Nehemiah Curnock in Vol. I of Wesley's *Journal* (1909, pp. 106-65), and a facsimile of the opening page is given there (p. 107). Curnock claims that the document was 'drafted for' and 'undoubtedly sent to' Wesley's brother Samuel; at the turn of this century, it was owned by Mr. Andrews, of an 'old Devonshire family' in Exeter (pp. viii, xi). This document seems now to have disappeared. It is difficult to be absolutely sure of the contents of the document since Curnock conflated it (mainly within square brackets) with the published text of the *Journal*. Certainly it differed in many details from the three presently accessible MS copies.

One quite reliable copy among the extant transcripts is in an unknown hand, in one of the many manuscript volumes prepared for the Earl of Egmont. It now resides in the Special Collections of the University of Georgia Libraries, Athens, Georgia. Volume 14201 in the collection forms part of the Egmont Papers, purchased from the estate of Sir Thomas Philipps at Sotheby's sale in 1946. It includes a transcript of Ingham's own voyage journal (pp. 421-64) as well as of Wesley's (pp. 257-86), entitled, 'A Journal of the Passage from England to Georgia by the Revd. Mr. John Wesley'. We are grateful to the University of Georgia for giving us permission to reproduce this transcript of Wesley's journal.

The other two extant transcripts have undoubted affinities with the document in the Egmont papers. One, with text equally reliable to the Egmont copy, is in the Rawlinson MSS (Rawl. D. 1348) in the Bodleian Library, Oxford. It comprises twenty-three quarto pages, with a separate title-page prefixed: 'A Journal of a Voyage to Georgia by the Rev. Mr. John Wesley, M.A. and Fellow of Lincoln College in Oxford'. Variant readings from the Egmont papers are minor, including two editorial footnotes, as well as what may have been occasional editorial comments.

Another similar transcript is somewhat more elaborate in presentation, but not as trustworthy as the Egmont or Rawlinson copies. This document is housed in John Wesley's New Room in the Horsefair, Bristol, England. It is in two distinct hands, the second appearing only on pp. 20-25 of thirty-two quarto pages. 'Mr. John Westley's Journal of his passage from England to Georgia' occupies pp. 1-27, and is followed by some selections from Benjamin Ingham's own voyage journal and the beginning of a letter from him to Thomas Broughton and the Oxford Methodists. There are a few clear errors (e.g., the opening date of Oct. 4). The copy is heavily edited, evincing dozens of minor omissions, many changes of phraseology, and a handful of attempts to smooth away what seemed to the amanuensis Wesley's infelicities (e.g., his reference on Nov. 9 to the gay young woman whose seriousness was removed by 'good company', which a scribe innocent of satire altered to 'bad company'). In general, however, it confirms the text of the other extant copies.

The available sources may be summarized thus:

(G) 'A Journal of the Passage from England to Georgia; Egmont

Papers, MS. 14201, pp. 257-86; Univ. of Georgia, Athens, Georgia.

(I) Curnock, Wesley's *Journal*, I.106-65; a conflation of Ingham's copy (whereabouts not known) and Wesley's published *Journal.*

(N) 'Mr. John Westley's Journal of his Passage'; 27 pp.; John Wesley's New Room in the Horsefair, Bristol.

(R) 'A Journal of a Voyage'; Rawlinson MSS, D.1348 (fols. 290-302), 23 numbered pages; Bodleian Library, Oxford.

In our transcription of the voyage journal we have used the Egmont document (G) as the primary text, and have incorporated within square brackets the more important variants from the Rawlinson copy (prefixed by R), the New Room copy (N), and Curnock's transcript (I).

(b) The Georgia Ministry, Mar. 7, 1736–Dec. 15, 1737

Much more complex are Wesley's own manuscripts surviving from his stormy ministry in Georgia. Here it seems desirable to list and characterize the five major documents under the letters which will be used for reference in transcribing selections from them. It is essential to realize the apparent purpose for which each document was prepared, so that the resultant composite does not appear unduly disjointed. All five documents are in the Wesley manuscript collection (JW.MSS) in the Methodist Archives of The John Rylands University Library of Manchester.

(A) March 1736–Mar. 12, 1737 (JW.MSS.III.5); 68 numbered paragraphs on 44 pages, transcribed in England, March 13, 1738; an account of Wesley's relations with Sophy Hopkey, written apparently for close friends or family members; this document provides the basic text for the first year of our transcript, with variants added from the other documents in square brackets.

(B) March 1736–Oct. 25, 1737 (JW.MSS.IV.2); 74 numbered sections on 69 numbered pages, entered mostly on the rectos of 66 leaves; space is left for additions (and some later documents are added) but the narrative ends in Sept. 1737; this was prepared by Wesley as a legal brief (referred to in the diary as 'Miss Sophy's Case' or 'My Case') for his trial on charges brought by the Grand Jury.

(C) Aug. 20–Sept. 8, 1736 (JW.MSS.III.13); fragment of a draft MS journal on versos of leaves numbered 148-60; contains pastoral activities and reflections (mostly at Frederica), reported to friends in England (quoted by Whitefield).

(D) Sept. 8, 1736–Dec. 16, 1737 (JW.MSS.III.4); 85 numbered pages written variously on the rectos and/or versos of 51 leaves; 'Journal' inscribed by Wesley on the front page; contains a few emendations and was probably intended by Wesley as a fair copy to be circulated; this document provides the basic text for our transcript from March 13–Dec. 16, 1737, with variants added from (B) and (E).

(E) Sept. 13, 1736–Dec. 14, 1737 (JW.MSS.IV.1); 55 numbered pages on 29 leaves (three blank versos); inscribed by Wesley at the front, 'No. 3. To Dec. 14, 1737', and with a note at the end, 'It goes on in the bound (Nicodemus) book'; surely a fair copy, with few signs of emendation; shorter and apparently later than (D), with some deletions and many variant readings, mostly descriptive or editorial insertions (many of which parallel the published journal).

The basic text of the MS Journals transcription below, then, consists of document (A) for the first year (March 1736–March 1737), followed by document (D), with significant variant readings from the other documents identified and added in square brackets.

Wesley's Diaries, Oct. 17, 1735–Aug. 21, 1738

Wesley's private diaries differ from the journals (both MS and published) in several ways. The diaries were essentially private documents, not primarily intended to be read by others. They contained a great deal of information that would have been of interest only to Wesley—records of hourly self-examination, notations of readings, evaluations of conversations, regular analysis of religious disposition, and many other details that understandably never made their way into any narrative account intended for public circulation (cf. his own comment to this effect also in the Preface [¶1] to the first published extract of his Journal, above).

The diaries were daily records of activities, written at the time and on the spot. There is no hindsight, no editorializing, no propaganda; they were not intended as reflective, apologetic, or narrative documents. In the first instance, the material within the diaries provided a record by which Wesley could measure his spiritual growth. With time, these notebooks also became a useful framework and source of details for his narrative journal accounts. The cryptic entries taken together form a veritable data-bank; there are, however, few 'quotable quotes' within this mass of information.

Wesley started keeping his diary at Oxford during Lent of 1725, more than ten years before his trip to Georgia. He was inspired by a suggestion in Jeremy Taylor's *Rule and Exercises of Holy Living*, which he was reading in preparation for the episcopal examination requisite to deacon's orders. 'Care of our time', Taylor's first rule, prompted such disciplines as keeping a diary. This practice would have seemed fully appropriate to Wesley. The eighteenth century was an age of diarists, many of whom (like his own parents) saw the Christian diary as a means of promoting personal piety.

The purpose of the diary, then, was more than to provide a foothold for the memory. Not only did a carefully kept record of activities and attitudes provide a means by which to measure spiritual growth, but the very process of keeping such a record would make one more likely to 'redeem the time'. The daily, even at times hourly, process of introspection gave both the impulse toward improvement and the means to measure one's movement toward perfection.

Wesley' changing method of diary-keeping, using various systems of coded entries, was intended to provide some measure of secrecy as well as economy. In the earliest diary, a natural desire for privacy led him to develop and use a cipher to cover entries that might be considered controversial, peculiar, or too personal for prying eyes. Abbreviations and symbols quickly worked their way into the diaries, as did various ways of using number schemes. What began as a collection of brief entries for each day (a line or two) soon grew to a standard three-line entry by 1729, marked by heavy use of abbreviations. In the late spring of 1732, the entries expanded dramatically, and the method adjusted to accommodate Wesley's desire for fuller records.

By January 1734, in the midst of his most introspective period of meditative piety, the whole format of the diaries shifted to provide a full page for each day's entry. Columns were drawn on the right-hand side of the page to receive specific information beside each hour's record of activities—temper of devotion (rated on a scale from 1 to 9, 'dead' to 'highest zeal'), recollection (rated according to six 'degrees of attention'), resolutions broken, resolutions kept (referenced by letters and numbers to lists of resolutions), and blessings. A 'temper of devotion' rating of 7 was about as good as Wesley would score himself, 4 was about the minimum; 6 seems to have been an acceptable level.

This 'exacter' form of diary, as the Oxford Methodists called it, is still being used by Wesley while in Georgia. The annotations in the right-hand columns are never quite so extensive as in the 1734–35 Oxford diaries, but the framework of the system is still there and occasionally used. The columnar format often allows for daily summaries at the end of each day's entry. The bottom of many pages contains Wesley's notes gathered under three heads: 'P', for God's providential activities (such as the weather, matters of health, pastoral success, etc.); 'M', for works of God's mercy (such as being freed from temptation or preserved from a particular sin); and 'G', for evidences of divine grace (such as the level of his devotion, ability to convince others, or presence of lively zeal, etc.).

In 1735 and 1736 Wesley also began to incorporate shorthand into his diary method. While at Oxford, he had both used and taught James Weston's method (published as *Stenography Compleated; or, The Art of Short-Hand Brought to Perfection*). Fortunately for the present editor, Wesley soon dropped this complicated system, and in Georgia followed his brother Charles's suggestion to use the simplified method developed and taught by their friend John Byrom (later published as *The Universal English Short-Hand*, 1767). After December 1736 the diary entries follow the same basic pattern as before, but now most of the entries are in shorthand. Even those activities that had long been indicated by simple abbreviations are now entered in shorthand: 'p' (private prayer), 'rt' (religious talk), 'm' (meditated), and so forth.

Before leaving Georgia, Wesley begins to abandon the column format, reverting to the paragraph style that had served him earlier at Oxford. The shorthand persists, however, and is the predominant style of entry throughout the remainder of his diaries; that is, to within a week of his death in 1791.

The notebooks containing the diaries were purchased by Wesley as 'paperbooks', then bound in leather to his specifications. Some were used for other purposes: extracts of books, copies of correspondence, collections of poetry or prayers, drafts of writings. The information for the diaries was kept on scrap paper, then entered into the volume at regular intervals, depending on how detailed the material was. These occasions are usually noted: 'writ diary'. Occasionally, obvious mistakes are made—days are reversed in order (in the shorter format), misdated (sometimes for as long as a week at a time), accidentally duplicated, or omitted.

The diaries from 1742 to 1783 are missing, as are the diaries for some parts of 1727–29, 1734, 1737, and 1738. It seems unlikely that these are gaps in Wesley's diary-keeping. More likely, these portions fell victim to destruction before or after Wesley's death (apparently his wife was not without blame in this regard, as perhaps also John Pawson, one of his preachers who succeeded him at City Road Chapel), or were separated from the others and lost in the process of transmission over the years, either by intentional gift or accidental loss. The shorter gaps may have resulted from Wesley's own neglect to transfer his diary notes into the notebook. In any case, we are fortunate to have about twenty-five years of detailed private diary from Wesley's pen to accompany the journals, manuscript and published. The three types of documents complement each other nicely—each has its own kind of detail; each has its own way of providing a window into Wesley's life and thought.

The diaries give the impression of completeness and accuracy, a plethora of detailed activities noted by the hour, the half-hour, the quarter-hour, and even occasionally to the nearest ten-minute interval. The reader should not be misled by this appearance of precision; life is neither scheduled nor lived in neat quarter-hour segments, not even

Wesley's. His entries, it will be noted, also include some catch-all references, such as 'necessary business', 'walked', 'in town', 'at home'. It is usually difficult to tell what specific activities these entries might include; necessary business, for instance, could include cleaning up, doing household chores, shaving, preparing for guests, building bookshelves, or any one of a number of other 'necessary' but seemingly insignificant activities. Occasionally Wesley also listed activities as filling much more time than would normally be expected, such as 'ejaculatory prayer' for a quarter-hour (short, sentence prayers that would usually take just a few minutes), 'dressed' for a half-hour, 'thought' for a half-hour or more. In some instances, the *Journal* mentions activities that are not recorded specifically in the diary.

What we have then is a detailed, but approximate, record of Wesley's activities, recalled and recorded in such a fashion as to give a good impression of how each day was spent. Even in the simpler forms that start and end the series of diaries, though, we get an amazing picture of his energy and drive: an incomparable record of reading, preaching, travelling, writing, and publishing; seemingly endless notations of conversations, devotional activities, self-examination, and administrative duties; helpful notes on controversies, health, and even the weather. The diaries are more than a list of notes, however. They are the manifestation of 'method'. Behind the seeming monotony of repetitive entries lies an approach to life that can be ferreted out through careful examination of patterns and can be studied by analyzing changes in these patterns. Much analytical work remains to be done in this regard, and we hope the publication of these documents will assist that endeavour.

In some cases, entries are so specific as to tempt one to hope for precision. For instance, at times of Morning or Evening Prayer (especially at Oxford and in Georgia), Wesley frequently notes specific parts of the service in the Book of Common Prayer (1662), showing which he used, and in what order. A rather full listing might read 'r e c a p p s h s l 1 2 c 1 2 3 4 x s c p t b', and would indicate 'read ejaculations [i.e., scripture sentences], prayer of confession, absolution, Lord's Prayer, Psalm, scripture (First Lesson), hymn (*Te Deum*, etc.), scripture (Second Lesson), litanies (numbered), collects for the day (numbered), expounded, sang, collect (or creed), Lord's Prayer, thanksgiving, blessing'. The meaning of letters serving multiple purposes (c, s, p) is sometimes unclear, depending upon the order and context. The impression of accuracy and detail is enhanced by Wesley's frequent notation of his 'degree of attention' for each discrete section of the service by the inclusion of a symbol over many of the separate parts. Even more intriguing is the fact that the list of sections varies, often including separate parts of the service of Holy Communion (usually indicated simply by 'D'), leading one to suspect that these lists might be a good clue to Wesley's experimentations with the prayer service during his early years.

Another indication of precision in Wesley's diary method is his frequent notation of 'resolutions broken' (or 'kept'). Although the transcription in this volume does not include most of those entries, it does list those instances where Wesley himself felt they were significant enough to list them in a daily summary: 'preserved from w2', 't.5 for fifteen hours'. The symbol 'w2' is the second question relating to Wednesday's virtues, mortification and self-denial: 'Have I watched for and used all opportunities of self-denial?; 't.5' is the fifth question for Thursday's virtues, resignation and meekness: 'Have I been cheerful (not light), mild, and courteous in all I said or did?' 'w4/1' is the first aspect of the fourth question for Wednesday's virtue: 'Have I *felt*, entertained, or appeared to approve any un[chaste] thought?' These examples in the diary of careful self-examination reach a peak in 1734/35, and although they never completely disappear from Wesley's diary, they become less frequent as the years pass. The method of self-examination itself, however, persists in the life of the Methodists, as seen in various lists of rules by which Wesley and his followers guided their activities in the societies, classes, and bands.

The diaries are singularly unique documents; there were no copies made by Wesley, much less his friends. Consequently, the loss of some of these manuscript diaries over the years has left noticeable gaps in the private record of Wesley's daily activities. It does free us from the problem of variant readings for these documents. The diary material used in this volume can be described briefly as follows:

> Georgia Diary 1, Oct. 17, 1735–April 30, 1736; on 174 numbered pages, inscribed by Wesley on the front leaf in Greek, Ὁ Χριστοῦ Στρατιώτης, Θεοδρόμος Ἄοκνος . . . [several phrases from Ignatius' Epistle to Polycarp]; some additional notes at front and back in both Charles's and John's hand on unnumbered pages; Vol. XI in the Colman Collection, MA.
>
> Georgia Diary 2, May 1, 1736–Feb. 11, 1736/37; on 176 numbered pages, inscribed by Wesley on the front leaf, 'Pray without ceasing!'; some additional notes in Charles's and John's hand at front and back on unnumbered pages; in Special Collections, Woodruff Library, Emory University, Atlanta, Georgia.
>
> Georgia Diary 3, Feb. 12–Aug. 31, 1737; on pages numbered 43-188 (not in one series); additional documents and notes at front and back in Wesley's hand (resolutions, 'Of the Weekly Fasts of the Church', etc.) and other hands ('The Primitive Communicant', letter to Dr. Burton); Vol. XII in the Colman Collection, MA.

London Diary 1, April 1, 1738–Oct. 14, 1739 (with gaps from May 1–Sept. 16, and Nov. 10-21, 1738; on 88 mostly unnumbered leaves, and not in consecutive order; additional notes at front and back in Wesley's hand; Vol. XVII in the Colman Collection, MA.

The text of the diaries in this Appendix is printed in correlation with the text of the MS journals, and continues as far as the text of the published *Journal* contained for this volume.

Styling

The styling of the documents in this Appendix generally follows the method used for the published Wesley text; that is, the spelling and punctuation are usually modernized without comment, generally following the *OED*. Names of persons and places, often spelled phonetically by Wesley, have been made to conform to present standards, when known: names determined by recognized authorities, places according to the present spelling.

The complexity of the diaries presents a special challenge in styling; the method of transcription we have followed is intended to protect the integrity of the documents while assisting the reader. Abbreviations are extended without the use of brackets except in cases of uncertain meaning. A few common abbreviations are retained, without using a period (Mr, Mrs, St, etc, Jun, Dr). A small number of frequently used abbreviations are retained to save repetitious use of space ('E' for ejaculatory prayer, 'e c a p p . . . ' for parts of the Prayer service; 'w2' for his question about self-denial, and similar entries). The cross symbol (+), difficult to transliterate (representing some positive spiritual blessing, usually in association with 'lively zeal'), has been retained on each occasion of its appearance. In a few instances where headings in the daily summaries are missing but implied ('Providence', 'Grace'), they are added without brackets. Wesley's summary of his hourly ratings of 'temper of devotion' on an ascending scale is designated to the specific times (e.g., 'Grace: 7,2. 6,14' is extended to 'Grace: 7 rating twice [5 to 6 am, 4 to 5 pm]; 6 rating fourteen times') so that the reader can tell Wesley's self-rating for each hour. Punctuation has been minimized: commas are used between parts of an entry that are closely related; semicolons between less-related parts (e.g., '9.15 At home; dressed; Charles came, read Kempis, religious talk'). Abbreviations characterizing conversations often include one or more modifiers, which are included in parentheses, so that 'rtn' becomes 'religious talk (necessary)'. Marginal notes have been incorporated into the text (within parentheses) at the appropriate place, such as, '3.30 Sophy came, necessary talk (she very open)'. Shorthand entries are not differentiated from others.

Most of Wesley's entries were made in, or implied, past tense: prayed, transcribed, walked, rode, made, christened, preached, and the like. In some cases, other forms have been changed to conform to the past tense: 'sing' or 'sung' becomes 'sang'; 'eat' (sometimes understood as past tense in the eighteenth century) becomes 'ate'. Some forms of the day are retained, such as 'writ' (wrote).

The transcription is not absolutely complete. Most of the repetitive entries indicating the results of hourly self-examination have been omitted, although notable entries of this sort have been included from time to time, especially if Wesley has recognized them as especially important in some way, such as by noting them in a daily summary. Wesley's habit of recording activities in hourly segments starting rather faithfully with the beginning of every hour is not always followed; if an activity goes over into the next hour without any change or any intervening activity, the next entry noted in our transcription is the next new activity. Such repetitive entries (e.g., '9 Read Clement. 10 Read Clement. 11.00 Read Clement. 11.15 Necessary business') are simplified without losing any of the sense ('9 Read Clement. 11.15 Necessary business'). There is enough monotony in the present transcription to allow the heavily methodical flavour of the document to come through to the reader without further punctuating the style with its own frequent repetitions.

Neither the MS journals nor the diaries have been extensively annotated in this Appendix. Editorial insertions have been placed within square brackets; appropriate notes from these materials have been inserted in the annotations to the *Journal* under the corresponding dates. The following glossary is provided to assist the reader with terms that might be unfamiliar in their usage here.

Glossary

+ —an indication by Wesley of some positive spiritual virtue or blessing; perhaps 'contrition', as in Benjamin Ingham's key to the Wesleyan symbols.

Ate—transcription of 'eat' (arch. past tense); usually not at a common meal.

Breakfast—the first meal of the day, ending the fast; usually early in the morning, but on fast days at three or six o'clock in the afternoon.

Called—awakened.

Came home—returned to the abode of the day.

Dinner—the noon meal.

Dressed—changed clothes, often into clerical dress.

Ejaculatory prayer ('E')—short prayers or 'ejaculations' of praise or petition, often focusing on the main virtues; used hourly.

Garden—sat or walked in a small park, usually for meditation, prayer, or reading.

Good talk—conversation that was 'useful', the general tone or substance of which is often indicated (religious, various, etc.).

Greek Testament—read the New Testament in Greek.

Learned talk—conversation about scholarly topics.

Meditated—reflected closely upon particular virtues or other set topics, at times noted; frequently accompanied by self-examination.

Necessary business—a chore or errand such as sorting papers, preparing for a meal, shopping, etc.

Necessary talk—conversation indispensable to the furtherance of some particular action; may be further qualified (religious, various, etc.).

Prayed—probably refers to extemporary prayer, at times alone, at times with another person.

Prayer—probably refers to the use of written prayers from one of several collections of such, published and manuscript.

Private prayer—a period of prayer, read or spontaneous, by an individual either alone or in a group; similar to 'prayed'.

Rating—self-evaluation as to 'temper of devotion', on a scale of 1 to 9 (5 to 6 representing the transition to the higher, more acceptable part of the scale).

Read Prayers—use of the Book of Common Prayer for Morning and Evening Prayer, either in private devotions or in public worship; the parts of the service are sometimes indicated by the following letters, in various sequences that may indicate different adaptations:

    e—scripture sentences or ejaculations
    c—prayer of confession
    a—absolution
    p—Lord's Prayer
    p—psalm
    s—scripture (First Lesson)
    h—hymn (Te Deum, etc.)
    s—scripture (Second Lesson)
    l—litanies (numbered)
    c—collects (numbered)
    i—intercessory prayer
    x—expounded (sermon)
    D—Eucharist or Holy Communion
    s—sang
    c—creed
    p—Lord's Prayer

t—prayer of thanksgiving

b—blessing

Read—may imply 'read together' or 'studied'.

Religious talk—conversation characterized by spiritual or religious concerns, the nature of which is often indicated (useful, necessary, etc.).

Sacrament—the sacrament of the Lord's Supper.

Sermon—when following 'read Prayers' usually may be read 'preached', though at times may simply indicate attendance at a preaching service.

Set out—began a trip, often on foot.

Supper—the evening meal.

t.5—indication of Wesley's fifth question relative to Thursday's virtues, resignation and meekness: 'Have I been cheerful (not light), mild, and courteous in all I said or did?'

Various talk—conversation that covers a number of topics, the prevailing tone or subject of which is often described (useful, religious, etc.).

Visited—made a pastoral call upon someone.

w2—indication of Wesley's second question relative to Wednesday's virtues, mortification and self-denial: 'Have I watched for and used all opportunities of self-denial?'

w4/1—indication of the first aspect of Wesley's fourth question relative to Wednesday's virtues: 'Have I *felt*, entertained, or appeared to approve any un[chaste] thought?'

Walked—often a solitary perambulation for exercise or meditation; 'walked with' might also be read 'went with'.

Writ diary—transcribed notes of daily or hourly recollection into diary.

Writ notes—gathering of material for a document to be written, or summary reflections upon an event that has recently transpired.

1.:. Oct. 17. 1735. Fr.

On board ye Simmonds, off Gravesend
5 ½ dr. p̄ wh-Ingh. 6. t of disposing our
7. buisin & Studies. 7. w to ye Rector, Mr
8 Hutchins, Sbm. 8½ tea. rt 9. nb ½ rpr
10¼ writ diar ½ b German Gramar. 12
12 p̄. German 2¾ p̄. F rt 4. b Deacon
5. w Delamotte &c 5. rt w Ambrosius
6 Tackner he resolved to be baptized!
7. ½ su. rt 7¼ d. rp betw decks. vis a sick
8. Moravian. rt 8½ rt. p̄. u 9¼

Sat. 18.

4 ½ dr. p̄. began Genesis 6. Deacon ¾ w to
7. V, Mr Sall Andrews, Sbm 8. F. w to Salm-
9. Clat. 10. Falcon w Tackner, baptized h. !
11. Delamott Ser. r Whiston's Catechism
1. ½ di 2½ on board. rt 3½ German. 4. Cbis
4 w to SH, Mr Vernon, Mr Hutcheson, m
5. m, Riv. 5½ t. 6¼ d ½ su. 7. German
7 w Tackner. rt p̄ 9¼

Su. 19

4. dr. p̄ Scripture. 6. Deacon. 7. Kempis
8. Xavier. t 10. rp. pr extempore. D. 3
11. Com. 12. Xavier. 1. di d. p̄. 2. r w Tackr
3. rp. exp. 4. An w Herndorf. 5. t. rt w
6 Mrs Tackner. ½ p̄. rt 6½ su. 7¼ An w O.
8. sung w Germans ¾ w O. An. p̄. 9.40.

MANUSCRIPT VOYAGE JOURNAL
October 14, 1735–February 16, 1735/36

Tuesday, October 14, 1735. About nine in the morning, Mr. Ingham, of Queen's College, Mr. Delamotte, son of a sugar merchant in London, aged twenty-one years (who had offered himself some days before, and showed an earnest desire to bear us company), my brother and myself, took boat for Gravesend. The design that moved us all to leave our native country was not to avoid want (God having given us plenty of temporal blessings), nor to gain riches and honour, which we trust he will ever enable us to look on as no other than dung and dross; but singly this—to save our souls, and to live wholly to the glory of God.

Mr. Burton, one of the Trustees, Mr. Morgan of Lincoln College, and Mr. Hutton, Jun., of Westminster, set out with us.

About four in the afternoon we found the *Simmonds* at Gravesend, and immediately went on board. My brother and I had a cabin allotted us in the forecastle, which had been designed for Mr. Hall [R—but he did not come]. Mr. Ingham and Mr. Delamotte had the next; we chose to be here for privacy, there being a partition between the forecastle and the rest of the ship.

Wednesday and Thursday we spent chiefly with Mr. Morgan and Mr. Hutton, partly on board, partly on shore, in exhorting one another to shake off every weight, and run with patience the race set before us [Heb. 12:1].

Friday, October 17. I began to learn German, in order to converse a little with the Moravians, twenty-six of whom we had on board, men who have left all for their Master, and who have indeed learned of him, being meek and lowly, dead to the world, full of faith and of the Holy Ghost.

GEORGIA DIARY 1
October 17, 1735—April 30, 1736

FRIDAY, OCTOBER 17. On board the *Simmonds*, off Gravesend. 5.30 Dressed; prayed; with Charles and Ingham. 6 Talk of disposing our business and studies. 7 Writ to the Rector [of Lincoln College], Mr. Hutchins, sister Emily. 8.30 Tea, necessary talk. 9 Necessary business. 9.30 Read Prayers. 10.15 Writ diary. 10.30 Began German Grammar. 12 Prayed; German. 2.45 Prayed; tea; religious talk. 4 Began Deacon with Delamotte, etc. 5 Religious talk with

Saturday, October 18. I baptized at his desire Ambrosius Tackner, aged thirty; he had received only lay baptism before. We dined on shore with Mr. Delamotte's father, who was come down on purpose to see him, and was not fully reconciled (which is the power of God) to what he at first vigorously opposed.

Sunday, October 19. The weather being fair and mild, we had the Morning Prayer on quarter-deck. I now began to preach extempore to a numerous and as it then seemed serious congregation. We then celebrated the Holy Eucharist, Ambrosius Tackner and two more communicating with us—a little flock which we did not doubt God would increase in due time.

Monday, October 20. My brother and I began to try how a vegetable diet would agree with us, which it has done hitherto perfectly well. In the afternoon Mr. Nitschmann, pastor of the Moravians, Mr. Van Hermsdorf, and Andrew Dober began to learn English. May God give us all not only to be of one tongue, but of one mind and one heart!

Tuesday, October 21. God sending us a fair wind, we set sail from

---

Ambrosius Tackner, he resolved to be baptized. 6.30 Supper, religious talk. 7.15 Writ diary; read Prayers between decks; visited a sick Moravian, necessary talk. 8.30 Religious talk; prayed; undressed. 9.15.

SATURDAY, OCTOBER 18. 4.30 Dressed; began Genesis. 6 Deacon. 6.45 Writ to Varanese [Sally Kirkham], Miss Sally Andrews, sister Emily. 8 Tea; writ to Salmon and Clayton. 10 Faulcon[er?] with Tackner, baptized him. 11 Delamotte Senior, read Whiston's *Catechism*. 1.30 Dinner. 2.30 On board; religious talk. 3.30 German. 4 Cabin; writ to sister Kezzy, Mr Vernon, Mr Hutcheson, my mother, Rivington. 5.30 Tea. 6.15 Writ diary. 6.30 Supper. 7 German; with Tackner, religious talk; prayed. 9.15.

SUNDAY, OCTOBER 19. 4 Dressed; prayed; Scripture. 6 Deacon. 7 Kempis. 8 Xavier; tea. 10 Read Prayers, preached extempore, Sacrament (three communicants). 12 Xavier. 1 Dinner; writ diary; prayed. 2 Read with Tackner. 3 Read Prayers, expounded. 4 Religious talk (necesssary) with Hermsdorf. 5 Tea; religious talk with Mrs Tackner. 5.30 Prayed; religious talk. 6.30 Supper. 7.15 Religious talk with Oglethorpe. 8 Sang with Germans. 8.45 With Oglethorpe, religious talk (necessary); prayed. 9.40.

MONDAY, OCTOBER 20. 4 Dressed; prayed; Scripture. 6 Deacon. 7 Xavier. 8 Tea; religious talk. 9 Transcribed letter. 10.15 Read Prayers; letter. 1 Xavier; necessary talk with Von Reck. 2.30 Dinner; Xavier. 4.30 German. 5 Began English with Nitschmann and Hermsdorf. 5.30 Writ diary; prayed. 6 Supper, religious talk. 6.45 English with Nitschmann and Hermsdorf. 7.15 They sang. 8 Prayers; religious talk; read Se[rmon?]. 9 Undressed; prayed.
[N.B.] Left off eating flesh.

TUESDAY, OCTOBER 21. 4.30 Dressed; prayed; Bible. 6 Deacon. 7.30 Religious talk (necessary) with Oglethorpe; tea; read Prayers. 10 German. 1 On board

Gravesend. When we were past half the Kentish [i.e., Goodwin] Sands, the wind failed us. Had the calm continued till the change of the tide, the ship had probably been lost. But the wind sprung up again shortly after, and carried us safe into the Downs. We began now to recover a little regularity of life. Our common way of spending our time was this: from four to five we used private prayer. From five to seven we read the Holy Scriptures, adding sometimes such treatises as give an account of the sense thereof, which was once delivered to the saints. At seven we breakfasted. At eight were the public prayers, at which were present usually between thirty and forty of our eighty passengers. From nine to twelve I commonly learned German, Mr. Delamotte Greek. My brother wrote sermons, and Mr. Ingham read some treatise of divinity, or taught the children. At twelve we met to give an account to one another of what we had done since our last meeting, and what we designed to do before our next. About one we dined. The time from dinner till four we spent with the people, part in public reading, part in reading or speaking to those severally of whom each of us had taken charge. At four we had Evening Prayer, and the children were instructed and catechized before the congregation, unless when the Second Lesson was explained, as it always was in the morning. Between five and six we joined in private prayer. From six to seven I read in our cabin to one or two of the passengers, and my brother to two or three more in theirs. At seven Mr. Ingham read to as many as desired to hear, which time I spent with the Germans in their public service. At eight we met again, to instruct and exhort one another, and between nine and ten we went to bed, where neither the roaring of the sea nor the motion of the ship could take away the refreshing sleep which God gave us.

———————

Captain Thomas [i.e., his ship], necessary talk. 1.30 Dinner; ended Xavier. 3 German; Hermsdorf and Nitschmann. 5.15 Tea. 5.30 Religious talk; prayed. 6 Supper; Prayers. 7 With Germans. 8.45 Meditated. 9.15 Prayed.

    Resolve: No tea in afternoon.

WEDNESDAY, OCTOBER 22. 5 Prayed; E; prayed. 6 Bible. 7 Deacon. 7.20 Necessary talk. 8 Prayed; German. 9 Tea. 9.45 Nitschmann. 10.45 German. 12.45 Prayed; German. 2.15 Nitschmann and Hermsdorf. 3 Prayed; bread and butter, religious talk. 3.30. German. 4.15 Read Prayers. 5 German. 6.15 Supper with all. 7 With Germans. 8.30 Quarter-deck; meditated; prayed. 9 Undressed.

THURSDAY, OCTOBER 23. 4 Dressed; prayed; Bible. 6 Deacon. 7 German. 7.30 Read Prayers. 8 Necessary talk (religious) with Oglethorpe; tea. 9.30 Nitschmann and Hermsdorf. 10.45 German. 12 Dinner; ended German Grammar. 2 Aboard Captain Thomas; visited sick woman, religious talk, prayed. 3 Religious talk with Von Reck. 4.30 At home; read Prayers. 5 Religious talk with Betty Tackner and Mr Hird. 5.45 Prayed. 6 Supper. 7 With Germans. 8 Deacon; prayed; undressed. 9.

Friday, October 24. Having a rolling sea, most of the passengers began to feel the effects of it. Mr. Delamotte's sickness was very violent, and lasted several days, Mr. Ingham's not half an hour. My brother's head ached pretty much. Hitherto it has pleased God that the sea has not disordered me at all; nor have I been hindered one quarter of an hour either from reading, writing, composing, or any other thing [I and R—business] I could have done on shore. During our stay in the Downs, some or other of us went, as often as we had an opportunity, on board the other ship which sailed with us, in which we found many persons glad to join in the prayers of the Church and to hear the Word of God explained.

Sunday, October 26. We had a new communicant.

FRIDAY, OCTOBER 24. 4 E; prayed alone. 4.45 Prayed with them. 5 E; prayed; Bible. 6 E; Deacon; prayed. 7 E; began Common Prayer with Deacon. 7.20 Writ diary. 7.45 Religious talk with Oglethorpe, he right. 8 Religious talk. 8.15 Read [Prayers] e c a p p etc. 9 E; German. 9.30 Aboard [Captain] Thomas, religious talk. 10 With the Salzburgers, prayed. 11 Read Prayers, preached. 12 E; visited; prayed; at home; writ diary. 12.30 German. 1 E; Nitschmann. 1.30 German. 2 E; German. 2.45 Prayed. 3 E; dinner; tossed; well. 4 Read Prayers; German. 5 German; they sick, I well. 6 E; tea; they idle talk; well. 7 E; with Germans. 8 E; Nalson; prayed; undressed.
> Providence: Quite well all day. Oglethorpe quite right. Prayed in the other ship. With the Salzburgers.
> Mercy: Preserved from intemperance, etc.
> Grace: Lively zeal twice [11 to 12 am, 7 to 8 pm].

SATURDAY, OCTOBER 25. 4 E; prayed with them. 4.15 Prayed alone. 5 E; Bible. 6 E; Deacon and Common Prayer. 7 E; Deacon and Common Prayer. 7.30 German. 8 E; read e c a p p s h s c p t b. 8.40 Tea, religious talk. 9 E; religious talk. 9.15 German. 9.30 In Captain Thomas, religious talk. 10 E; read Prayers, preached. 11.15 Visited Mrs Walker, religious talk (dispute). 12 E; religious talk; prayed. 12.30 At home; religious talk (necessary). 1 E; religious and useful talk. 1.30 Dinner. 2 E; dinner. 2.45 German. 3 E; German. 4 E; German. 5 E; read Prayers. 6 E; supper, religious talk. 7 E; Germans. 8 With Charles, etc; Charles perverse; prayed; Bible. 9 Undressed.
> Providence: Well. Prayed in other ship.
> Mercy: Preserved [from] intemperance [at supper].
> Grace: Lively zeal [10 to 11 am].

SUNDAY, OCTOBER 26. 4 E; prayed; prayer (private). 5 E; Bible; prayed. 6 E; Nalson; prayed. 7 E; dressed. 7.30 Necessary talk. 8 E; read Prayers; tea. 9 E; good talk. 9.45 In the other ship. 10 E; read Prayers, preached; at home. 11 E; religious talk. 11.30 Read Prayers. 12 E; preached, Sacrament (four communicants). 1 E; religious talk with Oglethorpe. 1.30 Dinner. 2 E; they good talk. 2.30 Religious talk with Charles, etc. 3 E; prayed; religious talk. 3.15 With men, religious talk. 3.30 Religious talk with Oglethorpe. 3.50 [Read] e c a p p s h s c p t b. 4.45 Religious talk, preached [?]. 5 E; prayed. 5.15 Religious talk.

Monday, October 27. Mr. Johnson complained to Mr. Oglethorpe that having the public prayer [I and R—prayers] in the great cabin was a great inconvenience to him. He said he could not bear to stay in the room when so many people were in it; and that he could not stay out of it while they were there, for fear of catching cold. After some dispute the matter was compromised, that the prayers in the morning (during which Mr. Johnson was in bed) should be read in the cabin, and the afternoon prayer [I and R—prayers] between decks (the quarter-deck being too cold). The fore hatchway was the best place we could find there, though indeed it was very dirty and very noisy, and so small it would not hold above half [I—a quarter of] our congregation, and so low none of them

---

5.30 Supper. 6 E; thought. 6.30 Read resolutions. 7 E; with Germans. 8 E; religious talk; prayed; undressed.

Providence: Well. Four communicants. Strengthened one another.

Grace: Convincing thrice [10 to 11 am, 3.30 to 5 pm].

Mercy: Lively zeal twice [10 to 11 am, 4 to 5 pm].

MONDAY, OCTOBER 27. 4 E; prayed; prayer (private). 5 E; religious talk. 5.15 Bible; rolling sea. 6 E; Deacon and Common Prayer; prayed. 7 E; religious talk with Oglethorpe (he right). 8 E; read Prayers; necessary business. 9 E; tea. 9.30 Began *Gesangbuch*. 10 E; German. 11 E; German. 12 E; German. 1 E; dinner; German. 2 E; German; writ diary. 3 E; German; religious talk with Lawley. 4 E; read Prayers. 4.45 Religious talk; Mr Johnson angry. 5 E; religious talk. 5.30 Mostly religious talk. 6 E; supper, they [had] various talk. 7 E; with Germans. 8 E. 8.15 With Charles, etc, religious talk. 8.45 Prayed; undressed.

Providence: Rolling sea, yet well. Oglethorpe right, Mr Johnson angry at our having Prayers.

TUESDAY, OCTOBER 28. 4 E; dressed; prayed; private prayer. 5 E; Bible. 6 E; Deacon and Common Prayer. 7 E; Common Prayer; dressed; necessary business. 8 E; Deacon. 8.30 Read Prayers. 9 E. 9.15 Tea; religious talk. 10 E; religious and useful talk. 10.30 German. 11 E; German; religious talk. 12 E; German. 1 E; German. 2 E; dinner; German. 3 E; religious talk with men. 4 E; religious talk. 4.30 Buried James Proctor. 5 E; religious talk. 5.45 Prayed. 6 E; supper, religious talk. 7 E; religious talk. 7.30 With Germans. 8 E; Gregory Lopez. 8.45 Undressed; prayed.

Providence: Well. Men affected.

WEDNESDAY, OCTOBER 29. 4 E; dressed; prayed. 5 E; Bible; prayed. 6 E; began Wall on Baptism. 7 E; Wall. 7.30 German; necessary talk with Oglethorpe. 8 E; German. 8.15 Read Prayers, preached. 9 E. 9.10 Breakfast. 9.30 German. 10 E; German. 11 E; German. 12 E; prayed; religious talk; German. 1 E; Life of Lopez. 2 E; Lopez; prayed. 3 E; religious talk. 3.45 Dinner. 4 E; with them. 4.30 Read Prayers. 5 E; necessary talk. 5.20 Prayed. 5.40 Supper. 6 E; religious talk. 7 E; with the Germans. 7.30 With Charles, etc. 8 E; religious talk; prayed; undressed.

Providence: Well. Rough Sea. Mr Johnson kind!

Grace: Lively zeal.

could stand upright. But these, and far greater inconveniences, vanish away before a desire to please God.

Friday, October 31. It pleased God that the wind came fair, and we sailed out of the Downs. At eleven at night I was waked by a great noise. Upon inquiry I found there was no danger, but the bare apprehension of it gave me a lively conviction what manner of men ought those to be who are every moment on the brink of eternity.

Saturday, November 1. We came to St. Helen's harbour, off the Isle of Wight.

Sunday, November 2. We passed the fleet at Spithead, and fell down into Cowes Road.

THURSDAY, OCTOBER 30. 4 E; dressed; prayed; private prayer (sea rough). 5 E; Bible; prayed. 6 E; Wall; prayed. 7 E; Wall. 7.15 German. 8 E; read Prayers, preached. 9 E; tea. 9.30 German. 10 E; German. 11 E; German. 12 E; prayed with Charles, etc, religious talk (necessary). 1 E; writ resolutions. 1.40 German. 2 E; German. 2.30 Dinner. 3.15 Under deck, religious talk; began Law; lively zeal, they affected. 4 E; read Prayers; prayed. 5 E; prayed. 5.30 Prayed; spoke to sailors. 6 E; religious talk. 6.30 Supper (preserved from intemperance). 7 E; with Germans. 8 E; read Law; prayed; undressed.

> Providence: Well. Sea more still. Began reading under deck. All seemed affected; sailors and cook seemed affected.
> Grace: Lively zeal [3 to 4 pm].

FRIDAY, OCTOBER 31. 4 E; dressed; prayed; writ diary; private prayer (wind faster). 5 E; Bible. 6 E; Wall. 7 E; Wall. 7.30 Necessary business; dressed. 8 E; read Prayers. 9 E; tea. 10 E; German. 11 E; German. 12 E; religious and useful talk with Oglethorpe. 12.30 With Charles, etc, prayed, religious talk. 1 E; religious talk. 1.45 Read under deck. 2 E; read [aloud]. 2.45 Prayed. 3 E; religious talk; dinner. 4 E; read Prayers; religious and useful talk with Oglethorpe. 5 E; prayed; supper, religious talk. 6 E; religious talk. 6.30 With Germans. 7 E; with Germans. 7.30 With Charles, etc, Law. 8 E; *Christian Perfection*. 8.30 Religious talk; prayed; undressed. 11 Waked by great noise; afraid to die!

> Providence: Well. Began *Christian Perfection* to them. They seemed affected [2 to 3 pm].
> Grace: Renewed resolutions. Lively zeal [1 to 3 pm].

SATURDAY, NOVEMBER 1. 4 E; dressed; prayed; private prayer. 5 E; Bible; writ diary. 6 E; Wall; prayed. 7 Prayed; Wall. 7.30 Dressed; German. 8 Prayed, c a p p s h s c p t b. 9 E; religious talk (necessary) with Oglethorpe. 9.15 Tea; various talk (religious). 10 E; German. 11 E; German. 11.45 Read Oglethorpe's letter. 12 Prayed; religious talk with Charles, etc. 1 Writ to my mother and Mr Vernon. 2 Dinner. 3 E; *Christian Perfection*. 4 E; read Prayers. 5 E; prayed; prayed. 6 Supper; religious talk. 7 With Germans. 8 Read resolutions to Charles, etc. 8.45 Prayed; undressed.

> Providence: Well. Resolved to Amend! [12 to 1 pm] Safe at St. Helen's.
> Grace: Lively zeal [3 to 4 pm].

SUNDAY, NOVEMBER 2. 4 E; dressed; prayed; private prayer. 5 E; sang; prayed.

5.45 Religious talk. 6 E; prayed; Johnson. 7 E; dressed; religious talk. 8 E; tea, they [had] various talk. 9 E; read Lopez (reproved the Captain). 10.15 Read Prayers. 11 Preached. 11.30 Religious talk with Mrs Mackay, interrupted. 12 E; religious talk; Delamotte, religious talk. 1 Dinner. 2 E; they various talk. 2.15 Lopez. 3 Read Prayers, preached. 4 On board Captain Thomas, read Prayers. 5 Religious and useful talk; at home; prayed. 6 Supper, religious talk. 7 E; with Germans. 8 Read Law; prayed; undressed.

Providence: Well. Reproved; they affected. Delamotte [between noon and 1 pm]!

Grace: Convincing twice [9 to 10 am, 3 to 4 pm].

Monday, November 3. 4 E; dressed; prayed; private prayer. 5 E; Bible; prayed. 6 E; necessary business. 6.15 Religious talk with Oglethorpe. 7 Religious talk. 7.30 Breakfast. 8 Read Prayers, preached. 9 Necessary business. 10 In the Isle of Wight with Charles, etc, necessary talk (religious). 11 Religious talk, very pleasant. 12 Newport; dinner. 1.15. Set out, religious talk. 2 Met Mr Oglethorpe, religious talk, sang. 3 Religious talk. 3.30 Captain Thomas', read Prayers. 4 Preached. 4.30 At home; read Prayers. 5 E; prayed. 5.45 Writ diary; supper; Mrs Mackay. 6 E; religious talk. 6.30 Writ notes. 7 E; with Germans. 8 E; religious talk with Charles, etc; prayed.

Providence: Well. Pleasant walk. Agreed with Charles, etc.

Grace: From 4 to 5 am, 7 rating.

Tuesday, November 4. 4 E; dressed; prayed; private prayer. 5 E; Bible; prayed. 6 E; prayed; Wall. 7 E; Wall. 7.15 Tea; necessary business. 8 Read Prayers; prayed; prayed. 9 E; transcribed names. 10 E; names. 10.15 German. 11 E; German. 12 E. 12.15 With Charles, etc, religious talk, prayed. 1 E. 1.15 German. 2 E; Dinner. 2.45 German. 3 E; religious talk with Hird and family, they affected. 4 Read Prayers, preached. 5 E; prayed; writ resolutions. 6 E; prayed; supper. 7 E; German. 8 E; began account of [Westley] Hall; prayed; undressed.

Providence; Well. Began visiting [3 to 4 pm]; they affected.

Grace: 7 rating twice [4 to 6 am].

Wednesday, November 5. 4 E; dressed; writ diary; prayed 1 3 2; private prayer. 5 E; Bible; prayed. 6 E; Wall.7 E; necessary business; tea. 8 E; Mr Oglethorpe, tea with women. 9 Read Prayers, preached. 10 E; began transcribing my sermon. 11 E; German. 12 E; German. 12.15 With Ingham, religious talk. 1 E; Religious talk with Davison, etc. 2 E; dinner, they various talk. 3 E; religious talk with Hird, etc. 4 E; read Prayers, preached (lively zeal). 5 Explained. 5.30 Necessary talk with Oglethorpe. 6 Necessary talk. 6.30 Supper. 7 E; German. 8 With Charles, etc, necessary business. 9 Prayed; undressed. 9.30.

Providence: Well. They affected [3 to 4 pm].

Grace: Lively zeal [4 to 5 pm]. Convincing [4 to 5 pm].

Thursday, November 6. 4 E; dressed; writ diary; prayed; prayed. 5 E; Bible. 6 E; Wall. 7 E; tea, religious talk. 7.45 Writ sermon. 8 Read Prayers, expounded. 9 E; transcribed sermon. 10 E; sermon. 10.30 German. 11 E; German. 12 E; German. 12.15 With Charles, etc, prayed, religious talk. 1 E; religious talk. 1.15 Sermon. 1.30 Dinner. 2 E. 2.15 Visited. 3 E; visited. 3.30 Read to them. 4 E; read Prayers, expounded. 5 E; private prayer; prayed. 6 E; supper, religious talk;

Sunday, November 9. A gay young woman, who casually heard me speaking to another of the nature of Christianity, appeared to be much surprised and affected; but good company soon restored her to her former gaiety. The wind was fair; but the man-of-war which was to convoy us not being yet ready, obliged us to wait for her. This was a glorious opportunity of building up our fellow-travellers in the knowledge of Christ, wherein they needed to be instructed little less than the savages of America. May he whose seed we have endeavoured to sow among them give it the increase in his due [I and R—good] time!

---

writ diary. 7 E; with Germans. 8 E; with Charles, etc, *Pietas Hallensis*. 8.45 Prayed.
  Providence: Well. Stormy [8 to 9 pm].
  Grace: 7 rating three times [4 to 6 am, 5 to 6 pm]. + [5 to 6 pm].

Friday, November 7. 5.45 Dressed. 6 E; prayed; Bible. 7 E; tea, religious talk. 7.30 Transcribed sermon. 8 Read Prayers. 9 E; expounded. 9.20 Sermon. 10 E; German. 11 E; German. 12 E; with Charles, etc, prayed, religious talk; explained with Captain. 1 E; religious talk. 1.30 Law to them. 2 Law; visited; prayed. 3 E; dinner. 3.45 Sermon. 4 Read Prayers, expounded. 5 E; expounded. 5.15 Prayed with Ingham, etc. 5.45 Lopez. 6 E; prayed; supper, religious talk. 6.45 With Germans. 7 E; with Germans. 8 E; read *Pietas Hallensis*; prayed.
  Providence: Well. Explained with Captain Cornish and Mr Johnson as to Prayers [noon to 1 pm].
  Grace: (con) [noon to 1 pm].

Saturday, November 8. 4 E; dressed; Deacon. 4.45 Private prayer. 5 E; Bible. 6 E; prayed; Wall. 7 E; prayed; tea. 7.30 Sermon. 8 E; read Prayers, preached, expounded. 9 E; sermon. 10 E; sermon. 10.30 German. 11 E; with Germans. 12 E; with Charles, etc, prayed, religious talk. 1 E; religious talk with men. 1.15 Sermon. 2 E; dinner. 2.30 Sermon. 3 E; read. 4 Read Prayers, expounded. 5 E; expounded. 5.30 Prayed; writ diary. 6 E; prayed; supper, religious talk. 7 E; with Germans. 8 E; *Pietas Hallensis*. 9 Prayed; undressed.
  Providence: Well.
  Grace: 7 rating three times [4 to 7 am].

Sunday, November 9. <4? E; dressed;> prayed 1, 2, 3; private prayer. <5 E;> Bible; prayed. <6> E; Wall. 6.30 Religious talk with Oglethorpe (he open). 7 E; tea. 7.30 Sermon. 8 Read Prayers, expounded. 9 E; sermon. 10 E; sermon; Mr Oglethorpe talked, waited. 11 Charles read Prayers, expounded. 12 Sacrament; prayed; sang. 12.30 Sermon ([cold] cured in a moment). 1 E; sermon. 1.30 Dinner. 2 E; dinner. 2.15 Sermon. 3 E; religious talk with [Will] Moore, etc; with Oglethorpe (all affected). 4 E; read Prayers, preached. 5 E. 5.15 Prayed; supper. 6 E; supper, religious talk. 6.45 With Germans. 7 E; with Germans. 8 E; prayed; *Pietas Hallensis*; prayed.
  Providence: Cold worse ['a cold' at 7 am]. Oglethorpe open (at 8). Much better of cold. All affected [at 3 pm]; Mrs Hawkins spoke to me.
  Grace: Lively zeal. 7 rating twice [5 to 6 am, noon to 1 pm].

MONDAY, NOVEMBER 10. 5 E; dressed; prayed 1, 2, 3. 5.30 Writ diary; prayed. 6 E; Bible; prayed. 7 E; tea; necessary talk with Oglethorpe. 8 Read Prayers, expounded. 9 E; sorted things. 10 E. 10.15 Transcribed sermon. 11 E; with Germans. 12.15 Religious talk with Charles and Ingham, prayed. 1 E; religious talk with [Von] Reck. 1.30 Dinner; ended sermon. 2 E; read. 3 E; read. 3.30 Religious talk with Hird[s] (they affected). 4 Read Prayers, expounded. 5.15 Prayed; necessary business. 6 E. 6.15 Supper, religious talk. 7 E; with Germans. 8 E; religious talk. 8.15 With Charles and Ingham, *Pietas Hallensis*. 9 Undressed.

Providence: No man-of-war come. Hird, etc, affected!

Grace: 7 rating once [5 to 6 am].

TUESDAY, NOVEMBER 11. 4 E; dressed; necessary business; prayed. 5 E; Bible. 6 E; prayed; Wall. 7 E; tea, religious talk. 7.30 Lopez. 8 E; e c a p p s h s c p t b, expounded. 9 E; German. 10 E; German. 11 E; with Germans. 12 E. 12.15 With Charles and Ingham, prayed, religious talk, prayed. 1 E; read. 2 E; Lopez; dinner. 3 E; religious talk with Hirds. 4 Read Prayers. 4.40 Expounded. 5 Expounded; prayed with Charles, etc. 6 E; religious talk; supper. 7 E; with Germans. 8 E; Francke. 9 Prayed; undressed.

Providence: Well. Hird, etc, affected.

Grace: 7 rating once [5 to 6 am].

WEDNESDAY, NOVEMBER 12. 4 E; dressed; writ diary; prayed; prayed. 5 E; Bible; prayed. 6 E; Wall. 7 E; tea, religious talk. 7.30 Religious talk with Oglethorpe. 8 Read Prayers, expounded. 9 E; began Lawrence with Ingham. 10 E; German. 11 E; with Germans. 12 E; prayed with Charles, etc, religious talk (lively zeal). 1 E; read (they affected). 2 E; Lawrence. 3 E; prayed; dinner, religious talk. 4 Read Prayers, expounded. 5 Religious talk with Mrs Tackner (she convinced and resolved to stay). 6 E; supper, religious talk. 7 E; with Germans. 8 E; Francke; prayed.

Providence: Well. Hird, etc, affected. Mrs Tackner convinced.

Grace: 7 rating four times [5 to 6, 8 to 10 am, noon to 1 pm]. t.5 for fifteen hours [all except 4 to 5 am]. Lively zeal twice [8 to 9 am and at noon].

THURSDAY, NOVEMBER 13. 4 E; dressed; prayed; private prayer. 5 E; Bible; prayed. 6 E; prayed; Wall. 7 E; tea. 7.30 Lawrence. 8 E; read Prayers, expounded. 9 E; Lawrence. 10 E; German. 11 E; with Germans. 12 E; prayed; religious talk. 1 E; read. 2 E; dinner. 2.45 Hird, religious talk. 3 E; religious talk. 4 Read Prayers, expounded (they affected). 5 E; religious talk; prayed; supper. 6 E; prayed; supper. 6.45 With Germans. 7 E; [with] Germans. 8 E; Francke. 9 Prayed; undressed. 9.15.

Providence: Well. Dispute with Hird [at 2 pm]; agreed. Read to all [at 4 pm], they seemed affected.

Mercy: Preserved from t.5 six times [noted once 4 to 5 am].

Grace: 7 rating thrice [4 to 6, 9 to 10 am].

FRIDAY, NOVEMBER 14. 4 E; dressed; prayed; private prayer. 5 E; Bible; prayed. 6 E; Wall; prayed. 7 E; tea, religious talk; Lopez (t.6 with Ingham). 8 E; read Prayers, expounded. 9 E; religious talk (necessary) with Oglethorpe. 9.30 Lawrence. 10 E; writ to Rivington. 11 E; with Germans. 12 E; prayed with Charles, etc, religious talk, prayed (all agreed). 1 E; read. 1.30 Religious talk

Sunday, November 16. Thomas Hird, Grace his wife, Mark his son, twenty-one, Phoebe his daugher, seventeen, who had been educated among the Quakers, were, at their earnest desire, and after frequent and careful instruction, received into the Church by baptism, whereby we gained four more serious and frequent [I and R—constant] communicants. Our custom had hitherto been, besides the Second Lesson, to explain part of the Common Prayer after service. But being informed, some of the people were tired with so much expounding, we proposed to them fairly to leave it off. This they utterly protested against, and desired us to go on as we began, which I did till we came out to sea.

---

with Mrs Tackner. 2 E; religious talk with Hird, etc. 2.45 Prayed (lively zeal, they affected). 3 E; dinner, religious talk. 4 Prayers, expounded. 5 Explained. 6 Supper, religious talk. 6.40 Necessary business. 7 E; with Germans. 8 E; necessary business. 9.15 Prayed.

Providence: Well. All agreed [at noon]; Hird, etc, agreed [at 2 pm].

Grace: Lively zeal [2 to 3 pm]. 7 rating thrice [4 to 6 am, noon to 1 pm].

SATURDAY, NOVEMBER 15. 4 E; dressed; prayed; writ diary; private prayer. 5 E; Bible; prayed. 6 E; Wall; prayed. 7 E; tea, religious talk; Lawrence. 8 E; read Prayers. 8.40 Lawrence. 9 E; Lawrence. 10 E; German. 11 E; with Germans. 12 E; with Charles, etc, prayed, religious talk. 1 E; read. 1.30 Lawrence. 2 E; dinner. 2.45 Lawrence. 3 E; religious talk with Hird, etc. 4 Read Prayers, expounded, lively zeal. 5 E; private prayer; prayed. 6 E; supper, religious talk. 6.30 Lawrence. 7 E; with Germans. 8 E; ended Lawrence. 8.30 Francke. 9 Prayed; undressed. 9.15.

Providence: Cold near gone.

Grace: Lively zeal [4 to 5 pm]. + [at 5 pm].

SUNDAY, NOVEMBER 16. 4.30 E; dressed; prayed. 5 E; prayed. 5.15 Bible. 6 E; Bible; prayed. 6.30 Necessary business. 6.45 Bible. 7 E; tea, religious talk. 7.30 Sang. 8 Baptized Thomas, Grace, Mark, and Phoebe Hird, religious talk. 9 E; read e c a etc, expounded; writ diary. 10 E; sang; Kempis; prayed. 11 E; read Prayers, preached (lively zeal). 12 Prayed, Sacrament, prayed. 12.30 Religious talk. 12.45 Lopez. 1 E; Lopez. 2 E; dinner, they [had] various talk. 3 E; religious talk with Hird, etc (they affected). 4 Read Prayers, expounded. 5 E; meditated; supper; prayed with Ingham (t.6 with Ingham). 6 E; supper; began Collier. 6.45 Necessary business. 7 E; with Germans. 8 E; read Collier's *Reasons*. 9 *Reasons*. 9.30.

Providence: Well. Baptized Thomas, Grace, Mark, Phoebe Hird. They affected [at 3 pm].

Grace: 7 rating seven times; + [at 10 am]. Lively zeal [at 11 am].

MONDAY NOVEMBER 17. 4 E; dressed; prayed; private prayer. 5 E; prayed; Bible. 6 E; Wall; prayed. 7 E; tea (no taste). 7.30 Wall. 8 Read Prayers, expounded. 9 E; Wall. 10 E; writ to Clayton, to Salmon. 11 E; with Germans. 12 With Ingham, prayed, religious talk. 1 E; dinner (all people angry); ended Collier's *Reasons*. 2

Wednesday, November 19. The man-of-war came, and the wind turned against us. Between twelve and one at night a gentleman who was disgusted at our occasioning (as he supposed) his maid to be set on shore, who was a known drunkard and suspected of theft and unchastity, waked us by dancing over our heads; but he begged our pardon the next day, and seemed convinced we had done him no wrong.

Thursday, November 20. We left Cowes, and at four in the afternoon anchored at Yarmouth; but the next day we were obliged to return to Cowes. During our stay in this harbour there were several storms, in one of which two ships that were in the road before Yarmouth, whence we were driven back, were stranded on the island.

E; Collier. 2.40 Hird, etc, read Wilson. 3 E; religious talk with Phoebe. 3.30 With them (they convinced and affected). 4 Read Prayers, expounded (lively zeal). 5 E; Charles came, prayed. 5.20 Private prayer; writ diary. 6 E; prayed; supper, religious talk. 7 E; with Germans. 8 E; Francke. 9 Prayed; undressed.
    Providence: Well. All the people angry at my expounding so often. All convinced and affected.
    Grace: Lively zeal [4 to 5, 7 to 8 pm]. + [at 7 pm].

TUESDAY, NOVEMBER 18. 4 E; dressed; prayed; private prayer. 5 E; prayed; Bible. 6 E; prayed; Wall. 7 E; tea. 7.30 Lopez. 8 E; read e c a p p s h s c p t b, expounded. 8.45 Religious talk (necessary) with Cooling and Walker, they seemed affected. 9 E; writ to mother. 10 E; German. 11 E; with Germans. 12 E; with Ingham, etc, prayed, religious talk. 12.30 With Oglethorpe, he necessary talk. 1 E; necessary talk. 1.15 Dinner. 1.45 Tackner, necessary talk. 2 E; meditated. 2.15 Hird, etc. 2.45 Mr Williams and wife, religious talk. 3 E; religious talk. 3.30 Read Prayers, expounded. 4 They [had] various talk. 5 Tea; they [had] various and useful talk. 6 E; writ diary; prayed. 6.40 With Oglethorpe, necessary talk. 7 E; with Germans. 8 E; ended Francke. 9 Prayed; undressed. 12.30 Waked by Mr Horton, etc.
    Providence: Well. Cooling, etc, affected. Waked [at 12.30 am].
    Grace: Lively zeal twice [2 to 4 pm]. Fervent in meditation [at 2 pm], zealous in prayer [at 6 pm]. 7 rating twice [5 to 6 am, 2 to 3 pm].

WEDNESDAY, NOVEMBER 19. 4 E; dressed; prayed; sang. 4.50 Slept (very heavy). 5 E. 5.15 Prayed; Bible. 6 E; Wall. 7 E; tea; necessary talk (religious) with Oglethorpe. 8 Read Prayers, expounded. 9 E; German. 10 E; writ to Mr Vernon. 10.30 German. 11 E; with Germans. 12 E; Hird, etc, Wilson, religious talk. 1 E; read Law. 2 E; with Ingham, etc, prayed, religious talk. 2.45 Prayed. 3 E; dinner. 3.30 Read Prayers. 4 Expounded. 5 E. 5.10 Private prayer; prayed; supper. 6 E; supper, religious talk. 7 E; with Germans. 8 E; began *Nicodemus*; prayed; undressed.
    Providence: Well.
    Grace: Lively zeal; 7 rating once [5 to 6 am].

THURSDAY, [NOVEMBER] 20. 4 E; dressed; prayed; private prayer (very heavy). 5 E; Bible; prayed. 6 E; Wall; prayed (Horton very angry). 7 E; tea; necessary talk

The continuance of the contrary winds gave my brother an opportunity to comply with the request of the minister of the place, by preaching three or four times at Cowes. The poor people flocked together in good numbers, and appeared extremely affected. We left a few books with the most serious of them, who expressed all possible thankfulness.

The next day [Friday, November 21] I visited one Mrs. Lawley, just recovering from a dangerous illness. She said she had a long time desired to receive the Lord's Supper, and desired to be instructed in the nature of it. I thought it would be of more service to her to be first instructed in the nature of the Christian religion, in which I spent an hour with her every day. She received it with gladness, and seemed every day more earnest to pursue the one thing needful.

Saturday, November 22. Many persons having endeavoured to sow dissension between us and Mr. Horton (whose maid was mentioned before), by representing us as dissemblers, backbiters, incendiaries, and what not, I came to an explanation [I and R—understanding] with him, wherewith he was at the present (blessed be God) fully satisfied.

---

with Oglethorpe. 8 E; read Prayers, expounded. 8.45 Necessary business. 9 E; German. 10 E; German; Vernon came. 11 E; with Germans. 12 E; religious talk with Ingham, etc. 1 E; dinner; read verses. 2 E; read. 3 E; visited Mrs Lawley. 3.30 Religious talk, Oglethorpe open, she affected. 4 Read Prayers, expounded. 5 E; expounded. 5.30 Prayed; Vernon came. 6 E; supper, religious talk (various) with Vernon. 7 E; with Germans. 8 E; religious talk. 8.15 With Ingham, etc, religious talk, prayer.

   Providence: Well. Mr Horton very angry. Vernon came [at 5.30 pm].

   Oglethorpe kind; Mrs Lawley affected.

   Grace: 7 rating once [5 to 6 am].

FRIDAY, NOVEMBER 21. 4 E; dressed; prayed. 4.50 Private prayer. 5 E; prayed; Bible. 6 E; prayed; Wall. 7 E; tea; necessary business. 8 E; read e c a p p s h s c l 1 2 3 4 t b, expounded. 9 E; writ to Mr Thomas Delamotte. 10 E; German. 11 E; With Germans. 12 E; with Charles, etc, prayed, religious talk. 1 E; read Law. 1.30 With Mrs Lawley. 2 E; religious talk. 2.30 Religious talk with Charles, etc, prayed. 3 E; dinner. 3.15 Religious talk with Hird, etc (they affected). 4 E; read Prayers, expounded. 5 E; expounded. 5.15 Prayed. 5.30 Private prayer. 5.45 Read resolutions. 6 E; prayed; supper, religious talk. 6.50 With Germans. 7 E; with Germans. 8 E; *Nicodemus*; prayed.

   Providence: Well. Hird, etc, affected.

   Grace: 7 rating thrice [4 to 7 am].

SATURDAY, NOVEMBER [22]. 4.15 E; prayed; private prayer (cold almost gone). 5 E; prayed; Bible. 6 E; prayed; Wall. 7 E; tea, necessary talk. 8 E; Cowes with Charles and Delamotte, walked, Lopez. 9 E; Lopez; Carisbrooke Castle. 10 Prayed; at Farmer's, tea, religious talk, they affected. 11 Prayed; Lopez. 12 Prayed; Lopez; religious talk. 12.45 Cowes; religious talk with many. 1.15

Sunday, November 23. We had twelve communicants. At night I was waked by the roaring of the wind, which plainly showed me I was not fit, because not willing to die.

Dinner. 2 E; writ diary; began Law with Mr and Mrs Lawley, they affected. 3 Law. 3.30 Religious talk with Hird, they affected. 4 Read Prayers, expounded. 5 Expounded. 5.15 With Oglethorpe. 5.30 Necessary talk with Horton, he open. 6 Prayed; supper, religious talk. 7 E; with Germans. 8 E; *Nicodemus*; prayed.
    Providence: Well. The women at Carisbrooke; at Cowes. Mr and Mrs Lawley. Hird and Phoebe affected. Horton open, friendly.

SUNDAY, NOVEMBER 23. 4 E; dressed; prayed. 4.30 Private prayer (cold better). 5 E; prayed; Bible. 6 E; Bible. 6.20 Hickes. 7 E; dressed; tea. 7.40 Sang. 8 Read e c a p p s h s c 1 2 3 4 t b, expounded. 9 E; religious talk (necessary). 9.30 Religious talk with Mark and Phoebe. 10 E; religious talk with Betty Hassel. 10.30 Meditated. 11 E; religious talk (necessary). 11.15 Read Prayers, interrupted. 12 Preached, Sacrament (twelve communicants). 1 E; religious talk with Ingham and Delamotte. 1.45 Thought (fell). 2 E; dinner. 2.30 Religious talk. 2.45 With Lawley, religious talk. 3 Read Law (lively zeal). 4 Read Prayers, expounded (Oglethorpe ill). 5 E; prayed. 5.15 Vernon came, religious talk. 6 E. 6.15 Supper, religious talk. 7 E; with Germans. 8 E; *Nicodemus*, prayed; undressed.
    Providence: Cold better. Mark, Phoebe, Betty, Mr Lawley, the Doctor, etc, seemed affected. Fell on my head. Oglethorpe very ill. Thomas, Grace, Mark, Phoebe Hird, Mr Tackner and Betty, Burk, and West communicated.   A storm! Afraid! Alas!
    Grace: Lively zeal [3 to 4 pm]. Meditated. 7 rating twice [5 to 7 am].

MONDAY, NOVEMBER 24. 4 E. 4.10 Dressed; prayed. 4.45 Private prayer. 5 E; prayed; Bible. 6 E; prayed; Wall. 7 E; tea; Horton came. 7.40 Religious talk; meditated. 8 Read e c a p p s h s c p t b, expounded. 9 E; writ to Thomas Delamotte. 10 E; letter. 10.30 German. 11 E; with Germans. 12 E; necessary talk with Mrs Tackner (she convinced). 12.30 Religious talk with Ingham, etc. 1 E; Law. 1.45 Dinner. 2 E; dinner. 2.30 With Lawley, read. 3 Law. 4 Read Prayers, expounded, interrupted. 5 Mr Oglethorpe sent, tea, prayed. 6 E; supper, religious talk. 7 E; with Germans. 8 E; *Nicodemus*; prayed.
    Providence: Well. Mrs Tackner resolved to stay. Mr Lawley affected.
    Grace: 7 rating twice [4 to 6 am].

TUESDAY, NOVEMBER 25. 4 E; dressed; prayed; private prayer. 5 E; prayed; Bible. 6 E; prayed; Wall. 7 E; tea; religious talk (necessary) with Oglethorpe, he open. 8 Read prayers, expounded. 9 E; expounded. 9.15 Necessary talk; necessary business. 9.50 Began *Nicodemus*. 10 E; *Nicodemus*. 11 E; with Germans. 12 E; religious talk with Ingham, etc; dinner. 1 E; Law to Mrs Lawley, etc. 2 E; meditated; religious talk with Charles. 2.45 Religious talk with Hird. 3 E; religious talk with Davison. 4 Read Prayers, expounded. 5 Private prayer. 5.25 Prayed; read resolutions; supper. 6 E; supper, religious talk. 6.50 German. 7 E; with Germans. 8 E; *Nicodemus*; prayed.
    Providence: Well; cold near gone. Mrs Lawley and Davison affected.

Friday, November 28. Mrs. Hawkins (the gay young woman mentioned before) was at Mrs. Lawley's cabin when I read Mr. Law, as she afterwards was several times. She was always attentive and often much amazed.

Oglethorpe quite open.

Grace: 7 rating twice [4 to 6 am]. Resolved to dine with Charles, etc.

[WEDNESDAY,] NOVEMBER 26. 4 E; dressed; prayed. 4.45 Private prayer. 5 E; prayed; Bible. 6 E; began Johnson; prayed. 7 E; tea; religious talk. 7.30 Lopez. 8 Read e and c 1 2 3 4 t b, expounded. 9 E; *Nicodemus*. 10 E; *Nicodemus*. 11 E; with Germans. 12 E; read Law, child cried, stopped. 1 E; with Mrs Lawley, read. 1.45 Lopez. 2 E; prayed; religious talk with Ingham, etc, prayed. 3 E; dinner, religious talk. 4 E; read Prayers; sang, expounded (preserved from laughing). 5 E; private prayer. 5.45 Prayed with Ingham and Delamotte. 6 E; supper, religious talk, prayed. 7 E; with Germans. 7.30 Lopez. 8 E; *Nicodemus*; prayed; undressed.

Providence: Well. Mrs Lawley, etc, affected. Child stopped.

Grace: Lively zeal thrice [4 to 5, 8 to 9 am, 1 to 2 pm]; (con) [at noon]; + [5 to 6 pm]. 7 rating five times [4 to 7, 8 to 9 am, 5 to 6 pm]. Fervent ejaculatory prayers twelve times [at every hour but 7 to 8 am, 3, 4, and 7 pm].

THURSDAY, NOVEMBER 27. 4 E; dressed; prayed. 4.30 Private prayer. 5 E; prayed; Bible. 6 E; prayed; Johnson. 7 E; Lopez; necessary business. 8 E; tea. 8.20 Read Prayers. 9 E; expounded. 9.20 *Nicodemus*. 10 E; *Nicodemus*. 11 E; with Germans. 12 E; Law. 12.30 Mrs and Mr Lawley. 1 E; Law. 1.30 With Ingham, etc, religious talk. 2 E; Lopez. 3 E; Lopez; dinner. 4 Read Prayers, expounded. 5 E; private prayer; prayed. 6 E; supper, religious and useful talk. 7 E; with Germans, religious talk. 8 E; *Nicodemus*, ended; prayed; undressed.

Providence: Well.

Grace: 7 rating thrice [4 to 7 am].

FRIDAY, NOVEMBER 28. 4 E; dressed; prayed; private prayer. 5 E; prayed; Bible. 6 E; prayed; Johnson's *Unbloody Sacrifice*. 6.30 Mrs Taylor, necessary talk. 7 E; tea, religious talk; Lopez. 8 Read Prayers, expounded. 9 Religious talk with Oglethorpe (he open and convinced). 10 E; *Nicodemus*. 11 E; *Nicodemus*. 12 E; took leave of Mr Johnson. 12.15 Law. 12.45 Religious talk with Tackner. 1 E; religious talk with Mr and Mrs Tackner and Betty, they seemed resolved. 2 E; religious talk with Ingham, etc, prayed. 3 E; dinner. 3.30 [Read] Law to Mrs Lawley and [Mrs] Hawkins, they affected. 4 Read Prayers, expounded. 5 E; private prayer; prayed. 6 E; supper, religious talk. 7 E; with Germans. 7.45 Religious talk. 8 E; religious talk. 9 Undressed. 9.15.

Providence: Well. Mrs Tackner opened herself. Reproved Oglethorpe, he open. Mr and Mrs Tackner, Mrs Lawley, etc, affected.

Grace: 7 rating twice [4 to 6 am]; 6 twelve times [6 to 11 am, noon to 6, 7 to 8 pm].

SATURDAY, NOVEMBER 29. 4 E; dressed; prayed; private prayer. 5 E; prayed; Bible. 6 E; prayed; *Unbloody Sacrifice*. 7 E; tea; Lopez. 8 Read Prayers, expounded. 9 E;

Sunday, November 30. It pleased God to visit her with sickness. I then began to hope he would perfect his work in her. During that whole time Mr. Johnson was more and more impatient of the contrary winds; and at last, on Monday, December 1, despairing, as he said, of their ever being fair while he stayed in the ship, he left it and took boat for Portsmouth in order to return to London. In the afternoon we had public prayers in the great cabin, one of the many blessings consequent on his leaving us.

Tuesday, December 2. Mrs. Moore, one of Mr. Oglethorpe's servants, being ill, I visited her, and found her very serious. She desired me to read some treatise I judged proper with her, which I gladly promised to do every day. I began with Mr. Norris on *Christian Prudence,*

Nicodemus; necessary talk (religious) with Oglethorpe (gave no ground). 10 E; *Nicodemus.* 11 E; with Germans. 12 E; Law; Mrs Lawley. 1 E; with Ingham and Delamotte, prayed, religious talk. 2 E; dinner, religious talk. 3 E; Hird, etc, religious talk (they affected, lively zeal). 4 Read Prayers, expounded. 5 E; private prayer; prayed. 6 E; supper, religious talk. 7 E; with Germans. 8 E; Law; prayed (Ingham zealous); undressed.

Providence: Well; necessary talk with Oglethorpe, gave no ground. Hird, etc, affected; Ingham zealous.

Grace: Lively zeal [3 to 4 pm]. 7 rating thrice [4 to 7 am].

Sunday, November 30. 4 E; dressed; prayed; private prayer. 5 E; prayed; Bible. 6 E; Hickes. 6.30 Patrick. 7 E; tea, religious talk; Lopez. 8 Read e c etc, 1 2 3 4 t etc, expounded (lively zeal). 9 E. 9.15 Visited. 9.45 Writ diary; Kempis. 10 E; Kempis; sang; Kempis. 11 E; necessary business; sang; Law. 12 E; Law. 12.30 Read Prayers. 1 E; Sacrament; writ diary. 1.30 Prayed. 1.45 Dinner. 2 E; Lopez. 2.30 With Mrs Lawley, etc (they seemed affected). 3 E; Law. 3.30 Necessary talk (religious) with Oglethorpe. 3.45 Prayed. 4 Read Prayers, expounded. 5 E; Oglethorpe [had] necessary talk with the women; prayed. 6 E; supper, religious talk; visited. 7 E; with Germans. 8 E; Law; prayed; undressed.

Providence: Well; Mrs Lawley, etc, seemed affected.

Grace: 7 rating five times [4 to 7, 8 to 9, 10 to 11 am]. Lively zeal thrice [8 to 9, 10 to 11 am, 4 to 5 pm].

Monday, December 1. 4 E. 4.15 Dressed; prayed. 4.50 Necessary business. 5 E; prayed; Bible. 6 E; prayed; Johnson. 7 E; tea, religious talk; Lopez. 8 E; read e c etc. 9 E; expounded; religious talk. 9.30 *Nicodemus.* 10 E; necessary business [until] 2 E; dinner, religious talk. 3 Religious talk with Oglethorpe. 4 Read Prayers, expounded. 5 E; visited. 5.15 Private prayer. 5.30 Prayed. 5.45 Writ diary; Prayers in cabin (!). 6 E; supper, religious talk (lively zeal). 7 E; with Germans. 8 E; prayed; Law; prayed; undressed.

[See summary (Grace) on December 3.]

Tuesday, December 2. 4 E; dressed; prayed; private prayer. 5 E; prayed; Bible. 6 E Prayed; Johnson. 7 E; tea, religious talk; Greek Testament. 8 Read Prayers, expounded. 9 E; *Nicodemus.* 10 E; *Nicodemus;* necessary talk with Sally

but never came to the end of it, for she recovered from her illness in a few days, and shortly after from her seriousness. By our stay at Cowes we gained likewise two new passengers, both serious, conscientious men.

Wednesday, December 3. I read the *Second Spira* to one of them (Mr. Reed), Mrs. Hawkins, and her husband. They were all affected for the present. God grant it may sink into their hearts!

[Andrews]. 11 E; necessary talk. 11.10 With Germans. 12 E; prayed with Mrs Moore; Law; religious talk with [Daniel] Arthur, he open. 1 E; religious talk with Charles. 1.30 Religious talk with Ingham, etc. 2 Dinner. 3 E; religious talk with Reed. 3.15 With Mrs Hawkins, he [Mr Hawkins] affected. 4 Read Prayers; religious talk with Mrs Mackay. 5 E; meditated; prayed. 6 E; supper, religious talk; visited. 7 E; with Germans. 8 E; Law; prayed; undressed; sermon.

[Grace: see summary on December 3.]

Wednesday, December 3. 4 E; dressed; prayed; private prayer (very heavy). 5 E; prayed; Bible; sang. 6 E; prayed; Johnson. 7 E; tea, necessary talk with Oglethorpe. 8 Read Prayers; began religious talk with James Billinghurst, he affected. 9 E; religious talk. 9.40 Necessary talk. 10 E; visited. 10.15 Lopez. 11 E. 11.15 With Germans. 12 E; religious talk with Mrs. Patterson. 1 E; religious talk (she seemed convinced). 1.30 Tract against Popery. 2 E; religious talk with Ingham, prayed; dinner. 3 E; with Mrs Lawley, Law. 4 Read Prayers, expounded. 5 Religious talk with Mrs Hawkins, prayed. 6 E; supper. 6.15 Read *Second Spira*. 7 With Germans. 8 E; Law; prayed; undressed.

Providence: Well; cold gone. Afternoon Prayers in cabin. [Daniel] Arthur open. Mr Reed, Mrs Mackay, Mrs Lawley seemed affected. Began with James Billinghurst and Mrs Patterson.

Grace: Lively zeal [6 to 7 pm on December 1]. Zealous in meditation; + [5 to 6 pm on December 2].

Thursday, December 4. 4 E. 4.10 Dressed; prayed 1 2 (little heavy). 5 E; prayed; Bible. 6 E; prayed; Johnson. 7 E; tea; Greek Testament. 8 E; read Prayers, expounded. 9 E; began with Jemmy Welch. 10 E; religious talk. 10.30 Walked with Charles, religious talk. 11 E; read *Answer to the Plausible Arguments*. 12 E; at Farmer's, religious talk, dinner. 1 E; religious talk; at Mr Wendover's, religious talk. 2 E; Law to Mrs Lawley, etc. 3 E; Law (they much affected). 3.45 Read Prayers. 4 E; read Prayers, expounded; necessary business. 5 E; sang; private prayer; prayed. 6 E; supper, religious talk. 7 E; with Germans. 8 E; Law; prayed. 9 Undressed.

Providence: Well. Mrs Hawkins, etc, much affected [at 3 pm].

Grace: 7 rating twice [5 to 7 am].

Friday, December 5. 4 E; dressed; prayed; private prayer. 5 E; prayed; Bible. 6 E; prayed; Johnson; religious talk, clear. 7 E; tea, necessary talk with Oglethorpe. 8 Read Prayers, expounded. 9 E; religious talk with James Billinghurst. 9.50 With Jemmy Welch. 10 E; with Jemmy Welch. 10.30 Began conversation with them. 11 E; with Germans. 12 E; Law, religious talk. 12.30 [Law] to Mrs Lawley (lively zeal, they affected). 1 E; Law. 1.30 Religious talk with Tackner (lively

Saturday, December 6. Alexander Craig, the second mate, an oppressive, insolent, turbulent man, who had before insulted and abused many of the passengers, affronted Mr. Oglethorpe himself to his face. The next day he was removed before the mast to the man-of-war. Praised be God for the deliverance of the [I and R—poor] people from an unrighteous and wicked man!

Sunday, December 7. We had fourteen communicants. In the evening we resolved to leave off suppers till we found some inconvenience from it, which hitherto we have not done. John Spurrell, a sailor belonging to the ship, began now to recover from an illness in which his life was despaired of. My brother attended him every day. His resolutions were a little shaken at first by the raillery of his companions, till it pleased God to touch the heart of one of them too, who has ever since gone on with him hand in hand.

---

zeal). 2 E; religious talk with Ingham, etc, prayed (lively zeal, they zealous). 3 E; dinner, religious talk. 3.45 Read Prayers. 4 Read Prayers, expounded; private prayer. 5 E; private prayer; sang; prayed. 6 E; prayed; supper, religious talk. 6.30 Visited, religious talk. 7 E; with Germans. 8 E; Law; prayed; undressed.

    Providence: Well; we clear about Tackner [Ingham, etc, at 2 pm]. All lively zeal [12 to 1 and/or 2 to 3]. James Billinghurst, Jemmy Welch, Mrs Lawley, Mrs Moore, and [Mrs] Hawkins seemed affected.

    Grace: 7 rating thrice [4 to 7 am]. Lively zeal thrice [noon to 3 pm]; (con) [6 to 7 pm].

SATURDAY, DECEMBER 6. 4 E; dressed; prayed; writ diary; prayed; private prayer (lively). 5 E; prayed; Bible. 6 E; prayed; Johnson. 7 E; tea, religious talk; Greek Testament. 8 E; read Prayers, expounded. 9 E; religious talk with James Billinghurst, with Jemmy Welch. 10 Writ conversations. 11 E; with Germans. 12 E; religious talk with Phoebe Hird. 12.30 Law. 1 E; religious talk with Ingham, etc. 2 E; dinner; read *Popish Tract*. 3 E; religious talk with Hird, etc (they affected). 4 E; read Prayers. 4.45 *Popish Tract*. 5 E; private prayer; sang; prayed (Craig beat by Oglethorpe). 6 E; supper, religious talk. 6.30 Religious talk with Mrs Moore. 7 E; with Mrs Perkins; with Mrs Lawley, religious talk. 8 E; with Germans, religious talk; prayed; undressed.

    Providence: Well; lively. Phoebe Hird affected. [Alexander] Craig beat by Oglethorpe.

    Grace: 7 rating thrice [4 to 7 am].

SUNDAY, DECEMBER 7. 5 E. 5.15 Dressed; prayed; private prayer. 6 E; Hickes; dressed. 7 E; religious talk (necessary). 8 E; read Prayers, expounded. 9 E; Lopez. 9.40 Necessary talk (religious) with Oglethorpe. 10 E; tea, religious talk with Oglethorpe. 11 E; religious talk; meditated. 11.30 Read Prayers. 12 E; Preached, Sacrament (fourteen communicants). 1 E; dinner, religious talk. 1.45 With Mrs Lawley, etc. 2 E; Law, religious talk (all serious). 3 E; sang; *Popish Tract*. 4 E; necessary talk with Captain Cornish. 4.30 Read Prayers. 5 E; expounded. 5.20 Sang; prayed. 6 E; supper, religious talk. 6.30 Law to Mrs

Wednesday, December 10. About eight in the morning we set sail from Cowes, at three in the afternoon passed the Needles. Those ragged rocks, with the waves dashing at the foot of them, and the white side of the island rising perpendicular from the beach, gave a noble idea of him that spreads out the earth and holds the water in the hollow of his hand [cf. Isa. 40:12; 48:13].

Lawley [etc] (they affected). 7 E; with Germans. 8 E; religious talk. 8.30 Religious talk with Ingham, etc. 9.15 Prayed; undressed.

Providence: Well. Fourteen communicants. Mrs Lawley, etc, seemed affected.

Grace: 7 rating twice [5 to 7 am]. Resolved to leave off supper.

Monday, December 8. 4 E. 4.15 Dressed; writ diary; prayed. 5 E; prayed; Bible. 5.45 Read notes. 6 E; prayed; Johnson. 7 E; tea, religious talk; Greek Testament. 8 Read Prayers, expounded. 9 E; religious talk with James Billinghurst, with Jemmy Welch. 10 E; necessary talk with Oglethorpe. 10.15 Writ conversations. 11 E; with Germans. 12 E; necessary talk with Oglethorpe. 12.30 Religious talk with Mrs Patterson. 1 E; religious talk with Ingham, etc. 1.45 Dinner. 2 E. 2.15 Meditated; began Norris with Mrs Moore. 3 Norris. 4 With Oglethorpe, necessary talk. 4.15 Read Prayers, expounded. 5 Expounded. 5.15 Religious talk (necessary) with Oglethorpe. 6 Law to Mrs Lawley, etc. 7 Oglethorpe sent for me, necessary talk (religious) with Vernon. 8 Necessary talk with Oglethorpe and Lawley. 9 Undressed; necessary talk. 9.30.

Providence: Well; lively [4 to 5 am]. Mrs. Lawley, etc, serious [6 to 7 pm].

Grace: 7 rating once [6 to 7 am].

Tuesday, December 9. 3 Prayed. 3.40 Dressed; writ diary. 4 Prayed; private prayer. 4.40 Writ resolutions. 5 Prayed; Bible. 6 Prayed; religious talk; Johnson. 7 Prayed; tea; Greek Testament; Lopez. 8 Read Prayers, expounded. 9 Necessary talk (religious) with Oglethorpe. 9.45 With Weston. 10 Prayed; writ Catechism. 11 Prayed; with Germans. 11.45 With Mrs Mackay, religious talk (lively zeal, she affected). 12 Prayed, religious talk. 12.30 Law. 1 Prayed; religious talk with Ingham, etc. 2 Prayed; Lopez; necessary talk with the Captain; with Oglethorpe. 3 Dinner; religious talk with Mrs Moore. 4 Read Prayers, expounded. 5 Expounded. 5.30 Prayed. 6 With Mrs. Lawley, etc; tea, religious talk; Law; Mrs Hawkins open. 7 With Germans. 8 Law; prayed; undressed.

Providence: Well. Mrs Mackay and Mrs Hawkins [11 to noon].

Grace: Lively zeal [11 to noon]. N. B. No hourly prayers like ejaculatory prayers!

Wednesday, December 10. 4 E; dressed; prayed. 4.50 Prayed; sang. 5 E; prayed; Bible. 6 E; prayed; Johnson. 7 E; tea; Lopez; Greek Testament. 8 E; read Prayers; religious talk with William Weston; sailed! 9 E; with Jemmy Welch. 9.15 Catechism. 10 E; Catechism. 11 E; Mrs Hawkins and Mrs Lawley came, religious talk (they much affected). 12 E; Law; religious talk. 1 E; Norris to Mrs Moore. 2 E; religious talk (necessary) with Ingham, Oglethorpe, etc; prayed. 3 E; dinner, religious talk with Oglethorpe. 4 Read Prayers, expounded. 5 E. 5.15

Today I took an opportunity of speaking home to Mrs. Hawkins on the nature of Christianity. She listened with great attention, answered readily to all the questions I proposed, and afterwards said, with many tears, 'My mother died when I was only ten years old. Some of her last words were, "Child, whatever you do, fear God; and though you lose me, you shall never want a friend." I have now found one when I most needed and least expected it.'

From that time till the fourteenth, being in the Bay of Biscay, the sea was very rough. Mr. Delamotte and many others were now more seasick than before; Mr. Ingham, a little; I, not at all. On the fourteenth we had a calm, which was very agreeable to the sick, who now recovered apace.

Oglethorpe opened himself; prayed (zealous); prayed. 6 E; with Mrs Lawley and Hawkins, religious talk, Law (she in tears). 7 With Germans. 8 With Oglethorpe, he open! O God. 9 Religious talk with Oglethorpe. 9.20 Undressed. 10 [To] sleep (not sick).

>Providence: Sailed from Cowes; not sick. Mrs Lawley much affected. Mrs Hawkins twice in tears. Oglethorpe opened his heart. O God!

>Grace: + [twice 4 to 6 pm]. Lively zeal [4 to 5 pm]. c [con?; 4 to 5 pm].

Thursday, December 11. 3.40 E; writ diary. 4 E; private prayer (sea rough; well!). 5 E; prayed; Bible. 5.40 Sleepy (well!). 6 E; prayed; Lopez. 7 E; tea, religious talk; Lopez. 8 Prayed; visited; Lopez; in the Bay of Biscay. 12 Visited; Lopez. 2 Dinner. 3 Visited. 4 Read Prayers; necessary talk (religious) with Oglethorpe. 6 Visited. 7.45 Lopez. 8 Prayed; writ diary; undressed. 9 To bed. 11 To sleep.

Friday, December 12. 4 E; dressed; prayed; sang. 5 E; prayed; Bible; very rough [sea]. 6 E; prayed; Johnson. 7 E; Johnson. 8 Prayed; useful and necesary talk. 9 E; necessary talk (religious) with Oglethorpe. 10 Visited; with Mrs Moore, tea, religious talk. 11 E; religious talk. 11.30 Lopez. 12 E; on quarter-deck with Oglethorpe, etc, religious and useful talk. 1 E; religious talk; writ diary; Lopez. 2 E; Lopez. 3 E; dinner, religious talk with Mrs Lawley. 4 E; religious talk with Mrs Hawkins (she in tears, lively zeal). 4.45 Read Prayers. 5 E; Lopez; writ diary; prayed. 6 E; with Oglethorpe; journal. 7 E; religious talk with Reed. 7.30 With Mr and Mrs Hawkins. 8 Religious talk with Davison, etc. 8.45 Undressed.

>Providence: In the Bay of Biscay. Quite well! [noted at 4 am and 8 pm]. Mr and Mrs Hawkins and Mr Reed affected. She in tears. Lively zeal [4 to 5 pm].

Saturday, December 13. 5 E. 5.15 Dressed; writ diary; prayed. 6 E; Johnson. 7 E; Johnson; tea. 8 E; Lopez. 8.15 Read Prayers; necessary talk. 9 E; Lopez. 10 E; Lopez, ended. 11 E; visited. 12 Law. 1 E; visited. 1.15 Law. 2 E; dinner; meditated. 3 E; meditated. 3.15 Religious talk with Mr Reed and Mrs Hawkins. 4 Religious talk (necessary) [with] Mrs Hawkins; read Prayers. 5 Meditated; religious talk; prayed. 6 E; visited; with Mr and Mrs Hawkins, tea, religious and useful talk. 7 Religious talk. 7.45 With Oglethorpe, he open. 8 Religious talk with Mrs Hawkins and [Mrs] Welch. 9 Undressed.

>Providence: Quite well, off Cape Finisterre. Mr and Mrs Hawkins affected [at 7 pm]. Oglethorpe quite open, half resolved to communicate.

SUNDAY, DECEMBER 14. 4 E. 4.15 Dressed; prayed; writ diary. 5 E; prayed; Bible. 6 E; religious talk; sang; dressed. 7 E; breakfast, religious talk with Oglethorpe. 8 Religious talk with Oglethorpe. 8.30 Read Prayers. 9 Good talk with Oglethorpe. 10 Religious talk with Mrs Ward. 10.30 Kempis. 11 E; necessary talk; read Prayers, preached. 12 E; Sacrament. 12.30 Religious talk with Reed. 1 E; visited. 2 E; dinner; Lopez. 3 E; religious talk with Tackner, etc. 4 Read Prayers, expounded. 5 E. 5.15 Read sermon to Mrs Hawkins, etc, they affected. 6 On quarter-deck; prayed; sang; religious talk. 7 With Oglethorpe, etc, necessary talk. 7.30 With Germans. 8 With Germans. 8.30 With Charles and Ingham, religious talk, prayed.

Providence: Well; dead calm. Mrs Hawkins, etc, affected. Oglethorpe quite open, but deferred Sacrament.

Grace: Lively zeal [4 to 5 pm].

MONDAY, DECEMBER 15. 4 E. 4.15 Dressed; prayed; necessary business; (rough [sea]). 5 E; prayed; Bible. 6 E; prayed; Johnson. 7 E; Johnson, religious talk. 8 E; religious talk with Oglethorpe. 8.30 Tea. 9 E; read Prayers, expounded. 9.30 Religious talk with Oglethorpe. 10 E; religious talk with Mrs Lawley and Mr Reed (lively zeal). 11 E; religious talk with them. 11.45 With Mrs Hawkins, etc. 12 E; religious talk with Mrs Mackay; with them (lively zeal). 1 E; religious talk with Charles, etc, Delamotte open. 2 E; they [had] good talk; dinner. 2.45 Religious talk with Reed. 3 Norris with Mrs Moore, etc. 4 Read Prayers, expounded. 5 Read Law to Oglethorpe, etc. 5.45 Prayed. 6 Prayed; meditated. 7 E; with Germans. 8 Religious talk with Ingham and Charles, Law, all angry. 9 Stormy, quite well, slept sound!

[Providence:] Delamotte open.

Grace: Lively zeal twice [10 to 11 am, noon to 1 pm]. 7 rating thrice [5 to 7 am].

TUESDAY, DECEMBER 16. 4 E; dressed; prayed (a storm). 5 E; prayed; Bible (very heavy). 6 E; prayed; Johnson. 7 E; Johnson. 8 E; breakfast, necessary talk (religious). 9 E; meditated. 9.30 Writ on Sacrament. 10 On Sacrament. 11 E; ended on Sacrament. 12 E; good talk. 12.30 Visited. 1 E; visited. 2 E; religious talk with Charles. 2.30 With Mrs Lawley. 3 E; religious talk with Reed. 3.30 With Mrs Lawley. 4 E; with Mrs Hawkins, religious talk; dinner. 5 Mostly religious talk with Oglethorpe, etc. 7 Mostly religious talk with Oglethorpe. 9 Prayed; undressed.

Providence: Storm; well!

Grace: 7 rating once [4 to 5 am].

WEDNESDAY, DECEMBER 17. 6.30 Dressed; prayed. 7 E; prayed; Johnson. 8 E; coffee, religious talk. 9 Religious talk (necessary). 9.30 Read Prayers. 10 E; Johnson. 11 E; Johnson. 12 E; visited. 1 E; visited. 2 E; with Charles, etc, religious talk. 3 Dinner. 3.30 Religious talk with Phoebe Hird. 4 Religious talk. 4.30 Read Prayers. 5 Religious talk with Mrs Hawkins (she open). 6 Religious talk; prayed. 7 With Germans. 8 With Oglethorpe, mostly religious talk. 9 Prayed; undressed.

On Thursday, December 18, one Mrs. Welch, who was believed to be at the point of death, being big with child, in a high fever, and quite wasted with a cough, was by Mr. Oglethorpe removed into his own cabin (he ordering a hammock to be hung up for himself). She earnestly desired to receive the Holy Communion [R—before she died], and from the moment of her communicating she began to recover, and is now in good hopes of a safe delivery.

Sunday, December 21. We had fifteen communicants, on Christmas Day nineteen.

THURSDAY, DECEMBER 18. 4 E; dressed; prayed; sang. 5 E; prayed; Bible. 6 E; prayed; Johnson. 7 E; prayed; Johnson; coffee. 8 E; read Prayers; religious talk (necessary) with Oglethorpe. 9 Religious talk with Oglethorpe. 11 E; religious talk. 11.45 Johnson. 12 E; visited. 2 Dinner. 3 Necessary business; necessary talk (religious). 4 Sacrament with Mrs Welch (she dying); meditated. 5 Prayed; meditated. 6 Read Scriptures to Oglethorpe (he affected; lively zeal). 7 He read Scriptures, religious talk. 8 Religious talk.
    Providence: Phoebe Hird, Oglethorpe affected. Well. At the point of death, Mrs Welch.
    Grace: +, zealous meditation [4 to 5 pm]. Lively zeal [6 to 7 pm].

FRIDAY, DECEMBER 19. 4 E; dressed; prayed. 4.30 Slept. 5 E; read resolutions; private prayer. 6 E; meditated. 6.40 Religious talk with Oglethorpe. 7 E; religious talk; coffee. 8 Visited all. 9 E; necessary talk. 9.15 Visited. 10 Prepared for the sick. 10.30 Johnson. 11 E; Johnson. 11.45 Prepared. 12 E; prepared. 12.45 With Germans. 1 E; with Germans; delivered gruel. 1.45 Law. 2 E; Law; dinner. 2.45 Religious talk with Charles, etc. 3 E; religious talk. 3.15 Read Law to them. 4 Read Prayers; with Oglethorpe and Mrs Welch, good talk. 5 They [had] good talk. 5.20 Prayed. 6 E; Johnson. 7 With Germans. 7.45 With Oglethorpe, necessary business. 8 With Charles, [etc], religious talk; private prayer; undressed. 9.15.
    Providence: Well. In four hours got gruel for the people.
    Grace: 7 rating thrice [5 to 7 am, 11 to noon]; lively zeal twice [5 to 7 am]. Resolved on more self-denial!

SATURDAY, DECEMBER 20. 4 E. 4.30 Dressed; prayed (heavy). 5 E; Bible; private prayer (heavy). 6 E; religious talk. 6.30 Johnson. 7 E; tea, good talk (necessary, religious). 8 Read Prayers. 8.45 Dressed. 9 With Oglethorpe on board [Captain] Thomas. 10 Necessary talk. 10.30 Came back; Johnson. 12 E; Johnson to Hird, etc (they serious). 1 E; dinner. 2 Religious talk to Mrs Welch. 3 Read Law to them, Oglethorpe, good talk. 4 Read Prayers; religious talk with Delamotte. 5 Private prayer; meditated. 6 Read to Mrs Lawley, etc. 7 With Germans. 8 Religious talk with Oglethorpe. 8.15 Religious talk with Charles and Ingham. 8.45 Prayed.
    Providence: Well; a calm. All better [noon to 1 pm].
    Grace: 7 rating thrice [5 to 6 am, 2 to 3 pm, 5 to 6 pm]. Lively zeal [2 to 3pm].

SUNDAY, DECEMBER 21. 4 E; dressed; prayed; private prayer; Oglethorpe's birthday. 5 E; prayed; Bible. 6 E; Hickes. 7 E; religious talk with Oglethorpe;

tea; Kempis. 8 Read Prayers, expounded. 9 E; Johnson. 10 E; religious talk with Tackner (he affected). 10.30 Read Law to them. 11 E; read Prayers, preached. 12 Sacrament; Kempis; Oglethorpe there. 1 E; dinner. 2 E; religious talk with Mrs Welch and Hawkins (lively zeal). 3 E; religious talk with Reed, Phoebe Hird, and Betty Tackner (they affected). 4 Read Prayers, expounded. 4.45 Meditated. 5 Meditated; private prayer. 5.40 Prayed with Delamotte and Ingham. 6 Religious talk with Mrs Mackay. 7 With Germans (sleepy). 8 Religious talk with Charles and Ingham. 9 Prayed; undressed.

Providence: Well, lively; Oglethorpe's birthday. 15 at Sacrament, Oglethorpe; a calm. Tackner, Phoebe Hird, etc, affected.

Grace: Lively zeal [2 to 3 pm]. 7 rating six times [4 to 7 am, 9 to 10 am, noon to 1, 5 to 6 pm], 6 nine times [all other hours except 1 to 2 pm, 7 to 8 pm]. Convincing in expounding [4 to 4.45 pm].

MONDAY, DECEMBER 22. 4 E; dressed; prayed; slept; (wind). 5 E; prayed (heavy); Bible. 6 E; necessary business; Johnson. 7 E; necessary talk; German. 8 Read Prayers; German. 9 E; Johnson with Ingham. 10 E; Johnson; religious talk with Oglethorpe (gained no ground). 11 E; religious talk. 12 E; visited. 1 Dinner. 2 Religious talk with Mrs Welch, Oglethorpe, etc (they much affected); writ diary. 3 E; religious talk with [Daniel] Arthur, etc. 4 Read Prayers; religious talk. 5 E; prayed; sang. 5.30 Religious talk with Mrs Mackay. 6 Religious talk with Reed. 6.45 Mrs Lawley came, religious talk (she affected). 7 With Germans. 8 Religious talk; prayed; undressed.

Providence: Oglethorpe much affected. Mrs Lawley affected.

Grace: [no entry].

TUESDAY, DECEMBER 23. 4 E; dressed; writ diary; prayed; private prayer. 5 E; prayed; Bible. 6 E; prayed; Johnson. 7 E; religious talk (necessary) with Oglethorpe; breakfast. 8 Read Prayers; Johnson. 9 E; Johnson. 10 E; Johnson. 10.30 Religious talk with Mrs Hawkins (she affected). 11 E; with Germans. 12 E; began Brevint to Reed and Mrs Lawley. 1 Dinner. 1.45 Johnson. 2 E; Johnson. 3 E; religious talk with Betty Hassel (she convinced). 3.45 With Oglethorpe. 4 Read Prayers; with Mrs Welch. 5 With Mrs Welch, good talk. 5.30 Prayed. 6 Read to Mrs Lawley, etc. 7 With Germans, religious talk. 8 Religious talk with Charles and Ingham. 9 Prayed; undressed.

Providence: Mrs Hawkins open and affected. Betty Hassel convinced.

Grace: 7 rating twice [4 to 6 am].

WEDNESDAY, DECEMBER 24. 4 E; dressed; prayed. 5 E; prayed; Bible. 6 E; prayed; Bible. 7 E; prayed; Bible. 8 E; read Prayers; Johnson. 9 E; religious talk with Mrs Hawkins (gained no ground). 9.30 Ended Johnson. 10 E; Johnson. 10.30 Meditated. 11 E; with Germans. 11.45 Religious talk with Mrs Hawkins (she affected). 12 E; religious talk; read Nelson to them. 1 Religious talk with Betty Hassel and Phoebe Hird; meditated. 2 Religious talk with Charles, etc; prayed. 3 Dinner, religious talk. 3.30 Religious talk with Oglethorpe. 4 E; religious talk; read Prayers. 5 E; meditated; prayed. 5.30 Prayed with Ingham; sang. 6 E; read to Mrs Lawley. 7 With Germans. 8 E; religious talk with Charles and Ingham; prayed; undressed.

Providence: Well; Mrs Hawkins affected.

Grace: 7 rating four times [4 to 7 am, 5 to 6 pm].

Saturday, December 27. I endeavoured to reconcile Mrs. Moore and Mrs. Lawley with Mrs. Hawkins, with whom they had had a sharp quarrel. I thought it was effected; but the next day showed the contrary, both Mrs. Moore, Mrs. Lawley, and their husbands being so angry at me that they resolved (and prevailed on some others to do the same) never to be at prayers more.

CHRISTMAS DAY [THURSDAY, DECEMBER 25]. 4 E; necessary business. 4.20 Prayed; private prayer (heavy). 5 E; prayed; Bible. 6 E; prayed; Bible; dressed. 7 E; Quesnel. 7.30 Kempis. 8 Read Prayers; Kempis. 9 Kempis. 10 Kempis. 10.30 Necessary business; Kempis. 11 Read Prayers, preached. 12 Sacrament (nineteen communicants). 12.20 Religious talk with Reed, Phoebe Hird, Betty Hassel, Francis Brooks. 12.45 Religious talk. 1 Dinner. 2 E; they [had] good talk. 2.40 Religious talk with Perkins. 3 Religious talk with Patterson. 4 Read Prayers, expounded; religious talk with Mrs Mackay. 5 Religious talk; prayed; sang. 6 Religious talk with Reed, etc. 7 With Germans. 8 Religious talk with Oglethorpe (he affected); feverish. 9 Undressed; could not sleep till 12.

Providence: Well; nineteen communicants. Francis Brooks affected, and Oglethorpe.

FRIDAY, DECEMBER 26. 5 E; dressed; prayed; Bible. 6 E; Bible; prayed. 7 E; dressed; necessary talk (religious). 8 Read Prayers. 9 Began treatise on Sacrament. 10 On Sacrament. 12.30 Religious talk with Mrs Mackay. 1 Dinner. 2 E; with Mrs Welch and Hawkins, religious talk. 3 Religious talk with Hodgkinson and Heddon. 4 Read Prayers. 4.45 Meditated. 5 E; religious talk with Mrs Welch and Hawkins. 5.30 Prayed; sang. 6 E; Mrs Lawley not [come]; meditated; religious talk with Mrs Hawkins, etc (they affected). 7 E; with Germans. 8 E; religious talk with Ingham. 8.45 With Charles; prayed; undressed. 9.30 To sleep.

Providence: Well. Mrs Hawkins and Welch affected. Mrs Lawley and Moore unaffected, lukewarm! Heddon serious!

SATURDAY, DECEMBER 27. 4 E. 4.15 Dressed; prayed; private prayer. 5 E; prayed; Bible. 6 E; prayed; Bible. 7 E; meditated; religious talk with Mrs Moore. 8 Read Prayers; writ resolutions. 9 Germans. 10 Religious talk (necessary) with Oglethorpe; tea. 11 Religious talk with Mrs Hawkins, Mrs Welch, and Oglethorpe (Mrs Hawkins convinced). 12 Religious talk. 12.30 Dinner. 1.15 Religious talk with Mrs Welch and Hawkins (they affected). 2 Religious talk with them, close (they affected). 3 Religious talk with Oglethorpe. 3.30 Read Prayers. 4 Expounded. 4.15 Puffendorf. 5.30 Religious talk with Mrs. Hawkins. 5.45 Prayed. 6 Sang; prayed; reconciled Mrs Moore and Hawkins. 7 Religious talk with them. 7.30 With Germans. 8.15 With Charles and Ingham, religious talk; religious talk with Oglethorpe. 9 Undressed.

Providence: Well. Mrs Hawkins convinced. She and Mrs Moore reconciled. Close with Mrs Welch and Mrs Hawkins. Oglethorpe convinced and affected.

SUNDAY, DECEMBER 28. 6 E; dressed; prayed; Job; (sickish). 6 E; dressed; religious talk; Bible. 8 Religious talk. 8.15 Read Prayers. 9 E; Patrick with Reed, etc; tea;

[Tuesday, December 30.] Being informed Mrs. Lawley was ill, I hoped she might be in a milder temper, and therefore spent some time with her, and told her of her alteration [cf. I and R—the alteration of her behaviour] since her being acquainted with Mrs. Moore. As soon as I was gone, she told all and more than all that I said, who from that hour counteracted us publicly and privately to the utmost of their power.

---

meditated. 10 Kempis. 11 Read Prayers, preached. 12 Sacrament (fourteen communicants). 12.15 Patrick with them; religious talk with Reed. 1 Dinner. 2 E; with Mrs Welch, religious talk; religious talk with Delamotte. 3 Religious talk with Patterson. 3.30 With Horton. 4 Read Prayers, expounded (lively zeal). 5 Kempis; prayed; sang. 6 Meditated; prayed; sang. 7 With Germans. 8 Sang; prayed. 8.30 Religious talk with Oglethorpe and Charles. 9 Religious talk (necessary) with Oglethorpe. 10.30 Undressed.

Providence: Well. Fourteen communicants!

Grace: Lively zeal (4 to 5 pm). Attentive meditation (6 to 7).

MONDAY, DECEMBER 29. 4 E. 4.15 Dressed; prayed. 4.50 Religious talk with Mrs Lawley. 5 E; prayed; Bible; religious talk. 6 E; Bible. 7 E; religious talk with Oglethorpe; coffee. 8 Read Prayers, expounded. 9 German. 10.30 Read sermon to Mrs Hawkins, she affected. 11 Sermon. 11.30 German. 12 With Germans. 12.45 Dinner. 1.30 German. 2 Religious talk with Mrs Welch, Sacrament. 3 Religious talk with Mrs Tackner; read Prayers. 4 Religious talk with Charles, etc. 4.30 Sang. 5 Religious and useful talk with Mrs Hawkins (5.15) and Oglethorpe. 5.45 Prayed. 6 Sang; meditated (called for Mr Hawkins). 7 With Germans. 8 Religious talk with Charles, etc; prayed; undressed.

Providence: Well; Sacrament! Mrs Hawkins affected till Oglethorpe came!

TUESDAY, DECEMBER 30. 4 E. 4.15 Dressed; prayed; called upon Mrs Hawkins, asleep; prayed. 5 E; prayed. 5.15 Bible. 6 E; prayed; Bible. 6.30 Religious talk with Mrs Hawkins (she affected). 7 Religious talk with Mrs Hawkins (she seemed more affected); coffee. 8 Read Prayers, expounded; writ diary. 9 E; German. 11.45 Religious talk with Charles, etc. 12 With Germans. 1 E; dinner; German; meditated. 2 E; religious talk with Reed, etc (he open). 3 Religious talk with Patterson, Phoebe Hird, etc. 4 Read Prayers; meditated. 5 Religious talk with Oglethorpe. 5.30 Prayed with Ingham, sang. 6. Began *Theologia Germanica*; tea. 7 With Germans. 8 Prayed with Charles, etc, religious talk. 9 Prayed; undressed. 11 To sleep.

Providence: Mrs Hawkins much affected. Reed open. Met with Charles, etc [at 11.45 am].

Grace: Lively zeal [7 to 8 pm]. 7 rating once [4 to 5 am]; 6 sixteen times [the rest of the day, although 10 to 11 am is noted as five].

WEDNESDAY, DECEMBER 31. 4.15 Necessary business; prayed. 5 Prayed; Bible. 6 Prayed; Bible. 7 Necessary business; German. 7.30 Read Prayers. 8.15 German. 9 Necessary business. 9.15 Saw five blooded. 10 Saw two more. 10.30 German. 11.15 Religious talk with Mrs Lawley; with Mrs Hawkins (gave no ground). 12 Religious talk with Ingham and Delamotte. 12.30 German. 1 E; German. 2 Dinner. 2.45 Meditated; prayed. 3 Religious talk with Mrs Moore

Thursday, January 1 [1735/36]. We celebrated the Holy Eucharist, and had fifteen communicants. May the New Year bring a new [I and R—heart] and a new life to all those who seek the Lord God of their fathers!

(she angry); with Mrs Hawkins; with Oglethorpe. 4 Read Prayers, expounded. 4.45 Necessary talk (religious) with Oglethorpe, Mrs Lawley, and Mrs Moore. 5 Oglethorpe, necessary talk with them. 5.30 With Mrs Hawkins, read Law. 6.45 Necessary talk with Mrs Mackay (she affected). 7 With Germans. 8 Prayed with Ingham, etc; religious talk; prayed.

Providence: Well. Mrs Hawkins affected. Mr and Mrs Moore very angry at me.

[Grace]: Gave no ground with Mrs Lawley!

THURSDAY, JANUARY 1. 4 E. 4.30 Dressed; prayed. 5 E; prayed; Bible. 6 E; Hickes. 7 E; necessary talk. 7.30 Read Prayers. 8 E; read Prayers, expounded. 8.30 Tea. 9 Read Patrick to them, religious talk. 10 Read Prayers, Sacrament. 10.30 Saw blooded. 11 Saw them. 11.30 Religious talk with Mrs Mackay. 12 Religious talk with her and Mrs Hawkins. 1 Religious talk with Charles; meditated. 1.40 Dinner. 2 E; dinner. 2.15 Religious talk with Alexander [Grimaldi], Reed, and Franks. 3 E; with Mrs Welch, etc; with Mrs Lawley. 4 E; read Prayers, expounded. 4.30 Meditated. 5.15 Mrs Hawkins came to me, various talk (close). 6 Prayed; sang; meditated; religious talk. 7 With Germans. 8 With Oglethorpe, religious talk (necessary). 9 Religious talk (necessary); undressed.

Providence: Well; Sacrament, fifteen communicants. Mrs Hawkins came from Oglethorpe to me. She seemed more affected.

Grace: 7 rating thrice [4 to 6 am, 5 to 6 pm]; 6 nine times.

FRIDAY, JANUARY 2. Προσεύχεσθε ἀδιαλείπτως ['pray without ceasing'; abbreviated at top of page through January 5]. 4 E. 4.30 Dressed; writ diary. 5 E; prayed; private prayer. 5.45 Bible. 6 E; Bible. 7 E; necessary business. 7.30 Read Prayers. 8 E; read Prayers. 8.30 German. 9 German; necessary talk with Oglethorpe. 10 German. 11 E; with Germans. 12 E; religious talk with Reed and Mrs Hawkins. 1 Religious talk with Mrs Welch and Mrs Hawkins. 2 Religious talk with Charles, etc; necessary business; prayed. 3 Dinner. 3.30 Writ diary; necessary talk (useful and religious). 4 Read Prayers. 4.45 *Theologia Germanica.* 7 Prayed; sang; meditated. 7 E; with Germans. 8 With Mrs Mackay; tea. 8.15 Religious talk with Charles, etc. 9.30 Prayed; undressed.

Providence: Well. Mrs Hawkins could not come all day.

Grace: 7 rating thrice [4 to 6 am, 5 to 6 pm].

SATURDAY, JANUARY 3. 4 E. 4.15 Dressed; prayed. 5 E; prayed; Bible. 6 E; prayed; Bible. 7 E; religious talk (necessary). 7.15 Read Prayers, expounded. 8 E; tea with Captain [Thomas], good talk. 8.45 German. 9 E; German; religious talk with Oglethorpe. 10 E; German. 11 E; with Germans; meditated. 12 E; religious talk with Charles, etc. 1 E; dinner. 1.45 Prayed. 2 E; began catechizing six children. 3 E; religious talk with Phoebe Hird and Betty Hassel. 3.15 With Francis Brooks. 4 E; read Prayers, expounded. 4.30 Religious talk with Mrs Welch and Mrs Hawkins (lively zeal). 5 Read Mr Moore's letters. 6 Read letters. 7 With Germans. 8 Religious talk with Ingham. 8.45 Good talk with Mr

Hawkins. 9 Religious talk with Mrs Hawkins. 10 Religious talk with Mrs Hawkins; undressed.

Providence: Well. Began catechizing six children. Phoebe Hird, Betty Hassel, and Francis Brooks seemed affected.

Mercy: Preserved from w4 twice [9 to 11 pm].

Grace: 8 rating once [4 to 5 am]; 7 thrice [5 to 7, 10 to 11 am]; 6 eight times. Lively zeal thrice [10 to noon, 4 to 5 pm]. Fervent meditation [11 to noon].

Sunday, January 4. 5 E; dressed; prayed; writ diary. 6 E; sang; Bible; sang. 7 E; necessary talk (religious) with Oglethorpe, tea. 8 Read Prayers, expounded. 9 E; Kempis. 9.30 Patrick. 10 E; sang. 10.30 Kempis. 11 Read Prayers, expounded, Sacrament (sixteen communicants). 12 E; Patrick. 12.30 Religious talk with Charles, etc. 1 E; religious talk with the doctor of Mrs Hawkins; prayed; dinner. 2 E; catechized. 3 E; religious talk with Mr and Mrs Hawkins (she angry at him). 4 Read Prayers, catechized; religious talk (necessary) with Oglethorpe. 5 E; *Theologia Germanica*. 6 E; with Mr and Mrs Hawkins, religious talk (they seemed affected). 7 With Germans (very heavy). 8 Religious talk with Charles, etc; prayed. 9 Undressed. 9.30.

Providence: Not sickish. Sixteen communicants. Mrs Hawkins very angry. He and she affected.

Grace: 7 rating once [5 to 6 pm].

Monday, January 5. 4 E; dressed; prayed; private prayer. 5 E; prayed; Bible. 6 E; prayed; Bible. 7 E; German. 7.30 Read Prayers. 8 E; prayed. 8.15 German. 9 E; German; tea. 10 E; German. 11 E; German. 11.30 With Germans. 12 E; religious talk with Germans. 12.30 With Mrs Hawkins (gave no ground, she angry). 1 E; dinner. 1.30 Catechized. 2 E; catechized. 2.45 Religious talk with them. 3 E; religious talk with Mrs Hawkins (she more affected). 3.45 Sang. 4 E; read Prayers; catechized. 5 E; writ Catechism. 6 E; Catechism. 6.30 Sang. 7 With Germans. 8 Religious talk with Charles, etc. 8.45 Sang. 9.15 [To bed]. 12.30 Waked by a squall, afraid. 1.30 To sleep.

Providence: Well; Mrs Hawkins quite angry; she right, and she and Mr Hawkins more affected.

Grace: 7 rating thrice [4 to 6 am, 3 to 4 pm]; 6 ten times. Convincing [4 to 5 pm]. Preserved from w4/1.

Tuesday, January 6. 4 E. 4.30 Dressed; writ diary; prayed. 5 E; prayed; Bible; sang. 6 E; prayed; Bible; sang. 7 E; read Prayers, expounded; religious talk with Hodgkinson (he convinced). 8 E; German; breakfast. 9 E; German. 10 E; German. 11 E; with Germans. 12 E; religious talk with Ingham, etc. 1 E; dinner; catechized. 3 Religious talk with Reed and Mrs Hawkins. 4 Read Prayers, expounded. 5 Religious talk with Oglethorpe. 6 Meditated; prayed; sang. 7 E; with Germans. 8 Religious talk with Mrs Hawkins. 8.30 With Charles, etc. 9 E; religious talk (necessary) with Mrs Hawkins. 10 E; religious talk (necessary) with Mrs Hawkins. 11 With Heddon. 11.30.

Providence: Hodgkinson seemed convinced. Mrs Hawkins serious and open.

Grace: 7 rating twice [4 to 6 am].

Wednesday, January 7. 4 E. 4.15 Dressed; prayed (very heavy). 4.45 Slept. 5 E; prayed; Bible. 6 E; religious talk with Ingham and Charles; necessary business.

7 E; read Prayers, expounded. 8 E; religious talk with Ingham. 8.45 Religious talk with Charles. 9 E; German. 10 E; German. 11 E; with Germans. 12 E; with Oglethorpe, necessary talk (religious). 1 E; religious talk with Charles, etc. 2 E; catechized; prayed with Charles, etc. 3 Dinner, religious talk. 4 Read Prayers, expounded. 5 Began *Serious Call* with Mrs Hawkins (she affected). 5.30 Prayed with Delamotte. 6 Writ Catechism. 6.30 Meditated. 7 E; with Germans. 8 With Charles, etc; Mr Horton, necessary talk (religious). 9 Necessary talk (religious) with Mr and Mrs Lawley; undressed.

Providence: Well; Mrs Hawkins affected.

Grace: 6 rating thirteen times [every hour except 9 to 11 am, 3 to 4, 6 to 8 pm].

THURSDAY, JANUARY 8. 4 E. 4.15 Dressed; writ diary; prayed. 5 E; prayed; Bible; sang. 6 E; prayed; Bible. 6.30 Breakfast; necessary business. 7 E; read Prayers, expounded. 8 E; German. 9 E; German. 10 E; German. 11 E; with Germans. 11.45 Religious talk. 12 E; religious talk with Delamotte, etc. 12.45 *Theologia Germanica*. 1 E; dinner; read Law below (lively zeal). 2 E; catechized. 3 E; religious talk with Harding. 3.30 With Mrs Welch and Mrs Hawkins (she affected). 4 Read Prayers, expounded. 5 [Read] Law to Mrs Hawkins and Welch. 5.30 Prayed. 6 Necessary and useful talk with Oglethorpe. 7 E; with Germans. 7.45 Meditated. 8 E; prayed; meditated. 9 Mr and Mrs Hawkins came, good talk; undressed.

Providence: Well; resumed reading Law to them. Harding convinced. Mrs Hawkins affected.

Grace: Lively zeal [1 to 2 pm]. 7 rating twice [5 to 6 am, 5 to 6 pm]; 6 eleven times.

Resolved: To be more zealous and active, especially from 5 to 10.

FRIDAY, JANUARY 9. 4 E. 4.15 Dressed; writ diary; prayed; called. 5 E; prayed; Bible; sang. 6 E; prayed; Bible; sang. 6.45 Dressed. 7 E; read Prayers, expounded. 7.45 Began Indian Dictionary. 8 E; Dictionary. 9 E; Dictionary. 10 E; Dictionary. 10.30 German. 11 E; with Germans. 12 E; Law. 12.30 Religious talk with Charles, etc. 1 E; religious talk. 1.30 Catechized. 2 E; religious talk with Mrs Tackner. 2.45 Prayed. 3 E; dinner. 3.30 Religious talk (necessary) with Mr Hawkins. 4 E; read Prayers, expounded. 5 E; *Theologia Germanica*. 5.45 Necessary talk; prayed. 6 E; religious talk with Ingham and Delamotte. 6.30 With Francis Brooks (he affected). 7 E; with Germans. 8 E; necessary talk with Mr and Mrs Hawkins. 8.30 Religious talk with Ingham, etc. 9 Religious talk with Oglethorpe. 10.15.

Providence: Well; Francis Brooks affected.

Grace: 7 rating once [5 to 6 am].

SATURDAY, JANUARY 10. 4 E; dressed; prayed for Mrs Hawkins. 4.30 Prayed. 5 E; prayed; Bible; sang. 6 E; prayed; Bible. 7 Read Prayers, expounded. 7.40 German. 8 E; tea. 8.15 German. 9 E; German. 10 E; German. 10.30 Religious talk with Reed. 11 E; shaved; religious talk with Mrs Mackay (she seemed affected). 12 E; religious talk with Ingham and Delamotte. 12.40 Dinner. 1 E; dinner; writ diary. 1.30 Read Law. 2 E; religious talk with Phoebe Hird and Betty Hassel, and catechized. 3 E; catechized; religious talk with [Daniel] Arthur; with Mrs Hawkins. 4 E; read Prayers, expounded. 5 E; religious talk with them; with Mrs Welch and Mrs Hawkins, prayed. 6 E; began reading

Sunday, January 11. We had twenty-one communicants. In the afternoon [R—Mr. Reed] and Mrs. Hawkins, between whom some of their neighbours had endeavoured to sow dissension, explained themselves to each other, and came to a thorough reconciliation.

Monday, January 12. Mrs. Hawkins expressed a desire of receiving the Holy Communion. Several [R—persons] being apprised of it, warned me of her insincerity, and laid many crimes to her charge, of which I informed her. In the evening she replied clearly and calmly to every article of the charge, and that with such an appearance of innocence as to most particulars, and of an entire change of the rest, that I could no longer doubt of her sincere desire to be not only almost but altogether a Christian. She accordingly received the Holy Communion the Sunday following, and at every opportunity since. 'The right hand of the Lord still hath the pre-eminence, the right hand of the Lord bringeth mighty things to pass' [Ps. 118:16 (BCP)].

Country Parson to Arthur and Francis Brooks. 7 E; German. 8 E; religious talk with Charles, etc, they angry. 9 E; prayed; religious talk with Delamotte. 10 Undressed.

> Providence: Well. Charles and Ingham angry at me! Mrs Mackay, Phoebe Hird, Betty Hassel, [Daniel] Arthur, Francis Brooks, Mr Delamotte seemed affected.

> Grace: 6 rating seventeen times [every hour but 7 to 8 pm].

SUNDAY, JANUARY 11. 4 E; dressed; writ diary; prayed. 5 E; prayed; Bible; sang. 6 E; Bible. 6.15 Hickes. 7 E; read Prayers, expounded. 8 E; German. 9 E; tea; Kempis. 10 E; Patrick; *Theologia Germanica*. 11 E; read Prayers, preached, Sacrament (twenty-one communicants). 12 E; Patrick with them; private prayer. 1 Religious talk with Oglethorpe. 1.10 *Theologia Germanica*. 1.30 Dinner. 2 E; prayed with Mrs Welch. 2.15 Catechized. 2.45 Meditated. 3 E; religious talk with Mr Reed and Mr and Mrs Hawkins, they reconciled. 4 Read Prayers, expounded. 5 Religious talk with Mrs Hawkins (close, she affected). 5.30 Prayed; supper. 6 E; read to [Daniel] Arthur and Francis Brooks. 6.45 Religious talk with Heddon. 7 E; with Germans (sleepy). 8 Religious talk with Charles, etc. 9 Religious talk with Reed. 9.15 Meditated; prayed. 9.45 Undressed.

> Providence: Well. Twenty-one communicants. Mr, Mrs Hawkins and Reed reconciled. Religious talk, close; Mrs Hawkins affected; [Daniel] Arthur and Francis Brooks affected.

> Grace: 7 rating twice [10 to 11 am, noon to 1 pm]; 6 fifteen times [all but 7 to 8 pm].

MONDAY, JANUARY 12. 4.45 Dressed; prayed; writ diary; Bible. 6 E; sang; Bible. 6.30 German. 7 E; read Prayers, expounded. 8 E; tea. 8.30 German. 9 E; transcribed Catechism for children. 10 E; Catechism. 11 E; Catechism. 12 E; prayed; religious talk with Charles, etc. 1 E; dinner; *Theologia Germanica*. 1.30 Religious talk with Hird. 2 E; catechized. 2.45 Meditated. 3 E; religious talk with Patterson (he serious). 4 Read Prayers, expounded. 4.45 Religious talk

Wednesday, January 14. Mr. Oglethorpe taking up Gother's *Sinner's Complaints to God*, light[ed] upon a part of it which relates to forgiveness. We then put him in mind of one of his servants, who had injured him some time before. He forgave him from that hour.

---

with Mrs Hawkins (she affected much). 5 E; religious talk. 5.45 Tea. 6 E; religious talk with Sally [Andrews]. 6.30 Read to Arthur and Francis Brooks (they seemed affected). 7 E; with Germans. 8 E; Religious talk with Nitschmann. 8.30 With Delamotte, [religious talk] of Mrs Hawkins. 9 E; necessary talk with Brownfield of Mrs Hawkins, he open, against her. 10 Necessary talk with Horton of Mrs Hawkins. 11 Religious talk with Mrs Hawkins, she in tears. 12 Religious talk. 1.15 Undressed.

> Providence: Well; Mr Patterson serious. Sally [Andrews], [Daniel] Arthur, Francis brooks seemed affected. Brownfield, Delamotte, and Horton against Mrs Hawkins' communing. Mrs Hawkins deeply affected and open.

> Grace: 6 rating seventeen times [all but 9 to 10, 11 to noon, 5 to 6 pm].

TUESDAY, JANUARY 13. 4 E; dressed; prayed. 4.45 Religious talk with Charles of Mrs Hawkins. 7 E; read e c a p p s h s c p t b, expounded (lively zeal). 8 E; tea. 8.30 Religious talk with Charles of Mrs Hawkins. 8.45 Religious talk with Oglethorpe of Mrs Hawkins. 9 E; religious talk with Oglethorpe of Mrs Hawkins, (10.30) of Georgia. 11 Religious talk of Negroes. 11.45 Religious talk with Mrs Welch. 12 Prayed; religious talk with Charles, etc. 12.30 Religious talk with Charles of Mrs Hawkins. 1 E; dinner; *Theologia Germanica*. 2 E; religious talk with Mrs Welch and Mrs Hawkins. 2.30 Catechized. 3 E; read Patrick to Mrs Welch and Mrs Hawkins. 4 Read Prayers, expounded. 5 E; religious talk with Mrs Hawkins. 6 Necessary talk with Mr and Mrs Hawkins. 6.45 Religious talk with Mr Hawkins, they very angry! 7 With Germans (sleepy). 8 With Oglethorpe, religious talk. 8.30 With Charles, etc, religious talk (lively zeal). 9 Talk with Delamotte of Mrs Hawkins. 9.45 Undressed.

> Providence: Well; Mrs Hawkins quite angry; gave no ground.

> Grace: 7 rating once [7 to 8 am]; 6 fourteen times [all but 4 to 5, 6 to 8 pm]. Lively zeal twice [7 to 8 am, 8 to 9 pm].

WEDNESDAY, JANUARY 14. 4 E. 4.30 Dressed; writ diary; prayed. 5 E; prayed; Bible. 5.45 Slept. 6 E; slept. 6.20 Dressed; German. 7 E; read Prayers, expounded; necessary talk (religious) with Reed. 8 E; German; tea; planned letters. 9 E; German, with them. 10 With Germans. 12 E; *Theologia Germanica*; religious talk with Mrs Hawkins and Welch. 1 E; religious talk with Charles, etc. 1.30 Catechized. 2 E; religious talk. 2.45 Prayed. 3 E; dinner; religious talk with Mrs Welch and Hawkins. 4 Read Prayers, expounded. 5 Religious talk with Mrs Welch and Hawkins. 6 Religious talk. 6.15 Read to [Daniel] Arthur and Francis Brooks. 7 With Germans. 8 With Charles, etc, prayed, religious talk. 9 With Oglethorpe and Charles, religious talk, Oglethorpe forgave Alexander [Grimaldi]. 10.15.

> Providence: Well; Mrs Hawkins quite cool; Oglethorpe forgave Alexander Grimaldi.

> Grace: Lively zeal to be a Christian [3 to 4 pm].

Thursday, January 15. Complaint being made of the unequal distribution of the water, Mr. Oglethorpe appointed new officers for it. At this the old ones were highly disobliged at us, to whom they imputed the change. But 'the fierceness of man shall turn to thy praise' [Ps. 76:10 (BCP)].

Saturday, January 17. The people began to be very impatient at the contrary winds. At seven in the evening their impatience was quieted by a storm. It rose higher and higher till nine. The sea broke over us from [R—stem] to stern; and part of it burst through Mr. Oglethorpe's cabin, where three or four of us were sitting with a sick woman, and covered her all over. A bureau sheltered me from the main shock. Mr. Oglethorpe removed Mrs. Welch once more into his own bed. I laid me down in the great cabin, very uncertain whether I should wake alive, and much ashamed at my unwillingness to die. O how pure in heart must he be who would rejoice to appear before God at a moment's warning! Towards the morning God rebuked the winds and the sea, and there was a great calm [Matt. 8:26].

THURSDAY, JANUARY 15. 5 E. 5.30 Dressed; prayed; writ diary. 6 Private prayer; prayed. 6.30 dressed; meditated. 6.45 Read e c a p p s h s c p t b, expounded (lively zeal). 8 E; raisins. 8.30 German. 9 E; German. 10 E; German. 10.30 *Theologia Germanica*. 11 E; religious talk with Mrs Hawkins and Welch. 11.30 Prayed with Charles, etc, religious talk. 12 Inquired of the water; necessary talk with Oglethorpe. 1 New orders. 1.20 Dinner; *Theologia Germanica*. 2 E; meditated. 2.15 [Read] Law to them. 2.45 Catechized. 3.15 Read Gother to Mrs Hawkins and Welch, religious talk. 4 Read c a p p s h s c p t b. 4.45 *Theologia Germanica*. 5 *Theologia Germanica*; read to [Daniel] Arthur and Francis Brooks. 6.30 With Germans. 7.15 Meditated. 7.45 With Ingham, etc, religious talk. 9 Religious talk (necessary) with Oglethorpe. 9.15 *Theologia Germanica*. 9.45 Religious talk with Mrs Hawkins. 11 Religious talk (necessary). 12.

Providence: Well; new officers for water. Mrs Hawkins open and affected.
Grace: 7 rating once [7 to 8 am]; 6 sixteen times [all but 10 to 11 pm]. Lively zeal, convincing [7 to 8 am].

FRIDAY, JANUARY 16. 4 E; dressed; prayed. 5 E; Bible; prayed. 5.30 slept. 6.30 Religious talk with Mrs Hawkins (she affected). 7 Read Prayers; meditated. 8 E; *Theologia Germanica*. 8.30 Sorted books. 10 Tea; religious talk with Mrs Welch and Hawkins. 10.45 Necessary business. 11 sorted. 12.15 Prayed; religious talk. 1 E; religious talk with Delamotte. 1.30 Read Law. 2 E; catechized. 2.30 Prayed; dinner, religious talk. 3 E; read Law to Mrs Welch and Hawkins (Mrs Hawkins sleepy). 3.45 Read e c a p p s h s x c p t b. 4.45 Necessary talk with Oglethorpe. 5 Oglethorpe read the Charter. 6 Charter. 7 With Germans. 7.45 Religious talk with Charles, etc. 8 *Theologia Germanica*. 9 Ended it; undressed. 10.

Providence: Well; Mrs Hawkins in good temper. Mrs Perkins pacified.

SATURDAY, JANUARY 17. 4 E; dressed; private prayer; prayed. 5 E; prayed; Bible; sang. 6 E; prayed; Bible. 7 E; read e c a p p s h s c p t b. 7.45 *Theologia Germanica*. 8 E; *Theologia Germanica*; sang. 9 E; tea; German. 10 E; with Germans. 11 E;

Sunday, January 18. We returned thanks to God for our deliverance, of which some few appeared duly sensible; the rest like true cowards (of whom were most of the sailors) denied we had been in any danger. I could not have believed that so little good would be done by the terror they were before in. But for the future I will never believe them to obey God out of fear who are deaf to all the motives of love.

---

with Germans. 11.45 Necessary business. 12 Prayed with Charles, etc, religious talk (necessary). 12.45 Religious talk with Mrs Mackay. 1 E; religious talk (necessary). 1.45 *Theologia Germanica.* 2 E; dinner. 2.30 Catechized. 3 E; [read] Law to Mrs Welch and Hawkins. 4 Read Prayers, expounded. 5 Mrs Lawley, Hawkins, and Oglethorpe, religious and useful talk. 6 Mostly religious talk; stormy! 7 With Germans. 8 Religious talk with Ingham, etc. 8.30 Religious talk with Mrs Hawkins. 9 Religious and useful talk; a storm, sea broke in to us. 10 Prayed; religious talk; afraid to die; stormy still. 11 Prayed; religious talk. 11.30 Lay on the boards; slept. 12 Stormy still, afraid! 1 Lay on Mrs Welch's bed, she in Mr Oglethorpe's; calmer.

Resolved: Not to please myself in eating or drinking; thankfulness no reason!

SUNDAY, JANUARY 18. 7 Dressed; prayed; meditated (lively zeal); dressed. 8 Religious talk with Charles; prayed; meditated. 9 Religious talk; read Kempis to them; religious talk with Betty Hassel. 10 Religious talk with Betty Hassel; meditated. 11 Read Prayers, preached. 12 Sacrament (twenty-three communicants); religious talk with Mrs Hawkins (resolved not to praise myself! she much affected); prayed; writ diary. 1 Prayed; meditated; slept. 2 Dinner. 3 Catechized; religious talk with them. 4 Read Prayers, expounded; religious talk with Mrs Hawkins (she much affected). 6 *Country Parson* with [Daniel] Arthur and Francis Brooks, religious talk (close). 7 With Germans. 8 Religious talk with Charles, etc. 9.15 Undressed.

[MONDAY,] JANUARY 19. 5.30 Dressed; prayed. 6 Prayed; meditated. 6.45 Dressed. 7 Read Prayers, expounded; sorted. 9 Tea; sorted; prayed. 10 Sorted. 10.15 Began Account of Voyage. 11.45 Prayed with Charles, etc. 12 Religious talk. 12.30 [Read] Law to them. 1 Account; dinner; Account. 2 Necessary business. 2.30 Catechized. 3 Read Letter on Education to Mrs Welch and Hawkins; Oglethorpe came, religious and useful talk. 3.45 Read e c a p etc. 4.40 Religious talk with Mr Hawkins, he very serious. 5 Mrs Hawkins came to me, began Prayers to her. 5.45 Necessary talk. 6 Read to [Daniel] Arthur and Francis Brooks. 6.30 German. 7.15 Religious talk with Mrs M[ackay]. 7.30 With Charles and Delamotte. 8 Necessary talk (religious) with Oglethorpe. 9.30 Read the Prayers to Mrs Hawkins. 10.30.

TUESDAY, JANUARY 20. 5 Dressed; prayed; Bible (lively zeal). 6 Religious talk with Mrs Hawkins; prayed. 7 Read c a p p s h s x c p t b. 8 Read resolutions to Charles, etc. 9 Writ Account of Voyage. 12 Religious talk with Charles, etc, [read] Law to them. 1 Account. 1.30 Dinner. 2 Account. 2.30 Catechized. 3 Account. 4 Read c a p p s h s x c p t b; Account. 5.15 Meditated; prayed. 6 Slept. 6.15 Meditated; necessary talk with Catherine [Harling, Mr Hawkins' maid].

Friday, January 23. In the evening God visited us with a second storm. In the morning it increased so that we were obliged again to drive before the wind. I could not but say to myself, How is it that thou hast no faith? [cf. Mark 4:40]—being still unwilling to die. About one in the afternoon, almost as soon as I was gone out of the great cabin door, the sea did not break as usual, but came smoothly with a full tide over the side of the ship. I was covered in a moment from head to foot, being quite vaulted over with water, and so stunned that I scarce expected to lift up my head again till the sea should give up her dead. But it was the will of God, I should receive no hurt at all. About midnight the storm ceased.

6.30 Read to [Daniel] Arthur and Francis Brooks. 7 With Germans. 7.45 With Charles, etc, religious talk. 9 Undressed; prayed.
    Providence: Well, though stormy.
    Grace: Lively zeal, 7 rating once [both between 5 and 6 am].

WEDNESDAY, JANUARY 21. 4 E; dressed; writ diary; prayed. 4.40 Slept (a calm). 5 E; prayed; Bible; sang. 6 E; prayed; Bible. 6.30 Read c a p p. 7 E; s h s c p t b. 7.30 Account. 8 E; Account. 9 E; with Mrs Mackay, tea, religious talk. 10 E; Account; writ to brother Samuel. 11 E; letter. 12 E; letter. 12.30 Prayed with Charles, etc, religious talk. 1 Writ resolutions. 2 Catechized. 2.30 Prayed; dinner. 3 Religious talk with Mrs Welch and Hawkins. 3.45 With Perkins. 4 Necessary talk (religious). 4.30 Oglethorpe, good talk (he seemed convinced). 5 Oglethorpe [had] religious talk (necessary) with the people. 6 He [had] religious talk (necessary). 7 With Germans. 8 Religious talk (necessary) with Charles, etc. 9 With Oglethorpe. 9.45 (Stormy).
    Providence: Well.
    Grace: 7 rating twice [4 to 6 am].

THURSDAY, JANUARY 22. 4 E; dressed; prayed; private prayer. 5 E; intercession. 6 Germans; read Prayers. 7.30 Necessary talk with John Brownfield. 8 Tea. 8.15 Religious talk (necessary) with John Brownfield. 9.45 Ended letter. 10 E; writ to Mr Vernon. 11 [Writ] to Mr Hutcheson; prayed. 12 Religious talk with Charles, etc. 1 Ended letter. 1.15 Slept. 1.30 Dinner. 2.15 Account. 2.45 Religious talk with Mrs Welch. 3 Read Law to Mrs Welch and Mrs Hawkins (they convinced). 3.45 Meditated. 4 E; meditated. 4.15 Read c a p p s h s x c t b. 5 Religious talk with Catherine. 5.15 With Mrs and Mr Hawkins (all seemed affected). 6 Meditated; *Country Parson* with [Daniel] Arthur (he open). 7 With Germans. 7.45 Religious talk with Oglethorpe, etc. 8 Religious talk with Oglethorpe; with Delamotte, etc. 9 Necessary talk (religious) with Oglethorpe; could not talk with Mrs Hawkins. 10 Necessary talk (religious).
    Providence: Fair wind; well. John Brownfield convinced. Mrs Welch and Mrs Hawkins convinced. Catherine and Mr Arthur open.

FRIDAY, JANUARY 23. 5.30 Dressed; prayed; cabin; Mrs Hawkins (she would not come). 6 Sang; German. 7 Meditated. 7.15 Read c a p p s c 1 2 3 4 t b. 8 E; writ to Sir John [Philipps]. 9 Writ letter; coffee. 10 Letter. 11 E; German; meditated.

Sunday, January 25. While the calm continued, I endeavoured to prepare myself for another storm. At one our third storm began. At four it was more violent than any we had had before. The waves of the sea were now mighty, and raged horribly [cf. Ps. 93:5]. They rose up to the heavens above, and seemed to cleave even down to hell beneath [cf. Ps. 107:26]. The wind roared about us, and—what I never heard before or since—whistled distinctly, as if it had been a human voice. The ship not only reeled to and fro with the utmost violence, but shook and jarred with so unequal and grating a motion that one could with great difficulty keep one's hold of anything, nor stand a moment without it. Every ten minutes came a shock against the stern or side of the ship, which one would think should dash it into a thousand pieces. In the height of the storm a child, privately baptized before, was publicly received into the Church. It put me in mind of Jeremiah's buying land when the

---

12 Read Law to them. 12.30 Necessary business. 1.30 Religious talk with Alexander. 2 Religious talk with Francis Brooks. 2.15 Necessary talk (religious) with Charles; prayed. 3 Dinner. 3.30 Religious talk with Mrs Welch and Hawkins. 4 Read Prayers, expounded. 4.45 Religious talk (necessary) with Catherine. 5.30 Prayed (Mrs Hawkins not [there]). 6 *Country Parson* with [Daniel] Arthur (Francis Brooks not [there]). 7 With Germans. 7.45 Von Reck's journal. 8 Mostly religious talk with Oglethorpe, etc. 9 Religious talk with Oglethorpe of Indians. 9.45 Undressed. 11 Very stormy all night; less afraid than before!

Providence: Well; stormy. Mrs Hawkins did not come twice; why so? see Thursday [January 22 at] 9 [pm]. Francis Brooks said he would not come.

SATURDAY, JANUARY 24. 4 E. 4.30 Dressed; prayed (stormy). 5 E; Bible; Prayed; sang. 6 E; Bible; prayed; sang. 6.45 Bread and cheese. 7 Read Prayers; ended Von Reck's journal. 8 E; transcribed Account of Voyage. 9 E; Account. 10 E; Account (we drove). 11 Prayed (storm greater; afraid!). 12 Prayed with Ingham; religious talk with Charles, etc. 1 Washed all over, undressed. 2 Dinner, mostly religious talk (storm rather abated). 3 Explained with Horton (he convinced). 4 Religious talk; prayed. 4.45 Religious talk with Mrs Hawkins, ill. 5 Religious talk with Mr and Mrs Hawkins (they seemed affected). 6 *Country Parson* with [Daniel] Arthur and Francis Brooks. 6.45 Slept. 7 With Germans. 8 Religious talk with Charles, etc. 9 Writ diary; undressed. 9.45 (Stormy still). 12 Calm returned.

Providence: A storm; well; drove; afraid of death. The sea covered me [at 1 pm]. Explained with Mr Horton, he convinced. Mr and Mrs Hawkins seemed affected. Francis Brooks came [at 6 pm].

Grace: 7 rating thrice [4 to 6 am, 11 to noon]; 6 nine times [all but 7 to 8, 10 to 11 am, 1 to 2, 7 to 8 pm].

SUNDAY, JANUARY 25. 4 E. 4.30 Dressed; prayed; writ diary (calm). 5 E; prayed. 5.20 Slept. 6 E; prayed; dressed; necessary business. 7 E; read Prayers. 8 Tea; sang. 9 E; prayed; sang. 10 E; read Patrick to them. 10.30 Slept. 10.45 Kempis.

Chaldeans were at the point of destroying Jerusalem, and seemed a pledge of mercy which God designed to show us, even in the land of the living.

We spent three or four hours after prayers with Mr. Oglethorpe in conversing suitably to the occasion, confirming one another in a calm expectation of the wise, holy, gracious will of God. A storm did not appear to me so terrible a thing as it had done before. Blessed be a God who alone does wonders, and is able mightily to deliver his people!

At seven I went to the Germans. In the midst of a psalm, wherein we were mentioning the power of God, the sea broke over, covered the ship, and split the mainsail. Many of the English screamed out. The Germans looked up, and without intermission sang on. From them I went to their crying, trembling neighbours, and found myself enabled to speak with them in boldness, and to point out to them the difference in the hour of trial betwixt him that feareth the Lord and him that feareth him not. At twelve the wind abated. That was the most glorious day I have hitherto seen.

Monday, January 26. We now enjoyed the calmer weather. I can conceive no difference comparable between a rough sea and a calm except that which is betwixt a mind calmed in faith and love, and one torn up by the storms of earthly passions.

---

11 Read c c c, preached, prayed, Sacrament (twenty communicants). 12 Sacrament; Patrick. 12.20 Meditated; prayed. 1 With Mrs Hawkins, religious talk, she worse; wind rose. 2 Dinner. 3 Mostly religious talk with Oglethorpe (storm, less afraid). 4 Read Prayers; religious talk with Oglethorpe, Charles, and Ingham (storm higher). 5 Religious talk (storm very high). 6 Religious talk with Charles (a little afraid). 7 With Germans; religious talk to people (convincing; not afraid; storm higher). 7.30 A wave covered the ship and split the mainsail. 8 Religious talk with Oglethorpe, etc (storm high). 9 Religious talk with Oglethorpe. 9.45 Slept (storm high). 10 Prayed; religious talk. 10.15 Slept. 10.30 Writ diary. 10.45 Slept (storm high). 11 Prayed; religious talk. 11.30 Undressed. 12 A little milder.

Providence: Well; twenty communicants. A great storm; mainsail split.

Grace: 7 rating four times [4 to 6, 9 to 10 am, 7 to 8 pm]; 6 sixteen times [the remainder]. Lively zeal [9 to 10 am]. Convincing [7 to 8 pm]. Less afraid.

MONDAY, JANUARY 26. 6 Dressed; religious talk with Mr and Mrs Welch (calmer [weather]). 7 Religious talk with Ingham and Delamotte (lively zeal). 8 Read Prayers, exhorted; religious talk. 8.45 Religious talk. 9 Religious talk with Mrs Hawkins, tea; visited all. 10 Began Nalson (lively zeal). 11 Visited Mrs Moore and Mrs Lawley, religious talk. 12 Religious talk (necessary) with Oglethorpe. 12.15 Read Law to them. 1 E; religious talk (necessary). 1.15 Shaved. 1.45 Religious talk with Hawkins. 2 E; religious talk; writ diary. 2.30 Nalson. 3 Dinner. 3.30 Nalson. 4 Read Prayers, expounded. 5 With Mrs Hawkins, Oglethorpe came, mostly religious talk. 6 Necessary talk with Oglethorpe;

Thursday, January 29. About seven in the evening we met with the skirts of a hurricane. The rain as well as the wind was exceeding violent, the lightning almost without intermission. Toward the end of it we had an appearance on each of our masts which the ancients called Castor and Pollux, the modern Romanists *corpus sanctum*. It was a small ball of white fire, like a star. The mariners say it seldom appears but either in a storm (and then it is commonly on the decks) or just at the end of one (and then it is usually seen on the masts or sails). Being below with the Germans, I knew nothing of the danger (God being merciful to me) till we were delivered out of it.

---

religious talk with [Daniel] Arthur, prayed. 6.45 With Germans. 7.45 Thought. 8 Religious talk with Charles and Ingham, Charles perverse. 9 Necessary talk with Charles, Charles perverse. 9.15 Undressed.

Providence: Well; calm.

Grace: 7 rating twice [10 to 11 am, 4 to 5 pm]; 6 thirteen times [all but 5 to 6 pm]. Lively zeal [7 to 8, 10 to 11 am]. Reflected on t.5 to Charles. Convincing [9 to 10 am].

TUESDAY, JANUARY 27. 4.45 Dressed; writ diary. 5 Prayed; read sermon. 6 German; necessary business. 7 Read Prayers, expounded. 8 Nalson; visited. 8.30 Necessary talk (religious) with Oglethorpe. 9 Tea, religious talk (necessary). 9.30 Religious and useful talk with Mr and Mrs Hawkins, she ill. 10 Read 'Battle of [the] Sexes'. 11 Religious talk (necessary) with Mrs Lawley. 12 Prayed with Charles, etc, religious talk. 1 Nalson. 1.45 Dinner. 2 Dinner. 2.30 Catechized. 3 Read Prayers with Mrs Hawkins (she open and affected). 4 Religious talk (necessary) with Brownfield. 4.15 Nalson. 4.30 Read Prayers. 5 Expounded. 5.30 Oglethorpe [gave] necessary talk to the people. 6.40 With Germans. 7.30 With Mrs Hawkins, talk of virtue (she better). 8 Religious talk, close. 9 Religious talk with Oglethorpe. 9.45 Undressed.

Providence: Well; calm. Mrs Hawkins open and affected.

Grace: 6 rating fourteen times [all but 7 to 8 am, 10 to noon, 9 to 10 pm].

WEDNESDAY, JANUARY 28. 5 Dressed; prayed (dead calm). 6 Nalson; prayed. 7 Read Prayers, expounded. 8 Writ alphabet. 10 Alphabet; (wind fair). 11 With Mrs Hawkins, Lawley. 12 Read Law to them. 1 Religious talk with Charles, etc. 2 Catechized. 2.30 Read Prayers; dinner. 3.15 With Von Reck, etc, they [had] good talk. 4 Read Prayers, expounded. 5 Necessary talk (religious) with Oglethorpe. 5.45 Prayed with Delamotte. 6 *Country Parson* with Francis Brooks, religious talk with Betty Hassel. 6.45 With Germans. 7.45 With Mrs Hawkins, religious and useful talk. 8 Religious talk with Charles and Delamotte. 8.45 Undressed.

Providence: Calm; wind fair; well.

Grace: 7 rating once [5 to 6 am].

THURSDAY, JANUARY 29. 4 Dressed; private prayer (heavy); prayed with Ingham (fair wind). 5 Prayed; read sermon. 6 Prayed; sermons. 6.45 Read c [a p p s h s], etc, expounded. 8 Tea; Nalson (lively zeal). 9 Began sermon on Single Eye. 10.30 Read Prayers to Mrs Hawkins (she seemed affected). 11.30 With Mrs

Friday, January 30. We had another storm in the night, which did us no other harm than splitting our foresail. I laid me down with my clothes on, the bed being wet, and God gave me sound sleep till the morning. I have not put them off since, nor propose [N and R—purpose] doing so any more till it is necessary to change them.

Sunday, February 1. The *Pomeroy* from Charleston came up with us,

---

Lawley, religious talk (she serious); Nalson. 12 Prayed with Ingham and Delamotte, religious talk. 12.30 Nalson. 2 Dinner. 2.45 Necessary talk with Robinson. 3 Religious talk with Alexander [Grimaldi] (he convinced). 4 Read Prayers, expounded. 4.45 Writ diary; sang. 5 Nalson; prayed. 6 *Country Parson* to [Daniel] Arthur and Francis Brooks, they serious (lightning and stormy). 7 With Germans (hurricane). 8 Mostly religious talk with Oglethorpe, etc. 9.30.

Providence: Well; wind fair. Mrs Hawkins affected; Mrs Lawley, [Daniel] Arthur, Francis Brooks serious. Alexander [Grimaldi] convinced of use of Public Prayers.

Grace: 7 rating twice [4 to 5 am, 1 to 2 pm]; 6 fourteen times [all but 8 to 9 pm].

FRIDAY, JANUARY 30. 4 Dressed; prayed; private prayer (heavy). 4.45 Slept. 5 Nalson; prayed (heavy). 5.45 Slept. 6 Nalson. 6.30 Writ diary; meditated; read c a [p p s h s], etc (stormy). 8 Writ Account [of Voyage]. 9 Nalson; prayed (heavy). 10 Nalson; sang. 11 With Mrs Hawkins, religious talk, could not speak home. 12 [Read] Law to them. 12.40 Nalson. 2 Nalson; dinner. 3 Oglethorpe, good talk. 4 Read Prayers; Nalson. 5 Prayed; Nalson. 6 Religious talk with Ingham and Delamotte (lively zeal). 7 With Germans. 7.45 With Mrs Welch and Mrs Hawkins (could not speak). 8 Religious and useful talk. 8.15 Religious talk with Charles, etc. 8.45 Prayed; undressed; storm.

Providence: Stormy; well.

Grace: Lively zeal [6 to 7 pm].

SATURDAY, JAN. 31. 4 Dressed; prayed (wind fair). 5 Prayed; Nalson. 6 Nalson; German. 7 Read Prayers. 7.45 Breakfast. 8 Writ sermon. 9 Tea; sermon. 10 Nalson. 11 Religious talk with Mrs Mackay. 11.30 [Read] Law to them (she serious). 12 Religious talk with Phoebe Hird, with Catherine (she serious). 12.30 Religious talk with Charles, etc. 1 Necessary talk with Horton. 1.15 Dinner. 2 Religious talk with Reed and Cooling. 3 Religious talk with Mrs Welch and Mrs Hawkins (she not affected). 4 Read Prayers; meditated; Mrs Hawkins not come. 5 Meditated; prayed with Ingham, etc. 5.45 Oglethorpe, good talk. 6 Religious talk with Delamotte. 6.30 With [Daniel] Arthur, Francis Brooks not [come]. 7 With Germans. 8 With Charles and Delamotte, prayed, religious talk; undressed.

Providence: Well; wind fair. Mrs Mackay serious; Phoebe Hird affected. Mrs Hawkins not affected, did not come; Francis Brooks did not come.

Grace: 7 rating once [10 to 11 am]; 6 fourteen times [all but 8 to 9 am, 7 to 8 pm]. + [10 to 11 am].

SUNDAY, FEBRUARY 1. 4 Dressed; private prayer (lively). 5 Prayed with Ingham; Hickes. 6 Sang; Bible. 6.15 German. 7 Read Prayers, preached. 8 Breakfast, bound for London. We were exceeding glad of so happy an opportunity of sending to our friends in England word of our safety.

Monday, February 2. About ten at night William Taverner, a lad fourteen or fifteen years old, came running to our cabin greatly affrighted at something which he said he had seen at the feet of his bed; he added that it looked at him continually unless when he was saying his prayers, and then he saw nothing of it. The rest of his account was very confused. He sat trembling and praying by our bedside till one in the morning, and has been utterly distracted ever since.

---

religious talk; German. 9 Nalson; religious talk with Oglethorpe. 10 [Read] Patrick to them; Kempis. 11 Read Prayers, preached. 12 Sacrament (twenty-two communicants); Patrick. 12.30 Nalson. 1 Read Nalson to Mrs Hawkins and Mrs Welch (they affected). 1.45 Nalson; writ diary. 2 Writ to brother Samuel, etc; ship came up to us. 3 They [had] good talk. 4 Dinner. 5 Read Prayers. 5.30 Meditated; prayed with Ingham. 6 [Read] *Country Parson* to [Daniel] Arthur. 6.45 With Germans. 7 Germans, religious talk with them. 8 Oglethorpe, good talk (necessary). 9.45 Undressed.

> Providence: Well. Mrs Hawkins affected with Nalson. She did not come [to the Sacrament?]. The *Pomeroy* from Charleston came up [2 to 3 pm].
> Grace: 7 rating twice [4 to 6 am]; 6 twelve times [all but 3 to 5, 8 to 10 pm]. Lively zeal [1 to 2 pm]. Twenty-two communicants.

MONDAY, FEBRUARY 2. 4.30 Dressed; writ diary; prayed. 5 Prayed with Ingham; Bible, stormy all day. 6 Prayed; Bible; breakfast. 7 Read Prayers, expounded. 8 Sermon. 10 Nalson. 10.45 Religious talk with Mr Patterson. 11 Necessary talk with Captain. 11.30 Prayed; sang. 12 Good talk with Oglethorpe. 1 Nalson. 2 Maimbourg. 4 Dinner, good talk. 5 Read Prayers; Oglethorpe, necessary talk. 6.15 Writ diary; meditated. 6.45 With Germans. 7.15 Religious talk with Ingham. 7.45 Good talk with Oglethorpe. 8 Captain Cornish came, necessary talk. 8.30 Necessary talk (religious) with Oglethorpe. 9 Undressed.

> Providence: Stormy all day; well. At noon ceased striving! O fool!

TUESDAY, FEBRUARY 3. 4.15 Dressed; writ diary; prayed. 5 Prayed with Ingham; Bible; sang. 6 German. 7 Read Prayers, expounded. 8 German. 9 Tea; religious talk with Oglethorpe. 10.30 Sermon. 11 Ended sermon. 12 Prayed with Ingham and Charles, religious talk. 12.30 Religious talk with Oglethorpe. 1 Religious talk (necessary). 2 Nalson. 2.30 Dinner. 3 Religious talk with Mr and Mrs Hawkins. 3.45 With Taverner, mad! 4 Meditated. 4.15 Read Prayers. 5 Expounded. 5.30 Mrs Hawkins not come; prayed. 6 [Read] *Country Parson* with Francis Brooks and [Daniel] Arthur (Francis Brooks serious). 6.45 Religious talk with Oglethorpe. 7 With Germans. 7.45 Writ diary. 8 Necessary and useful talk with Oglethorpe. 8.30 Religious talk with Mrs Hawkins (she right). 9.45 Undressed.

> Providence: Well; Will Taverner mad. Francis Brooks affected; Mrs Hawkins right.
> Grace: Lively zeal [5 to 6 pm]. 6 rating fifteen times [all but 1 to 2, 8 to 9 pm].

Wednesday, February 4. We had the welcome news that we were within soundings, having not twenty fathom water. About noon the trees of Georgia were visible from the mast, and in the afternoon from the main deck. In the Evening Lesson there were two verses which we could not help observing: 'A great door and effectual is opened; and there are many adversaries' [1 Cor. 16:9]; and 'as touching our brother Apollos, I greatly desired him to come unto you with the brethren, but his will was not to come at all at this time; but he will come when he shall have convenient time' [1 Cor. 16:12]. [R (referring to Apollos)—Mr. Wesley seems to have applied this to Mr. Hall before mentioned.]

Thursday, February 5. Between two and three in the afternoon God brought us all safe into the Savannah River. We cast anchor off the Isle of Tybee, which gave us a specimen of America. The pines, palms, and cedars, running in rows along the shore, made an exceeding beautiful prospect, especially to us who did not expect to see the bloom of spring in the depth of winter. The clearness of the sky, the setting sun, and the smoothness of the water conspired to recommend this new world, and prevent our regretting the loss of our native country.

Friday, February 6. About eight in the morning I first set my foot on American ground. It was an uninhabited island, but a few miles in

---

WEDNESDAY, FEBRUARY 4. 4.15 Dressed; private prayer. 5 Prayed with Ingham; Bible; sang. 6 German. 7 Read Prayers, expounded. 8 Corrected sermon; tea. 9 Sermon. 9.30 Corrected Account [of Voyage]. 12.30 Religious talk with Charles, etc. 1 Read Law to them. 2 Religious talk with Hughes, etc (they seemed affected). 2.45 Necessary talk with Oglethorpe. 3 Prayed; dinner. 3.30 Religious talk with Mrs Hawkins (she seemed affected). 4 Read Prayers, expounded. 5 Nalson; writ diary; private prayer. 6 Religious talk with Francis Brooks. 6.30 [Read] Norris with Oglethorpe. 7 With Germans. 7.45 With Oglethorpe, etc, he [had] idle talk. 8 Oglethorpe, much talk. 8.45 Necessary talk. 9.30 Religious talk with Mrs Welch and Hawkins. 10 Religious and useful talk. 10.45 Undressed.
>Providence: Well; Hughes and Sexton seemed affected. Saw land; read, 'A great door and effectual, etc' [1 Cor. 16:9].
>Grace: 7 rating twice [4 to 6 am]; 6 eleven times [all but 9 to noon, 2 to 3, 7 to 10 pm].

THURSDAY, FEBRUARY 5. 5.30 Dressed; prayed. 6 Prayed; German; read Prayers. 7 Read Prayers, expounded. 7.30 Account [of Voyage]. 8 Account; breakfast, could not get tea. 9 Account. 10 Account; tea. 11 Account. 2.30 Dinner; anchored at Tybee [Island]. 3 Dinner, necessary talk. 3.45 Religious talk. 4.45 Read Prayers. 5 Read Prayers, expounded. 5.45 Account. 7 With Germans. 8 Mr Oglethorpe talked to people; prayed; undressed; sleepy.
>Providence: Well; anchored at Tybee!

FRIDAY, FEBRUARY 6. 4.10 Dressed; writ diary. 4.30 Prayed. 5 Meditated; necessary business; religious talk with Charles, etc. 6 Necessary business. 7

A və. dr. ẋ½p̄   7   7. 2.   v

5. m. n̄b r̄ n[̄c   6   2.

6 n̄b.   6

7 n̄b. n̄F   5

8 n̄ on shore n ō. m̄pē 6 mark 6. Prep ded !

9 made a bridge   6

10 n̄[. r v̄ Acc̄ r̄ded   6

11 n̄b.   5

12 on board. r̄ n̄ Art   6

1 r̄n̄ Fraz̄, n̄ Heddon. 6 - Alex̄

2 dē. on shore. n̄r   6

3 n̄ n̄ MH. r̄F̄   6 Pa

4 n̄[̄c on B̄. r̄ F. All 5 μ̄ēᵈυon

5 n̄t.   5

6 n̄t̄r̄ n̄ Captain's   6 μ̄ open

7 n̄t̄r̄ n̄ yᵐ Th̄. Corn   6

8 n̄t̄n̄ C. Demps̄   6 --

9 u̅   7, 8, 6, 11, 12.

P. V. On shore in America

1 C. Tho. Corn. Demps̄ open

! Glorious Lesson !

1 MH aᵈ

extent, near Tybee, called by the English, Pepper Island. Mr. Oglethorpe led us through the moorish land on the shore to a rising ground, where we all kneeled down to return thanks to God, and beg the continuance of his fatherly protection over us. Mr. Oglethorpe then left us, and took boat for Savannah. When the rest of the people came on shore, we chose an open place surrounded with myrtles, bays, and cedars, which sheltered us both from the sun and wind, and called our little flock together. There were several passages in the Second Lesson (Mark 6) which were wonderfully suited to the occasion. Our Lord's directions to the first preachers of his gospel, the example of John the Baptist, their toiling at sea and deliverance—with these comfortable words, 'It is I, be not afraid' [Mark 6:50]—were all so manifestly spoken to us that we would not but make the application. God grant that, through patience and comfort of his Holy Word, we may ever hold fast the blessed hope of our calling!

Saturday, February 7. Mr. Oglethorpe having commissioned me and one more [John Brownfield of Bristol] to take care of the passengers in his absence, I find how hard it is to serve God without distraction in the midst of secular business. Happy are they who are delivered from this heavy cross, and so are they who bear it in the spirit of their Master. In the afternoon as we were coming from shore a shower of rain, common in these parts, overtook us, and before we could get one hundred yards

---

Necessary business; necessary talk. 8 Went on shore with Oglethorpe; read Prayers, expounded (Mark 6); Peeper Island. 9 Made a bridge. 10 With Charles, read the Account, sang. 11 Necessary business. 12 On board; religious talk with [Daniel] Arthur. 1 Religious talk with Frazer, with Heddon and Alexander. 2 Dinner on shore, necessary talk (religious). 3 Walked with Mrs Hawkins, religious talk (she affected). 4 Necessary talk. 4.30 Came on board; necessary talk; all μέϑυοι ['drunkards']. 5 Necessary talk. 6 Necessary talk (religious) with captains (they open). 7 Necessary talk (religious) with them (Thomas and Cornish). 8 Necessary talk with Captain Dempsey. 9 Undressed.

Providence: Well; Glorious lesson! [8 to 9 am]. Mrs Hawkins affected.

Grace: 7 rating once [4 to 5 am]; 6 eleven times [all but 7 to 8, 11 to noon, 4 to 6 pm]. s.1 [thankful?].

SATURDAY, FEBRUARY 7. 5.15 Necessary business; called people. 6 Necessary talk; necessary business. 7 Tea, necessary talk; writ diary. 7.45 Necessary talk; staved rum. 8 On shore; necessary talk; read Prayers, expounded. 9 Necessary business. 11 Necessary talk with Brownfield. 11.20 Prayed; sang. 12 On board; necessary talk; dinner. 1 On shore; meditated; prayed. 2 Read Norris to Delamotte, Mr and Mrs Hawkins. 3 Tea, mostly religious talk. 4 Good talk (necessary). 5 In the woods with Mrs Hawkins, religious talk. 6 Took boat; hard rain; necessary talk; very wet. 7 Mr Vanderplank, Spangenberg, etc, necessary talk; read letters. 8 With Germans; religious talk with Spangenberg. 9 Necessary talk with Ingham, B[rownfield], etc. 9.50 Undressed.

Providence: Well; saw Spangenberg.

wetted us all from head to foot. I found no ill effects of it at all. What can hurt those whom it pleases God to save?

Before Mr. Oglethorpe left Savannah, one Mrs. Stanley, an experienced midwife, came to him, and said she heard several women on board were near their time. He told her he believed not, but that he should be glad, nevertheless, if she would go down with him and examine a pretended midwife who was on board the *Simmonds*. Accordingly he returned in the evening with her and Mr. Spangenberg, who had conducted the first company of the Bohemian Brethren to Georgia. He told me several particulars relating to their faith and practice and discipline, all of which were agreeable to the plan of the first ages, and seemed to show that it was their one care, without desire of pleasing or fear of displeasing any, to retain inviolate the whole deposition once delivered to the saints. [R—At nine, Mr. Oglethorpe went back to Savannah.]

Sunday, February 8. I asked Mr. Spangenberg's advice with regard to myself. He told me he could say nothing till he had asked me two or three [R—one or two] questions. 'Do you know yourself? Do you know Jesus Christ? Have you the witness of the Spirit in your heart?' After my answering these, he gave me several directions, which may the good God who sent him enable me to follow.

Monday, February 9. Mrs. Welch was safely brought to bed by Mrs. Stanley. On this occasion I received a fresh proof how little extraordinary providences avail those who are not moved by the ordinary means he hath ordained to devote their whole souls to his service. Many burials and some deaths I have been present at, but I

SUNDAY, FEBRUARY 8. 4.45 Dressed; (well); prayed. 5 Prayed; meditated; writ diary. 6 Meditated; dressed. 7 Necessary talk; breakfast. 8 Religious talk with Spangenberg (excellent man). 9 Necessary talk (religious). 9.30 Read Prayers. 10 Preached. 10.15 Meditated; read Patrick to them. 11 Patrick; religious talk. 11.30 Read Prayers, preached. 12 Sacrament. 12.30 Meditated. 1 Religious talk with Spangenberg of myself. 2.30 Meditated; prayed. 3 Dinner. 4 Read Prayers, expounded. 5 Meditated; prayed; sang; tea. 6 Meditated; sang [supper?] with Spangenberg; Oglethorpe came. 7 With Oglethorpe, necessary talk; necessary talk (religious) with Spangenberg. 8 Necessary talk with Oglethorpe, etc. 9 Necessary talk; undressed. 9.45.

Providence: Mr Spangenberg a wise man; advised me as to myself!

Grace: 7 rating four times [11 to noon, 1 to 2, 5 to 7 pm]; 6 eleven times [all but 6 to 8 am]. + twice [5 to 6 am, 6 to 7 pm]. Meditated fervently [at 5 pm]; lively zeal [4 to 5 pm]. Resolved: To follow Christ.

MONDAY, FEBRUARY 9. 2 With Mrs Welch; gave things; prayed (zealous); made coffee. 3 Slept. 5.30 Religious talk with Volmar (gained no ground). 6 Necessary business. 6.15 Prayed; necessary talk; read Prayers, expounded. 7 Necessary business; writ diary. 7.20 Breakfast for them; tea. 8 Necessary business. 8.30

never yet knew a soul converted by the sight of either. This is the second time I have been witness (there being only a door between us) of one of the deepest distresses that life affords. The groans of the sick person had very short intermissions, and how were these filled up by these assistants? With strong cries to God? With counselling her that was encompassed with sorrows of death to trust in him? With exhortations to each other to fear him who is able to inflict sharper pains than these? No; but with laughing and jesting, at no time convenient, but at this least of all. 'Verily, if they hear not Moses and the prophets, even the thunder of his power they will not understand [cf. Luke 16:31; Job 26:14].

In the afternoon, the boat being not yet come which was to carry Mr. Spangenberg and his people to Savannah, we took a walk on the shore, in which time I had an opportunity of learning several particulars both with regard to himself and the Church at Herrnhut. The account he gave of himself was this, viz.:

I was left without father and mother when I was ten years old. From that age to eighteen I lived without the fear of God. I was sent to the University of Jena, where I spent some time in learning tongues, and the vain philosophy which I have been labouring ever since to forget. Here it pleased God, by some who preached his word with power, to overturn my heart. I threw away all learning but what tended to save my soul. I shunned all company. I retired into a desert, and resolved to spend the remainder of my life there. For three days I found great comfort here, but the fourth it was otherwise. I then went to ask the advice of an experienced Christian. When I came to him I could not speak. But he saw my heart, and advised me to go back to my house and follow the business Providence should assign me. I went back to my house, but was fit for nothing. I could neither do any business nor join any conversation. All I could say to them who spoke to me was, Yes, or No. Many times I could not say that, nor understand what they said to me. All my friends and acquaintance

On shore; necessary talk. 9.30 Meditated. 10 Meditated; Bible; Kempis. 11 Necessary talk with Captain Thomas' men; Mrs Welch delivered. 12 On board; necessary business. 12.30 Writ diary; religious talk. 1 Dinner. 2 On shore with Spangenberg, religious talk. 3 Religous talk with him. 4.30 Religious talk of myself, close. 5 Tea, useful and necessary talk. 6 Read Prayers, expounded; writ diary. 6.45 Necessary talk. 7 With Germans. 8 Necessary talk. 8.30 Prayed; sang (lively zeal). 9 Undressed.
  Providence: Well; Mr Spangenberg clear. Mrs Welch brought to bed by midwife, come last night from Savannah.
  Grace: 7 rating thrice [2 to 3, 10 to 11 am, 4 to 5 pm]; 6 eleven times [all but 11 am to 2 pm]. + thrice [2 to 3, 10 to 11 am, 4 to 5 pm]. Zealous in meditation twice [9.30 to 11 am]. Lively zeal [8 to 9 pm].

looked upon me as dead, came no more to me, nor spoke nor thought of me.

When I began to recover, I set upon teaching some poor children. Others joined with me, and then taught more, till there were about forty of us, and three hundred of the children. I was now desired by several universities to accept of the place of professor of divinity or philosophy. But I utterly refused it, and begged of God with my whole heart that I might not be famous, but very little and unknown. After I had spent some years in this employment, Professor Breithaupt of Halle died. That university by their letters earnestly pressed me to accept of his professorship. I thought God called me thither, and therefore went. I had not been there long before the directors of the University found many faults with my behaviour and preaching. They grew more and more dissatisfied, and after half a year wrote a petition to the King of Prussia to displace me; he sent an order to the Commander of Halle, in pursuance whereof I was warned (without any hearing) to leave the city in forty-eight hours. I retired to Herrnhut, to Count Zinzendorf, whom I had known for several years. I wrote to the directors that I desired to know my crimes; but they never sent an account. I could easily have cleared myself by a public defence from all imputations they had cast upon me; but I feared it might lessen the success of their ministry, therefore chose to be silent.

Count Zinzendorf is about thirty-six years old. He has been full of the love of God from a child, insomuch that he has sometimes owned he has never felt the love of the world one quarter of an hour in his life. The Church in Herrnhut consists of near a thousand persons gathered out of all parts in Germany. They all hold fast the discipline, as well as the faith and practice, of the apostolical age. I was desired by the Brotherhood last year to conduct about fifteen of them to Georgia, where one lot of land was assigned them near the town of Savannah, and another in the country; and with them I have stayed ever since.

I then asked him whither he was to go next. 'I have some thoughts to go to Pennsylvania, where are about one hundred of my countrymen driven by persecution out of their own country, who have neither means of subsistence where they are nor money to transport them to Georgia. If it pleases God that I shall be useful to them, I shall be glad; and if not, I shall be glad. What he will do with me I know not, nor whither he will send me next, I know not. I am blind. I am a child. It is all one to me. My Father knows; and I will go whithersoever he calls.'

I asked Mr. Spangenberg of Mrs. Hawkins's case, and desired his advice how to behave towards her. He answered, 'My dear brother, I believe our friend Kempis advises well, *Omnes bonas mulieres devita, easque Deo commenda* ['Fly from all good women, and recommend them to God'; cf. Kempis, I.viii]. Not that I would advise you to give her up quite, but to converse much may be dangerous either to her or you. It may be best to speak to her seldom, and in few words, and earnestly to pray God to do the rest.'

TUESDAY, FEBRUARY 10. 5.30 Necessary talk (religious); prayed. 6 Prayed (zealous) with Mrs Welch; necessary business. 6.20 Writ diary; tea, religious talk. 7.30 Read Prayers, expounded (lively zeal). 8 Writ Account. 10 Necessary talk; necessary business. 10.30 Account. 1 Meditated; religious talk with Charles. 1.30 Dinner. 2.15 Necessary talk with Mrs Hawkins. 2.30 Religious talk with Charles. 3 On board Captain Thomas', [ship], necessary talk; on board Captain Diamond's [ship]. 4 On shore; necessary talk with James Billinghurst. 5.15 On board; read Prayers, expounded. 6 Meditated; prayed. 7 With Hermsdorf, sang (he very zealous). 8 Religious talk (necessary) with Charles, etc. 9 Religious talk with Mrs Hawkins, close (she affected); undressed.

> Providence: Mr Hermsdorf very zealous. Explained with Mrs Hawkins, she seemed affected.
>
> Grace: Lively zeal [7 to 8 am].
>
> [N.B.:] A poor, careless, lukewarm day!

WEDNESDAY, FEBRUARY 11. 6 Dressed; prayed with Delamotte; necessary business. 7 Necessary talk. 7.15 Read Prayers, expounded. 8 With Hermsdorf, sang. 9 Tea. 9.30 Meditated. 10 On shore; meditated; prayed (zealous). 11 Bible. 12 Necessary business. 12.30 Meditated. 2 On board; necessary talk; writ diary. 2.30 Religious talk. 2.45 Dinner. 3 On shore; religious talk with Ingham. 4 Sat with Mrs Hawkins, religious and useful talk (did nothing!). 5 Religious and useful talk with Mrs Hawkins, gained no ground. 6.30 On board; read Prayers, expounded. 6.45 Meditated. 7 With Hermsdorf, sang. 8 Good talk with Horton, etc; prayed; undressed.

> Providence: Meditated, etc; nothing, but God all! With Mrs Hawkins too long, therefore did nothing.
>
> Grace: Fervent in meditation, zealous in prayer [10 to 11 am].

THURSDAY, FEBRUARY 12. 4.30 Dressed; religious talk with Charles, etc. 5 Prayed; Bible. 6 With Mrs Welch; tea, useful and necessary talk; writ diary. 7 Read Prayers, expounded. 7.45 With Hermsdorf, sang. 8.30 On shore; thought. 9 Meditated. 10 Greek Testament (sins of thought). 12 Necessary talk with Captain Cornish (he convinced). 12.45 Meditated. 1 Dinner. 2 On shore; religious talk; meditated. 3 Greek Testament. 4 Religious talk with Tackner (he convinced); with Mrs Tackner, etc (she gave no ground). 5 Meditated. 5.30 On board; tea, necessary talk. 6 Prayed with Ingham, etc. 6.30 Read Prayers, expounded; meditated. 7 With Hermsdorf, Dober there, sang. 7.45 Religious talk. 8 Religious talk with Charles. 8.30 Religious talk with Mrs Hawkins, etc. 9 Religious talk with Mrs M[ackay]. 9.30 Undressed; Mr Oglethorpe came, on shore with him, necessary talk. 10 Necessary talk (religious) with Spangenberg, necessary talk with them. 11 Good talk with them. 12.30.

> Providence: Captain Cornish convinced; Mr Tackner convinced.
>
> Grace: preserved from sins of thought [10 to 11 am].

Friday, February 13. We received information that Tomochichi and his beloved men were coming to see us. They sent us down a side of venison before them. This morning in the course of reading were these words: 'I will save you, and ye shall be a blessing. Fear not, but let your hands be strong. Thus saith the Lord of hosts, It shall come to pass that there shall come people, and the inhabitants of many cities. And the inhabitants of one city shall go to another, saying, Let us go speedily to prayer before the Lord, and to seek the Lord of hosts. I will go also. Yea, many people and strong nations shall come to seek the Lord of hosts. Thus saith the Lord of hosts: In those days it shall come to pass that ten men shall take hold of the skirts of a Jew, saying, We will go with you, for we have heard that God is with you' [Zech. 8:20-22].

Saturday, February 14. In our course of reading were these words: 'By the blood of thy covenant I have sent forth thy prisoners out of the pit wherein there is no water. Turn ye to the stronghold, ye prisoners of hope. Even today do I declare, I will render double to you' (Zech. 9:11-12). 'From the rising up of the sun unto the going down of the same my name shall be great among the Gentiles, and in every place incense shall be offered to thy name, and a pure offering' (Mal. 1:11).

One of the Psalms for the day was the seventy-second, a glorious prophecy of the propagation of the Kingdom of Christ. The Second Lesson was Mark 13, containing both our Lord's directions to the first publishers of his gospel, and a plain description of the treatment which all who published it were to expect from those who received it not.

FRIDAY, FEBRUARY 13. 5.30 Dressed; prayed. 6 Prayed; with Spangenberg, sang. 7.15 Read Prayers. 7.30 With Spangenberg, etc. 8 Necessary and useful talk. 9 Tea, good talk (necessary and religious). 9.30 Religious talk with Oglethorpe (he open). 10 Necessary talk (religious). 10.15 Writ for Mr Oglethorpe. 4 Dinner. 5 Religious talk with them, with Oglethorpe; read Prayers. 6 Oglethorpe, good talk. 6.40 Tea. 7 Meditated; they [had] mostly religious talk. 7.45 Sang with Germans. 8.30 Religious talk with Charles. 9 Prayed.

Providence: Well; Oglethorpe open and friendly [9 to 10 am].

SATURDAY, FEBRUARY 14. 4 Prayed. 4.30 Slept (sick). 5 Bible; prayed. 7 Sang with Spangenberg. 7 Necessary talk (religious) with Oglethorpe; tea. 8 Necessary talk (religious). 8.30 Writ diary; necessary business. 9 Read Prayers, expounded. 10 Necessary business. 11 Writ Account. 12.30 Meditated. 1 Dressed. 1.15 With Tomochichi, religious talk. 2.15 Writ Account. 4 Dinner; Mr Spangenberg and Hermsdorf. 5 Religious talk. 5.30 Read Prayers. 6 Expounded; religious talk with Spangenberg. 7 Writ diary; necessary talk with Mr Hawkins; prayed with Mrs Welch. 8 Religious talk (necessary) with Oglethorpe and Mrs Welch.

Providence: Tomochichi came.

About one, Tomochichi, Toonahowi, Sinauky, and the Mico or King of the Savannah nation, with two of their chief women and three of their children, came on board. Tomochichi, Sinauky, and Toonahowi were in an English dress. The other women had on calico petticoats and coarse woollen mantles. The Savannah king, whose faced was stained red in several places, his hair dressed with beads, and his ear with a scarlet feather, had only a large blanket which covered him from his shoulders to his feet. Sinauky brought us a jar of milk and another of honey, and said she hoped when we spoke to them we would feed them with milk, for they were but children, and be sweet as honey towards them.

At our coming in they all rose, and Tomochichi, stepping forward, shook us by the hand, as did all the rest, women as well as men. This was the more remarkable because the Indians allow no man to touch or speak to a woman, except her husband, not though she be ill and even in danger of death. When we were all sat down, Tomochichi spake (by his interpreter, one Mrs. Musgrove) to this effect:

> I am glad to see you here. When I was in England, I desired that some might speak the *Great Word* to me; and my nation then desired to hear it. But since that time we have been all put into confusion. The French have built a fort with a hundred men in one place, and a fort with a hundred men in it in another. And the Spaniards are preparing for war. The English traders, too, put us into confusion, and have set our people against hearing the great word. For they speak with a double tongue; some say one thing of it and some another. But I am glad you are come. I will go up and speak to the wise men of our nation; and I hope they will hear. But we would not be made Christians as the Spaniards make Christians: we would be taught first, and afterwards baptized.

All this he spake with great earnestness, and much action both of his hands and head, and yet with the utmost gentleness [I and R—and softness] both of tone and manner. I answered in a few words: 'There is but One, he that sitteth in heaven, who is able to teach man wisdom. Though we are come so far, we know not whether he will please to teach you by us or no. If he will teach you, you will learn; but we can do nothing.' We then saluted them all as before, and withdrew. Having a few moments to myself, before we went in to the Indians, I took down my Greek Testament, which opened on these words: Ὑμεῖς μιμηταὶ ἐγενήθητε τῶν ἐκκλησιῶν [R adds—τῶν ἐν τῇ Ἰουδαίᾳ, etc. These words are 1 Thess. 2:14-16. So much of that place as was here quoted would run thus: "Ye are become followers of the churches of Judea, for ye also have suffered like things of your own countrymen, even as they have of the Jews; who have persecuted us, and forbid us to speak to the Gentiles that they might be saved."]

Sunday, February 15. Another party of the Indians of the Savannah nation came down; they were all tall, graceful, well-proportioned men, and had a remarkable softness in their speech and gentleness in their whole behaviour. In the afternoon they all returned home except the Mico and two others, who stayed to go with Mr. Oglethorpe, and hunt for him at the Altamaha River.

Monday, February 16. About six in the evening Mr. Oglethorpe set out for the new settlement. He took with him about fifty men of our two ships, besides Mr. Ingham, Mr. Hermsdorf, and three Indians. These five [R—six] went with Mr. Oglethorpe in the scoutboat, the rest in a sloop hired on purpose.

[N—'Memorandum. Here ends Mr. Wesley's Journal in MS, with which Mr. Ingham's agrees so far as to the circumstances of the voyage and landing—and proceeds as to himself in the following manner, viz.' There follow, pp. 28-32, selections from Ingham's journal, Feb. 16-24, as found in Luke Tyerman, *The Oxford Methodists* (London, Hodder and Stoughton, 1873), pp. 76-78.]

Sunday, February 15. 4.30 Meditated; prayed. 5 Prayed; religious talk; tea. 6 Religious talk. 6.15 Spangenberg came, sang, religious talk. 7 Religious talk; writ diary. 8 Read Prayers, expounded. 9 Meditated; dressed. 10 With Mrs Welch, religious talk, necessary talk. 11 Read Prayers, preached. 12 Sacrament (thirteen communicants). 12.30 Writ diary; religious talk with Spangenberg. 1 Religious talk with Spangenberg, sang. 2 Religious talk with Spangenberg, etc. 3 Took leave of Tomochichi. 3.15 Sang. 3.30 Dinner. 4 Religious talk, all open and friendly. 5 [Read] Patrick to them; read Prayers, expounded. 6 In Great Cabin, meditated, necessary talk. 7 Prayed with them; sang. 7.45 Meditated. 8 Great Cabin, necessary talk. 9 Religious talk with Spangenberg; prayed. 9.45.

Providence: Took leave of Tomochichi. We all open and friendly.

Grace: 6 rating fourteen times [all but 3 to 4, 6 to 7, 8 to 9.45 pm].

Monday, February 16. 4 Dressed; prayed; private prayer. 5 Bible; sang; religious talk (t.6/1 with Ingham). 6 Mr Spangenberg came, tea, religious talk. 7 Necessary talk (religious) with Oglethorpe (he convinced and friendly); read Prayers. 8 Writ for Oglethorpe. 12.30 [Writ] Account. 1 Writ for Oglethorpe. 2 Dinner; religious talk (necessary). 3 Writ for Oglethorpe. 4.30 Necessary talk. 5 Necessary talk (religious). 6 Religious talk. 6.30 Oglethorpe went (to Altamaha); necessary business. 7.30 Read Prayers; religious talk. 8 Religious talk. 9 Necessary talk (religious). 10 Religious talk with Mrs Hawkins. 10.30 Undressed.

Providence: [Well;] Oglethorpe open and friendly and convinced. Mrs Hawkins seemed affected.

[N.B.:] A hurrying day.

Tuesday, February 17. 4.15 Prayed; meditated. 5 Prayed with Delamotte; religious talk. 6 Tea, religious talk. 7 Read Prayers, expounded. 8 Necessary talk; necessary business. 9 Necessary business; writ diary. 9.30 Writ Account.

10.30 Necessary business. 11 Account; good talk with Captain Dempsey. 12 Prayed with Delamotte and Charles, religious talk. 1 Dinner. 2 Meditated. 2.15 Religious talk with James Billinghurst. 3 Religious talk with Mr Faulcon[er?]. 3.15 Religious talk. 3.30 Religious talk with Mrs Hawkins and Mrs Welch. 5 Read Prayers, expounded. 6 Sang with Delamotte, prayed, religious talk. 7 Necessary talk with Vanderplank; supper. 8 Greek Testament. 8.30 Religious talk with Captain Deliegec; necessary talk. 9 Necessary talk. 9.30 Prayed. Providence: Well.

James Billinghurst affected, and Mr Faulcon[er?]! Mrs Welch angry at me.	Never make yourself familiar, cheap.

Grace: + [2 to 3 pm].

WEDNESDAY, FEBRUARY 18. 5 Prayed; meditated; private prayer. 6 Mr Richards came, religious talk, Greek Testament. 7 Read Prayers, expounded. 7.45 Tea. 8 Religious talk. 8.30 Account. 9.30 Meditated; prayed. 10 Religious talk with James Billinghurst, Frances Hird, and [John] Cousins, began Bible with them. 11 Religious talk. 11.30 Meditated; sang. 12 Religious talk with Charles, prayed. 12.30 Meditated; prayed (very cold). 1 Religious talk with Chance, etc (they affected). 2 Religious talk with Charles. 2.30 Tea. 3 Delamotte came, religious talk; writ diary. 4 Meditated; sang; prayed (lively zeal). 5 Meditated; sang; prayed (lively zeal). 5.45 Necessary talk. 6 Read Prayers, expounded. 6.45 Necessary talk. 7 German Psalms. 8 Religious talk with Charles, etc, prayed. 9 Lay on the ground, slept pretty well.
    Providence: Began Bible with children. Slept on the ground, pretty well.

THURSDAY, FEBRUARY 19. 3.30 Dressed; prayed. 4 Tea; dressed. 5 Necessary business. 5.30 Set out in the boat, mostly religious talk. 6 Mostly religious talk; hard gale. 10.15 At Savannah, stayed in boat. 11.15 Set out; Greek Testament. 1 Religious talk (necessary). 1.30 At the Cowpen; necessary talk with Mrs Musgrove. 2 At the Indian Town, king not there; necessary talk. 2.30 Met him. 3 Greek Testament. 3.30 At Mr Causton's, good talk. 4 Tea; Mr Spangenberg came, religious talk. 5 Walked with him in the garden; Mr Quincy came, religious talk. 6 Necessary talk (religious) with John Brownfield. 6.30 Mr Quincy's; tea, good talk. 7.15 With Germans, sang, religious talk. 8 Religious talk. 8.45 Mr Causton's, sang. 9 Sleepy, they [had] good talk. 12 Set out in boat; slept.
    [N.B.:] Beware America—be not as England!

FRIDAY, FEBRUARY 20. 4 On board; lay down. 6.30 Dressed; necessary business. 7 Read Prayers, expounded. 7.45 Got tea for them. 8 Tea, they [had] various talk. 9 Meditated; Charles came, religious talk; writ diary. 10 Meditated; prayed. 11 German. 11.30 Meditated; prayed (lively zeal). 12 Religious talk with Delamotte. 12.45 Bible with James Billinghurst and Cousins (friendly, he zealous). 1.15 Religious talk with John Welch; with Mrs Lawley (she affected). 2 Religious talk with Delamotte, prayed. 3 Dinner, religious talk. 4 Greek Testament. 5 Religious talk with Mrs Welch and Mrs Hawkins (they affected), tea. 5.30 Read Prayers, expounded. 6 Expounded. 6.30 Necessary talk. 6.45 Prayed with Delamotte. 7 Sang; German. 8 Religious talk with Charles and Delamotte. 9 Religious talk with Mrs Hawkins (she affected). 9.40.

SATURDAY, FEBRUARY 21. 4 Prayed. 4.30 Prayed with Delamotte. 5 Meditated; private prayer. 6 Religious talk; tea (preserved from intemperance). 7.15 Read Prayers, expounded. 8 Necessary talk with Vanderplank, etc. 9 Greek Testament; necessary talk. 10 Greek Testament. 10.30 Began Greek Testament with Charles and Delamotte. 11 Sent for by Mrs Hawkins, religious talk. 12 Religious and useful talk. 12.45 Religious talk with Charles and Delamotte. 1 Dinner. 1.40 Writ diary; religious talk with Charles and Delamotte. 2 Religious talk with Mrs Welch, Mr Welch, Mr Tackner. 3 Religious talk with Phoebe Hird and Betty Hassel. 3.30 Tea; religious talk with John Hughes. 4 With Mrs Hawkins, religious talk. 4.15 Good talk. 5 Good talk with him. 5.20 Meditated. 5.30 Necessary talk with Charles. 6 Read Prayers. 6.30 Necessary talk (religious) with Vanderplank; sang. 7 Sang; meditated; prayed. 8 Religious talk with Charles, etc. 8.45 Sang.

Providence: Well. Lost myself by w2 with Mrs Hawkins [4 to 5 pm].

Grace: Attentive in meditation [5 to 6 am]; 7 rating once [5 to 6 am]; 5 twice [noon to 1, 6 to 7 pm]; 4 twice [4 to 6 pm].

SUNDAY, FEBRUARY 22. 4 Prayed; meditated; prayed with Delamotte. 5 Sang; religious talk. 6 Religious talk; tea. 7 Read Prayers, expounded. 8 Religious talk with Charles and Delamotte. 8.15 Sang; prayed. 9 Prayed. 9.30 Baptized Mary Welch by trine immersion! 10 Patrick; religious talk with Phoebe Hird; sang. 11 Read Prayers, preached. 12 Sacrament (twelve communicants). 12.30 Sang. 1 Slept. 1.15 Nalson. 1.45 Dinner. 2.30 Necessary talk with Charles and Delamotte. 3 Religious talk with Alexander [Grimaldi], Mr Allen. 3.45 Read Prayers. 4 Read Prayers, expounded. 4.30 Meditated; read Patrick to them. 5 Prayed; sang. 5.30 Religious talk with Mrs Hawkins (she serious). 6.15 Necessary talk with Charles and Delamotte. 7 Religious talk, prayed. 7.45 Charles and Delamotte went to Savannah. 8 Necessary business; meditated; prayed.

Providence: Baptized Mary Welch by trine immersion. Twelve communicants.

Mercy: Preserved from w4/1, w2 with Mrs Hawkins! [5 to 6 pm].

Grace: 6 rating fourteen times [all but 2 to 3, 6 to 8 pm].

MONDAY, FEBRUARY 23. 4.15 Dressed; private prayer. 5 Prayed; private prayer. 5.45 Tea; read Clarendon. 6.45 Sang. 7 Read Prayers, expounded. 8 Necessary talk. 8.15 Necessary business. 8.45 Writ diary. 9 Translated German Psalms. 10 Psalms; necessary talk (religious). 10.45 Psalms. 11.30 Read Law to people (eleven there). 12 Religious talk with them. 12.15 Meditated; sang. 1 Dinner. 1.30 Religious talk with Mrs Welch. 2 On shore with Mrs Hawkins; began Scougal (she serious). 3 Scougal; religious talk. 4 Religious talk. 4.45 On board; writ diary. 5 Read Prayers, expounded. 5.45 Tea. 6 German; meditated; prayed. 7 Writ German. 8.30 Meditated.

Providence: Well; Mrs Hawkins serious; immediately in light company, all vanished.

Grace: 7 rating once [4 to 5 am]; preserved from w4/1 [3 to 4 pm?].

TUESDAY, FEBRUARY 24. 5 Prayed; private prayer; necessary business. 6 Tea, religious talk; prayed; Colonel Bull came. 7 Read Prayers, expounded. 7.45 Writ German. 8 Read account of the children in Herrnhut. 11 Read Law. 11.45

Religious talk with children (they affected; lively zeal). 12 Religious talk with children, sang. 12.30 Religious talk (necessary) [with] Delamotte. 1 Dinner. 2 On shore with Delamotte, religious talk. 3 Nalson; religious talk. 4 Religious talk (necessary); on board. 5 Read Prayers, expounded; prayed; sang. 6 Writ Account; Mr Oglethorpe came. 7 Necessary talk with him. 7.30 Religious talk (necessary) with Delamotte. 8.30 Necessary business; prayed.

Providence: All affected with Law. Mr Oglethorpe came safe.

Grace: Lively zeal [11 to noon].

WEDNESDAY, FEBRUARY 25. 5 Prayed; sang; prayed. 6 Tea, religious talk. 6.45 Religious talk (necessary) with Oglethorpe. 7 Read Prayers, expounded. 8 Religious talk with Hird, Tackner, John W[elch] (they affected). 9 Religious talk with Mr Williams, Bainer, Mrs Hird (they affected). 10 Religious talk with Taverner, Mary, Mr Welch, Phoebe, Frances Hird, Jerry Faulcon[er?]. 11 Mr Faulcon[er?]. 11.30 Read Law. 12 Religious talk with Mrs Taverner, Mr Davison, Mr Dobree, Will Hassel, Betty Hassel (they affected). 1 Religious talk with Mrs Welch. 1.30 With Mrs Proctor; with Esther Rogers (they affected). 2 Religious talk with Mr and Mrs Allen, etc (they affected). 2.30 Religious talk with Mr Delamotte; prayed. 3 Tea, religious talk; writ diary. 3.45 Religious talk with Will Proctor (he seemed affected). 4 Shaved; meditated; prayed. 4.30 Religious talk with Will Dobs, Goldwire, John Walker, Mrs Perkins (they affected). 5 Read Prayers, expounded (lively zeal). 6 Religious talk with Mrs Walker (she affected). 6.30 Prayed; sang. 7 Read Law (they affected). 7.45 Necessary business. 8 Nalson. 8.30 Religious talk; prayed. 10 Mr Spangenberg and Nitschmann came, with them, necessary talk (religious). 11.45 Lay on the ground.

Providence: Spoke to forty, all affected.

Grace: Lively zeal [5 to 6 pm].

THURSDAY, FEBRUARY 26. 4 Prayed with Spangenberg. 4.30 Began Account. 5 Account; religious talk. 6 Tea, religious talk. 7 Read Prayers, preached. 8 Necessary business. 8.30 Prayed. 9 Necessary business, religious talk. 9.45 Mrs Hawkins came, told her of all her faults, advised against light company (she affected and resolved). 11 Set out with Spangenberg, Nitschmann, etc, religious talk. 12 Read Account of the Brethren. 1.45 Savannah; at the Germans'; writ diary. 2 Dinner, religious talk. 3 Religious talk; set out with Spangenberg, Nitschmann, and Dober. 4 At the Cowpen, saw ground for house. 5 Tea, religious talk with Spangenberg, etc. 6 Religious talk. 7 Mostly religious talk with them. 9 Sang; mostly religious talk. 11 Prayed; lay down.

FRIDAY, [FEBRUARY] 27. 5 Prayed; sang; religious talk. 6 Set out; necessary talk (religious and useful). 8 At Savannah, with Germans; breakfast on Indian corn. 9 Sorted books and clothes. 1.30 With Spangenberg, talk of mystic divinity, he is a mystic. 3 Tea, talk of ministry, he denies the [Apostolic] succession, religious talk. 5.30 Meditated (zealous). 6 Sang. 6.15 With Spangenberg, talk of Mr Gambold, read Whitefield's Case. 7.45 With the Germans, sang. 8.45 Writ diary; undressed; prayed. 9.

SATURDAY, FEBRUARY 28. 5.30 Prayed; meditated. 6 Sang with them. 7 Tea (preserved from intemperance), talk of mystics with Spangenberg and Nitschmann. 8 Religious talk. 8.30 Religious talk with Spangenberg. 9 Began

German Grammar with him. 10.30 Sorted things; Mr Quincy came. 11 Sorted. 12 Garden; meditated; sang. 1 Meditated. 1.15 Grammar. 1.45 Dinner. 2.15 Writ diary. 2.30 Walked with Delamotte, began *Light of the World.* 3 *Light of the World.* 5 At Mr Quincy's, necessary talk (religious), tea. 6 Walked; meditated; sang. 7 With Germans, they ordained. 8.15 They sang. 9 Tea, religious talk; prayed. 10.

SUNDAY, FEBRUARY 29. 5.30 Prayed; dressed. 6 Sang with Germans. 6.45 Prayed. 7 Religious talk with Spangenberg. 7.30 Hird and Davison came; at Mr Quincy's, tea, necessary talk. 8 Necessary talk; necessary business. 8.30 Necessary talk with Spangenberg. 9 Religious talk with Spangenberg and Nitschmann and Dober. 10 Took boat; Greek Testament. 1 Meditated; Greek Testament. 1.45 On board; dinner. 2 Necessary talk (religious) with Charles. 2.30 Necessary talk with Oglethorpe. 5.30 Read Prayers, expounded (all sailors there, they affected; lively zeal). 6.15 Read letters from Oxford, they zealous; prayed; meditated. 7 Religious talk with sailors, with Mrs Allen, etc (they affected). 8 Religious talk with Charles and Delamotte. 9 Religious talk. 9.30 Prayed.

MONDAY, MARCH 1. 5.30 Prayed; sang. 6 Prayed with Charles and Delamotte. 6.30 Greek Testament, necessary business. 7 Necessary talk with Oglethorpe. 7.15 Read Prayers below, expounded (they affected; lively zeal). 8.15 Necessary business; necessary talk. 8.45 Necessary talk with Oglethorpe. 9 Writ for Oglethorpe; necessary talk; tea. 10 Writ for Oglethorpe. 10.45 With Mrs Welch, religious talk. 11 Religious talk; writ for Oglethorpe. 12 Writ for Oglethorpe. 2 Religious talk with Mrs Welch and Mrs Hawkins. 2.30 Dinner. 3.15 Meditated. 3.30 Mrs Hawkins came, religious talk (she deeply melancholy). 4 Religious talk, she would not speak, in despair! (gained no ground). 5 Read Prayers, expounded. 6 Prayed with Charles and Delamotte; sang; writ diary. 6.30 Prayed for Mrs Hawkins, necessary talk. 7 Religious talk with Mr Hawkins, prayed for Mrs Hawkins. 8 Necessary talk. 8.30 Meditated; prayed. 9 Prayed for Mrs Hawkins; meditated (O Jesu!). 10 Religious talk with Hird. 10.15 Talk with Oglethorpe of Mrs Hawkins, he can't guess. 11 Religious talk. 11.30.

Providence: Mrs Hawkins melancholy! Would not speak!

Grace: 7 rating twice [5 to 6 am, 9 to 10 pm]; 6 twelve times [all the rest that are noted, no ratings between 10 am and 3 pm].

Convincing, + [9 to 10 pm].

TUESDAY, MARCH 2. 5.30 Sang; prayed for Mrs Hawkins. 6 Prayed with Delamotte; tea; writ diary; Bible. 7 Read Prayers, expounded below. 8 Writ conference with Mrs Hawkins. 9 Religious talk with her (she deeply afflicted). 11.30 Religious talk with Levally. 11.50 Prayed for Mrs Hawkins. 12.30 Prayed; sang; religious talk. 1 With Oglethorpe, etc, he [had] necessary talk. 2 Dinner, religious talk with them. 3 Religious talk with Mr Spangenberg of Mrs Hawkins, he hopes for her. 4 Read Prayers, expounded; religious talk. 5 Religious talk; tea. 6 Religious talk. 6.30 Prayed with Delamotte and Spangenberg; sang. 7 Necessary talk. 7.15 Prayed for Mrs Hawkins. 7.45 Charles came, necessary talk. 8 Religious talk. 8.30 With Mrs Welch and Mrs Hawkins, Francis Moore, religious talk. 9 Religious talk with Mrs Hawkins and Mrs Welch. 9.45 Mrs Hawkins in a fever, mild but utterly inconsolable, took solemn leave!

Providence: Mrs Hawkins inconsolable.

Grace: 7 rating thrice [noon to 1, 7 to 8, 9 to 10 pm]; 6 thirteen times [all but 2 to 3 pm]. Convincing twice [noon to 1, 7 to 8 pm].

WEDNESDAY, MARCH 3. 3.30 Dressed; prayed for Mrs Hawkins. 4 Writ second conferences; prayed; tea. 5 Tea; sang; prayed; writ diary. 6 Religious talk with Mrs Hawkins, she sad but mild (I hope for her). 7 Religious talk with her (she softened). 7.30 They took boat, prayed for them. 8 Prayed for them. 8.30 Meditated; religious talk. 9 Religious talk. 9.30 Writ journal. 1.30 Meditated; prayed. 2 Tea, religious talk. 3 With Mr Oglethorpe, necessary talk (religious). 4.15 Set out in canoe (wind high). 5 Religious talk with Delamotte; left Mr Spangenberg. 6 Prayed; meditated (wind fell). 7 Religious and useful talk (bitter cold). 8 Savannah; sang with Germans. 8.45 Necessary talk. 9 Sang; prayed; (hard frost). 10.

THURSDAY, MARCH 4. 5.30 Dressed; prayed; (sharp frost). 6 Dressed; necessary business; writ diary. 6.45 Tea. 7 Necessary talk with Nitschmann. 8 Religious talk with Frazer (he affected); necessary business. 9 Garden, prayed for Mrs Hawkins; meditated. 10 Read Tauler's Life. 12 Religious talk with Delamotte (friendly); necessary business. 12.45 Dinner. 1.15 Necessary business; writ diary. 1.45 Necessary talk with Nitschmann. 2.15 Read Boehme's Life. 3 Meditated. 3.30 Began visiting parish. 4 Mrs Bradley's, necessary talk. 4.30 Religious talk with Delamotte. 5 Trustees' Garden, religious talk. 5.15 Necessary talk. 5.30 Prayed; sang. 6 Began Ludolf. 6.30 Hows came, religious talk. 7 Tea, religious talk; writ diary. 8 With Germans, sang (sleepy). 8.45 Necessary business; prayed.

Providence: Well; Frazer affected; Delamotte open and friendly.

FRIDAY, MARCH 5. 5.15 Dressed; sang with Germans (sleepy). 6 Necessary business; prayed; writ diary. 7 Revised Prayerbook; tea, religious talk. 8 Revised Common Prayer book. 8.40 Prayed; sang. 9 Looked over Psalmbook. 10 Psalmbook. 12 Prayed with Delamotte; ended Psalmbook. 1 Meditated; Tauler. 2 Tauler. 2.30 Writ diary; prayed. 3 Tea, religious talk. 4 Ludolf. 6 Mr Causton's with Nitschmann, necessary talk. 7.15 Ludolf. 8 Sang; prayed.

SATURDAY, MARCH 6. 4 Dressed; prayed with Delamotte. 4.30 Private prayer. 5 Prayed. 5.15 With Germans. 5.45 Began teaching them English. 6.45 Tea. 7 Tea, religious talk. 7.30 Ludolf. 8 Ludolf; writ diary; ended Ludolf. 9 Writ Journal. 1.30 Dinner. 2 German with Töltschig, etc. 3 German. 3.15 Began Drake with John [Regnier?]. 4.30 Sang; prayed with Delamotte. 5 Sang. 5.30 Mr Quincy's, necessary talk (religious). 6 Buried a child; tea, necessary talk (religious). 7 Mostly religious talk. 7.15 Journal. 8 Sang. 8.45 Prayed.

3. to & fro betn ye Door & ye Garden. I saw
She wanted to speak to me, but remem=
berd my Resolution & professed, that, "To
converse wth her only in Mr D's presence."
Yet after a what struggle, the Evil Soul pre
vaild in me, & I went. Immediately, she
catch'd hold of both my Hands, & in ye most
engaging Gesture, Look & Tone of Voice said
"You never denied me any thing I desired
yet, & You shan't deny me what I am going
to desire now". I said, "No I won't; what is
it?" She answerd, "Don't say any thing to her
yt offerd me ye Letter ye other day. My refusing it has given her pain enough already"
I replied, "I won't. And if you had told me
of it before, I would'nt have told yr Uncle
of it, as Mr Williamson did." She said, "Did
he? Well, I find what you have often said
is true. There is no trusting any but a Xti:
an. And for my part I am resolved never to trust
any one again who is not so." I look'd upon her, & sh'd have said too much, had we
had a moment longer. But in yt instant
Mrs C. call'd us in. So I was once more
"snatch'd as a brand out of ye "Fire."

MANUSCRIPT GEORGIA JOURNAL
March 7, 1735/36–December 16, 1737

'The Lord knoweth the thoughts of man, that they are but vain' [Ps. 94:11 (BCP)].

'O give me not up unto mine own heart's lust, neither let me follow my own imagination' [cf. Ps. 81:12 (BCP)].

[B—It was not my desire, but the desire of the Trustees, disappointed of another minister, which induced me to take charge of Savannah till I could pursue my first design. And [the] very day I entered on this charge I told you that offences would come; indeed I expected greater, long before this day.]

At my first coming to Savannah, in the beginning of March 1736, I was determined to have no intimacy with any woman in America. Notwithstanding which, by the advice of my friends, and in pursuance of my resolution to speak once a week at least to every communicant apart from the congregation, on March the 13th, I spoke to Miss Sophy Hopkey, who had communicated the Sunday before, and endeavoured to explain to her the nature and necessity of inward holiness. On the same subject I continued to speak to her once a week, but generally in the open air, and never alone [B—always in [the] presence of Miss Fawset].

***

SUNDAY, MARCH 7. 4 Dressed; prayed with Delamotte. 4.30 Private prayer. 5 Prayed; Journal. 5.45 Sang. 6.30 Dressed. 7 Tea, religious talk (necessary). 7.45 Von Reck came, religious talk. 8 Necessary business. 8.45 Quesnel. 9 Greek Testament; meditated. 10 Mr Quincy read Prayers (lesson!). 11 Prayers. 11.30 Preached on 1 Corinthians 13 (lively zeal). 12 Prayers; necessary talk. 12.20 Necessary talk. 12.30 Dinner. 1 Religious talk with boys. 1.30 Meditated. 2 Mr Quincy read Prayers, preached. 3 Preached. 3.30 Meditated. 3.45 John Brownfield and Mr Christie came, religious talk. 4 Religious talk (necessary) with John Brownfield (he open); tea. 5 Walked with Von Reck, religious talk (he open and affected). 6 Visited Mr Dearn, he talked much, prayed. 6.20 Religious talk with Cawtrey. 6.30 Garden, meditated. 7.15 Journal. 7.45 Religious talk. 8 With Germans, sang. 8.45 Undressed.

Providence: Luke 18, lesson. Mr Brownfield and [Von] Reck affected. All the children serious [6 to 7 pm].

Grace: 7 rating once [4 to 5 am]; 6 thirteen times [all but 6 to 7, 8 to 9 am, noon to 1 pm]. Lively zeal [11 to noon].

Convincing [11 to noon, 2 to 3 pm].

I had a good hope that herein I acted with a single eye to the glory of God and the good of her soul, both because I did not act by my own judgment and because, though I approved of Miss Sophy's constant attendance both at the morning and evening service, and at the Holy Communion, yet I had a particular dislike to her person, and a still greater to her common behaviour, which was reserved, I thought, even to affectation.

[B—Soon after, being at Mr. Causton's house, Mrs. Causton, when I went out of the room, said, 'There goes a husband for my Phiky' (her common title for Miss Hopkey). And in June following she told me, 'Sir, you want a woman to take care of your house.' I said, 'But women, madam, are scarce in Georgia. Where shall I get one?' She answered, 'I have two here. Take either of them. Here, take Miss Fawset.' I said, 'Nay, madam, we shan't agree. She is too merry for me.' She replied, 'Then take Phiky; she is serious enough.' I said, 'You are not in earnest, madam!' She said, 'Indeed, sir, I am; take her to you, and do what you will with her.']

In April, by the advice of Mr. Delamotte, who thought common civility required it, after we had been walking some time, I asked her and her companion Miss Fawset to step in and breakfast with me. Immediately after breakfast they went. Though I hope my eye was single in this too, yet I doubt whether it was not a step too far, as tending to a familiarity which was not needful.

From the middle of May till the end of June, I was at Frederica. After I was returned to Savannah, in the beginning of July, Mrs. Causton earnestly [B—expressed with many tears] desired me to talk to Sophy by herself, who (she said) was utterly ruined, being in love with and resolved to marry a notorious villain, one Mellichamp, then in prison at Charleston for forgery. She added, 'Sophy minds nobody but you; if you will be so good as to step into the garden, I will send her to you.' I went, and soon after, Miss Sophy came, all in tears, and with all the signs of such a distress as I had never seen. She seemed to have lost both comfort and hope. I stayed with her about an hour. At the end of which she said she was resolved to seek comfort in God only, and through his help to tear from her heart an inclination which she knew did not tend to his glory.

I was deeply affected with her distress, which I saw was beyond all utterance; and yet more with the manner in which she bore it, betraying no kind of impatience, making no complaint, saying nothing weak or womanish, taking the whole blame upon herself, owning the providence of God in all, and acknowledging the goodness as well as justice of that providence.

My friends believed it was now my duty to see her more frequently than before; in compliance with whose advice I accordingly talked with her once in two or three days [B—often alone]. In all those conversations I was careful to speak only on things pertaining to God. But on July [23?], after I had talked with her for some time, I took her by the hand and, before we parted, kissed her. And from this time I fear there was a mixture in my intention, though I was not soon sensible of it.

MONDAY, MARCH 8. 5.15 Dressed; prayed; necessary talk with Hows; religious talk. 6 Read Prayers at Court-house (four persons there). 6.30 Writ diary; necessary business. 7 Tea; journal. 9.15 Necessary talk with Mr Quincy. 9.30 With Franck, he worse. [9.] 45 Necessary business. 10 Mr Quincy's, necessary talk; Drake's *Anatomy*; (sins). 11 Sorted things. 12.45 Dinner. 1.30 Bible with Nitschmann, etc. 2.30 Drake with John [Regnier]. 3 Drake; Franck died. 4 Garden; meditated (fervent); prayed. 5 Necessary talk with Delamotte. 5.15 Prayed. 5.30 Mr Causton, necessary talk (religious). 6 Read Prayers, expounded (lively zeal, convincing). 6.30 Mr Quincy's; supper, religious talk. 7.30 Franck buried. 8 Garden, meditated. 8.30 Sang with them. 9 To bed.

TUESDAY, MARCH 9. 4.45 Dressed; prayed. 5 Garden; prayed; sang; meditated (fervent). 6 Read Prayers, expounded. 6.20 Mr Quincy's, tea, religious talk. 7 Writ diary; Mr Causton came, necessary talk. 7.30 Garden, Greek Testament. 9 Set out; necessary talk; necessary talk (religious) with Mr Quincy, Delamotte, Nitschmann, Anton [Seiffert]. 10 Necessary talk. 11 Mrs Musgrove's, necessary talk; saw the ground. 12 Necessary talk. 12.30 Dinner. 1 Necessary talk. 1.30 Set out; necessary talk (religious). 2 Necessary and useful talk. 3 Necessary talk (religious). 3.30 Mr Quincy, necessary business; writ diary. 4 John Brownfield and Mr Hodgkinson; tea, religious talk (necessary). 5 Necessary business. 5.30 Garden; prayed; meditated. 6 Meditated. 6.15 Necessary talk. 6.30 Read Prayers, expounded. 7 Religious talk with Mrs Dearn (she serious); meditated; prayed. 8 Necessary talk with Germans. 8.30 Sang. 9.30.

WEDNESDAY, MARCH 10. 4 Garden; meditated; prayed. 5 Slept. 6 With Germans, necessary talk with them. 7 Prayed with Delamotte. 7.15 Writ diary; Greek Testament. 8 Greek Testament. 9 Greek Testament; dressed. 10 Read Prayers. 11 Read Prayers, preached (thirty at Court-house). 12 Necessary talk (religious) with John Desborough, Ellen Dean, Mrs Hows. 12.30 Writ diary. 12.45 Prayed. 1 Religious talk (necessary) with boys. 1.30 Slept; necessary talk with Julie. 2 Greek Testament. 2.15 Read Prayers, preached (thirty there). 3 Preached; tea; religious talk. 4 Walked with Delamotte, religious and useful talk. 5 Von Reck came, religious talk. 6 Sang; meditated; prayed. 7 Mr Dearn's, religious talk; meditated. 6 Necessary talk with John [Regnier]; sang. 9.15 Prayed.
 Providence: Well; about thirty at Court-house [11 am].
 Grace: 7 rating once [4 to 5 am]; 6 thirteen times [all but 4 to 6 pm].

THURSDAY, MARCH 11. 4 Meditated; prayed; sang. 5 Meditated; prayed. 5.45 Sang with Germans (sleepy). 6 Read Prayers, expounded. 6.30 Religious talk with Mrs Dearn; necessary business. 7 Necessary talk. 7.45 Necessary talk with Delamotte. 8 Von Reck and Apee came; tea, religious talk. 9 Garden, religious talk (Appee struck). 10 [Read] Drake with John [Regnier]. 11 Garden; Greek Testament. 12 Greek Testament; meditated. 1 Dinner. 1.45 Bible with

Nitschmann, etc. 2.15 Drake. 2.45 Slept. 3 Visited Mrs Loyd, religious talk; Mrs Bradley, necessary talk. 4 Walked; meditated; Greek Testament. 5 Meditated; Greek Testament. 5.45 Mr Quincy, necessary talk. 6 Writ diary; meditated; prayed. 6.45 Read Prayers. 7 Expounded. 7.30 Mr Quincy's, religious talk (close). 8 Sang. 8.30 With Germans, sang. 9 Prayed. 9.15.
　　Providence: Mr Appee struck! Fervent exposition, close.
　　Grace: 7 rating twice [4 to 5 am, noon to 1 pm]; 6 eleven times [all but 7 to 8 am, 1 to 3, 8 to 9 pm].

FRIDAY, MARCH 12. 5 Garden; prayed; meditated. 5.40 Sang with Germans (sleepy). 6 Sang; writ diary. 6.30 Meditated. 7 Garden; sang; Greek Testament. 8 Sang; Greek Testament. 9 Greek Testament; bread and butter; dressed. 10 Read Prayers, expounded; baptized John Bradley by immersion! 11 Read Prayers. 11.15 Religious talk with Mr Vat. 12 Religious talk (necessary). 1.15 Meditated; prayed for Oglethorpe, etc. 2 Visited Mr Watkins. 2.45 Tea, religious talk. 3.15 Mr Appee and Von Reck, religious talk (they very serious). 4 Religious talk. 5.30 They went; prayed with Delamotte. 5.45 Garden; prayed. 6 Greek Testament. 7 Read Prayers; writ to Bolzius and Gronau. 8 Sang. 9 Prayed.

SATURDAY, MARCH 13. 4 Private prayer; prayed with Delamotte. 5 Greek Testament; sang with Germans. 6 Read Prayers. 6.30 Von Reck came; tea, talk of Ebenezer. 7 Talk of Ebenezer and Mr Vat (he open). 8 Necessary talk (religious). 8.30 John Brownfield came, necessary talk (religious, he open). 9.30 Mr Causton's, religious talk with Miss Sophy and Miss Fawset. 10 Visited Mr Flower, prayed. 11 Necessary talk with Mr Pury; necessary business. 12 Garden; Greek Testament. 1 Greek Testament; meditated. 1.30 Dinner. 2 Bible with Germans. 3 Visited Ellen Dean, religious talk. 3.40 Garden; Greek Testament. 4 Greek Testament; writ to Count Zinzendorf. 5 Writ to Bolzius. 5.30 Writ diary; Von Reck came, religious talk; tea. 6 Mr Appee came, religious talk. 7 Read Prayers, expounded. 7.30 Religious talk with Dean, etc. 8 Necessary business. 8.15 Sang.
　　Providence: Von Reck and Brownfield open.
　　Grace: 7 rating once [4 to 5 am]; 6 twelve times [all but 10 to noon, 6 to 8 pm].

SUNDAY, MARCH 14. 4 Religious talk with Nitschmann. 5 Transcribed to Count Zinzendorf. 5.40 Prayed. 6 Dressed; necessary business; sang. 7 Mr Quincy's; tea, necessary talk (religious). 8 Writ to Varanese, to Mrs Skinner. 9 Garden; Kempis; meditated. 10 Read Prayers. 11 Mr Quincy preached; prayed. 12 Sacrament (eighteen communicants, they affected). 12.45 Walked with Miss Sophy and Miss Fawset, religious talk. 1.20 Dinner. 1.45 Writ diary. 2 Necessary business; read Prayers. 3 Expounded. 3.45 Transcribed letters. 5 Prayed with Delamotte. 5.15 Walked with him, religious talk. 6 Mr Quincy's, Mr Amatis came and Miss Dearn, they [had] necessary talk. 7 Buried; supper. 7.15 Mr Loyd's, religious and useful talk. 8 Garden; meditated. 8.30 Sang with Germans. 9.30 Prayed.
　　Providence: Well; Miss Sophy and Miss Fawset much affected. Eighteen communicants.
　　Grace: 6 rating thirteen times [all but 6 to 9 am, 4 to 5, 6 to 7 pm].

MONDAY, MARCH 15. 5.30 Prayed; meditated. 6 Read Prayers, expounded; necessary business. 7 Writ resolutions. 7.30 Mr Quincy's necessary business. 8 Company came; tea, necessary talk. 9 He [Quincy] went; placed books. 10 Cleaned things in my house. 11 Cleaned and sorted. 12 Sorted. 1 Necessary business. 1.30 Dinner. 2 Necessary business in my house. 6 Necessary business; religious talk with them. 6.45 Supper. 7 Read Prayers, expounded; necessary and religious talk. 8 Sang. 9 Necessary talk; necessary business; writ diary.

TUESDAY, MARCH 16. 4 Prayed with Delamotte; private prayer (sleepy). 5 Religious talk; private prayer. 5.30 Sang with Germans (sleepy). 6 Read Prayers, expounded; necessary business; tea. 7.15 At home; necessary business. 8 Necessary business; writ diary. 8.45 Necessary talk with John [Regnier]. 9 Necessary business. 9.30 Writ journal. 10.30 James Betty of the Uchee town, religious talk, he seemed affected. 11 Garden; read tracts. 12.45 Dinner. 1.15 Read German with them. 2 Sorted seeds. 3 Necessary business in garden. 3.30 Von Reck and Gronau, religious talk. 4 Necessary talk with Mrs Dearn. 4.45 Garden; read tracts. 6 Necessary business; Greek Testament. 6.45 Buried. 7 Read prayers, expounded. 7.45 Sang with Germans. 8.45 Dober and Töltschig with us, necessary talk (religious). 9 Necessary talk. 9.15 Began Echard's *Ecclesiastical History*. 10 Undressed.

Providence: Mr Gronau with me. James Betty seemed affected; well.

WEDNESDAY, MARCH 17. 4.30 Prayed with Delamotte, religious talk. 5 Private prayer with Germans. 6 At home; necessary talk (religious); necessary business. 7 Unpacked books; writ diary. 8 Books; bread and butter. 9 Writ to Rivington; dressed. 10 Read e c a p p s h s c 1 2 3 4 t b, expounded. 11 Necessary talk (religious) with Millidge, etc. 11.30 Writ to Mr Vernon. 12 Writ to sister Nancy, to Salmon. 1 [Writ] to Iliffe. 1.30 Necessary business. 2 Garden; read tracts. 3 Tea; religious talk. 3.45 Mr Appee, religious talk. 4 Tea, religious talk. 4.30 Garden with him, religious talk (close, he *in Orco*). 5 Religious talk (he open). 5.45 Prayed for him; writ diary. 6 Garden; meditated; prayed; sang. 7 Prayed; meditated. 7.30 Read Prayers, expounded. 8 Visited Mr Dearn, necessary talk (religious); prayed. 8.15 With Germans, sang. 9 Echard; prayed. 9.45.

Providence: Well; Appee *in Orco*, but hopes.

Grace: 7 rating once [6 to 7 pm]; 6 twelve times [all but 6 to 8, 10 to 11 am, 2 to 4 pm].

THURSDAY, MARCH 18. 5 Prayed with Delamotte; sang with Germans. 6 Read Prayers, expounded; walked with Miss Sophy and Miss Fawset, religious talk. 7 With Germans; breakfast (began sassafras), religious talk. 8 Writ to my mother and brother Samuel. 9 [Writ] to sister Kezzy and sister Lambert. 10 [Writ] to Mr Burton and Brown. 11 Read tracts. 12 Read tracts; prayed; writ diary. 12.40 Dinner. 1 Bible with Germans. 2 Necessary talk with John Brownfield; Drake with John [Regnier]. 3 Tracts; garden, worked. 4 Garden, worked; tracts. 5 Tracts. 5.30 Meditated; prayed with Delamotte. 6 Supper; Echard. 7 Read Prayers, expounded; with Germans; garden, meditated. 8 They sang. 9 Echard. 9.45 Prayed.

Providence: Well; began drinking sassafras.

FRIDAY, MARCH 19. 4.45 Prayed; married John Brownfield. [5.] 45 Echard. 6.40 With Germans, breakfast. 7 At home; necessary business. 7.30 Read tracts. 8 Writ to Wogan, to R Wood. 9 Letter; writ diary. 9.30 Writ to Mr Wogan, Mr Clayton. 10 Read Prayers, expounded. 11 Prayers. 11.30 To Clayton. 1 Ended letter. 1.15 With Germans and read Psalms. 2 Psalms. 2.15 Saw Rüscher and came home (they dissected). 3.15 Tea, religious talk. 4 Echard. 4.30 Mr Appee came, religious talk; tea. 5 Garden with him, religious talk (close, he serious). 5.45 Buried. 6 Garden; necessary business. 6.30 Writ diary; religious talk (necessary) with them. 6.45 Echard. 7 Greek Testament. 7.15 Read Prayers, expounded. 8 With Germans, they buried Rüscher; sang. 9 Sang. 9.15 At home; Echard. 9.45 Prayed.

Providence: Mr Appee serious; Rüscher buried.

Grace: 7 rating twice [5 to 6, 8 to 9 pm]; 6 ten times [all but 7 to 9, 10 to noon, 1 to 2 pm]. + and lively zeal [8 to 9 pm].

SATURDAY, MARCH 20. 4 Prayed with Delamotte; private prayer. 5 Sang with Germans; sang (lively zeal). 5.45 Necessary talk. 6 Read Prayers, expounded. 6.20 Religious talk with Mrs Smith; with Germans; breakfast. 7 Writ to Horne; necessary talk with them. 8 [Writ] to Broughton; religious talk with them. 9 Writ to Morgan; religious talk with Mrs Dean, etc. 10 Writ to Sally Andrews, to Mrs Musgrove; writ diary. 10.45 Necessary business. 11.30 Set out; read tracts with Delamotte. 12 Tracts; sang. 1 Mrs Musgrove's, she not [there]; tea. 2 Set out; tracts; religious talk. 3.30 At home; Mr Causton; read letters from Oglethorpe, necessary talk. 4 Dr Tailfer came; tea, religious talk of episcopacy. 5.15. He went; Echard; writ diary. 5.45 Garden; meditated. 6 Mr Simms [Symes?] came, necessary talk; prayed with Delamotte; Echard. 7 Greek Testament; read Prayers, expounded. 8 With Germans, sang. 8.45 Echard. 9.30 Prayed.

Providence: Well; Dr. Tailfer serious; boatmen serious.

Grace: 7 rating once [4 to 5 am]; 6 thirteen times [all but 3 to 6, 7 to 8 pm].

SUNDAY, MARCH 21. 4 Prayed with Delamotte; German; private prayer. 5 Sang. 5.15 Walked; meditated. 5.45 Sang with Germans. 6.30 Shaved; tea. 7 Tea, necessary talk (religious). 7.30 At home; necessary business. 7.45 Necessary business. 8 Dressed. 8.30 Garden; sang; Greek Testament. 9 Meditated on sermon; prayed; sang with Delamotte. 10 Sang; read e c a p p s h s c 1 2 3 4 t b. 11 C cc, sang, preached, prayed. 12 Prayed, Sacrament (fifteen communicants), prayed. 12.45 Dinner. 1 Dinner; sang. 1.30 Slept; meditated. 2 Meditated. 2.10 Read e c a p p s h s, catechized, p t b, sermon. 3.45 Necessary talk (religious). 4 Writ to Oglethorpe, to Charles. 5 Mr Gough came, religious talk. 5.15 Letter. 6 Supper, Echard. 6.30 Garden; meditated; sang. 7 Meditated. 7.30 Writ diary; Echard. 8 With Germans, sang. 8.45 Echard. 9 Echard; prayed. 10.

Providence: Well; fifteen communicants.

Grace: 7 rating once [8 to 9 am]; + [7 to 8 pm]; lively zeal [8 to 9 pm].

MONDAY, MARCH 22. 4.30 Prayed with Delamotte; private prayer. 5 Meditated. 5.30 With Germans, sang (sleepy). 6 Read Prayers, expounded. 6.30 Tea, religious talk. 7 Religious talk; necessary business. 8 Writ to Charles. 9 [Writ] to Mr Sarney. 10 [Writ] to the Rector. 11 Garden; read tracts; necessary talk. 12 Tracts. 12.45 Dinner. 1 Dinner; read Bible with Germans. 2 Necessary business. 2.30 Necessary talk with Mr Causton. 3 At Captain Watson's, necessary talk (strange!). 4 Necessary talk (religious). 4.30 Set out with

Delamotte, necessary talk. 5.10 At the plantation, necessary and useful talk. 6 Set out, necessary talk. 6.30 At home; tea, religious talk. 7 Greek Testament; read Prayers; religious talk with Mrs Dearn. 8 With Germans, sang (sleepy). 8.45 Echard. 10 Ended first volume; prayed. 11.

Providence: Necessary talk with Captain Watson, strange things, if true.

TUESDAY, MARCH 23. 5 Dressed; with Germans, sang. 6 Read Prayers, expounded; walked with Misses [Hopkey and Fawset] (they very serious). 7 They came with me; tea, religious talk (they seemed affected). 8 Sorted books. 9 Sorted. 10 Writ diary; writ to Sir John Philipps. 11 Tracts. 12 Meditated. 12.30 Dinner. 1 Bible with Germans. 1.45 Necessary talk with Töltschig. 2 Began Waterland on *Importance of Trinity*. 3.30 Writ catalogue of the people for John Millidge. 5.40 Garden; Mr Appee came, read *Phaedo*. 6 Read Plato; tea, religious talk (he much affected). 7 Necessary talk (religious). 7.15 Read Prayers, expounded. 7.40 With Germans, necessary talk. 8 Sang. 9 Echard. 9.30 Prayed.

Providence: Well; Miss Sophy and Miss Fawset serious and affected. Mr Appee much affected.

WEDNESDAY, MARCH 24. 4.30 Prayed with Delamotte; meditated. 5 Meditated. 5.15 Sang with Germans (lively zeal). 6 Read German; tea, good talk. 7 At home; necessary business; writ notes. 7.30 Waterland. 9 Mr Causton and Vat came, necessary talk. 9.30 Writ to Von Reck. 9.45 Dressed. 10 Read Prayers, expounded. 11 Read Prayers. 11.30 Garden; sang; Waterland. 12 Sang; Waterland. 1 Prayed for Mrs Hawkins and Oglethorpe. 12.30 Slept; ended Waterland. 2 Visited Mrs Mellichamp, Mr Dearn, necessary talk (religious). 2.50 Writ diary. 3 Dinner, religious talk; necessary business (sleepy). 4 Garden; began Arndt. 5 Arndt; meditated; prayed. 6 Echard. 6.45 Mrs Dearn, religious talk (she very serious). 7.15 Read Prayers, expounded; prayed; sang; Bible. 7.45 With Germans, sang. 8.45 Echard; prayed. 9.45.

Providence: Well.

Grace: Lively zeal [5 to 6 am].

THURSDAY, MARCH 25. 4 Prayed; private prayer. 5 Slept. 5.15 With Germans, sang. 6 Meditated; tea. 7 At home; necessary business. 8 Dressed; [read] Hickes with Delamotte; meditated. 9 Writ of the Moravians. 10 Meditated; read c a p p s h s c. 11 P t b; sang; sermon; prayed. 12 Sacrament; prayed. 12.30 Dinner, good talk. 1 Bible with Germans. 1.30 Writ of the Moravians. 2.45 Visited Mr Dean (ill, he affected). 3 Prayed with him, began Common Prayer. 3.30 Necessary talk (religious) with Mrs Gilbert. 4 Writ of Moravians. 5 Arndt. 5.40 Prayed with Delamotte. 6 Tea, religious talk. 6.30 Echard. 7 Greek Testament; read Prayers, expounded. 8 Sang with Germans. 9 Echard. 9.30 Prayed.

Providence: Mr Dean ill, serious, affected.

Grace: 6 rating thirteen times [all but 7 to 8 am, noon to 2, 6 to 7, 9 to 10 pm].

FRIDAY, MARCH 26. 4 Prayed with Delamotte; private prayer. 5 With Germans. 5.45 Writ for them. 6 Breakfast with Delamotte; writ for Germans. 7 Dressed; writ diary. 7.30 Sowed seaway beans. 8 Sowed. 9.15 Dressed. 9.30 Arndt. 10 Greek Testament; read c a p p s h s x, sang. 11 C p 1 2 3 4 t b. 12 Visited Mr Dean, prayed, Common Prayer. 12.30 Sowed. 1 Sowed; writ for Germans. 2 Transcribed in German. 3 Necessary business. 3.15 Tea, religious talk. 4

Garden; Arndt. 6 Prayed with Delamotte. 6.15 Echard. 6.30 Appee came, religious talk (he very serious). 8 With Germans, sang. 7 Read Prayers, expounded, religious talk (necessary). 9 Echard. 9.30 Prayed.

Providence: Well; Appee very serious.

Grace: 7 rating once [4 to 5 am].

SATURDAY, MARCH 27. 4 Prayed with Delamotte; private prayer (lively zeal). 5 Meditated; with Germans, sang; read Prayers. 6 Expounded; necessary business in garden. 7 Tea; read Greek with Delamotte. 8 Greek. 9 Sang; Arndt. 10 Arndt. 10.45 Religious talk (necessary) with Appee. 11 Arndt; writ to Charles. 12 [Writ] to Mrs Hawkins. 12.45 Dinner. 1.15 Necessary business. 2 Catechized children. 3 Visited Dean, prayed, Common Prayer. 4 With Germans, they meeting. 4.45 At home; necessary talk. 5 Tea, religious talk. 5.30 With Germans, they read letters [aloud]. 6 Sang; letters. 7 Quite faint. 7.15 Read Prayers, expounded. 7.45 Religious talk with Gough. 8 Religious talk on lay-baptism. 8.30 With Germans, sang. 9.30 Writ diary.

SUNDAY, MARCH 28. 4.30 Prayed (lively zeal). 5 Private prayer; meditated. 5.30 Sang with Germans. 6 [Read] Hickes with Delamotte; necessary business. 7 Hickes. 7.15 Tea, religious talk. 8 Dressed. 8.15 Garden; sang; Greek Testament; Arndt. 9 Arndt; Hickes with Delamotte. 9.30 Arndt. 10 Read e c a p p s h s c 1 2 3 4 t b. 11 Prayed, c, preached; prayed. 12 Sacrament (fourteen communicants); prayed. 12.30 Dinner. 1 Arndt. 1.30 Slept; Greek Testament. 2 Read c a p p s h s c p t b; catechized. 3 Preached; Bible. 3.45 Visited Peter Wright, religious talk. 4 Religious talk; prayed; religious talk to his companions (he affected, they serious). 4.30 Arndt. 5 Walked; Arndt. 6 Arndt. 6.15 At home; prayed with Delamotte. 6.30 Tea, religious talk. 7 Echard. 7.45 Meditated. 8 Sang with Germans. 8.45 Echard. 9 Echard; prayed. 9.30.

Providence: Well; fourteen communicants. Peter Wright much affected, his companions serious.

Grace: 7 rating five times [4 to 5, 7 to 8, 10 to noon, 2 to 3 pm]; 6 eleven times [all but 7 to 8, 9 to 10 pm].

MONDAY, MARCH 29. 4 Prayed. 4.30 Slept. 5 Meditated; with Germans. 6 Read Prayers, expounded; prayed with Peter Wright; necessary talk with Mr. Causton. 7 Breakfast; necessary business. 8 Writ to Mr Erasmus Phillips; necessary business. 9 Sealed letters; writ to Mr Hawkins. 10 Arndt. 12 Arndt; prayed. 12.45 Dinner. 1 Read Bible with Germans; translated for them. 2 Ended Arndt. 2.30 Mr Campbell came, religious talk. 3 Religious talk (necessary); writ diary. 4 Garden; Arndt. 5 Arndt; prayed with Delamotte. 6 Echard; supper; Echard. 7 Meditated; read Prayers; expounded; necessary talk. 8 Sang with Germans (lively zeal). 9 Prayed.

Providence: Mr Campbell came, he open and friendly.

Grace: 6 rating twelve times [all but 7 to 10 am, 1 to 2, 6 to 7 pm]. Lively zeal [8 to 9 pm].

TUESDAY, MARCH 30. 3 Uninterrupted thunder and lightning. 5 Prayed with Germans, sang. 6 Meditated; read Prayers, expounded; with Peter Wright, religious talk, prayed (he very serious). 7 Breakfast, religious talk. 7.15 Mr Ingham came, religious talk of Savannah. 8 Religious talk of Frederica. 9.15 Causton came, necessary talk of Frederica. 11.20 With Germans, necessary talk (religious); religious talk with Ingham and Delamotte. 12 Writ diary; prayed with Ingham and Delamotte. 12.30 Dinner. 1 Religious talk with Töltschig and Anton [Seiffert]. 1.30 Necessary talk with Ingham. 1.45 Necessary talk. 2 With Mr Appee, necessary talk; Mr Causton's, necessary talk; with Peter Wright; prayed, religious talk. 3 With Josua Stringer, prayed; at home; tea. 4 Mr Vernon came; Mr Causton's, necessary talk (religious). 5 Walked with Ingham, talk of Frederica. 6 At home; prayed; supper; Garden; meditated. 7 Meditated; read Prayers, expounded. 8 With Germans, sang (zealous). 9 Prayed; undressed.

Providence: Mr Ingham came; talk of [Frederica]! βοήθει μοι ['Help me'].

Grace: 7 rating twice [7 to 9 pm]; 6 fourteen times. Meditated [7 to 8 pm]; lively zeal [8 to 9 pm]; + [6 to 7, 8 to 9 pm].

WEDNESDAY, MARCH 31. 4 Prayed with Ingham and Delamotte; necessary business. 5 Bread. 5.30 Religious talk with Ingham. 6 Mr Causton came, necessary talk. 6.30 Mrs Mellichamp, religious talk. 7 Necessary business; writ diary. 8 Writ to Mr Bolzius and Von Reck. 9 Letter. 9.30 Garden; Greek Testament; prayed for Oglethorpe. 10 Read Prayers, expounded. 11 Prayed. 11.15 Religious talk with Miss Sophy and Miss Fawset; writ diary. 12 Writ journal; prayed. 1 Journal. 1.15 Garden; meditated; prayed. 3 Prayed with Ingham; bread. 4 Garden; ended Arndt; sang; prayed (lively zeal). 5 Sang; prayed; meditated. 6 Writ diary; prayed with Ingham and Delamotte; walked with Ingham, religious talk. 7 Garden; Greek Testament, read Prayers, expounded. 8 With Germans, sang. 9 Prayed.

Providence: Wind against, could not go.

Grace: 7 rating twice [4 to 6 pm]; 6 twelve times [all but 7 to 8, 10 to noon]; lively zeal [4 to 5 pm].

THURSDAY, APRIL 1. 4 Prayed with Ingham and Delamotte; private prayer. 5 Private prayer; religious talk. 5.45 Read Prayers, expounded. 6 Read Prayers; religious talk. 6.30 Bread. 7 Greek with Delamotte. 8 Writ German Catalogue. 9.30 Prayed; reviewed brother Samuel's *Poems*. 10 *Poems*, prayed for Oglethorpe and Mrs Hawkins. 11 *Poems*; prayed for Mrs Hawkins and Oglethorpe. 12 Bread; religious talk. 1 Garden with Mr Ingham, read journal. 2 Meditated; sang. 2.30 Mr Campbell came, necessary talk (religious). 3.30 Visited Miss Bovey, religious talk; company came. 4 Mostly religious talk. 4.30 Walked; sang; meditated (lively zeal). 5 Sang; meditated (lively zeal). 5.30 At home, Appee there, religious talk. 6.30 He went; supper. 7 Greek Testament; read Prayers, expounded. 8 With Germans, sang (lively zeal). 8.45 Prayed for Mrs Hawkins. 9 Prayed with them.

Providence: Wind against us.

Grace: 7 rating twice [4 to 5 am, 5 to 6 pm]; 6 eleven times [all but 7 to 10 am, 7 to 8 pm]. Meditated attentively twice [4 to 6 pm]; lively zeal twice [thrice: 4 to 6, 8 to 9 pm].

FRIDAY, APRIL 2. 4 Prayed with them. 4.30 Prayed for Oglethorpe and Mrs Hawkins. 5 Meditated; prayed for myself, Mr Oglethorpe, and Mrs Hawkins. 6 At home; garden; began *Solid Virtue*. 7 *Solid Virtue* (wind fair, yet they will not go). 8 Breakfast, religious talk. 8.30 *Solid Virtue*. 9 Prayed with them. 9.15 Slept. 9.30 Greek Testament; meditated. 10 Necessary business. 10.30 Read Prayers, expounded. 11 Read Prayers. 11.30 *Solid Virtue*. 12 Prayed with them for

Oglethorpe and Mrs Hawkins. 12.15 *Solid Virtue*. 1 Garden, *Solid Virtue*; sang. 2 Meditated; *Solid Virtue*; sang. 3 Prayed with them; bread, religious talk; writ diary. 4 Echard. 5 Ended Echard. 6 Garden; sang; Greek Testament; meditated. 7 Meditated; read Prayers, expounded. 8 With Germans, sang. 9 Prayed.

Providence: Wind fair, ship not go.

SATURDAY, APRIL 3. 4.15 Prayed with Ingham and Delamotte; private prayer. 5 With Germans, sang [lively]. 5.45 Read Prayers. 6 Expounded; bread; necessary talk with Töltschig. 7 Garden, sang; *Solid Virtue*. 8 Sang; *Solid Virtue*. 9 *Solid Virtue*; sang. 10 *Solid Virtue*; sang. 11 Prayed for myself. 11.15 Prayed for Oglethorpe, for Mrs Hawkins. 12 Dinner, religious talk. 12.30 Visited Mr Dearn, necessary talk. 1 Made his will. 1.30 At home; mended. 2 Catechized. 3 Mr Vat came, necessary talk. 3.45 Mended. 4.15 Ended *Solid Virtue*. 5.45 Prayed with Ingham. 6 Supper; buried; supper, religious talk. 7 Greek Testament; read Prayers, expounded (lively zeal). 8 With Germans (lively zeal); writ diary; prayed.

Providence: Wind fair, ship not go.

Grace: 7 rating twice [4 to 5, 11 to noon]; 6 twelve times [all but 6 to 7 am, 1 to 2 pm]. Lively zeal [twice, 7 to 9 pm].

SUNDAY, APRIL 4. 5 Meditated; sang with Germans. 5.45 Meditated. 6 Garden, Greek Testament; meditated. 7 Bread, religious talk; dressed; necessary business. 8 Kempis. 10 Read Prayers (boat not ready). 11 Preached, Sacrament. 12 Bread; prayed for Oglethorpe and Mrs Hawkins; necessary business. 1 At the bluff, boat not ready; religious and useful talk. 3 In the piragua; began *Light of the World*. 4 Set out with Delamotte and Mr Mackay (thunder and lightning, flies!). 5 Religious talk; good talk. 6 Bread, religious talk (necessary); read Prayers. 8 To bed (hard rain!).

MONDAY, APRIL 5. 4 Prayed for Mrs Hawkins and Oglethorpe. 4.30 Slept. 5 Prayed; sang; *Light of the World*; bread. 7 Mr Lacy's, he walked with us, good talk (flies, pleasant!). 8 Tea, good talk. 9 Walked with Delamotte, religious talk; writ diary. 9.30 Walked, religious talk (all civil to me!); prayed. 11 At Mr Lacy's, good talk. 11.30 Bathed. 12.15 Walked with Delamotte, religious talk; prayed for Oglethorpe and Mrs Hawkins. 1 Mr Lacy's, Mr Delegal, good talk. 2 Dinner. 2.45 Good talk. 3 Religious talk with two Swiss; tea, idle talk. 4 Set out, various and useful talk (all kind!). 5 Skidaway, religious talk (necessary) with them. 5.45 On board. 6 Sang; writ diary. 6.30 Prayed for Mrs Hawkins and Oglethorpe; sang. 7 Thought; necessary talk; [at the] shoals. 8.30 Slept. 10.30 Rose; necessary talk. 11 At anchor; slept. 1.30 Fell overboard, swam, unhurt!

TUESDAY, APRIL 6. 5 Various talk; prayed. 6 Bread. 6.30 On shore; read *Light of the World*; sang with Delamotte, alternè. 9 Religious talk with James; read; sang, alternè. 10 Religious talk; prayed. 11 On board; letter from Charles; dinner. 12 Writ diary; read Antoinette Bourignon. 4 On shore. 4.30 On board; read Antoinette Bourignon. 5 Private prayer; sang. 6 Supper. 6.30 On shore with Delamotte, religious talk. 7 On board; meditated; read Prayers. 8 Lay on deck (flies!).

WEDNESDAY, APRIL 7. 5 Prayed; sang. 6 Prayed. 6.15 Bread. 6.45. Read Antoinette Bourignon; sang. 9 On board; Mr Delegal; ate fish. 10.30 On shore, with Delamotte. 11 Read Antoinette Bourignon; religious talk. 2 Rain, flies. 2.15 On board; Antoinette Bourignon; writ diary. 3 Bread; Antoinette Bourignon. 5 Prayed; private prayer. 6 Prayed; sang; prayed for Ingham; Antoinette Bourignon; prayed for Mrs Hawkins. 8 Read Prayers. 8.15 Lay down.

THURSDAY, APRIL 8. 5 Private prayer. 6 Antoinette Bourignon; breakfast; Antoinette Bourignon; sang. 8 Read Prayers (all there, seemed affected); Antoinette Bourignon. 9 Necessary business. 10.15 Writ diary; Antoinette Bourignon, ended. 12 Dinner; began the Epistles; meditated. 5 Prayed; Kempis. 6 Sang. 6.30 Prayed for Savannah and Frederica; prayed for myself (+). 8.15 On board them. 8.30 Read Prayers. 8.45 Lay down.

FRIDAY, APRIL 9. 4.30 Prayed; prayed for Oglethorpe, etc. 6 Breakfast. 6.15 Greek Testament; sang, alternè. 8.15 Read Prayers; religious talk with Mr Mackay. 9 Read Parnell to him, he fell asleep. 10 Greek Testament; sang. 12 Sang with Delamotte; sang; prayed; meditated; slept. 1 Greek Testament; sang. 3 Dinner. 3.15 Greek Testament; sang. 4.15 Meditated. 5 Prayed; sang; prayed. 6 Greek Testament; sang; prayed. 7 Private prayer. 8 Read Prayers (wind contrary!).

SATURDAY, APRIL 10. 5 Private prayer; prayed. 6 Breakfast, religious talk. 6.30 Greek Testament; sang. 7 Religious talk with Nowell. 7.45 Greek Testament; religious talk with them; Greek Testament; sang. 10 Shaved. 10.15 Greek Testament; sang. 12 Dinner, religious talk. 12.30 Necessary talk. 1 Storm; religious talk with Delamotte, etc. 2 Wind for us! 3 Dinner. 3.15 Writ diary; necessary business. 4 Meditated; prayed; religious talk with soldier, etc. 5 Opened Bible and Kempis; prayed for Oglethorpe, Mrs Hawkins, etc. 5.30 At Frederica; Mr Oglethorpe came on board and received us with the utmost love, saluted Mrs Hawkins. 6 Religious talk with Charles of Frederica. 7 He read Prayers, expounded; Mrs Hawkins there. 7.30 Religious talk with her, she quite cold and reserved (no. 1). 8.30 With Oglethorpe, he quite open and friendly. [9] Horton came, friendly. 9.30 Storehouse; prayed.

SUNDAY, APRIL 11. 4.30 Rose; religious talk with Delamotte (lively zeal). 5 With Charles; walked; prayed; read his diary! 6 Diary! 7 Religious talk. 7.30 Religious talk with them (they all civil!). 8 Read Prayers, expounded. 9 At Mrs Welch's, religious talk, coffee (she open). 10 At Charles'; writ diary. 10.45 Religious talk (necessary). 11 Charles read Prayers, preached (lively zeal). 12 Sacrament (+). 12.30 Sang with Charles and Delamotte, religious talk (necessary). 1 Writ conference with Mrs Hawkins; dinner; visited Betty Hassel. 2 Walked; meditated; prayed for Mrs Hawkins. 2.30 With Charles, read his diary. 3.30 Walked; meditated; prayed for Mrs Hawkins. 4 Meditated. 4.30 Read Prayers (lively zeal; convincing). 5 Expounded; prayed. 5.30 Walked with Charles, diary. 6.30 With Mrs Welch, she open. 7 With Charles; bread, religious talk; he read diary. 8 Walked with Horton, necessary talk of Mrs Hawkins. 9 Necessary talk of her, of Oglethorpe. 10 Came home; sang; guardhouse; prayed with Delamotte. 11.

Providence: [Well]; heard Charles' diary!!!! All civil; how long? Mrs Welch seemed open.

Grace: Something like faith. + [noon to 1 pm]; lively zeal twice [4 to 5, 11 to noon]; convincing [4 to 5 pm].

MONDAY, APRIL 12. 5 Charles', necessary business; necessary talk (religious). 6 Walked with him and Delamotte; prayed. 6.30 Heard diary. 7.30 Charles'; meditated. 8 Walked with Mrs Welch, talk of Mrs Hawkins (she quite open). 9 Miss Perkins', chocolate, religious talk (necessary). 10 Mr Oglethorpe called me in Mrs Hawkins' tent; tea, he read letters. 11 Read Prayers, expounded. 12 Writ diary. 12.15 Diary; religious talk with Delamotte. 12.45 Religious talk with Charles. 1 Writ diary; writ conference with Mrs Welch; Mrs Hawkins beat her boy. 2 Conference. 2.15 Visited Betty Hassel, religious talk, prayed; walked; meditated. 3 Meditated. 3.15 Charles', Horton came, necessary talk; Oglethorpe came from Mrs Hawkins, very angry! 4 Coffee. 4.15 Walked with Mrs Welch, religious talk (no. 2; she quite open!!!!). 5 Religious talk, she resolved to change. 6 Religious talk. 6.30 Sang; writ diary. 6.45 Meditated. 7 Read Prayers, expounded; Oglethorpe came, necessary talk (religious) with him (no. 3; he open). 8 Necessary talk (religious) with Charles. 8.30 Necessary talk (religious) with Horton. 10 With Delamotte, religious talk. 10.45 Lay down.

Providence: Mrs Welch open! Resolved to change. Oglethorpe friendly, soft. Horton seemed friendly and serious. Oglethorpe came out of the Hawkins' very angry. Why?

Grace: 6 rating eighteen times [every hour]. Lively zeal twice [2 to 3, 7 to 8 pm].

TUESDAY, APRIL 13. 5.30 Walked with Charles; prayed. 6 Charles read diary. 6.30 Writ diary; necessary talk with Mr Hawkins, he very angry at Charles. 7 Began account of Mrs Welch. 7.30 Mr Welch's, Mrs Hawkins', good talk (necessary, religious); tea. 8 Tea, mostly religious talk (she exceedingly civil). 9 Account. 10 Ended account. 10.15 Greek Testament; meditated (fervent). 11 Meditated. 11.15 Writ account of Mrs Hawkins. 11.45 Meditated. 12 Dinner, religious talk. 1 Visited Betty Hassel, religious talk. 1.30 Mr Welch's, religious talk with him (he seemed open and affected). 2 Bible. 2.30 Meditated; prayed for Mrs Hawkins, etc. 3 Meditated. 4 Walked with Mrs Welch, talk of Mrs Hawkins, of Sacrament (no. 4; seemed open). 5 Religious talk. 5.30 Mrs Hawkins', company came, religious talk. 6.30 Bread. 6.45 Prayed; Mrs Hawkins there (Mrs Welch open). 7 Charles read Prayers, expounded. 7.30 Necessary talk with Mrs Hawkins (no. 5; she very angry). 8 She milder, necessary talk (seemed open). 9 Necessary talk. 9.30 Oglethorpe came, necessary talk (religious). 10 Went; met Oglethorpe, talk of Mrs Hawkins, etc (seemed open). 11 Talk of the trial, he calm (no. 6; seemed open, O God!). 12 Storehouse; lay down.

Providence: Mrs Hawkins civil. Mr Welch seemed open and affected. Mrs Welch seemed open and affected; not at Prayers. Mrs Hawkins at Prayers; she open and milder. Oglethorpe seemed open; O God, in thy Light let us see light.

WEDNESDAY, APRIL 14. 5.15 Prayed; religious talk (necessary) with Delamotte. 6 Walked; talk of Oglethorpe and Mrs Hawkins. 7 Religious talk (necessary). 7.30 Meditated; writ diary. 8 Bread; writ diary; necessary talk (religious). 8.45 Necessary talk (religious) of Oglethorpe. 9 Writ account of conference with Mrs Hawkins; dressed. 10 Mr Hird's, necessary talk (religious). 11 Charles read Prayers, expounded. 11.45 Religious talk with him. 12 Walked with Charles, religious talk (necessary) of Mrs Welch, etc (dark). 1 Greek Testament; meditated; prayed. 2 Meditated; prayed. 2.30 Religious talk with Charles. 3

Bread, religious talk. 3.30 Visited Betty Hassel. 4 Mrs Welch's, necesssary talk of her dissembling (no. 7). 5 Mrs Hawkins came, religious talk (necessary) (no. 8; she seemed open). 6 Religious talk (she seemed open). 7 Read Prayers, expounded; good talk with Oglethorpe. 8 Walked with Charles, religious talk (necessary). 8.45 Sang. 9 Necessary talk with Reed. 9.15 Necessary talk (religious) with Delamotte.

Providence: Mrs Hawkins came to me at Mrs Welch's. God will reveal all! Grace: 6 rating fourteen times [all but 8 to 11 am].

THURSDAY, APRIL 15. 4.45 Prayed. 5 Meditated; private prayer. 5.45 Prayed with Charles. 6 Writ account of conference; bread ([cast] lots). 7 Account. 8 Account. 9 Prayed; writ diary; sang; meditated. 10 Walked; Greek Testament; meditated. 11 Read Prayers, expounded; necessary talk with Oglethorpe. 12 Mrs Hawkins', talk of Charles, religious talk (necessary) (gained no ground). 1 Mr Hawkins came, necessary talk. 1.30 Dinner. 2 Visited Mrs Hird, etc. 3 Visited Mrs Calwell. 4 Visited Mrs Perkins. 4.20 With Mrs Welch, Mrs Hawkins came, religious talk. 5 Mr Hawkins came, they [had] good talk; he went; they serious. 6 Religious talk. 6.45 Read Prayers (lively zeal). 7 Expounded; religious talk. 7.30 Charles', religious talk (necessary); sang. 8 Religious talk with Mark Hird. 8.15 With Davison (they seemed affected). 9 With Oglethorpe, necessary talk. 9.15 Walked; sang; prayed; meditated (zealous). 10 With Mr and Mrs Welch, religious talk. 10.30 Walked with Delamotte; to bed. 11 Flies. 12.15 To sleep.

Providence: Lots; well; no sleep for flies. Talk with Mrs Hawkins, gained no ground. She open to Mrs Welch's, they seemed serious. Mark Hird, Davison, Mr and Mrs Welch seemed affected.

Grace: Lively zeal [6 to 7]; zealous meditation [9 to 10 pm]. 7 rating once [9 to 10 pm]; 6 fourteen times [all but 7 to 9 am].

FRIDAY, APRIL 16. 5 Prayed; prayed with Charles; private prayer. 6 Prayed; sang; Greek Testament. 7 Bread, religious talk; writ diary. 7.45 Religious talk with Delamotte. 8 Greek Testament; meditated; sang. 9 Visited Mrs Robins; religious talk with Phoebe Hird (+ ; they affected); walked; meditated (zealous). 10 Walked with Charles, religious talk (necessary). 10.45 Necessary business; Charles read Prayers. 11 Prayers, expounded. 11.30 Necessary talk with them. 11.45 Religious talk with Delamotte. 12 Walked; Greek Testament; meditated; prayed for Oglethorpe, etc. 1 Visited Mr Tackner, Betty Hassel; Mrs Perkins. 2 Religious talk with Mrs Perkins. 2.45 Charles', necessary talk. 3 Dinner, religious talk (necessary). 4 Mrs Welch's, Mrs Hawkins and Calwell, they [had] various talk. 4.45 Mrs Hawkins went; religious talk with Mrs Welch (no. 9). 5.15 Walked; meditated. 6 Meditated; prayed. 6.30 Mrs Hawkins and Welch came to me; Mrs Welch went; began necessary talk (religious) with Mrs Hawkins (she open). 7 Read Prayers, expounded. 7.30 With Oglethorpe, necessary talk (religious), explained fully (no. 10). 8 Necessary talk (religious); he and Mrs Hawkins seem innocent!!! (he seemed open). 9 Necessary talk (religious) with Mrs Welch, she fainting; with Mrs Hawkins, she very angry! 10 Religious talk (necessary) with Charles. 10.45 Lay down.

Providence: Mrs Robins and Phoebe Hird affected. Mrs Welch and Mrs Hawkins came to me in the field. Mrs Hawkins and Oglethorpe seem innocent! Amen! She quite angry; Mrs Welch in a swoon; news of the

Spirit's coming. Oglethorpe seemed quite open and in an excellent temper.

Grace: 7 rating once [5 to 6 am]; 6 thirteen times [all but 10 to noon, 2 to 4 pm]. + / Open my eyes [9 to 10 am].

SATURDAY, APRIL 17. 5 Private prayer; prayed with Charles; meditated; (afraid!). 6 Religious talk with Charles; sang. 6.30 Dressed. 7 With Oglethorpe, writ for him; meditated; writ diary; (not afraid!). 8 Writ for Oglethorpe. 10.30 Mrs Hawkins', Oglethorpe there, religious talk (necessary) (she very angry and sad!). 11 Read Prayers, expounded. 11.15 Religious talk (necessary) with Charles. 12 Necessary talk (religious) with Mrs Welch. 12.30 At home; writ account of conference with Oglethorpe. 1 Oglethorpe came, religious talk (necessary). 2 Religious talk (useful and necessary). 3 Religious and useful talk; with Mrs Welch, mostly religious talk. 4 With Oglethorpe, dinner, necessary and useful talk. 5.30 Account. 6 Walked; meditated; prayed. 6.45 With Mrs Welch, religious talk. 7 Charles read Prayers, expounded; necessary talk (religious) with Mrs Perkins. 8.30 Mr Hawkins', necessary talk; at home, religious talk. 9 With Oglethorpe. 9.30 Charles', religious talk; with Delamotte; lay down.

SUNDAY, APRIL 18. 5 Meditated; prayed; prayed with Charles. 6 Religious talk with Charles and Delamotte; went to Oglethorpe, he busy. 7 With Mrs Perkins, Mr Hawkins. 7.50 Mrs Hawkins', necessary talk (religious) (she very angry!). 8 Read Prayers, expounded, Sacrament. 9 Expounded them. 9.15 With Oglethorpe, company there; religious talk with Charles, etc. 10 Stayed for Oglethorpe's letters. 10.30 Set out in Mr Houston's boat. 11 They [had] good talk. 1 Dinner, good talk (hard rain); meditated. 5.30 On Sapelo; could not get fire. 6 Got fire; supper. 7 Set out; slept; thought; slept.

MONDAY, APRIL 19. 12 [midnight] On ground. 6 Bread and cheese, mostly religious talk; (fair!). 7 Got off; writ conference with Oglethorpe, with Mrs Hawkins, with Mrs Welch. 10 Writ diary; Greek Testament; slept. 11 Greek Testament. 12 Dinner, good talk. 1 Greek Testament; slept. 2 Overtook Dorman, Indian traders there. 3 Religious talk. 4 Walked with Delamotte, religious talk. 5 On board, mostly religious talk. 6 Set out. 8 Very dark; lost ourselves; flies. 11 Came to Hussebaw; made fire; sick. 12.15 Lay on the ground!

TUESDAY, APRIL 20. 4.30 Set out. 6 Overtook Dorman, good talk. 7 Tea, good talk. 8 Greek Testament. 9 Religious talk with traders. 10.30 Ate oysters; set out (hard rain!). 2 Thunderbolt; Mr Lacy not [there]; eggs, good talk. 4.15 Set out with Delamotte and Mr Houston; meditated; religious talk (necessary) with Delamotte. 6.15 At Savannah! Mr Quincy with us, religious talk; tea. 7.45 Read Prayers, expounded. 8.30 With Germans (sleepy). 9.15 At home; religious talk with Ingham; prayed. 10.

WEDNESDAY, APRIL 21. 5 With Germans, necessary talk (religious). 5.30 Garden; prayed; meditated. 6 Revised papers. 7 Dressed; walked with Ingham; read papers as to Frederica. 8 Papers. 9 Bread; Mr Vat came, necessary talk. 10 Writ diary; Mr Quincy, necessary talk. 11 Necessary talk (religious). 11.15 Read Prayers, Ingham expounded. 12 Prayers. 12.15 Writ to Charles. 1 Writ to Mr Hawkins. 2 Writ to Oglethorpe; necessary business. 3 Necessary business. 3.30 Bread; prayed; religious talk. 4 Religious talk. 4.30 Mrs Causton's, talk with her of Miss Sophy. 5 Religious talk with Miss Sophy; tea. 6 Necessary talk with Mrs Causton; at home; prayed with Delamotte. 7 Greek Testament; meditated. 8 Read Prayers; expounded; with Germans, sang (sleepy). 9 With Germans. 9.30 Prayed; lay down.

Providence: Mr, Mrs Causton open. Miss Sophy open and much affected. Ingham dead! O Jesus!

THURSDAY, APRIL 22. 4.45 Prayed; meditated; prayed. 6 Transcribed Charles' journal. 7 Bread, religious talk; transcribed journal. 9 Writ journal. 10 Garden; Greek Testament; sang; meditated. 11 Meditated. 11.15 Read Prayers, expounded. 12 Prayers. 12.15 Journal; Robert Rose came, religious talk. 1 Journal. 2.15 Garden; meditated; sang; Kempis. 3 Prayed with Delamotte and Ingham; bread, religious talk. 4 Visited Mr Dearn, religious talk; prayed. 4.30 Journal. 5.45 Walked; meditated. 6 Prayed; meditated. 6.30 Delamotte came, necessary talk (religious). 6.45 At home; John Brownfield, religious talk. 7.15 Religious talk (necessary) with Miss Fawset (she quite open and affected). 8 Religious talk. 8.15 Read Prayers, expounded. 8.45 With Germans (sleepy). 9.45.

Providence: Much easier. Peter Wright relapsed; Mr Dearn in good temper. John Brownfield seemed open and affected. Miss Fawset seemed quite open and affected.

GOOD FRIDAY [APRIL 23]. 4.45 Prayed; prayed with Delamotte; private prayer (lively zeal). 6 Journal. 6.30 Greek Testament. 7 Journal. 7.45 Meditated. 8 Greek Testament; journal. 9 Dressed; Kempis. 10 Read Prayers. 11 Ingham read Prayers; preached. 12 Preached, Prayers. 12.15 Prayed with Delamotte; garden; sang. 1 Meditated; prayed. 1.30 Mr Dearn's, Sacrament. 2 Journal. 2.20 Meditated; read Prayers, Mr Ingham expounded; prayed. 3.45 Dinner. 4.20 Journal. 5 Walked; Kempis; meditated. 6 Kempis; sang; meditated. 7 At home; Mr Loyer came, religious talk; prayed with Delamotte; journal. 8 With Germans (sleepy). 9 Prayed.

EASTER EVE [APRIL 24]. 4.15 Private prayer; prayed with Delamotte; private prayer. 5 Journal. 5.30 Garden, necessary business. 6 Bread; began Fleury; sang; journal. 7 With Mr Causton, necesssary talk. 8.30 Journal. 9 Necessary business; Greek Testament; sang. 10 Journal. 11 Read Prayers, expounded. 12 Ingham read prayers. 12.20 Walked with Miss Sophy and Miss Fawset, religious talk (they seemed much affected and open). 1 Journal; Fleury. 4 Bread; visited Mr Brownfield, Mr Dearn. 5 Visited Mr Loyer. 5.30 Greek Testament; Kempis. 6.30 Journal. 7.15 Meditated. 7.30 Read Prayers, expounded. 8 With Germans (not sleepy). 9 Necessary talk (religious). 9.30 Lay down.

Providence: Well; Miss Sophy and Miss Fawset open and affected! Not sleepy with Germans!

Grace: 7 rating once [4 to 5 am].

ʽΗ ʽΕορτη˙ ['The Feast Day', EASTER, APRIL 25]. 12 [midnight] Sang; Hickes (lively zeal); (thunder and lightning). 1 Slept. 5 Sang; prayed with Delamotte; sang. 6 Tea, religious talk (Ingham zealous). 7 Dressed. 8 Religious talk with John Brownfield (he very serious). 8.20 Greek Testament; sang (zealous). 9 [Read] Hickes with them. 9.40 Sang. 10 Read Prayers. 11 Preached; prayed. 12 Sacrament (thirty-five communicants). 12.30 Dinner. 1 Writ names; writ diary.

1.30 Greek Testament. 2 Greek Testament; sang. 2.30 Read Prayers. 3 Read Prayers, preached. 4 Preached. 4.15 Meditated; religious talk. 5 Visited Mr Dearn; Hickes with Delamotte. 5.30 Fleury. 6 Sang, religious talk. 6.30 Walked; Fleury. 7 Fleury. 7.30 At home; meditated; religious talk with Ingham. 7.45 Meditated. 8 With Germans (sleepy). 9 Sang.

Providence: Well; Ingham zealous; John Brownfield very serious.

Grace: 7 rating six times [midnight to 1, 5 to 6, 8 to 11 am, 3 to 4 pm]. + [8 to 9 am].

MONDAY, APRIL 26. 4.15 Prayed; dressed. 5 Necessary business; prayed with Delamotte. 6.30 Set out; religious talk; sang; religious talk. 8 Mrs Musgrove's, necessary talk; tea. 9 Religious talk. 9.30 Religious talk with her brother. 10 Set out; religious talk (necessary). 11 At home; writ diary; necessary business; Ingham read Prayers. 12.45 Set out with Delamotte, religious talk. 1.30 Thunderbolt; Mr Lacy very ill; religious talk. 3 Dinner; tea; prayed with him, religious talk. 4.45 Set out; religious talk. 6.30 At home; writ diary; necessary business. 7 Prayed; supper. 7.45 Read Prayers (many there, not at the ball). 8 Expounded; with Germans. 9.30 Prayed; lay down.

TUESDAY, APRIL 27. 4.30 Prayed. 5 Writ journal. 5.30 Necessary business. 6.30 Set out; Fleury. 8.30 Mr Lacy's, he better; religious talk; all servants came in; read Prayers, expounded. 9.30 Set out; Fleury; lost. 10 Ran. 11 At home; dressed; read Prayers, expounded. 12.15 Writ diary; dinner; read notes. 1 Writ journal. 3.15 Began Mr Hall's case. 3.30 Mr Parker came, religious talk (open). 4.30 Tea; religious talk. 5 Mr Causton came, religious talk (necessary) (he seemed affected much). 6.30 Mr Parker went; necessary talk with Mr Causton. 6.45 Writ diary. 7 Sang; religious talk. 7.45 Read Prayers. 8 Expounded; with Germans. 9.30 Prayed.

WEDNESDAY, APRIL 28. 4 Private prayer; prayed with Delamotte. 5 Began account of Mr Hall; dressed. 6 Set out; began Fleury's *Catechism*. 8 Mr Lacy's, he better; religious talk (he seemed affected); tea. 8 Servants came; read Prayers, expounded (eleven there, all seemed affected). 10 Set out; Fleury. 12 At home; writ diary; Fleury. 12.45 Dinner, religious talk. 1 Writ account of Mr Hall. 4 Mr Causton came, necessary talk. 4.45 Account. 5 Garden; meditated; private prayer; sang. 6 Prayed; sang. 6.40 Mr Causton's, necessary talk with him. 7 Necessary talk (religious) with Miss Fawset and Miss Sophy. 7.45 Read Prayers, expounded. 8.15 With Germans (sleepy). 9 Religious talk with Ingham. 9.45.

THURSDAY, APRIL 29. 4.15 Private prayer; prayed with Delamotte. 5 Dressed; read Prayers, expounded; read resolutions. 5.45 Set out with Delamotte; Fleury. 6 Fleury; religious talk. 6.45 Mr Lacy's; religious talk. 8 Read Prayers, expounded; tea, religious talk. 9 Set out; religious talk; Fleury; religious talk (necessary). 11 At home; set out with Mr Ingham and Miss Fawset, religious talk with her; met Mrs Musgrove. 12 Writ diary; dinner, religious talk. 1 Account of Hall. 4 Mr Butler, necessary talk (he much afraid!). 4.15 Account. 5 Visited Josua Stringer, religious talk (he seemed affected). 5.30 Meditated; prayed. 6 Mr Causton came, necessary talk; Mr Butler, necessary talk. 7 Supper; good talk with Mr Brownfield. 7.45 Read Prayers. 8 Read Prayers, expounded; with Germans. 9 Prayed. 9.20.

FRIDAY, APRIL 30. 4.15 Private prayer; prayed with Delamotte. 5 Hall's account. 6.30 Bread. 7 Account. 8 Ended account. 9 Read Ingham's journal. 10 Read my journal. 10.45 Read Prayers. 11 Prayers, expounded. 11.45 With Mr Causton, necessary talk. 12.15 Set out with Ingham (strong tide against us), religious talk. 1 Read Hall's case; religious and useful talk. 3.30 Mrs Musgrove's; she and Miss Fawset in the woods, found them. 4 Religious talk with Tomochichi; religious talk with Miss Fawset (she affected). 5 Necessary talk; tea. 5.30 Set out; religious talk. 7.45 At home; supper. 8 Read Prayers, expounded; with Germans. 9.30 Prayed; lay down.

GEORGIA DIARY 2

May 1, 1736—February 11, 1736/37

SATURDAY, MAY 1, 1736, Old Style. 4.30 Private prayer; prayed with Delamotte. 5 Writ to Oglethorpe; necessary talk. 6 Letter; breakfast. 6.45 Letter. 7 Ended letter; necessary business. 8 Shaved; writ letter for Oglethorpe. 9 Garden, Kempis; sang. 10 Read Prayers. 11 Preached, Sacrament (twelve communicants); at home; prayed. 12 Dinner; writ letter for Oglethorpe. 1 Letter for Oglethorpe. 2 Catechized children; letter. 3 Letter. 4 Visited Josua Stringer, Mr Jackson. 5 Necessary business. 5.15 Garden; sang; meditated; prayed with Delamotte. 6 supper, religious talk; Fleury. 7 Mr Causton, necessary talk (religious). 8 Read Prayers, expounded; with Germans; sleepy. 9.15 Prayed. 9.30.

Providence: Well. Twelve communicants. Mr Jackson seemed serious.

Grace: 7 rating once [4 to 5 am]; 6 seven times [5 to 7, 9 to 11 am, 4 to 6, 7 to 8 pm]; 5 nine times. Attentive in meditation [5 to 6 pm]. Lively zeal [4 to 5 am].

SUNDAY, MAY 2. 4.45 Private prayer; prayed with Delamotte; letter for Oglethorpe. 6 Letter. 7 Töltschig and Anton [Seiffert], tea, religious talk (necessary). 8 Talk of parish. 8.45 They went; dressed. 9 Dressed. 9.15 Greek Testament; meditated. 9.45 Read Prayers. 10.45 Preached. 11 Preached; Sacrament. 11.45 Religious talk with Miss Sophy (she seemed affected). 12 Writ notes; writ diary. 12.20 Dinner, religious talk. 1 Writ letter for Oglethorpe; Greek Testament. 2 Letter. 2.15 Read Prayers. 3 Preached. 3.45 Letter. 5 Letter; prayed with Delamotte. 6 Supper, religious talk; ended letter; read letter. 7 Mrs Causton's, religious talk (necessary). 8 German; sleepy. 9 Religious talk. 9.30 Prayed. 10.

Providence: Well. Töltschig and Anton [Seiffert], religious talk, close. Miss Sophy seemed affected.

Grace: 7 rating twice [10 to noon]; 6 twelve times [4 to 6, 7 to 10 am, noon to 8 pm]; 5 thrice [6 to 7 am, 8 to 10 pm]. Convincing [2 to 4 pm].

MONDAY, MAY 3. 4 Private prayer; dressed (very heavy). 5 Prayed with Delamotte; read Prayers, expounded (twenty there). 5.45 Töltschig, German. 6 German. 7 Breakfast; Mr Causton came, necessary talk. 8 Necessary talk; tea. 9 With Germans, began learning. 10 Learning. 10.30 At home; religious talk with

Ingham; began *General Grounds of Grammar*. 11 *Grounds*. 11.30 With Germans. 12.30 Dinner. 1 *Grounds*. 3 Ended *Grounds*. 4 Sang; Kempis; sang; Kempis. 5 Translated *Grounds*; prayed with Delamotte. 6 Töltschig came; supper; German. 7 Began Greek Testament with Ingham and Delamotte. 7.45 Read Prayers. 8 Expounded. 8.30 With Germans. 9.30 Prayed.

Providence: Töltschig at Public Prayers.

Grace: 7 rating once [4 to 5 pm]; 6 eight times [4 to 7, 9 to 10 am, 5 to 9 pm]; 5 eight times [7 to 9, 10 am to 4 pm].

Mercy: [cipher entry, meaning unclear].

TUESDAY, MAY 4. 4 Private prayer; prayed with Delamotte. 5 Read Prayers, expounded (twenty-five there); writ German. 6 German. 6.15 Breakfast. 6.45 With Germans. 7 Germans. 11 Trustees' Garden; *Ecclesiastical History*, Hebrew Psalm. 12 Fleury's *History*. 12.30 Dinner. 1 German. 1.45 Slept. 2 German. 3.30 Mrs Musgove and Miss Fawset, mostly religious talk. 4 Garden with Miss Fawset, religious talk. 4.30 Tea, religious talk (necessary). 5 Religious talk with Miss Fawset (she seemed affected). 5.45 Mostly religious talk. 6.30 Supper. 7 Read Greek Testament with them. 7.45 Read Prayers. 8 Expounded. 8.20 With Germans, sang. 9.30 Prayed.

Providence: Well. Miss Fawset seemed affected.

Grace: 7 rating once [4 to 5 am]; 6 nine times [5 to 11 am, 4 to 5, 7 to 9 pm]; 5 six times [11 am to 1 pm, 2 to 4, 5 to 7 pm]; 4 once [1 to 2 pm].

Mercy: Preserved from w4 [2 to 3 pm].

WEDNESDAY, MAY 5. 4 Private prayer; prayed with Delamotte (lively). 5 Sorted papers. 5.45 Necessary business (colic). 6 Tea, religious talk; sorted. 7 Sorted. 7.45 Writ diary; necessary business. 8 With Germans. 10 Combed; dressed. 11 Read Prayers, expounded; Ingham read Prayers. 12 Religious talk with Mrs Parker of baptizing her child, gave no ground! 12.30 Dinner, religious talk (colic). 1 Began writing German. 2 Writ German. 3 Translated German Psalms. 4 Visited Mr Dearn [?], Mr Jackson. 5 Necessary business. 5.15 Sorted letters. 6 Von Reck came, religious talk (necessary), tea. 6.30 He went; religious talk with Ingham. 7 Greek Testament. 7.45 Read Prayers. 8 Expounded. 8.30 With Germans. 9 Germans. 9.15 Garden; meditated; prayed. 10.

Providence: Colic. Gave no ground with Mrs Parker. Well after dinner.

Grace: 7 rating once [4 to 5 am]; 6 thirteen times [5 to 7, 8 to 11, noon to 1, 3 to 10 pm]; 5 four times [7 to 8, 11 to noon, 1 to 3 pm].

THURSDAY, MAY 6. 4 Private prayer; Greek Testament. 5 Read Prayers, expounded; Mr Lacy there, religious talk with him (t.5 to Delamotte). 6 Mr Lacy, tea, religious talk (necessary). 7.30 Mr Von Reck, Junior, tea, religious talk. 8 Religious talk, close. 9 With Töltschig. 11.15 Necessary business; writ diary. 11.30 Fleury. 12 Fleury; dinner, religious talk. 1 Sorted letters. 2.30 Translated German. 6 Supper, religious talk. 6.45 Walked; Greek Testament. 7 Meditated. 7.30 Read Prayers, expounded. 8 Read Prayers. 8.15 With Germans. 9.30 Writ diary; religious talk with Delamotte. 10.

Providence: Well.

Grace: 7 rating once [4 to 5 am]; 6 seven times [5 to 7, 8 to 10, 11 to noon, 6 to 8 pm]; 5 nine times [7 to 8, 10 to 11 am, noon to 6 pm].

FRIDAY, MAY 7. 4.15 Private prayer; dressed; prayed with Delamotte. 5 Set out; translated hymns from German. 6 Translated. 7 Mr Lacy's, he not [there]; writ verses; religious and useful talk with her [Mrs. Lacy]. 8 Tea, religious and useful talk. 8.30 Read Prayers, expounded. 9 Expounded. 9.20 Verses. 9.40 Set out and translated. 10 Translated. 11.20 At home; writ verses; shaved. 12 Sang; dinner, religious talk; writ diary. 1 Mr [Von] Reck, necessary talk (religious; he seemed affected). 2 Writ to Oglethorpe. 3 Letter. 3.15 Visited Mrs Rivett, necessary talk (words!). 4 Necessary talk (religious); visited Jackson, religious talk; Josua Stringer, prayed, religious talk. 5 Sang; private prayer. 6 Fleury; supper. 6.45 Necessary talk. 7 Greek Testament; read Prayers. 8 Expounded. 8.30 With Germans (lively zeal). 9.15 Religious talk with Töltschig; writ diary. 9.45 Religious talk with Delamotte.

Providence: Mr Von Reck seemed affected.

!Mrs Smith spoke to me of Delamotte.

Grace: 7 rating twice [4 to 5 am, 5 to 6 pm]; 6 eleven times [5 to 7, 8 to 9 am, noon to 5, 7 to 10 pm]; 5 five times [7 to 8, 9 to noon, 6 to 7 pm]. Lively zeal [1 to 2, 8 to 9 pm].

SATURDAY, MAY 8. 4.15 Private prayer; sang; prayed with Delamotte; (well). 5 Read prayers, expounded. 5.40 Miss Mellichamp came, necessary talk. 6 Necessary talk (religious). 6.20 Physic; Mr Von Reck and his brother, tea, religious talk. 7 Mr Appee, religious talk. 7.30 Garden; necessary business. 8 Fleury. 10.30 With Mrs Smith, religious talk (close, she affected). 11 Religious talk with her (she seemed much affected). 11.30 Fleury. 12 Dinner, religious talk; Fleury. 1 Fleury. 1.30 Baptized Stephen Landry. 2 Religious talk; meditated. 2.30 Necessary business. 3 Writ diary; Fleury. 4 Ended Fleury. 5 Sang; private prayer. 5.40 Sang. 6 Garden; necessary business. 6.40 Supper, religious talk. 7 Greek Testament; meditated. 7.45 Read Prayers. 8 Expounded. 8.45 Germans (convincing). 9 Germans. 9.30 At home; religious talk; writ diary. 9.45 Prayed. 10.

Providence: Close religious talk with Mrs Smith, she seemed much affected.

Grace: 7 rating twice [4 to 5 am, 5 to 6 pm]; 6 seven times [5 to 8 am, 6 to 10 pm]; 5 nine times [8 am to 5 pm]. Convincing [8 to 9 pm].

SUNDAY, MAY 9. 4 Garden, private prayer (very heavy). 5 Prayed with Delamotte; necessary business. 5.30 Sang; necessary talk (religious). 6 Transcribed letter to Oglethorpe; tea, religious talk. 7 Dressed; necessary business. 8 Read Prayers in the Court-house (thirty-three there). 9 Expounded; prayed. 9.40 Letter. 10 Much tired, sleepy. 10.15 Sang. 10.30 Religious talk with Ingham, agreed. 11 Read Prayers, preached. 12 Sacrament (eighteen communicants). 12.30 Writ notes; dinner. 1 Dinner. 1.15 Sang; Greek Testament. 2 Meditated. 2.15 Read Prayers. 3 Preached. 4 Mr Quincy came, necessary talk, tea. 5 Necessary talk. 5.45 He went; sang. 6 Sang; meditated. 6.30 Walked; meditated (fervent). 7 Meditated. 7.15 Religious talk with Delamotte. 7.45 With Germans. 8.40 At home; religious talk. 9 Prayed.

Providence: Well; Ingham and I agreed. Began reading Prayers in the Court-house: 33 at 8 am, about 90 at 11 am, and 120 at 2 pm.

Grace: 7 rating twice [4 to 5 am, 7 to 8 pm]; 6 twelve times [5 to 7, 8 am to 4, 6 to 7, 8 to 9 pm]; 5 twice [7 to 8 am, 4 to 5 pm]. + [7 to 8 pm]; fervent in meditation [6 to 7 pm]. Lively zeal [7 to 9 pm].

MONDAY, MAY 10. 4 Private prayer (lively zeal); John came, necessary talk (heavy); Greek Testament. 5 Greek Testament; read Prayers, expounded (lively zeal). 6 Breakfast on bread; German. 7 Religious talk with Töltschig. 7.45 German. 10 Writ to Oglethorpe. 11 Visited the sick. 11.45 Sang with Delamotte; letter from Charles, Oglethorpe innocent! 12 Dinner on bread, religious talk. 12.45 Writ to Mr Burton. 1 Letter. 1.30 Transcribed letter to Oglethorpe. 3 Visited Mrs Loyd, religious talk; Mr Brownfield, religious talk (necessary). 4 Visited Mrs Johnson, Mrs Bradley, Mr and Mrs Smith. 5 Visited Mrs Moore, christened her sick child. 6 Sang with Delamotte; supper, religious talk. 7 Greek Testament; meditated. 7.45 Read Prayers (sixty there). 8 Expounded; with Germans. 9.15 Garden, meditated. 9.30 Prayed.

    Providence: Letter from Charles, Oglethorpe innocent! Sixty at Evening Prayers.

    Grace: 7 rating once [4 to 5 am]; 6 eleven times [5 to 9, 10 am to 1, 3 to 4, 5 to 6, 7 to 9 pm]; 5 five times [9 to 10 am, 1 to 3, 4 to 5, 6 to 7 pm]. + [5 to 6 am]; lively zeal twice [4 to 6 am].

TUESDAY, MAY 11. 4 Private prayer (heavy); meditated; Greek Testament. 5 John came. 5.15 Read Prayers, expounded. 5.45 Mrs Dearn came, religious talk (she very serious). 6 Breakfast, religious talk; writ to Charles. 7 Letter. 7.30 With Germans. 10 Translated German. 11 Visited Mrs Rivett, Mr Causton, necessary talk (religious) with her. 12 Religious talk with Miss Sophy. 12.40 At home; dinner; sang; religious talk. 1.15 Transcribed letter to Oglethorpe. 3.15 With Ingham and Delamotte, prayed, sang, religious talk. 4 Visited Mr Woodruff, religious talk; Mr Watkins, religious talk (necessary). 5.15 Writ diary [summary?]. 5.30 Private prayer; sang. 6 Mr Causton came, tea, necessary talk. 7 Greek Testament. 7.30 Meditated. 7.45 Read Prayers. 8 Expounded. 8.30 With Germans. 9 John came; meditated, prayed. 9.30.

    Providence: Mrs Dearn open! Mrs Rivett convinced. Miss Sophy serious and open. Began meeting with Delamotte and Ingham.

    Grace: 6 rating eleven times [4 to 6, 10 am to 2, 3 to 6, 7 to 9 pm]; 5 six times [6 to 10 am, 2 to 3, 6 to 7 pm].

WEDNESDAY, MAY 12. 4 Private prayer; meditated; John came. 5 Set out; translated German. 7 Mr Lacy's, he better, religious and useful talk; tea. 8 Religious talk with him. 8.30 Religious talk with Chapman, he convinced. 9 Religious talk with Chapman. 9.30 Set out; verses. 10 Chapman overtook me, religious talk. 11 At home; they at children; writ verses. 12 Dinner, religious talk (necessary). 1 Transcribed letter to Oglethorpe. 3 Sang with Ingham and Delamotte. 3.30 Visited Mrs Mellichamp, religious talk (necessary). 4.30 At home; necessary talk with Delamotte. 5 Walked; meditated; Greek Testament; sang. 5.50 At home; prayed. 6 Ended letter. 6.30 Supper, religious talk. 7 Necessary business. 7.30 Meditated. 7.45 Read Prayers. 8 Expounded; with Germans. 9.15 Necessary talk.

    Providence: John Chapman half convinced.

    Grace: 6 rating nine times [4 to 6, 8 to 11 am, 2 to 4, 5 to 6, 7 to 8 pm]; 5 eight times [6 to 8, 11 am to 2, 4 to 5, 6 to 7, 8 to 9 pm].

THURSDAY, MAY 13. 4.30 Private prayer; prayed with Delamotte. 5 Read Prayers, expounded. 5.45 Read letter to Oglethorpe. 6.15 Necessary business. 6.30 Mr

Quincy came, religious talk (necessary). 7 Tea, religious talk (necessary). 8 With Germans. 10 Writ German. 11 Walked; began Archbishop Sharp's *Sermons*. 12 Sang, with Delamotte; dinner, religious talk. 1 German; reviewed papers. 2 Scheme of our Saviour's Life. 3 Greek Testament. 3.30 Sang; prayed with Ingham and Delamotte. 4 Visited Josua Stringer, prayed, religious talk; Mrs Rivett, necessary talk; Mrs Smith, religious talk. 5 Religious talk. 5.20 Sang; prayed; prayed with Delamotte (lively zeal). 6 Supper, religious talk. 6.30 Read *Art of Surgery*. 7 Greek Testament. 7.30 Meditated. 7.45 Read Prayers. 8 Expounded. 8.45 With Germans; sleepy. 9 With Germans. 9.20 Necessary talk (religious); John came. 9.45 Prayed.

Providence: Mrs Smith and Johnson very serious.

Grace: 6 rating thirteen times; 5 five times [6 to 9 am, 6 to 7, 9 to 10 pm].

FRIDAY, MAY 14. 4 Private prayer. 5 Prayed with Delamotte; John came, private prayer. 6 Bread; Archbishop Sharp. 6.30 German. 10 Sharp. 11 Read Prayers, expounded. 11.45 Mr Ingham read Prayers. 12 Preached. 12.10 Dinner; Gother. 1 Francke. 2 Mrs Dean came, very angry, necessary talk (religious) of her son. 2.30 With Mr Dean, necessary talk (religious), gave a little ground. 3 Francke. 3.30 Visited Josua Stringer and Mr Jackson, religious talk. 4 Religious talk with El[len?] Dean (gained a little ground). 4.30 At home; Gother. 5 Mr Brownfield, religious talk (necessary). 5.30 Mr Quincy came, necessary talk (religious); tea. 6 Necessary talk (religious); Mr Quincy went. 7 Necessary talk (religious) with John Brownfield. 7.45 Read Prayers. 8 Expounded. 8.30 With Germans, sang. 9 Religious talk (necessary); prayed. 10.

Providence: Well; quarrel between Mrs Dean and son, she very angry; gained a little ground. Gained little ground with Eleanor [Ellen?]. John Brownfield quite open.

Grace: 7 rating twice [4 to 6 am]; 6 twelve times [6 to 11 am, noon to 6, 8 to 10 pm]; 5 thrice [11 to noon, 6 to 8 pm].

SATURDAY, MAY 15. 4 Private prayer; sang. 5 Prayed with Delamotte; read Prayers. 5.45 Walked with Miss Sophy, religious talk. 6 She open, religious talk. 6.30 Tea, religious talk; Ingham very angry. 7 German. 10 Sharp; John came. 11 Sharp. 12 Gother; dinner, religious talk. 1 Sharp; with Germans, sang. 2 Francke. 3.15 With Ingham and Delamotte, prayed, religious talk. 4 Mr Causton came, necessary and useful talk. 5 Tea, necessary and useful talk. 5.45 Prayed. 6 Prayed with Delamotte; private prayer; Greek Testament (lively zeal). 7 Garden; private prayer; shaved. 8 Read Prayers, expounded; religious talk with Mr and Mrs Smith. 9 With Germans. 9.45 Writ diary.

Providence: St Anthony's Fire; smarted much.

Grace: 7 rating thrice [4 to 5 am, 6 to 8 pm]; 6 eight times [5 to 7, 10 am to 2, 3 to 4, 8 to 9 pm]; 5 seven times [7 to 9 am, 2 to 3, 4 to 6, 9 to 10 pm]. Lively zeal [6 to 7 pm].

SUNDAY, MAY 16. 4 Private prayer; meditated; private prayer for mother, etc; (pain). 5 John came; sang; read resolutions; (easier). 6 Read resolutions. 6.30 Tea, religious talk (lively zeal). 7 Religious talk. 7.15 Prayed; meditated; sang. 8 Read e c a p p s h s, expounded; Ingham read Prayers, 1, 2, 3, 4. 9 Thanksgiving, blessing. 9.30 Sang; meditated. 10 John came, [read] Hickes with them. 10.45 Ingham read c, c, c, sang. 11 Preached. 11.45 Prayed. 12 Sacrament (twenty-one communicants). 12.30 Sang; dinner, religious talk. 1 Sharp; sang.

2 Greek Testament; sang. 2.45 Read c a p. 3 [Read] p s h s; christened; sang. 4 Ingham read p t b, preached. 4.45 Writ notes. 5 Greek Testament. 5.30 Visited Mrs Smith, both very serious, religious talk. 5.45 Prayed. 6 Sang, religious talk. 6.30 Sharp. 7.30 With Germans; meditated; sang. 8 Sang. 8.30 John. 8.45 Necessary talk; necessary business. 9 Charles came; tea, talk of Frederica. 10 Physic.

Providence: In pain; easier. Mr and Mrs Smith very serious.

Grace: 7 rating once [4 to 5 am]; 6 sixteen times [5 am to 8 pm, 9 to 10]; 5 once [8 to 9 pm].

MONDAY, MAY 17. 4 Private prayer; prayed with Delamotte and Charles. 5 John came; read Prayers, expounded. 6 Garden with Charles and Ingham, religious talk (necessary) of Frederica. 7 Religious talk (necessary). 8 German. 9 Sharp. 11 Ended second volume. 12 Sang with them; dinner, religious talk. 1 Necessary business. 3 Religious talk with Ingham, etc. 4 Mr Causton's, necessary talk; visited Mr Smith, religious talk; prayed. 5 Mr and Mrs Dearn came, mostly religious talk; tea. 6 Religious talk. 6.30 Religious talk with Mrs Dearn (she much affected). 7 Greek Testament. 7.30 With Miss Bovey; John Brownfield came, mostly religious talk, not close. 8 Read Prayers, expounded. 8.45 With Germans. 9 They prayed for me. 9.30 John came; necessary business. 10 Prayed.

Providence: [blank].

TUESDAY, MAY 18. 4.15 Private prayer; necessary business; John came. 5 Read Prayers, expounded. 5.45 Prepared. 6 Necessary business. 6.45 Mr Causton and Miss Sophy came, religious talk. 7 Tea, necessary talk (religious). 8 Percy came, necessary talk. 8.30 Set out with Ingham, Delamotte, and Charles, religious talk. 9 Religious talk. 11 Mr Lacy's, religious and useful talk. 11.45 Read Prayers, expounded. 1 Religious talk with Chapman, gave no ground. 1.15 Dinner, good talk. 2.30 Charles in the woods! 3 Coffee. 4 Charles and Ingham walked, we with them, religious talk. 5 Religious and useful talk. 6. Walked with Delamotte. 7 Religious talk; supper; prayed. 7 At home; religious talk; close with Mr Lacy (he seemed affected). 8 Read Prayers, expounded (all seemed affected). 9 Supper, religious talk (necessary). 10.30 Prayed.

WEDNESDAY, MAY 19. 4.15 Prayed; walked; private prayer. 5 Translated German. 7 At home; coffee; mostly religious talk. 8 Good talk. 8.30 Writ diary; transcribed verses. 9 Transcribed verses and necessary papers. 10 Mostly religious talk. 10.30 Walked with Mr Lacy, good talk. 11 Good talk (necessary) with him. 11.40 Meditated. 12 Dinner, religious talk. 1 Religious and useful talk. 2 Charles and Delamotte came, they dined, good talk (various). 3 Sick, vomited. 4 Sick, vomited. 5 Better; piragua came. 5 Set out in our boat; supper, religious talk, sang. 7 Writ diary; Skidaway; Mrs Mouse's, tea, religious talk. 8 Read Prayers, expounded (nine there). 9.30 Set out; rain went off. 10 Slept.

THURSDAY, MAY 20. 3.30 Rowed, religious talk; (well). 4 Rowed, religious talk. 5 Rowed, prayed, religious talk. 5.30 At All-honey; tea. 6 Mostly religious talk; Mr Delamotte dressed me. 7 Set out; translated German. 9 Began De Renty. 10 De Renty. 11 Washed feet; verses; lay by. 12 Dinner; very hot; religious talk. 1 Set out, read Renty; (wind rose). 2 Renty; (very rough). 3.15 On Millikin's Island; necessary business. 4.15 Greek Testament; supper, religious talk; (no water). 5 Religious talk. 5.45 Set out; verses; (water rough! afraid!). 6 Verses; St Catherine's Sound; (rough). 7 On the sand; religious talk (afraid). 8 Religious talk. 9.30 On St Catherine's, could not find water. 10 Boat. 10.30 Found water. 11.30 Lay on shore.

Grace: 6 rating twelve times [3 am to 3 pm, 6 to 8]; 5 five times [3 to 6 pm, 8 to 10].

FRIDAY, MAY 21. 5 Necessary business; tea; (my boil better). 6 Walked with Delamotte. 6.30 Walked; meditated. 7 Meditated; prayed. 8 Greek Testament. 9 Greek Testament; read Prayers, expounded; meditated. 10 Set out; writ diary; translated German. 11 Translated German. 12 Dinner. 1 Slept. 2.45 Rowed (sea rough, wind high!). 4.30 Delamotte's Island; made fire. 5 Tea, religious talk; religious talk; prayed; sang. 6 Read Prayers, expounded (twenty there); religious talk. 7.45 Set out (rough). 9 Lay by near the Sound, could not go on!

SATURDAY, MAY 22. 4 Rowed; private prayer; sang. 5 Private prayer. 5.30 Sapelo [Island]; necessary business; tea, religious talk; writ diary. 7.45 Prayed. 8 Slept. 9.30 Set out; on ground; transcribed verses. 12.45 Dinner. 1 Writ diary; read Renty. 3 Translated German. 3.30 Wind rose. 4 Doboy Sound, very rough, high sea; prayed. 5 In the creek; sang. 5.15 Sang. 6.15 Good talk (religious, necessary). 9.30 In St Simons River; supper! 10 Slept.

SUNDAY, MAY 23. 5.30 Dressed. 6 Frederica; Mr Oglethorpe sent for us; talk of the Spaniards; all well, he very open. 7 Talk of Miss Fawset, of Savannah; tea. 8 Talk of Miss Sophy. 8.30 Dressed; at Mrs Welch's, necessary talk, she much afraid. 9 Read Prayers, expounded (three there, then nineteen). 10 Religious talk (necessary) with Mr Horton; with Delamotte (he quite open). 10.30 Writ diary. 11 Necessary business; Kempis. 11.30 Read Prayers, preached. 12 Preached, Sacrament. 12.50 Religious talk with Mrs Hird. 1 Religious talk; meditated. 1.30 Dinner with Oglethorpe. 2 Dinner, good talk. 2.45 Religious talk with Reed. 3 Writ diary; Appee came, religious talk. 4 Read Prayers, expounded. 4.45 Religious talk with Appee (he quite open). 5 Tea, religious talk. 6 Religious talk. 6.30 Miss Fawset, religious talk. 7 Religious talk. 7.30 At home; private prayer; necessary business. 8 The Germans came, sang. 9 Sent for by Mrs Welch, necessary talk. 9.30 Mr Hawkins, necessary talk. 10 Mr Oglethorpe's, Mr Mackay there, they [had] necessary and useful talk. 11 They [had] necessary and useful talk. 12 He went; read Journal to Oglethorpe (he quite open).

MONDAY, MAY 24. 12 Read Journal to Oglethorpe (he quite open). 1 Talk of Mrs Welch and Mrs Hawkins (he open and friendly). 2 Talk of Savannah and Frederica (he convinced). 3 Talk of his life, etc (he affected). 4 Slept. 5.15 Rose; private prayer; necessary talk with Delamotte. 6 Religious talk with Delamotte; examined with Francis Moore. 7 With Delamotte, religious talk. 7.30 Writ diary. 7.45 Necessary business. 8 Mrs Welch's; tea, religious and useful talk. 9 Sang; Greek Testament. 10 Visited the sick (all seemed affected). 10.45 Sang. 11 Read Prayers, expounded (twenty there). 12 Visited Betty Tackner, talked of her marriage (gained no ground). 1 Necessary talk (religious) with them. 2 Dinner, they [had] various talk. 3 Various talk. 3.30 Walked; Greek Testament; meditated. 4 Meditated; necessary talk (religious) with Betty Tackner; children seized, gained no ground! 5 Mr Calwell's; Mr Appee and Delamotte, religious and useful talk; tea. 6.15 Sang; writ diary; necessary talk; writ to Charles. 7

Walked; meditated; necessary talk (religious). 8 Read Prayers, expounded (Mrs Hawkins there); walked; meditated. 9 Meditated; prayed. 9.30 Lay without bolster.

Tuesday, May 25. 4.15 Private prayer; meditated; (a flux). 5 Private prayer; meditated; necessary talk (religious) with Oglethorpe. 6 Necessary talk. 6.30 Walked with Betty Hassel, necessary talk (religious); necessary talk (religious) with Mrs Tackner. 7 At home; Mrs Welch came; tea, religious talk; Mrs Patterson came, religious talk. 8 Mr Tanner came, good talk. 8.45 Necessary business. 9 Walked; Gother. 10 Writ diary [summary?]. 10.15 Writ notes. 10.30 Visited the sick. 11 Read Prayers, expounded (twelve there). 12 Dinner, religious talk. 12.30 Necessary business. 12.45 Gother. 1 German; slept; German. 2 German. 2.45 With Oglethorpe, they [had] necessary talk. 3 They [had] necessary talk; religious talk with Mr Appee (he very serious). 4 With Mrs Welch, talk of Oglethorpe, herself, Mrs Hawkins (dark). 5 Talk of Mrs Hawkins, religious talk. 5.30 Sang; prayed. 6 Delamotte came; supper; walked, religious talk with Delamotte (Oglethorpe not gone). 7 Necessary and useful talk with them. 8 Read Prayers, expounded (Mrs Hawkins and Mrs Welch there). 8.30 Religious talk with Tackner. 9 Religious talk with her. 9.30 Prayed; lay down.

Grace: 6 rating fifteen times; 5 thrice [8 to 9 am, 4 to 5, 7 to 8 pm].

Wednesday, May 26. 4.40 Prayed with Delamotte. 5 Gother. 5.30 Prayed for Frederica. 6 Mr Oglethorpe sent for me, necessary talk of Mrs Lawley. 6.45 Tea. 7 Mrs Welch came, and Mr Appee, religious talk (they seemed affected); writ diary. 8 German; sang; Greek Testament. 9 Visited the sick. 10 Visited Mr Hird, Calwell, etc, religious talk (necessary). 11 Read Prayers, expounded. 12 Necessary talk with Mr Hird; dinner, religious talk. 1 German. 2 Visited (all seemed affected). 3 Visited. 4 Mrs Patterson's, Mrs Hird came, religious talk; tea. 5 Mr Mackay came, religious and useful talk. 5.45 At home; Mr Horton came, necessary talk. 6 Necessary talk. 6.45 Mrs Calwell, talk of Mrs Hawkins. 7 Necessary talk (religious); supper. 8 Read Prayers, expounded; necessary talk with Delamotte. 8.45 Necessary talk (religious) with Mrs Patterson. 9 Necessary talk (religious) of Mrs Hawkins (Question? If she in love?). 9.30 Lay down. 12 Fleas, no sleep. 12 Slept.

Grace: 6 rating fourteen times; 5 twice [6 to 8 pm].

Thursday, May 27. 4.15 Private prayer; sang. 5 Prayed with Delamotte; physic. 5.30 Talk of Mrs Hawkins (clear). 6 Mr Horton came; tea, mostly religious talk. 7 Greek Testament. 7.45 Slept. 8 Greek Testament; sang; Mrs Welch came, said Mrs Hawkins wanted to talk with me. 9 Sang; meditated. 9.30 *Canones critici*. 10 *Canones*. 10.30 Mr Reed and Lawley, they [had] various talk. 10.45 Meditated. 11.15 Read c p p s c x p t b. 12 Gother. 12.15 Mr Welch's, dinner, mostly religious talk. 1 Religious and useful talk with Davison. 1.30 Slept. 2 German. 3.30 Visited sick. 4 Mrs Patterson came, religious talk (she very serious); tea. 5 Visited Mr Lascelles. 5.15 Walked; Kempis. 6 Necessary talk (religious) with Hird. 6.15 Kempis; supper. 7 Kempis; sang. 7.45 Read Prayers, expounded. 8 Buried Leary. 8.30 Necessary talk (religious) with Mrs Calwell. 9 At home; necessary talk (religious) with Mr Reed. 9.45.

Grace: 6 rating thirteen times; 5 four times [6 to 7, 10 to noon, 9 to 10 pm].

FRIDAY, MAY 28. 4 Private prayer. 5 Kempis; sang; prayed with Delamotte. 6 Greek Testament; prepared; sent for Mrs Hawkins; Greek with Delamotte. 7 Gother for him; German. 8 Tea, religious talk (she not come). 8.30 Read the last prayer by Mr [Michael] Germain. 9 He recovered; visited sick. 9.30 German. 10 Dressed; necessary business; sang. 10.30 Kempis (lively zeal). 11 Kempis. 11.15 Read c p p s h s c 1 2 3 4 t b (convincing). 12 Religious talk with Moore (he serious). 12.30 Dinner, religious talk of Mrs Hawkins. 1 Necessary talk (religious). 1.30 Visited Moore, necessary talk (religious). 2 Gother. 3 Sent for Mrs Hawkins, she would not come; necessary talk at Mrs Parker's. 3.40 German. 4 Tea with Reed, religious talk. 4.30 Visited. 5 Walked, Kempis. 6 Meditated. 6.15 Greek Testament; religious talk; sang. 7 Sang. 7.15 Necessary talk with Mrs Welch; meditated. 8 Read Prayers, expounded (seven there). 8.30 Meditated; with Mrs Calwell, necessary talk of Mrs Hawkins. 9 Meditated; necessary talk (religious) with Delamotte; prayed. 10.

Grace: 7 rating twice [5 to 6 am, 5 to 6 pm]; 6 twelve times [4 to 5, 6 to noon, 2 to 3, 4 to 5, 6 to 8, 9 to 10]; 5 four times [noon to 2, 3 to 4, 8 to 9].

SATURDAY, MAY 29. *Salutem solam <tuam> cogitem <et quae Dei sunt> curem* ['Think only of your salvation, and care for the things of God'; cf. Kempis, I.xxiii.8]. 4 Private prayer; thought of Mrs Hawkins. 5 Kempis; yet thought of Mrs Hawkins. 6 Greek Testament; Greek with Delamotte. 7 Mrs Patterson's; talk of Mrs Hawkins; Mrs Welch came, religious talk; tea. 8 Religious talk (necessary). 8.30 Writ journal. 10 Visited. 10.15 Mrs Patterson's; Mrs Hawkins there, she would not explain. 11 Read Prayers, expounded (five there). 12 Journal. 12.30 Dinner, religious talk. 1 Journal. 2.30 Visited. 3 Mrs Patterson's, Mrs Hawkins there; tea, religious talk (necessary), interrupted thrice (she seemed open). 4 At home; Mrs Calwell and Mrs Welch; tea, religious talk. 5 Mrs Welch went; talk of Mrs Hawkins. 5.30 Walked, Kempis. 6 Kempis; religious talk with Davison and Moore. 6.30 Shaved; supper. 7 Kempis; buried (Germain). 7.45 Meditated. 8 Read Prayers, expounded (one there). 8.30 At home; religious and useful talk. 9 Mostly religious talk. 9.45.

Grace: 6 rating twelve times; 5 six times [7 to 9 am, 1 to 3, 5 to 6, 9 to 10 pm].

SUNDAY, MAY 30. 5 Sang; private prayer; meditated; (well). 6 Tea, religious talk (very zealous, lively zeal; +). 7 Greek Testament; meditated; sang. 8 Slept. 8.15 Writ diary; read e c p p s h s x c [9 am] 1 2 3 4 t b (five there). 9.15 Walked; Greek Testament. 10 Greek Testament; Kempis. 11 Meditated. 11.15 Read Prayers, preached (convincing; twenty-five there). 12 Sacrament (ten communicants). 12.30 Writ diary; looked for dinner. 1 Dinner at the fort. 1.30 Greek Testament; slept. 2 Greek Testament; sang. 3 Read e c p p s h s c p sang t b. 4 Walked, Kempis; prayed. 5 Kempis; meditated; religious talk with Phoebe Hird; sang with Delamotte. 6 At home; supper, religious talk. 6.45 Walked; read Mr Hawkins' Case to Delamotte. 7 Religious talk. 7.15 Mrs Calwell's, necessary talk (religious). 8 Mrs Hawkins at her door, asked me to come in (open); Mr Hawkins came, necessary talk; ate peas; they very civil. 9 Necessary talk. 9.30 At home; religious talk; Fort; prayed. 10.

MONDAY, MAY 31. 4.15 Private prayer; meditated. 5 Private prayer; sang; necessary business. 6 Writ journal. 7 Mr and Mrs Hawkins, tea, good talk (necessary and religious), they very civil and serious and open! 8 Mr Horton came, necessary talk. 9 They went; visited; Mrs Patterson's; walked. 9.30 At home; journal. 11 writ diary; read c p p s h c p t b. 12 Christened Thomas Meyer. 12.30 Dinner, religious talk. 1 Visited Allen, etc (all affected, lively zeal). 2 Visited. 2.30 Journal. 3.45 Visited Lascelles, made his will. 4.15 Mrs Patterson, tea, religious talk (necessary). 5 Religious and useful talk (necessary). 6 With Lascelles, necessary talk. 6.30 At home; sang; religious talk. 7 Walked; Kempis; meditated. 8 Read Prayers; religious talk with Delamotte. 9 Religious talk with Delamotte.

TUESDAY, JUNE 1. 4.30 Private prayer. 5.45 Prayed with Delamotte. 6 Meditated; tea with Delamotte, religious talk. 7 Mr and Mrs Hawkins, Mr and Mrs Patterson, tea, mostly religious talk. 8 Mr Hawkins went; mostly religious talk. 8.45 Mrs Hawkins went; mostly religious talk. 9 Necessary talk; necessary business; sang. 10 Necessary business; journal. 11 Read Prayers, expounded (Mrs Hawkins there, very serious). 11.45 Dinner. 12 Dinner, religious talk. 12.45 Necessary business. 1 Journal. 1.30 Visited. 2 Ended journal. 3 Necessary business. 3.15 Visited. 4 Mrs Patterson's, she not [there]; walked with Delamotte, religious talk. 4.30 Greek Testament; sang. 5 Mrs Patterson's, Mr and Mrs Hawkins, Mr Reed, Delamotte, religious and useful talk; tea. 6 They all went; examined with Mrs Hawkins (she much affected and open). 7 Religious talk. 8 Read Prayers, expounded (nine there, Mrs Hawkins). 8.30 Religious talk (necessary) with Mrs Calwell. 9 Necessary talk (religious). 9.45 Prayed; slept sound.

WEDNESDAY, JUNE 2. 4.15 Private prayer. 5 In the water; dressed. 6 Necessary business; journal. 7 Necessary talk with Mr Horton, etc. 7.45 Walked. 8 At the Acre Lot with Mr and Mrs Horton, Mrs Patterson, Mrs Hird, and Delamotte; tea. 9 Walked; good talk. 9.30 Mrs Hird's, examined with her. 10 Examined; religious talk. 10.30 Greek Testament. 11 Read Prayers (Mrs Hawkins not [there]); dinner, religious talk. 12 Dressed; necessary business. 12.30 Visited Walker (+). 1 Religious talk. 2 Visited Bennet. 2.30 Mr Perkins, company. 3 Necessary talk. 3.45 With Lascelles, religious talk, prayed (+). 4 Mrs Calwell's, necessary talk; tea. 5 With her and Mrs Robinson, necessary talk (religious, gained little ground). 6 Sang; writ diary. 6.15 Walked, Kempis. 7 Meditated. 7.30 Met Mrs Parker, necessary talk (religious). 7.45 Meditated. 8 Read Prayers, expounded (Mr Horton and Mrs Hawkins there). 8.30 Necessary talk with Mr Horton. 9 Met Mrs Patterson and Mrs Hawkins, they [had] various talk. 9.30 Mrs Hawkins', religious talk with her (she not much affected). 9.45.

HOLY THURSDAY [JUNE 3]. 4 Private prayer. 5 Necessary talk with Mr Horton; walked. 5.45 At home; tea, religious talk. 6 Religious talk. 6.30 Meditated on sermon (+). 7 Meditated on sermon (attentive meditation, lively zeal). 8 Mr Hawkins', Mr Horton, etc, there, religious and useful talk. 9 At the house; meditated on sermon. 10 Meditated. 10.15 Dressed; meditated. 10.45 Read e c p p s h s c p t b (Mrs Hawkins there). 11 Christened person; Sacrament (five there). 12.30 Necessary talk with Delamotte; necessary business. 1 Mr Patterson's. 1.15 Mr Meyer's, christening, much company. 2 They [had] much talk. 2.30 Mr Hird's, good talk. 3 Saw house, necessary talk. 4 With workmen. 4.40 Writ diary; walked, meditated; visited. 5 Meditated. 6 Kempis. 6.30 Tea with Mrs Calwell; walked; prayed. 7 Mrs Patterson and Mrs Hawkins came, religious talk. 8 Read Prayers, expounded (Mrs Hawkins came). 8.30 Mrs

Hawkins and Patterson came, good talk. 9 Mostly religious talk; writ diary. 9.30 Necessary talk (religious) with Delamotte; prayed. 10.

Friday, June 4. 4 Private prayer. 5 At the house; prayed. 6 At home; journal. 7 Greek with Delamotte. 7.15 Mr and Mrs Hawkins, etc; tea, good talk. 8 Good talk (necessary). 8.45 House; prayed. 9 House. 9.45 Journal. 11 Read Prayers, expounded (Mrs Hawkins not [there]). 12 Dinner, religious talk. 12.40 Gother. 1 Slept. 1.30 Visited. 2.30 House. 3 House; necessary talk (religious) with Mrs Lascelles; Mrs Robinson's; walked; meditated. 4 Tea, religious talk (necessary). 5.15 House; supper. 6 Walked, Kempis. 7 Necessary talk with Mrs Patterson (she out of humour); with Mr and Mrs Hawkins. 8 Read Prayers, preached. 8.30 Mrs Patterson's, Mr and Mrs Hawkins there, good talk. 9 Good talk; prayed. 10.

Saturday, June 5. 4.15 Private prayer. 4.30 House. 4.45 Set out with Mr Hawkins, good talk. 5 Good talk; met Mr Lawley and Hird. 6 Fished. 7.15 Religious talk with Mr Hawkins. 8.15 Dressed; Mr Hawkins', Mr and Mrs Patterson, etc; tea, mostly religious talk. 9 Good talk (necessary and religious). 9.45 House. 10.30 Greek Testament. 11 Greek Testament; read Prayers, expounded. 12 Wrote diary; German. 1 Mrs Hawkins', company there; dinner, they [had] various talk (religious). 2 Good talk. 2.30 House, worked. 3 Worked. 4 With Mrs Hawkins, religious talk, close (she quite reserved!). 5 Walked with her to the Acre Lot; Mr Horton there; tea, mostly religious talk. 6 Walked, good talk (various). 7.15 At home; supper. 8 Read Prayers, expounded. 8.30 Mrs Hawkins sent for me, mostly religious talk. 9 They [had] various talk. 9.45 Prayed.

Providence: [blank]
Grace: 6 rating nine times [4 to 6, 7 to 8, 10 am to 2, 4 to 5, 8 to 9 pm]; 5 nine times.

Sunday, June 6. 4.15 Private prayer. 5 Prayed with Delamotte; dressed; sang. 6 Kempis; sang. 7 Mrs Patterson's, much company; tea; Mrs Hawkins there, religious talk (necessary). 8 Read Prayers, expounded (thirteen there). 9 Expounded. 9.30 Visited. 10 Sang; Greek Testament. 11 Read Prayers, preached (Mrs Hawkins not there, twenty-five there). 12 Sacrament (nine there). 12.30 Dinner, religious talk. 1 Religious talk with Reed. 1.30 Visited Levally. 2 Visited (convincing; +; lively zeal). 3 Read Prayers, expounded (twenty-six there). 4 Walked, meditated; writ diary. 4.30 Tea, religious talk. 5.45 With Mrs Hawkins, prayed for her (she seemed sick). 6 Walked; sang; Kempis; sang. 7 Kempis. 7.30 Religious talk with Delamotte. 8 Walked, meditated. 8.15 Religious talk with Mr and Mrs Calwell. 8.45 Mrs Patterson's, mostly religious talk. 9 Mrs Hawkins', religious talk (she quite open and seemed much affected!). 10 Religious talk. 10.45 Prayed.

Providence: Mrs Hawkins open, resolved, affected!!!
Grace: 7 rating five times [4 to 5, 6 to 7, 10 to 11 am, 2 to 3, 6 to 7]; 6 fourteen times; all [either six or seven]!

Monday, June 7. 4 Private prayer. 4.45 House, no men. 5 Sought them; necessary talk (religious) with Von Reck. 5.30 Sang. 6 Von Reck and brother and Ausperger came, tea, religious talk. 7 House, necessary talk. 7.45 Mrs Hawkins', religious and useful talk. 8 Read Mr Hawkins' Case, religious and useful talk. 9 Religious and useful talk (she open and seemed affected). 10.30 Visited. 10.45 Writ diary; Greek Testament. 11 Read c p p s h s c p t b, expounded (Mrs Hawkins there). 12 Dinner, religious talk. 12.20 Writ to Charles. 1 Necessary talk. 1.30 Necessary talk with Mrs Welch. 2 Visited. 3 With Mr Horton, etc, necessary and useful talk. 3.30 House. 3.45 Necessary talk. 4 Sent for, to Mr Heddon's, Mrs Hawkins and company there; tea. 5 Good talk. 5.30 Religious talk with Weston (close, he seemed affected). 6 House. 6.40 Walked; meditated. 7 Meditated. 7.50 Necessary talk. 8 Read Prayers, expounded; Mr Horton took Mrs Hawkins; meditated. 9 Meditated. 10 Could not sleep for flies, etc.

Grace: 7 rating once [4 to 5 am]; 6 twelve times [5 am to 1 pm, 2 to 3, 7 to 10]; 5 five times [1 to 2, 3 to 7 pm].

TUESDAY, JUNE 8. 4 Private prayer. 5 Slept. 5.30 Prepared. 6 Necessary business. 6.15 Mrs Hawkins and Mrs Patterson, Mr Hawkins, mostly religious talk (she very open!). 7 Religious talk. 7.30 All went; house. 8 House. 8.15 Journal. 9 Visited. 9.45 Greek Testament. 10 Mrs Hawkins, she in a passion, utterly unreasonable! 11 Read Prayers, expounded. 12 Dinner. 12.30 Visited. 2 Gun; slept. 2.45 Meditated. 3 Visited Lascelles, Sacrament. 3.30 Journal. 4 Mr Horton came; tea, necessary talk; Mrs Perkins came, good talk. 5 Walked; meditated; Mrs Hawkins would not [come]. 6 Kempis. 7 Religious talk (necessary) with Mr Dyson. 7.30 Greek Testament; meditated. 8 Read Prayers, Mrs Hawkins there, religious talk with her (she quite open, company came!). 9 Horton, etc; supper, they [had] good talk. 10 Mrs Patterson came, they [had] necessary talk. 11.

Grace: 7 rating once [4 to 5 am]; 6 eleven times [5 to 7, 9 am to 3, 5 to 7, 8 to 9 pm]; 5 seven times [7 to 9 am, 3 to 5, 7 to 8, 9 to 11 pm].

WEDNESDAY, JUNE 9. 4 Private prayer. 5 Dressed. 5.15 Private prayer; sang; prayed for Mrs Hawkins. 6 Tea, religious talk; Mrs Calwell's, necessary business. 7 Necessary business; meditated. 7.45 Journal. 8.30 Mrs Hawkins', Mrs Patterson there, mostly religious talk. 9 Mostly religious talk. 10 Visited; meditated. 10.45 Sang. 11.15 Read Prayers, expounded. 12.15 Dinner, religious talk. 1 House, worked. 2 Worked. 2.30 Visited. 3 Visited; Journal. 4 Tea with Delamotte and Reed, religious talk. 4.45 Horton came. 5 Writ to Charles and Oglethorpe. 6 Walked with Mrs Hawkins, Mrs Calwell, and Mrs Perkins, they [had] good talk. 7 Mostly religious talk. 7.45 Necessary talk with Delamotte. 8 Read Prayers, expounded; visited. 9 Visited. 9.15 Religious talk with Delamotte. 10.15.

Grace: 7 rating twice [4 to 6 am]; 6 five times [10 to 11 am, 4 to 6, 8 to 10 pm]; 5 eleven times [6 to 10, 11 am to 4, 6 to 8 pm].

THURSDAY, JUNE 10. 4.15 Private prayer. 5 Private prayer; prayed with Delamotte; dressed. 6 Necessary business; Account of People. 6.30 Mr and Mrs Hawkins, Mrs Calwell, religious and useful talk. 7 Mostly religious talk with Mrs Hawkins and Delamotte. 8 Mostly religious talk. 8.30 House. 9.30 Visited Mrs Patterson, ill; Mrs Hawkins there, religious and useful talk. 10 Good talk. 10.15 Greek Testament; dressed. 11 Read e c p p s h s c p t b (Mrs Hawkins not [there]). 12 Dinner, religious talk. 12.45 House. 1 House, worked. 2 Worked; necessary business. 3 Mrs Patterson's, Mrs Hawkins there; visited. 4 At home; tea; Mrs

Patterson came. 5 Mrs Calwell, Mr and Mrs Lawley, religious talk. 6 Religious and useful talk. 7 Supper. 7.15 Walked; meditated (attentive, fervent zeal). 8 Read Prayers, expounded (Mrs Hawkins not [there]). 8.45 Mark Hird, began singing. 9 Religious talk. 9.15 Walked with Delamotte, religious talk. 10.15.

Grace: 7 rating once [4 to 5 am]; 6 nine times [5 to 7, 11 am to 2, 5 to 6, 7 to 10]; 5 eight times [7 to 11 am, 2 to 5, 6 to 7 pm].

FRIDAY, JUNE 11. 4 Private prayer; necessary talk with Mr Hawkins (heavy). 5 Private prayer; (physic!). 6 Private prayer; German; sang. 7 Tea, religious talk. 7.15 Mrs Welch came, good talk. 7.45 Translated German. 8 Gother. 8.30 German. 10 German, dressed. 11 Read Prayers, expounded (Mrs Hawkins sad). 12.15 Began dinner; sent for, to the Fort, mostly religious talk with Mr Hawkins, etc. 1 With Mrs Hawkins (she angry); Mr Hawkins would not come. 2 Dinner with her, religious and useful talk (she milder). 3 Mr Hawkins came (she very angry), they quarreled. 4 He went; tea (she a little milder). 5 He came (she very angry); quarrel, alas! 6 Mostly religious talk with her, she could not hear (gained no ground). 7 Supper; walked; meditated. 8 Read Prayers, expounded. 8.45 Mrs Patterson, religious talk (close). 9 Religious talk. 9.30 Prayed.

Grace: 7 rating twice [4 to 6 am]; 6 ten times [6 to 10, 11 am to 3, 8 to 10 pm]; 5 six times [10 to 11 am, 3 to 8 pm].

SATURDAY, JUNE 12. 4.30 Private prayer. 5 Prayed with Delamotte; private prayer. 6 German; Greek Testament. 7 Tea, religious talk. 7.30 Mr and Mrs Hawkins came, good talk; tea. 8 Mostly religious talk. 8.45 Began *Christian Perfection*. 9.15 Necessary talk with Mr Horton. 9.30 Mr Hawkins', necessary talk. 9.45 Set out. 10 Good talk (necessary). 11 Prayed. 11.15 Read Prayers, expounded (Mrs Hawkins there). 12 Expounded. 12.15 Mr Hawkins'; dinner, mostly religious talk. 1 Mostly religious talk. 2.30 Visited (+; lively zeal). 4 Mrs Lawley's. 4.15 Mr Hawkins', Mrs Patterson, etc; tea, religious talk. 5 Mostly religious talk. 6 Walked; meditated; Kempis. 7 Kempis; meditated. 8 Read Prayers; expounded (Mrs Hawkins not [there]). 8.45 Sang with Delamotte, etc. 9 Supper, religious talk. 9.15 Walked with Delamotte, religious talk. 10 Mrs Hawkins came, invited me, religious talk (close). 10.15 Mr Hawkins, religious and useful talk. 11.

Grace: 7 rating twice [4 to 6]; 6 thirteen times [6 to 8, 9 to 10, 11 am to 2, 3 to 5, 6 to 11 pm]; 5 four times [8 to 9, 10 to 11 am, 2 to 3, 5 to 6 pm].

WHITSUNDAY [JUNE 13]. 6 Private prayer; tea, religious talk. 7 Dressed; meditated; private prayer; tea, religious talk. 8 Meditated. 8.15 Read Prayers, expounded (fifteen there). 9 Read Prayers. 9.30 Meditated; slept. 10 Greek Testament; meditated. 11 Meditated. 11.15 Read Prayers, preached (Mr Moore there, and thirty!). 12 Sacrament (twelve there). 12.30 Dinner, religious talk. 1 Religious talk. 1.15 Visited Tackner and Mr Calwell (they affected). 2 Walked; Kempis; meditated. 3 Read Prayers, expounded (thirty-seven there). 4 Mrs, Mark, Phoebe Hird, Betty Hassel came; tea, religious talk; sang. 5 Began *Christian Perfection*; sang. 5.45 Writ for Lascelles. 6 Walked; meditated; Kempis. 7 Kempis. 7.30 Mr Hawkins', necessary talk. 7.45 At home; prayed with Delamotte. 8 Supper, religious talk. 8.30 Mrs Hawkins' (she angry at me), religious and useful talk. 9 Religious and useful talk (gained no ground). 9.45.

Grace: 7 rating once [7 to 8 am]; 6 fifteen times.

MONDAY, JUNE 14. 4.15 Private prayer; 4.45 Religious talk with Delamotte. 5 Prayed with Delamotte. 5.15 Religious talk with Mr Patterson, with the Scotch [sic]. 6 Journal. 7 Mrs Patterson came, religious talk; tea. 8 Journal. 9 Sent for by Mr Tackner, religious talk, prayed. 9.45 German. 10 Translated German. 10.15 Law. 11 Meditated. 11.15 Read c p p s h s c p t b. 12 Dinner, religious talk. 12.30 Gother. 1 Visited Mrs Perkins, Mrs Calwell, Mrs Walker (lively zeal). 2 Religious talk (lively zeal); Andrew [and] Mrs Lascelles. 3 Nailed pales. 4 Prepared; prayed; Kempis. 5 Mrs Hawkins, Mr and Mrs Calwell; tea, religious and useful talk (Mrs Hawkins in good humour). 6 Mostly religious talk. 6.30 Walked with her, religious talk (close). 7 Religious talk. 8 Read Prayers, expounded. 8.45 Mr Hird, etc, sang. 9 Mrs Hawkins', supper, good talk (various). 10.15.

> Grace: 7 rating once [4 to 5 am]; 6 fifteen times [5 am to 5 pm, 6 to 9 pm]; 5 twice [5 to 6 pm, 9 to 10]. Light with Mrs Hawkins! *Cave!* ['Beware!']

TUESDAY, JUNE 15. 4.30 Private prayer; necessary talk. 5 Prayed with Delamotte; called Mr Hawkins, necessary talk. 6 Walked with Mr and Mrs Hawkins, good talk. 6.30 Religious and useful talk with Mrs Hawkins (she resigned!). 7 Mostly religious talk with her. 7.30 Delamotte and Mr Hawkins came; tea, necessary talk. 8 Necessary and useful talk. 9 Made arbour. 10 Visited. 10.15 Slept. 10.30 Greek Testament. 11 Read Prayers, expounded. 12 Dinner, religious talk. 12.30 Read journal to Delamotte. 1 Visited. 3 Mrs Hawkins' (she angry), religious talk (gained no ground). 3.15 Necessary business. 4 Worked. 4.15 Gother. 5 Religious talk. 5.15 Tea, religious talk. 5.45 Walked; religious talk. 6 Religious talk (necessary). 6.30 Gathered flowers. 7 Religious talk. 7.15 Met Mr and Mrs Hawkins, good talk. 7.45 Read Prayers. 8 Prayers, expounded. 8.30 Sang with Mark Hird, etc. 8.45 Mr Hawkins', they [had] good talk. 9.15 Supper, mostly religious talk. 10 Mr Hawkins went; religious talk (necessary) with Mrs Hawkins (close), she utterly renounced my friendship. Be it so!!

> Grace: 6 rating thirteen times [4 to 7, 10 am to 3, 4 to 6, 8 to 10 pm]; 5 six times.

WEDNESDAY, JUNE 16. 4 Private prayer; thought of Mrs Hawkins. 5 Writ to her. 6 Letter. 6.30 Tea, religious talk. 7 Letter. 9 Letter, ended. 10 Greek Testament. 11 Meditated; sang. 11.30 Read Prayers, expounded. 12 Visited Davison, Mrs Hawkins, company there (could not speak). 1 Took my leave of her. 1.15 Visited; prayed; sang. 2 Mr Reed, Delamotte, and Davison; sang; prayed; [read] Mr Law, religious talk; sang. 3 Mr Walker came, religious talk; he went; sang. 3.30 Tea, religious talk. 4 Religious talk (lively zeal). 4.30 Walked; sang. 5 Sang; meditated; thought of Mrs Hawkins. 6 Kempis; prayed for Oglethorpe, Mrs Hawkins, etc. 7 Meditated. 7.30 With Delamotte, religious talk. 7.45 Read Prayers (Mrs Hawkins there). 8 Read Prayers, expounded. 8.30 Phoebe, etc, sang. 9 Mrs Patterson, necessary talk (religious).

> Grace: 7 rating twice [1 to 2, 6 to 7 pm]; 6 fourteen times; 5 twice [9 to 10 am, 9 to 10 pm].

THURSDAY, JUNE 17. 4.15 Private prayer; prayed with Delamotte. 5 Slept. 6 Sang; religious talk. 6.30 Mrs Patterson and Mrs Calwell came, religious talk. 7 Tea, religious and useful talk. 8 Religious and useful talk. 8.15 Sang; necessary business; Greek Testament. 9 Mrs Calwell's (Mrs Hawkins came), necessary talk; walked, Law. 10 Law; meditated. 11 At home; talk of Mrs Hawkins with

Delamotte. 11.15 Dressed. 11.30 Read Prayers (six there). 12 Expounded. 12.15 Dinner; prayed; religious talk of Mrs Hawkins. 1 Necessary talk. 1.15 Visited Davis, Mr and Mrs Ward, religious talk. 2 Visited Faulconer, Heddon, etc, Mrs Lawley. 2.45 Journal. 3.45 Mrs Calwell's, Mrs Hawkins there, but went immediately; necessary talk of her. 4 Necessary talk (religious), Delamotte came; tea, necessary talk (religious). 5 Necessary talk (religious). 5.45 Walked; sang; reproved. 6 Sang; meditated. 7 Meditated. 7.15 Supper, necessary talk (religious). 8 Read Prayers, expounded. 8.30 Mark Hird, etc, sang. 9 Mrs Patterson's, company, they [had] good talk. 9.30 At home; necessary talk (religious); prayed. 10.

Grace: 6 rating sixteen times; 5 once [8 to 9 pm].

FRIDAY, JUNE 18. 4.40 Prayed with Delamotte; (well). 5 Private prayer; meditated; (well). 6 Meditated. 6.15 Breakfast. 6.20 Translated German. 7.30 Greek Testament. 8 Necessary talk with Horton; chocolate. 9 Religious talk (necessary) with Delamotte. 9.30 Meditated; sang. 10 Necessary talk with Hird. 10.30 Writ to Mrs Hawkins. 11 Necessary talk (religious). 11.15 Read Prayers, expounded; with Mrs Calwell. 12 Necessary talk with them. 12.15 Necessary talk (religious) of Mrs Hawkins. 12.45 Visited. 2 Mr Davison, Walker, Mark Hird; prayed; Law, religious talk; sang (lively zeal; +). 3 Mrs Calwell came; tea, religious talk. 4 Religious talk. 4.15 Walked; religious talk with Mr Hird. 4.45 Meditated. 5 Law; sang. 6 Delamotte came, religious talk. 7 At home; necessary talk (religious); dressed. 8 Read Prayers, expounded (Mrs Hawkins there); Phoebe Hird, etc. sang. 9 Mrs Calwell's, religious talk (necessary). 9.45 Talk of Mrs Hawkins with Delamotte. 10.

Grace: 7 rating once [2 to 3 pm]; 6 thirteen times [4 to 8, 9 to 11, noon to 2, 3 to 7, 8 to 10 pm]; 5 thrice [8 to 9, 11 to noon, 7 to 8 pm].

SATURDAY, JUNE 19. 4 Dressed. 4.15 At the bluff to take boat; Mr Oglethorpe came, necessary talk with him and Mr Horton; necessary talk with Mr Horton (he affected). 5 Necessary talk (religious) with Burk, of Savannah, alas! 5.15 Necessary business; prayed. 6 With Mr Horton, etc; necessary talk of Savannah. 7 Mrs Calwell's, went with Mr Hawkins, necessary talk. 7.45 Mrs Calwell's, tea, religious talk. 8 Religious talk. 8.30 Mrs Hawkins came; examined with her (she open and serious). 9 Necessary talk. 9.15 Necessary talk with Mr Horton. 9.45 Walked; Law. 10 Law. 11 Read Prayers, expounded (three there). 11.45 Necessary talk with Patterson. 12 Dinner, religious talk. 12.45 Visited Davison. 1 Visited Moore, Ward. 1.20 Writ notes. 2 Mark Hird came; sang; Law. 3 Sang. 3.15 Slept. 3.45 With Mr Oglethorpe, etc; dinner. 4 Dinner, they [had] various talk. 5 Mrs Calwell's, necessary talk (religious). 5.30 Walked; Law. 6 Law. 6.40 Delamotte came, religious and useful talk. 7 At home; necessary talk. 7.15 Mr and Mrs Hawkins came, necessary talk. 8 Read Prayers, expounded (Mrs Hawkins and Oglethorpe there; 31st Job). 8.45 Visited with Oglethorpe. 10 He talked to the Bailiffs. 11 He necessary talk to them.

Grace: 6 rating sixteen times [4 am to 4 pm, 5 to 6, 7 to 9 pm]; 5 four times [4 to 5, 6 to 7, 10 to 11 pm].

SUNDAY, JUNE 20. 6 Prayed with Delamotte; dressed; religious talk. 7 Mr Hawkins'; tea, religious talk. 8 Read Prayers, expounded (thirteen there). 9 Prayers. 9.30 Thought on sermon. 10 Thought; sang. 11 Read Prayers, preached (about forty there). 12 Sacrament. 12.30 Religious talk with

Oglethorpe, necessary talk. 1 Mr Calwell's, Mr and Mrs Hawkins there; dinner, good talk (necessary and religious). 2 Mostly religious talk. 2.15 Greek Testament. 3 Read Prayers, expounded (Oglethorpe there, about forty-four). 4 With Oglethorpe; necesssary talk with Francis Moore; supper. 4.45 At home; Mark Hird, etc, religious talk. 5 Tea, religious talk; sang; religious talk. 6 Walked; Law. 6.45 Delamotte came, religious talk. 7 Visited Ward. 7.30 Walked with Delamotte, religious talk. 8 Mrs Patterson's, religious talk. 8.15 Mrs Hawkins', Mrs Calwell there, religious talk (they angry). 9 Religious talk. 9.15 Religious talk with Mrs Calwell (she affected). 9.45.

Grace: 6 rating fifteen times; 5 once [1 to 2 pm].

MONDAY, JUNE 21. 4.45 Prayed with Delamotte. 5 Private prayer; meditated; sang. 6 Journal. 7 With Oglethorpe and Francis Moore, necessary talk; Mr and Mrs Hawkins at my house. 8 With Oglethorpe and Mrs Hawkins and Horton; tea, necessary talk. 9 Necessary talk. 10 At home; writ diary; Greek Testament; Journal; prayed. 11 Meditated. 11.15 Workmen; spoke to Oglethorpe; read Prayers, expounded. 12 Dinner, religious talk. 12.45 Visited Mrs Calwell, religious talk (necessary). 1 Visited Faulconer, Heddon, etc; White (all seemed affected). Necessary talk with Mr Hawkins. 2.15 Religious talk with Mrs Hawkins (she quite open and affected). 2.30 Visited. 4 Walked with Mr and Mrs Hawkins, religious talk. 4.30 Tea, religious and useful talk. 5 Good talk. 5.30 Religious talk with Mrs Hawkins (she affected); at home; house. 6 Religious talk (she affected). 6.15 Oglethorpe came, he [had] necessary talk. 6.45 Buried Lascelles. 7 Talked to them. 7.15 Mrs Hawkins', Oglethorpe there, he [had] necessary talk. 7.30 Supper, religious talk. 8 Read Prayers, expounded (Oglethorpe there). 8.45 Mark Hird, etc; sang; religious talk. 9 With Mrs Calwell, necessary talk (religious). 9.45 Prayed; necessary talk.

Grace: 6 rating fourteen times [4 to 6, 10 am to 10 pm]; 5 thrice [7 to 10 am].

TUESDAY, JUNE 22. 4.15 Private prayer; prayed with Delamotte. 5 Private prayer. 6 Packed. 6.45 Necessary talk with Horton (he very angry). 7 Necessary talk. 7.15 Mrs Calwell and Mrs Hawkins, tea, mostly religious talk. 8 Good talk (necessary and religious). 8.30 Journal. 10.30 Greek Testament. 11 Read Prayers, expounded; dressed. 12 Religious talk; dressed. 12.20 Mr Hawkins', religious talk (necessary) with him. 12.30 Dyson came, various talk. 12.45 Mrs Hawkins came, various talk. 1 Necessary talk. 1.30 Dinner, necessary talk. 2 Visited Mrs Levally, Welch, etc (they seemed affected). 3 Mrs Hawkins', necessary talk; visited Mrs Davison, religious talk. 3.30 Religious talk with Reed. 4 Necessary talk with Davison (gained no ground). 4.30 Visited. 5 Walked; Law; meditated. 6 Necessary talk with them. 6.30 Religious talk with Mrs Patterson (she in good temper); (lively zeal). 7 Religious talk; supper. 7.45 Read Prayers (Mrs Hawkins ill). 8 Expounded; Mark Hird, etc, sang. 9 Religious talk with Betty Hassel. 9.15 Necessary talk with Oglethorpe (gained no ground). 10.30 Sins of thought.

Grace: 7 rating twice [4 to 6 am]; 6 ten times [actually eleven, 6 to 7, 9 to noon, 2 to 3, 4 to 10 pm]; 5 six times [actually five, 7 to 9 am, noon to 2, 3 to 4 pm].

WEDNESDAY, JUNE 23. 4.45 Prayed with Delamotte; private prayer. 6 Journal. 7.30 Tea, religious talk. 8 Religious talk. 8.30 With Oglethorpe, talk of Savannah. 9 Mostly religious talk. 10 Religious talk of himself. 10.45 Mr Hawkins', necessary talk (religious; he quite open and affected). 11.15 Read Prayers, expounded (five there). 12. Religious talk with Delamotte. 12.30 Slept. 1 With Oglethorpe, writ for him. 2.15 Necessary business for him. 2.45 Mr Hawkins' (she in bed), necessary and useful talk. 3.15 Visited. 3.30 At home; tea, religious talk. 4 Mrs Calwell came, talk of Mrs Hawkins. 4.45 Packed. 5.30 Visited. 6 Sat by Mrs Hawkins (she very angry; gained little ground). 7 At home; meditated; Greek Testament; meditated; Mark Hird, etc; ill; religious talk; prayed. 8 Read Prayers, expounded; Mr Hird, etc; sang; religious talk. 9 Religious talk. 9.15 Mr Calwell's, necessary talk (religious). 9.30 Mrs Hawkins' (she very sad), prayed for her. 10 Mrs Patterson's; Mrs Calwell's, necessary talk (religious); faint. 10.15 Mr Hawkins' (she very sad). Oglethorpe there; religious talk with Mr Hawkins of her; took leave (she very soft); prayed. 11 In the piragua; prayed; slept. 12 Set out.

THURSDAY, JUNE 24. 4.40 Private prayer; Law (Houston and Tanner with us). 6 Writ to Mrs Hawkins. 7 Tea, they [had] necessary talk. 8 Letter. 11 Religious talk with Núñez. 11.30 Transcribed letter. 12.30 Dinner. 1 They [had] various talk. 1.30 Transcribed letter. 2 Ended letter. 2.30 Writ to Mr Calwell. 3.30 Tea. 4 Religious talk with Delamotte. 4.30 Law. 5 Meditated. 5.15 Sang. 6 Supper. 6.30 Meditated. 7 Private prayer; meditated. 8.30.

FRIDAY, JUNE 25. 4.30 Fitzwalter's boat came, went in it; Mr Colliton, Reeves, and Yoakley there, good talk. 8.30 Chocolate Island; breakfast; chocolate. 11 Sang. 11.30 With them, necessary and useful talk. 12.30 Set out. 3 Very hot. 8 Dog Island; necessary talk; supper, mostly religious talk. 11.

SATURDAY, JUNE 26. 4 Called them; chocolate. 5.15 Set out, mostly religious talk. 10 Thunderbolt; religious talk with Colliton, with Reeves (they convinced); tea. 11.15 Set out with Fitzwalter, religious talk (he seemed affected). 1 At home; religious talk with Charles; dinner. 2.30 With Oglethorpe, necessary talk (religious); read letter from Spangenberg (Oglethorpe open). 5 Visited. 6.30 Tea with Charles, etc, religious talk. 8 Read Prayers, expounded. 8.45 With Germans. 9.30 Oglethorpe's, read notes. 10 Oglethorpe came, religious talk (necessary). 12. Lay down.

SUNDAY, JUNE 27. 5 Private prayer; dressed; meditated. 6 Read Prayers, expounded (twenty there). 7 Necessary business; religious talk. 7.30 Tea, religious talk. 8 Religious talk; writ diary; read journal to Charles and Ingham. 9 Journal. 10 Greek Testament; religious talk. 10.30 Oglethorpe forbid prayers because Indians coming! 11 With him, spoke not. 11.30 Religious talk with Ingham. 12 With Germans; dinner, religious talk. 1 Religious talk. 1.30 At home; necessary talk (religious) with John and Indians. 2 Necessary business; religious talk; meditated. 3 Indians came; tea. 4 Indians. 5 Read Prayers, Charles preached (Oglethorpe and fifty there). Walked with Oglethorpe, religious talk (necessary; lively zeal). 6.45 Meditated. 7 With Germans, religious talk. 8 Supper with them, sang. 9 At home; religious talk; prayed. 9.30 Lay down in the garden.

Grace: 6 rating fourteen times [all but 3 to 5 pm].

MONDAY, JUNE 28. 4.15 Private prayer; meditated. 5 Read Prayers, expounded; necessary business. 6 Necessary business; removed to the Germans. 7 Necessary business. 7.30 Indians came. 8 Indians. 8.30 Necessary business;

necessary talk with Ingham of the alphabet. 9 Necessary talk with Ingham and John; all agreed. 10 Began Spanish. 11 Spanish. 12 Dinner, sang with Germans. 1 Spanish. 2 Meditated; thunder; slept. 3 At home; tea, religious talk (quite dispirited!). 4 Religious talk. 5 Religious talk; necessary business. 6 With John Brownfield, read journal. 7 Journal. 7.45 Read Prayers. 8.30 With Germans. 9 Religious talk with Ingham and Delamotte (they very zealous). 9.30 Prayed.

TUESDAY, JUNE 29. 4 Private prayer; prayed with Ingham and Delamotte (very heavy). 5 In the water (heavy). 6 With Germans; tea; John Brownfield came. 7 Read journal to him, religious talk. 8.15 With Oglethorpe, company there, they [had] necessary talk. 9 With Captain Watson, necessary talk. 10 Necessary talk (religious; I know nothing!). 10.30 Dressed; Charles read Prayers. 11 Preached; Sacrament (fourteen communicants). 12 With Germans; dressed. 12.30 Necessary business (very heavy). 1 Necessary business; necessary talk; writ diary (very heavy). 2 John Brownfield came, religious talk (necessary); (courage!). 3 Talk of Savannah (God help!). 4 Tomochichi, etc, religious talk; tea. 5 Mr Causton came, garden with him, necessary talk (he affected, sad!). 6 Meditated; supper; Von Reck, necessary talk. 7 Necessary talk; garden, meditated. 7.45 Read Prayers. 8 Expounded. 8.30 With Germans, sang (lively zeal). 9 At home; prayed. 9.15.
  Grace: 6 rating nine times [4 to 6, 7 to 8, 9 to 10, 11 to noon, 2 to 4, 5 to 6, 8 to 9 pm]; 5 eight times [6 to 7, 8 to 9, 10 to 11, noon to 2, 4 to 5, 6 to 8].

WEDNESDAY, JUNE 30. 5 Private prayer; physic; meditated (lively). 6 Garden; walked, Sharp's *Sermons*; tea with Delamotte, religious talk. 7 Garden; sang; *Sermons*. 8 Sang; *Sermons*. 9 Religious talk with John (thought of going to Choctaws). 10 Greek Testament; religious talk; meditated; prayed. 11 Read Prayers, expounded. 12 Religious talk with Miss Sophy at Mr Causton's (she affected). 12.30 Necessary talk. 1 Dinner, good talk (necessary); Colonel Blake. 2 With Oglethorpe, necessary talk; with Germans. 3.15 At home; religious talk with Ingham and Delamotte. 4 Religious talk (necessary); 5.30 Walked with Ingham and Delamotte, religious talk. 6 Religious talk (gained no ground with Ingham). 7 Religious talk. 7.45 Read Prayers. 8 Expounded. 8.30 With Germans. 9 Religious talk (clear; not go yet). 10.
  Grace: 6 rating twelve times [5 to 11 am, noon to 2, 4 to 5, 6 to 7, 8 to 10 pm]; 5 five times [11 to noon, 2 to 4, 5 to 6, 7 to 8 pm].

THURSDAY, JULY 1. 4.45 Dressed; read Prayers, expounded (very heavy). 5.30 Slept. 6 With Oglethorpe, could not speak. 6.30 At home; tea, religious talk with Delamotte. 7 Necessary talk; with Germans; writ diary. 7.45 Spanish. 9 Spanish; (sins of thought, sins). 10 Walked, meditated; Kempis; sang. 10.30 Mr Parker came, walked with him, necessary talk. 11 At his lot, mostly religious talk. 12 Set out with him, religious and useful talk. 12.30 At home; dinner, religious talk. 1 Necessary talk (religious). 1.30 Meditated; slept. 2 Visited Mrs Smith, Mr Dearn (he civil). 3 At home; religious talk with Ingham and Delamotte. 4 At the Indian Talk. 5 At the Talk. 6 At home; supper, religious talk. 7 Garden, meditated; Greek Testament. 8 With Germans. 9 Prayer; religious talk. 9.30.
  Grace: 6 rating eleven times [4 to 7, 10 am to 1, 2 to 6, 7 to 9 pm]; 5 five times [7 to 10 am, 1 to 2, 6 to 7 pm].

FRIDAY, JULY 2. 4 Private prayer; slept. 5 Private prayer; Germans', Gother, sang. 6 Translated verses; sang; Spanish; (lively zeal). 7 Verses; sang; Spanish. 8 Verses; sang; Spanish. 9 Sang; Spanish; verses. 10 Verses; sang. 10.30 Meditated. 10.45 Read Prayers. 11 Expounded, Ingham read Prayers. 12 Visited Betty Wright, etc. 1 Writ letter for Charles. 2 Letter. 3 Prayer with them; tea, religious talk (necessary). 4 Letter. 4.30 Sang. 5 Verses; sang. 6 Walked, rain; Germans', sang, Kempis, prayed. 7 At home; supper, religious talk (necessary). 8 With Germans, sang, religious talk with them. 9 Prayed.

Grace: 7 rating thrice [4 to 6 am, 6 to 7 pm]; 6 nine times [6 to 11 am, noon to 1, 3 to 4, 5 to 6, 8 to 9]; 5 five times [11 to noon, 1 to 3, 4 to 5, 7 to 8].

SATURDAY JULY 3. 4.30 Private prayer. 5 Private Prayer. 5.30 Read prayers, expounded; physic. 6 Dr Núñez, religious talk. 7 Tea, religious talk. 7.30 Oglethorpe sent for me, religious talk with him. 8 Religious talk; he writ a letter for me to the Bishop of London. 9 At home; tea, religious talk; dressed. 10 Oglethorpe sent for me; to court, Indians there. 11 Necessary talk. 12 Captain Watson came, tried. 1 He was heard. 2 Oglethorpe took leave of Indians. 2.30 Oglethorpe's with Chigilly and Malachi, dinner, religious and useful talk. 3 Religious talk with them. 4 Necessary talk; company came. 4.45 At home; Appee there; garden, religious talk. 5 Religious talk with him. 5.15 Private prayer; sang. 6 Supper, religious talk. 7 Visited James [Burnside]. 7.30 Miss Bovey's, mostly religious talk. 8 Religious talk (they seemed affected). 8.30 With Germans, sang. 9 Religious talk with them. 9.30 Necessary talk.

Grace: 6 rating thirteen times [4 to 9, 10 am to 4, 5 to 6, 7 to 9]; 5 four times [9 to 10 am, 4 to 5, 6 to 7, 9 to 10 pm].

SUNDAY, JULY 4. 4.15 Private prayer. 5 Kempis; sang. 5.45 Dressed. 6 Necessary talk with Charles. 6.15 Read Prayers, expounded. 7 Tea, religious talk. 8 Mr Colliton came, various and useful talk; Chigilly, necessary talk with them. 9 Necessary talk with them. 9.45 Garden, Greek Testament. 10 Greek Testament; meditated. 11 Ingham read Prayers, preached (lively zeal). 12 Sacrament (seventeen communicants). 12.15 Prayer with Delamotte. 12.30 Dinner, religious talk. 1 Religious talk. 1.30 Writ to Rivington. 1.45 Read Sermon. 2 Greek Testament. 3 Visited Peter [Wright?]. 3.20 Religious talk. 4 Ingham read Prayers, christened. 5 Preached. 5.30 [Read] Hickes with Delamotte. 6 Supper, religious talk. 7 Mostly religious talk. 7.30 Visited Mrs Smith; walked, meditated. 8 Germans'; sang; religious talk. 9 Necessary talk. 9.30.

Grace: 7 rating once [4 to 5 am]; 6 twelve times [5 to 8, 9 am to 3, 4 to 6, 7 to 9 pm]; 5 four times [8 to 9 am, 3 to 4, 5 to 7 pm].

MONDAY, JULY 5. 4 Sang; garden; slept. 5 Sang; read Prayers; (very happy). 6 Germans'; writ notes; sang. 6.30 J Wedge came, necessary talk (religious). 7 Religious talk with Margaret Walmsley. 7.30 At home; tea, religious talk. 8 Sent for by Captain Watson, necessary talk (religious; he seemed much affected). 9 Letter from Mrs Hawkins. 9.30 Transcribed Herbert. 10 Sang; Herbert; sang. 11 With Delamotte, read notes. 11.30 Necessary business; Mrs Pember's, religious talk. 12 Necessary talk with Butler. 12.15 At home; necessary business. 12.30 Dinner, necessary talk (religious). 1 Dinner. 1.15 Visited. 3 At home; writ to Mrs Hawkins. 4 Walked with Charles, necessary talk (religious). 5 Mrs Parker's, necessary talk, religious talk. 5.45 At home; prayed. 6 Supper.

6.45 Religious talk. 7 Religious talk (necessary and useful). 7.45 Read Prayers. 8 Expounded. 8.15 Visited; Germans'; sang. 9 Religious talk with them. 9.30. Grace: 6 rating ten times [4 to 7, 8 am to 1, 2 to 3, 8 to 10 pm]; 5 seven times [8 to 9 am, 1 to 2, 3 to 8 pm].

TUESDAY, JULY 6. 4 Sang; slept. 4.30 Prayed with Delamotte; (very heavy). 5 Read Prayers, expounded; walked with Miss Sophy, Miss Fawset, religious talk (not close!). 6 Religious talk. 6.15 At home; with Miss Sophy and Miss Fawset; tea, religious talk. 7 Religious talk with Charles; Germans'; writ diary. 8 Writ to Mrs Hawkins; sang. 9 Letter; sang. 10 Transcribed letter. 11.30 Garden; walked; sang. 12 Dinner, religious talk. 1 Writ for Charles (lively zeal). 2 Abridged Carolina Papers. 3 Abridged. 4 Mr and Mrs Parker came, mostly religious talk; tea. 5 Good talk (necessary). 5.30 Writ diary; necessary talk; prayed. 6 Supper, religious talk. 6.30 Abridged. 7 Walked; Greek Testament; meditated. 7.45 Read Prayers. 8 Expounded. 8.20 With Germans. 9 Prayed; could not sleep. 9.45.

Grace: 6 rating eleven times [4 to 6, 8 to 10, noon to 2, 5 to 10 pm]; 5 six times [6 to 8, 11 to noon, 2 to 5 pm].

WEDNESDAY, JULY 7. 4 Private prayer (heavy). 4.45 Lively private prayer. 5 In the water with Charles and Delamotte. 6 Prayed with Delamotte; breakfast; necessary business. 7 Cleaned and catalogued books. 8 Catalogued. 9.15 Dressed. 9.30 Writ diary; slept; transcribed verses. 10 Transcribed verses; sang. 11 Read Prayers, expounded. 12 Read Prayers. 12.15 Sang. 12.40 Visited; lightning (not afraid!). 1 Visited Betty Wright; prayed; religious talk. 2 Visited Mrs Mellichamp, necessary talk. 3 At home; sang; dinner, religious talk. 4 Read for Charles. 4.30 Writ for Charles. 5 Sang; prayed. 5.30 Slept. 5.40 Greek Testament; sang. 6 Miss Bovey's, Mrs Vanderplank there; they [had] various talk. 7 They [had] various talk. 7.40 Prayers (they there), expounded (lively zeal; convincing). 8 Read Prayers. 8.15 With Germans; sang; religious talk. 9 Religious talk with Delamotte; prayed. 9.30.

Grace: 7 rating twice [4 to 5 am, 5 to 6 pm]; 6 seven times [6 to 7, 11 am to 2, 3 to 4, 8 to 10]; 5 nine times [5 to 6, 7 to 11 am, 2 to 3, 4 to 5, 6 to 8 pm].

THURSDAY, JULY 8. 4 Garden; private prayer (lively; well!). 5 Read Prayers, expounded (ten there); garden; necessary business. 6 Necessary business in garden; necessary talk. 7 Tea, necessary talk. 8 Cleaned, etc, books. 9 Necessary business in garden. 9.45 Germans'; writ diary. 10 Sang; writ diary; transcribed verses. 11 Visited. 11.45 Verses. 12 At home; Mr Parker there; dinner, necessary talk (useful and religious). 1 Oglethorpe sent for me, religious talk (necessary). 2 Oglethorpe, necessary talk with them. 3 He [had] necessary talk. 3.30 Took boat with him, necessary talk (religious). 4.30 Tomochichi's, he very ill; necessary talk. 5 Talk with Oglethorpe of Mellichamp and Parker (I convinced). 6 Ingham and Mrs Musgrove came, necessary talk. 6.30 Took boat; religious talk. 7 Oglethorpe ill for grief, religious talk. 7.45 Read Prayers. 8 Expounded. 8.15 At home; supper; Mrs Smith, good talk. 8.45 Germans'; sang. 9.15 At home; garden; religious talk with Delamotte (lively zeal). 9.30.

Grace: 7 rating once [4 to 5 am]; 6 seven times [5 to 6, 10 to noon, 1 to 2, 4 to 5, 7 to 8, 9 to 10]; 5 nine times [7 to 10 am, noon to 1, 2 to 4, 5 to 7, 8 to 9 pm]; 4 once [6 to 7 am].

FRIDAY, JULY 9. 4 Private prayer; sang; (very lively; well!). 5 Prayed; private prayer; sang. 6 Breakfast. 6.30 Germans'; transcribed verses. 7 Verses; sang. 8 Sang; verses; sang (lively zeal). 9 Sang; verses; sang; prayed (convinced). 10 Garden, meditated. 11 Read Prayers, expounded (eleven there). 12.15 With Oglethorpe, necessary talk. 1 Necessary talk. 1.30 Visited. 2.45 Read resolutions. 3 At home; read resolutions. 3.30 Dinner, religious talk. 4 Visited. 5.30 Necessary business; prayed with Delamotte. 6 With Delamotte; supper, religious talk. 7 Sent for by Oglethorpe, religious talk (necessary). 7.45 Read Prayers, expounded. 8 Read Prayers. 8.15 Germans'. 8.45 Mrs Smith, religious talk (necessary); ate fish. 9.15 Garden; religious talk with Delamotte; prayed. 10.

Grace: 7 rating twice [4 to 6 am]; 6 ten times [6 to noon, 2 to 3, 4 to 5, 9 to 10 pm]; 5 six times [noon to 2, 3 to 4, 6 to 8 pm].

SATURDAY, JULY 10. 4 Private prayer. 4.45 Oglethorpe came, religious talk (lively zeal; well!). 5 Read Prayers, expounded (twelve there); Oglethorpe came home with me; garden; religious talk, he right. 6 Religious talk (necessary); tea. 7 Necessary talk (religious). 8 Walked with Oglethorpe, necessary talk (religious). 8.30 At home; house; tea, they [had] necessary talk; prayed for Oglethorpe. 9 Religious talk (necessary) with him. 10 Religious talk (necessary). 12.30 At home; dinner, religious talk (necessary; he quite right and serious). 1.30 Writ diary; verses; prayed. 2 Visited. 3 With Germans, religious talk (necessary); sang. 4 Mr Parker came; necessary talk (religious). 4.30 Greek Testament; dressed. 5 Read Prayers, expounded. 5.15 Necessary talk with Mr Dyson. 6 Supper. 6.15 At the court; Miss [Becky] Bovey died, saw her! 7 Court. 7.15 Miss [Margaret] Bovey's; violent storm; prayed with Oglethorpe. 8 Religious talk with Miss Bovey; prayed. 8.30 German. 9 Religious talk with Delamotte and Charles. 9.45.

Grace: 7 rating once [4 to 5 am]; 6 ten times [5 to 7, 8 to 9 am, 2 to 3, 4 to 10 pm]; 5 seven times [7 to 8, 9 am to 2, 3 to 4 pm].

SUNDAY, JULY 11. 4.30 Private prayer (lively). 5 Private prayer; prayed with Ingham; sang. 6 Read Prayers, expounded (nineteen there). 7 Garden, thought on sermon. 8 Tea, religious talk. 9 Writ on Miss Bovey. 10.15 Miss Bovey's, religious talk with Mrs Weddal. 11 Ingham read Prayers, preached; Sacrament (eighteen communicants). 12 Sang; dinner, religious talk. 12.45 German; writ. 1 Writ on Miss Bovey. 3.45 Religious talk with Delamotte. 4 Religious talk with Oglethorpe. 4.45 Religious talk with Charles and Ingham. 5 At Miss Bovey's funeral; no talk. 5.45 Read Prayers. 6 Read Prayers, preached. 7 Buried Miss Bovey, spoke. 7.30 Supper, religious talk (necessary). 8 Good talk. 8.15 German. 8.45 Garden, meditated. 9 Religious talk with Ingham; prayed. 9.20.

Grace: 7 rating twice [actually thrice, 4 to 6 am, 6 to 7 pm]; 6 eleven times [6 am to 2, 4 to 6, 7 to 8 pm]; 5 thrice [2 to 4, 8 to 9 pm].

MONDAY, JULY 12. 4 Walked; private prayer (lively). 5 Read Prayers; religious talk (necessary) with Miss Sophy; meditated. 6 Tea, religious and useful talk. 7 German. 8 Sent for by Oglethorpe; religious talk (lively zeal; convincing). 9 Necessary talk (religious). 10 Began methodizing his business. 11 Necessary talk (religious). 12 Company came; writ to Mr Appee. 1 Writ to Mr Calwell; they [had] necessary talk. 2.15 Dinner, good talk. 2.45 Necessary talk with

Delamotte and Charles. 3 Writ to Calwell. 3.30 Writ diary; visited. 4 Visited. 4.30 Meditated; private prayer. 5 Prayed. 5.15 Supper. 5.30 Visited. 6.15 Miss Bovey's, religious talk (she in excellent temper!). 7 Religious talk (she seemed much affected). 8 Read Prayers, expounded. 8.30 Germans'. 9 Religious talk with Germans. 9.30 At home.

Grace: 7 rating twice [4 to 5, 8 to 9 am]; 6 twelve times [5 to 6, 7 to 8, 9 am to 1, 3 to 9 pm]; 5 four times [6 to 7 am, 1 to 3, 9 to 10 pm].

TUESDAY, JULY 13. 4 Private prayer. 4.15 Slept. 4.30 Prayed; dressed. 5 Read Prayers, expounded (thirteen there). 5.30 Read Charles' letter to Oglethorpe. 6 Tea, religious talk; Mrs Lacy came, religious and useful talk. 7.30 Read letter. 7.45 Oglethorpe's, he asleep; meditated; prayed. 8 With Oglethorpe, necessary talk (religious); letters. 9 Sorted letters. 9.45 At home; necessary talk; sang. 10 Writ for parish. 11 Visited. 12 Dinner, religious talk; read letters. 1.15 Visited. 3 At home; religious talk with Ingham and Delamotte. 3.45 Visited. 4.30 Mrs Causton, etc, came; religious talk; tea. 5 Religious talk with Miss Sophy, much talk. 6 Supper, necessary talk (religious). 7 Meditated; prayed; necessary talk; ate with Ingham. 8 Read Prayers, expounded. 8.30 Germans, religious talk. 9 Religious talk (necessary) with Delamotte; prayed. 9.30.

Grace: 7 rating once [4 to 5 am]; 6 six times [11 to noon, 1 to 3, 4 to 5, 8 to 9 pm]; 5 eleven times [6 to 11 am, noon to 1, 3 to 4, 5 to 8, 9 to 10 pm].

WEDNESDAY, JULY 14. 4.30 Prayer; dressed; (lively). 4.45 Read Prayers (eleven there). 5 Expounded. 5.15 Oglethorpe's; private prayer. 5.45 Read letters. 6 Letters. 8 Tea. 8.15 Writ to Mrs Hawkins. 9 Letter. 10 Oglethorpe's; necessary business. 11 Writ for him. 1.30 Dinner. 2 Necessary talk. 2.30 Writing interrupted by visitor. 3 Writ; interrupted. 4 Writ; interrupted. 5 Writing. 5.45 At home; dressed. 6 Supper. 6.15 Miss Bovey's, Miss Sophy there; tea, religious talk. 7 Began Young's *Last Day*. 7.45 Oglethorpe came; necessary talk (they much affected). 8 Read Prayers, expounded; Miss Bovey's, ended [Young]. 9 Religious talk on dress and company (close). 9.45 At home; prayed.

Grace: 6 rating ten times [4 to 7, 9 to noon, 6 to 10 pm]; 5 eight times [7 to 9 am, 12 to 6 pm].

THURSDAY, JULY 15. 4.15 Prayer; called Oglethorpe (he not ready). 4.45 Read Prayers. 5 Expounded; transcribed [letter] to Mrs Hawkins. 6 Transcribed. 6.30 At home; tea, religious talk. 7 Oglethorpe's; writ for him. 8 Tea; writ for him. 9 Writ. 11 Necessary talk. 11.30 Visited. 12 Dinner, religious talk; meditated. 1.15 Visited Mrs Smith, necessary talk (religious and useful); Mrs Bush, religious talk. 2 Visited Mr Gilbert (close, he deeply serious). 3 At home; transcribed [letter] to Mr Appee; writ diary. 4 Visited Johnson, religious talk with him. 5 Mr Ducat; at home; tea, necessary talk. 6 Garden with Delamotte; prayed. 6.15 Miss Bovey's, company there, necessary and useful talk. 7 Read my sermon (she in tears). 7.45 Read Prayers, expounded. 8 Expounded. 8.30 Germans. 9 Religious talk with them. 9.30 Prayed.

Grace: 6 rating nine times [4 to 5, 6 to 7, 11 to noon, 2 to 3, 6 to 9]; 5 nine times [5 to 6, 7 to 10 am, noon to 2, 3 to 4, 5 to 6].

FRIDAY, JULY 16. 4.15 Private prayer; read Prayers. 5 Expounded; letter. 6 Oglethorpe's; writ for him. 7 Writ. 8 Writ; tea. 9 Writ. 1.30 Dinner. 2 Necessary talk (useful and religious). 3 Writ. 4 Sorted papers. 4.30 At home; private prayer; meditated. 5 Meditated; prayed with Delamotte. 5.30 Oglethorpe sent for me; writ for him. 6 Writ. 6.30 Miss Bovey's, religious talk. 7 Religious talk (close). 8 Read Prayers, expounded; Germans'. 9 Religious talk. 9.15 Prayed.

SATURDAY, JULY 17. 4.30 Prayed; read Prayers, expounded. 5.15 Private prayer; meditated. 6 Oglethorpe's; he asleep; writ verses. 6.30 Prayed. 7 Verses. 7.45 Tea. 8 Petitions. 12.15 Sorted them. 1 Sorted. 1.30 Dinner. 2 Necessary talk (religious). 2.30 Visited Gilbert. 3 At home; religious talk; writ diary. 3.45 Writ notes. 4 Visited. 5 Mr Causton's, necessary talk (religious). 5.30 At home; tea, religious talk. 6 Necessary business. 6.15 Miss Bovey's, Miss Sophy there; tea, religious talk. 7 Religious talk (close; she affected). 8 Read Prayers, expounded; Germans, necessary talk with them. 9 Necessary talk. 9.15 At home; necessary talk (religious); prayed. 9.30.

Grace: 6 rating ten times [4 to 8 am, noon to 1, 3 to 8 pm]; 5 eight times [8 to noon, 1 to 3, 8 to 10 pm].

SUNDAY, JULY 18. 4 Private prayer. 4.30 Slept. 4.45 Private prayer; (lively). 5 Private prayer; dressed. 6 Necessary business. 6.15 Read Prayers, expounded. 7 Ingham read Prayers. 7.15 Religious talk; tea. 8 Religious talk. 8.45 Walked, Greek Testament. 9 Meditated; religious talk with Delamotte. 9.45 At Mrs Pember's. 10 Married her and Sir Francis Bathurst. 10.30 Read Prayers. 11 Sermon; Sacrament (seventeen communicants). 12 Writ diary; dinner, religious talk. 1 Garden, Greek Testament. 2 Catechized. 3 Visited. 3.30 Read prayers, catechized (sixty there). 4 Sermon. 4.45 Prayed. 5.15 Supper, religious talk. 5.45 Miss Bovey's; tea, religious talk. 6 Religious talk (she affected). 7 Scougal. 8.15 Germans'. 9 At home; garden; meditated; Scotsman came. 9.30 Charles came.

Grace: 7 rating once [4 to 5 am]; 6 fourteen times [5 to 7, 9 am to 9 pm]; 5 thrice [7 to 9 am, 9 to 10 pm].

MONDAY, JULY 19. 4.30 Private prayer (lively zeal). 5 Read Prayers, religious talk with Ingham, etc. 6 Oglethorpe not up (Miss Bovey up); necessary talk (religious). 7 Writ verses; read resolutions. 7.45 Germans'; meditated. 8 Oglethorpe's; religious talk with Miss Fawset. 8.30 At home; Mr Andrews, necessary talk; tea. 9 Necessary talk. 9.20 Mr Oglethorpe's; necessary business. 10 Writ for him. 11 Petitions; interrupted. 12 Petitions; interrupted. 1 Writ for him. 1.15 Dinner, good talk (necessary). 2 Petitions. 3 Writ for him. 4 Sorted papers. 4.30 At home; writ diary; visited. 5 Visited. 5.40 Miss Bovey's, Mr Burnside there; religious talk. 6 Miss Sophy, religious talk (she not go to Ball). 7 Scougal; religious talk. 8 Read Prayers, expounded. 8.30 Germans; Ingham left us. 9 Religious talk with Germans. 10 Religious talk with Delamotte; sang (lively zeal).

Grace: 7 rating once [4 to 5 am]; 6 eight times [7 to 8, 9 to 11 am, 5 to 10 pm]; 5 nine times [5 to 7, 8 to 9, 11 am to 5 pm].

TUESDAY, JULY 20. 4 Private prayer (lively zeal). 5 Read Prayers, expounded; religious talk with Miss Sophy (Miss Bovey up). 6 Writ journal. 7 Tea, religious talk; journal. 8 Journal. 9 With Chickasaws, religious talk. 10 Writ our conference. 11 Writ. 12 Visited; dinner, religious talk. 1 Writ. 1.45 Read it to Germans. 2 Visited. 3.45 Religious talk with Charles and Delamotte; religious talk. 4.30 Visited. 5 Chickasaws' last audience. 6 At home; supper. 6.15 Miss

Bovey's, Miss Hopkey there, religious talk. 7 Scougal. 8 Read Prayers, expounded. 8.45 Germans. 9 Religious talk with them. 9.45 Religious talk.
  Grace: 7 rating once [4 to 5 am]; 6 twelve times [5 to 11 am, noon to 1, 2 to 4, 5 to 8 pm]; 5 four times [11 to noon, 1 to 2, 4 to 5, 8 to 10 pm].

Wednesday, July 21. 4.30 Sang; private prayer. 5 Read Prayers, expounded; necesssary talk with Mr Causton. 6 Necessary business; writ notes. 6.30 Religious talk with Miss Sophy. 6.45 Oglethorpe's, necessary talk. 7 Religious talk (necessary) with him. 8 Petitions; tea. 9 Company came; necessary talk (religious) with Mrs Causton. 10 Necessary talk with Charles and Delamotte; writ to Mrs Hawkins. 11 Read letters. 12 Journal; writ to Mrs Hawkins. 1 Journal. 3 Tea, religious talk. 4 Dressed; garden, read Heylyn; prayed. 5 Prayed; visited. 5.45 Miss Bovey's, tea; Miss Hopkey there, religious talk. 6 Religious talk; Miss Núñez came, religious talk. 7 Religious talk. 7.30 She went; religious talk (close). 8 Read Prayers, expounded. 8.45 Germans'. 9 Sang; religious talk; at home; prayed. 10.
  Grace: 7 rating once [4 to 5 am]; 6 ten times [5 to 6, 7 to 9, 11 am to 1, 3 to 6, 7 to 8, 9 to 10 pm]; 5 seven times [6 to 7, 9 to 11 am, 1 to 3, 6 to 7, 8 to 9 pm].

Thursday, July 22. 4.30 Private prayer. 5 [Read] Prayers, expounded; note to Miss Bovey. 6 With Oglethorpe; writ for him. 7 Writ. 7.30 Tea. 8 Writ. 11 Petitions; writ. 12 Writ. 12.45 Dinner. 1 Dinner; religious talk with Oglethorpe. 2 Religious talk (necessary). 2.30 Company came; necessary business. 3 Mr Johnson came, good talk (necessary). 4 Mr Causton's; visited. 5 Visited. 5.40 Miss Bovey's, religious talk; tea. 6.15 Called; meditated. 6.30 Buried. 7 Miss Bovey's; Scougal. 7.30 Charles came; at home; supper, religious talk. 8 Read Prayers, expounded. 8.45 Germans. 9 Religious talk. 10.

Friday, July 23. 4.30 Private prayer. 5 Read Prayers, expounded. 5.45 Miss Sophy; garden, religious talk. 6 Religious talk (she open and affected). 6.30 Oglethorpe's; religious talk (necessary); tea. 7 Religious talk (necessary); necessary talk. 8 Writ. 9 At home; writ to Mr Hutcheson. 10 To Mr Vernon. 11 Oglethorpe's; necessary talk. 1.30 Dinner. 2.30 Company; necessary talk. 3 Necessary and useful talk. 3.45 Meditated. 4 At home; meditated; dressed; writ diary. 4.45 Prayed. 5.15 Ate, religious talk. 5.45 Visited. 6 Miss Bovey's; tea, religious talk; Scougal. 7 Scougal. 8 Read Prayers, expounded; Oglethorpe's; necessary talk (religious). 9 Necessary talk (religious). 10.45.
  Grace: 7 rating once [4 to 5 am]; 6 seven times [6 to 7 am, 4 to 10 pm]; 5 eleven times [5 to 6, 7 am to 4, 10 to 11 pm].

Saturday, July 24. 4.45 Private prayer. 5 Private prayer; read Prayers, expounded; Oglethorpe's; necessary talk. 6 Necessary talk; at home; Oglethorpe came; tea, good talk. 7 Court-house with Oglethorpe; none came. 8 Writ notes; necessary business. 9 Court-house. 1 At home; dinner; writ notes. 2 Visited. 3.30 Oglethorpe's; they [had] necessary talk. 4 They [had] various talk. 5 Mr Causton's; Mr Jeffrey's; necessary talk (religious). 6 Buried. 6.15 Miss Bovey's; tea, religious talk. 7 Garden, religious talk with (she very zealous). 8 Read Prayers, expounded; Oglethorpe's; at home; supper, necessary talk. 9 Necessary talk (religious). 9.30 Prayer.
  Grace: 7 rating once [5 to 6 pm]; 6 six times [4 to 6 am, 2 to 4, 6 to 8 pm]; 5 eleven times [6 am to 2, 4 to 5, 8 to 10 pm].

July 26. I set out for Charleston. In my journey, hearing Mr. Mellichamp was gone to Savannah, I was deeply concerned, having often heard her say that she hoped God would keep him out of her sight, at least till her mind was stronger, for if she was to see him then, she could deny him nothing. I prayed earnestly that he who alone was able, would snatch her out of the fire. And he did indeed stir up his power and save her with a great deliverance.

SUNDAY, JULY 25. 4.30 Private prayer. 5 Private prayer; prayed with Delamotte. 6 Dressed; [read] Prayers, expounded (Miss Bovey there and nineteen!). 7 Tea with Oglethorpe; letters. 8 Writ for him. 9 Writ. 10.45 [Read] Prayers (Oglethorpe there and seventy!). 11 Charles preached; Sacrament (Miss Bovey there and seventeen). 12 Transcribed letter; writ for Oglethorpe. 1 Writ. 1.30 Dinner, necessary talk (religious). 2.30 Writ for him. 3 Writ. 4.30 Read Prayers. 5 Charles preached; necessary business. 6 Writ diary [summary]. 6.20 Miss Bovey's; Oglethorpe there; tea, religious and useful talk. 7 Religious and useful talk. 9 Oglethorpe went; religious talk; supper, religious talk (close). 10 Religious talk. 10.45 At home.

MONDAY, JULY 26. 4.45 Private prayer. 5.15 Read Prayers, expounded (Miss Bovey there!); necessary business. 6 Oglethorpe's; letters; tea; letters. 7.30 Germans'; religious talk; necessary business. 8 Miss Bovey's; religious talk; Oglethorpe's; letters; necessary business; necessary talk. 12 At the bay. 12.30 Set out; dinner; (wind contrary). 1 Read Account of Carolina. 3.30 Bathed. 4. Ate; Account. 6.30 Supper. 8.30 Slept.

TUESDAY, JULY 27. 5.30 Prayer; sang. 6 Read Law. 5.45 Set out; writ diary. 7 German, Law, alternè. 10 Harris'; religious talk; tea. 11 With sick woman; religious talk; read Prayers, expounded. 12 Walked with Charles; meditated; religious talk. 1 Religious and useful talk. 1.45 Dinner. 2 Necessary and useful talk. 3 Necessary talk. 3.15 Set out; sang; Law. 5 Private prayer; sang. 6 Supper, necessary and useful talk. 8 Rowed. 9.

WEDNESDAY, JULY 28. 5.30 Private prayer. 6 Law. 7 Hilton Head; tea, necessary talk. 8 Walked; sang; Law. 9 Read Prayers, expounded (Mrs Dawson much affected). 9.45 Boat. 10.15 Set out; sang; Law. 12 Melon. 12.30 Sang. 1 Read Law to them; sang; Law. 3 Melon; good talk (various). 4 Law; sang. 6 Ate, necessary talk (useful and religious). 7.30 Beaufort; Mr Woodward and the Committee, necessary talk. 8 Serjeant's with them; necessary and useful talk. 9.15 Supper, necessary and useful talk. 11 To bed.

THURSDAY, JULY 29. 4.30 Meditated. 5 Tea, mostly religious talk. 6.30 Set out (wind fair); sang; Law. 7 Writ diary; German; Law. 11 St Helena River (wind!). 12.15 Dinner (well); St Helena Sound (storm, sail broke!). 3 Safe on shore; religious talk with Charles; sang; Law; writ diary. 5 Sang; private prayer. 6 Supper, necessary and useful talk. 7 Rowed, necessary and useful talk. 9 Slept.

FRIDAY, JULY 30. 4.30 Private prayer. 5 Private prayer; sang, necessary talk (religious); (wind fair). [6] Began Macarius. 6.30 Bennett's Point; Macarius. 7 Tea, necessary talk (religious); Macarius. 8 Macarius; read Prayers, expounded. 8.45 Boat; Macarius; sang. 9 Macarius; sang; writ diary. 10 Macarius; sang; (rain). 11 Sang; Macarius (rain). 12 Various and useful talk. 12.30 Bread and butter, mostly religious talk; (mast fell!). 1 Macarius; sang. 2 Macarius. 3 Macarius; good talk; (we lost ourselves!). 4 Macarius; (found our way!). 5 Rowed. 6 Private prayer; sang. 6.30 Supper; writ diary. 7 Meditated; prayed; they [had] various talk. 8 They [had] various talk. 8.30 Lay down.

Grace: 6 rating eleven times [4 to noon, 1 to 2, 4 to 5, 6 to 7 pm]; 5 six times [noon to 1, 2 to 4, 5 to 6, 7 to 9 pm].

SATURDAY, JULY 31. 1 Meditated; private prayer. 2 Slept. 4.30 Private prayer. 5 Private prayer; meditated; necessary talk. 6 Sang; Macarius. 7 Ate, necessary talk; Macarius. 8 Macarius. 9 Lady's Island; tea, necessary talk; Dog [Island], man surly!. 10 Set out; Macarius; sang. 12 Necessary business; Macarius. 12.30 Writ diary; necessary business; thought on sermon. 2.30 Stonobridge; walked with Charles, Macbain, and Mr Sweeny. 3 Necessary talk (religious). 3.30 Wallis'. 3.45 Set out. 5 Macbain tired. 6 Ashley; Mr Guy's; necessary talk (religious). 6 Sarreau's; necessary talk; Mrs Bellinger's; necessary talk. 7 Set out with horses; religious talk (necessary) with Mr Smith. 10 Charleston; Mr Eveleigh in bed; inn. 11 Prayed.

SUNDAY, AUGUST 1. 5 Private prayer; meditated. 6 Dressed; barber; necessary business. 7 Mr Eveleigh's; necessary talk; tea. 8 Necessary talk; at our lodging; necessary talk. 9 Mr Garden's, religious talk (necessary). 9.30 At home; thought. 10 [Read] Prayers. 12 Preached (about three hundred there). 1 Sacrament (about fifty [there], one Negro woman). 1.30 Necessary business. 2 Tea, religious talk; necessary business; writ diary. 3 Writ notes. 4 [Read] Prayers; Judge Trot's; tea, mostly religious talk. 6.30 Necessary talk with them. 8.30 At home; sang; religious talk. 9.30 To bed. 11 Called by La-rong.

MONDAY, AUGUST 2. 12 At La-rong's. 12.15 Set out; good talk. 4 Made fire; tea, various talk; they went. 5 Set out. 7 Mr Waring's, they at Prayers. 7.30 Religious talk (necessary). 8 Tea, mostly religious talk. 8.30 Set out. 11 Colonel Broughton's; necessary talk (religious). 1 Dinner, religious talk. 2.30 Set out; meditated; (very hot, handkerchief). 4 The tavern; tea; (horse tired!). 5 Set out; led my horse; thirsty! 10 At quarter-house, they would not let me in! 11.30 Mr Barton's, they let me in! necessary talk; supper.

TUESDAY, AUGUST 3. 5 Dressed; necessary talk; set out; private prayer. 6.30 Met Mr Dwight; he lent me his horse. 7.30 At home; necessary talk (religious); tea. 8 Necessary business in town. 10 Packed. 11 Mr Garden's; necessary talk (religious); Colonel Fenwick's; necessary talk; Jenys', he not [there]. 12.30 Mr Garden's; necessary talk (religious). 2 Dinner, necessary talk (religious). 3.30 Judge Trot's; necessary talk (religious and learned). 4.30 Caught in storm; at home; necessary business. 5 Tea, necessary talk; necessary business; writ diary. 6.15 Necessary business. 8 Supper; necessary business. 10 Prayed.

WEDNESDAY, AUGUST 4. 3 Called; necessary business. 4 Set out with Charles and Appee; religious talk. 5.30 Quarter-house; tea, religious talk. 7 Set out with Charles; religious talk. 9 Mr Guy's, mostly religious talk; tea. 10 Mrs Bellinger's, necessary talk (religious). 11.30 Walked in their garden. 12.30 Mr Garden's; good talk. 1.30 Dinner. 3 Mrs Bellinger's; mostly religious talk. 4 He came; necessary talk; tea. 6.30 Set out with Charles. 8.30 Charleston; Mr Jenys not come. 9 Mr Lynthwait's; supper, religious talk; Appee came. 10.15.

THURSDAY, AUGUST 5. 4.45 Set out. 7 Mr Bellinger's; tea, religious talk (useful and necessary). 9.45 Set out with him on his horse. 12 Wallis'; Mr Bellinger went back; set out with Will Bellinger; good talk. 4.30 Ponpon. 5 Dinner. 5.45 Set out. 7.30 Ashepoo Ferry; supper. 10 To bed.

FRIDAY, AUGUST [6]. 4.30 Called; breakfast. 6.30 Set out. 8.3 Jehu Barton. 9 Melon; necessary talk. 10 Set out. 10.30 Cumbahee Ferry; necessary talk with Mr Bull's overseer. 12.15 Set out with him. 2 Mr Griffith's; good talk (necessary). 2.30 Set out. 7.30 Beaufort; Serjeant's. 8 Supper. 8.30 Mr Jones'; religious talk. 9.30 At home; necessary talk. 10.

SATURDAY, AUGUST 7. 5.45 Necessary business; necessary talk; writ diary. 7 Mr Jones'; religious talk; tea. 9 At Inn. 10 Religious talk with him. 10.45 Set out; read Miller's *Propagation of Christianity*; (wind high against us!); dinner. 7 Mrs Dawson's; religious talk; supper. 8 Set out; private prayer; necessary talk (religious). 9.30 Storm; could not bear up; lay by.

SUNDAY, AUGUST 8. Set out; private prayer; read Ostervald's *Catechism*; breakfast; Ostervald. 10 Tybee Creek; lay by; religious talk. 12 Set out; slept; mostly religious talk. 4 Savannah; at home; dressed; dinner, religious talk. 5 Prayed with Delamotte. 5.30 Miss Bovey's; religious talk; company came. 7 Religious talk; tea. 7.30 They went; religious talk (she right). 8 Garden with her; religious talk. 8.30 Germans'; religious talk (necessary); religious talk (necessary) with Delamotte. 9 Miss Bovey's; supper, religious talk. 10.

MONDAY, AUGUST 9. 4.30 Garden; private prayer; sang (lively; well). 5 Private prayer; dressed; prayed with Delamotte; read Prayers (fourteen there). 6 Tea, religious talk. 7 Journal; sang. 8 Journal. 11 Visited. 12 Dinner, religious talk. 1 Visited (lively zeal, they affected). 2 Visited (lively zeal, they affected). 3 Religious talk. 3.10 Mr Houston came; necessary talk; tea. 4 Necessary talk; necessary business. 5 Packed; necessary business. 6 Prayed with Delamotte. 6.15 Miss Bovey's; tea, religious talk. 7 Began journal to her. 7.15 Read Prayers, expounded. 8 With Germans. 8.15 Miss Bovey's, journal; supper. 9 Journal. 11 Journal; religious talk. 11.45.

Grace: 7 rating once [4 to 5 am]; 6 thirteen times [5 to 9, 10 am to 4, 6 to 9 pm]; 5 six times [9 to 10 am, 4 to 6, 9 to 11 pm].

TUESDAY, AUGUST 10. 5 Private prayer; read Prayers; expounded (twelve there). 6 Necessary business; religious talk with Mr Woodruff; tea, religious talk with Delamotte. 7 With Mr Causton, necessary talk; necessary business with boatmen. 10 Miss Bovey's, religious talk. 10.30 Set out with Jemmy Billinghurst, religious talk. 11 Hard rain. 1 At Thunderbolt; Mrs Causton there, religious talk (necessary). 3 Dinner. 4 Set out; sang. 6 Skidaway; tea, religious talk (necessary). 7.30 Garden; meditated; sang. 8.30 Sang; read Prayers, expounded (eight there). 10.15.

Grace: Meditated! [at 7.30 pm].

WEDNESDAY, AUGUST 11. 2.45 Called them. 3 Set out; slept. 4.30 German; Law; ((breakfast)). 8 Pine Island; tea. 9 Set out; *Serious Call*; sang. 12 Dinner; German; *Serious Call*. 6 Wind high, could not cross St Catherine's Sound. 9 Lay down.

Of this, when I came to Frederica, August 13, Mr. Oglethorpe gave me a large account. At the same [time], he said he wished I would spend as much time with her as I could. For this he gave two reasons: her deep distress, wherein none but me, under God, could comfort her, and her earnest desire to be fully instructed in the duties of a Christian life. From him I went to her, at Mr. Hird's, and talked with her near an hour. I told her I would now lay aside the reserve I had used with her at Savannah, being convinced that God had in a peculiar manner committed her to my charge; that therefore in all my intercourse with her I should look upon her as one of my sisters, and omit nothing in my power which might be conducive to her giving herself up to God. I was both pleased and surprised with the good sense, piety, and gratitude of her reply.

[B—The time I was with her was spent chiefly in reading. The books I now read and explained to her were, first, *A Collection of Prayers;* next, *Tracts on the Presence of God;* and then, Dr. Cave's *Primitive Christianity.*]

THURSDAY, AUGUST 12. 3.30 Walked; meditated. 4.30 Set out; slept. 5.30 Law; prayed; sang. 7 On St Catherine's Island; tea. 8 Walked; Law; sang; prayed. 11.30 Dinner. 12 Walked; Law. 2 Tea. 3 Set out. 6.30 Clark's Bluff; supper. 7 Walked; sang; meditated. 9.45 Called; set out.

FRIDAY, AUGUST 13. 5.30 Law; prayed; sang. 7 Breakfast; Law; prayed; sang. 12 Dinner. 3 German; Law. 4 Ended Law. 6 Frederica! 7 With Oglethorpe, talk of Miss Sophy, religious talk. 9 Mr Hird's with Miss Sophy, religious talk (she quite right). 10 Prayer with Jemmy Billinghurst.

SATURDAY, AUGUST 14. 4 Private prayer; meditated (zealous). 5 Prayer with Jemmy Billinghurst; necessary business. 6 Read Prayers, expounded (ten there). 6.45 With Oglethorpe, necessary talk (religious; he open and friendly). 7 Hird's; tea, religious talk (necessary). 8 Calwell's, necessary business; at home; necessary business. 9 Mrs Hawkins', necessary talk (religious; I not as before!). 10 Necessary business. 11 Writ diary. 11.15 Shaved; necessary business. 12 Mr Hird's, religious talk (necessary); Oglethorpe there; he went; dinner, religious talk. 1 Read *Collection* to Miss Sophy. 2 Religious talk with Mark Hird. 3 Visited Robinson! (lively zeal!). 4 At home; tea with Miss Sophy, religious talk. 5 Walked; prayed; meditated. 6 Walked with Miss Sophy, read prayers to her. 7 Read Prayers, expounded (ten there); necessary business; writ diary. 8 [At] Mr Hird's, religious talk (necesssary); Miss Fawset ill; supper. 9 Talk of Mr Moore, etc (they very angry!). 10.

Providence: Well.

Grace: Zealous meditation, + [4 to 5 am].

SUNDAY, AUGUST 15. 5 Prayed; meditated. 6 Read Prayers, expounded (eight there). 7 Religious talk with Dobree. 7.30 At Mr Hird's, religious talk (necessary). 8 Tea, religious talk (necessary). 9.15 Dressed; sang; meditated. 10 Meditated; sang. 10.30 Meditated. 10.45 Read Prayers (twenty-six there). 11 Preached, Sacrament (ten there; lively zeal). 12 Walked; meditated. 12.30 Dinner, religious talk. 1 At home with Miss Sophy, read my journal. 2 Journal. 4 Read Prayers, expounded. 5 Mark Hird, Mrs, Mr Hird, Mr Tackner, Miss

Monday, August 16. I was seized with a fever. At hearing of this [B—after my second fit], she expressed much concern, saying, 'If Mr. Wesley dies, I shall lose the only friend I ever had in the world.' She desired me the next day, if it returned, to send for her immediately. I did so, and she instantly came, sat by my bed, read several prayers, and prepared whatever I wanted with a diligence, care, and tenderness not to be expressed [B—and would not leave me till the fit was over].

Sophy, Miss Fawset with me; sang; Law; sang (they seemed affected). 6 Tea, religious talk. 6.45 Walked with Miss Sophy and Miss Fawset, mostly religious talk. 7 Supper, religious talk (necessary). 8 Religious and useful talk. 9.30 Lay down.

N.B. Too long with them.

Monday, August 16. 5 Private prayer. 5.30 Necessary business; prayed. 6 Read Prayers, expounded. 6.30 Miss Hopkey, ended journal. 7 Tea, religious talk; read Prayers (nine there). 8 Read *Collection*. 8.30 Mrs Calwell's, religious talk; writ diary. 9 Walked to Mrs Hawkins', she not [there], visited (lively zeal), not well. 10 At home; shook, headache; sang; slept. 11 Hot fit; sang; meditated; slept. 12 Hot fit. 12.15 Writ diary [summary?]. 12.30 Began to sweat; writ diary. 1 Sweat; slept. 1.45 Cooler. 2 Slept. 2.30 Robinson, religious talk. 3 Religious talk. 3.30 Miss Sophy and Mrs Hird; sang; Law; sang. 4 Tea, religious talk. 5 Religious talk; writ diary. 5.15 Prayed with Miss Sophy and Mark Hird. 5.30 Read resolutions. 6 Walked with Miss Sophy; read prayers with her. 7 Read Prayers, expounded (twenty-two there). 7.30 Miss Sophy, etc; sang. 7.45 Necessary business. 8 Mrs Hird's, religious talk; supper, necesssary talk (religious), Mrs Robinson there. 9 Necessary talk of enemies. 9.30 To bed.

Tuesday, August 17. Prayed; private prayer. 6 Read Prayers, expounded (seven there). 6.30 Miss Sophy and Mrs Robinson, religious talk, tea. 7 Religious talk (necessary). 7.15 Walked; necessary talk with Dawson. 8 Necessary talk with Mrs Patterson. 9 Writ diary; *System of Theology*. 10 *British Theology*. 11 A little cold. 12 A little hot. 1 Sweat, headache. 2 Sweat; Mr Hawkins came, necessary talk (he seemed open!). 3 Mark Hird, Robinson, Miss Sophy, Miss Fawset; sang; Law; sang; they went to Mrs Hawkins. 4 Mrs Lawley came; tea, necessary talk of her case. 5 Mrs Hird and Mrs Robinson came, necessary talk (religious). 6 Mrs Hird's, bread and butter. 7 Read Prayers, expounded; Miss Sophy, etc, came; sang. 8 Mrs Hird's, necessary talk (religious). 8.45 Supper. 9 Religious talk (necessary). 10.30 Prayed.

Wednesday, August 18. 5 Private prayer; necessary business. 6 Read Prayers, expounded (seven there). 6.30 Miss Sophy and Miss Fawset, religious talk. 7 Religious talk. 7.30 Necessary business; *British Theology*. 8 Combed; sang; necessary business; writ diary. 9 *British Theology*. 9.30 Strong shaking. 10 Miss Sophy came, religious talk; cold fit. 11 Hot fit; religious talk. 12 Sweat; religious talk; Miss Sophy read Prayers. 1 Religious talk; sweat. 2 Religious talk; cooler. 3 Mark Hird; read resolutions. 3.15 Robinson came; sang; Law. 4 Sang. 4.15 Mrs Hird's; dinner. 5 Dinner. 5.45 Walked with Miss Sophy and Miss Fawset, religious and useful talk. 6 Tea, religious talk. 6.50 Meditated. 7 Read Prayers,

Thursday, [August] 19. Being a little recovered, I resumed the *Collection of Prayers for Every Day in the Week*. I had begun to read and explain them to her the day after I came to Frederica. And one of these we read every morning after breakfast till Wednesday, [August] 25. On which, having ended them, I began ((Dr. Heylyn's)) the *Devotional Tracts on the Presence of God*. I was quite surprised to find in one of so little experience a taste for the noblest passages in them. Those thoughts, she often said, gave her comfort and ease in the bitterest of afflictions. Twice or thrice after our reading I kissed her; but I ((soon)) immediately condemned myself as having done foolishly, being convinced (and the more so because she seemed not displeased) that it was not expedient either for her or me.

In private she commonly employed herself in Mr. Law's *Serious Call* and *Christian Perfection*. She made no objection to the strictness of either, being fully convinced, as she frequently said, that 'as there is no happiness but in holiness, so the more holiness the more happiness.'

[C—. . . (that) I had heard of him [Hawkins?], to which he gave me a satisfactory answer. And at parting, we agreed that neither, for the future, should believe or relate anything of the other till he had first mentioned it to [him] himself.

[Friday, August 20. Mr. Oglethorpe returned. Between five and six in the evening I called at Mr. Hawkins's for my decoction of the bark. He was not at home. She desired me to sit down, and sat down by me. I told her 'the being ill-treated by those from whom I expected it had given me

---

expounded; at home; sang. 8.15 Took vomit. 9 Vomit; writ diary. 9.40 Religious talk. 10 Supper. 10.15 Lay down.

THURSDAY, AUGUST 19. 5.15 Private prayer; dressed. 6 Read Prayers, expounded (seven there); necessary business. 7 Mrs Hird's; tea, religious talk. 8 Read Herbert to them. 8.30 Mr Calwell's, necessary talk (religious). 9.45 At home; necessary business. 10 Necessary business. 11 Sang; Herbert; thought. 12 With Miss Sophy and Miss Fawset; read letters to and from Morgan. 1 Dinner; letters; writ to Francis Moore. 2 At home; Miss Sophy, etc; sang; Law; sang. 3 Necessary business; necessary talk (religious) with Miss Sophy, etc. 4 Went to Francis Moore, necessary talk, he seemed convinced. 5 Tea, necessary and useful talk. 6 At home; meditated; private prayer. 6.45 Read prayers. 7 Expounded (sixteen there); at home; sang. 7.30 Mrs Hird's, necessary talk (religious) with Mr Hird. 8 Supper; read Morgan's letters. 9 Read Letters. 10.30.

FRIDAY, AUGUST 20. 4.45 Private prayer. 5.15 Slept. 5.45 Read Prayers, expounded (ten there). 6 Miss Sophy, religious talk; tea. 7 Read Mr Hawkins' case. 8 Mr Hawkins', company there; writ diary. 9 At home; transcribed Herbert. 10 Herbert. 11.15 Walked; read *Negro's Advocate*. 12 *Negro's Advocate*. 1.45 At home; Miss Sophy and Mark Hird; sang. 2 Law; sang. 3 Tea, religious talk (necessary). 4 With Miss Fawset; with Oglethorpe; they [had] various talk. 5

little concern. But it had grieved me to find Mr. Hawkins joining with them, whom I used to look upon as my friend.' She asked how he had treated me ill. I answered, 'By exposing my brother's paper, which as a friend he should have shown to me only.' She said, 'All the women in the town are uneasy and affronted at the two Greek words there. They think them a general reflection on them all. Pray tell me, who do they mean?' The substance of my answer was: (1) What my brother says is not said by me; neither am I accountable for it; (2) This was writ before we had explained, when all things were dark; he is now of a quite different opinion; (3) I take him to mean by those words only two persons, you and Mrs. Welch.

[She started up, said I was a villain, a scoundrel, a pitiful rascal, with several titles of the same kind. In the midst of her speaking, Mr. Hawkins came in. She told him I said that dog my brother meant her by those damned words. Upon which he immediately joined her, bestowed much of the same sort of eloquence both upon him and me, only intermixed with more oaths and imprecations. I was much grieved, and indeed could not refrain [from] tears. I know not whether they interpreted this as fear, but they rose in their language, and told me they would uncase [i.e., unfrock] us both: him for adultery (the terms they used were coarser), the consciousness of which, they said, forced him to run away to England; and me for what was as bad, or worse. I replied, the sooner the better, and that I would go to Mr. Oglethorpe just now. I did so, and gave him a plain relation of what had occurred. After prayers, they came too; but were so warm and used such language in the very relating their case, that Mr. Oglethorpe was obliged to check them more than once. After a long hearing, Mr. Oglethorpe said (1) That my brother had been guilty of an indiscretion in writing that paper; (2) That this was not imputable to me, who was no way accountable for what he said; and that therefore, (3) They had done very ill in abusing me in a manner no way justifiable or excusable. With this reprimand he dismissed them.

[Saturday, August 21. I spent an hour with Mr. Horton, and laboured to convince him I was not his enemy. But it was labour in vain; he had heard stories which he would not repeat, and was consequently

---

They [had] various talk. 5.30 Mrs Hawkins, she very abusive. 6 Mr Hawkins came, both very abusive; adieu! 6.30 Necessary talk with Oglethorpe of them. 7 Read Prayers, expounded (twenty-one and Oglethorpe there). 7.30 Mr and Mrs Hawkins came to Oglethorpe and me; they complained; they abusive! 8 Necessary talk with them and Oglethorpe. 8.30 Gained no ground; necessary talk (religious) with Oglethorpe. 9 Oglethorpe sent for Horton; he accused me! 9.30 Mrs Hird's, necessary talk (religious). 10.

SATURDAY, AUGUST 21. 5 Private prayer; slept. 5.45 Read Prayers. 6 Expounded. 6.30 Necessary business; writ diary. 7 Hird's; tea, necessary talk (religious);

immovable as a rock. Many things indeed he mentioned in general, as that I was always prying into other people's concerns, in order to set them together by the ears; that I had betrayed everyone who had trusted me; that I had revealed the confessions of dying men; that I had belied everyone I had conversed with: himself, in particular, to whom I was determined to do all the mischief I could. But whenever I pressed him to come to particulars, he absolutely refused it. I asked him what motive he thought I had to proceed thus. He said he believed it was a pure delight in doing mischief, and added, 'I believe in a morning when you say your prayers you resolve against it; but by that time you have been abroad two hours, all your resolutions are vanished, and you can't be easy till you are at it again.'

[Here Mrs. Welch coming up, asked, with a curse, what I meant by saying she was an a[dulteress?], and entertained me and a pretty many other auditors with such a mixture of scurrility and profaneness as I had not heard before. God deliver thee from the gall of bitterness and the bond of iniquity!

[I now found what remained was, to look upon my (once) acquaintance, as well as my late friend, as dead, and so neither to speak of them. But on Sunday the 22nd, between three and four in the afternoon, Mrs. Hawkins sent me by her maid a note wherein she desired to speak with me upon an affair of importance. I paused a little, and then asked the servant whether she knew what her mistress wanted. She said, No; upon which I replied, 'If a parishioner desires my company, I must go; but, be sure, stay you within, all the time I am at your house.'

[When I came in she said, 'Sir, sit down.' I sat down on the bedside. She stood close to me, with her hands behind her, and said, 'Sir, you have wronged me, and by God I will shoot you through the head this moment with a brace of balls." I catched hold of the hand with which she presented the pistol, and at the same time, of her other hand, in which

---

Vanderplank came, good talk (various). 8 Necessary talk (religious). 8.30 Necessary talk with Horton, he quite angry, gained no ground. 9 Mrs Welch came, she quite scurrilous and profane; with Francis Moore, he open and friendly. 10 Sang; writ diary. 10.30 Writ journal. 11 Journal. 12.15 Hird's; dinner, necessary talk (religious). 1 Necessary talk (religious); writ diary; sang. 2 Miss Sophy and Miss Fawset; sang; Law. 3 Mrs Calwell sent for me, necessary talk (religious). 3.30 At home; necessary talk. 4 Tea, religious talk; Vanderplank came, mostly religious talk. 4.45 Writ diary; walked; sang. 5 Sang; read *Humble Heart*; sang. 6 Oglethorpe's, necessary talk (religious). 7 Read Prayers, expounded. 7.30 Miss Sophy, etc; sang; necessary talk (religious). 8 Hird's; began Cave. 9 Supper, good talk. 10.

   Grace: 6 rating nine times [5 to 6, 8 to noon, 2 to 3, 5 to 8 pm]; 5 eight times [6 to 8 am, noon to 2, 3 to 5, 8 to 10 pm].

she had a pair of scissors. On which she threw herself upon me, and forced me down upon the bed, crying out all the while, 'Villain, dog, let go my hands,' and swearing bitterly with many imprecations both on herself and me, that she would either have my hair or my heart's blood. I was very unwilling either to cry out, which must publish to all the world what for her sake I desired should be more private; or to attempt rising by force, which considering the posture in which she lay could not have been done without hurting her. Just then the maid came in, whom she ordered to reach a knife, swearing, she would be the death of her if she did not. The woman stood trembling, not knowing what to do. Her two boys came in next, whom she bid to hold my hands and I desired to take hold of their mistress. But they did not dare to do either.

[Then came in Mr. Davis, the constable, and Mr. Reed, who on my desire were going to take her by the arms, when Mr. Hawkins came in, asked what that scoundrel did in his house, and commanded them, at their peril, not to touch his wife. Upon this encouragement, she struggled again to get her hands loose; but not being able, seized on my cassock with her teeth, and tore both the sleeves of it to pieces, and then fixed upon my arm, four men (for Mr. Robinson and Ward were now come) standing by, and not daring to hinder her. I then spoke to Mr. Hawkins, who, seeing the company increase, took her round the waist, and lifted her up.

[I went to Mr. Oglethorpe, and gave him a simple narration of what had happened. He sent for them both, and for Mr. Horton. She defended all, saying he had not done her justice for the wrong she had received, and therefore she had done herself justice. After a long hearing, her husband and she, promising better behaviour for the future, were dismissed.

[I thought here had been a full end of all, but every hour brought me fresh reason to believe the contrary. Mr. Hawkins related what had

---

SUNDAY, AUGUST 22. 5 Private prayer; prayed. 6 Read Prayers, expounded (sixteen there). 7 Mr Reed, Miss Sophy and Miss Fawset, tea, religious talk (necessary). 8 They went; necessary talk with Reed. 8.30 Read *Contrite Heart.* 9 *Contrite Heart*; meditated on sermon; sang. 10 Sang; dressed; religious talk to Pouvroy, etc. 11 Read Prayers, expounded (thirty-two there). 12 Sacrament. 12.15 Prayed; sang with them; religious talk. 12.30 Dinner. 1 Dinner, good talk. 1.45 Walked with Miss Sophy and Miss Fawset, religious and useful talk. 3 Religious and useful talk, writ diary. 3.30 Sang; Mrs Hawkins sent for me; all gazed!!! 4 With Mr Oglethorpe, told him all; he sent for Mr and Mrs Hawkins, necessary talk. 4.30 Mr Horton came, necessary talk, 5 Necessary talk. 5.30 They went; necessary talk (religious). 5.45 Mrs Lawley's, tea, necessary talk. 6 Read Prayers, expounded (fifty there). 7 Miss Sophy, etc; sang; Law; sang. 8 Hird's, Davison, etc, came; supper, necessary talk. 9 Necessary talk. 9.30 Mark Hird and Mr Reed lay in my house; prayed. 9.45.

passed wherever he came, in such a manner as he judged proper. Mrs. Hawkins did the same. A report likewise went through the town that I designed to steal away in the night. Many advised me very seriously not to go; others came to take their leave. Finding how things were managed, early in the morning I sent Mr. Oglethorpe the following letter:

[Aug. 23

Sir,

I choose to write rather than speak, that I may not say too much. I find 'tis utterly impossible anything should be kept secret unless both parties are resolved upon it. What fell out yesterday is already known to every family in Frederica; but to many it has been represented in such a light that 'tis easy to know whence the representation came. Now, sir, what can I do more? Though I have given my reputation to God, I must not absolutely neglect it. The treatment I have met with was not barely an assault; you know one part of it was felony. I can't see what I can do but desire an open hearing in the face of all my countrymen of this place. If you (to whom I can gladly entrust my life and my all in this world) are excepted against as partial, let a jury be empanelled, and upon a full inquiry determine what such breaches of the law deserve. I am, sir, your obliged and most obedient servant.

[Mr. Oglethorpe sent for Mr. Horton, who came from him to me; spoke largely of the necessity of union among ourselves, now we were surrounded with enemies; of the many divisions already in the town, and the probability that this would increase them. He then informed me that he was ordered nevertheless, if I insisted on it, to open a court, but he thought (to speak freely) it would be much better to terminate things in a more friendly manner. I told him I had no desire of doing any hurt either

---

MONDAY, AUGUST 23. 5 Private prayer; religious talk with Mark Hird; read Prayers, expounded. 6 Miss Sophy and Mr Reed, religious talk; writ to Oglethorpe. 7 Tea, religious talk. 8 Religious talk (necessary). 8.30 Writ journal. 9 Journal. 10 Mrs Welch came, necessary talk. 10.30 Journal. 11 Journal; writ diary; Mr Reed came. 12 Mr Horton came, necessary talk. 12.15 Sang; Mr Horton, necessary talk. 12.45 Hird's, necessary talk (religious). 1.15 Oglethorpe sent for me; necessary talk of Mrs Hawkins. 2.15 Dinner with him, he [had] necessary and useful talk. 3.15 At home; Robinson, etc; sang; Law; sang. 4 Religious talk (necessary) with Miss Sophy. 4.30 Reed came, religious talk. 5 Hird's, religious talk (necessary), tea. 6 At home; prayed; meditated. 7 Read Prayers, expounded. 7.30 Miss Sophy, etc; sang; Mr Oglethorpe sent for me; Mr and Mrs Hawkins there, necessary talk. 8 Mr Oglethorpe tried to reconcile. Alas! 9 They seemed reconciled. 9.15 Hird's; necessary talk (religious). 10.

Grace: 6 rating eleven times [6 to 8, 9 to 11, noon to 1, 3 to 4, 6 to 10 pm]; 5 seven times.

to Mr. or Mrs. Hawkins, but that I must secure myself against future insults and put a stop to their misrepresentations of what was past. He said he would talk with them on those heads, and return to me with their answer. This he soon did, assuring me in their name that I should have no further reason of complaint.

[At one Mr. Oglethorpe sent for me, and talked fully upon the same subject; and at eight again, at which time I found Mr. and Mrs. Hawkins sitting with him. For above an hour was he labouring to reconcile us. No! I had obliged them beyond all reconciliation. The wrongs I had done might be forgiven (for indeed they were none at all); but my friendship never can till the day of their death. However, something like an agreement was patched up, one article of which was, that we should speak to each other no more. Blessed be God, who hath at length given me a full discharge, in the sight of man and angels, from all intercourse with one 'whose heart is snares and nets, and her hands as bands' [Eccles. 7:26].

TUESDAY, AUGUST 24. 5.30 Dressed; read Prayers, expounded (ten there). 6 Miss Sophy; read sermon. 7 Mrs Calwell came, tea, religious talk (necessary). 7.30 Read sermon (she affected). 8 Writ journal. 10 Indian came; dressed; Miss Sophy, etc; prayed; sang. 11 Read Prayers, preached (twenty-four there). 12 Sacrament (eight communicants). 12.15 Miss Sophy, etc; sang. 12.30 Hird's; dinner. 1 Rain; religious talk. 2 Religious talk (much). 3 Religious talk. 3.15 At home; sang. 3.30 Writ diary; read Prior; meditated. 4 Visited. 4.15 Hird's; tea, religious and useful talk. 5 Walked; prayed; private prayer; meditated. 6 Walked and meditated. 6.30 Meditated. 6.45 Read Prayers (Miss Sophy not there!). 7 Expounded; Mark Hird, etc; sang. 7.30 Religious talk with him; supper. 8 Journal. 9.15.

WEDNESDAY, AUGUST 25. 5 Prayed; religious talk with Mark [Hird]. 5.45 Read Prayers. 6 Expounded. 6.15 Religious talk with Miss Sophy. 6.45 Heylyn's *Tracts*. 7 Tea; Heylyn; religious talk (she much affected). 8 Necessary talk. 8.30 Oglethorpe's, necessary talk (religious). 9 Necessary talk (religious). 11.15 Writ account. 12.15 Miss Sophy came; Heylyn. 1.30 Visited. 2.20 [Read] Heylyn to Miss Sophy; religious talk. 3 Miss Fawset came; prayed; Mrs Hird's, religious and useful talk. 4 Dinner, mostly religious talk. 5 Prayed; meditated. 6 Walked with Miss Sophy and Miss Fawset, read journal. 6.45 Read Prayers (thirty there and Mr Horton!). 7 Expounded; sang with them. 7.45 Hird's, religious and useful talk. 8 Tea, mostly religious talk. 9 Necessary talk (religious). 9.30.
    Grace: 6 rating six times [5 to 8 am, 1 to 3, 5 to 6 pm]; 5 eleven times.

THURSDAY, AUGUST 26. 5 Private prayer; prayed; meditated. 5.45 Read Prayers. 6 Read Prayers, expounded (ten there). 6.15 Miss Sophy; Heylyn. 7 Ausperger and Reed, necessary talk (religious), tea. 8 Necessary business. 8.30 Transcribed hymns. 10.30 Read letters. 12.30 Hird's, dinner. 1 Good talk (necessary). 1.30 Visited. 2 At home; Mark Hird, etc; sang; prayed; sang. 3 Miss Sophy came; Heylyn. 4 Hird's; walked with them to Reed's lot; tea; much talk (religious). 5 Necessary and useful talk. 6 Necessary talk (religious). 6.20

[August 27. Father Don Antonio de Arredondo came to St. Simons from the Havana, to treat with Mr. Oglethorpe. He said he had full powers from the king his master to conclude as he judged convenient. Capt. Gascoigne set up tents for him and his attendants, on Jekyll Island, over against St. Simons. The ship lay in the river between. Mr. Oglethorpe came down to him from Frederica every day, for six or seven days successively, after which he returned to the Havana.

[Saturday the 28th, I began to set apart, out of the little stock I had, such books as were of most general use, toward a library at Frederica. At eleven, while I was with Mrs. Patterson, who was dangerously ill, Mrs. Hawkins came in and sat down; but I exchanged not a word with her, good or bad. In the afternoon I walked with Mark Hird to the fort where the Independent Company is placed, on the other side of the island. Above five we set out homeward; but the night overtaking us, and my guide knowing little more of the way than myself, we were soon lost in the woods. It was a starlight night, but neither of us knew which way the town lay. We walked, however, straight forward, and crept where we could not walk, till between nine and ten o'clock; when being heartily tired and thoroughly wet with dew, we lay down and slept till morning.

Meditated; prayed. 7 Read Prayers, expounded (thirty there); sang. 8 Supper; Cave. 9 Religious talk. 9.30.

FRIDAY, AUGUST 27. 5 Prayed; sick; slept. 5.45 Read Prayers. 6 Expounded; Miss Sophy and Reed, mostly religious talk, tea. 7 Walked with Reed; made arbour. 8 Arbour. 9 Arbour; meditated. 10 Religious talk (necessary). 10.30 Hird's, religious talk. 11 Meditated; religious talk; visited. 12 Visited; read letters. 1 Visited. 2 With Miss Sophy, Mark Hird, etc; sang; Law; prayed. 3 Read resolutions. 3.15 Hird's; dinner, mostly religious talk. 4 Visited Mrs Patterson (she very ill); Hird's, good talk. 5 Prayed; private prayer; meditated. 6 Walked with them, mostly religious talk. 7 Read Prayers, expounded (twenty-six there); sang. 7.45 Hird's, necessary talk. 8 Tea, mostly religious talk; Cave. 9 Oglethorpe sent for me; necessary talk of the Spaniards. 10 Hird's, necessary talk; could not sleep for Pouvroy. 11.45.
    Grace: 6 rating nine times [5 to 6, 9 to 10, 11 am to 3, 5 to 6, 7 to 8, 9 to 10 pm]; 5 nine times.

SATURDAY, AUGUST 28. 5 Private prayer; meditated. 5.50 Read Prayers. 6 Expounded; prayed. 6.15 [Read] Heylyn to Miss Sophy. 7 Walked to Reed's lot with them; Oglethorpe sent for me; read letters. 8 Necessary talk (religious) with him. 8.30 At home; letters. 9 Transcribed hymns. 10 Sorted books for library. 11 Books. 11.15 Visited Mrs Patterson; Mrs Hawkins came in. 12 Hird's, religious talk; dinner. 12.45 Set out with Mark [Hird], religious talk. 1 Religious talk. 2 Walked, mostly religious talk; bemired. 3 Lost; religious talk (necessary). 4 At the fort; good talk (necessary) with Delegal, Junior. 5 Set out; religious talk. 5.45 Bemired. 6. Lost; prayed; found way. 7 Lost; prayed; found way; lost again. 8 Walked; tired. 9 Lay down by wood; slept sound.

[About daybreak on Sunday [the] 29th, we fixed on one of the brightest stars, and resolved to steer straight towards it as long as it appeared. About six we lost sight of our star, but found ourselves in the Great Savannah by Frederica. By this good providence God has I hope delivered me from another fear, that of lying in the woods, which I find by experience is (in fair weather, and to a person in tolerable health) a mere 'lion in the way' [Prov. 26:13].

SUNDAY, AUGUST 29. 4.45 Prayed; set out; religious talk; sang; (well). 6 At home; dressed. 6.30 Read Prayers, expounded (ten there). 7 Hird's; Oglethorpe sent, with him, necessary talk (religious), tea. 8 Writ for him. 10 At home; religious talk with Mrs Sweeny (gained no ground); Greek Testament; dressed. 11 Read Prayers, preached (thirty-two there). 12 Sacrament. 12.30 Hird's, dinner. 1 Necessary talk (useful and religious). 2 Mostly religious talk. 2.15 At home; slept. 2.45 Reed came, religious talk. 3 Religious talk; Miss Sophy came, religious talk; Heylyn. 4 Read Prayers, expounded (thirty there). 5 Miss Sophy, etc, came; sang; Law; sang. 6 Tea, religious talk. 6.45 Prayed with Mark [Hird]. 7 Hird's, religious talk (necessary); supper; Cave. 8 Cave. 9 Cave; prayed. 9.30.

Grace: 6 rating thirteen times [4 to 8, 11 am to 1, 2 to 7, 8 to 9.30 pm]; 5 three times.

MONDAY, AUGUST 30. 5.30 Private prayer; meditated. 6 Read Prayers, expounded (five there); Miss Sophy; Heylyn. 7 Mrs Calwell came, tea, necessary talk (religious). 8 Oglethorpe's, necessary talk; read letters. 9 Hird's, necessary business. 9.30 At home; necessary business. 10.30 Read verses on death. 11 My father on death. 12 Religious talk with Jemmy [Billinghurst]. 12.30 Hird's, necessary talk (religious). 1 Dinner, mostly religious talk. 2 Walked with Mr Hird, necessary and useful talk. 2.45 At home; Mark and Miss Sophy came. 3 Prayed; religious talk; prayed. 4 Walked with Miss Sophy, etc, to Mrs Calwell's lot, good talk (much). 5 Tea, they [had] much talk; rain (very wet). 6 Hird's; at home; meditated; prayed. 7 Read Prayers, expounded; sang. 7.45 Walked with Miss Sophy, religious talk. 8.15 Supper; Ausperger came, necessary talk. 9 Necessary and useful talk. 9.30.

Grace: 6 rating six times [5 to 8, 11 to noon, 3 to 4, 6 to 7 pm]; 5 ten times; four rating once [5 to 6 pm].

TUESDAY, AUGUST 31. 5.15 Necessary talk; slept. 6 Read Prayers, expounded (six there); with Miss Sophy; Heylyn. 7 Robinson came; tea, necessary talk (religious). 8.30 Writ diary; necessary business. 9 Transcribed verses. 10 Altered verses. 12 Hird's, good talk (necessary). 1 Dinner, mostly religious talk. 2 Read poem on death; at home. 3 Mr Reed, necessary talk (religious); Miss Sophy came; sang; Law. 4 Sang; Hird's; tea, they [had] various and useful talk. 5.15 Necessary business. 5.45 Prayed. 6 Marked Psalms and Hymns. 7 Read Prayers, expounded; Quesnel; sang. 8 Hird's; supper; Cave. 9 Mostly religious talk. 9.30.

Grace: 6 rating nine times [5 to 6, 9 to noon, 2 to 7 pm]; 5 eight times.

WEDNESDAY, SEPTEMBER 1. 5 Prayed; private prayer; meditated. 5.45 Read Prayers (seven there). 6 Expounded. 6.15 Miss Sophy came, religious talk. 7 Hird's,

[I was now in hourly expectation of setting out for Savannah. Mr. Reed promised to read Evening Prayers in my absence, and five or six persons agreed to spend an hour together every day in singing, reading, and exhorting one another. At last, on Thursday, September 2, the sloop sailed.]

After giving [Miss Sophy] in writing, as she desired, a few advices relating to the presence of God, I left Frederica, September 2, not doubting but he who had begun a good work in her would establish her heart unblameable in holiness, unto the day of the Lord Jesus. I then found I had not only a high esteem but a tender affection for her: but it was as for a sister, and this I thought strictly due both to her piety and her friendship.

[C—About ten on Sunday morning [September 3], we were at Skidaway; whence, after reading Prayers and preaching to about half a dozen people, I set out for Thunderbolt, and thence for Savannah in the afternoon.

---

mostly religious talk. 7.45 Tea, religious talk. 8 Tea, religious and useful talk; necessary business. 9 At home; necessary business; writ diary. 9.30 *Contrite Heart*. 11.30 Visited Davison and Calwell. 12 With Oglethorpe, necessary talk (religious). 1 With Captain Dempsey, necessary talk; (sins!!!). 1.45 Dressed; *Contrite Heart*. 2 Miss Sophy, Robinson, Mark [Hird]; sang; Law; sang. 3 Hird's, tea, religious talk. 4 Visited Mrs Patterson. 4.30 Necessary talk (religious). 5 Walked; prayed; meditated; prayed. 6 Quesnel. 6.45 Read Prayers (twenty-five there). 7 Expounded. 7.15 Sang; Hird's, necessary and useful talk. 8 Sang; good talk (much and religious). 10 Mostly religious talk. 10.15 Prayed. Grace: 6 rating nine times [5 to 7, 10 to noon, 2 to 7 pm]; 5 seven times; 4 once [10 to 10.15 pm].

THURSDAY, SEPTEMBER 2. 5 Prayed; meditated; private prayer. 6 Read Prayers, expounded (eight there) religious talk with Miss Sophy. 7 Hird's, tea, religious talk (necessary). 8 With Oglethorpe, necessary talk (religious). 8.30 At the bluff. 9 Walked; began Worthington on resignation. 10 Hird's; read Worthington to Miss Sophy. 11.15 Miss Fawset came, religious talk. 11.30 Dinner. 12 Set out in the sloop; Worthington. 1 Religious talk with Mr Stuart. 2 Worthington. 3.45 Writ diary. 4 Began Spanish Grammar. 6.45 Supper. 7 Sang; private prayer; meditated. 8 Mostly religious talk. 8.45 Prayed with them. 9.

FRIDAY, SEPTEMBER 3. 4.30 Private prayer; sang. 5 Prayed; read Worthington. 7 Spanish. 9 Tea; Spanish. 11 Writ diary. 12 Worthington. 1 Religious talk with Stuart. 1.30 Ended Worthington. 2. Watts. 3.30 Bread and cheese. 4 Watts; prayed. 6 Tea; private prayers. 7 Mostly religious talk; read Prayers. 9.

SATURDAY, SEPTEMBER 4. 5.15 Private prayer; sang. 6.30 Dr Knight's *Sermons*. 7.30 Writ diary. 9 Tea; Knight; sang. 11.30 Dinner; Knight; sang. 2 Wind contrary. 3 Slept. 3.15 Ended Knight. 4 Began Potter on *Church Government*. 5 Sang; prayed. 5.30 Tea. 6 Religious talk. 7 Afraid. 10 Very sick! 11 Vomited, purged. 12 Little better.

[September 6. Many complaints being made of what had been done in my absence by Mr. Dyson, Chaplain of the Independent Company, who had now been at Savannah several weeks, I went to his lodgings, and taxed him, (1) with baptizing several strong, healthy children in private houses, which was what I had entirely broke through; (2) with marrying several couple[s] without first publishing the banns, which he knew was contrary to the rubric and canon both; and (3) with endeavouring to make a division between my parishioners and me, by speaking against me before them, both as to my life and preaching. The two last charges he denied, but owned the first, promised never to do it again, and did the very same thing the next day. O discipline! Where art thou to be found? Not in England, or (as yet) in America.]

[B—On [September] the 7th, I writ a letter to Miss Sophy, showed it to Mr. and Mrs. Causton, and then sent it. I desire that letter may be read in court.]

SUNDAY, SEPTEMBER 5. 6.45 Prayed. 7 Bishop Potter. 7.30 Tea. 8 Potter; sang. 9 Potter. 9.30 Skidaway boat came, walked with them. 10 Mrs Mouse's, necessary talk (religious). 10.45 Read Prayers, expounded (nine there). 11.15 Mrs Mouse's. 11.30 In boat. 12 In the sloop, read Potter. 1.45 Thunderbolt; dinner, necessary talk (religious) with Mrs Lacy. 2 Savannah; dressed; read Prayers, expounded (forty there!). 5.15 Mr and Mrs Causton came, necessary talk (religious) with her. 5.45 Tea, religious talk (necessary). 6.30 Prayed with Delamotte. 6.45 Garden with him and Ingham, necessary talk (religious); sang. 7.30 Germans', sang. 8.30 At home; garden with Ingham and Delamotte, religious talk. 9.15 Prayed.

MONDAY, SEPTEMBER 6. 4.30 Private prayer. 5.15 Read Prayers, expounded (seventeen there; +; lively zeal). 6.15 Bread and butter, religious talk. 7 Read letters; Delamotte pressed to go home. 8 Letters, religious talk. 8.45 Miss Bovey's, tea, religious talk (necessary), (she right). 10 At home; prayed with Delamotte; necessary business. 11 Necessary business. 12 Prayed with Delamotte; bread and butter, religious talk. 1 Religious talk (necessary). 1.30 Visited John Brownfield, necessary talk (religious). 2 Visited; German. 2.45 Writ diary. 3 Prayed with Delamotte; Miss Bovey's; French. 4 Read the Prayers. 4.45 Company came, went. 5 Religious talk (close); tea. 6 Prayed with Delamotte; supper, religious talk. 7 Meditated. 7.15 Read Prayers, expounded (twenty-four there). 7.45 Germans'; sang. 8 Sang. 8.30 Read journal to them. 9 Journal. 9.30 At home; prayed.
   Grace: 5 rating five times [10 to noon, 1 to 2, 3 to 4, 9 to 10 pm; 6 for the rest, though not summarized in this note].

TUESDAY, SEPTEMBER 7. 5 Private prayer. 5.40 Prayers, expounded. 6.15 Necessary business; bread and butter, religious talk. 7 Religious talk (necessary). 7.30 Necessary talk (religious) with Mr Causton. 8 Necessary talk with Mrs Causton. 8.30 Mr Dyson's, necessary talk (religious). 9 Tea, necessary talk. 9.30 Necessary talk with Mrs Causton; at home; writ diary. 10 Necessary

[C—September 8, Wednesday. Mr. Von Reck and his brother came to town, in order to their passage to Europe. Neither of them was well recovered from the fever. The next morning I desired them to make use of our house while they stayed. On Friday we began our Morning Prayers at quarter past five, an hour we hope to adhere to all the winter. Between fifteen and twenty persons constantly attend them, besides the children, and the rest of our own family.

[I had often observed that I scarce ever visited any persons, in health or sickness, but they attended Public Prayer for some time after. This increased my desire of seeing not only those who were sick, but all my parishioners as soon as possible at their own houses. Accordingly I had long since begun to visit them in order from house to house. But I could not go on two days, the sick increasing so fast as to require all the time I have to spare (which is from one in the afternoon till five). Nor is even that enough to see them all (as I would do) daily. So that even in this town (not to mention Frederica and all the smaller settlements) here are above five hundred sheep that are (almost) without a shepherd. He that is unjust must be unjust still; here is none to search out and lay hold on the *mollia tempora fandi* ['favourable opportunities for speech', Virgil, *Aeneid*, iv.293-94], and to persuade him to save his soul alive. He that is a babe in Christ may be so still; here is none to attend the workings of grace upon his spirit, to feed him by degrees with food convenient for him, and gently lead him till he can follow the Lamb wherever he goeth.

---

business. 11 Meditated on letters. 12 Dinner, religious talk (necessary). 12.45 Visited Thomas Mellichamp. 1 Necessary talk (religious); visited Betty Wright. 2 Visited Mrs Causton, etc; necessary talk with Mr Causton. 3.15 At home; prayed. 3.30 Miss Bovey's, French. 4 Read *Collection*, religious talk (she affected). 5 Tea; company came, good talk. 6 At home; prayed with Delamotte; supper, religious talk; meditated. 7 Read Prayers, expounded. 7.45 German. 8 German; writ to Mr Hird, to Miss Sophy. 9 Letter. 9.30 Mr Causton's, necessary talk. 10.15 At home.

WEDNESDAY, SEPTEMBER 8. 5 Private prayer; meditated. 5.30 Read Prayers, expounded (fifteen there). 6 Necessary talk (religious) with Ingham, etc; breakfast. 7 Writ to Oglethorpe; necessary business. 8 Writ to Charles. 9 Writ to Mrs Hutton; prayed with Ingham and Delamotte. 10 [Writ] to Mr Newman. 11 Began to brother Wright [Hetty Wesley's husband]; writ diary. 12 Prayed with Delamotte and Ingham; visited. 1 Visited. 1.45 Wright's, dinner. 2 Visited. 2.45 Prayed with Delamotte and Ingham. 3 Bread and butter, religious talk. 3.45 Miss Bovey's, French. 4 Read Prayers; tea, mostly religious talk. 5 Mostly religious talk. 5.30 Meditated; sang. 6 Meditated; private prayer. 6.45 Necessary talk; meditated. 7 Read Prayers, expounded (thirty there). 7.45 Germans', sang. 8 Sang. 8.20 At home; tea, religious talk. 9 Mostly religious talk.

Grace: 6 rating eight times [7 to 9 am, noon to 3, 6 to 7, 8 to 10 pm]; 5 nine times.

Does any err from the right way? Here is none to recall him: he may go on to seek death in the error of his life. Is any wavering? Here is none to confirm him. Is any falling? There is none to lift him up. What a single man can do is not seen or felt. Where are ye, who are very zealous for the Lord of Hosts? Who will rise up with me against the wicked? Who will take God's part against the evildoers? Whose spirit is moved within him to prepare himself for publishing glad tidings to those on whom the Sun of Righteousness never yet arose, by labouring first for these his countrymen, who are else without hope, as well as without God in the world? Do you ask what you shall have? Why, all you desire: food to eat, raiment to put on, a place where to lay your head (such as your Lord had not), and a crown of life that fadeth not away! Do you seek means of building up yourselves in the knowledge and love of God? I call the god whom we serve to witness, I know of no place under heaven where there are more, or perhaps so many, as in this place. Does your heart burn within you to turn many others to righteousness? Behold, the whole land, thousands of thousands are before you! I will resign to any of you all or any part of my charge. Choose what seemeth good in your own eyes. Here are, within these walls, children of all ages and dispositions. Who will bring them up in the nurture and admonition of the Lord, till they are meet to be preachers of righteousness? Here are adults from the farthest parts of Europe and Asia, and the inmost kingdoms of Africa. Add to these the known and unknown natives of this vast continent, and you will indeed have a great multitude which no man can . . .]*

THURSDAY, SEPTEMBER 9. 4.45 Private prayers; meditated; prayed with them; read Prayers, expounded. 6 Bread and butter, religious talk. 7 Writ to brother Samuel; necessary business. 8 Letter. 9 Visited Mr Von Reck, religious talk (necessary); chocolate. 10 Necessary talk with Mr Causton; at home, necessary business. 11 Necessary business; prepared. 12 Cleaned. 1 Necessary talk; meditated. 1.15 Dinner. 2 Visited. 3.45 Miss Bovey's, French. 4 Read Prayers. 4.45 Read poem on death. 5 Poem; tea, religious talk. 6 Religious talk. 6.15 At home; with Von Reck, religious talk; tea. 7 Read Prayers, expounded (thirty-five there). 7.45 Germans', sang. 8 Sang. 8.30 With Von Reck, religious talk. 9 Necessary talk (religious). 9.30 Prayed.

Grace: 5 rating eleven times [7 am to 1, 3 to 8, 9 to 10 pm]; 6 six times.

FRIDAY, SEPTEMBER [10]. 5 Private prayer; read Prayers, expounded (fifteen there). 6 Writ to sister Patty. 7 Necessary business; tea with Von Reck, mostly religious talk. 8 Mostly religious talk. 8.45 Prayed with Delamotte. 9 Writ to Whitefield. 10 [Writ] to Clayton. 11 Visited. 12 Walked; meditated. 12.30 Visited. 1 Visited. 2.45 At home; dressed; prayed. 3 Dinner, necessary talk (religious). 3.30 Miss Bovey's, Mrs Weddal there, they [had] various talk. 4 Tea, religious talk; they [had] various talk. 5 They [had] various talk. 6 At home;

---

*End of document C; for this as a call to the Oxford Methodists, see *Letters* (25:471-73, 516 in this edn.).

[D—Monday, September 13. I [E—We] began reading over Bishop Beveridge's *Pandectae canonum conciliorum*. Nothing could so effectually have convinced me that both Particular and 'General Councils may err and have erred'; and of the infinite difference there is between the decisions of the wisest men and those of the Holy Ghost recorded in his Word [E—the oracles of God].

---

supper, mostly religious talk. 7 Read Prayers, expounded (thirty there); German. 8 German. 8.15 Religious talk with Töltschig. 8.30 Meditated; religious talk; at home (lively zeal [at some point during this hour]). 9 Garden with Delamotte, religious talk; prayed. 9.40.

Grace: 6 rating nine times [5 to 7, 10 am to 3, 8 to 10 pm]; 5 eight times.

SATURDAY, SEPTEMBER [11]. 4.15 Private prayer. 5 Meditated; read Prayers, expounded (eighteen there). 6 Writ to Mr Vernon. 6.30 Visited Dean. 7 At home; tea, religious and useful talk. 7.45 Letter. 8 Writ to Mr Thorold. 8.45 Letter. 9 Necessary talk (religious) with John. 9.30 Letter. 10.15 Smith came, religious talk. 10.30 Visited. 12.15 Dinner, good talk with Von Reck. 1 Mostly religious talk; slept. 1.45 Catechized children. 2.30 Visited. 4 Miss Bovey's; read Prayers; tea, religious talk. 5 Religious talk. 5.30 Walked; meditated. 6 At home; tea, mostly religious talk. 7 Read Prayers, expounded; German. 8 German; meditated; religious talk with Delamotte; prayed. 9.15.

SUNDAY, SEPTEMBER 12. 4.45 Private prayer; meditated; prayed with Delamotte. Read Prayers, expounded (twenty-five there). 7 Greek Testament. 7.45 Coffee, mostly religious talk. 8 Mostly religious talk. 8.30 Walked; prayed; meditated. 9 Meditated; prayed; sang. 10 Mr and Mrs Smith came, mostly religious talk; meditated; dressed. 10.45 Read Prayers. 11 Read Prayers, preached (thirty-five there). Sacrament. 12 Sacrament (thirteen there). 12.15 Religious talk with William Wallis. 12.45 Dinner. 1 Dinner, good talk. 1.30 [no entry]. 2 Catechized. 2.30 Walked; meditated. 3 Walked with Delamotte, religious talk. 4 Read Prayers (fifty there); catechized. 5 Prayers. 5.30 Mrs Gilbert's; prayed; sang; *Country Parson*. 6 *Country Parson*; sang. 6.30 Tea; Ingham, religious talk. 7 Germans', necessary talk (religious). 8 At home, religious talk. 9 Prayed.

Grace: 6 rating thirteen times [5 to 7, 8 to 10, 11 am to 1, 2 to 9 pm]; 5 three times.

MONDAY, [SEPTEMBER] 13. 4.10 Prayed with Delamotte; began *Codex canonum*. 5 Meditated. 5.15 Read Prayers, expounded (eleven there). 6 Hair cut. 6.45 At home; tea. 7 Tea, mostly religious talk. 8 Writ journal. 10 Marked journal. 12 Dinner. 12.45 Marked. 1.20 Visited. 4 Miss Bovey's; Mr Houston, necessary talk; tea. 5 Began Fleury's *Moeurs des Israelites*. 5.45 Walked; meditated. 6 At home; necessary talk. 6.15 Burial. 6.45 Tea, mostly religious talk. 7 Read Prayers, expounded; Germans'. 8 German. 8.30 Necessary talk with Mr Parker. 9 Necessary talk (religious) with Delamotte and Ingham. 9.45 Prayed.

Grace: 6 rating ten times [4 to 7, 8 to 10 am, noon to 1, 3 to 4, 5 to 6, 7 to 10 pm]; 5 eight times.

TUESDAY, SEPTEMBER 14. 4 Prayed with them; private prayer. 5 Private prayer. 5.15 Read Prayers, expounded (fourteen there); read Psalms. 6 Psalms. 7.30

Tea, good talk (necessary and religious). 8 Letters. 10 Sang; meditated; sang. 11 Meditated; Sacrament with Mr Charles. 12 At home; dinner, religious and useful talk. 1 Visited. 3.30 Miss Bovey's, French. 4 Mrs Vanderplank came, tea, good talk (necessary). 5 Good talk (necessary). 5.30 Began Law. 6 Walked; meditated; supper, necessary talk (religious). 7 Read Prayers, expounded; German. 8 German; necessary talk.

WEDNESDAY, SEPTEMBER 15. 3.45 Prayed with Delamotte; private prayer. 5 Private prayer; read Prayers, expounded (eighteen there). 6 Necessary business; coffee. 6.20 Writ diary. 7 Garden; necessary business. 8 Necessary business in garden. 9.45 Writ notes. 10 Writ to sister Emily and Rivington. 11 Garden; sang; meditated. 12 Visited. 1 Visited; prayed. 1 Visited; prayed. 3 At home; dinner, religious and useful talk. 4 Necessary business. 4.30 Miss Bovey's, Mrs Vanderplank came; tea; garden, good talk. 5 Good talk. 5.30 Religious talk; they went. 6 Meditated; prayed. 6.30 Von Reck came, religious and useful talk. 7 Read Prayers, expounded; Germans'. 8 Germans'. 8.30 German with Von Reck. 9 Various talk; prayed. 9.20.

Grace: 7 rating once [4 to 5 am]; 6 six times [7 to 8, 10 am to 1, 6 to 7, 8 to 9 pm]; 5 ten times.

THURSDAY, SEPTEMBER 16. 4 Prayed with Delamotte; private prayer. 5 Dressed; read Prayers, expounded. 6 Tea, religious talk. 7 Writ to Mr Horne, sister Kezzy. 8 [Writ] to my mother, sister Ellison, sister Nancy. 9 [Writ to] Serena, Hervey. 10 Sorted Letters. 11 Letters. 12. Dinner, necessary talk. 1 Visited. 3.30 Miss Bovey's, French. 5 tea, religious talk; Law. 5.45 At home; prayed with Ingham and Delamotte. 6 Supper, religious talk; meditated. 7 Read Prayers, expounded. 7.45 German; sleepy. 8 German. 8.30 Religious talk with them. 8.45.

FRIDAY, SEPTEMBER 17. 5 Dressed; read Prayers, expounded (twenty there). 6 At home; letters. 7 Coffee, religious talk. 8 Writ to Mr Burton. 9 Letter. 10 Writ to Aspasia, to Selima. 11 Religious talk (necessary) with Ingham. 11.45 Visited Charles and Dean. 12 Visited Joubert. 1 Visited Duché, Richard Norwood. 2 Visited Desborough, Goldwire; at home; tea, religious talk. 3 Miss Bovey's, French; Law. 4 Religious talk, tea; Law. 5 Religious talk. 5.20 At home; necessary talk; writ diary. 5.40 Prayed with Delamotte and Ingham. 6 Walked; meditated. 7 Read Prayers, expounded; German. 8.30 Necessary talk. 9 Prayed.

Grace: 6 rating eleven times [6 to 8, 11 am to 8 pm]; 5 five times.

SATURDAY, SEPTEMBER 18. 4 Prayed with Delamotte; private prayer. 5 Private prayers; dressed; read Prayers, expounded (twenty-two there). 6 Tea, religious talk. 7 Read Fleury's *Catechism* to Ingham. 8 Causton's, necessary talk. 8.30 Religious talk (necessary) with Mr Causton (he convinced). 9 Necessary talk (religious) with Mrs Causton (she convinced). 9.30 At home; transcribed verses. 10 Ended verses; writ diary. 11 Translated Greek, German; sang. 12 Dinner, religious and useful talk. 1 Visited Mrs Smith. 2 Catechized. 2.45 Mr Causton and Henry Parker, good talk (necessary). 3.30 Miss Bovey's, French. 4.45 Tea, religious talk. 5 Religious talk; Law. 5.45 At home; meditated. 6 Supper, religious talk. 7 Read Prayers, expounded (twelve there). 7.45 Communicants came, began Patrick. 8 Patrick; religious talk; sang; prayed (lively zeal). 8.30 Read my mother's letter. 9 Religious talk. 9.15 Prayed.

[Monday, September 20. We ended those that are called the Apostolical Canons; of which Bishop Beveridge observes, that they are the decrees of the several synods which met at several places and on several occasions in the second and third age after Christ; and are therefore called apostolical because partly grounded upon, partly agreeing with, the traditions they had received from the apostles.

[He further observes that as they were enacted by different synods, so they were collected by different persons, till about the year 500, John, Bishop of Constantinople, placed them in the head of the canons which he then collected into one code; since which time they have been in force in the Eastern Church. But then he adds (*Cod. canonum*, p. 159), 'They contain that discipline which was in the Church when they were collected, not when the Council of Nice[a] sat, for then [E—many parts of it were useless and] they were obsolete.]

Grace: 7 rating once [4 to 5 am]; 6 eight times [5 to 6, 8 to 9, 11 to noon, 1 to 3, 5 to 7, 8 to 9 pm]; 5 eight times.

SUNDAY, SEPTEMBER 19. 4 Dressed; slept; prayed with Ingham. 5 Private prayer; dressed. 6 Read Prayers, expounded. 7 Tea, religious talk. 8 Garden; meditated on sermon. 9 Meditated. 9.30 Garden; dressed; garden; sang. 10 Ephraem Syrus. 10.30 Necessary talk (religious). 10.45 Read Prayers. 11 Preached, Sacrament (sixteen communicants). 12 Prayed. 12.15 Dinner, religious talk. 1 Religious talk; visited. 2 *Canones apostolici*. 2.30 Catechized boys. 3 *Canones*; necessary talk. 3.45 Read Prayers (sixty there). 4 Read Prayers, catechized; prayed. 5 Visited Potter, religious talk; prayed with Delamotte. 6 Supper, religious talk. 7 Company came, good talk. 7.15 German. 8 Read *Apostolic Canons*. 8.45 Garden; religious talk (close). 9.15 Prayed.
Grace: 6 rating fifteen times; 5 twice [6 to 7 am, 3 to 4 pm].

MONDAY, SEPTEMBER 20. 4 Prayed with Delamotte; private prayer; writ notes (heavy; well). 5 Meditated; read Prayers, expounded (twenty-one there). 6 Tea, religious talk. 7 Transcribed journal. 8 Journal; with Von Reck. 10 Journal; with Von Reck. 10 Journal; necessary talk. 11 Garden; German. 12.15 Dinner, religious and useful talk. 1 Necessary business. 1.20 Visited Andrews, etc. 2 Visited Dean, Desborough, Potter. 3 Dressed; Miss Bovey's, French. 4 French. 4.30 Mr Houston came, good talk; tea. 5 Religious talk. 5.30 Necessary business; prayed with Delamotte. 6 Supper, religious talk. 6.45 Garden; meditated. 7 Read Prayers, expounded (thirty there); communicants [came], Patrick. 8 Sang; prayed. 8.30 *Canons*. 9 *Canons*; prayed. 9.30.
Grace: 6 rating ten times [4 to 7, 8 to 9, 11 to noon, 2 to 3, 5 to 9 pm]; 5 eight times.

TUESDAY, SEPTEMBER 21. 4 Prayed with Delamotte; private prayer (very heavy). 5 Dressed; read Prayers, expounded (twenty-three there). 6 Tea, religious talk. 7 Journal. 9 Garden; meditated on sermon; sang. 10 Meditated; dressed; German. 10.45 Read Prayers (seventeen there). 11 Preached, Sacrament (no wine there!). 12 Prayed. 12.15 Dinner, mostly religious talk. 1 Visited Smith,

[B—September 23. I writ a second letter to [Miss Sophy], showed it to Mr. and Mrs. Causton, and then sent it. I desire that letter may be read in court.

Andrews, Clancey, Martin. 2 Visited Richard Dean, Charles, Fall[owfield?]. 3 Visited Par[nel?], Potter, Desborough, Deikin, Smith. 4 Miss Bovey's, Law; tea, religious talk. 5 Religious and useful talk. 5.45 At home; prayed with Delamotte. 6 Supper, religious talk. 7 Read Prayers, expounded; Germans'. 8 German. 8.30 Councils; prayed. 9.15.

WEDNESDAY, SEPTEMBER 22. 4 Prayed with Delamotte; slept (very heavy and sick). 5 Dressed; read Prayers, expounded. 6 Coffee; journal 7 Journal. 11 Garden; sang; meditated. 12 Dressed; visited Michel and Rigden. 1 Visited Mr ———, Mercer, Wright. 2 Mr Causton's, necessary talk; visited Mrs Gilbert, James Dean. 2.30 At home; journal. 3 Dinner. 3.30 Miss Bovey's, French. 4 French; tea, mostly religious talk. 5 Law. 5.30 At home; necessary talk with Von Reck, Junior; meditated. 6 Buried; Mrs Hows, etc, began Clement. 7 Read Prayers, expounded (thirty-five there). 7.30 German. 8.30 *Canons*. 9.15 Prayed.
 Grace: 6 rating nine times [5 to 6, 11 am to 4, 6 to 9 pm]; 5 seven times. Lively zeal, + [8 to 9.15 pm].

THURSDAY, SEPTEMBER 23. 4 Private prayer; prayed (very lively). 5 Dressed; meditated; read Prayers, expounded (thirteen there). 6 Tea; necessary business. 7 Journal; writ to Miss Sophy. 8 Mr Causton's, necessary talk (useful and religious); tea. 9 Journal. 9.45 Writ on mystics. 10 Mystics. 11 Walked; meditated; sang. 12 Writ [on] mystics. 12.30 Dinner, good talk. 1 Necessary and useful talk. 1.15 Dressed. 1.30 Visited. 3 Miss Bovey's, French. 4 Tea, religious talk (necessary). 5 Law. 5.45 Christened. 6.15 Supper, religious and useful talk. 7 Read Prayers, expounded (twenty there). 7.30 Germans'. 8 Matthew Barisch buried. 8.30 *Canons*. 9.30 Prayed.
 Grace: 7 rating once [4 to 5 am]; 6 eleven times [5 to 6, 7 to 8, 9 to noon, 1 to 3, 4 to 6, 7 to 9 pm]; 5 five times.

FRIDAY, SEPTEMBER 24. 4 Prayed with Delamotte; slept (very heavy). 5 Slept. 5.15 Read Prayers, expounded (sixteen there). 6 Coffee, religious talk. 6.30 Mystics. 9.45 Mrs Causton's, necessary talk. 10 Mystics; necessary talk. 11 Mystics. 11.30 Necessary talk. 11.40 Garden; meditated. 12 Visited. 1 Letter. 1.30 Visited. 2 Visited Mrs Brownfield. 2.40 At home; writ to Rivington. 3 Dinner, mostly religious talk; Ingham came. 3.30 Miss Bovey's, French. 4 Law; tea, religious talk (she sad). 5 Religious talk. 5.15 At home; writ to Mr Laserre of Charleston. 6 Necessary business. 6.15 Churchyard; meditated (no corpse). 7 Read Prayers, expounded; buried. 7.45 German. 8.15 *Canons*. 9.15 Prayed. 9.30.
 Grace: 6 rating eleven times [5 to 9, 11 am to 2, 4 to 5, 6 to 9]; 5 five times [9 to 11 am, 2 to 3, 5 to 6 pm; no rating noted 4 to 5 am].

SATURDAY, SEPTEMBER 25. 4 Prayed with Delamotte and Ingham; private prayer. 5 Read Prayers, expounded; meditated (heavy). 6 Tea, religious talk. 7 Mystics. 10 Garden; read mystic papers. 11 Mystic papers. 12 Dinner, good talk; shaved. 1 Visited. 2 Catechized. 2.30 Slept. 2.45 Visited. 5 Mr Causton, Christie,

Parker; tea, necessary talk (religious). 6.45 Visited. 7 Read Prayers, expounded (twenty-four there); communicants [came], Patrick. 8 Sang; prayed. 8.20 Garden; meditated; prayed.

Grace: 7 rating once [4 to 5 am]; 6 eight times [6 to 8, 10 to 11 am, 1 to 4, 7 to 9 pm]; 5 eight times.

Sunday, September 26. 4 Prayed with Delamotte and Ingham; slept. 5.30 Dressed; meditated. 6 Read Prayers, expounded (twenty-four there). 7 Tea, religious talk; meditated. 8 Read *Canons*. 10 Garden; sang; meditated; sang. 10.45 Read Prayers. 11 Preached, Sacrament (ten there); sang; prayed. 12 Dinner, religious talk; *Canons*. 1 *Canons*. 2 Catechized. 3 Read Prayers (fifty there); catechized. 4 Preached. 4.15 Visited. 5 Private prayer. 5.30 Tea, religious talk. 6 Religious talk. 6.30 Garden, religious talk with Delamotte. 7 Germans'. 8 Writ diary; religious talk with Ingham and Delamotte. 9 Prayed.

Grace: 6 rating twelve times [5 to 6, 7 to 8, 10 am to 1, 2 to 8 pm]; 5 four times [no rating noted 4 to 5 am].

Monday, September 27. 4.15 Prayed with them; private prayer. 5 Meditated; read Prayers, expounded (nineteen there). 5.45 Prayed. 6 Burnside, religious talk, tea (he seemed affected). 7 Mystics. 8 Religious talk with Mrs Musgrove. 8.30 Mystics (lively zeal; +). 9 *Canons*. 11 Walked; James' *Corruptions of the Fathers*. 12 Dinner, religious talk; *Canons*. 1 *Canons*. 1.30 Visited. 2 Visited. 3 Miss Bovey's, French. 4 Vanderplank came, tea, good talk (various). 5 He went; religious talk. 5.30 Necessary talk with Von Reck; necessary talk (religious) with Delamotte. 6 Supper, religious talk. 6.30 Causton's, necessary talk. 6.50 Meditated. 7 Read Prayers, expounded (thirty there); Germans'. 8 Germans'. 8.15 *Canons*. 9 Prayed.

Grace: 7 rating once [4 to 5 am]; 6 ten times [5 to 7, 11 am to 3, 5 to 9 pm]; 5 six times.

Tuesday, September 28. 4.15 Prayed with Delamotte; private prayer. 5 Meditated; read Prayers, expounded (sixteen there). 6 Tea, religious talk. 6.45 *Canons*. 9.45 Trustees' Garden; began German Grammar. 10 Grammar; sang. 11 James; sang; writ diary. 12 Dinner; writ notes. 1 Writ notes. 1.20 Visited. 3 Miss Bovey's, French. 4.15 Tea, religious talk; Mr Houston came. 5 At home; prayed with Delamotte. 5.15 Religious talk with the boys. 5.30 Garden; private prayer; sang. 6 Sang with boys; supper, religious talk. 6.30 Causton's, necessary talk; meditated. 7 Read Prayers, expounded; communicants came, Patrick; prayed; sang. 8 *Canons*; prayed.

Grace: 7 rating twice [4 to 5 am, 5 to 6 pm]; 6 fourteen times.

Wednesday, September 29. 4.15 Prayed with Delamotte; private prayer. 5 Meditated; read Prayers, expounded (seventeen there). 6 Read Prayers. 6.15 Burnside came, religious talk. 7 Tea, religious talk (necessary). 7.45 Began translating German dictionary. 9.45 Garden. 10 Meditated; sang. 11 Read Prayers, ((expounded)) preached (twelve there). 12 Dinner, religious talk; writ for sick. 1 Visited. 4 Miss Bovey's, Law; tea, religious talk. 5 At home; Von Reck there, necessary talk. 5.30 Writ diary; private prayer; prayed with Delamotte. 6 Supper; visited. 7 Read Prayers, expounded (seventy there); buried Lady [Martha] Bathurst. 8.15 *Canons*; prayed. 9.30.

Grace: 7 rating once [4 to 5 am]; 6 fourteen times; 5 twice [8 to 10 am]. [Lively zeal, convincing, 7 to 8 pm].

THURSDAY, SEPTEMBER 30. 5 Dressed; read Prayers, expounded. 6 Writ notes; tea, religious talk. 7 Religious talk. 7.30 Dictionary. 11 Garden; James. 12 Dinner; Von Reck came, necessary talk. 1 Necessary business. 1.30 Visited Judith Cross, Charles, Dean. 2 Visited Mr Jones, Duché, James Dean, Pury. 3 Miss Bovey's, French. 4 Law; tea, religious talk (close). 5 Religious talk. 5.30 Meditated; prayed. 6 Sang; supper, religious talk. 6.45 Meditated. 7 Read Prayers, expounded (thirty-five there); Germans'. 8 German; *Canons.* 9.30 Prayed.

Grace: 6 rating nine times [6 to 8 am, 1 to 3, 4 to 9 pm]; 5 seven times.

FRIDAY, OCTOBER 1. 4 Prayed with them; private prayer (lively). 5 Dressed; read Prayers, expounded. 6 German; coffee. 7 German. 11 Garden; sang; meditated. 12 Meditated. 12.30 Visited Mrs Brownfield, necessary talk (religious, she quite open); Mr Joy, religious talk. 1 Necessary talk (religious). 1.45 Visited Mr Vanderplank (she seemed affected). 2 Religious talk; prayed; Cuthbert's (close, they affected). 2.30 Prayed; necessary business. 3 Tea, religious talk. 3.15 Miss Bovey's, French. 4 Tea, religious talk. 5 Prayed with Delamotte; garden; sang; private prayer. 6 Sang; German. 6.45 Meditated. 7 Read Prayers, expounded; German. 8 German. 8.15 *Canons.* 9.15 Prayed; writ diary.

Grace: 7 rating twice [4 to 5 am, 4 to 5 pm]; 6 twelve times; 5 thrice [5 to 6, 9 to 11 am]. [Lively zeal, 4 to 6 pm; convincing, noon to 3, 4 to 5 pm.]

SATURDAY, OCTOBER 2. 3.30 Prayed; German (very lively; the cold). 4 Prayed with Delamotte; sang; private prayer (very lively). 5 Meditated; read Prayers, expounded; German (very lively). 6 Tea, religious talk. 6.30 German. 8 German (sins!!!). 10.30 Trustees' Garden; meditated; sang. 11 Meditated; sang. 12 Dinner, religious talk; German. 1 Visited. 4.45 German. 5 Prayed with Delamotte; sang; private prayer. 6 Sang; supper, religious talk (lively zeal). 7 Read Prayers, expounded (twenty-two there); communicants came, Patrick; sang (lively zeal; +). 8 Prayed. 8.15 Garden; meditated; sang (lively zeal; +).

Grace: 7 rating five times [4 to 5 am, 5 to 9 pm]; 6 eight times [3 to 4, 5 to 7, 11 am to 4 pm]; 5 five times.

SUNDAY, OCTOBER 3. 3.45 Prayed with them; sang (very lively). 5 Sang. 5.15 Patrick; Hebrew; dressed. 6 Read Prayers, expounded; sang; Ingham read [aloud]. 7 Garden; meditated. 7.30 Tea, religious talk (lively zeal). 8 Religious talk; Mr Wightman came, religious talk; Patrick; sang with Delamotte. 9 Trustees's Garden; Patrick; meditated. 10 At home; dressed; religious talk. 10.45 Ingham read Prayers. 11 Preached (seventeen there), Sacrament (lively zeal). 12 Writ diary; writ notes. 12.15 Dinner, religious talk. 1 Sang; private prayer. 1.45 Catechized. 2.45 Sang; religious talk. 3 Read Prayers (fifty there); catechized. 4 Ingham read [aloud]. 4.30 Walked with them, religious talk; sang (lively zeal). 5 Religious talk; sang. 5.30 At home; prayed with Delamotte; private prayer. 6 Sang; tea, religious talk. 7 Germans', religious talk with them. 8 *Canons.* 8.30 Verses on death. 9.15 Prayed.

Grace: 7 rating five times [3 to 8, 9 to 10 am]; 6 twelve times.

MONDAY, OCTOBER 4. [4] Prayed with them; Hebrew; sang; German (lively; well; lively zeal). 5 Meditated; read Prayers, expounded (twenty there). 5.45 Began cutting trees. 6.15 German. 6.45 Tea, religious talk. 7 Religious talk. 7.15 German. 10 Necessary talk with Mrs Causton. 10.30 German. 11 Trustees' Garden; James. 12 Dinner, religious talk. 12.45 German. 1 Visited. 3 Miss

Bovey's, French. 4 Tea, religious talk; Law; (she very serious). 5 Law. 5.15 Meditated; prayed with Delamotte. 5.30 Religious talk with Jemmy Billinghurst; sang with boys. 6 Supper; *Canons.* 7 Read Prayers, expounded. 7.30 Germans'. 8 *Canons,* ended them. 9.15 Prayed.

Grace: 7 rating twice [4 to 5, 8 to 9 am]; 6 ten times [5 to 8, 9 am to 1, 3 to 6 pm]; 5 five times.

TUESDAY, OCTOBER 5. 4 Prayed with Delamotte; Hebrew; German; (lively; well). 5 Meditated; read Prayers, expounded; felled [trees]. 6.15 Tea, religious talk. 6.45 German. 7 German; necessary talk. 8 German. 9 German; necessary talk with Delamotte. 10 German. 11 Trustees' Garden; James; sang. 12 Dinner, religious talk. 12.45 Set out with Delamotte and Jane Bradley, good talk. 1 Mostly religious talk. 2 German. 2.15 At the plantation; religious talk with Jane [Bradley], etc; read Prayers. 3 Set out; German verses; religious talk. 4 Miss Bovey's, French. 4.45 Houston came, good talk (necessary), tea. 5 Good talk. 5.15 Prayed with Delamotte; sang. 5.40 Religious talk with Carter; writ diary [summary?]; sang. 6 Supper, religious talk (necessary). 6.40 Mr Causton's, necessary talk. 7 Read Prayers, expounded. 7.45 German. 8.30 Began Cotelerius. 8.30 Prayed.

Grace: 6 rating thirteen times; 5 four times [10 to 11 am, noon to 2, 8 to 9 pm].

WEDNESDAY, OCTOBER 6. 4 Prayed with Delamotte, slept (sick). 5 Dressed; read Prayers, expounded. 6 Felled [trees]. 6.45 Tea, religious talk. 7 German. 11.15 Garden; meditated. 11.30 Visited. 12.45 At home; necessary talk. 1 Visited. 2.15 Writ notes. 2.30 Prayed with Delamotte; tea, religious talk. 3 Religious talk. 3.15 Miss Bovey's, French. 4 Tea, necessary talk (religious). 5 Law. 5.15 Prayed with Delamotte. 5.30 German. 5.45 Sang; religious talk with Cousins. 6 Religious talk with Mellichamp; walked; meditated. 7 Read Prayers, expounded; necessary talk with Mr Causton. 7.30 Mrs Gilbert, etc; Clement; sang. 8 German. 8.45 Ate, religious talk. 9.15.

Grace: 6 rating twelve times; 5 four times [5 to 6, 10 to 11 am, 3 to 5 pm; no rating noted 4 to 5 am]. [Lively zeal from 11 am to 2 pm.]

THURSDAY, OCTOBER 7. 4.15 Prayed with Delamotte; Hebrew; German. 5 Dressed; read Prayers, expounded (eleven there). 6 Felled [trees]. 6 Felled. 6.15 German. 6.30 Tea, religious talk (necessary). 7 German. 9 German; necessary talk with Mr Causton. 10 German. 11 Trustees' Garden; James. 12 Dinner; Ingham came, religious talk. 1 Visited. 2.30 Necessary business. 3 Miss Bovey's, French. 4 French; tea, religious talk. 5 Religious talk. 5.15 Prayed with Ingham and Delamotte (Ingham very zealous). 5.30 German; sang. Supper, religious talk; christened; meditated. 7 Read Prayers, expounded (twenty-seven there); Germans'. 8 Religious talk with Germans. 8.15 Writ German. 9.15 Prayed.

Grace: 6 rating twelve times; 5 four times [5 to 6, 7 to 8, 10 to 11 am, 2 to 3 pm].

FRIDAY, OCTOBER 8. 4.20 Prayed with them; Hebrew; Greek. 5 Private prayer. 5.20 Read Prayers, expounded (ten there). 6 Felled [trees]. 6.30 Coffee, religious talk. 7 German. 7.30 Necessary business. 8 German. 8.30 Necessary business for Delamotte and Ingham. 9 Taught school; prayed; German. 10

Spaniard came; writ certificate; German. 11 German. 11.45 Necessary talk with Ingham. 12 Garden; meditated; visited Hazelfort, he very serious; visited. 1 Visited. 2.30 At home; tea, religious talk. 3 Religious talk. 3.15 Miss Bovey's, French; Mrs Weddal came. 4 Good talk (necessary and religious), tea. 5 Mr ((Edgcomb)) Mackintosh, good talk. 5.30 At home; prayed with Ingham; writ diary. 6 Sang; ate, religious talk. 6.30 Walked; meditated. 7 Read Prayers, expounded (thirty there). 7.30 Germans' (sleepy). 8 German. 8.30 Garden; meditated; sang; prayed. 9.10.

Grace: 6 rating thirteen times; 5 four times [8 to 9, 10 to noon, 4 to 5 pm].

SATURDAY, OCTOBER 9. 4 Prayed with Ingham; Hebrew; German. 5 Dressed; read Prayers, expounded (twelve there); necessary business. 6 Prepared for them. 6.30 Tea with Ingham and Delamotte, religious talk. 7 Religious talk. 7.30 German. 8 Necessary business, sorting books. 9 Sorted. 10 Packed. 11 Mrs Causton's, necessary talk. 11.45 Writ notes. 12.30 Walked; meditated. 1 Dinner, religious talk. 1.45 Catechized (could not speak). 2.30 Slept. 2.45 Visited. 3 Visited (mostly religious talk). 5.10 Prayed with Delamotte; necessary business; sang. 6 supper, religious talk; prayed with Delamotte; religious talk (lively zeal). 7 Read Prayers, expounded; communicants [came], Patrick; sang; prayed (lively zeal). 7 Prayed. 8.15 Meditated; transcribed verses; prayed.

Grace: 6 rating seven times [4 to 6 am, noon to 2, 6 to 9 pm]; 5 ten times. Preserved from w4 [10 to 11 am].

SUNDAY, OCTOBER 10. 4 Prayed with Ingham; German. 4.45 Slept. 5.45 Dressed; read Prayers, expounded (twenty there). 7 Necessary talk. 7.30 Tea, religious talk. 8 Garden; meditated; necessary business. 9 Meditated. 9.30 Ephraem Syrus (+). 10.30 Read Prayers (forty there; lively zeal). 11 Preached. Sacrament (sixteen there). 12. Prayed. 12.15 Dinner, religious talk with Ingham. 12.45 Ephraem. 1 Ate with Ingham. 1.30 Catechized. 2.30 Ephraem. 2.45 Religious talk (necessary). 3 Read Prayers; catechized. 4 Prayed. 4.15 Necessary business; necessary talk. 4.30 Miss Bovey's, religious talk. 5 Religious talk, tea (close, she affected; lively zeal; +). 5.30 Garden; private prayer; sang. 6 With Delamotte; tea, religious talk. 7 Germans'; religious talk. 8 Ephraem Syrus; prayed with Delamotte.

Grace: 7 rating twice [9 to 10 am, 7 to 8 pm]; 6 eleven times; 5 twice [5 to 8 am].

MONDAY, OCTOBER 11. 4 Prayed with Ingham; German; private prayer; (very lively; well). 5 With Delamotte; read Prayers, expounded; visited Mr Mercer (convincing). 6 Sacrament with Ingham and Delamotte; tea, necessary talk (religious). 7 Necessary business; necessary talk; writ for Miss Bovey. 8 Dr Núñez came, necessary talk. 8.40 Visited Mr Desborough, Duché, Jones (convincing). 9 In school; prayed; writ for Miss Bovey. 10 Transcribed verses for Miss Bovey; necessary talk with Delamotte; writ diary. 11 Necessary business; necessary talk. 12 Dinner with Delamotte; prayed; religious talk. 1 School; visited Hazelfort. 2 School; religious talk. 3 Miss Bovey's, French. 4 Tea, religious talk. 5 Religious talk. 5.15 At home; prayed with Ingham; private prayer; sang. 6 Supper; Mr Bolzius came, necessary talk (religious). 7 Read Prayers, expounded (twenty-one there). 7.30 Germans'. 8 With Delamotte, necessary talk. 8.30 Ephraem. 9.30 Prayed.

Grace: 6 rating eleven times [4 to 7, 9 to 10 am, noon to 6 pm]; 5 seven times.

[Tuesday, October 12, about five in the evening, being to set out for Frederica the next day, I asked Mr. Causton what commands he had to Miss Sophy. Some of his words were as follows: 'The girl will never be easy till she is married.' I answered, 'Sir, she is too much afflicted to have a thought of it.' He replied, 'I'll trust a woman for that. There is no other way." I said, 'But there are few here whom you would think fit for her.' He answered, 'Let him be but an honest man, an honest, good man. I don't care whether he has a groat. I can give them a maintenance.'

[I asked, 'Sir, what directions do you give me with regard to her?' He said, 'I give her up to you. Do what you will with her. Take her into your own hands. Promise her what you will; I will make it good.']

[D—Wednesday, October 13. I set out for Frederica, and came thither early on Saturday morning the 16th] with that unlimited commission from Mr. Causton. [D—I met Mark Hird on the bluff, who gave me a melancholy account of the state of things there. The Public Service had been long discontinued, and from that time everything was grown worse and worse. Mr. Tackner had thrown off the form as well as the power of godliness, and so had most of his neighbours who had ever any pretension to it.

[Even poor Miss Sophy was scarce the shadow of what she was when I left her.] Harmless company had stole away all her strength. Most of her good resolutions were vanished away. [D—I endeavoured to

---

TUESDAY, OCTOBER 12, 1736. 4.15 Private prayer. 5 Meditated; read Prayers, expounded; necessary talk. 6 Tea with Ingham, religious talk. 6.30 German. 7 With Delamotte; with Ingham, necessary talk; necessary business. 8 German; prayed with Delamotte; necessary business for him. 9 School; Ephraem. 9.45 The Manlys and Rigdens (convincing); prayed. 10 School; James. 10.40 Trustees' Garden; James. 12 At home; dinner, necessary talk (religious) with Delamotte. 1 School; ended James. 1.30 Slept. 1.45 Visited Mrs Smith (convincing); prayed. 2 Visited Mrs Potter. 2.30 Catechized. 3 Mr D[elamotte?], necessary talk (religious). 3.15 Miss Bovey's, French. 4 Tea, religious talk. 5 Religious talk. 5.15 Necessary talk with Mr Causton. 5.30 Prayed with Delamotte. 5.45 Prayed; sang. 6 Meditated; supper, good talk (necessary) with Delamotte. 7 Read Prayers, expounded (twenty-two there); German. 8 Religious talk with Delamotte; read Ephraem to him. 9.15.

Grace: 7 rating once [4 to 5 am]; 6 eleven times; 5 five times [7 to 8, 11 to noon, 2 to 3, 6 to 8 pm].

WEDNESDAY, OCTOBER 13. 4 Private prayer with Delamotte; necessary talk (religious). 5 Meditated; read Prayers, expounded (twelve there). 5.30 Necessary business. 7 Miss Bovey's; chocolate, religious talk. 8 Mr Bellinger, Junior, necessary and useful talk. 8.30 Necessary business. 9 Necessary talk with Delamotte. 9.45 Necessary business; writ diary. 10 Necessary business. 10.30 Visited Mrs Parker, Charles, Dean. 11 Mrs Lion [?], Vanderplank, Causton, Cross. 11.45 At home; necessary talk. 12 Necessary business for Delamotte. 12.30 Bluff. 1 Causton's; necessary talk; dinner. 2 Bluff. 2.30 With

convince her of it, but in vain; and to put it effectually out of my power so to do,] and to complete her destruction, she was resolved to return to England [D—immediately. I was at first a little surprised, but I soon recollected my spirits, and remembered my calling. 'Greater is he that is in you than he that is in the world' [1 John 4:4].

Non me, qui caetera, vincet
Impetus, at rapido contrarius evehar orbi.]
['The force which overcomes others will not overcome me;
I shall ride out the swift circuit of the universe.'
(Ovid, *Metamorphoses*, ii.72-73)]

I reasoned with her much, but with no success; she could not see she was at all changed, and continued fixed in her resolution of leaving America with the first ship that sailed. I dropped the argument for the present, finding the veil was upon her heart. I begged of her to pray earnestly to God that he would direct her to what was best. I then read to her some of the most affecting parts of the *Serious Call* and of Ephraem Syrus [B—and *Paradise Lost*. But I expressly desired we might leave out the love parts of that poem, because (I said) they might hurt her mind].

Delamotte, necessary talk; set out with Jemmy [Billinghurst]; read Potter. 3 Potter. 4.45 Mrs Lacy's, necessary talk. 5 Necessary talk (various and useful). 5.30 Tea. 6 Boat; sang; private prayer (no words). 7 Private prayer. 7.30 Mr Mouse's, supper, mostly religious talk (no wind). 8 Read Prayers; Mr Griffith's, religious talk (no words). 9 Set out; sang. 9.30 Mrs Mouse came; sailed; meditated (no words). 10 They [had] mostly various talk; sang; private prayer; meditated (no words). 11.30.
　　Grace: 7 rating once [6 to 7 pm]; 6 ten times.

THURSDAY, OCTOBER 14. 3.30 Called them; slept (fair wind). 5 Private prayer; sang (no words). 6 Private prayer; Potter (no words). 7 Potter (no words). 8 Potter. 11 Ended Potter. 11.45 Dinner (words). 12.15 Writ diary; private prayer; slept. 1 German. 2 Mr Clark's bluff; writ diary; tea, mostly religious talk. 3 Walked; meditated; sang. 4 Patrick. 5 Read Prayers, expounded. 5.15 German. 5.45 Supper. 6.15 Sat with them; good talk (words).
　　Grace: 7 rating twice [3 to 5 pm]; 6 six times [5 to 8 am, noon to 1, 5 to 6 pm]; 5 five times [no rating noted 3 to 5 am, 1 to 2 pm].

FRIDAY, OCTOBER 15. 3.30 Called them; slept; private prayer. 6 Private prayer; on shore; Patrick (calm). 7 Boat; Rogers on the Thirty-Nine Articles. 8 Rogers; Patrick (no words). 9 Rogers (words). 10 Rogers. 10.45 Writ diary [summary?] (words). 11 Ended Rogers; Patrick. 12 Patrick. 1 *Country Minister's Advice*. 2 Patrick. 3 Dinner; Patrick. 4 Ended Patrick. 4.30 German. 5 Writ diary; German; rowed. 6 Landed; supper; prayed (words). 7 Various and useful talk (words); slept.
　　Grace: 7 rating thrice [6 to 7 am, 2 to 4 pm]; 6 six times; 5 four times [9 to 11 am, 6 to 8 pm].

[D—Observing there were several Germans in Frederica who, understanding no English, were utterly cut off from the Public Service, on Monday, [October] 18, I desired them to meet at my house, which they did every day at noon from thence forward. We first sung a German hymn, then read a chapter in the New Testament, which I explained as well as my little skill in the tongue would allow, and then after a second hymn and the Lord's Prayer, I concluded with the Blessing.]

SATURDAY, OCTOBER 16. 3.30 Frederica; met Mark Hird, necessary talk (religious); alas! 4 Necessary talk (religious); ah my friend! 5 Religious talk. 5.15 Slept. 6.15 Dressed; read Prayers, expounded (nine there). 7 With Miss Sophy, religious talk (necessary; she half open, not affected!). 8 Mrs Hird's, tea; Miss Fawset, Mouse, etc, necessary talk (religious and useful). 9.30 Walked with Robinson, religious talk (he seemed affected). 10 Religious talk. 10.45 At home; necessary talk. 11 Walked; Heylyn; sang. 12 With Miss Sophy, necessary talk (religious). 12.45 Dinner with Miss Sophy, Miss Fawset, Mrs Mouse. 1.15 In Mark's hut with Miss Sophy, necessary talk of Miss Fawset in vain. 2. Religious talk of her going to England (gained no ground). 3 Religious talk of her present state (gained no ground; she not convinced, not affected). 4 Walked; private prayer for Miss Sophy; Heylyn. 5 At home; Ausperger, necessary talk (religious); necessary business. 6 Writ diary; necessary talk. 6.15 Bread and butter, mostly religious talk with Ausperger. 7 Read Prayers, expounded. 7.30 Nine came; Ephraem Syrus. 8 Sang. 8.15 Necessary business. 8.30 Hird's, necessary talk with him. 9 Necessary talk (religious). 9.30 Lay down.

Grace: 7 rating twice [11 to noon, 4 to 5 pm]; 6 fifteen times.

SUNDAY, OCTOBER 17. 4.30 Prayed with Mark; meditated; private prayer. 5 Private prayer. 6 Dressed. 6.15 Read Prayers, expounded (fourteen there). 7 Read Prayers. 7.15 Religious talk with Miss Fawset (she seemed affected); religious talk with Weston. 8 Hird's, tea, mostly religious talk. 8.45 At home, necessary business. 9 Necessary business. 9.20 Meditated; sang. 10 Tackner and Mark came, religious talk (they zealous); prayed. 10.30 Sang; necessary business. 11 Read Prayers, preached (forty-six there, Mr Dyson read), Sacrament. 12 They came; sang; religious talk with Miss Sophy and Miss Fawset (they seemed affected); dressed; religious talk. 1 Ephraem Syrus; sang. 2 Sang; Ephraem. 2.45 Read Prayers. 3 Read Prayers, expounded. 3.45 Miss Sophy, etc; Ephraem. 4 Ephraem; sang. 4.45 Tea, religious and useful talk. 5.15 Walked with Miss Sophy, religious talk (gained little ground). 6 Supper. 6.30 Germans came (fourteen of us), sang. 7 Read Epistle to Timothy; sang. 7.30 Necessary talk (religious) with Ausperger. 7.45 Walked; meditated. 8 Private prayer; meditated. 9 Patrick. 9.30.

Grace: 7 rating once [8 to 9 pm]; 6 seventeen times.

[MONDAY,] OCTOBER 18. 4 Private prayer for myself. 5 Private prayer for my mother, etc. 6 Dressed; read Prayers, expounded. 7 Religious talk with Miss Sophy. 7.30 Hird's, tea with him, religious talk. 8 Cleaned my house. 9 Cleaned; necessary talk (religious) with Hird; German. 10 German. 11.30 Meditated. 11.45 Dinner. 12 Germans came (ten of us), sang; Bible; sang; dinner. 1 Mrs

In the evening of Tuesday the 19th, [I] asked [Miss Sophy] if she was still determined to go to England. On her answering, 'Yes', I offered several arguments drawn from the topics of religion against it. But they did not appear to make any impression. Then I pressed her upon the head of friendship, upon which she burst into tears and said, 'Now my resolution begins to stagger,' as it did more and more every day. [D—I began with earnestly crying to God to maintain his own cause; and then reading to a few who came to my house in the evening one of Ephraem Syrus's exhortations, as I did every night after; and by the blessing of God, not without effect. My next point was to divert Miss Sophy from her fatal resolution of going to England, in which, after several fruitless attempts, I at length prevailed; nor was it long before she more than recovered the ground she had lost.]

Calwell came, necessary talk (religious); Mrs Parker, necessary talk (religious), they friendly! 2 Ephraem. 2.45 Walked. 3 Miss Sophy came; Heylyn; prayed. 4 Heylyn; sang; prayed. 5 Walked; meditated; sang; private prayer. 6 Hird's, with Miss Sophy; tea, religious and useful talk; writ diary; read Prayers. 7 Read Prayers, expounded. 7.20 Five came, Ephraem. 8 Ephraem; sang. 8.15 Law with Miss Sophy. 9 With Miss Sophy in her hut, religious talk. 10.20 Writ diary [summary?]. 10.30.

    Grace: 7 rating four times [4 to 6 am, 3 to 5 pm]; 6 eleven times; 5 thrice [6 to 7, 11 to noon, 7 to 8 pm].

TUESDAY, OCTOBER 19. 5 Private prayer. 5.30 Slept. 5.45 Private prayer. 6 Dressed; read Prayers, expounded. 7 Miss Sophy; prayed; Heylyn. 7.45 Hird's, began Milton with him. 8 Tea with them. 8.30 Milton. 9.30 At home; necessary talk; necessary business. 10 German. 11 Walked; Heylyn. 11.40 Dinner. 12 German. 12.30 Ephraem. 2.15 Miss Sophy came; Law. 3 Talk of her going to England (gained no ground). 4 In her hut; Milton. 5 Walked; meditated; private prayer; (lively zeal). 6 Tea with Miss Sophy, mostly religious talk; with Dorman, necessary talk. 7 Read Prayers, expounded. 7.30 They came; Ephraem; sang. 8 Religious talk with Miss Sophy of going (she doubted). 9 She went; private prayer for her (lively zeal; convincing). 9.30.

    Grace: 6 rating twelve times; 5 five times [6 to 7, 9 to 10 am, 3 to 4, 6 to 8 pm].

WEDNESDAY, OCTOBER 20. 4.30 Private prayer. 6 Dressed; read Prayers, expounded. 7 Miss Sophy came to me, Law, religious talk (she affected much). 8 Hird's; tea, religious and useful talk (necessary). 9.15 Visited Mr Lawley, necessary talk. 9.45 Writ diary. 10 German. 11 Heylyn. 12 German; Ephraem. 1 Ephraem. 1.30 Visited. 2.45 Necessary business. 3 Hird's; Miss Sophy, company came; tea, various talk (words). 4 Various talk. 4.30 Walked; meditated; sang; (words). 5 Law; sang; private prayer; (lively zeal and +). 6 Writ to the Trustees. 6.30 Read Prayers (twenty-eight there). 7 Miss Sophy, etc; Ephraem; sang. 7.45 Hird's, religious talk. 8 Supper, religious and useful talk. 9 Religious and useful talk.

    Grace: 7 rating twice [11 to noon, 7 to 8 pm]; 6 nine times; 5 seven times [8 to 10 am, 3 to 4, 6 to 7, 8 to 10 pm].

[Saturday 23. Between five and six in the evening Mr. Oglethorpe returned from the southward. I was in the fort with Mr. Horton when he came. He ran to Mr. Horton, kissed him, and expressed much kindness to him, but took no notice of me, good or bad, any more than if I had not been in the room. I was not surprised, having long expected it.]

On Saturday evening I told [Miss Sophy of] the unusual coldness with which Mr. Oglethorpe had then received me, and added, 'Now, Miss Sophy, you may go to England, for I can assist you no longer. My interest is gone.' She answered, 'No, now I will not stir a foot.' I said, 'If Mr. Oglethorpe advised you to go, he may be displeased.' She replied, 'Let him be pleased or displeased. I care not.' And then, turning to me with the utmost earnestness, she said, 'Sir, you encouraged me in my

---

[THURSDAY,] OCTOBER 21. 5 Private prayer; meditated. 6 Dressed; read Prayers, expounded. 7 Religious talk with Miss Sophy; Hird's; tea, religious talk. 7.45 Law. 8.30 At home; German. 9 German; writ diary. 9.30 Ephraem. 10 German. 10.30 Walked; Heylyn. 11 Heylyn. 11.30 Dinner. 12 German. 12.30 Visited. 1.45 Necessary business. 2 Ephraem. 4 Miss Sophy came, Law. 4.20 Walked; Milton. 5 Prayed with her. 5.15 Private prayer. 6 Tea with her, religious talk. 6.30 Read Prayers, expounded (twenty there). 7 They came; Ephraem; sang. 8 Miss Sophy; Law, religious talk; prayed. 9 Writ diary.

Grace: 6 rating fourteen times; 5 twice [6 to 7 am, 6 to 7 pm].

[FRIDAY,] OCTOBER 22. 3 Private prayer; (well). 4 Slept. 5 Private prayer; religious talk with Mark. 6 Dressed; read Prayers, expounded (eight there). 7 Prayed with Mark and Miss Sophy; tea, religious talk. 8 Law. 9 At home; German. 10.15 Ephraem. 11 Necessary business. 11.15 Six Germans. 11.45 Necessary business. 1 Visited Davison. 2 Religious talk. 2.45 Mr Lawley (he and Graham seemed affected). 3 Hird's; Miss Sophy and Mrs Mouse; tea, religious talk. 4 Religious talk. 4.15 Walked with Miss Sophy, religious talk. 4.30 Sat; read Law. 5.10 Prayed. 5.30 Walked; private prayer. 5.45 At home; Ephraem. 6.30 Read Prayers, expounded (twenty-five there). 7 Miss Sophy, etc; read Ephraem; sang. 7.30 Supper with Miss Sophy. 7.45 Law. 8.45 Hird's, religious talk. 9 Mostly religious talk. 9.45 At home; Mr Graham came. 10 Slept.

Grace: 7 rating twice [4 to 6 pm]; 6 fourteen times; 5 twice [8 to 10 pm].

SATURDAY, OCTOBER 23. 6 Private prayer; read Prayers, expounded (nine there). 7 Miss Sophy; prayed; Law. 8 Hird's; tea, religious talk. 8.45 Milton. 10.30 At home; German. 11.30 Mr Hird's, he asleep; necessary talk (religious) with Miss Phoebe. 12 Ephraem. 12.30 With Miss Sophy and Miss Fawset, religious and useful talk. 1 Dinner, Milton. 2 Visited. 2.30 Ephraem. 3 Hird's; religious talk with Miss Sophy. 4 Tea with Miss Fawset, etc. 4.45 With Mr Horton, necessary talk (he very ill, and open!). 5 Necessary talk. 5.30 Oglethorpe came, he [had] necessary talk (cold and strange!). 6 At home; necessary talk with Vernon. 6.15 Read Prayers, expounded (twenty-two there). 7 Ephraem. 7.45 Religious talk (necessary) with Miss Sophy (excellent woman!). 8 With Miss Fawset, etc; tea, religious talk. 9 Writ diary. 9 Prayed; could not sleep. 11.

greatest trials. Be not discouraged in your own. Fear nothing. If Mr. Oglethorpe will not, God will help you.'

The next morning I had a long conversation with Mr. Oglethorpe, in consequence of which I told her, 'Miss Sophy, Mr. Oglethorpe thinks it best that you should return to Savannah immediately. She fell into a great passion of tears, and said she could not bear the thoughts of it [B—she was deeply concerned and utterly averse to it]. I talked with her near an hour, told her Mr. Causton's engagement to make good whatever I should promise her, so that she had only to make her own terms, and left her a little more composed.

Monday, October 25. [D—I set out for Savannah with Miss Sophy.] I asked Mr. Oglethorpe in what boat she should go. He said, 'She can go in none but yours, and indeed there is none so proper.' I saw the danger to myself, but yet had a good hope I should be delivered out of it, (1) First, because it was not my choice which brought me into it; (2) Because I still felt in myself the same desire and design to live a single life; and (3) Because I was persuaded, should my desire and design be changed, yet her resolution to live single would continue.

We set out about noon. The afternoon, and so the greatest part of the following days, we spent partly in using Bishop Patrick's prayers, partly in reading the first volume of Fleury's History of the Church—a book I

SUNDAY, OCTOBER 24. 3.30 Private Prayer. 4 Private prayer; prayed with Mark. 5 Slept. 6 Dressed; read Prayers (eighteen there). 7 Expounded; prayed. 7.30 Prayed with Miss Sophy and Mark; religious talk (necessary) with Miss Sophy. 8 Tea, religious talk (necessary). 9.45 Oglethorpe's, necessary talk (religious). 11 Read Prayers, preached (thrity-four there). 12 Sacrament; prayed with Miss Sophy, etc. 12.45 Religious talk (necessary) with Miss Fawset (she convinced). 1 Dinner, religious talk (necessary) with Miss Sophy (she grieved). 2 Religious talk (necessary); prayed. 3 At home; Ephraem. 3.30 Read Prayers (fifty there). 4 Expounded; Miss Sophy, etc; Law; sang. 5 Prayed with Mark and Miss Sophy; necessary business. 6 Hird's; tea, necessary talk (religious). 7 Miss Phoebe's, necessary talk (religious). 7.30 Germans (eleven came), sang, etc. 8 Hird's; mostly religious talk with Miss Sophy, etc. 9.30.

Grace: 7 rating once [3.30 to 5 am]; 6 twelve times; 5 four times [actually three, 6 to 7, 8 to 10 pm].

MONDAY, OCTOBER 25. 4.45 Private prayer. 5 Prayed; meditated; necessary business. 5.45 Married Mr Weston and Miss Fawset. 6 Religious talk. 6.15 Read Prayers, expounded. 7 Hird's, necessary talk (religious); tea; company came. 8 Necessary business. 9 Necessary business; necessary talk. 10 With Oglethorpe, he [had] necessary talk. 11.30 Set out with Miss Sophy, religious talk. 1 Prayed with Miss Sophy; began Fleury. 3.15 Landed; tea, mostly religious talk. 4 Set out; Fleury; prayed. 5 Rowed. 5.45 Religious talk with Miss Sophy. 6 Thought. 7 Doboy [Sound], landed. 7.30 Supper; read Prayers. 9 Lay by Miss Sophy. 1 Sins of thought.

chose for her sake chiefly, as setting before her such glorious examples of faith and patience in the sufferings of those ancient worthies 'who resisted unto blood, striving against sin'.

In the evening we landed on an uninhabited island, made a fire, supped, went to Prayers together, and then spread our sail over us on four stakes, to keep off the night dews. Under this on one side were Miss Sophy, myself, and one of our boys who came with me from Savannah; on the other, our boat's crew. The northeast wind was high and piercingly cold. And it was the first night she had ever spent in such a lodging. But she complained of nothing, appearing as satisfied as if she had been warm upon a bed of down.

I can never be sensible enough of the exceeding goodness of God, both this night and the four following, all which we spent together, while none but the All-seeing Eye observed us. To him alone be the praise that we were both withheld from anything which the world counts evil. Yet am I not thereby justified, but must justify God for whatever temporal evils may befall me on her account. What though I was innocent of the great offence? Yet as St. Cyprian observes on almost a parallel occasion (*Ep. ad Pomponium*, ¶3): 'Certe ipse complexus, ipsa confabulatio et osculatio, quantum dedecoris et criminis confitetur!' ['Assuredly the fact of lying together, embracing and kissing, constitutes a confession of unseemly misbehaviour.']

The next morning [October 26], as we crossed Doboy Sound, the wind being high and the sea rough, I asked her, 'Miss Sophy, are not you afraid to die?' She answered calmly, 'No, I don't desire to live any longer. O that God would let me go now! Then I should be at rest. In this world I expect nothing but misery.'

In the evening, the wind being contrary, we landed on the south end of St. Catherine's Island. And here we were obliged to stay till Friday, so that I had time to observe her behaviour more nearly. And the more I observed, the more was I amazed. Nothing was ever improper or ill-timed. All she said and did was equally tinctured with seriousness

---

TUESDAY, OCTOBER 26. 6 Prayed; tea, religious talk; read Prayers. 7 Set out; prayed with Miss Sophy; Fleury. 8 Prayed with Miss Sophy; religious talk; Fleury. 9 Prayed with Miss Sophy; Fleury. 10 Writ diary; prayed; Fleury. 10.30 Rowed. 11 Prayed with Miss Sophy; Fleury. 12 Dinner. 12.30 Landed on Sapelo [Island]. 1 Set out; Fleury; prayed with Miss Sophy. 2 Fleury. 4.15 St Catherine's [Island], north end; walked with Miss Sophy, religious and useful talk. 5 Tea, good talk, oysters. 6 Good talk (various and religious). 7.30 Read Prayers; necessary and useful talk. 8.30.

Grace: 6 rating nine times; 5 six times [2 to 4, 5 to 9 pm].

WEDNESDAY, OCTOBER 27. 12 [midnight] Religious talk with Miss Sophy. 1 Slept. 6.15 Drowsy, necessary talk (religious); writ diary (no words [every hour until 11 am]). 7 Tea, religious talk; read Prayers. 8 Fleury. 9 Walked with Miss Sophy;

and sweetness. She was often in pain, which she could not hide; but it never betrayed her into impatience. She gave herself up to God, owning she suffered far less than she deserved. On Wednesday in the afternoon we fell into a conversation on 'lying in order to do good.' She owned she used to think there was no harm in it and that she had herself sometimes done it [B—many times, particularly] to me, [B—in the case of the Miss Fawset.] But added, she was now convinced, no lying was lawful [B—excusable], and would therefore watch against all kinds of it for the future [B—do so no more].

On Thursday [October 28], in the afternoon, after walking some time, we sat down in a little thicket by the side of a spring. Here we entered upon a close conversation on Christian holiness. The openness with which she owned her ignorance of it, and the earnest desire she showed for further instruction, as it much endeared her to me, so it made me hope she would some day prove an eminent pattern of it.

On Friday morning [October 29], we ventured to set out, though the wind was very high. The waves dashed over the boat every moment, and the cold was extremely piercing. She showed no concern, nor made any complaint, but appeared quite cheerful [B—easy] and satisfied.

It was not without some difficulty that in the afternoon we landed on St. Catherine's again. Observing in the night, the fire we lay by burning

---

prayed; religious talk. 10 Religious talk. 10.30 Fleury. 11 Fleury; writ diary. 11.30 Prayed; Fleury. 12 Mostly religious talk. 1 Fleury. 12.30 Walked; prayed with Miss Sophy; religious talk. 2 Religious talk; prayed with her. 3 Religious talk (necessary). 3.30 Tea, religious talk. 4 Necessary business. 4.40 Fleury. 5 Walked with Miss Sophy, religious talk. 5.45 Supper. 7 Good talk (religious and much); read Prayers. 8.

Grace: 6 rating eleven times; 5 thrice [noon to 1, 3 to 4, 7 to 8 pm].

THURSDAY, OCTOBER 28. 6.45 Private prayer; tea; read Prayers. 8 Fleury. 9 Walked with Miss Sophy, mostly religious talk. 10 Walked; religious talk; sang. 10.45 Fleury. 12 Dinner; Fleury. 1 Fleury. 1.30 At the well, religious talk. 2 Religious talk (she very serious and affected; lively zeal). 3 Religious talk; tea, necessary talk. 4.15 Writ diary; walked; private prayer; meditated. 5 Meditated; private prayer (lively zeal). 6 Supper, good talk (various and religious). 7 Read Prayers; mostly religious talk. 8 Lay down. 11 Sins.

FRIDAY, OCTOBER 29. 6.30 Meditated; necessary business. 7 Tea, religious talk (necessary). 8 Read Prayers; religious talk. 9 Religious talk (necessary). 10 Set out; good talk (necessary); wind stormy (words). 3.15 St Catherine's; tea, religious talk (necessary). 4 Religious talk (necessary). 4.30 Walked; meditated; private prayer. 5 Writ diary; Fleury. 5.30 Necessary business; religious talk. 6 Supper; much talk (religious). 7 Read Prayers; religious talk (much); lay down. 11 Religious talk with Miss Sophy; expounded [examined?] (excellent woman). 12 Religious talk (close); sang.

Grace: 6 rating seven times [8 to 10 am, 3 to 6, 11 pm to 1 am]; 5 nine times.

bright, that Miss Sophy was broad awake, I asked her, 'Miss Sophy, how far are you engaged to Mr. Mellichamp?' She answered, 'I have promised either to marry him or to marry no one at all.' I said (which indeed was the expression of a sudden wish, not of any forward design) [B—a sudden wish of what I knew could never be], 'Miss Sophy, I should think myself happy if I was to spend my life with you.' She burst out into tears and said, 'I am every way unhappy. I won't have Tommy, for he is a bad man. And I can have none else.' She added, 'Sir, you don't know the danger you are in. I beg you would speak no word more on this head.' And after a while, 'When others have spoke to me on this subject, I felt an aversion to them. But I don't feel any to you. We may converse on other subjects as freely as ever.' Both my judgment and will acquiesced in what she said, and we ended our conversation with a Psalm.

On Saturday [October 30], in the afternoon we landed on Bear Island, and walked together for near two hours. Here again Miss Sophy expressed the strongest uneasiness and an utter aversion to living at Mr. Causton's, saying, with many tears, 'I can't live in that house; I can't bear the shocks I meet with there.' I said, 'Don't be uneasy, Miss Sophy, on that account. If you don't care to be at Mr. Causton's, you are welcome to a room in our house; or, which I think would be best of all, and your aunt herself once proposed, you may live in the house with the Germans.' She made little reply. About five we took boat again, and in the evening came to Rotten Possum, another uninhabited island about thirty miles from Savannah. Here our provisions failed, neither could we find any firewood, except one old stump of a tree, nor so much as two or three stakes to prop up our sail. Miss Sophy hung her apron on two small sticks, which kept off a little of the north wind from her head, and lay down on the ground under the canopy of heaven, with all the signs of perfect content.

On Sunday, October 31, we came to Thunderbolt. Here we agreed that I should walk to Savannah, and meet her at the landing; that she

---

Saturday, October 30. 5.30 Private prayer; tea, religious talk; read Prayers. 7 Set out; Fleury; prayed. 1 Bear Island; dinner; writ diary. 1.15 Meditated; private prayer. 2.30 Religious talk (necessary) with Miss Sophy. 3.30 Tea, religious talk (necessary; she grieved!). 4 Necessary talk. 4.15 Set out; rowed. 5.15 Private prayer; prayed with Miss Sophy. 6 Private prayer. 6.30 Slept. 7 Slept; private prayer; necessary talk (religious). 8 Rotten Possum; tea, necessary talk; read Prayers. 9 Lay down.

[Sunday,] October 31. 1 Set out; private prayer; slept. 5.15 Skidaway; Mr Wattle's, necessary talk (useful and religious). 6 Mr Griffin's, religious talk. Wattle's, tea. 7 Mr Mouse's, good talk (necessary and religious). 8 Good talk (necessary and religious); breakfast. 9 Read Prayers. 9.30 Set out; religious talk.

should stay at my house while I went to Mr. Causton's and obtained for her such conditions as she desired, and [B—that, those being obtained, I would afterward go with her to Mr. Causton's house.] But I, by a mistake, not meeting her at the landing, she went to Mr. Causton's directly. About five Mr. Causton came to my house, [B—invited me to his,] largely professed his obligations to me, and repeated again and again, whatever I desired with regard to Sophy, he would consent to. After talking again with her upon it, I desired, (1) That [B—whereas she complained of want of retirement,] she should come to my house [B—till 10] every morning and [B—a short time after Prayers in the] evening; (2) That at his house she should come into no company but by her own choice; (3) That she should be no more upbraided with Mellichamp, nor should he be mentioned before her.

Monday, November 1. She was eighteen years old, and from the beginning of our intimate acquaintance till this day, I verily believe she used no guile: not only because even now I know no instance to the contrary, nor only because the simplicity of her behaviour was a constant voucher for her sincerity, but because of the entire openness of all her conversation, answering whatever questions I proposed without either hesitation or reserve, immediately and directly. Another thing I was much pleased with in her was that whenever we were conversing or reading there was such a stillness in her whole behaviour, scarce stirring hand or foot, that she 'seemed to be all but her attention dead' [cf. Congreve, 'On Mrs. Arabella Hunt, Singing']. Yet at other times she was all life—active, diligent, indefatigable—always doing something, and doing with all her might whatever her hand found to do. For indeed if the weakness of her body did not, her sense of honour would not hinder her doing anything.

10.30 Thunderbolt; necessary talk (religious). 11 Tea, religious talk (necessary). 12 Read Prayers. 12.30 Set out; mostly religious talk. 1 Good talk (necessary and religious). 2 Mostly religious talk. 2.30 At home; religious talk (necessary) with Delamotte; (sins). 3 Religious talk (necessary) with Mrs Musgrove; tea; walked in Trustees' Garden; meditated. 4 Private prayer; sang; Miss Sophy came not to meditate! 5 At home; religious talk. 5.15 Mr Causton came, necessary talk (religious). 5.30 Necessary talk; necessary business. 6 Necessary business. 6.30 Miss Bovey's, necessary talk (religious). 7 Religious talk. 7.30 German. 8 Religious talk. 8.30 At home; necessary business. 9 Prayed.

Grace: 6 rating five times [5 to 6, 9 to 10 am, 3 to 5, 7 to 8 pm]; 5 eleven times.

MONDAY, NOVEMBER 1. 4 Private prayer. 5 Necessary talk; read Prayers, expounded. 5.45 With Miss Sophy, necessary talk. 5 Necessary talk (religious). 6.45 At home; necessary talk with Miss Sophy. 7 Tea, they [had] good talk. 7.30 Garden with Miss Sophy, religious talk. 8 Prayed with her; walked with Ingham

Nor did she at all favour herself on account of that weakness; as she could not remove, she would not indulge it. Softness and tenderness of this kind she would not know, having left the delicacy of the gentlewoman in England. She utterly despised those inconveniences which women of condition in Europe would think worse than death. With bread to eat and water to drink, she was content. (Indeed she never used any drink beside.) She was patient of labour, of cold, heat, wet, of badness or want of food. And of pain to an eminent degree, it never making any alteration in her speech or behaviour; so that her frequent headache was only to be discerned by her paleness and the dullness of her eyes.

As little of a gentlewoman as she was in delicacy and niceness, she was still less so, if possible, in love of dress. No philosopher would have defined her ζωὸν φιλόκοσμον ['natural regard for appearance']. Though always neat, she was always plain. And she was equally careless of finery in other things. It was use she considered, not show. Nor novelty either, being as little concerned for new as for fine or pretty things. The same disregard she had for what are called diversions, such as balls, dancing, visiting; having no desire either to see or be seen, unless in order to be wise and better.

Not that her love of retirement or want of curiosity was owing, as some supposed, to want of sense. Her constant, even seriousness was very far from stupidity. Indeed her understanding was not of a piece with her years. Though unimproved, it was deep and strong. It reached the highest things and the lowest. It rose to the greatest, yet stooped to the least. With fine sense she had a large share of common sense, and particularly of prudence, suiting herself readily to all persons and occasions, nature in her supplying the place of experience. Her apprehension was so quick that there was scarce ever need to repeat a thing twice to her, and so clear as to conceive things the most remote from common life without any mistake or confusion. But she was by no means fond of showing her sense, seldom speaking when she could

---

and Delamotte, necessary talk (religious). 9 Necessary talk (religious). 10 Religious talk with Mrs Gilbert; read Prayers. 1 Preached, Sacrament. 12.15 Prayed with Ingham and Delamotte; writ diary. 12.45 Meditated. 1 Dinner, good talk. 2 Visited Mrs Parker, Hazelfort; prayed; religious talk. 3 Visited John Brownfield, mostly religious talk; necessary business. 4 Miss Bovey's, Houston came; tea, mostly religious talk. 5 At home; prayed with Delamotte; writ diary. 5.30 Tea, religious talk (close). 6 Religious talk. 6.45 Sang with Delamotte; read Prayers. 7 Read Prayers, expounded; religious talk (necessary) with the Germans. 8 German. 8.15 Miss Sophy, read John Valdesso. 9 Religious talk; Sophy went; prayed. 9.30.
    Grace: 6 rating ten times [4 to 5, 10 am to 1, 2 to 3, 4 to 7, 8 to 10]; 5 eight times.

decently avoid it, and then in few words, but such as were clear and pertinent, and contained much in little compass. One reason of her speaking so seldom was the mean opinion she had of herself, particularly of her own understanding, which was also the great cause of her constant eagerness for instruction. And indeed, for improvement of every kind, as she was very sensible of her want of all. Hence too it was that she was so teachable in things either of a speculative or practical nature; so readily convinced of any error in her judgment, or oversight in her behaviour; and so easily persuaded to lay aside her own designs or measures, and pursue those which others advised. Indeed one would almost have thought she had no such ingredient in her nature as self-will.

As her humility was, so was her meekness. She seemed to have been born without anger. Her soul appeared to be wholly made up of mildness, gentleness, long-suffering. Then especially, when she had to do with those who had injured her beyond the manner of men. She stayed for no entreaty before she forgave. But of one thing she was not easily convinced: that anyone needed her forgiveness, or had done ill either to her or any other. She was very difficultly induced to believe any evil which she did not see. And even when she could not help believing, still she took care 'to speak evil of no man' [Titus 3:2].

And as her greatest enemies, so much more the greatest strangers had a share in her goodwill and affection. She was a friend to humankind. To whoever was distressed she was all sympathy, tenderness, compassion. But to any whom she particularly called a friend her behaviour can only be conceived, not expressed. Such was the spirit of gratitude that ran through it, such the softness, the sweetness of every part of it; yet still preserving in all that yielding easiness, a modesty pure as the light.

The temper of her heart toward God is best known by him 'who seeth in secret' [Matt. 6:4, etc.]. What appeared of it was a deep, even reverence, ripening into love, and a resignation unshaken in one of the severest trials which human nature is exposed to. The utmost anguish never wrung from her a murmuring word: she saw the hand of God and was still. She said indeed, 'If it be possible, Father', but added, 'Not as I will, but as thou wilt!' [cf. Mark 14:36].

Such was the woman, according to my closest observation, of whom I now began to be much afraid. My desire and design still was to live single. But how long it would continue I knew not. I therefore consulted my friends, whether it was not best to break off all intercourse with her immediately. Three months after, they told me 'It would have been best.' But at this time, they expressed themselves so ambiguously that I understood them to mean the direct contrary, viz., that I ought not to break it off. And accordingly she came to me (as had been agreed) every morning and evening.

The time she was at my house was spent thus. Immediately after breakfast we all joined in Hickes's *Devotions*. She was then alone till eight. I taught her French between eight and nine, and at nine we joined in prayer again. She then read or wrote French till ten. In the evening I read to her and some [B—several] others, select parts of Ephraem Syrus, and afterwards Dean Young's and Mr. Reeves's *Sermons*. We always concluded [B—our reading] with a Psalm.

This I began with a single eye. But it was not long before I found it a task too hard for me to preserve the same intentions with which I began, in such intimacy of conversation as ours was. My greatest difficulty was while I was teaching her French, when being obliged (as having but one book) to sit close to her, unless I prayed without ceasing I could not avoid using some familiarity or other which was not needful. Sometimes I put my arm round her waist, sometimes took her by the hand, and sometimes kissed her. To put a short stop to this, on November 10, I asked her to step into my garden, and told her, 'Miss Sophy, I am going to use such a freedom with you as scarce ever man used with woman before. I have often desired that you would treat me as I do you—tell me of what you dislike in my behaviour. But you never have, to this day. At least now tell me, and I will alter it.' She said, 'Indeed, sir, I have seen nothing yet to tell you of. When I do, I promise you I will speak.' I replied, 'Why then, Miss Sophy, I must tell you plainly, what I dislike in it myself. I converse with you, not to please myself, but to help you. I desire to converse, not as a lover, but a friend. And so I have often told you. But some parts of my behaviour might make you question my sincerity. Those I dislike, and have therefore resolved never to touch you more.' She appeared surprised and deeply serious, but said not one word.

For ten days I kept firm to my resolution; but on November 20, as we sat together, I took her by the hand (though I was convinced it was wrong), and kissed her once or twice. I resolved again and relapsed again several times during the five or six weeks following. And on December 28, when I set out for Frederica, I found the effects of it, being thoroughly unwilling to leave her, and not soon recovering from the heaviness consequent upon it.

TUESDAY, NOVEMBER 2. 4 Prayed with Delamotte; private prayer. 5 Necessary business; read Prayers, expounded. 5.45 Miss Sophy came; tea. 6 Religious talk. 7 Letter to Trustees. 8 Began French with Miss Sophy. 9 French; prayed with her and Delamotte. 10 Writ French. 11.15 Trustees' Garden; walked; French; sang. 12 At home; sang with Delamotte; writ diary; dinner, necessary talk (religious). 1 Abridged French; visited Kelly. 2 Visited Potter; necessary business; necessary talk. 3.15 Miss Bovey's, French. 4 Tea, religious talk. 5 Mrs Joubert, religious talk. 5.15 At home; prayed with Delamotte. 5.30 Private prayer; sang. 6 Supper. 6.30 Meditated. 6.45 Read Prayers. 7 Expounded;

German. 8 Miss Sophy and Miss Bovey, began Ephraem Syrus. 9 Private prayer. 9.15.

Grace: 7 rating once [4 to 5 am]; 6 eight times [5 to 7, 8 to 9, noon to 1, 2 to 3, 4 to 6, 8 to 9 pm]; 5 eight times.

WEDNESDAY, NOVEMBER 3. 4.45 Private prayer. 5 Necessary business; read Prayers, expounded (very lively). 6 Miss Sophy came; coffee, religious talk. 7 Writ French. 8 Abridged French Grammar. 9 Prayed with Delamotte and Miss Sophy; French; writ diary. 10 French. 11 Trustees' Garden; meditated; prayed for Oglethorpe and myself (c and lively zeal). 12 At home; necessary business; visited Mrs Weddal, etc. 1 Visited Charles, etc. 2 At home; French. 3 Dinner, religious talk. 3.30 French. 4 ((Edgcomb)) Mackintosh came, mostly religious talk, tea. 4.45 Thompson, religious talk. 5 At home; prayed with Delamotte; private prayer; sang. 6 Garden; meditated. 6.30 German. 7 Read Prayers, expounded. 7.45 Miss Bovey and Miss Sophy came, Ephraem Syrus. 8 Ephraem; sang. 8.45 Religious talk (necessary) with Miss Sophy (I fear for her!). 9.15 At home; prayed with Delamotte. 9.30.

Grace: 7 rating twice [11 to 12 am, 8 to 9 pm]; 6 eleven times; 5 four times [4.45 to 6, 7 to 9 am, 2 to 3 pm].

THURSDAY, NOVEMBER 4. 3.40 Private prayer. 4 Meditated; private prayer. 5 Necessary business; read Prayers, expounded. 5.45 Miss Sophy came; tea. 6 Tea, religious talk; prayed with them. 6.45 French. 7 French; prayed with them. 9 French. 10 Mr Causton's, necessary talk (religious) with him. 11 Trustees' Garden; read *The Poor Planter's Physician*. 12 Dinner, necessary talk (religious); writ notes. 1 Visited. 2.15 French. 3 Miss Bovey's; Mrs Montagut there; mostly various talk. 4 Good talk (various and religious); tea. 5 At home; prayed with Delamotte. 5.30 Walked to the churchyard, no burial; meditated. 6 Supper, religious talk. 6.30 German. 7.15 Read Prayers, expounded (thirty-five there). 8 Miss Bovey and Miss Sophy came; Ephraem; sang. 9 Walked with Miss Sophy, religious talk (she quite open and affected); prayed. 9.30.

Grace: 7 rating once [8 to 9 pm]; 6 ten times; 5 seven times [9 am to 1, 2 to 4, 7 to 8 pm].

FRIDAY, NOVEMBER 5. 4 Prayed with Delamotte; slept; (very heavy). 5 Prayed; necessary business; read Prayers, expounded (thirteen there). 6 Prayed with them; coffee, religious talk. 7 Religious talk. 7.15 French. 9 Prayed with them; French. 10 French. 11 Read Davies to Miss Sophy. 11.30 Writ diary; visited Mrs Smith, Clancey. 12 Visited Manly, Campbell. 12.15 French. 2.45 Tea. 3 Tea, religious talk. 3.30 Miss Bovey's, French. 4.45 Tea, religious talk (necessary). 5 Religious talk. 5.15 Prayed with Delamotte. 5.30 Ephraem. 5.45 Sang with boys. 6 Ephraem. 6.30 Germans'; they supping; ate; meditated. 7 Read Prayers, expounded; Germans'. 8 Miss Bovey and Miss Sophy; Ephraem; prayed; sang. 8.45 Walked with Miss Sophy, religious talk (she zealous). 9 Religious talk. 9.15 At home; prayed.

Grace: 7 rating once [8 to 9 pm]; 6 thirteen times; 5 five times [5 to 6, 8 to 11 am, 2 to 3 pm; no rating noted 4 to 5 am].

SATURDAY, NOVEMBER 6. 4 Prayed with Delamotte; Hebrew; private prayer. Necessary business; read Prayers, expounded. 5.45 Miss Sophy; tea. 6 Tea, religious talk; [read] Hickes with them; writ diary. 7 French. 9 Prayed with them; French. 10 French. 11 Trustees' Garden; Kempis. 12 At home; garden; necessary business. 12.30 Dinner, religious talk. 1 Indians came, they dined. 1.45 Set out; religious talk. 2 Religious and useful talk. 3 Good talk; read Brerewood. 3.45 Mr Lacy's, good talk. 4. Good talk; tea, good talk. 5 Set out; religious talk; private prayer. 6 Religious talk; private prayer. 6.30 At home; tea, religious talk (necessary). 7 Read Prayers, christened, expounded. 8 Miss Sophy, etc; Patrick; prayed; sang; religious talk with Miss Sophy. 9 Religious talk. 9.15 Prayed.

Grace: 7 rating once [4 to 5 am]; 6 six times [6 to 7, 11 am to 1, 2 to 3, 5 to 6, 8 to 9 pm]; 5 ten times.

SUNDAY, NOVEMBER 7. 4 Prayed with Ingham and Delamotte. 4.30 Slept. 5.15 Dressed; necessary business. 6 Read Prayers, expounded (twenty there). 7 Tea, religious talk (necessary). 8 Garden; Greek Testament. 9 Ephraem. 9.30 Trustees' Garden with Ingham, religious talk (close; lively zeal). 10 Religious talk. 10.45 Read Prayers. 11 Read Prayers, preached (forty-five there), Sacrament (twelve there). 12 Sacrament. 12.30 Germans'; dinner. 1 Dinner, religious talk (necessary). 1.45 Necessary business. 2 Catechized. 2.30 Slept. 2.45 Religious talk with Delamotte. 3 Read Prayers; catechized. 4 Read Prayers. 4.15 Religious talk (necessary). 4.30 Ephraem. 5 Ephraem; prayed with Delamotte; religious talk; sang. 6 Miss Sophy came; tea, no talk. 6.45 German. 7 German, religious talk with them. 7.30 With Miss Sophy; Ephraem. 8 Religious talk with Miss Sophy. 9.15 Prayed; necessary talk. 9.30.

Grace: 7 rating twice [4 to 5, 9 to 10 am]; 6 twelve times; 5 four times [noon to 2, 4 to 5, 9 to 10 pm].

MONDAY, NOVEMBER 8. 4 Prayed with Delamotte; Hebrew; German; private prayer (lively). 5 Necessary business; read Prayers, expounded (twenty there). 6 Miss Sophy; tea, religious talk. 7 Began German Grammar. 9 Grammar; prayed with them. 10 Trustees' Garden; Hickes' *Christian Priesthood*. 11 Hickes. 12.30 Dinner, mostly religious talk. 1 Necessary business. 1.20 Visited James Smith, Betty Wright. 2 Visited Mrs Wilder [?], Vanderplank. 3 Miss Bovey's, French. 4 Tea, religious talk. 4.45 At home; religious talk with Delamotte. 5 Prayed with Delamotte; buried; sang. 6 Sang; Ephraem. 6.45 Meditated. 7 Read Prayers, expounded (thirty there); German (very sleepy). 8 At home; Miss Bovey, Miss Sophy; Ephraem; sang. 9 Necessary talk (religious). 9.15 Prayed.

Grace: 7 rating twice [4 to 5 am, 8 to 9 pm]; 6 ten times; 5 five times [5 to 6, 7 to 9, 10 to noon].

TUESDAY, NOVEMBER 9. 4 Prayed with Delamotte; not well, slept. 5 Necessary business; read Prayers, expounded (twenty there); Miss Sophy, tea, religious talk. 6 Religious talk, tea. 7 German. 8.45 Visited Mrs Potter. 9 Shaved; necessary business; necessary talk. 10 Took boat; Hickes. 11.15 Irene; prayed; religious talk (necessary). 12 Cut down trees. 1 Mrs Musgrove came, religious talk. 1.30 Tomochichi and Sinauky came; dinner. 2 Dinner, religious talk (useful and various). 3 Tea, religious talk (necessary); sang with Ingham; with Germans. 4.15 Set out; good talk. 5 Good talk (necessary). 5.45 At home; necessary business. 6 Supper; Clement. 6.30 German. 7 Read Prayers, expounded (twenty-seven there). 8 Miss Sophy and Miss Bovey, Ephraem; sang. 8.40 Religious talk with Miss Sophy. 9 Religious talk. 9.30.

Grace: 6 rating eleven times; 5 six times [9 to 10 am, 1 to 3, 4 to 6, 7 to 8 pm].

[D—Friday, November 12. By a careful inquiry of many persons, I came to the full knowledge of a strange piece of history. Mr. Tailfer, a surgeon of Edinburgh, debauched the only child of one Mr. Uré, a lawyer, his distant relation. He then persuaded her to sign a writing which she had never read, and to go over with him to America. [E—She did so, partly out of fear of her father, but chiefly out of love to him.] When she came hither [E—(having been brought to bed in Carolina)], he treated her as a common servant; and not only so, but beat her, and that very frequently to such a degree that the scars made by the whip were plainly to be seen a year after. The fault commonly was that the child she had had by him cried [E—when he had company]. After he

---

WEDNESDAY, NOVEMBER 10. 4 Prayed with Delamotte; slept. 5 Necessary business; read Prayers, expounded (nineteen there). 6 Religious talk with Miss Sophy; coffee, religious talk (necessary); prayed with them. 7 German. 8 German; French with Miss Sophy. 9 Prayed with them; German. 10 German; resolved not to touch Miss Sophy, told her so. 10.30 Hickes; Trustees' Garden. 11 Trustees' Garden; Hickes; sang. 12 Hickes; sang. 12.30 Visited Hazelfort, religious talk. 1 Visited Mr Rigden, religious talk; Dean, religious talk; Charles, prayed; Parker, religious talk, prayed. 2 Visited Mr Wright, necessary talk. 2.30 Dressed; necessary business; prayed. 3 Tea with Delamotte, religious talk. 3.30 Miss Bovey's, French. 4.15 Tea, religious talk; read mother's letters. 5 She affected, religious talk. 5.15 Prayed with Delamotte; Ephraem. 6 Ephraem. 6.30 Germans'. 7.15 Read Prayers, expounded (thirty there). 8 Miss Bovey and Miss Sophy, read a sermon, sang. 8.45 Walked with Miss Sophy, religious talk. 9.15 Prayed.
Grace: 6 rating eleven times; 5 five times [5 to 6, 8 to 9 am, 5 to 8 pm].

THURSDAY, NOVEMBER 11. 4 Prayed with Delamotte; Hebrew; German (very lively; well). 5 Necessary business; read Prayers, expounded (eighteen there). 6 Miss Sophy, Mr Causton and Williamson came, good talk (necessary and religious); tea. 7 Writ to Mr Regnier. 7.15 With John Brownfield, religious talk, prayed. 8 Letter to Verelst. 9 To Charles; writ diary. 10 Trustee's Garden with Miss Sophy, religious talk, read resolutions. 11 Walked, Hickes. 12 Dinner, religious talk; meditated. 1 Meditated; Ephraem. 2 Ephraem. 2.45 Mr Reed came, necessary talk. 3 Robinson came, necessary talk. 3.15 Visited. 3.30 Miss Bovey's, French. 4.15 Tea, religious talk (close). 5 Mr Causton's, necessary talk with Miss Sophy. 5.15 Ephraem. 5.45 Sang. 6 Supper, necessary talk. 6.30 Germans'. 7 German. 7.15 Read Prayers, expounded. 8 Miss Sophy, Robinson, and Reed; Ephraem; sang. 8.40 Garden with Miss Sophy, religious talk. 9 Good talk (necessary and religious) with Robinson. 9.45.
Grace: 7 rating once [4 to 5 am]; 6 nine times [7 to 8, 10 to 11 am, noon to 5, 7 to 9 pm]; [5] eight times.

FRIDAY, NOVEMBER 12. 4.15 Private prayer; prayed with Delamotte; Hebrew; German. 5 Necessary business. 5.15 Read Prayers, sang, expounded, [collects] 1 2 3 4 t b. 6 Robinson, Reed, Miss Sophy; coffee, necessary talk (religious). 7 Writ to Lord Percival, to Mr Carter of Eton. 8 Oglethorpe came, necessary talk

had kept her thus for about two years, and she had borne a second child [E—(the first being dead)], he married, and sold her to one of the Indian traders.

[The facts he allowed and defended [E—when I met him and her] before Mr. Oglethorpe (only he said he had given, not sold her); who after a full hearing determined that she should be set at liberty [E—with an allowance of food out of the public store)], to work for herself and the child.

(religious). 9.30 Prayed with Miss Sophy. 9.45 Began with Dr Tailfer. 10 Necessary talk with Mrs Causton; with them; with Mrs Mouse. 11 Oglethorpe's, he [had] various talk to others; meditated; at home; dressed. 12 Mr Brownfield, religious talk, Sacrament. 12.30 Mr Trip's, Rachel Uré, and Mrs Mouse, necessary talk (religious). 2 Visited Mrs Potter, prayed; Mrs Lion, necessary talk (religious). 2.30 At home; Ephraem. 3 Tea, necessary talk (religious). 3.30 Miss Bovey's, Mr Dempster and Houston there, good talk. 4 Tea, good talk. 4.15 French, religious and useful talk. 5 Religious talk. 5.15 Prayed with Delamotte; with Oglethorpe, talk of Dr Tailfer; Piva's [?], necessary talk. 6 Writ to Oglethorpe. 6.15 Necessary talk (religious) with Mrs Mouse. 6.30 Germans'. 7 Read Prayers, expounded. 7.30 Oglethorpe's; meditated; private prayer. 8 Dr. Tailfer came with Oglethorpe, talk of his maid. 9 Talk of her. 9.45 Rachel came, necessary talk. 10 Necessary talk (religious). 10.45 At home; lay down.

Grace: 7 rating twice [4 to 5 am, 7 to 8 pm]; 6 thirteen times; 5 four times [5 to 9 am].

SATURDAY, NOVEMBER 13. 4 Hebrew; German; private prayer. 5 Necessary business; read Prayers, expounded, s p t b (fourteen there). 6 Reed, Robinson, Miss Sophy; tea, religious talk (necessary). 7 Writ to Mr Carter of Eton. 8 Mrs Causton's, necessary talk (religious); tea. 9 Prayed with them; writ to brother Samuel. 10 Religious talk (necessary) with Miss Bovey. 10.15 Garden with Miss Sophy, religious talk (necessary; she quite open!). 11 Trustees' Garden; Hickes; private prayer. 12 At home; garden; Hickes; religious talk with Delamotte. 1 Dinner. 1.30 Garden; meditated. 2 Catechized. 3 Ingham came, necessary talk. 3.30 Visited. 4 Visited John Brownfield. 4.45 At home; walked with Delamotte, religious talk. 5 Religious talk; prayed; sang. 5.40 Necessary business; supper. 6 Supper. 6.15 Germans'. 7 Read Prayers, expounded (eighteen there). 8 At home; Miss Sophy, etc; Patrick, religious talk; sang; prayed. 8.45 Mr Causton's. 9 Necessary talk with Mr Causton. 9.45.

Grace: 7 rating three times [4 to 5 am, 2 to 3, 8 to 9 pm]; 6 nine times; 5 six times [8 to 9 am, 1 to 2, 3 to 5, 7 to 8, 9 to 10 pm].

SUNDAY, NOVEMBER 14. 4 Private prayer; prayed with them. 4.15 Slept. 4.45 Hebrew; (well; lively zeal). 5 Hickes with them; Bible. 5.30 German; necessary business; dressed. 6 Read e c p p s h s x p 1 2 3 4 t b (twenty there). 7 Miss Sophy, Mrs Musgrove, etc; tea, religious talk. 8 Garden; meditated on sermon. 9 Hickes with them; dressed; walked; meditated. 10 Walked; meditated; religious talk with Robinson. 10.45 Read Prayers. 11 Read Prayers, preached (forty there), Sacrament (fifteen there). 12 Religious talk with Miss Sophy. 12.20 Writ diary; writ notes; necessary business. 1 Dinner. 1.45 Meditated. 2 Catechized. 2.30 Necessary business. 2.45 Garden; meditated. 3 Heylyn; sang. 4 Religious talk; Heylyn; visited Mrs Potter. 4.30 Read Prayers (fifty there). 5 Catechized; read Prayers. 5.45 Miss Sophy, Mr Houston, Gilbert, etc; read Young's sermon. 6 Sermon, religious talk, sang. 7 Tea, good talk. 7.30 Germans', necessary talk. 8 Writ diary; good talk with Delamotte. 9 Prayed.

Grace: 7 rating twice [4 to 5 am, 2 to 3 pm]; 6 fourteen times; 5 thrice [1 to 2, 7 to 9 pm].

MONDAY, NOVEMBER 15. 4 Prayed with them; Hebrew; German. 5 Necessary business; read Prayers, expounded; Miss Sophy, etc. 6 Tea, necessary talk (religious and useful); prayed with Miss Sophy. 7 Ended to Charles. 8 Revised letter to Oglethorpe. 9 Prayed with Miss Sophy; letter. 10 Letter. 10.45 Miss Bovey's, necessary talk. 11 Trustees' Garden; Sydenham's *Processus*; German. 12 Dinner, good talk. 12.45 Necessary talk with Reed. 1.15 Visited Mr Gilbert. 2 Mrs Cross, necessary talk; Mrs Desborough, religious talk. 2.30 Writ for Mrs Lion. 2.45 Mrs Lion's, necessary talk. 3 Miss Bovey's, French.4 Miss Sophy came; tea, religious talk. 5.45 Buried. 6 Supper, mostly religious talk. 6.45 German. 7.30 Read Prayers, expounded (twenty-six there). 8 Young's sermon, sang, religious talk with her. 9.15 Prayed; lay down. 10 Mr Wheeler [?] came, necessary talk for Reed.

Grace: 7 rating once [4 to 5 am]; 6 nine times [7 to 8, 11 to noon, 1 to 6, 7 to 9 pm]; 5 seven times [no rating noted 9 to 10 pm].

TUESDAY, NOVEMBER 16. 4 Prayed with them; Hebrew; German; (colic). 5 Necessary business; read Prayers, expounded. 6 Miss Bovey's, Miss Sophy there, French. 7 Coffee, religious talk (necessary). 7.45 Oglethorpe's; private prayer. 8 Necessary talk (religious) with Ingham. 8.30 Necessary talk (religious) with Oglethorpe. 9.30 At home; necessary business. 10 Necessary business; writ notes. 10.45 Read notes. 11 Necessary business; necessary talk. 11.30 Set out with Ingham and Delamotte, religious talk. 12.45 [At] Irene, prayed. 1 Felled trees. 1.30 Dinner, religious talk. 2 Trees. 3.45 Tea, religious talk. 4.45 Set out; necessary talk (religious). 5 Necessary talk (religious); writ diary. 6 Supper; German. 7 Read Prayers, expounded (thirty there). 8. Miss Sophy came; read sermon, religious talk. 9.15 Prayed.

Grace: 6 rating ten times; 5 seven times [5 to 6, 8 to 11 am, 3 to 4, 5 to 6, 7 to 8 pm].

WEDNESDAY, NOVEMBER 17. 4 Prayed with Delamotte; slept. 5 Meditated; read Prayers, expounded (twenty there). 6 Miss Sophy; coffee, religious talk, prayed with them. 7 Transcribed letter to Oglethorpe. 12 Letter; writ diary. 12.30 Visited Mr Houston, James Smith, necessary talk. 1 Letters. 2 Mrs Musgrove came, necessary talk (useful and religious). 2.45 She went; tea, religious talk. 3.15 Meditated; Oglethorpe sent for me, necessary talk. 4 Mr Bailey's; buried Mr Tolmie. 5 John Brownfield's, necessary talk. 5.15 Buried a child; John Brownfield's, necessary talk. 6 Oglethorpe's; John Brownfield's; Oglethorpe's, necessary talk. 7 At home; writ diary. 7.15 Read p s p p t b (twenty-six there). 8 Miss Sophy, etc; sermon, religious talk, sang. 8.45 Necessary talk (religious). 9 Mostly religious talk. 9.30 Prayed.

Grace: 6 rating thirteen times; 5 four times [11 to noon, 1 to 3, 9 to 10 pm]. C[composed] for Oglethorpe [9 to 10 am].

THURSDAY, NOVEMBER 18. 4 Prayed with Delamotte; Hebrew; German. 5 Necessary business; read Prayers, expounded; religious talk with Miss Sophy, etc. 6 Tea, religious and useful talk; prayed with Miss Sophy and Delamotte. 7 Transcribed letter. 7.15 Necessary talk with Mr Causton. 7.45 Letter. 11 Read Bishop of London's letter for Negro's book on confirmation. 12 Christened Elizabeth Elbert. 12.15 Dinner, good talk; sang. 1 Ended letter. 2 Transcribed letter. 3.40 Dressed. 3 Miss Bovey's, Miss Sophy there, French. 4 Tea, religious talk. 5.15 Necessary talk; German. 5.45 Sang with them. 6 Supper. 6.15 Oglethorpe's, necessary talk. 6.30 Germans'. 7 Read Prayers, expounded; Miss Sophy came, etc. 8 Sermon; sang. 8.45 Prayed.

Grace: 7 rating once [4 to 5 am]; 6 eight times [6 to 7, 10 to noon, 2 to 3, 4 to 7, 8 to 9 pm]; 5 eight times.

FRIDAY, NOVEMBER 19. 5.30 Necessary business; read Prayers. 6 Expounded, read Prayers. 6.30 Miss Sophy, etc; coffee, religious talk. 7 Religious talk. 7.30 Prayed; necessary business; read notes. 8 Read letter to Oglethorpe to Delamotte and Miss Sophy; necessary talk. 8.45 French. 9 Sang; transcribed letter. 10 Transcribed letter. 12.30 Mr Brownfield, necessary talk. 1 Letter. 1.45 Tea. 3 Tea, religious talk; Miss Sophy came. 4 Miss Bovey's, French; tea, good talk. 5 Mostly religious talk. 5.30 Necessary talk with Robinson; necessary talk with Oglethorpe, (sins during hour). 6 Necessary talk with Dobree; with Oglethorpe. 6.15 Necessary talk; German. 7 Read Prayers, expounded (lively zeal; +). 8 Sermon; sang; read notes; prayed (lively zeal). 9 Private prayer; necessary talk; prayed. 9.30.

Grace: 7 rating twice [7 to 9 pm]; 6 five times [6 to 7, 9 to 10 am, 3 to 4, 6 to 7, 9 to 10 pm]; 5 ten times.

SATURDAY, NOVEMBER 20. 4 Prayed; private prayer. 5 Necessary business; read Prayers, expounded; Miss Sophy, religious talk. 6 Tea, mostly religious talk; necessary talk with Mr Causton. 7 Necessary talk with him; with Dobree, necessary business; with Oglethorpe. 8 Oglethorpe's, necessary talk; Mr Bradley's, necessary talk. 9 Miss Bovey's, necessary talk (religious); Oglethorpe's, necessary talk (religious). 10 At home; necessary business. 12 Dinner, religious talk. 12.45 Letter. 1 Necessary business. 5 Ended transcribing letter. 6 Supper; necessary talk (religious). 6.45 Germans'. 7 German; read Prayers, expounded (six there). 8 Began Dr Bray's circular letters. 9.15 Prayed.

Grace: 7 rating once [4 to 5 am]; 6 six times [5 to 6, 8 to 10, noon to 1, 5 to 6, 8 to 9 pm]; 5 ten times.

SUNDAY, NOVEMBER 21. 4 Prayed with Delamotte; garden; meditated; slept. 5 Private prayers; meditated; slept; necessary business. 6 Read Prayers, expounded (fifteen there). 7 Miss Sophy; tea, religious talk; prayed with them. 8 Necessary business; writ notes; dressed. 9 Trustees' Garden with Delamotte, religious talk of catechumens. 10 Religious talk; necessary business. 10.30 Read c c c; sang. 11 Preached (eighteen there), Sacrament, p b (ten there); sang. 12 Writ notes. 12.15 Dinner, religious talk. 1 Writ catechumens. 1.30 Writ to Sir John Philipps. 2 Catechized. 2.45 Miss Bovey's (she at Prayers), necessary talk (religious). 3 Read Prayers (forty there); catechized. 4 Read Prayers. 4.20

[Tuesday, [November] 23. Mr. Oglethorpe sailed for England. In the evening I buried Mrs. Musgrove's only son, who would probably have been quite lost in grief, but that God diverted her from it by the pain of a violent rheumatism.

Walked with Miss Sophy, religious and useful talk; sang. 5 Mrs Gilbert, Potter, etc, came; prayed; read sermon. 6 Sang; Prayers. 6.15 Tea, mostly religious talk. 7 Germans', religious talk. 7.30 Religious talk with Delamotte. 8 Read Dr Bray to Miss Sophy and Delamotte, religious and useful talk. 9.15 Prayed.
Grace: 6 rating fourteen times; 5 thrice [8 to 9 am, 4 to 5, 6 to 7 pm].

Monday, November 22. 4 Prayed with Delamotte; Hebrew; German. 5 Necessary business; read Prayers, expounded. 6 Tea, religious talk; Miss Sophy not with us. 7 Mr Causton's, necessary talk; prayed with them. 8 Miss Bovey's, Mr Bryan, necessary talk (religious). 9 French with Miss Sophy. 9.30 German, necessary talk. 10 German. 11 Garden; German. 12 Writ diary; dinner, religious talk. 1 Dressed; visited Mrs Smith, Potter. 2 At home; Ephraem Syrus. 1.45 German Grammar. 3.30 Miss Bovey's, French. 4 Tea, religious talk of Oglethorpe. 5 Private prayer. 5.30 Prayed; sang with boys. 5.45 Meditated (lively zeal and +). 6 Meditated, religious talk; German. 7 Writ diary, religious talk. 7.15 [Read] p s p p b. 7.45 Mr Potter and Miss Sophy. 8 Read Ephraem; sang. 8.30 Religious talk; read Mr Hall's case. 9 Hall's case. 9.30.
Grace: 7 rating once [5 to 6 pm]; 6 ten times [4 to 5, 6 to 7, 8 to 9, noon to 3, 4 to 5, 6 to 9 pm]; 5 rating six times; 4 once [10 to 11 am].

Tuesday, November 23. 4 Prayed with Delamotte; Hebrew; German. 5 Necessary business; read Prayers, expounded. 6 Miss Sophy; tea, religious talk; Hickes. 7 Writ to brother Samuel. 8 With Miss Sophy, French. 9 French; necessary talk (religious). 9.30 Letter. 10 Garden; German Grammar; necessary talk with Mrs Dean, etc. 11 Mr Bryan came, religious talk (necessary). 12 Writ diary; dinner, religious talk. 1 Letter. 2.45 Visited. 3 Miss Bovey's, mostly religious talk; Miss Sophy, French. 4 Company came, tea (Mr Ingham came). 5 Buried Ned Musgrove, etc. 6 Religious talk, supper; German. 7 Read Prayers, expounded. 8 Miss Bovey, etc; sermon; sang. 8.45 Mr Causton's, necessary talk; ate. 9 Good talk. 9.45 At home.

Wednesday, November 24. 1 Tea; prayed; necessary business; tea. 2 Pushed off boat. 2.30 Set out. 3 On ground; waded; got off. 4 Rowed; religious and useful talk; sang. 5 Rowed; good talk (necessary and religious). 6 Good talk; (very rough). 9 On ground at Dokumé, waded, got off. 10 Rowed, over the marsh on Tybee; James Dean, etc, there. 11 Walked to Tybee; in the lighthouse. 12 Walked back; sea overtook us; oysters; good talk. 3 Good talk; Mr Hows came; slept. 4.15 Set out; mostly religious talk. 8.30 Mr Causton's, necessary talk (religious). 9.15 At home; tea, necessary talk (religious). 9.45.
Grace: 6 rating thrice [1 to 2, 3 to 5 am]; 5 fifteen times.

Thursday, November 25. 4.30 Prayed with Ingham; necessary business. 5 Necessary business; read Prayers, expounded. 6 Miss Sophy; tea, religious talk; prayed with them. 7 Set out with Miss Sophy, etc; read Bray; sang. 8 Religious talk; Bray. 8.30 Mrs Musgrove's, she ill; read Bray to all. 9 Religious talk;

religious talk with Mrs Musgrove. 10 Ingham; read Prayers, expounded; Bray. 11 Tea, religious talk (necessary). 11.45 Walked with Ingham and Delamotte, necessary talk. 12 Necessary talk. 1 Necessary talk (religious); Bray. 1 Mostly religious talk. 3.30 Dinner. 4.15 Set out; religious talk. 5.45 At home; writ diary; necessary talk (religious). 6 Tea, religious talk. 6.45 German. 7 German; read Prayers, expounded. 8 Miss Sophy, Miss Bovey, John; sermon; sang. 9.15 Prayed.

Grace: 6 rating eleven times; 5 six times [5 to 6, noon to 4, 7 to 8 pm].

FRIDAY, NOVEMBER 26. 4 Prayed with Delamotte; German. 5 Necessary business; read Prayers, expounded. 6 Miss Sophy; coffee, religious talk. 7 Prayed with them; Spanish Grammar. 8 Spanish; necessary talk with them. 8.30 French with Miss Sophy. 9 Spanish; Hickes with them; writ diary. 10 Spanish. 2 Dressed; meditated; necessary talk. 2.40 Tea, religious talk. 3.20 Miss Bovey's, religious and useful talk. 5 Burnside came, mostly religious talk. 5.30 At home; religious talk; sang. 6 Religious talk; German. 7.15 Read c p s c t b (twenty-five there; lively zeal). 8 Miss Bovey and Miss Sophy; Reeves; sang. 9.15.

Grace: 6 rating eight times; 5 nine times [5 to 6, 7 am to 2, 3 to 4 pm].

SATURDAY, NOVEMBER 27. 4 Prayed with Delamotte; German; private prayer. 5 Necessary business; read Prayers, expounded. 6 Miss Sophy, tea, religious talk. 7 Hickes; writ diary. 7.15 Spanish. 8 Sang; Spanish. 9 Prayed with Miss Sophy; Spanish. 10 Garden; Dr Bray's tracts. 11 Tracts, necessary talk. 12 Gilpin's *Life*. 1 Dinner, necessary talk (religious); Gilpin. 2 Catechized. 2.45 Mr Brownfield's, necessary talk. 3 Walked with Delamotte, religious talk. 4.45 At home; necessary talk (religious). 5 Private prayer. 5.30 Prayed with Delamotte. 5.45 Sang. 6 Tea, religious talk. 6.40 Letter. 7 Read Prayers, expounded. 7.45 Miss Sophy, etc, Patrick. 8 Patrick; sang; prayed; read sermon to Miss Sophy. 9 Necessary talk (religious); prayed. 9.45.

Grace: 7 rating twice [4 to 5 am, 5 to 6 pm]; 6 ten times; 5 four times [5 to 7, 11 am to 1 pm].

SUNDAY, NOVEMBER 28. 4 Prayed with Delamotte; German. 5 Private prayer; slept; necessary business; dressed. 6 Read Prayers, expounded (twenty there). 7.15 Miss Sophy; tea, religious talk. 8 Hickes. 8.15 Garden; thought on sermon. 9 Hickes; Trustees' Garden; Gilpin. 10 Gilpin; sang. 10.40 Read Prayers. 11 Preached (thirty-seven there), Sacrament (fourteen there); sang. 12 Prayed. 12.15 Dinner, religious talk. 1 Bray's tracts. 1.30 Garden; Gray. 2 Catechized. 2.45 Slept. 3 Read Prayers (forty-five there); catechized. 4 Prayers. 4.15 Walked with Miss Sophy and Delamotte, religious talk; sang. 5 Mrs Gilbert, etc; sang; prayed; sermons. 6 Sang; prayed. 6.30 Tea, religious talk. 7 Germans'; meditated. 8 Read letters to Miss Sophy and Delamotte; prayed.

Grace: 6 rating sixteen times; 5 once [6 to 7 am].

MONDAY, NOVEMBER 29. 4 Prayed with Delamotte; German; private prayer. 5 Necessary business; read Prayers, expounded. 6 Miss Sophy; Mr Campbell came, religious talk. tea. 7 Spanish. 8 French with Miss Sophy. 8.45 Spanish. 9 Prayed with her; Spanish. 10 With Miss Sophy, Spanish. 10.30 Spanish. 12.40 Visited Ross; prayed, religious talk (lively zeal). 1 Visited. 1.30 Spanish. 2 Garden; meditated. 2.45 Tea. 3 Miss Bovey's, read letter to Oglethorpe. 4 Mostly religious talk, tea; Mrs Weddal came. 5 Private prayer; meditated

[In the beginning of December I advised Miss Sophy to sup earlier, and not immediately before she went to bed. She did so; and on this little circumstance [E—(for by this she began her intercourse with Mr. Williamson)] what an inconceivable train of consequences depend! [E—None but the Uncreated Eye can see to the end of them!] Not only 'All the colour of remaining life' for her [Prior, *Solomon*, ii.235]; but perhaps all my happiness, too, in time and in eternity!

(zealous). 5.45 Sang; necessary business. 6 Ate; Germans'. 7 Read Prayers, christened, expounded (lively zeal). 8 Miss Sophy came; (Miss Bovey not [there]); sermon; sang. 9.15.

Grace: 7 rating thrice [4 to 5 am, 5 to 6, 8 to 9 pm]; 6 six times [6 to 8, 9 to 10 am, 2 to 3, 6 to 8 pm]; 5 eight times. Lively zeal [7 to 8 pm].

TUESDAY, NOVEMBER 30. 4 Prayed; private prayer. 5 Necessary business. 5.15 Read Prayers, expounded. 6 Prayers. 6.15 Miss Sophy, Mr Burnside, religious talk, tea. 7 Hickes; German. 8 German. 8.45 Prayed with them. 9 Trustees' Garden; sang; thought on sermon. 10 Thought. 10.50 [Read] c c c, sang, preached (twenty-one there), Sacrament. 12. Sang, p b. 12.15 Dinner, good talk. 1 Good talk. 1.15 German (sins!!!). 2 Meditated; visited Watkins, religious talk. 3 Trustees' Garden; read letters from Charles (lively zeal!). 4 Private prayer; meditated. 5 Churchyard; meditated; buried Ross. 6.45 At home; sang; tea. 6 Bolzius came, religious talk; tea. 7 Religious talk. 7.15 Read Prayers, expounded (thirty-five there). 8 Miss Sophy, etc; sermon; sang. 8.45 Writ diary.

Grace: 7 rating thrice [4 to 6, 9 to 10 am]; 6 eleven times; 5 twice [noon to 2 pm]. Sins [1 to 2 pm].

WEDNESDAY, DECEMBER 1. 4 Prayed with Delamotte; German; (mild frost). 5 Dressed; read p s x p s p b (eighteen there). 6 Miss Sophy, coffee, necessary talk (religious). 7 Hickes; German. 8 French. 8.30 German. 9 Prayed with them; German. 10 German. 12 Garden; read letter from Watkins; meditated. 1 Visited Mrs Mellichamp, religious talk. 2 Mr Causton's, necessary talk (religious) with him. 3 Necessary talk. 3.30 Miss Bovey's, French. 4.15 At home; tea, necessary talk (religious). 5 Prayed with Delamotte; garden; private prayer; meditated. 6.45 Sang. 6 Ended Dr Bray. 6.45 German. 7.15 Read Prayers, expounded (thirty-five there). 8 Miss Sophy, etc; sermon; sang. 9.15 Prayed.

Grace: 7 rating once [4 to 5 am]; 6 twelve times; 5 four times [5 to 7 am, 4 to 5, 7 to 8 pm].

[THURSDAY,] DECEMBER 2. 4 Prayed with Delamotte; German; private prayer; (sharp frost). 5 Necessary business; read Prayers, expounded. 5.45 Miss Sophy; tea, religious talk. 6 Tea, religious talk; Hickes. 6.45 German. 7.45 Causton's, necessary talk. 8 Necessary talk; tea. 9 Necessary talk. 9.30 Writ to Charles. 10 Writ to Rivington, Laserre, Eveleigh. 12 Dinner, necessary talk; necessary business. 1 Necessary business; necessary talk; dressed. 1.45 Visited. 2.45 Writ to Watkins. 3 Necessary business. 4 Miss Bovey's; tea, religious talk. 5.15 Read notes. 5.30 Prayed with Delamotte; sang. 6 Supper, religious talk; Germans'. 7

Garden; meditated. 7.15 Read Prayers, expounded. 8 Miss Bovey and Miss Sophy, sermon, sang. 8.45.

Grace: 7 rating once [4 to 5 am]; 6 six times [6 to 7 am, 2 to 3, 4 to 7, 8 to 9 pm]; 5 nine times; 4 once [1 to 2 pm].

[FRIDAY,] DECEMBER 3. 4 Prayed; private prayer; German; (sharp frost). 5 Necessary business; read Prayers, expounded (thirteen there). 6 Coffee, religious talk; Hickes. 7 German; (milder). 8 French with Miss Sophy. 8.30 German. 9 Moses Núñez came, Spanish; (mild). 10 German. 12 Garden; meditated; sang; slept; dressed. 12.45 Visited. 1 Visited (all open). 2 Garden; meditated; prayed; sang. 2.45 Miss Bovey's, French. 3.30 At home; tea, religious talk. 4 In town; necessary business. 5 With Mr Hermsdorf, necessary talk (religious). 5.15 Prayed with Delamotte; writ notes; sang. 6 Buried; Germans'. 7 At home; necessary business. 7.15 Read Prayers, expounded (thirty-five there). 8 Miss Bovey, etc; sermon; sang. 9 Necessary talk; necessary business; prayed. 9.30.

Grace: 7 rating once [4 to 5 am]; 6 nine times; 5 six times [7 to 11 am, 7 to 8, 9 to 10 pm].

SATURDAY, DECEMBER 4. 4 Prayed; German; private prayer; (very warm). 5 Necessary business; read prayers, expounded; (cloudy). 6 Miss Sophy; tea, religious talk. 7 Writ for Watkins; German. 8 German; French with Miss Sophy. 9 Prayed; German. 10 Necessary talk with Mr Causton. 11 Trustees' Garden; meditated. 12 At home; Ingham; dinner, necessary talk (religious). 1 Necessary business; catechized. 2 Garden with Ingham and Delamotte, religious talk; religious talk with Ingham. 4 With Germans; sang; prayed, etc; (rain). 5 sang; prayed. 5.30 At home; religious talk. 6 Tea, religious talk. 6.30 Germans'. 7 Ingham read Prayers. 8 Mr Hows, etc; Patrick; sang; prayed. 8.30 Mr Causton's; tea, religious talk (necessary). 9.15 Prayed.

Grace: 7 rating once [4 to 5 am]; 6 ten times [9 to 10, 11 to noon, 1 to 9 pm]; 5 six times.

SUNDAY, DECEMBER 5. 4 Prayed; German; private prayer; garden; (mild). 5 Private prayer. 5.15 Slept. 5.45 Dressed. 6 Read Prayers, sang, Ingham read litany, etc (twenty-five there). 7 At home; tea, religious talk; Hickes. 8 Garden; thought on sermon; Hickes with them. 9 Religious talk (necessary). 9.30 Trustees' Garden; Kempis. 10.15 Read Prayers, preached (thirty there). 11 Sacrament. 11.45 Writ diary; religious talk. 12 Dinner, necessary talk (religious). 12.45 Walked with them, religious talk; (warm). 1 Religious talk; sang; (windy). 2 Catechized. 2.30 Read resolutions. 2.45 Read Prayers (sixty there); catechized. 4 Garden; meditated. 4.30 Mr Hows, etc; sang; sermon. [5.]20 Sang; prayed; sang (lively zeal). 6 Garden with Miss Sophy, religious talk. 6.15 Supper, mostly religious talk. 6.40 Germans'. 7.15 With Miss Sophy, garden, religious talk (necessary). 8 Read *Nicodemus*. 9.15 Prayed.

Grace: 7 rating thrice [4 to 5 am, 4 to 6 pm]; 6 twelve times; 5 once [1 to 2 pm?].

MONDAY, DECEMBER 6. 4 Prayed with them; German; (mild, windy). 5 Necessary business; read Prayers, expounded (thirteen there); Miss Sophy came. 6 Tea, religious talk (necessary); Hickes. 7 German. 8 With Miss Sophy; French; necessary talk; German. 9 Prayed with them; began shorthand. 10 Shorthand.

[Thursday, [December] 9. Hearing a poor woman was dangerously ill, I went to her immediately. She told me she had long wanted to speak with me, and had sent several messengers—who never came—that she had many things to say. But the time was past, for her weakness now prevented her saying more; and on Friday the 10th, God required her soul of her.

10.45 Garden; shorthand. 11 Shorthand; German. 12 Mostly religious talk; dinner, mostly religious talk; (mild, rain). 1 Good talk (necessary and religious). 1.30 Visited Mrs Smith, Junior, religious talk. 2 Visited Kelly Potter, religious talk, prayed. 3 Ephraem [Syrus]. 4 Miss Bovey's; tea, religious talk. 6 At home; private prayer; prayed with Delamotte. 5.45 Sang; Mr Causton's. 6 Tea, religious talk (necessary and useful). 7 At home; necessary talk; read Prayers, expounded (thirty-five there). 8 Miss Bovey, etc, sermon, sang. 9 Prayed; (warm, stormy, and rain). 9.15.

    Grace: 7 rating once [5 to 6 pm]; 6 ten times; 5 six times [5 to 7, 8 to 9, 10 to 11 am, 1 to 2, 7 to 8 pm].

TUESDAY, DECEMBER 7. 4 Prayed with Delamotte; German; (warm, rain). 5 Necessary business; read Prayers, expounded. 6 Tea, necessary talk (religious). 6.45 Ended German Grammar; garden; (rain). 7 Read notes. 7.30 Abridged *Nicodemus*. 10 Shorthand; necessary talk. 11.15 Garden; Dr Bray. 12 Meditated; dinner, necessary talk (religious). 1.30 Visited; (mild, fair). 2 Visited. 3 Miss Bovey's, French. 3.45 Tea, good talk. 4 Good talk (various and religious). 4.45 At home; Ingham there, religious talk. 5 Christened; prayed with Ingham and Delamotte. 6 Supper, religious talk (necessary); German; (full moon). 7.15 Read Prayers, expounded (thirty there). 8 Miss Bovey, etc; sermon; sang. 9 Prayed; (cold).

    Grace: 6 rating eight times [4 to 5, 8 to 9, 10 to 11 am, 2 to 4, 5 to 6, 7 to 9 pm]; 5 nine times.

WEDNESDAY, DECEMBER 8. 4.15 Prayed; garden; private prayer; (frost). 5 Necessary business; read Prayers, expounded (fourteen there). 6 Miss Sophy; coffee, religious talk (close). 7 Hickes; *Nicodemus*. 8 French with Miss Sophy; *Nicodemus*. 9 Prayed with them; *Nicodemus*. 9.30 Shorthand. 11 Dr Bray; Trustees' Garden. 12 Necessary business; necessary talk. 12.30 Visited. 1.30 Writ for boys. 2 Miss Bovey's, French. 3 Prayed with Delamotte; tea, religious talk (necessary). 4 Garden; read tracts. 5 Religious talk with Carter; prayed with Delamotte. 5.30 Buried; religious talk with Jemmy. 6 Ate; read tracts; Germans'. 7 Germans'; read Prayers, expounded (thirty-two there). 8 Miss Sophy, etc; sermon; sang. 9 Tracts. 9.30 Prayed; slept; Miss Sophy came for Tom Causton; lots; kept him; (cool, fair).

    Grace: 6 rating sixteen times; 5 twice [5 to 6, 8 to 9 am].

THURSDAY, DECEMBER 9. 4.15 Prayed with Delamotte; German; garden; private prayer; (frost). 5 Necessary business; read Prayers, expounded. 5.45 Walked with Mr Causton, religious talk (necessary) of Tom. 6 Tea, religious talk (necessary). 7 *Nicodemus*. 8 Read Blair's [sermon] on our Lord's sermon. 9 Set out with Miss Sophy and Delamotte, necessary talk (religious). 11.30 Mrs

[Sunday, December 12. I read the Proclamation against Profaneness to a numerous congregation. The Acts of Parliament appointed to be read in churches were read on the following Sunday, and have since been put in execution by those Ministers of God here who bear not that character in vain.

Musgrove's, she better; Mrs Salter there, necessary talk (religious).12 Ingham read Prayers, expounded; walked; religious talk with Ingham and Delamotte. 2 With Mrs Musgrove, read *Account of Florida*. 2.30 Dinner. 3.15 Religious talk. 3.30 Set out; necessary talk (religious). 4 Irene; tea, religious talk (necessary). 5 Set out; religious and useful talk. 6 At home; visited Mrs Clark; tea, religious talk. 7 Read Prayers, expounded. 8 Visited Mrs Clark; tea, religious talk. 7 Read Prayers, expounded. 8 Visited Mrs Clark; Miss Bovey, etc, sermon, sang. 9 Religious talk; prayed. 9.30 (Sharp frost).

FRIDAY, DECEMBER 10. 4.15 Prayed; German; (very sharp frost). 5 Necessary business; read Prayers, expounded (twelve there). 6 Miss Sophy, religious talk, coffee. 7 Hickes; shorthand. 8 Religious talk with boys; with Miss Sophy; prayed with them. 9 Shorthand; *Nicodemus*. 10 *Nicodemus*. 11 Trustees' Garden; tracts. 12 At home; read to boys, religious talk, prayed. 12.45 Dressed; (sharp frost). 1 Visited Mrs Clark, Watkins. 2 Miss Bovey's, French. 3 At home; tea, religious talk. 4 Read Entick's book. 5 Prayed with Delamotte. 5.20 Private prayer. 5.45 Sang with boys; read notes. 6 Read notes; Germans'. 7 Read Prayers, expounded (twenty-five there); visited Mrs Clark. 8 Visited Mrs Woodruff; at home; Miss Bovey, Miss Sophy, sermon, sang. 9 Religious talk (necessary); prayed. 9.15 (Very sharp frost).
Grace: 6 rating ten times; 5 seven times [7 to 8, 9 to noon, 2 to 5 pm].

SATURDAY, DECEMBER 11. 4 Prayed with Delamotte; German; (very sharp frost). 5 Necessary business; read Prayers, expounded; visited Mrs Woodruff. 6 At home; tea, religious talk; Hickes. 7 Shorthand. 8 French with Miss Sophy; shorthand. 9 Prayed with them; *Nicodemus*. 10 *Nicodemus*. 10.40 Visited. 11.15 Garden; read Calveto. 11.45 Dinner. 12.30 Set out; Nelson's *Address*. 1 Nelson; sang; (very sharp frost). 2 Nelson. 2.45 Mr Lacy's, necessary talk (religious). 3 Tea, mostly religious talk. 3.45 Set out; religious talk. 4 Mostly religious talk. 5.30 At home; Mr Clark's, necessary talk (religious); necessary talk (religious) with Mr Bradley. 6 Tea, mostly religious talk. 7 Read Prayers, expounded (fifty there); buried Mrs Clark; (dark). 8 At home; religious talk with Bob Bradley; Miss Sophy, etc, came, Patrick, prayed, sang. 9 Prayed; (very sharp frost).
Grace: 6 rating ten times; 5 seven times [8 to 11 am, 1 to 3, 4 to 5, 6 to 7 pm].

SUNDAY, DECEMBER 12. 4 Prayed; German; (very sharp frost). 5 Read resolutions; dressed. 6 Read Prayers, expounded (twenty there). 7 Miss Sophy; tea, religious talk; Hickes. 8 Thought on sermon. 9 Trustees' Garden with Ingham, religious talk, prayed. 10 At home; necessary business. 10.30 Read Prayers. 11 Preached (thirty there), Sacrament (thirteen there); at home; prayed with them. 12 Dinner, religious talk; Ingham went; (sharp frost). 1 Religious talk with John. 2 Catechized. 3 Read Prayers, read the *Proclamation of Profaneness* (seventy there). 4 Prayers. 4.20 Visited. 4.45 At home; Mr Hows, etc. 5 Sang, read sermon, prayed, sang. 6 Tea, religious talk. 6.45 German; (+). 7.30 Meditated (lively zeal). 8 Began Dr Owen (excellent; lively zeal). 9 Religious talk; prayed. 9.15 (Sharp frost).

Grace: 7 rating twice [7 to 9 pm]; 6 thirteen times; 5 twice [6 to 7 am, 6 to 7 pm].

MONDAY, DECEMBER 13. 4 Prayed; German; (frost). 5 Necessary business; read Prayers, expounded (seventeen there). 6 Owen; tea, religious talk. 7 Hickes; *Nicodemus*; (milder, frost). 8 French; shorthand; prayed with them. 9 Writ to Mr Butler. 10 *Nicodemus*; writ diary. 11 Trustees' Garden; Kempis; meditated (lively zeal; +). 12 Dinner, religious talk; (mild, frost). 1 Garden; meditated. 1.30 Visited Mr Simms [Symes?], Mrs Gilbert. 2 Visited Mrs Vanderplank, religious talk (necessary). 3 At home; *Nicodemus*. 4 Miss Bovey; tea, religious talk. 5 Garden, private prayer, sang. 5.30 Necessary talk. 5.45 Sang; Mr Causton's. 6 Tea, necessary talk (religious and useful). 7 Meditated; read Prayers, expounded (thirty-three there). 8 Miss Bovey's, sermon, sang. 9 Religious talk (necessary); prayed. 9.30.

Grace: 7 rating twice [11 to noon, 5 to 6 pm]; 6 thirteen times; 5 thrice [5 to 6, 9 to 10 am, 6 to 7 pm].

TUESDAY, DECEMBER 14. 4 Prayed; German; necessary business; (mild, fair). 5 Meditated; read Prayers, expounded. 5.45 Miss Sophy not [come]; Mr Campbell came, Owen. 6 Tea, religious talk (necessary). 6.45 At his lot; necessary talk. 7 Shorthand. 7.15 *Nicodemus*. 8.30 French with Miss Sophy; *Nicodemus*. 9 Necessary talk; prayed with them; *Nicodemus*. 10 *Nicodemus*. 11 Trustees' Garden; Kempis; slept; prayed for Oglethorpe. 12 Necessary talk with Delamotte; dinner, mostly religious talk; (warm, cloudy). 1 Dressed; visited Watson. 2 Visited Mrs Parker, Deikin. 3 Miss Bovey's, French. 4 Ephraem [Syrus]. 5 Private prayer; prayed. 5.30 Religious talk with Tom Causton. 5.40 Sang; *Nicodemus*; (warm, rain). 6 Tea, religious talk (necessary). 6.30 Germans'; sleepy. 7 Germans'; read Prayers, expounded (thirty there). 8 Miss Bovey, etc, sermon, sang. 9 Necessary talk; prayed. 9.30 (Warm).

Grace: 6 rating twelve times; 5 six times [8 to 11 am, noon to 1, 6 to 7 pm].

WEDNESDAY, DECEMBER 15. 4 Prayed; German; necessary business; (south wind, warm, cloudy). 5 Meditated; read Prayers, expounded (fourteen there). 6 Miss Sophy, Owen; tea, religious talk. 7 Religious talk; Hickes. 7.15 *Nicodemus*. 8 French. 8.30 *Nicodemus*; prayed with them. 9 *Nicodemus*; writ diary. 10 Shorthand; religious talk with Miss Sophy. 11 Trustees' Garden; Kempis; meditated. 12 Necessary business; dressed. 12.30 Visited; (mild, fair, south wind). 2 *Nicodemus*. 3 Mrs Causton's, necessary talk (religious). 4 Tea, necessary talk (religious). 5 Private prayer; prayed; meditated. 5.40 Sang; *Nicodemus*. 6 Necessary talk (religious) with Delamotte; German; sleepy. 7 Meditated; read Prayers, expounded (forty there). 8 Mr Hows, etc, sermon, sang. 9 Religious talk; prayed. 9.30 (Mild, fair, south wind).

Grace: 6 rating thirteen times; 5 five times [5 to 6, 9 to 10 am, 3 to 5, 6 to 7 pm].

THURSDAY, DECEMBER 16. 4 Prayed; private prayer; German; necessary business; (mild, fair, windy; well). 5 Meditated; read e c s, expounded, p b; Owen; (cold, north wind). 6 Tea, religious talk. 7 Hickes; *Nicodemus*; necessary talk with Mrs

Gilbert. 8 French. 8.30 Shorthand; prayed with Miss Sophy. 9 *Nicodemus.* 11 Trustees' Garden; Kempis; meditated. 11.45 *Nicodemus.* 12 *Nicodemus*; dinner, religious talk (necessary). 1 Visited Mrs Gilbert, Cross, Smith, Senior; (cold, north wind). 2 Visited Mr Henry Parker, religious talk. 3 *Nicodemus.* 3.40 Miss Bovey's, mostly necessary talk. 4 Mostly religious talk, tea. 5 Prayed; slept; sang. 6 Supper, necessary talk (religious); German. 7 Religious talk; read Prayers, expounded (thirty there); (calm). 8 Miss Bovey, etc, sermon, sang. 9.15 Prayed; (light frost).

Grace: 7 rating once [4 to 5 am]; 6 nine times [6 to 7, 9 to noon, 1 to 3, 4 to 5, 7 to 8]; 5 seven times.

FRIDAY, DECEMBER 17. 4 Prayed; garden; private prayer; (cold, no fire, no wind). 5 Meditated; read p b, expounded, 1 1 2 t b. 6 Owen; coffee, religious talk. 7 Mostly religious talk. 7.30 *Nicodemus.* 8 French. 8.30 Shorthand; prayed. 9 *Nicodemus.* 10 *Nicodemus*; religious talk to boys. 11 *Nicodemus.* 12 Read to boys; prayed; dressed. 1 Visited Miss Ann, religious talk of popery (she serious and convinced). Miss Bovey's, French. 3 Prayed; tea, religious talk (necessary). 4 Read resolutions. 4.15 *Nicodemus.* 5 Meditated. 5.15 Prayed with Delamotte. 5.30 Meditated; sang; ate. 6 Plato; Germans'. 7 German; read Prayers, expounded. 8 Miss Bovey, etc; Plato. 9 Plato; sang. 9.30 Prayed.

Grace: 7 rating once [4 to 5 am]; 6 eleven times; 5 six times [5 to 6, 7 to 10, 11 to noon, 7 to 8 pm].

SATURDAY, DECEMBER 18. 4 Prayed; German; (cold). 5 Meditated; read Prayers, expounded (thirteen there); Owen. 6 Owen; tea, religious talk; Hickes. 7 *Nicodemus.* 8 Walked toward Irene with Delamotte; swamp; (cold). 9 Walked; came to the spring; swamp. 10 Walked. 10.30 At home; *Nicodemus.* 11 Ingham came; ended *Nicodemus.* 11.15 Scheme for Psalms. 12 Psalms; necessary talk (religious) with Ingham; dinner; (cool, cloudy). 1 Necessary talk (religious). 2 Walked, necessary talk (religious). 3 Dr Hirsh: tea, necessary talk (religious). 4.30 Scheme for Psalms. 5 Prayed with them, religious talk, sang. 6 Tea; German. 7 Read Prayers, expounded (twenty-five there; lively zeal; +). 8 Mr Hows, etc, Patrick, sang, prayed; Psalms. 10 (Mild, rain).

Grace: 6 rating nine times; 5 eight times [5 to 6, 7 to 8, 9 to 11 am, noon to 2, 3 to 5 pm].

SUNDAY, DECEMBER 19. 4 Prayed; German; Psalms; (mild, rain, south-east [wind]). 5 German; ended scheme; dressed. 6 Read Prayers, expounded (fourteen there). 7 Tea, religious talk; Hickes. 8 Thought on sermon. 9 Hickes. 9.15 Religious talk. 9.20 Sang; writ resolutions. 10 Necessary talk (religious); resolutions. 10.15 Meditated. 10.30 Read e c c (twenty-one there). 11 Sermon, p, Sacrament, s p b (thirteen there). 12 Necessary business; dinner, necessary talk (religious). 1 Scheme for hymns. 2 Catechized; scheme. 3 Read Prayers, catechized, expounded (twenty-one there). 4 Prayers, 4.15 Mr Hows, etc, sang, began *Christian Perfection.* 5 Prayed; sang. 5.15 Prayed with Miss Sophy. 5.30 Necessary business; writ diary. 5.45 Scheme. 6 Tea, religious talk; Germans'; sleepy. 7 Germans'; sleepy. 7.30 Scheme. 8 Owen. 8.45 Scheme. 9.15 Prayed (lively zeal).

Grace: 7 rating thrice [9 to 10, 11 to noon, 5 to 6 pm]; 6 eleven times; 5 twice [noon to 1, 7 to 8 pm].

[Thursday, [December] 23. We [E—Mr. Delamotte and I] set out for the Cowpen by land, having a guide with us who had gone that way before. After about three hours' walking we came to a creek which our guide had forgot; but there was no remedy but wading through! An hour or two after, we came to a cypress swamp, through which likewise we were to walk, the water being about breast-high. By that time we had gone a mile or two beyond it, we were all out of our knowledge, and out

---

Monday, December 20. 4 Prayed with Delamotte; writ diary; read resolutions; German. 5 Dressed; read Prayers (twelve there). 6 Owen; tea, religious talk. 7 Scheme for hymns (+). 8 Scheme; prayed with them. 9 Transcribed hymns (+). 12 Transcribed; dressed. 1 Visited. 3 At home; tea, religious talk. 4 At Miss Sophy's; tea, religious talk. 5 Mr Burnside came, religious talk. 5.20 At home; meditated; writ diary; sang. 5.45 Sang with the boys. 6 Prayed; hymns; Germans'. 7 Read Prayers; prayed. 8 Sir Francis Bathurst, Miss Bovey, etc, began *Nicodemus*; sang. 9 Writ diary; prayed; necessary talk (religious). 9.30.
Grace: 6 rating eighteen times.

Tuesday, December 21. Prayed with Delamotte; German. 5 Necessary business; read Prayers (fifteen there). 6 Mr Campbell; Owen; tea, religious talk. 7 At his house. 7.30 Hymns. 8 Hymns; writ diary. 8.30 Dressed. 9 Walked; thought upon sermon. 10 At home; thought. 10.30 [Read] Prayers. 11 Preached (thirty there), Sacrament (thirteen there); prayed; (sins of thought!). 12 At the guardhouse with the magistrates. 1 At Mr Causton's; with the magistrates there, necessary talk (religious). 2 Dinner, good talk. 3.15 At home; religious talk with Delamotte. 4 Hymns. 4.30 Walked with Delamotte, religious talk. 5 Prayed with Delamotte; meditated. 5.40 Sang; writ diary. 6 Tea, religious talk; Germans'; sleepy. 7 [Read] Prayers, expounded (twenty-two there; lively zeal). 8 Miss Bovey and Miss Sophy, *Nicodemus*, prayed, sang; writ diary.
Grace: 6 rating fifteen times; 5 twice [noon to 1, 2 to 3 pm].

Wednesday, December [22]. 4 Prayed with Delamotte; German; dressed. 5 Necessary talk (religious); read Prayers, expounded (twelve there); Mrs Brownfield. 6 Owen; coffee, religious talk. 7 Hymns. 8 French. 8.30 Hymns; prayed with them. 9 Hymns. 10 At Miss Bovey's. 10.30 Set out with Delamotte and James Smith. 11 Walked; sang; walked; religious and useful talk; wet. 1.30 At the creek, in deep. 3 At the cypress swamp; above our middle. 4 Walked; wet, cold. 5 At the hut. 5.30 Stopped, sat. 6 Sharp frost, tinder wet, alas! 7 Lay down all together; very sharp frost; slept. 9 Waked by frost and cramp many times. 10 Heavy dew, froze over; ground and cloths wet beneath; almost dispirited.

Thursday, December 23. 6 Rose; prayed; (sharp frost); set out; swamps; (well!). 7 At Captain Williams', all there very kind; ate. 8.30 Set out. 9 Mrs Musgrove's (she better!), Ingham there, necessary talk (religious), coffee. 12 Read Prayers, expounded. 12.15 Set out; Irene; sang; religious talk. 1.45 Dinner, religious talk (necessary). 2.15 Tea, religious talk (necessary). 4.15 Set out. 5.15 At home; necessary business; prayed. 6 Tea, Williamson came, necessary talk (religious). 6.45 Germans'. 7.20 Read Prayers, expounded (thirty-three there). 8 Miss Bovey, etc, *Nicodemus*, sang. 9 Mr Causton's, ate, religious talk (necessary). 9.40.

of all path. However, we went on till past sunset, and then sat down in a pine-grove [E—on the driest spot we could find], intending [E—after a while] to make a fire and stay there till morning. But finding our tinder was all wet, we considered what to do next. I was for walking still, but both my companions, being faint and tired, were for lying down, which accordingly we did, about six o'clock. It was a sharp frost, and [the] ground we lay on being very moist and our clothes wet before we lay down, we were in a few hours frozen over [E—as hard as the tree we lay against]. However, I slept pretty quietly till near six in the morning. There fell a heavy dew in the night [E—which covered us over], so that when we rose the side that had been uppermost was white as snow. In less than [an] hour we came to a plantation, and after resting a little, to Mrs. Musgrove's. Nor did any of us receive any hurt at all, but came home in the evening in perfect health.

FRIDAY, DECEMBER 24. 4.30 Prayed with Ingham; necessary business. 5 Necessary business; read Prayers, expounded (eighteen there). 6 Miss Sophy; Owen, religious talk, coffee. 7 Hickes; hymns. 8 Hymns; prayed with them. 9 Hymns. 9.45 Writ diary. 10 Religious talk with Miss Sophy (she quite silent). 10.30 Visited. 12 At home; transcribed hymns. 1 Hymns. 3 Prayed with them; tea, religious talk. 4 Walked with Delamotte, religious talk. 5 Prayed with Delamotte; meditated. 5.40 Sang with boys. 6 Hymns. 6.30 Germans'. 7 Read Prayers, expounded (lively zeal; +). 8 Miss Bovey, etc, *Nicodemus*; prayed; sang (lively zeal). 9 Religious talk (necessary); prayed. 9.30.

Grace: 7 rating twice [4 to 6 pm]; 6 fourteen times; 5 twice [5 to 6 am, 2 to 3 pm].

SATURDAY, DECEMBER 25. 4 Rose; prayed with them; German; dressed. 5 Read Prayers, expounded. 6 Owen; tea, religious talk. 7 Hymns; prayed with them. 8 Hymns. 9 Thought upon sermon. 10 Meditated; dressed. 10.30 Read Prayers. 11 Preached (fifty there), Sacrament (eighteen there). 12 Prayed. 12.15 At home; prayed; Mr Causton's, Miss Bovey there, mostly religious talk. 1 Dinner, religious and useful talk (necessary). 2 Necessary and useful talk. 3 Read Prayers, expounded (sixty there; convincing). 4 Read Prayers. 4.15 Mr Hows, etc, sang, Law, sang, prayed. 5 Sang. 5.30 They went; tea with Miss Sophy, religious talk. 6.15 Germans'; buried. 7 Mrs Dearn's, religious talk (she open, seemed convinced). 8 At home; religious talk. 9 Prayed.

Grace: 6 rating thirteen times; 5 four times [noon to 3, 8 to 9].

[SUNDAY] DECEMBER 26. 4 Prayed with Ingham; hymns; meditated. 5 Meditated; hymns; dressed. 6 Read Prayers, expounded. 7 At home; tea, religious talk. 8 At the bluff, no one came. 8.30 Religious talk with Charles, and walked with [him]; prayed with Delamotte. 9 Married George Roan; religious talk. 10 Dressed; read Prayers. 11 Preached (forty there), Sacrament (twenty-one there). 12 Prayers. 12.20 At home; prayed; German's; dinner. 1 Necessary talk (religious); read letter from Spangenberg. 2 Letter. 2.45 At home; necessary talk. 3 Read Prayers, expounded (sixty there). 4 Walked with Miss Sophy, religious talk. 4.20 At home; Mr Hows, etc; sang; Law. 5 Sang; prayed; sang. 5.30 Necessary

[Tuesday, [December] 28. Mr. Delamotte and I with a guide set out for Frederica by land. We stayed that night and the next morning at the Cowpen, and in the evening came to Fort Argyle. It [E—is a small square wooden building, standing] pleasantly on the high bank of the River Ogeechee, having woods at a little distance on every side. Here we were obliged to stay till the next afternoon. Then we went on to Canoochee River, over which we swum our horses by the side of the small canoe in which we crossed it ourselves. On the side of it we made a fire, set up our blankets for a tent, and commended ourselves to God till morning.

[The next day, after riding through woods between thirty and forty miles, we made a good fire, and cheerfully ended the Old Year.

---

business; necessary talk (religious). 6 Hermsdorf came; tea, mostly religious talk. 6.30 Germans'; sleepy. 7.30 Writ notes; writ diary. 8 Hymns. 8.20 Owen. 9 Religious talk (necessary); prayed. 9.20.

Grace: 7 rating once [4 to 5 am]; 6 thirteen times; 5 thrice [1 to 3, 6 to 7 pm].

MONDAY, DECEMBER 27. 4 Prayed; hymns. 5 Dressed; read Prayers; expounded. 6 Owen; tea, religious and useful talk. 7 Prayed with them; hymns. 8 Talk of the Germans; prayed. 9 Hymns. 10 Dressed; writ diary; meditated. 10.30 Read Prayers. 11 Read Prayers, preached (twenty-six there), Sacrament; prayers. 12 At home; prayed; dinner, religious talk. 1 Garden; meditated; religious talk with Delamotte of Frederica. 2 Religious talk of it with Germans. 2.45 Meditated; prayed. 3 Read Prayers, expounded. 4 Mr Causton's, religious talk (necessary). 5 Tea, religious talk (necessary). 5.15 Prayed; religious talk (necessary); buried. 6 Supper; German. 7 Miss Bovey and Miss Sophy, read Mr Morgan's letters. 9 Letters, writ diary. 9.45.

TUESDAY, DECEMBER 28. 4 Prayed with Delamotte; writ Spangenberg. 5 Dressed; read Prayers, expounded. 6 Miss Sophy; tea, necessary talk (religious). 7 Prayed with them; letter. 8 Letter. 9 Letter; necessary business. 10 Necessary business. 10.45 Read Prayers. 11 Read Prayers, preached (twenty-three there), Sacrament (seventeen there). 12 Necessary business; Causton's, necessary talk. 12.45 Miss Bovey's, religious talk. 1 At home; dinner; necessary business. 2 Boat with Delamotte, etc, necessary talk (religious and much). 4 Mrs Musgrove's with Ingham, religious talk (necessary). 5.15 Tea, religious talk. 6.15 Supper, religious talk (necessary). 7.30 Ingham read Prayers, expounded; packed. 9.15 Slept.

WEDNESDAY, DECEMBER 29. 6 Private prayer. 6.45 Packed. 7.30 Writ diary; necessary business. 8 Read Prayers, expounded; coffee. 9.30 Packed; necessary business. 10 Necessary business; necessary talk. 11.30 Set out, northwest. 12 West; southwest; private prayer. 1 West; south-southwest; west. 3 Over first swamp; southwest. 4.30 River swamp; southeast; east. 5 South-southeast. 5.30 Past the swamps. 6 Ferried; at the Fort Ogeechy. 7 Mr Finlay's, supper, mostly religious talk; read Prayers, expounded. 8.45 At Mr Fitchet's; slept.

[Saturday, January 1, 1737. Our provisions fell short, but having some dried bear's flesh, which we had reserved for such an occasion, we boiled it in the evening, and found it very wholesome (though not very agreeable) food.

[On Sunday, January 2nd, we came to the Scotch settlement at Darien [E—about twenty miles from Frederica], where I was surprised to hear an extemporary prayer and a written sermon. Are not then the words we speak to God to be set in order at least as carefully as those we speak to our fellow-worms! One consequence of this manner of praying is that they have Public Service only *once* a week. Alas, my brethren! I bear you record, 'Ye have a zeal for God, but not according to knowledge!' [Rom. 10:2].

[Yet it must be owned that in all instances of personal or social duty this people utterly shames our countrymen: in sobriety, industry, frugality, patience; in sincerity and openness of behaviour; in justice and mercy of all kinds, being not content with exemplary kindness and friendliness to one another, but extending it, to the utmost of their ability, to every stranger that is within their gates.

[Mr. Macleod, their minister, is a serious, prudent, resolute, and (I hope) a pious man.

[On Monday evening I set out from Darien in a piragua, it being about twenty miles by water from Frederica. Wednesday, January 5, in

---

THURSDAY, DECEMBER 30. 6 Tea, necessary talk (religious). 7 Read Prayers, expounded. 7.30 Walked with Finlay, necessary talk (religious). 9 Fort; sixty Indians came, necessary talk (useful and religious). 11.30 Dinner. 12 Walked; meditated; private prayer. 1.45 Set out [with Cook]; south; south-southwest. 3 At Canoochee Ferry, boat not come. 5 Fire. 5.30 Boat came, ferried. 6.30 fire. 7 Made camps. 8 Supper; read Prayers, expounded. 8.45 Rain.

FRIDAY, DECEMBER 31. 6 Tea, read Prayers; necessary business. 8.15 Set out; south-southwest; private prayer. 12.20 [At] the branch; dinner. 1 Set out; south by east to south by west; private prayer. 5.15 Bee tree; camped. 6 Tea, religious talk (close with Will Francis, he open); read Prayers. 8.30.

SATURDAY, JANUARY 1 [1736/37]. 5.30 Prayers; tea; they sought horses. 7.30 They found them! 8 Set out; northeast. 9 East; east by south; private prayer. 11 Southeast; private prayer. 12.15 Yamasee. 1 Camp; dinner. 1.30 Set out; west; north; southwest. 4 Past first swamp. 6 Camped; tea; ate bear. 8 Rained; read Prayers. 8.15.

SUNDAY, JANUARY 2. 5 Tea; read Prayers; (ill!). 7.30 Set out; private prayer; south by west; five swamps, six ponds. 11.30 Darien, Mr Mackintosh's, they very civil. 12 Prayers, sermon. 1.30 Mr Mackintosh's; dinner; walked with Mr Macleod, religious talk. 3 Tea, religious talk. 4 Walked with Delamotte and Macleod to the fort, religious talk. 5.15 Mr Monroe, Macleod, and Mrs Patterson there, religious talk. 7.45 Mrs Mackintosh's; supper; sang; Ingham prayed extempore! 8.30 Mr Macleod's; to bed.

the afternoon, we came thither, and took up our quarters at Mr. Hird's. Most of those we met with were, as we expected, cold and heartless. I could not find one who retained his first love. 'O send forth thy light and thy heat, that they may guide them, and lead them unto thy holy hill!" [cf. Ps. 43:3 (BCP)].

When Mr. Delamotte and I came to Frederica we lodged at Mr. Hird's. There they were talking of [Miss Sophy] almost continually, and frequently saying how glad they should be if I would marry her. I found this had a great effect upon me, and one day seriously checked them, saying, 'Why do you talk so idly? You know she is resolved "not to marry at all".' 'Why, she told me,' said Phoebe Hird, 'she would never marry any but Tom Mellichamp—unless it was a very religious man. But when I asked her, what if Mr. Wesley would have her, she smiled, looked down, and said nothing.' I told Mr. Delamotte when we were alone that now I perceived myself to be in real danger, since it was probable, even from that little circumstance, that the marriage stopped not at her but at me.

MONDAY, JANUARY 3. 6.45 Walked; meditated; prayed. 7.45 Writ diary. 8.15 Monroe's, Mr Macleod, etc; tea, religious talk (necessary). 9.30 Mr Macleod's; read Catechism of Assembly. 11 Mr Macleod came, religious talk. 12 Slept. 1 Mr Mackintosh's; headache; dinner. 2 Necessary talk (useful and religious). 2.30 Writ diary; began Haliburton's life; slept. 4.45 Monroe's; tea, mostly religious talk (necessary). 7.30 Captain Mackintosh's; supper. 9 Set out with Mr Humble, Delamotte, etc. 9.30 In the piragua; read Prayers. 10.

TUESDAY, JANUARY 4. 6.45 Windbound; read Prayers; tea, necessary talk. 8 Haliburton. 12 Dinner; Haliburton. 5.30 Tea, religious talk (necessary). 6 Private prayer. 7 Read Prayers; meditated. 8.30 Cold; not so ill.

WEDNESDAY, JANUARY 5. 4.15 Private prayer; meditated. 6.45 Read Prayers. 7 Dressed; tea; Fleury. 11 Religious talk. 1.45 Frederica; Mr Hird's, all well, he not [there?]. 2 Dinner, necessary talk (religious). 3.30 Walked with Delamotte, religious talk. 5 At home; necessary business; prayed with Delamotte. 6 Supper; read Prayers, expounded (they with us; sixteen there), sang. 7.15 Hird's, necessary talk (religious). 8 He came, necessary talk (religious). 10.15 Mark's house; prayed ['necessary talk' overwritten].

THURSDAY, JANUARY 6. 4 Prayed with Delamotte; meditated; private prayer. 5 Hymns. 6.30 [Read] Prayers, expounded (eleven there). 7.30 Tea. 8 Tea, religious talk (necessary). 9 Haliburton's. 11 Haliburton's life; read notes. 12 Life. 1 Dinner, religious talk (necessary). 2 Visited. 4 Haliburton. 5 Prayed with Delamotte; [meditated?]; prayed. 6 Tea, religious talk. 6.45 Read Prayers (eighteen there). 7 Expounded; at home; Law; sang. 8 Haliburton. 9 Hird's, necessary talk (religious); prayed. 9.30.

FRIDAY, JANUARY 7. 4 Prayed with Delamotte; meditated. 5 Haliburton. 6.45 Read Prayers. 7 Expounded; prayers. 7.30 Haliburton. 8 Coffee, religious talk. 9 Haliburton. 12 Visited. 1 Haliburton. 3 Tea, religious talk. 3.40 Haliburton.

[B—On January 10, I writ to Miss Sophy. I desire that letter may be read in court.]

4.40 Walked; meditated (+). 5 Meditated. 5.15 Haliburton. 5.45 Prayed with Delamotte (lively zeal). 6 Religious talk. 6.45 Read Prayers. 7 Expounded; sang; Law. 7.45 Haliburton. 9 Hird's, religious talk. 9.20 Prayed.

Grace: 7 rating once [4 to 5 am]; 6 twelve times; 5 four times [9 to 11 am, 1 to 3 pm].

SATURDAY, JANUARY 8. 4 Prayed with Delamotte; meditated; writ diary. 5 Haliburton. 6.45 Read Prayers (eight there). 7 Expounded. 7.15 Haliburton. 8 Hird's; tea, much talk (religious). 9 Haliburton. 11.45 Walked. 12.15 Dinner, necessary talk. 1 Necessary and useful talk. 1.30 Haliburton. 4.30 Walked; meditated (+). 5.30 Delamotte, religious talk; private prayer. 6 Tea, necessary talk (religious). 6.45 [Read] Prayers (fourteen there). 7.15 Law; sang. 8 Haliburton. 9 Good talk (necessary and religious) with Mrs Hird. 9.45 Prayed.

SUNDAY, JANUARY 9. 4.30 Private prayer. 5 Haliburton. 6 Dressed; necessary talk (religious). 7 Read Prayers, expounded (twelve there). 8.15 Mr Weston's, useful and necessary talk. 9 Tea, religious talk. 10 Meditated. 10.30 Read Prayers. 11 Sermon (seventeen there), Sacrament (six there). 12 Prayed with Delamotte; Haliburton. 1 Haliburton. 2 Dinner. 2.45 Haliburton. 3 Read Prayers, expounded (forty-four there). 4.15 Haliburton. 5 Prayed with Delamotte; private prayer. 6 Haliburton; tea, religious talk. 7 Haliburton. 9 Religious talk; prayed. 9.20.

Grace: 7 rating once [5 to 6 pm]; 6 ten times; 5 five times [8 to 9 am, 1 to 3, 4 to 5, 8 to 9 pm].

MONDAY, JANUARY 10. 4.45 Prayed with Delamotte; Haliburton. 6 Haliburton. 7 Read Prayers, expounded (eight there); necessary business. 8 Mr and Mrs Weston; tea, necessary talk. 9 He went; necessary and useful talk. 10 Delamotte went; necessary and useful talk. 10.30 Haliburton. 12 Writ diary. 12.15 Dinner. 1 Mrs Weston, necessary talk. 1.30 Haliburton. 3 Necessary talk with Hows; necessary talk. 3.30 Haliburton. 4 Haliburton; necessary talk; meditated. 5 Meditated; private prayer with Delamotte; writ diary. 6 Writ to Mr Causton; supper. 7 [Read] Prayers; Law; sang. 7.45 Writ to Miss Sophy. 8 Haliburton. 9 Haliburton; private prayer. 9.30.

Grace: 6 rating eight times; 5 eight times [8 to noon, 1 to 4].

TUESDAY, JANUARY 11. 4.30 Prayed with Delamotte. 5 Haliburton. 7 [Read] Prayers. 7.30 Haliburton. 8 Mrs Hird; tea, religious talk. 8.30 Haliburton. 9 Greek with Delamotte. 9.30 Haliburton. 10 Haliburton; writ diary. 10.30 Haliburton. 12 Walked; Haliburton. 1 Dinner, mostly religious talk. 1.45 Haliburton. 2 Visited. 3 Haliburton. 5 Private prayer. 6 Haliburton; supper. 7 Read Prayers; read; sang. 8 Haliburton. 8.30 Religious talk with Phoebe; with Delamotte. 9.20 Private prayer.

Grace: 6 rating fifteen times; 5 twice [1 to 2, 7 to 8 pm].

WEDNESDAY, JANUARY 12. 4.15 Prayed with Delamotte; private prayer. 5 Haliburton. 7 [Read] Prayers (six there); Haliburton. 8 Coffee, religious talk. 9 Haliburton. 10 Greek; Haliburton. 11 Writ diary; visited. 12 Walked; read.

12.15 Haliburton. 3 Prayed with Delamotte; tea, religious talk. 4 Haliburton. 5 Prayed with Delamotte; private prayer. 6 Haliburton; supper. 7 Read Prayers (nine there); sang. 7.30 Haliburton. 8 Mr Hird came, religious talk (he right). 9.30 Prayed.

Grace: 7 rating once [5 to 6 pm]; 6 eleven times; 5 six times [6 to 7, 9 to 11 am, 1 to 3 pm].

THURSDAY, JANUARY 13. 4.30 Prayed with Mr Hird, Mark, and Delamotte. 5 Haliburton. 6 The same, necessary talk; recollected. 6.45 Read Prayers (six there). 7 Expounded; Haliburton; tea, religious talk. 8 Haliburton. 10 Writ diary; Haliburton. 11 Haliburton; walked. 12 Dinner; good talk. 1 Haliburton. 5 Prayed with Delamotte; private prayer. 5.45 Supper. 6 Haliburton; read Prayers (fourteen there). 7 Law; sang. 7.30 Mr Hird, mostly religious talk. 9.30 Prayed.

Grace: 6 rating eight times [4 to 6, 7 to 8, 10 to noon, 4 to 6, 7 to 8 pm]; 5 ten times. Preserved from w 4/1 [no time indicated].

FRIDAY, JANUARY 14. 3.30 Private prayer. 4 Private prayer; prayed with them. 5 Haliburton. 6 The same. 6.40 Read Prayers. 7 Expounded (six there); Haliburton. 8 Coffee, religious talk; Haliburton. 11 Walked; Haliburton; meditated. 12 Visited. 12.30 Haliburton. 2 Haliburton, necessary talk (religious). 3 Tea, religious talk. 3.40 Haliburton. 5 Prayed; private prayer. 5.40 Religious talk with Mark, he affected. 6 Haliburton; supper. 7 Read Prayers, expounded (twelve there); read; sang. 8 Haliburton. 8.45 Hird, religious talk. 9 Mark. 9.15 Prayed.

Grace: 7 rating thrice [3 to 5 am, 5 to 6 pm]; 6 eleven times; 5 thrice [5 to 7 am, 2 to 3 pm].

SATURDAY, JANUARY 15. 4.45 Prayed with them; Haliburton. 6 The same. 6.45 Read Prayers. 7 Tea, religious talk; Haliburton. 8 Ended it. 9 Walked; Watts' hymns. 12 Writ diary; Watts' Psalms. 1 Dinner, mostly religious talk. 2 Ended Psalms. 3 Walked; meditated on sermon. 4 Meditated; sang. 5 Prayed with Delamotte; private prayer. 6 Transcribed Watts; tea, necessary talk (religious). 7 Read Prayers; religious talk; read; sang. 8 Watts. 9.30 Prayed.

Grace: 7 rating twice [4 to 6 pm]; 6 eleven times; 5 four times [6 to 7 am, 1 to 2, 5 to 7, 9 to 10 pm].

SUNDAY, JANUARY 16. 4 Prayed with Delamotte; private prayer. 5 Watts. 6 Dressed; Watts. 7 Read Prayers (fifteen there). 8 Tea, religious talk. 9 Watts. 10 Meditated upon sermon. 10.45 Read Prayers. 11 Sermon (twenty-five there), Sacrament (eight there). 12 Watts. 2 Dinner, mostly religious talk. 3 Read Prayers (thirty there). 4.15 Watts. 4.30 Walked; meditated; sang. 5 Private prayer; prayed with them. 6 Watts; tea, mostly religious talk; Watts. 7 Mr Hird, religious talk. 8 Mostly religious talk. 9.15 Prayed.

Grace: 7 rating twice [4 to 5 am, 5 to 6 pm]; 6 twelve times; 5 thrice [7 to 8 am, 2 to 3, 8 to 9 pm].

MONDAY, JANUARY 17. 3.15 Watts. 4 Private prayer; prayed with them. 5. Watts. 7 Read Prayers (five there). 7.30 Tea, mostly religious talk. 8 Watts. 11.15 Writ diary. 11.30 Watts. 12 Private prayer. 12.45 Watts. 1 Dinner, mostly religious talk. 2 Cut wood. 3 Watts. 4.30 At Mr Perkins', good talk. 5 Tea, good talk; prayed with Delamotte. 6 Supper; Watts; meditated. 7 Read Prayers (fifteen

[D—Tuesday, [January] 18. At night we had as sharp a frost as any I ever remember in England. We lay in a very small room, and had a fire all night, notwithstanding which, not only all the water in the room was frozen, but our ink too, which stood on a table almost close to the fireside.

---

there); read; sang. 7.45 Watts. 8.45 Religious talk with Mark. 9.15 Private prayer.

Grace: 6 rating nine times; 5 eight times [7 to 8, 9 to 10 am, 1 to 5, 6 to 8 pm.]

TUESDAY, JANUARY 18. 4.30 Necessary business; prayed with them. 5 Watts. 6 Watts; dressed. 6.45 Read Prayers (five there). 7 Tea, religious and useful talk. 7.30 Watts. 11 Visited Stabler and Mrs Loope. 12 Watts. 1 Dinner. 1.30 Hymns. 3 Mrs Robinson's, tea, necessary talk (religious). 4 Necessary talk (useful and religious). 4.30 Buried. 5 Private prayer; prayed. 6 Tea, necessary talk. 7 Read Prayers (six there). 8 Hymns. 9.15.

Grace: 6 rating nine times [4 to 8, 9 am to 1, 4 to 6, 7 to 8 pm]; 5 eight times.

WEDNESDAY, JANUARY 19. 4.15 Private prayer; (very sharp frost, rain; well). 5 Hymns. 6 Prayed with Delamotte; dressed; hymns. 7 Read Prayers; coffee. 8 Hymns. 12 Visited. 1.15 Hymns. 2.30 Necessary business. 3 Prayed; tea, religious talk. 4 Religious talk with Mrs Hird. 4.45 Necessary business. 5 Prayed with Delamotte; private prayer; religious talk with Mark. 6 Religious talk; supper. 6.45 Read Prayers (ten there). 7 Expounded; read; sang. 7.30 Mark, religious talk. 9.40 Private prayer; meditated. 9.15 Prayed.

Grace: 7 rating once [4 to 5 am]; 6 eight times [5 to 8, 9 to 10 am, noon to 1, 3 to 4, 5 to 8 pm]; 5 eight times.

THURSDAY, JANUARY 20. 4.30 Private prayer. 5 Private prayer; prayed with them; necessary talk (religious). 6 Necessary talk (religious); private prayer. 6.45 Read Prayers (eight there). 7.15 Tea, necessary talk (religious). 8 German; hymns. 10 Walked; read Haliburton; sang. 11 Read; sang. 11.45 Hymns. 12 The same. 1 Dinner, mostly religious talk. 2 German; necessary business; meditated. 3 Necessary business. 3.30 Mrs Calwell and Mrs Weston, religious talk. 4 Tea, good talk. 5 Prayed with Delamotte; private prayer. 6 Supper, religious talk. 7 Read Prayers (thirteen there); read; sang. 8 Pierce upon infant communion. 9.15 Prayed.

Grace: 6 rating nine times; 5 nine times [actually seven, 6 to 10 am, 1 to 2, 3 to 5 pm].

FRIDAY, JANUARY 21. 4.30 Private prayer. 5 Private prayer; prayed with them. 6 Religious talk with Delamotte; read Prayers. 7 Married Ward and Mary Truby. 7.45 Coffee. 8 Writ Journal. 12 Prayed with Delamotte; walked; meditated. 1 Meditated; private prayer. 2 At home; journal. 3 Tea, religious talk. 3.45 Journal; (lively zeal, s.2). 4.45 Meditated (lively zeal). 5 Prayed with Delamotte; private prayer. 6 Supper; Pierce. 7 Read Prayers (sixteen there); read; sang. 8 Hird, religious and useful talk. 9.15.

Grace: 6 rating ten times [4 to 6, 7 to 8, 9 am to 2, 3 to 8 pm]; 5 seven times.

[Saturday, [January] 22. I came to the speech of poor Mr. Tackner, who told me the occasion of his breaking with Mark Hird [E—renouncing the only Christian friend he had], owned himself to blame, and expressed an earnest desire of a thorough reconciliation. This was, by the blessing of God, effected the next day, and they joined together in the Sacrifice of Thanksgiving.

[On Sunday morning I spoke to two or three who were going a-shooting; but they made light of it, and went on. I then represented it to the magistrates, who two days after directed an order to the constables, to be more watchful in preventing this and all other profanation of the Lord's Day.

[Tuesday the 25th. Being on board a sloop which lay in the river, I

SATURDAY, JANUARY 22. 3.15 Private prayer. 4 Private prayer; meditated. 4.30 Journal; prayed. 6 Journal; dressed. 6.45 Read Prayers (eight there). 7 Tea, necessary talk. 8 Journal. 10 Religious talk with Tackner (he convinced and affected). 11 Necessary talk with Mrs Hird; journal. 12 Meditated; sang. 1 Dinner, mostly religious talk. 2 Mostly religious talk; necessary business. 3 Visited; Mrs Calwell, Allen. 4 Calwell; tea, religious talk. 4.30 Walked; meditated; sang. 5 Sang; prayed with Delamotte; necessary business. 6 Supper, necessary talk (religious). 7 Read Prayers (twenty there); read; sang. 8 *Life of Mahomet.* 9.15 Prayed.

Grace: 7 rating once [3 to 4 am]; 6 seven times [4 to 5, 10 to 11, noon to 1, 3 to 6, 7 to 8 pm]; 5 nine times.

SUNDAY, JANUARY 23. 5 Prayed with them; private prayer. 6 Dressed; necessary business; necessary talk. 7 Read Prayers (twelve there). 8 Tea, necessary talk (religious). 9 Meditated upon sermon. 10 Meditated; religious talk. 11 Read Prayers, sermon (thirty-one there, all the Scotch), Sacrament (eight there). 12.15 At home; prayed with them. 12.45 Dinner. 1 Dinner, good talk. 2 Religious talk with Mr White. 2.15 Walked; meditated; sang; religious talk with Delamotte. 3 Read Prayers (thirty-four there). 4 With Mr Macleod; tea, religious and useful talk. 5 Mostly religious talk. 6 With them at Mr Hird's. 7 Supper; Mr Perkins. 8 Mostly religious talk. 9.15.

Grace: 6 rating nine times [5 to 8, 9 am to 1, 2 to 3 pm]; 5 eight times.

MONDAY, JANUARY 24. 4.30 Sick; prayed with Delamotte. 6 *Life of Mahomet.* 7 Read Prayers; Mr Macleod; tea, mostly religious talk. 8 Mostly religious talk. 9 *Life of Mahomet.* 10.45 Meditated. 11 Packed. 12.15 Mr Hird's, necessary talk. 12.45 Dinner, good talk (necessary and religious). 2 Storehouse, necessary business. 3 Mrs Patterson; necessary talk with Penrose. 3.30 At home; Pierce. 5 Private prayer; Patrick. 5.30 Private prayer. 5.45 Mrs Hird came, tea. 6 Tea, religious talk; Pierce. 7 Read Prayers; religious talk; prayed. 8 Hird's; Mr Dyson there. 9.15 Necessary business; religious talk with Mark and William. 10 Delamotte came.

TUESDAY, JANUARY 25. 5.30 Prayed with them. 6 Meditated. 6.45 Read Prayers, expounded. 7.30 Tea, religious talk. 8 Writ resolutions. 9.30 Walked;

heard Mr. Mellichamp was on his journey to Savannah, and therefore determined to be there myself as soon as I could. At noon the next day I left Frederica. Having procured a very celebrated book there, Machiavelli's *Works*, I set myself to consider it in my passage. I weighed thoroughly the sentiments that were less common, compared one passage with another, and endeavoured, with all the reason and coolness I was master of, to form an impartial judgment of the whole. And my cool judgment is, that if all the doctrines of devils which have been committed to writing since letters were in the world were collected together in one volume, it would fall far short of this; and that should a prince form himself by the maxims of this book, so calmly recommending hypocrisy, treachery, lying, robbery, and murder of all kinds, Domitian or Nero would be an angel of light compared to that man.

---

meditated; private prayer. 10.45 Read Prayers, sermon (sixteen there), Sacrament (four there). 12.15 At home; prayed; read. 1 In Captain Ellis' sloop with Dyson and Macleod. 2 Dinner, good talk. 3.30 Heard of Mellichamp; met Mr Horton, he very civil; necessary and useful talk. 4.15 Walked with Delamotte, necessary talk (religious) of Miss Sophy, prayed for her. 5 At home; company, necessary talk (religious); tea. 7 Read Prayers, expounded (eighteen there); religious talk; sang. 8 Necessary talk with Hird, Horton, Penrose, etc. 9.45.

WEDNESDAY, JANUARY 26. 4 Private prayer; prayed. 6 Walked; meditated; private prayer for Miss Sophy. 6.45 Read Prayers (ten there). 7.15 Necessary talk. 9 At home; tea, necessary talk (religious) with Hird; necessary business; necessary talk (religious). 10.30 In Penrose's boat; began Machiavelli's works. 12 Set out; Machiavelli. 5 Rowed. 6 Private prayer; prayed. 6.45 Slept. 7.45 Doboy Sound; fog; ate. 10.

THURSDAY, JANUARY 27. 6.15 Prayed; private prayer. 7 Machiavelli; ate. 11.30 Stormy; Sapelo [Island]; meditated. 1 Dinner; Machiavelli [and] Patrick alternè. 5 Private prayer; tea; necessary business. 7 Supper, they [had] good talk. 9.15 Prayed with them.

FRIDAY, JANUARY 28. 6.30 Private prayer. 7 Necessary business; read Prayers with them; tea; good talk; Machiavelli. 12.45 Ate. 2.15 Set out; driven back again. 5 Landed; rained hard; religious talk with Peter. 7 Fair; supper, mostly religious talk (not close). 9 Read Prayers.

SATURDAY, JANUARY 29. 6 Private prayer; necessary and useful talk. 8 Tea. 9 Machiavelli [and] Patrick alternè. 1.30 Meditated. 2 Dinner; meditated. 3.15 Wind came, fair; thick fog. 4 Set out. 5 Patrick; private prayer. 6 Came back. 8 Supper. 9.30 Read Prayers; hard rain.

SUNDAY, JANUARY 30. 4 Private prayer; rained through tent. 6 Private prayer; sang. 6.30 Tea. 7 Patrick; meditated; sang; private prayer. 11.30 Dinner; Patrick. 1.15 Set out; meditated; private prayer. 4 Patrick; sang. 5.45 Supper. 7 Slept. 11 Storm; private prayer!

[After having been detained several days on Sapelo Island by mists and contrary winds, at last on Monday, January 31, I came to Savannah.]

Finding Miss Sophy was with Mrs. Musgrove at the Cowpen, a place where I doubted she would learn little good, I went up thither the same evening. She took boat and came down with me immediately, as it was not her custom to deny me anything. For indeed from March 13, 1736, the day I first spoke to her, till that hour [B—to March 12, 1737 (the day she married Mr. Williamson)], I cannot recollect so much as a single instance* of my proposing anything to her, or expressing any desire, which she did not fully [B—immediately] comply with. [*B—(except that one on February 15, the day after I told her my resolution not to marry') . . . Perhaps what occurred on Thursday, February 3 may be thought one more exception.]

[D—Tuesday, February 1. Being the Anniversary Feast on account of the first convoy's landing in Georgia, we had a sermon and the Holy Communion. The next morning, being informed of Miss Bovey's design to marry shortly, I went to her and told her with all plainness my thoughts of Mr. Burnside and of the whole affair. Though we did not entirely agree in our judgment, she took it as it was intended. Here is one woman in America in whom to this day I have found no guile.]

I was now in a great strait. I still thought it best for me to live single, and this was still my design, but I felt the foundations of it shaken more and more every day. Insomuch that on Thursday, February 3, I again used the familiarities [with Miss Sophy] I had resolved against. And likewise again hinted at a desire of marriage, though I made no direct proposal. For indeed it was only a sudden thought, which had not the consent of my own mind. Yet I firmly [B—verily] believe, had she closed

---

MONDAY, JANUARY 31. 2 Necessary talk; slept. 6 Private prayer; Skidaway; tea, necessary talk. 8.30 Set out; wind contrary; landed; private prayer. 12 Thunderbolt. 12.45 Set out; meditated; private prayer. 2.45 At Germans', necessary talk; dressed. 3.30 Mrs Causton's, necessary talk of Miss Sophy, she at the Cowpen. 4 Set out; religious talk. 5.15 At the Cowpen, religious talk, tea. 6.45 Necessary talk with Ingham. 7 Supper, religious talk (necessary). 8 Read Prayers, expounded. 8.30 Set out with Miss Sophy, religious talk with her (she quite open and affected). 9.30 Mr Causton's, necessary and useful talk. 10 Prayed.

TUESDAY, FEBRUARY 1. 4.15 Necessary business. 5.30 Read Prayers (thirteen there). 6.15 Miss Sophy, religious talk of Mellichamp. 7 Mr Causton's; tea, mostly religious talk. 8.30 Necessary business. 10.45 Read Prayers, preached (thirty-three there), Sacrament (thirteen there). 1 Necessary business. 2 Sent for to Penrose's; much company; dinner. 3.15 Necessary business. 4.45 Visited Simms. 5 Meditated; private prayer. 6 Supper; Germans'. 7.15 Read Prayers (twenty-three there). 8.15 Miss Bovey, etc; began Haliburton's life. 9.30 They went.

with me at that time, my judgment would have made but a faint resistance. But she said, she thought it was best for clergyman not to be encumbered with worldly cares; and that it was best for her too to live single, and she was accordingly resolved 'never to marry [B—while she lived]'. I used no argument to induce her to alter her resolution.

Upon reflection, I thought this a very narrow escape; and after much consideration I went [on Saturday, February 5] to Mr. Töltschig, the Pastor of the Moravians, and again desired his advice, whether I had not

---

WEDNESDAY, FEBRUARY 2. 5 Necessary business; read Prayers. 6 Miss Sophy came, necessary talk (religious). 7.15 Necessary business. 8 Miss Bovey's (she not convinced). 8.30 Necessary business; necessary talk (religious) with Miss Sophy. 10 Meditated. 10.45 Read Prayers, preached, Sacrament. 12.30 Dinner. 1 Necessary business. 5 Buried (+); meditated. 6 Sang; supper. 6.45 Germans' (lively zeal; +). 7.15 Read Prayers (lively zeal). 8.15 Mr Hows, etc. 9 Prayed.

[THURSDAY,] FEBRUARY 3. 4 Private prayer; meditated. 5 Necessary business; read Prayers. 6 Miss Sophy; Owen, religious talk, tea. 7 Hickes; necessary business. 8.15 French with Miss Sophy, religious talk. 9.15 She went (sins!); necessary business. 12 Dinner; read resolutions; necessary business. 1.30 Set out; religious talk. 2 Mr Potter's, religious talk; prayed. 2.30 Set out. 3 Visited; Miss Bovey's, necessary talk (religious); tea, religious talk (close); Campbell's, religious talk. 5 Sang; meditated. 6 Supper; German. 7 Read Prayers; Miss Bovey, etc. 9.30.

[FRIDAY,] FEBRUARY 4. 4 Private prayer; sang; Hebrew. 5 Religious talk; read Prayers, expounded. 6 Miss Sophy; Owen, tea, religious talk. 7 Hickes; necessary business. 8 French. 9 Necessary business. 12.30 Nelson with boys; prayed. 1 Necessary business. 2 Miss Bovey's, Miss Sophy there, mostly religious talk; coffee. 3.15 French. 4 At home; necessary business. 4.15 Garden; Mr Burnside came, talk of the banns (gained no ground). 4.45 Meditated. 5 Miss Bovey's, religious talk of banns (gained little ground). 5.45 Private prayer for them. 6. Supper; prayed. 7 Read Prayers. 8 Miss Bovey, etc, read, sang. 8.45 Necessary business. Garden; meditated; private prayer. 9.30.

SATURDAY, FEBRUARY 5. 4 Private prayer. 5 Religious talk; read Prayers. 6 Miss Sophy; Owen; tea, religious talk. 7 Meditated; necessary business. 8 French; necessary talk (religious). 9 Necessary business; Mrs Vanderplank's, religious talk. 10 Walked; meditated. 11.30 Meditated; private prayer. 11.45 With Töltschig and John, talk of Miss Sophy. 12.30 Dinner with them. 1.15 Visited Mrs Ann, Simms! 2 Catechized. 2.45 Set out, read Gask's sermon. 3.30 Mr Potter's; read Prayers; religious talk; set out; meditated. 4.45 Garden; meditated; necessary talk; religious talk. 5.15 Ingham and Delamotte, necessary talk (religious). 5.30 Prayed; sang. 6 Tea, they [had] religious talk against Miss Sophy. 6.45 Germans'. 7.15 Read Prayers; Mr Hows, etc. 8.45 Delamotte and Ingham went to Germans; private prayer. 10.45 Lots; went to them; they for it. 12.15 Prayed.

best, while it was yet in my power, break off so dangerous an acquaintance. He asked, 'What do you think would be the consequence if you should?' I said, 'I fear her soul would be lost, being surrounded with dangers, and having no other person to warn her of and arm her against them.' He added, 'And what do you think would be the consequence if you should not break it off?' I said, 'I fear I should marry her.' He replied short, 'I don't see why you should not.'

I went home amazed to the last degree, and it was now first that I had the least doubt whether it was best for me to marry or not. Which I never before thought would bear a question. I immediately related what had occurred to Mr. Ingham and Delamotte. They utterly disapproved of Mr. Töltschig's judgment, and in the evening went, as I desired they would, and talked largely with him and Anton [Seiffert] (the Moravian bishop) about it. It was near midnight when I went to them [Ingham and Delamotte], but even then they did not seem to be fully agreed. [B—They earnestly advised me against having any such thought.] Mr. Ingham still insisted I had not sufficient proof of her sincerity in religion, since the appearance of it might be owing partly to an excellent natural temper, partly to her desire of marrying me. I asked, how he could reconcile such a desire with what she had said on Thursday. He said, 'Very well. [B—Those words were not to be minded.] She would soon recall those words if I made a direct [B—serious] proposal.'

[B—And that they judged better than me may appear not only from Mrs. Causton's declaring at this time that Sophy was now resolved to marry none but a clergyman, but from her own confession since, that if Mr. Wesley had ever proposed marriage to her, she could not have refused him.

[If it be asked, why I did not propose it, though I had so great a regard for her, I answer, for three reasons chiefly: (1) Because I did not think myself strong enough to bear the temptations of a married state; (2) Because I feared it would have obstructed the design on which I came, the going among the Indians; and (3) Because I thought her resolved not to marry, were it only on Mr. Mellichamp's account.]

[D—One of the most remarkable dispensations of providence toward me which I have yet known began to show itself this day. For many days after I could not at all judge which way the scale would turn. Nor was it fully determined till March 4, on which God commanded me to pull out my right eye. And by his grace I determined so to do, but being slack in the execution on Saturday, March 12, God being very merciful to me, my friend performed what I could not.

[I have often thought, one of the most difficult commands that ever was given was that given to Ezekiel concerning his wife. But the difficulty of obeying such a direction appeared to me now more than ever before. When, considering the character I bore, I could not but perceive that the word of the Lord was come to *me* likewise, saying, 'Son of man, behold I take away from thee the desire of thine eyes with a stroke; yet neither shalt thou mourn, nor weep, neither shall thy tears run down' (Ezek. 24:16).]

[Mr. Ingham] added, that I could not judge coolly of these things while I saw her every day, and therefore advised me 'to go out of town for a few days'. I clearly saw the wisdom of this advice; and accordingly went to Irene the next day [Sunday], four miles from Savannah. But first I writ two or three lines which I desired Miss Bovey to give Miss Sophy. They were, I think, in these words:

Feb. 6

I find, Miss Sophy, I can't take fire into my bosom, and not be burned. I am therefore retiring for a while, to desire the direction of God. Join with me, my friend, in fervent prayer, that he would show me what is best to be done.

When I came to Irene, I did not dare to ask counsel of God immediately, being 'a man of so unclean lips' [Isa. 6:5]. I therefore set aside Monday the 7th for self-examination, adding only that general prayer, whenever thoughts arose in my heart concerning the issue of things: 'Lord, thou knowest! If it be best, let nothing be able to hinder; if not, let nothing be able to effect it.' And this exercise I continued for several hours, with some measure of cheerfulness. But towards evening God hid his face, and I was troubled. My heart sunk in me like a stone. I felt how bitter a thing it is for a spirit of an unbounded appetite to be left a prey to its own desires. But it was not long. For I no sooner stretched

---

SUNDAY, FEBRUARY 6. 5 Private prayer; sang with them; read Prayers. 7.15 Mr Causton's, religious talk (necessary), tea. 8.30 Came home; religious talk with them. 8.45 Walked; meditated (zealous). 9.45 Religious talk with Delamotte; necessary business. 10.15 Read Prayers, sermon, Sacrament (lively zeal; +); religious talk. 1 Dinner. 1.30 Sang; writ note to Miss Sophy. 2 Miss Bovey's, religious talk of Miss Sophy. 2.30 Read Prayers, expounded (seventy there). 4. Religious talk; Mr Hows, etc; sang; read; prayed. 5.30 Religious talk with Will Francis. 5.45 Tea with Mrs Musgrove and Miss Sophy, religious talk. 6 Mr Causton came, necessary talk. 6.30 Miss Bovey's, religious talk. 7.15 Necessary business; read Prayers. 8 Set out with Mrs Musgrove, religious talk. 9 Irene; religious talk with Peter. 9.30 Private prayer (zealous).

MONDAY, FEBRUARY 7. 4 Private prayer; sang. 5 Private prayer; they came; Testament; sang; prayed (lively zeal). 6 Religious talk; rice. 6.45 Set out with Tookuthli. 7.20 Cowpen; read Prayers, expounded; religious talk with Mrs Musgrove. 8 Set out; meditated; private prayer. 8.45 At home; private prayer; Haliburton; private prayer; sang; meditated. 3 Sang; private prayer; meditated (sad!). 4 Haliburton (sadder). 5 Private prayer (comforted!). 6.30 Religious talk with our boys. 7 Peter came; prayed, etc. 8 Writ Account of Miss Sophy. 9.

forth my hands to heaven and bewailed my having departed from him, than God sent me help from his holy place, and my soul received comfort.

The next morning, Tuesday the 8th, I was obliged to go down to Savannah. There I stayed about an hour. And there again I felt and groaned under the weight of an unholy desire. My heart was with Miss Sophy all the time. I longed to see her, were it but at a distance and for a moment. And when I was called to take boat, it was as the sentence of death; but believing it was the call of God, I obeyed. I walked awhile to and fro on the edge of the water, heavy laden and pierced through with many sorrows. There, one came to me and said, 'You are still in doubt what is best to be done. First then cry to God that you may be wholly resigned, whatever shall appear to be his will.' I instantly cried to God for resignation. And I found that and peace together. I said, Sure it is a dream. I was in a new world. The change was as from death to life. I went back to Irene wondering and rejoicing; but withal exceeding fearful, lest my want of thankfulness for this blessing, or of care to improve it, might occasion its being taken away.

I was now more clear in my judgment every day. Beside that I believed her resolved never to marry, I was convinced it was not expedient for me, for two weighty reasons: (1) Because it would probably obstruct the design of my coming into America, the going among the Indians, and (2) Because I was not strong enough to bear the complicated temptations of a married state. Of this I informed my friends at my return to Savannah

---

TUESDAY, FEBRUARY 8. 4 Private prayer. 4.45 Account (very heavy). 5.30 Peter. 6.15 Rice. 6.45 Set out. 7.30 Mrs Musgrove's, religious talk; read Prayers; set out. 9 At home; necessary business. 9.30 Mr Burnside came; set out with him, mostly religious talk. 12.30 At home; dinner, necessary talk (religious) 1. Religious talk with the Germans. 2 At the boat; John came, religious talk (easy!). 3 Set out. 4.45 Irene; religious talk; private prayer. 6.15 Supper. 6.30 Sang; (easy). 7 Peter; sang, etc; private prayer. 9.

WEDNESDAY, FEBRUARY 9. 4 Private prayer; sang. 5 Peter. 6 Set out. 6.30 Lost. 8 Mrs Musgrove's, religious talk, tea; read Prayers. 9 Religious talk with her (she open). 10 Walked. 11.45 At home; private prayer. 12 Private prayer; dinner; necessary business; private prayer (easy, fearful). 2 Haliburton; sang; private prayer. 3 Writ notes. 3.30 Mrs Musgrove and Deikin, religious talk, tea. 4.30 Read death of Haliburton. 6 Necessary business. 6.30 Prayed; good talk. 7.15 Peter. 7.45 Private prayer. 8 Writ notes. 9.30.

THURSDAY, FEBRUARY 10. 4 Private prayer. 5 Peter. 6 Private prayer; sang. 7 Necessary business. 7.30 Prayed. 8 Meditated; private prayer. 9 Breakfast; private prayer; meditated. 10 Necessary business; private prayer; helped Peter. 12 Meditated; prayed; sang; necessary talk (religious); prayed; sang. 4 Tea, religious talk. 5.15 Read Greek Testament; meditated. 6 Sang; prayed. 7 Peter came. 8 Prayed; sang. 9.30 Bolzius, necessary talk (religious), tea. 11.

on Saturday, February 12. And on Monday the 14th, about seven in the morning, I told her in my own garden, 'I am resolved, Miss Sophy, if I marry at all, not to do it [B—at least] till I have been among the Indians.' [B—Nor have I, to my knowledge, said anything contrary to this, either to her or any other, from that hour.]

The next morning she told me, 'People wonder what I can do so long [B—so many hours in a day] at your house. I am resolved not to breakfast with you any more. And I won't come to you any more alone.' The day following she said, 'I don't think it signifies for me to learn French any longer.' But she added, 'My uncle and aunt, as well as I, will be glad of your coming to our house as often as you please.' I answered, 'You know, Miss Sophy, I don't love a crowd, and there is always one there.' She said, 'But we needn't be in it. We may be in the garden, or under the shed, or anywhere.'

FRIDAY, FEBRUARY 11. 5 Prayed. 5.45 Peter. 6 Sang; prayed; Greek Testament; set out. 7 Blazed. 8 Mrs Musgrove's; read Prayers; tea, religious talk. 10 Set out; blazed. 11 At home. 1 Greek Testament; meditated; sang. 1.30 Helped Peter. 3.30 Tea; helped him to fence. 7 Prayed; sang; meditated. 7.15 Peter. 8 Writ Account of Miss Sophy. 9.

GEORGIA DIARY 3
February 12–August 31, 1737

SATURDAY, FEBRUARY 12. 4.30 Prayed. 5 Private prayer; Peter. 6 Rice; account of myself. 7 Set out; meditated. 7.45 Musgrove's; meditated. 8 Prayed; tea, religious talk (she serious). 9 Set out; mended the way. 10 Mended. 11 Mended; meditated. 12 At home; dinner; necessary business; dinner. 1 Mr Burnside and Gronau, necessary talk (religious). 1.30 He went, religious talk with Gronau. 2 Tea, religious talk. 3 Set out; sang; meditated. 4 Meditated. 4.30 Savannah; necessary business. 5 Dressed; meditated; private prayer. 6 Ingham and Delamotte, religious talk, tea. 7 Read Prayers, exhorted. 7.45 Mr Hows and the rest, Patrick. 8 Religious talk; prayed; sang. 8.30 Religious talk. 9 Religious talk; prayed. 9.40.

SUNDAY, FEBRUARY 13. 4 Prayed with Delamotte; private prayer. 5 Private prayer; sang; dressed. 6 Read Prayers (twenty-five there). 7 Miss Sophy, tea; Mr Causton, religious talk (necessary). 8.15 He went; sang; meditated upon sermon. 9 Meditated; Causton, necessary talk; prayed. 10.15 Dressed. 10.30 Read Prayers. 11 Sermon (fifty there), Sacrament (eighteen communicants). 12.15 Writ; dinner, religious talk. 1 John came, religious talk. 2 Read Prayers, spoke upon rubrics (eighty there). 3.30 The people came; sang; read. 4 Sang, prayed, sang; visited. 5 Tea, mostly religious talk (Miss Sophy not affected). 5.45 Religious talk with Delamotte. 6 Meditated; private prayer. 6.30 Walked;

Germans'. 7 Religious talk with them. 8 Religious talk; they open. 9 Religious talk with Delamotte; prayer. 9.30.

Grace: 7 rating twice [4 to 5 am, 8 to 9 pm]; 6 fourteen times; 5 twice [7 to 8 am, 5 to 6 pm].

MONDAY, FEBRUARY 14. 4 Private prayer. 5 Private prayer; read Prayers (fifty-two there). 6 Mrs Musgrove and Miss Sophy, Owen, tea, religious talk. 7 Necessary business; necessary talk. 8 Explained with Miss Sophy. 8.45 Private prayer; uneasy (lively zeal) [pointing hand in margin]. 9 Necessary talk with Delamotte; writ diary; more uneasy; O Lord, help! 10 Deciphered Charles' letter. 11 Letter. 11.30 Meditated; private prayer (uneasy; +). 12 Dinner; private prayer. 1 Visited (lively zeal; convincing). 2 Visited. 4 Walked; Greek Testament. 5 Sang. 5.30 At home; prayed with Delamotte. 5.45 Mr Causton's. 6 Stated our account. 6.30 Tea, religious talk. 7 Necessary talk (religious); read Prayers, exhorted. 8 Miss Bovey, Haliburton; sang. 9 Religious talk (necessary). 9.15 Prayed.

Grace: 7 rating once [4 to 5 am]; 6 fourteen times; 5 twice [5 to 6 am, 7 to 8 pm].

TUESDAY, FEBRUARY 15. 4 Private prayer; Hebrew. 5 Private prayer; read Prayers. 6 Miss Sophy and Mrs Musgrove, Owen, tea, religious talk (close!). 7 Writ to the Trustees. 8.15 Religious talk with Miss Sophy. 8.30 Writ to Dr Bray's associates! 9 To the rector. 10 To Dr Cutler. 11 Writ diary; walked; sang; meditated; Kempis. 12 Dinner, necessary talk (religious). 12.30 Necessary business; private prayer. 1 Visited. 2.30 Miss Bovey's, religious talk. 3 Miss Sophy and Mrs Musgrove, tea, mostly religious talk. 4.30 They went; necessary talk (religious). 5 Necessary talk (religious). 5.40 At home; private prayer; sang. 6 Supper, necessary talk (religious). 6.40 Germans'. 7 Germans'; read Prayers. 8 Miss Sophy, etc; Haliburton; sang. 9 Writ diary. 9.15 Necessary talk; prayed. 9.30.

Grace: 7 rating once [4 to 5 am]; 6 thirteen times; 5 four times [5 to 6 am, 5 to 6, 7 to 8, 9 to 10 pm].

WEDNESDAY, FEBRUARY 16. 4 Prayed with Delamotte; Hebrew; private prayer. 5 Private prayer; prayed [read Prayers?]. 6 Miss Sophy, she would not stay; meditated; private prayer; tea. 7 Writ letters to Mr Burton. 8 To Mr Brown. 9 To Hutchings and Morgan. 10 To Whitefield; writ diary. 11 Garden; meditated; sang. 12 Visited. 1 Mr Campbell, Mrs Gilbert, Miss Sophy; sang; prayed; sang; prayed; sang. 2 Garden; religious talk; she quite open (gained no ground). 2.45 Meditated; she would breakfast with me no more! 3 Tea, religious talk. 4 Walked; meditated; sang. 4.30 Mr Potter's, necessary talk (religious). 5 Set out; meditated; sang. 6 Prayed with Delamotte. 6.15 Necessary business. 7 Read Prayers. 7.45 Miss Sophy, etc; read. 8 Read; sang; religious talk. 9 Religious talk; read a letter. 9.15 Prayed.

Grace: 7 rating twice [4 to 5 am, 1 to 2 pm]; 6 twelve times; 5 thrice [10 to 11 am, 6 to 8 pm].

THURSDAY, FEBRUARY 17. 4 Prayed; Hebrew; sang; private prayer. 5 Private prayer; read Prayers (Miss [Sophy,] eighteen there). 6 Tea, John not come, religious talk. 6.30 At the Germans', writ for them. 7 Writ for them to Mr Causton. 8 Writ. 9 Religious talk with them. 10 Religious talk, they open. 11

On Saturday, [February] 19, I called upon her at Mr. Causton's, and we walked together in the garden. She did not seem to be affected with anything I said, but was in such a temper as I never saw her before: sharp, fretful, and disputatious. Yet in an hour she awaked as out of sleep, told me she had been very ill all day, and indeed scarce in her senses, and feared she had given a sufficient proof of it in her behaviour, which she begged I would not impute to her, but solely to her disorder.

Transcribed my letter. 11.45 Meditated. 12 Dinner, religious talk; writ diary; dressed. 1 Visited. 2 Miss Bovey, French. 3 Mrs Causton's, good talk. 3.30 Necessary talk with him. 4 Tea. 4.15 French with Miss Sophy, religious talk. 5 Mr Finlay's, necessary talk (religious); tea. 6 Necessary talk (religious). 6.45 Germans'. 7 Read Prayers (fifty there). 8 Miss Sophy, etc; read; sang. 9 Necessary talk (religious). 9.40.

Grace: 6 rating ten times; 5 eight times [5 to 6 am, noon to 8 pm].

FRIDAY, FEBRUARY 18. 4 Prayed; Hebrew; private prayer. 5 Private prayer; read Prayers (eighteen there, Miss [Sophy]). 6 Tea. 6.30 Writ to Chapman. 7 To Horne. 8 To Hervey. 9 Prayed with Delamotte; letter to Sarney. 10 To Mr Jones of Beaufort. 11 Writ diary; dressed; Greek Testament. 12 Read to the boys; prayed. 12.30 With Mr Brownfield, necessary talk (religious). 1 Necessary talk (religious). 2.20 Mrs Gilbert's. 3 Tea, religious and useful talk. 4 Greek Testament. 5 Meditated; sang. 5.30 Brownfield; necessary talk (religious); tea. 6 Necessary talk (religious). 7 Read Prayers, exhorted (forty-five there). 8 Miss Bovey, etc; read; sang. 8.45 Machiavelli. 9 The same. 9.30 Writ diary. 9.45 Prayed.

Grace: 7 rating once [4 to 5 am]; 6 twelve times; 5 five times [5 to 6 am, 1 to 2, 3 to 4, 6 to 7, 9 to 10 pm].

SATURDAY, FEBRUARY 19. 4 Prayed; private prayer. 4.30 Slept. 5 Read Prayers (twenty-three there); private prayer. 6 Tea, religious talk (necessary). 6.30 Machiavelli. 7 The same. 9 Prayed with Delamotte; the same. 10.45 Writ diary; dressed. 11 Walked; meditated; sang. 12 Dinner, necessary talk (religious). 1 Visited. 2 Visited; catechized boys. 3 Visited; Miss Bovey's, necessary talk (religious); necessary business. 4 Set out; Greek Testament. 4.30 Mr Peters, religious talk; read Prayers. 5 set out; meditated; Greek Testament. 5.30 Mr———; religious talk with Miss Sophy (she not affected!). 6.15 At home; tea, religious talk. 7 Meditated; sang; read Prayers. 8 Mr Hows, etc; read; sang; prayed. 8.45 Meditated; private prayer; (lively zeal; +). 9 Meditated; private prayer. 9.30 Religious talk with Delamotte; prayed; (lively zeal).

Grace: 7 rating twice [8 to 10 pm]; 6 eleven times; 5 five times [6 to 7, 9 to 11 am, noon to 1, 3 to 4 pm].

SUNDAY, FEBRUARY 20. 4 Prayed; private prayer (lively zeal). 5 Private prayer; sang; dressed. 6 Read Prayers (thirty-five there). 7 Tea, religious talk. 8 Walked; meditated upon sermon. 9 Meditated; religious talk with Delamotte; religious talk with Mr Christie. 10 Necessary talk (religious). 10.30 Read Prayers. 11 Sermon (sixty there). 12 Sacrament (eighteen communicants). 12.30 Prayed; dinner. 1 Necessary business; German. 2 Read *Canons*. 2.15 Writ diary. 2.30 Read Prayers (one hundred there). 3 Catechized. 4 Garden with Miss Sophy, religious talk. 5 Mrs Gilbert, etc; sang; read; sang; prayed; sang. 6 Tea, religious talk. 7.15 Sophy went; Germans'; sleepy. 8.15 Religious talk with Ingham and Delamotte. 8.30 Writ diary. 8.45 Necessary talk (religious); prayed. 9.

Grace: 7 rating thrice [4 to 6, 11 to noon]; 6 thirteen times; 5 once [7 to 8 pm].

MONDAY, FEBRUARY 21. 4 Sang; meditated; prayed with them; private prayer; meditated; (heavy rain). 5 Private prayer; read Prayers (thirty there). 6 Mr Causton, religious talk with him. 6.30 Tea, necessary talk (religious). 7.30 Töltschig, necessary talk (religious). 8.30 Mr Causton went; necessary talk (religious). 9 Haircut. 9.45 Writ to Mr Horton. 10 Letters. 11 Walked; meditated; private prayer. 12 Dinner, religious talk. 1 At Miss Sophy's acre lot; necessary talk (religious) with Mr Causton, with Mrs Causton. 2 Tea, they [had] necessary and useful talk. 3 Necessary talk. 3.30 Writ to Mr Hird. 3.30 Visited. 4 Set out; Greek Testament; Mr Peter's; read Prayers. 5 Greek Testament; meditated. 5.45 At home; Mr Ellis, necessary talk, tea. 6 Religious talk with Ingham; necessary business. 7 Read Prayers (very heavy). 8 Miss Bovey, etc; read; prayed; sang. 9 Sang; meditated; prayed. 9.30.

Grace: 6 rating twelve times; 5 six times [8 to 11 am, 1 to 3, 6 to 7 pm].

TUESDAY, FEBRUARY 22. 4 Private prayer; sang; writ diary. 5 Private prayer; read Prayers (twenty-two there). 6 Tea, religious talk with them. 7.45 With Kitty (open, lively zeal). 8 Religious talk with them. 8.30 Writ for Miss Sophy. 9 Religious talk with Töltschig. 9.30 Writ for her. 10.30 Walked; meditated. 11 Meditated; sang. 12 Dinner, mostly religious talk; dressed. 1 Visited. 2 Miss Bovey's, French, religious talk. 3 At Mr Causton's, company, good talk, tea. 4 With Mr Causton, necessary talk of his letters. 5 Necessary talk (religious). 6 Necessary talk. 6.15 At home; necessary talk; supper. 7 Meditated; read Prayers (forty there). 8 Miss Sophy and Miss Bovey; read; sang. 9 Necessary talk (religious). 9.15 Prayed.

Grace: 7 rating once [4 to 5 am]; 6 thirteen times; 5 thrice [2 to 4, 5 to 6 pm].

ASH WEDNESDAY, FEBRUARY 23. 4 Private prayer; sang; prayed with them. 5 Private prayer; read Prayers (twenty-five there). 6 Read Prayers. 6.40 Necessary business. 7 With Mr Watson, tea, necessary talk; strange! 8 Mr Causton came, went with him, necessary talk; letters. 9 Meditated; sang; meditated. 10 Meditated. 10.30 read Prayers (twenty-two there). 11 Sermon, Sacrament (thirteen communicants). 12 Writ diary; walked; meditated; sang. 1.15 Visited. 2 with Mrs Núñez, religious talk. 3 Mr Campbell's, religious talk. 4 Tea, religious talk. 4.30 At home; religious talk. 4.45 Meditated. 5 Meditated; prayed with them. 5.50 Writ diary; private prayer. 6 Walked; meditated; sang, etc. 7 Read Prayers (fifty there). 7.40 Miss Sophy; read. 8 Sang, religious talk. 8.30 Meditated; private prayer. 9 Meditated. 9.30 Prayed.

Grace: 7 rating twice [4 to 5 am, 6 to 7 pm]; 6 fourteen times; 5 twice [6 to 7, 8 to 9 am].

THURSDAY, [FEBRUARY] 24. 4 Prayed with them; private prayer; sang; (hard rain). 5 Private prayer; read Prayers (fifteen there). 6.20 Religious talk. 6.45 Mr and

[D—Thursday, [February] 24. We agreed that Mr. Ingham should set out for England; chiefly that he might confer with our friends there, and endeavour to bring over some of them to help us. And on Saturday the 26th, a passage offering to Pennsylvania, where he was to call on Mr. Spangenberg to go with him, he embraced the opportunity, and embarked about three in the afternoon. May God give him a happy return!

[By Mr. Ingham, I writ to the Founders of Parochial Libraries, who sent one hither in the latter end of the last year. The latter part of the letter was as follows:

[Our general method (of catechizing) is this: A young gentleman who came with me teaches between thirty and forty children to read, write, and cast accounts. Before school in the morning and after school in the afternoon, he catechizes the lowest class, and endeavours to fix something of what they have said in their understandings as well as their memories. In the evening he instructs the larger children. On Saturday in the afternoon I catechize them all. The same I do on Sunday, before the Evening Service; and in the church, immediately after the Second Lesson, a select number of them having repeated the Catechism and been examined in some part of it, I endeavour to explain at large and enforce that part, both on them and the congregation.

[Some time after the Evening Service, as many of my parishioners as desire it meet at my house (as they do likewise on Wednesday evening) and spend about an hour in prayer, singing, reading a practical book, and mutual exhortation. A smaller number (mostly those who desire to communicate the next day) meet here on Saturday evening; and a few of these come to me on the other evenings, and pass half an hour in the same employments.]

Thursday, [February] 24. Mentioning at Mr. Causton's that either Mr. Ingham or I must go to England, Miss Sophy fixed her eyes upon me all the time I spoke, changed colour several times, and then broke out, 'What! Are you going to England? Then I have no tie to America left.' Mrs. Causton said, 'Indeed, I think I must go too. Phiky, will you go with me?' Miss Sophy answered, 'Yes, with all my heart.' Mrs. Causton added, 'Last night you said you would not.' She said, 'True; but now all the world is alike to me.'

Mrs Vanderplank's. 7 Tea; religious talk (necessary). 7.45 Writ sermon. 9.15 Meditated and sermon. 9.45 Mr Causton's, necessary talk (religious). 10.15 Necessary talk (religious) with Delamotte. 10.30 Read Prayers (thirty there). 11 Sermon, Communion (fourteen communicants); prayed. 12 Writ diary. 12.15 Dinner, mostly religious talk. 1 Writ to Oglethorpe. 2 Transcribed. 3 Mr

Walking home with her from my house in the evening, I asked her, 'Miss Sophy, what did you mean this afternoon by saying, If I went to England you had no tie to America left?' She answered with tears, 'You are the best friend I ever had in the world. You showed yourself a friend indeed at a time when no one else would have afforded me any more than common pity.' I said, 'You would hardly confess this if the Trustees should be set against me, and take away all I have here.' She replied with much earnestness, 'Indeed I would; and you or your friends can never want while I have anything.'

Saturday, [February] 26. Calling at Mr. Causton's, she was there alone. And this was indeed an hour of trial. Her words, her eyes, her air, her every motion and gesture, were full of such a softness and sweetness! I know not what might have been the consequence had I then but touched her hand. And how I avoided it I know not. Surely God is over all!

Sunday, [February] 27. After all the company but Miss Sophy was

---

Causton's, necessary talk (religious). 4 Tea; mostly religious talk of going to England; Miss Sophy much affected! 5 Religious talk. 6.15 At home; religious talk; tea. 7 Read Prayers; Miss Bovey, etc. 8 Read; sang. 8.45 Necessary talk (religious) with Miss Sophy, she owned her friendship! 9 Writ to my brother Charles.

Grace: 6 rating seventeen times; 5 twice [3 to 5 pm].

FRIDAY, FEBRUARY 25. 4 Private prayer; writ sermon; prayed. 5 Private prayer. 5.15 Read Prayers. 6 Tea, religious talk. 7 Sermon. 8 Sermon; transcribed letter. 9 Sermon. 11 Sermon; dressed. 12 Writ notes. 1 Read to boys. 1.20 Sermon. 2 Miss Bovey's, necessary talk (religious). 3 Delamotte and Ingham, Miss Sophy, tea, religious talk. 4 French. 4.45 Necessary talk (religious) with Miss Sophy. 5.15 Necessary business; private prayer; writ notes. 6 Tea, religious talk. 7 Read Prayers. 7.45 Miss Bovey, etc; read. 8 Read; sang. 9 Writ hymns. 10 Hymns. 10.30.

Grace: 6 rating eleven times; 5 eight times [8 to 11 am, noon to 3, 9 to 10.30 pm].

SATURDAY, FEBRUARY 26. 4 Private prayer; meditated; Greek Testament; prayed. 5 Private prayer; read Prayers (twenty-eight there). 6 Tea, religious talk. 6.45 Sermon. 12 Writ diary; dinner, religious talk. 1 Religious talk with them. 2 Germans, necessary talk (religious). 2.45 Ingham went. 3 Mr Causton's, Miss Sophy only, necessary talk (religious); French. 4 French, necessary talk (religious); tea; Mr Williamson, mostly religious talk. 5 Mostly religious talk. 5.30 At home; meditated. 6 Tea, religious talk; writ diary. 7 Meditated; read Prayers (thirty-five there). 7.45 Hows, etc; read. 8 Sang; religious talk; prayed. 8.30 Necessary business; prayed.

Grace: 6 rating ten times; 5 seven times [5 to 6, 8 to noon, 3 to 5 pm].

SUNDAY, FEBRUARY 27. 4 Private prayer; prayed; sang; necessary business. 5 Private prayer; dressed. 5.45 Read Prayers (thirty-five there). 7 Tea, religious

gone, Mr. Delamotte went out and left us alone again. Finding her still the same, my resolution failed. At the end of a very serious conversation, I took her by the hand and kissed her twice; and perceiving she was not dis[pleased], I was so utterly disarmed that this hour I should have engaged myself for life had it not been for the full persuasion I had of her entire sincerity; in consequence of which I doubted not but she was resolved (as she had said) 'never to marry while she lived'.

A moment's reflection when she was gone convinced me that I had done foolishly, and I once more resolved, by God's help, to be more wary for the future. Accordingly, though I saw her every day in the following week, I touched her not. Yet on Thursday evening after we came from her, Mr. Delamotte was deeply concerned. I had never seen him in such uneasiness before. He said, with many tears, he found we must part, for he could not live in the house when I was married to Miss

---

talk. 8 Married Mr Neal and Mrs Amatis. 8.45 Meditated. 9. Meditated upon sermon. 9.45 Sleep. 10 Meditated. 10.30 Read Prayers (fifty there). 11 Sermon. 12 Communion (fourteen communicants). 12.30 Dinner. 1 Writ Fleury. 2 Religious talk with Mrs Vanderplank; read Prayers (fifty-five there). 3 Catechized. 4 Mr Hows, etc; sang; read; sang; prayed; sang. 5 Mrs Adkin and Miss Sophy; tea, religious talk. 6 Religious talk (necessary) with Miss Sophy; (!) 6.30 She went; Hermsdorf, religious talk of the Germans. 7 Germans'. 7.45 At home; religious talk (necessary) with Hermsdorf. 8 Necessary talk (religious). 8.30 He went; necessary talk (religious); prayed.

Grace: 7 rating twice [4 to 6 am]; 6 twelve times; 5 thrice [6 to 7 am, 6 to 7, 8 to 9 pm].

MONDAY, FEBRUARY 28. 4 Private prayer; sang; writ diary. 5 Private prayer; read Prayers (eighteen there). 6 Tea; read resolutions. 7 Writ notes. 8 Translated logic. 11 Logic. 12 Walked; meditated; sang; (lively zeal). 1 Dressed; Fleury. 2 Fleury's *Catechism*. 2.30 Visited (lively zeal). 3 Tea, religious talk. 4 Set out; Greek Testament. 4.30 Mr Potter's, necessary talk (religious). 5.15 Set out; private prayer. 6 Meditated; private prayer; religious talk with Delamotte (lively zeal). 7.15 Read Prayers (thirty-five there; lively zeal). 8 Miss Bovey, etc; read; sang. 9.20 Necessary business; prayed. 9.35.

Grace: 7 rating once [7 to 8 pm]; 6 thirteen times; 5 four times [8 to noon].

TUESDAY, MARCH 1. 4 Prayed; Greek Testament; Hebrew; private prayer; (well). 5 Private prayer; read Prayers (twenty-three there). 6 Tea, religious talk. 6.45 German Dictionary. 7 German; (sins; I know not how!!). 8 German. 9 Prayed with Delamotte; German. 10 German. 11.30 Dressed. 11.45 Walked; meditated. 12 Meditated; sang. 1 Visited (convincing; lively zeal). 2 Miss Bovey's, religious talk. 2.45 Walked with her to Miss Sophy's lot. 3 They [had] mostly religious talk. 3.45 French. 4.30 Logic. 5 Tea, religious talk. 6 Necessary talk (religious). 6.30 Germans'. 7 Read Prayers (thirty-eight there). 8 They here, read Hammond's life; sang. 9 Mr Causton's, religious talk; Bolzius there. 10 Prayed.

Grace: 7 rating once [4 to 5 am]; 6 sixteen times; 5 once [6 to 7 pm].

Sophy. I told him I had no intention to marry her. He said I did not know my own heart; but he saw clearly it would come to that very soon, unless I broke off all intercourse with her. I told him, this was a point of great importance, and therefore not to be determined suddenly. [B—Imagining me not to be fully fixed, [he] desired me once more to weigh thoroughly the whole affair.] He said I ought to determine as soon as possible, for I was losing ground daily. I felt what he said to be true, and therefore easily consented to set aside the next day for that purpose.

This was Friday, March 4. Having both of us sought God by deep consideration, fasting, and prayer, in the afternoon we conferred together, but could not come to any decision. We both apprehended Mr. Ingham's objection to be the strongest—the doubt whether she was what she appeared. But this doubt was too hard for us to solve. At length

---

WEDNESDAY, MARCH 2. 4 Prayed; Hebrew; Greek Testament; writ diary. 4.45 Private prayer; (well). 5 Read Prayers. 6 Coffee, religious talk. 6.45 German. 7.45 Mr Causton's, necessary business. 8 Garden with her [Miss Sophy?], religious talk. 9 German. 9.45 Bolzius, religious talk. 10 German. 12 Walked; meditated; sang. 1 Religious talk with Delamotte. 1.15 Visited. 2.50 German. 3 Tea, religious talk. 3.40 German. 4.30 Greek Testament. 5 Private prayer; meditated; sang. 6 Meditated; [writ] account; (lively zeal). 6.30 Germans'. 7 Read Prayers (Miss Sophy there). 8 Mr Hows, etc; read; sang. 8.45 Account. 9.40 Read Prayers.

Grace: 7 rating twice [4 to 5 am, noon to 1]; 6 fifteen times; 5 once [5 to 6 am].

THURSDAY, MARCH 3. 4 Prayed; Greek Testament; Hebrew; writ diary; private prayer; (well). 5 Private prayer; read Prayers (Miss Sophy there). 6 Tea, religious talk. 6.30 Writ to Laserre of Charleston. 7 Writ to the Bishop of London. 8 German. 9 Miss Sophy, logic. 9.45 Religious talk (necessary). 10 German. 12 Walked; read Wake's Epistles. 1 Wake's Epistles. 1.45 Visited. 2.30 Miss Bovey's, French. 3 At Miss Sophy's lot; French. 4 Delamotte, logic. 5 Williamson; tea, mostly religious talk. 6 Mostly religious talk. 6.30 At home; meditated; German. 7 Religious talk with Töltschig. 7.30 Read Prayers (lively zeal). 8 Miss Bovey, etc, read Tilly's sermon; prayed; sang; writ diary (lively zeal). 9 Talk with Delamotte of Miss Sophy, he sad. 9.45 Private prayer. 10.

Grace: 7 rating once [4 to 5 am]; 6 fourteen times; 5 thrice [5 to 6, 11 to noon; 5 to 6 pm].

FRIDAY, MARCH 4. 4 Prayed; Hebrew; private prayer. 5 Private prayer. 5.10 Read Prayers (lively zeal). 6 Mr Lacy, tea, religious talk. 7 Garden, religious talk. 7.30 Writ to the Trustees; he quite melted. 8 Writ to them. 9 Wake's Epistles. 10 Letter. 10.30 Mr Causton's garden, religious talk (necessary) with him. 11 Necessary talk (religious). 11.15 Wake. 12 Read to boys; prayed. 12.30 Visited. 1 Visited Captain Austin[?], necessary talk (religious). 2 Necessary talk (religious). 3 At home; Mr Campbell; prayed; tea, religious talk. 4 Religious talk with Delamotte of Miss Sophy. 4.30 Writ lots; private prayer. 5 Private prayer. 5.20 Prayed with Delamotte; lots; prayed; think of it no more!! 6 Sang with boys;

we agreed to appeal to the Searcher of Hearts. I accordingly made three lots. In one was writ, 'Marry'; in the second, 'Think not of it this year.' After we had prayed to God to 'give a perfect lot', Mr. Delamotte drew the third, in which were these words: 'Think of it no more.' Instead of the agony I had reason to expect, I was enabled to say cheerfully, 'Thy will be done.' We cast lots once again to know whether I ought to converse with her any more. And the direction I received from God was, 'only in the presence of Mr. Delamotte'. [Cf. B—I [weighed thoroughly the whole affair] on Friday, and the resolutions I then formed and immediately acquainted [Delamotte] with were, (1) to think of marriage no more; (2) to speak no more with her alone.]

I saw and adored the goodness of God, though what he required of me was a costly sacrifice. It was indeed the giving up at once whatever this world affords of agreeable ((or desirable)), not only honour, fortune, power (which indeed were nothing to me, who despised them as the clay in the streets), but all the truly desirable conveniences of life: a pleasant house, a delightful garden, on the brow of a hill at a small distance from the town; another house and garden in the town; and a third a few miles off, with a large tract of fruitful land adjoining to it. And above all, what to me made all things else vile and utterly beneath a thought, such a companion as I never expected to find again, should I live a thousand years twice told. So that I could not but cry out:

O Lord God, thou God of my fathers, plenteous in mercy and truth, behold I give thee not thousands of rams or ten thousands of rivers of oil, but the desire of my eyes, the joy of my heart, the one thing upon earth which I long for! O give me wisdom which sitteth by thy throne, and reject me not from among thy children!

[D—Today I writ to the Trustees an account of our year's expenses, from March 1, 1736, to March 1, 1737. Which (deducting extraordinary expenses [E—such as repairing the parsonage house and journeys to Frederica]) amounted to £44. 4s. 4d. At the same time I accepted of the £50 a year sent by the Society [for the Propagation of the Gospel] for my maintenance, which indeed was in a manner forced upon me, contrary both to expectation and desire.

[From the direction I received from God this day [see diary, below], touching an affair of the last importance, I can't but observe (as I have done many times before) the entire mistake of many good men, who assert that God will not answer your prayer unless your heart be wholly resigned to his will; therefore, I durst not depend on my own judgment. And for this very reason I cried to him the more earnestly to supply what was wanting in me. And I know, and am assured, that he 'heard my voice, and did send forth his light and his truth' [Ps. 43:3].]

On Monday the 7th, Mr. Causton asked me to walk with him to his plantation, four miles from Savannah. [D—I plainly felt that, had God given me such a retirement with the companion I desired, I should have forgot the work for which I was born, and have set up my rest in this world.] I was quite struck with the pleasantness of the situation: the hill, the river, the woods were too delightful, and shot a softness into my soul which had not left me when at our return he asked me to drink a dish of tea at his house. Soon after I came in, Miss Sophy went out and walked to and fro between the door and the garden. I saw she wanted to speak to me, but remembered my resolutions. Especially that, 'to converse with

---

Germans; sang, etc; religious talk (lively zeal). 7 Read Prayers. 8 Miss Sophy, Mr Campbell; read; prayed; sang. 8.45 necessary business. 9 Prayed.

Grace: 7 rating twice [4 to 5 am, 5 to 6 pm]; 6 fourteen times; 5 once [2 to 3 pm].

SATURDAY, MARCH 5. 4 Prayed; Greek Testament; Hebrew; private prayer; (little lively, well). 5 Private prayer; read Prayers. 6 Tea, religious talk. 6.30 Wake. 11 Visited Mrs Gilbert, Mrs Causton. 12 Visited. 12.30 Dinner, mostly religious talk. 1 Visited. 1.45 Necessary business. 2 Catechized. 2.30 Miss Bovey's, good talk. 3 At the lot, Mr Causton, necessary talk. 4 Tea, mostly religious talk. 4.45 Mr Causton went; logic. 5 Logic; prayed. 6 Religious talk; met Mrs Causton, Mellichamp come; Germans'. 7 Read Prayers (forty there). 8 Mr Hows, etc; read; sang; prayed; writ diary. 9 Necessary talk (religious). 9.30 Prayed.

Grace: 7 rating once [4 to 5 am]; 6 twelve times; 5 five times [7 to 10, am 2 to 3, 9 to 10 pm].

SUNDAY, MARCH 6. 4 Prayer with Delamotte; private prayer; Hebrew; slept. 5.15 Meditated; read Prayers (thirty-five there). 6 Read Prayers. 7 Tea, religious talk. 8 Necessary talk with Mr Causton, with Mrs Causton. 8.30 Meditated upon sermon. 9 Meditated upon sermon. 10 Dressed; meditated. 10.30 Read Prayers (fifty there). 11 Sermon. 12 Communion. 12.30 Dinner. 1 Fleury. 2 Read Prayers (fifty-five there); catechized. 3 Read Prayers. 3.30 Hows, etc; sang; read. 4 Sang; prayed; sang. 5 Tea, religious and useful talk. 6 Religious talk. 6.30 Germans'. 7 Writ to Hird, Mrs Weston, Mrs Robinson. 8 Writ. 8.30 Mr Causton's, necessary talk. 9.15 Prayed.

Grace: 7 rating once [4 to 5 am]; 6 twelve times; 5 four times [6 to 7 am, 2 to 3, 7 to 9 pm].

MONDAY, MARCH 7. 4 Prayed; Hebrew; private prayer; (well). 5 Read Prayers. 6 Tea, religious talk. 6.30 Wake. 7 Wake; dressed. 7.45 Went with Mr Causton. 8 Necessary talk (religious). 9 They [had] necessary talk. 10 At the 500 acre lot, cut trees. 11 Felled [trees]. 12 Walked with him, good talk. 1 He blazed. 1.30 Delamotte came; dinner. 2 Walked; he directed the workmen. 3 Walked. 4 Set out. 4.45 Lost. 5 Walked. 6 At Mr Causton's, necessary talk (religious) with Miss Sophy. 7 Tea; read Prayers (fifty there). 8 They came; began Wake; sang. 8.45 Necessary talk (religious). 9.15 Prayed.

Grace: 7 rating once [4 to 5 am]; 6 seven times; 5 nine times [9 am to 1 pm, 2 to 4, 5 to 7 pm].

her only in Mr. Delamotte's presence'. Yet after a short struggle the Evil Soul prevailed in me, and I went. Immediately she catched hold of both my hands, and with the most engaging gesture, look, and tone of voice said, 'You never denied me anything I desired yet, and you shan't deny me what I am going to desire now.' I said, 'Miss Sophy, I won't; what is it?' She answered, 'Don't say anything to her that offered me the letter the other day. My refusing it has given her pain enough already.' I replied, 'I won't, and if you had told me of it before, I wouldn't have told your uncle of it, as Mr. Williamson did.' She said, 'Did he? Well, I find what you have often said is true. There is no trusting any but a Christian. And for my part I am resolved never to trust anyone again who is not so.' I looked upon her, and should have said too much, had we had a moment longer. But in the instant, Mrs. Causton called us in. So I was once more 'snatched as a brand out of the fire'.

Tuesday, March 8. Miss Sophy [B—and Mr. Delamotte] breakfasting with me, I asked her what she now thought of Mr. Mellichamp. She said, 'I thank God, I have entirely conquered that inclination.' After some serious conversation interposed, I said, 'I hear Mr. Williamson pays his addresses to you. Is it true?' She said (after a little pause), 'If it were not I would have told you so.' I asked, 'How do you like him?' She replied, 'I don't know; there is a great deal in being always in the house with one. But I have no inclination for him.' I said, 'Miss Sophy, if you deceive me, I shall scarce ever believe anyone again.' She looked up at me and answered with a smile, 'You will never have that reason for distrusting anyone. I shall never deceive you.' When she was going away she turned back and said, 'Of one thing, sir, be assured. I will never take any step in anything of importance without first consulting you.'

She went, and I saw myself in the toils. But how to escape I saw not. If I continued to converse with her, though not alone, I found I should love her more and more. And the time to break it off was past; I felt it was now beyond my strength. My resolutions indeed remained. But how long? Yet a little longer, till another shock of temptation, and then I well knew

---

TUESDAY, MARCH 8. 4 Prayed; writ diary; German. 5 Private prayer; read Prayers. 6 Miss Sophy; tea, necessary talk (religious). 7 Prayed with them. 7.15 Wake. 8 Clement. 9 At Mrs Montagut's, necessary talk. 9.30 Clement. 10 The same. 1.15 Walked; meditated; (sins; I therefore not worthy of her!!!). 2 Sang; meditated. 2.15 Lively. 3 Tea, religious talk. 3.30 Mrs Nel[son], necessary talk (religious). 4 At the lot, religious talk (necessary). 4.30 French; Mrs Parker came. 5 Tea, mostly religious talk. 5.30 Logic. 6 Necessary talk (religious). 6.15 Meditated. 6.40 With Germans. 7 Read Prayers. 8 With Mrs Causton, she very angry at Miss Sophy; read letter from Me[llichamp]; necessary talk with Mrs Ann. 9 Mr Causton's' supper, necessary talk (religious); all confused. 10.30. Grace: 6 rating ten times; 5 nine times [5 to 8, 9 to 10 am, noon to 1, 4 to 6 pm]. 11 Miss Sophy engaged. Alas! [line added later by Wesley]

they would break in sunder, as a thread of tow that has touched the fire. I had many times prayed that if it was best our intercourse should break off and I could not do it, she might. But this too I saw less and less reason to expect. So that all these things were against me. And I lay struggling in the net: nay, scarcely struggling—as even fearing to be delivered.

After Evening Prayers, Miss Bovey came (as usual) to my house with Miss Sophy, who was in the utmost consternation. She begged me to go and pacify her aunt. I went, and found Mrs. Causton in great disorder, with an open letter in her hand, which she gave me to read, telling me she had just then intercepted it. It was writ by Mr. Mellichamp to Miss Sophy. I told her, I hoped things were not so ill as she apprehended, and when she was a little more composed, went, at her desire, to make some further inquiry. In half an hour I returned, and found Mrs. Causton chiding Miss Sophy very sharply. Some of her expressions were: 'Get you out of my house; I will be plagued with ye no longer.' And turning to me she said, 'Mr. Wesley, I wish you would take her. Take her away with ye.' I said, 'Miss Sophy is welcome to my house, or anything that I have.' Miss Sophy answered only with tears. About ten I went home, though with such an unwillingness and heaviness as I had scarce ever felt before.

[Cf. D—March 8. Miss Sophy engaged herself to Mr. Williamson, a person not remarkable for handsomeness, neither for genteelness, neither for wit or knowledge or sense, and least of all, for religion.]

The next morning, Wednesday, March 9, about ten, I called on Mrs. Causton. She said, 'Sir, Mr. Causton and I are exceedingly obliged to you for all the pains you have taken about Sophy. And so is Sophy too; and she desires you would publish the Banns of Marriage between her and Mr. Williamson on Sunday.' She added, 'Sir, you don't seem to be well pleased. Have you any objection to it?' I answered, 'Madam, I don't seem to be awake. Surely I am in a dream.' She said, 'They agreed on it

---

WEDNESDAY, MARCH 9. 4 Private prayer; prayed; writ diary. 4.45 Private prayer. 5 Meditated; read Prayers. 6 Coffee, religious talk. 6.30 Clement. 7 Necessary talk (religious) with Mrs Ann. 7.45 With Mrs Bush. 8 Necessary talk (religious). 8.30 Clement. 9.45 Logic. 10 Mrs Causton's, necessary talk with her; Miss Sophy to be married! 11 ((Erased material)); amazed; in pain, prayed; meditated. 12 At the lot, necessary talk (religious) with her; I quite distressed! 1 Necessary talk (religious); confounded! 2 Took leave of her. 2.30 At home; could not pray! 3 Tried to pray; lost; sunk! 4 Bread, religious talk with Delamotte; little better! 5 Mr Causton came, necessary talk; tea. 6 Kempis; Germans; easier! 7 Read Prayers. 8 Miss Sophy, etc. 8.30 Necessary talk (religious) with her. 8.45 With Delamotte; prayed.

No such day since I first saw the sun!
O deal tenderly with thy servant!
Let me not see such another!

last night between themselves, after you was gone. And afterward Mr. Williamson asked Mr. Causton's and my consent, which we gave him. But if you have any objection to it, pray speak. Speak to her. She is at the lot. Go to her. She will be very glad to hear anything Mr. Wesley has to say. Pray go to her and talk with her yourself.' I said, 'No, madam, if Miss Sophy is engaged [B—to Mr. Williamson], I have nothing to say. It will not signify for me to see her any more.· I then offered to go; but she pressed me to stay, at least till the rain was over. The burden of her conversation was still, 'Why are you uneasy?' and 'Go and talk with her yourself.'

[B—If I may speak what was then the utmost thought of my heart, it was that] I doubted whether all this were not artifice, merely [B—purely] designed to quicken me [B—and that as much engaged as she was, had I only said, 'I am willing to marry her myself,' that engagement would have vanished away]. But though I was uneasy at the very thought [B—mention] of her marrying one who I believed would make her very unhappy [B—thoroughly miserable], yet I could not resolve to save her from him by marrying her myself. [B—This was the only price I could not pay, and which therefore I never so much as hinted at in any of those following conversations wherein I so earnestly endeavoured to prevent that unhappy union.] Besides, I reasoned thus: 'Either she is engaged or not; if she is, I would not have her if I might; if not, there is nothing in this show which ought to alter my preceding resolution.'

Thus was I saved purely by my ignorance, for though I did doubt, I would not believe. I thought it unkind and unjust to believe an artifice of which I had not full proof. O let no one ever fear the being lost by thinking no evil! Had I known the snare, I had perished thereby. All the world could not have saved me. Had I then seen the real case to be this—'She is engaged', but conditionally only; 'Mr. Williamson shall marry her, if you will not'—I could not have stood that shock. I should have incurred any loss rather than she should have run that hazard of losing both her body and soul in hell.

From Mrs. Causton I went home full of perplexity. After some time spent in prayer, [B—a little before twelve] I desired Mr. Delamotte to go to the lot, and ask if my company would be agreeable. In the meantime, seeing nothing but clouds before me, I had recourse to the oracles of God. I received two answers. The first was, 'Blessed be thou of the Lord, my daughter; for thou hast showed more kindness in the latter end than at the beginning' [Ruth 3:10]. The other (which was part of the morning lesson on Saturday, August 27, following the court-day on which I expected my trial) was in these words: 'If I be an offender or have committed anything worthy of death, I refuse not to die. But if there be none of these things whereof these accuse me, no man may deliver me unto them' [Acts 25:11].

Soon after Mr. Delamotte came back, I went. Mr. Williamson and she were together [B—there alone]. She began with her usual sweetness: 'Why would you put yourself to the trouble of sending? What need of that ceremony between us? You know your company is always welcome to me.' Then silence ensued, which Mr. Williamson broke thus: 'I suppose, sir, you know what was agreed on last night between Miss Sophy and me?' I answered, 'I have heard something, but I could not believe it unless I should hear it from Miss Sophy herself.' She replied, 'Sir, I have given Mr. Williamson my consent—unless you have anything to object.' It started into my mind, 'What if she mean, Unless *you* will marry me?' But I checked the thought with, 'Miss Sophy is so sincere, if she meant so, she would say so.' And replied, 'If you have given your consent, the time is past. I have nothing to object.' Mr. Williamson desired me, if I had, to speak, and then left her and me together. 'Tis hard to describe the complication of passions and tumult of thought which I then felt. Fear of her approaching misery, and tender pity; grief for my own loss; love, shooting through all the recesses of my soul, and sharpening every thought and passion. Underneath these was a faint desire to do and suffer the will of God; which, joined to my doubt whether that proposal would be accepted, was strong enough to prevent my saying plainly (what I wonder to this hour I did not say), 'Miss Sophy, will you marry me?' As soon as I could speak, I reminded her [B—in the mildest terms I could] of her resolution, 'if she married at all, to marry none but a religious man', and desired her to consider whether Mr. Williamson was such. She said she had no proof to the contrary. I told her that was not enough. Before she staked so much upon it, she ought to have full, positive proof that he was religious. She said again, 'I no otherwise consented, than if you had nothing to object.' Little more was said [cf. B—I don't remember that anything more was said], tears in both supplying the place of words. [B—But I do remember that I made no proposal of marriage directly or indirectly, nor said one syllable, good or bad, about fasting or going to the Indians.] More than an hour was spent thus.

About two, Mr. Williamson came again. I think it was just as he came she said, 'I hope I shall always have your friendship.' I answered, 'I can be still your friend, though I should not stay in America.' She said, 'But I hope you won't leave us.' I said, 'I can't at all judge how God will dispose of me.' She added, 'However, you will let me have your correspondence.' I replied, 'I doubt, it cannot be.' I then exhorted them both to assist each other in serving God with all their strength; and her in particular to remember the many instructions and advices I had given her. I kissed them both and took my leave of her, as one I was to see no more.

I came home and went into my garden. I walked up and down, seeking rest but finding none. From the beginning of my life to this hour, I had not known one such as this. God let loose my inordinate affection upon me, and the poison thereof drank up my spirit. I was as stupid as if but half awake, and yet in the sharpest pain I ever felt. 'To see her no more!' That thought was as the piercings of a sword. It was not to be borne—nor shaken off. I was weary of the world, of light, of life. Yet one way remained: to seek to God, a very present help in time of trouble. And I did seek after God, but I found him not. I forsook him before; now he forsook me. I could not pray. Then indeed the snares of death were about me; the pains of hell overtook me. Yet I struggled for life, and though I had neither words nor thoughts, I lifted up my eyes to the Prince that is highly exalted, and supplied the place of them, as I could, στεναγμοῖς ἀλαλήτοις ['with groanings which cannot be uttered' (Rom. 8:26)]. And about four o'clock he so far took the cup from me that I drank so deeply of it no more.

Soon after, I writ a note to Mr. Causton [B—which, if he has read to any, I desire may be read to all here], who came to me about five o'clock, and told me [B—frankly and openly], 'I don't approve of this match. Mr. Williamson asked my consent this morning, but I have neither denied nor given it. Indeed I have often promised Sophy, so she would not have Mellichamp, she should have whom she would beside. But what passed between her and you at the lot?' I told him without any disguise. He said, 'If you loved her, how could you possibly be so overseen as not to press her, when she was so much moved?' [B—(The plain reason of which strange proceeding as it must doubtless have appeared to all who understood not my principles of acting, was that I did not act from a design to marry her myself, but only to hinder her marrying him.)] He added, 'I will tell her my thoughts of it [cf. B—of Mr. Williamson and this match] once more, and if you please, so may you. But if she is not then convinced, I must leave her to herself.'

Had he then said plainly, 'If you please you may have her still; but if you won't, another will,' I know not what might have been the event; or had Mr. Delamotte left us alone when she came to my house [B—at my desire] after Evening Prayers. Mr. Williamson begged her not to stay after the rest of the company. But she did, very readily. He walked to and fro on the outside of the house, with all the signs of strong uneasiness. I told her, 'Miss Sophy, you said yesterday, you would take no step in anything of importance without first consulting me.' She answered earnestly, and many times over, 'Why, what could I do? I can't live in that house. I can't bear these shocks. This is quite a sudden thing. I have no particular inclination for Mr. Williamson. I only promised, if no objection appeared. But what can I do?' Mr. Williamson coming in abruptly, took her away, and put a short end to our conversation.

However, in the morning [Thursday, March 10], I called once more at Mr. Causton's and desired to speak with her. Mr. Williamson told me, 'Sir, you shall speak with her no more till we are married. You can persuade her to anything. After you went from the lot yesterday she would neither eat nor speak for two hours, but was crying continually, and in such an agony she was fit for nothing.' I said, 'Tomorrow, sir, you may be her director, but today she is to direct herself.' I desired a piece of paper [B—pen and ink], and writ these words: 'Miss Sophy, will you see me or not?' Mr. Causton had Mrs. Causton carry it up, and Miss Sophy immediately came down. We went into the garden, and I asked, 'Are you fully determined?' She said, 'I am.' I replied, 'Take care you act upon a right motive. The desire of avoiding crosses is not so. Besides, you can't avoid them. They will follow and overtake you in every state.' Mr. Williamson then coming to us, I advised them to have the banns regularly published, exhorted them to love and serve God, and told them they might always depend on my friendship and assistance, and went home easy and satisfied.

In the afternoon Mr. Delamotte and I went to them at the lot, where I read them Bishop Hall's 'Meditation on Heaven', during which Miss Sophy fixed her eyes on Mr. Williamson and me alternately for above half an an hour, with as steady an observation as if she had been drawing our pictures. Mr. Williamson afterwards told me, he should always be glad of my advice, and hoped I would still favour them with my conversation, which he should look upon as a particular happiness both to her and him. I answered, 'I hope we shall all be happy [B—happy together] in the place we have been reading of.' Of which indeed I had so strong a persuasion that I returned rejoicing and wondering at myself [B—not only contented but joyful]. The next morning she set out for Purrysburg, and on Saturday, March 12, 1737, was married there

---

THURSDAY, MARCH 10. 5 Private prayer; read Prayers. 6 Mr Causton's; Miss Sophy, necessary talk; prayed; Mr Vanderplank's, tea, necessary talk (religious). 6.30 Mr Causton's, she [Mrs Causton had] necessary talk; prayed; necessary talk with Mr Causton. 7 Necessary talk with Mr Williamson; necessary talk (religious) with Miss Sophy; she vexed! 8 At home; easier; necessary talk (religious) with Delamotte; private prayer. 9 Prayed with Delamotte; writ diary; private prayer; sang. 10 Read Prayers; sang; meditated; writ diary. 11 Read; private prayer. 11.45 Walked. 12 Private prayer; sang. 1 Visited (lively zeal). 2 Bread. 2.30 At the lot; read Hall; prayed; meditated (lively zeal). 3 Hall (lively zeal); I sad (!). 4 Tea, religious talk. 5 Religious talk. 5.30 At home; private prayer; sang; cheerful. 6 Sang with boys; writ diary. 6.30 Germans'. 7 Religious talk with them. 7.30 Read Prayers. 8 Miss Sophy, etc; began Worthington; prayed; sang; pained! 9 Walked home with Miss Sophy; religious talk (necessary); Miss Boyse, necessary talk (religious). 9.30 Prayed; pain!

Grace: 7 rating thrice [8 to 9, 10 to 11 am, noon to 1]; 6 eleven times; 5 twice [5 to 7 am].

[D—as were Miss Bovey and Mr. Burnside], this being the day which completed the year from my first speaking to her! [END OF DOCUMENT A; BEGIN D AS STANDARD TEXT] 'What thou dost, O God, I know not now; but I shall know hereafter' [cf. John 13:7]. O give her not up yet to a strong delusion, that she should believe a lie!

FRIDAY, MARCH 11. 4 Private prayer; sang; (pain). 5 Private prayer; read Prayers. 5.45 Coffee. 6 Coffee, religious talk. 6.30 Mr Hows, necessary talk (religious). 7 Necessary talk (religious) with Mr Causton. 7.30 German Dictionary; (light came!). 8 German. 9 Mr Thicknesse, necessary talk. 9.45 German. 10 German; (much more pain!). 11 Walked; began [book of] Job; private prayer; (much pain, lively zeal, easier!). 12 Kempis. 12.30 Religious talk to boys. 1 Mr Brownfield, necessary talk (religious). 3 Tea, necessary talk (religious). 4 Walked. 4.45 Mr Causton's, necessary talk with him. 5 Tea, necessary talk (religious). 6 Meditated; private prayer; Germans'. 7 Religious talk; read Prayers (fifty there; convincing). 8 Germans'; talked of Miss Sophy. 9 Religious talk. 9.30 Prayed.
Grace: 7 rating five times [4 to 5, 8 to 9, 10 am to 1 pm]; 6 thirteen times.

SATURDAY, MARCH 12. 4 Sang; private prayer; (easier). 5 Private prayer; read Prayers. 5.45 Mr Causton came, necessary talk. 6 Tea, necessary talk (religious). 7 Mr Causton's, read letters. 8 Tea, mostly religious talk with Mrs Causton. 9 German; (pain). 10 Necessary talk. 10.15 Sang; German. 10.45 Walked; meditated; (lively zeal, more pain). 11 Kempis; sang; meditated. 12 Necessary talk with Mrs Bush. 12.30 Job. 1 Dinner. 1.15 Necessary talk (religious) with Captain Austin [?]. 1.45 Catechized. 2.30 Writ my will. 3 Mrs Bush; tea, necessary talk (religious). 4 Will. 5 Testament; with Germans. 6 Greek Testament; Germans'. 7 Read Prayers. 8 Mr Hows, etc; read; prayed; sang. 8.45 Writ diary. 9 Mr Causton's, necessary talk. 9.30 Private prayer; prayed.
Grace: 7 rating thrice [4 to 5, 10 to noon]; 6 fifteen times. Today Miss Bovey and Miss Sophy were married at Purrysburg!!!

SUNDAY, MARCH 13. 4 Private prayer; sang; meditated; (lively, they came at 3; well). 5 Private prayer. 5.30 Read Prayers (forty there, Miss Sophy). 6.30 Tea, religious talk. 7 Necessary talk (religious) with Thicknesse. 7.30 Meditated upon sermon. 8 Meditated. 8.30 Fleury. 9 Private prayer; meditated. 10 Fleury. 10.20 Private prayer. 10.30 Read Prayers (sixty there). 11 Read Prayers, sermon (Miss Sophy and Mrs Burnside not [there]; lively zeal!). 12 Delamotte. 12.15 Dinner, necessary talk (religious). 1 Catechized. 1.45 Job; (pain!). 2 Meditated. 2.15 Read Prayers (Miss Sophy there); read; sang; prayed. 3 Read Prayers. 3.15 Religious talk with Mr Burnside. 3.30 Mr Hows, etc. 4 Sang. 4.20 Slept. 4.30 Writ notes; walked with Delamotte, religious talk; (pain!). 5 Religious talk. 5.15 Tea, religious talk; (pain!). 6 Meditated; Germans. 7 Hermsdorf, religious talk. 8 Germans', religious talk. 9.15 Prayed; (easier).
Grace: 7 rating twice [4 to 5, 9 to 10 am]; 6 twelve times; 5 thrice [5 to 7 am, 2 to 3 pm].

MONDAY, MARCH 14. 4 Private prayer. 4.15 Prayed with Delamotte. 4.30 Private prayer; (easier!). 5 Private prayer; read Prayers. 5.45 Tea, religious talk. 6.30 German. 8.30 Mrs Smith's; religious talk. 9 Mrs Burnside's, religious talk

[B—Tuesday the 15th. I invited Mr. Williamson to my house, whom I was surprised to find exceeding angry. He told me (among other warm things) that I hated both him and his wife; that he had looked upon her as his wife for above six weeks; that she herself had not only declared she would never come within my house; but begged of him not to do it, nay, not to go out alone, for she believed if Mr. Delamotte or I caught him, we should murder him. I desired to talk with her myself, but he said, 'She would never consent to it.' So we parted as we met.

(necessary). 10 German. 11 Dressed; Mr Peterson, necessary talk (religious). 12 Walked; Kempis. 1 Writ prayers. 2 Visited. 3 Dinner, necessary talk (religious). 3.40 Writ prayers; (easier). 4 Walked; Greek Testament; private prayer. 5 Germans'. 6 Religious talk; meditated. 6.40 Germans'. 7.15 Read Prayers (Miss Sophy there, lively zeal, pain). 8.15 Read Pope's Epistles (uneasy!). 9 Writ diary; necessary talk (religious); prayed. 9.30.

    Grace: 7 rating thrice [4 to 5, 7 to 8 am, noon to 1]; 6 thirteen times; 5 twice [3 to 4, 9 to 10 pm].

TUESDAY, MARCH 15. 4 Sang; prayed; Greek Testament; private prayer; (easier). 5 Read Prayers (Miss Sophy, neither there!). 5.45 Tea. 6 Tea; Mr Bolzius, necessary talk (religious). 7 Writ to Mr Chiffele; to the Bishop of London. 8 Mr Causton's, necessary talk; necessary talk with her. 9 Writ to Miss Bovey. 9.45 Writ [extract of] Fleury. 10.30 Account of Miss Sophy. 11.45 Dressed. 12 Miss Burnside, religious talk. 1 Account of Danish mission[aries]; prayed. 2 Visited Betty Wright, religious talk, prayed. 2.30 Mr Bolzius, religious talk. 3 Dinner, religious talk. 3.30 Account of mission[aries]. 4 Greek Testament; private prayer. 4.30 Mr Causton and Williamson, tea. 5 Garden with Williamson, necessary talk, he very angry!! 6 Necessary talk (religious) with him and Mr Causton. 6.30 Necessary talk (religious). 6.45 Germans. 7 Germans; read Prayers (Miss Sophy). 8 Mr Campbell; read; sang. 9 Writ diary; prayed. 9.30.

    Grace: 7 rating twice [4 to 5 am, 1 to 2 pm]; 6 twelve times; 5 four times [5 to 6, 8 to 9 am, 7 to 8, 9 to 10 pm].

WEDNESDAY, MARCH 16. 4 Sang; prayed; Greek; private prayer. 5 Read Prayers (forty there, Sophy). 6 Religious talk. Writ to Mrs Burnside. 7 German. 9 Prayed; German. 10 German. 10.30 Account of missionaries; (+). 11.30 Walked; prayed. 12 Prayed; meditated. 12.45 Mr Campbell and Mrs Gilbert; sang. 1 Prayed; sang. 1.20 They went; writ diary; visited. 2 Visited. 2.30 Account of missionaries. 3 Tea, religious talk. 4 Mr Peterson, necessary talk (religious). 4.30 Mrs Burnside's, religious talk (necessary). 5 He came; tea, necessary talk (religious). 6 Germans'. 7.30 Read Prayers. 8 Mr Hows, etc; read; sang; prayed; writ to Mr Causton. 9 Writ diary; religious talk; prayed.

    Grace: 7 rating once [4 to 5 am]; 6 sixteen times; 5 once [5 to 6 am].

THURSDAY, MARCH 17. 4 Sang; Greek; prayed; private prayer. 5 Read Prayers (forty there); Mr Craus, tea, religious talk. 6 Tea, religious talk. 6.30 German. 7 German; necessary talk with Mr Causton; German. 8 Sang; necessary talk with Delamotte; transcribed hymns. 9 Hymns; necessary talk (religious) with Mr Woodruff. 10 Hymns. 11 Dressed; [read] Missionaries. 11.30 Mr Burnside,

[Saturday, [March] 19. He told me I should talk with her, if I would. Accordingly in the evening I met her at Mrs. Burnside's. Only we three were present. I taxed her with insincerity before and ingratitude since her marriage. As to the first, she said, 'I was never insincere to you. On the noon of that day when the letter was taken, I told Mr. Williamson I should be glad to serve him as a friend, but was resolved never to admit him as a lover.' After more to the same effect, she said, 'I own, I could not have denied you, had you pressed me to marriage at any time when my temper was ruffled.' As to the second, she said, 'It was not you but Mr. Mellichamp's friends who I feared might hurt Mr. Williamson. Indeed many instances of their anger and resentment have been related to me since my marriage. But I could hardly believe them. Nor could they ever provoke me to say anything disrespectful of you. The most I have ever said was, 'Well, whatever he may say or do, now or hereafter, I will always own, the man has been my friend, and done me more service than any person living.'

[I believed what she said, and received her as a communicant the next

---

necessary talk (religious). 12 Dinner. 12.30 In the boat. 2.15 Walked, could not pass the creek. 3 In the boat. 5.30 At the Cowpen; necessary talk (religious); religious talk. 6 Tea. 6.15 Set out. 7.45 At home. 8 Read Prayers (fifty there). 8.30 Mr and Mrs Burnside. 8 Read Worthington. 9 Tea, necessary talk (religious); necessary business; prayed. 10.

Grace: 7 rating once [4 to 5 am]; 6 nine times; 5 eight times [actually seven, noon to 7 pm].

Friday, March 18. 4.45 Private prayer. 5 Read Prayers; writ diary. 6.15 Wake. 6.30 Coffee. 6.45 Wake. 9 Prayed with Delamotte; Wake. 10 Wake. 11 Dressed; walked; gathered. 12 Private prayer; meditated. 12.30 Religious talk with boys; sang; prayed. 1 Visited. 2 Mrs Burnside's, French. 3 Mostly religious talk, tea. 4 Religious and useful talk. 5 Bread; meditated; sang; Greek Testament. 6 Meditated; sang; Germans. 7 Germans', read Prayers. 8 Mr Burnside, etc; read; sang; writ diary.

Grace: 6 rating twelve times; 5 four times [4 to 5 am, 2 to 5 pm].

Saturday, March 19. 4 Prayed; Greek Testament; meditated. 5 Read Prayers; Mr Williamson, necessary talk (religious). 6 Tea. 6.30 He went; religious talk. 6.45 Wake. 7 Hymns. 9 Made verse. 10 Verse. 11 Writ verse. 11.30 Mrs Woodruff's, necessary talk (religious); Mrs Burnside's, necessary talk (religious). 12 Dinner, necessary talk. 12.45 Verse. 1 Visited; (he seemed affected). 2 Catechized. 2.30 Verse. 4 Garden; Greek Testament. 4.40 Mrs Burnside's, religious talk. 5 Tea, religious talk; Miss Sophy not come. 6 At home; supper. 6.30 Mrs Burnside's, Miss Sophy there, necessary talk (religious)! 7 Necessary talk (religious), she open, blameless. 7.30 Read Prayers. 8.15 Mrs Hows, etc; read; prayed; sang. 8.45 Religious talk. 9 Writ diary. 9.20 Necessary talk (religious); prayed. 9.30.

Grace: 6 rating sixteen times; 5 twice [5 to 6 am, 9 to 10 pm].

day, being March the 20th. The Communion ended, I spoke to her in the street, and exhorted her 'not to be weary of well-doing'. Before we parted she told me plainly, 'Mr. Williamson thinks it makes me uneasy, and therefore desires me to speak to you no more.'] Ah, poor Sophy! If this is the beginning, what will the end be!

[B—A day or two after, I related this to Mr. and Mrs. Burnside, and told them God would expect at their hands the service which I could perform for her no longer. And from this time to the 8th of April I conveyed by them the several advices she seemed to stand the most in need of, for which they had always thanks, at least, and fair promises.]

SUNDAY, MARCH 20. 4 Sang; prayed with Delamotte; Greek Testament; (not easy). 5 Private prayer; slept. 5.30 Read Prayers. 6.45 John [Regnier?], religious talk; tea; 7 Religious talk; necessary business. 8 Walked; meditated upon sermon; sang. 9 Dressed. 9.20 Fleury; slept. 10 Sang. 10.30 Read Prayers (fifty there). 11 Sermon (lively zeal). 12 Sacrament; religious talk with Miss Sophy. 12.30 Delamotte. 1 Fleury; catechized. 2 Meditated. 2.15 Read Prayers (eighty there). 3.15 Mr Hows, etc; read; sang; prayed; sang. 4 Ned Parker; tea, necessary and useful talk. 5 Walked; sang; meditated; private prayer. 6 Religious talk with Charles. 6.15 Sang; Germans'. 7.15 Mr Causton's, necessary talk; read letter. 8 Necessary talk. 8.30 Religious talk with Delamotte; necessary talk; Delamotte. 9.15.

Grace: 6 rating fourteen times; 5 thrice [6 to 7 am, 4 to 5, 8 to 9 pm].

MONDAY, MARCH 21. 4.15 Private prayer; Greek Testament; private prayer. 5 Read Prayers (forty there); Mr Causton came, necessary talk. 6 Mr Vanderplank's, necessary talk. 6.40 Writ to Mr Chiffele. 7 Letter. 8 Necessary talk; read letters. 8.30 Mr Causton's, necessary talk. 9 Account of Miss Sophy. 1.45 Fleury. 2.15 Mr Watson's, necessary talk. 3 Account. 3.30 Tea, religious talk (necessary). 4 Mr and Mrs Burnside, tea, religious talk (necessary). 5 Walked with them, to her lot, mostly religious talk. 6 Religious talk. 6.30 Germans. 7 Read Prayers. 8 Mr Campbell; read; sang. 9 religious talk; prayed. 9.20.

Grace: 7 rating once [4 to 5 am]; 6 eleven times; 5 five times [6 to 7, 8 to 9 am, 2 to 4, 5 to 6 pm].

TUESDAY, MARCH 22. 4.45 Private prayer; sang. 5.15 Read Prayers. 5.45 Tea. 6 Religious talk. 6.15 Account. 8 Walked; verse; sang. 9 Made verse; sang. 10 Verse; sang. 11 Verse; writ them. 12 Writ them; dressed. 12.45 Visited. 2.45 Transcribed. 3 Tea, religious talk. 3.40 Logic. 4 Transcribed. 4.45 Walked; sang. 5 Walked; sang; private prayer; Greek Testament. 6 Meditated. 6.15 Germans'. 7 Meditated; read Prayers. 8 Mr Burnside, etc; read; sang. 8.30 Fleury. 9 Fleury. 9.15 Necessary talk (religious); prayed. 9.30.

Grace: 7 rating once [5 to 6 pm]; 6 fifteen times; 5 once [7 to 8 am].

WEDNESDAY, MARCH 23. 4 Private prayer; prayed; Greek Testament; sang; private prayer. 5 Read Prayers. 5.45 Fleury. 6 Coffee, religious talk. 6.30 Account of Miss Sophy. 7 Walked; verse. 8 Verse. 10 Account. 12 Dressed. 12.15 Visited

Thursday, [March] 24. About nine in the morning a fire broke out in the house of Mr. [E—Robert] Hows, a tithing-man, which in less than an hour consumed it and all that was in it, except two saws. The wind carried the flame from the neighbouring houses, so that it spread no farther. The next day a collection was made for him in the town, in which the willingness of the people to give [E—a little] out of the little they had [E—to relieve a necessity which they apprehended greater than their own] was really surprising. Only one gentleman (so called, by the courtesy of England) said he thought the helping one another was giving a bad example, and therefore he would not be concerned in it.

Mrs Brownfield, she quite open! 1.15 Visited. 2 Mr Burnside's, French. 3 Tea, religious talk. 3.45 At home; tea, religious talk. 4.15 Greek Testament. 4.30 Verse 5.15 Garden; sang; meditated; private prayer. 6 Germans. 7 Read Prayers. 8 Mr Hows, etc; read; sang; prayed. 8.30 Necessary talk (religious). 9 Necessary talk (religious); prayed. 9.30.

Grace: 7 rating once [4 to 5 am]; 6 fifteen times; 5 once [11 to noon].

THURSDAY, MARCH 24. 4 Sang; prayed; hymns; private prayer. 5 Read Prayers. 5.30 Tea, religious talk. 6 Religious talk. 6.30 Mr Causton's, necessary talk. 7 Necessary talk (religious); tea. 8 Necessary talk (religious). 9 Read. 9.30 Walked; verse 10 Verse. 11.30 Account. 1 Visited Mr Ratford. 2 Religious talk. 2.45 Necessary business. 3 Tea, religious talk (necessary); account. 4 Read logic. 4.30 Hymns. 5 Sang; private prayer; Greek Testament. 6 Germans. 7 Germans; read Prayers. 8 Mr Burnside, etc; read; sang. 8.30 Necessary talk (religious). 9.30 Prayed.

Grace: 7 rating twice [4 to 5 am, 5 to 6 pm]; 6 twelve times; 5 four times [6 to 9 am, noon to 1 pm].

FRIDAY, MARCH 25. 4 Private prayer; sang; Greek Testament. 5 Read Prayers. 6 Mr Causton came, necessary talk. 7.15 Meditated upon sermon. 8 Made collection for Mr Hows. 9 Collection. 9.45 Dressed. 10 Meditated; private prayer. 10.30 Read Prayers (twenty there). 11 Sermon, Sacrament (thirteen communicants). 12 Dinner, necessary talk (religious). 12.45 Collected. 3 Mr Burnside's, tea, religious talk. 4.15 Collected. 6 Meditated; private prayer; Germans'; (lively zeal). 7 Read Prayers. 7.45 Mr Burnside; read (lively zeal). 8 Read; sang. 8.15 Mr Causton's; necessary talk (religious); supper; they all free. 9 Necessary talk (religious). 9.45 Private prayer.

Grace: 7 rating once [4 to 5 am]; 6 twelve times; 5 five times [6 to 7 am, noon to 1, 4 to 6, 9 to 10 pm].

SATURDAY, MARCH 26. 4.30 Sang; writ diary; private prayer. 5 Read Prayers. 5.45 Tea. 6 Tea, religious talk. 6.30 Hymns. 8 Mrs Vanderplank, necessary talk (religious). 9 Collection. 10 Hymns. 11 Mrs Burnside's, read account of Sophy. 12 Religious talk. 12.30 Dinner. 1 Dressed. 1.15 Set out; Account of the Mission[aries]. 2 Account, religious talk. 3 Mr Lacy's, he bitter; tea, necessary talk (religious). 4 Necessary talk. 4.15 Set out, religious talk (necessary). 5 Private prayer; meditated. 6 At home; tea, necessary talk (religious) with Mr

Campbell; buried. 7 Necessary talk (religious). 7.15 Read Prayers. 8 Mr Hows, etc; read; sang; prayed. 8.45 Necessary talk (religious) with Delamotte. 9 Necessary talk (religious); prayed. 9.40.

Grace: 7 rating once [4 to 5 am]; 6 fifteen times; 5 twice [7 to 8, 9 to 10 am].

Sunday, March 27. 4 Sang; private prayer; dressed; writ diary; (well). 5 Private prayer. 5.30 Read Prayers (Miss Sophy there). 6.40 Tea, religious talk. 7.15 Hymns. 8 Married; [read] Patrick upon the Bible. 9.15 Meditated upon sermon. 10 Meditated. 10.30 Read Prayers (fifty there). 11 Sermon, Sacrament. 12 Dinner, religious talk. 12.45 Hymns. 1 Garden; meditated; 1.30 Catechized. 2 Necessary talk; dinner. 2.30 Read Prayers. 3.45 Mr Hows, etc; read; sang. 4 Prayed; sang; read. 5 Sang; religious talk. 5.30 Ate, religious talk. 6 Meditated. 6.30 Germans. 7 Religious talk. 7.15 Meditated. 8 Meditated; sang; private prayer. 9 Prayed.

Grace: 7 rating once [4 to 5]; 6 fifteen times; 5 once [6 to 7 am].

Monday, March 28. 4 Sang; prayed. 4.30 Letter. 4.45 Private prayer. 5 Read Prayers. 5.30 Writ to Mrs Hutton. 6 Letter. 6.45 Fleury. 7 Tea, religious talk. 7.30 Writ to James Hutton. 8 Mr MacQueen and Bailey, tea, necessary talk (religious). Writ to Mr Wogan. 11 To brother Samuel. 12 To brother Samuel; writ diary. 12.30 Dressed; visited. 1 Visited Mrs Brownfield. 2 Mr Vanderplank's, Mrs Causton sent for me, necessary talk (religious). 3 At home; tea, religious talk (necessary). 4 Visited. 5 Read hymns. 5.25 Greek Testament; sang. 5 Meditated; sang; Germans'. 7.15 Read Prayers. 8 Mrs Vanderplank, etc; read; sang. 8.30 Fleury. 9 Religious talk; prayed. 9.20.

Grace: 7 rating once [4 to 5 am]; 6 twelve times; 5 four times [6 to 7, 8 to 9, 11 am to 1 pm].

Tuesday, March 29. 4 Private prayer; sang; Greek Testament. 5 Read Prayers; necessary business. 5.45 Fleury. 6.15 Mrs Vanderplank, tea, necessary talk (religious). 7 Writ to Mrs Chapman. 8 Writ. 9.30 Transcribed letter. 11 Walked; sang; meditated. 12 Meditated. 12.15 Dressed; necessary business. 12.45 Visited. 2.45 Necessary business. 3 Mrs Causton came; tea, necessary talk (religious). 4 Garden with her, talk of Miss Sophy. 5 Mostly religious talk. 5.30 She went; bread. 5.45 Meditated. 6 Private prayer; sang. 6.45 Germans' (lively zeal). 7.15 Read Prayers (Miss Sophy there). 8 Mr Burnside, etc; writ diary. 8.45 Fleury. 9.30.

Grace: 7 rating twice [4 to 5 am, 6 to 7 pm]; 6 eleven times; 5 five times [9 to 10 am, noon to 1, 4 to 6, 9 to 10 pm].

Wednesday, March 30. 4.45 Private prayer. 5 Read Prayers; writ diary. 6 Coffee; transcribed letter. 7 Writ to our Society [SPCK]. 8 Writ to Sir Erasmus Philipps. 9 Transcribed. 11 Walked; Kempis. 12 Dressed; necessary talk (religious). 12.30 Visited. 2 Mrs Burnside's, necessary talk (religious); French. 3 Tea, religious talk. 4 Necessary talk (religious) with Delamotte; logic. 4.30 Writ diary; meditated; Greek Testament. 5 Private prayer. 5.40 Mrs Ann, religious talk. 6 Religious talk (necessary). 6.40 Germans'. 7 Read Prayers. 7.45 Mr Hows, etc. 8 Read; sang; prayed. 8.30 Mrs Causton's, necessary talk (religious); all pleased! 9 Necessary talk (religious); less open.

Grace: 6 rating fifteen times; 5 twice [4 to 5 am, 9 to 10 pm].

Thursday, March 31. At his own repeated desire, I visited one who had long sat in the seat of the scorner. Nor am [I] without hopes that one of that character will at length find the wisdom he seeks.

April 1, being Friday, and once a day from that time, I visited a young gentleman who by a happy misfortune had gained both leisure and inclination to think more deeply on Christianity than he had before done. O fair blossoms! But who can tell whether any fruit will be brought to perfection?

Sunday [April] 3 and every day in the Great and Holy Week, we had

---

THURSDAY, MARCH 31. 4.20 Sang; private prayer. 5 Read Prayers. 5.30 Tea, religious talk. 6 Writ to the Trustees; writ diary. 7 Writ for the people [see Apr. 6]. 8.30 At Mr Young's, necessary talk (religious). 9.15 Mr Causton's, necessary talk. 9.30 Letters. 10 Writ for people. 11 Walked; religious talk. 11.15 Sang; meditated. 12 Visited. 1 Visited; ate. 2 At home; writ for people. 3 Dinner, necessary talk (religious). 3.45 Writ. 4.30 Bathed. 5 Mostly religious talk. 5.30 Sang with Delamotte; private prayer. 6 Mr Brownfield's, necessary talk; tea. 7 Germans'. 7.30 Read Prayers. 8 Mrs Burnside, etc. 8.30 Mr Causton's, necessary talk; ate. 9 They [had] good talk. 10.15 Prayed.

Grace: 6 rating fourteen times; 5 four times [1 to 2, 5 to 7, 9 to 10 pm].

FRIDAY, APRIL 1. Ἀπό σοῦ, Σῶτηρ ['Because of you, Saviour']. 4 Prayed; private prayer; writ diary. 5 Read Prayers. 5.40 Writ to Mr Horton. 6 Coffee, religious talk. 6.45 Writ to Mr Hird. 7 Visited Mr Grant, religious talk; prayed. 8 Mr Causton's, necessary talk. 8.15 Writ to Mr and Mrs Weston. 9 Buried; visited. 9.45 Necessary business. 10 Letters. 11 Religious talk with William Williamson. 11.30 Kempis. 12 Private prayer for Miss Sophy, etc. 12.30 Religious talk with boys; prayed. 1 Writ heads of divinity. 2 Mrs Burnside's, necessary talk (religious); French. 3 Tea, religious talk. 4 Read notes. 5 Private prayer; sang. 5.45 Religious talk with Mrs Ann. 6.30 Germans; sleepy. 7.15 Read Prayers. 8 Mrs Burnside, etc. 8.30 Writ diary.

Grace: 7 rating once [4 to 5 am]; 6 twelve times; 5 four times [5 to 6, 8 to 9, 10 to 11 am, 4 to 5 pm].

SATURDAY, APRIL 2. 4 Private prayer; sang; prayed with Delamotte. 4.30 German; hymns. 5 Read Prayers. 5.30 Tea, religious talk (necessary). 6 Mr Kent, necessary talk; tea. 6.45 Writ heads of divinity. 7 Heads. 8 Visited Mr Grant; read; prayed. 9 Heads. 11.40 Dinner. 12.15 Set out; private prayer. 1 Private prayer. 2.15 Thunderbolt, necessary talk (religious). 3 Coffee, necessary talk (religious). 3.45 Set out; private prayer. 4 Private prayer; made verse. 5 Religious talk with Fitzwalter. 5.40 At home; necessary business. 6 Tea; Germans'. 7 Read Prayers; Mr Hows, etc; read; supper; transcribed verses for Miss Sophy. 9 Mr Causton's; he not [there]; religious talk with Miss Sophy, Mrs Causton, Mr Williamson. 10 Could not sleep. 11 Mrs Brownfield came; could not sleep. 12.

Grace: 6 rating fifteen times; 5 thrice [5 to 7 am, 2 to 3 pm].

SUNDAY [APRIL 3]. Ἡ Μεγάλη καὶ Ἁγία Ἑβδομάς ['The Great and Holy Week']. 4 Private prayer; slept. 5 Dressed; read Prayers (thirty there). 6.30 Tea, at least twelve communicants. Monday the 4th, I began to learn Spanish in order to converse with my Jewish parishioners, some of whom have more of the mind that was in Christ than most of those that call him Lord.

---

religious talk. 7 Writ verse. 8 Meditated upon sermon. 9 Meditated upon sermon. 10 Religious talk. 10.15 Private prayer. 10.30 Read Prayers. 11 Sermon (seventy there). 12 Sacrament. 12.30 Dinner. 1 Garden; sang; meditated. 2 Catechized. 2.30 Read Prayers (ninety there). 3 Catechized; read Prayers. 4 Mr Hows, etc. 5 Tea, religious talk. 6 Mr Causton's, company came, they [had] necessary talk. 7 They necessary talk. 9 They necessary talk; supper, religious talk (necessary).

Grace: 6 rating [twelve times]; 5 five times [4 to 7 am, 7 to 9 pm].

MONDAY, APRIL 4. *Silentium meum loquitur* ['My silence speaks'; Kempis, III.xxi.4]. 4 Private prayer; sang. 5 Read Prayers. 6 Mr Finlay, tea, necessary talk (religious). 7 Transcribed ((hymns)) journal. 8 Visited Mr Grant, religious talk; prayed. 9 Meditated upon sermon; Fleury. 10 Meditated; read Prayers (thirty-five there). 11 Sermon. 12 Sacrament. 12.30 Read with boys. 1 Religious talk; slept. 1.30 Visited. 2.15 Mr Brownfield's, necessary talk (religious). 3.15 At home; tea, religious talk. 4 Fleury. 5 Walked; Greek Testament; sang; meditated. 6 Sang with Delamotte; necessary talk with Dr Núñez; Germans. 7.15 Read Prayers. 8 Mr Campbell; read; sang. 9.15.

Grace: 7 rating once [4 to 5 am]; 6 fourteen times; 5 twice [6 to 7 am, 2 to 3 pm].

TUESDAY, APRIL 5. 4.30 Sang; private prayer. 5 Read Prayers. 6 Tea, religious talk. 6.45 Journal. 8 Visited; (lively zeal). 9.15 Meditated upon sermon. 10 Dressed; meditated. 10.30 Read Prayers. 11 Sermon. 12 Sacrament (Miss Sophy not there!). 12.15 Necessary business; read to boys. 1.15 Walked; Spanish. 2 Kempis. 2.45 Spanish. 3 Mr Brownfield; tea, necessary talk (religious). 4 Necessary talk (religious) for Miss Sophy. 5 Necessary talk (religious) for Mrs Perkins. 6 Necessary talk (religious). 6.30 Meditated; Germans'. 7.15 Read Prayers; christened. 8.15 Mr Campbell; read; sang. 9 Mr Causton came; necessary talk (religious). 10.

Grace: 6 rating fifteen times; 5 thrice [4 to 6, 9 to 10 pm].

WEDNESDAY, APRIL 6. 4 Private prayer; German; sang; dressed. 5 Read Prayers (twenty-seven there). 6 Coffee, religious talk. 6.30 Journal. 8 Visited Mr Grant; religious talk; prayed. 9 Meditated upon sermon. 10 Meditated. 10.30 Read Prayers (twenty-seven there). 11 Sermon. 12 Sacrament. 12.15 Read hymns; read to boys. 1 Writ a prayer. 2 Mrs Burnside's, read; meditated upon heaven. 3 Tea, mostly religious talk. 4 Mostly religious talk. 4.30 Dr Núñez', began Spanish. 5 Spanish. 6 Mr Causton's, necessary talk; tea. 7 Necessary talk. 7.15 Read Prayers. 8.15 The people; read; sang; prayed. 8.45 Writ diary.

Grace: 7 rating once [4 to 5 am]; 6 thirteen times; 5 thrice [3 to 6 pm].

THURSDAY, APRIL 7. 4 Sang; private prayer; German; Greek Testament. 5 Read Prayers (eighteen there). 6 Tea, religious talk. 6.45 Journal. 7 Journal. 8 Visited Mr Grant, etc. 9.15 Meditated upon sermon. 10 Dressed; meditated; private

[B—But finding little effect from [the Burnsides], April the 8th, being Good Friday, I spoke to [Mrs. Williamson] myself, under Mr. Causton's shed. This was our third conversation since her marriage, and lasted near half an hour—but no private one, four or five persons being in the house, within sight of us, and if they pleased, hearing too. She professed large obligations to me. I exhorted her to fulfil all righteousness. And before we parted, in consequence of a conversation I had had with Mrs. Burnside concerning her, I gave her that much-controverted advice, which, fairly represented, I will avow before all the world: 'In things of an indifferent nature, you can't be too obedient to your husband. But if his will should be contrary to the will of God, you are to obey God rather than man.' It may be observed that this day, of her own free choice, she fasted till the evening.

---

prayer. 10.30 Read Prayers. 11 Sermon (twenty-six there), Sacrament. 12 Sacrament. 12.15 French. 2 Spanish. 3 Tea, religious talk. 4 Will Parker, necessary talk. 4.45 Mr Burnside, mostly religious talk. 5 Tea, good talk. 5.45 At Dr Núñez'. 6 Spanish. 6.45 Germans'. 7.30 Read Prayers. 8.15 Mrs Burnside, etc; read; sang. 9.15 Prayed.

Grace: 7 rating once [4 to 5 am]; 6 thirteen times; 5 thrice [4 to 7 pm].

GOOD FRIDAY [APRIL 8]. 4 Private prayer; slept. 4.40 Private prayer; dressed. 5 Read Prayers. 6 Mr Causton's, necessary talk (religious) with him. 7 Tea, mostly religious talk (necessary); religious talk with Miss Sophy; Is all well? 8 Meditated upon sermon. 8.30 Religious talk with Mrs Ann; writ diary. 9 Meditated upon sermon. 10 Dressed; meditated. 10.30 Read Prayers. 11 Sermon (forty-five there). 12 Sacrament (twenty-one communicants). 12.30 Religious talk with boys. 1 Mr Causton sent for me; alarming necessary talk (religious). 2 Necessary talk (religious). 2.30 Meditated. 2.40 Read Prayers. 3.30 Religious talk; prayed. 3.45 Mr Weston's, necessary talk (religious). 4.15 Mr Causton's, Captain Gray and Indians [there]. 5 Garden; private prayer. 5.20 Tea, necessary talk (religious). 6 Religious talk with Mrs Causton. 6.40 Germans'. 7 Germans'; Indians came. 8 Mr Burnside's, necessary talk (religious); ate. 9 Religious talk; prayed. 10.

Grace: 6 rating fifteen times; 5 thrice [7 to 8 am, 6 to 7, 8 to 9 pm].

EASTER EVE [APRIL 9]. 4.15 Private prayer; sang; private prayer. 5 Read Prayers (twenty-three there). 6 Mr Finlay, tea, religious talk. Meditated and sermon. 7 Walked; meditated upon sermon. 8 Meditated. 8.30 Visited Grant, religious talk; tea. 9 Religious talk; prayed. 9.30 Necessary business. 10 Dressed; private prayer. 10.30 Read Prayers (twenty-three there). 11 Sermon. 12 Sacrament. 12.45 Religious talk with Miss Sophy; Mr Causton's, religious talk. 1 Read with boys; prayed. 1.30 Visited; (lively zeal). 2 Fleury. 2.45 Necessary talk (religious). 3 Writ French. 4 Spanish. 4.45 [Read] Hickes with Delamotte. 5 Hickes. 5.15 Rachel [Uré], necessary talk (religious). 6 Tea, necessary talk (religious). 6.40 Germans'. 7 Germans', read Prayers (Miss Sophy there, Kὲ!). 8.15 Mr Hows, etc; religious talk. 9.15 Prayed.

Grace: 7 rating once [4 to 5 am]; 6 sixteen times.

[The next day, after the Communion, I spoke to her again in the street to the same effect, which was our fourth conference. She now told me, in so many words, 'Mr. Williamson is not unwilling I should talk with you because he thinks it makes me uneasy, but because he is afraid it would make me too strict.' When we came to Mr. Causton's she said, 'There is company in the house; I will go in this way,' and went in at the yard-gate, while I went in directly at the fore door, as usual. As for the assertion of my thrusting her in, she herself knows that from March 12, the day of her marriage, till this hour, I have not touched the hem of her garment.

[April 10, being Easter Day, one of Mr. Causton's servants, whom I knew to have been particularly intimate with Miss Sophy, coming to my house on a message, we fell into a remarkable conversation concerning her. The substance of what she said was this:

[In the beginning of November, when you came back with her from Frederica, Mr. Williamson renewed his courtship. For about a month she slighted it, saying, 'I love Mr. Williamson very well, but not for a husband.' But in December she began to seek his company, sitting near him and talking familiarly with him.' She often said, 'Mr. Williamson has very good sense,' and 'Mr. Williamson is a man of a mighty good temper.' After a while she would not eat without him, but if he didn't come at the beginning of breakfast, dinner, or supper, appeared uneasy, and sent all the servants, one after another, to find him. They commonly sat up together after the family was in bed, one or two nights a week. This made her not wake in a morning. If I called her, she rose; if not, she missed prayers. About three weeks before the marriage Mrs. Causton knew of it, but didn't like it at all. A fortnight before the letter was taken she told me, 'Now, Agnes, I have given my consent. I will marry Mr. Williamson.' Eight days before she said, 'Well, now I am resolved to marry Mr. Williamson.' But all this time she frequently said, 'I won't let Mr. Wesley know anything

---

Easter Day [April 10]. ʽΗ ʽΕορτη ['The Feast Day']. 4.15 Private prayer; sang; Hebrew. 5 Dressed; private prayer. 5.30 Read Prayers (thirty-three there). 6.30 Tea, religious talk. 7.15 Meditated upon sermon. 8 Paustoobee came, sang; private prayer. 8.30 Mrs Gilbert's, religious talk. 9 Meditated upon sermon; dressed; private prayer. 10 Private prayer. 10.30 Read Prayers. 11 Sermon (forty there), Sacrament. 12 Sacrament. 12.15 Mr Burnside's, necessary talk; dinner. 12.50 Writ diary. 1 Garden; meditated; private prayer. 1.45 Catechized. 2 Religious talk with Delamotte. 2.30 Read Prayers. 3.30 Mr Hows, etc; sang; read. 4 Sang; prayed; sang. 4.30 Walked; sang. 5 Meditated. 5.30 At home; tea, religious talk. 6 Religious talk; prayed. 7 Germans'. 7.30 Necessary talk with Agnes! 8 Meditated. 8.30 Writ account of Agnes. [9.] 15 Necessary talk with Delamotte.
Grace: 7 rating once [4 to 5 am]; 6 fifteen times; 5 once [6 to 7 am].

of it; for I know he will be against it.' One night in the week before the letter was taken, they sat up together in the yard till four in the morning. Three days before, she said, 'All is agreed on, but I won't marry just yet, for fear of Mr. Wesley.' That night she said, 'Well, now all the world shall not hinder my having Mr. Williamson.' The next night she said, 'I have given my full consent,' and for two hours she cried bitterly. The morning they went to Purrysburg I told her, 'Miss Sophy, you will never be happy at heart.' She clasped me round my neck, cried, and said, 'No, Agnes, I never expect it.']

Tuesday, April 12. Being determined, if it were possible, to put a stop to one of my neighbours of Carolina [E—the minister of Purrysburg], who had married several of my parishioners without either banns or license, and, as I was informed, designed to do so still, I set out for Charleston in a sloop. We passed the bar on Wednesday, and on Thursday morning landed there. I went to Mr. Garden, the minister of Charleston and Commissary for the Bishop of London, and related Mr. Ch[iffelle]'s behaviour to him. He assured me, he would effectually prevent anything of that kind for the future, said that he believed no other clergyman in the province would be guilty of such irregularity, but that, however, he would caution them against it at the General Meeting of the clergy, which was to be the week following.

MONDAY, APRIL 11. 4 Private prayer; sang. 5 Read Prayers. 6 Necessary talk with Mr Causton. 6.15 Tea, Tomochichi, etc; necessary talk (religious). 7 Necessary talk with Mr Causton, etc; necessary talk with Töltschig. 8 Read sermon; necessary talk with Mr Smith, etc. 9 Necessary talk with Levinson; dressed; writ diary. 10 Meditated. 10.30 Read Prayers. 11 Sermon (forty there), Sacrament. 12 Sacrament. 12.15 Religious talk with Mr England. 12.30 Dinner. 1 German. 3 Dr Núñez', Spanish. 4 Religious talk 5.15 At home; religious talk. 5.30 Meditated; Mr Campbell; tea, religious talk. 6 Religious talk. 6.30 Meditated; private prayer. 7 Germans. 7.45 Read Prayers. 8.30 Mrs Burnside, etc; read, prayed; sang. 9 Writ diary.

Grace: 7 rating once [4 to 5 am]; 6 eleven times; 5 five times [5 to 6, 7 to 10 am, 2 to 3 pm].

TUESDAY, APRIL 12. 4 Private prayer. 5 Read Prayers. 5.45 Necessary business. 6.15 Mrs Vanderplank; tea, religious talk. 7.15 Mr Causton's, necessary talk (religious). 8 Packed; necessary talk. 10 Dressed; necessary business. 10.30 Read Prayers. 11 Preached, Sacrament. 12.15 Necessary business. 12.30 Mrs Burnside's, religious talk (necessary); dinner. 2.30 Necessary business; Mr Causton's. 3 In the sloop; Mrs Neal; fair wind; (!) 4.30 Set out; Mrs Tisdale, Phil Thicknesse. 5 Private prayer; sang. 6 Sang. 7.30 Tybee bar; slept.

WEDNESDAY, APRIL 13. 5 Private prayer; necessary talk; sang. 6 Read sermon; sang. 7 Read sermon on Robert Boyle, Patrick. 8 Charleston bar; wind contrary; sermon; (!). 10 Slept; Patrick. 11.30 Sailed; wind contrary. 1 Dinner; read

Friday, [April] 15. I walked over to Ashley Ferry, twelve miles from Charleston, and thence in the afternoon went with Mr. Guy, the Minister of Ashley, to Colonel Bull's seat, two miles further. This is the pleasantest place I have yet seen in America, the orchard and garden being full of most of those sorts of trees, and plants, and flowers, which are esteemed in England, but which the [E—indolence and] laziness of the Americans seldom suffers them to raise.

On Sunday, April 17, Mr. Garden desired me to preach for him, which I did on those words of the Epistle for the day, 'Whatsoever is

---

[Robert] Welsted *De Aetate vergente*. 5 Private prayer; sang; read Prayers. 6 Expounded; writ diary. 7 Mostly religious talk. 8.30 Slept.

THURSDAY, APRIL 14. 5 Necessary talk (religious); private prayer. 6.30 Charleston; Mr Eveleigh's, good talk (various) with him. 7.30 Tea; Mrs Matthews, etc. 8 Necessary talk with Mr Timothy. 8.30 Mr Laserre's, necessary talk. 9 With Mrs Laserre, etc, necessary talk (religious). 10 Necessary business in town. 10 Mr Garden's, necessary talk (religious). 1 Dinner. 2 Religious talk. 3 Judge Trot's, necessary and useful talk. 4 Tea; Mr Braithwaite, etc, necessary talk. 5 Saw the silkworms, necessary talk. 7 Good talk (necessary, religious). 7.45 At home; good talk (necessary). 8 Supper; they [had] good talk (idle). 9 Prayed.

FRIDAY, APRIL 15. 4.45 Dressed; private prayer. 5.15 Set out; read Kidder's *Demonstration of the Messiah*. 9 Mr Guy's, tea, necessary talk (useful, religious). 10.30 Mr Bellinger came, necessary and useful talk. 12.30 Mr Bellinger's, necessary and useful talk. 1.15 Dinner, good talk. 3 Mr Guy's, mostly religious talk. 3.30 Set out; mostly religious talk. 4 Colonel Bull's, Dr Bull and Mrs Bull and Misses, good talk (necessary); tea. 5.30 Walked in the garden, good talk (necessary). 6 In the house; good talk; syllabub. 7 Miss Charlotte played on spinet. 9.15 Supper, necessary and useful talk. 10.30 Religious talk, close, they seemed affected! 12 Set out; at Mr Guy's. 12.30.

SATURDAY, APRIL 16. 5.15 Dressed; necessary talk with Mr Guy. 5.45 Set out; Kidder. 6 Kidder. 7.45 Meditated. 8 Mr Loyd's; tea, necessary talk. 9 Writ diary; writ notes; shaved. 9.45 Dressed. 10 Meditated; necessary business. 11 With Thicknesse, writ for him. 11.30 Mr Garden's, necessary talk (religious). 11.45 Judge Trot's, good talk. 12.45 Mr Braithwaite came. 1 Set out with him; necessary talk. 1.30 At his house; necessary and useful talk. 3 Dinner, good talk (necessary, religious). 5 Set out; necessary and useful talk. 5.45 Judge Trot's; good talk; meditated. 6.15 Necessary talk with them. 6.45 Mr Eveleigh's; necessary talk (religious). 8 At home; supper. 9 Prayed. 9.15.

SUNDAY, APRIL 17. 5 Private prayer; sang. 6 Necessary business; writ diary; private prayer. 7 Meditated on sermon. 7.45 Tea, mostly religious talk. 8.15 Meditated. 8.45 Writ to Charles. 9 Letter. 9.15 Meditated. 10 Read Prayers. 11.30 Preached. 12 Preached, read Prayers [Sacrament?]. 1 Mr Laserre's; dinner, mostly religious talk. 2 Mostly religious talk. 3 Read Prayers. 4 Mr Garden preached. 5 Judge Trot's; religious and useful talk (learned). 6 Tea,

born of God overcometh the world. And this is the victory which overcometh the world, even our faith' [1 John 5:4]. To the plain account of the Christian religion which these words naturally led me to give, I heard but one objection (which indeed was made by a man of character and education): 'Why, if this be Christianity, a Christian must have more courage than Alexander the Great.'

Monday, [April] 18. I had a conversation of some hours with Mr. Garden, whom I found (very different from the representation I had heard) to be a man not only of ((very)) extensive knowledge, both as to things, books, and men, but (as far [as] I can judge) of an excellent spirit.

Tuesday, [April] 19. I went on board again. That evening we could not get out of the harbour. The next morning we sailed a few leagues, but [E—meeting with stormy and contrary winds,] the wind changing and rising much in the evening, we were forced to drive all night. The next night, Thursday the 21st, we with much difficulty got back to Charleston.

I was now resolved to use more freedom of speech than before, and not to be ashamed of the gospel of Christ. And this, by God's assistance, I did this evening, as well as the remaining days I spent here, whatever company I was in.

---

mostly religious talk (learned). 6.45 Writ diary. 7 Writ to my mother. 7.30 Mr Laserre's, religious talk (necessary, useful). 8 Religious and useful talk. 9.45 Supper. 10.15 Mostly religious talk. 11 (Preserved from sins of thought.)
    Grace: 7 rating once (4 to 5 am]; 6 thirteen times; 5 five times [1 to 3, 5 to 6, 9 to 11 pm].

MONDAY, APRIL 18. 5 Private prayer; transcribed hymns. 6 Hymns. 7.45 Necessary business. 8 Mr Garden's; religious talk. 9 Tea, read resolutions; religious talk. 10 Good talk (learned, religious). 11 Read Account of Indian Christians. 12 At Mr Eveleigh's; necessary talk. 1 Dinner, they [had] idle talk; (preserved from idle talk). 2 Good talk. 3 At home; slept; Account of Indians. 4.15 Private prayer; meditated. 4.45 Mr Laserre's; necessary business. 5 Necessary talk. 5.30 With Mrs Laserre, etc; tea, company there, mostly religious talk. 6 Mostly religious talk. 7 Writ to Mr Guy, Mrs Laserre. 6.40 Meditated. 7.15 Supper, good talk (necessary). 9 Good talk (necessary); corrected proof. 9.45.
    Grace: 6 rating eleven times; 5 six times [10 to 11 am, 1 to 3, 6 to 7, 8 to 10 pm].

TUESDAY, APRIL 19. 5 Private prayer; sang. 6 Transcribed German Grammar; (sins). 7 German. 7.15 Sang; journal. 8 Tea; saw the fort. 9 Mr Timothy's, Garden, etc. 10 *Clavis linguae sententiae*. 11 On board; read Italian Grammar. 12 Italian. 12.30 Writ diary; dinner. 1 Italian. 3 At Sutherland's Fort; necessary talk; company; meditated. 4 Tea, mostly religious talk. 5 On board; ended Italian Grammar. 6 Supper. 6.30 Private prayer; sang. 8 Lay down.

WEDNESDAY, [APRIL 20]. 4.45 Sang; private prayer. 6.30 Ate; Gother; sang. 9 Gother; sang. 9.30 Slept. 10 Gother; sang. 12 Dinner, mostly religious talk.

Friday, April 22. I met the clergy of the province at Mr. Garden's, who severally assured me they would never interfere with me in anything, nor (in particular) marry any persons of our province without a letter from me desiring them so to do. At eleven we all went to church together; nor was I ever more sensible of the comfort of joining with the assembly of the faithful than now that I had been some days secluded from it. In the afternoon we met again, where was such a conversation for several hours, on Christ our righteousness and our example, with such seriousness and closeness as I never heard in England in all the Visitations I have been present at.

Saturday, [April] 23. Mentioning to Mr. Thompson, the minister of Ponpon [E—forty miles south of Charleston], my being disappointed of a boat, he offered me one of his horses, if I would go by land, which I willingly accepted. He went with me half the way, and sent his servant to guide me the other twenty mile[s] to his house. Finding a young Negro there, who seemed more sensible than the rest, I asked her how long she had been in Carolina. She said, two or three years, but that she was born in Barbados, and had lived there in a minister's family from a child. I

12.45 Gother; sang; wind contrary, very high. 3.30 Slept. 5 Gother; sang. 6 Supper. 7 Meditated; private prayer. 8 Lay down; wind high; affected!

THURSDAY, [APRIL] 21. 3.30 Private prayer; sang; Gother. 6 Breakfast; Gother; German. 12 Dinner; Judge Trot's; German. 6.15 Charleston. 6 Mr Loyd's, Mr Guy and Mr Jones, mostly religious talk (necessary). 7 Mrs Laserre's, religious and useful talk, they affected! 10.15 Mr Loyd's, mostly religious talk. 10.30.

FRIDAY, [APRIL] 22. 5.15 Private prayer; meditated. 6 Saw the fort. 6.30 Necessary talk with Mrs Matthews. 7 Necessary talk with Mrs Delegal; tea, necessary talk (religious). 8 Mr Garden's, necessary talk (religious). 8.30 Necessary business. 9 Mr Garden's, the clergy there, they [had] necessary talk (religious). 10.30 At Church. 11.30 Mr Garden's, religious talk; (lively zeal; +). 12 Religious talk. 12.30 Necessary business. 1 Dinner, religious talk. 2.30 Necessary business; writ diary. With the clergy, religious talk. 6.30 Writ diary; Mrs Laserre's; company there, religious talk; (lively zeal). 8.30 Mr Carr's, Mr Guy not there; Mr Loyd's; supper. 9 They [had] good talk. 10 Prayed.
Grace: 6 rating sixteen times; 5 once [9 to 10 pm].

SATURDAY, [APRIL] 23. 5 Private prayer; dressed. 6 Journal; Mrs Delegal sent, I could not go with her! 7 Necessary talk with Mr Thompson and Guy; necessary business. 8 Mr Garden's, necessary talk (religious). 8.15 Mrs Laserre's, Mrs Delegal there, could not speak! 9 With Mr Guy, Thompson, and [Walter] Ord. 9.15 Set out; religious talk. 11.30 Mr Bellinger's, necessary talk. 12 Mr Guy's; necessary talk (religious). 1 Set out with Mr Thompson; religious talk. 2.30 Wallis'; dinner, necessary talk (religious). 3.45 Set out with Tom; thought. 7 [At] Ponpon; Mr Thompson's; necessary talk; meditated. 7.45 Tea, religious talk with Nanny. 8 Religious talk, she affected! 8.45 Writ diary; private prayer. 9 Meditated; religious talk; private prayer. 10.

asked whether she ever went to church there. She said, 'Yes, every Sunday—to carry her mistress's children.' I asked what she had learned at church. She said, nothing; she had heard much, but she didn't understand it. 'But what did your master teach you at home?' 'Nothing at all.' 'Nor your mistress?' 'No.'

I asked, 'But don't you know that your hands and feet, and this you call your body, will turn to dust in a little time?' She answered, 'Yes.' 'But there is something in you that will not turn to dust, and this is what they call your soul. Indeed you can't see it, though it is within you, as you can't see the wind, though it is all round about you. If you hadn't a soul, you could no more see or hear or feel than this table can. What do you think will become of your soul when your body turns to dust?' 'I don't know.' 'Why, it will go out of your body, and go up there above the sky, and live always. God lives there. Do you know who God is?' 'No.' 'You can't see him, any more than you can see your own soul. But it is he that made you and me, and all men and women, and all beasts and birds, and all the world. It is he that makes the sun to shine, and the rain to fall, and the ground to bear corn and fruits. He makes all these for us; but what do you think he made me and you for?' 'I can't tell.' 'He made you to live with himself, above the sky. And so you will in a little time—if you are good. If you are good, when your body dies, your soul will go up, and want nothing, and have whatever you desire. No one will beat or hurt you there. You will never be sick any more. You will never be sorry for anything, nor afraid of anything. I can't tell you how happy you will be there; for you will be with God.'

The attention with which this poor creature received instruction is inexpressible. The next day she remembered all I had said, readily answered the questions I proposed concerning it, and said she would ask him that was above the sky to show her how to be good.

Sunday, April 24. I preached twice at Ponpon Chapel, on the former part of the thirteenth of the First Corinthians. And before the morning sermon (as Mr. Thompson had desired, great part of the congregation being Dissenters) used an extempore prayer. O how will even the men of Carolina rise up in the Judgment against this generation, and condemn it! They came, many of them eight, ten, twelve miles, to hear the gospel. Ye hear it not, when it is preached at your own doors!

———————

Sunday, [April] 24. 5.15 Private prayer; sang; necessary business. 6 Journal. 7.15 Tea; meditated on sermon. 9 Dressed. 9.15 Set out; religious talk with Tom. 10 Read Prayers, preached (seventy there); (lively zeal). 1 At home; Mr Edy; dinner, useful and necessary talk (religious). 2 Set out; read Prayers, preached. 4 At home; journal. 5.15 Walked; meditated; sang; private prayer. 6.15 Tea; journal; religious talk with Nanny. 8.30 Mr Thompson and Edy came! 9 Mostly religious talk. 10.

Monday, [April] 25. Mr. Thompson sent his servant with me to Mr. Bellinger's, at Ashepoo Ferry, who the next day went with me himself to one Mr. Palmer's, five mile[s] short of his own plantation at Tillifinny. Thither we came on Wednesday the 27th, and there the rain kept us till Friday. Here I met an old Negro who was tolerably well instructed in the principles of Christianity [E—who was almost a Christian], and who, as well as his fellow Negroes and a half-Indian woman, seemed earnestly desirous [E—and very capable] of further instruction. He said, 'When I lived at Ashley Ferry, I could go to church every Sunday. But here we are buried in the woods; though if there was any church within five or six miles, I can't walk, but I would crawl thither.'

Mr. Bellinger sent a Negro lad with me on Friday, who conducted me safe to Purrysburg in the evening, a town the most without the

---

MONDAY, APRIL 25. 4.30 Necessary business; tea, necessary and useful talk (religious). 6 Set out with Mr Edy, mostly religious talk. 8 Mr Webster's, good talk (necessary); tea. 9 Mr Bellinger's, he there, good talk (necessary). 12 Mr Gerardeau's; slept; good talk (various). 1.30 Dinner; walked; read *Paradise Regained*. 5 At Ashepoo; Milton. 6 Mr Bellinger came. 7.30 Mr Gerardeau's, good talk. 8.30 Supper. 9.45 Lay down.

TUESDAY [APRIL] 26. 5 Private prayer. 5.45 Dressed. 6 Tea, mostly religious talk. 7.30 At Ashepoo; they [had] necessary talk. 9 Set out with Mr Bellinger; hard rain. 11.30 Combahee. 11.45 Set out; mostly religious talk 3 Mr Hugh Bryan's; dinner, necessary talk (useful, religious). 5 Set out, he with us; necessary talk (religious). 6.30 Mr Palmer's, necessary talk (useful, religious); stormy. 8.15 Supper, mostly religious talk (necessary). 10.

WEDNESDAY [APRIL] 27. 4.30 Called; necessary talk; meditated. 6 Set out with Mr Bellinger and Palmer. 8 At Chulifinny [now Tillifinny]; writ diary; milk. 8.45 Transcribed journal. 9 Sick; slept. 10 Journal. 11 Walked; meditated. 12.30 Slept. 1 Journal. 2.15 Walked; sang; meditated. 3 Dinner; journal. 3.45 Walked; sang. 4 Meditated; Milton; sang. 5.30 Mr Bellinger came; supper. 6 Walked, mostly religious talk. 7 At home; mostly religious talk. 7.45 Mostly religious talk. 9.

THURSDAY [APRIL] 28. Private prayer; necessary talk (religious) with Mr Bellinger; hard rain. 7 Breakfast; journal. 10.30 Necessary talk (religious) with Mr Bellinger; journal. 12.15 Dinner, necessary and useful talk; journal. 2 They set out; walked; meditated; sang; Milton. 3 Journal. 4 Walked; sang; Milton. 5 Journal. 6 Walked; sang; private prayer. 7 Religious talk with Negroes, they seemed affected. 7.30 Supper. 8 Religious talk. 8.30 Private prayer. 9.

FRIDAY [APRIL] 29. 4.15 Called; private prayer; breakfast. 5.45 Set out; thought; sang. 7.45 At Tillifinny Creek, could not pass; religious talk with Negro. 9 Meditated; religious talk; sang. 10 Set out; meditated. 7.15 Purrysburg; Mr Nutman's; necessary talk; walked; necessary and useful talk. 8.30 Supper, good talk. 9.30 Private prayer.

appearance of a town I ever saw, with no form or comeliness or regularity. This lad, too, I found both capable and desirous of instruction. And I can't but think, the easiest and shortest way to propagate Christianity among the American Negroes would be, first, to find out some of the most serious planters, and then, having inquired which of their slaves were best inclined, to go to them from plantation to plantation, teaching some to read, and instructing others without, as in particular cases should appear most expedient. Three or four gentlemen I have met with between Charleston and Purrysburg who would be exceeding glad of such an assistant, who might pursue his work with small expense, and with no more hindrances than must everywhere attend a ((servant of Christ)) preacher of the gospel.

Saturday, April 30. I took boat, and before noon came safe to Savannah. Here I found things in a better state than could be expected. Those who desired to be followers of Christ had not made my absence an excuse for the neglect of assembling themselves together, and by the blessing of God on their endeavours, most of them were more steadfast and zealous of good works than when I left them.

SATURDAY, APRIL 30. 4.15 Called; private prayer; sang; tea. 6 Set out; meditated; sang. 9.30 Mrs Matthews'; necessary talk (religious) with Mrs Deikin; dressed. 11 Set out; meditated. 12 Mr Causton's; necessary talk; at home; religious talk with Delamotte; dinner. 1 Fleury. 1.45 Catechized. 2.30 Walked with Delamotte, religious talk. 3 Religious talk of Carolina. 4 Mr Brownfield's, necessary talk (religious). 5 At home; prayed with Delamotte; necessary business; Greek Testament. 6 Tea, religious talk; Mrs Ann came, religious talk (she zealous). 7 Meditated; read Prayers, expounded (lively zeal, forty there). 8 Mr Hows, etc; Brevint; prayed; sang. 8.45 Germans'. 9 Mr Burnside's, religious talk. 9.30 They zealous; (lively zeal).

SUNDAY, MAY 1. 4.30 Private prayer; prayed with Delamotte. 5 Shaved; read Prayers (thirty there). 6.30 Writ diary; tea. 7 Mr Foster, necessary talk (religious); necessary business. 7.45 Sang. 8 Walked; meditated upon sermon. 9 Transcribed prayers. 10 Meditated; sang. 10.30 Read Prayers (sixty-five there). 11 Sermon. 12 Sacrament. 12.30 Dinner, religious talk. 1 Fleury. 1 Catechized; meditated. 2.30 Read Prayers (fifty there). 3 Catechized. 4 Mr Hows, etc. 4.45 Visited. 5 Prayed; sang. 5.30 Mr Causton, necessary talk (religious). 6 Necessary and useful talk; tea. 7 Germans. 8 Walked; meditated. 9.15.
Grace: 7 rating once [4 to 5 am]; 6 fifteen times; 5 once [6 to 7 pm].

MONDAY, MAY 2. 4 Private prayer; prayed; writ prayers. 5 Read Prayers. 5.30 Tea, religious talk. 6.30 Writ to Charles. 7 Writ to Mr Laserre. 8 To Mrs Laserre and Miss Molly. 9 Fleury; slept. 10 Fleury. 10.30 Walked; read. 11 Read. 12 Dinner, mostly religious talk. 1 Visited. 2.15 Spanish. 3.30 Mr Grant, religious talk. 4 Religious talk; tea. 5 Religious talk. 5.15 Mrs Gilbert, religious talk. 5.30 Religious talk with Mr Grant. 6 Religious talk. 6.15 He went; supper. 7 Meditated; read Prayers; (lively zeal). 8 Mrs Burnside, etc. 8.30 Read. 9 Necessary talk (religious). 9.30 Prayed.

Tuesday, May 3. I walked to the three hundred acres of land which [is] here set apart for glebe, and believed it would be worth while to make a small garden upon a part of it, which would enable either me or my successor without any expense to give many of these poor people a

---

TUESDAY, MAY 3. 4 Private prayer; prayed; Hebrew; German. 5 Read Prayers. 5.45 Tea. 6 Religious and useful talk. 6.30 Journal. 9 Mr Bradley's, necessary talk; coffee. 10 Necessary talk. 11 At home; necessary business; writ German; Mr Bradley's. 12 Dinner, good talk (necessary). 1 German; religious talk with Will Wallis. 2 Mr Brownfield, necessary talk (religious). 3 Mr Jones', walked with him and Mr Bradley. 4 Walked round the glebe. 6 Walked, necessary talk. 6.45 Mr Bradley's; tea. 7 Meditated; read Prayers, expounded. 8 Mr Burnside, etc; read; sang; letter. 9 Necessary talk (religious) with Mr Hermsdorf; with Töltschig. 10.
  Grace: 7 rating once [4 to 5 am]; 6 nine times; 5 eight times [9 am to 1, 3 to 6 pm].

WEDNESDAY, MAY 4. 4 Private prayer; prayed. 5 Read Prayers. 6 Necessary talk; chocolate. 7 Hermsdorf came, mostly religious talk; tea. 7.45 Journal. 8 Journal. 9 Italian Grammar. 10 With Hermsdorf; at Mr. Causton's; necessary talk. 11 Italian, etc. 12 Dinner; necessary business; sins!!! 1 Walked; sang; meditated; (+). 2 Visited; (lively zeal, convincing). 3 At home; Italian. 4 Italian. 4.30 [Read] Wheatley on Common Prayer. 5 Private prayer; sang. 5.45 Mrs Ann; tea. 6 Rachel came, necessary talk; religious talk with Mrs Ann. 7 Meditated; read Prayers. 8 Mr Hows, etc. 8.45 At Mr Burnside's, religious talk. 9 Supper, religious talk. 10.30.
  Grace: 6 rating eleven times; 5 seven times [6 to noon]; 4 once [noon to 1 pm].

THURSDAY, MAY 5. 4.15 Private prayer; prayed. 5 Read Prayers. 5.45 Mr Grant. 6 Tea, religious talk. 7 Journal. 10 Journal; slept. 11 Walked; read. 12 At home; dinner, mostly religious talk. 12.45 Journal. 1 Italian. 2 Visited Mrs Turner, etc. 3 Visited Mr Piercy. 3.30 Necessary talk. 3.45 Visited Fitchet. 4 Mr Grant's, religious talk; tea. 5 Religious talk. 5.30 At home; meditated; private prayer. 6 Greek Testament; supper, religious talk. 7 Read Prayers. 8 Mr Burnside, etc; journal. 9 Played upon the flute. 9.30.
  Grace: 6 rating thirteen times; 5 five times [5 to 7, 10 to 11 am, noon to 1, 9 to 10 pm].

FRIDAY, MAY 6. 4 Private prayer; prayed. 4.40 Slept. 5 Read Prayers. 5.45 Tea, religious talk. 6.30 Journal. 8 E; journal. 10.30 Necessary business. 11 Walked; [read] Bedford on Sir Isaac Newton's Chronology. 12 Bedford. 12.30 Dinner, religious talk. 1 Necessary talk; necessary business. 1.30 Visited. 3 Mr Burnside's, mostly religious talk; tea. 4 Religious talk. 4.30 Walked with Delamotte to the glebe, necessary talk. 5 Necessary talk. 6.15 Visited. 6.30 Supper, necessary talk (religious). 7 Meditated; read Prayers. 8 Mr Burnside, etc. 8.45 Mr Burnside's, religious talk. 9 Supper, mostly religious talk. 9.30 Prayed.
  Grace: 7 rating once [4 to 5 am]; 6 nine times; 5 eight times [7 to 9, 11 to noon, 3 to 7, 9 to 10 pm].

sort of relief, which in summer especially is very acceptable to them.

Saturday, May 7. I took a walk to Hampstead, a little village of ten families about five miles south of Savannah. But I found no one there with whom I could talk, they not understanding mine ((High)), nor I their ((Low)) Dutch. From thence I went to Highgate, a [E—village a] mile west of Hampstead, having the same number of families. But neither could I converse with these, who spoke French only, except one family. Till the inhabitants of these villages have learnt English, that objection does not affect them which lies so strong against the rest, viz., that by placing them so distant from any other minister, and in so small numbers that they can't expect one of their own, you compel them to be without Public Worship, and in effect, to be without God in the world.

[B—Although some time had passed since these passages [with Mrs. Sophy Williamson] had occurred, yet I was in doubt whether I could admit her to the Communion till she had in some manner or other owned her fault, and declared her repentance of it. I doubted the more because I was informed she had left off fasting, and because she neglected all the Morning Prayers, though still acknowledging her obligation to both, which made a wide difference between her neglect and that of others. But after much consideration I resolved to take Mr. Delamotte's advice, and to bear with her till I had spoke to her once more.

SATURDAY, MAY 7. 4 Private prayer; meditated. 5 Prayed. 5.15 Read Prayers; (lively zeal). 6 E; tea, religious talk. 6.30 Writ diary; Mrs Causton's; necessary talk (religious). 7 E; mostly religious talk; tea. 8 Journal; E. 9 E; Prayed; journal. 10 E; writ to Mr Laserre, Mark Hird, Mrs Dalton. 11 E; sang; read Bedford; sang. 12 E; dinner, religious talk. 1 Set out; read Account of Hutcheson's Works. 2 Account; sang. 3 Account; religious talk. 3.30 Highgate, Mr Brown's, good talk. 4 Good talk (necessary); tea. 5 Set out; read Account; sang. 6 Ended Account; religious talk. 6.30 At home; tea, religious talk (necessary). 7 Meditated; private prayer. 7.30 Read Prayers; (lively zeal, 2). 8 Mr Hows, etc; read; sang; prayed. 8.45 Mrs Gilbert, etc. 9 They explained. 9.30 Prayed.

Grace: 7 rating once [4 to 5 am]; 6 thirteen times; 5 four times [5 to 6, 7 to 8 am, 3 to 5 pm].

SUNDAY, MAY 8. 4.30 Private prayer; sang; (well). 5 Dressed; writ diary; private prayer. 5.15 Read [Prayers] c p p s h s c 1 2 3 4 t b. 6.45 Chocolate. 7 Religious talk. 7.30 At Mrs Gilbert's, all there, religious talk. 8 They friends. 8.45 Meditated upon sermon. 9 Meditated. 9.45 Dressed; (Mr Delamotte [has] ague). 10 Necessary talk with Delamotte; meditated. 10.30 Read Prayers. 11 Sermon (fifty there). 12 Sacrament. 12.20 Religious talk with Mr Hows. 12.30 Dinner. 1 Fleury. 2 Catechized; meditated. 2.30 Read [Prayers] e c a p p s h s. 3 [Read Prayers] x c p t b. 3.30 Mr Hows, etc; read; sang. 4 Sang; prayed; sang. 4.30 With Delamotte, necessary talk (religious). 5.15 Mr Grant's; Mrs Burnside, etc; tea, religious talk. 6 Religious talk. 6.45 Germans'; sang. 7 Sang, etc. 7.30 At home; prayed; private prayer; (lively zeal). 8 Private prayer. 8.30

With Delamotte; necessary business. 9 Necessary business. 9.30.
Grace: 7 rating once [4 to 5 am]; 6 sixteen times; 5 once [9 to 10 pm].

MONDAY, MAY 9. 4.15 Private prayer; writ diary. 5 Read [Prayers] p s x p p t b.
5.45 Religious talk with Mr Campbell; tea, religious talk. 6.30 Journal. 7 E;
journal. 8 E; journal; prayed with Delamotte. 9 E; journal. 10 E; journal. 10.30
Visited Fitchet, Mrs Turner, Cross. 11 Visited. 11.15 Walked; read. 12 Dinner,
religious talk; writ diary. 1 Journal. 1.30 Visited; (convincing). 1 Dr Núñez';
visited. 3 Walked with Delamotte and boys to the glebe. 4 Felled trees. 5 Felled;
walked. 6 Tea, religious talk; Greek Testament. 7 Meditated; buried. 7.30 Read
Prayers. 8 Mr Grant; verses upon death. 9 Verses. 9.30 Prayed.
Grace: 7 rating once [4 to 5 am]; 6 twelve times; 5 five times [8 to 10 am, 4
to 6, 9 to 10 pm].

TUESDAY, MAY 10. 4.15 Private prayer. 5 Read [Prayers] p s p s p t b. 5.30
Necessary business. 6 Tea. 6.15 Journal; religious talk (necessary). 7 Journal. 8
Journal; necessary talk. 9 E; journal, necessary talk. 9.30 Prayed with boys,
heard them. 10 E; journal. 11 E; journal. 12 E; dinner; read *Apparatus Biblicus*. 1
Necessary business. 1.30 Visited; (convincing). 2 Visited; catechized. 3
Catechized. 3.15 Necessary business. 4 Writ notes. 4.15 Necessary business in
Garden. 5 Mr Brownfield came, tea, mostly religious talk; Mr Grant, religious
talk. 6 Read Letter to Mr Morgan. 7 Religious talk; meditated; read Prayers. 8
Mrs Burnside, etc; read; sang; religious talk with Töltschig. 9 Journal. 9.30
Private prayer.
Grace: 7 rating once [4 to 5 am]; 6 seven times [7 to 8, 9 to 10 am, 1 to 3, 6
to 9 pm]; 5 ten times.

WEDNESDAY, MAY 11. 4 Private prayer. 5 Read [Prayers] p s x p p t b (twenty-eight
there). 6 E; journal. 6.15 Tea, religious talk (necessary). 7 E; Mr Causton,
necessary talk. 7.15 Journal [E on the hour]. 11 E; walked; read. 11.45
Necessary talk. 12 Dinner; with Germans. 1 Set out; *Apparatus Biblicus*. 2 Felled
trees with boys. 2.45 *Apparatus*. 3.15 At home; necessary talk. 3.30 Mrs
Burnside's, tea, religious talk. 4 Religious and useful talk. 4.30 *Apparatus
Biblicus*. 6 Ended it. 6.15 At home; tea, religious talk (necessary). 6.45
Meditated. 7.30 Read Prayers. 8 Expounded. 8.15 Mrs Gilbert, etc; read; sang;
prayed. 8.45 Writ diary.
Grace: 7 rating once [4 to 5 am]; 6 nine times; 5 seven times [6 to 8, 11 to
noon, 2 to 4, 5 to 7 pm].

THURSDAY, MAY 12. 4 Sang; private prayer. 4.30 Slept. 4.45 Read. 5 Read
[Prayers] p s x s i p t b (twenty-nine there, Miss Sophy there!). 6 E; Mr Grant;
tea, religious talk. 7 E; journal. 8 E; journal. 9 E; journal. 10 E; sorted papers. 11
E; necessary business. 11.45 Dinner. 12 E; prayed; dinner, necessary talk
(religious). 12.45 Writ Miss Sophy's Case. 1 E; Writ Miss Sophy['s Case; E on
the hour]. 3.15 Visited. 4 E; visited. 4.20 Miss Sophy['s Case]; (convincing). 5
E; tea, religious talk. 6 E; read 6.30 Meditated; read Wheatley. 7 E; meditated;
[read Prayers] c p s h c p t b x (twenty-one there); hard rain. 8 E. 8.15 Miss
Sophy's [Case]. 9.15 Prayed.
Grace: 6 rating twelve times; 5 five times [11 am to 1, 2 to 3, 4 to 5, 8 to 9 pm].

FRIDAY, MAY 13. 4.30 Private prayer; sang; meditated. 5 [Read Prayers] p s x p t b.
6 E; Case of Miss Sophy. 7 E; Case; tea, religious talk. 8 E; Case. 9 E; Case. 10
E; Case. 11 E; Case. 11.15 *Origines Sacrae* of Stillingfleet. 12 E; Stillingfleet.

[My journey to Charleston delayed this for a while, but on Monday, May 16, I did speak to her under the shed at Mr. Causton's from seven till Evening Prayers. This was our fifth conversation, in which I earnestly exhorted her to avoid all insincerity as she would avoid fire; to hold fast all the means of grace; and never to give way to so vain a thought as that she could attain the end without them. I hoped my labour was not in vain, for she promised fair and appeared deeply serious.]

12.30 Dinner, religious talk. 1 E; Case. 1.15 With Germans. 1.45 Case. 2 E; Case. 3 E; prayed; Mr Burnside's, tea, religious and useful talk. 4 E; read Herbert. 4.45 Case. 5 E; private prayer. 6 E; Will Williamson, necessary talk. 6.30 Greek Testament; supper. 7 Supper, religious talk. 7.30 Read Prayers. 8.15 E; Case. 9.15.

 Grace: 7 rating twice [4 to 5 am, 5 to 6 pm]; 6 ten times; 5 five times [9 to 11 am, 2 to 4, 8 to 9 pm].

SATURDAY, MAY 14. 4 E. 4.30 Sang; private prayer. 5 E; read [Prayers] p s p x p t b. 5.45 Necessary business. 6 E; tea, religious talk (necessary). 6.30 Case. 7 E; Case. 8 E; Case. 8.30 Necessary talk. 9 E; prayed with Delamotte; Case. 10 E; Case; dressed. 11 E; visited. 12 E; dinner; Germans'. 1 E; set out; Stillingfleet. 2 Felled trees. 3 Felled. 4.45 Set out; Stillingfleet. 5 Private prayer; religious talk with Jo[hn?] Simms. 5.30 At home; sang; private prayer. 6 E; tea, religious talk. 6.30 Greek Testament; meditated; (lively zeal). 7 E; religious talk with Mrs Burnside; meditated. 7.30 Read Prayers, expounded; (lively zeal; convincing). 8 Mr Hows, etc; read; prayed; sang. 8.45 Religious talk with Mr Charles; (lively zeal). 9.15 Writ diary; prayed. 9.30.

 Grace: 7 rating once [8 to 9 pm]; 6 eleven times; 5 six times [5 to 7, 8 to 9 am, 2 to 5 pm].

SUNDAY, MAY 15. 4 Private prayer; meditated; dressed; (well). 5 Read Prayers (thirty there). 6 E; Read Prayers; writ diary. 6.30 Case. 6.45 Chocolate, religious talk. 7 E. 7.15 Case. 7.30 Walked; meditated upon sermon. 8 E; Kempis. 9 E; Case. 9.30 Fleury; dressed. 10 E; sang; private prayer; read Prayers (sixty there). 11 Sermon, Sacrament. 12 Sacrament. 12.15 Dinner, mostly religious talk. 1 Meditated; Fleury; sang. 2 Meditated; sang; private prayer. 2.30 Read Prayers (sixty there). 3.45 Mr Hows, etc; sang. 4 Read; sang; prayed; sang. 4.30 Will Williamson, religious talk. 5 Tea, religious talk. 6 E; Case. 6.45 Meditated. 7 E; Germans'. 7.45 Religious talk with Delamotte; (ate). 8 Religious talk. 8.30 Read letters. 9 Letters. 9.15.

 Grace: 6 rating seventeen times; 5 once [noon to 1].

MONDAY, MAY 16. 4 Sang; private prayer. 5 Read Prayers. 5.45 Necessary talk. 6 Tea, religious talk. 6.30 Case. 7 E; Case. 8 E; Case. 9 E; ended it. 9.30 Mr Causton's, necessary talk. 10 Necessary talk; Miss Sophy came; private prayer for her. 11 Necessary talk. 11.15 Necessary business; dinner, religious talk. 12 Read. 1 Visited. 1.45 Fleury; (convincing). 2 E; Fleury. 3 E; set out; read Hopkins' *Sermons*. 4 E; felled. 5 E; Private prayer; thought. 5.45 At home; necessary business. 6 E; read. 6.30 Tea, religious talk. 6.45 Mr Causton's, necessary talk. 7 Religious talk with Miss Sophy, she very serious. 7.30 Read

Wednesday, [May] 18. I discovered the first convert to Deism here. It was one who had been exemplarily religious, but who indulged himself in harmless company till he first lost his zeal, and then made shipwreck of his faith. I have since found several others who have been attacked, but as yet have maintained their ground, though I doubt the devil's apostles are too zealous and vigilant and active to let them long halt between two opinions [cf. Kgs. 18:21].

Prayers (lively zeal). 8 Mrs Burnside, etc; read; sang (lively zeal). 8.45 At Mrs Burnside's. 9 Religious talk; supper (lively zeal). 10 Religious talk. 10.30.

Grace: 6 rating thirteen times; 5 six times [7 to 10 am, noon to 1, 4 to 6 pm].

TUESDAY, MAY 17. 4.30 Private prayer; slept. 5.15 Read Prayers. 6 Tea, religious talk. 6.45 Hopkins. 7 E; Hopkins. 7.45 Walked with Mr Causton and Grant. 8 Mostly religious talk. 9.15 At Hogstead, necessary talk (religious) with Mrs Causton, etc. 10 Tea; religious talk with Agnes. 11 They fished. 11.30 Kempis. 12 They fished, etc. 1 Dinner, they [had] necessary and useful talk (various). 2 They went; mostly religious talk with Mrs Causton. 3 Mostly religious talk. 4 They came; tea, mostly necessary talk (religious). 4.45 Set out; necessary talk (religious) with Grant. 5 Religious talk with Fitzwalter; good talk (necessary). 6.15 At home; religious talk Greek Testament; writ diary. 7 E; private prayer; religious talk (necessary). 7.30 Read Prayers. 8 Expounded. 8.15 Mrs Burnside, etc; read; sang. 9 Prayed.

Grace: 6 rating twelve times; 5 four times [noon to 2, 4 to 6 pm].

WEDNESDAY, MAY 18. 4 Slept. 4.30 Read; (heavy). 5 Read Prayers. 5.30 Tea, religious talk (necessary). 6 Transcribed Fleury. 7 E; Mr Brownfield's, necessary talk (religious). 8 Necessary talk (religious); tea. 9 Necessary talk (religious). 9.30 Necessary talk (religious) with Rachel. 10 Writ account of Savannah. 11 Account. 11.45 Dinner. 12 Dinner; Germans'. 1 Visited Fitchet. 1.15 Duché, Dr Garret there. 2 Dispirited. 2.30 Mrs Burnside's, religious talk; French. 3.15 Tea, religious talk. 4 Walked; read Hopkins; private prayer. 5 Felled. 5.30 Walked; Greek Testament. 6 Necessary talk. 6.15 Read; religious talk. 6.45 Mr Grant, religious talk; tea. 7 Religious talk. 7.30 Read Prayers. 8 Mr Hows, etc. 8.50 Played the flute. 9.15 Prayed.

Grace: 6 rating thirteen times; 5 four times [5 to 6, 8 to 10, 11 to noon].

ASCENSION DAY [THURSDAY] MAY 19. 4 Private prayer; dressed. 5 Read Prayers (twenty-four there). 6 E; Mr Brownfield came; tea, religious and useful talk. 7 E; mostly religious talk. 7.30 Walked; meditated. 8 E; meditated. 9 E; meditated. 9.30 Hopkins. 10 E; dressed; read Prayers (twenty-four there). 11 Sermon, Sacrament. 12 Dinner. 12.30 Germans'. 1 E; visited. 1.15 Journal. 2 E; journal. 2.30 Visited. 3 Visited, etc. 4 E; journal. 5 E; private prayer; sang. 6 E; sang; read. 6.30 Supper, religious talk. 7 E; Greek Testament; meditated. 7.30 Read Prayers. 8 E; Mrs Burnside, etc; sang.

Grace: 7 rating once [5 to 6 pm]; 6 fifteen times; 5 once [6 to 7 am].

FRIDAY, MAY 20. 4 E; private prayer; read. 5 Read Prayers. 5.45 Mr Brownfield and Grant. 6 E; tea, religious talk (necessary). 6.45 Journal. 7 E; journal. 8 E; writ. 9 E; journal. 10 E; journal. 10.30 Visited. 11 E; prayed; visited. 11.45

Wednesday, [May] 25. I was sent for by one who had been a convert to the Church of Rome, but desired to return to the Church of England. Upon this occasion I can't but observe the surprising infatuation that reigns in England, and especially in London. Advice upon advice did we

---

Dinner. 12 E; Germans. 12.30 Walked; read. 1 E; read; felled. 1.45 Read. 2 E; read. 2.30 Mrs Burnside's, French. 3 Tea, religious talk. 4 E; read Clark's *Lives*. 4.30 Felled. 5 E; private prayer; sang. 6 E; supper. 6.15 Read; Greek Testament. 7 E; meditated; private prayer. 7.30 Read Prayers. 8 Mrs Burnside, etc; read; sang. 8.45 Writ diary.

SATURDAY, MAY 21. 4 E; private prayer; prayed. 5 Read Prayers (twenty-six there). 5.40 Journal. 6 E; tea, religious talk. 6.45 Journal. 7 E; journal. 8 E; journal. 9 Sang. 9.15 Writ scheme for sermon; (lively zeal). 10 Sermon; dressed. 11 Visited. 11.30 Dinner. 12 E; Wheatley. 1 E; visited. 1.45 Catechized. 2.30 Visited. 3 Germans'; sang; Bible. 4 Sang; prayed. 4.45 At home; meditated; (lively zeal) 5 Meditated. 5.30 Germans'. 6.45 Tea, religious talk. 7 Greek Testament. 7.30 Read Prayers. 8 Mr Hows, etc; read; sang; prayed; religious talk.

Grace: 7 rating once [4 to 5 am]; 6 fourteen times; 5 twice [6 to 8 am].

SUNDAY, MAY 22. 4.15 Private prayer. 5 Read Prayers. 6.30 Will Williamson; tea, religious talk. 7 E; religious talk; writ diary. 7.30 Sermon. 8 E; sermon. 9 E; walked; meditated. 9.30 Religious talk with Mr Piercy. 10 E; dressed; sang; private prayer. 10.30 Read Prayers (sixty-two there). 11 Sermon, Sacrament. 12 Sacrament. 12.30 Dinner. 12.50 Read. 1 Garden; meditated; sang. 1.30 Catechized. 2 Meditated; sang. 2.30 Read Prayers (seventy-five there). 4 Mr Hows, etc. 5 Mr Campbell, etc; tea, religious talk. 5.30 Private prayer. 6 Visited. 6.30 Germans'; (lively zeal). 7.30 Meditated. 7.45 Mrs Burnside's, religious talk. 8 Religious talk; supper. 9 Religious talk; read. 10.15.

Grace: 7 rating once [4 to 5 am]; 6 sixteen times; 5 once [6 to 7 am].

[MONDAY] MAY 23. 4.30 Private prayer; dressed. 5 Read Prayers. 5.30 Mr Campbell, religious talk. 6 Tea, religious talk. 6.30 Fleury. 7 E. 7.15 Journal. 8 E; read; married Mr Foster. 9.15 Set out; Clark's *Lives*. 11.15 Thunderbolt; Mrs Lacy not [there]. 11.30 Set out; *Lives*. 1 Mr Causton's lot, religious talk with Mrs Causton. 1.15 Dinner. 2 Necessary talk (religious). 3 Fitzwalter came, religious talk; tea. 4 Religious talk. 5.15 Set out with him, religious talk, he seemed much affected. 5.30 *Lives*. 5.45 At home; tea, religious talk (necessary) with Mr Piercy. 7 Religious talk (necessary). 7.30 Read Prayers. 8.15 Mr Campbell, religious talk. 8.45 Mr Bolzius. 9.15 Prayed.

TUESDAY, MAY 24. 4.15 Prayed; private prayer. 5 Read Prayers. 5.45 Religious talk with Charles. 6.15 Tea, religious talk (necessary). 7 E; writ diary; journal. 8 E; journal. 9 E; private prayer; journal; dressed. 10 E; visited. 11.30 Dinner, religious talk. 12 Religious talk of doing good, Delamotte not convinced. 1 E; journal. 2 E; visited. 2.45 Read. 3 E; prayed; set out with Delamotte, religious talk; felled. 4 E; prayed; felled. 4.30 Walked, religious talk; felled. 5 E; private prayer; prayed with Delamotte. 5.30 Tea, religious talk. 6 E; Bolzius came, religious talk. 6.45 Read. 7 E; Greek Testament. 7.30 Read Prayers. 8.15 Mrs

receive there to beware of the increase of popery, but not one word do I remember to have heard of the increase of infidelity. Now this overgrown zeal for Protestantism, quite swallowing up zeal for our common Christianity, I can't term anything better than infatuation, for these very plain reasons: (1) Because as bad a religion as popery is, no religion at all is still worse, a baptized infidel being twofold more a child of hell than the fiercest Papist in Christendom; (2) Because as dangerous a state as a Papist is in, with regard to eternity, a Deist is in a far more dangerous state, if he be not rather an assured heir of damnation; and (3) Because as difficult as it is to recover a Papist, 'tis far more difficult to recover an infidel. This I speak from the strongest of all proofs, experience. I never yet knew one Deist re-converted; whereas, even in this place, I do not know of more than one Papist remaining, except an Italian or two, whom I cannot yet speak to.

Friday, May 27. Hearing just before Evening Prayers that Mrs. Causton was taken dangerously ill at Hogstead, as soon as Prayers were over Mr. Delamotte and I walked over thither. We found her something better, with Mr. Causton and all her family about her; all of whom took the visit as it was intended, and professed much obligation to us.

Burnside, etc. 8.45 Religious talk. 9 Writ diary; religious talk; prayed.

WEDNESDAY, MAY 25. 4 E; private prayer; prayed; (heavy). 5 Read Prayers. 6 E; tea, religious talk. 7 E; necessary talk. 7.15 Journal [E on the hours]. 10.30 Visited Mrs Fallowfield, religious talk. 11 E; religious talk (she seemed open and affected). 11.45 Journal. 12 E; dinner; journal. 1 Visited. 2 E; prayed; Mrs Burnside, French. 3 Delamotte came; tea, religious talk. 4 Religious talk. 4.45 Read. 5 E; walked; prayed; private prayer. 6 Private prayer; prayed; buried. 7 Religious talk with Charles Carter. 7.30 Read Prayers. 8.15 Mr Hows, etc. 8.45 Religious talk.

THURSDAY, MAY 26. 4.30 Private prayer; prayed. 5 Read Prayers (twenty-six there); religious talk with Mr Tisdale. 6 Tea; Mrs Antrobus. 7 Journal. 9 Writ diary. 10 Dressed; visited Mr Bradley. 11 Religious talk. 11.30 Dinner. 12 Germans'; writ diary. 1 Visited Mrs Britain, etc; (preserved from sins of thought). 2 Walked; necessary talk. 2.45 Felled. 4.45 Walked; Greek Testament. 5 Meditated. 5.45 At home; necessary business. 6 Read. 6.15 Delamotte; tea, religious talk. 7 Meditated; religious talk with Ned Desborough. 7.30 Read Prayers. 8.15 Mrs Burnside, etc; read; sang; prayed. 9 Necessary business; writ diary; religious talk; prayed. 9.30.

Grace: 6 rating thirteen times; 5 five times [7 to 10 am, 2 to 4 pm].

FRIDAY, MAY 27. 4.15 Private prayer; prayed with Delamotte. 5 Read Prayers. 5.30 Mr Causton, necessary talk (religious); tea. 6 Necessary talk (religious). 7 E; writ to Hird. 8 Mr Turner came, walked with him, religious talk, he open! 8.30 Mr Bradley's, necessary talk (religious), he open! 10.30 At home; writ to Mr Hutchins. 11 Letter. 11.30 Dinner, religious talk. 12 Religious talk. 12.15 Germans'; writ diary; religious talk; (preserved from sins of thought). 1 Visited.

May 29, being Whitsunday, four of our scholars, after having been daily instructed for several weeks preceding, were at their earnest desire, frequently expressed, admitted to the Lord's Table. I trust their zeal will stir up many to adorn the gospel of our Lord Jesus Christ in all things.

---

2 Mrs Burnside's. 3 Tea, religious talk (necessary). 4 Writ diary; sins!!! 5 Mr Buckley came, good talk; tea. 6 Writ diary. 6.15 Religious talk with Delamotte. 6.30 Walked; meditated; private prayer; (lively zeal). 7 Meditated; visited Mrs Vanderplank; prayed. 7.30 Read Prayers. 8.15 Set out with Delamotte, Duke [Cannon], religious talk. 9 Religious talk. 9.45 Mrs Causton's, she better. 10 Good talk; ate. 10.30 Set out. 12.15 At home.

   Grace: 6 rating twelve times [actually thirteen]; 5 eight times [actually five, 5 to 6 am, 1 to 2, 3 to 6 pm].

SATURDAY, MAY 28. 4.45 Private prayer. 5 Read Prayers (twenty-seven there); necessary talk (religious). 6 Mr Grant, necessary talk (religious); tea. 7 E; necessary talk (religious). 7.30 Necessary business; writ diary. 7.45 Necessary business. 8 Slept. 9 Prayed with Delamotte; E; Fleury. 10 E; meditated; sang. 11 With Mrs Turner, Sacrament; visited Mrs Bradley; prayed. 12 E; dinner; Germans'. 1 E; lay down; catechized; religious talk. 2 E; Mrs Ann, religious talk. 2.30 Writ notes [?]. 3 E; visited Mrs Fallowfield, religious talk (she open). 4 Washed. 5 Tea, religious talk. 5.45 Prayed with Delamotte. 6 Religious talk with Mr Mercer. 7 Necessary talk (religious); meditated. 7.15 Buried. 7.30 Read Prayers, expounded (convincing). 8 Read. 8.15 Mr Hows, etc; religious talk; read; prayed; sang. 9.15 Prayed.

   Grace: 6 rating thirteen times; 5 twice [6 to 8 am].

WHITSUNDAY, MAY 29. 4.30 Sang; dressed (colic, easier). 5 Read Prayers (thirty-one there). 6.15 Mr Campbell, religious talk. 6.45 Will Williamson, religious talk. 7 Anton [Seiffert] and Töltschig, religious talk; tea. 8 Meditated upon sermon; religious talk with John Dodding, etc. 9.15 Meditated; sang; necessary business. 10 Read Prayers. 11 Sermon, Sacrament (four new communicants!). 12 Dinner, religious talk (necessary) with John. 1 Religious talk with Charles. 1.30 Catechized. 2 Meditated; religious talk. 2.30 Read Prayers (sixty there). 3.45 Hows, etc. 4 Prayed; sang. 4.30 Mrs Bush, religious talk; tea. 5 Religious talk. 5.30 Walked; prayed. 6 Private prayer. 6.30 Germans'. 7.15 Prayed with Delamotte, religious talk. 7.45 Mrs Burnside's, religious talk. 8 Read *Song of the Three Children.* 9 Supper, religious talk. 9.45 Religious talk with Mr Grant.

   Grace: 6 rating sixteen times; 5 twice [5 to 6 am, noon to 1].

MONDAY, MAY 30. 4.30 Sang; dressed; read Prayers (thirty-four there). 6 Mr Hows, religious talk; tea. 7 Writ diary; necessary business. 7.30 Fleury. 9 Sang; meditated upon sermon. 10 Catechized; dressed; meditated. 10.30 Read Prayers (thirty-seven there). 11 Sermon, Sacrament. 12 Sacrament (Miss Sophy not there!). 12.15 Religious talk; dinner; writ; meditated. 1 Religious talk with Tom Turner; catechized. 2 Religious talk with Agnes; necessary business; Fleury. 3 Fleury; meditated. 3.45 Mrs Ann came, religious talk. 4 Mr Grant's, with him at Dr Núñez'; tea, religious talk (necessary). 5 Spanish. 6 Supper;

Saturday, June 4. God showed me yet more of the greatness of my deliverance, by opening to me a new and unexpected scene of Miss Sophy's dissimulation. O never give me over to my own heart's desires, nor let me follow my own imaginations!

---

walked; Greek Testament; prayed. 7 Meditated; private prayer. 7.30 Read Prayers. 8 Read Prayers; Mrs Burnside, etc. 8.45 Writ diary.
  Grace: 6 rating fourteen times; 5 thrice [7 to 8 am, 4 to 6 pm].

TUESDAY, MAY 31. 4 Private prayer; slept. 5 Read Prayers (twenty-nine there). 6 Tea; Mrs Manly, necessary talk (religious). 7 Meditated upon sermon; necessary business. 8 Necessary talk with Duke Cannon; meditated. 9 Meditated; school, catechized. 10 Dressed; read Prayers (thirty-one there). 11 Sermon, Sacrament. 12 At home; Mrs Burnside's; dinner, religious talk. 1 Religious talk. 1.45 Fleury. 2 Visited. 4 Dr Núñez', Spanish. 5 Mr and Mrs Burnside, tea, religious talk (necessary). 6.15 Supper; Greek Testament. 7 Prayed; meditated. 7.30 Read Prayers. 8.20 Religious talk. 9.20 Prayed.
  Grace: 6 rating seventeen times.

WEDNESDAY, JUNE 1. 4.15 Colic; sleep. 5 Read Prayers; writ notes. 6 Tea, religious talk. 6.30 Writ Grammars. 11 Grammars. 12 Visited Mrs Manly; Mr Bush. 1 Visited. 2 Mrs Burnside's, French. 3 Necessary talk (religious); tea. 4 Mr Grant; Dr Núñez, necessary talk; Spanish. 5 Spanish. 6 Walked; prayed; meditated. 7 Meditated; sang. 7.30 Read Prayers. 8.15 Mr Hows, etc. 8.45 Religious talk (necessary) with Mrs Pensyre. 9 Necessary talk (religious). 9.15.
  Grace: 6 rating ten times; 5 seven times [4 to 5, 7 to noon, 5 to 6 pm].

THURSDAY, JUNE 2. 4 Private prayer; sang; prayed; (lively!). 5 Read [Prayers] p s x p p b. 5.30 Tea, religious talk. 6 Grammars. 11 Dressed. 11.30 Dinner. 12 Germans'. 12.30 Visited. 2.30 Grammar. 3 Visited; Mrs Minas. 4 Dr Núñez', Spanish. 5 Necessary talk (religious). 5.15 Writ diary; Mr Grant, tea, religious talk. 6 Religious talk. 6.30 Meditated; necessary talk (religious). 7 Religious talk with Mrs Ann. 7.30 Read Prayers. 8 Mrs Burnside, etc. 8.30 Mrs Burnside's, necessary talk (religious). 9 Supper, religious and useful talk.
  Grace: 7 rating once [4 to 5 am]; 6 eleven times; 5 six times 6 to 9, 11 to noon, 4 to 5, 9 to 10 pm].

FRIDAY, JUNE 3. 4 Private prayer; slept. 5 Read Prayers. 5.45 Tea. 6 Mrs Ann, religious talk. 6.30 Grammars. 7 Grammars. 9 Prayed with Delamotte; Grammars. 10 Dressed; visited. 11.30 Mrs Fallowfield, she very serious. 12 Visited; prayed with boys. 1 Grammars. 1.20 Visited. 2 Mrs Burnside's, French. 3 Dinner, mostly religious talk. 4 Dr Núñez', not [there]; Mr Bradley's, good talk (necessary). 5 Good talk (necessary). 6 Writ diary; Greek Testament; meditated; (very heavy). 7 Meditated; sang. 7.30 Read Prayers; (very heavy). 8.15 Necessary business; sang. 8.30.
  Grace: 6 rating ten times; 5 five times [4 to 6 am, 3 to 6 pm].

SATURDAY, JUNE 4. 4.45 Sang; dressed. 5 Read Prayers. 5.30 Tea, religious talk. 6 Grammars. 9 Grammars; prayed with Delamotte. 10 Grammars. 10.30 Dressed; Mrs Brownfield's, necessary talk (religious). 11.15 Writ diary. 12 Dinner, necessary talk (religious) with Mr Brownfield. 1.15 Set out; verses. 3

[B—I continued to hope [my labour with Miss Sophy was not in vain], without speaking to her any more, till Saturday, June 4, when going to speak to Mr. Brownfield, and not finding him at home, I fell into a conversation with Mrs. Brownfield upon Mrs. Williamson. She told me, 'Mr. Brownfield warned me of her long ago, in words to this effect: "Polly, have a care of Miss Sophy; she is above your match."' She went on:

[On Sunday [February 27], sennight before the stir about the letter was, I dined at Mr. Causton's, and being after dinner in the garden with Miss Sophy, I taxed her with her inconstancy to Tom Mellichamp. She said she was not inconstant to him, but loved him as well as ever, and would come to my house on Tuesday to speak to me about him. On Tuesday [March 1] she came, and desired me to send a letter for her to Dolly Mellichamp, to give poor Tommy an opportunity of clearing himself. I told her, 'I would not do it for the world without first asking Mr. Brownfield's advice.' Which when I did, his advice was to have nothing at all to do with it. The next day she came to me, crying and saying, 'I am ruined; my uncle says they have put Tommy in jail again.'

[What could I do now? 'Go, and tell her of her fault between me and her alone' [cf. Matt. 18:15]? So I should have chosen, either as a friend or a pastor; but being cut off from this, all that remained was to inquire of others as diligently as I could, whether this were not a false accusation. First, then, I asked Mr. Brownfield to tell me frankly how far one might depend on Mrs. Brownfield's word. He answered, 'Perhaps she may not tell you all the truth she knows; but be assured, she will tell you nothing but the truth.' I asked him next if he had ever advised her to have a care of Miss Sophy. He said he had, and repeated the words. I inquired further if she had ever asked his advice about sending a letter from Miss Sophy to Dolly Mellichamp. He said yes, and he had advised her to have nothing at all to do with it.

[I could think of but one thing more, which was to hear what Mrs. Causton, who knew her best, had to say in her defence. I went therefore to Hogstead, where she was, and told her so much of my objections against Mrs. Williamson as I could without betraying my authors to the resentment of the family. She strenuously maintained that Mrs. Williamson had never said anything false, or dissembled with me at all.

———————

Mrs Causton's, necessary talk (religious) with Agnes and Rachel. 4 Tea, necessary talk (religious). 5 Set out; verses. 6.30 At home; religious talk with Delamotte and Töltschig; tea. 7 Writ diary; sang; meditated. 7.30 Read Prayers. 8.15 Mrs Ann, etc. 8.40 Mr Causton's. 9 Writ verses, etc. 9.45 Prayed.

Grace: 6 rating eleven times; 5 six times [6 to 10 am, 4 to 6 pm].

Some of her words, which she spoke leaning her head back and lifting up both her hands, were: 'By the Lord God, Sophy is as innocent as a newborn child. And I know she has as great a value for you as for any person alive except Mr. Williamson.'

I related this to Mr. Delamotte, and at his instance consented still to admit her to the Holy Communion.]

Sunday, June 5. I baptized Richard Turner, aged forty, and his son Thomas, aged fourteen. About this time we observed the spirit of God to move upon the minds of many of the youth [E—children] of this place. Who knows but some of them may work together with him till they come to the measure of the stature of the fullness of Christ!

Tuesday, June 7. I writ to my sister Kezzy, and made her an offer of living with me here. But upon reflection I was in doubt whether I had

---

TRINITY SUNDAY, JUNE 5. 4.30 Sang; dressed; read Prayers (thirty-four there); Richard and Thomas Turner baptized!. 6.30 Tea, religious talk. 7.30 Walked; meditated upon sermon. 8 Meditated. 9 Sang; writ diary; Mr Grant, religious talk. 10 Religious talk; sang. 10.30 Read Prayers (seventy there). 11 Sermon. 12 Sacrament (twenty-seven communicants). 12.45 Dinner. 1 Fleury; catechized. 2 Christened Thomas P[ensyre?]!; religious talk with Will Williamson, Mrs Gilbert, etc. 2.30 Read Prayers. 3 Prayed; catechized. 3.45 Mr Hows, etc. 4 Prayed; sang; religious talk. 5 With Bob Bradley and John Millidge [boys]; tea, religious talk. 6 Religious talk with Delamotte; read letters. 6.30 Religious talk with Töltschig. 7 Sang. 7.30 Mr Burnside's, religious talk. 8 Supper, religious talk. 9.15 Prayed.

Grace: 6 rating sixteen times.

MONDAY, JUNE 6. 4.15 Sang; private prayer; dressed; (rain). 5 Read Prayers. 5.45 Necessary talk with Brownfield. 6 Tea, religious talk. 6.45 Writ diary. 7 Grammars. 10 (Sins!!!); slept; read letters from England. 11.45 Dinner. 12 Religious talk. 12.15 Germans'. 1 Visited. 3.30 Writ verse. 4 Dr Núñez', Spanish. 5 Religious talk. 5.30 Necessary talk. 5.45 Prayed with Delamotte. 6 Supper, religious talk. 6.30 Greek Testament. 7 Religious talk with Bob Bradley; meditated. 7.30 Read Prayers. 8 Mr Campbell, religious talk; sang; religious talk. 9.

Grace: 6 rating fourteen times; 5 thrice [7 to 10 am].

TUESDAY, JUNE 7. 4.15 Sang; private prayer; dressed. 5 Read Prayers (twenty-seven there). 5.45 Tea, religious talk. 6.30 Grammars. 7 Writ to my sister Kezzy. 8 Writ to Mr Butler. 8.45 At Mr Causton's, he not [there]. 9 At Mr Burnside's, he not [there]. 9.15 Necessary business. 10 With Mr Causton, necessary talk; necessary business. 11 Garden; verses. 12.40 Dinner. 1.15 Necessary business; visited. 2 Visited. 3.30 Necessary business. 3.45 Dr Núñez', Spanish. 4 Spanish; necessary talk. 5 Hebrew with them. 5.30 At home; necessary business. 6 Tea, religious talk (necessary). 6.45 Greek Testament. 7.15 Meditated; private prayer. 7.30 Read Prayers; letters from England! 8.30 Mrs Burnside, etc. 9 Religious talk; prayed. 9.30.

Grace: 6 rating fourteen times; 5 four times [9 to 11 am, 4 to 6 pm].

done well, considering the slippery ground on which I stand. However, I leave the whole matter in God's hand; let him order for us what is best!

Friday 10. I buried the only child of a fond parent, who had been snatched away from him in a moment, falling into a well, and being stifled there, before those with whom he had been just playing could help him. A happy misfortune, I trust, to his father, who sees and adores the hand of God therein, and, 'humbled in the dust, Now owns with tears the punishment was just' [Parnell, *The Hermit*, 237-38].

Saturday, June 11. Having been desired some time before by Mr. Causton to hear what the people had to say against him, that he might have an opportunity either of clearing himself or removing the complaint, I told him plainly some of the things they complained of. He

---

WEDNESDAY, JUNE 8. 4 Private prayer; sang. 5 Read Prayers. 5.40 Necessary business. 6 Mrs Ann; coffee, religious talk. 6.30 Sorted books. 7 Sorted; cleaned. 8 Grammars. 9 Prayed; ended Grammars. 10 Dressed; visited Mrs Fallowfield, religious talk. 11 Mrs Charles'; Mrs Dean; necessary talk. 12 Mr Coates, necessary talk. 1 Writ resolutions. 2 Mrs Burnside's, French. 3 Prayed; tea, good talk. 4 Dr Núñez', Spanish; English with Miss Sypera [Núñez]!! 5 Necessary business. 5.30 Prayed; meditated. 6 Mr Grant, religious talk. 6.45 Walked; sang. 7 Sang; meditated. 7.30 Read Prayers. 8.15 Sang; Hows, etc.

Grace: 7 rating once [4 to 5 am]; 6 fourteen times; 5 twice [3 to 5 pm].

THURSDAY, JUNE 9. 4 Private prayer; sang. 5 Read Prayers. 5.45 Tea, religious talk. 6 Necessary business. 8 Necessary business; necessary talk with Miss Rivett. 9 Necessary business. 9.30 Prayed with Delamotte; necessary business. 10 Necessary business; Mr Bolzius. 11 Necessary business. 11.30 Necessary talk; necessary business. 12 Dinner, religious talk (necessary). 1 Set out with Mr Bolzius, religious talk. 2 Read his journal. 2.45 Mrs Causton's, Mr Causton there, necessary talk (religious). 3 Mostly religious talk; tea. 3.45 With Mr Causton, necessary talk (religious) of himself. 5.15 Set out; necessary and useful talk. 6 Necessary talk (religious). 6.40 Meditated. 7 Sang; meditated. 7.30 Read Prayers. 8 Religious talk with Mr Grant; at Mrs Ann's with Mrs Fallowfield, religious talk! 9 Religious talk; prayed. 9.30.

Grace: 7 rating once [4 to 5 am]; 6 eleven times; 5 six times [6 to 8, 10 to noon, 5 to 7 pm].

FRIDAY, JUNE 10. 4.30 Private prayer; sang. 5 Read Prayers. 6 Mr Bradley's, religious talk. 7 Writ of Count Zinzendorf; read German. 8 Writ to Mr Hird; to Mark [Hird]. 9 To Mr Newman; Mr Verelst. 10 Writ to Mr Horton. 11 Writ to Charles; religious talk. 12 Prayed; visited. 1 Visited Mrs Weddal. 2 Mrs. Burnside's, French. 3 Tea, religious talk. 4.30 Dr Núñez', Spanish. 5 Mr West's, religious talk; buried his son; religious talk with him!! 6 Prayed with Delamotte. 6.30 Meditated; sang. 7 Verses. 7.30 Read Prayers; (lively zeal). 9 With Germans; sang; religious talk.

Grace: 6 rating fourteen times; 5 thrice [5 to 6, 7 to 8 am, 4 to 5 pm].

SATURDAY, JUNE 11. 4.15 Private prayer; sang. 5 Read Prayers (twenty-three there). 6 Tea, John came, religious talk. 7 Necessary talk; Mr Causton's,

could not bear it, but turned full upon me, said he was surprised I of all people should join with his enemies, [E—and fully convinced me of what I had often heard before, but never would believe, that he could not bear plaindealing,] and said many other warm things to my great surprise, though I had been warned before that thus it would be. I was first prompted to say in my heart, 'Now I may be excused from speaking on this head any more.' But I soon recollected that my commission is, to speak 'whether men will hear or whether they will forbear' [Ezek. 2:5, etc.].

---

necessary talk of the people's accounts, he very affected! 8 In the store, necessary talk. 9 At home; Töltschig and Antone; explained with them. 10 Dressed; meditated on sermon. 10.45 Read Prayers. 11 Preached, Sacrament. 12.15 With Germans; dinner, read Bible. 1 Bible; religious talk; sang. 2 Catechized. 2.30 Walked with Mr Burnside, necessary talk (religious). 3 Felled at the lot. 4 Walked; religious and useful talk (necessary). 5 At home; Mr Gray and Burnside, religious talk; tea. 6 Visited Mrs Bradley, prayed; Mrs West, religious talk; (they affected!). 7 Meditated; Greek Testament. 7.40 Read Prayers. 8.15 Mr Hows, etc. 9 Mr Grant, religious talk (he seemed zealous). 10 Prayed.

Grace: 6 rating fourteen times; 5 four times [5 to 6, 8 to 9 am, 2 to 4 pm].

SUNDAY, JUNE 12. 4.30 Sang; private prayer; dressed. 5 Read Prayers (twenty-seven there). 6.15 Will Williamson and Mr Griffin, religious talk (necessary). 7.30 Writ diary; meditated. 8 Walked; meditated upon sermon. 9 Meditated; sang. 10 Sang; dressed; read Prayers. 11 Sermon, Sacrament. 12 Sacrament; dinner; Fleury. 1 Fleury; religious talk. 2 Catechized. 2.30 Read Prayers (sixty there). 3 Mr Hows, etc. 3.45 Mr Grant's, religious talk; Mr Burnside's, Mr Bailey. 5 Tea, religious talk (necessary). 6 Mostly religious talk. 7 Visited Mr West, religious talk (close, he zealous); Mrs Bradley; prayed. 8 At home; supper; Mr Grant; read account of Miss Sophy. [9] Account. 9.45 Prayed.

Grace: 6 rating fifteen times; 5 thrice [5 to 6 am, 5 to 7 pm].

MONDAY, JUNE 13. 4 Sang; prayed. 4.45 Read Prayers. 5.30 Verse. 6 Walked; verses. 7 Verses. 8 Mr West's; tea, religious talk. 9 Prayed with her (they zealous). 9.15 Writ to Mrs Skene. 10.15 Writ diary; visited Fitchet. 11 Mrs Fallowfield. 11.30 Dinner. 12 Necessary talk (religious); Germans'; Mr Gronau, religious talk (he very zealous); sang. 1 [Read] Bible with them; sang. 2 Sang. 2.30 Mrs Dixon, religious talk (she seemed affected). 3.30 Mr Grant's, necessary talk. 4 Dr Núñez', Spanish. 5 Dr Smith, necessary talk (religious). 5.15 Sang; religious talk. 6 Supper, religious talk. 6.30 Walked; meditated; Mrs Bradley died! 7 Writ to Mrs Burnside, Mr Burnside, Mr Hows, Mrs Hows (convincing); private prayer. 7.40 Read Prayers; (sultry!). 8.15 Writ to Mr Bradley; writ diary. 8.30 Watts; (convincing). 9.15 Necessary talk (religious); private prayer; prayed.

Grace: 6 rating seventeen times; 5 once [9 to 10 am].

TUESDAY, JUNE 14. 4 Private prayer; sang. 5 Read Prayers. 5.40 Watts. 6 Chocolate, religious talk; writ to Clayton. 7 To Clayton. 7.30 To Mr Hall. 8.30

Mr Causton's, they [had] necessary talk. 10 Necessary talk (religious) with him, he not open. 10.45 Visited. 11 Visited Mr West. 11.15 Letter; dinner. 12 Germans'. 12.30 Necessary talk with Janet Rogers. 1 Slept. 1.15 Visited (convincing). 3 Mr Grant, necessary talk. 3.30 Dr Núñez', Spanish. 4.30 Sang. 5 Mr Grant; tea, mostly religious talk. 5.45 Meditated. 7 Mr Bradley; read Prayers. 8 Buried Mrs Bradley (lively zeal). 9 Sang; writ diary. 9.30.

Grace: 6 rating fifteen times; 5 thrice [6 to 7, 9 to 10 am, 3 to 4 pm].

WEDNESDAY, JUNE 15. 4 Private prayer; sang. 5 Read Prayers; Mrs Dean; tea, necessary talk (religious). 6 Necessary talk (religious). 6.45 Mr Dean's, necessary talk (religious). 7 Religious talk with Dr Garret. 7.30 Mr Causton's, etc. 8 At home; necessary business. 9 Necessary business. 10 Necessary business. 11 Necessary business; religious talk with Will Williamson, etc. 12 Prayed; necessary business. 12.45 Germans'. 1 Germans'; visited. 1.40 Germans. 2 Mrs Burnside, French. 3 Tea, religious talk. 4 Necessary business; necessary talk. 4.30 Dr Núñez. 5 Necessary business. 5.30 Sang. 6 Mrs West, religious talk; tea. 7 Buried. 7.30 Read Prayers. 8 Mr Hows, etc. 8.45 Religious talk.

Grace: 6 rating thirteen times; 5 four times [6 to 7, 8 to 10 am, noon to 1 pm].

THURSDAY, JUNE 16. 4 Private prayer; prayed with Delamotte. 5 Read Prayers; tea, religious talk. 6 Religious talk. 6.30 Necessary business. 7.15 Writ to James Hutton. 8 To Selima. 9.45 Dressed. 10 VisitedMr Bradley (convincing). 11 Visited Mr Fallowfield. 11.30 Dinner (convincing). 12 Germans'. 12.30 Mr Hows, etc; sang; prayed; sang. 1 Necessary talk (religious). 1.15 Germans'. 2.15 Visited. 2.45 Writ verse. 3 Mr Grant's, religious talk. 3.45 Dr Núñez. 4 Spanish. 4.15 At home; Spanish; tea. 5 With Mrs Fallowfield, religious talk (she very zealous). 6 Sang; Greek Testament. 7 Meditated; sang. 7.30 Supper. 8 Mrs Burnside. 8.45 Verse. 9.30 Prayed.

Grace: 6 rating seventeen times; 5 once [6 to 7 am].

FRIDAY, JUNE 17. 4 Dressed; sang; prayed; (lively zeal). 5 [Read Prayers] p s x, sang, p b. 6 Mr Grant, religious talk; coffee. 7 Verse. 8 Verse; prayed with Delamotte. 9 Verse. 9.30 Slept; verse. 10 Visited. 11 Mr Causton's, necessary talk (religious). 12 He [Mr Causton], etc, necessary talk. 1 At home; verse. 2 Mrs Burnside's, French. 3 Tea, religious talk. 4.15 Dr Núñez', Spanish. 5 Prayed; Mrs Causton came, good talk; Mr Causton's, tea. 6 Good talk (necessary, religious). 6.45 Mr West's. 7 Meditated; read Prayers. 8.15 Mr Burnside, etc. 9 Mrs Burnside's, supper, religious talk. 10 Religious talk (they zealous). 10.45.

Grace: 7 rating once [4 to 5 am]; 6 fifteen times; 5 trice [noon to 1, 5 to 7 pm].

SATURDAY, JUNE 18. 4 Private prayer; slept; sang. 5 Read Prayers; John came; chocolate. 6 Religious talk. 6.30 Necessary talk with Delamotte. 7 Fleury; writ diary. 7.30 Necessary business. 8 Fleury; verse. 9 Verse. 10.30 Set out with Delamotte, religious talk. 11 Walked; religious talk (necessary). 12 Necessary talk (religious). 2 At home; dinner. 3 Necessary business; necessary talk. 4 Mr Causton's, necessary and useful talk; tea. 5 At home; tea, religious talk. 5.30 Greek Testament. 6 Prayed with Delamotte; sang; writ diary. 7.30 Prayed;

meditated. 7.45 Meditated; buried; read Prayers. 8 Mr Hows, etc; sang; Mr Bradley. 9.15 Toothache.

Grace: 7 rating once [6 to 7 pm]; 6 eight times; 5 seven times [5 to 8, 11 am to 2, 3 to 5 pm].

SUNDAY, JUNE 19. 4 Private prayer; prayed with Delamotte; slept. 5 Read Prayers (twenty-three there; sleepy). 6 Mr Grant; tea, religious talk. 7 Necessary business. 7.30 Walked; meditated upon sermon. 8 Meditated. 8.30 Verse. 10 Dressed; sang; meditated. 10.30 [Read Prayers] p c c, sang (fifty-five there). 11 Sermon; prayed. 12 Sacrament, sang, prayed (twenty-four communicants); dinner. 1 Sang. 1.30 Visited. 1.45 Necessary business. 2 Sang; meditated. 2.30 [Read Prayers] p a p p s h b c a c p t b. 4 Mr Hows, etc. 4.30 Verse. 5 Garden; meditated. 5.15 Tea, religious talk. 5.45 Prayed with Delamotte. 6 Rachel came, necessary talk (religious). 6.45 Germans'. 7.30 Visited Mr Vanderplank. 8 Mr Gilbert's, necessary talk (religious). 8.45 At home; Mr Grant, religious talk. 9 Mostly religious talk. 9.30 Prayed.

Grace: 6 rating seventeen times; 5 once [5 to 6 am].

MONDAY, JUNE 20. 4 Private prayer; sang; private prayer. 5 Read Prayers. 5.30 Mr Campbell, religious talk; tea. 6 Began English Grammar. 7 Grammar. 8.45 Necessary talk; visited. 9 Visited. 9.30 Grammar. 11 Visited Mr West, religious talk; walked with him. 12 At his lot, religious talk. 12.30 At home; dinner, necessary talk (religious). 1 Germans'; read; sang. 2 Visited Mrs Bush. 3 Dr Núñez', he not [there]; necessary talk with Miss Sypera [Núñez]. 4 Necessary talk. 4.30 Visited Mrs Turner, religious talk; prayed. 5 With Mrs Charles, necessary talk (religious). 6 Tea, religious talk; meditated. 7 Sang; meditated. 7.30 Read Prayers. 8 Read Prayers; Mrs Burnside, etc.

Grace: 7 rating once [4 to 5 am]; 6 ten times; 5 six times [5 to 6, 7 to 10 am, 1 to 2, 3 to 4 pm].

TUESDAY, JUNE 21. 4 Private prayer; sang; prayed with Delamotte. 5 Read Prayers; Mrs Ann, tea. 6 Necessary talk (religious). 6.30 Grammar. 7 English Grammar. 8.15 Mr Causton's, necessary talk; tea. 9 At home; meditated; Grammar. 10 Grammar. 11 Sang. 11.45 Dinner. 12.30 Visited. 1 Germans'. 2 Visited. 3.30 Dr Núñez'. 4.30 Visited. 4.45 Private prayer. 5 Sang; private prayer. 5.45 Tea, religious talk. 6 Walked; sang; private prayer. 7 Meditated; sang. 7.30 Read Prayers. 8 Mrs Burnside, etc. 8.45 Mr Causton's, necessary talk. 9 Supper, necessary talk (religious). 10 Necessary talk (religious). 10.30.

Grace: 7 rating twice [4 to 5 am, 5 to 7 pm]; 6 eight times; 5 eight times [6 to 8, 9 to 11 am, noon to 1, 9 to 11 pm].

WEDNESDAY, JUNE 22. 4.30 Meditated; private prayer. 5 Read Prayers. 5.45 Coffee. 6.15 Sermon. 7 Grammar. 9.15 Slept. 9.30 Sang. 10 Dressed; visited; Mr Bradley. 11 Necessary talk with him. 12 Necessary talk (religious); dinner, necessary talk. 1 At home. 1.30 Germans. 2 Mrs Burnside's, French. 3 Tea, religious talk. 4 Dr Núñez'. 5 Sang. 5.30 Prayed with Delamotte. 6 Mr Vanderplank's; Mr West, necessary talk (religious). 7 Meditated. 7.30 Read Prayers. 8 Mr Hows, etc. 9 Prayed; could not sleep.

Grace: 7 rating once [5 to 6 pm]; 6 eleven times; 5 five times [7 to 9 am, noon to 1, 3 to 5 pm].

Saturday, 25. Mr. Causton was seized with a fever. I attended him every day, and had a good hope from the manner wherein he bore it, and the thankfulness he showed for my attending him, that it would be a blessing both to him and his dependents.

THURSDAY, JUNE 23. 4.15 Prayed; private prayer. 5 Read Prayers; Mr Griffith, religious talk; tea. 6 Walked to lot with Mr Griffith. 7 Worked. 9 At home; prayed; visited. 10 Visited. 12 Dinner; Germans. 1 Grammar. 1.30 Germans'. 2.30 Visited. 3 Dr Núñez. 4.15 Writ. 4.30 Sang. 5.45 Tea, religious talk. 6.30 Walked; meditated. 7 Meditated. 7.30 Private prayer. 7.45 Read Prayers. 8.30 Mrs Burnside; Watts. 9.30.

Grace: 6 rating sixteen times; 5 twice [7 to 9 am].

FRIDAY, JUNE 24. 4 Private prayer; sang; prayed with them. 5 Read Prayers. 6.15 Tea, religious talk. 7 Writ sermon. 10 Sermon; dressed. 10.45 Read Prayers. 11 Read Prayers; Sermon. 12 Sacrament. 12.45 At home. 1 Dined with the Free Masons. 2 Writ diary; Watts. 3 Watts. 3.30 Mrs Burnside's, Mr Andrews, tea, good talk. 4.30 Necessary business. 5 Private prayer; sang; meditated. 6 Supper. 6.15 Walked; private prayer; sang. 7 Mr Piercy, Mr Causton and Mr Anderson, necessary talk; read Prayers. 8 Read Prayers; Mr Campbell, etc. 8.45 Religious talk. 9.15 Necessary talk (religious); prayed.

Grace: 7 rating once [4 to 5 am]; 6 twelve times; 5 five times [6 to 7, 9 to 10 am, 2 to 5 pm].

SATURDAY, JUNE 25. 4 Private prayer; sang; prayed with them. 5 Read Prayers; tea; necessary business. 6 Tea, necessary talk (religious). 6.45 Grammar. 7.30 Walked; verse. 8 Walked; verse. 9 Verse; visited. 10 Verse; religious talk with James Smith (gained no ground). 11 Religious talk (gained no ground). 11.30 Dinner. 12 Dinner, religious talk (necessary). 12.45 Visited; prayed. 1 Mr Bradley, necessary talk. 1.15 Set out with Mr Brown, good talk. 2 Mostly religious talk. 3 Highgate, necessary talk; tea, necessary talk. 4 Visited Mrs Landry, good talk (necessary, religious). 5 Mr Brown's, necessary talk. 5.15 Set out, necessary and useful talk (religious). 5.30 He went back. 6 Verses. 6.30 At home; religious talk; tea. 7 Meditated; prayed. 7.45 Read Prayers. 8.30 Mr Hows, etc. 8.45 Mr Causton's, he better. 9 Mostly religious talk; ate.

Grace: 6 rating ten times; 5 seven times [5 to 7 am, noon to 4, 5 to 6 pm].

SUNDAY, JUNE 26. 4.15 Dressed; sang; prayed; (heavy). 5 Read Prayers (thirty-four there). 6 Tea, religious talk (lively zeal). 7 Walked; meditated upon sermon. 8 Sang; writ verse. 9 Verse; slept; writ diary; writ verse. 10 Dressed; [read Prayers] c c c p (fifty there). 11 Preached, p p, Sacrament. 12 Dinner, religious talk. 1 Fleury. 2 Catechized. 2.30 Read Prayers (sixty there). 3 Catechized; prayed. 3.30 Mr Hows, etc. 4 Prayed; sang. 4.45 Mr Causton's, religious talk (necessary); tea; he very ill. 5 Religious talk (necessary). 6 Visited Mrs Antrobus; Germans'; (lively zeal). 7.15 Buried; Mrs Burnside's, religious talk (close; lively zeal!). 8 Religious talk. 9 Supper, religious talk (necessary).

Grace: 7 rating once [7 to 8 pm]; 6 sixteen times; 5 once [noon to 1].

MONDAY, JUNE 27. 4.30 Private prayer; prayed. 5 Read Prayers. 5.30 Tea, religious talk. 6.45 Grammar. 8 Grammar. 10.30 Visited Mr Dearn (convincing). 11 Visited. 11.45 Dinner. 12 Dinner, religious talk (necessary); Germans'; writ diary. 1 Visited. 2 Visited Mr Causton (too long!). 3 Visited Mrs Burnside (too long). 4 Dr Núñez; visited; (convincing). 5 Sang. 5.15 Mr Bolzius; tea, religious talk. 6 Walked; meditated; sang. 7 Meditated; private prayer. 7.30 Read Prayers. 8 Buried; religious talk with Mr Campbell (he open!). 9 Prayed.

Grace: 6 rating thirteen times; 5 four times [6 to 8, 9 to 10 am, 3 to 4 pm].

TUESDAY, JUNE 28. 4.30 Private prayer; dressed. 5 Read Prayers (twenty-seven there). 5.30 Coffee. 6 Grammar. 9 Collected hymns. 10 Hymns. 11 Visited Mrs Molton (she not affected). 12 Religious talk with Will Williamson. 12.30 Visited. 1.45 Mr Causton's (he better). 2 Necessary talk (religious and useful). 2.45 Visited Mrs Burnside, religious talk. 3 At home; tea, religious talk. 4 Dr Núñez. 5 Sang. 6 Walked; meditated; sang. 7 Meditated; private prayer. 7.30 Read Prayers. 8.15 Sang; religious talk. 8.30 Verse. 9 Prayed; lay down; buried.

Grace: 7 rating once [5 to 6 pm]; 6 fourteen times; 5 three times [7 to 9, 10 to 11 am].

WEDNESDAY, JUNE 29. 4.15 Private prayer; sang. 5 Read Prayers (twenty-five there). 6 Writ. 6.45 Tea, religious talk (necessary). 7 Meditated upon sermon. 7.30 Verse. 8 Verse, necessary talk. 9 Verse. 10 Dressed. 10.15 Collect, collect, collect, Sermon, sang. 11 Sacrament; prayed; religious talk. 12 Necessary talk (religious); dinner. 1 Germans. 2.30 Visited. 3 Mrs Burnside's, religious talk (necessary); tea. 4 Religious talk. 4.15 Visited. 4.45 Necessary business. 5 Sang; private prayer. 6 Supper, religious talk. 6.30 Walked, religious talk. 7 Meditated. 7.15 Religious talk. 7.30 At Mrs Burnside's; meditated. 8 Read Prayers. 8.30 Buried; Mr Hows, etc; sang. 9 Writ diary; verse. 9.30.

Grace: 7 rating once [5 to 6 pm]; 6 eleven times; 5 six times [6 to 7, 8 to 11 am, 12 to 1, 3 to 4 pm].

THURSDAY, JUNE 30. 4.15 Private prayer; prayed; sang; private prayer. 5 Read Prayers. 5.40 Tea, religious talk. 6 Necessary talk (religious). 6.30 Walked with Delamotte; verse; at the lot. 7 He worked. 8 Verse. 9 In school; necessary business; writ verse. 10 Necessary business; verse. 11 Verse. 11.30 Dinner. 12 Germans'; visited. 1.15 Germans'. 2 Writ verse. 3 Visited. 3.30 Dr Núñez'. 4 At home; necessary business; writ verse. 5 Sang; walked. 6 Tea; meditated. 7 Meditated; read Prayers. 8.15 Religious talk; sang. 8.45 Verse. 9.15 Prayed.

Grace; 6 rating twelve times; 5 five times [6 to 8, 11 to noon, 4 to 6 pm].

FRIDAY, JULY 1. 4 Called; slept; prayed; (very heavy). 5 Read Prayers; coffee; (very heavy). 6 Religious talk. 6.15 Began Wake. 8 Mr Causton's, necessary talk. 8.15 Wake. 9 Prayed; Wake. 9.30 Visited. 12.15 Prayed. 12.30 Slept. 12.45 Visited. 2 Mrs Burnside's, French. 3 Tea, religious talk. 3.30 Mrs Fallowfield, religious talk. 4 Garden with her, religious talk (she much affected!). 4.45 Dr Núñez, necessary talk. 5 Mr Causton's, tea, necessary talk (religious). 6 Necessary business for the burial. 7 Meditated; read Prayers. 8 Buried [Mr John Dearn]; Mrs Burnside's, religious talk (very zealous; convincing). 9 Supper, religious talk. 10.15.

Grace: 7 rating once [8 to 9 pm]; 6 sixteen times; 5 once [5 to 6 am].

[B—But a new hindrance [to admitting Mrs. Williamson to Holy Communion] now occurred: she would not admit herself. Looking over the register, I found she had absented from it five times in April and May only; and in this month, June, four times more, viz., the 11th, 12th, 24th, and 29th. To clear up all which difficulties at once, I determined to speak to her again. Accordingly, as we returned from church,] Sunday, July 3, immediately after the Holy Communion, I reproved Mrs. Williamson for her insincerity and other faults. She absolutely denied that she was in any fault, and was very angry at me for thinking so [E—for telling her of it]. [B—I said, 'Mrs. Williamson, have you any reason to believe that from the day I first saw you till this hour, I have dissembled with you?' She answered, 'Indeed, I don't believe you have. But you seem to think I have dissembled with you.' I told her, I did so, and began to explain with her upon it. But the more I spoke, the more angry she appeared, till after a few minutes she turned about and went abruptly away, thus putting an end to our sixth and last conversation.

[Being unwilling to trust my own judgment, I went to Mr. Burnside, told him the case, and asked how he thought I ought to act. He answered plainly, 'Sir, the case is clear. While things appear to you as they do now, you can't admit her to the Holy Communion. The consequences of rejecting her you know. But be they what they will, that doesn't alter your duty.' Hereon I determined to do what I judged my duty, but with all the mildness and prudence God should give me. And therefore the next day [Monday, July 4] I went once more to Mr. Causton's, to give Mrs. Williamson another opportunity either of clearing herself or owning her fault. But she said nothing at all. Mrs. Causton, indeed, desiring me to take a walk in the garden, talked largely of Sophy's innocence; told me she was exceedingly grieved for what had passed the day before, and added more than once, 'Can't you write to her and tell her what you dislike?' I answered, 'Yes, I will.'] I did so on Tuesday. The effect was not what I expected. However, [E—if she die in her iniquity,] 'I have delivered my own soul' [Ezek. 14:14].

SATURDAY, JULY 2. 4.30 Private prayer; sang. 5 Read Prayers. 5.30 Munster. 6 Mrs Ann, necessary talk (religious). 7 Clement; religious talk. 8 Religious talk; necessary talk (religious) with boys. 9 Necessary talk (religious) with Delamotte; prayed; writ to Mr Baker. 10 Writ. 10.30 Visited. 11.30 Dinner. 12 Germans', necessary talk. 1 Necessary talk (religious). 1.30 Germans. 2 Catechized; religious talk. 3 Slept; visited. 4 Visited. 4.45 Sang. 5 Prayed; sang. 5.45 Tea, religious talk. 6 Religious talk. 6.30 Walked; private prayer. 7 Greek Testament. 7.30 Read Prayers. 8 Mr Hows, etc; (lively zeal).
   Grace: 6 rating thirteen times; 5 four times [5 to 7, 11 am to 2 pm].

SUNDAY, JULY 3. 4.15 Private prayer; sang. 5 Read Prayers (thirty-one there). 6 Tea, religious talk. 7 Meditated upon sermon. 7.30 Fleury. 8.30 Garden; sang. 9 Kempis. 9.30 Private prayer. 10 Dressed; read Prayers. 11 Sermon (fifty-five

[B—But first on Tuesday, July 5, I writ the following note to Mr. Causton:

[Sir,
To this hour you have shown yourself my friend; I ever have and ever shall acknowledge it. And it is my earnest desire that he who hath hitherto given me this blessing would continue it still.

But this cannot be unless you will allow me one request which is not so easy an one as it appears: 'Don't condemn me for doing in the execution of my office what I think it my duty to do.'

If you can prevail upon yourself to allow me this, even when I act without respect of persons, I am persuaded there will never be, at least not long, any misunderstanding between us. For even those who seek it shall, I trust, find no occasion against me, except it be concerning the law of my God.

[An hour or two after, I sent the following note to Mrs. Williamson, which I wrote in the most mild and friendly manner I could, both in pursuance of my resolution to proceed with all mildness, and because (Mrs. Causton told me) she was so much grieved already:

[If the sincerity of friendship is best to be known from the painful offices, then there could not be a stronger proof of mine than that I gave you on Sunday, except this which I am going to give you now, and which you may perhaps equally misinterpret.

---

there), Sacrament. 12 Sacrament. 12.30 Religious talk with Miss Sophy; dinner. 1 Mrs Burnside's, religious talk. 1.45 Necessary business. 2 Religious talk. 2.30 Read Prayers; (extremely hot!). 3.30 Mr Hows, etc. 4 Sang. 4.15 Mrs Mouse, religious talk (not close); tea. 5 Mrs Ann, religious talk. 5.30 Private prayer; prayed. 6 Supper, religious talk. 6.30 Germans'. 7.15 Visited. 7.45 At home, religious talk with Mr Brownfield. 8 Religious talk. 9.15 Prayed.

Grace: 7 rating once [9 to 10 am]; 6 fifteen times; 5 once [4 to 5 pm].

MONDAY, JULY 4. 4 Private prayer; slept; prayed. 5 Read Prayers. 5.30 Necessary business; tea. 6 Tea, religious talk. 6.30 Clement. 9 Sang with Delamotte; Clement. 9.30 Visited. 11.30 Dinner. 12 Slept; visited. 1 Germans. 2 Visited. 3 Visited; Dr Núñez. 4 Fleury. 4.45 Visited. 5 Sang; meditated. 5.30 Mr Causton's, necessary talk (religious); tea. 6 Necessary talk (religious) with Mrs Causton of Miss Sophy. 7 Mrs Burnside's, necessary talk (religious). 7.30 Read Prayers. 8 Mrs Burnside, etc; meditated. 9.20 Prayed.

TUESDAY, JULY 5. 4 Private prayer; prayed. 5 Read Prayers; necessary business. 6 Tea, necessary talk (religious). 7 Writ to Mr Causton. 8 Writ to Miss Sophy. 9 Transcribed. 10 Mr Brown, necessary talk. 11 Germans'. 11.30 Mrs Burnside's, necessary talk of Miss Sophy. 12 Dinner, necessary talk. 1 Germans. 2 Dressed; Mr Bradley's, necessary talk. 3.45 At home; necessary business. 4 Mrs Burnside and Mrs Fallowfield, tea, religious talk. 5.30 Walked

Would you know what I dislike in your past or present behavior? You have always heard my thoughts as freely as you asked them. Nay, much more freely. You know it well. And so you shall do, as long as I can speak or write.

In your present behaviour I dislike, (1) Your neglect of half the Public Service, which no man living can oblige you to; (2) Your neglect of fasting, which you once knew to be a help to the mind, without any prejudice to the body; (3) Your neglect of almost half the opportunities of communicating which you have lately had.

But these things are small in comparison of what I dislike in your past behaviour. For, (1) You told me over and over, you had entirely conquered your inclination for Mr. Mellichamp. Yet at that very time you had not conquered it. (2) You told me frequently, you had no design to marry Mr. Williamson. Yet at the very time you spoke, you had that design. (3) In order to conceal both these things from me, you went through a course of deliberate dissimulation. O how fallen! How changed! Surely there was a time when in Miss Sophy's lips there was no guile.

Own these facts, and own your fault, and you will be in my thoughts as if they had never been. If you are otherwise minded, I shall still be your friend, though I can't expect you should be mine.

To Mrs. Williamson, July 5th

[The next day [July 6], Mr. Causton came to my house with Mr. Parker and Mr. Recorder [Thomas Christie]. He complained I had sent him a letter he could not understand, and added with much warmth, 'How could you possibly entertain such a thought of me as that I should oppose you in executing any part of your office?' I said bluntly, 'Sir, what if I should [believe] it the duty of my office to repel one of your family from the Holy Communion?' He made a large reply, one part of which was, 'If you repel me or my wife, I shall require a legal reason. But I shall trouble myself about none else. Let them look to themselves.']

in garden, religious talk. 6 In the arbour, religious talk. 7 Supper, religious talk. 7.15 Meditated. 7.30 Read Prayers. 8.15 Mrs Burnside, Mrs Fallowfield, etc.
Grace: 6 rating thirteen times; 5 four times [6 to 7 am, noon to 1, 2 to 4 pm].

WEDNESDAY, JULY 6. 4 Private prayer; dressed; prayed with Delamotte. 5 Read Prayers; necessary business. 6 Coffee, religious talk. 6.15 Set out; verse. 7 Verse. 8 Read Archbishop Ussher. 8.15 Thunderbolt; necessary talk (religious); tea. 9 Read Prayers, preached. 10 Set out; verse. 11 Verse. 12.20 Writ verse. 2 Mrs Burnside's, French. 3 Tea, religious talk. 4 At home; Mr Causton's, Christie and Parker, necessary talk (religious); tea. 5 Necessary talk (religious). 5.30 Ate. 6 Meditated; sang; private prayer. 7 Religious talk. 7.30 Read Prayers. 8 Visited; Mr Hows, etc. 8.45 Religious talk. 9.15.
Grace: 6 rating fourteen times; 5 thrice [noon to 1, 3 to 4, 5 to 6 pm].

Thursday, [July] 7. I was unawares engaged in a dispute with Dr. Núñez, a Jew, concerning the Messiah. For this I was afterward much grieved, lest the truth might suffer by my weak defence of it.

Saturday, [July] 9. A Frenchman who had been taken prisoner by the Chickasaws, and lived among them for some months, gave us a particular and [E—strange but] (it seems) just account of many things which have been very variously related. He said.

A few years past the Chickasaws and French were good friends. The French were then mingled with the Natchez Indians, whom they used as slaves, sending them where they pleased, beating them frequently [E—continually], and taking away their wives or children continually. The Natchez at last made a general rising, and took all the French among them prisoners. But soon after, a French army set upon them, killed many, and made the rest slaves. Among those who were killed were some Chickasaws, whose death the Chickasaw nation resented; and watching their opportunity, fired a volley of shot into a French boat, which was going by them [B—through their

---

Thursday, July 7. 4.15 Meditated upon sermon. 5 Read Prayers, Sermon. 6 Mr Causton, Parker, and Gronau, tea, necessary talk (religious). 8 Necessary talk; necessary business; Clement. 9 Clement. 12 Dinner. 12.30 Clement. 1 Visited. 3.15 Dr Núñez (could not answer him!). 4.45 Read. 5 Private prayer; sang. 5.45 Prayed with them. 6 Tea, religious talk; Mrs Mouse came and Mrs Ann, necessary talk (religious). 7 Walked; meditated. 7.30 Read Prayers; (lively zeal; convincing). 8.15 Sang; visited. 9 Ate, religious talk. 9.30 Prayed.
Grace: 7 rating once [5 to 6 pm]; 6 fifteen times; 5 twice [7 to 9 am].

Friday, July 8. 4 Private prayer; dressed; prayed. 5 Read Prayers. 5.45 Coffee, religious talk. 6.15 Writ to Mr Garden. 7 Writ to Mr Butler. 7.3 Wake. 8 Wake; writ diary. 9 Writ verse; dressed. 9.45 Visited. 11.45 Germans (sins!!!). 12.15 Swept. 12.45 Private Prayer. 1 Sang; meditated; private prayer. 2 Mrs Burnside's, French. 3 Tea, religious talk. (necessary). 4 Visited. 5 At home; Mrs Ann and Mrs Fallowfield, tea, religious talk. 6 Religious talk; prayed with her. 6.30 Walked; private prayer; meditated. 7 Meditated. 7.30 Read Prayers. 8.15 Mrs Burnside, etc. 9 Mrs Burnside's, religious talk, supper. 10 Religious talk (necessary). 10.30.
Grace: 6 rating sixteen times; 5 twice [11 to noon, 3 to 4 pm].

Saturday, July 9. 4.30 Private prayer. 5 Read Prayers (twenty-three there); tea, religious talk. 6 Religious talk. 6.30 Necessary business. 7 At the court. 8 Court. 10.30 Mrs Fallowfield's, religious talk. 11 Religious talk. 12 At home; dinner. 1 Germans'. 2 Catechized. 3 Visited. 3.45 At Mr Emery's, necessary talk. 4 The Frenchman, necessary talk (religious). 5 Set out; private prayer. 5.30 At home; Mrs Lacy. 5.35 Writ diary. 6 Tea, religious talk. 6.15 Necessary talk (religious). 6.45 Walked; meditated. 7 Meditated; sang. 7.30 Read Prayers. 8.15 Mr Hows, etc. 8.45 Verses.
Grace: 6 rating fifteen times; 5 twice [6 to 7 am, noon to 1 pm].

country] laden with ammunition to the northward, killed all the men but two, took those prisoners, and seized upon the lading. The French resolved upon revenge, and orders were given for many Indians and several parties of white men to rendezvous on the 26th of March, 1736, near one of the Chickasaw towns. The first of these, consisting of fifty men, came thither some days before the time. They stayed there till the 24th, but none came to join them. On the 25th they were attacked by two hundred Chickasaws [E—(who are about nine hundred fighting men in all)], whom they attempted to break through. Five or six and twenty of them did so; the rest were taken prisoners. The prisoners were sent two or three to a town to be burnt; only the commanding officer, and one or two more, were put to death on the place of the engagement, and I and one more were spared [E—saved by the warrior who took us].

The manner of burning them [E—the rest] was, by holding lighted canes to their arms or legs or several parts of their bodies, and then for a while taking them away, lest they should die too soon. They likewise stuck burning splinters of wood into their flesh all round, in which condition they kept them from morning till evening. But they commonly beat them before they burn them. I saw the priest that was with us carried to be burnt, and from head to foot he was all black [E—as black as your hat] with the blows they had given him.

I asked him as to their manner of life. He said, 'They do nothing but eat and drink and smoke from morning to night, and almost from night to morning. For they frequently rise at any hour of the night when they wake, and after eating and drinking as much as they can, go to sleep again.'

Monday, July 11. Mrs. Williamson miscarried: as Mrs. Causton told one, because of my chiding her eight days before; as she told another,

---

Sunday, July 10. 4.15 Private prayer (colic!). 5 Read Prayers (ill). 6.15 Tea, religious talk. 7 Fleury. 9 Meditated; transcribed. 10 Dressed; [read Prayers] c c c, sang. 11 Sermon (sixty there), p, Sacrament, p b, sang. 12 Fleury. 12.15 Mr Bradley's, dinner. 1.30 Catechized. 2 Necessary business. 2.30 Read Prayers. 3.30 Mr Hows, etc. 4 Read; prayed; sang. 4.40 Slept. 5 Tea, religious talk. 6 Walked; meditated; sang. 6.45 Germans'; (lively zeal). 7.15 Religious talk with Delamotte; Mr Burnside's, religious talk. 8 Religious talk. 9.15 Prayed.

Grace: 6 rating fifteen times; 5 twice [6 to 7 am, 1 to 2 pm].

Monday, [July] 11. 4 Private prayer; prayed; dressed. 5 Read Prayers (thirty-two there); tea, religious talk. 6.15 Polycarp. 8 The same. 9 Fleury. 10 Charles Charles [*sic*] came, French. 11 French. 11.45 Dinner. 12.15 Walked. 1 Peter Emery's, necessary talk (religious). 1.30 Germans'. 2 Visited. 3 Dr Núñez'. 4 Mr West's, necessary talk (religious; they seemed affected). 5 Writ diary; private because of my unkind letter; as she herself said, because of the hurry and concern which Mr. Williamson's illness threw her into.

Tuesday 12. I read Dr. Humphreys' *Account* of the proceedings of the Society of Propagating [i.e., the Propagation of] the Gospel; concerning which I could not but observe, (1) That nine out of ten [E—a great majority] of the missionaries sent into America have died before the end of the fourth year; (2) That out of that vast number not above two (or three at most) are mentioned who were not 'well spoken of by all men'. If these then were the disciples of Christ, the scandal of the cross is ceased! Concerning the conversion of the heathen, I could not but say in my letter to Dr. Humphreys:

> Where is the seed sown, the *sanguis martyrum* ['the blood of the martyrs']? Do we hear of any who have sealed the faith with their blood in all this vast continent? Or do we read of any church flourishing in any age or nation without the seed first sown there? Give me leave, sir, to speak my thoughts freely. When God shall put it into the hearts of some of his servants, whom he hath already delivered from earthly hopes and fears, to join hand in hand in this labour of love; when out of these he shall have chosen one or more to magnify him in the sight of the heathen by dying, not with a stoical or Indian indifference, but blessing and praying for their murderers, and praising God in the midst of the flames, with joy unspeakable and full of glory; then the rest, 'waxing bold by their sufferings' [see Phil. 1:14], shall go forth in the name of the Lord God, and by the power of his might cast down every high thing that exalteth itself against the faith of Christ. Then shall ye see Satan, the grand ruler of this New World, as lightning falls from heaven! Then even these lands shall be full of the knowledge of the Lord, as the waters cover the seas.

---

prayer; prayed. 6 Supper. 6.30 Walked; private prayer. 7 Meditated. 7.30 Read Prayers. 8.15 Mrs Burnside, etc; writ diary.

Grace: 6 rating fifteen times; 5 twice [10 to 11 am, noon to 1 pm].

TUESDAY, JULY 12. 4 Private prayer; dressed. 5 Read Prayers (thirty-two there); Munster. 6.15 Mrs Musgrove and Bush; tea, mostly religious talk. 7 Mostly religious talk. 7.20 Polycarp. 8 The same. 9 Fleury. 10 Dressed; writ diary; Charles came, French. 11 Buried; Germans. 12 Dinner, religious talk. 12.30 Set out, read Humphreys' *Account*. 1 Read. 2.45 Mr Burnside's, necessary talk. 3 Necessary talk; tea. 4 Necessary talk. 4.15 Set out, read. 5 Read, ended it. 6 At home; tea, religious talk. 7 Buried; religious talk. 7.30 Read Prayers. 8.15 Mrs Burnside, etc. religious talk.

WEDNESDAY, JULY 13. 4.15 Private prayer; prayed. 5 Read Prayers (twenty-five there). 5.45 Coffee, religious talk. 6 Writ hymns. 7 Spanish. 7.30 Hymns. 8 Hymns; Mrs Ann, necessary talk. 9 Sang with Delamotte; hymns. 10 Jacob Charles, French. 10.30 Visited. 11.45 Germans'. 12 Visited. 1 Dressed. 1.15

Sunday, July 17. I had occasion to make a very unusual trial of the temper of Mr. Bolzius, pastor of the Salzburgers, in which he behaved with such lowliness and meekness as became a disciple of Jesus Christ.

Germans'. 2 Mrs Burnside's, French. 3 Tea, good talk. 4 At home; ate. 4.30 Walked. 5 Private Prayer. 5.30 Lot, religious talk; private prayer. 6 Necessary talk; private prayer. 6.30 Sang; meditated. 7 Meditated. 7.30 Read Prayers. 8 Mr Hows, etc, necessary talk (religious); writ diary.

Grace: 7 rating once [4 to 5 am]; 6 fourteen times; 5 twice [3 to 5 pm]..

Thursday, July 14. 4 Private prayer; dressed. 5 Read Prayers (twenty-five there). 5.30 Tea, religious talk. 6.15 Hymns. 6 Mr Causton, Mr Bolzius, tea, necessary talk. 10 Hymns. 12 Germans'. 12.15 Dinner. 12.45 Hymns. 1 Germans'; hymns. 1 Visited. 2.45 Hymns. 3 Dr Núñez'. 3.30 Hymns. 5 Sang; private prayer. 6 Sang; Bolzius; tea, religious talk. 7 Religious talk; meditated. 7.30 Read Prayers. 8.15 Mr Bolzius, religious talk. 9.30 Prayed.

Grace: 6 rating sixteen times; 5 twice [9 to 10 am, noon to 1].

Friday, July 15. 4 Private prayer; prayed. 5 Read Prayers (twenty-nine there); writ diary; Hebrew. 6 Mr Bolzius; tea, necessary talk. 6.15 Hymns. 9 Sang with Delamotte; hymns. 10 Hymns 10.30 Dressed; hymns. 11 Jacob Charles, French. 11.30 Hymns. 12 Read with boys; prayed. 12.30 Hymns. 1 Germans'. 2 Mrs Burnside's, religious talk, French. 3 Tea, religious talk. 4 Dr Núñez'. 4.40 Hymns. 5 Necessary talk with Mr Brown. 5.30 Sang. 6 Mr Bolzius, tea, religious talk; buried. 7 Meditated. 7.30 Read Prayers. 8.15 Mrs Burnside. 8.45 Mrs Burnside's, religious talk. 9 Supper, religious talk. 10 Prayed.

Grace: 6 rating sixteen times; 5 twice [6 to 7, 11 to noon].

Saturday, July 16. 4.15 Private prayer. 4.30 Prayed; dressed. 5 [Read Prayers] p s x p s p t b. 5.45 Necessary talk. 6 Tea, religious talk. 6.30 Hymns. 7.15 Mr Bradley, necessary talk. 8 Necessary talk (religious). 9.45 Hymns. 10 Jacob Charles, French. 10.30 The Frenchman, necessary talk. 11 Mrs Brown, necessary talk; dinner. 12 Hymns. 12.15 Mrs Gilbert, etc; sang; prayed; sang; religious talk. 1 Catechized. 1.45 Religious talk with Leah [Minas?]. 2 Hymns. 3 Visited Mrs Causton's, necessary talk (religious). 4 Mrs West, good talk (necessary). 5 At home; tea, religious talk; meditated. 6 Walked; meditated. 7 Read Prayers. 7.45 Set out, necessary talk (religious). 8 Religious talk; sang; religious talk. 9 Religious talk. 10 Cowpen; christened. 10.30 Set out, necessary talk (useful and religious). 1 At home.

Sunday, July 17. 4.30 Private prayer; dressed. 5 Read Prayers (twenty-eight there). 6 Tea, religious talk; garden, necessary talk (religious) with Mr Bolzius. 7 Necessary talk (religious). 8 Religious talk of the Communion (lively zeal). 9.30 Meditated. 10 Meditated; read Prayers (fifty there). 11 Sermon; Sacrament. 12.15 Dinner. 1 Slept. 1.15 Read Prayers (fifty-five there). 3.45 Mr Hows, etc. 4 Prayed; sang; read. 4.45 Mrs Fallowfield, religious talk; tea. 5 Garden, religious talk. 6 Religious talk. 6.45 Supper, religious talk. 7.15 With Mrs Ann (she quite open!). 8 Religious talk. 9.30 At home.

Grace: 6 rating eighteen times.

Monday, July 18. 4.15 Private prayer. 5 Read Prayers (twenty-six there); tea,

Saturday, [July] 23. The strange esteem which Mr. Causton seemed to show for us, by which means we had nothing without but ease and plenty, occasioned my expressing myself thus in a letter to a friend: 'How to attain to being crucified with Christ I find not, being in a

_____

religious talk (necessary). 6 Necessary talk (religious). 7 Fleury. 9 Necessary business. 10 Visited. 12 Spanish; dinner, necessary talk (religious). 1 Will Williamson, necessary talk (religious). 1.30 Germans'; Mr Charles sent for me. 2 Mr Bradley, etc, necessary talk (they not very affected!). 3 They [had] necessary talk; he went. 4 Tea, necessary talk (religious; all civil); prayed for Miss Sophy. 5 Sang; private prayer for Miss Sophy; sang; (lively zeal; convincing). 6 Tea, religious talk; meditated. 7 Verse. 7.30 Read Prayers; Mrs Burnside, etc; verse. 9.15 Prayed.

Grace: 7 rating once [5 to 6 pm]; 6 eleven times; 5 four times [5 to 7, 9 to 10 am, noon to 1 pm].

TUESDAY, JULY 19. 4 Private prayer; prayed. 5 Read Prayers; Hebrew. 6 Tea, religious talk; hymns. 7 Hymns; writ diary. 10 Visited. 12 Dinner, religious talk. 1 Hymns; visited. 3 Hymns. 4.30 Mr D[ean?] and Mrs Causton, tea, religious talk (necessary). 5 They went; sang; private prayer. 6 Supper, religious talk; meditated. 7 Read Prayers. 8 Sang; with Mrs Gilbert, religious talk; Mrs Ann, religious talk. 9 Religious talk; prayed. 10.

WEDNESDAY, JULY 20. 4 Private prayer; slept. 5 Read Prayers; tea. 6 Hymns. 8 Mr Jones, mostly religious talk; hymns. 9 Hymns. 11 Visited. 12.30 Hymns. 1 Necessary talk. 2.15 Mrs Burnside's, French. 3 Tea, religious talk. 4 Dr Núñez'. 5 Mrs Fallowfield, religious talk. 6 Tea, religious talk. 7 Meditated; read Prayers. 8 Mr Hows, etc. 8.45 Heard their complaints. 9.30 Prayed.

[THURSDAY] JULY 21. 4 Private prayer; prayed. 5 Read Prayers (thirty-five there); tea, religious talk. 6.30 Hymns. 7 Necessary talk (religious) with Mrs Ann. 8.45 Hymns. 9.30 Jacob Charles and the Frenchman, talked French. 10.15 Hymns. 10.45 Visited. 11 Visited. 11.30 Ended hymns. 12 Dinner. 12.45 Writ diary; dressed. 1 German; necessary talk. 2 German. 2.30 Visited. 3 Núñez'. 4 Walked with Delamotte, religious talk; lot. 5 Walked; read; religious talk. 6 Tea, religious talk. 6.30 Writ diary. 7 Sang; meditated. 7.30 Read Prayers. 8 Sang; necessary talk (religious); religious talk (necessary). 9.15 Prayed.

Grace: 6 rating sixteen times; 5 once [twice, noon to 1, 8 to 9 pm].

[FRIDAY] JULY 22. 4 Private prayer; prayed. 5 Read Prayers; tea. 6.15 Necessary business; necessary talk. 7 Writ to Dr Humphreys; necessary talk (religious). 10 Dressed; visited Mrs Fallowfield. 12.45 Writ to Dr Humphreys. 1.45 Visited. 2 visited. 2.30 Mrs Burnside's. 3 Tea, religious talk. 4 Necessary talk (religious). 5 Sang; meditated; sang. 6 Sang; meditated; sang. 7 Meditated; read Prayers. 8 Mrs Burnside, etc. 8.40 Mrs Burnside's, religious talk. 9 Supper; mostly religious talk. 9.45.

SATURDAY, JULY 23. 4.15 Meditated; private prayer. 5 Read Prayers (thirty-four there). 5.30 Tea, religious talk. 6 Writ to Dr. Cutler. 8 Writ to the Society for Propagating the Gospel. 10 Visited. 12 Dinner, religious talk. 1 Fleury. 2 Catechized; visited. 4.20 Fleury. 5 Sang; meditated; sang. 6 Tea, religious talk.

condition which I neither desired nor expected in America—in ease and honour and abundance. A strange school for him who has but one business, Γυμνάζειν εἀυτὸν πρὸς ἐυσέβειαν ['to exercise himself in godliness'; cf. 1 Tim. 4:7].

Wednesday, July 27. In the evening I met once more with that good soldier of Jesus Christ, Mr. Spangenberg. Saturday the 30th, I began taking a more exact account of my parishioners, by going from house to house [E—to every house]. By the best computation I can make, there are now in the town of Savannah five hundred and eighteen souls, one hundred and forty-nine of whom are under sixteen years of age. About one hundred and eighty of the adults are, or are called, of the Church of England.

6.30 Meditated; sang. 7 Meditated; sang. 7.30 Read Prayers. 8 Mr Hows, etc. 8.45 Necessary talk (religious) with Mrs Ann. 9.30 Prayed.

Sunday, July 24. 4.30 Dressed; meditated. 5 Read Prayers (thirty-one there). 6 Tea, religious talk. 7 Meditated upon sermon; religious talk. 10 [Read Prayers] sang, c c c p s, Sermon (sixty-four there). 11 Sermon, p p, Sacrament, s p b. 12.30 Dinner, religious talk. 1 Religious talk. 1.30 Catechized. 2.15 Meditated; read Prayers (seventy there). 3.30 Mr Hows, etc. 4.30 Religious talk. 5 Tea, religious talk; religious talk with many. 6 Germans'. 6.45 Necessary talk (religious); (lively zeal). 7 At home, religious talk (lively zeal). 8 Religious talk (necessary). 9 Prayed.

Monday July [25]. 4 Private prayer; prayed. 5 Read Prayers (thirty-six there). 6 Tea, religious talk. 7 Visited. 8 Mrs Anderson's, necessary talk (religious). 9 Visited. 9.30 At home; meditated. 10.30 Read Prayers (thirty-six there). 12.30 Dinner. 1 Writ notes. 2 Visited. 3.15 Dr. Núñez'. 4 Writ notes. 4.30 Mr Gough, religious talk; tea. 5 Tea with Delamotte, religious talk. 6 Mrs Fallowfield came, religious talk. 6.45 Religious talk with Mrs Ann; meditated. 7 Germans'; read Prayers. 8.15 Sang; writ diary. 9.

Tuesday, July 26. 4 Private prayer; prayed. 5 Read Prayers; tea, religious talk. 7 Transcribed letter. 8 Mr Causton, good talk (necessary, religious). 9 Visited. 11 Writ notes. 12 Germans'. 12.30 Dinner. 1 Germans'. 2 Visited. 4.30 Mr Causton's, necessary talk; tea. 6 At home; Mr Anderson, religious talk. 7 Germans'; read Prayers. 8 Mrs Burnside; supper, necessary talk (religious). 9.30 Writ diary.

Wednesday, July 27. 4.30 Private prayer; dressed. 5 Read Prayers (forty there); tea, religious talk; Wake. 7 Wake; dressed. 10 Visited. 12 Germans; necessary business; necessary talk. 1 Writ notes. 2 Visited. 2.15 Mrs Burnside's. 3 Tea, religious talk. 4 Dr Núñez'. 4.30 Mrs Pensyre, religious talk. 5 Ate. 5.30 Walked; meditated; sang. 6 Meditated. 6.30 Mr Anderson, mostly religious talk. 7 Germans'; read Prayers. 8 Mr Turner, etc. 8.40 Meditated. 9.30 Mr Spangenberg came.

Thursday, July 28. 4 Private prayer; prayed. 5 Read Prayers (twenty-eight there); tea, religious talk. 6 Began translating *Moeurs des chrétiens*. 10 Jacob

Sunday, [July] 31. Having been long in doubt concerning the principles of the Moravian Brethren, at Mr. Spangenberg's desire, I proposed to them the following queries, to each of which is subjoined the substance of their answer:

1. What do you mean by conversion? 'The passing from darkness into light, and from the power of Satan unto God' (Acts 26:18).
2. Is it commonly wrought at once, or by degrees? 'The design of passing thus from darkness into light is sometimes wrought in a moment (Acts 16:27), but the passage itself is gradual' (Acts 2:37).
3. Ought we so to expect the Holy Ghost to convert either our own or our neighbour's souls as to neglect any outward means? 'Many things are mentioned in Scripture as helps to an entire conversion: so, reading the Scripture (2 Chr. 34:14), hearing it (Acts 16:14), fasting (Joel 2:12), self-examination (Lam. 3:40), the instructions of experienced persons (Acts 2:37), fervent prayer. None therefore ought to neglect any of these when it is in their power to use them.'
4. Ought we so to expect the Holy Ghost to interpret Scripture to us as to neglect any outward means? Particularly, inquiring into the sense of the Ancient Church? 'The Scripture is clear, in all things necessary to be known. And the more obscure parts of it will be made

---

Charles, French. 10.30 Visited (convincing; lively zeal). 12 Germans'; dinner. 1 With Spangenberg, religious talk. 3.15 At home; Mr Anderson; tea, religious talk. 6 Ate. 6.15 Sang; private prayer. 7 Germans'; read Prayers. 8 Mrs Burnside, etc. 8.45 Religious talk; read.

FRIDAY, [JULY] 29. 4 Private prayer; prayed. 5 Read Prayers (thirty there); tea. 6 Fleury. 10 Visited. 12 Germans'; writ diary; religious talk with John. 1 Writ Spangenberg and Töltschig. 2.15 Mrs Burnside's. 3 Tea, religious talk. 4 Religious talk with Delamotte. 4.30 Necessary talk (religious). 5 Walked; meditated; sang. 7 Germans'; read Prayers. 8 Sang; ate, religious talk. 8.30.

SATURDAY, JULY 30. 4 Private prayer; prayed. 5 Read Prayers (thirty there); tea, religious talk. 6 Account of parish. 8 Mr Bradley, necessary talk. 9 Germans', necessary talk (religious). 11.30 Sang, etc. 12.15 Dinner, religious talk. 1 Catechized. 2 Visited. 3.45 At home; necessary talk (religious). 4 Writ for Germans. 5 Tea, necessary talk. 6 Walked; meditated; sang. 7 Germans'; read Prayers. 8 Mrs Gilbert, etc. 8.30 Mr Bradley's, prayed. 9 Made his will. 10.30 At home.

SUNDAY, JULY 31. 4.30 Private prayer; dressed. 5 Read Prayers (thirty-one there). 6.30 Tea, religious talk. 7.30 Writ for Germans. 9 Meditated upon sermon. 10 Religious talk; read Prayers. 11 Sermon. 12 Sacrament. 12.15 Dinner, religious talk. 1 Catechized. 2 Slept; read Prayers. 3.45 Mrs Gilbert, etc; (Miss Sophy mis[carried, on July 11]). 4.30 Tea, religious talk. 5.30 Walked; meditated; private prayer. 6.30 Buried; necessary talk (religious). 7.45 Mrs Burnside; supper, mostly religious talk. 9.30 Prayed.

plainer by prayer, meditation, temptation, and experience, and by comparing them with the plain parts. We wish the writings of the Ancient Church, especially of the apostolic age, were more valued, and neither despise nor neglect them, where there is opportunity of reading and comparing them with the Scripture.'

5. What is the Visible Church? 'Where there is a society of men united together, in apostolical order and discipline, and endued with the spirit of Christ, there is a Visible Church. Such was once that of Rome, Corinth, and others.'

6. What is faith? ''Ελπιζομένων ὑπόστασις, ἔλεγχος πραγμάτων οὐ Βλεπομένων' ['The substance of things hoped for, the evidence of things not seen'; Heb. 11:1].

7. Does it precede or follow the use of the means of grace? 'It (ordinarily) cometh by hearing.'

8. Is faith perfected by good works, or only shown thereby? 'By works faith is made perfect.'

9. Do you believe those called Athanasian, the Nicene, and the Apostles' Creed to be agreeable to Scripture? 'We do, if they are rightly understood.'

10. Do you believe the Mosaic precepts concerning unclean meats to be binding? 'No further than is expressed, Acts 15'.

11. Is it lawful to bear arms, or to defend one's life by force? 'No.'

12. To put offenders to death? 'Yes.'

13. To go to law? 'No.'

14. To be a magistrate? 'Yes.'

15. To swear when required by a magistrate? No answer (their judgment is, no).

16. Is celibacy a state more advantageous for holiness than marriage? 'Yes, to them who are able to receive it.'

17. Are the ministrations of a man not episcopally ordained valid? [No answer.]

18. Does the wickedness of a man episcopally ordained make his ministrations invalid? 'I dare neither affirm nor deny either of these questions universally.'

19. About what age do you commonly begin to instruct children in religion? 'From their mother's womb.'

20. About what age do you commonly confirm, and begin to instruct and prepare them for the Lord's Supper? 'We instruct children in Christianity from their infancy, but so as to regard their understanding rather than memory. I have known a child of eight years old admitted to communicate, and a man of seventy not yet admitted.'

21. Is the Lord's Supper a means of grace? 'Yes.'

22. About what age do you commonly admit children to join with

you in Public Prayer? 'We do not so much regard the natural as the spiritual life.'

23. What qualifications do you require in them before you admit them to communicate? 'To know, to love, and to follow Christ.'

24. Are all the brethren and sisters constant in attending the Public Prayers? 'Everyone may be present at the daily prayers, but [one] is not compelled.'

25. When any are absent, are they themselves or the rulers of the church the judges of the cause of their absence? 'The overseers of the church inquire the cause of them, and admonish them, if they suspect slackness.'

26. Do you prefer extemporary to set forms of prayer in public? 'Our hymns are forms of prayer. For the rest, everyone speaks as he is moved by the Holy Ghost.'

27. How do you interpret that command of our Lord, 'Ye, when ye pray, say, Our Father'? 'As a command to avoid vain repetition in prayer.'

28. Do your Public Prayers contain the four parts required by St. Paul (1 Timothy, chap. 2, ver. 1)? 'No.'

29. Have you any joint intercession for enemies? 'No, but we pray daily for all men.'

30. Of the few prayers recorded in the New Testament, are the greater part addressed to Christ, or to the Father through Christ? 'We believe the Son equal with the Father.'

31. Have you any fixed or joint fasts? 'No, but we appoint them frequently.'

Monday, August 1. I set out with Mr. Spangenberg for Ebenezer. In the evening we came to the Old Town, which is more pleasantly situated than any settlement I have yet seen in Georgia. But the soil is exceedingly barren [E adds—sand], and likewise liable to be overflowed upon any sudden or violent rain. New Ebenezer is about six miles distant from it, lying upon a high bluff, close to the river [E adds—Savannah]. Here is some fruitful land, but not much, the pineland bearing scarce anything. The industry of the poor people is quite surprising; their huts are neatly and regularly built, and there is not a foot of land between them but is improved to the best advantage, and planted with what is suitable to it. On one side of the town is a pretty large field of Indian corn; on the other are several well-cleared plantations [E—belonging to particular persons, pretty well cleared, fenced, and planted]. All which

---

MONDAY, AUGUST 1. 4.15 Private prayer; prayed. 5 Read Prayers; tea, necessary talk. 6.30 Dressed; Fleury. 8.30 Set out with Spangenberg, etc, necessary talk (religious). 10.30 Landed at Augustin's; walked, necessary talk (religious). 6 Old Ebenezer, necessary talk (religious) with boys. 7 Set out, necessary talk (religious). 9 New Ebenezer, necessary talk (religious). 11.

together one would not imagine [E—scarce think possible] to be the work of such a handful of people in one year.

I was much pleased with the plainness of dress of Mrs. Bolzius and Mrs. Gronau; but more with what little I saw of their behaviour. It appeared to be their delight as well as their custom to be servants of all. The hospitality, openness, and piety of their husbands could not be less [E—was equally] agreeable.

They proposed to Mr. Spangenberg in the most mild and friendly manner the objections they had against him. Most of them fall in with the preceding questions. The rest, relating chiefly to the Count's exposition of Scripture and method of Public Prayer, fully convinced me that he likewise is but a man [E—and not either wiser or better than the apostles]. O thou Giver of every good and perfect gift, how will men so full of faith and love adorn the gospel of thy Christ, when thou shalt give them a due reverence for the good old paths, and the openness and plainness of speech which he used in whose lips was no guile! [E reads—which becometh his disciples!]

Wednesday, August 3. We returned to Savannah. On Friday the 5th, I gave Mr. Causton an account of our journey. On Sunday the 7th, I repelled Mrs. Williamson from the Holy Communion, for the reasons specified in my letter of July 5th, as well as for not giving me notice of her design to communicate, after having intermitted it for some time. I foresaw the consequences well; but remembered the promise in the Epistle for the day. 'God is faithful, who will not suffer you to be

---

TUESDAY, AUGUST 2. 5.30 Dressed; walked with Bolzius, religious talk. 8 At home; tea, religious talk. 10 Sang with Gronau; slept. 11 Religious talk with Bolzius and Spangenberg. 11.30 Dinner. 12.30 Religious talk with them. 4 They [had] necessary talk (religious). 5 Set out, necessary talk (religious) with Spangenberg and Gronau. 8 At Purrysburg; supper, religious talk. 9 Slept.

WEDNESDAY, AUGUST 3. 12 [midnight] Set out; steered. 1.15 Slept. 3.30 Steered. 4 Rowed. 6 At home; tea, religious talk. 7 Religious talk with Delamotte. 8 Visited. 10 Slept; writ diary. 12 Germans'. 1 Read notes. 1.45 Germans', religious talk; ate. 3 Mrs Burnside's, religious talk; tea. 5 At home; Greek Testament; meditated; Gronau came; tea, religious talk. 6.15 Walked; meditated; sang. 7 Germans'. 7.45 Read Prayers. 8.15 Mrs Gilbert, etc; writ diary. 9.

THURSDAY, AUGUST 4. 4 Private Prayer; dressed; slept. 5 Read Prayers (thirty-three there); tea, religious talk. 6 Fleury. 7 Walked; worked; Greek Testament. 9 At home; Greek Testament. 11.30 Germans'; dinner, religious talk. 1 Greek Testament; Germans. 2 Visited. 3.30 Dr Núñez'. 4 At home; Mrs Fallowfield, etc; tea, religious talk. 5 Religious talk with her. 5.30 Visited. 5.45 Greek Testament. 6 Supper, religious talk. 6.30 Walked; meditated. 7 Germans'; read Prayers. 8 Mrs Burnside and Fallowfield; Germans. 9.30 Prayed.

tempted above that ye are able, but will with the temptation also make a way to escape, that ye may be able to bear it' [1 Cor. 10:13].

[B—From [July 6] till August 7 (part of which she was ill), neither Mrs. Williamson spoke to me nor I to her; though she had several opportunities of doing it. So that I was surprised as well as much grieved to be then reduced to the necessity of telling her in the church (indeed so softly that none heard it but herself, and in the mildest manner I was master of), 'I can't administer the Holy Communion to you before I have spoken with you.' Behold how much matter a small fire kindleth!

[From Mrs. Williamson's marriage till April 12, on which day I set out for Charleston, few days passed in which Mr. or Mrs. Causton was not at mine, or I at Mr. Causton's house. It was the same thing from my return thence till August 7th. And, whether I was present or absent, no terms of respect were judged too high for me, no professions of friendship too strong. Indeed, I was often utterly ashamed at them, especially at those which Mrs. Causton used on all occasions. March 29, drinking tea at my house, after talking at least an hour and a half in praise of Mrs. Williamson, she said (and to the same effect she spoke two or three months after, both at her house in town and at Hogstead, 'Why couldn't you have told me you liked her? Oh! I should have been too happy!' And on Monday, May 23, speaking at Hogstead on the same head, after expressing several times her wish that I had married her, she added, 'What could I do more? I bid you take her, take her away with ye.' I answered, 'Madam, I told her she was welcome to my house.' She said again, 'Ay, but you didn't take her.'

[In the beginning of June, I was occasionally saying to Mr. Causton, 'I find, sir, people now speak to me of you more freely than before Miss Sophy's marriage. But I seldom think it worth my while to hear them.' He said, 'Indeed I think it would. I wish you would hear all they have to say. And what if you should *seem* to be of their opinion?' I was shocked at the thought, and spoke a few words, to which there was no reply. Thursday, June 9, I told him several things I heard, which he bore with tolerable calmness. But on Saturday, June 11, when I spoke again on the same head, he turned full upon me, told me he didn't expect such usage from me of all men, reproached me for taking part with his enemies, meddling with things foreign to my office, making parties, and inflaming things instead of composing them. Yet in three or four days the storm blew over, and he behaved to me as before. July 6th he used a little sharpness again. But that too ended in perfect harmony. Accordingly, July 7th I breakfasted with him; the 14th he drank tea with me, as did Mrs. Causton on the 16th. On the 18th he sent for me, and I stayed with him near four hours. The 19th they both drank tea at my house. A day or two [later] I offered mine and Mr. Delamotte's service, to transcribe for him anything which required haste, or which he could not trust to common transcribers. The 26th he came to my house, told me he would accept of my kind offer, and desire[d] Mr. Delamotte to write some accounts for him. After some other conversation he began to complain very bitterly against Mr. Williamson. He added, 'Since happiness is the end of marriage, where that can't be attained, the marriage is certainly null and void, and consequently both parties at liberty to marry where they can be happy. Why now,' says he, 'there is poor Sophy. She can never be happy with that man—.' I cut him short by saying, 'I grant unhappy couples are at liberty to live asunder. But not to marry elsewhere. There is no law of God or man which will justify that.' He answered, 'If there is not a law for it, there ought to be, that the community may not lose so many children.'

[In the afternoon I went to him to fix the time and manner of our journey to Ebenezer. He first proposed setting out with me that night, but afterward desired to put it off till Monday. On Sunday evening (the 31st) he came to my house, and said business prevented his going, but he had sent his horse for me, and desired I would not think of walking. After my return, on Friday, August 5, I waited on Mr. Causton and gave him an account of my journey. And thus far there was no complaint, but I was received by them all as one who had done all things well.

[On Sunday evening (the 7th) Mrs. Williamson, in conversation with Mrs. Burnside, expressed much anger at my repelling her from the Holy Communion. Mrs. Burnside told her, 'You was much to blame, after receiving that letter from Mr. Wesley, to offer yourself at the Table before you had cleared yourself to him. But you may easily put an end to this, by going to Mr. Wesley now, and clearing yourself of what you are charged with.' She replied, 'No, I will not show such a meanness of spirit as to speak to him about it myself, but somebody else shall.'

FRIDAY, AUGUST 5. 4 Private prayer; sang. 5 Read Prayers; tea, religious talk. 6 Greek Testament; Mr Causton's, necessary talk. 7 Walked; Greek Testament; worked. 8.45 Greek Testament. 9.30 Visited. 11.45 Germans'. 12.30 Greek Testament; Fleury. 2 Mrs Burnside's, French. 3 Tea, religious talk. 4 Dr Núñez'. 5 Walked; Greek Testament; sang. 6.45 Germans'. 7.30 Read Prayers. 8.15 Mrs Burnside. 8.45 Visited. 9 Mrs Burnside, religious talk. 10.30.

SATURDAY, AUGUST 6. 4.30 Private prayer; sang. 5 Read Prayers (twenty there); tea; Mr Spangenberg, religious talk (clear, lively zeal). 7 Fleury. 9 Sang with Delamotte; visited. 10.30 Read German. 11.15 Slept. 11.30 Writ diary; Germans'. 12 Dinner, religious talk. 1 Read German. 3 Necessary business. 4.45 Meditated. 5.15 Mr Spangenberg, religious talk; tea. 6 Mr Brownfield, Mrs Ann, religious talk (lively zeal). 7 Germans'; read Prayers. 8.15 Mrs Gilbert, etc. 9 Spangenberg, religious talk. 9.30 Mrs Fallowfield, necessary talk (religious). 10.45.

SUNDAY, AUGUST 7. 4.30 Private prayer; dressed. 5 Read Prayers. 6.15 Spangenberg and Eckstein, tea, religious talk. 9.30 Meditated upon sermon. 10.30 Read Prayers, Sermon (sixty there). 11.30 Sacrament, Miss Sophy

[The next day, August 8, the following warrant was issued out by Mr. Recorder:

[Georgia
Savannah S[essions]s
To all Constables, Tithingmen, and others, whom these may concern:
You, and each of you, are hereby required to take the body of John Wesley, Clerk;
And bring him before one of the bailiffs of the said town, to answer the complaint of William Williamson and Sophia his wife, for defaming the said Sophia and refusing to administer to her the sacrament of the Lord's Supper in a public congregation without cause; by which the said William Williamson is damaged one thousand pounds sterling. And for so doing this is your warrant, certifying what you are to do in the premises.
Given under my hand and seal the 8th day of August, *Anno Dom.* 1737.

Thomas Christie]

After Evening Prayers we joined with the Germans in one of their Love-feasts. It was begun and ended with thanksgiving and prayer, and celebrated in so decent and solemn a manner as a Christian of the apostolical age would have allowed to be worthy of Christ.

[B—Tuesday, [August] 9. Mr. Jones the Constable served this warrant, and carried me before Mr. Bailiff Parker and Mr. Recorder.] Mr. Williamson's charge against me was: (1) That I had defamed his wife; (2) That I had causelessly repelled her from the Holy Communion. [B—Mr. Williamson, after much reviling, inserted on the edge of the warrant, that I had endeavoured to alienate her affections

---

repelled! 12.15 Dinner, religious talk. 1 Catechized. 2 Meditated. 2.30 Read Prayers. 3.30 Mrs Gilbert, etc. 4.30 Mr Spangenberg spoke. 5 Tea, religious talk. 6.30 Buried. 7 Germans'; religious talk with Delamotte. 9 Prayed.

MONDAY, AUGUST 8. 4 Private prayer; sang. 5 read Prayers (twenty-five there; heavy); tea, religious talk. 6.15 Fleury. 8 Read notes; necessary talk. 9 Sang with Delamotte; Fleury. 11 Visited; writ diary. 11.45 Germans. 12.30 Dinner. 1 Fleury; necessary talk (religious) with them. 2 Visited. 3.30 Dr Núñez'. 4.45 At home; private prayer. 5 Tea, religious talk. 5.45 Mrs Fallowfield, necessary talk (religious). 6.30 Mrs Turner, talk of Mrs Causton, they very affected! 7 Meditated. 7.30 Read Prayers. 8 Germans', Agape; sang; prayed; ate; sang; prayed. 10.

TUESDAY. AUGUST 9. 4.30 Private prayer. 5 Read Prayers (thirty there); Fleury. 6 Mrs Ann, religious talk; tea. 7 The Constable came with a warrant. 7.30 Before the Magistrates, necessary talk (convincing!). 8 Writ to the Trustees. 8.30 Visited; prayed; sang; (lively zeal). 9 Mr Young came, religious talk. 9.20 Mr

from him.] [E—Being required to plead to the warrant,] [B—this charge, and that of defaming her, I denied. As to the other,] being purely ecclesiastical, I could not acknowledge their power to interrogate me. [B—Mr. Parker endorsed the warrant, whereby I was ordered to appear at the next Court holden for the town.

[Soon after I was gone home, Mr. Williamson posted up the following advertisement:

[Province of Georgia
Savannah S[session]s
Whereas there is an Action for Defamation and several other Notorious Offences brought against John Wesley of this Town, Clerk, by William Williamson, wherein there is One Thousand Pounds Damages charged against the said John Wesley.

This is to give notice to all whom it may concern, that if any person or persons whatsoever shall carry or convey, or be in any wise aiding or assisting in carrying or conveying the said John Wesley out of this Province, till he hath fully answered the Actions above mentioned, He, She, or They so doing will be prosecuted for the said Damages according to Law.

If anyone takes down this Advertisement they will also be prosecuted by me, William Williamson.]

The Evening Lesson was the eleventh chapter of the Epistle to the Hebrews. O may I ever 'have respect unto the recompense of reward, and esteem the reproach of Christ greater riches than the treasures of Egypt' [cf. Heb. 11:26]!

[B—The next day Mr. Jones (who had before told Mr. Coates in the fullness of his heart, 'Mr. Causton is at the bottom of all this, but will be seen in it as little as possible') brought me the following letter from him:

[Savannah, Aug. 10, 1737
Sir,
I have heard of a difference between you and Mr. William Williamson, touching matters which (I am informed by the magistrates) you say are ecclesiastical;

Spangenberg, religious talk (necessary); (lively zeal). 10 Religious talk. 10.15 Fleury. 10.45 Visited; private prayer. 11.30 Writ diary; Germans'. 12.30 Dinner. 1 Spangenberg, religious talk. 2.15 Visited; necessary talk (religious). 3 Dr Núñez'. 4 Visited. 4.15 Walked; Greek Testament; meditated. 4.45 Delamotte came, religious talk (necessary). 5.15 Tea, religious talk; meditated; sang. 6 Meditated; sang. 6.45 Germans'. 7.30 Read Prayers; (lively zeal). 8.15 Mrs Burnside, etc. 8.45 Mrs Fallowfield, necessary talk (religious). 9 Mrs Burnside's; they quite open and friendly; supper. 10.30 Prayed.

WEDNESDAY, AUGUST 10. 4.30 Private prayer. 5 Read Prayers (thirty there); tea,

As there is no ecclesiastical court in this Province,

To preserve the character of Mrs. Sophia Williamson my niece, who has received her education by my means;

To prevent the bad effects your behaviour in this case may have on the minds of ill-disposed people, who doubtless will be glad to embrace such an opportunity as this appears to be;

To prevent all manner of misunderstanding whatever, and for the sake of yourself, religion, and justice, I desire that you would meet me at four of the clock in the court-house and in the presence of all Christians (who think it proper to be there), make known the reasons why you refused the Sacrament of the Lord's Supper to my said niece, to the intent that the differences may be rightly understood, and if not accommodated, a case may be agreed upon, to be laid before the Trustees.

As this, sir, is sincerely offered, upon the principles of a Christian in a private capacity, and with a just regard to the friendship which has, till this affair, subsisted between us, I hope I need not doubt your concurrence, and am, sir, your humble servant,

T. Causton

P.S. If the time fixed does not suit you, be pleased to appoint your own.]

I could not assent to this on several accounts, as (1) because 'All the people' were not proper judges of ecclesiastical matters; (2) because I was unwilling to expose her; (3) because I foresaw Mr. Causton himself would probably be insulted by the people.

[B—On this letter I must observe:

[First, that I was surprised at the civility of it, till Mr. Causton informed me he had sent it to the Trustees, and that he wrote it with that design.

[Secondly, that I never received from Mr. Causton any proposal of accommodation before or besides this.

[Thirdly, that there is gross prevarication in the very first words of it: 'I have heard of a difference—'.

---

necessary talk (religious). 6.45 Walked; German. 8.30 At home; necessary talk; necessary business. 10 Visited. 11 Buried. 11.15 At home; letter from Mr Causton; went to Mr Spangenberg, necessary talk (religious), answered it. 12 Sang with Germans; religious talk with Delamotte; prayed. 1 Ephraem Syrus. 1.15 Necessary talk; meditated. 2 Mrs Burnside's, read *Nicodemus*. 3 Tea, religious talk (necessary); buried. 3.30 At home; sang. 4 Sang; Spangenberg went away; sang. 5 Tea, religious talk (necessary); sang. 6.30 Meditated; sang. 7 Germans'; Mr Causton came, he very angry; read Prayers. 9 Mr Burnside's, religious talk; ate. 10.30.

[Fourthly, that the same artful disingenuity runs through the whole, particularly in talking 'of the bad effects of my behaviour', whereas my behaviour this whole week was to sit still, to be quiet and mind my own business, speaking to few persons at all, to fewer upon this affair, and enlarging upon it to none.

[Lastly, that the whole sole crime which is here charged upon me, as causing a breach in that friendship between Mr. Causton and me, which [he] himself here testifies 'subsisted till this affair' is 'the refusing the Sacrament of the Lord's Supper to Mr. Causton's niece'.

[My short answer was:

[Sir:
I apprehend many ill consequences that may arise from a public conversation on this subject. Why may not a case be agreed on in a more private manner, to be laid before the Trustees? I am, sir,
Your Humble servant,
John Wesley

[As this was the first proposal of accommodation I made, so it might fairly have been the last, considering the use which [was] made of it, contrary to all rules both of generosity and common justice. Before this I was accused of refusing a private conference, 'a plain proof', says Mr. Causton, 'of his spite and malice.' Now I was accused of *desiring* a private conference, 'a plain proof', says the same Mr. Causton, 'Of his guilt'. To one, Mr. Anderson (at Mr. Burnside's), Mr. Causton says, 'I was for a private conference before a few friends; but Mr. Wesley would not agree to it.' To another, Mr. Delamotte (at his own house), Mr. Causton says, 'No, I will have nothing private: the more public the better.' This hour, 'tis said: 'If it had not been mere spite and malice, why did he not repel her at first, as soon as she was married? The delaying it so long plainly shows the principle on which it was done.' The next: 'If he had repelled her at first, as soon as she was married, everyone would have seen it was mere spite and malice; but the putting off so long, that was the devil, the subtlety of the devil.'

[I was now the constant subject of conversation at Mr. Causton's, where the account given of me to all company was, that I 'was a sly hypocrite, a seducer, a betrayer of my trust, an egregious liar and dissembler, an endeavourer to alienate the affections of married women from their husbands, a drunkard, the keeper of a bawdy-house, an admitter of whores, whoremongers, drunkards, ay, and of murderers and spillers of blood to the Lord's Table, a repeller of others out of mere spite and malice, a refuser of Christian burial to Christians, a murderer of poor infants by plunging them into cold water, a Papist, if not a Jesuit, or rather, an introducer of a new religion, such as nobody ever heard of; a proud priest, whose view it was to be a bishop, a spiritual tyrant, an arbitrary usurper of illegal power; a false teacher enjoining others under peril of damnation to do what I would omit myself, to serve a turn; a denier of the King's supremacy, an enemy to the colony, a sower of sedition, a public incendiary, a disturber of the peace of families, a raiser of uproars, a ringleader of mutiny'—in a word, such a monster 'that the people would rather die than suffer him to go on thus'.]

About seven, Mr. Gough, the officer on duty, rung the bell for the relieving the guard. It was soon rumoured abroad that this bell rung for my trial, which occasioned a vast concourse of people [E—the people flocked together to the court-house in great numbers]. Soon after [E—(a little before I returned from the Germans)], Mr. Causton came to my house [cf. B—Coming home in the evening, I found Mr. Causton (with Mr. Parker and Jones) at my house], from whose behaviour I clearly saw that whatever the most vindictive temper could contrive and lawless power execute, that I was to expect [cf. E—whose whole behaviour showed that he was determined to push things to the utmost extremity]. [B—He broke out, 'Wesley, I am ashamed of this. I could not have believed it of thee. Why is all this uproar?' I told him I knew of none. 'Yes,' says he, 'there is; but I'll not endure it. The court-house is full of people.' (Which was true, and occasioned by a report of my being to be tried, and this was accidentally confirmed by Mr. Gough's ringing the bell to relieve the guard, the drummer being out of the way.) He went on: 'I have been insulted in the streets, I have been called Judas to my face. And why must one of my family be the first to be repelled from the Holy Communion?' He added many reproaches and upbraidings. The sum of my answer was, 'I am sorry if there has been any disturbance, and will do all that in me lies to preserve peace and the respect due to all magistrates, whom I reverence as the Ministers of God.'] I determined, however, God being my helper, to follow the directions he gave in the Lesson for the day: 'Let us lay aside every weight, and run with patience the race that is set before us; looking unto Jesus, the author and finisher of our faith; who for the joy that was set before him endured the cross, despising the shame, and is set down at the right hand of the throne of God' [Heb. 12:1-2].

[B—Thursday, August 11. Mr. Causton came to my house again, soon after Morning Prayers. We went into the garden.] His language was now rougher than before. [B—He said many times, 'Wesley, thou art a villain,' and added, 'I came to speak on another subject. But I no

---

THURSDAY, AUGUST 11. 4.30 Private prayer; sang. 5 Read Prayers; Mr Causton came, he very angry! necessary talk. 6.30 Tea, necessary talk. 7.15 Writ to Miss Sophy; Fleury. 11 Visited. 11.45 Sorted letters. 12 Necessary talk (religious); dinner, necessary talk. 1 Letters. 3 Visited; Dr Núñez'; visited. 5 Töltschig came, necessary talk (religious); tea. 6.15 Meditated. 6.30 Sang. 7 Germans'. 7.30 Read Prayers. 8 Mrs Burnside, etc, religious talk (necessary) with Delamotte. 9.15.

sooner saw thy house than I was enraged at thee. Make an end of this matter. Thou hadst best. I have drawn the sword, and I will never sheathe it till I have satisfaction. Let me know the reason why my niece must be used thus. You don't repel the drunkards and whoremongers that come to your house, though they come only for a piece of bread. This is all spite and malice, because she wouldn't have you. But let me tell you, it was not the part of an honest man to propose marriage to her without my consent.' I told him, 'Sir, I think I had your consent. But I never did propose marriage to her, nor ever coolly intended it.' He said, 'Then you intended worse. Wesley, this has very much the look of Father Girard's story. But I will put a stop to your proceedings. I will support you in your arbitrary dealings no longer. I will oppose the pride of priests wherever I am. You are introducing I know not what new religion among us. You refused Christian burial to Paul Cheesewright. Mr. Gilbert made complaint on it to me. But I told him, I was no judge of such matters, and sent him to Mr. Oglethorpe, who likewise told him he had nothing to do with ecclesiastical matters.' I answered, 'Why then, sir, what have we to do but to refer this matter to the Trustees' determination?' He replied, 'No, I won't stay for that. I know their dilatory manner. I will have a speedier redress.' Many reproaches followed, with such a turn put upon everything I said that I was obliged to say plainly, 'Sir, if you thus wrest and pervert my words, even before my face, I must never speak to you again without witnesses. But if you come in at one door, I will go out at the other.'

[Soon after he added,] 'I will not rest till I have revenge [E—till I have satisfaction; B—till this is over.] Give your reasons before the whole congregation.' I told him, 'Let her offer herself on Sunday and I will.' [B—'Sir, if you insist upon it, I will; and so you may be pleased to tell her.' He said, 'No, I won't tell her. She won't believe me. Write to her and tell her so.' I said, 'I don't think it safe to write. I don't know what construction you may put upon it.' He said, 'Tell her it was my desire.' I said, 'I will; and let all things rest till Sunday.']

And at his desire, I assured her of it under my hand. [B—After he went, I writ the following note, the second and last proposal of accommodation I have made:

[To Mrs. Sophia Williamson.

At Mr. Causton's request I write once more. The rules whereby I proceed are these:

'So many as intend to be partakers of the Holy Communion, shall signify their names to the curate at least some time the day before.' This you did not do.

'And if any of those . . . have done any wrong to his neighbours by word or deed, so that the congregation be thereby offended, the curate . . . shall advertise him, that in any wise he presume not to come to the Lord's Table until he hath openly declared himself to have truly repented' [BCP, Communion, first rubrics].

If you offer yourself at the Lord's Table on Sunday, I will advertise you (as I have done more than once) wherein you 'have done wrong'. And when you have 'openly declared yourself to have truly repented', I will administer to you the mysteries of God.

August 11, 1737   John Wesley]

But nothing followed except more threats and ill language. [B—Mr. Delamotte carrying this, Mrs. Williamson insisted she had done nothing amiss. Mr. Causton said, 'I am the person that is injured. I am ill used. The affront is offered to me, and I will espouse the cause of my niece. It will be the worst thing Mr. Wesley ever did in his life, to fix upon my family. She shall not offer herself on Sunday. She shall never communicate with him more. Neither will I as long as I live; nor shall any of my family.' After many other sharp words he added, 'But I have made his character public to all the world. I have sent it to England already; and I will publish it in every newspaper in England and America. I am injured, and I will have satisfaction, if it be to be had in the world.' 'And I', said Mr. Williamson, 'will never leave him to my life's end.']

In the Evening Lesson were those comfortable words: 'I will never leave thee nor forsake thee. So that we may boldly say, The Lord is my helper. I will not fear what man shall do unto me' [Heb. 13:5-6].

Friday, August 12, and the following days, Mr. Causton read to as many as conveniently he could [E—to very many persons], all the letters which I had writ to him or Miss Sophy, from the beginning of our acquaintance; not indeed throughout, but selecting such parts of each as might best bear an ill construction, and inserting here and there a few words to make things more clear to the apprehension of the hearers. The rest of the family, in the meantime, were very [E—equally] industrious in convincing all they could speak to, 'that Mr. Wesley had done this merely out of revenge, because Sophy would not have him'. I sat still and (I thank God) easy at home, having committed my cause to him, and remembering his word (which was read this night): 'Blessed is the man that endureth temptation; for when he hath been tried he shall

---

Friday, August [12]. 4 Private prayer. 5 Read Prayers (twenty-five there); tea, religious talk. 6 Writ Account of Mr Causton, etc. 9 Sang with Delamotte; sang. 10 Mrs Fallowfield, religious talk; prayed. 11 Germans'; my hair cut. 12 Sang, etc. 12.30 At home; Mrs Ann, religious talk; prayed. 1 Visited. 2 Mrs Burnside's, *Nicodemus*. 3 Tea, religious talk (necessary). 4 Dr Núñez'; visited. 5 Sang. 6 Meditated; religious talk; Germans'; read Prayers. 8 Mrs Burnside, etc; at Mrs Burnside's; supper, religious talk (necessary). 10.

receive the crown of life, which the Lord hath promised to them that love him' [Jas. 1:12].

Saturday, August 13. Calling on one who was acquainted with my whole intercourse with Miss Sophy from the beginning, I found Mr. Causton had, notwithstanding this, quite won him over from his former conviction [E—convinced him that I was wholly in the wrong]. I said little to him, finding him deeply prejudiced against me, knowing the time was not yet come—and indeed doubting whether God did not see it to be best for me to be condemned and despised of all men.

I was at first afraid that those who were weak in the faith would be turned out of the way hereby; at least so far as to neglect the public worship, by attending which they were likely to suffer in their temporal concerns. But I feared where no fear was: God took care of this likewise, insomuch that on Sunday, [August] 14, we had a greater number than usual [E—than had been for some months] present at the early prayers [E—Morning Prayers]. Many could not but observe those remarkable words in the First Lesson: 'Set Naboth on high among the people; and set two men, sons of Belial, before him, to bear witness against him, saying, Thou didst blaspheme God and the King' [1 Kgs. 21:9-10]. No less remarkable were those in the Evening Lesson [E—concerning Ahab and Micaiah]: 'I hate him, for he doth not prophesy good concerning me but evil' [1 Kgs. 22:8]. O may I ever be able to say with Micaiah, 'What the Lord saith unto me, that will I speak' [1 Kgs. 22:14]; and that, though I too should be 'put in prison and fed there with bread of affliction and with water of affliction' [1 Kgs. 22:27].

Monday, August 15. Mr. Causton desired Mr. Burnside, one who had been employed two years and a half in casting up and transcribing

---

Saturday, August [13]. 4 Sang; private prayer. 5 Read Prayers; writ account; visited. 6 Tea, necessary talk of Mr Causton. 6.30 Account. 10.45 Visited. 11.30 Writ notes. 12 Dinner, talk of Mr Causton; writ notes. 1 Catechized. 1.40 Slept. 2 Visited Mr Brownfield, etc. 4.45 Religious talk with Delamotte. 5.45 Sang; prayed with Delamotte. 6 Tea, religious talk; buried. 7.15 Meditated. 7.30 Read Prayers. 8 Mrs Gilbert, etc. 8.45 German. 9.30 Necessary talk of Mr Causton. 10.

Sunday, August 14. 4.15 Private prayer. 5 Read Prayers (thirty-one there). 6 Mr Dyson, mostly religious talk. 7 Meditated upon sermon. 8 Read the last prayer by Robert Patterson [?]; necessary talk (religious). 8.45 Dressed. 9 Walked; meditated; sang. 10 Meditated; private prayer. 10.30 Read Prayers, Sermon. 12 Sacrament. 12.15 Dinner, religious talk; catechized. 2.15 Read Prayers. 3.45 Mrs Gilbert, etc. 4.45 To Mrs Fallowfield. 5.30 Tea, religious talk. 6.30 Germans; buried. 7 At home, religious talk with Delamotte. 9.30 Prayed.

Monday, August 15. 4.15 Private prayer. 5 Read Prayers; tea, religious talk. 6 Set out with John, religious talk; Kempis. 7.30 Cowpen; set out, ate. 8.45 Irene;

accounts for the Trustees, to sign a certificate containing three heads [E—asserting]: (1) That Mrs. Williamson had been for ten months last past as constant a communicant as any other; (2) That he could conceive no reason why she should be now repelled; (3) That she was and had been of an unblameable behaviour. Mr. Burnside said he could not sign it with a safe conscience, knowing it to be false. Upon which Mr. Causton, after many severe reproaches, discharged him from his employment, and told him he hoped he would never expect any more favours from him.

Notwithstanding this example made of the first refuser, I do not hear of any more than two of between twenty and thirty communicants with whom Mr. Causton had any better success [E—whom either fear or favour could induce to sign that paper]. However, names of some sort or other must be had; and a good number was accordingly procured to a paper the very first article of which was shamelessly false (for she had omitted communicating nine times in three months), and which, had it been ever so true, not one of them was able to testify. [Cf. E—A good number of persons, most of whom had never communicated at Savannah, and not one constantly, certified that 'Mrs. Williamson had communicated as constantly as any other for ten months'—particularly several that lived out of town.]

All this week Mr. Causton employed his utmost power and art and application to prepare the persons who form the Grand Jury here [E—(which was another material point)] against the next court-day, which was Monday the 22nd instant. He was talking with some or other of them day and night. His table was open to all. Whatever they pleased to have from the stores was delivered. Old misunderstandings were forgot. And nothing was too much to be done or promised to those who a week before could not procure a morsel of bread. This evening was the last time Mr. Causton was at church, or any of his family, Mrs. Causton openly declaring she would come there no more while I stayed at Savannah.

Tuesday, [August] 16. [B—Being informed that two of the communicants had been induced to sign this certificate, to prevent others from being] ensnared or offended by the reports so carefully

---

religious talk (necessary); sang. 11.30 Set out; Kempis. 12.45 At home; dinner; dressed. 1.45 Visited. 2.15 Töltschig and Antone, necessary talk. 3 Necessary talk with Mr Mercer; with Germans. 3.45 Writ notes. 4.45 Sang; meditated; private prayer for Mr Causton, Miss Sophy. 6 Tea, necessary talk; meditated; Germans'; read Prayers. 8.15 Mrs Fallowfield, etc. 9.30 Mr Burnside's, necessary talk (religious); supper. 10.30 Prayed.

TUESDAY, AUGUST 16. 4.15 Private prayer; read Prayers; religious talk with Mr and Mrs Vanderplank. 6 At home; tea, necessary talk. 10 Writ my Case. 10.30 Germans; read it. 12 Mrs Gilbert, etc; prayed. 12.30 Case; transcribed. 5 Mr

propagated, I complied with the request of [B—((my friends))] several of them, drew up a short relation of the case [E—of what had occurred between Mrs. Williamson and me], and read it after Evening Prayers were ended, in the open congregation. And this evening I suppose it was that poor Mrs. Williamson was induced to swear to and [E—sign The Memorable Affidavit]:

Province of Georgia, Savannah S[ession]s

Sophia Christiana Williamson, the wife of William Williamson of Savannah aforesaid, maketh oath that about twelve months since, she was committed to the care of Mr. John Wesley, the Missionary residing in this province, by her relations, which care the said John Wesley discharged with a great deal of seeming fidelity for two or three months. And this deponent further said, that after the said three months, the said John Wesley began to use his endeavours to alienate the affections of the said deponent from her said relations; and often in very pathetic terms urged to her the necessity of her forsaking them, and leaving their house, in order to cohabit with him, alleging that he, the said John Wesley, would maintain her; and basely insinuating that she ne'er could make so good a progress to salvation while she lived with them as she could if she lived wholly with him.

And this deponent further saith, that the said John Wesley, finding all the aforesaid arguments and persuasions ineffectual, he the said John Wesley frequently made several overtures of marriage to this deponent, without acquainting her relations thereof, as they have [B—since] informed this deponent. And the better to induce this deponent thereto, he the said John Wesley often alleged that he could easily alter anything in his way of life that was disagreeable to her; though he the said John Wesley had always prescribed to this deponent the same way of life he then led as the only means of obtaining salvation: to corroborate which he always added, that he endeavoured to imitate the Primitive Fathers, who were strict imitators of the life of Christ. And this deponent further saith that the said John Wesley further added, that whereas he had no settled habitation, and in regard this deponent might not like his present wandering way of life, he would procure to himself the settlement of Savannah, and used other arguments which this deponent cannot at

---

Brownfield's, necessary talk (religious; gained little ground!). 6.15 At home; necessary talk (religious); tea; Mr Gronau came, necessary talk (religious). 6.45 Germans'. 7.30 Read Prayers; read my Case! 8.30 Mrs Burnside, etc. 9 Writ to the Trustees, to Mr Burton. 9.30 Mr Gronau, religious talk. 10.15 Lay down; slept very sound!

present recollect, whereby he gave this deponent to understand that he would lay aside his former intentions of going among the Indians, in case this deponent would approve of him for a husband.

And this deponent further saith that about three days before her marriage with the said William Williamson, the said John Wesley came to this deponent, and urged very much to know whether this deponent had not been over-persuaded or forced to agree to the said marriage, and whether it might not still be prevented. Adding again, that if there was anything in his way of life by which he gave this deponent to understand he meant fasting, and the other severe mortifications, which he the said John Wesley, and she this deponent, by his injunction had then strictly practised for about six months, which she this deponent had any dislike to, he the said John Wesley would make all those things easy to her, in case she would consent to marry him.

And this deponent further saith, that ever since her marriage with the said William Williamson, he the said John Wesley hath taken all opportunities in her husband's absence to persecute this deponent, and to force his private discourse to her, wherein he hath often terrified her with the danger her soul would be in if she did not continue to spend her time and converse with him the said John Wesley in the same manner she did before marriage.

And this deponent further saith, that particularly about three months since, the said John Wesley, being at this deponent's house among other company, who were then busy with this deponent's uncle, he the said John Wesley took an opportunity to follow this deponent to the back door, and there told this deponent that it was necessary for the benefit of her soul that he should still continue to converse with her; that she must not mind what the world said on such an occasion, and that she must contrive some opportunity or proper times for him to converse with her. To which this deponent answered, she wondered he could desire such a thing when he knew this deponent's husband had so often forbid him, and she had so often refused him so to do.

Signed by Sophia Christiana Williamson.
Sworn before me, this 16th day of August, 1737.
Henry Parker
Transcribed from the copy taken and attested by Mr. Burnside.

A case hitherto full as deplorable as that of Theomachus! God forbid it should have the same event!

[B—If the former part of this narrative does not give sufficient light to the matter of this affidavit, it may be further explained by certificates following, all which the certifiers are ready to give upon

[Whereas an affidavit dated Savannah, Aug. 16, 1737, and signed by Sophia Christiana Williamson, doth assert, 'That Mr. John Wesley, Missionary at Savannah, did frequently make several overtures of marriage to the said Mrs. Williamson, and used many arguments to induce her to it, all which proposals she rejected':

This is to certify, that I, James Burnside, of Savannah aforesaid, did in January and February last, hear William Williamson, now the husband of the said Sophia, express much apprehension because Mr. Wesley (as he supposed) did court Mrs. Williamson; that I always desired him to lay aside such apprehensions as utterly groundless.

I further certify, that on or about the 14th of March last past, the said Mr. Williamson did affirm to me, he had heard his said wife declare that 'if Mr. Wesley had ever proposed marriage to her, she could not have refused him'.

And I further certify, that I never at that or any other time till August 7 last past, heard Mrs. Williamson give any intimation of her having any objection to any part of Mr. Wesley's behaviour; and that till then I never heard Mr. Williamson make any other objection to Mr. Wesley but 'his being too strict, and making Sophia so'. In witness whereof I have subscribed my name,

James Burnside

[Whereas an affidavit has been signed by Mrs. Sophia Christiana Williamson, asserting 'that Mr. John Wesley, Minister of Savannah, had pressed her to cohabit with him, and upon her refusal made several overtures of marriage to her, and to induce her to it offered to leave off fasting, and to lay aside his design of going among the Indians':

This is to certify that I, Margaret Burnside, wife of James Burnside of Savannah aforesaid, was intimately acquainted with Mrs. Williamson for about twelve months preceding the date of the said affidavit, and had very many opportunities of knowing her judgment, particularly on this head; both by her coming, generally five afternoons in a week, to my house for several months, to read French and drink tea there with Mr. Wesley; and by our going together to his house, generally four evenings in a week.

And I do hereby certify that at all times, and on all occasions during our acquaintance, particularly from November 1, 1736, to March 12, 1737, Mrs. Williamson expressed the highest esteem for Mr. Wesley, and freely owned her great obligations to him. And in all this time she not only never gave the least intimation of her disliking any part of his behaviour, but did constantly, both by word and deed, in his presence and in his absence, show an entire approbation thereof.

I do further certify, that on Sunday, February 6, Mr. Wesley desired me to give Mrs. Williamson a note, signifying the reason of his then going out of town, upon reading which she expressed a very great concern, saying, It was strange, she could never have a friend, but something happened to deprive her of that blessing; and in the whole turn of her behaviour showing a settled esteem of Mr. Wesley, and a deep sense of her obligations to him.

I do further certify, that on March 19, Saturday, in the evening, Mr. Wesley did at my house and in my hearing, mildly reprove Mrs. Williamson for several faults, particularly insincerity; that in her whole answer she made no kind of objection to anything he had said or done before her marriage, but on the contrary, professed (as usual) a great esteem for him, and approbation of his behaviour; that part of what she said was to this effect: 'I believe it is better for you as it is; but I own, if you had pressed me to marriage at any time when my mind was ruffled, I could not have denied you.' And afterwards she spoke these or the like words: 'Many instances of your anger and resentment have been related to me since my marriage. But I could hardly believe them. Nor have I ever been provoked to say anything disrespectful of you. The utmost I have ever said was, Well, whatever he may say or do, now or hereafter, I will always own, the man has been my friend, and done me more service than any other person living.'

I do further certify, that I have frequently conversed with Mrs. Williamson since her marriage, and in many of those conversations, as occasion offered, she professed much esteem for Mr. Wesley, and many obligations to him.

And, whereas that affidavit asserts that Mr. Wesley offered to leave off fasting in compliance with Mrs. Williamson, I do further certify, that Mrs. Williamson told me after her marriage, that she herself continued to practise it; and that even when she discontinued it, she still owned it to be a duty, but said she thought a wife ought to have no will of her own, and therefore omitted it in compliance with her husband, who did not approve of it.

And I further certify, that on Sunday, August 7 last past, Mrs. Williamson came to me, and expressed much anger at Mr. Wesley, for having that day repelled her from the Holy Communion; that I said, 'You was very much to blame, after receiving a letter from Mr. Wesley, wherein he accuses you of several things, to offer yourself at the Holy Table before you had cleared yourself to him. But you may easily put an end to this by going to Mr. Wesley and clearing yourself now of what you are charged with'; and that she replied, 'No, I will not show such a meanness of spirit as to speak to him about it myself, but somebody else shall.'

And the above-written certificate I am ready to attest upon oath,

Margaret Burnside

[B—Savannah, October 25, 1737

[Whereas it is asserted in an affidavit dated at Savannah in Georgia, August 16, 1737, and signed by Sophia Christiana Williamson, 'that about twelve months before, she was committed to the care of Mr. John Wesley, Missionary at Savannah', this is to certify that the manner wherein Mrs. Williamson (then Hopkey) was committed to Mr. Wesley's care was as follows:

[In July 1736, Mrs. Causton earnestly begged Mr. Wesley to talk with her niece, Miss Hopkey, who was 'utterly ruined, being in love with and resolved to marry a notorious villain'. Mr. Wesley did so, and continued so to do once or twice a week till his journey to Charleston. The same request was made by Mr. Causton three months after, and seconded by Mr. Oglethorpe.

[Secondly, whereas it is asserted that Mr. Wesley did use his endeavours to alienate the affections of Miss Hopkey from her relations, I do further certify that Mr. Wesley has, to my personal knowledge, used his utmost endeavours to reconcile her affections to them, when they were in fact alienated from them by their harsh treatment of her.

[3. Whereas it is asserted that 'Mr. Wesley did basely insinuate that Miss Hopkey could not make so good a progress toward salvation while she lived with them as she could if she lived wholly with him', this is to certify that it was I, Charles Delamotte, who did, not basely insinuate, but frankly declare to Mr. Wesley several times (and I know not but I might to Miss Hopkey) that it was my judgment and Mr. Ingham's, she could not be so good a Christian *in* that family as *out* of it. And I did accordingly mention to Mr. Wesley several times, her having (if she chose it) a room in his house. But his answer was, he thought it much better for her to be (as Mrs. Causton herself had once proposed) at the Germans'.

[4. Whereas it is asserted that Mr. Wesley 'offered to maintain Miss Hopkey', I do further certify that after his return from Frederica with her, Mr. Wesley did inform me of his having offered so to do. Once on Bear Island, and before that, in Frederica, when Miss Hopkey, declaring she must go to England, as expressing some doubt whether her friends there would receive her. Mr. Wesley spoke to this effect: 'Miss Sophy, if you must go to England, though your aunt should not receive you, you shan't want there. I have enough in England to maintain you, and what I have, you are welcome to.'

[5. Whereas it is asserted that Mr. Wesley, finding all his arguments and persuasions ineffectual, did, without acquainting her relations, frequently make several overtures of marriage to Miss Hopkey, I do further certify, (1) That both Mr. and Mrs. Causton had often declared to Mr. Wesley and me, 'Whoever, except

Mellichamp, has Sophy's consent, has ours'; whence I apprehended Mr. Wesley to have been at full liberty, had he so pleased, to make any overtures without further ceremony; (2) That from the whole tenor of Miss Hopkey's behaviour while she was for several months several hours a day at Mr. Wesley's house, I am well assured there would not have needed many arguments or persuasions to have made such an overture from Mr. Wesley effectual; (3) That to my certain knowledge Mr. Wesley did never intend to marry her, or any other, since our first landing in America; (4) That when I imagined his resolution to be a little shaken, I pressed him to adhere to it, and gave him several reasons why it was not best for him to marry anyone now, and not her in particular; (5) That Mr. Ingham joining with me herein, he did entirely agree with us; and soon after, viz., on March 4, resolved 'never to speak to Miss Hopkey' but in my company.

[6. Whereas it is asserted that Mr. Wesley 'always prescribed to Mrs. Williamson the same way of life he then led, as the only means of obtaining salvation'; I do further certify that I have heard Mr. Wesley declare to Miss Hopkey over and over that the way of life he then led was not the only means of obtaining salvation; that he did not prescribe or advise it to her; and that the chief reason why he himself did many things was to prepare for what he came into America for, the going among the Indians.

[7. Whereas it is asserted that 'Mr. Wesley and Mrs. Williamson by his injunction did strictly practise for about six months before her marriage, fasting and other *severe mortifications*, and that nevertheless he often alleged, he could easily alter these things in case she would consent to marry him'; I do further certify, that I have heard Mr. Wesley declare to Mrs. Williamson on all occasions, during the whole time she came to his house, that he believed fasting an unalterable duty, incumbent both on married and unmarried Christians; that nevertheless he always advised both Mrs. Williamson and me to judge for ourselves concerning the manner and measure of it; that the manner wherein Mrs. Williamson practised it during the time she breakfasted at Mr. Wesley's, was by drinking three or four dishes of coffee in a morning, dining at three, and supping at eight or nine; that Mr. Wesley has many times advised her to eat something at breakfast, saying, 'Miss Sophy, it is your duty not to injure your health.' That Mr. Wesley has practised no other severe mortifications (as they are called) unless lying on the ground can be called so; nor could I ever know or learn any which Miss Hopkey practised, either by Mr. Wesley's injunction or without it, except the *severe* mortification of drinking tea without sugar; but neither was this by his advice or injunction, for I have heard him press her to drink sugar more than once, to which she always replied, 'Indeed, sir, I don't choose it.'

[8. Whereas it is asserted that 'Mr. Wesley promised Mrs. Williamson he *would procure* to himself the settlement of Savannah, and lay aside his intentions of going among the Indians', I do further certify, that Mr. Wesley needed not to promise he *would* procure that settlement, for he had it already, by an express instrument brought with him under the Trustees' hand and seal; that nevertheless he had declared to Miss Hopkey on all occasions, that he would never lay aside his design of going among the Indians; and that the last time he declared this, February 14, she was so well convinced thereof that she plainly told him the very next day, people wondered why she was so much at his house, and she would come thither no more alone.

[9. Whereas it is asserted that 'about three days before her marriage, Mr. Wesley urged to know whether it might not still be prevented', I do further certify (as I am able to do, from having been a witness to all Mr. Wesley's conversation and behaviour at that time) that the reason why he desired to prevent it was not because he designed to marry her himself, but because he judged she would be very unhappy if she married Mr. Williamson.

[10. Whereas it is asserted that ever since her marrige, Mr. Wesley has taken all opportunities of forcing his discourse to Mrs. Williamson, and has urged to her that it was necessary for her salvation for him to converse with her as before (although her husband had often forbade him to converse with her, and she had often refused him so to do); and particularly about three months since, Mr. Wesley being at Mr. Causton's house, among other company, 'took an opportunity to follow her to the back door', I do further certify, (1) That this back door is in the same room with the fore door (the very room wherein the company was), being opposite to it at the distance of about five yards; (2) That he never conversed with her at all since her marriage without pre-consulting me; (3) That it was I who believed it necessary for her salvation to converse with her pastor sometimes, though not as before her marriage; (4) That when he was twice determined to give her up and speak to her no more, I persuaded him to speak to her again; (5) That all this time I never heard or suspected, either that Mr. Williamson had forbid Mr. Wesley speaking to his wife in whatever manner he judged proper (the contrary whereof I had heard him say expressly, both before and after marriage), or that Mrs. Williamson had refused him so to do, having myself seen her walking up and down on the outside of the house when Mr. Wesley was within, as I apprehended from a desire he should speak to her.

[And this I am ready to attest upon oath.
Witness my hand, Charles Delamotte]

Wednesday, [August] 17, and the following days, I possessed my soul in patience, casting all my care on God, and speaking very sparingly, lest I should speak amiss. On Thursday or Friday the panel for the Grand Jury [E—to the number of twenty-six] was delivered [B—by the Recorder] to the officers. [B—Most of these were summoned that same day.] But [E—the next day], after the persons first empanelled were summoned [B—the list was called in by the Recorder, and] twenty-four more were added to the number. [B—(But no seal was ever affixed to that warrant wherein these twenty-four men were added.)] This Mr. Causton considered would add weight to everything transacted by them, which would then appear to be the general sense of the people. Besides that so many being engaged in the same work would encourage one another to take bolder steps than a few would venture on. [B—The reason of this unusual step may appear, if it be considered that a majority of the first twenty-six were not only Englishmen, but members of the Church of England, and many of them constant attenders of the church service; whereas of the forty-four who afterwards met, one was a Frenchman, who understood no English, one a professed infidel, three Anabaptists, and sixteen or seventeen Presbyterians, most of them of the Scotch nation. Now if these two and twenty (few of whom, unless by great accident, ever set foot within the church door) could gain but one man of the rest to their side, they secured a majority.]

I was now informed that Mr. Causton intended to proceed on three or four several [E—distinct] indictments [E—against me]. But whether it were so or no, I was not careful [E—I took no thought]; being instructed by the Lesson for this evening: 'Behold the husbandman waiteth for the fruit of the earth, and hath long patience for it. Be ye also patient. Stablish your hearts, for the coming of the Lord draweth nigh' [Jas. 5:7-8].

WEDNESDAY, AUGUST 17. 4.15 Private prayer. 5 Read Prayers. 5.40 Tea, religious talk. 6.15 Fleury. 7 Mrs Fallowfield's, necessary talk (religious); Mrs Charles', necessary talk (religious). 8.30 Fleury. 11 Visited; Mrs Burnside's, *Nicodemus*; Mr Anderson came, religious talk (necessary); tea. 5 At home with him, necessary talk (religious). 5.45 Germans'; Mr Burnside, necessary talk (religious). 6.15 Meditated; Germans'; read Prayers; Mrs Gilbert, etc, religious talk. 8 With John Lyndal, necessary talk; with Mrs Fallowfield, necessary talk. 10.

THURSDAY, AUGUST 18. 4.15 Private prayer; read Prayers; necessary talk; Mr Mercer's, necessary talk; tea. 7.15 Set out. 8 Lost; Gesangbuch; met Mr Fallowfield, necessary talk; German. 10 Writ the Case. 12 Dinner, necessary talk. 12.45 Case. 4.15 Visited; met Mr and Mrs Matthews (they affected!), necessary talk. 5.15 Visited the Captain, necessary talk. 6 Tea, religious talk (very lively); Germans'. 7.30 Read Prayers. 8.15 Campbell, necessary talk; sang. 8.30 Christened John Mac[kay]. 9 Mr Bradley's, necessary talk. 9.45 Necessary talk. 10.

Saturday, August 20. In the afternoon, remembering the former kindnesses of Mr. Causton and Miss Sophy, I was strongly moved to pray for them with my might, with earnest cries and many tears. O think not then that 'God hath forgotten to be gracious, or that he will shut up his loving-kindness in displeasure' [cf. Ps. 77:9 (BCP)].

Sunday, [August] 21. God gave us a day of rest. On Monday morning the Lesson was the twentieth chapter of the Acts, a great part of which by the grace of God I could with confidence apply to myself. When the court was met, Mr. Causton gave a long charge to the Grand Jury, to maintain their rights and privileges, and not to suffer any person to infringe their liberty, or usurp an illegal authority over them [cf. B—to beware of spiritual tyranny, to insist upon their ecclesiastical rights and privileges, to oppose the new, illegal authority which was erecting among them, and suffer no one to lord it over their consciences]. Forty-four jurors were then sworn, a great majority of whom were well prepared for their work, either by previous application from Mr. Causton or by avowed enmity to me or to the Church of England. Mrs. Williamson's affidavit [of August 16] was next read, of which I desired a copy. Mr. Causton answered that I might have one from any of the newspapers [B—in America], for it [E—was sent and] would be printed in them all immediately.

Then the court [E—Mr. Causton] delivered to the Grand Jury the

---

FRIDAY, AUGUST 19. 4.30 Private prayer. 5 Read Prayers; writ Case. 8 Mr Bradley and Kent, good talk (necessary). 9 Sang; Case. 11 Visited. 3 Mrs Burnside's, necessary talk (religious); tea; Mrs Fallowfield. 5 Visited; private prayer, religious talk. 5.30 Necessary talk. 6.30 Meditated; private prayer; buried. 7.30 Read Prayers (thirty-three there). 8 Mr Burnside, etc. 8.45 Mr Burnside's, religious talk (necessary); supper. 10.

SATURDAY, AUGUST 20. 4.30 Private prayer; sang. 5 Read Prayers (twenty-five there); tea, religious talk. 6 Case. 10.10 Mrs Gough, talk of Sacrament. 11 Mr Coates came, necessary talk. 11.30 Germans'. 12 Dinner; religious talk (necessary); Case. 1 Case. 3 Private prayer for Miss Sophy and Mr Causton (lively zeal; convincing); necessary business. 4 Mr Gilbert and Campbell, necessary talk. 5 Tea, religious talk (necessary). 6 Meditated; Germans. 7.30 Read Prayers (thirty there). 8.15 Mrs Gilbert, etc. 8.30 Visited. 9 Mrs Burnside's, necessary talk (religious). 10.

SUNDAY, AUGUST 21. 4.30 Private prayer; sang. 5 Read Prayers (thirty-one there). 6 Tea, religious talk. 6.30 Fleury. 7.30 Walked; sang; meditated upon sermon. 9 Fleury. 9.15 Sang. 9.30 Frenchman came, necessary talk; Fleury. 10 Meditated; read Prayers (fifty there). 11 Sermon, Sacrament (twenty-five communicants). 12 Writ diary. 12.15 Dinner, religious talk; sang. 1 Catechized. 1.15 Slept. 2 Sang; read Prayers (fifty-five there). 3.30 Mrs Gilbert, etc. 4.30 Visited. 5.45 At home; tea, religious talk. 6.30 Germans'. 7.30 Mr Bradley and Brown, necessary talk. 8.30 Necessary talk (religious) with Delamotte. 9.15 Prayed.

following paper [B—worthy to be had in remembrance to all posterity] [E—which was unluckily entitled]:

A list of Grievances presented by the Grand Jury
for Savannah, this [blank] day of August, 1737

That whereas the Colony of Georgia is composed of a mixed number of Christians, members of the Church of England and Dissenters, who all or most part willingly would attend divine ordinances and communicate with a faithful pastor of the Established Church; The Rev. Mr. John Wesley, who for the present serves the cure of Savannah, has not as the law directs emitted any declaration in this place of his adherence to the principles of the Church of England. We have the more reason to complain of grievance, that the said Rev. Person (as we humbly conceive) deviates from the principles and regulations of the Established Church, in many particulars inconsistent with the happiness and prosperity of this Colony, as

Prima, by inverting the order and method of the Liturgy;

Secondly, by changing or altering such passages as he thinks proper in the Version of Psalms publicly authorized to be sung in the Church;

3. By introducing into the church and service at the altar, compositions of Psalms and Hymns not inspected or authorized by any proper judicature;

4. By introducing novelties, such as dipping infants, etc., in the Sacrament of Baptism, and refusing to baptize the children of such as will not submit to his innovations;

5. By restricting the benefit of the Lord's Supper to a small number of persons, and refusing it to all others who will not conform to a grievous set of penances, confessions, mortifications, and constant attendance of early and late hours of prayer, very inconsistent with the labours and employments of this Colony;

6. By administering the Sacrament of the Lord's Supper to boys ignorant and unqualified, and that notwithstanding of their parents and nearest friends remonstrating against it, and accusing them of disobedience and other crimes, etc.;

7. By refusing to administrate the Holy Sacrament to well-disposed and well-living persons, unless they should submit to confessions and penances for crimes which they utterly refuse, and whereof no evidence is offered;

8. By venting sundry uncharitable expressions of all who differ from him, and not pronouncing the benediction in church until all the hearers except his own communicants are withdrawn;

9. By teaching wives and servants that they ought absolutely to

follow the course of mortification, fastings, and diets of prayers prescribed by him, without any regard to the interest of their private families, or the commands of their respective husbands and masters;

10. By refusing the Office of the Dead to such as did not communicate with him, or leaving out such parts of that service as he thought proper;

11. By search into and meddling with the affairs of private families, by means of servants and spies employed by him for that purpose, whereby the peace both of public and private life is much endangered;

12. By calling himself, 'Ordinary', and thereby claiming a jurisdiction which we believe is not due to him, and whereby we should be precluded from access to redress by any superior jurisdiction;

We do with all respect and difference [deference?] to the person and character of the Rev. Mr. John Wesley, present these our grievances; not from any resentment, but allarnarly that such relief may be afforded in time coming as shall be judged necessary for the interest of peace and religion in this province.

[B—N.B. 'Allarnarly' is a Scotch law-term for 'only'.]

[E—Every one of the thirteen [particulars was] either so palpably false or so uncouthly worded that even *that* jury could not digest any as there proposed, though they never brought them in (as they ought to have done), *Ignoramus* ['we do not know'].

[For three days that small number of the jurors who were unbiased withstood the multitude. But they were then outfaced and outvoted.]

This odd presentment was at first both opposed and defended with much warmth. But it was soon agreed to lay it aside; perhaps not so much for the notorious falsehood of many parts as for the extreme uncouthness of the whole.

[B—As many of these grievances (so called) as there was any shadow of proof for (to procure which no art or pains were wanting) were put into a little better dress by the majority of the Grand Jury, and on Thursday, September 1, delivered to the court [see below].]

They examined Mrs. Williamson in the afternoon [of August 22], and

---

MONDAY, AUGUST 22. 4 Private prayer; slept; sang. 5 Read Prayers (twenty-seven there). 5.30 Tea, religious talk. 6 Case. 9 In the Court. 10 Case. 12 Dinner. 12.30 Miss Sophy went to the Grand Jury, prayed (zealous) for her. 1 Case. 2.30 Mr Gilbert, necessary talk. 3 Case. 3.45 Mr Burnside's, they serious. 4 Read Case; tea; Mrs Montagut came, good talk. 5 Private prayer; sang. 6 Meditated; buried; tea, religious talk. 7 Germans'; read Prayers (forty there). 8 Mrs Burnside, etc. 8.45 Mrs Ann's. 9.15.

afterward Mr. Causton, and Mrs. Causton on Tuesday [August 23]. Mrs. Williamson declared, she had no objection at all to my behaviour before her marriage; Mr. Causton that he should not have denied if I had ever asked his consent to marry her; and Mrs. Causton that it was at her request I wrote the letter to Mrs. Williamson of July 5th.

On Wednesday, [August] 24, the Grand Jury inquired into the ecclesiastical grievances. This likewise occasioned warm debates, but the majority, being sure men, prevailed at length, and carried all their points [E—his points (i.e., Mr. Causton's)]. So that on Thursday [August 25], Mr. Causton had the joy of a complete victory. It was now therefore time for God to arise, and to take the wise in their own craftiness. And that his hand might be the more remarkably visible there, he chose Mr. Causton himself for his instrument. Who, being informed, they were falling on other matters beyond his instructions, went to them [E—went directly into the room where they were consulting], and behaved in such a manner that in one quarter of an hour he turned two-and-forty of the forty-four into a fixed resolution to inquire into his whole conduct [E—into civil grievances too]. They entered directly upon the examination of witnesses on that head, and

---

TUESDAY, AUGUST 23. 4 Sang; writ to Mr Hird; sang. 5 Read Prayers (thirty-five there); tea, religious talk. 6 Case. 8.45 Company, good talk. 9.15 Case. 9.45 Visited. 10 Case. 10.45 Slept. 11 Case. 11.30 Germans. 12.15 Dinner, religious talk. 12.45 Case. 1 Fleury. 1.15 Case. 4.15 Mr Watson's, necessary talk. 5.15 Sang; private prayer. 6 Tea, religious talk. 6.30 Sang; Germans'. 7.30 Read Prayers (thirty there). 8 Mrs Burnside, etc. 8.30 Buried. 9 Prayed.

WEDNESDAY AUGUST 24. 4 Private prayer; sang. 5 Read Prayers. 5.30 Tea, religious talk. 6 Case. 8.45 Sang; 9 Meditated upon sermon; dressed. 10 Sang; read Prayers, Sacrament. 12 Mr Bolzius, necessary talk; Mrs Burnside's, dinner, read Case. 2.30 At home; Case. 4 Mrs Fallowfield's, religious talk, read Case. 5.30 Sang; visited John Lyndal. 6 Tea, religious talk. 6.30 Germans'. 7.15 Read Prayers; Mrs Burnside, etc. 8.15 Case. 9.15 Prayed.

THURSDAY, AUGUST 25. 4 Sang. 5 Read Prayers; tea, religious talk (necessary); Mr Hows. 6 Case. 9 Necessary talk; Case. 11.45 Dinner; Germans'. 12.45 Case. 3.30 Mr West's, necessary talk (religious). 4 Case. 4.30 Walked; sang. 6.30 At home; tea. 6.45 Germans'. 7.15 Read Prayers. 8 Necessary talk with Mr Vanderplank. 8.30 At home; Mr Hows, etc, necessary talk; sang; read notes. 8.45 Meditated. 9 Mrs Burnside's, necessary talk (religious). 10.30.

FRIDAY, AUGUST 26. 4.30 Sang. 5 Read Prayers; Mr Gilbert, necessary talk; tea. 7 Case. 9.30 Mrs Fallowfield's, religious talk, read Case. 10.45 At home; ended it. 11.45 Meditated. 11.45 Read to boys; prayed; sang. 1 Case. 2.15 Mrs Burnside's, read Case. 3 Tea; Mrs Fallowfield, religious talk. 4 Visited. 5 Walked; meditated; sang. 6.30 Germans'. 7.15 Read Prayers. 8 Mrs Burnside, etc. 8.45 Mrs Burnside's; (lively zeal). 9 Supper, religious talk; necessary talk. 10.

continued so to do all Friday. On Saturday [August 27], Mr. Causton, finding all his arts ineffectual, and that they were resolved to go through with their work, adjourned the Court till Thursday following; and spared no pains to bring them in the meantime to another mind. But the jurors he had added for my sake gave such spirit to the rest that all his labour was in vain.

Thus far however he prevailed, that on Thursday, September 1, the Grand Jury delivered two presentments into Court containing ten indictments against me. They were read in court as follows:

SATURDAY, AUGUST 27. 4.30 Sang. 5 Read Prayers (twenty-six there). 5.40 Tea, religious talk. 6 Fleury. 7 Mr Bradley's, necessary talk. 8 Fleury. 9 Walked; verse. 9.30 Worked. 10.30 Walked; verse. 11 Visited. 12 Dinner, good talk. 1 Catechized. 2 Mrs Vanderplank's, read Case. 4 Necessary talk; walked; verse. 5 Verse; sang. 5.45 At home; Mrs Ann; tea, religious talk (necessary). 6.45 Germans'. 7.15 Read Prayers. 8 Mr Hows, etc. 8.30 Necessary talk (religious). 9 Prayed.

SUNDAY, AUGUST 28. 4.15 Private prayer; read Homily. 5 Read Prayers. 6.15 Tea, religious talk. 6.45 Fleury. 7.30 Walked; sang. 8 Meditated upon sermon. 8.30 Mr Brownfield's, necessary talk. 9.15 Meditated; sang. 10.15 Read Prayers (sixty there), Sermon, Sacrament (twenty-six communicants). 12 Dinner, necessary talk (religious). 1 Catechized. 2 Meditated; read Prayers (sixty there). 4 Mr Hows, etc. 5 Visited. 5.30 Tea, religious talk. 6 Meditated; Germans'. 7.15 Walked with Delamotte, religious talk; sang. 8.30 At home; necessary talk (religious). 9 Prayed.

MONDAY, AUGUST 29. 4 Private prayer; sang. 5 Read Prayers (twenty-eight there); tea, religious talk (necessary). 6.15 Writ journal. 10 Visited Mrs Campbell, Mrs Symes, etc. 11.45 Dinner, religious talk; Germans'. 12.30 Journal. 3.15 Walked to the lot, worked. 6 Supper, religious talk; Germans'. 7.15 Read Prayers. 8 Mrs Burnside, etc. 8.45 Mrs Burnside's, religious talk; ate. 10 Prayed.

[TUESDAY,] AUGUST 30. 4.30 Sang; private prayer. 5 Read Prayers (thirty there); tea; Mrs Ann, necessary talk. 6.15 Journal. 9.15 Read letter from Count Zinzendorf; dressed. 10 Visited. 12 Dinner; Germans. 12.45 Journal. 2.45 Visited; Dr Núñez'; visited. 4 Mr Bradley's, good talk; tea. 5 Sang; meditated. 6 Tea, religious talk. 6.30 Germans'; (lively zeal). 7 Visited Mr Vanderplank; read Prayers. 8 Mrs Burnside, etc. 8.30 Read resolutions; verse. 9.

WEDNESDAY AUGUST 31. 4 Private prayer; sang. 5 Read Prayers (twenty-five there); tea, religious talk; (sins). 6 Journal. 9 Prayed with Delamotte; journal. 10.30 Visited. 11.45 Germans; journal. 1 Fleury. 2.15 Mrs Burnside's, necessary talk (religious). 3 Tea, necessary talk. 3.45 Núñez', Spanish. 4 Dispute! 4.40.

Savannah S[ession]s

Whereas several disputes have happened within the town and county of Savannah concerning matters of religion and morality, and whereas it is [B—to be] apprehended that many ill consequences may attend evil proceedings in affairs of this solemn nature;

Therefore we, the Grand Jury of the said town and county, being duly sworn on the 22nd of this month, think it our duty as much as in us lies, to prevent the bad impressions which may be made upon the minds of well-disposed persons through the artful misrepresentations of ill-designing people. And having carefully examined several persons and papers, do upon our oaths present John Wesley, Clerk, of the said town and county, for that he, the said John Wesley, did after the 12th day of March last, privately force his conversation to Sophia Christiana Williamson, wife of William Williamson of the said town and county, contrary to the express desire and command of him the said William Williamson, and also the repeated promises of him the said John Wesley. And did likewise after the date aforesaid write and privately convey papers to the said Sophia Christiana Williamson, contrary to the desire and command of him the said William Williamson; which proceedings did occasion much uneasiness between the said William Williamson and Sophia Christiana Williamson, his wife; contrary to the peace of our Sovereign Lord the King, his crown and dignity.

True Bill.

[We] do also present the said John Wesley, for that he did on or about the 7th of this instant August refuse the Sacrament of the Lord's Supper to the said Sophia Christiana Williamson, without any apparent reason for so doing, much to the disquiet of the mind of the said Sophia Christiana Williamson, and to the great disgrace and hurt of her character, from which proceeding, we conceive that he the said John Wesley, did assume an authority contrary to the laws established, and to the peace of our Sovereign Lord the King, his crown and dignity.

August 23, 1737   True Bill.

Savannah

Whereas the Colony of Georgia is composed of a mixed number of Christian members of the Church of England and Dissenters, who all or most part would willingly attend divine ordinances and communicate with a faithful pastor of the Established Church; and whereas great uneasiness hath been occasioned among many well-disposed persons, being members of the Church of England and Dissenters in the town and county of Savannah in the Colony aforesaid, by reason of sundry wrong proceedings in the form of divine service and administration of Sacraments in the said town of Savannah;

We the Grand Jury of the said town and county, being duly sworn on the 22nd of this month, think it our duty as much as in us lies to prevent the bad impressions which may be made upon the minds of well-disposed persons through the artful misrepresentation of ill-designing men; and having carefully examined several persons, do upon our oaths present John Wesley of the said town and county, Clerk, for that he the said John Wesley hath not since his arrival at this town emitted any public declaration of his adherence to the principles and regulations of the Church of England, contrary to the laws established, and to the peace of our Sovereign Lord the King, his crown and dignity.

A True Bill.

[We] do also present the said John Wesley, for that he hath for many months past since his said arrival, divided on the Lord's Day the Order of Morning Prayer, appointed to be used in the Church of England; he the said John Wesley only reading the said Morning Prayers and the Litany at five or six of the clock, and wholly omitting the same between the hours of nine and eleven of the clock, the customary time of public Morning Prayer; contrary to the peace of our Sovereign Lord the King, his crown and dignity.

A True Bill.

[We] do also present the said John Wesley, for that he did on or about the month of April 1736 refuse to baptize otherwise than by dipping the child of Henry Parker of the said town and county, unless the said Henry Parker or his wife would certify that the [B—their] said child was weak and not able to bear dipping; he the said John Wesley adding to his refusal that unless the said parents would consent to have their said child dipped, it might die a heathen, contrary to the peace of our Sovereign Lord the King, his crown and dignity.

A True Bill.

[We] do also present the said John Wesley, for that notwithstanding his having administered the Sacrament of the Lord's Supper to William Gough of the said town and country some time in or about the month of March 1736, he the said John Wesley did within one month after the said date refuse the Sacrament of the Lord's Supper to him the said William Gough; saying, he heard the said William Gough was a Dissenter, contrary to the peace of our Sovereign Lord the King, his crown and dignity.

A True Bill.

[We] do also present the said John Wesley, for that he did in the latter end of June 1736 refuse reading the Office of Burial of the Dead over the body of Nathanael Polhill, only because the said Nathanael Polhill was not of the said John Wesley's opinion; by means of which refusal the said Nathanael Polhill was interred without the appointed Office for the Burial of the Dead, contrary to the peace of our Sovereign Lord the King, his crown and dignity.

A True Bill.

[We] do also present the said John Wesley, for that on or about the tenth day of this month, he the said John Wesley in the presence of Thomas Causton of the said town and county did presumptuously call himself Ordinary of this place, assuming thereby an authority which we apprehend did of no right belong to him, contrary to the peace of our Sovereign Lord the King, his crown and dignity.

A True Bill.

[We] do also present the said John Wesley, for that he did on or about the Tuesday in Whitsun Week last, refuse William Aglionby, of the said town and county, to stand godfather to the child of Henry Manly; he the said John Wesley giving no other reason for the said refusal than that the said William Aglionby had not been at the Communion Table with him the said John Wesley; notwithstanding he the said William Aglionby hath received the Sacrament of the Lord's Supper, contrary to the peace of our Sovereign Lord the King, his crown and dignity.

A True Bill.

[We] do also present the said John Wesley, for that he did in or about the month of July last part, baptize the child of Thomas Jones of the said town and county, having only one godfather and one godmother; notwithstanding that Jacob Matthews and Mary his wife, near relations of the said child, did offer to stand godfather and godmother at the same time, contrary to the peace of our Sovereign Lord the King, his crown and dignity.

August 31, 1737   A True Bill.

[The above text of the indictments is taken from D and B; cf. E, which gives the following summary: . . . ten indictments against me, asserting that I had broken the laws of the realm, 'contrary to the peace of our Sovereign Lord the King, his crown and dignity',

1. By writing and speaking to Mrs. Williamson against her husband's consent.

2. By repelling her from the Holy Communion.

3. By dividing the Morning Service on Sunday.

4. By not declaring my adherence to the Church of England.
5. By refusing to baptize Mr. Parker's child by sprinkling unless the parents would certify it was weak.
6. By repelling Mr. Gough from the Holy Communion.
7. By refusing to read the Burial Service over Nathanael Polhill, an Anabaptist.
8. By calling myself Ordinary of Savannah.
9. By refusing to receive William Aglionby as a godfather, because he was not a communicant.
10. By refusing Jacob Matthews for the same reason.]

September 2, Friday. The Court sat again. I then spoke to this effect: 'As to nine of the ten indictments against me, I know this Court can take no cognizance of them, they being matters of an ecclesiastical nature, and this not being an ecclesiastical court. But the tenth, concerning my speaking and writing to Mrs. Williamson, is of a secular nature; and this therefore I desire may be tried here, where the facts complained of were committed.' Little answer was made, and that purely evasive—in which for the present I acquiesced.

In the afternoon I moved the Court again for an immediate trial at Savannah, that those who were, or might be, offended, might 'clearly see' (so I concluded what little I said) 'whether I had done any wrong to anyone, or whether I had deserved the thanks of Mrs. Williamson and Mr. Causton and all his family'.

In Mr. Causton's answer, which was full of civility and respect [B—which was another civil refusal], was one very unguarded expression: 'Perhaps things would not have been carried so far, had you not said that afternoon, you believed if Mr. Causton appeared, the people would tear him to pieces; not so much out of love to you as out of hatred to him for his abominable practices.'

Saturday, September 3. I was seized with a violent flux [E—occasioned by feeding on damaged flour], which so weakened me before evening that I had much ado to get to church. But when I was there God renewed my strength, so that I did not shorten the service. The next day I was much better, and in two days more it pleased God to restore me to perfect health.

Wednesday, [September] 7. Mr. Dyson, Chaplain to the company of soldiers at Frederica [on St. Simons], called at a house where I was and said that he had now authority from the magistrates to perform ecclesiastical offices at Savannah, and should begin so to do the next day, by reading prayers, preaching, and administering the Sacrament. On Thursday the 8th at nine the first bell was accordingly rung, upon which I wrote and sent by Mr. Delamotte the following note:

To the Magistrates of the town of Savannah.

[September] 8, 1737

Gentlemen,

If you are not apprised that Mr. Dyson intends this day publicly to perform several ecclesiastical offices in Savannah, and (as he says) by your authority, I do now apprise you thereof, and am, gentleman, your humble servant,

John Wesley

Mr. Delamotte delivered it to Mr. Recorder. However, at ten the bell rung again, and Mr. Dyson entered upon his office by reading prayers and preaching in the church to Mrs. Causton (Mr. Causton being walked out of town), Mr. Williamson, Mrs. Williamson, and eight or ten more. He told the congregation he should do so every Thursday; that he had intended likewise to administer the Lord's Supper, but some of his communicants were indisposed; and that he would administer Baptism also to as many as he was desired.

On Friday the 9th, Mr. Delamotte believed it would be proper for me to go myself for England, chiefly to prevent or remove the misrepresentations which Mr. Williamson and his wife (who were to go in the next ship) might spread abroad. I begged advice of him who had hitherto directed me, and received the two following answers (the one I interpreted as a personal caution, the other as foretelling the event of things): 'He went out and found one of his fellow-servants which owed him an hundred pence. And he caught him by the throat, saying, "Pay me that thou owest" [Matt. 18:28]; 'Cast out the scorner, and contention shall go out; yea, strife and ((debate)) reproach shall cease' [Prov. 22:10].

Saturday, September 10. Having consulted my friends, I laid aside the thoughts of going to England, thinking it more suitable to my calling still to commit my cause to God, and not to be in haste to justify myself—only to 'be always ready to give to any that should ask me, a reason of the hope that is in me' [cf. 1 Pet. 3:15].

After explaining to the congregation on Sunday, [September] 11, those words of our blessed Master, 'It must needs be that offences will come' [Matt. 18:7]. I read to them a paper which I had read before, on March 10, 1736 [E—March 7th], being the day I entered upon my ministry at Savannah. I had then apprised them [E—therein] of the offences that must needs come, and forewarned them of the [E—particular] occasions, as, (1) That I must admonish every one of them not only in public, but [E—in private too] from house to house; (2) That I could admit none to the Holy Communion without previous notice; (3) That [E—both for my own and their convenience,] I should divide the Morning Service on Sundays, in compliance with the first design of the church; (4) That I must obey the rubric by dipping all children [E—in Baptism] who were well able to endure it [E—unless the parents certified, they were not able to endure it]; (5) That I could admit none who were not communicants to be sureties in Baptism; (6) That in general, though I had all the ecclesiastical authority which was entrusted to any within this province, yet I was only a servant of the Church of England, not a judge, and therefore obliged to keep to her regulations in all things.

I made a short application, to remind them that all the offences lately taken had sprung, directly or indirectly, from one or other of these occasions. Excepting only one, 'the not declaring my adherence to the principles and practices [E—regulations] of the Church of England'; which, being a charge I had not the least suspicion of, I could not guard against.

Monday, [September] 12. I was desired to read over the following paper [B—signed by ten or twelve of the Grand Jury], designed to be sent to England immediately:

To the Honourable the Trustees for Georgia.

Whereas two presentments have been made, the one of August 23rd, the other of August 31st, by the Grand Jury for the town and county of Savannah in Georgia, against John Wesley, Clerk;

We whose names are underwritten, being members of the said Grand Jury, do humbly beg leave to signify our dislike of the said presentments; being by many and divers circumstances thoroughly persuaded in ourselves, that the whole charge against Mr. Wesley is an artifice of Mr. Causton's, designed rather to blacken the character of Mr. Wesley than to free the Colony of religious tyranny, as he was pleased in his charge to us to term it. But as these circumstances will be too tedious to trouble your Honours with, we shall only beg leave to give the reasons of our dissent from the particular bills.

With regard to the first bill, we do not apprehend that Mr. Wesley acted against any law by writing or speaking to Mrs. Williamson; since it does not appear to us that the said Mr. Wesley has either spoke in private or wrote to the said Mrs. Williamson since March 12, except one letter of July 5, which he wrote at the request of her aunt (as a pastor) to exhort and reprove her.

The second we do not apprehend to be a true bill, because we humbly conceive Mr. Wesley did not assume to himself any authority contrary to law. For we understand, every person intending to communicate should 'signify his name to the curate at least some time the day before'; which Mrs. Williamson did not do, although Mr. Wesley had often in full congregation declared he did insist on a compliance with that rubric, and had before repelled divers persons for non-compliance therewith.

The third we do not think a true bill, because several of us have been his hearers when he had declared his adherence to the Church of England in a stronger manner than by a formal declaration, by explaining and defending the Apostles', the Nicene, and the Athanasian Creeds, the Thirty-nine Articles, the whole Book of Common Prayer, and the Homilies of the said Church; and because we think a formal declaration is not required but from those who have received institution and induction.

The fact alleged in the fourth bill we cannot apprehend to be contrary to any law in being.

The fifth we do not think a true bill, because we conceive Mr. Wesley is justified by the rubric, viz., 'If they (the parents) certify that the child is weak, it shall suffice to pour water on it,' intimating (as we humbly suppose), it shall not suffice if they do not certify.

The sixth cannot be a true bill, because the said William Gough, being one of our members, was surprised to hear himself named without his knowledge or privity; and did publicly declare, it was no grievance to him, because the said John Wesley had given him reasons with which he was satisfied.

The seventh we do not apprehend to be a true bill, for Nathanael Polhill was an Anabaptist, and desired in his lifetime that he might not be interred with the Office of the Church of England; and further, we have good reason to believe that Mr. Wesley was at Frederica, or on his return thence, when Polhill was buried.

As to the eighth bill we are in doubt, as not well knowing the meaning of the word 'Ordinary'. But for the ninth and tenth, we think Mr. Wesley is sufficiently justified by the Canons of the Church, which forbid any person to be admitted godfather or godmother to any child before the said person has received the Holy Communion; whereas William Aglionby and Jacob Matthews had never certified [B—to him] that they had received it.*

This was signed by twelve of the Grand Jurors [E—of whom three were constables, and six more tithingmen; who consequently would have made a majority had the jury consisted (as it regularly should) of the eleven tithingmen and four constables.]

On Thursday, September 15, Mr. Bradley desired me to step with him to Mr. Causton's, to be a witness to the conclusion of a conference at the beginning of which I was present by Mr. Causton's desire, July 18. I was very averse to such a work, but believed I could not honestly decline it, though I knew an artful man would some way turn it to my disadvantage [E—Mr. Causton would certainly take some advantage

---

*Document B ends at this point.

against me from it]. And so (I was some weeks [E—about a month] after informed) he has done, by sending two or three affidavits to the Trustees; in which I suppose (for a copy of them he refused) he has turned the tables, and accused me of the incivility which I then received from him.

Friday, September 30. Having ended the Homilies, I began reading Dr. Roger's [E—eight] sermons on the Christian Revelation to the congregation, hoping they might be a timely antidote against the poison of infidelity, which was [E—now] with great industry propagated among us; it being about this time that Mr. Causton read a clause of the Trustees' Charter to [E—put new life into] the two fathers of the unfaithful, to show them that if they would hold a meeting [E—and preach there] under the name of Quakers, I could not hinder them.

October 6, Thursday. Two of the communicants on whose account much suspicion, animosity, and dissension had arisen among the rest, gave glory to God by clearly and openly declaring what had passed between them, and referring the whole to their pastor and a select number of their brethren, whereby peace and unity were restored and established. [E—By this Christian method all misunderstandings were cleared, and peace and unity re-established.]

Friday, [October] 7. I consulted my friends, whether God did not call me to England, not on my own account, but for the sake of the poor people. They judged [E—they were unanimous], after considering the thing deeply, that I 'ought to go, but not yet'.

Tuesday, [October] 11. I went to Ebenezer to inquire of Mr. Bolzius and Gronau whether I could do them [E—the Salzburgers] any service if God should prosper me in my journey. If 'the hand of the diligent [E—still] maketh rich' [Prov. 10:4], this poor people [E—indefatigable labourers] can't be long in the present distress. On Wednesday evening I came back to Savannah.

Thursday, [October] 13. I inadvertently mentioned Mr. Causton's desiring me to write the Trustees an account of the Scotch at Savannah. A Scotch gentleman who was present acquainted his countrymen with it, who seemed at first to resent it highly. But Mr. Causton flatly denying it, they appeared pretty well satisfied.

Saturday, [October] 15. Being at Highgate, a village five miles from Savannah, consisting chiefly [E—(all but one)] of French families, I offered to officiate [E—read Prayers] with them (if they desired it) in French every Saturday in the afternoon. They embraced the offer gladly, and I promised with God's leave to begin the week following.

Thursday, [October] 20. A Court was held, in order to pass sentence on Capt. Watson, who had been two years eleven months confined as a lunatic. But oppression had not yet made him mad. He offered to prove by witnesses [E—the surviving jurors] then in Court that the verdict on which this sentence was to be grounded had never been given, and was entirely different from that verdict which the jury on Nov. 20, 1734, had delivered to the Court in writing. But his witnesses were not suffered to speak, and he was remanded to his confinement.

Saturday, [October] 22. I read prayers in French to the villagers of Highgate, and in German to those of Hampstead. We began and ended the service at both places with a Psalm, the Scriptures [E—a chapter in the New Testament] being read and prayers used between them.

Sunday, October 23. Having ended Fleury's *Manners of the First Christians*, we began to instruct the children in public as well as private, in a short paraphrase of our Lord's Sermon on the Mount.

Saturday, [October] 29. One or two of the French of Savannah were present at the prayers at Highgate. The next day I received a message from their whole body, that whereas I read prayers at Highgate to those who were but few in number, they hoped I would do the same at Savannah, where there was a large congregation who did not understand English. I told them I would willingly do it, if they would come every Sunday at one in the afternoon. This day [Sunday 30th] I began so to do.

Monday, [October] 31. The Grand Jury sitting in the court-house, we had the Evening Prayers in the school, which held upwards of thirty persons conveniently. The rest stood without, but I hope not so far off as to fail of that blessing which God giveth to all that diligently seek him.

November 1, Tuesday. Col. Stephens arrived, by whom I received a benefaction of ten pound sterling—after having been for several months without one shilling in the house, but not without peace, health, and contentment.

Thursday, [November] 3. Being informed [E—by one who heard him] it was Mr. Hugh Anderson who had asserted [E—affirmed] that I went from house to house to stir up the people to mutiny, and that I had publicly affirmed [E—declared] myself to be the Bishop and Ordinary of this place, I took an opportunity this day 'to desire the Court, he might either prove or retract those assertions'. But Mr. Causton said 'it was not a proper time [E—place]'. So I acquiesced, and let the matter sleep.

Friday, November 4. Mr. Burnside having let his house in town, as resolving immediately to remove into the country so soon as he had a small hut built, I invited him and his family to stay at my house in the meantime. The next day, Mr. Watson was set at liberty, after a confinement of two years, eleven months, and nineteen days. And on Sunday the 6th [having had regular notice and] being fully satisfied of his integrity [E—persuaded of his good intention], as well as [E—sound] understanding (though he neither denied nor disguised the faults he had before been guilty of), I admitted him to the Holy Communion.

November 11. [blank page]

November 22, Tuesday. Mr. Causton desired to have a conference with me, wherein he said he doubted not but he should clear up all the misunderstandings which had been between us. Accordingly at three in the afternoon I went to him. He spoke many fair words [E—said many civil things]—but I now knew their sterling value. He likewise read me the affidavits made September 15, in one of which it was expressly asserted [E—roundly affirmed] that I had 'assaulted [E—abused] Mr. Causton in his own house, calling him liar, villain, and so forth'. But he assured me, none of these affidavits was gone to the Trustees. And it was true, for he had sent only the copies. It was at this conversation Mr. Anderson told me, I had been reprimanded in the last Court for an 'enemy to and hinderer of the public peace'. We all parted, in appearance, friends.

The next morning I went to Mr. Causton's again, and told him I did not think it proper for a hinderer of the public peace to stay in the place where he was so, and that I designed to set out for England immediately. I posted up an advertisement to the same effect, and then quietly prepared myself for my journey.

Wednesday, November 30. I went to Mr. Causton's once more, to desire money for the expenses of it. The same evening two children were baptized, as were three more the day following (the youngest two years and a half, the eldest six years old), whose parents had been Anabaptists.

Friday, December 2. I proposed to set out for Port Royal about noon, the tide then serving. But about ten the magistrates sent for me, and told me I should not leave [E—they would not suffer me to go out of] the Province till I had entered into recognizance to appear at the Court, and answer to the allegations laid against me. I replied, I had appeared at four Courts successively, and had openly desired a trial, but was refused it. [E—But as they had now referred (the allegations) to the Trustees, to the Trustees I desired to go.] They said, however, I must give security to appear again. I asked, What security? After a long consultation together [E—about two hours], they agreed upon [E—the Recorder showed me] a kind of bond that I would appear at Savannah when I should be required, under fifty pound penalty. But the Recorder added, I must likewise give bail to answer Mr. Williamson's action of one thousand pound damages. I then began to see into their design of spinning out time and doing nothing, and so told him plainly: [E—'Sir, all this is mere trifling.] I will sign neither one bond nor the other. [E—You use me very ill, and so you do the Trustees too.] You know your business, and I know mine.'

In the afternoon the magistrates published an order requiring all officers [E—and sentinels] to prevent my going out of the Province, and forbidding any person whatever to be in any wise aiding or assisting me so to do. Being now only a prisoner at large, in a place where I well knew [E—by experience] every day would give fresh opportunities of procuring evidence for words I never spoke and actions I never did, I saw clearly I had nothing more to do but to fly [E—escape] for my life. And the tide serving as soon as Evening Prayers were over, I shook off the dust of my feet, and left Savannah, after having preached the gospel there (with much weakness indeed, and many infirmities) one year and nine months. 'Oh that thou hadst known, at least in this thy day, the things which make for thy peace!' [cf. Luke 19:42].

Saturday, December 3. We came to Purrysburg, early in the morning. Here I endeavoured to procure a guide to Port Royal, whither we hoped to walk before evening. But none being to be had, we set out, with the best directions we could procure, an hour before sunrise. In half an hour we lost the path; an hour after we came to a plantation, where a lad undertaking to guide us for a mile and a half, led us just so much out of the way [E—entirely the wrong way], and then delivered us to an old Frenchman [E—who promised to set us right], by whom we were brought into a little blind path, running along a line of blazed trees, which he said would lead us directly [E—in five or six hours] to Port Royal. In this we walked (being four in all, two [E—((two)) one] of whom intended to go for England with me, and the other [E—others] to settle in Carolina), till about eleven we came into a large swamp, without path or blaze, where we wandered up and down near three hours. About two we got out, found a blaze, and traced it till it divided into two, one of which we followed through an almost impassable thicket, the briars of which dealt but roughly both with our clothes and skin, till [E—about a mile beyond it] we came to the end of the blaze. We then prayed to God to direct us, and forced our way through the thicket once more, searched out the other blaze, and traced that till it came to an end too. It now grew toward sunset, so we sat us down on the ground, faint and weary enough. Indeed, had the day continued we could not have gone much farther, having had no sustenance since five in the morning, except about a quarter of a pint of rum and a cake of gingerbread, which Mrs. Burnside had persuaded me to take with me. A third part of this we had divided among us for dinner; another third we took for our supper, and the rest we reserved for the next day. Our worst want was that of water, having met with none all day. I thrust a cane we had into the ground, and drawing it out found the end moist; upon which two of our company fell to digging with their hands, and at about three foot depth found good water. We thanked God, drank, and were much refreshed. The night was sharp, and we had no means of making a fire. However, there was no complaining [E—among us]. But after we had commended ourselves to God, we lay down close together, and (I at least) slept till the morning.

Sunday, December 4. God renewed our strength, so that we arose neither faint nor hungry [E—nor weary], and having committed ourselves to his protection, and drank each of us a draught of water, set forward [E—resolved to make one trial more to find a path] for Port

Royal. We steered by the sun, as near as we could, east. But finding neither path nor blaze, and the woods growing thicker and thicker, we judged after an hour or two's trial it was our best course to return, if we could, by the way we came. The day before I had broke, though I knew no reason why, many young trees almost all the way we went. These we found a great help in many places, where neither blaze nor path was to be seen. At twelve we ate the remainder of our cake, and meeting some moist ground, dug as before and found water. Between one and two, God brought us safe to Benjamin Arieu's house, the old man whom we had left the day before.

I read French prayers in the evening to a numerous family, a mile from Arieu's, one of whom undertook to guide us to Port Royal, which he said was between forty and fifty miles off. In the morning [December 5], we set out, but took care to carry a good loaf of bread with us. About sunset we asked our guide if he knew where he was, who frankly answered, No. However, we pushed on, sometimes *in* a path and sometimes *out*, till about seven we came to a plantation, which indeed was many miles wide of that we designed to go to. But here we got good potatoes and a lodging; and the next evening [E—after many difficulties and delays] we got to Port Royal.

Wednesday, December 7. We walked to Beaufort, on the other side of Port Royal Island. Here we met with many of our old neighbours of Savannah, who appeared heartily glad to see us. Our interview much resembled that of persons who having by different ways escaped out of a common shipwreck, naturally relate to each other the fears and dangers they have gone through, and the means of their deliverance from them.

Both this and the following day the gentleman who invited me to his house gave me a lively idea of the old English hospitality. Yet observing the elegance and more than neatness of everything round about him, I could not but sigh to myself and say, *Heu delicatum discipulum duri magistri!* ['Alas! the disciple's ease compared with the Master's suffering!']

On Thursday morning Mr. Delamotte came, with whom on Friday, [December] 9, I set out for Charleston by water. In the evening (the wind having been against us all day) we were hospitably entertained at Mr. Cockram's plantation. I can't say so of the poor folks at whose plantation we landed the next day; who however at last gave us a few bad potatoes, of which they plainly told us we robbed the swine. The wind continuing contrary, we could but just reach Johns Island on Monday the 12th in the morning. Here we were obliged to stay till noon. Our provisions falling short, we desired of Mr. G——— a little meat or drink of any sort, either with or without price; and with much difficulty obtained some potatoes, and liberty to roast them in a fire which his Negroes had made a distance from the house.

Early on Tuesday, December 13, [E—after a slow passage by reason of contrary winds and some conflict with hunger as well as cold,] we came to Charleston, where I expected trials of a quite different nature—and far more dangerous, contempt and hunger [E—want] being easy to be borne. But who can bear respect and fullness of bread [E—abundance]!

December 14, Wednesday. Being desired by Mr. Garden's assistant to read [E—public] prayers, I was much refreshed by those glorious prophecies and promises which were exhibited to us both in the seventy-second Psalm and the fortieth chapter of Isaiah. Amen! May those 'who trust in the Lord renew their strength' [cf. Isa. 40:31], and 'let all the earth be filled with the glory of his majesty'! [cf. Ps. 72:19]

In the afternoon, visiting a poor man who in all probability had not many days to live, we found him still full of the freshest advices, domestic and foreign, and busy in settling the affairs of Muscovy and Persia [E—the affairs of the Czarina, Prince Thamas, and the Ottoman Porte]. Surely the notion of the Platonists is right [E—Who then can deny]:

> *Quae cura nitentes*
> *Pascere equos, eadem sequitur tellure repostos.*
> ['The same care they took (while alive) in feeding their sleek steeds,
> attends them still, buried though they be.'
> Virgil, *Aeneid*, vi. 654-55.]

For if a soul, quivering on the verge of life, has still leisure [E—for these impertinencies] to amuse itself with battles and sieges, why may not the same dreams continue, even in the sleep of death?*

Thursday, December 15. I began to feel the effects of ease and harmless conversation, having no spirit left in me. So that I should have fallen an easy prey to any temptation which had then attacked me. But the next [day, December 16], it pleased God to give me new life; and I again rejoiced in his strength, and felt a good hope that I should continue to watch and pray, and not enter into temptation.

---

*End of document E.

LONDON DIARY 1
April 1-30, 1738

SATURDAY, APRIL 1. 4.30 Prayed; writ sermon. 6 Read Prayers; sermon. 7 Coffee; sermon. 8 Read Prayers. 9 Charles read his journal, prayer; sang. 12.15 Dinner; read my sermon. 1 At Mr Fox's. 2 Castle; read Prayers. 3 With Charles, he read his journal; tea. 5 Garden; meditated; read Prayers; sang; (preserved from sins in thought). 6 Charles read his journal. 8 Shaved; Washington's, Bible. 9 Sang; read *The Angelical Life*; prayer. 11.15 Religious talk; prayer. 12 Prayer. 12.30 Lay down.

EASTER DAY [APRIL 2]. 5.45 At home; prayed; necessary talk; prayer. 6.45 Tea, religious talk. 8 Dressed; read Prayers. 9 Preached, Communion (all serious, all stayed). 10.15 With the Rector, he kind. 10.30 With Charles, religious talk, he read his journal. 12.15 Prayer; religious talk; dinner. 1 Mr Fox's, sang, read, prayer. 2 Castle, read Prayers, sermon. 3.35 Carfax, read Prayers. 4 Preached (all serious; convincing). 5 At home; tea, religious talk. 6 Mr Vesey's, tea, necessary talk. 6.30 Mr Fox's. 7.30 At home; sang; they read. 9 Prayer. 9.30.

MONDAY, APRIL 3. 4 Necessary business; tea, religious talk. 6 Set out with Mr Fox. 7 A stranger, necessary talk (religious). 8 We parted; read Scriptures. 11.30 Mrs Pocock's, religious talk; tea. 1.30 Dinner; talked of Georgia. 3 Set out. 7 At Dummer. 7.15 Read Prayers. 8 Mr Pike. 8.30 He went, religious talk; tea. 9.30 Prayer. 9.45.

TUESDAY, APRIL 4. 4 Prayer; prayed. 5 Read Prayers. 5.45 Set things in order; prayer. 8 Tea; writ diary. 9 Journal; prayer. 11 Miss Molly and Stephen Kinchin, necessary talk (religious). 11.30 Bible; sang; prayer. 12.15 Dinner, necessary talk. 1 Talked of logic. 2.30 All walked, necessary talk (religious). 3.15 Visited. 4.30 At home; read journal to them. 5 Religious talk; prayed; meditated. 6 Tea, religious talk. 6.45 Read Prayers. 7.30 Read journal. 9.15 Prayer.

WEDNESDAY, APRIL 5. 4 Prayer; prayed; sang. 5.15 Read Prayers. 6 Prayer; Bible; Mr Terry came; tea, religious talk. 8 Began logic with them; prayer; sang. 11 Walked; necessary talk (religious). 12 Dinner, necessary talk. 1 Religious talk with Miss Molly. 2.30 Read French with Stephen. 3.30 Prayer; visited. 5 Prayed; sang. 6 Tea, religious talk. 6.30 Read Prayers. 7.15 At Fisher's, sang, Bible. 8.45 At home; necessary talk; prayer. 9.30.

THURSDAY [APRIL] 6. 4 Prayer; prayed; sang. 5 Read Prayers. 5.45 Necessary business. 6.15 Tea, religious talk; Bible; sang; prayer. 7 Writ logic; read it. 9 Prayer; read sermon to Miss Molly. 10.15 Religious talk; read Prayers. 11.30 They went; walked; read *Desideria*. 1.45 Mr Kinchin, set out, necessary talk (religious). 3 Woodmancott, necessary talk; ate. 4.15 Tea, religious talk. 5.15 Prayer (lively zeal). 5.30 Set out with Miss Molly, etc, religious talk. 6.30 At home; tea, religious talk, read Prayers. 7.15 Necessary talk (religious); writ diary. 7.45 Began Mr de Renty. 9 Prayer; ended *Desideria*. 9.30.

FRIDAY [APRIL] 7. 4 Prayer; prayed; meditated. 5 Read Prayers. 6 Tea, religious talk; prayer; sang. 8 Necessary business. 8.30 Read to Miss Molly. 10 Stephen, necessary talk (religious) upon Mr Clayton. 11 Prayed; religious talk. 12 Dinner, necessary talk. 12.30 Read Morgan's letters. 3 Visited. 4 Writ to Miss Molly. 3.45 Catechized children. 5 Prayer; prayed; meditated. 6 Mr Pike, necessary talk (religious); tea; private prayer. 7 Stephen read Mr Clayton's letters. 8 Religious talk. 8.30 Read to Miss Molly, religious talk; prayed. 9.30.

SATURDAY, APRIL 8. 4 Prayer; prayed. 5 Read Prayers. 6 Tea, religious talk; Bible. 8.15 Prayer; sang. 9 Prayer; logic; writ diary. 11 Walked, necessary talk (religious); sang. 12.15 Dinner. 1 Read Haliburton. 2 Visited. 4 Writ to Miss Molly. 5 Prayer; walked; meditated. 6 Tea, religious talk. 6.45 Read Prayers. 7.30 Necessary talk with Dame. 8 Fisher's. 9 Prayer; necessary talk. 9.45.

SUNDAY [APRIL 9]. 4.30 Prayed. 5 Meditated; necessary business. 6 Prayer; tea, religious talk. 7 Bible; sang. 9 Meditated upon sermon. 10.30 Read Prayers. 11.30 Preached, Sacrament. 1.15 Prayer; dinner, religious talk. 2 Read Haliburton. 2.30 Sang; Bible; prayer. 3 Meditated. 3.15 Read Prayers; catechized. 4.15 Prayer; necessary talk (religious); sang; tea; Bible. 6.30 At Goody Fisher's. 7 Read Bible; prayer; sang. 8.30 At home; ended Haliburton. 9 Prayer; religious talk with Miss Molly. 9.45.

MONDAY [APRIL 10]. 4.15 Prayer; meditated. 5 Read Prayers; tea, necessary talk (religious). 6.30 Miss Molly ill, sat [with] her. 11 Mrs Terry, necessary talk; translated Sanderson. 12.30 Dinner; Sanderson. 1.30 With Miss Molly and Mrs Terry. 2 She went; religious talk with Miss Molly. 5 Mrs Kinchin, necessary talk (religious). 6.45 Read Prayers. 7.30 Necessary talk. 8.15 With Miss Molly, etc, necessary talk (religious). 11.45.

TUESDAY, APRIL 11. 4.30 Prayer; dressed. 5 Read Prayers. 6 Bible; necessary business. 7 Tea, necessary talk (religious). 8 Sanderson; Miss Molly came, she little better, necessary talk (religious). 10 Read De Renty to them. 11.30 Set out; meditated; prayed. 2 At Stockbridge; dinner, religious talk to hostler. 2.30 Set out; meditated; prayer. 5 At Sarum; necessary talk of Miss Molly. 6 Necessary talk; tea, religious talk. 7 Prayer; necessary talk (religious). 9 Supper. 10.30 Necessary talk (religious) with my sister. 11.30.

WEDNESDAY [APRIL] 12. 3.45 Necessary talk; tea, religious talk to Alice. 4.30 Went for my horse. 5 Set out; lost. 7.45 Stockbridge; religious talk to all; (lively zeal). 8.45 Set out; prayed; sang; meditated; religious talk to a stranger. 11.45 Woodmancott; Miss Molly there; necessary talk (religious); tea. 1.30 Dinner; she worse; necessary talk (religious). 4.30 She told her story, was very ill. 5.30 Prayer. 5.45 Set out. 6.30 Dummer; tea, religious talk; read Prayers. 7.30 Heard letters; at Goody Fisher's; read; sang; prayers. 9 Lay down.

THURSDAY, APRIL 13. 5 Dressed; read Prayers. 6 Writ diary. 6.30 Set out; read Isaac Mills. 7.15 Woodmancott; necessary talk (religious). 8 Miss Molly; necessary talk (religious). 9 Prayers; tea, religious talk. 10 Logic. 11 De Renty; necessary talk (religious). 2 Dinner. 3 Logic, necessary talk; prayer. 4.30 Necessary talk (religious); prayer. 5.45 Set out. 6.45 At home; meditated. 7 Read Prayers; tea, necessary talk (useful, religious); writ diary. 8.45 Prayer. 9.

FRIDAY [APRIL] 14. 4.45 Prayed; read Prayers. 6 Prayer; necessary business. 6.45 Set out. 7.30 Woodmancott; necessary talk (religious). 8 With Miss Molly, religious talk. 9 Tea, necessary talk (religious). 10 Prayer; Haliburton. 11.30 French. 1 Walked; meditated. 1.15 Dinner. 2 Set out with James Kinchin, religious talk. 3.30 Winchester; with Dr Combes, necessary talk of Miss Molly; read Prayers. 4.45 At Mr Gatter's[?], necessary talk. 5 Set out; necessary talk (religious). 6.30 Woodmancott; necessary talk; Miss Molly very ill. 7.30 Set out. 8.15 Dummer, Mr Terry's, old Mr Terry there, necessary talk (religious). 9.30 Prayer.

SATURDAY [APRIL] 15. 5 Read Prayers; prayer. 6 Set out; meditated. 7 Woodmancott; necessary talk; necessary talk (religious). 8 Tea, necessary talk (religious). 8 Prayer; read Haliburton. 10.30 Mr Lawrence, he will not bleed Miss Molly, necessary talk. 1 Dinner; necessary talk; Miss Molly very ill; writ diary. 3 Necessary talk (religious). 5 Prayer; necessary talk (religious); she very ill. 7 Set out; meditated; read. 8 At home; tea, religious talk. 8.30 At Goody Fisher's, read; prayer. 9 Prayer. 9.30.

SUNDAY, APRIL 16. 4.45 Prayer; dressed; prayer; Bible; meditated. 6.15 Set out; meditated upon sermon. 7 Woodmancott; writ diary. 7.15 Tea, religious talk. 8.30 Popham; read Prayers. 9.30 Sermon, Sacrament. 11 Dummer; read Prayers, Sermon. 1.15 Woodmancott; dinner, necessary talk (religious). 2 Meditated. 2.45 Read Prayers; Sermon. 4.15 Necessary talk (religious); Miss Molly ill. 5 Set out with Stephen and Jimmy, religious talk. 7 Goody Fisher's. 7.15 Read; sang; prayer. 8 Tea, necessary talk (religious). 8.30 With old Mr Terry, religious and useful talk. 10.15 Prayer.

MONDAY [APRIL] 17. 4.30 Prayer; prayed. 5 Read Prayers; prayer; Bible. 6.15 Set out; meditated. 7 Woodmancott, religious talk to Stephen, to Miss Molly, to Jimmy. 8 Tea, necessary talk (religious). 9 Prayer. 9.15 Set out with Stephen and Charles, religious talk. 12 At Mrs Pocock's; dinner, mostly religious talk. 1.30 Set out, religious talk to Stephen. 2 Newbury; we parted; meditated; read Scriptures; meditated. 7 Mr Sarney's, necessary talk (religious) with Charles; supper, necessary talk (religious) with Charles. 8 Washington, etc, necessary talk (religious). 9 Prayer; necessary talk (religious). 10.

TUESDAY [APRIL] 18. 5 Read Prayers; dressed. 6 Garden; meditated; read Prayers. 7 At home; tea, religious talk. 8 Necessary talk. 9 Sang with Charles; necessary business; necessary talk. 9.30 Set out; began Life of A. M. Schurman. 3 At the lot upon the hill, religious talk. 3.15 Set out. 4 Read Mr Kirby. 5.30 Mr Crouch's; ate, necessary talk. 6 Writ to Miss Molly. 7 Necessary talk (religious). 8.30 Supper, religious talk. 9.30 Prayer. 10.

WEDNESDAY, APRIL 19. 5 Prayed. 5.15 Set out; ran. 7.15 Beaconsfield; tea, religious talk. 8 Set out; read Schurman. 4 At James Hutton's. 5 Went with him to Mr Hutton's; at Westminster, necessary talk (religious); tea. 7.15 At home; Mr Shay and Clark, religious talk; supper, religious talk; prayer. 9.45.

THURSDAY [APRIL] 20. 5 Prayed. 5.30 Writ to Charles Kinchin. 6 Prayer; writ. 7.15 Read Prayers; tea; Mr Broughton, etc. 9 Writ to Charles Delamotte, to Mrs Burnside. 11.30 To Molly Kinchin; dressed. 1 Set out with James Hutton, etc. 1.45 At Mr Stonehouse's, dinner, talk of the mystics! 4 Read Prayers; tea,

8.
21. 1738.

4 ½) ᒣ,) 6. S. Anthol... 3,

8 V; ; , 9. h, ;

9 12½ h, , 2. A . Brown

2 = ½ , 3¾ , , ..¾

4 43, , 5½ 7 ,

6. h, C ½ A, . , ?

7. 8. U , , , 10½

7, 22.

5 ½), 6 7¾ 3, 8. V, , A

9. ¼ A, 10. 7 , ½ ,

11. , 3¾ 7 , 12¾ A, 6, Bohl

2 3¾ ½ , 4 C V, 7

5 5½ Böhler's, , A 6

7 ½ h, , A 9¾ 6 ½

23.

4 ¾), 6. St Ann.. 3, , 9. ,

10. A 10. Wapping, 3, 12½

2 6, A 2½ S. Helen.. 3, 4¾ 7 h

5 Böhler Faj... 0.

religious talk. 5.30 Set out. 6.15 Mr Bray's; sang. 6.30 Gutter Lane; sang; read; prayer. 8 At home; supper. 8.30 Jane D[elamotte?], necessary talk (religious). 9 Religious talk; prayer. 10.

FRIDAY, APRIL 21. 4.30 Meditated upon sermon; prayed. 6 St Antholin's, read Prayers, preached. 8 Mr Bray's, religious talk; tea; prayer. 9 At home, necessary talk (religious); at Mr Hutton's, necessary talk (religious). 12.30 At home; necessary business. 2 Writ to Mr Brown of Highgate. 2.30 Tea, religious talk. 3.15 Walked; meditated (lively zeal). 3.45 At Mr Hutton's, necessary talk (religious) with Charles. 4 Read Prayers; sang; necessary talk (religious). 5.30 Set out; meditated. 6 At home; necessary talk (religious) with Mr Shay. 6.30 Writ. 7 Supper; Captain Coram, necessary talk. 8 Mr Broughton, etc; sang; Bible; sang; prayer. 10.30.

SATURDAY [APRIL] 22. 5.30 Prayed. 6 Prayer; religious talk. 7.15 Read Prayers. 8 Mr Clark's, tea, religious talk; prayer. 9.15 Writ. 10 Set out. 10.30 Mr Hutton's, Charles not there; meditated. 11 Charles came, necessary talk. 11.45 Set out; meditated. 12.45 Writ. 1 Dinner; Böhler, religious talk. 3.15 Slept. 3.30 Tea, religious talk. 4 At Dr Cosburn's, necessary talk of Miss Molly. 5.30 At Böhler's, sang, he read letters. 7.30 At home; supper writ to Charles Kinchin. 9.15 Writ diary. 9.30.

SUNDAY [APRIL] 23. 4.45 Prayed; meditated. 6 At St Ann's, read Prayers, preached, Sacrament. 9 Mrs West's, tea, religious talk. 10 Wapping, read Prayers, preached. 12.30 Mr Parker's, prayer, dinner, religious talk. 2.30 St Helen's, read Prayers, preached. 4.45 At home; Böhler, etc; convinced that faith c[onvert]s at once. 6 Tea; sang; (+). 7 Religious talk to Böhler; prayer. 7.30 Mr Hutton's; sang; prayer. 9 Religious talk with Metcalf. 9.30 Prayer. 10.30 At home.

MONDAY [APRIL] 24. 5 Prayed. 6.30 Read Prayers; Mr Broughton's. 7 Religious talk to Metcalf; tea, religious talk. 8 Learned to sing. 9 Mr Broughton's, religious talk. 10 At home; necessary talk. 11 Islington, read Prayers. 12 Religious talk with Mr Stonehouse; (lively zeal). 1 Dinner, religious talk; set out; religious talk to Mr Clark. 2 At home; necessary talk. 3 Set out; read *The Way to the Sabbath of Rest*. 6.30 Blendon; necessary talk (religious) with Mr Broughton. 7.30 Miss Hetty sang; religious talk to Mrs Delamotte, Miss Betty[?], and Charles; sang; religious talk. 8.30 Supper, religious talk. 10.30 Mr Piers went; prayer. 11 Sang. 11.30.

TUESDAY [APRIL] 25. 4.45 Prayed; with them; sang; prayer; read; sang. 7 Meditated; religious talk; tea; sang. 8 Set out; with Mr Broughton, religious talk; meditated. 10 Necessary talk with John Delamotte. 11.15 At home; religious talk with Böhler; (+, lively zeal). 12 Set out; meditated. 1 Islington; Mr Hall and Sister Patty there; necessary talk (religious). 2.45 Set out; meditated. 3.15 At home; Miss Clagget there; Böhler; religious talk; tea. 6 St Helen's, read Prayers, preached. 8 At home; writ to Mr Kinchin, to Mr Clayton. 10 Necessary talk (religious). 10.30.

WEDNESDAY, APRIL 26. 5 Prayed; writ. 6.30 Religious talk; sang. 7 Hervey and Metcalf, tea, religious talk. 8 Read Prayers; necessary business. 10.30 At Mr Broughton's, necessary talk. 12 At the Trustees' House. 12.45 Left my papers;